P9-CLJ-488

BREWER'S DICTIONARY OF 20TH-CENTURY PHRASE AND FABLE

BREWER'S DICTIONARY OF 20TH-CENTURY PHRASE AND FABLE

Houghton Mifflin Company · Boston

First US edition 1992

Houghton Mifflin Company
Two Park Street
Boston
MA 02108

Library of Congress Catalog Card Number 91–29299
CIP Data is available.

ISBN 0–395–61649–2

Compiled and typeset by Market House Books Limited, Aylesbury
Printed and bound in Great Britain by
Mackays of Chatham PLC, Chatham, Kent

CONTENTS

ACKNOWLEDGEMENTS

EDITORS

(Market House Books Ltd)

David Pickering

Alan Isaacs

Elizabeth Martin

CONTRIBUTORS

Callum Brines

John Daintith

Rosalind Fergusson

Robert Hine

Amanda Isaacs

Heather Jargus

Elizabeth Kirkpatrick

Jonathan Law

Kate Reddick

Kathy Seed

John Wright

PREFACE

The first edition of Dr Ebenezer Cobham Brewer's *Dictionary of Phrase and Fable* was published in 1870. By the time a second edition had appeared in 1895, the publisher was able to claim sales of 100,000 copies – no mean achievement in an age in which only a small proportion of the population was able to benefit from secondary or higher education.

Clearly his formula of combining what was then called philology with classical, Celtic, and Norse mythology, all embellished with a wide range of literary allusion, was a winner. As John Buchanan-Brown says in his Introduction to the 14th (1989) edition:

> 'The *Dictionary* undoubtedly owed its popularity to the way in which its subject-matter, whether by intuition or by conscious design, responded to the needs of a reading public created by nineteenth-century conditions. From the rapidly growing towns and cities emerged a class of reader, literate if not educated in the academic sense, which looked beyond the pure entertainment of novels and poetry, the utility of self-education and the moral uplift of religious books to the satisfaction of simple intellectual curiosity. This is that spirit of enquiry which at one end of the scale leads to pure scholarship and at the other to the acquisition of what some would stigmatize as totally useless information.'

Revisions and updated editions of Dr Brewer's *Dictionary*, which have appeared at regular intervals, have attempted to acknowledge the most striking developments in the language of the contemporary age without destroying the balance and charm of the original. However, it has become increasingly apparent that developments in this century, being both rapid and voluminous, would justify an account in their own right; and hence a purely 20th-century version was conceived.

The brief for the new book has been much the same as that which Dr Brewer set himself in the 1860s, except that this book takes 1900 as its starting-point, thus excluding any entry that does not truly belong to the 20th century. The compilers have attempted to pick up the threads of Dr Brewer's approach to his subject matter in the original volume, finding modern equivalents for – and developments of – the phrases and myths that first attracted him. Inevitably, this is not a Victorian book, but what it does share with the original is a taste for the unusual, even the bizarre, in language and event, as well as an enthusiasm for providing interesting information not available in conventional dictionaries and encyclopedias.

Since 1900 there has been a positive avalanche of new phrases in the English language. It has not been possible to include them all. What has been achieved is a selection of the most evocative and interesting words and phrases, choosing especially those about which there is something worthwhile to say. The selection has been made from the English spoken on both sides of the Atlantic, as well as in Australia and New Zealand.

Because the 20th century is not especially known for its fables, it has been necessary to interpret this word in the broader sense of 'myths'; these range from famous murders and military disasters to political scandals and legendary film stars. The 20th century is by no means short of myths, as the browser in this compilation will soon discover. Numerous quotations and copious anecdotal material have been included, in order to make *Brewer's Dictionary of 20th-Century Phrase and Fable* entertaining as well as informative. Because the 20th century has seen the most far-reaching developments in science in the whole history of mankind, it has been thought worthwhile to include a number of entries recording the milestones along this most exciting of routes.

The editors will welcome any correspondence on the individual entries in this book, or suggestions for new entries in subsequent editions.

ABBREVIATIONS

Arab.	Arabic	Ital.	Italian
Austr.	Australian	Jap.	Japanese
Dan.	Danish	Lat.	Latin
Dut.	Dutch	Port.	Portuguese
Fr.	French	Russ.	Russian
Ger.	German	Sans.	Sanskrit
Gr.	Greek	Sp.	Spanish
Heb.	Hebrew	Swed.	Swedish
Hind.	Hindustani	Turk.	Turkish

CROSS-REFERENCES

These are indicated in the text by the use of SMALL CAPITALS.

A

A A former category of film classification indicating that in the opinion of the British Board of Film Censors a film was suitable for being shown to adults and children over 14 years of age and to children below that age only if accompanied by an adult. The symbol was first introduced in the UK in 1914 and finally dropped in the 1980s.

AA A former category of film classification indicating that in the opinion of the British Board of Film Censors a film was not suitable for being shown to children under 14 years of age. An abbreviation for Accompanied by Adult, the classification was introduced in 1970 and dropped in the 1980s.

A-bomb *See* ATOM BOMB; NUCLEAR WEAPON.

A-effect (Ger. *V-Effekt*, *Verfremdungseffekt*) Alienation effect. The term coined by the playwright Bertolt Brecht (1898–1956) for his technique of deliberately distancing both actors and audience to his plays by various alienating devices, thereby controlling the degree to which they identify with the drama. Brecht's intention was to jolt the sensibilities of all participants in order to sharpen their objectivity and awareness. He achieved this A-effect in several ways, including the use of third person narrative, past tense, unusual or subversive design, and spoken stage directions embodied in the production. For example, an actor may step out of character during a scene to address the audience.

A-Line *See* DIOR.

A side The most commercially promising side of a pop-music single disc, *i.e.* the recording intended to enter the CHARTS. A 'double A side' single is one with potential chart material on both sides. *See also* B SIDE.

A_2 The virus identified as the cause of ASIAN FLU.

A6 murder The controversial murder case involving James Hanratty, a petty burglar, who in 1962 was convicted of murdering office worker Michael Gregston. The body of Gregston was discovered in a lay-by on the A6 at Deadman's Hill near Bedford, in August 1961. Hanratty was convicted largely on the strength of his identification by Gregston's girlfriend, Valerie Storie, who had been seriously wounded by the couple's attacker. Hanratty was hanged on 4 April, in spite of doubts about his conviction expressed by some. Concern over the outcome of the case contributed to the abolition of the death penalty in the UK.

aardvark British student pun of the late 1980s for hard work.

Abadan Crisis A political dispute between the UK and Iran following the nationalization of the Iranian oil industry in 1951. This threatened the interests of the Anglo-Iranian Oil Company (later renamed British Petroleum), which operated the large refinery at Abadan. The UK retaliated with a blockade of Iran, thereby damaging the Iranian economy. The crisis was resolved by the formation in 1954 of an international consortium of oil companies (including Anglo-Iranian) to run the Iranian oilfields.

Abbey Theatre A Dublin theatre, opened in 1904, renowned for staging works by contemporary Irish playwrights, including Yeats, Synge, George Russell (known as AE), and Lady Gregory. The Abbey Theatre was built at the instigation of Annie Horniman (1860–1937) and became the home of the Irish National Dramatic Society. A fire destroyed the original building in 1951 but a new playhouse was subsequently built, opening in 1966.

ABDA American, British, Dutch and Australian Command – the short-lived Allied command set up under Wavell (1883–1950) in the Pacific in early 1942.

Abdication Crisis The constitutional dispute between the uncrowned King Edward VIII and the British Establishment; it was caused by the king's intention to marry the American twice-divorced Mrs. Wallis Simpson. Edward had been an intimate friend of Mrs. Simpson for some years before acceding to the throne after the death of his father, George V, on 20 January 1936. In the ensuing months he continued to escort Mrs. Simpson while she awaited her divorce from her second husband, Ernest Simpson. This was granted in October, and the couple hoped the final hurdle to their marriage had been cleared.

However, they reckoned without the Establishment. Prime Minister Baldwin, prodded and supported by various prominent figures alarmed by the constitutional implications, informed the king that marriage to Mrs. Simpson was unacceptable while he remained on the throne. Reaction among the British public was mixed. The king had been a popular figure noted for his concern for the unemployed and the poverty of the 1930s. But opposition to divorce was still widespread, a moral position staunchly upheld by the Church of England, especially by the Archbishop of Canterbury, Cosmo Lang, who who came out as a strong supporter of Baldwin.

With no hint of compromise from his prime minister, the king relinquished the throne on 11 December, to be succeeded by his brother, George VI. In a radio broadcast to the Commonwealth on the night of his abdication, the ex-king gave a moving account of his reasons for leaving: "... I have found it impossible to carry the heavy burden of responsibility and to discharge my duties as king as I would wish to do without the help and support of the woman I love."

Edward was created Duke of Windsor and given the title Royal Highness, although this was refused his wife after their marriage on 3 June 1937 in Paris. The Abdication, a mountain in Britain's moral landscape, retains its fascination for successive generations; at its heart it contains the dilemma of an individual torn between love and the highest office in the land.

> Well, Mr. Baldwin! *This* is a pretty kettle of fish!
> QUEEN MARY, speaking to the prime minister.

Aberfan disaster A tragedy that befell the mining village of Aberfan in Mid Glamorgan on 21 October 1966. A vast tip of colliery waste slid downhill engulfing part of the village, including the school. 116 of the 144 lives lost were children. The disaster prompted an urgent review of the siting and maintenance of similar tips.

Abgrenzung (Ger. demarcation) The former policy of separation of the German Democratic Republic and the Federal Republic of Germany following the creation of two German states after World War II. Deeply resented by many Germans in both countries, it was finally and comprehensively dropped as official policy in 1990, when the two states reunited.

able. able and willing to pull his weight President Theodore Roosevelt's summary of the ideal American in a widely reported speech of 1902. The oft-repeated sentiment in full ran thus:

> The first requisite of a good citizen in this Republic of ours is that he shall be able and willing to pull his weight.

ableism Discrimination on the grounds of able-bodiedness. Employers are accused of ableism when they discriminate in favour of hiring an able-bodied person for a job rather than a person with a physical or mental handicap who could have done the job equally well. The word is formed on the same basis of racism and sexism.

ABM Anti-Ballistic Missile. A weapon designed to shoot down an incoming enemy missile. ABMs were developed and deployed by America and the Soviet Union in the 1960s and early 1970s to preserve a retaliatory capacity even in the event of a first strike by the other side. The menace from ABMs was effectively neutralized by the SALT I accord (*see* SALT) in 1972.

Abominable Snowman Name, popularized by Eric Shipton's Everest Expedition of 1951, for the yeti, a rare, elusive, and supposedly bearlike animal of the Himalayas. Sir Edmund Hillary found the alleged footprints of a yeti in 1960 and explained its elusiveness thus: "There is precious little in civilization to appeal to a yeti." *See also* BIGFOOT.

above-the-line Advertising expenditure on which a commission is payable to an advertising agency. This includes all mass-media advertising. **Below-the-line** advertising, on which no commission is payable, includes direct mail, free samples, and point of sale material. The distinction is arbitrary but reflects the way in which company profit and loss accounts are prepared, with a horizontal line separating entries that show how the profit or loss is calculated (above the line) from those that show how it has been used or distributed (below the line).

Absurd, Theatre of the A form of drama that jettisons the conventions of narrative plot and characterization to reflect the dramatist's belief in the meaninglessness of human existence. Absurdist theatre was first fully realized in Ionesco's *The Bald Prima Donna* (1948) and Beckett's *Waiting for Godot* (1952). In the latter work, two tramps wait in vain for the mysterious Godot, who never appears. Like all absurdist works, it hovers inconsequentially around the concepts of isolation, futility, and self-deception. The tramps' predicament is universal and the play's title has come to stand for that predicament. In his later works, Beckett reached the frontiers of the absurdist's world, with characters in bizarre settings and the minimal use of speech. For instance in *Happy Days* (1960), the main character, Winnie, is gradually immersed in sand, while *Breath* (1969) runs for just 30 seconds and includes sounds of both birth and death. Many of Harold Pinter's works, such as *The Room* (1957) and *The Caretaker* (1960), are described as absurdist or neo-absurdist.

abuse A well-established word that has taken on a new lease of life in the 20th century. It has acquired a sinister relevance in such combinations as **alcohol abuse**, **drug abuse**, **solvent abuse** (*see* GLUE SNIFFING), and CHILD ABUSE. The US psychiatrist Thomas Szasz (1920–) described **self-abuse** (masturbation) as "the primary sexual activity of mankind . . . ", concluding that "in the nineteenth century it was a disease; in the twentieth it's a cure."

Abwehr The German military intelligence service. It was led from 1935 by Admiral Wilhelm Canaris, who saw its authority increasingly curtailed before and during World War II. Hitler favoured the rival intelligence organizations, the SD (*Sicherheits-dienst*) and the SS (*Schutzstaffel*). As a consequence, the Abwehr became a focus of opposition to Hitler. Several of its leaders, including Canaris, were implicated in the 1944 plot to overthrow the Führer, and Hitler ordered that it be merged with the SD in February 1944.

Abyssinia! A catchphrase, dating from the time of the Abyssinian War (1935–36), to mean 'I'll be seeing you'.

ACAB All Coppers Are Bastards. An abbreviation much used in the 1950s and 1960s in graffiti and in slogans on clothing, as well as in chants at demonstrations and football matches.

acanthaster The **crown-of-thorns** starfish, which in the latter part of the 20th century was discovered to be posing a major threat to the survival of the world's coral reefs because of the destruction of its natural predator, the Pacific triton, by shell collectors. Feeding on coral, the acanthaster is capable of destroying 50 years worth of coral growth overnight; Australia's Great Barrier Reef is particularly at risk with a consequent significant loss in tourist revenue being reported in the 1980s.

Acapulco Gold A type of marijuana with golden leaves grown in the region around Acapulco, Mexico, and much prized for its potency. It was imported into America, particularly California, from the late 1960s.

ACAS Advisory Conciliation and Arbitration Service. In the UK, a government QUANGO set up in the 1970s to attempt to resolve industrial disputes before major damage could be done to the economic interests of the country.

accepted pairing In advertising, an admission that a rival's product has a particular strength in order to highlight the superior quality of that feature in one's own product.

accommodation collar US slang for an arrest made for motives not related to the alleged offence itself. Such an arrest is often made to meet a demand for police action and in the knowledge that the charges will fail for lack of evidence.

according to plan A catchphrase derived from communiqués issued during World War I, when the phrase became associated with official attempts to cover up military blunders and setbacks. It was thus employed ironically to describe things that did *not* go according to plan.

AC/DC Bisexual. The expression originated in America by analogy with electrical devices adaptable for either alternating or direct current. It became popular in the UK during the 1960s and early 1970s. Bisexual people are also said to 'swing both ways'. The sexual imagery of electricity is further elaborated in the tradition of 'male' and 'female' connectors in wiring etc.

ace The number one on playing cards or dice, from *as*, the Latin unit of weight. In World War I the French word, *as*, was applied to an airman who had brought down ten enemy aeroplanes; it was imported in its English equivalent, *ace*, and later extended to any especially expert flier, golfer, etc. Anything excellent or outstanding can now be referred to as 'ace'.

> Liverpool . . . the city of the Beatles, *Brookside* and an ace football team is poised to storm back into fashion.
>
> *The Independent*, 16 March 1991.

ace in the hole US expression for a reserve, often hidden, advantage or strength that is held until needed, especially for a crisis or opportunity, as in 'his friendship with the chairman is his ace in the hole'. It became popular in the 1920s and was derived from stud poker. A similar expression is 'ace up one's sleeve'.

acey-deucy US slang for partly good partly bad, or slightly dubious. Derived from a card game in which aces are high and twos (deuces) are low, it pre-dates World War II but is still sometimes heard.

acid A slang name for LSD.

acid bath murders The gruesome series of murders committed by John George Haigh in the 1940s. Haigh was arrested in 1949 for the murder of an elderly widow, Mrs Durand-Deacon, whom he had killed and whose body he dissolved in a bath of sulphuric acid. Haigh confessed to the crime, and to the murder of seven other people, two of which were fictitious. He claimed to have drained the blood from his victims prior to dissolving them, and to have drunk a cupful of blood from each. His plea of insanity was dismissed and he was hanged. The bath he used is preserved in Scotland Yard's Black Museum.

acid head One who is addicted to, and probably often mentally incapacitated by, LSD.

acid house or **house** A style of synthesized music with a repetitive hypnotic beat, originating from America and associated with the taking of hallucinogenic drugs, especially ECSTASY. As its popularity spread in the UK during the late 1980s, thousands of young people (many wearing 'A-c-e-e-e-d' T-shirts) congregated in deserted warehouses and club venues for all-night acid-house parties. These were frequently raided by the police in search of drugs, although party organizers and acid-house fans have always denied any drug connection. *See also* ORBITAL.

acid pad A place, particularly someone's home, where LSD, and probably other drugs, are regularly used.

acid rain Originally a term used to describe the heavily polluted rainfall in the Manchester area in the 19th century. Then, as now, it refers to rain containing sulphuric and nitric acids formed from sulphur dioxide and nitrogen oxides present in the atmosphere as a result of burning fossil fuels on an industrial scale. The combustion of petrol and oil in vehicles without cleaning the exhaust gases now also contributes these acid-forming oxides to the environment. It is believed that acid rain can destroy crops, trees, and fish as well as causing damage to buildings. In 1985, 19 countries agreed to reduce their emissions of sulphur dioxide by 30% by 1993.

acid rock A type of rock music popular in the 1960s and early 1970s involving amplified electronic effects and bizarre lighting, suggestive of disorientating hallucinatory drugs.

ack. ack-ack Slang from World Wars I and II meaning anti-aircraft guns (from signalling code for AA).

ack emma *See* PIP EMMA.

ackers (Egypt. *akka* currency unit) Money. This word has been used by the British forces and the working class since the 1920s, but re-emerged in the 1980s along with other humorous synonyms for money including **spondulicks** and **rhino** in the speech of middle-class imitators.

ACORN A Classification of Residential Neighbourhoods, a directory of 39 different neighbourhoods in the UK, used by companies selling goods or services on the assumption that the inhabitants of particular neighbourhoods are likely to have similar interests and disposable incomes. It is much used by door-to-door and telephone salespeople offering swimming pools, double glazing, insurance, finance, etc. It also provides information on which areas to omit in a sales drive.

acqua alta (It. high water) Italian term used of the water that periodically floods central Venice. The city was badly damaged in such floods in November 1966. In the late 1960s, in an attempt to prevent further inundations (and to halt the city's rapid deterioration in the late 20th-century from air pollution), UNES-

CO launched a programme of scientific and technical research. A series of flood barriers is also planned for the city. The *Venice in Peril* campaign aims to promote the city's protection.

Acrobat The codename for a British offensive into Tripolitania, N Africa, in late 1941. The plan to capture Tripoli was frustrated by Rommel, and by January 1942 the British, led by Auchinleck, were forced to retreat.

acrophobe A person who is afraid of heights. The name became increasingly relevant in the 20th century with the building of SKYSCRAPERS.

action. action level The amount of a toxic or other undesirable substance in a foodstuff that warrants official investigation in America.

Action Man A nickname acquired by Prince Charles in the years before his marriage to Lady Diana Spencer in 1981. Derived from the tradename of a toy soldier figure, it referred humorously to the prince's adventurous lifestyle, which included service in the Royal Navy and various sporting interests.

action painting A term coined by the US art critic Harold Rosenberg in 1952 to describe works produced by a group of Abstract Expressionists, the best known of whom were Jackson Pollock and Willem de Kooning. The style is characterized by dynamic spontaneous gestures, spilling, spattering, and dripping paint onto canvas laid on the floor. The finished work is intended to reflect a creative interplay between the artist and his materials, free from the constraints of preconceived form or subject matter. It placed more value in the act of creation rather than in the final product.

> On the floor I am more at ease, I feel nearer, more a part of the painting, since this way I can walk around it, work from the four sides and literally be 'in' the painting.
>
> JACKSON POLLOCK, in 1947, quoted in Tomassoni's *Pollock* (1968).

> Abstract Expressionism was invented by New York drunks.
>
> JONI MITCHELL, interview on BBC television, 1985.

action replay The repetition of a section of a TV broadcast, usually in SLOW MOTION, to analyse a key moment in a sports event such as a goal, winning putt, etc.

Actors' Studio The New York-based workshop for professional actors founded in 1947 by Elia Kazan, Robert Lewis, and Cheryl Crawford. Under the artistic direction of Lee Strasberg (from 1948), the Studio became known as the US home of the acting technique known as the METHOD and nurtured many leading theatre and film stars, including Marlon Brando. The Studio is primarily a forum for exploration and experimentation, away from the pressures of commercial production. The costs are met by voluntary subscription, and membership is by invitation following audition.

actress. as the actress said to the bishop An expression added to what seems a perfectly straight-forward innocent remark to create a sexual double entendre. Typical examples might include "I never knew I had it in me" or "I'd bend over backwards to please you". The phrase was popular in the RAF in the 1940s, although its origin is said to be Edwardian. An alternative form of this expression is **as the art mistress said to the gardener**, which was popularized by the British actress Beryl Reid when playing the part of Monica in the BBC radio series *Educating Archie* (broadcast in the 1950s).

AD Drug Addict. An abbreviation used mostly in America by both drug addicts and the police. It is formed by taking the first two letters of addict, or by reversing the initial letters of the two words, thereby distinguishing it from DA for District Attorney. DA, however, was the more fashionable expression in the UK in the 1960s.

ad. admass Coined by J. B. Priestley in *Journey Down a Rainbow* (1955) to describe the vast mid-20th-century proliferation of commercial advertising and high-pressure salesmanship, especially in America. The word has now come to mean the vast mass of the general public to which advertisers address their publicity.

adperson An employee in the advertising business.

advertorial An article in a newspaper or magazine that appears to be editorial matter but on closer examination, is intended to promote a particular product or service. *See also* PLUGUMENTARY.

Ada A computer-programming language developed for the US Department of Defense. It was named after Augusta Ada Lovelace, daughter of Lord Byron, wife of the Earl of Lovelace, and co-worker of Charles Babbage (1792–1871), the British mathematician. Babbage is given credit for the invention of computers as he built a calculating machine regarded as the forerunner of the electronic computer. The machine is preserved, unfinished, in the Science Museum in London.

Adam *See* ECSTASY.

Adams, Bodkin *See* BLUEBEARD OF EASTBOURNE.

ADAPTS Air Deliverable Antipollution Transfer System. A system of dealing with oil pollution employed by the US coastguard. The system relies upon entrapping the oil with inflatable nylon bags and then pumping it off the water.

admiral. Admiral's Cup The trophy presented by the Admiral of the Royal Ocean Racing Club to the winners of the biennial series of races for yachts in the 29–60 foot class. The three-boat teams compete in five races along the English Channel, including the famous FASTNET Race. The competition was inaugurated in 1957, when a British team won the trophy.

The Admiral of the Atlantic salutes the Admiral of the Pacific A telegram from the German emperor Wilhelm II to Czar Nicholas II in 1905. Sent during a naval exercise, it reflected Germany's determination to assert itself as a world power, a desire that contributed to the outbreak of World War I.

advance man A public relations officer who paves the way for a politician on a campaign tour. The term was formerly used of publicity agents for touring circuses and similar entertainment troupes.

adventure playground A children's playground furnished with climbing frames and other equipment, especially designed to encourage exploration and develop physical skills.

AE The pseudonym of the Irish poet and playwright George William Russell (1867–1935). It was derived as a contraction of his one-time signature 'aeon'. Russell's output was considerable and varied and includes several volumes of poetry and the play *Deirdre* (1902). He also helped found Dublin's ABBEY THEATRE.

aequorin A secretion produced by the jellyfish *Aequorea aequorea*. Its luminous qualities make it useful in microscopy.

aerial ping-pong A facetious name for Australian Rules Football, in which much of the game is played in the air because of the high jumps and kicks involved in the style of play.

aero-. aerobics (Gk. *aer* air, *bios* life) Programmes of exercise designed to improve the body's uptake of oxygen and thus benefit general health. Aerobic exercises first became popular in the 1960s and soon won converts throughout the western world; noted proponents of the system have included the film actress Jane Fonda.

aerogram An airmail letter in the form of a sheet of thin paper which can be folded and posted overseas.

aerophobe A person who is petrified of air travel. The term was first coined in the 1960s.

aerosol A type of pressurized spray can much used in perfumery, polishes, paints, etc. until the 1980s. The use of chlorofluorocarbons (*see* CFC) as propellants in aerosols caused concern when it was alleged that the proliferation of such substances in the atmosphere was damaging the OZONE LAYER. New NONAEROSOLS were developed in response to public doubts.

Aertex A type of fabric woven into a pattern of small squares and widely used for clothing in the mid-20th century. Originally a tradename (belonging to William Hollins and Company), constructed from the words *airy* and *texture*, it is now used loosely for any material of a similar kind; the fabric itself was first invented in 1888.

aestheticienne A female beautician; an anglicized form of the French *esthéticienne*, which has the same meaning. There has always been a marked French influence on the beauty and fashion worlds of the UK and America and this tendency, with its overtones of Parisian elegance and luxury, increased as the cosmetics industry became more competitive and more profitable in the 1960s.

affluence. Affluent Society A phrase, popular from the later 1950s, denoting the overall growth in material prosperity of British society. It is measured by the increasingly widespread ownership of cars, television sets, washing machines, refrigerators, etc. in a society further cushioned by its 'free' social services. J. K. Galbraith's *The Affluent Society* was published in 1958.

affluenza A new coinage derived by combining affluence and influenza to describe a condition originating in America and affecting those who have so much money and so many possessions that their mental health has suffered. The resulting psychological changes and disturbances are seen as the symptoms of affluenza.

Afghanistanism Journalists' slang for unusual interest in events in remote parts of the world over and above happenings at home. The term was first used in the 1950s but acquired new relevance when Soviet troops invaded Afghanistan in 1980.

Africa. Afrikaans A language of South Africa that has evolved from the Dutch originally spoken by 17th-century settlers and their descendants, the Afrikaaners. It had become distinct as a spoken language by 1800, and in 1925 was made an official South African language (with English).

Afrika Korps The combined force of two armoured divisions and one infantry division that was led to devastating effect by Erwin Rommel (*see* DESERT FOX) as part of the German offensive in North Africa during World War II. Formed in Feburary 1941, the Korps enjoyed a string of military successes until halted and ultimately repulsed at ALAMEIN. The Korps finally surrendered in May 1943, although Rommel had been ordered home by Hitler in March.

African. African lager Guinness. So called in some London pubs in the 1970s, because the most popular beer in the pubs of Southern England was lager and Guinness is black.

African National Congress *See* ANC.

African woodbine A cannabis cigarette, a reefer, a joint. Woodbines are a cheap brand of cigarettes that were especially popular in the 1950s and 1960s.

Afro A large spherical bushy haircut of tight curls popular with Black people in the 1960s and 1970s, also imitated by Whites during this period.

Afroism Sympathy with the culture and interests of Black Africa. In some definitions it includes the promotion of BLACK POWER.

Afro-Saxon Any Black person who is seen as a collaborator with the white community.

after. afterbirth (1) Army and school slang for rhubarb, used in both the UK and America. (2) A rare US expression for excessive paperwork.

after you, Claude – no, after you, Cecil The catchphrase of the broker's men Cecil and Claude in the BBC radio comedy 'ITMA', which was very popular during the 1940s.

Agadir Crisis The dispute between France and Germany triggered by the despatch of the German warship *Panther* to the Moroccan port of Agadir in July 1911. Germany held that this was needed to protect German interests in response to the arrival of French troops in Morocco. The affair raised tensions throughout Europe but was settled by an agreement signed between France and Germany on 4 November. However, hostility between the two nations remained, while the crisis served to strengthen Franco-British relations.

ageism Discrimination on the grounds of age, usually referring to the older rather than the younger members of the community. Coined by Dr. Robert Butler, director of the Institute of Aging, by analogy to racism, the term is most commonly applied in the field of employment. Discrimination on the grounds of age is particularly prevalent in times of wide unemployment as in the 1980s in the UK.

agenbite of inwit Remorse of conscience. The phrase was popularized in the 20th century by James Joyce in the novel *Ulysses* (1922) and was widely heard in the UK in the 1960s. Joyce in turn derived it from a medieval manuscript, the *Ayenbite of Inwyte*.

Agent Orange A defoliant used in jungle war, especially by US forces in the VIETNAM WAR, during which it gained its name as its containers had orange rings painted round them. It is highly toxic to humans. Chemically it consists of 2,4,5-trichlorophenoxyethanoic acid. Less toxic versions were **Agent Blue, Agent Purple,** and **Agent White.**

aggiornamento (It. bringing up to date) The liberalization of policy that was officially sanctioned in the Roman Catholic church in the 1960s. It was the main feature of the Vatican Council of 1962–65 and the result of pressure by Pope John XXIII and Pope Paul VI to reform the church in line with developments in the modern world. It included reform of the liturgy and promotion of the ecumenical movement.

aggro Aggressive trouble-making; in the 1960s and 1970s aggro was associated with thuggish behaviour, football hooliganism, etc., but in later usage it was employed in the less threatening sense of mild irritation, as in 'I don't need this kind of aggro'.

agit-. agitpop The use of pop music to put across a political message. The pop star Billy Bragg, for example, has used his music to espouse many left-wing causes. The word derives from the Russian AGITPROP.

agitprop (Russ. *agitatsiya propaganda* agitation propaganda) A term coined by Georgy Plekhanov and later elaborated by Lenin in *What Is To Be Done* (1902). 'Agitation' implied the use of political slogans and half-truths to exploit mass grievances and mould public opinion while 'propaganda' meant to employ rational, scientific, and historical arguments to enlighten the educated and provide for the political training and indoctrination of Communist party members. In 1920 the Department of Agitation and Propaganda was established by the Central Committee of the CPSU; in its various forms it has controlled internal and external Soviet Communist party propaganda ever since. The term is also used more loosely to refer to any dramatic, literary, or artistic work, both at home and abroad, intended to promote Communist ideology.

Agnewism The policies and political ideas espoused by the US vice-president Spiro T. Agnew (1918–). Agnew was particularly noted for his attacks on the critics of the president, Richard Nixon, and for his support of law and order. He resigned his office in 1973 after a federal tax case and was given a fine and a suspended prison sentence.

agony. agonizing reappraisal The process of restarting a project from scratch because its first realisation has been a failure. The term first appeared in a speech made by John Foster Dulles, US Secretary of State, at a NATO meeting in 1954. In common with many clichés it had a short vogue before proving to be ephemeral.

agony aunt A woman who conducts an advice column or page in a newspaper or magazine (especially a women's magazine) and often appears on television or radio answering correspondents who seek help with their problems. Most of the letters are from girls and women and are mainly concerned with family relationships, marital problems, sex, and boy friends. The male equivalent is, inevitably, an **agony uncle**.

agony column Originally, a column in a newspaper containing advertisements for missing relatives and friends. Now commonly applied to the columns in which an AGONY AUNT offers advice.

agronomics The branch of economics that is concerned with agriculture and the agricultural distribution and management of land. The related discipline of **agronomy** is concerned with crop production in relation to soil management and the cultivation of land. The commercial aspects of farming are sometimes summarized as **agribusiness**.

AGS Abort Guidance System. A FAIL-SAFE mechanism that comes into operation when the primary guidance system of a spacecraft fails.

aha reaction A term used in psychology for a sudden insight in solving a problem. First heard in the 1970s, it replaced such earlier equivalents as the **aha experience** and the **ah-ah experience**, heard in the 1940s and 1950s.

ahh Bisto! A trade slogan for gravy browning. It was first used by the Cerebos company in an advertising campaign of 1919. The name 'Bisto' is said to have been derived from the additional slogan 'Browns, Seasons, Thickens in One'. Two cartoon characters who appear in advertising for the product became known as 'the Bisto kids'.

AI Artificial Insemination. This involves semen from a male being injected into a female to cause pregnancy. The technique was developed by Soviet livestock breeders in the early 20th century and is now widely used in the agricultural industry, especially for breeding cattle, as it enables rapid improvements in the genetic quality of a herd and better control of venereal disease. With the development of research to solve the problems of human infertility, the practice of AI was extended to humans (*see* AID; AIH; IVF; SPERM BANK).

AID Artificial Insemination by Donor. AID is used in cases in which the male of a couple trying to conceive is infertile and semen from an unidentified doner is injected into the female partner. Because of the similarity between the abbreviations AID and AIDS, the name for this procedure was changed to *donor insemination*, the abbreviation DI thus avoiding any possible association with the disease. *Compare* AIH.

Aids Acquired immune deficiency syndrome, a condition resulting from infection by the human immunodeficiency virus (HIV), first identified in 1983. The virus creates a deficiency of the white blood cells that combat infection and so renders the body vulnerable to a wide range of infections and other disorders, such as pneumonia and cancer, which are then frequently fatal. The virus is transmitted by blood, semen, or vaginal fluids. Originally those most at risk were thought to be homosexual or bisexual men; drug-users who injected drugs intravenously, often with dirty needles; haemophiliacs and others who had received transfusions of contaminated blood or of coagulation factor VIII before the risk was identified in 1986; those who had had casual sexual relationships in sub-Saharan Africa, where the virus is thought to have originated; and the babies of infected mothers. Now, however, as the disease has spread further into the community, HIV is known to be spread also by heterosexual intercourse, particularly by infected men to women. These findings have resulted in the advocacy of CONDOMS to promote safer sex. There have also been campaigns to reduce promiscuity and drug abuse, although these are thought to have been only partially successful.

Aids terrorists People who know that they are infected with HIV but deliberately have unprotected sex with unsuspecting partners. The intention of the Aids terrorist is to take revenge on the rest of humankind for being infected by the virus.

AIH Artificial Insemination by Husband (*see* AI). This is usually used in cases in which a couple are unable to have children because the male is unable to have normal sexual intercourse, usually because of impotence: semen from the husband (or male partner) is then injected into the woman. *Compare* AID.

aikido (Jap.) A Japanese martial art that became popular in the western world in the late 20th century. An ancient Japanese form of self-defence, it demands great mental concentration.

AIM American Indian Movement. A US pressure group founded by American Indians in 1968 in an attempt to defend their civil rights. The organization seeks to redress wrongs done to Indians by the state in the 19th and 20th centuries.

Aim Archie at the Armitage Australian slang meaning to urinate (of males). Armitage ware is a well-known brand of lavatory bowl. This phrase is a later version of 'point Percy at the porcelain', taken from the cartoon series *Barry McKenzie* by Barry Humphries, which appeared in the magazine *Private Eye* in the UK in the 1970s.

air. **airbag** An inflatable plastic bag that is designed to prevent passengers in a car from hitting the windscreen in the event of an accident. The bag inflates instantly from its storage position beneath the dashboard.

air bridge An airline route between two airports that provides a regular link between them. *See also* BERLIN AIRLIFT.

aircraft By the end of the 19th century two things had happened to bring man close to his dream of creating a heavier-than-air machine. The first was a sufficient grasp of aerodynamics to understand that emulating the wing-flapping of birds was not the way to do it; the second was the advent of Otto's internal-combustion engine to provide the power required. It was the WRIGHT BROTHERS who made use of Otto Lilienthal's gliding experience and Otto's engine to introduce the powered flight that has revolutionized not only travel and warfare in this century, but also international relations and the world economy; indeed, it has had repercussions in almost every field of human activity. Despite rapid developments in the early years of the century – only six years separate the Wright Brothers' first twelve-second trip in 1903 and Blériot's cross-channel flight in 1909 – until World War I a 'flying machine' was still regarded as something of a circus attraction; few would have predicted the major role aircraft play in modern life. The war, in which aircraft were used initially for reconnaissance and then as bombers and then as fighters to destroy the bombers, was a great stimulus to technical innovation, forcing governments to take the potential of aviation seriously (*see* FOKKER; HANDLEY PAGE BOMBER; SOPWITH CAMEL). Public fascination with flying remained strong in the inter-war era, owing largely to a succession of record-breaking flights, such as those by LINDBERGH and Amy Johnson (*see* QUEEN OF THE AIR). The 1920s and 1930s also saw the development of commercial civil aviation, although the first transatlantic service was not introduced until 1939. In World War II heavy bombers inflicted unprecedented levels of devastation on civilian populations, but airpower did not play the decisive role that many had predicted. The main post-war development has been the advent of the jet engine and the virtual disappearance of the propeller from modern commercial aeroplanes. Jets have enabled very large aircraft (*see* JUMBO JET) to fly faster, more economically, and high enough to be above the weather. CONCORDE, the only supersonic commercial plane in service, flies from London to New York in three hours – a trip that took 2–3 weeks by sailing ship. The shrinking of the world into a GLOBAL VILLAGE has enabled the average UK family to spend their annual holiday in the Mediterranean, Africa, or America, which would have been undreamt of only 70 years ago. *See also* ALCOCK AND BROWN; HURRICANE; MACH NUMBER; SPITFIRE.

air cushion vehicle *See* HOVERCRAFT.

air-dance A euphemism for death by hanging used by police and criminals alike in the UK before the abolition of capital punishment in 1965.

air hall A temporary plastic structure erected over outdoor swimming pools, tennis courts, etc. to guarantee good playing conditions in any weather.

airhead Every age has a series of disparaging terms for someone who is a fool – at least in the opinion of the user of the word. Airhead came to prominence in the UK in the 1980s and is clearly based on the suggestion that the person so described has a head full of air where his brain should be.

airlift An organized manoeuvre to transport troops or stores to a destination by air. *See* BERLIN AIRLIFT.

airmiss A near collision by two or more aircraft flying at less than a prescribed distance apart.

air piracy The seizing of an aircraft by hijackers, also called **skyjacking** (*see* HIJACK).

airplane cloth A type of strong unbleached linen originally used for airplane wings in World War I. It was not long before the cloth, made in various gauges and colours, came to be used for clothing and other fashion items.

airspace Radio-frequency channels used for broadcasting.

AI radar Aircraft Interceptor radar. A British radar system developed during World War II to enable fighter pilots to intercept enemy aircraft at night. Ground control used high-power radar installations to direct fighters to positions close to the enemy craft, where the pilot could pick up the enemy plane on his own low-power cockpit radar. The first victim of the system was a German Ju-88, shot down in July 1940.

aisle sitters US theatre critics. In the UK, an 'aisle' usually refers to the passage between the pews of a church; in America the phrase is applied to any kind of gangway in public buildings, aircraft, trains, etc. In a theatre, an aisle sitter can escape from a boring play before the end or leave to send copy to his newspaper without disturbing other theatregoers.

aka Also known as. An abbreviation used in America for an assumed name, particularly a false name used by criminals (as *alias* is used in the UK).

Akela The adult leader of a Cub Scout troop, derived from the name of the leader of a wolf pack in Kipling's *Jungle Book*. Cub Scouts greet their leader with the shout 'Akela we will do our best'. *See* BOY SCOUTS.

Alain-Fournier Pseudonym of Henri-Alban-Fournier (1886–1914), French writer whose only completed novel *Le Grand Meaulnes* (1913; *The Lost Domain*, 1959) is a classic evocation of the yearning to recapture the cherished landscape of childhood. The novel is an entrancing blend of nostalgia and realism, set in rural France in the 1890s, in which the hero spends his life searching for a house and a beautiful girl, encountered as an adolescent running away from home. The heroine is modelled on a girl, Yvonne, whom the novelist met briefly in 1905. Fournier was killed in the first Battle of the Marne and his body was never recovered. *Le Grand Meaulnes* created a literary sensation when 'rediscovered' in the 1980s.

> I like the marvellous only when it is strictly enveloped in reality; not when it upsets or exceeds it.
> ALAIN-FOURNIER, in a letter of 1911.

Alamein, Battles of El- Two battles fought during World War II near El-Alamein, some 60 miles W of Alexandria in Egypt. The first Battle of El-Alamein took place during July 1942, when Britain's Eighth Army (*see* DESERT RATS) finally succeeded in halting the eastward advance of

Rommel's AFRIKA KORPS. Rommel's forces were weary and in need of re-supply after their rapid advance, while the British, under Claude Auchinleck, had the benefit of fresh troops and equipment.

In August of that year, General Bernard Law Montgomery replaced Auchinleck as British commander, and during September and October British and other Allied forces were greatly reinforced. The second Battle of El-Alamein started on 23 October 1942 with the launch of the British offensive. Rommel, returning from convalescence in Austria, reached the front on October 25 and directed a skilful defence, inflicting heavy casualties on the British. However, the numerical superiority of the British tanks and their secure supply lines eventually told, and Rommel began his retreat from El-Alamein on 4 November. Soon, as a famous communiqué of the time put it, Rommel was 'motoring westwards in top gear'. El-Alamein proved to be a decisive turning-point in the Allies' North African campaign.

> Before Alamein we never had a victory. After Alamein we never had a defeat.
>
> WINSTON CHURCHILL, *The Hinge of Fate*, ch. 33.

Alamogordo The US air base in New Mexico where the first atomic bomb was detonated on 16 July 1945.

alas, my poor brother A catchphrase borrowed from a Bovril advertisement in the 1920s. The exclamation, with its echoes of Hamlet's famous line, is uttered by a bovine lamenting the transformation of an erstwhile sibling into a tin of the beefy beverage.

Alaska highway A scenic route covering 2451 km (1523 miles) through the Yukon between Dawson Creek, British Columbia and Fairbanks, Alaska. The highway was built in 1942 by US Army engineers as an overland military supply route to Alaska.

Albanization The voluntary political and economic isolation of a country. Albania has been noted for deliberately avoiding contact with the West, the other members of the Communist bloc, and later, even China (its former ally). Its isolation and its siege economy have resulted in its widespread poverty.

Albert A character invented by Stanley Holloway (1890–1982) in one of his comic verse monologues; he was swallowed by a lion and lived to tell the tale. *Albert's Reunion* (1978) describes a further encounter with the beast:

> You've heard of Albert Ramsbottom
> And Mrs Ramsbottom and Dad
> And the trouble the poor lion went to
> Trying to stomach the lad.

Alcatraz A small island in San Francisco Bay and the site of an infamous top-security prison. The island became a US possession in 1851 and was shortly after made the home for a military correction centre. The military prison erected in 1909 was transferred to the federal prison authorities in 1933. Until its closure in 1963, Alcatraz held some of America's most notorious criminals, including Al CAPONE and Machine-Gun Kelly. The regime was harsh: inmates were kept in solitary confinement in cells measuring 2.7 m by 1.5 m (9ft by 5ft). Escape was made virtually impossible by the freezing waters and dangerous currents surrounding the island. One inmate, the murderer Robert Strand, studied birds during his incarceration and was the subject of the 1961 film, *The Birdman of Alcatraz*. The empty prison buildings are now a tourist attraction.

Alcock and Brown The pioneering aviation partnership consisting of Captain John Alcock (1892–1919) and Lieutenant Arthur Whitten Brown (1886–1948), which in 1919 achieved the first air crossing of the Atlantic. The challenge was set by a *Daily Mail* offer of £10,000; Alcock and Brown, both heroes of World War I, were recruited by Vickers to fly a converted Vimy bomber from Newfoundland to Ireland. After months of preparation they set off (accompanied by Brown's toy cat Twinkletoes). During the next 16 hours 27 minutes they were beset by thick fog, lost all radio contact, survived an engine fire, were caught in a storm, were forced to climb out on the wing to free the air intakes of snow, and finally crash-landed in a peat bog, which they mistook for a field. Both fliers were knighted within the week and hailed as national heroes. Sadly, Alcock died in an air accident six months later; Brown was shattered by the news and never flew again.

Alcoholics Anonymous An organization founded in 1935 by two Americans to help alcoholics control their addiction. The stockbroker William Griffith Wilson ('Bill W') and the surgeon Robert Holbrook Smith ('Dr. Bob S') originated the now famous programme of self-help based on small groups of sufferers sharing their experiences and giving mutual support. No fees are paid and members are known only by their first names and initial of their surnames. The British offshoot of AA was founded in 1947; there are now over 2300 groups in the UK.

Aldeburgh A small coastal town in Suffolk that hosts an annual music festival established by Benjamin Britten, Peter Pears, and their friends in 1948. The festival developed out of Britten's association with the English Opera Group, a small troupe of singers and musicians for whom many of his works were written. Aldeburgh and the nearby Maltings at Snape became an important venue for introducing Britten's new operas to the public.

Aldermaston Marches A series of Easter protest marches (1958–63) sponsored by CND close to the site of the Atomic Weapons Research Establishment at Aldermaston, Berkshire. At their peak they attracted between 50,000 and 150,000 supporters.

Aldis lamp A portable lamp for signalling in Morse code, named after its inventor A. C. W. Aldis.

Aldwych farce One of a series of plays written by Ben Travers (1886–1980) and staged at the Aldwych Theatre, London, between 1925 and 1933. The series began with *A Cuckoo in the Nest* (1925) and featured a regular cast headed by Robertson Hare, Mary Brough, Tom Walls, and Ralph Lynn.

aleatorism The incorporation of an element of chance in the performance of music.

A level The advanced level of the General Certificate of Education. It is higher than the ordinary level and GCSE. A levels came under increasing criticism from reformers in the 1980s and early 1990s as being too specialized but the examinations have been defended by Conservative government ministers as the 'Jewel in the Crown' of the British secondary education system; they remain the only route to university entrance. However, to broaden the curriculum of sixth formers, in 1989 AS-level (advanced supplementary level) were also introduced.

Alexander technique A form of physiotherapy based on the teachings of F. M. Alexander (d. 1955) which emphasises the importance of correct physical posture in maintaining good health.

Alexandra Day A day in June when rose emblems are sold for the hospital fund inaugurated in 1912 by Queen Alexandra (1844–1925), Danish consort of Edward VII, to celebrate the fiftieth year of her residence in England.

Alexbow A form of ship's bow that was designed in 1968 to facilitate a vessel's progress through ice by lifting the ice upwards. It was named after its Canadian inventor, Scott Alexander.

alfalfa US prison slang for tobacco, money, or marijuana. Alfalfa is a plant commonly used as cattle food.

'alf a mo, Kaiser Catchphrase from a British recruiting poster of World War I, depicting a British soldier pausing for a cigarette before resuming the fight.

Al Fatah (Arab. the victory) One of the most powerful factions of the PLO. Under its leader Yassir Arafat (1929–) it has organized the guerrilla campaign against Israel despite suffering many internal divisions. It was founded in the late 1950s.

Alf Garnett The central character in BBC TV's comedy series 'Till Death Us Do part' (first seen in 1967) and its sequels. Played by Warren Mitchell (1926–), Alf Garnett was soon established as the archetypal working-class bigot – patriotic, racist, sexist, arrogant, and reactionary. He found a US counterpart in ARCHIE BUNKER.

Algeciras Conference A conference of European powers held in the Spanish port of Algeciras in 1906 to settle the issue of Moroccan sovereignty. France wanted to establish a protectorate over Morocco, a move strongly opposed by Germany. Tension had been increased in 1905 by a visit to Morocco by Kaiser Wilhelm II. The Conference ended in March, guaranteeing Moroccan independence and ensuring free access for all nations but giving a special role to France and Spain in policing.

Algerie française (Fr. Algeria is French) The rallying cry of the colonial French in Algeria who opposed moves to Algerian independence during the 1950s and early 1960s.

Algol ALGOrithmic Language. A high-level computer programming language developed in the 1950s (and issued in 1960) for mathematical and scientific problems.

Algonquin Round Table A group of noted US wits who met regularly to dine and exchange witticisms at New York's Algonquin Hotel in the interwar years. They included Dorothy Parker and Robert Benchley. On one occasion Dorothy Parker left her place at the Round Table saying "Excuse me, I have to go to the bathroom." After a pause, she added "I really have to telephone, but I'm too embarrassed to say so."

Alice blue A pale-blue shade named after Alice Roosevelt Longworth (daughter of Theodore Roosevelt), who was particularly fond of it. Joseph McCarthy wrote a song called 'Alice Blue Gown'.

> In my sweet little Alice blue gown
> When I first wandered out in the town...

Ali shuffle The fleetness of foot in the ring for which the former world heavyweight boxing champion Cassius Clay (later MUHAMMED ALI) became famous.

> Float like a butterfly
> Sting like a bee.
> MUHAMMED ALI, summarizing his boxing style.

aliyah (Hebrew. ascent) The mass immigration of Jews from all over the world to Israel after the new state won independence in 1948. *See* OLIM.

Alka-Seltzer An effervescent antacid preparation. Actually a tradename belonging to Miles Laboratories and made with medicinal mineral water from Nieder-Selters in Germany, the product's name is now often applied to any similar preparation.

all. all because the lady loves Milk Tray A highly successful trade slogan used in advertising campaigns for Cadbury's Milk Tray chocolates. Television adverts for the product, featuring a black-clad stuntman who performed various daring feats to deliver a box of chocolates to the lady in question, have been much parodied but have remained substantially unchanged for 20 years or more.

All Blacks The New Zealand International Rugby Union Football team (so-called from their all-black strip), which first played in England in 1905.

All Souls' Parish Magazine *The Times* was so nicknamed during the editorship (1923–41) of G. G. Dawson, Fellow of All Souls College, Oxford. He and some of his associates, who were also fellows of the college, frequently met there for discussions.

all systems go A catchphrase of the 1960s and 1970s, meaning a state of readiness for imminent action. It derived from its use during the launch of US space missions to indicate that all the craft's components were working normally. As interest in space flight waned by the end of the 1970s, so did the use of such phrases.

all-terrain vehicle or **ATV** A motor-vehicle that is specially designed for rapid transport over rough ground. ATVs include such vehicles as **dune-buggies**, intended chiefly for recreation; others include **snowcats** and various **moon buggies**.

all the president's men *See under* PRESIDENT.

allergy A medical condition in which the body reacts abnormally to a certain foreign substance, known as an **allergen**. Although the condition has been known since World War I, people have become more aware of its existence and importance since the 1960s. Hayfever, asthma, and such skin disorders as dermatitis are well-known conditions caused by allergic reactions, but the late 20th-century interest in ALTERNATIVE MEDICINE has revealed many more, some of then related to diet. A major problem with allergies is the length of time required to identify the causative allergen, since all potential allergens (of which there are vast numbers) must be separately tested. The ultimate allergic response was identified in the 1980s – **total allergy syndrome**, a debilitating illness ascribed to an allergy to a combination of various fabrics, chemicals, foodstuffs, etc. Sufferers are sometimes described as 'allergic to the 20th century'.

alley cat A pejorative term for a person of either sex who favours a wild and promiscuous street life, used often in the phrase 'to have the morals of an alley cat'. It was originally a pre-World War II US expression, but has been heard in the UK and Australia since the 1960s.

Allies Those countries allied against Germany in World War I, notably the UK, France, Italy, Russia, and America; in World War II those 49 nations allied against the AXIS states, including the UK and the Commonwealth countries, America, the Soviet Union, China, and France.

alligator In Black US JAZZ slang, a white musician, dancer, or fan of jazz music (first heard in the 1930s).

alligator shoes Shoes that gape at the toes in a manner reminiscent of an alligator's jaws. The name is a facetious reference to the extremely expensive and fashionable shoes made from that creature's skin.

See you later, alligator A catchphrase that was first heard in America in the 1930s. As the title of a ROCK 'N' ROLL hit by Bill Haley and the Comets, the phrase won an even wider audience. The usual response was 'In a while, crocodile'.

Ally Pally A familiar and affectionate name for the Alexandra Palace in North London, which became the site of the world's first television transmitter when it was acquired by the BBC in 1936. It opened in 1863 but burnt down and was rebuilt in 1873; in World War I it was used as a barracks. In 1956 it witnessed the first experiments with colour television. It was devastated by another disastrous fire in July 1980, but much of it has been rebuilt and it now contains a skating rink and a winter garden.

alone. I want to be alone Catchphrase associated with the Swedish-born US film actress Greta Garbo (Greta Gustafson; 1905–90). She said the words in *Grand Hotel* (1932) and, in conjunction with her aloof beauty and reclusive lifestyle, they became one of the best known of all cinema legends.

> Garbo's temperament reflected the rain and gloom of the long dark Swedish winters.
>
> LILLIAN GISH.

You're never alone with a Strand Trade slogan associated with a much-acclaimed but commercially disastrous advertising campaign of 1960. The aim of the slogan, commissioned for the launch of the cheap new Strand cigarette, was to identify with contemporary rebellious and rejected youth. The cigarette failed to sell but the advert, and the actor (Terence Brook) who appeared in it, were greatly admired.

Alte, der (Ger. The Old Man) The nickname given to Konrad Adenauer (1876–1967), who was one of the chief architects of postwar Germany. His nickname referred to the fact that when he became Chancellor he was already 73 years of age.

alternative A buzz-word, common in the later part of the 20th century, to describe anything that offers an alternative to the usual or conventional form of that thing. **Alternative lifestyle** and **alternative comedy** are examples of this usage.

alternative energy Energy derived from sources other than conventional finite mineral resources and therefore sometimes called renewable energy sources. Their attraction is that they conserve resources of fossil fuels, do not involve the dangers of nuclear power, and cause no pollution. Alternative energy sources include HYDROELECTRIC POWER, SOLAR POWER, WIND POWER, TIDAL POWER, WAVE POWER, GEOTHERMAL ENERGY, and BIOMASS energy. It has been estimated that with the appropriate expenditure on research and development, some 20% of the UK's energy requirements could be met by renewable sources by 2025.

alternative medicine or **complementary medicine** A treatment for physical or mental illness that exists outside conventional medical practice. It is usually sough by patiants suffering from cancer, back pain, migraine, allergies, etc., in which orthodox medicine has failed to produce a cure or to alleviate symptoms.

Its methods include acupuncture, AROMATHERAPY, faith healing, herbalism, homeopathy, hypnosis, naturopathy, osteopathy, and REFLEXOLOGY. The effectiveness of such therapies, which is largely unamenable to scientific assessment, is controversial. Alternative medicine is often known as **fringe** or **unorthodox medicine**. *See also* HOLISTIC MEDICINE.

Alternative Services Book The controversial plain-English alternative forms of service of the Church of England published in 1980.

Since the 1960s *The Book of Common Prayer* has been increasingly displaced by alternative forms of service commonly known as Series 1, Series 2, and Series 3. The *Alternative Services Book* of 1980 contains three alternative forms of Communion Service; namely, revised versions of Series 1 and 2 (largely based on the *Book of Common Prayer*) and the more controversial Series 3 (Revised) in modern English. The other services are all in the Series 3 idiom, those for the Visitation and Communion of the Sick being dropped. None of the readings (formerly called *lessons*) is from the Authorized Version of the Bible and perhaps more properly it should have been called "The Replacement Service Book", although this was not supposed to be the intention.

alternative society Any society based on a set of values that do not conform with those of conventional society.

Altmark, The In the Royal Navy an opprobious synonym for a ship or an establishment with a reputation for very strict discipline. It derives from a famous naval exploit of February 1940 when Captain Philip Vian, commanding the destroyer HMS *Cossack*, entered Norwegian territorial waters to effect the release of 299 British prisoners of war from the German auxiliary-cum-prison ship *Altmark*, which had taken refuge in Josing Fjord. The boarding party was led by Lieutenant Bradwell Turner whose cry "The Navy's here!" was widely imitated for years afterwards as a reassurance to anyone in trouble.

Alzheimer's disease A degenerative disease of the brain first described by the German neurologist Alois Alzheimer (1864–1915) in 1906. It causes speech disturbance, symptoms of senility (though it may occur in middle age), and ultimately a total collapse of mental activity of any kind. Its cause is uncertain but it is possibly a result of a slow-acting virus, a genetic factor, or an environmental toxin. No cure in known.

AM Amplitude Modulation. *See* FM.

Amami night. Friday night is Amami night A trade slogan of the 1920s. Advertising hair products, it capitalized upon the current practice of washing one's hair on Friday night ready for the weekend.

amateur. amateur night A poor or half-hearted effort, often with reference to athletic performance or sexual skills. The term originated in US theatres and cabaret establishments that featured amateurs, usually in a talent-spotting competition once a week. The Apollo in Harlem still holds such contests; former winners include JAZZ singers Ella Fitzgerald and Sarah Vaughan.

It is beginning to be hinted that we are a nation of amateurs A much-repeated phrase from a speech made by the former prime minister (1894–95) Earl of Rosebery when he was rector of Glasgow University in 1900. It was subsequently quoted with scorn in German diplomatic circles and still reappeared as a political goad at the end of the century.

amber. amber gambler A driver of a motor vehicle who habitually fails to heed the amber traffic light (meaning caution, coming after green for 'go' and before red for 'stop') and speeds through as the lights change to red. The dangers of 'amber gambling' have been the subject of periodic public information campaigns in the press and on television.

amber nectar Australian euphemism for beer or lager. It was first adopted in the UK in the 1970s from the cartoon series *Barry McKenzie* by Barry Humphries, which appeared in the magazine *Private Eye*. It became much more widely used, especially by young middle-class people, in the 1980s after the phrase was used in a TV advertisement for an Australian lager that featured the MACHO Australian actor Paul Hogan.

ambivalent A modern euphemism for bisexual.

Ambridge The fictional village whose inhabitants' lives are chronicled in the BBC radio serial *The* ARCHERS. The village was based on a composite of real-life Inkberrow, Hanbury, and other villages in E Worcestershire, not far from where the programme is recorded in Birmingham. Coach tours now offer excursions round the 'actual' locations of events portrayed in the programme.

ambulance. ambulance chaser A lawyer who rushes to the scene of an accident in the hope that he will be able to retain the victim as a client in the event of any claim for compensation. Now heard on both sides of the Atlantic, the equivalent form in the UK was formerly **accident tout.**

ambulance stocks Stocks or shares that a broker recommends to a client in the hope that they will restore the client's confidence in him. If a portfolio has been performing below expectations, the broker may suggest purchasing ambulance stocks, which can be relied on to enliven his client's holdings – at least in the short term.

Ameche An alternative name for a telephone, which came into vogue in the 1940s. It became popular after the success in 1939 of the film *The Story of Alexander Graham Bell*, in which the lead role was played by the US actor Don Ameche (1908–).

Amerasian A person of mixed US and Asian parentage. First coined in the mid-1960s, the term was later used specifically of someone born during the VIETNAM WAR to a Vietnamese mother with a US serviceman as the father. A resettlement programme instituted in 1982 led to many Amerasians moving to America.

America's Boy Friend The nickname acquired by the matinée idol Charles 'Buddy' Rogers (1904–) in the 1920s. His films included *This Reckless Age* (1932) and *Once in a Million* (1936); he was married to Mary Pickford (*see* WORLD'S SWEETHEART), who was also known as **America's Sweetheart**.

American. American Caesar The nickname acquired by General Douglas MacArthur (1880–1964). First bestowed in the 19th century upon Ulysses S. Grant, the title was given to MacArthur as his reputation as a determined and controversial commander grew in World War II; he finally fell from grace after the KOREAN WAR, when he clashed with President Truman and was dismissed (1951).

American Dictator *See* BOSS, THE.

American Dream, The A phrase epitomizing the democratic ideals and aspirations on which America had been founded: the American way of life at its best.

> It [the American dream] has been a dream of being able to grow to fullest development as man and woman, unhampered by the barriers which had slowly been erected in older civilizations, unrepressed by social orders which had developed for the benefit of classes rather than for the simple human being of any and every class.
>
> J. T. ADAMS: *The Epic of America, Epilogue* (1938).

American Legion The US armed forces veterans' organization. It was established in 1919 to serve the interests of US servicemen returning from the war in Europe and now includes veterans of World War II, the KOREAN WAR, and the VIETNAM WAR. The Legion administers programmes of rehabilitation and welfare for veterans and their families, as well as promoting the rights of veterans and campaigning on defence and security issues. There are some 2.5 million members worldwide.

American sock US slang for a CONDOM.

American Workhouse, The A name given to the Park Lane Hotel, London, by taxi-drivers because of its popularity with wealthy Americans; hence, in general, any hotel offering luxurious accommodation.

Amethyst, HMS The British frigate that made a daring escape along the Yangtze River in July 1949 to evade Chinese Communist forces. The acting commander, Lieutenant-Commander J. S. Kerans, navigated the damaged *Amethyst* in a 140-mile sprint for safety, under cover of darkness and running the gauntlet of hostile shells, to rejoin the British Fleet south of Woosung.

AMGOT Allied Military Government of Occupied Territory. An organization formed in 1943 to administer territories as they were liberated from AXIS forces. It first operated in Sicily, under the leadership of Major General Lord Rennell.

ammunition. Praise the Lord and pass the ammunition The reaction of the US naval lieutenant Howell Maurice Forgy (1908–) when PEARL HARBOR came under attack from the Japanese in 1941. The attack meant that US military involvement in the war in the Far East was inevitable. A derivative phrase was used in London under attack from BUZZ BOMBS in World War II: "Praise the Lord and keep the engines running." (When the engine stopped the bomb fell to earth and exploded.)

Amnesty International (AI) An international organization founded in 1961 and devoted to informing public opinion of violations of human rights and campaigning for the release of political prisoners. From its London headquarters AI maintains contact with human rights activists all over the world, and through regular newsletters, annual reports, travelling exhibitions, newspaper and television campaigns, etc., encourages public scrutiny and condemnation of regimes guilty of torture and political oppression. Particularly effective is the process for supporting 'prisoners of conscience' by 'adoption groups' who send Christmas cards and correspondence to individual prisoners and also bombard guilty governments with letters of protest until the victims are released. AI's logo is a candle wrapped in barbed wire. The organization was awarded the Nobel Peace Prize in 1977.

amniocentesis The extraction of a sample of the amniotic fluid surrounding a foetus for diagnostic purposes. With the aid of an ultrasound scan, a hollow needle is inserted through the abdominal and uterine walls and a sample of the fluid, which contains foetal cells, is taken. The chromosomes from the cell nuclei can then be tested for various congenital abnormalities, such as Down's syndrome and spina bifida. Because of the chance of miscarriage (one in 100 women) the test is only carried out routinely on women at risk of Down's syndrome (women over 35) or those who have a family history of inherited disease.

Amos 'n' Andy The most successful US radio programme; a 1930s comedy series about the tribulations of two Black characters, who were actually played by White actors – Freeman Gosden as Amos and Charles Correll as Andy. The popularity of the 15-minute programmes each weekday forced department stores to broadcast them and cinemas to switch off projectors and switch on radios. Television's commercial debut at the 1939 World's Fair in New York was an Amos 'n' Andy test programme using actors with blacked faces. With Black actors, it became a hit on early 1950s television but was cancelled after protests that its portrayal of Blacks was unrepresentative.

Amritsar Massacre A bloody incident in modern Indian history, in which 379 Indian demonstrators were shot dead by British troops commanded by General Reginald Dyer in the city of Amritsar, Punjab. On 13 April 1919 an estimated 10,000 people packed into the walled square of Jallianwala Bagh to protest at the extension of emergency powers by the British colonial government. Dyer ordered his men to fire on the unarmed crowd, making the square a death trap. Apart from the dead, an estimated 1200 were injured. Dyer was castigated by a commission of inquiry but his action was supported by the British House of Lords. The incident prompted Mahatma Gandhi to institute a campaign of civil disobedience against the British. In 1984 another 1000 people died in Amritsar when Sikh extremists seized and held the Sikh shrine, the Golden Temple, until it was stormed by the Indian army. As a reprisal, Sikh members of the prime minister's bodyguard murdered Indira Gandhi later that year.

amscram Scram, go away. An example of pig Latin or back slang that survives, although it is now rarely used. It was first heard in America, before World War II, but has been heard since the 1950s in Australia as well as the UK.

Amundsen Sea Part of the South Pacific Ocean in Antarctica off Byrd Island, named after the Norwegian explorer Roald Amundsen (1872–1928), who in 1911 became the first man to reach the South Pole.

amusement arcade An indoor gallery of coin-operated games machines found in most city centres and seaside resorts throughout the UK and abroad.

anabolic steroid A steroid compound used to promote the growth of tissue. Male sex hormones (androgens) are naturally occurring anabolic steroids. Synthetic forms are used to promote weight gain in debilitating diseases and sometimes in the treatment of breast cancer. They are also used by athletes and in horseracing to enhance performance, although these uses are now banned by athletic authorities and racing bodies as they can cause liver damage. Many authorities, including the International Olympic Committee, require samples of athletes' urine to prove them free of anabolic steroids.

Anastasia Anastasiya Nikolayevna (1901–18), Grand Duchess of Russia and youngest daughter of Tsar Nicholas II and Alexsandra Fyodorovna. Anastasia was almost certainly executed by the BOLSHEVIKS in a cellar in Ekaterinburg with the rest of her family. However, several women have insisted that they were the Tsar's daughter who escaped murder and have claimed the Romanov fortune, deposited in Swiss banks. The most renowned of these claimants called herself Anna Anderson (1902–84), although critics alleged she was a Pole. Her suit was rejected by the West German Federal Supreme Court in 1970 and the remaining Romanov fortune was awarded to the Duchess of Mecklenberg. In the film version (1956) of a TV play *Anastasia* by Marcelle-Maurette based on the case, Ingrid Bergman won an Academy Award in the title role.

Anatomic Bomb The nickname given to the voluptuous Italian film actress Silvana Pampanini (1927–), who appeared in light comedies in the 1950s.

ANC African National Congress. A Black nationalist organization in S Africa, which aims to promote Black interests. Opposed to APARTHEID, it was banned in South Africa in 1960 for its adoption of violence but finally won recognition in 1990. Its deputy president, Nelson Mandela, was imprisoned as an ANC activist from 1964 to 1990.

anchor man (1) A presenter of a television programme, who coordinates film footage, live interviews, and reports both inside and outside the studio. In America the increasing tendency is for the anchor man or woman to be chosen for their appearance, while in the UK they are usually journalists. (2) In the 1920s, the student who graduated with the lowest grade in his class at the US Military and Naval Academies.

Anderson shelter An air-raid shelter provided for the protection of British civilians during the BLITZ. It was named after its designer, Dr David A. Anderson, but the name is associated by many with the then Home Secretary, Sir John Anderson, who ordered their construction and distribution in 1938. They comprised 14 corrugated iron sheets and when erected measured 6 feet high by 4½ feet by 6½ feet. The shelter was buried 4 feet deep, and the top was covered by soil. Sheltering inside was like "being entombed in a small dark bicycle shed, smelling of earth and damp", according to the historian Norman Longmate. *See also* MORRISON SHELTER.

Andromeda strain A type of microorganism, hitherto unidentified by scientists, which would have disastrous effects for human beings if it became prevalent in the universe. A novel, by the US author Michael Crichton gave rise to the expression. The novel centres on a dangerous unknown type of bacteria brought to earth by a returning space probe.

Andy Capp A cartoon character (created by Reg Smythe) that first appeared in the *Daily Mirror* in 1958. Capp is a determinedly lazy working-class Geordie, apparently permanently attached to his flat cap. He is something of a national institution.

angel. angel dust A powdered form of the drug PCP (phencyclohexylpiperidine, or phencyclidine), which is used in veterinary medicine as an anaesthetic. The powder, often homemade, can be sniffed or smoked to produce extreme psychological and physical effects, ranging from hallucinations to uncontrolled violence. As it was so easy to produce it became a serious problem in America in the late 1970s, especially among poor teenagers. Angel dust has now been largely superseded by CRACK. Its use never caught on elsewhere.

Angel of Death Name by which the German medical scientist Josef Mengele (1894–*c.*1979) became known for the atrocities committed under his orders at AUSCHWITZ concentration camp, where he was camp doctor from 1943 to 1945. His barbarous medical experiments on live camp inmates accounted for many of the 400,000 deaths (mostly of Jews) in which he was subsequently held to be involved. He vanished after the defeat of Nazi Germany and was rumoured to be living in South America: it is thought he died from drowning in Brazil in 1979. A body was identified as his in 1985. Acquaintances of his in South America said he refused to accept any blame for the crimes he had committed.

Angels of Mons The 3rd and 4th Divisions of the Old CONTEMPTIBLES, under the command of General Dorrien-Smith, were sorely pressed in the retreat from Mons (26–27 August 1914). Their losses were heavy and that they survived at all was by some attributed to divine intervention. Arthur Machen, writing from Fleet Street, described with great verisimilitude how St George and the Angels, clad in white and with flaming swords, held back the might of the German First Army. Although Machan later admitted he had made the story up, many soldiers gave eyewitness accounts of an army of angels at Mons.

angels on horseback A savoury dish first created in the early 20th century; it consists of oysters rolled in bacon and served on toast, either as the culminating delicacy of a dinner menu or as a supper dish. It is a translation of the French *anges à cheval*; probably a Gallic invention, contrasting the celestial flavour of the oyster with the more mundane saddle of the bacon, astride the vehicle provided by the toast.

angry. angries *See* ANGRY YOUNG MEN.

Angry Brigade A radical group with anarchist sympathies, who were involved in sporadic violence, such as bombings and firearm attacks, in the UK in the late 1960s and early 1970s. Some of the leaders of the group were imprisoned for a bomb attack on the home of the Secretary of State for Employment in 1971.

Angry Young Men or **Angries** A name applied to certain British dramatists of the 1950s, particularly John Osborne, from whose play *Look Back in Anger* (1956) the term was derived. They were characterized by dissatisfaction with established social, moral, political, and intellectual values, although their protest looked vague and moderate in comparison with the radicalism of the 1960s. By association it is also applied to some American writers of protest.

> In the absence of any really firm standards among those whom they sought to replace the temptation to exploit the gullibility of the public and those who were supposed to guide them was too strong for many of the 'Angry Young Men' to resist.
>
> BORIS FORD, *The Modern Age*, Pt. III, *The Novel Today*.

animal. animal, vegetable, or mineral Catchphrase associated with the BBC radio quiz programme 'Twenty Questions' (1947–76). The phrase had previously been used in America in a radio quiz (1946), although it had more distant origins in a parlour game dating back to the 18th century.

Animal Farm A satirical 'fairy story' by George Orwell (1903–50) of totalitarianism of the Soviet kind under Stalin. A modern fable in which the pigs, by cunning, treachery, and ruthlessness, lord it over the more honest gullible hardworking farm animals. It was first published in 1945.

animal house US student term for an extremely dirty and uproarious college fraternity house. Originally popular in the late 1950s, its use was revived in the 1978 film *National Lampoon's Animal House*, which starred John Belushi.

animal liberation or **animal rights movement** A protest movement founded to protect animals from exploitation by humans. Since the 1970s such groups as the Animal Liberation Front have adopted violent methods, including CAR BOMBS, arson, and breaking into scientific research establishments, as part of their campaigns to exert pressure on those alleged to subject animals in their care to cruelty. *See also* LEAGUE AGAINST CRUEL SPORTS.

Animated Meringue A nickname given to the romantic novelist Barbara Cartland (1901–). It was bestowed upon her by the humorist Arthur Marshall; she responded by sending him a telegram of thanks.

ankle-biter A child, especially a toddler. Used in both a friendly and a mock unfriendly way in the UK and Australia in the 1970s and 1980s.

A Noddo Duw a Noddir (Welsh. Who supports God will be protected) The motto chosen by the photographer Antony Armstrong-Jones on becoming Earl of Snowdon. His marriage to Princess Margaret in 1960 ended in divorce in 1978.

anointing of the sick A sacrament of the Roman Catholic church and Eastern Orthodox church that, before 1972, was known as the sacrament of extreme unction. The name was changed to avoid the implication of the somewhat alarming ancient name for this rite, which suggested that it was only performed on patients *in extremis*, for whom there was no hope of recovery.

anorak A disparaging student name for a fellow student who habitually wears this particular garment and is considered dull, boring, and unfashionable. Used in the UK from the 1980s, it gave rise to the expression 'anorak rock' in the music press to describe a type of guitar music favoured by these people.

anorexia nervosa A psychological disorder chiefly afflicting teenage girls, in which the patient refuses food (even to the point of death) and experiences considerable emotional distress. The condition, often inspired by a girl's conviction that she is overweight or by an unstable family background, came into the public eye for the first time in the 1970s and 1980s. Treatment involves hospitalization, psychotherapy, sedation, and intensive nursing. *See also* BULIMIA.

Anschluss, The (Ger. union) In a modern historical context it refers to the takeover of Austria by Germany in March 1938.

answer is a lemon, the A catchphrase, probably originating in America in the early 1900s, meaning that a response to a question or proposition is rejection or rebuttal. It was current in the UK in the 1920s but is now obsolete. In America a lemon also describes a dud or worthless object, as in 'he ended up dancing with a real lemon'.

Antarctic Treaty A treaty signed in 1959 between 12 nations, including the UK, that restricts activities in the Antarctic to those that are peaceful ones, such as scientific research. The treaty also lays down certain conditions, such as prohibiting all new claims on the continent, forbidding its use for nuclear explosions, and banning the dumping of wastes. The treaty also provides for periodic meetings of the signatories to resolve any difficulties arising.

Anthony. Anthony dollar A US dollar coin that was introduced in 1979 in honour of the US suffragette leader Susan B. Anthony (1820–1906).

Anthony Eden Popular name for the style of black homburg hat worn by Sir Anthony Eden (later Lord Avon) when he was Foreign Secretary in the 1930s. It was an unusual departure from the near-uniform bowler hat that was then fashionable in Whitehall.

Anthroposophical Society An organization founded in 1912 by the Austrian philosopher and scientist Rudolph Steiner (1861–1925), to promote **anthroposophy**. This philosophy, influenced by theosophy, was formulated by Steiner to develop latent human faculties to enable the facets of a spiritual world to be experienced. The society's original headquarters, the twin-domed wooden Goetheanum (named after Goethe) in Dornach, Switzerland, were burnt down in 1922 and replaced by a concrete building. The British offshoot of the Society was founded in 1923. It shares the universal Steiner aim of 'a union of human beings who desire to further the life of the soul, both in the individual and in society at large, based on a true knowledge of the spiritual world.'

anti-. anti-art Art that does not conform to the conventions of any recognized artistic schools.

Anti-Comintern Pact An agreement signed between Germany and Japan on 25 November 1936, expressly to oppose the activities of the COMINTERN – the Communist International. For Japan, the pact gave a fillip to her expansionist plans and helped bolster the Japanese invasion of China the following year, when Italy also became a signatory. This foreshadowed the 1940 TRIPARTITE PACT between the three countries. Other nations regarded the pact as an ominous development.

anti-roman *See* NOUVEAU ROMAN.

antiscience Opposition to scientific projects that conflict with humanitarian interests.

antiworld A theoretical world composed of antimatter. No such astronomical body has yet been positively identified.

antsy Restless, agitated, or nervous. The word originates from the expression **to have ants in one's pants**, the obvious inference being that if one has ants in one's pants one cannot comfortably sit still. Antsy originated in America in the late 1960s; it was later used to imply sexual restlessness or lustfulness.

Anual The site of the Spanish garrison in Morocco that was overwhelmed by Abd al-Krim al-Khattabi, leader of the Berbers, in September 1921. The victory prompted his announcement of the formation of a Berber state in the Riff Mountains. The rebellion was eventually suppressed by Spanish and French forces.

Anvil Codename for the proposed Allied landing in S France in 1944. The operation caused friction between the Allies, although a force of mainly US troops did eventually land, on 15 August, near St Raphael (by which time the operation had been renamed **Dragoon**).

anything. anything can happen and probably will Catchphrase associated with the enormously successful BBC radio series 'Take It From Here' (1948–59). Other catchphrases to emerge from the programme included "Black mark, Bentley!", "oh, Ron . . . yes, Eth?", and "wake up at the back there!"

anything goes A catchphrase meaning 'anything is permissible', used in America from the 1930s. *Anything Goes* was the title song of the 1934 Cole Porter musical, chosen intentionally to reflect the liberated moral climate of the times:

> In olden days, a glimpse of stocking
> Was looked on as something shocking,
> But now, Heaven knows,
> Anything goes.'

any time, any place, anywhere Trade slogan associated with Martini. It was coined in the 1970s.

Anzac A word coined in 1915 from the initials of the Australian and New Zealand Army Corps. It was also applied to the cove and beach in GALLIPOLI on which they landed.

Anzac Day 25 April, commemorating the landing of the Anzacs in GALLIPOLI in 1915. Sometimes also called the **One Day of the Year**.

Anzac Pact The agreement between Australia and New Zealand in 1944 to cooperate in their policies with regard to armistices with the AXIS powers, the postwar settlement, and in certain other matters.

ANZAM Australia, New Zealand, and Malaysia – the name given to a defence strategy for SE Asia agreed in 1949 between the UK, Australia, and New Zealand.

Anzio Site of the bridgehead established by seaborne British and US troops on the Italian coast 30 miles S of Rome in January 1944. Progress of the Allied forces was frustrated for four months by German resistance at **Monte Cassino**. British and Polish troops finally captured the monastery ruins and the Allies were able to break out from Anzio to join with the Fifth Army advancing from the south.

AOK A US abbreviation for *all systems OK*. It is used to indicate that something is in good working order.

apartheid (Afrikaans. apartness) The policy of racial segregation operated by the government of South Africa. Introduced in 1948 by the National Party to describe the extension of the already widespread practice of segregation, apartheid was codified in a series of legislative measures. These included the Population Registration Act (1950) dividing South Africans into Bantus (Blacks), Coloureds (mixed race), and Whites – the category Asians (Indian and Pakistani) was added later; The Group Areas Act (1951), which designated separate residential and business sections in urban areas, enforced by the 'pass' laws requiring non-Whites to carry documents authorizing their presence in restricted areas; and other laws banning mixed marriages, establishing separate education, and prohibiting non-White participation in government. The policy also promoted tribal organizations, and from 1970 enforced membership of a 'homeland', effectively disbarring the Black majority from South African citizenship. Internal opposition to apartheid from the outlawed African National Congress (ANC) and external pressure through sanctions and international isolation led to the gradual weakening of the policy during the 1980s. In 1990 the government legalized the ANC and began negotiations with its charismatic deputy leader Nelson Mandela for dismantling apartheid.

APB All-Points Bulletin. In the jargon of the US police force, a message sent to all cars, patrolmen, etc. in a particular area, often beginning with the words: 'Calling all cars'.

ape. apehangers The very high handlebars on motorbikes and bicycles that were popular in the 1950s with BIKERS in America and later in the UK, where the term was adopted by both rockers (*see* MODS AND ROCKERS) and school children.

go ape To enter a state of wild excitement, originally US slang but now heard elsewhere as well.

aperturismo The liberalization of Spanish politics following the death of General Franco in 1975. The term was first used in Italy in the 1960s to mark certain relaxations in Catholic thinking. *See also* AGGIORNAMENTO.

Apollo moon programme The US space programme that culminated on 20 July 1969 with the successful first manned moon landing. The most significant missions in the programme were:

Apollo 7 (1968) first manned Apollo flight
Apollo 8 (1968) first manned moon orbit
Apollo 9 (1969) lunar module tested in earth orbit
Apollo 10 (1969) rehearsal of moon landing
Apollo 11 (1969) first manned moon landing
Apollo 12 (1969) second moon landing
Apollo 13 (1970) aborted after explosion
Apollo 14 (1971) third moon landing
Apollo 15 (1971) fourth moon landing
Apollo 16 (1972) fifth moon landing
Apollo 17 (1972) last moon landing

apparatchik An official of a Communist party administration (Russ. *apparat*); more loosely any bureaucrat or functionary of a public or private organization.

apple. Apple Corps The company founded by the BEATLES in 1968 to produce and market the group's records and other merchandise. The company's headquarters were in elegant Savile Row offices and became a focus of the counterculture of the 1960s. The Beatles' records were released on the company's 'Apple' label, although the attempt to merge fashionable values of love and peace with commerce often proved chaotic. John Lennon described the venture as an attempt "to wrest control from the men in suits". The Beatles' last public performance took place on the roof of the Apple Building on 30 January 1969.

apple polisher A sycophant or toady. Derived from the idea of the model pupil presenting the teacher with a polished apple every day. The expression is common throughout the English-speaking world and is sometimes used as a verb.

apples a pound pears A parody of the often unintelligible cries of fruit and vegetable sellers, apparently dating from the 1920s.

applesauce An Americanism with meanings ranging from nonsense to exaggeration, to lies, to pretentious language, depending on the context. Its origin lies in the story (possibly apocryphal) that the keepers of small hotels were in the habit of serving large quantities of applesauce with their main courses to augment their small portions of meat or other expensive foods.

après. après la guerre A catchphrase from World War I used ironically to mean 'never', probably coined by soldiers caught in the seemingly unending stalemate of trench warfare. The true nostalgia of the phrase was expressed in the contemporary song *Après la Guerre*:

> Après la guerre finie
> Oh, we'll go home to Blighty
> But won't we be sorry to leave chère Germaine
> Après la guerre finie.

après moi le deluge (Fr. after me, the deluge) The motto of 617 squadron of the RAF. A reference to Louis XV of France's comment anticipating the French Revolution, the motto was chosen after the squadron's celebrated role in the DAMBUSTERS raid of 1943. The squadron's badge depicts a wall pierced by lightning.

après-ski Social entertainment and relaxation after a day's skiing at a winter sports resort. For some the après-ski activities are more important than the actual skiing.

APT Advanced Passenger Train. A new generation of high-speed intercity trains that British Rail intended to introduce in the 1980s. The programme was dogged by technical problems and the APT was withdrawn. *Compare* TGV.

aqua-. aquaplaning (L. *aqua*, water; *plane*, to glide, from L. *planum*, flat surface) The uncontrollable sliding of a vehicle on a wet road, which results when a layer of water builds up between the moving tyres and the road surface to such an exent that the tyres lose direct contact with the road. Since this phenomenon was first recognized in the early 1960s, measures investigated to combat it have included inserting narrow channels in the road for water to escape and improving the road-holding capacity of tyres. In America the phenomenon is called **hydroplaning**.

aquatel A marina that includes various facilities, such as restaurants and shops for the use of travellers by boat. It is derived from the words *aquatic* and *hotel*. An alternative name is **boatel**.

Aquarius, the age of An astrological period, lasting 2000 years, that is supposed to start at the end of the 20th century. In the 1960s the new age, with its promise of more liberal values and a new optimism, was anticipated enthusiastically by proponents of the permissive society (*see* NEW MORALITY).

Arab. Arab League An organization of Arab states founded in 1945 with the aim of fostering economic, political, and cultural cooperation throughout the Arab world. The League has experienced division on many issues, notably the status of Israel, the formation of a Palestinian state, the Lebanese civil war of the 1970s and 1980s, and the crisis precipitated by Iraq's invasion of Kuwait in 1990.

Arab Legion A British-led force, created in 1920 by Lt. Col. G. F. Peake ('Peake Pasha'), from villagers of Transjordan in order to protect the region from raiding Bedouin tribes. From 1939 it was led by Major (later General) John Bagot Glubb ('Glubb Pasha') (1897–1986), who oversaw its expansion during World War II into a considerable and effective fighting unit. Glubb was dismissed by the 20-year-old King Hussein of Jordan in 1956, in part to quash rumours that the Legion's by now legendary commander was in *de facto* control of Jordan.

Arab Revolt An uprising against occupying Turks declared in June 1916 by Hussein, Shereef of Mecca. The revolt united Arabian tribes, encouraging them to fight for independence from the Ottoman Empire; it was supported by the British and French. T. E. Lawrence (*see* LAWRENCE OF ARABIA) was active in the campaign, advising Hussein's third son, Feisal.

Arab Union A short-lived agreement for the union of Jordan and Iraq signed in February 1958. It was dissolved by Jordan's King Hussein in the following August following the overthrow of Iraq's King Feisal.

Arcadia The first Washington Conference between Franklin D. Roosevelt and Winston Churchill, which took place at the White House in December 1941 and January 1942. It established joint agreement on the war strategy and created ABDA.

Archer London street slang for £2000. It originated in the East End and is named after Jeffrey Archer, the novelist, playwright, and former deputy chairman of the Conservative party, who resigned from this post after being accused of paying a prostitute, Monica Coughlan, hush money of £2000. In 1987 he won a libel action against *The News of the World*, who published the story, and received a large sum of money in damages. An Archer is sometimes also called a Jeffrey.

Archers, The The 'everyday story of country folk' broadcast several times a week on BBC Radio Four. This national institution began on 1 January 1951; the only member of the cast to have stayed with the programme all the way through has been Norman Painting (1924–), who plays Phil Archer, head of the family at the centre of the events in the fictional village of AMBRIDGE. The Post Office produced a special set of stamps in 1989 to mark the 10,000th episode of this the longest-running of all radio serials. *See also* AMOS 'N' ANDY; BLUE PETER; CORONATION STREET; DESERT ISLAND DISCS; SOOTY.

Archibald. Archibald, certainly not! The title of a music-hall song by Lee St John, made famous by George Robey. From before World War I until the 1920s it was a catchphrase used as a mock rebuff for sexual advances.

Archie Bunker In US and Canadian slang the typical prejudiced working-class man. The name was taken from a TV character with such attitudes, who appeared in the comedy series *All in the Family*, based on the British original *Till Death Us Do Part*. *See also* ALF GARNETT.

Archies In World War I anti-aircraft guns and batteries were thus nicknamed – probably from Archibald, the hero of one of George Robey's songs (*see* ARCHIBALD, CERTAINLY NOT!).

arcology A self-contained city or other environment. Designs for such structures have included cities under the sea and in space. The term arcology was coined by the architect Paolo Salieri from the words *architectural* and *ecology*.

Arcos Raid A British police raid on the Soviet trade delegation, Arcos, which took place on 24 May 1927. Documents seized were claimed to prove that Soviet diplomats were engaged in spying but no real evidence was actually found. However, the incident provided a pretext for the UK to sever diplomatic relations with the Soviets, Soviet diplomats being expelled from London.

Ardennes Offensive *or* **Battle of the Bulge** In World War II, the advance by German forces in the Ardennes region of Belgium that succeeded in breaking through Allied lines (in an attempt to reach the coast at Antwerp). The surprise attack started in foggy conditions on 16 December 1944 and by the end of the month a German salient (or 'bulge') up to 60 miles deep had formed. By the end of January 1945 the offensive had been repulsed and the Germans driven back to their original positions. The squandering of resources in this last offensive of the war hastened Germany's defeat.

area code In America and Canada a telephone dialling code used in long-distance calls. *See also* STD; ZIP CODE.

argie British slang for an Argentinian. It was used especially in the tabloid press and by the armed forces during the FALKLANDS CONFLICT in 1982.

Ariel A series of six UK satellites launched in America between 1962 and 1979 to carry scientific instruments into space. The first Ariel, launched on 26 April 1962, was the UK's first space satellite.

aristo-pop Pop music dominated by high-earning groups and individuals who invest the money produced by pop music in various other profitable schemes. The **pop aristocracy** are the singers and musicians involved in these ventures.

ark A large greenhouse-type structure in which a self-sufficient environment can be created, allowing food, etc., to be grown in otherwise hostile surroundings. Such self-contained environments are being developed for use in arid climates and possibly as life-support systems in space. The more complex versions can be used to provide several microclimates in which a wide range of habitats can be created.

Arkle A near-legendary steeplechaser that captured the heart of the nation by his exploits on the race track. Trained by Tom Dreaper and ridden by Pat Taafe, the gelding won three Cheltenham Gold Cups, the King George VI Chase, and the Irish Grand National, among other famous victories. His owner, the Duchess of Westminster, never allowed him to race in Aintree's fearsome Grand National. His racing career was ended by injury in December 1966.

armchair quarterback or **Monday morning quarterback** Someone who lacks knowledge or active involvement in a particular subject but still freely offers opinions and criticisms. Other versions include 'armchair sportsman' and 'armchair traveller', all being derived from 'armchair general', a World War II term still in common use. The 'Monday morning' version refers to fans who point out mistakes made in weekend American football matches.

Armenteers *See* MADEMOISELLE FROM ARMENTEERS.

Armistice Day 11 November (or the Sunday nearest to that date), the day set aside from 1919 to 1945 to commemorate the fallen in World War I, marked by a TWO-MINUTE SILENCE at 11 a.m. and appropriate civil and religious ceremonies. The armistice ending the war was signed at 11 o'clock on 11 November 1918. In 1946 the name was changed to REMEMBRANCE DAY. In America and Canada, 11 November is a legal holiday, its name being changed to *Veteran's Day* in 1954.

Armstrong murder A notorious 1922 case in which Herbert Rowse Armstrong, a retired army major and solicitor of Hay-on-Wye, was convicted of murdering his wife and of attempting to murder a fellow solicitor in the town, Oswald Martin. Armstrong slowly poisoned his wife with small repeated doses of arsenic but his exploits aroused the suspicions of a local doctor, who reported Armstrong to the authorities.

Arnhem A city in the Netherlands and the site of a disastrous battle for a strategic bridge across the Rhine during September 1944. The mass parachute drop of the First British Airborne Division was part of a larger Allied assault on key river crossings. However, the planned reinforcements by a British armoured division, failed to arrive as they were unable to break through German lines; in addition, bad weather prevented air reinforcement and German resistance was well organized. The British reached the northern end of Arnhem bridge but their heavy casualties made retreat inevitable. Some three-quarters of the 10,000-strong British force were killed or captured, and the defeat dashed hopes of a speedy Allied advance before the winter.

aromatherapy The use of plant extracts and fragrant oils to sooth tension and promote health, beauty, and mental well-being. Aromatherapy is part of the ALTERNATIVE MEDICINE movement favouring natural remedies for common physical and mental ailments.

arse bandit British abusive male term for a homosexual, used especially by soldiers and schoolboys.

art. Art Deco The decorative style of the 1920s and 1930s in painting, glass, pottery, silverware, furniture, etc. It is distinguished by bold colours, ornateness, geometrical lines, and lack of symmetry. It takes its name from the *Exposition Internationale des Arts Décoratifs et Industriel Modernes* held in Paris in 1925. It is in deliberate contrast to the earlier (1890–1910) Art Nouveau.

art trouvé (Fr.) Found art. Not the direct creation of the artist but adapted from 'found' or natural objects, which have been primarily shaped by circumstances, nature, and the elements. Items found on the seashore are obvious examples of the raw material of *art trouvé*.

Arthur Rank A bank. A British working-class rhyming-slang expression based on the name of the industrialist and film magnate J. Arthur Rank (1888–1972).

artificial intelligence The study of ways in which a computer can be built and programmed to perform tasks that, in a human being, would require intelligence. The idea of 'thinking machines' was first put forward by the mathematician Alan Turing (1912–54) who suggested what is known as the **Turing test**. In this, a person sits in a room and is told that he can communicate with a separate room through a computer keyboard. In the other room there is either a person or a computer programmed to answer questions. The subject asks a number of questions and receives replies. Would he be able to tell whether the other room contained a person or a computer? If, after a number of trials, the subject thought that the computer was a person, then it can be argued that the machine was thinking. Answering questions in a sensible way is only one part of intelligence and a considerable amount of work has gone into the study of artificial intelligence since the 1950s. At one level, this simply consists of problem solving. Programs, known as 'expert systems', have been written to perform tasks that need logical analysis of a large amount of data – as in medical diagnosis. Programs for playing games, such as chess, have also been produced. More difficult is the production of programs that actually 'think' – for example, in solving or even postulating mathematical theorems. Even more contentious is the idea, put forward by some, that it might in principle be possible for a computer to experience emotions.

Arvin Army of the Republic of (South) Vietnam.

Aryan myth The doctrine propounded by the NAZIS that power was the prerogative of the Nordic-Aryan race because of its 'pure' blood. Other races were, by virtue of their 'impurity', inferior and fit only for subservient roles in society. In particular, the Jewish-Semitic race was regarded as a destructive force – a 'counter-race' – to be exterminated. Many of these ideas predated World War I, for example from the writings of Joseph A. de Gobineau and Houston Stewart Chamberlain, but during the 1920s and 1930s they were adopted by the Nazis to create a racist ideology of the most odious kind.

ASAT A type of satellite that is designed to destroy other orbiting satellites. Also called hunter-killer satellites, such satellites destroy their target by tracking it down and exploding in its vicinity. *See* STAR WARS.

ASDIC Admiralty Submarine Detection Investigation Committee, an early form of SONAR submarine detection that originated in 1917 and was used on British naval vessels towards the end of World War I.

ASH Action on Smoking and Health. A pressure group in the UK that promotes antismoking measures.

ash-can school A group of US painters active from *c.* 1908 to 1914, whose work concentrated on portraying the reality of urban street life. The leading member of the group was Robert Henri; other members included William James Glackens, John Sloan, George Benjamin Luks, and Everett Shinn, all of whom had worked as artist-reporters on the *Philadelphia Press*.

ashram In US slang of the 1960s a HIPPIE society or commune. It was originally a Hindu term for a hermitage or religious retreat.

Asian flu A strain of influenza caused by the myxovirus A_2, which is thought to have originated in China in early 1957 and by mid-year had circled the globe.

Aslan *See* NARNIA.

asleep at the switch A derisive nickname for the American Defense Medal, given to those in the armed forces on Pearl Harbor Day (7 December 1941). It derives from a US expression indicating a failure in alertness of mind or lack of awareness of threatened danger. This meaning was in turn derived from the railroads. 'To switch a train' is to transfer it to another set of rails by operating a switch. Failure to do this according to schedule might well lead to a catastrophe. *See* DEAD MAN'S HANDLE.

ASP Anglo-Saxon Protestant. A social category first identified in this way in America in the 1960s. *See also* WASP.

aspirin An analgesic in tablet or other form, consisting of acetylsalicyclic acid. The name began life in 1899 as a tradename belonging to the German firm of Bayer, but was later ruled to have passed into the public domain. The name was derived from the German title, *Acetylirte Spirsäure* (acetylated spiraeic acid).

Assassination is the extreme form of censorship Observation by George Bernard Shaw in his play *The Shewing-Up of Blanco Posnet*. *See* OSWALD, LEE HARVEY; SARAJEVO ASSASSINATION.

> They really are bad shots.
>
> CHARLES DE GAULLE, after surviving one of several attempted assassinations.

assemblage A work of art that consists of a collection of disparate items, such as pieces of wood and cloth, combined as a three-dimensional collage.

assertiveness training The promotion of a submissive individual's self-confidence so that he or she may adopt a more assertive role in normal social intercourse. Such courses of training, which include techniques ranging from provocation to mutual support, have become increasingly popular since World War II, especially among the business community and women's groups.

asset. asset-backed fund A fund in which money is invested in stocks and shares, property, works of art, etc., rather than being loaned to a bank to earn interest. In the second half of the 20th century inflation has been such a dominant influence on commercial activities that pension (and other) funds have needed to be asset-backed in order to keep pace with it.

asset stripping The practice of buying a company whose shares are valued at less than their asset value (i.e. the total value of a company's assets less its liabilities divided by the number of ordinary shares issued), with the object of selling off the company's most valuable assets and closing down the remaining shell or revitalizing its management and selling its shares at a profit. The practice was particularly prevalent in the UK and America in the decade following World War II, when rising property values made the shares of many companies look very cheap. Although the asset stripper and his associates may make enormous profits from these deals, many of the employees may lose their jobs, the other shareholders may come off badly, and the interests of the suppliers, customers, and creditors may be totally ignored. For these reasons asset stripping is now strongly deprecated by governments and company accountants have a responsibility for seeing that the assets of a business are not undervalued in their accounts.

Astaire, Fred Frederick Austerlitz (1899–1987), the near-legendary US stage and film dancer. Although his career began inauspiciously with his first audition verdict "Can't act. Can't sing. Slightly bald. Can dance a little", he went on to delight two generations of filmgoers with his effortless and inventive dance routines. Both Balanchine and Nureyev described him as the world's greatest dancer; the film critic C. A. Lejeune said of him ". . . in his loose legs, his shy grin, or perhaps the anxious diffidence of his manner, he has found the secret of persuading the world". In many of his films he was partnered by the almost equally legendary Ginger Rogers (1911–), who danced with him in the 1935 musical film *Top Hat*, when they were probably both at their peak.

Asterix The diminutive Gallic warrior who is the hero of the comic strip adventures originally created by Goscinny and Uderzo in 1959. With his friend Obelix, he has survived multiple translations (the English versions have been much admired), extensive commercialization, and weak imitations in the cinema and on television, to become one of the widest-read and most erudite of modern cartoon characters.

astro-. astrobug A sample of bacteria or other microscopic organisms that is sent into space for experimental purposes.

astrodome (1) An indoor stadium with a translucent domed roof. The first was built in Houston, Texas in 1965, and covers a playing area large enough for baseball and American football. The plastic-panelled dome has a span of 196m (642 ft), has seating for 66,000 people in six tiers, and the interior is air-conditioned to 23 °C. (2) The transparent observation canopy on the upper side of an aircraft fuselage.

astromonk Any one of several monkeys sent into space in the 1950s and 1960s in order to observe the likely effects of such travel upon man.

astronaut (Lat. *astrum*, star; *nauta*, sailor) One who voyages in space. This word, first used in 1929, emerged from the realms of science fiction after the first manned spacecraft flight by Major Yuri Gagarin of the Soviet Union in April 1961. The first non-Soviet astronaut was the American Allan Bartlett Shepard (1923–), who completed a 15-minute space flight in May 1961, 23 days after Gagarin's flight. *See* COSMONAUT.

Astroturf Trademark for a type of artificial playing surface used for football pitches, etc. Such pitches were first introduced in America in the 1960s; the name is derived from the Astrodome indoor ball park in Houston, where the first such pitch was laid.

Aswan High Dam A dam 111 m (364 ft) high across the Nile at Aswan, Egypt, financed by the Soviet Union, and completed in 1970. The creation of its reservoir, **Lake Nasser**, entailed the resettling of 90,000 Egyptian peasants and Sudanese Nubian nomads as well as the repositioning of the ancient Egyptian Temple of Abu Simbel. The dam allows the annual Nile flood to be controlled for irrigation and to generate prodigious amounts of electricity. It lies four miles upstream from the earlier Aswan Dam (1902), once one of the largest dams in the world.

Atatürk Father of the Turks. A surname adopted in 1934 by Mustapha Kemal (1881–1938), the founder of modern Turkey, when all Turks were made to assume surnames. In World War I he held the DARDANELLES and subsequently ruthlessly set out to westernize the republic he had established in 1923. European dress was imposed, polygamy abolished, women enfranchised, and the Roman script replaced the Arabic.

ATB Advanced Technology Bomber. *See* STEALTH.

atheists. There are no atheists in foxholes Preaching a sermon during World War II, Father W. T. Cummings, a US army chaplain in Bataan, used the phrase "there are no atheists in foxholes", meaning that no one can deny the existence of God in the face of imminent death. This is, of course, the view of a theist and would be unlikely to be shared by an atheist.

athlete's foot Popular name for the skin condition tinea pedis affecting the feet and causing excessive itchiness between the toes. The expression was coined during the late 1920s in the course of an advertising campaign for a product used as a remedy for the condition. The origin of the term lies in the fact that the floors of gyms, sports halls, and swimming pools, where people often go barefoot, are obvious sources of the infection.

Atlantic. Atlantic Charter During World War II, President Roosevelt and Winston Churchill met at sea (14 August 1941) and made this eight-point declaration of the principles on which peace was to be based, consequent upon Allied victory. It can be compared with President Wilson's FOURTEEN POINTS.

Atlanticism The tradition of close cooperation in international affairs between America and the states of Western Europe.

Atlantic Wall The name given by the Germans in World War II to their defences along the Atlantic coast of Europe, built to resist invasion.

Battle of the Atlantic The German campaign waged against Allied shipping in the Atlantic during World War II in order to disrupt vital supplies to the UK. Ships of the Merchant Navy, crewed by volunteers and with Royal Navy escorts, braved the convoy routes from Canada and America and the risk of attack by German U-BOATS. The battle was most intense during 1940–43, but Britain's Atlantic lifeline was kept intact, greatly helped by technical improvements in radar and ASDIC to detect enemy vessels and by the increasing scale of US naval protection. By 1943 German U-boat losses had reached unsustainable levels and the threat to shipping was on the wane.

Atlas, Charles Stagename of Angelo Siciliano (1894–1974), who became famous after winning 'The World's Most Perfectly Developed Man' title in a US body-building contest in 1922. He consolidated upon this success by launching mail-order body-building courses under the slogan 'You too can have a body like mine'. Charles Atlas himself was a fine advertisement for such courses, having been a 'seven stone weakling' until he devised his body-building technique, called 'Dynamic Tension', after watching a lion flexing its muscles at the zoo.

atom. atom bomb (A-bomb) The first such bombs were developed by America and dropped on **Hiroshima** and **Nagasaki** in August 1945, bringing World War II to an end. With an explosive power equivalent to 20,000 tons of TNT they devastated these two Japanese cities. *See* MANHATTAN PROJECT; NUCLEAR WEAPON.

> The Bomb brought peace but man alone can keep that peace.
> WINSTON CHURCHILL, speech, 16 August 1945.

atomic pile *See* NUCLEAR REACTOR.

There is no evil in the atom, only in men's souls Remark made in 1952 by the US statesman Adlai Stevenson (1900–65). It has since been quoted many times by defendants of various nuclear programmes. *See* MANHATTAN PROJECT.

attaboy An exclamation of enthusiastic approval or encouragement, originating in America and widely used in the 1930s by young people in the English-speaking countries of the British Commonwealth.

attention all shipping The words with which gale warnings and other items of maritime meteorological information are preceded in broadcasts by BBC radio.

Attila. Attila of Sunnybrook Farm *See* WORLD'S SWEETHEART.

Attila the Hen Nickname for Margaret Thatcher. *See* IRON LADY.

ATV *See* ALL-TERRAIN VEHICLE.

Aubrey holes A series of 56 holes that mark the outer ring of the stones at Stonehenge. They were named in 1959 in honour of the antiquarian and diarist John Aubrey (1626–97), who was the first to identify them.

Auk, The Nickname of Field-Marshall Sir Claude Auchinleck (1884–1981).

aunt. Aunt Edna A fictional theatregoer who represents the typical English audience. Conceived by Terence Rattigan as the epitome of the matinée audience he had to please, she became a widely recognized personalization of all the forces that the new rebellious (kitchen-sink) generation of writers of the 1950s sought to displace. Rattigan introduced her in his preface to the second volume of his *Collected Plays* (1953):

> A nice respectable, middle-class, middle-aged maiden lady, with time on her hands and the money to

help her pass it . . . Let us call her Aunt Edna . . . Aunt Edna is universal . . . She is also immortal.

Auntie A popular nickname for the British Broadcasting Corporation (BBC). It was acquired by the corporation in the 1950s when the apparently more adventurous commercial TV stations first started transmitting in the UK. The BBC responded, however, by adopting the nickname as a compliment rather than a criticism. The comedian Arthur Askey claimed to have first used the name for the BBC. The Australian Broadcasting Commission shares the same nickname. *See also* BEEB.

Aunt Jane US slang for any enthusiastic Black female member of a church congregation, noted for her uninhibited participation in religious services. *See also* AUNT TOM.

Aunt Nelly Belly. A British rhyming-slang term, also heard in Australia, current in the 1950s when 'belly' was still considered an unmentionable word by many people.

Aunt Tom A derogatory expression for a woman who does not agree with the philosophy of WOMEN'S LIB and does not support its aims. It comes from Harriet Beecher Stow's *Uncle Tom's Cabin*, whose chief character epitomized the servility of Blacks to the White establishment. An Aunt Tom is considered to be too servile to men to seek her independence from a society that is perceived as male-dominated. Other variants with the same meaning have included **Aunt Jane**, **Aunt Jemima**, and **Aunt Thomasina**.

au pair (Fr. on equal terms) A foreign girl who is given free board and lodging (and sometimes a small amount of cash) in return for help around the house, looking after children, etc. The practice of taking in au pairs by middle-class families as a substitute for domestic servants became widespread after World War II; it was originally a German idea.

Auschwitz or **Auschwitz-Birkenau** The largest of Nazi Germany's CONCENTRATION CAMPS, situated near the Polish town of Oswiecim in Galacia. The complex, commanded by Rudolf Franz Hoess, consisted of three camps: the first, reserved for mainly Polish prisoners-of-war, was established by Heinrich Himmler in April 1940; Auschwitz II, or Birkenau, was added in October 1942, and became the main extermination centre with large 'bathhouses' (disguised gas chambers) which could hold 2000 people at a time, cellars (*Leichenkeller*) for storing corpses, and ovens for cremating the remains; Auschwitz III was established in May 1942 to furnish the nearby chemical and synthetic rubber manufacturer I. G. Farben with slave labour. Jews were rounded up and transported by rail from every corner of Europe. On arrival the young, old, and infirm were 'selected' for immediate extermination, while the rest earned brief respite from death in the labour gangs. Estimates of the numbers of men, women, and children who perished in this camp alone from gassing, medical experiments (*see* ANGEL OF DEATH), and forced labour vary between one and four million.

It was a denial of God, it was a denial of man. It was the destruction of the world in miniature form.
RABBI HUGO GRYNN, Auschwitz survivor, BBC interview 1982.

Aussie A familiar name given to Australians during and after World War I. Their own colloquial term was DIGGER.

Austin 7 *See* BABY AUSTIN.

Australia. Australia for the White Man Slogan used by the Australian newspaper *The Bulletin* from 1908 to 1960, emphasizing its support for the WHITE AUSTRALIA policy.

Australian Novel, the Great The almost mythical work of fiction that has been anticipated from various Australian novelists of the 20th century. The phrase originated in the first half of the century, inspired by Australia's relatively undistinguished cultural history; however, towards the end of the century the works of such writers as Patrick White (winner of the NOBEL PRIZE for Literature in 1973) had done much to render the phrase irrelevant, although it is still used as a spur to write even finer novels.

Well, good luck to you, lad! I'm going to write the Great Australian Novel.
PATRICK WHITE, *The Vivisector*.

auteurism A style of direction that developed in the cinema in the 1960s. It hinged upon the director exercising strong personal leadership in all aspects of movie-making.

auto. autobahn A German, Austrian, or Swiss motorway.

autochondriac A facetious and usually derogatory term for a person who is obsessed with the condition or appearance of his or her car. The autochondriac is constantly hearing potentially damaging noises when driving the car and frequently sees scratches, imaginary or otherwise, on the car's paintwork.

autocide Deliberate self-destruction achieved by crashing one's car. From *automobile* and *suicide*.

autocondimentation A circumlocution for seasoning one's food with pepper and salt at table. It is sometimes used facetiously but originated as a quasi-scientific term in the course of research into eating habits. Many people, particularly the British, automatically add seasoning at the table before tasting the food set before them.

autocue A device, hidden from the audience, that displays a text to a speaker or performer as a memory aid. They are used mainly by politicians and television presenters to enable them to be word-perfect. Closely related is the **Teleprompter**, which scrolls words on a screen and is usually situated below the television camera that the television performer is addressing.

autogiro An aircraft with a freely rotating horizontal wing to provide lift and a motor-driven propeller for forward motion. It was superseded by the helicopter after World War II, which, having a motorized rotor, is capable of vertical takeoff and landing.

autoimmune disease Any disease characterized by the body's antibodies attacking its own cells and tissues.

automatic pilot or **autopilot** A device that controls an aircraft or other vehicle without the need for human intervention. Modern computerized autopilots can execute complex manoeuvres, flight plans, and even landings and takeoffs. The manufacturers of these systems claim they are FAIL-SAFE and that there is no need for concern about computer error. Such devices can also control ships, submarines, missiles and spacecraft.

automobilia The collecting of artefacts connected with cars and motoring.

autopia An area of a city dominated by the needs of the motorist, as opposed to those of any other transport system or, indeed, those of pedestrians. From *auto* and *utopia*.

autopista (Sp.) Motorway.

autoput (Serbo-Croat) Yugoslavian name for motorway.

autoroute (Fr.) Motorway.

Auto State, The An alternative modern nickname to 'the Wolverine State' for Michigan, home of the Ford Motor Company.

Auxis *See* BLACK AND TANS.

avant-garde (Fr. vanguard) In the forefront of new ideas or techniques, especially used of writers, artists, musicians, etc. The term was coined in the 1900s and was subsequently particularly associated with the more adventurous European cinema directors.

avenue-tank US Black slang, first heard in the 1940s, for the double-decker buses used on New York's 5th Avenue.

aversion therapy A method used in psychiatry to break a patient's harmful habit or addiction. Often used in relation to drug-taking, alcohol, or smoking, it can include the use of mild electric shocks and the prescribing of drugs that will produce unpleasant effects if combined with alcoholic drink, heroin, etc. *See also* BEHAVIOUR THERAPY.

avoid five o'clock shadow Trade slogan adopted by Gem Razors and Blades in America in the 1930s. This was apparently the first time the phrase 'five o'clock shadow' (for the growth of a beard at the end of the day) was ever heard.

Avon calling A catchphrase adopted by door-to-door salesmen of Avon cosmetics. One of the best known of all commercial slogans of the 20th century, it was actually first used in America in 1886.

AWACS Airborne Warning and Control System. A sophisticated radar and communications system installed in converted Boeing 707s, with a far greater range than ground-based radar stations. AWACS can detect potentially hostile air or ground activity and coordinate the necessary offensive and defensive measures.

awayday (1) An excursion or outing. (2) A single dose of LSD or other hallucinogenic drug (a pun on TRIP). Both senses derive from the cheap one-day excursion ticket, using this name, which is available on British Rail.

awful. ooh you are awful Catchphrase popularized in the 1970s by a drag character called Mandy in a TV comedy series starring the comedian Dick Emery (1917–83). The usual continuation of the phrase, accompanied by a clout with a substantial handbag, was "but I like you".

axe Slang term for any musical instrument, particularly an electric guitar.

> He . . . performing a Peter Green instrumental which allowed him to stray up his fret board and pull axe-hero grimaces.
>
> *The Independent*, 31 January 1991.

Axis The Rome–Berlin Axis: the alliance of the Fascist states of Germany and Italy (October 1936), described by Mussolini as "an axis round which all European states animated by the will to collaboration and peace can also assemble". It became the **Rome–Berlin–Tokyo Axis** in 1937. *See also* FASCISM; PACT OF STEEL.

axle grease US Black slang for heavy-duty hair oil.

aye, aye, that's yer lot A catchphrase associated with the comedian and variety artist Jimmy Wheeler, who in the 1940s and 1950s used it to sign off at the end of his routine.

ay thang yew A rendering of 'I thank you' and one of the many catchphrases of the British comedian Arthur Askey (1900–82), who first introduced it to a wide audience in the BBC radio show 'Band Waggon', which started in 1938. The phrase was apparently borrowed from London's bus conductors, thanking their customers for buying a ticket.

Azania An alternative name for South Africa, sometimes used by nationalists in that country. It was originally the name of an Iron Age civilization that occupied the area between 500 A.D. and 1500 A.D. Evelyn Waugh used the name Azania for the imaginary African kingdom in his novel *Black Mischief* (1932).

Aztec two-step An attack of diarrhoea. The term was coined in America, where holiday-makers visiting Mexico would often find themselves doing an agonized hobble, not unlike a dance-step, to the nearest lavatory. It became a fashionable expression during the late 1970s. *See also* MONTEZUMA'S REVENGE.

B

B. **B-road** In the UK, a secondary road.

BA US slang for an aggressive person, someone with a 'bad attitude': a 'bad ass'. These initials were used for the name of the aggressive Black hero B. A. Barracas, played by Mr T, in the popular TV series *The A-Team* in the 1980s.

B and D A British and Australian slang expression meaning bondage and discipline, used by prostitutes to describe the services that they offer.

B and K Abbreviation for the Soviet statesmen Nicolai Bulganin (1895–1975) and Nikita Khrushchev (1894–1971). It was used in newspapers during their visit to the UK in 1956. At the time, Bulganin was the Soviet prime minister and Khrushchev, who subsequently ousted Bulganin, was the first secretary of the Communist Party.

B and S Brandy and soda.

B and T British schoolboy abbreviation for **bum and tit**, popular in the 1970s. The expression usually refers to photographs of young ladies showing either or both.

B-girl A US slang word for a prostitute who frequents bars in search of clients.

B-movie A motion picture made as a companion to a 'main feature' in a double-bill programme at the cinema in the 1930s to 1950s. B-movies were made on low budgets, usually with lesser-known stars and often with slight plots. Although many were derided for their feeble special effects and wooden acting, several famous actors who featured in B-movies later became stars, including the future US president Ronald Reagan.

B side The **flip side** of a pop-music single disc, *i.e.* the reverse side of the record-ing intended to enter the CHARTS.

B-52 (1) A US heavy bomber (also called the **Stratofortress**) first built by Boeing in the 1950s. With eight engines and the capacity to carry nuclear weapons, the B-52 was acknowledged the most powerful bomber in the world and was still in service in the 1990s. (2) A BEEHIVE hairstyle of the early 1960s, named after the heavy bomber.

Baader-Meinhof gang *See* RED ARMY FACTION.

Ba'athists Members of a radical Islamic Arab movement (the Arab Socialist Ba'th Party) founded in Damascus in 1943. They advocate the formation of a single socialist Arab nation and hold power in both Syria and Iraq (*see* BUTCHER OF BAGHDAD). Ba'th (also spelled Ba'ath) means 'renaissance'.

Babar the Elephant A character in a series of illustrated childrens' books created in 1931 by the French writer and illustrator Jean de Brunhoff (d. 1937). The books have been translated into English and many other languages.

Babbitt The leading character in Sinclair Lewis's novel of this name (1922). He is a prosperous 'realtor' or estate agent in the Western city of Zenith, a simple likeable fellow, with faint aspirations to culture that are forever smothered in the froth and futile hustle of US business life. Drive (which takes him nowhere), hustle (by which he saves no time), and efficiency (which does not enable him to do anything) are the keynotes of his life. Babbitt in present usage typifies the businessman of orthodox outlook and virtues, with no interest in cultural values. *See also* MAIN STREET.

Babe, The George Herman Ruth (1895–1948), US professional baseball player. He earned his nickname in his first team, when he was only 19. He was also called the **Bambino**, by his fans of Italian origin. *See also* MURDERERS' ROW.

Babi Yar A ravine N of Kiev in the Ukraine, which in World War II became the site of a mass grave for over 100,000 victims of NAZI exterminations. Most of the victims, killed between 1941 and 1943, were Jews (*see* HOLOCAUST) who were unjustly blamed for a bomb attack on German troops stationed in Kiev. When the

Nazis retreated, the site of the mass grave was concealed and Babi Yar only came to international attention in 1961 with the publication of a poem of the same name by the acclaimed Soviet poet Yevgeny Yevtushenko. Dmitry Shostakovich subsequently set the poem to music and incorporated it in his 13th symphony (1962); both artists were reprimanded by the authorities who were reluctant to draw attention to Jewish victims of the Nazis. A memorial erected on the site in 1966 omitted any acknowledgement of the Jews killed there.

babushkaphobia A woman's aversion to her grandchildren. Although properly a fear of grandmothers (Russ. *babushka*, grandmother), this term is confusingly used to describe a rejection of the traditional role of grandmother. It reflects the view held by increasing numbers of women in the latter part of the 20th century who, having raised a family, wish to re-establish careers and enjoy their independence free from the constraints of baby-minding and child-rearing.

baby. **baby Austin** The nickname for a small seven-horsepower family car (the **Austin 7**), first produced in 1921 by the British engineer and industrialist Herbert Austin (later Baron Austin; 1866–1941) at his Longbridge works in Birmingham. Following the lead of Henry Ford in America, the Austin 7 was the first mass-produced car to be manufactured in Europe and greatly influenced British light-car design. *See also* TIN LIZZIE.

baby battering *See* CHILD ABUSE.

baby boom An increase in the birth rate, especially the sharp increase in Europe and America after World War II, when servicemen returned to their wives. Children born in this period are often known as **baby boomers**.

baby bust A sudden marked decline in the birthrate; a 1980s colloquial term modelled on BABY BOOM. The post-World War II baby boom was followed in Western countries by a fall in the birthrate, which began in the mid-1960s. The adverse economic and social implications of this trend included an overall shift in the age structure of society, a declining workforce, and a potential reduction in consumer markets.

baby in a microwave *See* URBAN LEGENDS.

baby-kisser A politician, so called from the 1940s onwards for the ubiquitous photographs issued during election campaigns of politicians making the acquaintance of various younger members of their constituencies in the belief that this will help endear them to the voting public. *See also* PHOTO CALL.

baby-sitting (1) Staying with someone to care for them and guide them whilst they are taking illegal drugs, particularly hallucinogens. (2) A journalistic term for guarding an informant in order to prevent other journalists from picking up the story.

Babylon (1) British slang for a White racist society, the UK, or a place of exile for a social group. Originally the word, with all its biblical connotations, was used by the RASTAFARIANS but its usage has spread through the widespread popularity of REGGAE music to both Black and White youth. (2) **The Babylon** The police force; the instrument of authority in a racist society. A more specific application of the word, now also used by White youths.

back. **backbeat** In JAZZ, a secondary rhythm.

backdoor (1) British slang meaning to commit adultery. (2) British slang meaning to betray or deceive. (3) A method by which the Bank of England injects cash into the money market by buying Treasury bills at the market rate.

backdoor man (1) US slang expression for a secret lover, particularly a married woman's secret lover, which came originally from Black jargon of the 1950s. It implies that the lover leaves by the back door as the husband arrives home at the front door. 'Back Door Man' is a well-known song recorded by The Doors in 1968. (2) A heterosexual man who practises anal intercourse. (3) Australian slang for a homosexual.

backdoor work A euphemism for anal intercourse.

back end A late stage in the processing of nuclear fuel in which used fuel is separated into recyclable uranium and plutonium and radioactive waste. The phrase has since been applied to the final stage of any project (especially in a financial context).

Backfire bomber A NATO codename assigned to the Soviet-made Tupolev V-G swing-wing long-range bomber that was first deployed in the 1970s.

back-gate parlor US prison slang dating from the 1940s referring to death in prison.

backgrounder US journalistic slang for a political briefing given by government officials.

backroom boys The unpublicized scientists and technicians in World War II, who contributed so much to the development of scientific warfare. The term has since applied generally to any anonymous workers. The phrase comes from a speech by Lord Beaverbrook on war production (24 March 1941): "To whom must praise be given . . . to the boys in the backroom." Lord Beaverbrook no doubt used the phrase remembering Marlene Dietrich's song 'See what the boys in the backroom will have', from the film *Destry Rides Again* (1939); this connection is all the more likely as Beaverbrook is reported to have once said that Marlene Dietrich in her fishnet stockings in *The Blue Angel* was a greater work of art than the Venus de Milo. Nigel Balchin provided a further tribute to these workers in his novel *The Small Back Room* (1943).

back-seat driver One who gives a car driver advice and instructions from the back seat.

backstage The area behind the stage in a theatre, including the wings, the dressing-rooms, etc. In a 20th-century refinement of the word, it came to signify a film or stage show (often a musical) based upon life 'backstage'.

backs to the wall Originally, on the defensive against odds. Someone beset with foes tries to get his back against a wall to prevent attack from behind. A modern refinement of the phrase gives it sexual connotations, making it a warning that one is in the presence of a homosexual.

> Every position must be held to the last man: there must be no retirement. With our backs to the wall, and believing in the justice of our cause, each of us must fight on to the end.
>
> DOUGLAS HAIG, ordering his troops to resist a German attack in World War I.

back to basics Back to the first principles of something, a phrase first heard in the 1950s.

back to square one Back to where one started from. Popularized from the early days of broadcast commentaries on football matches when, in order to make the course of the game easier to follow, a diagram of the pitch, divided into numbered squares, was printed in radio programmes. Possibly derived from earlier board games.

back to the drawing board Rethinking the whole design or concept. Probably the phrase was first used by aircraft designers when a concept, or even a whole design for a new plane, was shown to be faulty and had to be rethought.

bacteriophobia An unreasoning fear of bacteria. Sufferers are obsessed with avoiding 'dirt' of any kind in case of contamination; they wash themselves frequently. Such behaviour is often interpreted as evidence of a guilt complex and is sometimes called the **Lady Macbeth syndrome**.

bad Good. Originally a Black US slang expression. Probably deriving from its ironic use by JAZZ musicians in the 1950s, it became much more widely used by the young in the UK, as well as America, in the 1970s and 1980s through the popularity of Black music in general and Michael Jackson's album *Bad* in particular. Whether it is being used in its literal sense or in this slang sense is largely distinguished by pronunciation. Bad in this sense is pronounced 'b-a-a-d'. The superlative form is **baddest**. *See also* WICKED.

> She had on a little black cocktail number and the baddest suede, pointy, red shoes you ever saw.
>
> BEN ELTON, *Stark* (1989).

bad actor A harmful substance, especially a poisonous plant. This meaning dates from the 1970s; in US Black slang of the 1940s the term was used of any person (or animal) causing a nuisance.

bad news A difficult or disliked person; a troublemaker. Originally a US expression, it has been used in the UK since the 1960s.

Badminton horse trials A competition held annually in April in the park of Badminton House, the seat of the dukes of Beaufort in Avon (formerly Gloucestershire). It is a three-day event consisting of a dressage stage, a speed and endurance stage over steeplechase and cross-country courses, and a showjumping stage on the final day. The trials were started in 1952 with the intention of raising the standards of British horsemanship.

Baedeker Raids A phrase used in Britain to describe the German air attacks on 29th April 1942 (in reprisal for British raids on Cologne and Lübeck). These reprisals were deliberately targeted on historic monuments such as those listed in the Baedeker series of guidebooks for tourists (*e.g.* Bath, Canterbury, Norwich).

Bafta award One of several awards presented annually to the film and TV industry by the British Association of Film and Television Arts.

bag. baggies US surfing jargon dating from the 1960s for the wide long shorts worn by surfers.

bag lady A female tramp, a vagrant, characterized by her assortment of plastic carrier bags that contain her worldly possessions. The euphemism originated in the 1970s in America but is now used in the UK and elsewhere; it has also come to be used to describe a very untidy unkempt woman.

bag man (1) A US underworld expression of the 1920s and 1930s for the man sent by the big gangsters to collect extortion payments. (2) A male tramp, a vagrant, characterized by his assortment of plastic carrier bags.

bagpipe (1) US slang dating from the 1940s for a vacuum cleaner. (2) To indulge in sexual activity specifically involving stimulation of the armpit.

bag system A public welfare scheme promoted in Australia during the GREAT DEPRESSION. Under its terms the unemployed were given a bag of essential groceries on each dole day.

not one's bag Not what one specializes in. This sense originated in US jazz slang, meaning a personal style of playing, *e.g.* 'playing in a big band was not his bag'. This usage widened in America and crossed the Atlantic with the wider meaning.

bagel The Yiddish name for a hard round roll, simmered in hot water before baking and then glazed with egg white. They are eaten with LOX and cream cheese, especially by Jews in New York City. The Yiddish word is derived from the German *Beugel*, a round loaf. Although bagels were well known to European Jews, and were traditionally served with hard-boiled eggs after a funeral, their association with lox and New York Jews is a 20th century phenomenon.

Baghdad Pact A treaty for military and economic cooperation originally signed in 1955 between Iraq and Turkey. It was later joined by Iran, Pakistan, and the UK. In 1959 Iraq withdrew, America became an associate member, and the organization was renamed the **Central Treaty Organization** (CENTO). After the fall of the Shah of Iran in 1979, Iran withdrew from the pact and the organization was dissolved.

Bahasa Indonesia (Malay. *bahasa*, language) A form of Malay widely used as a trade language in SE Asia and adopted as the official language of Indonesia in 1972.

Bailey bridge In World War II a metal bridge of great strength made of easily portable sections and capable of speedy erection. It was invented by the British engineer D. C. Bailey. Bailey bridges were a major factor in enabling the Allies to advance so rapidly, especially in NW Europe.

bait and switch An advertising ploy in which a customer is first lured by a cheap product and then persuaded to buy a more expensive product that has obviously superior features.

Bakelite The tradename for a phenol-formaldehyde resin invented in 1908 by Leo Bækeland (1863–1944), a US chemist of Belgian birth. While searching for a substitute for shellac, which was then being used for making records for the emerging gramophone industry, he investigated the phenol-formaldehyde resins that had been discovered in 1871 by Karl Baeyer. By choosing appropriate formulation and reaction conditions he discovered a hard resin that could be both cast and machined and had unusually good electrical properties. The result, patented under the name Bakelite, formed the basis of the vast plastics industry. Shellac, however, continued to be used for 78 rpm records, until the advent of extended-play (45 rpm) and long-playing (33 rpm) records in the 1950s, which were both made from vinyl plastics.

Baker. Baker day In the British educational system the informal name for a day devoted to the training of teachers. It was named after the Secretary of State for Education Kenneth Baker (1935–), who in the educational reforms of the 1980s introduced several such days each year.

Baker Street Irregulars The group of young boys that Sherlock Holmes used to gain information about London's underworld in the novels of Sir Arthur Conan Doyle (1859–1930). The name has been taken by a US appreciation society dedicated to studying the Sherlock Holmes novels. It was also used by the **Special Operations Executive (SOE)** – a British secret-service organization set up (1940) during World War II to train agents working in occupied territories. The SOE took the name because its original headquarters were in Baker Street (and Sherlock Holmes' rooms were at 221b Baker Street).

balance of terror The role of nuclear weapon arsenals in maintaining stable international relations, a refinement of the more traditional phrase 'balance of power'.

Balearic A form of DISCO music that became popular in the 1980s. Its name was derived from the Balearic Islands (especially Majorca and Minorca), popular with British holiday-makers, where there are numerous discos.

Balenciaga The Spanish fashion house founded by Cristóbal Balenciaga (1895–1972). Its style of elegant suits and evening dresses was enormously popular in the 1950s but fell from fashion in the 1960s.

Balfour. Balfour declaration A statement made by the British Conservative statesman Arthur Balfour (1848–1930) in 1917 (when he was foreign secretary) regarding the establishment of a national Jewish state in Palestine. The promise to support the setting up of such a state was made in a letter from Balfour to the Zionist leader Lionel Walter Rothschild (2nd Baron Rothschild; 1868–1937), and was conditional on the fact that the rights of existing non-Jewish residents in Palestine should be maintained and that the rights of Jewish residents in other countries should also be respected. The declaration was repudiated by the British Government in 1939. *See also* MCMAHON LETTERS; SYKES-PICOT AGREEMENT.

Balfour's Poodle The House of Lords. From 1906 Balfour, as the Conservative leader, exploited the Conservative majority in the House of Lords to block the legislation of the Liberal government, which had an overwhelming majority in the Commons. When the Lords rejected the Licensing Bill of 1908, Henry Chaplin MP claimed that the House of Lords was the "watchdog of the constitution", to which Lloyd George replied, "You mean it is Mr Balfour's poodle! It fetches and carries for him. It barks for him. It bites anybody that he sets it on to!"

Balkan. Balkan League A military alliance formed (1912) between Bulgaria, Serbia, Greece, and Montenegro to wage war against Turkey. *See* BALKAN WARS.

Balkan Pact A military treaty (1954) between Greece, Turkey, and Yugoslavia. Although never formally cancelled, the three members have quietly forgotten its existence.

Balkan Wars Two military conflicts occurring just before World War I in the Balkans. The first (1912–13) was between the members of the BALKAN LEAGUE and the Ottoman Empire. The Empire was forced to give up most of its European territories. The second Balkan War was between members of the Balkan League – Bulgaria was defeated by Serbia, Greece, and Romania in a quarrel about the distribution of territory gained in Macedonia during the first war. At the same time, the Turks regained part of Thrace.

ball. ballpark figure An estimate, usually of a financial quantity, upon which no great reliance should be put. A ballpark is a large stadium in America in which baseball is played. The original reference, 'in the same ballpark', means that two figures are roughly of the same magnitude as they fall within the same ballpark.

ballroom without a parachute In US Black slang, a place in which marijuana is habitually smoked but in which there is currently no marijuana available. *See also* BALLOON ROOM.

balls Testicles. The word has acquired two slang meanings on both sides of the Atlantic. 'Don't talk balls' means 'don't talk rubbish'. **Balls** as a single expletive also means 'Rubbish, I don't agree'. On the other hand 'He doesn't have the balls for it' means 'He doesn't have the courage'. The term **balls-up**, used for something that has gone hopelessly awry, was first heard in the 1930s.

Ballets Russes The enormously influential ballet company founded in Paris in 1909 by Sergei Diaghilev (1872–1929). It acquired almost legendary status under the choreographers Fokine, Massine, Balanchine, and Nijinsky before it was finally disbanded on Diaghilev's death.

balloon. balloon angioplasty A surgical operation in which a blocked coronary artery (which supplies blood to the heart) is stretched by inserting into it a plastic cylinder (*balloon*), which is then inflated.

balloon astronomy The use of special balloons carrying sophisticated cameras and other scientific equipment in making examinations of astronomical features from high altitudes, where the earth's atmosphere is very thin.

balloon cloth A type of cloth first used in hot-air balloons and dirigibles, but later adapted for use in the clothing industry.

balloon pump A pump used in heart surgery to imitate the pulsating action of the heart, first used in the 1960s.

balloon room In US Black slang, a place in which marijuana is smoked. *See also* BALLROOM WITHOUT A PARACHUTE.

When the balloon goes up When trouble breaks out. The phrase was first used in World War I, referring to the launching of observation balloons shortly before an attack.

bally British euphemism for 'bloody', now rarely heard except among middle- and upper-class elderly people. It was very popular in the pre-World War II period.

ballyhoo A fuss, cacophony of raised voices, etc. In the film industry the word (Irish in origin) acquired the more specialized sense of publicity for a film that is put out without linking it in any way to the actual merits of the film itself. *See also* HYPE.

Balmain A fashion house founded by the French couturier Pierre Alexandre Balmain (1914–82) in 1935.

Balt Australian slang of the 1950s for a new Australian, an immigrant. Originally the term was specifically applied to immigrants from the Baltic States, but was later more widely applied.

Baltic Exchange A market in the City of London for buying and selling freight space for goods to be transported by sea or air. It also deals in chartering ships and aircraft. In addition the market deals with some commodities – grain, potatoes, and meat. Forward freight is dealt with by the *Baltic International Freight Futures Exchange* (*BIFFEX*). The name comes from the fact that in the 18th century most of its business involved trade in grain through Baltic ports.

Bambi A small deer, the eponymous star of a feature-length Walt Disney cartoon film (1942) based on the novel by Felix Salten (1869–1945).

Bambi Project A US defence project for orbital satellites armed with missiles designed to intercept intercontinental ballistic missiles at take-off. The project was suspended in 1964, but was a forerunner of the STAR WARS programme.

Bamboo Curtain The veil of secrecy and mistrust drawn between the Chinese Communist bloc and the non-Communist nations. It was named by analogy with the IRON CURTAIN. *See also* GARLIC WALL.

ban The restriction of political activity imposed on certain Black dissidents in South Africa under the Internal Security Act of 1977. 'Banned' people were prevented from appearing in public or expressing political opinions.

Banaban A native of Ocean Island in the SW Pacific. Inhabitants of the island were engaged in a lengthy battle for compensation from the British government in the late 1970s for damage done to their home during extensive mining for phosphates (1900–79) culminating in their resettlement on Rabi Island in Fiji during World War II; they were finally awarded £5 million.

banana (1) A fool. This now obsolete sense in the UK is still sometimes heard in the shortened form 'nana' among children as a mild insult. (2) British slang meaning penis. Sometimes used in the expression 'turn my banana'. (3) US slang for a light-skinned Black woman. Used by Black men, it can have either appreciative or derogatory overtones.

banana belt An area in North America that is popular for winter holidays due to its mild climate (warm enough for bananas to be grown). It is also used of other similar regions.

banana boat *See* COME OVER WITH THE ONION BOAT.

banana republic Any state that is dependent on one particular agricultural product, such as bananas. Usually applied to the nations of South America or Africa, the phrase has overtones of bureaucratic inefficiency, impoverishment, and easily bribed leaders. *Bananas* (1971) was a film starring Woody Allen about such a state.

Yes, we have no bananas Nonsensical catchphrase of the 1920s. It was taken from the chorus of a song (1923) by Frank Silver and Irving Cohn.

> I would rather have been the Author of that Banana Masterpiece than the Author of the Constitution of the United States. No one has offered any amendments to it. It's the only thing ever written in America that we haven't changed, most of them for the worst.
>
> WILL ROGERS; *The Illiterate Digest* (1924).

The phrase was revived in the UK during World War II, when it became particularly appropriate as bananas disappeared completely from the shops. At the end of the war there were 5-year old children who had never seen a real banana.

band. **band-aid** To fix something on a temporary basis, from the tradename for an adhesive plaster. In 1984 the name **Band Aid** was adopted by the organizers of a fundraising effort launched by the pop music community to help the starving in Ethiopia and Sudan; the pun reflects what they obviously considered an inadequate response to a serious problem. Nevertheless, their recording of 'Do They Know It's Christmas' became the UK's biggest-selling single ever, raising about £8M. The success of the campaign inspired several similar organizations with the same aims, including the **Comic Relief** events, in which leading comedians urge the public to support worthy causes by buying red plastic noses, etc. *See also* LIVE AID; TELETHON.

bandmoll US name for a GROUPIE.

bandog A cross between a PIT BULL TERRIER and a mastiff, ROTTWEILER, or similarly aggressive breed. These crosses became a subject of public concern in the 1980s when British media attention was focused on attacks on children by these dogs.

Bandung Conference A conference (1955) that took place between 29 African and Asian states at the city of Bandung in West Java, Indonesia. A strong stance against colonialism was taken and a policy of non-alignment between the Western and Communist blocs agreed.

bandy A British working-class term of abuse used by men to describe a woman who is alleged to be 'bandy-legged' from having sex frequently. It was used by London mods (*see* MODS AND ROCKERS) and SKINHEADS in the late 1960s.

bang (1) To have sex. A widely used slang word since the 1960s but more common in the UK and Australia than in America. *See also* GANG-BANG. (2) US slang for a big thrill. (3) A drug abuser's term, dating from the 1940s, for an injection of illegal drugs, particularly heroin or morphine. (4) Archaic Australian slang for a brothel. (5) **bang like a shithouse door (in a gale)** An Australian expression meaning to be an enthusiastic sexual partner. It was popularized by the comic cartoon strip *Barry McKenzie* (by Barry Humphries) in the magazine *Private Eye* in the 1960s.

banger (1) British slang for a sausage, current since the 1940s, supposedly derived from the noise of the sausage skin popping while it cooks. **Bangers and mash** (sausages and mashed potato) is a favourite British dish. (2) An affectionate term for an old decrepit car.

banjo'd, banjoed (1) British slang meaning completely drunk, or stoned, under the influence of drugs. It is probably a corruption of *banjaxed*, an Irish word meaning totally overcome, and was used mainly by young people in the 1980s. (2) An army expression of the 1970s and 1980s for defeated, again probably related to banjaxed. There may also be a connection with an archaic slang usage of banjo meaning a shovel or weapon.

bank. **bankable** Any project or person thought likely to succeed and thus to prove financially profitable, applied chiefly to film stars and other celebrities since the 1960s.

Bankers' Ramp An alleged conspiracy by British bankers (1931) to discredit the Labour government of the time by undermining the economy.

bank rate *See* MINIMUM LENDING RATE.

Bantustan An area in South Africa set aside by the government for Blacks, who are allowed limited self-government. A number of these areas (also called *Bantu Homelands*) have been created, the first being Transkei in 1963 (received full independence in 1976). The name comes from combining *Bantu* – the indigenous people inhabiting the area, with *-stan*, from Pakistan – taken as an example of a state formed from an existing state (Pakistan being a state formed from India).

banzai (Jap. forward) Japanese battlecry, uttered in frontal attacks on enemy troops in World War II. As a traditional greeting its original meaning was 'May you live forever'.

bar. **bar code** A machine-readable code consisting of a series of parallel lines, of varying thickness, that can be read by a laser scanner. Bar codes are widely used for coding products for sale to enable faster processing of goods at the checkout. Known as **EPOS** (electronic point of sale), this system enables stock figures to be reduced automatically as sales are made and a warning system to be activated as stocks fall below a specified figure. Such codes are also used to programme video cassette recorders etc.

bar fly A US slang expression of the 1930s for a man or woman who frequents cheap bars. It was the title of a 1987 film with a script by Charles Bukowski.

barb British drug-abusers' slang first used in the 1950s for a barbiturate.

Barbarossa The German code name for the invasion of the Soviet Union in 1941. The name was taken from the nickname of the Holy Roman Emperor Frederick I (*c.* 1123–90).

> When Barbarossa commences, the world will hold its breath and make no comment.
>
> ADOLF HITLER.

barber. Every barber knows that That is already common knowledge. A primarily US comment implying that chat between customers and their barbers is so continuous, intimate, and diverse that barbers may be expected to be extremely well informed, especially in the fields of gossip and rumour.

Barbican A development in the City of London, originally planned in 1955 to replace bombed parts of the City. Officially opened in 1982, it contains many private flats as well as an exhibition gallery, theatre complex, cinemas, etc. The name comes from a London street on the site named after a barbican (watch tower) in the old city walls.

barbie An Australian slang abbreviation for barbecue, dating from the 1960s, that has become widely used in the UK, especially by YUPPIES. Its use in the UK coincided with the arrival of Australian SOAP OPERAS on British TV.

Barbie doll A US slang term for an empty-headed but sexually attractive young woman. *Barbie* is the tradename for a plastic doll with a woman's figure, long combable hair, and a wardrobe of glamorous clothes. *See also* ACTION MAN.

Barbour The tradename of a typically green waxed cotton coat or jacket manufactured by J. Barber and Sons Ltd of South Shields, Tyne and Wear, established 1880. This hard-wearing waterproof and windproof article of clothing, the traditional outdoor wear of the county set and gentleman-farmers, was in the 1980s enthusiastically adopted by YUPPIES weekending in the country. Its almost cult popularity, coupled with its practicality, gave rise to a host of cheaper imitations.

Barcelona chair A simple yet elegant chair with a stainless steel frame designed by Ludwig Mies van der Rohe in 1929. First seen on show in Barcelona, it had a fundamental effect upon contemporary design.

barefoot doctor A medical practitioner who works in remote areas of the world, usually for international charity organizations. It is a rough translation of the Chinese phrase *chijiao yisheng* – many peasant doctors being literally barefooted.

bariatrics (Gr. *barós,* weight) The branch of medicine dealing with the treatment of obese patients; it developed as a distinct speciality in the 1960s. *See also* BULIMIA.

barmy army Nickname sometimes given to any semi-organized group, usually of football supporters or pop music fans.

barrel. Political power grows out of the barrel of a gun One of the political maxims proposed by Mao Tse-Tung in 'Problems of War and Strategy'. Typical of his philosophy of enforcing communist doctrine by military power, it acquired an ironic echo in the practice of HIPPIES all over the world who, when confronted by armed troops at various peace demonstrations, 'spiked' the soldiers' guns with flowers.

Baruch plan A plan, put forward in 1946, in which America agreed to destroy its stock of nuclear weapons and fissionable material provided that an international body was set up to prevent the spread of these weapons and to control the use of nuclear power. The plan, which was rejected by the Soviet Union, was proposed by Bernard Baruch (1870–1965), who was advisor to the US president and was involved in formulating US policy on atomic energy.

base Crack. An abbreviation of *freebase*, which is a method of smoking purified cocaine. It became part of British drug abusers' jargon in the late 1980s.

base rate *See* MINIMUM LENDING RATE.

bash (1) A party. (2) British term for a homeless person's shelter, made of cardboard and plastic sheeting.

> I live in a bash – a room made of pallets and cardboard, with blankets for doors.
>
> Homeless person quoted in *The Independent on Sunday*, 20 January 1991.

Basic Beginners All-purpose Symbolic Instruction Code, a computer-programming language using common English terms.

Basic English A fundamental form of English, consisting of a selected vocabulary of 850 words, designed by the British scholar C. K. Ogden in 1926–30 as a common first step in the teaching of English and as an auxiliary language. The name comes from the initials of the words British, American, Scientific, International, Commercial.

basilect A dialect that is treated with scorn by users of that language. The word was coined by the US linguist William A. Stewart in 1964.

Basin Street A street in the red-light district of New Orleans, which was possibly the original home of JAZZ music. The well-known *Basin Street Blues* was composed by Spencer Williams in 1928: 'Basin Street is a street where Black folk meet'.

basket case (1) US slang for someone with both arms and legs amputated. (2) Someone who is mentally incapacitated. Patients in mental hospitals are often taught basket-weaving skills. (3) A nervous wreck. Originally a US expression. (4) A journalist's expression for a ruined project. Derived presumably from the idea that it is fit only for the wastepaper basket.

basse couture (Fr. low sewing) In the clothing industry, any garment that fails to meet the standards set by leading fashion designers.

Bataan A peninsula in the Philippines, which witnessed some of the fiercest fighting in the Pacific theatre of World War II. US and Philippine forces surrendered to the Japanese here in 1942 after a heroic defence lasting three months; many thousands of prisoners subsequently died on a long 'death march'. Bataan was retaken by US forces later in the war. *See also* CORREGIDOR.

batch-process A manufacturing process in which the product is made in a series of separate batches, rather than continuously.

bath. Bath Festival An annual festival of 18th-century music founded in Bath in 1948. It ceased in 1956 after financial difficulties and was revived three years later by Yehudi Menuhin. It subsequently expanded into a festival of the arts, with painting exhibitions, poetry readings, etc. Many notable performers have appeared in the festival.

bathroom record A more than usually lengthy record played by a DISC JOCKEY to allow him time to visit the bathroom (*i.e.* lavatory) between announcements.

To take an early bath To retire early to the players' dressing-room after being sent off the field (or injured) during a match of football, rugby, etc. The term is used more widely of any situation in which someone is obliged to retire from the 'field of play' before its conclusion. In US slang, 'to take a bath' means to suffer any defeat.

bathyscape A vessel designed by Auguste Piccard (1884–1962) and his son Jacques Piccard (1927–) to enable them to explore the depths of the oceans. In 1960, in the bathyscape *Trieste*, they reached a depth of 10,917 metres (about 6.8 miles).

batman (Fr. *bat*, pack-saddle) Originally a soldier in charge of a **bat-horse** (pack-horse) and its load of officer's baggage. The name came to denote an army officer's servant in World War I through its inaccurate use by non-regular wartime officers.

It also now denotes a person at an airport or on an aircraft carrier who wields a pair of lightweight bats to direct the pilot in moving the aircraft on the ground (or deck).

Batman US COMIC STRIP hero who first appeared in 1939. The **Caped Crusader** of Gotham City fought such criminal arch-fiends as The Joker and The Penguin, first in newspapers, then on television, and in the cinema (1943, 1966, and 1989). A number of catchphrases associated with his adventures became common parlance, especially among children. His accessories include the **Batmobile** and the **Batboat**, while **Robin** (the **Boy Wonder**) was his crime-fighting colleague in some adventures.

Battenberg The original name of the Mountbatten family. Prince Louis of Battenberg (1854–1921) took the name of Mountbatten in 1917 because of anti-German prejudice during World War I. *See also* WINDSOR.

battered baby *See* CHILD ABUSE.

battle. Battle Act An act passed in America (1951) to prohibit aid being given to nations under Soviet influence. It was named after Senator Battle, who proposed it.

Battleaxe Codename for an abortive attack by British tanks against Rommel's forces in 1941 on the Egypt–Libya border.

battle bowler A nickname given in World War I to the soldier's steel helmet or tin hat. In World War II it was also called a 'tin topee'.

battle cruiser Cockney rhyming slang for a boozer, a pub. It dates from the 1940s.

Battle of Britain The attempt by the German Luftwaffe in their prolonged attack on SE England (August–October 1940) to defeat the RAF, as a prelude to invasion of the British Isles. The RAF managed to defeat the enemy, largely as a result of the heroism of the young fighter pilots of HURRICANES and SPITFIRES, whom Churchill described as the FEW. The name of the battle arose from Churchill's earlier speech (18 June 1940)—"What General Weygand called the 'Battle of France' is over. I expect that the Battle of Britain is about to begin."

Battle of Flowers An annual flower festival that takes place in St Helier, Jersey, in July. It involves a procession of flower-decorated floats and culminates in a flower-throwing contest; it was inaugurated in 1902 to mark the coronation of Edward VII and Queen Alexandra.

batty Crazy. Possibly derived from the phrase 'to have bats in the belfry', first heard in the 1900s.

baud A unit measuring the rate at which information can be transmitted. It is equal to one unit of information per second, where the unit is a bit, digit, or symbol depending on the system. The **baud rate** measures the speed at which a computer transfers data. The unit is named after J. M. E. Baudot (1845–1903), a French inventor who patented (1874) a telegraph code (the **Baudot code**) based on sets of binary digits to replace Morse code.

Bauhaus A school of architecture and design founded by the German architect Walter Gropius (1883–1969) in 1919. From 1925 to 1932 it was housed in an influential building in Dessau designed by Gropius. The full name was *Staatliches Bauhaus* (Public House of Building) – 'Bauhaus' was coined by inverting the German word *Hausbau* (building of a house). The Bauhaus school stressed the teaching of art and crafts and emphasized the mass manufacture of well-designed functional objects. The school was immensely important for its influence on 20th-century design. It was forced to close in 1933 by the NAZIS. Other influential members of the school were the artists Wassily Kandinsky (1866–1944), Paul Klee (1879–1940), and László Moholy-Nagy (1895–1946) and the architect Ludwig Mies van der Rohe (1886–1969). *See* BARCELONA CHAIR.

Bay of Pigs An abortive attempt (17 April 1961) to invade Cuba made by about 1500 expatriate anti-Castro Cubans. The invasion forces were trained and financed by the CIA and landed at several sites in the south of the island, in particular Bahia de los Cochinos (the Bay of Pigs). Inadequately supported by the US military, the invaders were no match for Castro's forces and by 19 April 1100 men had been captured. They were later 'ransomed' for $53 million worth of aid. *See also* CUBAN MISSILE CRISIS.

bazaari (Pers. bazaar) An Iranian shopkeeper. The bazaaris played a key role in the Iranian Revolution of 1979.

bazooka US infantry light rocket-firing tube used as an anti-tank weapon in World War II. It was then applied to the British **PIAT** (projection, infantry anti-tank) and the German *Panzerfaust*. The name was possibly derived from its earlier use for a comedian's trombone-type wind instrument (perhaps modelled on the *kazoo*, a submarine-shaped toy producing sounds of the 'comb and paper' variety).

To be bazookaed To be in a tank struck by such a weapon and thus metaphorically to be 'scuppered', put out of action, done for.

bazumas Female breasts. Probably a corruption of *bosoms*. *See also* MAZUMA.

BBC British Broadcasting Corporation. It was set up in 1922 and became a public body under royal charter in 1927, with responsibility to parliament. Under such directors-general as John Reith (later 1st Baron Reith; 1889–1971), the BBC acquired an international reputation for its professionalism, high moral standards, and lack of political bias. Its role in World War II further added to its high standing, although commercial pressures following the introduction of independent television companies in the 1950s together with rapid social changes led to a gradual evolution in both style and in its broadcasting philosophy. *See also* AUNTIE; BEEB; WORLD SERVICE.

BBC English *See* RECEIVED PRONUNCIATION.

be. be-in In the 1960s, an informal gathering of people in a public place at which participants are encouraged to act without inhibitions or regard for conventional modes of behaviour. *See also* LOVE-IN; SIT-IN.

Be Prepared The motto of the BOY SCOUTS, chosen in 1908.

beach. **beachball** A method of escape from an orbiting spacecraft to another spacecraft in the event of an emergency. It consists of a circular 'bubble', which is connected to the larger craft's life-support system.

beach bunny A girl who parades herself on the beach wearing a skimpy BIKINI.

Beachcomber Pen name of the writer of a humorous column, *By The Way*, in the *Daily Express*. Originally started by D. B. Wyndham-Lewis (who later wrote a column under the name *Timothy Shy* for the *News Chronicle*), it was continued by J. B. Morton (1893–1979). Morton created a number of fantastic characters including Mr Justice Cocklecarrot and the famous Dr Strabismus (Whom God Preserve) of Utrecht, noted for crossing a salmon with a mosquito so that fishermen could have a bite every time. Beachcomber's humour was an early example of the type of comedy exemplified by the GOON SHOW and, later, by MONTY PYTHON'S FLYING CIRCUS.

beach music A pop music genre combining elements of SOUL with RHYTHM AND BLUES. Its origins lie in the Black culture of America's SE coastal states, particularly South Carolina. Well established in this region and intermittently popular on both sides of the Atlantic, beach music enjoyed a revival when the shag, an American dance linked with the music, became a focus of media attention in 1987.

beam. **beamer** YUPPIE word for a BMW car.

beam me up, Scotty A catchphrase derived from the TV science-fiction series *Star Trek* (1966–69). To 'beam someone up' was to transfer them as 'matter' from one location to another (usually from a planet's surface to the orbiting starship *Enterprise*); 'Scotty' was the chief engineer on the *Enterprise*. *See also* BOLDLY.

beam weapon A laser developed for use in various advanced weaponry systems. One highly specialized possible application is as a component of America's STAR WARS programme.

bean. **beanbag** A large pellet-filled cushion, commonly found in fashionable living-rooms in the 1960s and 1970s. The theory behind the beanbag was that it would mould itself to the shape of the person who sat in it. It does not, however, provide support.

Beanz Meanz Heinz A slogan used in the 1960s to sell Heinz Baked Beans.

bear A policeman. This nickname originated in America in posters advertising 'Smokey the Bear' in the uniform of a ranger; it was picked up by CB users in the 1970s.

The Bear *See* STORMIN' NORMAN.

beard (1) Slang for a HIPPIE or intellectual. (2) US slang for a chaperone.

beast. **Beast 666** Aleister Crowley (1876–1947), who earned the epithet the **Wickedest Man in the World** for his practice of the black arts and his advocacy of drugs and satanic sexual rituals. He chose his name from the bible:

> Let him that hath understanding count the number of the beast: for it is the number of a man: and his number is six hundred threescore and six.
>
> *Revelation*, 13

Beast of Belsen In World War II the name given to Joseph Kramer, commandant of the infamous BELSEN concentration camp.

Beast of Bolsover Dennis Skinner (1932–), Labour MP for Bolsover (Derbyshire). Describing himself in *Who's Who* as coming from 'good working-class mining stock' and having been himself a miner for 21 years, he was given his nickname by lobby correspondents for his aggressive behaviour in parliament. As a result of persistent and noisy interruptions, he was several times asked to leave the Chamber by the Speaker.

Beast of Exmoor A mysterious puma-like creature that captured British newspaper headlines in 1983. The 'Beast' was sighted several times on the Somerset–Devon boundary and was blamed for the deaths of over 200 sheep in the area. Panic over the animal, which was described as some kind of large cat, led to a Royal Marines team equipped with night sights being detailed to find it: they failed but sightings of the creature gradually tailed off.

The Beast of Exmoor was in fact only one of many such unidentified animals reported throughout the country in modern times, with similar press attention being given to big cats in Surrey, Derbyshire, Dorset, Buckinghamshire, Dyfed, Hertfordshire, Powys, and Essex in 1983 alone. One, caught in a trap in Scotland in 1980, did actually turn out to be a puma, which had presumably escaped from a zoo.

don't let's be beastly to the Germans The title of a song (1930) by Noël Coward, which became a catchphrase in the pre-World War II period, often used ironically.

beat (1) A member or follower of the **Beat Generation** of the 1950s. Coined by the writer Jack Kerouac, the word first appeared in John Clellon Holmes's novel *GO*, to describe a group of US writers including Kerouac, Allen Ginsberg, and William Burroughs, whose writings told of their experiments with drugs, sex, religion, and politics. In the UK in the early 1960s the beats were a youth group who adopted these liberal ideas and a bohemian lifestyle; as the decade progressed, they became known as HIPPIES. (2) An abbreviation for BEATNIK. (3) A slang word for exhausted.

beat group A type of pop group of the 1950s and 1960s, characterized by a marked emphasis on rhythm or beat.

Beatles British POP group of the 1960s, also known as the **Fab Four**, that attained near-mythical status before finally disbanding in 1970. Comprising John Lennon (1940–80), Paul McCartney (1942–), George Harrison (1943–), and RINGO Starr (1940–), the group established a cult following (called **Beatlemania**) during appearances at the **Cavern Club** in Liverpool in 1962. Lennon was moved to remark that in their heyday they were "more popular than Jesus Christ". The unrivalled sequence of hit records that followed in the next eight years included the singles 'She Loves You' (1963), 'Yellow Submarine' (1966), 'Penny Lane' (1967), 'Hey Jude' (1968), and 'Long and Winding Road' (1970) and the albums *Help* (1965), *Sergeant Pepper's Lonely Hearts Club Band* (1967), and *Let It Be* (1970). A host of legends surrounded the band, many of them associated with the rumour that McCartney had died. The group's impact was immeasurable; their music – with its shades of ROCK 'N' ROLL, PSYCHEDELIC experience, and Indian mysticism – was widely taken to summarize the mood of the SWINGING SIXTIES. Although there were connections with the drug culture of the time (*see* MANSON GANG), the establishment had to recognize their achievement and worldwide popularity. In 1965 they were awarded MBEs (which John Lennon returned in protest against the UK's involvement in the Biafran War of Independence). *See also* APPLE CORPS.

beatnik A 'beat' person of the 1960s, one who lived a beat life. Socially, politically, intellectually, and artistically beatniks stood apart, flouting all or most of the established conventions and values, this being emphasized by their typically unconventional dress and slovenliness. The word probably derives from BEAT and the Russian suffix ***nik*** (as in SPUTNIK).

> The Russian-sounding suffix . . . hinted at free love and a little communism (not enough to be threatening), as well as a general oafishness.
>
> JOYCE JOHNSON, *Minor Characters* (1983).

If you can't beat 'em, join 'em A catchphrase, dating from the 1940s, that offers advice to those who do not have the resources to destroy their enemies. It implies that being a member of an alliance is preferable to being a loser. It is often used in a political context.

Beatty In lower-deck naval slang, an officer. It comes from Earl Beatty (1871–1936), a British admiral who took part in the battle of JUTLAND and was later first sea lord.

beauty In nuclear physics, a FLAVOUR of QUARK.

beautiful people Slang for the most fashionable (usually wealthy) trend-setting members of society; heard in the 1960s.

beautility A design philosophy in which beauty and utility are given equal consideration.

becquerel The international unit of radioactivity adopted in 1976. A replacement for the CURIE, it was named after the French physicist Antoine H. Becquerel (1852–1908).

beaver (1) In the 1920s and 1930s anyone wearing a beard. In this period beards were so rare that a person with one was in danger of having 'beaver' shouted at him in the street by schoolchildren. (2) A woman's pubic hair, *e.g.* "She has shaved her beaver."

The Beaver Name given in journalistic circles to Lord Beaverbrook (William Maxwell-Aitken; 1879–1964), Canadian-born politician and newspaper magnate. He served in a number of capacities in World War I and as Minister of Aircraft Production in World War II (*see also* BACKROOM BOYS), being responsible for stepping up the output of the SPITFIRE fighter and Whitley bomber. He became Minister of Supply in 1941.

bebop A syncopated style of modern JAZZ accompanied by nonsense words. It became popular in the 1940s.

bebop glasses Sunglasses, as worn by JAZZ musicians in the 1940s.

bed. bed of nails A self-inflicted awkward situation. Derived from the Indian fakir's spiked bed, it was first used in a modern context of the Labour government in 1966.

beddo A bed that can be adjusted by electronic means. Such beds, which can be raised, lowered, rotated, etc., were popular in Japan in the 1960s and 1970s.

bedsit A combined bedroom and sitting-room, constituting a cheap form of accommodation designed for occupation by students, etc.

bee. beehive A dome-shaped hairstyle of the late 1950s and early 1960s, achieved by backcombing and the application of lacquer.

bee's knees A superlative situation, a phrase widely heard in the 1920s. In the 1970s it became the name of a popular US cocktail, made of lemon juice, gin, and honey.

Beeb An affectionate term for the BBC, the British Broadcasting Corporation.

Beeching's axe Cuts in the services of British Rail (then British Railways) made as a result of a report by Dr. Beeching (later Lord Beeching; 1913–85). Beeching was brought in by the government in 1960 as a successful industrialist from ICI to 'make the railway service profitable'. In 1961 he was put in charge of British Railways and in 1963 he put forward a report (*The Reshaping of British Railways*) that recommended closing 2128 stations, cutting the rail network by 25%, and the loss of over 65,000 jobs. Although Beeching was sacked by the government in 1964, major cuts were made in the rail network a few months later following his recommendations.

beef. beefalo A breed of beef cattle developed in America in the early 1970s by crossing domestic cattle with buffalo. The resultant hybrids, some three-eighths of whose genetic make up is of buffalo origin, yield a low-fat protein-rich meat.

beef mountain *See* CAP.

where's the beef? A political slogan associated with the US Democratic politician Walter Mondale in 1984. The phrase, which in a political context implies a lack of substance in a rival's promises and was used during Mondale's campaign to be nominated Democratic presidential candidate, originated in an advertising campaign for Wendy hamburgers. Mondale won the Democratic nomination but was defeated in the presidential election by Ronald Reagan.

beer. beer and sandwiches The fare that was offered to trade union leaders at 10 Downing Street in informal talks with the Labour government during the 1960s and 1970s. Such 'beer and sandwich' sessions were ridiculed by the Conservatives as indicative of the extraordinary influence the trade unions were alleged to have on the government of the day.

beer-hall Putsch *See* MUNICH PUTSCH.

beer is best An advertising slogan of the 1930s.

only here for the beer A trade slogan used in the UK for Double Diamond beer in the 1970s.

Beetle The name given (because of its bulbous shape) to a car first made by Volkswagen in Germany in 1935. Designed by Ferdinand Porsche on Hitler's instructions as a peoples' car, it became the best-selling car ever made. Production finally ceased in the 1980s. *See also* PORSCHE.

BEF British Expeditionary Force, the seven British regiments (160,000 men; six infantry regiments and one cavalry regiment) sent to France at the start of World War I in 1914. Known as the Old Contemptibles (*see* CONTEMPTIBLES, OLD), they suffered heavy losses at the hands of the Germans and had to be heavily reinforced. A second BEF was formed in 1939, when 10 divisions were sent to France at the start of World War II. After the Germans outflanked the MAGINOT LINE they had to be evacuated from DUNKIRK and other ports between 26 May and 4 June 1940, when 338,226 Allied troops were brought back to the UK.

before you came up A World War I put-down used by a veteran soldier to an inexperienced one, who had only recently joined up or come up to the front line. It implied that the recipient of the remark was totally ignorant of, and unlikely to be able to cope with, the rigours of life in the trenches: "I'd stuck my bayonet up 25 Jerries before you came up". Variants included "before your number was dry" (on your kitbag) and "before you knew what a button-stick was".

Befrienders International *See* SAMARITANS.

behaviour. behaviour therapy A method of treating patients with psychological disorders in which undesirable patterns of behaviour are replaced with less damaging new ones.

behaviourism A school of psychology founded by the US psychologist J. B. Watson (1878–1958) and advocated by the US psychologist B. F. Skinner (1904–90). Behaviourist psychologists stress observable behaviour and the effect of conditioning.

Bekaa Valley or **Beqaa Valley** A valley in S Lebanon between the Lebanon and the Anti-Lebanon Mountains, which has been the scene of many armed clashes in that country's modern history. In 1982 it witnessed heavy fighting between Israeli and Syrian forces.

Belau A republic consisting of a group of islands in the W Pacific Ocean, which achieved independence in 1981. It was formerly a UN Trust Territory.

Belgrade Theatre A civic theatre founded in Coventry in 1958 – the first new British theatre to be opened after World War II. It was named in recognition of a gift of timber from Belgrade, Yugoslavia, that was used in its construction.

believe it or not! The slogan associated with the US cartoon strip of the same title created by Robert Leroy Ripley (1893–1949) in 1923. The strip, which later spawned a radio and TV series and even a museum at Niagara Falls, presented extraordinary facts and tales, all allegedly true.

Belisha beacon An amber-coloured globe mounted on a black and white banded pole, the sign of a pedestrian crossing. Named after Leslie Hore-Belisha, Minister of Transport (1934–37), who introduced them.

Bell A series of early US experimental rocket planes designed to test high-speed flight at high altitudes. The Bell XS-1 was the first plane to achieve supersonic flight, piloted by Charles Yeager at 670 mph on 14 October 1947.

bell-bottoms A style of trousers that became popular in the 1960s and 1970s. Not dissimilar to the trousers traditionally worn in the navy, they flared out at or below the knee. Other names included **bells** and **flares.**

Belleau Wood A forest in N France, in which US Marines halted a German attack on Paris in 1918. It was in the fighting here that Dan Daly, a sergeant in the US Marines, uttered the immortal rallying cry: "Come on, you sons of bitches! Do you want to live forever?"

Belle Époque (Fr. beautiful period) The period in Europe from the turn of the century up to the start of World War I, in which the affluent lived in great comfort and style.

belly. belly bomber US slang for a heavily spiced extremely hot-tasting burger. A 1980s example of FAST FOOD in America, the bite-size burgers are eaten in rapid succession, producing the impression of a series of small explosions within the stomach.

belly landing The landing of an aircraft on its fuselage without the use of its landing gear. This was a not uncommon occurrence with fighter planes in World War II. Sometimes the retractable undercarriage was damaged in combat, sometimes it jammed for mechanical reasons, and sometimes the pilot forgot to lower it.

belly up In US slang, to go bankrupt (by allusion to dead fish).

Bélmez, Faces of The unexplained appearance of ghostly faces on the kitchen floor of a house in the S Spanish village of Bélmez, that caused a sensation in August 1971. The faces, which all wore unutterably sad expressions, resisted all attempts to erase them and terrified the occupants of the house, who eventually ripped up the floor and replaced it with concrete. Three weeks later the faces reappeared. An official inquiry was launched and investigators soon discovered the house stood over a medieval cemetery. The kitchen was sealed but new faces appeared elsewhere in the house and ultrasensitive microphones recorded strange cries of torment. Scientists photographed the faces but were unable to explain their origin. The faces eventually disappeared of their own accord.

below-the-line *See* ABOVE-THE-LINE.

Belsen A German CONCENTRATION CAMP during World War II, situated near the village of Belsen (north of Hanover). It was also called *Bergen–Belsen* from the nearby village of Bergen. 37,000 people died of starvation or disease here, including the Dutch diarist Anne Frank (1929–45). The commandant, Josef Kramer, was known as the BEAST OF BELSEN. Belsen was one of the first camps to be liberated (by the British in 1945) and the world was shocked by films of emaciated prisoners and of troops using bulldozers to move piles of naked corpses into mass graves.

Ben Barka disappearance An unsolved mystery surrounding the disappearance of the Moroccan opposition politician Mehdi Ben Barka (b. 1920) in Paris in October 1965. Ben Barka had been exiled to France and was last seen in October 1965 being driven away in a French police car. It is generally assumed that he was murdered by Moroccan agents with the connivance of the French secret service.

bender (1) A period of heavy drinking, or a wild spree. It is possibly derived from the euphemism 'to bend the elbow' meaning to drink alcohol heavily, but it may also be derived from the mid-19th century phrase 'hell-bender' meaning any exciting or outrageous event. (2) British slang for a homosexual. A euphemism for submitting to buggery, it is used less frequently now than it was in the 1960s. (3) British slang for an improvised tent-like structure made from hazel saplings bent into a semicircle and covered with a tarpaulin. Originally the name for the tents of travellers and gypsies, the word came into more common usage in the 1980s with the wide media coverage of the peace camp set up in 1981 by women, who camped in benders outside the US base at GREENHAM COMMON.

Benelux The customs union (1948) of the three countries Belgium, The Netherlands, and Luxemburg. They joined the EUROPEAN COMMUNITY in 1958, but the term is still used of these three countries.

Benghazi. **Benghazi cooker** An Australian name in World War II for a contrivance for heating water, made from a can containing petrol-soaked sand.

Benghazi Handicap or **Benghazi Derby** The Allied retreat to TOBRUK in 1941, which was carried out in a state of considerable confusion and haste and involved elements of the British and Australian forces.

Benidormification or **Benidorming** The over-commercialization of once tranquil or exclusive holiday resorts. The exploitation of such places accompanied the rise of mass tourism and the package-holiday industry. The word, coined in the late 1980s, is based on the Spanish coastal resort of Benidorm, whose mass market appeal, particularly among the British, turned a small fishing village into a sprawling development of high-rise apartment blocks and hotels, bars, discos, and FAST FOOD outlets.

benign neglect Doing nothing in the belief that an already difficult state of affairs will deteriorate if a more positive course is followed. The term was first heard in America in the 1970s in reference to race relations.

Benioff zone A layer beneath the earth's crust that is closely linked with volcanoes and earthquakes etc. It was named in 1968 after the US seismologist Victor Hugo Benioff (1899–).

Bennery A set of left-wing policies associated with the political aims of the British Labour MP Tony Benn (Anthony Neil Wedgwood Benn; 1925–). As secretary of state for industry in 1974–75, he pressed for increased nationalization of various industrial concerns and more government intervention in private companies.

bennie A Benzedrine pill. Benzedrine is a tradename for an amphetamine widely used and frequently abused from the 1940s to the 1960s. *See also* BUBS.

Berchtesgaden *See* EAGLE'S NEST.

Bergen–Belsen *See* BELSEN.

berk or **burk** A fool. A mild term of abuse widely used in the UK and Australia since the 1960s. It is derived from the Cockney rhyming slang Berkeley or Berkshire hunt for cunt, the secondary meaning of which, in the late 19th century and early 20th century, was a fool.

Berlin. **Berlin airlift** An operation by the UK and America to supply by air (the so-called **airbridge**) the city of West Berlin with food and other essential supplies between 26 June 1948 and 12 May 1949; a total of 195,530 flights was made. It was in response to the **Berlin blockade**, an attempt by the Soviet authorities to isolate West Berlin by blocking road and rail routes through the Soviet-occupied zone (later East Germany). A wide range of aircraft were used, many of them belonging to small companies that had been set up after the war by ex-RAF pilots. The Berlin airlift enabled these companies to grow into fully fledged airlines.

Berlin by Christmas The cry of Allied servicemen at the start of World Wars I and II. In both cases the optimism evaporated rapidly. **Berlin or bust** was a more realistic variant, introduced by US soldiers when America joined in both wars.

Berliner Ensemble A theatre company founded in Berlin in 1949 by the German playwright Bertolt Brecht (1898–1956). After Brecht's death, it was taken over by his widow Helene Weigel (1900–71). The company devoted itself to producing Brecht's plays or adaptations before diversifying from the 1970s.

Berlin Wall A wall built through Berlin in 1961 by the East German government to prevent the increasing flow of refugees from the Eastern sector to the West. It was heavily guarded by the East Germans and generally regarded as a symbol of Communist repression. Many East Germans were shot trying to escape over it. The Soviet policy of GLASNOST, introduced in 1986, led to the liberalization or breakdown of Communist regimes in eastern Europe: demolition of the wall began in 1989, heralding the unification of Germany in October 1990. German entrepreneurs subsequently set up a flourishing trade in pieces of demolished wall. *See also* CHECKPOINT CHARLIE.

Ich bin ein Berliner! (Ger. I am a Berliner!) A declaration by John F. Kennedy made during a speech in West Berlin in June 1963. One of the most famous political statements of the century, it was designed to underline America's commitment to West Berlin's independence from the Communist bloc, although wags pointed out that the strictly correct translation was: "I am a hamburger!"

> All free men, wherever they may live, are citizens of Berlin. And therefore, as a free man, I take pride in the words *Ich bin ein Berliner*.
>
> JOHN F KENNEDY.

Bermuda. Bermuda shorts Knee-length brightly coloured summer shorts that presumably originated in Bermuda but became widely fashionable in the 1980s.

Bermuda Triangle or **Devil's Triangle** A triangle of sea in the West Atlantic ocean, covering 3,900,000 sq km (1,500,000 sq mi) between Bermuda, Florida, and Puerto Rico. Within this area numerous ships and aircraft have unaccountably disappeared without trace. Some have attributed these disappearances to the prevalent severe weather or dangerous sea currents, others say that no more mysterious losses have occurred here than elsewhere, while others have suggested that the area is subject to more sinister forces of unknown origin. The myth began in 1945, when five US torpedo-bombers vanished without trace; the wrecks of these aircraft were thought to have been located off Florida in 1991, but these turned out not to be the missing flight, thus leaving the myth intact.

Bertie Edward VII (1841–1910; reigned 1901–10). His mother, Queen Victoria, called him Bertie, but his subjects had other nicknames for him, including **Tum-Tum** for his corpulence and **Edward the Caresser**, for his behaviour with girls. He was also known, respectfully, as **Edward the Peacemaker**, for his skill in creating the ENTENTE CORDIALE with France, but less respectfully by the homophone **Edward the Piecemaker**, for his affair with Lily Langtry.

Berufsverbot (Ger. prohibition of vocation) The exclusion of political radicals from holding offices in the German civil service: a policy pursued by West Germany in the 1970s.

best. best by taste or **best by test** Originally an advertising slogan for Cola soft drinks, first used in the immediate post-war years; it became a US catchphrase for something regarded as highly desirable.

best-case scenario Jargon for the best possible outcome of a situation.

best of British (luck) Originally a World War II catchphrase used with irony to mean, 'if you think you can do it you get on with it, but leave me out'. At that time the war was going badly for the Allies and British luck was down. After the war, particularly in the 1960s and 1970s, the phrase was often shortened to **and the best of British**; it was then used rather less ironically and carried little more meaning than 'good luck'.

the best car in the world A slogan associated with the cars manufactured by Rolls-Royce in the UK. Among other slogans used to sell Rolls-Royce models was the famous boast "at 60 miles an hour the loudest noise in this new Rolls-Royce comes from the electric clock", which was actually an extract from an article in *The Motor*. The reaction of a Rolls-Royce official on reading the report was: "We really ought to do something about that damned clock."

beta-blocker A drug that blocks the stimulation of the beta receptors of the sympathetic nervous system by adrenaline. These drugs are therefore used to reduce high blood pressure, treat angina, and control abnormal heart rhythms. Beta blockers in common use include propranolol, oxprenolol, and metoprolol.

better. a better 'ole The catchphrase of **Old Bill**, a walrus-moustached disillusioned old soldier in World War I, created by Captain Bruce Bairnsfather (1887–1959), artist and journalist, in his publications *Old Bill* and *The Better 'Ole*. Cowering in a muddy shell-hole in the midst of a withering bombardment, he says to his grousing pal Bert, "If you know of a better 'ole, go to it."

Betty Boop A US cartoon character created by Max Fleischer in 1915. She was based on the real 'boop-a-doop' singer Helen Kane. The popularity of the Betty Boop cartoons was increased after they attracted the attention of US censors; careful examination of surviving cartoons reveals the occasional lifted skirt or dropped shoulder-strap that the US censors missed.

Bevanite A supporter of the left-wing Labour MP and former minister of health, Aneurin ('Nye') Bevan (1897–1960).

Beveridge Report A report produced in 1942 by the British economist William Henry Beveridge (later Lord Beveridge; 1879–1963). Entitled *Report on Social Insurance and Allied Services*, it led to the creation of the WELFARE STATE. Although the Labour government implemented many of the measures proposed by the report, and took the credit for these measures, Beveridge himself was a member of the Liberal party.

Beverly Hills A town in SW California, close to Los Angeles. It has become the home town of many of America's leading media celebrities, including many stars of the cinema world. Tourists can be taken on coach tours of the area, being shown the often palatial houses belonging to their screen idols.

Bevin Boys Nickname for the young men directed to work in coal mines under the Emergency Powers (Defence) Act (1940). Ernest Bevin (1881–1951) was Minister of Labour and National Service at the time and according to this edict one in ten men called up between the ages of 18 and 25 were sent down the mines. The scheme started in 1943 and continued after the war.

bewdy Newk! A catchphrase adopted in Australia to promote a nationwide health campaign in the 1970s, in which armchair sports fans were encouraged to participate actively in sport. The slogan originated in the admiring comments of a typical sports fan seen in the campaign watching the Australian tennis player John Newcombe on his television.

Beyond the Fringe An influential satirical revue staged in London in 1960. The 'Beyond the Fringe' team included Peter Cook and Dudley Moore as well as Jonathan Miller and Alan Bennett and several other young ex-Cambridge University undergraduates who were to dominate British comedy for the next 20 years or more. Cook and Moore later produced another touring show called 'Behind the Fridge'.

Bhangra A form of pop music combining Western rock music with Punjabi folk music, popular with the Indian community in the UK.

Bhopal An Indian city, the capital of Madhya Pradesh, with a population of 672,000 (1981). It became headline news in December 1984 when over 2500 people were killed by an escape of highly poisonous methyl isocyanate gas from its US-owned Union Carbide factory. Local medical facilities collapsed when some 50,000 others, temporarily blinded or disabled by the gas, sought help. A lengthy battle for legal compensation ensued.

Biafra An eastern region of Nigeria in which the Ibo people unilaterally declared independence in 1967. The state was not recognized by the Nigerian government, which finally forced it to surrender early in 1970, after the Ibo people had been decimated.

biathlon (1) An athletic event combining cross-country skiing with marksmanship. It was first included in the Winter Olympic Games in 1960. (2) An athletic event that consists of running and swimming contests, introduced in 1968.

Bible. Bible Belt A range of US states in the South, in which the people are said to be characterized by Protestant fundamentalist ideals, strict morality, narrow-mindedness, and racial intolerance.

Bible-thumper or **Bible-basher** An enthusiastic evangelist, who makes frequent reference to the Bible itself.

bidonville (Fr. tin-can town) A shanty town built of metal from tin cans and other refuse materials.

big. Big Apple US 20th-century slang for New York City. It is thought to have originated among Black JAZZ musicians who first used the phrase to mean any big city, perhaps because going to a big city offered the opportunity for 'a bite of the apple', that is, a chance of success.

big band A band of musicians, usually more than 15 in number, that played the form of JAZZ known as SWING in the 1930s and early 1940s. Functioning largely as dance bands, they made use of saxophones and several trumpets (or cornets) and trombones to provide colourful orchestration in place of the earlier solo improvizations. The US big bands included those of Glenn Miller, Benny Goodman, Artie Shaw, and Duke Ellington. Smaller and less glamorous big bands in the UK were led by Geraldo, Ambrose, and Joe Loss.

Big Bang (l) An explosion of a superdense mass of matter some 20×10^9 years ago, in which the universe is believed to have originated. Evidence for this event is thought to lie in the continuing expansion of the universe, as first suggested by the US astronomer Edwin Hubble (1889–1953) in 1929, from his observation of the REDSHIFT of the light from distant galaxies. (2) The upheaval on the London Stock Exchange (LSE) in October 1986, when the whole manner of trading was changed. The major changes were the abolition of jobbers, who were replaced with MARKET-MAKERS, and the abolition of fixed commissions charged by brokers. These changes were introduced in return for the government's undertaking not to prosecute the LSE under the Restrictive Practices Act. As a result of the Big Bang, the LSE was modernized by the extensive use of computers and broadened to become an international market. *See also* CHINESE WALL.

Big Bertha The nickname for the large howitzers used by the Germans against Liège and Namur in 1914. Made at the Skoda works, they were mistakenly thought to be a product of Krupps, the German armament firm, hence the allusion to Frau Bertha Krupp. In 1918 Paris was shelled from a range of 76 miles by the 142-ton 'Paris' gun to which the name Big Bertha was again applied. In US slang a 'Big Bertha' is a fat woman.

Big Bill William Hale Thompson (1867–1944), three-times mayor of Chicago, who was noted for his anti-British views. He once threatened to punch George V on the nose if he ever visited Chicago. *See also* WOBBLIES.

Big Brother is watching you Authority, totalitarian and bureaucratic, has you under its observation from which there is no escape. One of the telling phrases from George Orwell's *Nineteen Eighty-Four* (1949). The allusion was to the Soviet Union but its application is not without significance in other modern states.

> The posters that were plastered everywhere—BIG BROTHER IS WATCHING YOU the caption said, while the dark eyes looked into Winston's own.
>
> *Nineteen Eighty-Four*: Pt.I, i.

big C Cancer. This phrase received wide coverage when used by the US actor John Wayne (1907–79) to express his determination to cope with his cancer.

big crunch The theory that the universe will eventually collapse into a small compact core.

Big Cyril Cyril Smith (1928–), Liberal MP for Rochdale. A vast man, weighing some 25 stones, who became a popular media personality in the 1980s.

Big Daddy (1) Stage name of Shirley Crabtree (1936–), British wrestler and media personality. (2) Idi Amin (1925–), who as President of Uganda (1971–79) repressed the Ugandan people and instituted his own bizarre and cruel personality cult; he was finally ousted by Tanzanian forces. (3) Lyndon B. Johnson (1908–73), US president (1963–69).

Big Eight The eight largest firms of international accountants in the world: Arthur Andersen; Coopers and Lybrand; Deloitte Haskins and Sells; Ernst and Whinney; Peat Marwick Mitchell; Price Waterhouse; Touche Ross; and Arthur Young.

big enchilada A VIP. The phrase became popular from its use in the WATERGATE tapes to describe the US attorney-general. An *enchilada* is a Mexican dish of a tortilla filled with meat and dressed with chili sauce; the link is obscure.

Big Five (1) The five countries taking part in the Paris Peace Conference in 1919 following World War I: the UK, France, Italy, Japan, and America. (2) In the UK, the five large clearing banks (Barclays, Lloyds, Midland, National Provincial, and Westminster). The National Provincial and Westminster banks merged in 1968, at which point the Big Five became the **Big Four**.

Bigfoot A postulated 'apeman' of the mountains of the Pacific Northwest of America, of which several sightings are alleged to have been made in the 20th century. Indistinct photographs suggest a tall hairy creature with long arms and a slightly pointed head; it is said to leave huge footprints, 43 cm (17 in) long. Also known as the **Sasquatch** (from a Salish Indian word, *saskehavas*, meaning hairy men), it was first promoted by the news media in the early 1970s, though the legend probably dates back to the late 1920s. Links are made between this monster and the ABOMINABLE SNOWMAN of the Himalayas.

Big Four *See* BIG FIVE.

Big Gooseberry Season The SILLY SEASON, the dead season during the summer holidays, when newspapers are glad of any subject to fill their columns; monster gooseberries exhibited at local fruit and vegetable shows will do for such a purpose.

Big Green Nickname of Dartmouth College in New Hampshire. One of the eight prestigious IVY LEAGUE colleges, which are the US equivalent of OXBRIDGE in the UK.

Big-hearted Arthur Arthur Askey (1900–82). The British comedian and music-hall artist, who endeared himself to the wartime British public with his radio show *Bandwagon*. He referred to himself as Big-hearted Arthur in the first edition of *Bandwagon* (in 1938) and was known by this name thereafter.

big house US underworld slang for a prison, particularly a federal prison, which came into common parlance with the 1930 OSCAR-winning film of that name, starring Wallace Beery.

Big Look A fashion in women's clothes of the 1970s, which was based on loose-fitting designs.

Big Mac (1) Tradename for the best-known item of food on the menus of McDonald's FAST FOOD outlets, consisting of a large hamburger. *See also* MCDONALD'S. (2) The Municipal Assistance Corporation, which was founded in 1975 to cope with New York City's huge debt problem.

big O A euphemism for an orgasm, especially a female orgasm.

Big One Nickname given in America to Ringling Brothers Circus and Barnum and Bailey's Circus when they merged in 1907. The 'Big One' finally ceased operations in 1956.

big-stick diplomacy Backing negotiations or policy with the threat of military force. The term was popularized by Theodore Roosevelt's declaration in 1900 that he had always been fond of the West African proverb "speak softly and carry a big stick". He used such tactics successfully (1902–04) in the Alaskan boundary dispute and the second Venezuelan crisis.

Big Three The heads of government of America, the UK, and the Soviet Union – Roosevelt, Churchill, and Stalin, respectively – at the time of the YALTA CONFERENCE in 1945, when they met towards the end of World War II to agree upon the postwar occupation of Germany.

Big Wind or **Windy** US slang for Chicago, referring to the high winds that come off Lake Michigan on which the city stands.

Biggles The hero of several popular adventure stories by Captain W. E. Johns. He was based upon Air Commodore Cecil George Wigglesworth (1893–1961), who was Air Officer Commanding Iceland during World War II and who served alongside Johns in World War I. Biggles made his first appearance in *The Camels are Coming* (1932).

bike. biker A motorcycle rider, or member of a motorcycle gang. Originally a US expression, its usage has been widespread in the UK since the late 1960s.

on your bike! A peremptory dismissal, which is as old as the bicycle itself; it enjoyed a new lease of life after the Conservative politician Norman Tebbitt (1931–) obliquely referred to it in a much-discussed speech at the party conference of 1981.

> I know all about these problems. I grew up in the thirties with an unemployed father. He didn't riot. He got on his bike and looked for work. And he found it!

Bikini An atoll in the Marshall Islands, the scene of US nuclear weapon testing in 1946 (and 1954). It has given its name to a scanty two-piece bathing outfit for women, apparently likening the devastating effects of an atomic explosion to the supposedly over-powering effect caused by a woman wearing a bikini.

Biko Affair The scandal that evolved from the death in custody of Steve Biko (1946–77), a leader of the Black Consciousness Movement in South Africa and founder (1968) of the South African Students Organization (SASO). An active opponent of APARTHEID, he was arrested in September 1977 and died of injuries sustained while in police custody six days later. World condemnation of this event made Biko an international symbol of the anti-apartheid struggle and a folk hero among South African Blacks.

Bill. **Old Bill** *See* 'OLE, A BETTER.
the Bill or **the Old Bill** The police. A British working-class slang expression that has crept into common parlance since the 1970s and 1980s with the advent of several TV police dramas (including one called *The Bill*). Its derivation is obscure but could be related to the weapon the policeman used to carry.

Billings method A method of family planning devised by Drs. John and Evelyn Billings in the 1960s. It involves daily examination of the cervical mucus in the vagina in order to observe changes in mucal consistency, which enables those days on which ovulation occurs to be identified. On these days intercourse is avoided if the woman does not wish to become pregnant or encouraged if she does. Many women regard the procedure as unacceptable; as a form of contraception it is regarded as unreliable.

Billy. **Billy Graham crusades** A number of crusades for Christianity undertaken by the US evangelist Billy Graham (1918–) in many countries. The meetings are characterized by a high level of pre-publicity and are held in large stadiums. Members of the audience are invited to come forward and publicly to 'take a decision for Christ'.
Billy Williams's Cabbage Patch The English Rugby Football Union's ground at Twickenham, the headquarters of the game, also known as *Twickers*. Popularly so-called after W. (Billy) Williams (1860–1951), who discovered the site and through whose persistence the ground was acquired in 1907; also from the ground's former partial use as a market garden. The first match was played there on 2 October 1909. The nearby *Railway Tavern* changed its name to *The Cabbage Patch* in the early 1970s.

bimbo An empty-headed but sexually attractive and glamorous woman. The word originated in America around 1915–20 but in this sense, which is widely used in tabloid journalism, did not become current until the 1980s, when it spread from America to the UK and Australia. It is sometimes also applied to sexually attractive but brainless men (sometimes in the form **himbo**). Originally, a bimbo (probably derived from the Italian *bambino*, a child) was a stupid, contemptible, and often disreputable man; later, in the 1920s, it was used as slang for a prostitute. A combination of these senses seems to have led to its current usage. A **bimbette** is a younger version of a bimbo.

> We want to love women in a way that doesn't condescend. We don't just love bimbos.
>
> LEE EISENBERG, *The Independent on Sunday*, 9 December 1990.

binary weapon A nerve gas, the potential lethal effects of which are released when two relatively harmless chemicals are mixed as the projectile in which they are carried reaches its target.

Binet test A series of intelligence tests devised in 1903 by the French psychologist Alfred Binet (1857–1911), who based them on the responses of his two daughters to his use of objects and pictures to assess intelligence and aptitude. They have since been adapted for use in many countries, the Stanford-Binet test (prepared at Stanford University, California, in 1916) being the best-known revision.

Bing *See* OLD GROANER.
Bing Boys The nickname of the Canadian troops in World War I from the name of their commanding officer, Lord Byng of Vimy. Also from the revue, *The Bing Boys Are Here*, which opened at the Alhambra in Leicester Square, London, in 1915.

bingle Australian slang for a car crash. Earlier meanings of the word included a skirmish (in World War II) and damage done to a surfboard.

bingo A game of chance, in which players have to fill in a certain sequence of numbers on a card as they are announced by the 'bingo-caller'; the first to complete his sequence is the winner. The game had its origins before World War I, other names being 'Keno', 'Beano'. 'Loo', 'Housey Housey', or 'Lotto'. Many British cinemas were converted to bingo halls in the 1960s when the game was at its most popular.

bint (Arab. *bint*, a daughter, a young woman). A rather derogatory expression for a woman, used by British troops serving in Egypt from the 1920s to the 1960s. It is now rarely used.

bio-. **bioastronomy** The search for life elsewhere in the universe. Deep-space probes have been fitted with equipment to detect living processes on other planets but have so far had no success; some carry information about the probe's origins and about the earth and its inhabitants.

biodegradable Describing substances that can be degraded (*i.e.* broken down into their constituents) by bacteria or other biological agents. The term was originally applied to sewage but in recent years it has been used in connection with the disposal of other pollutants: with growing concern about the build-up of domestic and industrial waste and the persistence in the environment of pesticides, there is increasing pressure for the development of packaging and products that are biodegradable. *See also* PHOTODEGRADABLE.

biofeedback A form of therapy in which patients learn to control unconscious physiological activities, such as heart rate and brain rhythms, with the aid of machines that monitor them. By relaxing and concentrating the mind on the activity in question, while receiving feedback from the machine on changes in the activity, patients can be taught to gain some control over these bodily functions. Biofeedback has been used with some success by practitioners of ALTERNATIVE MEDICINE to relieve migraine, tension headaches, and high blood pressure (hypertension); it is also said to have been helpful to cigarette smokers who want to reduce their smoking.

The techniques of biofeedback vary. In hypertension, for example, electrodes monitoring skin conductivity are taped to the patient's fingers. Damp hands (which are more conductive than dry hands) are associated with arousal and stress, factors also said to be a cause of raised blood pressure. By observing that the dial of the skin-conductivity meter is falling, the patients are taught to relax and their blood pressure falls.

biogas A mixture of methane and carbon dioxide gases produced by the action of bacteria on organic matter (sewage, household and industrial waste, etc.). Some THIRD WORLD countries, notably India, have been using biogas – generated in special biogas plants – as a source of energy since the 1970s. With existing reserves of fossil fuels likely to become exhausted within the next hundred years, and nuclear power stations still providing only a small proportion (some 5%) of the world's energy, developed countries have shown interest in ALTERNATIVE ENERGY sources. The large-scale production of biogas is one such solution that is being actively explored: it would serve the dual purpose of exploiting a potentially important energy source and of disposing of domestic and industrial waste.

Biograph Girl The nickname given to the US actress Florence Lawrence (1886–1938), who was a major star of the early silent cinema. Her films include *Resurrection* (1910) and *The Enfoldment* (1920).

biological clock The mechanism within living organisms that is assumed to control the timing of certain periodic changes of behaviour or physiology (*see* BIORHYTHM). These events, which include the annual migrations of birds and other animals, seem to occur more or less independently of changes in the environment: this has led biologists to postulate the existence of such a 'clock', although its method of working is not yet fully understood.

biomass The total weight of all the living organisms, or of one particular species, within a population or given area: biomass calculations are used in studies of energy flow within ecological communities. The term, which has been part of the vocabulary of ecologists since the 1930s, has come into wider and more general use in recent years in the concept of **biomass energy** – the energy derived from plants (*e.g.* sugar cane, trees) grown especially for this purpose; from sewage, farm, and domestic waste; and from other natural sources. These **biofuels** are becoming an important source of ALTERNATIVE ENERGY. *See* BIOGAS.

bionic Consisting of or possessing electronic or mechanical components whose design is based on that of comparable systems in living organisms. The term originated in the early 1960s with the evolution of **bionics** (from *bi(ological electr)onics*), the study and application of bionic systems, but became much more widely known in the 1970s in connection with the popular US TV series *The Six Million Dollar Man* (1973–78), starring Lee Majors as the eponymous 'bionic man' – an individual whose body parts had been replaced by electronic equipment, giving him superhuman strength and extraordinary powers. Since then the term has come into general use to denote superlative skill or performance.

biopic Biographical picture, a movie based on the life of a real person. Biopics have tended to be unpopular with film makers because they rarely make money. Perhaps this reputation reflects the rather poor showing that Hollywood made of its biopics in the 1930s and 1940s. For example, *Love Time* (1934; Schubert), *A Song* *to Remember* (1944; Chopin), *Song of Love* (1947; Liszt), *Song of my Heart* (1947; Tchaikovsky), and many others treated anecdotes in the lives of composers with a triviality reflected in their titles. Writers, scientists, inventors, and politicians have fared little better in the hands of producers. In fact, when Richard Attenborough tried to raise the money to fulfil a long ambition to make a biopic that truly followed the events in the life of Gandhi, he met with little sympathy. When, in 1982, his epic *Gandhi* finally emerged it did a great deal to repair the damage done to biopics by Hollywood's superficiality.

biorhythm A pattern of behaviour or a metabolic activity that occurs in regular cycles controlled by a BIOLOGICAL CLOCK within an organism, which operates independently of external factors. Examples are the 24-hour (**circadian**) rhythms of sleeping/waking and the annual rhythms of hibernation and migration that occur in many animals. This biological term has been debased by those who postulate that human behaviour is regulated by three biorhythms of physical, emotional, and intellectual activity: there is no evidence to support this assertion.

bippy. You bet your sweet bippy! A catchphrase popularized by the US TV comedy show *Rowan and Martin's Laugh-In* in the 1960s. It was usually spoken by Dick Martin.

Bircher *See* JOHN BIRCH SOCIETY.

Bird or **Yardbird** The nickname given to Charlie Parker (1920–55), the US Black JAZZ musician, who is now regarded as one of the most influential of all jazz performers.

birder A keen amateur ornithologist; a birdwatcher, especially one who is keen on spotting and identifying as many species as possible. **Twitchers** or **tickers** are birders who concentrate on spotting rare species, which they then tick off their list.

Birds Eye Tradename of a company noted for producing frozen foodstuffs. It takes its name from the US inventor Clarence Birdseye (1886–1956), who discovered (1915) that vegetables could be preserved by freezing them at low temperatures. He discovered this process while fur trading and trapping in Labrador. His own name was said to have been derived from an ancestor who was a page at the royal court who attracted attention when he shot a diving hawk through the eye with an arrow.

bird strike A collision between a flying bird and an aircraft. These collisions can be dangerous as the bird's body or feathers may block air intakes or lead to shattered windscreens, etc. Many airfields adopt various strategies to scare birds away.

Birmingham Six A group of six Irishmen who were imprisoned for 16 years for their supposed role in IRA pub bombings in Birmingham in which 17 people died in 1974. The heavy death toll in the attacks led to a public outcry for quick arrests. The six suspects were arrested and subsequently gaoled, although doubts were soon raised as to the quality of the evidence against them, which consisted of doubtful forensic evidence that their hands revealed traces of explosives. This evidence was later withdrawn as unsafe. There were also confessions by the men, which were later proved to have been extracted by dubious police methods. The police were also shown to have lied. Some, but not all, of this later evidence was available to the appeal court, which failed to quash their sentences. After intense public disquiet the Director of Public Prosecutions let it be known that he would not contest another appeal and the prisoners were released on 14 March 1991 amongst a storm of vituperation at the inadequacies of British criminal law and the judges in particular. The case was considered highly damaging to the reputation of the British legal system and reforms of police procedures and legal appeals were demanded. *See also* CHICAGO SEVEN; GUILDFORD FOUR.

Biro A ball-point pen using a quick-drying ink, which was invented in 1938 by the Hungarian inventor Laszlo Biró (1900–85). The word has now become a generic name for any ball-point pen.

birth. birth control The prevention of an unwanted pregnancy by 'natural' methods or by the artificial means that largely only became available in the 20th century. Long-practised 'natural' methods include *coitus interruptus* (removal of the penis from the vagina before ejaculation) and the rhythm method (in which ejaculation into the vagina is avoided except during the woman's so-called safe period).

Both these methods are unreliable, although they are the only ones permitted to members of the Roman Catholic Church (*see* HUMANAE VITAE). Artificial methods of birth control advanced in the 20th century have included the CONDOM, the diaphragm, or cap (a rubber disc fitted over the cervix of the womb), the IUD (intra-uterine device, a loop or coil inserted into the uterus by a doctor), and the PILL. In a world that is grossly overpopulated, prudent **family planning** using artificial contraception is an essential aspect of responsible parenthood. *See* STOPES CLINIC.

birth mother *See* GENETIC MOTHER; SURROGATE MOTHERHOOD.

bish-bash-bosh Quickly and efficiently. A fashionable expression amongst London YUPPIES in the mid 1980s.

Bishop of Fleet Street A nickname given to Hannen Swaffer (1879–1962) by his fellow journalists because of his pronouncements on public morality and his sombre eccentric clothes.

Bismarck A German battleship, named after Otto von Bismarck (1815–98), which sank the British ship HMS HOOD in May 1941. Three days later the *Bismarck*, which had threatened to terrorize shipping in the Atlantic, was sunk by the *Dorsetshire* after being seriously damaged by aircraft from the aircraft carrier *Ark Royal* and by the *King George V* and the *Rodney*. The wreck of the Bismarck, in its day the most powerful battleship afloat, was located and photographed in deep water in the 1980s.

Bismarck Sea A region of sea around the Bismarck Archipelago – a group of some 200 islands in the SW Pacific Ocean northeast of New Guinea. Here, in 1943, US aircraft operating from aircraft carriers destroyed a Japanese troop convoy bound for New Guinea (the *Battle of the Bismarck Sea*).

bistable *See* FLIP-FLOP.

bistro A British restaurant that prides itself on its 'continental' style, especially reminiscent of France, where a *bistro* is any café offering relatively low-priced food.

bit A unit of computer information; an abbreviated form of 'binary digit'.

bit of fluff *See under* FLUFF.

bit of rough British slang for a lover, of either sex but usually a man, either from a lower social class or with rough manners. It was used in a friendly way in the 1980s and derives from the term 'rough trade', meaning an uncouth male lover, either homosexual or heterosexual.

Bitch of Buchenwald or **Witch of Buchenwald** Ilse Koch (d. 1967). The hated wife of the Commandant of the German concentration camp at BUCHENWALD during World War II. A woman of unspeakable cruelty, she and her husband epitomized the degradation of the German people during the NAZI regime.

bite. To bite the dust or **the ground** To fall, to be struck off one's horse, to be vanquished. The phrase 'another Redskin bit the dust' was derived from Wild West stories.

bitser or **bitsa** A mongrel. An Australian word based on the idea that the animal's pedigree is made up of bits of this and that. It can be applied to anything made up of component parts.

bivvy British army and BOY SCOUT slang meaning to bivouac, to make camp.

blabber Australian slang for a TV remote-control device, presumably because of its ability to control the volume.

black. Any colour, so long as it's black Henry Ford's famous reply to queries about the colour range in which the Model T was available (*see* TIN LIZZIE).

Black and Tans The name of a pack of hounds in County Limerick, subsequently applied to the irregulars enlisted by the British government in 1920 to supplement the Royal Irish Constabulary. This force was so called from their mixed black and tan uniforms (there being a shortage of proper police uniforms). The force (subsequently reinforced by an Auxiliary Division of irregulars – the **Auxis** – who were not theoretically members of the RIC) was deeply resented and was accused of brutality in its attempts to suppress Irish nationalists (*see* BLOODY SUNDAY); they were withdrawn in 1921. Later the Irish used the name indiscriminately for all the armed constabulary.

black bag job US slang for an undercover operation carried out by a government agency. This phrase dates from the WATERGATE scandal of 1972.

Blackboard Jungle Schools in downtown New York in which delinquency is rife and discipline is difficult to impose. The name is taken from the title of a novel by Evan Hunter published in 1954 and filmed in 1955, based on a New York school, which was a savage indictment of certain aspects of the US state educational system.

black bombers British slang for the very strong black amphetamine capsules containing Durophet that were popular with drug abusers in the 1960s and early 1970s.

Black Bottom In US slang, that part of a city in which the bulk of the Black population lives. It is also the name of a dance once popular in Black circles.

black box (1) An aircraft's FLIGHT RECORDER. (2) Any device, real or conceptual, that takes input and produces output, but whose internal workings are invisible to the outside world; often used in computer programming. (3) British derogatory slang of the 1980s for a Muslim woman wearing the traditional shapeless black ankle-length garment, the *burka*.

Black Caucus In America, an organization of supporters of Black civil rights in Congress, founded in 1967.

black-coated workers Prunes. This euphemism for the prune in its laxative capacity was popularized by Charles Hill, the BBC's radio doctor of the 1940s.

Black consciousness A movement in South Africa that has as its aim the overthrow of APARTHEID and the establishment of equal civil rights for South African Blacks.

black economy That part of the economic activity of a country that does not feature in national statistics because it is undisclosed. The reasons for its non-disclosure are either because it involves money earned but not returned to the tax authorities, which therefore escapes taxation, or money earned but not disclosed by those claiming state benefits. In command economies (*e.g.* in former communist regimes) the black economy is believed to be very large but in mixed economies it is also thought to be of significant proportions, although by its nature it is unmeasurable.

black flag To show a black flag to a particular driver during a motor race means that he must immediately drop out of the race; this is usually done after some serious infringement of the rules of motor-racing.

Black Friday 15 April 1921 was Black Friday for the British Labour Movement when the threatened GENERAL STRIKE was cancelled. *See also* RED FRIDAY.

Black Hand (1) The popular name of the Slav secret society largely responsible for contriving the assassination of the Archduke Franz Ferdinand on 28 June 1914 (*see* SARAJEVO ASSASSINATION). This was the event that precipitated World War I. (2) A criminal society, once active in New York, largely made up of Italians.

black hole A hypothetical object in space that is believed to result from the gravitational collapse of a massive star at the end of its life, first postulated by the German astronomer Karl Schwarzchild (1873–1916) in 1916. Because the escape velocity from the object is equal to the speed of light, no radiation can escape from it and what goes on inside its boundary, called its **event horizon**, is theoretically unknowable. No black hole has been identified, although it has been postulated that they are the power sources of QUASARS.

black is beautiful Slogan adopted in the 1960s by supporters of Black civil rights in America in an attempt to destroy the negative associations that the word 'black' had had until then. The slogan was coined by Stokely Carmichael in 1966 and taken up by Martin Luther King the following year.

black knight *See* WHITE KNIGHT.

black market A World War II phrase to describe illicit dealing in rationed goods and used subsequently for any illegal dealing. *See* UNDER THE COUNTER.

black-out (1) Originally, a period in the theatre when the whole stage is in darkness. This usage first occurred in the 1920s. (2) A World War II air-raid precaution. From the outbreak of war against Germany (3 September 1939) until 23 April 1945 (coastal areas, 11 May), it was obligatory throughout Great Britain to cover all windows, skylights, etc., before dark so that no gleam of light could be seen from outside. Moving vehicles were only allowed to use masked lights. (3) A complete loss of consciousness.

black mist (Jap. *kuro kiri*) Translation of a Japanese term denoting corruption in business or politics. Several major scandals of this nature have disrupted Japanese life since the 1960s; the black mist referred to is the usual attempt made to disguise such corruption.

Black Monday Either of the two Mondays in the 20th century on which the New York Stock Exchange opened very considerably below its level on the previous Friday. The first WALL STREET CRASH occurred on Monday 28 October 1929, when the 13% knocked off the Dow Jones Industrial Average led to the GREAT DEPRESSION of the 1930s. The second Black Monday occurred on 19 October 1987, when the Dow Jones Average fell by an alarming 23%. Although Wall Street's collapse in both cases triggered falls in stock-market prices throughout the world, in the 1987 crash careful management of international finances managed to avoid a serious slump and prices gradually recovered.

Black Muslims A popular name for the Nation of Islam, a Black US sect noted for its unorthodox beliefs and fierce racial ideology. The movement dates from about 1930 when Wallace Fard Muhammed, acclaimed by his followers as the incarnate Allah sent to liberate the Black race from oppression, built a mosque in Detroit (he disappeared shortly afterwards in mysterious circumstances). Under Fard's successor, Elijah Muhammed, the sect developed its characteristic doctrine of racial separation, preaching that White society was the creation of devils and doomed to imminent destruction. The Black Muslims came to national prominence in the 1960s, owing mainly to their charismatic spokesman Malcolm X and the recruitment of such figures as the boxer Cassius Clay (Muhammed Ali). In the 1970s and 1980s the movement repudiated its more extreme beliefs, merging eventually with the Islamic mainstream.

Black Panther (1) The name given by the popular press to the British murderer Donald Neilsen. After a nine-month search he was finally caught and convicted of the murder of Lesley Whittle and three sub-post office officials in 1975. The name reflects his use of a black hood to conceal his identity. (2) A member of a US Black militant organization of the late 1960s, briefly notorious for such demands as the release of all Black prisoners from US gaols and for staging a series of dramatic shootouts with the police. Although the origins of the name are disputed, it seems to have arisen from the panther symbol used by a group of BLACK POWER candidates who fought elections in Alabama in 1966. A Black Panther Party emerged in California the following year under the leadership of Huey Newton and Eldridge Cleaver, preaching total separation from White society and urging Blacks to take up arms in 'self defence'. By the 1970s the movement had been seriously weakened by internal rifts and the arrest, defection, or death of its leading members.

Blackpool illuminations The annual display of elaborate street lighting that stretches for over 9 km (6 m) along the front at Blackpool. Consisting of 375,000 lamps, the lights go on in the autumn and extend the 'season' by several weeks, attracting many thousands of visitors to the town. They were first erected in 1912 for a visit by Queen Victoria's daughter Princess Louise and (with a break during World War II) became an annual event from 1925.

Black Power A slogan first used by the US Black leader Stokely Carmichael in about 1966 and subsequently adopted by a variety of Black and radical organizations. The phrase implies a rejection of both integration as a political goal and of the pacifism of the CIVIL RIGHTS MOVEMENT led by Martin Luther King.

Black September A Palestinian terrorist group founded in 1972. It was named in commemoration of the Jordanian expulsion of Palestinians in September 1970. The seizure of Israeli athletes (and the subsequent killing of most of them) during the Olympic Games of 1972 was staged by the group, as well as various sky-jackings and assassinations.

Blackshirts Mussolini's Italian Fascists, named after the distinguishing garments they wore. Similar shirts were adopted by the British Union of Fascists under Sir Oswald Mosley (*see* MOSLEYITES). Also a name for the German SS or *Schutzstaffeln*, led by Himmler. *See* BROWN SHIRTS; FASCISM.

Black Sox scandal A notorious bribery scandal that shook the US baseball world in 1920. Members of the Chicago White Sox team had been bribed to 'throw' a game in the 1919 World Series. At the subsequent trial the accused players were acquitted due to lack of evidence. However, the newly appointed first commissioner of baseball realized the threat to the sport's reputation and banned those involved from baseball for life. When news of the scandal first broke, supporters were stunned. One small boy approached his favourite star and tearfully begged him to 'say it ain't so, Joe'. His words are now one of the best known quotations in baseball history; it is also used ironically in other situations in which a hero is suspected of having done something awful.

black spot A stretch of road that has become notorious for the frequency of car accidents occurring there. The phrase is now also used in other contexts, including areas of high unemployment.

blag (1) British slang meaning to rob, or a robbery. A familiar expression since the 1970s from its use in TV crime dramas. (2) To scrounge, or the spoils from scrounging. The derivation of both these meanings is obscure.

Blake. Blake, Nicholas The pseudonym used by the British poet C. Day Lewis (1904–72) as the author of some 20 crime novels published between 1935 and 1968. The future poet laureate turned to crime fiction when he found himself unable to pay for urgently needed repairs to his house: the pseudonym was the idea of his literary agent, worried that publication under his own name could threaten Day Lewis's literary reputation. Those who knew Blake's identity (a closely guarded secret) may have seen in the novels' main protagonist, the sleuth Nicholas Strangeways, a likeness to Day Lewis's friend and fellow poet W. H. Auden.

Blake case The trial in 1961 of the British DOUBLE AGENT George Blake, who while working for MI6 claimed to have betrayed some 400 of his East European contacts to the KGB. Blake received a 42-year sentence, at the time the longest ever handed down by a British court. In the event, he spent less than five years in prison, escaping from Wormwood Scrubs in 1966. Bewildered officials found only an improvised rope ladder, constructed from 20 size 13 knitting needles, and a single pink chrysanthemum. It transpired that this coup had been masterminded not by a crack team of Soviet agents but by two CND activists, Michael Randle and Pat Pottle, who considered Blake's sentence excessive. It was suggested in Blake's defence that he was brainwashed by Communist agents while held captive in Korea during the 1950s. Blake denied this, offering instead the excuse that he only passed names to the KGB on the understanding that no one would be harmed.

In 1991 Randle and Pottle were tried for their part in the escape; although they admitted their role, they pleaded not guilty on the humanitarian grounds that Blake's sentence was excessive—a plea that the jury accepted. This perverse acquittal perhaps reflected the jury's contempt for British justice after the BIRMINGHAM SIX and GUILDFORD FOUR affairs.

Blanco White *See under* WHITE.

Blandings, Empress of A prize sow belonging to Lord Emsworth, the master of Blandings Castle: the true heroine of the Blandings novels of P. G. Wodehouse.

bland out To lose personality, to become conventional.

blanket protest Prison protests in which prisoners vandalize and deface their own cells and clothes and dress only in blankets. Such protests became a regular occurrence in British prisons holding Irish terrorists in solitary confinement in the 1970s and 1980s.

Blast A magazine of the literary and artistic avant-garde founded in 1914 by Wyndham Lewis and Ezra Pound. Subtitled 'the Review of the Great English Vortex', the journal was a vehicle for VORTICISM. Although shortlived, it became notorious for its provocative rhetoric and experimental typography.

Blaue Reiter (Ger. blue riders) A German school of expressionist artists started in 1911 by the Russian painter Wassily Kandinsky (1866–1944) and the German Franz Marc (1880–1916). It was later joined by the Swiss artist Paul Klee (1879–1940) and others. The artists were a breakaway group from an organization formed in 1909 – the *Neue Kunstlerver-einigung* (New Artists' Association). In explaining the name, Kandinsky said: "We both liked blue and Marc liked painting horses". (Marc's best-known painting is *Blue Horses* (1911), in the Walker Art Center, Minneapolis).

blaxploitation The exploitation of sympathy for Black civil rights by aiming one's product, usually a movie or play, specifically at a Black audience.

bleeper A small electronic device that alerts the wearer to contact his base by telephone. They are much used by medical staff.

Blessed Margaret *See* IRON LADY.

Blighty Soldier's name for England. It was widely current in World War I but was also well known to soldiers who had served in India long before. It is derived from the Hindi *bilayati*, foreign, from Arab. *wilayet*, provincial, removed at some distance. Its use during World War I is illustrated by three popular songs of the time: 'There's a ship that's bound for Blighty', 'We wish we were in Blighty', and 'Take me back to dear old Blighty, put me on the train for London town'.

Blighty one In the two world wars, a wound that is not very serious but still serious enough to mean that the sufferer will be returned to BLIGHTY to recuperate.

blikkeys A US slang term for the soap flakes that some drug dealers pass off as CRACK in order to deceive addicts.

blimp Originally an observation balloon in World War I. 'Colonel Blimp' was created by David Low, the cartoonist, between the wars, to embody the elderly dyed-in-the-wool Tory, opposing all and any change. A *blimp* has come to mean an elderly reactionary 'gentleman' of somewhat limited intelligence. Barrage balloons over London and other cities in World War II were also called blimps.

blind trust A trust fund that takes over the money and financial affairs of a politician or other person in a position of influence. 'Blind' implies that the individual has no knowledge of how the money is invested, and consequently cannot be accused of using his or her position for private gain.

blissed out To be in a state of euphoria after a religious experience. Probably of US origin, the expression is derived from the alternative religious cults that arose in the 1960s. It can also be used in the wider sense of being extremely happy.

Blitz The bombing of London and other targets in the UK by the German Luftwaffe in 1940 as a precursor to the planned invasion of Britain (*see* BATTLE OF BRITAIN). The name was derived from the German word *Blitzkrieg* (lightning war), which in World War II was applied to the German strategy of making a rapid advance after initial strikes by aircraft, tanks, etc. The tactic was hugely successful in the invasion of Poland, France, and the Low Countries. The Blitz on London, however, never achieved its prime objective of terrifying the population into submission. In fact, it hardened the resolve of those subjected to its nightly harassment to destroy Nazi Germany. 'London can take it' and 'business as usual' were the slogans commonly chalked up on the walls of buildings damaged in the bombing of the previous night.

blitzed Very drunk or stoned.

blob (1) British slang for a road accident victim, a corpse. It is mostly used by the police, ambulance men, and vagrants. Hence **blobwagon**, ambulance. (2) An ulcer. (3) A breast, or testicle.

block (1) Head. British slang word used in such well-known aggressive phrases as 'to knock someone's block off'. (2) **The block**. Solitary confinement in prison.

block association In America, a group of residents in a small area (*e.g.* a city block) who organize themselves to promote or defend the interests of the area. The equivalent in the UK is a RESIDENTS' ASSOCIATION.

blockbust To force property values in a particular area to plummet by spreading rumours that Black people or other 'undesirables' are about to move in.

blockbuster A massive bomb, first developed in World War II, that is capable of destroying a whole block of houses. A blockbuster later became anything large and successful, especially a lavish musical or big-budget film.

Blonde Bombshell Jean Harlow (1911–37), the US film actress and sex symbol, who starred in such films as *Hell's Angels* (1930), *Dinner at Eight* (1933), and *Bombshell* (1933). Jean Harlow's short life ended tragically with kidney failure. The phrase has since been used of any attractive blonde, particularly those with an explosive personality.

blood. blood, toil, tears and sweat The words used by Winston Churchill in his speech to the House of Commons on becoming prime minister, 13 May 1940. "I would say to the House, as I have said to those who have joined this Government, I have nothing to offer but blood, toil, tears and sweat." Churchill had a number of possible sources of inspiration for his famous phrase. In his *Anatomie of the World*, John Donne, says, "Mollifie it with thy teares, or sweat, or blood", and Lord Byron has:

> Year after year they voted cent per cent,
> Blood, sweat, and tear-wrung millions—why? for rent!
>
> *The Age of Bronze*, xiv, 621.

Gladstone's speech in Westminster Abbey (22 February 1866) commemorating Lord Palmerston includes reference to "the unhappy African race, whose history is for the most part written in blood and tears".

Blood and Guts Nickname given by the soldiers in World War II to the US General George Smith Patton (1885–1945).

Bloody Mary A drink consisting of a mixture of vodka and tomato juice, usually with small amounts of other ingredients, such as Worcester sauce, Tabasco, celery salt, or lemon juice. Originating in the 1950s, its name comes from the nickname of Mary I (1516–58), the Roman Catholic Queen of England (1553–58), noted for her persecution of Protestants. Bloody Mary was also a character in the popular Rodgers and Hammerstein musical *South Pacific* (1949). A **Bloody Maria** is a similar drink made with tequila rather than vodka ('Maria' being the Spanish equivalent of 'Mary'). In recent health-conscious times, a **Virgin Mary** (a Bloody Mary without the vodka) has made its appearance.

Bloody Sunday (1) 22 January 1905. A deputation of workers led by Father Gapon marched to the Winter Palace in St Petersburg to present a petition to the Czar. They were attacked by troops and hundreds of unarmed peasants were killed. (2) 21 November 1920. The IRA killed 11 Englishmen thought to be spies; the BLACK AND TANS responded by killing 12 spectators at a football match in Croke Park, Dublin, the same afternoon. (3) 30 January 1972. The dispersal of anti-internment marchers in the Bogside, Londonderry, by British troops, during which 13 civilians were killed.

Bloomsbury Group A group of writers, artists, philosophers, and economists who, from about 1904, met regularly mostly at the Bloomsbury homes of Clive and Vanessa Bell (née Stephen) in Gordon Square or that of Virginia and Adrian Stephen in Fitzroy Square. Virginia Stephen married Leonard Woolf and, as Virginia Woolf, became the group's best-known writer. Others prominent in the circle were Roger Fry, Duncan Grant, J. M. Keynes, David Garnett, Lytton Strachey, and to a lesser extent E. M. Forster. Seeing themselves as advocates of a new rational civilized society, many of them had met at Cambridge University and were influenced by *Principia Ethica* (1903), by the Cambridge philosopher G. E. Moore (1873–1958). The group had lost its cohesion by the end of the 1920s. After World War II interest in the activities of the group reached a high level, with biographies, autobiographies, and other books, plays, and films contributing to a burgeoning Bloomsbury industry.

blooper US slang term for a mistake. The equivalent of the British 'bloomer'. Presumably *blooper* is a combination of 'bloomer' and 'oops'.

blotto Drunk. Used since the early years of the 20th century, it conveys both the ideas of blotting things out and absorbing liquid (like blotting paper).

blow (1) US slang meaning to leave. (2) To perform fellatio. A **blow job** is an act of fellatio. (3) To smoke, particularly cannabis, or to inhale or snort cocaine. (4) US slang expression meaning to be repellent: 'his cooking really blows'. (5) In JAZZ slang, to play in a jam session. (6) To fart. (7) Cannabis. A user's term common in the UK and America. *See* POT. (8) Tobacco. A prison jargon term. (9) Cocaine.

blow away (1) Slang, originally US, meaning to kill someone. (2) To be deeply impressed by someone or something.

> Liza was so beautiful. She just blew me away.
> *The Sun*, 26 March 1991.

blowdown A sudden dangerous break or explosion of a cooling pipe in a nuclear reactor. *See also* MELTDOWN.

blow-dryer A hand-held electrical device that blows hot air, used to dry and style the hair.

blower British slang for the telephone, first heard in the 1940s. It probably derives from the action of blowing down an old telephone before speaking, or from the now archaic meaning of to blow, to talk.

blow one's mind To be utterly amazed, astounded by something, originally by using LSD or other hallucinogenic drugs.

Blowpipe A British-made portable short-range missile used against aircraft.

blowser Rarely used British slang of the 1980s for a glue-sniffer.

blow-your-mind roulette A reckless game played in the 1960s in which drugtakers pool all their pills and scatter them on the floor. The lights are then turned out and participants grab whatever pills they can find.

Bloxham tapes A series of recordings of 'psychic regressions' made by subjects under hypnosis by the Welsh psychic researcher Arnall Bloxham in the 1960s. Among the most remarkable recordings were an English teenager's description of her previous life in a prehistoric society, another woman's recollection of her life as the daughter of Charles I and Queen Henrietta Maria during their exile in France, and – most remarkably – a woman who told in detail of her death during a massacre of Jewish inhabitants of the city of York in the Middle Ages, after she was found hiding in a church vault. Few of Bloxham's subjects pretended to the kind of detailed historical knowledge they communicated under hypnosis and several of the stories were subsequently supported by archaeological finds. The account of the massacre in York, for instance, was scorned by historians who said that the church named had no crypt: shortly afterwards workmen stumbled upon a hitherto concealed vault. It was exactly as Bloxham's patient had described it.

bludger (Austr.) Originally (19th century) a pimp, but later any scrounger or one profiting without risk. In World War I *to bludge on the flag* meant 'to slack' in the army.

blue (1) Australian slang for a violent argument or fight. (2) British drug-users' slang from the 1960s for a blue amphetamine tablet containing drinamyl. (3) A policeman. This primarily US usage comes from the colour of the uniform. The British equivalent is 'the boys in blue'. (4) Australian slang for a red-headed man.

Bluebeard Nickname of Henri Landru, a Frenchman guillotined in 1922 for the murder of 10 women and one of their sons. Unlike the Bluebeard of legend Landry did not actually marry any of his victims but he did make their acquaintance by advertising for a wife in the lonely-hearts columns of newspapers. Rather than keeping their bodies in a mysterious locked room, a practice that led to the downfall of his predecessor, he disposed of their remains in the stove of his country villa. A man of great charm, he was the inspiration behind Charles Verdoux, the dapper murderer in Charlie Chaplin's 1947 film *Monsieur Verdoux*.

Bluebeard of Eastbourne Nickname given by the press to Dr John Bodkin Adams in 1956, after he was suspected of poisoning a number of his patients in Eastbourne. It was thought unlikely to have been merely coincidence that the doctor appeared as a beneficiary in the wills of several of his deceased women patients. In December 1956 he was arrested for the murder of Edith Morrell, who had left the doctor a Rolls-Royce. A sensational trial ensued, in which Adams was acquitted for lack of evidence. In 1957 the **Tucker Report** into the case recommended new rules governing press reports of murder trial proceedings. Many legal experts remained unconvinced of Adams's innocence, believing the press indirectly protected an infamous poisoner.

Bluebell girls A troupe of dancers originally formed before World War II at the Folies Bergère in Paris. They were first organized by a dancer from Liverpool, Margaret Kelly, whose nickname 'Bluebell' (from the colour of her eyes) provided the name of the troupe. The group still performs in Paris variety theatres. Bluebell girls, many of whom are British, are noted for their height, statuesque figures, exotic costumes, and their elaborate semi-nude dance routines.

Bluebell line A railway line in Sussex between Haywards Heath and Horsted Keynes. Closed by British Railways in 1960, it was reopened by a group of enthusiasts. The name comes from the story that the guard used to stop the train to allow the passengers to pick bluebells.

Bluebird The name given to a series of racing cars, speedboats, and hydrofoils used by Sir Malcolm Campbell (1885–1948) and his son Donald Malcolm Campbell (1921–67) to set various world speed records on both land and water between 1927 and 1967. Donald was killed when the last Bluebird, a turbo-jet hydroplane, somersaulted and capsized during his attempt to break the water-speed record on Coniston Water.

Blue Bird of Happiness An idea elaborated from Maeterlinck's play of that name, first produced in London in 1910. It tells the story of a boy and girl seeking "the blue bird" that typifies happiness.

blue cheer A US drug-user's term of the 1960s and 1970s for LSD. This probably derives from the colour of the tablets or from their ability to drive away 'the blues'.

blue flu In America, organized absenteeism by policemen or (sometimes) firemen pretending to be sick as a way of taking industrial action. The expression came into use in the late 1960s and was used throughout the 1970s. *See also* YELLOW FLU.

blue helmet A member of the UN peacekeeping forces, who wear distinctive light blue headgear, including helmets.

blue meany A mean person. The term derives from the villains, blue and grotesque cartoon characters, in the animated BEATLES film *Yellow Submarine* (1967).

Blue Monkey The nickname given to the Marquis Luis Augusto Pinto de Soveral (d. 1922), from his swarthy complexion and blue-black hair. Portuguese ambassador to London almost continuously from 1884 to 1909, and an intimate of King Edward VII, he was noted for his wit, discretion, and ability as a raconteur. He held a unique position in Edwardian society, being known at the German embassy as 'Soveral-Uberall' (Soveral-the-supreme).

blue movies Sexually explicit films not available for public showing. There is some controversy over the traditional connection between sexual activity and the colour blue. The connection is, however, common to many cultures around the world. The Chinese, for instance, always painted their brothels blue. In the Christian world, a link has been suggested with the tradition that associated the Devil with the colour blue (possibly because brimstone burns with a blue flame). Perhaps the most likely explanation, however, is the association between the censor's **blue pencil** (a concept that originated with military censors in the last century) and the obliteration of any material unsuitable for innocent eyes. **Blue jokes** would fit most convincingly with this etymology.

Blue Orchid A member of the Royal Australian Air Force in World War II, so called because of their uniform, which was considered more glamorous than those of the other services.

Blue Peter Classic British children's television programme, first broadcast in 1958. Hosts of this magazine, familiar to several generations of children, have included Valerie Singleton, Christopher Trace, and John Noakes, together with a long sequence of cats, dogs, tortoises, etc. Among the near-legendary phrases associated with the programme are 'Here's one I made earlier' and 'sticky-backed paper'. The programme has staged a long series of charitable appeals on behalf of such worthy causes as guide dogs for the blind, inshore lifeboats, and provision of improved facilities for mentally ill children in Romania.

Blue Riband of the Atlantic The liner gaining the record for the fastest Atlantic crossing is said to hold the 'Blue Riband of the Atlantic' and from 1907 to 1929 it was held by the Cunard liner *Mauretania*. It then passed to the *Europa* (1930) and *Bremen* (1933) of Germany, to the *Rex* of Italy (1933), and to the French liner *Normandie* in 1935. It was next held by the British QUEEN MARY from 1938 until its capture by the US-owned *United States* in 1952. A trophy offered in 1935 by H. K. Hales (1868–1942) was first accepted by the United States Lines in 1952. The average speed of the *Mauretania* was 17.4 knots, that of the *United States* 35.69 knots. A claim by the businessman Richard Branson that he had won the title for his powerboat crossing in 1986 was dismissed on the grounds that only non-powerboats not specifically designed to win the award are eligible. In 1990 the Hales Trophy was sent to the UK after the catamaran ferry *Hoverspeed Great Britain* crossed in record time, but the organizers of the Blue Riband award refused to call it holder of the Blue Riband itself as the boat was not in regular Atlantic service.

Blue Riders *See* BLAUE REITER.

blue rinse A dyeing process in which a bluish tinge is imparted to grey hair, much favoured by women of a certain age. The **blue-rinse brigade** comprises the elderly well-groomed socially active women in any community.

blues An early 20th-century form of US folksong derived from the songs expressing the unhappiness of the Black man in the Deep South. Blues usually consist of 12 bars in 4/4 time made up of three 4-bar phrases. They are characterized by the use of **blue notes** (flattened thirds, fifths, and sometimes sevenths). They can be vocal or instrumental and have had an enormous influence on JAZZ and ROCK. *See also* RHYTHM-AND-BLUES.

Blues and Royals The informal name acquired in 1969 by the Royal Horse Guards (the Blues) and the Royal Dragoons (the Royals) when they amalgamated to form the Royal Horse Guards and 1st Dragoons.

blueshift A change in wavelengths to shorter wavelengths (*i.e.* to the blue end of the visible spectrum) for light or other radiation emitted by an object moving towards the observer. It is the opposite of a REDSHIFT in astronomy.

Blue Shirts An Irish Fascist organization under General Eoin O'Duffy, former Commissioner of the Garda, which developed from the Army Comrades Association in the early 1930s. A Blue Shirt battalion led by O'Duffy fought for General Franco in the Spanish Civil War (1936–39). *See also* FASCISM.

blues rock A style of popular music of the 1970s that combined rock with elements of BLUES music.

Blue Water School Nickname of a group of influential officials in the British Admiralty who, between the two world wars, argued in favour of building large ships to be deployed in distant parts of the world. A result of this policy was that, at the start of World War II, Britain had no landing craft.

bluie or **bluey** (1) British slang term for a five-pound note that was doomed to become obsolete when the old blue five-pound notes were phased out in 1990. (2)

Slang for an airmail letter, usually written on thin blue paper.

blurb A publisher's note on the dustjacket or cover of a book purporting to tell the potential purchaser what the book is about and how good it is (with favourable press comment if it is a reprint). The word was coined by the US novelist Gelett Burgess (1866–1951) in 1906 to publicize one of his own books; he subsequently defined blurb as "self praise, to make a noise like a publisher". The original instance of blurb consisted of a paragraph of nonsensical text under a picture of a pretty girl, who Burgess dubbed 'Belinda Blurb'.

BMEWS Ballistic Missile Early Warning System; a system set up by America with large radar installations at Clear in Alaska, Thule in Greenland, and Fylingdales in Yorkshire.

BMX Bicycle Motorcross, a bicycle designed to be used for stunt riding or on an obstacle course. Small versions with high handlebars were very popular with children until they were largely replaced by MOUNTAIN BIKES in the late 1980s.

BO *See* BODY ODOUR.

Boanerges The nickname given by the adventurer and writer T. E. Lawrence to the Brough Superior motorbike on which he was killed in an accident (trying to avoid cyclists) on a Dorset road in 1935. The name, meaning 'sons of thunder', was taken from the biblical tale of James and John, the sons of Zebedee, who wanted to call down "fire from heaven" to consume the Samaritans for not 'receiving' the Lord Jesus (*Luke* ix, 54; *Mark* iii, 17). Lawrence's motorbike was little damaged and is still extant and in working order. In a similar context, the vintage car that serves as the mascot of the engineering department of the Imperial College of Science, Technology and Medicine is also called Boanerges.

boat. boater A flat-topped shallow-crowned straw hat, usually trimmed with a band of ribbon, popular in late-Victorian and Edwardian England and still seen until the early 1930s at cricket matches, picnics, and boating parties (hence the name). It is the established headgear of Harrow School and was formerly much favoured by butchers and fishmongers.

boat people Refugees from Vietnam who, following the Chinese invasion (Feb–Mar, 1979), escaped the country in small, often unseaworthy, boats across the South China Sea. Many died in the attempt, and those that did survive had difficulties in finding a country that would give them asylum. In the late 1980s increasingly large numbers of boat people, fleeing from the Communist regime in Vietnam, arrived in Hong Kong; there the authorities were forced to detain them in large squalid camps and to consider forcible repatriation.

bob A short haircut, popular among fashionable young women of the 1920s, particularly after the British actress Beatrice Lillie (1898–1989) had her hair cut this way. Variants of the style included the Irene Castle bob (Irene Castle was a popular dancer of the period).

Bob-a-Job-Week An imaginative way of raising funds by self-help, instituted by the BOY SCOUTS in 1949. All kinds of jobs were undertaken, some for their publicity value, for the payment of one shilling. It became an annual effort but with the declining value of the 'bob' and the advent of DECIMAL CURRENCY, *Scout Job Week* took its place in 1972, largely to encourage patrons to give a fairer return for the work done.

bobby-sox Long white cotton socks or ankle socks worn by teenage girls in America in the early 1940s. Hence the name for the young females themselves, **bobby-soxers.**

Bob Hope Dope, *i.e.* cannabis. This British slang term using the name of the British-born US comedian (1903–) was probably coined by middle-class cannabis users in imitation of cockney rhyming slang and is therefore pronounced with a self-conscious cockney-dropped 'H'.

Boche Derogatory term for a German or (in the phrase 'the Boche') Germans collectively. It was used in World Wars I and II and was applied especially to German soldiers. It comes from the French word *alboche*, which is probably a blend of *allemand* (German) and *caboche* (pate, head).

bodbiz *See* SENSITIVITY TRAINING.

bodgie Australian slang of the 1950s for an uncouth youth, the equivalent of the British TEDDY BOY.

body. body art A fashion for decorating the human body with painted designs and displaying or photographing the result. It was popular during the 1960s and early 1970s.

body bag A plastic or rubber container with a zip fastener, used to transport a corpse. Body bags first attracted public attention during the VIETNAM WAR, when tens of thousands of young US servicemen were sent home in body bags.

body building A system of diet and exercise designed to increase muscle size. The 'sport' developed before World War II; in competitive body-building men compete for such titles as 'Mr Universe'. Women also compete for similar titles. Doubts have been expressed by medical organizations about the wisdom of adopting these punishing regimes, which sometimes include the taking of ANABOLIC STEROIDS.

body count The number of dead in a military operation or other incident, or simply the number of people present at a particular event or location.

body line In cricket, fast bowling at the batsman rather than the wicket, with the intention of forcing him to give a catch while defending himself. The accurate but dangerous bowling of Larwood and Voce in the infamous **Body Line Tour** of 1932–33 won the Ashes for England, but roused a storm of indignation in Australia that led to a modification in the laws of cricket. *See also* BOUNCER.

body odour or **BO** The name given in 1933 to any offensive body smell, chiefly that caused by stale sweat. The phrase was coined in a US publicity campaign for Lifebuoy soap.

body-popping A dance popular in the 1980s, in which sequences of jerky movements are employed.

body scanner In popular usage, any of several pieces of medical equipment that reveal the internal structure of the body and are widely used in diagnosis. The term was coined in the 1970s, when it was used synonymously with the CT SCANNER (originally called a 'CAT scanner'); since then it has been used, together with **body scan** and **body scanning**, in connection with several other techniques, including the ULTRASOUND SCANNER, used especially to monitor pregnancy; and magnetic resonance imaging (MRI), utilizing the phenomenon of nuclear magnetic resonance. The advantage of all these techniques over conventional X-ray examination is that they can 'scan' the soft tissues, producing images in different planes of the body. *See also* BRAIN SCANNER.

body shop The job centre, the employment agency. It is used in America and the UK and reflects the depersonalized atmosphere in such places. In the UK it is an ironic contrast to the **Body Shop** chain of stores, which sell environmentally friendly cosmetics.

body worker US slang for a prostitute.

Boer Wars or **South African Wars** The two wars (1880–81 and 1899–1902) in which the Boers of the Transvaal challenged British rule in South Africa. The first war resulted in the Transvaal regaining its independence; the second ended in the re-establishment of British supremacy. The Second Boer War saw the humiliation of the British Army by Boer guerrillas on several occasions and British victory was only secured after harsh measures, including the confining of Boer women and children in CONCENTRATION CAMPS, where 20,000 died. The ugliness of the war has been seen by some historians as a forewarning of the brutality of subsequent 20th-century conflicts, especially the two world wars. *See also* MAFFICKING.

boffin A nickname used by the RAF in World War II for research scientists or BACKROOM BOYS. It passed into general use in the 1940s. It is said to derive from the practice of a certain scientist, who gave his colleagues Dickensian nicknames, Mr. Boffin being a character in *Our Mutual Friend*. There is also a family of HOBBITS called Boffins.

boffo A US slang term from the theatrical world meaning excellent. Apparently derived from 'box office' (*i.e.* box-office success), it is widely used by journalists.

Bofors gun An automatic double-barrelled anti-aircraft gun used in World War II. It was named after Bofors, a town in Sweden where it was first made.

Bogart To monopolize the joint, to fail to pass on the cannabis cigarette to the next person. This expression, used in HIPPIE circles in the late 1960s, was obviously inspired by the popular screen image of the actor Humphrey Bogart with a cigarette permanently hanging from his lip. It was widely used after the 1969 film *Easy Rider* featured a song by the Holy Modal Rounders called 'Don't Bogart that Joint'.

Bogey Humphrey Bogart (1899–1957), the US film star whose portrayal of tough gangsters with a gentle heart endeared him to audiences throughout the world. In *Casablanca* (1942), described by a critic as "one of the outstanding entertainment experiences of cinema history", he establishes his persona with the line:

I stick out my neck for nobody. I'm the only cause I'm interested in.

His other films include *Angels with Dirty Faces* (1938), *The Maltese Falcon* (1941), and *The African Queen* (1952). *See also* PLAY IT AGAIN, SAM.

boiler A woman. British offensive slang used by young working-class males to describe an unattractive and unintelligent woman. In the pre-World War II period the word was usually used to describe an older woman with roughly the shape of a boiler or possibly one resembling a boiling chicken, *i.e.* one too old and tough to roast. The phrase **dodgy boiler** implies that the woman in question could be a transmitter of sexual diseases.

boldly. To boldly go where no man has gone before Slogan that was part of the introduction to the popular US TV space adventure series *Star Trek*. The mission of the Starship *Enterprise* to explore deep space attracted millions of regular viewers, although its expressed aim 'to boldly go' became probably the most ridiculed split infinitive of the 20th century. *See also* BEAM ME UP, SCOTTY.

Bolero Codename for the initial planning stage (started in 1942) for a second front in Europe during World War II.

bollock A ball, *i.e.* a dance. A jokey upper-class British use of the word by boys as well as girls without any embarrassment, in such phrases as 'hunt bollocks' and 'charity bollocks'.

bolo (or **bola) tie** A string or narrow leather necktie with a decorative metal clasp, associated with Western-style US dress. It is named after the *bola* – a missile used by South American gauchos, consisting of two or more weights on the end of cords thrown to entangle the legs of the quarry.

Bolshevik or **Bolshevist** Properly a member of the Russian revolutionary party under Lenin that seized power in 1917 with the objectives of establishing a socialist and then a communist state in Russia. The Bolsheviks were so called from the fact that at the party conferences of 1902–03 the Leninists were the majority group (*Bolsheviki* = majority). The defeated minority were called MENSHEVIKS. In later usage a Bolshevik was any communist, especially one from the Soviet Union.

Bolshie or **Bolshy** A contraction of BOLSHEVIK. It is used to denote a person with 'red' or revolutionary tendencies, but is often extended to include any troublemaker. *See also* LOONY LEFT.

bomb (1) British slang for adorning a building, railway carriage, etc., with graffiti. (2) To be badly received by an audience or to fail at some test.

It was a set up. If I had to go to a club and genuinely bomb, I'd faint. I do have an embarrassment threshold.

RUBY WAX, *Daily Telegraph*, 19 January 1991.

ban the bomb! Slogan adopted by CND in the late 1950s.

Bomb Alley A region of Kent and Sussex between London and the English coast in the path of the BUZZ BOMBS aimed at London in 1944 during World War II. The area suffered extensive damage from bombs that fell short of their target or were shot down en route to London. The term 'Bomb Alley' has also been applied to other heavily bombed areas in an attacking flight path.

bomber (1) A capsule or pill containing amphetamines. (2) A large and very strong joint, or cannabis cigarette. (3) A graffiti vandal.

Bomber Command A command of the RAF in World War II used to carry out bombing raids on enemy territory. *See* BOMBER HARRIS.

Bomber Harris Nickname of Sir Arthur Travers Harris (1892–1984), who as commander-in-chief of BOMBER COMMAND from 1942 to 1945 advocated a controversial strategy of heavy bombing of German industrial cities. As a result of this controversy, Harris was the only leading British wartime leader who did not subsequently receive a peerage.

bomber jacket A strong well-padded short jacket that became a popular item of casual wear after World War II, during which such jackets were worn by the crews of air-force bombers.

bona British working-class slang exclamation of approval mainly used in London in the 1980s. It possibly derives from the Latin *bona fide* meaning real, in good faith, or from the Spanish *buena* and the Italian *buona* meaning good.

Bond, James A British secret agent created by the author Ian Fleming (1908–64). Commander Bond (with the code name 007) appeared in 12 novels and 7 short stories. The exploits of this archetypal hero – suave, resourceful, sexually attractive, and high-living – have been the subject of a series of spectacular films (the **Bond films**). Bond's name was taken by

Fleming from that of an ornithologist who lived near his home in Jamaica. His adventures were loosely based on those of the British spy Sidney Reilly and the double-agent Dusko Popov, both notorious womanizers.

bondook British army slang from the GULF WAR of 1991 for a weapon, of obscure derivation.

Bones *See* OLD BLUE EYES.

bong A water-pipe used for smoking cannabis. It is smaller than a hubble-bubble and became a typical accessory for drug users in the 1960s and 1970s. The word is used throughout the English-speaking world.

bonk To have sexual intercourse. It became a popular euphemism for 'fuck' in the late 1970s and 1980s. Because it is devoid of the aggressiveness associated with 'fuck' as a swearword, it can be used more comfortably for an act of love. 'Bonk' was originally early 20th-century slang for a hit; the sexual sense probably arose by analogy. *See* BONKERS.

> Council watchdogs bugged a couple's flat after neighbours complained they were bonking too noisily.
>
> *The Sun*, 15 March 1991.

bonkers Crazy, mad. Common in the UK since the 1960s, it was used in the 1920s to mean slightly drunk. The origin of its present usage is unclear, but could be related to the idea of being deranged from a *bonk*, a hit on the head (*bonce*).

Bonneville salt flats An area in NW Utah in America, where several land-speed records have been broken since it was first identified as suitable for this purpose in 1935. The flats are the dried bed of an ancient lake.

Bonnie and Clyde The US robbers Bonnie Parker (1911–34) and Clyde Barrow (1909–34) whose trail of violence and larceny across Texas, Oklahoma, New Mexico, and Missouri (1932–34) captured the US public imagination. Barrow was a small-time car thief before he met Parker in 1930; after his release from a jail sentence (1930–32) they embarked upon a series of raids on minor banks and gas stations until betrayed by a confederate and killed in a roadblock ambush by police. Their short, violent, but flamboyant lives formed the basis for a major film called *Bonnie and Clyde* (starring Warren Beatty and Faye Dunaway) in 1967, by which time the real outlaws had acquired semi-legendary status.

boo US slang for marijuana.

boo-hurrah theory The philosophical theory, also known as emotivism, that moral statements are not true in any other sense than that they express the feelings of the person making them. Thus, the statement 'charity is good' merely means that the person saying it thinks that being charitable is desirable.

boob (1) A fool, an idiot. An inoffensive shortened form of booby. (2) An inoffensive term for a mistake, a blunder. (3) Socially acceptable slang for a female breast.

boob tube (1) A tight-fitting strapless top for women, *i.e.* a tube to contain the breasts. (2) In US and Canadian slang, a television set.

booby hatch Slang for a mental hospital, derived from the traditional meaning of 'booby' as 'fool'. In the UK the phrase acquired added significance by its relation to **Colney Hatch**, a village near Barnet where a mental hospital was built in 1851.

booby trap An explosive device that is set to go off without warning, often when it is touched. Such devices were used in World War I and reached new levels of sophistication in World War II when the Japanese even booby-trapped corpses. The IRA and other terrorist organizations have also made use of booby-trapped devices. Originally, a 'booby trap' was simply a practical joke.

boofer US slang for a buyer of illegal drugs.

boogie To dance to popular music, especially at a DISCO. To boogie was a common expression in the 1970s and was clearly derived from the earlier BOOGIE-WOOGIE.

boogie box A portable tape recorder. The term was originally used by young Blacks in the 1970s as a synonym for GHETTO-BLASTER. It was adopted by a wider spectrum of British teenagers in the 1980s.

boogie-woogie A style of piano playing. The left hand maintains a heavy repetitive pattern of eight beats to the bar over which the right hand provides a syncopated improvisation. Probably developed in the Middle West by JAZZ musicians early in the 20th century, it owes its name to Clarence 'Pinetop' Smith's *Pinetop's Boogie-Woogie* (1928). It did not become popular, however, until the 1930s. *Boogie* in US slang is a negro performer and *woogie* a rhyming additive. *See also* BLUES; RAGTIME; SWING.

Booker Prize An annual prize for a British, Commonwealth, or Irish work of fiction first awarded in 1969. It was founded by the British engineering and trading company Booker McConnell in conjunction with the Publishers' Association and is selected by a panel appointed by the Book Trust. The prize is currently £20,000. Past winners include William Golding (1980), Salman Rushdie (1981), Kingsley Amis (1986), and Kazuo Ishiguro (1989).

boom. boom boom In US Black slang of the 1940s, a cowboy movie and hence also a gun.

boom corridor A strip of land under the flight path of a supersonic plane, within which the sonic boom can be heard. The term came into use with the advent of the Anglo-French supersonic airliner CONCORDE (1969) – in particular, in connection with designated flight paths that caused minimum inconvenience.

boomerang kid A young adult who leaves the family home but soon returns to it, rather than set up a new home on his or her own. The phenomenon was said to be on the increase in the 1980s.

boondock US slang meaning to court sexually. It is derived from *bundok* in Tagalog, the language of the Philippines, meaning mountain, an isolated place. This usage presumably reflects the idea of an isolated place being sought by courting couples. It came to be used by the US armed forces during World War II. Hence, the use of the word **boondocks** for any remote place.

boondoggling The useless spending of money, usually with reference to the US government's expenditure in the 1930s to combat the GREAT DEPRESSION. It apparently derives from the Scottish word *boondoggle*, meaning a marble received as a gift.

boot. bootleg An unauthorized recording of pop music, distributed or sold in breach of copyright. The recordings may be made by smuggling tape recorders into concerts.

bootlegger One who traffics illegally in alcoholic liquor, derived from the smuggling of flasks of liquor in the legs of smugglers' boots.

Bootlegging became a major racket in America during the years of PROHIBITION (1920–34). Criminal elements took over and the profits from bootlegging enabled rapid and dangerous growth of the underworld to take place under such gangsters as CAPONE. *See also* RUM RUNNERS.

bootstrap In science and technology, a system that is self-acting or self-sufficient in some way. For instance, in computer science a **bootstrap program** is a short program used to load the operating system and start up the system. The word can also be used as a verb: 'to bootstrap a computer'. In nuclear physics, a **bootstrap theory** is a self-consistent theory in which fundamental nuclear particles are interconnected – composed of each other, rather than made up of more fundamental entities such as QUARKS. Such uses of the word come from the phrase 'pulling oneself up by one's own bootstraps'. Possibly this originated with a story by the German writer Rudolph Raspe (1737–94) in which his hero Baron Munchhausen boasted that he once found himself trapped in quicksand, lifted himself by his bootstraps, and carried himself to firm ground.

bop A style of JAZZ music that replaced BEBOP in the 1940s. Its distinguishing features were rapid singing and dance rhythms. Subsequently the word came to be used for any dance to jazz or pop music.

Borley Rectory Reputedly 'the most haunted house in England', a former rectory in the village of Borley, Essex. It laid claim to a ghostly nun, a headless coachman, and various other poltergeist manifestations. It was investigated by the Society for Psychical Research but burned down shortly after (1929). The house's reputation was largely contrived by the journalist and psychic researcher Harry Price, who was suspected of faking some of his 'evidence'. When the house burned down ghostly faces were seen in the windows: since then reportings of strange happenings in the church opposite have led to speculation that the house's ghostly inhabitants have found a new home nearby.

born. born 1820 – still going strong Trade slogan associated with Johnnie Walker whisky. It was coined in 1910; 1820 was the year the company was founded.

born-again Christian A person who has experienced a spiritual conversion and become an ardent and often evangelizing

Christian. The epithet 'born-again' is usually, but not always, religious. For example, a **born-again golfer** is one who, having played golf occasionally for many years, becomes an ardent player on retirement.

boroscope A fibre-optic probe used to investigate otherwise inaccessible places, such as those in complex machinery.

Borstal A former British institution for the detention and rehabilitation of offenders between the ages of 15 and 21. Youths could be detained for up to two years with a subsequent 'parole' period of two more years. The Borstal system was introduced in 1908 and named after the first such prison at the village of Borstal, near Rochester in Kent. Borstals were abolished in 1983; offenders under 21 years of age are now sentenced to 'detention in a young offender institution'.

bosey (Austr.) In cricket, another name for a googly, so named from its inventor, the English bowler B. J. Bosanquet, who toured Australia in 1903–04. The term was also applied in World War II to a single bomb dropped from a plane.

Bosnywash In America, the thickly populated and affluent eastern region of the country. It comes from the names of the three main cities in the region: *Bos*ton, *NY* (New York), and *Wash*ington. *See also* CHIPPITTS; SANSAN.

boss Excellent. This sense, used widely in the English-speaking world, originated among the Black youth of America in the 1960s.

Boss, The (1) Franklin D. Roosevelt (1882–1945), US president, also known as the **American Dictator**, the **New Deal Caesar**, the **Sphinx**, **Franklin Deficit Roosevelt**, and **Houdini in the White House**. *See* FDR. (2) Bess Truman (1885–1982), wife of the US president Harry S. Truman. (3) Bruce Springsteen (1949–), US rock star. (4) Margaret Thatcher. *See* IRON LADY.

bossa nova (Port. new voice) A type of dance music, based on the SAMBA, that originated in Brazil but subsequently became popular throughout the West.

Boston Strangler A mass-murderer who killed at least 11 women in Boston, Massachusetts, in the period 1962–64. He is thought to have been Albert DeSalvo, who was sentenced to life imprisonment in 1967 for other offences involving sexual assault.

Botswana A country in S Africa formerly under British control as *Bechuanaland*. The name Botswana was adopted when it gained full independence in 1966.

bottle (1) Courage, nerve. A British slang expression usually used in such phrases as 'to lose one's bottle' and 'his bottle's gone' but also, more positively, in 'I admire his bottle.' The origin of bottle in this sense is somewhat devious; in cockney rhyming slang 'bottle and glass' means arse. 'Arse' is a taboo word for bottom, and bottom has an old-established sense meaning courage. It only came to be widely used in its present sense in the 1970s, probably influenced by criminal and police speech in TV crime dramas. In 1985 it was used in the advertising slogan for milk, 'Milk has gotta lotta bottle'. It is usually pronounced with a medial glottal stop in an imitation of cockney speech. (2) British slang for the money collected by street buskers. (3) To injure by thrusting a broken bottle into someone. (4) **To bottle out**. To lose one's nerve.

> He was there on the big occasion and had the guts not to bottle it.
>
> *The Independent*, 5 January 1991.

(5) **To hit the bottle**. To drink heavily.

bottle bank A large container provided by local authorities in a public place to enable members of the public to dispose of their used glass bottles for recycling. Three such containers are often provided, one for colourless glass, one for brown or amber glass, and one for green glass.

bottleneck (1) A style of pop guitar playing in which a small length of tubular metal or other device worn on the player's finger is pressed on the strings and moved to produce a gliding sound. It is so called because originally the neck of a glass bottle was used. This style of playing is also called **slide** or **slide guitar**. (2) A road that is frequently clogged with traffic.

bottle party A party to which guests are expected to bring a bottle of an alcoholic drink.

bottom line The main point of an argument or problem, or the basic characteristic of something. The phrase became popular during the 1970s, possibly because of its use by the US secretary of state Henry Kissinger (*see* SHUTTLE DIPLOMACY). He spoke of 'the bottom line' as the eventual outcome of a negotiation – disregarding the intermediate arguments or rights and wrongs of the situation. The phrase, in its figurative sense, predates the 1970s and refers to the last line on a financial statement summarizing the net profit or loss of a company.

Bottomley case A fraud case involving Horatio Bottomley (1860–1933), former Liberal MP and editor of the magazine *John Bull*. In 1922 he was sentenced to 7 years' imprisonment for his part in issuing bogus *victory bonds*.

bouffant A ladies' hairstyle, common in the 1960s, in which extra height and breadth are given by back-combing. It comes from the French *bouffer*, to puff up.

Boulder Dam *See* HOOVER DAM.

boulevard cowboy or **boulevard westerner** In US slang, a reckless taxi-driver of the type encountered in New York, Chicago, and other major cities.

Boulwarism US colloquialism for collective bargaining, named after Lemuel Boulware, labour relations chief of General Electric in the 1950s.

bounce. bouncer In cricket, a deliberately short-pitched ball intended to bounce high enough to reach the batsman at around head height. The increasing use of the bouncer to intimidate batsmen, considered by many as 'ungentlemanly', led in the 1970s to the use of protective headgear by many professional cricketers.

Bouncing Czech A media name for the publisher Robert Maxwell (Robert Hoch; 1923–). He is more familiar as **Captain Bob**. Born in Czechoslovakia, he was destined for a local rabbinical school but with the advent of World War II he escaped from occupied Europe to serve as a captain in the British Army, becoming head of the press section of the German department of the Foreign Office in Berlin (1945–47). In the postwar years he built a remarkable network of publishing businesses, culminating in the acquisition of the *Daily Mirror*. He was also Labour MP for Buckingham (1964–70).

Bourbaki, Nicolas A contemporary French mathematician noted for the presentation of mathematics in an original fashion, stressing its axiomatic structure. In fact, Bourbaki is not a person but a pseudonym for a group of mathematicians who came together in 1939 to write a treatise *Eléments de Mathématique*. They took the name from a French general who, in the Franco–Prussian war of 1870–71, valiantly but unsuccessfully tried to break the Prussian line.

bovine spongiform encephalopathy *See* MAD COW DISEASE.

bovril Australian slang for 'rubbish', derived from the tradename of a beef extract, which was itself coined by combining the Latin word *bos* (ox) with *vril* (a magical fluid with extraordinary properties in the novel *The Coming Race* (1871) by Edward Bulwer-Lytton). The word 'bovril' was also used as a euphemism for a brothel in the 1930s.

bovver Trouble, aggravation. A British aggressive slang word widely used by young males, especially SKINHEADS. This spelling is an imitation of bother, a euphemism for extreme aggravation, spoken with a London accent. The classic skinhead taunt was 'You want bovver?' to provoke a fight.

bovver boots Heavy boots worn as part of SKINHEAD dress in the late 1960s. They were usually either ex-army boots or DOC MARTENS.

bovver-boy (1) British slang expression for a provocatively aggressive youth, especially a SKINHEAD. (2) A trouble-shooter. A humorous extension of the original meaning.

bowl game An American football game between winning teams of leagues held after the end of the league season. *See* ROSE BOWL.

box (1) The anus. An old male homosexual term that came to be used again in the 1970s. (2) The male genitals. A British schoolboy and male homosexual usage based on the cricket box, a protective shield worn over the genitals whilst playing cricket. (3) The female genitals. This is mainly an Australian usage. (4) A coffin. (5) A safe. A term from the criminal world. (6) **the box**. The TV. A British colloquialism. (7) A guitar. Originally a Black US musician's term of the 1950s, it was taken up by British rock musicians in the 1960s. (8) A portable tape recorder. US slang from the 1970s.

Boxers A branch of the White Lotus sect in China which played a prominent part in the rising against foreigners in 1900 and was suppressed by joint European action. The Chinese name was *I Ho Chuan* or 'Righteous Harmony Fists', implying training for the purpose of developing righteousness and harmony.

open the box One of the two choices available to participants in the British television quiz *Take Your Pick*, first screened in 1955. If the contestant elected to open the box he took a gamble on the value of what was inside; the alternative was to 'take the money' the contestant had already won and leave the box unopened.

boy. Boy Orator of the Platitude *See* MAN ON THE WEDDING CAKE.

Boy Scouts A successful youth movement started by General Sir Robert Baden-Powell (Lord Baden-Powell of Gilwell) in 1908. The aim was to train boys to be good citizens with high ideals of honour, service to others, cleanliness, and self-reliance, based essentially on training in an outdoor setting. The movement became worldwide with a membership now of over 14 million young people. A complete Scout Group now consists of Cub Scouts (formerly Wolf Cubs), age 8 to 11; Scouts, 11 to 16; and Venture Scouts (formerly Rover Scouts), 16 to 29. These new designations, as well as that of **Scout Association**, were introduced in 1967. The first Girl Scouts were admitted in 1990. *See also* GIRL GUIDES.

Boy Wonder *See* BATMAN.

Boycs Nickname of Geoffrey Boycott (1940–) British cricketer who played for Yorkshire (1962–86) and England (1964–74, 1977–81).

bozo A fool, a stupid fellow. An inoffensive US slang term, originally dating from the 1920s but now heard frequently in the UK and Australia. It has often been applied to Ronald Reagan, US president (1981–89). The derivation is uncertain.

bra (Fr. *brassière*) A support for a woman's breasts, which takes its name ultimately from the French *bra* (arm). It was invented by a US debutante, Mary Phelps Jacob, with the assistance of her French maid, initially with two handkerchiefs and a ribbon. Her friends applauded her idea and she finally sold the patent in 1914 for $15,000. In the 1960s the garment became a feminist symbol of women's subjugation to men on the grounds that it was worn solely to satisfy male ideals of female beauty. Perhaps inspired by mass burnings of army draft cards during the VIETNAM WAR, female supporters of feminism were exhorted to burn their bras.

Brabazon A huge airliner built (1949) by the Bristol Brabazon company, run by Lord Brabazon of Tara (1884–1964). It was withdrawn in 1952. Lord Brabazon was the first British citizen to fly in the UK, in 1909.

Brabham A type of racing car designed and built by the former Australian racing driver John 'Jack' Brabham (1926–). He started making cars in 1962 and in 1966 became the first driver to win the motor-racing championship in a car of his own construction.

Bradbury A £1 note, issued by the Treasury in the period 1914–28, bearing the signature of J. S. Bradbury (first Baron Bradbury), who as Joint Permanent Secretary to the Treasury began the issue.

Brahms and Liszt Cockney rhyming slang for pissed (meaning drunk). It has been heard since the 1930s but has been in much wider use since the 1970s, promoted by the popularity of such TV situation comedies as *Only Fools and Horses*.

brain. brain death The state that exists when the region of the brain that controls vital activities, such as breathing and eye reflexes, ceases to function. Traditionally, a person was pronounced dead when his heart stopped beating and his breathing ceased. However, the use of mechanical ventilators to maintain respiration in brain-damaged patients can also enable the heart to continue beating after natural breathing has ceased; the presence of a heartbeat is no longer a valid criterion for establishing death. In such cases, if two doctors agree that vital brain function has nevertheless ceased, the patient is declared 'brain-dead' and organs for transplantation may be legally removed before the heart has stopped beating.

brain drain A drift abroad (from the early 1960s) of British-trained scientists, technologists, doctors, and university teachers (especially to America), attracted by higher salaries and often better facilities and funding for their work. *See also* BRAWN DRAIN.

brain gain An increase in the pool of skilled or professional workers in a country as a result of immigration. It is thus the opposite of BRAIN DRAIN.

brain scanner Any of several pieces of medical equipment used to detect abnormalities within the brain. These include the CT SCANNER and the **PET scanner** (positron emission tomography scanner). *See also* BODY SCANNER.

brainstorm In business or marketing, to assemble a group of people to tackle a problem together by pooling their ideas. Brainstorming became an accepted business technique in America in the 1930s.

Brains Trust Originally the name 'Brains Trust' was applied by James M. Kieran of the *New York Times* to the advisers of F. D. Roosevelt in his election campaign; later it was used of the group of college professors who advised him in administering the NEW DEAL. In Britain it became the name of a popular BBC programme in which well-known public figures (including Prof. C. E. M. Joad, Commander Campbell, and Julian Huxley) aired their views on questions submitted by listeners. Now in general use for any such panel of experts or team which answers questions impromptu.

brainwashing Persuading a person to discard his own opinions in favour of a set of ideas not his own. This is sometimes achieved by various subtle psychological methods, such as repeating an idea continuously while the person concerned is in a weakened state. These processes were a favourite theme of adventure films and novels throughout the century; in real life, brainwashing techniques were widely employed in the KOREAN WAR and have since been used by various repressive regimes.

brand. brand awareness The extent to which members of the public are aware of a particular consumer product, the yardstick that determines what kind of advertising a particular product requires.

Brands Hatch British motor-racing circuit near Farnham, Kent, which was opened in the 1920s for use by motorcycles; from 1949 it was also used to stage car races. The British driver Jim Clark won the first Grand Prix to be held here (1964).

Brand X Any unidentified competitor's product used as an example of an inferior alternative to a product being advertised. It first appeared in television advertisements in the late 1960s in which the virtues of named products, particularly soap powders, were compared with the failings of the unnamed competitor, Brand X.

branwagon An allegedly healthy diet based on high-fibre foods, such as bran, that was enthusiastically adopted by increasing numbers of health fadists in the West during the 1980s. 'Jumping on the branwagon' was a fairly obvious variant of 'jumping on the bandwagon'.

Brasília The capital of Brazil; a new city built on the country's central plateau. Building was started in 1960 on a site chosen in 1956, the principal architect was Oscar Niemeyer (1907–). Within 30 years the population was approaching half a million.

bratpack A group of young US film stars who emerged in the 1980s. Their exuberant lifestyles were seen by the media to be reminiscent of those of previous generations in the film world; they included Emilio Estevez (1962–) and Tom Cruise (1962–).

Braun, Eva Adolf Hitler's mistress from 1933 until their marriage, the day before their joint suicide on 30 April 1945. Her contribution to Hitler's life was said to be domestic rather than sexual; she was never seen in public with him and apparently had no influence on his monstrous political aspirations or his seduction of 80 million Germans into implementing them.

Brave New World A novel (1932) by the British author Aldous Huxley (1894–1964) with a bleak view of what the future had in store. In Huxley's Brave New World human embryos are produced and grown under laboratory conditions and pre-designed and conditioned to perform certain tasks in society. The title comes from Shakespeare's *Tempest*, in which Miranda says:

> O brave new world that has such people in it.

The phrase is now used of any new real or hypothetical society that bears similarities to Huxley's invention.

brawn drain The emigration of athletes and manual workers to other countries in search of better rewards. *See also* BRAIN DRAIN.

Brazilian Bombshell Carmen Miranda (1913–55). The Portuguese singer who wore strange flower- and fruit-laden hats when singing South American songs in her many wartime films.

bread Money. A 1960s version of the earlier euphemism 'dough' and widely used in HIPPIE jargon as well as working-class speech. It now sounds rather outdated and has been replaced by such words as **dosh.**

breadhead A disparaging slang expression for someone who is only interested in money and getting rich, a capitalist. It was common in the HIPPIE era of the 1960s and 1970s, when such an attitude was much frowned on, and is still in use.

break A short solo improvisation in JAZZ music.

breakaway furniture In the film industry, furniture that is designed to break easily, thus avoiding injury in the barroom brawls typical of the WESTERN and other violent movies.

break dance A dance craze of the 1980s, the distinguishing feature of which was the use of energetic acrobatic movements.

breaker A person using a CITIZENS' BAND radio. In America, the term was used from about 1963 and derives from the idea that the person broadcasting was 'breaking in' to other people's conversations. CB radio spread to the UK in the 1970s and originally was illegal because it was said to interfere with the short-range radio communications of the emergency services. Enthusiasts in the UK thought of themselves as 'breakers' in the sense that they were breaking the law.

breakfast of champions US trade slogan associated with *Wheaties* breakfast cereal, extolling its stamina-giving qualities. Kurt Vonnegut (1922–) wrote a novel under the same title in 1973.

breathalyser A device used by the police to estimate the amount of alcohol that a driver has recently consumed. This is done by asking the driver to blow into the device so that the amount of alcohol in the breath can be measured, which reflects the amount of alcohol in the blood. The legal limit in the UK and America is 80 milligrams of alcohol in 100 millilitres of blood. Drivers with a higher concentration of alcohol in their blood are liable to prosecution. The original breathalysers relied on a colour change in potassium dichromate crystals as a result of contact with alcohol in the driver's breath. More modern devices are electronic. Portable instruments used at the roadside give a red warning light if the limit is exceeded. Drivers who fail the preliminary test are taken to a police station and tested on a more accurate instrument, which gives a digital readout. They may then have to submit to a blood or urine test. *See also* EYELYSER.

Brechtian Describing the style of theatre, in particular EPIC THEATRE, associated with the German dramatist Bertolt Brecht (1898–1956).

brekkers *See* HONKERS.

Brenda *Private Eye's* nickname for Elizabeth II.

Bren-gun A World War II light machine gun, fired from the shoulder. Originally made in Brno, Czechoslovakia, it was then manufactured in Enfield, England. *Bren* is a blend of Brno and Enfield.

Brenner express A regular night train from Munich to Rome that passes through the Brenner Pass on the Austro-Italian border.

Brest-Litovsk Treaties Treaties in 1918 towards the end of World War I between the Ukraine and Germany and between Soviet Russia and Germany. The treaties were annulled after the defeat of Germany. They were signed at Brest-Litovsk, a port now in the Soviet Union, which changed its name to Brest in 1921.

Bretton Woods Conference A conference, attended by America, the UK, and Canada, held (1944) at the town of Bretton Woods in New Hampshire, America, leading to the establishment of the International Monetary Fund (IMF) and the World Bank.

Brezhnev Doctrine The policy, associated with the Soviet president Leonid Brezhnev (1906–82), that authorized the Soviet Union to intervene in the domestic affairs of satellite states in defence of socialism.

Brian A bore, a dull or unintelligent person. The name was supposed to typify a tediously hard-working lower-class male in the 1970s and 1980s; it was used in such phrases as "Well, Brian . . . ", at the start of a tedious explanation, in an imitation of the well-known sports commentator Brian Moore. This usage culminated in the contentiously comic film about the life of Christ, called *The Life of Brian*, made by the team of MONTY PYTHON'S FLYING CIRCUS.

Brideshead *See* FLYTE, SEBASTIAN.

Brides in the Bath A famous British murder case (1915) in which G. J. Smith was convicted of murdering three woman whom he had bigamously married and later drowned in the bath.

Bridge Club The four main participants in the KENNEDY ROUND of economic negotiations in the 1960s: America, the UK, the EEC, and Japan.

Brighton trunk murders Two unrelated murder cases that captured national headlines in 1934. The first case began with the discovery of a dismembered body in a trunk at a left-luggage office in Brighton.

Subsequently, another body was found in a second trunk at the home of a petty criminal, Tony Mancini. Mancini was charged with the murders but, after a brilliant defence by the advocate Norman Birkott, acquitted, although he did subsequently admit in a newspaper (in 1976) that he had killed one of the deceased. For a time after the trial Mancini toured with a travelling fair as 'The Infamous Brighton Trunk Murder Man', pretending to cut off the head of a pretty girl with a fake guillotine. The first trunk, chief item of evidence in a crime that was never solved, is now an exhibit in Scotland Yard's Black Museum.

bright young things A phrase coined by the novelist Barbara Cartland (1902–) to describe the young socialites of the years following World War I. Their reaction to the horrors of the war was to dance the night away in a riot of frivolous parties in an attempt to pretend that it had never happened. *See also* FLAPPER.

brill A British teenager's word for excellent, wonderful. A shortened form of *brilliant*, it has been used since the 1970s.

brilliant pebbles A space warfare strategy, in which large numbers of small but sophisticated missiles would be deployed in orbit to keep watch for and then destroy any hostile missile that came in range. A refinement of the STAR WARS project launched in the 1980s, the 'brilliant pebbles' concept started life as a far grander scheme based on bigger intercepting missiles, called **smart rocks.**

brinkmanship A term coined by the US politician Adlai Stevenson in 1956 (though he disclaimed originality), with reference to the policy of J. Foster Dulles in leading to the brink of war but not to war itself. It has since been used of any strategy that risks disastrous consequences if it goes slightly wrong. *See also* LIFEMANSHIP.

Brisbane Line A plan of defence that was put forward by the military to the Australian government in early 1942, when a Japanese invasion seemed imminent. The suggestion that the plan intended to concentrate on defending only the most crucial areas of the country, implying that all of Australia north of Brisbane would be surrendered, caused considerable public concern.

Britain. Britain can take it A slogan publicized by the British government in the early part of World War II; it was intended to cement the national resolve in the face of enemy attacks. In fact, the public reacted badly to this piece of somewhat Victorian jingoism and the slogan was dropped in late 1941.

I'm backing Britain A slogan briefly and enthusiastically adopted by the British public in 1968, often in the form of stickers or posters, designed to encourage people to make special efforts in the national interest, particularly by doing extra work for no payment. It was coined by five female typists in Surbiton, who were determined to do something to bolster national pride and improve the country's economic position by working an extra half hour a day free; unfortunately the slogan did not survive to the end of the decade.

Britannia (1) A long-range turboprop airliner made by the Bristol Brabazon company and introduced in 1957. It was driven out of service by competition from jet airliners, particularly the Boeing 707. (2) A range of gold coins that was introduced in the UK in 1987 as a rival to the KRUGERRAND of South Africa.

British. British Academy A learned society founded in 1901 to promote the study of the humanities in the UK, including language, literature, archaeology, philosophy, economics, etc.

British Antarctic Territory A British colony established in 1962, consisting of the South Orkney and South Shetland Islands and part of the continent of Antarctica.

British Army of the Rhine (BAOR) British forces stationed in West Germany in the post-World War II period as part of the NATO defence against any Soviet attack. The unification of Germany in 1990 and the thawing of relations between the West and the Soviet Union led to major reassessments of the BAOR's role.

British Boxing Board of Control An organization, founded in 1929, responsible for the regulation of boxing in the UK. It replaced the former *National Sporting Club*.

British Broadcasting Corporation *See* BBC.

British Commonwealth of Nations A loose association of 50 nations established in 1931 under the Statute of Westminster. Member states, formerly part of the British Empire, include approximately 25% of the world's population and recognize the British monarch as the head of the Commonwealth. After World War II the name was changed to the **Commonwealth.**

British Council A government-supported body founded in 1934 to promote British culture and the teaching of English abroad.

British disease An uncomplimentary term used abroad with reference to the prevalence of strikes and INDUSTRIAL ACTION in the UK during the 1970s. *See also* ENGLISH DISEASE.

British Gazette A government newspaper produced during the first few days of the GENERAL STRIKE in 1926. The editor was the then chancellor of the exchequer, Winston Churchill.

British Legion The *Royal British Legion*, an organization set up in 1921 by the merger of other ex-servicemen's associations. It acts as a social and welfare organization for both ex-servicemen and women and for those still serving in the armed forces. *See also* REMEMBRANCE DAY.

British Library A national institution created in 1972 from the amalgamation of the British Museum Library, the National Central Library, and the National Lending Library for Science and Technology. The library's proposed premises in Euston Road, London, were long a subject of debate; construction of the building only started in the late 1980s, based on designs by Colin St John Wilson.

British Lions The name given to the Rugby Union team selected from the players of England, Scotland, Wales, and Ireland to represent the British Isles in international matches abroad.

British Union of Fascists A right-wing political party founded by Sir Oswald Mosley (1896–1980) in 1932. *See also* BLACKSHIRTS.

Brixton briefcase British slang expression for a portable tape player, a GHETTO-BLASTER. Brixton is a district in London with a large Black population.

Brockton Blockbuster Nickname given to the US world heavyweight boxing champion Rocky Marciano (1923–69) whose home town was Brockton, Massachusetts.

bromide (1) A small dose of potassium bromide given as a sedative. In World War II the tea served in servicemen's canteens was said to be laced with bromide to reduce the men's libidos. (2) A person who makes soothing trite remarks. It was used in this sense by Gelett Burgess (1866–1951) in his novel *Are You a Bromide?* (1906). (3) The soothing remark itself.

Bronx cheer US slang for a 'raspberry', a noise made with the tongue and lips as a sign of contempt. The Bronx is a largely working-class district of New York City.

Brookhaven National Laboratory A US research establishment at Upton, Long Island, New York, noted for work on high-energy particle physics.

Brooklands A former car-racing circuit near Weybridge in Surrey. It was opened in 1907 and closed down in 1946. It was famous for its steeply banked bends, which enabled cars to corner at high speeds.

brothel creepers British slang of the 1950s for suede shoes with thick crepe soles as worn by TEDDY BOYS. **Brothel stompers** is the US equivalent.

Brother, can you spare a dime? The title of a song with lyrics by Edgar Harburg (1896–1981) composed in the 1930s during the GREAT DEPRESSION. A British film made in 1975 used the same title to give a semi-documentary picture of the US Depression, in which many formerly prosperous citizens were reduced to beggars. The phrase remains characteristic of the period.

brown. Brown, Rosemary British medium, who attracted attention in the 1960s when she claimed to be in communication with Igor Stravinsky, Franz Liszt, Beethoven, and Chopin. In her home in Balham, S London, Mrs Brown took down by dictation entire new musical works from these composers, despite having only a rudimentary knowledge of music theory. The subsequent publication of some of these pieces, which included a 40-page Schubert sonata, songs by Schubert, and Beethoven's 10th and 11th symphonies confounded music critics who had to admit they have all the hallmarks of each composer's style. No one ever succeeded in proving that Mrs Brown was faking the works; among those convinced that she was passing on genuine compositions from beyond the grave were Richard Rodney Bennett and the pianist Hephzibah Menuhin (sister of the violinist Yehudi). Bennett remarked: "I couldn't have faked some of the Beethoven myself."

Brown Bagger A serious student who is only interested in his course of study, especially at university. The epithet derives from the brown attaché case in which students (especially non-resident students) used to carry their books.

> A "Brown Bagger" I must explain, is a peculiar person; he is one who arrives at 10 a.m. (or earlier) and leaves at 5 p.m., takes no active part in the social life of the college, works at home or elsewhere on Boat Race and Athletic Days when the college is shut and perhaps knows only by hearsay where the Union is.
>
> *Westminster City School Magazine*, Dec 1930

In America a *brown bagger* is a workman who takes his lunch from a brown-paper bag rather than use the cafeteria; one who similarly takes his own liquor to a club or restaurant, usually where alcoholic drinks are not available.

Brown Berets A US organization of Mexicans seeking to defend the interests of the Mexican community in America, named after the brown berets they wear.

Brown Bomber The US boxer Joe Louis (1914–81), who was undefeated heavyweight champion of the world from 1937 until his retirement in 1949. On his return in 1950 he was defeated by Ezzard Charles. He began his career in 1934, winning 27 fights, all but four by knockouts.

browned off A slang phrase (derivation uncertain) widely current in World War II, signifying 'fed up' or 'bored stiff'. *Cheesed off* is a similar expression.

brown goods Any electronic product that is housed in a wood, or imitation wood, cabinet. *See also* WHITE GOODS.

brownie points An imaginary award for doing the right thing, or a good deed, in order to impress somebody. Originally a US expression, it has become common in the UK since the 1970s. Some suggest it is based on the erroneous idea that Brownie guides are awarded points for good deeds; others prefer a derivation based on a points system for employees operated by US railway companies or on the concept of 'arse-licking'.

Brownies *See* GIRL GUIDES.

brown job An RAF name for a member of the army, *i.e.* a soldier in khaki.

brown-out In World War II, Australian slang for a partial BLACK-OUT, in which restricted lighting was allowed.

Brown Shirts Hitler's NAZI *Sturmabteilung* (stormtroopers) or **SA** formed in 1921. Under Ernst Röhm the Brown Shirts (so called from the colour of their shirts) attacked Nazi opponents until 1933, when Röhm was murdered on Hitler's orders and power passed to the SS. *See* KRISTALLNACHT; NIGHT OF THE LONG KNIVES.

brown sugar In America, slang term for a coarse low-grade variety of heroin originating in Asia.

Brücke, Die (Ger. the bridge) A school of German artists who came together (1905–13) to promote modern art. They included the expressionist and printmaker Ernst Kirchner (1880–1938). Die Brücke was noted for its emotional pictures in bright colours and for its influence on graphic art.

brunch A meal taken in the late morning, which replaces both breakfast and lunch.

Bruno US slang name for Brown University in America.

Brussels Treaty (1) A treaty signed in 1948 between the UK, France, and the BENELUX countries, originally for mutual defence. It led to the establishment of NATO (1949) and foreshadowed the Treaty of Rome leading to the EUROPEAN COMMUNITY. (2) A treaty by which the UK, Denmark, and the Republic of Ireland became members of the European Community in 1973.

brutalism A style of 20th-century architecture, also sometimes called new brutalism, first applied to the post-1930 work of LE CORBUSIER (1887–1965) and therefore regarded as an aspect of the **International Style** of architecture. Rugged monumental structures with raw untreated concrete and exposed services characterize the style.

Brylcreem Tradename for a hair preparation made by the Beecham Group. Combining the words 'brilliant' and 'cream', it was first sold in 1928 and became very popular amongst fashionable young men.

Brylcreem boys The RAF pilots who fought the BATTLE OF BRITAIN during the early part of World War II (*see* FEW, THE). The epithet was facetious, and usually envious of the glamour attaching to these young men. It was inspired by an advertisement for BRYLCREEM, showing a young RAF officer with shiny well-ordered hair, clearly intended to be seen as a copious user of the brand.

BSA Birmingham Small Arms. A former British engineering company (founded in 1873), noted for making bicycles, motorcycles, small cars, rifles, and air guns throughout the first half of the 20th century.

BSE Bovine spongiform encephalopathy. *See* MAD COW DISEASE.

BST (1) British Summer Time. The time set one hour ahead of GREENWICH MEAN TIME. It was adopted in the UK in 1916 and now lasts from the end of March until the end of October. (2) British Standard Time. The time, set one hour ahead of Greenwich Mean Time, that was adopted all the year round in the UK from 1968 to 1971. *See* DAYLIGHT SAVING. (3) *B*ovine *s*o-mato*t*rophin. A growth hormone of cattle, preparations of which are used to increase milk yield and beef production.

bubble. bubble dancing US Black slang from the 1940s, meaning to wash the dishes.

bubblegum A type of chewing-gum developed in the 1930s, that can be blown into large bubbles.

bubblegum music A simple packaged form of US popular music that appeared in the 1960s and was aimed at teenage and sub-teenage youngsters. It was so-called because its fans were expected to be bubblegum-chewers.

Bubbles Nickname given to the US soprano Beverly Sills (1920–).

bubble umbrella A type of umbrella with a dome shape surrounding the head and shoulders of the user and made of transparent plastic so that the user can see through. The use of such an umbrella by the Queen Mother to enable sightseers a clear view of her face was much applauded by her admirers.

bubs Acronym for bloody ungrateful bastards. A name given by British troops to Falkland Islanders, towards the end of the campaign against the Argentinian invaders (*see* FALKLANDS CONFLICT). Earlier in the campaign the troops called the Islanders **bennies**, an allusion to the simple-minded character of this name in the TV soap *Crossroads*. When admonished for using this uncomplimentary epithet, the British forces obstinately, and not with a great deal of subtlety, referred to them as **stills** (still Bennies). The response of the Islanders was to call their deliverers **whennies**, because so many of them referred to their earlier campaigns in such terms as: "When I was in Belfast . . . ", "When I was in Cyprus . . . ". Tired of this protracted repartee the British finally resorted to *bubs*.

Buchenwald A large Nazi CONCENTRATION CAMP set up in 1934 NW of Weimar. It held about 20,000 prisoners used as labourers in nearby factories. Although there were no gas chambers, many died through malnutrition, disease, and execution. Inmates were also used for medical research into vaccines and viral infections. The infamous sadistic Ilsa Koch, known as the BITCH OF BUCHENWALD, was the wife of the commandant in charge between 1939 and 1945.

Buchmanism *See* OXFORD GROUP.

buck. Buck Rogers A US cartoon hero, who appeared in his first comic strip in 1929. Originally the hero of Phil Nowlan's novel *Armageddon 2419*, he was an air-force officer who wakes up from a long sleep in the 25th century, in which he has numerous SCI-FI adventures. Various film and television versions of the Buck Rogers stories have been made.

buckshee Free, offered without charge. This word entered the language in the 20th century as a late import from the Indian Raj, when it was taken from *bak-sheesh*, meaning a tip or gift of alms (from Persian *bakhshīsh*, from *bakhshīdan*, to give).

The buck stops here A slogan popularized by US President Harry S. Truman, who had it written on a sign on his desk at the White House to remind him that he was ultimately responsible for all decisions; some years later President Jimmy Carter had the motto reinstated for the same purpose. The slogan may have been derived from a similar phrase used by poker players.

bucket. bucket shop A shop that offers discounted airline tickets, etc., often being able to do so by taking out minimal insurance, etc., and thus exposing the customer to some risk. The original 'bucket shops' sold alcoholic drinks in buckets in America and were often also on the fringe of the law. The term is also used of any business, especially a stockbroker whose standing and resources are open to question.

bucket trading An illegal practice on the stock exchange, which involves stockbrokers deliberately failing to obtain the best price possible for their clients. *See also* BUCKET SHOP.

Buckley's hope Australian slang for little or no chance at all, not a hope in hell. Often shortened to **Buckley's**. Buckley, apparently, was an escaped convict who, after 32 years on the run, gave himself up in 1955 to the authorities and then died the following year.

Buckmaster Divorce Act The name given to a British act of parliament, the *Matrimonial Causes Act* (1923). It made adultery sufficient cause for divorce by either party. Up to this time, a woman could not obtain a divorce on the grounds of adultery alone – cruelty or desertion had to be involved. The act is named after the Lord Chancellor of the time, Lord Buckmaster.

buddy US slang for a friend. Of 19th-century origin, it was adopted in the 1980s, in both America and the UK, as a specific term for a volunteer companion of an AIDS victim (*see* TERRENCE HIGGINS TRUST).

Budget leak tribunal An official tribunal that investigated (1936) allegations that details of the budget had been leaked to a private individual who had used the information to make money. The tribunal's report led to the resignation of the then colonial secretary J. H. Thomas.

bug. bugs bunny British underworld rhyming slang for money, common since the 1960s (derived from **Bugs Bunny**, Warner Bros famous wisecracking cartoon character).

bug smasher US airforce slang expression of contempt for a light aircraft, used since the 1950s.

Bulge, Battle of the *See* ARDENNES OFFENSIVE.

bulimia (Gr. *bous*, ox, *limos*, hunger) Compulsive and insatiable overeating. Originally known only as a neurological disorder, this condition, in the form of **bulimia nervosa**, became increasingly recognized during the latter part of the 20th century as a symptom of psychological disturbance, particularly affecting adolescent girls and popularly known as 'bingeing'. It is sometimes seen as a phase of ANOREXIA NERVOSA: the patient undergoes an orgy of overeating followed by drastic purging or self-induced vomiting.

bull. bulldog breed The British, especially with reference to their pugnacity. This phrase comes from Arthur Reece's music-hall song *Sons of the Sea, All British born* which had a tremendous vogue in late Victorian and Edwardian England. It came at the time of naval rivalry with the Kaiser's Germany and inspired the name of **Bulldog Drummond**, hero of the adventure novels of SAPPER.

Bullfrog of the Pontine Marshes A dismissive reference to Benito Mussolini (1883–1945) by Winston Churchill during World War II.

Bull Moose Nickname of US President Theodore Roosevelt (1858–1919).

> I am as strong as a bull moose.
>
> THEODORE ROOSEVELT, during 1900 vice-presidential campaign.

Bullamakanka Australian slang for any remote or backward place (there is no real place of the name).

bullet. bullet train A high-speed train developed in Japan since the 1970s. It proved capable of speeds over 125 mph.

Every bullet has its billet Nothing happens by chance and no act is altogether without effect.

bum. bum bag British slang for a small zipper bag attached to a belt worn around the waist with the bag part resting either at the back or in the front. Originally worn by skiers to hold their keys and money, they became part of street fashion in the late 1980s. They are worn by either sex and are a much safer alternative to a handbag, which can be snatched in the street. The US name is **fanny pack**.

bum's rush US slang to describe the forceable ejection of undesirables (bums), usually from a bar.

bump, bumpty-bump the bump In US Black slang, a phrase used by dancers in a dance involving the bumping of hips.

BUNCH Burroughs, Univac, NCR, Control Data, and Honeywell. After IBM and the Digital Equipment Corporation, this group of companies became the biggest-selling computer manufacturers in the 1980s.

Bundles for Britain An organization founded in America in January 1940, by Mrs. Wales Latham, to send parcels of comforts to Britain during World War II.

Bungalow Bill British slang for a rather unintelligent male, *i.e.* one 'with nothing going on upstairs', or a very sexually active male, *i.e.* 'one with a lot going on downstairs', or both. It was applied in 1987 in the tabloid press to the property developer Bill Wiggins, who was at the time the boyfriend of actress Joan Collins.

bunji-jumping British slang for the controversial practice of jumping from high places (such as bridges) while attached to an elastic line secured to the high place. It became popular in the late 1980s. Bunji is an adaptation of bungy, the playground word for an eraser, a rubber.

Bunny Nickname of the British comedy actor J. Robertson Hare (1891–1979), who became a star of the ALDWYCH FARCES of the 1920s and the 1930s.
bunny girl A somewhat scantily dressed waitress or attendant in certain night clubs and Playboy clubs, equipped with a fluffy tail and a headdress with long ears to suggest a rabbit.
bunnyhug A JAZZ dance that became popular in the early 20th century.

Bunter, Billy A fictional greedy fat public schoolboy (a pupil at Greyfriars School) created by the prolific writer Frank Richards (pen name of Charles Hamilton; 1876–1961) in the boys' comics *Gem* (1907–39) and MAGNET (1908–40). Billy Bunter was always in search of a chum who would advance him a small sum of money with which to buy tuck. The loan was always in anticipation of an expected postal order. A Billy Bunter is an epithet used of any grossly overweight young boy.

buppie A US slang term of the 1980s also heard in the UK for a Black YUPPIE.

Burgess and Maclean Two British foreign-office diplomats, Guy Burgess (1911–63) and Donald Maclean (1913–83), who were Soviet agents in the UK during World War II and the subsequent period of COLD WAR. Both were members of a group of privileged, mainly homosexual, young men recruited at Cambridge University in the 1930s. Burgess was an alcoholic and relatively minor official. Maclean, as a member of MI6 with access to classified information, was a more damaging agent. In 1951, both defected to the Soviet Union, having been warned by another intelligence officer, Harold (known as KIM) Philby (1912–88). Philby defected to the Soviet Union in 1963, when it was discovered that he was the so-called **third man** suspected in the affair. In 1979, the complicity of a **fourth man** in the ring was made public. He was Anthony Blunt (1907–83) – a distinguished art historian and surveyor of the queen's pictures – who had confessed to being an agent in 1964 following Philby's defection in return for a promise of secrecy and non-prosecution. Blunt was the man who arranged Burgess and Maclean's flight to the Soviet Union. Speculation still persists into the identity of a **fifth man** (the Soviet intelligence agencies speak of the *Magnificent Five*). *See also* FIFTH COLUMN.

Burgos government A rebel Spanish government set up in July 1936 by General Franco at Burgos, the former capital of Castile, at the start of the SPANISH CIVIL WAR.

Burma Road This great highway was made in 1937–39 to open up the western interior of China by communication with the sea, and ran from Lashio to Kunming in Yunnan, a distance of 770 miles. It was the chief highway for supplies to China during World War II until the Japanese cut it in 1941. It was recaptured in 1945.

burn The thrust produced by the ignition of a rocket engine.
burn, baby, burn A slogan adopted by militant Blacks after a riot in Los Angeles in 1965, in which 34 people died and a wide area was destroyed by arsonists.
burn rubber To leave somewhere so fast in a car that the tyres scorch on the road.

Burnham scale A scale of salaries and other benefits for school teachers in England and Wales, first instituted in 1924 and named after the former newspaper owner Viscount Burnham (1862–1933), chairman of the committee that originally set it up.

Bürolandschaft (Ger. office landscape) A style of open-plan flexible office design in which people work in areas delineated by small screens or rows of indoor plants, rather than by walls.

Burton. Gone for a Burton Absent, missing or lost (referring to persons or things), dead or presumed dead. Widely used by the services in World War II, it is of uncertain origin but it is sometimes claimed as an RAF coinage derived from the training of radio telegraph operators in Montagu Burton's clothing premises at Blackpool. Those who failed their tests were said to have 'gone for a Burton'; it was subsequently applied to those who were killed. It may also possibly be connected with Burton beer; the implication being that the absent person has gone for a drink. Another interesting suggestion is that when George Cadbury was standing for Birmingham Council in 1878 and supporting the temperance interest his opponent, Dr. Burton, was openly backed by the licensed victuallers. The Birmingham Post (22 July) reported: "During the whole of the polling day men were seen coming from Dr. Burton's committee room, and, parading Steward St with jugs of beer in their hands, on which were painted papers 'Vote for Burton'". This could have given rise to the expression 'he's gone for a Burton' when inquiring of someone's whereabouts.

bus. **busing** or **crossbusing** The practice of transporting Black children from one area to another so that they may attend schools in a predominantly White residential area, in pursuance of a policy of racial integration. The enforcing of such a policy in the southern US states in the 1950s provoked a violent backlash against the Black population.

busman's holiday A holiday spent doing very much the same thing as one does when working – an allusion to a bus driver taking a driving holiday. As the Prince of Wales says in Shakespeare's *Henry IV (part I)*:

> If all the year were playing holidays
> To sport would be as tedious as to work.

Busby's babes Members of the Manchester United football team managed by Sir Matt Busby (1946–69). *See also* MUNICH AIR CRASH.

business. **business as usual** *See* BLITZ.

business cycle *See* TRADE CYCLE.

business park An area, usually on the outskirts of a town, that is designated as a site for light industry etc.

businesspeak Jargon used in business and commerce. The term is one of a number coined with the suffix '-speak' and modelled on *Newspeak* and *Doublespeak* in George Orwell's novel *1984* (1949). There are perhaps two main styles of businesspeak: the 19th-century merchant's style, servile and garrulous, and the late 20th-century city whiz kid's double talk. An example of the former would be couched in terms of 'favouring us with an order from your good selves', while the latter might refer to SHARK REPELLENTS or a DEAD-CAT BOUNCE.

bust (1) An arrest, especially in connection with the possession of illegal drugs. Originally part of US criminal or street jargon in the late 1950s, it was adopted by the HIPPIES of the late 1960s and has since passed into everyday usage. (2) US teenage slang of the late 1980s for a great achievement. It derives from the basketball term for a good shot. (3) A wild party. (4) Australian slang for a robbery. (5) Slang for a break-out from prison. (6) To demote.

Butch Cassidy and the Sundance Kid The nicknames of two US bandits whose exploits have, with the help of John Foreman's excellent film with this title, become folklore. Butch Cassidy's real name was Robert Le Roy Parker (1886–1909) – he was called **Butch** for the very good reason that he was an ex-butcher. The Sundance Kid, real name Harry Longbaugh (1860–1909), established his reputation by robbing a bank in Sundance, Nevada. Most of the events portrayed in the film by Paul Newman as Butch and Robert Redford as the Kid were true, including their deaths in a shoot-out in Bolivia.

Butcher A name often given to unpopular and ruthless leaders. An early contender for the title was the Duke of Cumberland (1721–65), known as the **Bloody Butcher** for his cruel suppression of the Highlanders after the Battle of Culloden in 1746. 20th-century Butchers have included:

Butcher of Baghdad Epithet used for Saddam Hussein, president of Iraq, in the popular press in 1990 after his annexation of Kuwait and the atrocities performed there by his army of occupation. Hussein had previously established himself as a ruthless and aggressive dictator by his treatment of the Iraqi Kurdish minority and his attempted invasion of Iran.

Butcher of Broadway Nickname given to the US drama critic Alexander Woolcott (1887–1943), who was noted for his vitriolic reviews.

Butcher of Lyons The head of the German GESTAPO in Lyons (1942–44), Klaus Barbie (1913–), was notorious for his cruel murder of some 4000 people, including Jews, members of the French underground, and others. He also deported 7000 Jews to death camps. He was finally brought back to Lyons from Bolivia in 1987 and sentenced by a French court to life imprisonment.

Butcher of Tehran An acolyte of the Shah of Iran, General Gholam Ali Oveissi, earned the title by ordering his troops to open fire on the marching supporters of Ayatollah Khomeini in 1963 and again in 1978. He was shot in 1984.

Butler Act An act introduced in 1944 by the then minister of education R. A. Butler (1902–82) to reorganize British education. The act instituted the ELEVEN PLUS examination and divided schools into grammar, secondary modern, and technical schools.

Butlins A chain of holiday camps set up by the businessman Sir William ('Billy') Butlin (1900–80) in 1936. Holiday camps had been started earlier by J. Fletcher Dodd in 1906 at Caister-on-Sea in Norfolk. Butlin's achievement was to give them mass-appeal. His first camp was opened in Skegness in Lincolnshire in 1936; its success led to a chain of camps in which holiday makers lived in chalets but ate in large dining rooms. The first ones had an institutional air, involving communal meals and mass-entertainment organized by **redcoats**. Butlin advertised his camps in 1937 with the slogan, "Holiday with pay! Holiday with play! A week's holiday for a week's wage." Today, Butlins holiday camps are more luxurious and relaxed institutions catering particularly for families with children.

Butskellism The policies of the then chancellor of the exchequer R. A. Butler (1902–82) during the 1950s. The term was coined by the *Economist* to imply that there was little difference between Butler's type of conservatism and the socialism of his predecessor as chancellor, Hugh Gaitskell (1906–63).

butter. **butterfly effect** *See* CHAOS THEORY.
butter mountain *See* CAP.
buttie or **butty** British slang for a sandwich. Originally a Northern English, particularly Liverpudlian, dialect shortening of buttered bread, originating in the late 19th century, its usage became widespread in the 1960s.

buy. **to buy it** To pay with one's life; to die. Possibly of earlier origin, this usage became very common in World War II, especially among pilots in the RAF. "Old Bloggs bought it today" is a euphemism for "Bloggs was killed in combat today". The implication may be that he bought a place in eternity at the cost of his earthly life. This is perhaps connected with the US pilots' ironic euphemism **to buy the farm**, *i.e.* to retire for ever.

buzz (1) A rumour. (2) A moment of pleasure, as achieved by the use of drugs, music, or some other short-lived stimulation.
buzz bomb or **doodlebug** A German flying bomb used against London and SE England between June 1944 and March 1945. It was driven by a form of pulse jet, in which hinged air-intake flaps opened when the pressure of the air resulting from the bomb's passage through the atmosphere exceeded the pressure in the combustion chamber. The bombs were unguided and pointed in the direction of London from their launch site in N France with enough fuel to reach London. When the fuel was exhausted the engine cut out – a frightening sound for London's inhabitants, although it was said that if one heard the engine stop one was safe. They were called by the Germans **V1** weapons (V for *Vergeltungswaffe*, reprisal weapon).
buzz word A word that belongs to the contemporary jargon of a particular field of activity, especially of the business or technical world.

BYOG *See* PBAB.

bypass A main road built round a town or city to enable traffic to pass round the town without causing congestion within it. Bypasses began to be built in the 1930s in the UK as motor cars and road-haulage vehicles increased in number to such an extent that high streets designed for horse traffic in the middle ages became impassable. Many were widened into dual-carriageway roads in the post-war years.
bypass engines Jet engines in which some of the air from the compressor passes around the combustion chambers into the exhaust flow to provide extra thrust.
bypass surgery An operation to bypass a diseased or narrowed blood vessel. It is used very extensively and successfully in *coronary bypass grafts*, in which coronary arteries narrowed by atheroma are bypassed by healthy mammary arteries or saphenous veins from the leg of the patient.
by-pass variegated Name given to certain features of 20th-century architecture by the British cartoonist and writer Osbert Lancaster (1908–86).

byte A data-storage unit in a computer, comprising eight BITS treated as a single entity. It is probably an amalgamation of *bit* and *bite*.

C

C The code name used for the head of MI6. Made famous through the James BOND novels of Ian Fleming, it may have come from the founder of the SIS, Mansfield Cumming. Alternatively, it may stand for 'chief' or 'control'.

Cabbage patch *See* BILLY WILLIAMS'S CABBAGE PATCH.

Cabinet Office The branch of the British civil service responsible for the running of the Cabinet and Cabinet committees. It was started in 1916.

cable television A system using cables to relay television programmes to subscribers' homes. It was first used to improve network services in areas of poor reception. By the 1960s many areas in America had a master 'community antenna', which picked up signals from broadcasting stations and retransmitted them by coaxial cable. Modern systems, which increasingly use FIBRE OPTICS, offer a wide range of programmes, including those originated especially for cable TV or made by community groups; satellite channels can also be distributed through the cable system. In the 1990s, interactive services, such as home-banking, shopping, and accessing of data banks, were developed. Although many British towns and cities are wired for cable television, it is far less popular than in America.

Cad, the A nickname from the newspaper gossip columns for Peter Cadbury (1918–), entrepreneurial businessman and grandson of George Cadbury, the founder of Cadbury Bros., Bournville.

CAD Computer-Aided Design. The use of computers in the design of products, electronic circuits, buildings, etc. The computer can display plans, elevations, or isometric views using programs based on standard design criteria and the input of specific data relating to dimensions, tolerances, factors of safety, etc. These preliminary plans can then be modified by the designer on-screen. In some appropriate cases the CAD output can be used in computer-aided manufacture (**CAM**) of components of the design.

Caddy US slang for a CADILLAC car.

Cadillac A car manufactured by the Cadillac Motor Car Company of Detroit. The first Cadillacs appeared on the streets of America in 1903; the company itself was named after Antoine de la Mothe, sieur de Cadillac, the Frenchman who founded Detroit.

caff British slang for a café, especially a cheap one serving traditional fried food, as in the expression 'greasy caff'. The caff emerged as the meeting-place for young people in the 1950s and the word is still widely used. It is now sometimes pronounced 'cayf' to make the establishment sound more upmarket.

Cagoulard (Fr. hooded man) A member of a secret right-wing terrorist organization in France in the mid to late 1930s. The name derives from *cagoule*, a hooded sleeveless garment, originally a monk's cowl. The name 'cagoule' is now given to a light-weight, usually knee-length, anorak.

Caillaux affair A scandal that rocked French politics in 1914, following the shooting of the editor of *Le Figaro*, Gaston Calmette, by the wife of the French minister of finance, Joseph Caillaux. Calmette had threatened to publish letters between Caillaux and his mistress (whom he subsequently married). Madame Caillaux was acquitted at the ensuing trial, which provoked streetfighting between supporters of the political right, to which Caillaux then belonged, and the left.

Cairo. Cairo Conference A conference held in November 1943 between Churchill, Roosevelt, and the Chinese Nationalist leader Chiang Kai-shek (1887–1975), to establish the war policy of the Allies in the far East.

Cairo Fred A nickname given by the film industry to Omar Sharif (1932–), the

Egyptian film actor who was the leading star and male pin-up of the Egyptian cinema before becoming internationally famous in such major films as *Lawrence of Arabia* (1962) and *Doctor Zhivago* (1966). He was actually born in Alexandria rather than Cairo.

cakehole British vulgar slang for mouth, widely used in the 1950s and 1960s in the expression 'shut your cakehole' meaning shut up. It is still sometimes heard in the school playground.

calabash. goodnight Mrs Calabash – wherever you are A catchphrase used by the US comedian Jimmy ('Schnozzle') Durante (1893–1980) to end his radio and TV programmes in the 1940s and 1950s. 'Calabash' refers to 'empty head', from the hollow calabash gourd. It is thought that 'Mrs Calabash' was Durante's pet name for his first wife, who had died in 1943.

Calder Hall The world's first nuclear power station to feed appreciable quantities of electricity into a national grid. It was situated at Windscale (now SELLAFIELD) and was opened in 1956. It was fuelled by uranium slugs in aluminium cans in a graphite moderator. The coolant was carbon dioxide. The Calder Hall reactor combined power generation with plutonium production. It was the precursor of a programme of advanced gas-cooled reactors (AGRs) developed in Britain.

California. California, here I come Originally a reference to achieving success in the film business, it was the title of a song made popular by Al Jolson in the 1921 musical *Bombo*. It has since been said, on both sides of the Atlantic, by someone who believes he is on his way to success.

Californiate To spoil the landscape by unplanned building, industrialization, etc. The term was used in America in the 1970s and refers to the uncontrolled development of southern California. Sometimes **Californicate** is used (*California + fornication*).

call. call-and-recall A system in which those who require regular medical checkups, often for specific identified conditions, receive computer-generated reminders of the date of their next consultations. The system is particularly applicable to diagnostic tests used in preventive medicine. Call-and-recall frequently refers to smear tests for cervical cancer but also has relevance to other tests, such as mammography or blood-pressure tests, in which early detection can prevent death or serious illness.

call-back The recalling of a product in America by its manufacturer because of faults discovered after the product has been sold. The situation occurs most commonly with cars, when potentially dangerous defects can show up after a new model has been running on the road. Products may either be returned to the dealer for repairs to be carried out or may be withdrawn from sale altogether. In the UK, the term *recall* is more usual.

call bird A cheap article used in a shop to attract buyers in, in the hope that they will be tempted to make more expensive purchases.

call boy A male prostitute. The male equivalent of the CALL GIRL. *See also* RENT BOY.

call girl A female prostitute, usually an elegant and sophisticated one, who makes her assignations on the telephone. Originally, before telephones, the call girl worked from a call house, which was a low-class brothel.

call-in (US) *See* PHONE-IN.

calling all cars *See* APB.

call money (1) Money repayable on demand. Money invested with a bank may be placed on the money market, either for a fixed term or to be repaid when called for. (2) Money paid for a **call option** on a stock exchange or a commodity exchange, *i.e.* the cost of purchasing an option to buy certain shares or goods by a fixed date. A **put option** gives the buyer of the option the right to sell the shares or goods by a fixed date.

call off all bets Literally, to cancel all wagers in certain circumstances. A bookmaker, for example, might call off all bets if he suspected that some race or contest had been rigged. By extension, the phrase has been used to mean 'repudiating a complicated or disadvantageous agreement or problem'. In particular, in US Black slang of the 1940s, it meant 'to die' – perhaps the most effective way of calling off one's bets.

don't call us, we'll call you A phrase that is said to be used by theatre directors to say goodbye to unsuccessful applicants at auditions. The implication is that the auditionee need not bother to telephone to enquire about the result and that no call will be made. The phrase, which dates from the 1960s, is now used more widely, often in a jocular way, to get rid of someone offering to sell something or provide a service. It is often shorted to **don't call us**.

callanetics A system of exercises developed in the 1970s by the US writer on fitness Callan Pinckney. It aims to improve fitness and general muscle tone without the development of unsightly muscles. Callanetics came into public prominence in 1989 when the Duchess of York used the method to improve her figure after the birth of her first child, Beatrice. The name comes from 'Callan' plus '-etics', by analogy with 'athletics', and is possibly reminiscent of 'callisthenics'.

caló A form of Mexican Spanish using many slang terms and incorporating English words. Originally an argot used in the Mexican underworld, it is now in use by youths in SW America.

CAM Computer-Aided Manufacture. *See* CAD.

Cambridge Complex A group of research organizations associated with Harvard University, Cambridge, Massachusetts, and with the Massachusetts Institute of Technology.

Camden Town Group A school of post-impressionist painters founded in 1911 by the British artist Walter Sickert (1860–1905). It specialized in contemporary London scenes. In 1913, it amalgamated with other societies to form the LONDON GROUP.

Camelot The site of the mythical court of King Arthur and his knights of the Round Table. The name, with its romantic associations of chivalry and heroism, was applied to the administration (1961–63) of US President John F. Kennedy, whose glamorous image and youthful vigour inspired hopes of a golden age in America's history. At the time of Kennedy's inauguration, the Lerner–Loewe musical *Camelot*, loosely based on the Arthurian legend, had recently opened on Broadway.

camel walk A dance originating in the US Black community in the 1900s. It involved moving the back and shoulders in imitation of a camel.

camera-ready copy (CRC) The text of a page of a book, magazine, paper, etc., that has been set in type by a phototypesetter and has had any illustration material pasted on to it. The CRC is ready for photographing to obtain the film required to make the printing plates.

camouflage The various techniques used to conceal soldiers and military equipment and installations from the enemy. Until modern times the more conspicuous and dazzling a general could make his army, the more likely it was thought that his enemy would be cowed into submission before battle was joined. Thus, soldiers were often equipped with bright uniforms and tall hats; their presence was further advertised by the blaring of bugles, the rattling of drums, and the flying of colours. However, changes in battle strategy necessitated by advances in weaponry in the 19th century meant that there were advantages to be gained in a fighting unit being inconspicuous to his foe: with an accurate rifle a conspicuous soldier is easily shot. Early experiments with subdued colours for uniforms (such as the green jacket of the British Rifle Brigade in the Napoleonic Wars) had met with ridicule; however, by the end of the Victorian era, khaki had been adopted for most units of the British colonial forces. World War I hastened the development of camouflage techniques with the British, German, and US armies all adopting drab brown, green, or grey outfits; the light blue colour of French uniforms was blamed for increased casualties during the war. Similar thinking has since been applied to tanks, gun emplacements, aircraft, and ships (*see* DAZZLE SHIPS). Now every modern army has its specialists in the application of camouflage, which can be adapted according to the terrain in which it will be employed. The word camouflage itself was coined early in the century, from the French *camoufler* (to disguise).

camp Homosexual, displaying effeminate mannerisms of speech or gesture, acting in a self-consciously theatrical way. The term emerged from theatrical slang, meaning effeminate, after World War II. Although originally used to describe only male homosexuals, it can now be applied to either sex and has to some extent lost its sexual overtones. Its derivation is obscure; the two most likely sources are: from the French *camper*, to pose; or the 19th-century dialect word *kemp*, meaning uncouth.

camp about To joke around. A usage with no sexual overtones.

camp as a row of little pink tents Blatantly homosexual. A pun on the double meaning of *camp*; as a noun it refers to a site occupied by tents, as an adjective it is used to describe a man whose affected dress, mannerisms, and way of speaking are intended to convey that he is homosexual. A variant is 'bent as a lighthouse staircase'.

Camp David An official country retreat for US presidents in the Appalachian Mountains, Maryland. Originally named 'Shangri-La' by President F. D. Roosevelt, who established it in 1942, it was renamed by President Eisenhower, in 1953, after his grandson. It has been the site of a number of significant international meetings. The **Camp David agreement** of 1978 was arranged by President Carter, between the Israeli prime minister, Menachem Begin (1913–), and the Egyptian president, Anwar Sadat (1918–81). It led to a peace treaty between Israel and Egypt (1979).

camp it up To be theatrical and effeminate in an exaggerated way, as a male homosexual might act.

Campaign for Nuclear Disarmament *See* CND.

Campion, Albert A fictional detective created by the British writer Margery Allingham (1905–66). Campion first appeared in *The Crime at Black Dudley* (US title, *The Black Dudley Murder*; 1929), and continued his career through a further 21 novels. It is said that he was modelled on the author's husband, Philip Carter, who wrote two further novels featuring Campion after her death.

Campion is an archetypal upper-class 'silly ass' who gives a deceptive impression of vacuous inefficiency (similar to Bertie WOOSTER) and then surprises people with his insight and razor-sharp brain. He is similar to other 'gentleman amateurs', such as Lord Peter WIMSEY.

can. **can-do** A colloquial and voguish adjective, popular from the late 1980s, meaning willing and able to face situations, however challenging and arduous (*e.g.* a can-do entrepreneur). The expression reflects the Thatcherite ideal of free enterprise, which inspired the rise of small privately owned businesses. It is derived from an older expression **can do**, which was an affirmative reply to a request or command to do something, **no can do** being the facetious negative alternative.

canned laughter The recorded laughter superimposed on the soundtrack of a TV or radio programme, which has not been recorded in front of a live audience. Because the canned laughter is not always a response to something obviously funny, the term is frequently used derogatively.

canned music Music recorded and reproduced, as opposed to 'live music', *i.e.* played by musicians present in person. Canned music, like canned foods, can be stored and used when required. *See* DISC JOCKEY.

can of worms An unpleasant, difficult, or uncontrollable situation that is better left alone. Phrases such as 'don't open that can of worms' were first used in America in the 1950s; the phrase became popular in the UK in the 1970s.

Canal Zone or **Panama Canal Zone** The strip of land extending 8 km (5 miles) on either side of the PANAMA CANAL. In 1903 the USA acquired construction rights for the canal from the newly independent Panama, retaining sovereignty over the Canal Zone. The canal itself opened for shipping in 1914. In the 1960s anti-US riots led to a treaty negotiated by President Carter in 1978 in which jurisdiction over the Canal Zone passed to Panama in 1979, with sovereignty reverting to Panama in 2000.

canary (1) A female JAZZ singer accompanied by a jazz band (from the singing cage bird). (2) A person who gives information to the police about criminal activities. The term is usually used to describe criminals who, faced with prosecution, GRASS on their accomplices; *i.e.* they 'sing' to the police.

Canberra The UK's first twin-jet bomber. It was designed in the early 1950s by W. E. W. Petter as a replacement for the MOSQUITO. America later built it under licence as the Martin B57. The Canberra had a fairly low profile until the KOREAN WAR, after which it was used extensively in the NATO and CENTO theatres.

cancer stick British slang for a cigarette. It has been common since the 1960s, when the link between cancer and cigarette smoking was established.

candid camera An unseen camera used to photograph an unsuspecting subject. Candid-camera shots, which are often ridiculous, are much used in pictorial journalism.

candy US slang for illegal drugs. Originally used of cocaine and heroin, it then referred to marijuana or LSD on a sugar cube. It is now a general term for any illegal drug. **Nose-candy** is sniffed or snorted.

candyman US slang for a dealer in illegal drugs, especially heroin and cocaine. Originally part of Black street jargon, in which it could also have sexual connotations, the word became part of the addict's vocabulary and features in many blues songs.

Cannes Film Festival Founded in 1947 as a small film festival, this annual event, held in May, has become the most important of the international film festivals. Its various awards (including the PALME D'OR) cover both the official film programme and the fringe programme.

cannon fodder Originally young soldiers with little training, who were regarded as expendable in times of war. In the late 20th century the expression was also applied figuratively to young marketing managers, insurance salespersons, and anyone who could easily be replaced by their employers if they were unsuccessful in their appointed posts.

Canutism General resistance to inevitable change. The term comes from King Canute (or Cnut; *c.* 994–1035), who, according to legend, demonstrated the limit of his powers to his flattering courtiers by sitting on the sea shore and ordering the waves to recede.

CAP Common Agricultural Policy. A policy for food production first implemented by the EC in 1962 in order to support farmers and ensure a regular supply of reasonably priced foodstuffs. Part of the policy involves subsidies to farmers for modernization. More contentious is the use of a 'threshold price', below which certain foodstuffs (cereals, meat, eggs, fruit, etc.) cannot be imported into the EC. Moreover, there is a 'target price' for specified foodstuffs, which is considered to be a reasonable price for the producer. If the market price falls below this, the EC buys up surplus foodstuffs at an 'intervention price'. The system has been criticized because it is a way of paying farmers to produce food that nobody wants to buy, and has led to huge surplus stocks – the **butter mountain**, the **beef mountain**, and the **wine lake**. Some attempts have been made to impose production quotas on some foodstuffs. The CAP uses so-called **green money** (or **green currency**), which is the currencies of the EC member countries set at artificial exchange rates (based on the ECU), to protect farm prices from normal exchange-rate fluctuations. The **green pound** is the value of the pound sterling in green money.

Capcom or **CapCom** An acronym for *Capsule Communicator*, the person at a space centre on Earth, who maintains radio communication with the astronauts of a manned space flight. The capsule is the detachable pressurized compartment of a space vehicle in which the astronauts and instruments are housed. The term was coined *c.* 1970 during the US Apollo space programme (1961–72).

Cape. Cape Canaveral *See* CAPE KENNEDY.

Cape coloureds The population of mixed European, Hottentot, and Indian descent of Cape Province, South Africa. There are approximately 2,500,000 of which the majority are Christian; some 60,000 are Muslims (Cape Malays). Under the APARTHEID system of South Africa they are more highly regarded and awarded more privileges than the Bantu.

Caped Crusader *See* BATMAN.

Cape Kennedy After the assassination of US President Kennedy in 1963 Cape Canaveral in Florida was renamed Cape Kennedy. It reverted to its original name in 1973 in response to pressure from the local community. It is the site of operations for the US space programme under NASA.

capeesh US slang expression meaning 'do you understand?', from an anglicization of the Italian *capisci*.

capital. capitalist roader A person in China in the 1960s, accused of wanting to take the 'capitalist road' to a market economy, incentives, etc. *See* CULTURAL REVOLUTION.

capital levy A state tax on capital rather than income; it was first proposed in the British House of Commons in 1914. Capital levies are regarded by capitalists as a form of robbery and by socialists as a fair means of redistributimg wealth. A surtax surcharge imposed by the Labour government in 1968, which taxed the highest rate of income at over 100%, was the nearest the UK has come to a capital levy in the 20th century.

A **capital-gains tax** was imposed in the UK in 1965. This imposes a tax on any increase in capital or capital assets, with certain exceptions, such as the house one lives in. A similar tax is used in America and several other countries.

capital transfer tax *See* INHERITANCE TAX.

Capone, Al Alphonse Capone (1899–1947), notorious Chicago gangster and racketeer of Sicilian origin, nicknamed Scarface after a scar on his left cheek caused by a razor slash in a gang fight in his youth. He rose to power in the heyday of bootlegging in the 1920s and made himself master of the rackets in the city by organizing the killing of most of the rival gunmen. After the ST VALENTINE'S DAY MASSACRE of 1929, when seven rival gangster leaders were machine-gunned, he was left in supreme control of the protection racket, speakeasies, brothels, etc. The suburb of Cicero was completely dominated by him. He was imprisoned from 1931 to 1939 for tax evasion, the only charge that the police could sustain against him. He was released suffering from general paralysis resulting from advanced syphilis and died at the age of 48, a legendary symbol of evil. *See also* BOOTLEGGER; MAFIA.

Caporetto Yugoslavian name: Kobarid. A village now in NW Yugoslavia but part of Italy until 1947. It was the scene of an Italian military disaster in October 1917 during World War I, in which Italian troops were forced to retreat before an Austro-German offensive. The defeat prompted Italy's allies, France and Great Britain, to send support and finally to establish the Supreme War Council to unify the Allied war effort. *See also* ISONZO.

captive audience An audience that cannot easily escape some message being addressed to it. For example, advertisers are justified in assuming that a cinema audience is a captive audience, just as a preacher in a place of worship has a more-or-less captive audience in his congregation.

car The 20th century has often been called the age of the car, although the car was actually invented in the 19th century. However, Daimler's motorized dog cart bore about as much relation to the modern car as the WRIGHT BROTHERS' *Flyer* bears to CONCORDE. During the first decade of the century the spluttering horseless carriage came of age (*see* GREAT CAR RACE). By the start of World War I (often called the last of the horse wars) there were some 130,000 cars registered in the UK. But it was during the inter-war years that the car established itself as a reliable and comfortable way of moving from one place to another for anyone who did not wish to use public transport. Since the start of World War II, cars have not changed greatly; they are now slightly faster, slightly more economical in fuel, and slightly more reliable. Very roughly, a new car has always cost its owner about half his or her annual income; however, some two-thirds of new cars are now company cars, *i.e.* cars bought by companies for the use of employees in addition to their salaries. At the end of the 1980s 66% of UK homes owned one car, while over 20% had more than one car. The number of road vehicles registered in the UK in 1984 exceeded 24 million.

As mass-producers of carbon dioxide (*see* GREENHOUSE EFFECT) and lead (*see* LEAD-FREE) cars are the enemy of environmentalists, while as creators of urban congestion they have so far defeated the town planners. Yet for the man, and to a rather less extent, the woman in the street they mean much more than simply a means of transport. At once the car is a womb within which to seal oneself off from the outside world, a phallus with which to thrust oneself aggressively through it, and a symbol of the status, temperament, and aspirations of its owner.

> The car has become the carapace, the protective and aggressive shell, of urban and suburban man.
> MARSHALL MCLUHAN: *Understanding Media*.

carbecue A machine for demolishing old or wrecked cars. A US invention, the carbecue both crushes the vehicle and rotates it over a fire, the pressure and heat combined turning the vehicle into a solid mass of metal. The word, a blend of *car* and *barbecue*, was coined in the 1960s.

car bomb A car packed with explosives with a pretimed or remote-control detonator, left by terrorists close to a suitable target. Car bombs have been used extensively by the IRA since 1969.

car-boot sale A small local sale of second-hand goods held in a hired car park in which the goods are sold by individuals from the boots of their cars. It has tended to increase in scale and now often includes market traders, who set up stalls beside their cars.

car surfing Slang for riding on the roof of a moving car. An extremely dangerous craze among teenagers in the late 1980s, inspired by the US film *Teenwolf* (1985).

Great Car Race An epic round-the-world car race that captured worldwide attention in 1908. It required competitors to traverse North America, cross the ice of the Bering Straits, travel through Siberia and E Europe, and complete the course in Paris. Six massive cars, three French, one German, one Italian, and one from America, set off from Times Square, cheered on their way by a crowd of 200,000, on 12 February 1908. Over the next 11 days the cars fought a desperate battle with the elements, with unmade roads, and with mechanical breakdown. Crews had to repair bridges, pull cars out of swamps, brave blizzards and snowdrifts, and fill ditches before they could proceed; when the Bering Straits proved to be unfrozen they were forced to resort to travelling by ship. France's *Moto-Bloc* was defeated by mud in Iowa; a second French car, *De Dion*, was too battered to go further than Vladivostock, while the third French car *Sizaire-Naudin* withdrew after losing its differential gear on a rock. The three remaining cars, the German *Protos*, the Italian *Zust*, and the US *Thomas Flyer*, all finished. *Protos* arrived first but the honours went to the *Thomas Flyer* after taking into account time penalties: it had covered a total distance of 12,116 miles at a rate of 108 miles a day. Perhaps the most significant achievement of the race, however, was that it proved the potential of the motor vehicle as the transport of the future.

Caravelle A medium-range French jet airliner introduced in 1959. It was the first jet airliner in which the engines were mounted on the rear of the fuselage rather than on the wings.

carbon. carbon dating A technique for finding the date of specimens by measuring the amount of the radioactive isotope carbon-14 present. It can be used for items made from substances of organic origin (*e.g.* wood, cloth, etc.). There is a natural abundance of carbon-14 in the atmosphere, which is incorporated into living organisms by photosynthesis. On the death of the organism, this assimilation stops and the proportion of carbon-14 slowly falls at a known rate as a result of radioactive decay. This decay enables an estimate to be made of the age of the specimen. Carbon dating is extensively used for archaeological specimens and has been applied to such controversial articles as the TURIN SHROUD. It is also called **radiocarbon dating**.

carbon fibres Fine silky threads of pure carbon made by heating stretched threads of textile fibres. The crystal structure gives them immense strength enabling them to be used to produce composite materials with synthetic resins or other substances. They are found in aircraft, rockets, etc., and in such sporting equipment as tennis rackets and fishing rods.

carbuncular Describing buildings, architecture, etc., that are considered ugly or offensive. The term comes from a speech by the Prince of Wales in 1984 in which he described the proposed modern extension to the National Gallery in London as being "... like a monstrous carbuncle on the face of a much loved and elegant friend".

carcass trade Trade in reconstructing old dilapidated pieces of furniture by adding new veneer or new parts in order to pass them off as genuine antiques. The second part of the 20th century saw a rise in the demand for antiques as an investment and the carcass trade dishonestly capitalizes on this demand and the lack of knowledge of potential buyers.

card Slang for an eccentric fellow, a 'character'. Such a person is the hero of Arnold Bennett's novel *The Card* (1911).

CARD Campaign Against Racial Discrimination. An organization founded in London in 1964.

cardboard city An area in an inner city in which homeless people sleep rough, often using cardboard boxes as temporary shelters. In particular, it is an area around Waterloo station in London where such people spend the night.

card-carrying Denoting a person who is totally committed to a specified cause. It was originally used in the 1930s and 1940s to describe a member of the Communist Party, as opposed to someone who simply paid lip-service to its ideals and philosophy. An active supporter of the party would become a member, *i.e.* have a membership card, and could thus be described as card-carrying. In more recent times the expression has become more figurative; for example a card-carrying anti-vivisectionist would be a person deeply committed to the campaign against the use of animals in scientific and other research.

get one's cards To be dismissed from a job. The phrase dates from the 1940s and alludes to the National Insurance card and other documents that were held by the employer but owned by the employee.

When a person left a job the cards were returned. Thus, 'to give someone his cards' means to sack him. Alternatively, 'to be asked for one's cards' means to resign.

Cardin The name in *haute couture* that enlivened the years following World War II, when Europe was struggling to throw off the effects of austerity. Pierre Cardin (1922–) opened his fashion house in Paris in 1949, establishing a reputation in the 1950s for his long slim coats with large collars and his use of oriental styles. In the 1960s he entered the ready-to-wear market for women and produced a stylish range of clothes for men.

CARE Cooperative for American Relief Everywhere Inc. A relief organization that coordinates the sending of parcels of food and clothes to areas of need. It was founded in 1945 as the Cooperative for American Remittances to Europe; in 1952 its directors decided to broaden its scope beyond Europe and its name was changed accordingly.

carelessness kills *See* KEEP DEATH OFF THE ROAD *under* ROAD.

careless talk costs lives *See* BE LIKE DAD, KEEP MUM *under* DAD.

Carey Street A British colloquial term meaning bankruptcy. Carey Street is the London street in which the Bankruptcy Department of the Supreme Court was formerly situated.

Carlists Supporters of Don Carlos (1788–1855), second son of Charles IV of Spain, or his descendents as rightful kings of Spain. Carlist intrigues continued until the death of Don Carlos II in 1909 and in 1937 the Carlists supported General Franco's FALANGE, maintaining the present Carlist pretender, Carlos Hugo de Bourbón-Parma (1930–), as claimant to the throne.

Carlton Club meeting *See* CHANAK CRISIS.

Carnaby Street In the 1960s the much publicized clothing centre for fashion-conscious young men, situated east of Regent Street. It became associated with trendy unisex costumes and was somewhat showily refurbished by Westminster City Council in 1973, but its popularity had declined by 1975 when boutiques in King's Road, Chelsea, began to attract this type of trade.

carpet bombing Delivery by the postman of unsolicited (and mainly unwanted) advertising matter (*see* JUNK MAIL). It became increasingly prevalent from the 1970s.

carrots The myth that eating carrots enabled RAF pilots to spot enemy aircraft at night better than German pilots was put out deliberately at the beginning of World War II by the Ministry of Information. It is true that carrots do contain β-carotene, which forms vitamin A (retinol) in the human gut; moreover this substance is required for good night vision. However, the real reason for British pilots' superior ability to 'see' enemy aircraft was the well-developed British radar system. Work on this system started in 1935 and thanks largely to the work of Robert Watson-Watt (1892–1973) was functioning by the start of the war. The Germans had no comparable system until later in the conflict and the British wished to minimize its value.

carry. carry a torch To be in love with someone, the implication being that the emotion is long-standing and that it is either unrequited or undeclared. The torch may represent the flame of love. It is thought that the phrase **torch song**, signifying a love song, may have been coined by the US nightclub singer Tommy Lyman in the 1930s. The film *Torch Singer* (1933) was about an unmarried mother who sings in a nightclub, while *Torch Song* (1953) concerned a musical comedy star's love for a blind pianist; the play *Torch Song Trilogy* (1982) by Harvey Fierstein tackled homosexual love.

Carry on, London A catchphrase from the pre-war (1933) radio programme *In Town Tonight*. It was introduced by Eric Coates's 'Knightsbridge March' and an excerpt of the sound of London's traffic (always the same sound) being brought to a halt by a voice shouting 'Stop'. Interesting people who were visiting the capital were then introduced and interviewed. At the end of the programme the voice restored the traffic with the phrase 'Carry on, London', which in the BLITZ and later V2 and V1 attacks became a slogan expressing London-Can-Take-It Cockney defiance.

Carry On films A popular series of bawdy low-budget British farces, which began in 1958 with *Carry on Sergeant* produced by Peter Rogers and directed by Gerald Thomas. This team produced some two films every year (until 1974) using such comedians as Sid James, Kenneth Williams, Charles Hawtrey, Kenneth Connor, Hattie Jacques, Barbara Windsor, and Joan Sims. Never aspiring to be more than commercially successful, which they were, they became a British institution acquiring something of a cult status.

> Infamy! Infamy! They've all got it infamy!
> KENNETH WILLIAMS, as Julius Caesar in *Carry on Cleo*.

Carter, Nick A fictional US detective originally created in 1886 by publisher Ormond G. Smith and writer John Russell Coryell as a US counterpart to Sexton Blake. He first appeared in the novel *The Old Detective's Pupil* in which he was portrayed as a boyish clean-living all-American hero. Over 500 Nick Carter books were published, written by a stable of authors including William Wallace Cook and Johnston McCulley. He became so popular that a weekly magazine, *Nick Carter Detective Library*, was created; with films and radio plays his popularity survived two world wars. However, by the 1960s his popularity had begun to wane so the authors decided to change his persona. Nick Carter became a 'tough guy'. A television film featuring Nick Carter was produced in 1984.

cartoon Originally a preparatory sketch for a painting, fresco, tapestry, or other work of art. In the 19th century a cartoon became a humorous drawing in a newspaper or magazine, as pioneered by the satirical magazine *Punch*. Since the 20th century animated films have been known as cartoons. Mutt and Jeff were the earliest cartoon characters but Walt Disney (1901–66) with his MICKEY MOUSE (which began in the 1920s) established the genre.

carve. carve up (1) British slang meaning to spoil someone's chances, to have one's chances ruined, usually used in the passive form: 'he got carved up'. (2) To cut in front of another driver.

carving contest *See* CUTTING CONTEST.

Casablanca Conference A summit meeting held in Casablanca, Morocco, between Winston Churchill and Franklin D. Roosevelt during World War II. It decided on the invasion of Sicily, and unconditional AXIS surrender was first mentioned at this conference.

Casement diaries The diaries reputedly written by Sir Roger Casement (1864–1916), a British consular official in Africa and an Irish nationalist. In 1912 he retired to Ireland and during World War I attempted to obtain German support for Irish nationalism. He was arrested returning to Ireland in a German submarine and subsequently tried by the British for treason, found guilty, and hanged. The diaries, which contained detailed descriptions of homosexual practices, were not released until 1959, when their authenticity became a controversial issue.

cash. cash-and-carry A wholesale supplier who sells goods, usually groceries, etc., in fairly large-size packs to retail tradespeople and others engaged in small business enterprises rather than to members of the general public.

Cash and Carry Act A US act passed in November 1939, concerning the sale of arms to participants in World War II. The sale was permitted provided that the purchaser paid immediately and transported the arms himself.

cash cow A colloquial business name for a reliable and regular source of income, which requires very little effort or investment. It is usually a product with a brand name, well known in old-established markets.

cash in one's chips or **checks** Literally, to stop gambling and exchange one's chips for money. The phrase is used figuratively in two ways. First, it means to take what one has and stop; *i.e.* to 'cut and run'. More drastically, it means to die. To **throw in one's chips** implies that one has stopped playing for ever.

Cassandra Pseudonym under which Sir William Connor wrote a column for the *Daily Mirror* over many years. One of the most popular of such columnists, 'Cassandra' was one of the severest critics of P. G. Wodehouse's conciliatory stand towards Germany during World War II. The original Cassandra was a legendary prophet of woe, daughter of King Priam of Troy, who foretold the deaths of both her father and Agamemnon, her captor.

Cassino *See* ANZIO.

cast. a cast of thousands A jocular term implying that many people have been involved, as in 'this dictionary has been written by a cast of thousands'. It comes from the film industry, probably from the publicity for the first version of *Ben Hur* (1927), which boasted "a cast of 125,000". One of many apocryphal stories about the US film producer Samuel Goldwyn (1882–1974) is that he was filming *The Last Supper* and said, "only twelve disciples! . . . go out and get thousands!"

Castroism The form of communism developed in Cuba by the country's president Fidel Castro (1926–). It has also been called **Fidelism** and (the Spanish version) **Fidelismo**.

casual British slang of the 1980s for a member of a working-class subgroup of young people who wore expensive designer casual clothes in the US or Italian style and listened to lightweight disco and soul music. They were the late-1980s version of the earlier mods (*see* MODS AND ROCKERS) and exhibited the right-wing, materialistic, and self-absorbed attitudes so prevalent in that era. They were epitomized by the comic persona LOADSAMONEY, created by the comedian Harry Enfield.

cat (1) Originally, in the 1920s, Black musicians' jargon for a fellow musician, usually a man. The term implies approval, being used in such phrases as 'cool cat'. In the 1950s it became part of BEAT vocabulary. The phrase **hep-cat** (*see* HEP) was also used, and in the 1960s the word spread to the HIPPIE community. It is still a normal part of Black US speech, but can sound rather self-conscious when used by the British. (2) In America, the female genitals. *See* PUSSY. (3) In Australia, the passive partner in a male homosexual relationship. Possibly, it is a shortening of 'catamite'.

CAT (1) College of Advanced Technology. An educational establishment offering advanced courses in science and technology. In the 1960s, most were granted university status, with the right to confer degrees. (2) Computerized axial tomography or computer-assisted tomography. The abbreviation is used particularly in **CAT scanner**. *See* CT SCANNER.

Cat and Mouse Act Popular name for the Prisoners (Temporary Discharge for Ill-Health) Act of 1913, passed during the SUFFRAGETTES disturbances to avoid the imprisoned law-breakers from achieving martyrdom through hunger strikes. They were released on licence when necessary, subject to re-arrest if need arose. To **play cat and mouse** is to do what one likes with someone in one's power.

cat-o'-nine-tails A whip with nine lashes used for punishing offenders, briefly known as the 'cat'. Formerly used for flogging in the Army and Navy, it was not formally abolished as a civil punishment for crimes of violence until 1948.

cat's eye A reflector embedded in the road as a guide for motorists after lighting-up time or in fog.

Cat's Eyes A name applied to the World War II RAF fighter pilot Group Captain John Cunningham (1917–), noted for his successful night-time exploits.

cat's whisker In the original crystal wireless sets, the very fine wire that made contact with the crystal. *See also* THE CAT'S PYJAMAS.

the cat's pyjamas Something superlatively good; first rate; attractive. A US colloquialism in use by 1900 and current in the UK in the 1920s and 1930s. **The cat's whiskers** is used in the same way and with the same meaning.

catalytic converter A device fitted to the exhaust system of a car to convert the pollutant gases in the exhaust fumes into less harmful products. Used with unleaded petrol, metal catalysts, such as platinum and palladium, can eliminate 90 per cent of the carbon monoxide and unburnt hydrocarbons, which would otherwise be expelled into the atmosphere; they also reduce the levels of nitrogen oxides. Catalytic converters were introduced in America in the 1960s as a measure to combat air pollution and smog in cities; since 1975 all new cars sold in America have converters fitted (a requirement in the UK for new cars from 1992).

catastrophe theory A general theory of change based on mathematical theories of topology (the analysis of general geometrical form as opposed to particular shapes). If a system depends, for example, on four factors, then any state of the system can be represented by a point in four-dimensional space. The possible states of the system can be represented by a region in this space. Catastrophe theory deals with the classification of the forms of such regions, and the way in which one can turn into another. It correlates these with sudden discontinuous changes – 'catastrophes' – in the system. Originally, it was introduced in 1972 by the French mathematician René Thom (1923–) to explain biological differentiation (for example, how growing animal cells can suddenly start to develop into different organs). It has subsequently been applied to many other fields, including the stability of engineering structures on the one hand and the stability of international or personal relationships on the other.

Catch-22 Whichever alternative you choose you can't win – you lose either way. It is the title of Joseph Heller's book published in 1955. The story centres around Captain Yossarian of the 256th United States (Army) bombing squadron in World War II, whose main aim is to avoid being killed. The best way for a pilot to achieve this was to be grounded because of insanity. "There was only one catch and that was Catch-22 which specified that concern for one's own safety in the face of dangers that were real and immediate was the process of a rational mind. Orr was crazy and could be grounded. All he had to do was to ask and as soon as he did he would no longer be crazy and would have to fly more missions".

> How immediate is the response to a 999 call? The Catch-22 of the situation – as Chief Superintendent Eddie Gleeson of New Scotland Yard pointed out – is that the more violent and urgent the emergency, the less coherent the caller.
>
> *Sunday Telegraph*, 24 July, 1988

catenaccio A defensive formation used by soccer teams, consisting of four defenders, three mid-field players, and three forwards. The term is mainly used in Italy and means 'door bolt'; the more prosaic British equivalent is 'four-three-three'.

Caterpillar A type of tracked vehicle, such as a tractor, bulldozer, or tank. It was originally a tradename for such vehicles made by the *Caterpillar Tractor Company* of California, set up by the US industrialist Benjamin Holt in 1928.

Caterpillar Club An unofficial club started by the Irvin Parachute Company during World War II and still in existence; the caterpillar is the silkworm that supplied the material from which parachutes were formerly made. The company presented a small gold caterpillar pin to any RAF airman who had baled out in action and could supply the number of the parachute that had saved his life. Similarly the **Goldfish Club** existed for those who had been forced to use their rubber dinghies. Since then, similar clubs have been formed to encourage the wearing of protective clothing by industrial workers.

cathiodermie A deep-cleansing facial cosmetic treatment in which an electric current is passed through a specially prepared gel spread on the skin. The treatment was invented by René Guinot, the French cosmetologist.

cattle-trucked Rhyming slang for fucked, exhausted. *See also* CREAM-CRACKERED.

Caudillo (Span. leader) The title adopted by General Franco, head of the Falangist government in Spain, in imitation of Mussolini's DUCE and Hitler's FÜHRER. *See* FALANGE.

Cauldron, Battle of the A tank battle south of Tobruk during World War II (May, 1942). *See* ALAMEIN.

Cavell Memorial The statue of nurse Edith Cavell (1865–1915) near Trafalgar Square in London. She was executed by the Germans for helping Allied soldiers to escape from Belgium. The memorial is inscribed with her last words before the firing squad: "I realize that patriotism is not enough. I must have no hatred or bitterness towards anyone".

Cavendish Laboratory The physics laboratory at Cambridge University, founded in 1874 and named after the British scientist Henry Cavendish (1731–1810). In the 20th century, its director from 1919 until 1937 was the New Zealand physicist Ernest Rutherford (1871–1937). Here, in 1919, he first demonstrated the artificial disintegration of atomic nuclei (popularly known as 'splitting the atom'). Many other important discoveries have been made here.

Cavern Club *See* BEATLES.

CB Citizens' band radio. A short-wave short-distance two-way radio system available for use by the general public. CB radios are particularly used by motorists and truck drivers; in the early days, they were used to warn fellow drivers of traffic jams, radar traps, etc. In America, the *Citizens Radio Service* was established in 1945, but only became popular in the 1970s. In the UK, CB radio was illegal until 1981 because it was said to interfere with the radio transmissions of the emergency services. The use of CB radio declined during the 1980s. CB enthusiasts, who call themselves BREAKERS, have colourful pseudonyms (known as 'handles') and have developed their own slang.

CBS Columbia Broadcasting System. Founded in 1922 as a radio network, it became one of the main coast-to-coast TV networks in America.

CD *See* COMPACT DISC.

CD-ROM Compact-Disk Read-Only Memory. A computer storage device used to access large volumes of data, such as a dictionary, encyclopedia, or some other form of database. The present form of the CD-ROM is a 5-inch compact disk storing over 600 megabytes. The information on the disk is included during manufacture and cannot be altered or added to.

Ceefax (From *see* plus *facts*) An information service operated by the BBC since 1973, enabling pages of text to be displayed on a modified domestic television set. The information transmitted includes news flashes, market movements, weather reports, sports results, etc. The broadcast is transmitted with normal television programmes and makes use of two of the unused lines between picture frames. The required pages are selected for display by means of a keyboard. A similar system is operated by the Independent Broadcasting Authority under the name **Oracle**. The general name for such services is **Teletext**.

ceiling inspector A female sexual partner. An ironic description of the woman's view in the missionary position, especially if she has lost interest in what is going on. This expression is thought to have been coined by the Australian comic writer and actor Barry Humphries.

Celanese A tradename for a type of fabric made from acetate rayon. First introduced in the 1920s by the *British Celanese Company*, it was widely used in making ladies' underwear. The name comes from 'cellulose' (in wood pulp).

cell. **Cellnet** A tradename for a **cellular network** service operated in the UK jointly by British Telecom and Securicor. A cellular network enables mobile telephone users to be connected to the main telephone system. It consists of a large number of adjacent cells each containing a radio transmitter/receiver connected to the main telephone network. Mobile-telephone users have battery-operated radiotelephones in radio contact with the transmitter/receiver for the particular cell in which they are located. As the users move from one cell to another (by car, train, etc.) they are automatically switched to be in radio contact with the transmitter-receiver in the new area.

Cellophane A tradename for a transparent flexible material made from wood pulp and used for wrapping. Invented in France in 1869 by the Swiss chemist Jaques Brandenberger, it was first manufactured in 1913. The name, which is used generically in America, comes from 'cellulose' (in wood pulp) plus '-phane' (meaning transparent, by analogy with 'diaphanous').

cell therapy or **cellular therapy** A treatment to slow down and partially reverse the physical effects of ageing in human beings. It depends on the injection of preparations of young cells taken from the organs of embryonic animals, particularly sheep. Its popularity grew in the 1960s and early 1970s. In addition to its rejuvenating effects, the adherents of cell therapy also claim that it can cure many non-infectious illnesses. Scientifically controlled experimental studies have failed to provide any evidence in support of the claims made and the treatment is not accepted by the orthodox medical profession in Europe or America.

cellulite Lumpy fatty tissue beneath the skin, especially of the thighs and buttocks, that is said by some to be resistant to conventional dieting. The name was coined in the early 1970s by the French dietician Nicole Ronsard. Orthodox medical authorities have questioned the existence of cellulite as an entity distinct from normal subcutaneous fatty tissue.

Celtic. **Celtic Sea** Formally defined as "that part of the continental shelf lying between the 200 fathom contour, S. Ireland, the S.W. tip of Wales, Land's End, and Ushant". The term derives from the neighbouring Celtic areas – Brittany, Cornwall, Wales, and Ireland, and was first used by E. W. L. Holt in 1921.

Celtic Twilight The Irish literary revival of the late 19th and early 20th centuries. The phrase was adopted from the title of a collection of short stories by W. B. Yeats published in 1893, which illustrated the mysticism of the Irish and their belief in fairies. While many of the Irish literati, including Yeats himself and AE (George Russell), subscribed to the notion of Celtic Twilight it also attracted a great deal of criticism and ridicule. James Joyce was one of the most vociferous detractors of the theory dismissing it as "cultic twalette".

> In ancient shadows and twilights
> Where childhood has strayed,
> The world's great sorrows were born
> And its heroes were made.
>
> AE: *Germinal.*

Cenotaph (Gr. *kenos*, empty; *taphos*, tomb) A sepulchral monument raised to the memory of a person or persons buried elsewhere. By far the most noteworthy to the British is that in Whitehall, London, designed by Sir Edwin Lutyens, which was dedicated on 11 November 1920, to those who fell in World War I. It has since been adapted to commemorate the fallen of World War II. *See* ARMISTICE DAY; REMEMBRANCE DAY.

censor. deleted by French censor Phrase used by the US newspaper owner James Gordon Bennett II (1841–1918) during World War I to fill empty spaces left in his paper, the *New York Herald*, when news was lacking. *See also* GORDON BENNETT.

CENTO Central Treaty Organization. *See* BAGHDAD PACT.

central. central casting The casting department of a film studio, especially in America. Since the 1960s the expression has acquired the figurative sense of being stereotyped, as in such phrases as 'right out of central casting'. This is an allusion to the tendency of the larger Hollywood film studios to be unadventurous in their choice of plots, settings, and characters, preferring to follow the pattern of previous box-office successes.

Central Committee The main executive committee of the Soviet Communist Party, elected by the party congress. The main power resides in the POLITBURO and the Secretariat.

Central Intelligence Agency *See* CIA.

Central Office The headquarters of the British Conservative Party, situated in Smith Square, Westminster. *See also* TRANSPORT HOUSE.

Central Treaty Organization *See* BAGHDAD PACT.

centre. Centre 42 A cultural movement intended to make the arts more widely accessible, primarily through trade-union support and involvement. It was founded in 1961 by the playwright Arnold Wesker, who was also its artistic director until his decision to dissolve the movement in 1970.

centrefold An illustration folded into the centre of a magazine or book or occupying the two facing pages at the centre. Since centrefold illustrations were introduced in the 'girlie' magazine *Playboy*, the term has become synonymous with the picture of a nude female. More recently, the model herself has been referred to as a centrefold. *See also* PAGE-THREE GIRL; PIN-UP GIRL.

Centurion British 50-ton tank with a 76 mm gun. It was introduced in 1945 and considered comparable to the German Panther tank. It was rearmed in 1959 with a 105 mm gun. The tank has been used by the armies of several other nations, including Sweden and Switzerland.

century. Century of the Common Man The 20th century, the age of democracy. *The Century of the Common Man* (1940) was the title of a book by Henry A. Wallace, New-Dealer and US Vice-President (1941–1945) under F. D. Roosevelt. The phrase speedily became popular on both sides of the Atlantic and was much favoured by Nancy, Viscountess Astor.

go for the century To attempt to shear 100 sheep in a day; a phrase used by Australian shearers.

cereb US slang for a swot, derived from 'cerebral'. It can be pronounced 'see-reb' or 'sarebbe'.

CERN Conseil Européen pour la Recherche Nucléaire. The original name of the research centre for particle physics based in Geneva, which was formed in 1954 by most leading European nations. It operates a proton synchrotron with intersecting storage rings 300 metres in diameter and the Large Electron-Positron Collider built in a 5-mile tunnel under the Jura mountains. The centre has been renamed the **European Laboratory for Particle Physics**, but the acronym CERN is still used.

Certificate of Secondary Education *See* CSE.

c'est la guerre (Fr. it is the war) Originally a World War I French military catchphrase offered as an excuse for any failure to perform correctly. By 1915 it had been adopted by British soldiers but after the war its use declined until its revival in World War II. In this war it was widely used in a civilian context to account for anything that had changed as a result of the war.

CETA In America, an acronym for Comprehensive Employment and Training Act, an act of 1973 in which federal funds were made available to state and local-government organizations to provide jobs and training for the unemployed.

CFC Chlorofluorocarbon; one of a group of chemical compounds made from hydrocarbons by replacing some of the hydrogen atoms by chlorine and fluorine atoms. Such substances have been extensively used as propellants in AEROSOLS and as the working fluid in refrigerators. In the

1980s, conservation groups campaigned to ban their use because of their effect on the OZONE LAYER. *See also* HALON.

cha-cha-cha A 20th-century Latin-American ballroom dance.

Chaco War A bitter conflict between Bolivia and Paraguay over the disputed lowland plain known as Gran Chaco, which lies just east of the central Andes. After initial Bolivian successes in 1932, the Bolivian army, consisting largely of Indian conscripts, was repulsed by the Paraguayans; by early 1935 Paraguayan forces were making inroads into Bolivian territory and controlled most of the Chaco. A truce was called in June 1935, by which time some 100,000 men had died, many of disease. The treaty, signed at the Chaco Peace Conference in July 1938, gave the bulk of Gran Chaco to Paraguay.

Chad A character whose bald head and large nose were depicted appearing over a wall and inquiring, "Wot, no [word filled in to suit the circumstances]?", as a comment or protest against a shortage or shortcoming. Widely current during World War II, especially among the forces, Chad provided scope for humorous relief in many a difficult situation. It was the happy creation (1938) of the cartoonist 'Chat' (George Edward Chatterton). *See also* KILROY.

chain reaction Originally a chemical or nuclear reaction that creates energy or products, which in turn cause further reactions without a need for further energy input from outside. The concept in this sense emerged in the 1930s. In the 1970s it became part of the non-technical language, describing any series of events in which each event causes the next.

chair A late 20th-century neutered euphemism for a chairman or a chairwoman. For most of the 20th century females appointed to chair a committee, organization, bench, etc., were content to be referred to as chairmen and to be addressed as 'madame chairman'. However, with the growth of feminism in the 1960s a preoccupation with the etymology of words containing characteristically male sub-units led to the substitution of *-man* by *-person*. Thus, **chairpersons** and **spokespersons** made their appearance (though policepersons and seapersons did not). It was not long, however, before the predictable shortening took place and the chairperson became the chair. In this sense chair is used as an exact synonym for chairman or chairwoman. 'The chair asked for nominations' is a slightly different sense to 'questions should be addressed to the chair'. In the former the chair is a person, in the latter it is an office. The context will usually make it clear that it is not the piece of furniture that is being addressed.

Chairman Mao *See* LITTLE RED BOOK.

Challenger. Challenger disaster A tragic accident to the US SPACE SHUTTLE *Challenger*, which exploded shortly after take-off on 28 January 1986 at CAPE CANAVERAL. The disaster was later found to have been caused by leaking seals ('O rings') between stages of the rocket. All seven astronauts aboard were killed instantly, including the schoolteacher Christa McAuliffe, who had been selected as the first in a 'citizens in space' programme. Shown live on television and witnessed by the astronauts' families, the tragedy caused a massive shock, especially in America. President Reagan, speaking later, said that the crew had "touched the face of God". The Soviet space agency later announced that it was naming seven recently discovered asteroids after members of the crew.

Challenger tank British main battle tank, introduced in the 1980s after many years' development. Its effectiveness in battle was much speculated upon, particularly in view of the cost of the tank's manufacture, but it silenced most critics after performing well in the GULF WAR of 1991. It carries a 120-mm gun and is well-protected by Chobham armour.

Professor Challenger George Edward Challenger, a fictional professor created by Sir Arthur Conan Doyle in *The Lost World* (1912), and appearing in other stories. Challenger is a distinguished and adventurous zoologist and anthropologist with a fiery temper. He was possibly modelled on one of Doyle's fellow medical students, George Budd.

champagne socialists A derogatory term for those whose luxurious style of living and extravagant tastes do not conform to their declared left-wing political ideals.

Chanak crisis The crisis in October 1922 that caused the fall of Lloyd George's coalition government. It was started by the entry of the Turks into Chanak, on the Asiatic side of the Dardanelles, a neutral zone held by the British and the French. Their objective was to take part of Thrace from Greece. The Conservative members of Lloyd George's cabinet felt that he acted in favour of Greece by reinforcing the British garrison in Chanak. At the famous **Carlton Club Meeting**, on 19 October 1922, the Conservatives decided to withdraw from the coalition government, forcing Lloyd George's resignation as premier. This was the occasion for the formation of the **1922 Committee** of Tory backbenchers, who were determined that the leadership of the party should not take decisions without consulting them in the future.

Chanel The name under which a wide range of *haute couture* and beauty products have been marketed in the 20th century. The name is that of the Parisian couturier Coco Chanel (real name Gabrielle Chanel; 1883–1971), who started a fashion house in Paris in 1924. Her most characteristic innovations were her jersey suits, costume jewellery, colourful evening scarves, and perfumes, especially Chanel No 5. Although she retired before World War II she made a successful return to designing in 1954.

Channel. Channel Tunnel A rail link beneath the English Channel between the UK and France. The finance was raised by an Anglo-French consortium; construction began in 1987 and was due to be completed in 1993. The link actually comprises three tunnels: two carrying trains travelling one-way, with a third service and ventilation tunnel running between them. This massive engineering feat is a manifestation of the UK's closer connection with Europe; although the tunnel incorporates barriers to prevent rabid animals invading the UK from the Continent, this did not still criticism from those who felt threatened by the loss of the UK's island status.

The day the Channel caught fire A myth of World War II that spread rapidly through the UK in the darkest days of 1940. The defeat at DUNKIRK and rumours that the Germans were preparing to cross the Channel were severe tests of British morale; however, the populace was much cheered when it was rumoured that an attempted invasion had been foiled. The story, which circulated in September, was that the Channel had been drenched with petrol, which was ignited as the German invasion fleet approached. German bodies were reported to be choking the Channel and invasion had been averted. In fact the British had conducted experiments with submerged oil pipes but had realised that such a plan was not feasible. Nevertheless the story was widely repeated and for many months people recalled 'the day the Channel caught fire'.

chaos theory A mathematical theory of unpredictable behaviour of systems because of their sensitivity to the initial conditions or because there are so many factors influencing them. Even though the laws or rules governing the system's behaviour are well-understood, the behaviour of the system as a whole is 'chaotic' because it is so complex. It was originally developed as a theory of meteorology and illustrates the difficulty of weather forecasting. It has been said that a butterfly flapping its wings in South America can be the cause of a tornado in North America – the so-called **butterfly effect**. Chaos theory has been applied to many other branches of science and social science.

Chappaquiddick An island in new England, which in 1969 was the scene of a tragic car accident involving the US Senator Edward Kennedy, an incident that was to haunt his subsequent political career. Kennedy's car had crashed off a bridge into eight feet of water; a female passenger, Mary Jo Kopechne, aged 27, drowned. Controversy surrounded the senator's failure to save the girl, although he managed to escape from the car himself. Further controversy arose because he failed to inform the police immediately of the accident.

charismatic movement A Christian sect that emphasizes the charismatic gifts of speaking in tongues, healing by laying on of hands, and baptism by the Holy Spirit. Originally members of the Pentecostal Church, which developed from revivalist meetings in America in 1906, many later charismatics have preferred to remain in their own churches. Since the 1960s, therefore, many charismatics, who are also known as neopentacostalists, have also been found in Roman Catholic, Protestant, and Orthodox churches. In the Christian sense, charisma means a power or talent that is divinely bestowed upon a person, rather than the more general meaning of a power or talent for influencing people, which is usually cultivated.

charleston A ballroom dance popular *c.* 1923–27, which originated as a dance among Black Americans. Charleston is the name of a cotton-trading seaport in South Carolina, one-third of the population of which is Black. The charleston featured in the Black musical *Runnin' Wild* (1923) and with its 4/4 syncopated rhythm and kicking toe-in steps rapidly spread throughout the world.

Charlie (1) British slang for a fool, as in the expression 'a right Charlie'. It is derived from rhyming slang, Charlie Hunt for cunt, which originally meant fool in cockney jargon. (2) A euphemism for cocaine. It is the communications code name for its initial letter, C. (3) Slang name for the Vietcong used by US soldiers during the VIETNAM WAR. It comes from 'Victor Charlie', the code names for the abbreviation VC. (4) A slang euphemism for any unmentionable subject, as in the expression 'Charlie's come' to mean that a female's menstruation has started. (5) Australian rhyming slang for a girl, from Charlie Wheeler for sheila (a girl). *See also* CHECKPOINT CHARLIE.

Charlie Brown A cartoon character who appeared in the PEANUTS cartoon strip created by Charles M. Schultz in 1950. The character achieved great popularity, with his dog Snoopy and his friends Maisie and Linus. The cartoon strips had global syndication, animated cartoons appeared on television, and a host of ephemera was also produced. *See also* HAPPINESS IS... *under* HAPPY.

Charlie Chan Inspector Charles Chan, the fictional Chinese detective created by the US novelist and ex-journalist Earl Derr Biggers. He made his first appearance in 1925 in *The House Without a Key*. Chan lived in Honolulu with Mrs Chan and his many children. He was unfailingly dignified and polite, striving at all times to speak correct English. "You will do me the great honour to accompany me to the station, if you please", was his traditional mode of arresting criminals. He was sometimes accompanied in his work by his number one or number two son. Biggers created his gentle Chinese character as a protest against the identity of the Chinaman in America, which tended to be that of the laundry man. Eight books featuring Charlie Chan were published and over a dozen films starring Warner Oland as Charlie Chan appeared in the 1930s. Later films starred Sidney Toler and subsequently Roland Winters and Peter Ustinov.

Charlie Farnsbarns A person whose name one cannot remember, as in 'Mrs Thing', 'Old Whatsisname', 'Joe Bloggs', etc. It was used by the comedians Richard Murdoch and Kenneth Horne in their 1940s radio comedy *Much Binding in the Marsh*.

Charlie's Aunt A nickname of Princess Margaret. One of numerous nicknames used in the satirical magazine *Private Eye* (first published 1962), it is thought to have been coined (in allusion to the popular farce – *Charley's Aunt* (1892) – by Brandon Thomas) by the Princess herself who, of course, is the aunt of Prince Charles.

Charlie's dead A slang expression meaning that a woman's petticoat is showing, or that a man's trouser zip is undone. This expression is often heard in the school playground, where it has been current since the 1950s. The origin of the phrase and the identity of Charlie are unknown.

charm In physics, a property postulated to exist for certain QUARKS to account for the behaviour of some elementary particles. The term was first used in 1974 by the US physicist Sheldon Glashow (1932–), who used the word 'charm' because the symmetry of the theory was particularly pleasing. *See* ELEMENTARY PARTICLE.

Charter 77 A group of Czechoslovakian dissidents formed in Prague in 1977 (designated 'Year of Rights of Political Prisoners') to monitor abuses of human rights by the Czech authorities. The Charter itself demanded the adherence of the government to UN covenants and the Helsinki accords on human rights. During 1977 hundreds of signatures were collected from people of all classes, many of whom subsequently suffered harassment, imprisonment, or exile. One of those imprisoned, the writer Václav Havel, was elected President of Czechoslovakia in 1989.

charts Lists of best-selling records published regularly. The term is used in such phrases as 'in the charts' and 'top of the charts'. Originally used in the record industry, it was subsequently extended to other media, such as book sales or audiences for TV programmes.

chase the dragon (1) To smoke heroin. This expression came into use in the late 1970s with the arrival of cheap heroin in the UK. The drug is heated on a piece of aluminium foil and the fumes inhaled through a tube. Perhaps the imaginative name derives from 'chasing' the coils of smoke across the piece of foil. (2) To court death by taking heroin. This wider application was current among the upper- and middle-class drug users of the early 1980s.

chat. **chatline** A telephone service that offered the caller the facility of joining in a conversation with several other callers. The British Telecom version of this scheme, called Talkabout, was launched in 1983 but suspended in 1988. The disadvantages were that young people used the facility so frequently and for so long that their parents' telephone bills were unacceptably high; the service was also abused by making use of it as a dating agency or for pornographic purposes.

chat show A type of radio or television programme in which celebrity guests are invited to have light-hearted conversations with the presenter. Their content is usually somewhat trivial, hence 'chat'. These programmes are intended to appear natural and to be unrehearsed, although this is rarely the case.

> Genuinely spontaneous good talk is the rarest thing even in real life and almost unknown in the chat show.
>
> MAURICE WIGAN: *Sunday Times.*

chattering classes Newscasters, journalists, political pundits, and the like who talk about current political and social issues. More generally, the term is used to designate anyone who talks about such matters. The expression is slightly derogatory, conjuring up images of groups of pseudo-intellectuals having voluble, and perhaps superficial, discussions on subjects about which they have imperfect knowledge and no control.

Originally the term was coined in the first years of Margaret Thatcher's rule as a disparaging description of the liberal and left-wing middle-class intelligentsia who impotently raged about Thatcherism around the dinner tables of north London. It was popularized by the political correspondent Alan Watkins of the *Observer*, who widened its meaning to include people of all political complexions united only by their chattering.

> The Beatles, James Bond – that's the sort of thing we export to France best, while they send us their ideas. We do not even recognize our ideas merchants over here; we prefer to turn the spotlight on the glitterati, the chattering classes, the cognoscenti . . .
>
> *The Independent*, 20 March 1991.

chauffeur A person (male **chauffeur**, female **chauffeuse**) who is employed to drive another person's car. The word is derived from the French *chauffer*, to heat, and originally meant the stoker who fuelled the early steam cars and who occasionally took over from the driver. With the advent of the internal-combustion engine the stoker lost his job but the word remained – the chauffeur now being responsible for driving the vehicle and understanding enough about its engine to keep it running – no mean feat in the early days of motoring.

Che The name by which Ernesto Guevara (1928–67) was widely known. An Argentinian physician, writer, and guerrilla leader, he became a folk hero of socialist revolutionary movements. He joined Fidel Castro and played a prominent part in the Cuban Revolution, leaving Cuba secretly in 1965 to reappear attempting to instigate a revolt in Bolivia in 1966, where he was later wounded, captured, and shot by US-trained counter-insurgency forces. His book *Guerrilla Warfare* became required reading for all aspiring revolutionaries, while his face appeared on posters adorning private rooms throughout the western world.

cheap. **cheap money** or **easy money** A monetary policy in which interest rates are kept low to encourage economic expansion and investment by reducing the cost of borrowing. *See also* DEAR MONEY.

cheap shot In America, an unfair comment or action, especially one aimed at an easy target.

Checkpoint Charlie The nickname given by Allied forces to a checkpoint on the border between East and West Berlin before the demolition of the BERLIN WALL. It was situated at the junction of Friedrichstrasse and Zimmerstrasse and was important as the agreed crossing point for foreigners (*i.e.* non-Germans). As such, it served as a barometer indicating the political climate between East and West – at times of international tension the East German guards would cause long delays at the border. Checkpoint Charlie has been immortalized in many spy novels and films as the place at which intelligence agents were supposed to be exchanged. At the end of the COLD WAR (1990), when the Berlin Wall came down, Checkpoint Charlie was removed intact to be kept as a memento in a museum. The term has been extended to mean any crossing point between divided communities, for example, between Christian and Moslem quarters of Beirut in the 1970s and 1980s.

Cheeky Chappie The nickname of the music-hall comedian Max Miller (1895–1963). The epithet, which appeared on bills advertising his act from 1924, alluded to the risqué nature of his performance, in particular his use of the *double entendre*. Gags which came from his 'white book' were classed as 'clean', those from his 'blue book' as 'dirty'.

cheesecake An originally US description of a titillating photograph of a scantily clad female. It originated in the 1930s, when pin-up photographs became acceptable. The origin is obscure; possibly an analogy between the creamy white texture of the dessert and the bare flesh of the model. It might also suggest that the model is so delectable that she can be likened to a scrumptious slice of cheesecake. Two things have happened to the word since then: on the one hand its meaning has broadened to include the use of female sexual characteristics in advertising as well as female sexual attractiveness itself; on the other, it has been pounced on by feminists as sexist, derogatory, and offensive. A more sexual, rather than sexist, response from women has been an interest in **beefcake**, a photograph that displays men with muscular bodies.

Cheka The first political police agency of the Soviet Union, it was established by Lenin in December 1917 and originally known as Vecheka. It was intended to investigate any sabotage and counter-revolutionary activities. However, it took upon itself the arrest, imprisonment, and execution of anyone considered to be an enemy of the state. It was disbanded in 1922 to be replaced by the GPU. In 1923 this organization became the notorious OGPU.

Chelsea Flower Show A show held annually in May by the Royal Horticultural Society in the grounds of the Royal Hospital, Chelsea. Started in 1913, it has become the world's greatest horticultural show as well as something of a social event.

chemical warfare The use of chemical substances to kill or disable troops or civilians or to poison food or water. In spite of a declaration by the Hague Conference (1899) to ban them, Germany (a signatory) was the first to use poisonous gases in World War I. No chemical weapons were used in World War II, although Germany manufactured large quantities of the deadly nerve gases and stocks of these substances are now held by America and the Soviet Union. Chemical defoliants were used by America in Vietnam and toxic gases were used by Saddam Hussein of Iraq in the Gulf War against Iran and against his own Kurdish minority. The modern range of chemical weapons is very large, from the relatively humane tear gases and other incapacitating gases, to the horrific skin-burning (mustard) gases and the lethal nerve and respiratory gases.

cheque-book journalism A phrase introduced in the mid-1960s to describe the misuse of the wealth of the press to obtain the exclusive rights of stories from criminals and notorious persons generally, thus financially rewarding those whom society wishes to condemn. Although this practice has been criticized by the Press Council, many newspaper editors would defend it on the grounds that the press should be free to provide the public with what it wants to read. The freedom of the press is regarded in the UK as a highly valued privilege; it has to be accepted, in an imperfect world, that some undesirable results will flow from it.

Chequers The official country seat of British prime ministers, in Buckinghamshire near Princes Risborough. It was presented to the nation for this purpose by Sir Arthur and Lady Lee (Lord and Lady Lee of Fareham) in 1917 and first officially used by Lloyd George in 1921.

Chernobyl A town in the Ukrainian Republic of the Soviet Union that leapt into fame on April 26 1986, when the number 4 reactor in its nuclear power station blew up, causing some 250 deaths, the evacuation of 135,000 people from a 35 km (22 mile) zone surrounding Chernobyl, and increased levels of radioactivity in many parts of the world. Several countries placed restrictions on the import of food from Eastern Europe and considerable quantities of agricultural produce had to be destroyed. Heavy rain in Wales and parts of northern England coincided with the arrival of the radioactive cloud and sheep-grazing in Wales was affected. The fire in the reactor and the escape of radioactive materials was finally brought to an end by entombing the reactor in concrete. The world's worst nuclear accident, it was caused by an unauthorized experiment that went disastrously wrong, the poor single-shell design of the reactor building, and the slow reaction of the power-station staff to the early danger signs. Western countries issued reassuring statements regarding the safety of all non-Soviet double-shelled buildings, but immense damage was done to nuclear energy programmes throughout the world, many of which were cancelled or cut back as a result of public disquiet.

cherry. cherry farm A US colloquialism for a form of open prison in which the security is less than in other prisons and in which the prisoners carry out tasks of an agricultural nature. The implication is that the prisoners might as well be held in a cherry orchard.
cherry reds *See* BOVVER BOOTS.

Cheshire Homes Homes for the incurably sick founded by Group Captain Leonard Cheshire VC (1917–), who was so horrified at the bombing of NAGASAKI in 1945, at which he was an observer, that he devoted the rest of his life to the relief of suffering. There are 78 Cheshire Homes in the UK mainly offering residential care to severely disabled adults, although a small proportion also care for mentally handicapped adults. There are 170 Cheshire Homes in 47 countries overseas offering the same care as in the UK. The foundation that runs these homes is a charitable trust, which also runs Park House, Sandringham, a country-house hotel specially designed and equipped to provide holidays for disabled people. Cheshire's wife, Baroness Sue Ryder (1923–), runs a chain of charity shops to fund her own philanthropic work, which started with refugee relief after World War II.

Chesterbelloc The name by which the partnership between G. K. Chesterton (1874–1936) and Hilaire Belloc (1870–1953) was known. Both Roman Catholics and opponents of the socialism of G. B. Shaw and H. G. Wells, they collaborated on a number of humorous books in the early part of the 20th century, with drawings by Chesterton and text by Belloc.

Chetniks (Serb. *četnik*, from *četa*, troop) Members of the Serbian nationalist guerrilla bands which formed during World War II to resist the AXIS invaders. On the whole they fought Tito's communist guerrillas. Several factions evolved but the most important group was that based in Serbia led by Draza Mihajlovic. By the end of the war the Chetniks had greatly reduced in number and the remainder were captured and executed by Tito's partisans.

Chevy US slang for a Chevrolet car.

chew. chew up the scenery An originally US phrase coined by Dorothy Parker (1893–1967). In a review she so described one notorious piece of overacting. The phrase has since entered the general language meaning to dramatize events or oneself inappropriately.
chewy on your boot In Australian slang, a derisory call from the crowd to a player in Australian rules football kicking for goal. The hope is that the kicker will miss because he has 'chewy' (chewing gum) on his boot. The phrase is sometimes used more generally for any failure.

Chiantishire A facetious name, coined in the 1980s, for Tuscany, an area of Italy in which the wine Chianti is made. The name arose because of the number of British who purchased farmhouses in Tuscany, either as holiday homes or to live in permanently.

Chicago. Chicago piano A World War II naval nickname for an eight-barrelled pom-pom anti-aircraft gun. The allusion is to the Chicago of the gangsters (*see* CAPONE) and the hammer action of the piano, which the back-and-forth movement of the barrels resembled. Similarly, a four-barrelled pom-pom was called a **Chicago typewriter**.
Chicago Seven The people (originally eight) charged with violating the anti-riot provision of the 1968 Civil Rights Bill during the Democratic Convention in Chicago in August 1968. The charges stemmed from the rioting which ensued when police attacked hundreds of anti-war demonstrators. The label, used by their supporters and the press, set a trend for the naming of victims of legal systems on both sides of the Atlantic. Recent examples in the UK are the BIRMINGHAM SIX and the GUILDFORD FOUR.

chicane An obstacle on a racecourse, particularly an artificial bend introduced on motor-racing tracks. This sense arose in the mid-20th century. It is also a term used in bridge for a hand containing no trumps. Its general meaning is to practise *chicanery* (mean petty subterfuge, especially legal dodges and quibbles). 'Chicane' is a French word which originally meant a dispute in games, particularly mall, and originally the game of mall itself. It seems to derive ultimately from the Persian *chaugan*, the crooked stick used in polo.

chicano (From Sp. *majicano*, a Mexican) A US slang name for an American citizen of Mexican origin. The feminine equivalent is **chicana**.

chick (1) A girl, girlfriend. This word has been used for hundreds of years as a term of endearment, but reappeared in the late 1950s and early 1960s, becoming part of HIPPIE jargon in America and then in the UK. It sounded very dated in the post-feminist era and it is considered a rather pejorative term by women because of the sexual connotations. (2) A prostitute. (3) A rare term used among homosexuals to mean a male prostitute. In US usage it is specifically a passive homosexual partner. A prison term of the 1970s and 1980s.

chicken (1) Slang for a coward or cowardly. (2) Slang for a youth attractive to older homosexual males, known as **chicken-hawks**. This usage is part of US homosexual jargon as well as police and prison jargon. (3) Slang for an under-age girl used as a sexual partner in pornography.

chicken run US slang for a dangerous teenage game in which two drivers drive their cars towards each other to see which one will swerve aside first. The first one to do so is chicken, and the loser.

chicken switch The PANIC BUTTON in an aircraft that operates the ejector seat and enables the pilot to be parachuted safely to earth if something irrevocable has happened to the plane. Clearly, the moment at which to push the button is a matter of fine judgment. To push it too soon could jeopardize millions of pounds worth of aircraft unnecessarily and to push it too late could prove fatal. *See* CHICKEN.

play chicken To play a game in which people dare each other to do something dangerous, for example, to stand in the path of an oncoming train. The first one to withdraw to a position of safety is the chicken, and the loser.

Chicom In America, a derogatory term, used since the 1950s, for a Chinese communist.

Chief The head person or boss. In America, the title was applied particularly to Herbert Hoover (1874–1964), secretary of commerce (1921–28) and 31st US President (1929–33), in connection with his role as administrator of relief operations in Europe during and after World War I.

too many chiefs and not enough Indians or **all chiefs and no Indians** Originally a catchphrase that came from America, but now used universally in English-speaking countries. It is said when a situation arises in which there are too many bosses (perhaps because there have been too many promotions) and too few workers.

Chieftain British main battle tank. The first prototype was developed in 1959 and it entered service with the British Army in 1967, replacing the CENTURION. The Chieftain has also been used by the armies of Iran and Kuwait. It was superseded by the CHALLENGER in the 1980s.

child. **child abuse** In its broadest terms: any harm, physical or emotional, done intentionally to a child by its parents or other adults responsible for its wellbeing. This includes physical ill-treatment, sexual exploitation, and verbal or emotional assault. In the 1960s the **battered-baby** syndrome became a recognized medical condition and the 1970s witnessed growing awareness of the need to protect the rights and welfare of children. The ultimate abuse finds its expression in SNUFF MOVIES, in which the victim, usually a homeless adolescent, is tormented, literally to death. By the 1980s, the welfare of children so dominated the minds of the carers that the rights of the parents were sometimes overlooked. In the CLEVELAND AFFAIR, overenthusiastic reliance on controversial physical evidence and unsubstantiated testimonies of the children caused the health authorities to break up a number of families; this attracted strong criticism in a subsequent judicial enquiry. These and later cases of child abuse, or alleged child abuse, have revealed that the problem is complex, delicate, and not amenable to resolution by doctors or social workers who do not have the requisite good judgment and experience.

child-resistant Describing packaging, containers, etc., that are difficult for children to tamper with or open. For example, child-resistant containers, now commonly used for drugs, have tops that are not simply unscrewed, but involve two operations (*e.g.* pushing down and twisting). Their introduction in the 1970s was successful in reducing accidental poisoning of children, although many of these containers are also resistant to adults, particularly old people.

chillum A small cone-shaped pipe, usually made of clay but sometimes of wood or stone, used for smoking cannabis. The substance, either marijuana or a mixture of cannabis and tobacco, is packed on top of the 'chillum stone', a round object that fits into the narrowing end of the cone so that the contents are not sucked into the smoker's mouth. This is an anglicization of the Hindi *cilam* and has been widely used by cannabis smokers since the 1960s.

China syndrome A nuclear catastrophe, which derives from the film of the same name made in 1979, starring Jane Fonda and Jack Lemmon. It postulates that the heat generated by the breakdown of a nuclear reactor would make a hole right through the planet to China. The nuclear disaster at CHERNOBYL in the Soviet Union in 1986 heightened fears that the China syndrome might one day actually happen.

Chindit A corruption of *chinthe*, the lion-headed dragon gracing the outside of Burmese pagodas. It was adopted as the device of the troops of the 3rd Indian Division raised by Major-General Orde Wingate to operate in Burma behind the Japanese lines (1943–45). Supported by air drops, the Chindits sustained heavy casualties. Their bravery was never questioned but their military value has been. Wingate himself was killed in an aircrash in March 1944.

Chinese. Chinese restaurant syndrome A group of symptoms varying from sweating, burning sensations, headaches, and dizziness, to heart palpitations and temporary paralysis, first observed in the 1960s in some people after eating Chinese food. The symptoms are associated with an excessive intake of the food additive monosodium glutamate, a seasoning that intensifies the natural flavours of meat and vegetables and is commonly used in liberal quantities in Chinese restaurant cooking. The condition, thought to be an allergic reaction, is also called *Kwok's disease* after the scientist who made the connection with monosodium glutamate, Dr Robert Ho Man Kwok.

Chinese slavery Virtual slavery; excessively hard work for negligible rewards. The phrase became widely used as a political slogan by the Liberals from 1903, when Balfour's Conservative government (1902–05) introduced indentured coolies from China to combat the shortage of Kaffir labour in the Rand gold mines after the dislocation caused by the South African War. They were kept in compounds and only allowed out under permit.

Chinese wall A notional barrier to the passage of information between the parts of a business that might have conflicting interests. It is used mostly to refer to the barrier that should exist between the market-making part of a stockbroker's office and the brokers. For example, brokers should not be advising clients to buy a particular share because the market-making part of the firm want to sell it. The term arose after the BIG BANG of 1986, when the London Stock Exchange abandoned its two-function operation, with jobbers and brokers in separate firms. The amalgamation of these two functions into single firms necessitated the concept of a wall separating them in order not to compromise the interests of the customers. The wall was described as Chinese, either with reference to the Great Wall of China, and its former impregnability, or because Chinese walls are thought of in some contexts as being paper thin – a suitable analogue for a wall that is notional.

clever chaps (or **devils, buggers, etc.**) **these Chinese.** A catchphrase that seems to have originated in World War II, as a response to a complicated explanation that leaves the listener in a state of baffled incomprehension. It is probably a reference to what Westerners regard as the inscrutability of the Chinese. Later in the war, the Japanese sometimes replaced the Chinese as the source of oriental wisdom, but it was said in a more aggressive tone.

chinkie (1) British slang for a Chinese restaurant. (2) British slang for a Chinese meal. (3) British disparaging slang for a Chinese person.

chinless wonder A derogatory term to describe an upper-class young man who has a great deal of money, no responsibilities, and little in the way of brains or personality. There is a common belief that people with weak or receding chins have weak or receding personalities. The chinlessness is often ascribed to too much in-breeding in the aristocratic and upper classes. There is no evidence to support either proposition.

chip A small piece of silicon or other semiconducting material processed to hold a large integrated electronic circuit. The components of the circuit are formed by selectively diffusing the appropriate type of impurity into the semiconducting material. Connections between the components so formed are made by metallization. Very complex circuits can, in this way, be formed on a chip having only millimetre dimensions.

Chippitts In America, a name sometimes given to the northern industrial area of the country encompassing the cities of **Chi**cago and **Pitts**burgh. *See also* BOSNYWASH; SANSAN.

chippy (1) British slang for a fish and chip shop, common since the 1960s. (2) British slang for a carpenter. (3) US and Australian slang for a prostitute.

Mr Chips A fictional rather sad ageing schoolmaster, Arthur Chipping, who is the main character in *Good-Bye, Mr Chips* (1934) – a novel by the British writer James Hilton (1900–54). It is said that Hilton based the character on his father, who was a headmaster, and on his old classics master, W. H. Balgarnie. A 1939 film of the book featured Robert Donat; a musical remake in 1969 had Peter O'Toole in the title role. Graham Greene, the novelist, also the son of a headmaster, said of the 1939 film:

> The whole picture has an assurance, bears a glow of popularity like the face of a successful candidate on election day. And it is wrong to despise popularity in the cinema.

chips with everything Denoting a British working-class attitude in which all the food is served with fried potatoes and subsequently drenched with bottled sauce or vinegar. Originally the title of a play by Arnold Wesker (first performed in London in 1962), it is used as a catchphrase to describe the insularity of the British working-class tourist abroad and by extension to all those working-class eating habits that distinguish them from the middle classes. The middle-class evening meal is called dinner or supper, the working class have dinner in the middle of the day and tea in the evening, on returning home from work. The middle classes have a varied repertoire of food, now often influenced by continental cuisine; the working class have less adventurous appetites, and fried potatoes accompany almost all dishes. This is the theory, encapsulated in Wesker's play about class attitudes among National Servicemen in the RAF. *See also* SOCIAL CLASS.

chiropractic A form of ALTERNATIVE MEDICINE, not fully accepted by mainstream medicine, in which various diseases are treated by manipulation of the spine. It is based on the premise that many diseases are caused by misalignment of the skeletal bones (especially those of the spine), resulting in compression of the nerves, muscle spasms, etc.

chlorofluorocarbon *See* CFC.

chocaholic Someone addicted to chocolate. It is derived on the same basis as 'alcoholic'. Several of these words became common in the 1970s and 1980s. Other examples are **workaholic** and **carbaholic**, for those addicted to work and to carbohydrates, respectively.

choco A diminutive of *chocolate soldier*, an Australian colloquialism applied to militiamen and conscripts in World War II.

choose. I do not choose to run Phrase used to indicate that the speaker does not want to compete or participate. It was popularized by the US politician Calvin Coolidge (1827–1933), who became President in 1923. He was noted for his frugal unpretentious character and for a policy of general inaction on domestic and international issues. In 1927 he decided not to restand for the office and announced the fact in a characteristically short speech:

> I do not choose to run for President in 1928.

His decision not to seek re-election caused considerable puzzlement and reporters pestered him to explain more fully why he no longer wanted to be President. He replied:

> No chance of advancement.

His laconic utterances became famous and justified his nickname **Silent Cal**. It is said that a young lady sitting next to him at dinner told him that she had made a bet that she could get more than two words out of him. "You lose", said Coolidge.

Coolidge's unspectacular and retiring style, exemplified by his slogan 'keep it cool with Coolidge', did inspire some jibes. Alice Roosevelt (1884–1980) said: "He looks as if he had been weaned on a pickle", and Dorothy Parker (1893–1967), when told that he was dead, said: "How could they tell?"

chop (1) A cut-down customized motorcycle. An abbreviation of CHOPPER. (2) **the chop** The sack, the termination of employment, as in the expression **for the chop**, meaning likely to be sacked. Previously, especially in wartime, it could mean to be killed.

chop shop US slang for a workshop in which motorcycles and cars are customized or chopped. *See* CHOPPER.

chopshot Journalists' jargon for a picture of a death.

chopper (1) Slang for a helicopter, widely used since World War II and probably derived from a corruption of the word helicopter and a description of the sound and action of the rotor blades. (2) Slang for a customized motorcycle, especially one with high handlebars (*see* APEHANGERS) and extended front forks, as ridden by HELL'S ANGELS. It is an abbreviation of **chopped hog** and is sometimes shortened further to **chop**. Choppers became popular in the 1970s after they featured in the film *Easy Rider* (1964) with Peter Fonda. (3) A child's tricycle or bicycle designed to resemble a chopper motorcycle. They appeared in the 1970s. (4) British slang for a penis, dating from the 1940s and still in current use. (5) US slang for a submachine gun. Although no longer in current usage, this sense is widely known from films and crime fiction.

chozrim (Hebrew: returnees) Israeli citizens who emigrate from Israel and subsequently return. *See also* YORDIM.

Christian. Christian Action An interdenominational group, founded in 1940 by Canon Collins, to translate the teachings of Christ into practical action. The movement had close links with anti-apartheid groups and was involved with the Committee of 100, who founded CND.

Christian Aid An aid and development agency administered by the British Council of Churches, which finances projects in over 70 countries. Its annual income is used for long-term development in the poorest of Third World countries. This is channelled through local organizations to tackle the root causes of poverty, such as illiteracy, and to promote self-reliance and self-motivation against the forces of exploitation.

Christie murders A notorious series of murders committed by John Reginald Halliday Christie (1898–1953) in Rillington Place, Notting Hill Gate, London. Charged with the murder of his wife, he confessed to the murder of six other women and was hanged. His confession included the murder of the wife of Timothy Evans, who lived at the same address. Evans had already been hanged for the murder of his infant daughter and had been charged with murdering his wife. Public disquiet over these events led to a judicial enquiry in 1966, which found that Christie had probably murdered the infant Evans, but that Evans probably strangled his wife. Evans was given a posthumous free pardon for having been wrongly convicted of murdering his child. The evident frailty of human judicial procedures, so blatantly revealed by this case, convinced a majority of the members of the House of Commons (but not the public at large) that the death penalty, being unreversible, was an inappropriate punishment for anything and it ceased to be the punishment for murder in 1965.

Christingle A British Church of England service for children held around Christmas time, in which children donate purses of money for charity and are given a decorated orange with a lighted candle in it. The name comes from *Christmas* plus *ingle* (meaning 'fire' or 'flame'). Christingle services were popular in the early 1970s.

Christmas. Christmas Island (1) Kiritimati. A coral atoll of the Line Islands in the Pacific, halfway between Tahiti and Hawaii. The first British hydrogen bomb was exploded here in 1957. (2) An island in the Indian ocean discovered on Christmas Day 1643 by Captain Mynors. Annexed by Britain in 1888, it was occupied by the Japanese in World War II and transferred to Australia in 1958.

Christmas tree (1) Slang for an amphetamine spansule containing dinamyl, a pep pill. (2) Slang for an often large overdressed woman, especially one wearing too much large flamboyant jewellery.

Christopher Robin Son of the playwright and author A. A. Milne (1882–1956), who was immortalized in his father's books, *When We Were Very Young*, *Now We Are Six*, *House at Pooh Corner*, and *Winnie the Pooh*. The Pooh books charted the adventures of a young boy, Christopher Robin, and his 'friends' WINNIE THE POOH, Tigger, Piglet, Eeyore, Kanga, and Baby Roo. Milne is reputed to have based these characters on his son's favourite toys. The real Christopher Robin grew up to find his association with his father's book acutely embarrassing, although he eventually came to terms with his fictional self.

chubby chaser Slang name for someone sexually attracted to overweight people. **Chubby checker** has also been heard for a man who enjoys looking at overweight women (perhaps inspired by the name of the pop singer Chubby Checker (Ernest Evans), who originated the TWIST).

chunder In Australian slang, to be sick. It was popularized in the UK by the character Barry McKenzie in the *Private Eye* comic strip. The origin is uncertain. Possibly it is rhyming slang, Chunder Loo (spew), Chunder Loo being a comic character in an Australian boot-polish advertisement in the 1900s. Alternatively, it could simply be a shortening of the warning call 'watch under'.

Church Commissioners The body that administers the affairs and finances of the Church of England. Chaired by the Archbishop of Canterbury, it consists of the diocesan bishops together with other representatives and functionaries. It was formed in 1948 by amalgamation of the Ecclesiastical Commissioners (established 1836) and a charitable fund for impoverished clergy known as Queen Anne's Bounty (established 1704).

churn To encourage or coerce people to pay for additional unnecessary services in order to increase the final fee or commission. **Churning** is particularly associated with professional organizations, such as law firms, financial advisers, and medical practices.

chutzpah Audacity, cheek, nerve, of Yiddish origin, and pronounced 'hutspar'. Used in America by non-Jews since the 1960s, its use has been becoming more widespread in the UK since the 1970s. In his *The Joys of Yiddish* (1968), Leo Rosten defines chutzpah as the quality of a man who, having killed his mother and father, throws himself on the mercy of the court because he is an orphan.

CIA Central Intelligence Agency. A department of the US government set up by President Truman in 1947 to conduct intelligence operations outside America. Its clandestine overseas ventures are usually designed to undermine left-wing regimes, although it lost public support in the 1970s when US influence appeared to be diminished rather than enhanced by its activities. Its internal counterintelligence service, operated in conjunction with the FBI, now has to be sanctioned by the attorney general, since alleged abuses in the WATERGATE affair.

ciao An Italian word used as a greeting or as a farewell. It was adopted by English speakers in the 1960s but by the 1980s had become somewhat dated.

Cicero Pseudonym of Elyesa Bazna (1904–), who was born in Albania. He became a spy for NAZI Germany, using his employment as valet to the British Ambassador to Turkey as cover. He photographed secret documents from the embassy safe and is alleged to have passed details of the Normandy landings to the Germans. Cicero was not fully trusted by the Nazis and it is believed that much of his information was ignored. A film of Cicero's life, *Five Fingers*, based on his autobiography, was released in 1952.

Cinderella of the Arts A description of poetry, first used by the US poet and editor Harriet Monroe (1860–1936).

cinema. cinema novo (Portuguese: *cinema nôvo*, new cinema) A school of film-making in Brazil in the early 1970s, noted for fantasy and melodrama.

CinemaScope The first successful wide-screen film process, introduced by Twentieth Century-Fox in *The Robe* (1953). The system employed a special anamorphic lens to compress a wide picture onto a standard 35-mm frame. Projected through a complementary lens this gave an image width two and a half times its height. Although invented in the 1920s by Henri Chrétien, the process was not adopted by Hollywood until the 1950s, when it was used to help counter the growing threat from television. Other studios introduced their own versions of the system, variously called SuperScope, WarnerScope, and Panavision. Initially, however, many directors disparaged the process, despite the dramatic compositional possibilities it offers; however, later film makers, such as Stanley Kubrick in *2001: A Space Odyssey* (1968), made considerable use of its merits.

> There was a time when all I looked for was a good story, but nowadays everything has to look the size of Mount Rushmore, and the actors in close-up look as though they belong there.
>
> FRITZ LANG.

cinéma vérité (Fr. 'truth cinema') A technique of film making, developed in the 1960s, using handheld cameras and synchronous sound to record the authentic dialogue of real people in true-life situations. The aim was to convey reality, unedited and unrehearsed, but hopefully enhanced by the film maker's involvement. Classic examples of the genre include works by French film makers, such as Jean Rouch (*Chronique d'une Eté*; 1961), and the Americans Richard Leacock (*Primary*; 1960) and D. A. Pennebaker (*Monterey Pop*; 1968).

cinerama A cinema process in which three synchronized projectors each project one third of a film onto a wide curved screen, adding an extra dimension to audience involvement and enjoyment by the illusion of peripheral vision. The technique was invented by the New York photographer Fred Waller and given its first public viewing in *This Is Cinerama* (1952). The system's spectacular visual effects and stereo sound were restricted to travelogues until its first narrative use in *How The West Was Won* (1962). Because of the expense of the cumbersome projection machinery the system was superseded in the late 1960s by Panavision, which employed 70-mm precision lenses and Dolby stereo soundtracks to create similar wide-screen effects more efficiently.

circadian rhythm *See* BIORHYTHM.

circular file In America, slang term for the wastepaper basket, as in 'put it in the circular file'.

citizens' band *See* CB.

city. City of Dreadful Knights Cardiff. After World War I, Lloyd George, Prime Minister in the Coalition government, made many recommendations for the award of honours in what was considered to be a cynical and blatant fashion. In 1922 Lord Salisbury alleged that the government had fixed prices for the sale of titles, the money being put into party political funds. As a consequence, a Royal Commission was set up in 1922 to recommend future procedure. Three people connected with prominent South Wales newspapers were among the recipients of these honours, hence Cardiff was dubbed the 'City of Dreadful Knights', a punning allusion to *The City of Dreadful Night*, a poem by James Thomson (1834–82).

city technology college (CTC) A type of senior secondary school set up in urban areas in the UK, which provides a science-based education, as opposed to the more broadly based education available in other schools. They are financed jointly by industry and the government independently of Local Education Authorities. The late 1980s witnessed considerable controversy in education as the Conservative government introduced various changes. The establishment of CTCs was an attempt to make school pupils more interested in science and technology and to prepare them for careers in industry and science.

civex A US system for reprocessing nuclear fuel from fast-breeder reactors, developed in the late 1970s. The idea behind civex was that reactor technology could be sold to other countries but the reprocessing system did not allow the user to obtain pure plutonium for use in nuclear weapons. The term comes from *civ*ilian + *ex*traction, 'civilian' meaning 'non-military'.

Civic Trust An independent British charity founded in 1957 by Duncan Sandys, Minister of Housing and Local Government (1954–57), to promote high standards in architecture, civil planning, and to protect and improve the environment.

civil rights movement The movement founded in the 1950s in America to promote racial equality. The Commission on Civil Rights was created under the Civil Rights Act (1957) and then extended under the 1960 and 1964 acts. It had a watching brief on the development of equality for Blacks for voting registration and employment. The Commission was created in response to the agitation for civil rights in the 1950s and 1960s, largely led by Martin Luther King (1929–68). *See also* I HAVE A DREAM *under* DREAM.

> But in too many communities, in too many parts of the country, wrongs are inflicted on Negro citizens for which there are no remedies in law.
>
> JOHN F. KENNEDY; television address from the White House, June, 1963.

clam. clambake A colony of marine animals living on the ocean floor in an area in which the water is heated by an underground hot spring. The term is an extension of the US name for a beach picnic at which clams are baked.

clam diggers In America, trousers, similar to PEDAL PUSHERS, cut off below the knee, so-called because they were originally worn when digging clams.

Clapham. The man on the Clapham omnibus The man in the street. The image of this ordinary person travelling on an omnibus in Clapham was invented by a law lord, Lord Bowen, in 1903. While hearing a case for negligence, he said: "We must ask ourselves what the man on the Clapham omnibus would think."

In those days the omnibus was still horse-drawn and Clapham was a suburb that a judge might well regard as the epitomy of ordinariness – the home of common sense. In fact, this was not the Clapham omnibus's only claim to fame. Some 50 years earlier a young German chemist, Friedrich Kekulé von Stradonitz, was working as a laboratory assistant at St Bartholomew's Hospital in London. While asleep on the Clapham omnibus he fell into a dream that was to revolutionize organic chemistry: "... the atoms were gambolling before my eyes ... I saw how the longer ones formed a chain ... (and then) the cry of the conductor 'Clapham Road' awakened me from my dreaming ...". Kekulé's dream led to the elucidation of the structure of many organic molecules, notably that of benzene.

Since its years of Edwardian stolidity, Clapham has gone down and in recent years has come up again. With GENTRIFICATION and the advent of YUPPIES, it has acquired the joke pronunciation *clarms* (to rhyme with charms).

clapometer An instrument used in various British and US television talent shows to measure the volume or duration of audience applause in judging the result of the contest.

classism Discrimination against people on the grounds of class; the discrimination may be either against the lower or the upper classes. The word is formed by analogy with racism, sexism, and ageism. *See also* SOCIAL CLASS.

clause. Clause Four A clause in the constitution of the British Labour Party. It pledges the party to work for the common ownership of the means of production, distribution, and exchange. By 1954 Hugh Gaitskell, then the leader of the party, was already doubtful that such a pledge, with its communist overtones, made sense in the context of British social institutions. His attempt to remove this clause was defeated in 1960 by the inflexible socialist diehards in the party. The clause still remains in the constitution but most members of the Labour Party pretend that it doesn't.

Clause 28 A clause in the Local Government Bill (1988) that prevents local authorities in the UK from presenting homosexuality in a favourable light. The bill became law despite vociferous opposition from bodies defending homosexuality and the principle of free speech.

clay pigeon British bicycle or motorcycle couriers' slang for pedestrians. In the crowded London streets, in which motorcycles are often the only vehicles able to move, pedestrians, weaving their way across a road, may be surprised and knocked down by a hastening courier.

clean, bright, and slightly oiled An old army slogan that dates back to World War I and the condition in which a soldier was expected to keep his rifle. Between the wars 'slightly oiled' became an allusion to minor drunkenness. During World War II the slogan again reverted to its military usage and was celebrated as the title of a book of wartime short stories (*Clean, Bright and Slightly Oiled*; Gerald Kersh, 1946).

clearing house of the world A description of the City of London. It comes from a speech (1904) by the British politician Joseph Chamberlain at the Guildhall in London:

> ... provided that the City of London remains, as at present, the clearing house of the World.

Although London has been able to maintain this position for nearly a century, doubts are now being expressed about its ability to remain the financial centre of the world. There are several reasons for this possible change of status: the collapse of London as a port and with it its entrepôt trade; Mrs Thatcher's 11 years as prime minister, during which a disinclination to allow the UK to become too tangled with the rest of Europe allowed other more European-based financial centres, such as Frankfurt and Paris, to take priority over London; and the high rents and hopeless traffic jams that characterize the British capital.

Cleveland Affair During the period April to July 1987, 121 children in Cleveland in NE England were diagnosed by Doctors Marietta Higgs and Geoffrey Wyatt as having been sexually abused. These two paediatricians, working at Middlesbrough General Hospital, based most of their diagnoses on the controversial technique known as reflex anal dilation (RAD). The number of cases was quite extraordinarily high and the rights of the parents were uncaringly swept aside, with 67 of the children being made wards of court and some 85 children being separated from their families by place-of-safety orders. The uproar created by the unprecedented scale of the diagnoses led to the setting up of a judicial enquiry, conducted by Lord Justice Butler-Sloss. Her report, published on 6 July 1988, by which time 98 of the children had been returned to their families, was highly critical of all the agencies concerned. The two doctors were severely criticized for their overconfidence in the results of RAD; the police and the social services were criticized for the disagreements and poor communications between members of their staffs. In general, a large number of recommendations were made to prevent a recurrence of this tragedy and the poor judgment that caused it. *See also* CHILD ABUSE.

cliff-hanger Figuratively, a state of affairs producing anxiety. From the early serial adventure films in which the hero was often left hanging by his fingernails to the top of a cliff in order to whet the cinemagoer's appetite for the next instalment.

Clio A statuette awarded annually in America for outstanding achievement in a radio or television commercial; the advertising equivalent of the film industry's OSCAR. Awards are made in several categories for acting, writing, production, etc. Clio is the name of the Muse of history and was also adopted as a pseudonym by the English essayist and poet Joseph Addison (1672–1719).

clip joint Slang for any night club, bar, or restaurant with over-inflated prices in which people are 'clipped', a euphemism for swindled, out of their money. Originally a clip joint employed hostesses to invite male customers to buy them exorbitantly priced drinks in return for the promise of sexual favours, which were, in fact, rarely given.

clippie A popular nickname for bus conductresses during and just after World War II, since they clipped or punched the tickets.

Cliveden set The name given to the right-wing politicians and journalists who gathered for week-end parties in the late 1930s at Cliveden, the country home of Lord and Lady Astor near Maidenhead in Buckinghamshire. They were alleged to favour the appeasement of NAZI Germany. The name first appeared in *The Week*, but the legend seems to be largely supposition. A second Cliveden set emerged in the early 1960s, when John Profumo (1915–), secretary of state for war, met and had an affair with Christine Keeler, a call girl who was also the mistress of a naval attaché at the Soviet embassy. They were introduced by Lord Astor at Cliveden. *See also* PROFUMO AFFAIR.

clock (1) British slang meaning to look at, sometimes implying a defensive or aggressive look. It has been in use since World War II. (2) To put back the milometer on a car so that it shows a lower mileage than the car has actually covered; a practice frequently perpetrated by dishonest second-hand car dealers. Originally confined to car dealers' jargon, it is now in common usage, which reflects the extent of the practice. (3) British police slang for the 36-hour period of questioning that follows a caution to the suspect in a particular inquiry.

clockwork The mind or brain. The term was used in the 1940s in US Black slang.
clockwork orange A person who has been brainwashed to change his or her personality; particularly someone whose individuality has been suppressed by conditioning. The term comes from the title of a novel (1962) by the British writer Anthony Burgess (1917–), which was popularized by a film (1971) made by Stanley Kubrick. Burgess took his book title from an earlier cockney expression 'as queer as a clockwork orange'.

clone (1) A group of cells or organisms derived from a single ancestor, by any asexual means, and therefore genetically identical. The word, taken from the Greek *klōn*, twig, was first used at the beginning of the 20th century by botanists for a group of plants obtained by grafting from a single parent stock. Later it was applied to cell cultures and – most recently – to exact copies of a gene (**gene clone**) manufactured by techniques of GENETIC ENGINEERING. In a non-scientific context, 'clone' has passed into the general language as a colloquialism for a group of people with identical tastes, habits, etc. (2) Male homosexual slang used by gay men to describe a fellow gay man dressed in a recognizably homosexual fashion. Originating in the Castro Street area of San Francisco, the archetypal clone uniform consists of faded, but well cared-for, denims, leather caps and moustahces. (3) Slang for a person of either sex who slavishly follows a particular mode of fashionable dress, especially that of a pop star. For example, a 'Michael Jackson-clone'.
clone-zone Male homosexual slang from the 1970s, for the area of town in which gay men meet. *See also* CLONE.

close. closed shop. *See under* SHOP.

close encounter An encounter with extra-terrestrial beings. Such encounters can be subdivided into various classes. A close encounter of the first kind, for example, implies a simple sighting of a UFO, while a close encounter of the third kind involves communication with the beings in question. *Close Encounters of the Third Kind* was the title of a science-fiction film made by Steven Spielberg in 1977. *See also* FLYING SAUCERS.

close your eyes and think of England or **lie back, open your legs, and think of England** Advice given to newly wed girls in the days when they were assumed to have had no previous sexual experience nor any desire to participate actively in their first. It is unlikely to have been said by a lady-in-waiting to Queen Victoria, or by Mrs Stanley Baldwin about her own nuptials, in spite of rumours to the contrary. However, a Lady Hillingdon wrote in her *Journal* (1912) " . . . I endure but two calls a week [from her husband Charles] and when I hear his steps outside my door I lie down on my bed, close my eyes, open my legs and think of England".

closed. We never closed Slogan associated with the Windmill Theatre in London, which, under its proprietor Vivian Van Damm, was the only London theatre to remain open throughout the whole of the BLITZ in 1940. The Windmill specialized in nude revues and later became a proving ground for such comedians as Jimmy Edwards and Tony Hancock. It did in fact close in 1964 for conversion to a cinema and again in 1981 for further conversion.

closet queen, closet homosexual *See* COME OUT.

cloth-cap A British epithet for the working classes, as in "Private medical insurance is not used by cloth-cap employees". The expession derives from the cloth (or flat) caps worn by many outdoor workers in the UK and also by the older generation of British manual workers as part of their non-working attire. Although the cloth cap has come to symbolize a working man, it also happens to be worn by the upper classes when out shooting. Indeed, between August 10 and December 10, the moors abound with men in cloth caps and 12-bores under their arms (they invariably do have private medical insurance). A subtle distinction between the two types of cloth cap is that the upper classes often have them made from the same material as their jackets or suits, whereas the working man's cloth cap is purchased as a single item that does not need to match anything.

clotheshorse A derogatory term for a person who is extremely interested in fashion and invariably looks elegant in very fashionable expensive clothes. A clotheshorse, in this sense, is not expected to have outstanding intellectual powers. The expression derives from the wooden frame on which clothes can be hung to dry.

clown. send in the clowns A phrase said when something goes wrong meaning 'keep things going' or 'the show must go on' (*see* SHOW). It comes from the circus where, if there was an accident or other problem, the clowns were sent into the ring to divert the audience. The term dates from the 1930s. 'Send in the Clowns' was the title of an evocative popular song by the US composer Stephen Sondheim (1930–) in his 1973 musical *A Little Night Music*.

club. Club Fed US slang for a federal prison. A pun on the Club Med (Club Mediterranée) holiday villages, it thus perpetuates the image of the prison sentence as a holiday.

Club of Rome An international group of economists, businessmen, scientists, etc., formed in 1972 in Rome, who periodically issue reports about the state of the world, particularly on environmental and related issues.

clunk, click A catchphrase coming from the advertising slogan 'clunk, click, every trip', used in a series of British television advertisements (featuring the disc jockey and television presenter Jimmy Savile) in the 1970s to persuade people to use seatbelts. The 'clunk' was the sound of the car door closing and the following 'click' was the seatbelt being fastened. As a result of the campaign, some museum directors had problems with graffiti, 'clunk, click, every trip' being written on glass cases containing chastity belts.

cluster bomb A weapon consisting of a large number of individual bombs that are dropped in a single stick. Cluster bombing was commonly used in the VIETNAM WAR, and is particularly employed against civilians, using incendiary or fragmentation devices.

Clydesiders A loosely attached group of left-wing MPs representing Glasgow and

Clydeside constituencies, who enlivened British politics and parliament from 1922 until they were much diminished in numbers by the 1931 election. Notable among them were John Wheatley, Campbell Stephen, Emanuel Shinwell, and best known of all James Maxton, who became chairman of the Independent Labour Party. They were notable champions of the poor and unemployed.

CND Campaign for Nuclear Disarmament. An organization formed by Bertrand Russell and Canon John Collins, Dean of St Paul's cathedral, in 1958 to campaign for the UK to cease to be a nuclear power. Its mass demonstrations and annual ALDERMASTON MARCHES were a feature of British life in the late 1950s and 1960s. Its **Committee of 100**, which included Russell and Collins and a number of people prominent in the arts, favoured non-violent direct-action protests, which led to a split in the movement and its subsequent decline.

CND revived in the 1980s, with the proliferation of nuclear weapons, under the former Roman Catholic priest Bruce Kent (chairman) and Meg Beresford (General Secretary). Both of these officers resigned in 1990, after a sharp decline in membership as a result of improved relations between East and West.

coalition government A government formed by two or more rival parties, usually in times of crisis, when party differences are set aside. Examples in the 20th century are those of Liberals, Unionists, and LABOUR under Asquith 1915–16 (re-formed under Lloyd George 1916–22); Macdonald's NATIONAL GOVERNMENT, 1931–35; and Winston Churchill's Coalition Government, 1940–45.

Coathanger A colloquial Australian name for the Sydney Harbour Bridge, which (rather like a coathanger) arches 52 metres (170 ft) above the water.

Cobber Kain Nickname for Flying Officer E. J. Kain, DFC, the first New Zealand air ace, who was killed on active service in June 1940.

COBOL Common Business Oriented Language. A computer programming language invented in the 1950s by Commander Grace Hopper of the US Navy.

Cobra (1) An international art group founded in 1948 and named from the first letters of the cities Copenhagen, Brussels, and Amsterdam, the homes of its founders Asger Jorn (1914–73), Pierre Alechinsky (1927–), and Karel Appel (1921–), respectively. They aimed to revive a form of expressionism, their 1944 Amsterdam exhibition treating animals and insects in a free abstract style. The group was dissolved in 1951. (2) A German wire-guided antitank missile with a range of 1600 metres.

Coca-Cola A trade name for a fizzy dark-brown beverage that was registered as a tradename at the end of the last century but during the 20th century became one of the most widely advertised international products. Future archaeologists might be forgiven for thinking that the beverage had the properties of a panacea, so widely will remains of its advertising be found. In fact, it consists of a secret formula devised by a US druggist from Atlanta, Dr John S. Pemberton, using extracts of coca leaves and cola nuts. Originally the extract from the coca leaves included a minute quantity of cocaine – enough to enable the advertisers to claim that it was 'an esteemed brain tonic and intellectual beverage' – but all traces of cocaine were removed from the formula in 1905. Nevertheless, the alternative name 'Coke', even then a street name for cocaine, remained in common use. In the 1920s the Coca-Cola company engaged in a long battle in the courts to prevent another company, the Koke Company of America, from using the name Coke. They won their suit, the Supreme Court ruling that the name Coke was exclusively owned by the Coca-Cola Company, which eventually registered this alternative name in 1945. Representatives of the company are now extremely reticent if any suggestion arises that might link Coke with cocaine.

Because the second half of the name, *Cola*, is not registered by the Coca-Cola Company, another drugstore dispenser, Caleb D. Bradham, devised, registered, and marketed a successful rival to Coca-Cola. Called Pepsi-Cola, because it was alleged to relieve dyspepsia, this product is now marketed by Cadbury-Schweppes as a successful rival to Coca-Cola. *See also* PEPSIFICATION.

Cocacolaization The unwelcome influence of US culture, represented by the beverage COCA-COLA, on European habits and institutions. The word was a French coinage, in response to the impact that Coca-Cola had on the consumption of wine in Europe, even in France itself. *See also* PEPSIFICATION.

Coconut Grove fire A disastrous fire at the Coconut Grove night club in Boston in 1942. The fact that exit doors opened inwards contributed to the death toll of 487, making it one of the worst fire disasters in US history.

cocooning US YUPPIE slang of the late 1980s for leading an unadventurous life, typically staying at home with the family in the evenings, rather than socializing, and ignoring the problems of the outside world.

coelacanth *See* OLD FOURLEGS *under* FOUR.

cohab Short for 'cohabiter'; a person who 'cohabits', *i.e.* a sexual partner with whom one lives but to whom one is not married.

Cointelpro Counter-intelligence programme; a campaign mounted by the US FBI in the 1970s to discredit people or organizations that were regarded as subversive.

cojones Courage, guts, balls. The Spanish slang word for balls in both the literal and metaphorical senses, it has become widely known to English speakers through the works of Ernest Hemingway. It is pronounced 'co-honays'.

coke Slang for cocaine, used throughout the English-speaking world. *See* COCA-COLA.

Coke frame US slang of the 1940s for a girl's body. The term originated in Black slang and is derived from 'Coke' (COCA-COLA), because of the characteristic shapely contour of the traditional Coca-Cola bottle.

cold. catch a cold (1) Business slang meaning to suffer a financial setback, usually temporarily. (2) British army slang meaning to catch gonorrhoea. (3) Predominantly US slang meaning that a man has his trouser zip is undone. *See also* CHARLIE'S DEAD.

cold-calling The practice adopted by some salespersons of making unsolicited visits or telephone calls to people's homes or businesses with a view to selling them goods or services. The intention is to catch the targeted customers and use persuasive selling methods to get them to commit themselves to buying things that they would not otherwise have bought.

Cold Comfort Farm A phrase used to imply that a particular domicile is untidy and comfortless. It is from the humorous book (1932) of this title by Stella Gibbons.

> If she intended to tidy up life at Cold Comfort she would find herself opposed at every turn by the influence of Aunt Ada. Persons of Aunt Ada's temperament were not fond of a tidy life.
>
> STELLA GIBBONS; *Cold Comfort Farm*, Ch. v.

See also under NASTY.

cold faxing *See* JUNK MAIL.

cold fusion Nuclear fusion produced at low temperatures. All present sources of controllable nuclear energy are obtained by nuclear fission – a process in which heavy atomic nuclei are split with the release of energy. Fission needs expensive uranium fuel, which is not widely available. The opposite process, nuclear fusion, is the coming together of light nuclei, such as hydrogen or helium nuclei, to form heavier nuclei. This process also produces energy – it is the source of energy in the Sun and in the H-bomb (*see* NUCLEAR WEAPON).

The problem is that nuclear fusion reactions can only be induced at very high temperatures and it is difficult to control them and extract the energy in a usable form. Controlled high-temperature fusion would be an immense advance; the fuel, water, is cheap and in effectively unlimited supply. Many millions of pounds (and dollars and roubles) have been spent on research using such devices as Zeta and the tokamak (*see* NUCLEAR REACTOR), so far with no practical success.

Even better would be cold fusion – fusion induced without large initial inputs of energy. Various methods of achieving this have been tried. In 1989, two scientists, Martin Fleischmann and Stanley Pons, caused a considerable stir in the world of nuclear physics by announcing that they had produced cold fusion simply by passing an electric current through heavy water using special electrodes of platinum and palladium. Unfortunately, later work failed to confirm their results.

cold-meat party In America, a funeral; originally Black slang dating from the 1940s.

cold mooner A person who believes that lunar craters were formed by the impact of meteorites rather than as a result of volcanic activity. Cold mooners believe that the core of the moon is cold. *See also* HOT MOONER.

cold turkey Originally US drug addicts' slang for the effects of sudden withdrawal from hard drugs, especially heroin. This causes the addict to suffer goose pimples, hot and cold flushes, sickness, and considerable discomfort often likened to that of a bad attack of flu. The expression is now widely used and has, since the 1980s, been frequently heard in the more general sense of withdrawal from any usual activity. It probably derives from the appearance of the goose pimples and the sufferer's resemblance to pallid cold turkey meat.

Cold War A political and ideological conflict between nations carried on by means of propaganda, threats, economic sanctions, and subversion but stopping short of actual fighting. The term was first used in America in 1947 by Bernard Baruch (1870–1965), the US politician and economist, to describe the post-war conflict between America and her western allies on one hand, and the Soviet bloc on the other: "Let us not be deceived – we are today in the midst of a cold war."

The Cold War came to an end in 1990 as a result of the economic collapse of Communism in Eastern Europe and the cooperation of America and the Soviet Union over Iraqi aggression in Kuwait. A **Cold Warrior** (or **Cold War Warrior**) was a politician who actively promoted or supported the Cold War.

Cold War Witch *See* IRON LADY.

come in from the cold To come back from a lonely, isolated, or neglected position into a position of safety, favour, or recognition. The phrase was popularized by the title of a novel by the British writer John Le Carré (David Cornwell, 1931–), *The Spy Who Came in from the Cold* (1963), about a British agent in East Germany who wanted to return to the West.

Colditz A German town on the river Mulde in Saxony, with a castle built by Augustus II poised on a cliff above the town. This castle was used during World War II as a maximum-security prison for prisoners-of-war held by the Germans, who regarded escape from it as impossible. Several attempts were made, however, by British and other servicemen; some were successful, as related in the film *The Colditz Story* (1954) and a later (1972) TV series. The castle was subsequently converted into a tourist attraction.

collage (Fr. *coller*, to glue) A work of art made up wholly, or in part, from pieces of paper, cloth, or other materials stuck onto a flat backing. The technique was first used to real effect by the Cubists, who introduced everyday objects into their easel paintings, *e.g.* Picasso's *Still Life with Chair Caning* (1912); it was also a feature of DADAISM (in the form of photomontage), Abstract Expressionism, and the work of such pop artists as Jasper Johns. In his later works Matisse abandoned paint altogether, using instead pieces of brightly coloured paper.

collective bargaining The process by which the members of a workforce are represented by trade-union officials to negotiate wage rates, working conditions, pay settlements, etc. Collective bargaining provides one of the main reasons for joining a union. Alone, a worker has very little ability to stand up to management in such negotiations; as a member of a large body, with the sanction of industrial action at its disposal, workers are able to negotiate better wages and work conditions. Unfortunately the weapon is double-edged. If unions become too powerful they can force managements to make uneconomic settlements in collective bargaining that makes their products uncompetitive in world markets.

Collins Street Farmer Australian slang for a businessman who invests in farms or the farming industry. Collins Street is a principal business street in Melbourne.

Colombo Plan An agreement to foster economic development in South and South East Asia. There are annual meetings to discuss economic development plans, such as irrigation and hydroelectric schemes. There is a continuing body which helps to provide technical assistance. It was founded in 1951 at Colombo, Ceylon (now Sri Lanka).

Colonel Bogey One of the best-known military marches, composed by Major F. J. Ricketts, bandmaster of the Argyll and Sutherland Highlanders (and from 1926 of the Royal Marines). Ricketts named it after a colonel with whom he had played golf in 1913; the colonel had a habit of whistling two notes before he played a shot (instead of calling 'Fore!') – these became the first notes of the march. A 'bogey' in golf is the standard number of strokes a good player would take for a particular hole. Ricketts did not write words for his march, but various versions were known to soldiers in both world wars. Perhaps the best known in World War II began:

Hitler has only got one ball,
Göring has two but they are small,
Himmler has something similar,
And Goebbels has no balls at all.

Colorado beetle *Leptinotarsa decemlineata*, also known as the potato beetle or bug. The beetle is native to Colorado, USA, where it had become an important potato pest by 1874. It made its first appearance in the British Isles in 1933 and has since spread through Europe. It is 10 millimetres long, orange-red or yellow in colour with black stripes on its wing covers. One female can deposit 300–500 eggs on the underside of potato leaves; both the adults and the larvae eat the leaves and the larvae also consume the tubers.

colour. colour man In America, a broadcaster on radio or TV who gives interesting background information (*i.e.* variety or 'colour') during a public broadcast.

colour supplement A glossy magazine using coloured illustrations, issued with a newspaper. For many years these appeared only with the so-called 'quality' Sunday papers, such as the *Sunday Times* and the *Observer*. During the 1980s, however, the Sunday editions of tabloids also published their own colour supplements, while, in a new departure, *The Independent* and *The Times* now issue magazine supplements on Saturdays.

combat neurosis *See* SHELL SHOCK.

combo Combination. (1) A small group of JAZZ musicians, rather than a larger band. This term was widely used in the 1930s and 1940s. (2) In Australia, a slang name for a couple consisting of a White man and an Aboriginal woman.

comb-out A thorough clearing out from offices works, etc., of men of military age for service in the Army, in accordance with the Military Service Acts of World War I.

come or **come off** Slang for having a sexual orgasm. Although neither the experience itself nor the use of this term to describe it is restricted to the 20th century (citations go back to the 17th century), it is mainly in this century that orgasms have been openly talked and written about in contexts that are not pornographic. James Joyce, D. H. Lawrence, and Doris Lessing are only three of many 20th-century writers to have used the term freely in descriptions of sexual intercourse. Moreover, in the 19th century it was assumed, or appeared to be, that the experience was restricted to the male of the species. Once it became acceptable to discuss female orgasms, the editors of women's magazines of the late 1970s and 1980s found that descriptions of the experience, and how to achieve it, produced highly saleable copy. Unfortunately, the pendulum swung a little too far in the direction of liberalization, so that many women felt deprived if they failed to achieve an orgasm on every occasion that they made love.

come again? Please repeat what you have just said: I either didn't hear you or failed to understand you. Popular at various times in both the UK and America, it probably originated in America before World War I. Although it is acceptable in most contexts, it has a certain brusqueness that verges on the impolite.

come home all is forgiven The spoof text of an agony column advertisement from *The Times*. Perhaps some originals on these lines were actually published, by spouses seeking the return of a missing partner or by parents reversing a decision that an offspring should never darken their doorstep again. But it has gained wide currency in a humorous context.

come out Short for **come out of the closet**, to declare oneself a homosexual. In the days when homosexuality was a criminal offence, prudence led many gays to conceal the nature of their sexual interests. They became known as **closet queens** or **closet homosexuals**, the connection with the secrecy of the closet being obvious. As anti-homosexual laws were relaxed, the need for secrecy disappeared and gays were able to 'come out'. The expression is also used with no sexual connotations, to mean to state one's real position.

come over with the onion boat A derogatory reference to someone regarded as an unwelcome foreigner. It originated in the 1920s, with onion sellers who crossed the Channel from Brittany with their strings of onions and their bicycles, to hawk them round the towns and villages of southern England. "You don't think I came over with the onion boats, do you?" is a commonly used form, likely to be said by someone who wishes to establish his long residency in the British Isles, usually despite appearances to the contrary. Variations on this theme include 'came over with an icecream barrow' aimed at Italians, and 'came over with the banana boat' relating to those of African descent who arrived by ship from the Caribbean in increasing numbers after World War II.

come up and see me some time The sexual innuendo forever associated with Mae West (1892–1980). The line first appeared in the play *Diamond Lil* (1928) but probably gained wider currency from the film version *She Done Him Wrong* (1933), in which Mae West says to the young Cary Grant, "Why don't you come up some time and see me? I'm home every evening." It may be that the phrase was already used on the streets of New York before *Diamond Lil*, but it was certainly Mae West who immortalized it. The male counterpart, **come up and see my etchings**, is probably of earlier origin, though it has been treated as spoof melodrama – the villain seducing the innocent maiden – for most of this century.

come with me to the Casbah A line that Charles Boyer was supposed to have said to Hedy Lamarr in the film *Algiers* (1938). He didn't – any more than Humphrey Bogart said PLAY IT AGAIN, SAM in *Casablanca* (1942).

this is where we came in Phrase said when something, such as a discussion, project, etc., starts to repeat itself, implying that the process should cease. It dates from the 1920s when cinemas started to give continuous performances – *i.e.* the programme was repeated throughout the afternoon and evening. A couple might enter the cinema part-way through the main film and watch the rest of the film and, subsequently, the first part of the same film up to the point at which they came in. They would then leave.

COMECON Council for Mutual Economic Assistance. An association set up by Stalin in 1949 to promote economic development of the member countries, which included the Soviet Union and the other communist countries of Eastern Europe, except Yugoslavia. Until 1953 the organization was largely a propaganda vehicle used by Russia for the economic exploitation of its satellite states. In later years the organization began to promote genuine mutual economic cooperation and development. In 1989, after the political reforms in Eastern Europe, COMECON announced that it would take account of market forces.

Comet The first commercial jet airliner. Manufactured by the DE HAVILLAND AIRCRAFT COMPANY in 1952, Comet 1 was withdrawn after two tragic accidents, in which many people died, which were shown to have been caused by metal fatigue. De Havilland modified the design and introduced the extremely successful Comet 4, which entered service with BOAC in 1958.

comfortably. are you sitting comfortably? A catchphrase used to introduce a story or a speech, often used to imply that the story or speech will be quite a long one. The expression is a shortened form of "Are you sitting comfortably? Then I'll begin . . . ", which was used to introduce the story that was regularly featured in the BBC children's radio programme *Listen With Mother* (first broadcast in 1950).

comic strip A sequence of drawings relating a humorous or satirical story in cartoon style. They appear in newspapers and magazines and longer ones are published as comic books. The modern comic strip first appeared in the *New York World* in 1896; drawn by Richard Telton Outcault, it was called 'The Yellow Kid'. Its success encouraged many followers on both sides of the Atlantic during the 20th century. Notable are the American 'Krazy Kat' (1910) by Richard Herriman and 'Peanuts' (1922) by Charles M. Schulz; the originally British 'Andy Capp' (1957) by Reginald Smythe is known on both sides of the Atlantic. *See also* ASTERIX; CHARLIE BROWN; JANE; PIP, SQUEAK, AND WILFRED; RUPERT BEAR.

Cominform Communist Information Bureau. An international communist organization, set up in 1947 under Soviet control to publish propaganda to encourage international communist solidarity. It also coordinated the policies of the communist parties of countries not under Soviet control. The members of the Cominform were the Soviet Union, Bulgaria, Czechoslovakia, Hungary, Poland, Romania, Yugoslavia, France, and Italy. In 1948 Yugoslavia was expelled for its failure to follow Soviet instructions but the Cominform was dissolved in 1956 in order to improve relations with Yugoslavia.

Comintern Communist International. An organization of world communist parties founded by Lenin in 1919 as an early stage towards the worldwide revolution of the proletariat. It was dissolved by Stalin in 1943 as a gesture towards his wartime capitalist allies.

comix A spelling of 'comics' favoured in the 1970s and 1980s by originators of low-budget underground publications for young people.

commando (Port. *commandar*, command) Originally armed units of Boer horsemen, who were well known for their daring during the South African War (1899–1902).

> Lord Kitchener's relentless policy of attrition was slowly breaking the hearts of the commandos.
> DENEYS REITZ: *Commando*, ch. xxvi.

In World War II the name was adopted for the units of specially trained British assault troops formed from volunteers to undertake particularly hazardous tasks; the name was also used for a member of these units.

Committee. **Committee of 100** *See* CND.
1922 Committee *See* CHANAK CRISIS.

common. **Common Agricultural Policy** *See* CAP.
Common Cause A US political pressure group founded in 1970 to influence the government to respond to what it regards as the wishes and requirements of the people as a whole, rather than to factional interests.
Common Entrance The exam taken by British 13-year-old prep-school boys seeking entrance to a public school. The exam was instituted in 1903 and is still in force. Latin, which used to be a compulsory subject, is now optional.
Common Market The popular name for the European Economic Community, set up in 1957. *See* EUROPEAN COMMUNITY.

Commonwealth *See* BRITISH COMMONWEALTH OF NATIONS.
Commonwealth Day *See* EMPIRE DAY.

communications satellite An unmanned artificial earth satellite, usually in a geostationary orbit, *i.e.* one in which the satellite completes its orbit in 24 hours and thus appears to remain stationary in the sky above the same place on thc carth's surface. Three such satellites suitably placed can provide a worldwide communications link enabling television broadcasting, telephone communications, and computer data to be exchanged between any points on the earth. Radio signals from a transmitting station on earth are beamed to the satellite, which retransmits them to a receiving station out of normal ground-wave or sky-wave communication with the transmitting station. The first active communications satellite was the US **Telstar 1**, launched in 1962. There are now large numbers of these satellites serving both governments and commercial interests.

communist bloc or **Eastern bloc** After the Russian Revolution (1917) many socialist parties in Europe became communist parties, owing varying degrees of allegiance to the Soviet Communist Party. After World War II many countries in eastern Europe, with the aid of Soviet troops, became communist states. These states, which included Bulgaria, Czechoslovakia, East Germany, Hungary, Poland, and Romania, signed the WARSAW PACT in 1955. Albania was a member of this pact from 1955 until 1968, when it left. Yugoslavia is sometimes regarded as part of the communist bloc, but was not a signatory of the Warsaw Pact and managed to maintain an independent foreign policy. In 1989 mass unrest culminated in the communist parties in Poland, Hungary, Czechoslovakia, Bulgaria, Romania, and East Germany losing power. When, in 1990, the Soviet Communist Party lost its monopoly of power, the communist bloc ceased to exist.

community. **community charge** A British local tax introduced by the Conservative government in 1989 (Scotland) and 1990 (England and Wales) to replace the domestic rating system formerly used by local authorities. The community charge is a flat-rate charge on every adult in the community and has therefore been called a **poll tax** (from Middle English *polle*, head), like that first introduced in 1377 and periodically thereafter. The government claims that the tax is fairer than the rates, as everyone who benefits from the amenities provided by the local authority shares the bill for providing them, rather than the whole bill being paid by property owners. Opponents of the tax argue that as everyone pays the same amount, irrespective of means, its impact is severest on the poorer members of the community. Exemptions are made for very poor families. The unpopularity of the community charge contributed to the resignation in 1990 of Margaret Thatcher as prime minister, all three of the candidates to succeed her promising to make changes to it if elected.
community medicine The medical specialty concerned with maintaining the health of communities. Also known in the UK as public-health medicine, it did not emerge as a distinct branch of medicine until after World War II, with the introduction of the NATIONAL HEALTH SERVICE. It includes such aspects of health care as preventive medicine (immunization, BIRTH

CONTROL, health visiting, mass screening tests, etc.) and monitoring special groups of the population, notably young children and the elderly.

commuter Someone who regularly travels to a town or city centre to work. The word became common in the UK in the 1950s but has been popular in America since the late 19th century. It is derived from *commutation ticket*, the US equivalent of a British season ticket.

compact. compact disc (CD) A plastic disc upon which sound is recorded, especially used for recording music with high fidelity. A 120-mm diameter disc stores more than one hour of music. The disc is made by impressing one of its sides with the master disc, thus transferring to it a series of tiny pits of varying depth in an outward spiral. This is then coated with a layer of reflective aluminium and another layer of plastic. The disc is inserted into a CD player, in which a light beam from a low-intensity laser is alternately reflected and scattered by the pits; the light-sensor converts the varying light intensity into digital signals which are converted by the high-fidelity amplifiers into music. The master disc is created by a reverse process in which the minute pits are inscribed into the plastic disc by the laser of a digital recording instrument. The advantages of the system are that as nothing mechanically touches the surface of the disc during playback, it does not wear with use; also, as the pits are covered by a layer of plastic, they are unaffected by scratching the surface or by deposits of dust. These two factors ensure continued high-quality sound reproduction. *See also* CD-ROM.

compact video disc A development of the COMPACT DISC, which stores both sound and pictures. The term is abbreviated to CVD.

company. Company, the US slang name for the CIA, the Central Intelligence Agency. It is the word used by insiders.

company man *See* ORGANIZATION MAN.

comparative advertising In America, the name used for an advertising technique in which a competing product is mentioned by name and compared unfavourably with the advertised item. In the UK, information of this type is referred to as **knocking copy**. *See also* BRAND X.

compassion fatigue A reluctance to give money or goods to charity. As charities have increased in number and a large number of appeals have been made to the general public on television and radio as well as by the older methods of door-to-door and street collections, the increasing widespread exposure has produced a feeling of indifference in some sections of the public. The demand for money for charities in the 1980s was created partly by financial cut-backs in various social services. The people who were being asked for money frequently did not have much themselves and compassion fatigue may partly be caused by an inability, as well as a reluctance, to donate.

Compiègne The town in N France on the River Oise in which Joan of Arc was captured by the English in 1430. In the 20th century the Armistice ending World War I was signed by the Germans in a railway coach in a clearing in the forest of Compiègne on 11 November 1918. On Hitler's insistence the document acknowledging the defeat of France was signed on the same spot by Pétain and Hitler on 22 June 1940.

complement. complementarity principle *See* QUANTUM THEORY.

complementary medicine *See* ALTERNATIVE MEDICINE.

comprehensivization The replacement of a selective system of secondary education with a comprehensive system, *i.e.* one in which children of all academic abilities attend the same schools (although there may be streaming within the individual school). In the UK, comprehensive schools were introduced on a wide scale in the 1970s, replacing the higher-level grammar schools and the less academic secondary modern schools. This change was subsequently held responsible for a general decline in academic standards. Progress towards total comprehensivization was halted in 1979, when Local Education Authorities were no longer obliged to abolish selective schooling.

computer A device, developed from principles laid down in the 19th century by Charles Babbage (1792–1871), for storing and processing information at high speeds. Babbage's mechanical contrivance (which was never actually completed until the Science Museum built it in 1991) foreshadowed an electronic model, **ENIAC** (Electronic Numerical Integrator And Calculator), developed during World War II at the University of Pennsylvania. An enormous machine using 20,000 valves, it was designed to solve a specific problem related to high-altitude trajectories. Similar valve-based machines were subsequently built in the UK and France. However, the real computer revolution began in the 1950s and 1960s, when advances in information theory and the emergence of first the transistor and then the integrated circuit transformed computer design. The first computers were massive and expensive machines owned and run by large industrial, government, or academic institutions, but during the 1970s and 1980s, silicon-chip technology enabled extremely powerful desk-top machines to become available at a very moderate cost. The original ENIAC device used decimal arithmetic; however, subsequent transistor-based computers have been based on binary arithmetic in which 0 and 1 are the only digits. These are represented electronically as a closed pathway and an open pathway, respectively, the transistor thus functioning as an on-off switch. The instructions that enable a computer to function are known as its programs. In general, the programs are known as computer **software**, while the electronic equipment itself is its **hardware**.

By the 1980s computers had become so ubiquitous that they had transformed many aspects of everyday life. Records of almost every kind, from the stock of tomato soup in the local supermarket to the owner of every car on the road, are now computer-held. Many processes, from bringing down a Scud missile to typesetting a book, are computer controlled. Most calculations, from one's bank balance to the orbit of spacecraft, are performed by computers. Children are made familiar with computers at six or seven, secretaries have to be able to operate computerized WORD PROCESSORS, and doctors write their prescriptions on desk-top computers. Together with AIRCRAFT and the CAR, computers are perhaps the artefacts that have made the greatest impact on human beings in the 20th century. But like cars and aircraft, their use is not without problems. Stockbrokers, for example, can program their computers to sell securites if the price falls below a specified level. In a slump, such as occurred on BLACK MONDAY, the computers can automatically fuel the decline by selling at lower and lower prices until they are stopped by overwrought stockbrokers.

computer crime Illegal activity connected with computers, especially the practice of gaining access to a computer and modifying the data or program in order to transfer money for personal gain. The crime is also called **computer fraud**. Other activities connected with computers may also be illegal – for example, breaching computer security (*see* HACKER) or destroying data (*see* COMPUTER VIRUS; TROJAN HORSE).

computer dating Matchmaking using computers. Subscribers to a computer-dating agency send in details of their personal characteristics, interests, likes and dislikes, etc., which are stored in a computer and electronically matched with those of other subscribers in order to select a number of potentially suitable partners. Since the late 1960s many companies offering this type of introduction service have been set up across the world.

computer game Any of various games played using a computer program, in which the participant(s) can manipulate images on a video screen (they are sometimes called **video games**). Computer games became popular in the 1970s; an archetypal one was SPACE INVADERS.

computer model A theoretical mathematical description of a complicated system used with a computer in investigating and forecasting behaviour in economics, meteorology, etc.

computer virus or **electronic virus** A class of pernicious computer program designed to interfere with the operation of computer systems. Although differing in detail, all viruses share two characteristics. Once installed on a system they can lie dormant, undetected by the user, until triggered by a predetermined combination of circumstances – for example, a virus might bc so triggered to become operative when the computer is switched on when the date is Friday 13th. Their effects, once triggered, range from the trivial (*e.g.* printing a message on the screen) to the disastrous (*e.g.* destroying the data held on the computer's hard disks). Their second characteristic is that, while dormant, they can replicate and run themselves on other computers via networks or 'infected' disks – hence the analogy with viruses. Computer viruses appeared in the late 1980s; so far, they have mostly been practical jokes and not especially harmful, but the potential for a major disaster clearly exists. As with real viruses, measures can be taken to prevent infection (*e.g.* only buying floppy disks from reputable sources) and, once a new type of virus has been detected, classified, and analysed, an antidote can be developed – an ever more complex task as the authors of the viruses become more devious. Computer viruses have such unlikely names as 'Jerusalem B', 'Pakistani', and 'Stoned'.

concentration camp A prison in which political prisoners or people of a particular minority group are held without trial. The term originated during the second Boer War, when the British held a large number of Afrikaners in such camps.

In Germany, the rise of the Nazis from 1933 was accompanied by the establishment of concentration camps to imprison socialists and communists and later such minorities as homosexuals, gipsies, Roman Catholics, and Jews. German camps at DACHAU, BELSEN, RAVENSBRÜCK, and BUCHENWALD were augmented by the camps at AUSCHWITZ and TREBLINKA in German-occupied Poland during World War II. The cruelty of the German guards, their use of slave labour, the extreme malnutrition, and the medical experiments on living prisoners have made the German concentration camps the most notorious establishments in world history. The conversion of some of them into extermination camps in which over 20 million prisoners died of disease, starvation, or deliberate murder (including 6 million Jews; *see* HOLOCAUST) has left an ineradicable stain on German history.

conceptual art Art as idea as opposed to an artefact. The term was applied to a variety of genres developed in the 1960s, including MINIMAL ART, performance art (or HAPPENING), BODY ART, and LAND ART. Marcel Duchamp (1887–1968) was the major influence on the movement, which developed as a reaction to the marketing of both classic and radical art as commodities in the 1960s. Conceptual art was arbitrary, transitory, and deliberately insignificant; it was encouraged to be uncontaminated by the traditional burdens of meaning, context, and – above all – monetary value. A confused product of a confusing era, it succeeded admirably in avoiding any of these burdens.

concert. concert party *See* FAN CLUB.
concert pitch The pitch, internationally agreed in 1939, in which A has a pitch of 440 hertz, to which musical instruments are usually tuned.

Hence figuratively **to screw oneself up to concert pitch** is to make oneself absolutely ready, prepared for any emegency or anything one may have to do.

conchy *See* CONSCIENTIOUS OBJECTOR.

Concorde The first and only SUPERSONIC airliner in regular service; it is the fastest passenger aircraft in the world. Developed at considerable cost by an Anglo-French consortium consisting of Aérospatiale and the British Aircraft Corporation during the 1960s, it made its maiden flight in 1969 and entered commercial service in 1976. It cruises at Mach 2 (twice the speed of sound), carries 100–139 passengers, and can reach Paris from New York in three and a half hours flying at a height of 18,000 m. There are hopes of repeating the successful Anglo-French collaboration on a new supersonic airliner for the 21st century, Concorde 2. The first supersonic airliner to fly was the Soviet Tupolev Tu-144, in 1968 (often known in the west as **Concordski**). This aircraft, however, has not been in regular service since its crash at the Paris Air Show in 1973.

concrete. concrete music (Fr. *musique contrète*) A form of music introduced in 1948 by Pierre Schaeffer (1910–) in which natural or man-made sounds are recorded on tape and subsequently distorted to create a composition of concrete (real-life) sounds, as opposed to the abstract sounds made by musical instruments.
concrete poetry or **concretism** Poetry in which words, word elements, and individual letters are set down in patterns and shapes rather than in conventional linear arrangement, the meaning of the poem being conveyed by its visual form rather than semantically. It was an experimental art form dating from the late 1950s.

condo In America, short for 'condominium' – a block of apartments in which individuals own the separate apartments and share the upkeep of the common areas. The individual apartments are also known as 'condos'.

condom A sheath-like contraceptive made from thin rubber and fitted over the penis during sexual intercourse. The condom, thought to be named after Colonel Condom, a British Guards officer, who was anxious to protect his men from venereal disease, has been in use since the early 18th century. The popularity of the condom as a standard contraceptive device declined in the 1960s with the widespread availability of the contraceptive PILL for women. However, as the undesirable side-effects of the Pill became better understood, the popularity of the condom increased in the 1980s. At the same time it was discovered that barrier contraceptives provide some protection against the spread of AIDS by sexual intercourse as well as against other sexually transmitted diseases. The British government embarked upon an advertising programme to promote the use of condoms, especially in casual sex, as a means of controlling the spread of Aids. Increased use of the condom has led to many new nicknames for the device. To 'French letter', 'rubber', 'Johnny bag', and 'Wellie' may now be added 'American sock'.

condomania An apparent obsession, especially by the British media, with CONDOMS in the 1980s as a result of the concern over the spread of Aids by sexual intercourse and a consequent increase in the use of barrier contraceptives.

condom fatigue A weariness of hearing too much about CONDOMS – a reaction to CONDOMANIA. The excessive publicity given to condoms in the late 1980s led not only to lack of interest in them but to a diminishing concern about the spread of AIDS.

Confucius, he say A 1920s catchphrase used as an introduction to a witty piece of advice or a social comment disguised in broken English as if it was inadequately translated from the *Analects*, a collection of sayings and conversations attributed to the pre-Christian Chinese philosopher Confucius (*c.* 551–479 BC). For example: "Confucius, he say man speaking to God, he praying; God speaking to man, he nuts." This way of presenting a joke was popular in the 1920s and 1930s on both sides of the Atlantic; it now has a period feel to it, although it is still used.

connection Slang for a drug dealer or pusher. It originated in the US drug-users' jargon of the 1950s and 1960s but is now widely used, especially of heroin dealers. It was heard by a wider audience in the 1970s when the films *The French Connection I* and *II* came out.

connectionism An approach to the theory of the brain, especially memory, based on the idea that information is stored by processing units consisting of extended sets of connected neurones (neural nets). It was developed in the 1980s; analogous ideas have been used in computer science. *See* ARTIFICIAL INTELLIGENCE.

conscience. conscience investment An investment of money that is restricted to companies whose activities and attitudes are not held to be morally objectionable by the investor. Different people have conscientious objections to different things. Companies can be objected to on the grounds that their conditions of employment are discrimatory (*e.g.* racist, sexist, or ageist), that their products are injurious to health (*e.g.* tobacco and alcohol companies), that their products have led to the unnecessary death or suffering of animals, either in the manufacturing processes or in research (*e.g.* fur companies or some cosmetic companies), that they manufacture armaments, or that they have connections with countries whose political regimes are in some way repressive. Conscience investment is also known as *ethical investment*.

conscientious objector One who takes advantage of a conscience clause in an act of parliament and so evades some particular requirement of the law in question. Once specially applied to those who had a conscientious objection to vaccination, since World War I it has come to mean one who obtains exemption from military service on grounds of conscience. Such people are also called *CO*s or *conchies*.

consciousness raising (CR) The process of developing self-awareness, political awareness, social awareness, and other forms of 'awareness', often by such means as ENCOUNTER GROUPS.

conservation area An area of natural, historic, or architectural interest that has been so designated under the terms of the Civic Amenities Act (1967). Once designated a conservation area, planning control is imposed on any major changes in the area, such as tree-felling, demolition of buildings, etc. In some cases government grants and loans are available to help to preserve the amenities provided by the conservation area.

Conservative. Conservative Party The party of the traditionalist right in the UK. Based on the legacy of such statesmen as Burke, Peel, and Disraeli, it has in the 20th century generally championed evolutionary rather than revolutionary change: reform where necessary, but always within the existing framework of the state and society. This makes it attractive not only to those content with the existing order but also to those suspicious of the more radical policies of its political opponents (until the 1920s the LIBERAL Party, thereafter the LABOUR Party: it is a feature of the modern Conservative Party that it has always enjoyed considerable working-class support. Often the party has vigorously opposed certain measures, only to accept them once enacted; the PEOPLE'S BUDGET (1909), the curtailment of the power of the House of Lords (1911), Irish HOME RULE (1886–1922), and the WELFARE STATE (1945–51) are the principal examples. At the beginning of the century, the party was dominated by the landowners (including the aristocracy), whose overriding interest was the maintenance of the social and political hierarchy at home and the Empire's supremacy abroad. As the Liberal Party declined after World War I, many of its supporters, faced with the alternative of Labour's prescriptive egalitarianism, moved to the Conservatives, thus injecting into it such principles characteristic of 19th-century liberalism as personal freedom, equality of opportunity, and (in contrast to Labour's state corporatism) the merits of capitalism and free enterprise. At the end of World War II, the Conservatives were convincingly rejected by the British electorate. A new mood swept the country after the deprivations of six years of war: the have-nots now demanded a fairer share of the country's wealth and the idealists of the Labour Party gave it to them in the form of the welfare state. The Conservatives survived by adaptation; this they did by a combination of BUTSKELLISM and shrewd self-interest. However it was achieved, the Conservatives managed to alternate with Labour as the governments of the 1950s, 60s, and 70s. The adaptation involved a marked change in the Conservative Party itself. The Old Etonian leaders, Harold Macmillan and Alec Douglas-Home, were replaced by grammar-school educated Heath and Thatcher (*see* THATCHERISM). It was said that the Conservative Party had changed from the party of estate owners to the party of estate agents.

the Conservative Party at prayer A description of the Church of England. The phrase comes from a speech by the Congregationalist minister Agnes Maude Royden (1887–1967), who said in 1917:

> The Church should no longer be satisfied to represent only the Conservative Party at prayer.

constructive total loss An insurance term that was defined by the Marine Insurance Act (1906). It is an insured item, such as a ship or cargo, that is not totally destroyed or lost but is so badly damaged that it is not commercially worth repairing, *i.e.* the cost of repairing it could not be justified by its value after repair. For insurance purposes, therefore, it may be treated as a total loss.

constructivism Russian artistic movement founded between 1917 and 1920 by sculptors Vladimir Tatlin, Antoine Pevsner, and Naum Gabo. Their works, constructed from such modern materials as plastic, steel, and glass, were 'engineered' as a celebration of machinery and technology, as explained in Gabo's *Realist Manifesto* (1920). The name 'constructivist' is derived from this aspect of their work. Although proscribed under Stalin, the constructivist's functionalist and utilitarian creed spread to Europe and America, particularly influencing the BAUHAUS movement in Germany and the DE STIJL movement in Holland.

consumer. consumerism The protection and promotion of the consumer's interests. The term was first coined in the 1940s in America and became much used from the mid-1960s with increasing public demand for safety, quality, and choice in consumer goods. In America, the movement was also known as *Naderism*, after one of its most vociferous leaders, Ralph Nader (1934–), a US lawyer who spearheaded many campaigns aginst dangerous and defective goods and challenged the power of the producers. By the early 1970s the issue of consumers' rights had become firmly established in many European countries, including the UK. The theory advocating the economic desirability of a high rate of consumption of goods and services has also, since the 1960s, been called consumerism.

Consumers' Association The name by which the British *Association for Consumer Research* is widely known. The association, which is a registered charity, is independent of any business or company, thus allowing it the freedom to praise or criticize goods and services without bias, in fulfilling its purpose of protecting the consumer. It publishes a monthly periodical, *Which?*, in which detailed reports are printed of tests on various goods and services, often indicating a 'best buy'.

consumer terrorism The practice, occurring mainly in the 1980s, of introducing poison or other dangerous substances into consumer products, typically into foodstuffs on supermarket shelves. It is sometimes done for purely malicious reasons but often involves extortion of money from the food manufacturers. For example, in 1989, following the discovery of two jars of baby food containing broken glass, Heinz destroyed 50 million jars of food rather than give in to a blackmail demand. Similar demands were made at the time to pet-food manufacturers. The practice led to the introduction by some companies of so-called **tamper-proof** containers, which have an indicator on the lids that shows whether the container has been opened.

contact. **contact lens** A type of lens worn directly over the eye to correct long or short sight and astigmatism, and to provide protection in some disorders of the cornea. The first glass contact lenses were made by Adolf Fick in 1887, but the great discomfort these caused made them unpopular. Modern contact lenses, developed by Kevin Tuohy in 1948, are made of plastic and are shaped to fit the eyeball. These plastic lenses can be hard (corneal), gas-permeable (allowing oxygen to permeate the cornea), or soft (hydrophilic). They are widely used for cosmetic purposes.

contact magazine A publication in which those wishing to find partners for sexual activities can advertise.

Contemptibles, Old Member of the BEF (British Expeditionary Force) of 160,000 men that left Britain in 1914 to join the French and Belgians against Germany. The soldiers gave themselves this name from an army order (amost certainly apocryphal) said to have been given at Aix on 19 August by the Kaiser.

> It is my royal and imperial command that you exterminate the treacherous English, and walk over General French's contemptible little army.

It is said by some that actually he called the BEF "a contemptibly little army", which is not nearly so disparaging.

The surviving veterans held their last parade at the garrison church of All Saints, Aldershot, on Sunday 4 August 1974, in the presence of Queen Elizabeth II, who took tea with them before their final dispersal.

continuity man or **girl** The person who ensures that every detail of costume, scenery, etc., is correctly repeated on successive shots of a film. As scenes are not necessarily shot in sequence, it is essential to maintain this continuity. Sometimes, inevitably, errors occur. In *The King and I* (1956) Yul Brynner's ear-ring comes and goes in successive shots. In *Genevieve* (1953) Kenneth More's pint of beer becomes a half as he walks to his table. In *The Adventures of Robin Hood* (1938) Errol Flynn takes a bite from a whole leg of mutton; in the next shot he is holding only the bone. In *The Desk Set* (1957) a bunch of flowers held by Katharine Hepburn turns from white to pink in successive shots. In *Anatomy of a Murder* (1959) Lee Remick magically changes out of a dress into slacks as she leaves a café, while in one of the most celebrated films of all, *Brief Encounter* (1945), Celia Johnson manages to remain completely dry after running through a downpour.

Contra (from Lat. *contra*, against) A supporter of the dictatorial regime of the Nicaraguan President Anastasio Somoza (1925–80), who was deposed in 1979 by the SANDINISTA National Liberation Front led by Daniel Ortega. Based in Honduras and Costa Rica, the Contras organized a series of guerrilla attacks aimed at overthrowing Ortega's government. President Reagan, who accused the Sandinistas of aiding rebels attempting to overthrow the government of El Salvador, was widely censured for his active support of the Contras from 1986 onwards.

contraception *See* BIRTH CONTROL.

contraflow A much-disliked and sometimes hazardous system used on motorways or other dual-carriageway main roads in which one carriageway is under repair. Traffic in both directions then has to use the remaining carriageway, with vehicles travelling in opposite directions being separated by traffic cones.

contract An agreement to pay money to have someone killed. In the early 1960s it was restricted to US underworld slang but has subsequently, through the influence of books and films, become familiar on both sides of the Atlantic in such phrases as 'put out a contract on someone'.

contract marriage A marriage in which the partners agree to stay together for a certain period, possibly with an option to renew the contract at the end of the period.

contrail Condensation trail. A vapour trail left by a high-flying aircraft, which is caused by the condensation of water vapour from the products of combustion in the aircraft's exhaust. If the temperature is sufficiently low the water vapour freezes into tiny ice crystals.

control. Everything's under control Originally a 1930s catchphrase, this became very popular in World War II as a form of reassurance for every situation in which reassurance was required. It implied that the situation, however dire, was not out of hand – which did not have to be true.

conurbation A large densely populated area formed by the growth and merger of adjacent towns and cities. As human populations have grown, the prehistoric village developed into the town; by the middle ages, cities had appeared. The conurbation is a 20th-century phenomenon in which uncontrolled ribbon development along the roads between a large city and its satellite towns and villages swallowed up the intervening countryside. In 1770 Lambs Conduit Fields were fields on the outskirts of London. 50 years later these had been engulfed and Islington Fields, some 3 miles N, represented the N edge of the city. Now, the old towns of Watford in the NW and Orpington in the SE (some 30 miles apart) have all been swallowed by the conurbation.

convenience food Pre-packed or precooked food, such as frozen or COOK-CHILL dishes, which can be ready for eating with the minimum of preparation.

conventional Describing weapons, warfare, power stations, etc., that operate by any means other than nuclear reactions. The US president Lyndon Johnson said in Detroit in 1964:

> Make no mistake. There is no such thing as a conventional nuclear weapon.

cook (1) To play JAZZ in an inspired way; a Black US term originating in the 1930s. (2) To prepare heroin for injection by dissolving it in a spoon over a flame. Until the 1950s, a HEP person was sometimes referred to as a **cooker**, possibly because of one or other of the above senses.

cook-chill A method of catering, usually for the mass market, in which food is cooked, fast-chilled, and later reheated before consumption. The advantages are obvious from the point of view of large institutions, such as schools, hospitals, and airlines, but some food experts are concerned that the cook-chill method of catering can lead to the spread of diseases and disorders, such as listeriosis (*see* LISTERIA), unless exceptional care is taken with the hygiene, temperature control, and duration of shelf-life.

cool (1) Unflappable, unruffled by events, as in the phrase **stay cool**, meaning to keep calm. **To lose one's cool** is to become angry or emotional. (2) Good, marvellous, socially acceptable. This sense originated among the US JAZZ musicians of the 1930s when it was used to describe their particular brand of progressive jazz. It then became the keyword of BEAT culture of the 1950s and of the HIPPIES of the 1960s and 1970s for the coolly detached attitude to life that they espoused. The use of this sense as a term of approval reflected a detachment based on the credo that anything connected with the established order was so unacceptable that even living in poverty was better than becoming part of it. (3) Not found to be carrying illegal drugs when searched by the police. The opposite, therefore, of HOT.

cool it! An injunction to relax or calm down. Originating as a teenager's phrase in America in the 1950s, it reflected the laid-back BEATNIK way of life – **keeping one's cool** under all circumstances, especially as a response to parental exasperation. It spread to the UK in the 1960s, by when it was familiar in the form **cool it, man!**

cool jazz A style of JAZZ that originated in the late 1940s on the West Coast of America. Restrained and rhythmically relaxed, it reflected the use of the word 'cool' to mean sophisticated in an unenthusiastically elegant way.

cool out Caribbean slang meaning to relax. This expression is now quite widely used among Black and White people in the UK.

Coordinated Universal Time (UTC) *See* GREENWICH MEAN TIME.

Copenhagen interpretation *See* QUANTUM THEORY.

copy To receive a radio or other transmission successfully. The term was originally slang used by CB radio enthusiasts, but has come into more general use.

copycat murder A murder in which many of the details of the crime resemble those of another widely publicized recent murder. With members of the public avidly requiring the media to provide coverage of the macabre details of every murder committed, it is not entirely surprising that a murderous thought should occasionally be converted into an actual murder by some unbalanced person who has read such an account. A less well-known phenomenon is **copycat suicide**, in which a well publicized and often gruesome method of killing oneself sparks off a series of further deaths by similar means.

Coral Sea, Battle of the A naval and air engagement fought between US and Japanese forces between 4 May and 8 May 1942, during World War II.

Cordobes, El (Sp. man from Cordoba) The professional name of the Spanish bullfighter Manuel Benitéz Pérez (*c.* 1936–). At the height of his fame in the 1960s, he was the highest paid bullfighter in history and was idolized by the Spanish people. Famous for his daring and his rapid reflexes, he broke records for the number of bulls killed in the ring. He retired in 1972 but made a comeback seven years later.

co-residence Residence at an institution, especially a university, where men and women share the same building. Co-residence at British colleges became an issue in the 1970s.

Corfu incident In 1923 Italian forces under Mussolini bombarded and held Corfu in retaliation for the murder by Greek soldiers of an Italian delegation sent to define the Greek-Albanian border. Under pressure from Britain and France, the League of Nations managed to restore Corfu to the Greeks.

Corgi and Bess The nickname used in broadcasting circles for the Christmas message to the British nation made by Queen Elizabeth II. The annual event is broadcast on both radio and television with the televised version usually featuring one or more of the royal household's Welsh corgi dogs. The name is a pun on Gershwin's opera *Porgy and Bess* (1935).

Cornish pasties British pejorative slang of the 1980s for a style of shoes, particularly men's shoes, that are wide, solid, and sensible with heavy-duty stitching and thick crepe soles; the shoes are so-called because they resemble the eponymous meat and vegetable pies. They are often worn by such social sub-groups as 'alternative' or 'green' enthusiasts.

Cornwell Badge A badge awarded to BOY SCOUTS for an act of bravery or sustained brave conduct, for example in overcoming a physical handicap. It is given in honour of J. T. Cornwell, a 15-year-old boy in the Royal Navy who won the VC for outstanding bravery at the Battle of JUTLAND (1916). He died of his wounds one year after the battle.

Coronel A Chilean port off which a naval battle was fought in November 1914 during World War I. *See* FALKLAND ISLANDS, BATTLE OF THE.

Coronation Street A British television serial produced by Granada Television. Possibly the longest-running TV drama serial in the world, the first episode was shown on 9 December 1960; in 1990 the 2000th episode was broadcast. It deals with the lives of people living in a terraced street in an industrial area of Manchester in NW England. *See also* ARCHERS, THE.

corporate. **corporate advertising** Advertising that aims to promote and publicize not only a particular product but also the company or conglomerate of companies that manufactures it. In this way the company projects a desirable **corporate image** of itself – reflecting, for example, its concern for the environment or some other aspect of its outlook that is designed to attract public support.

corporate raider A company or person who purchases a significant number of shares in another company with a view to making a take-over bid.

correctional facility US euphemism for a prison, which was recommended in a 1970 report of a committee reviewing the US prison system. At the same time the prison guard became a **correctional officer**.

Corregidor An island at the entrance to Manila Bay, Luzon, in the Philippines. Because of their strategic positions, Corregidor and BATAAN were chosen by the American general, Douglas MacArthur, as the main defensive positions after the Japanese invasion of the Philippines in December 1941. After the fall of Bataan, on 9 April 1942, US and Philippino forces held out for 27 days on Corregidor under constant aerial and artillery bombardment, finally capitulating on 6 May. In March 1942, General MacArthur had left Corregidor with the pledge "I shall return". This pledge was redeemed when the island was recaptured by US forces in 1945. The island was designated a national shrine in 1954 and is the site of the Pacific War Memorial. The Malinta Tunnel, which served as hospital, shelter, and General MacArthur's headquarters, still survives.

corridors of power Collectively, the ministries in Whitehall and their top-ranking civil servants. The phrase was first used by C. P. Snow in his novel *Homecomings* (1956) and gained speedy acceptance. He used it as the title of a later novel, *Corridors of Power* (1964).

> Boffins at Daggers Drawn in Corridors of Power.
> *The Times* (Headline 8 April 1965)

corset In the UK, an economic measure to 'constrict' the growth of bank deposits (introduced by the government in the late 1970s in order to control the money supply).

Cosa Nostra *See* MAFIA.

cosmic string A theoretical one-dimensional warp, in the space-time continuum, of vast length and mass but of sub-microscopic thickness. Scientists have suggested that such warps are residues from the period during which the universe was in its infancy. The theory has been postulated that when cosmic strings form themselves into loops, these loops may form the basis of galaxies.

cosmo-. cosmodog A dog that has been sent into space for experimental purposes. In March 1966 two Soviet cosmodogs, Veterok and Ugolyok, were rocketed into orbit in Cosmos 110 and after 22 days in space were brought back safely back to earth. This created a record for living creatures in space.

cosmonaut (Gr. *kosmos*, universe; Lat. *nauta* sailor) Another name for an ASTRONAUT, used especially of Soviet astronauts. The first manned spaceflight was made by Major Yuri Gagarin of the Soviet Union in 1961. He landed safely after orbiting the earth in 89 minutes at altitudes ranging from 110 to 188 miles.

Cosmos A range of scientific and military SATELLITES put into orbit by the Soviet Union.

Costa (Sp. and It. coast) With the advent of cheap air travel and the relative affluence of the UK's working population, since World War II foreign travel has become increasingly common. Factory workers, who before the war were lucky to manage a few days in digs at damp and rather dreary British seaside towns, have since the war flooded to sunny Mediterranean coastal resorts, where large hotels catering for families have sprung up to accommodate them. Favourable rates of exchange with Spain have encouraged the Spanish tourist industry to specialize in providing traditional English fare and entertainments at their resorts, to ensure that the gastronomically cautious British will feel at home. The main Spanish resorts are situated on areas of coast line, which have been given these names:

Costa Brava The Mediterranean coast between France and Barcelona, including such resorts as Tossa del Mar, Blanes, and Palamos.

Costa Dorada The Mediterranean coast between Barcelona and Valencia, including Tarragona and Sagunto.

Costa Blanca The Mediterranean coast between Valencia and Alecante, including Javea, Denia, and Benidorm.

Costa del Sol The Mediterranean coast between Gibraltar and Malaga, including Marbella, Fuengirola, and Torremalinos.

Costa de la Luz The Atlantic coast between Gibraltar and Portugal in the Gulf of Cadiz.

The word *costa* is also used facetiously in English. For example, the S coast of England is sometimes called the **costa geriatrica**, because so many elderly people retire there. The Costa del Sol is also known as the **costa del crime**, as many British criminals who have escaped capture live there, exploiting loopholes in extradition arrangements.

cost-push *See* INFLATION.

cot death *See* SUDDEN INFANT DEATH SYNDROME.

cottage British and Australian slang for a public lavatory. It has been part of male homosexual jargon since the 1950s and 1960s as this was a typical pick-up place for male homosexuals before the anti-homosexual laws were relaxed in 1967.

> There are those people who would like to see public lavatories as cosy as cottages so they can loiter with new friends.
> *The Independent*, 3 November 1990.

Cotton Club The JAZZ club in Harlem, New York, which became the world's most famous venue for hot music in the 1920s. Among the many bands that played there perhaps the best-known was that of Duke Ellington. The inspired playing and the glamorous (and sometimes notorious) clientele have assured it a permanent place in the history of jazz.

couch potato US slang of the late 1980s for a lazy greedy person, whose favourite occupation is to lie in front of the TV all day eating and drinking. The expression is now used in most English-speaking countries. *See* EXERCISE IS BUNK.

Couéism A form of psychotherapy, dependent upon auto-suggestion, propagated by Emile Coué (1857–1926), a French pharmacist. The key phrase of his system was: "Every day, and in every way, I am getting better and better."

coughs and sneezes spread diseases An advertising slogan dating from the early part of World War II, in a campaign by the Ministry of Health to restrict the number of days lost by war workers as a result of minor ailments. Large amounts of money were spent to persuade the public not to sneeze on one another, especially in buses, tubes, and air-raid shelters. The associated injunction was "trap the germs in your handkerchiefs".

council. council house A house owned by a local town or district council, which is rented out, unfurnished, at a lower rent than it would command in the private sector. Council houses are much in demand and a waiting list exists for suitable and deserving tenants. Suitability is usually assessed by a points system. Controversially, the Conservative government, pursuing its policy of creating a property-owning democracy, began to sell off council houses in the 1970s, thus reducing the total stock of such dwellings.

Council of Europe A body constituted in 1949 to secure a greater measure of unity between the European countries, the member countries being the UK, France, Italy, Belgium, the Netherlands, Sweden, Denmark, Norway, the Republic of Ireland, Luxembourg, Greece, Turkey, Iceland, Germany, Austria, Cyprus, Switzerland, Malta, Portugal, Spain, and Liechtenstein. The Council consists of a Consultative Assembly, a Committee of foreign ministers, a Parliamentary Assembly (with members from national parliaments), and a European Commission investigating violations of human rights. It was founded at Strasbourg, where it still has its headquarters.

countdown The exact timing of the start of a crucial operation by counting backwards from a given number to zero. The word was coined by the German film director Fritz Lang for a rocket-launching scene in his science-fiction film *Frau im Mond* (The Woman in the Moon; 1929); after World War II it was used routinely in America in timing the launch of rockets and other missiles and – still later – in the US space programme. Its usage is now extended to general contexts in which critical timing is relevant.

counter. counterculture A culture with beliefs, values, and mores that are at variance with those of the established society. The word, which became current in the late 1960s with the advent of the HIPPIE movement, is applied to both a way of life that rejects the social norms and the people who adhere to it. Some aspects of the hippie counterculture, such as concern for the environment and the ethic of nonviolence, have since become more acceptable to western thinking. *See* ALTERNATIVE.

counter-intuitive Describing an idea, theory, proposal, etc., that (according to the speaker) seems unreasonable or unwise; literally, it goes against the speaker's intuition. It is bureaucratic jargon, originating in the US Pentagon, for something that no reasonable person would believe or support.

under the counter A phrase that became current in World War II, to denote a common practice of dishonest tradesmen. Articles in short supply were kept out of sight, or under the counter, for sale to favoured customers, often at enhanced prices. *See also* BLACK MARKET.

country. a country fit for heroes *See under* HERO.

country-and-western A form of US music based on the folk songs of the White rural South and West and ultimately derived from the musical tradition of the English settlers in the South. The first commercial recordings of Southern string-band music were made in the 1920s but the term 'country-and-western' did not appear until the 1960s, by which time some Western cowboy songs had been incorporated. Although embracing many regional styles, country-and-western is now most widely associated with sentimental, often mournful, ballads accompanied by electronically amplified string instruments, particularly guitars. Typical themes are love, divorce, and separation by distance from loved ones. The centre for country music is NASHVILLE, Tennessee.

Your Country Needs You A slogan used for recruiting British troops during World War I, used as the caption to a famous poster showing the then war secretary, Lord Kitchener of Khartoum (1850–1916), pointing at the reader (*see* KITCHENER'S ARMY). The powerful image was much copied elsewhere; in America a similar poster showed Uncle Sam pointing and saying "I want **you** for the US army". The caption became a catchphrase and exhortation to anyone who had a difficult or dangerous job to do for the public good. Despite the success of the recruiting campaign, Kitchener lost power in the early stages of the war, and time has not been kind to his reputation. Nevertheless, in the words of Margot Asquith:

> If Kitchener was not a great man, he was, at least, a great poster.

County Hall A large building on the S bank of the Thames by Westminster Bridge, designed by Ralph Knott for the London County Council and opened in 1933, although it was not completed until 1963, when it became the home of the GLC. When the GLC was abolished in 1986 the building became empty. Plans to convert it into a hotel came to nothing through failure to raise the necessary money. *See also* RED KEN.

Coupon Election The General Election of 1918, when Prime Minister Lloyd George and Chancellor of the Exchequer Bonar Law sent a certificate or coupon to all candidates supporting the continuation of the wartime coalition. The coupon scheme was an attempt to capitalize on Lloyd George's reputation as a war leader, it being calculated that any candidate who could produce this sign of the Prime Minister's endorsement would achieve favour with the electorate. The coupon was rejected by those Liberals who had resigned with Asquith in 1916 and by the Labour Party. As expected, the polls saw a decisive victory for those who accepted the coupon (known as *couponeers*).

Courtauld Institute of Art A gallery and college for the study of art donated to London University in 1931 by Samuel Courtauld (1876–1947), the great-nephew of the founder of the chemical manufacturing firm of that name. It was originally housed in his mansion in Portman Square, together with his collection of impressionist paintings. The collection, which has been augmented by several bequests, moved in 1958 to Woburn Square, and in 1990 to the west wing of Somerset House, which was formerly occupied by the General Register Office of births, marriages, and deaths.

cover. cover one's ass US slang meaning to concoct an excuse or alibi in advance in order to avoid taking the blame for something. The phrase originated in the 1960s among US troops in the VIETNAM WAR and later became part of general US slang; it became current in the UK in the 1980s.

cover the waterfront US expression meaning to discuss in depth, cover all aspects of a topic. It originates in the title of a book by Max Miller, a US journalist, in 1932, dealing with the exposure of corruption on the waterfront.

covert action or **covert operation** Secret and usually illegal activities by the police or the intelligence forces. *See also* COINTELPRO.

cow. cowabunga An Australian interjection expressing triumph or elation; originally a surfer's cry when riding a wave. The introduction of Australian soap operas to British television and the subsequent enthusiasm for the Australian life-style has led to its adoption by the youth culture in the UK. It also became a catchphrase of the TEENAGE MUTANT NINJA TURTLES.

> Cowabunga! Wanna get wised up on those big green guys who live in the sewers? Check out Sarah Edghill's awesome turtle guide and you'll be the coolest dude on the block!
>
> *TV Times* (17–23 November 1990)

cowboy (1) 1950s slang for a wild and irresponsible young man, usually said by an older man or a policeman. This usage reflects the image of the Western cowboy hero as well as the 1930s gangster's use of the word to mean undercover or illegal. (2) British slang for a bad workman, someone who does a slapdash or botched-up job, as in the phrase 'a cowboy builder'.

> A sign on the side of a builder's van read: Patel and Patel; Builders and Contractors – You've tried the cowboys, now give the Indians a chance.

cowhorns British slang for the high curved handlebars on a motorcycle or bicycle. A synonym for APEHANGERS.

coyote US slang of the 1970s and 1980s for an unscrupulous person who robs, or even kills, illegal immigrants who cross the border from Mexico into North America.

CR *See* CONSCIOUSNESS RAISING.

Crabb Affair The disappearance in 1956 of Commander Lionel 'Buster' Crabb, a frogman with the Royal Navy who, while apparently working independently, explored the underside of the Soviet cruiser, *Ordjonikidze*, in Portsmouth harbour. The cruiser was in Portsmouth having brought the Soviet leaders Bulganin and Khrushchev to England for an official visit. The British government persistently claimed that he had not been working for them but that he had drowned while involved in this exploit. However, reporters from *The Times* discovered that the hotel in which Crabb had stayed while working in Portsmouth had been visited by senior detectives, on the orders of the Chief Constable, where they had removed all record of Crabb's stay and told the staff not to discuss the matter. There were rumours that Crabb was alive behind the IRON CURTAIN. There was never any satisfactory explanation for the incident. Speculators suggested he had defected to the Soviet Union, drowned by accident, or been killed by British agents when it was realized that British interest in the visiting ships might prove embarrassing.

> It would not be in the public interest to disclose the circumstances in which Commander Crabb is presumed to have met his death.
>
> ANTHONY EDEN, May 1956 in reply to repeated opposition questions about the incident.

crack (1) Slang for a purified and highly addictive form of cocaine. The name probably reflects the crackling and fizzing noise the substance makes as it burns. A **crack house** is an establishment in which crack is made or smoked. *See also* ANGEL DUST. (2) British and Irish slang for what's happening now, the action, the news, as in the phrase 'What's the crack?' This is possibly derived from the verb **to crack on**, meaning to talk. (3) A slang word meaning to share out or split up.

crackback In American football, a block made at knee level, usually by a pass receiver blocking a defensive back from the blind side. It is a legal play, but often causes knee injuries.

cracker-barrel US slang meaning unsophisticated, rustic: used in such phrases as **cracker-barrel philosophy** or **philosopher**. It derives from the habit of people in rural areas or small towns of gathering around the cracker barrel (biscuit barrel) in the general store to exchange news and gossip, philosophize, etc.

Cracker Night Australian slang, originally for EMPIRE DAY (May 24), which was celebrated with fireworks (crackers) and bonfires, but later for Commonwealth Day and the Queen's birthday. However, the restrictions on the use of fireworks has meant that Cracker Night is now largely ignored.

get cracking Slang expression meaning to start to do something as quickly as possible, to get a move on. It originated as RAF slang in the mid-1920s, and was widely used during World War II.

Cranwell A village in Lincolnshire in which the Royal Air Force College (founded 1919) is situated. Cranwell bears roughly the same relationship to the RAF as Sandhurst does to the Army and Dartmouth does to the Navy.

crash (1) also **crash out**. A slang expression meaning to sleep, often after taking drugs. This was a very popular HIPPIE expression of the 1960s and 1970s, probably because smoking cannabis can induce sleep. Originally, it was World War II forces slang. A **crash pad** is a place to sleep overnight. (2) To come down from the 'high' of an illegal drug. (3) Short for **gatecrash**, that is to arrive uninvited at a party. This has been a popular form of entertainment with young people since the 1960s. (4) A sudden drastic failure of a COMPUTER system, usually resulting in the loss of data; also used in this sense as a verb.

crater US slang for die or become defunct. Originally, the verb was used in World War I meaning to destroy something by riddling it with craters, *i.e.* by shelling it.

Crawfie The name given by the media to Miss Marion Crawford, the governess of Queen Elizabeth and Princess Margaret. Her sentimental article 'The Little Princesses', published in the magazine *Woman's Own*, was regarded by the Palace as an indiscretion and she subsequently fell from favour.

crawl A list of titles, credits, etc., moving slowly down a screen, as at the end of a television programme.

crawler lane A traffic lane on an uphill section of a motorway, or other main trunk road reserved for slow-moving heavy traffic.

crazy. **Crazy Gang** A group of British music-hall comedians. Their comedy and variety act, which involved mixing with the audience and riotous impromptu routines, was highly successful. The Gang comprised three pairs of comedians: Bud Flanagan (1896–1968) and Chesney Allen (1894–1982), famous for their many songs, including 'Underneath the Arches'; Jimmy Nervo (1890–1975) and Teddy Knox (1896–1974); and Charlie Naughton (1887–1976) and Jimmy Gold (1886–1967). The Crazy Gang first appeared on the stage of the London Palladium in 1932 and starred there almost continuously until 1940. After the war Chesney Allen retired, and the Gang reformed at the Victoria Palace in 1947, with Eddie Gray, until they disbanded in 1962.

crazy like a fox The title of a book (1945, by S. J. Perelman); the phrase is an ironic corruption of 'cunning as a fox'. "Crazy! He's not crazy. He's crazy like a fox."

crazy mixed-up kid A US epithet used to describe the first post-war generation of teenagers. Relieved of the pressures of war, many teenagers found they could get away with doing very little by pretending to suffer from post-war trauma, resulting in confusion, especially in making moral distinctions, and mild psychological problems. Some crazy mixed-up kids extended their craziness and became HIPPIES; others abandoned it and became bank managers.

cream-crackered Rhyming slang for knackered, exhausted. *See also* CATTLE-TRUCKED.

creative. creative accounting A facetious expression indicating that some balance sheets or profit and loss accounts have been compiled in such a way that, without actually being fabrications, they present the information the accountant wishes to present but do not give a true indication of the state of the business concerned.

creative evolution The theory propounded by Henri Bergson (1901) in his book *L'Évolution creatrice* that a life force (ÉLAN VITAL) motivates a creative urge in man to accelerate his evolution, rather than waiting for what G. B. Shaw called the 'chapter of accidents' that brings about change in the form of natural selection, as set out in Darwin's theory of evolution. Modern biologists do not accept this concept.

creature-feature A mildly derogatory insult used in the school playground. It derives from the film-business term creature-feature, meaning a horror film.

cred Short for STREET CREDIBILITY.

credibility gap The discrepancy between what is claimed or stated to be the case, especially by those in authority, and what are the facts of the case. The phrase originated in America and is attributed to US President Gerald Ford in 1966, when he was a US Congressman, referring to the increasing involvement of America in the VIETNAM WAR, which was denied by Lyndon Johnson's administration.

credit Polonius's injunction "never a borrower or lender be" (*Hamlet*, I, iii) has not been taken very seriously in the affluent countries of the West during the second half of the 20th century. Credit is, in fact, the financial basis of much of this affluence. To buy a house, a newly married couple in the UK obtains credit from a building society, in which the house itself is the surety for the loan and a proportion of the couple's combined incomes is pledged to pay the interest and repayments for the next 25 years. If they have a car, it is likely that it, too, has been purchased on credit terms, *i.e.* a relatively small down payment and several years of pledged repayments. When the car is finally paid for it may well be virtually valueless. The furniture in the house, the television set, the cooker, and many other items that cost over £100 or so, will also often have been purchased on credit. The 20th-century philosophy is that one should enjoy the trappings of affluence while one is young. It may be a great comfort to be able to buy a washing machine for cash in one's 40s, but most families need one most when the children are small – and then it can only be afforded by borrowing.

This reversal of 19th-century frugality, which was based on the belief that one should only buy what one can pay for, has been encouraged by banks and credit companies for whom the credit boom has provided an enormously lucrative market. The high interest rates that consumers have to bear to enable politicians to maintain stable economies have brought such lavish profits to the lenders that they are able to be less than prudent in making their loans. Losses that arise when borrowers fail to make repayments are offset partly by repossession of the purchased items and partly by the large profits made on the satisfactory repayers. While many have benefitted by being borrowers, easy credit has also been a considerable source of distress for those who are dispossessed, especially those whose houses are repossessed by building societies when the unfortunate owners are made redundant and are unable to finance their mortgages.

credit card A plastic magnetized card usually issued free to creditworthy customers, representing the holder's right to credit from a particular finance company, bank, shop, etc. (with the amount of credit extended being dependent on the individual's CREDIT RATING). Their use has become widespread in the 1970s and 1980s, and they are indispensable for certain transactions, such as ordering goods by telephone, theatre bookings, and airline reservations. They can also be used to withdraw money from Automatic Cash Dispensing Machines. Some banks, however, now charge an annual fee to their cardholders, and retailers are now authorized to offer discounts to cash-paying customers. Both measures have reduced the advantage of paying for goods or services by 'plastic'. *See also* PIN.

credit rating The creditworthiness of an individual or company. Traditionally, banks have provided trade references in confidence but recently **credit reference agencies** have appeared, collecting information from such sources as bankruptcy proceedings, debt collectors, hire-purchase companies, etc., which they sell to anyone interested for a fee.

creep. CREEP An acronym used by critics for the *Committee to Re-elect the President* at the time of the WATERGATE affair. (The Committee itself preferred the abbreviation CRP).

creepshow Teenagers' slang meaning frightening or awful. Its use was inspired by the 1982 film of that name. It is an elaboration of the word creepy.

creep-up call The practice of tradesmen, deliverymen, and others who do not make their presence obvious to householders when they make a house call. For example, they may knock only very softly, then leave a note to say they have called but received no reply. In this way they can claim to have covered their quota of calls without having done the work.

crew (1) British slang for a gang of aggressive youths, such as SKINHEADS or football hooligans, that has been used since the 1960s by the youths themselves. (2) US slang of the 1980s for a group of young people, used primarily of musicians or dancers rather than hooligans.

crew cut A form of haircut popularized by US athletes, particularly college rowing teams, in the decade following World War II. The hair is cut very short all over and brushed upright on top, reminiscent of a hedgehog.

crinklie *See* WRINKLIE.

Crippen murder The murder of Mrs Crippen (Belle Elmor) by her husband Dr Hawley Harvey ('Peter') Crippen in 1910. Mrs Crippen was poisoned by means of hyoscine hydrobromide, after which her dismembered and filleted corpse was buried beneath the cellar of the family home in Holloway, North London. Crippen and his mistress, Ethel Le Neve, fled the country with Miss Le Neve disguising herself as a boy in the care of her uncle, 'Mr Robinson'. By a circuitous route they boarded the cargo ship *Montrose*, which was bound for Canada. However the captain of the ship suspected them of being Crippen and Le Neve and after a series of dramatic wireless messages from ship to shore and a chase across the Atlantic by Scotland Yard detectives, Crippen was arrested when the ship docked in Canada. Crippen is remembered for being the first person to be arrested by means of wireless telegraphy.

Cripps mission A mission to India in 1942, led by Sir Stafford Cripps (1889–1952), on behalf of Churchill's wartime coalition government. Threatened by Japanese invasion, India was offered by Cripps complete independence with dominion status after the war in exchange for immediate cooperation in resisting Japan and winning the war. Gandhi described the offer as "a post-dated cheque on a failing bank"; the offer was turned down by the Indian Congress Party and Gandhi and other Congress leaders were imprisoned until 1944, when they were released to discuss independence and partition.

Croix. Croix de Feu (Fr. fiery cross) An extremist Fascist movement formed in France by a Colonel de la Rocque. *See* FASCISM.

Croix de Guerre (Fr. cross of war) A French military decoration, instigated in 1915 for gallantry in battle. The different grades correspond to the level of the dispatch that records the courageous act for which it is awarded. A warship receiving the Croix may fly an appropriate pennant. During World War II several Croix were awarded: in 1939 (by the French government), in 1941 (by Pétain and the VICHY government), and in 1943 (by Giraud of the Free French in North Africa). In 1944 the French National Committee of Liberation declared that only the 1939 Croix was valid.

crooning A sentimental type of singing, which began in about 1929 and rapidly became popular. The singing is very soft "somewhere near the written notes, but preferably never actually on those notes" (Eric Blom), and its effects depend largely on electrical amplification.

crop circles Large circular or oval depressions that appear overnight in fields containing growing crops. There were over 100 sightings in the period 1988–90, mostly in S England, although there have been reports of similar phenomena in Japan, Italy, France, Canada, Brazil, Australia, and America. There has been much speculation as to their origins, with explanations ranging from UFO landings to stampeding hedgehogs. Although hoaxers were caught red-handed at one site in 1989, they cannot account for all examples of the phenomenon. The most rational explanation, and the one accepted by most scientists, is that the depressions are the result of air vortices.

cross. crossbusing *See* BUSING.

Cross of Lorraine The two-barred patriarchal and archiepiscopal cross, which was adopted as the emblem of the FIGHTING FRENCH during World War II because it had been the emblem of Joan of Arc.

Cross-roads of the Pacific A nickname of Honolulu, from its position on shipping and air routes.

Crouchback, Guy The divorced Roman Catholic hero of Evelyn Waugh's war trilogy *Sword of Honour*, comprising *Men at Arms* (1952), *Officers and Gentlemen* (1955), and *Unconditional Surrender* (1961). Both an observer and a participant in the dramatic events of the war and the matrimonial affairs of his friends, he epitomizes the patriot and gentleman that Waugh aspired to be.

crown-of-thorns starfish *See* ACANTHASTER.

crucial Slang for excellent. It is taken from the REGGAE jargon of Jamaica and was popularized in the UK by the Black comedian Lenny Henry, through his TV character Delbert Wilkins, who used the word incessantly.

crud (1) Dirt, filth, or rubbish; specifically, an unwanted residue or impurity arising from a process (as in a nuclear reactor). The word has its origins in the 14th century as a variant of *curds* (the residue that forms on top of curdled milk), from which it acquired this present sense after World War II. (2) An unworthy or despicable person. (3) A real or imaginary disease.

Cruelty, Theatre of A theory of drama proposed by the French director, actor, and writer Antonin Artaud (1896–1948) in his book *The Theatre and its Double* (1938; Eng. trans. 1958). Artaud was a leading exponent of SURREALISM and he sought to capture some of its theories, which he mixed with a smattering of Taoist principles and some aspects of Eastern dance drama, to create a primitive and ritualistic form of theatre. This was intended to be in direct opposition to the realistic theatre of the dominant rationalist culture. His aim was to shock his audiences into an awareness of basic primitive human nature by releasing feelings usually repressed in conventional behaviour. Playwrights Jean Genet and Joe Orton both experimented with the principles of a theatre of cruelty. The play *Marat/Sade* by Peter Weiss is generally considered to be the definitive example of Artaud's theory.

cruise. cruise missile A low-flying winged missile carrying a conventional or nuclear warhead and driven by an air-breathing turbofan; it has a speed of some 885 m.p.h. Such missiles are guided by an inertial system that is updated during flight by matching the contours of the land they overfly with the contour maps stored in their computer memories. They fly so low that they are difficult to detect by radar and therefore to destroy.

cruising Seeking a sexual partner in bars, etc., especially by a homosexual.

crumblie or **crumbly** (1) *See* WRINKLIE. (2) British slang for a parent. An inoffensive use of the word by upper- and middle-class children since the 1970s.

crunchie *See* LIPSTICK.

cry. cry all the way to the bank An originally US catchphrase that was popular in the 1950s and later in the UK. An ironic comment on someone who has foisted a lamentable creation on the world, it implies that the perpetrator has nevertheless made a great deal of money from it. It was probably said first by Liberace, when a critic had said unkind things about his music and his performance. A later sarcastic version is **laugh all the way to the bank**.

Cry Guy *See* PRINCE OF WAILS.

cryonics The practice of freezing a corpse in the hope of being able to bring it back to life at a future time. The idea of freezing a diseased human body until medical science developed a cure for the disease causing the death became quite popular in the late 1960s. In America, the practice has been carried out several times. The word comes from Greek *kruos*, cold, plus *-onics*, as in electronics.

cryptozoology The study of creatures whose existence has not been scientifically proved. Cryptozoology is concerned with such phenomena as the LOCH NESS MONSTER in Scotland, the Yeti in the Himalayas (*see* ABOMINABLE SNOWMAN), the Sasquatch (*see* BIGFOOT) in Canada, and other such creatures.

CSE Certificate of Secondary Education. A school examination taken at the age of about 16. It was introduced in 1965 as an alternative to the GCE examination for pupils who are less academically inclined. *See also* GCSE.

CS gas An extremely effective irritant gas (2-chlorobenzalmalononitrile) developed at the British government's chemical-weapon laboratory at Porton Down in the 1950s but first manufactured in the 1920s in America; it takes its name from the initials of the surnames of its US inventors, Ben **C**arson and Roger **S**taughton. It is now used for emergency crowd control. Dispersed in the form of smoke, CS gas causes gripping chest pains, streaming eyes and nose, salivation, coughing, and retching. These effects are instantaneous, although they are not lethal and do not persist.

CT scanner Computerized TOMOGRAPHY scanner. A type of BODY SCANNER that enables images of different planes of the body to be recorded, using low doses of X-rays. It is used for the diagnosis of tumours and other abnormalities affecting the soft tissues of the body. Also known by its original name, **CAT scanner** (computerized axial tomography scanner), but this is misleading as it implies – incorrectly – that images can be obtained only in the axial plane of the body.

Cuban missile crisis The crisis in October 1962 that was precipitated by the installation of Soviet rockets in Cuba; for thirteen days the world trembled on the brink of nuclear war. President Kennedy finally compelled Khrushchev, by means of a naval quarantine of Soviet shipments to Cuba, to remove the rockets. Why the Soviets should have taken the drastic step of placing rockets in Cuba after repeated US warnings that such an act would not be tolerated is still a matter of some controversy. The determination by the Soviet Union to match America in nuclear weaponry dates from this crisis.

> We're eyeball to eyeball and I think the other fellow just blinked.
>
> DEAN RUSK, US secretary of state on hearing that the Soviet ships had "stopped dead in the water".

> They talk about who won and who lost. Human reason won. Mankind won.
>
> N. S. KHRUSHCHEV after the crisis.

cube (1) British slang meaning even more unfashionable or out of date than a square person. A pejorative epithet of the 1950s, it is now itself out of date. (2) A lump of sugar with the hallucinogenic drug LSD on it. This was the way LSD was taken in the mid-1960s. A **cubehead** was a frequent taker of LSD in this form.

cubism The style of an early 20th-century school of painters who depict surfaces, figures, tints, light and shade, etc., by means of a multiplicity of shapes of a cubical and geometrical character. The name was given somewhat disparagingly by Henri Matisse in 1908. It was essentially abstract and divorced from realism. It rejected any attempt to depict actual appearances and turned its back on all accepted canons of art. Its chief exponents were Braque, Derain, Léger, and notably Picasso. *See also* DADAISM; FAUVISM; FUTURISM; ORPHISM; SURREALISM; SYNCHRONISM; VORTICISM.

cubist-realism A US form of cubism founded in about 1915, by Charles Demuth, Charles Sheeler, and other painters of the precisionist school. The movement embraced a less analytical and visually radical form of cubism, treating recognizably US themes without recourse to simultaneous multiple viewpoints or the fragmentation of reality and perspective.

cubscouts *See* BOY SCOUTS.

cuisine minceur *See* NOUVELLE CUISINE.

Culebra Cut *See* PANAMA CANAL.

Cullinan diamond The largest known diamond, named after the chairman of the Premier Mine, Johannesburg, where it was found in 1905. Its uncut weight was 3025¾ carats (about 1 lb 6 oz). It was presented to King Edward VII by the South African government and was cut into a number of stones (the largest weighing some 516 carats), which now form part of the Crown Jewels.

culture. cultural cringe An expression coined by the Australian writer Arthur Phillips in the early 1950s to denote the then common Australian habit of disparaging the Australian culture and venerating those of other countries, especially that of the UK. From the 1970s, however, Australians have been actively promoting their own culture.

Cultural Revolution The Great Proletarian Cultural Revolution took place in China in 1966 under the direction of Mao Tse-tung. Intended to invigorate revolutionary fervour and to avoid stagnation and revisionism, it involved replacing leaders of the old guard, abolishing the formal education system (many universities were closed), and mobilizing students as Red Guards. For ten years, until the death of Mao, there was social and political turmoil in which millions of urban 'bourgeois reactionaries' were sent to the country to be 're-educated' by manual labour.

culture shock The unpleasant feelings of alienation, rejection, withdrawal, etc., experienced by people when first confronted by cultures, customs, or tastes that are markedly different from their own. The phrase has become common since the mid-20th century; originally used only in an anthropological or sociological context, to describe the impact of a primitive culture on those from a more advanced one (and vice versa), it is now used in a much more general sense for the effect of anything unfamiliar (music, art, etc.) on those unprepared to accept it.

culture vulture A person who is excessively and indiscriminately interested in the arts. The phrase originated in the mid-20th century; **culture hound** and **culture-monger** are variants.

Two Cultures The existence in the UK, and to a great extent in W Europe, of two separate cultures with few points of contact between them; one based on the humanities and the other on the sciences. The phrase gained immediate popularity after C. P. Snow's Rede Lecture, subsequently published as *The Two Cultures and the Scientific Revolution* (1959). A useful comparison may be made with the ideas expressed in Matthew Arnold's *Culture and Anarchy* (1869) and his Rede Lecture entitled *Literature and Science* (1882).

when I hear the word culture, I reach for my revolver Remark often attributed to the German NAZI politician Herman Goering (1893–1946). The quotation is in fact by the German novelist and dramatist Hanns Johst:

> Whenever I hear the word 'culture' . . . I reach for my gun.
>
> *Schlageter*, I, 1.

Cuppie A devotee of yacht racing, often restricted to a person particularly interested in the social aspects of the sport. Since yacht racing tends to be associated with the wealthy middle classes, the word is often used derogatorily. It achieved popularity when the US entrants for the America's Cup Race were trying to regain the trophy and lost it to the Australian team in 1987. The publicity surrounding the event attracted many people, hitherto uninterested in the sport, who were attracted by its glamour. The word Cuppie clearly owes something to the existence of the word YUPPIE, although, unlike Yuppie, it is not an acronym.

curie The former unit of radioactivity, which has now been replaced by the BECQUEREL. The curie was named after the French scientist Pierre Curie (1859–1906), who with his Polish-born wife Marya Skłodowska (Marie Curie; 1867–1934) discovered radium and carried out a great deal of fundamental research into radioactivity. The element **curium** (atomic number 96) was named after the Curies jointly.

Curly Top A 1935 film featuring the US child star Shirley Temple (1928–), who was herself known by this nickname. The six-year-old starlet, with tight curls and an angelic smile, won her way into the hearts of mothers throughout the world. Regardless of colour or creed, each one of them saw in their own young daughters, a reflection of this winning little tap-dancing monster. Curly Tops, herself, had no such dreams:

I stopped believing in Santa Claus at an early age. Mother took me to see him in a department store and he asked me for my autograph.

With the passage of time, Shirley Temple ceased to be either a child or a star – a situation she coped with resourcefully. As Mrs Shirley Temple Black she became the US ambassador to Ghana and (from 1989) Czechoslovakia. *See also* ONE-TAKE.

Curragh mutiny A threat, in March 1914, by British cavalry officers stationed at The Curragh (a military training camp in County Kildare) to resign if they were called upon to coerce Ulster into the Irish Free State. This threat hardly constituted a mutiny; in fact, the real threat to Asquith's government lay with Sir Edward Carson and Bonar Law, who had said that they would lead the Unionists and Conservatives in armed resistance in order to keep Ulster out of an Irish Free State (*see* ULSTER VOLUNTEERS). Although Asquith was alarmed by the reaction of the cavalry officers, the problems of an imminent world war were more pressing.

curse of Tutankhamun A legend arising from the death of the 5th Earl of Carnarvon (1866–1923) during the excavations at Tutankhamun's tomb, which started in 1922. He died from pneumonia after an infection from a mosquito bite but Sir Arthur Conan Doyle, a convinced spiritualist, suggested that it might be attributed to elementals created by the priests of Tutankhamun. Coincidentally there was a power failure at Cairo when Carnarvon died and his dog in England expired at the same time. Carnarvon's associate, Howard Carter (1874–1939), died at the precise moment that one of the ancient trumpets found in the tomb was being blown for the first (and only) time since Tutankhamun's death. The English security guard who was detailed to sleep in the tomb every night for three years after it was opened always denied, however, that there was a curse and that the newspapers had invented the story of an inscription foretelling doom to grave robbers; he himself survived into his eighties.

Curzon line The demarcation line between Poland and the Soviet Union first proposed by the British Foreign Secretary Lord Curzon (1859–1925) in 1920 during the Russo-Polish war. Poland rejected the plan because they would lose 52,000 square miles of land. However, the Soviets claimed the land and in 1939 drove the Polish forces back, until they finally occupied all of the former state of Poland. At the YALTA CONFERENCE in 1945 the Curzon line was finally recognized as the Soviet Polish border, with some minor frontier adjustments that were made in 1951.

cushy Slang for easy or comfortable: applied to jobs, positions, etc. Anglo-Indian in origin, derived from the Hindi *khush*, pleasant, it became part of military slang in World War I, in which context it was also used to describe trivial wounds. In World War II, a cushy job was one that did not involve danger, or too much hard work.

custom clothes or **custom tailoring** The US equivalent of 'made to measure', or 'bespoke tailoring'. These terms were appearing in British fashion magazines by the 1960s.

customer. the customer is always right A phrase introduced into the retail trade in the 1930s by H. Gordon Selfridge (1856–1947), who came to the UK from America to start up the large department store that still bears his name. Mr Selfridge was to be seen in his store every day, up to the start of World War II – a familiar figure in silk hat and morning suit, with a flower in his buttonhole. A great salesman, he instructed his staff never to argue with or be disrespectful to his customers. Whatever the true rights and wrongs of the situation, it was to be assumed that the customer was always right.

cut (1) Musicians' slang for a record, or one track on a long-playing record. The verb, **to cut**, is used to mean making a record. (2) To dilute illegal drugs with another substance to increase the weight and thereby make more profit on the sale. (3) US euphemism for kill.

cut a rug 1940s slang meaning to dance vigorously, usually such lively dances as the JITTERBUG or the JIVE.

cutaways, cut-offs The fashionable long shorts made by cutting off blue jeans at the knee.

cut off at the pass To stop something at an early stage; to intercept. The phrase comes from US Western films in which a sheriff in pursuit of the baddies would often instruct his posse to "cut them off at the pass". It was used in 1973 by President Richard Nixon on the WATERGATE tapes, when he said that maybe the charge of obstruction of justice (a problem worrying his Special Counsel, John Dean) could be cut off at the pass.

cutting contest or **carving contest** A friendly contest between two or more JAZZ musicians playing the same piece of music, in which each takes it in turn to play a solo break, an improvised passage to demonstrate their technical virtuosity and musical inventiveness. The winner of the contest is the one that gains the most vociferous reaction from the audience.

Cuthbert A name coined by 'Poy', the cartoonist of the *Evening News*, during World War I for the fit men of military age, especially those in government offices, who were not called up for military service or who positively avoided it. These civilians were depicted as frightened-looking rabbits. *See also* COMB-OUT.

cyberphobia Fear of computers. This is formed from *kubernētēs*, steersman, which gave **cybernetics**, the science of control systems; hence the prefix *cyber-* to mean computer. To this is added *-phobia*, from Greek *phobos*, fear. Although young people who have grown up with computers have no fear or hostile feelings towards them, some older people feel threatened by something that they do not understand. For these people cyberphobia is a real experience.

cyclamates *See* DELANEY AMENDMENT.

cycleway A lane on a road reserved for cyclists.

D

D. D Day In World War II, the day appointed for the Allied invasion of Europe and the opening of the long-awaited second front. It was eventually fixed for 5 June 1944, but owing to impossible weather conditions, it was postponed at the last moment until 6 June. *See* OVERLORD.

D-notice Defence Notice. A British government notice to news editors not to publish items on specified subjects for reasons of security. First used in 1922, the D-notice has been strictly adhered to, enabling the UK to avoid press censorship.

D-ration An emergency ration distributed to US troops. It consists of concentrated chocolate and is one of the series of such rations designated by letters of the alphabet.

DA (1) British slang abbreviation of duck's arse, a man's hairstyle in which the hair is combed straight back and greased into a curl at the back of the neck, hence the resemblance to the rear end of a duck. It was very popular with the TEDDY BOYS of the 1950s and is still seen on elderly rockers. (2) Slang abbreviation of drug addict; it has been used by drug users themselves since the late 1960s.

dabs British criminal and police jargon for fingerprints. It has been used since the 1930s and is derived from the process of taking fingerprints, which involves pressing (dabbing) the fingers one by one onto an ink pad and then onto paper.

Dachau A small town 12 miles north of Munich, where the first of Nazi Germany's CONCENTRATION CAMPS was established, on 10 March 1933, only weeks after Hitler came to power. The main camp was supplemented by a network of smaller satellite camps throughout S Germany and Austria, all called Dachau. Of the estimated 260,000 prisoners who passed through the Dachau system, 32,000 died through overwork, malnutrition, disease, and as the result of medical experiments, although many more were sent to die in extermination camps, such as AUSCHWITZ in Poland. Dachau was the centre in which the most extensive programme of medical experiments on living prisoners was conducted, examining the effects of variations in atmospheric pressure, untried anti-malarial drugs, freezing, drinking seawater, starvation, and dehydration. After the war those doctors and scientists responsible were tried in the 'Doctors' Trial' at the NUREMBERG TRIALS, seven of the offenders being sentenced to death. *See also* HOLOCAUST.

Dacron Tradename for a synthetic polyester fibre made by the US company Du Pont. The British fibre TERYLENE is similar. The name was made up by comparison with NYLON.

dad. be like Dad, keep mum A slogan from the British Ministry of Information in 1941, which was responsible for wartime propaganda, exhorting people to remember national security and not to talk (keep mum) about matters of national security. Another similar slogan was **careless talk costs lives**. *See* KEEP IT DARK *under* DARK.

Dada Mama US Black slang from the 1920s for a drumroll.

Dad and Dave Two figures constituting a tradition in Australian humour; invented by A. H. Davis (Steele Rudd; 1868–1935). They first appeared in his humorous sketches, *On Our Selection* (1899), which deals with the hard lives of the small farmers of the period. Dad and Dave have since been widely used in Australian broadcasting serials.

daddy *See* SUGAR DADDY.

daddy week The employment of a band or other act by a theatre management, lasting for one week. It was named after Frank Schiffmann, manager of the Apollo Theater in Harlem, whose nickname was 'Daddy'.

Daddy, what did you do in the Great War? A slogan from a World War I recruiting poster showing a man obviously pondering how to answer the daughter on his knee. It became a catchphrase as 'What did you do in the Great War, Daddy?', and was used as the title of a US film in 1966, made by Blake Edwards and starring James Coburn.

Dad's Army Colloquial name for the HOME GUARD. It was also the title of a popular British television comedy series (1968–77) following the exploits of a bumbling platoon of the Home Guard in a small town in S England during World War II. The series won a BAFTA AWARD and was voted the Best Comedy Series in 1971; it starred such actors as Arthur Lowe, John Le Mesurier, Clive Dunn, and Ian Lavender.

dadaism An anarchic and iconoclastic art movement that began in Zürich in 1916, arising from the indignation and despair felt by so many artists and intellectuals in the aftermath of World War I. Its supporters sought to free themselves from all artistic conventions and what they considered to be cultural shams. Dadaism was influenced by CUBISM and FUTURISM and after about 1922 it was succeeded by SURREALISM. The name Dadaism was derived from *dada*, the French word for a hobbyhorse; it was selected by Tristan Tzara after opening a dictionary at random. Jean Arp (1887–1966) and Max Ernst (1891–1976) were among the leading dadaists. There was a similar movement in New York at the same time associated with Marcel Duchamp (1887–1968), Francis Picabia (1879–1953), and Man Ray (1890–1976). Visitors to a Dada exhibition in Cologne were actually invited to smash up the paintings on display. A plaque, showing a human navel, was unveiled at Zürich in February 1966, to commemorate the 50th anniversary of the movement. *See also* FAUVISM; ORPHISM; SYNCHRONISM; VORTICISM.

Daffy Duck A Warner Brothers cartoon character, said to have been modelled on Harpo Marx. He was one of the stable of characters created for the Looney Tunes and Merrie Melodies cartoons by the Warners team of animators, which included Tex Avery, Chuck Jones, and Robert Clampett. The cantankerous Daffy's first real appearances came in *Porky's Duck Hunt* (1937) and *A Wild Hare* (1940); his spluttering speech was articulated by Mel Blanc, who was the voice behind nearly all the Looney Tunes characters, including BUGS BUNNY, Elmer Fudd, and Sylvester the Cat.

daft. Ee, ain't it grand to be daft? The catchphrase used by Albert Modley (1901–79), the north country British comedian, who was known nationwide in the 1940s through the radio programme *Variety Bandbox*. In the 1930s and 1940s, the great age of the radio comedy, it was regarded as axiomatic that anything said in a north country accent was funny. The fallacy of this argument was revealed by the television programmes of the 1950s; first, north country comics did not necessarily look funny, and secondly, it was discovered that drama was more likely to be taken seriously if the characters had regional accents.

dagger-pointed goldies A style of shoe, popular in the 1940s, characterized by its yellow colour and pointed toe.

DAGMAR Defining Advertising Goals for Measured Advertising Results. The principle, which originated in America in the 1960s, in which the success or failure of an advertising campaign is measured against the objectives defined for it before it is embarked upon.

dagmars Round protuberances on the front of some US cars of the 1950s. The name was inspired by Jennie Lewis, a US actress in TV comedies who was known as 'Dagmar' and noted for her own round protuberances.

Dáil Éireann The lower chamber of the parliament of the Republic of Ireland. In Irish, *dáil* means assembly and *Éireann* means of Eire (the Irish Gaelic name for Ireland). There are 144 members of the Dáil, elected by proportional representation every five years. The first Dáil was set up in 1918 when 73 of the 103 MPs elected to represent Ireland in Westminster were Sinn Fein members, who refused to take their seats in the British parliament. The Dáil became the lower chamber of the Irish parliament in 1921, when the Irish Free State was set up. *See also* FIANNA FÁIL; FINE GAEL.

dailies *See* RUSHES.

dainties US and Australian euphemism for women's underwear.

daisy. daisy chain A form of group sexual activity. Each member of the chain sexually stimulates the next person in the group while simultaneously being stimulated by the previous person in the chain.

daisy-cutter In cricket, a ball that fails to rise when delivered, and in tennis a service which behaves similarly. In the 19th century a horse that lifted its feet very little above the ground was so described, and more recently it was applied colloquially by the RAF to a perfect landing.

Darling Daisy Frances, Countess of Warwick, adulterous wife of the 5th Earl of Warwick and for nine years mistress of King Edward VII, whom he often addressed as "My Darling Daisy wife" when writing to her. In 1914, she sought to increase her income by threatening to publish her memoirs, which would have included the late King's letters. This was prevented by three prominent courtiers acting on behalf of King George V.

Dakar expedition The abortive attempt by British and Free French forces to capture the port of Dakar, capital of French West Africa, that took place on 23 September 1940. The VICHY authorities who controlled Dakar refused to switch their allegiance, contrary to the expectation of the Free French leader, de Gaulle. The Dakar garrison fired on emissaries from the landing force and Vichy warships shelled the British vessels. The British called off the action when the scale of the opposition became apparent; de Gaulle's hopes of establishing a Free French enclave in West Africa were dashed by the expedition's failure.

Dakota The British name for the US-built Douglas DC-3 twin-engine aircraft, one of the stalwarts of the early days of commercial flying. Introduced in 1935, the Dakota established a reputation for reliability and low operating costs, playing a major role in the expansion of the airline business around the world. The original version carried 21 passengers and could cruise at 192 m.p.h. Military versions were widely used during World War II; after the war many were converted for passenger use. Nearly 11,000 Dakotas had been built when production ceased in 1946.

daks A slang name for any pair of trousers. *Daks* is a tradename for men's casual trousers manufactured by Simpsons, the clothing store in Piccadilly, London; the name was coined by the second son, Alexander, of the proprietor Simeon Simpson, in 1934 from a combination of 'dad' and 'slacks'. The slang use of the word is usually heard in the phrase 'to drop one's daks', which became popular after it appeared in 1960 as one of the catchphrases in *Barry McKenzie*, the cartoon strip created by Barry Humphries for the magazine *Private Eye*.

Dalcroze Institute of Eurhythmics *See* EURHYTHMICS.

Dalek *See* EXTERMINATE, EXTERMINATE.

dallymoney The US name for money ordered by a court to be paid to a former sexual partner by the other partner when it has been proved that he or she gave assurances of long-term affection and fidelity that have not been fulfilled. The word is formed from the combination of 'dalliance' and 'money' and was coined to rhyme with *alimony*, money paid by a spouse to a separated wife or husband, and **palimony**, money paid to an unmarried partner after the break-up of a long-term relationship.

Dalton. Dalton budget leak The incident as a result of which the British Labour Chancellor of the Exchequer, Hugh Dalton (1887–1962), was obliged to resign. Shortly before presenting his budget to the House of Commons on 13 November 1947, Dalton gave certain details of the budget to a lobby correspondent of *The Star*, one of London's evening papers. The paper was able to run a 'Stop Press' announcement of taxation changes before the House had been informed by the Chancellor. This grave breach of protocol left Dalton with no option but to tender his resignation to the prime minister, Clement Attlee. Dalton returned to the Cabinet in 1948, as Chancellor of the Duchy of Lancaster.

Dalton Plan A system of US high-school education developed by Helen Parkhurst (1887–1959) and named after the school in Parkhurst's birthplace, Dalton, Massachusetts, in which a pilot scheme was introduced in 1920. Influenced by the MONTESSORI METHOD, the Parkhurst system is based on learning 'contracts' in which pupils work on a particular topic for periods varying from one week to one month, organizing their own time and consulting books and teachers as necessary. The traditional classroom becomes a workshop, with the teacher in a supervisory role. Dalton schools were subsequently established in many European countries, as well as Japan and China.

Daltons The nickname, coined by the London Stock Exchange, for an issue of undated 2½% Treasury stock, authorized by Hugh Dalton in 1947, when he was Labour Chancellor of the Exchequer. The value of the stock dived shortly after issue due to loss of stock-market confidence in the government's financial strategy. *See also* DALTON BUDGET LEAK.

Dambusters The nickname of 617 Squadron of the RAF. On the night of 17 May 1943, the squadron, led by Wing-Commander Guy Gibson, attacked and destroyed the Mohne dam in the Ruhr valley and the Eder dam in the Eder valley, both highly important strategic targets in the German industrial heartland. The pilots flew low over the reservoirs behind the dams and dropped specially designed bombs at a precalculated height and distance. The so-called 'bouncing bombs' skimmed along the surface and exploded underwater at the base of the dam. The raid caused severe damage and high civilian casualties. The bombs were designed by the British aeronautical engineer Sir Barnes Wallis (1887–1979). In 1954 a popular account of the episode, and the scientific saga leading up to it, appeared in the film *The Dam Busters*, in which Michael Redgrave played the part of Barnes Wallis and Richard Todd was Guy Gibson; the film's stirring and much-admired musical theme (by Eric Coates) was called 'The Dambuster March'.

dancehall A US slang euphemism either for the place in which an execution takes place or the cell in which a condemned prisoner awaits execution. 'Dancehall' derives from old criminal slang **dance in the air**, meaning to be hanged. The allusion is to the dance-like foot movements of someone being hanged.

Dane, Clemence Pseudonym of Winifred Ashton (1888–1965), British playwright and novelist. She started acting under the stage name Diana Cortis in 1913, and published her first play, *A Bill of Divorcement*, in 1921. This was a sensitive study of a woman's deliberate estrangement and self-sacrifice prompted by her fear of hereditary madness. It received instant acclaim, and caused Dane to turn to writing full time. Later works include *Will Shakespeare* (1921), *Naboth's Vineyard* (1926), and *Wild Decembers* (1932), a portrayal of the Brontës. However, none matched the success of her first play. She took her pseudonym from the name of her favourite church, St Clement Danes in London's Strand.

dangerous age, An epithet that is usually presumed to refer to the age of 40, although in 1967 Dudley Moore starred in a film called *Thirty is a dangerous age, Cynthia*. It seems to have an air of sexual innuendo, implying that once this milestone has been reached the trammels of marital fidelity will be thrown off in an attempt to provide reassurance that one is still sexually attractive. *See also* LIFE BEGINS AT FORTY *under* FORTY; SEVEN-YEAR ITCH.

D'Annunzio raid The seizure of the city of Fiume (Yugoslavian name: Rijeka) in September 1919 by a force led by the Italian Fascist novelist and poet, Gabriele d'Annunzio (1863–1938). Fiume was a Hungarian port until 1919 when, as one of the spoils of war, it was claimed by both Italy and Yugoslavia. While it was still under the control of the LEAGUE OF NATIONS, D'Annunzio led some 2600 demobbed soldiers and fascists and took over the city, much to the delight of Italian nationalists and the embarrassment of the Italian government. He remained in control of Fiume until November 1920, when he was expelled following agreement between Italy and Yugoslavia. Fiume was briefly a free city, until its incorporation by Italy in 1923. As Rijeka, it finally became Yugoslavian in 1947, as reparation after World War II.

Danny the Red Nickname for Daniel Cohn-Bendit (1945–), a West German student in France who led a students' revolt at Nanterre campus in Paris in May 1968. He was later deported to West Germany.

DAP Draw A Person. A type of psychological test in which the subject has to make a drawing of a person. The psychologist, it is claimed, is able to draw conclusions about the personality of the subject from the type of drawing produced.

daps British slang for plimsolls or tennis shoes; it has been used, especially in Wales and SW England, since the 1960s. The derivation is uncertain, but it may be related to the verb to dap, meaning to bounce or skip.

Dardanelles (formerly Hellespont) A narrow strait in N Turkey linking the Aegean Sea with the Sea of Marmara. The straits have always been of strategic importance as the gateway to Istanbul and the Black Sea from the Mediterranean. In ancient history they were guarded by Troy from the Asian side (the straits are named after Dadanos, a former king of Troy). In the

4th century BC Alexander the Great crossed on a bridge of boats on his expedition against Persia. In April 1915 Anglo-French forces landed on the W and S sides of the GALLIPOLI peninsula guarding the straits, in a move to capture Istanbul and link up with Russian forces for an offensive in the east. The campaign, marked by ineptitude and indecisiveness on the part of the British commanders, quickly degenerated into a bloody stalemate and the Allied forces were forced to withdraw in January 1916.

dark. **dark matter** The hypothetical matter in the universe that cannot be observed by direct observation of the electromagnetic radiation it emits. Its existence is postulated to account for the **missing mass**, *i.e.* the difference that is believed to exist between the actual mass of the universe and that estimated by observations using all kinds of telescopes. Various exotic theories have been suggested to account for this dark matter, including BLACK HOLES, COSMIC STRINGS, etc.

dark star An invisible star, such as a component of a multiple star, the existence of which can only be deduced from infrared or radio emissions or from its observed gravitational effects.

keep it dark A slogan from World War II reminding people to remember national security and not unwittingly give away any information that would be useful to the enemy. In 1940 there was a variety show playing in London called *Shush, keep it dark*, and later there was a radio show featuring a character, Commander High-Price, whose catchphrase was "Hush, keep it dark". Echoes of the phrase were heard in 1983 when the Conservative candidate, Anthony Beaumont-Dark, used 'Keep it Dark' as his slogan during a successful campaign for re-election.

Darling. **Darling Daisy** *See* DAISY.

Darling of the Halls *See* PRIME MINISTER OF MIRTH.

Dartington Hall A community, near Totnes in Devon, founded in 1926 on enlightened social and economic principles. The founders were Leonard and Dorothy Elmhirst, who bought the Dartington estate in 1925. The following year they established Dartington Hall School, a coeducational day and boarding school organized on progressive lines. Pupils enjoyed considerable freedom and informality (for instance there were no compulsory games or uniforms) and were encouraged to pursue their own interests in both the arts and sciences. The Elmhirsts also founded a range of small-scale rural enterprises on the estate, such as joinery, sawmilling, cider-making, and poultry-breeding. All employees have access to the artistic and educational opportunities afforded by Dartington, with the aim of enriching the community spiritually as well as economically. Ownership of the estate was transferred to a trust in 1932. The Dartington Hall summer school for musicians has established an international reputation.

Dartington Hall School closed in 1986 after a series of sex and drugs scandals. The philosophy of the school is to be carried on in the new Schumacher College on the same site, named after the GREEN economist E. F. Schumacher (*see* SMALL IS BEAUTIFUL).

darts An indoor target game in which sharp weighted darts (also called 'arrows') are thrown at a circular marked board. The game evolved from military training in the Middle Ages, when 10-inch throwing 'dartes' for use in close range combat were thrown at archery targets or sawn-off tree trunks: however, the modern version of the game is less than a century old. In 1906 the first all-metal barrelled dart was patented in the UK and in a court ruling of 1908 the game was designated one of skill, not chance, and made legal in pubs. The National Darts Association was formed in 1962, and the game's most important tournaments, usually sponsored by the *News of the World*, used to be shown regularly on television sports programmes. In 1988, however, Independent Television decided to end its coverage of the game, one suspects because of its down-market image. The game is now played mostly in pubs, with a team consisting of the patrons of one local pub competing against a team from another local pub.

DAT Digital Audio Tape. A system for recording digitally encoded sound on magnetic tape. The format is similar to that of a recorded cassette but is capable of superior digital sound recording and reproduction. DAT technology is used widely in professional recording studios, although reasonably priced DAT machines have only recently become available to consumers. Widespread introduction of DAT machines was delayed by attempts to reach international agreement on measures to prevent wholesale copying and piracy of prerecorded DAT information and COMPACT DISCS.

database Organized information held on a COMPUTER in a form that enables it to be put to a number of different uses. The information has to be held in such a way that it can be easily retrieved. A special computer program, called a **database management system** (DBMS), is used for this purpose.

date mate (1) US teenage slang of the 1950s for a friend of the same sex who accompanies one on a double date. (2) Australian slang for a male homosexual partner. It is derived from the Australian slang usage of date, meaning anus, presumably from an association with the contoured skin of the fruit.

datum line A term used in surveying and engineering to describe a line from which all heights and depths are measured. The datum line upon which the Ordnance Survey maps of Great Britain were based until 1921 was the main sea-level at Liverpool. Since 1921 it has been the mean sea-level at Newlyn, Cornwall.

Davis. Davis apparatus More properly known as the Davis Submerged Escape Apparatus (DSEA). Designed by Sir Robert Davis, the Davis apparatus was introduced in the late 1920s to assist submarine crews to escape from stricken submerged vessels. It consisted of a mouthpiece and flexible tube attached to a rubber bag, which in turn was connected to a pressurized oxygen-filled container. The apparatus enabled the submariner to breathe during the ascent to the surface. However, the main drawback was the need to remove the mouthpiece on reaching the surface or risk suffocation. In 1946 the Royal Navy discontinued use of the DSEA during ascent, in favour of free escape following special training.

Davis Cup The trophy awarded to the winners of the International Lawn Tennis Championship. It was donated in 1900 for the inaugural contest between America and the UK by Dwight Filley Davis (1879–1945), who himself played for the US team in the opening contests. The competition now attracts some 60 nations. Each match comprises four singles and a doubles, and the eliminating round is played in three zones, American, European, and Eastern, with a zone final in each followed by an inter-zone final to decide the winner. In the 1980s the winners were: Czechoslovakia (1980); America (1981, 1982); Australia (1983, 1986); Sweden (1984, 1985, 1987) and West Germany (1988, 1989).

Dawes Plan A scheme for reorganizing reparation payments by Germany (*see* VERSAILLES TREATY), drawn up in 1924 by a committee headed by Charles Gates Dawes (1865–1951), a US brigadier-general. The scheme was devised in the wake of France's invasion of the Ruhr in 1923 following default on payments by Germany, with the intention of obviating such military sanctions in future. Central to the plan was the establishment of a German gold reserve based on an 800 million goldmark foreign loan and a system of reparation payments that would prevent currency depreciation and link payments to German industrial growth. The total amount of reparations payable was not fixed. The Dawes Plan was superseded in 1930 by the Young Plan. Dawes himself became Republican Vice-President (1925–29) and he was awarded the 1925 Nobel Peace Prize, jointly with Austen Chamberlain, for the Dawes Plan, which many regarded as having saved Europe from economic collapse.

dawk In America, a person who cannot make up his or her mind about whether to approve of a war or to campaign for peace. The term, a blend of DOVE and hawk, was coined by *Time* magazine in the late 1960s, during the VIETNAM WAR,to describe Republican politicians who approved of the war in principle but had to oppose it for political reasons.

dawn raid Business jargon for a sudden surprise attempt to buy a company's shares as soon as the stock market opens, in order to effect a takeover. The term became current in the early 1980s during the takeover boom in the City of London. The London Stock Exchange and Council for the Securities Industry subsequently introduced regulations to limit the amount of shares that can be acquired in this way although dawn raids can still be an option for those companies pursuing aggressive takeover strategies.

> Takeovers are for the public good, but that's not why I do it. I do it to make money.
>
> SIR JAMES GOLDSMITH, *Sunday Times*, 8 September 1985.

day. day care The practice of keeping old or ill people in homes or hospitals during the day, *i.e.* during normal working hours, so that the people looking after them can go out to work. In America, the term is also used for nursery schools for pre-school children.

day gig A daytime job taken by a musician who is obliged to do work outside the world of music in order to earn a living.

daylight saving The idea of making fuller use of the hours of daylight by advancing the clock originated with Benjamin Franklin, but its introduction was due to its advocacy from 1907 by William Willett (1856–1915), a Chelsea builder. It was adopted in 1916 in Germany, then in the UK, as a wartime measure, when clocks were advanced one hour. In the UK it became permanent by an Act of 1925. **Summer Time**, as it was called until 1939, and again in 1946 and from 1948 till 1959, began on the day following the third Saturday in April (unless that was Easter Day, in which case it was the day following the second Saturday in April). It ended on the day following the first Saturday in October. In 1961 Summer Time was extended by six weeks, beginning in March and ending in October, and similar extensions were made in 1962 and subsequent years. During World War II it extended from 25 February in 1940 and 1 January 1941–44, until 31 December. In 1945 it ended in October. **Double Summer Time** (*i.e.* two hours in advance of GMT instead of one hour) was in force during 1941–45 and 1947 to save fuel. *See also* GREENWICH MEAN TIME.

In America, **Summer Time** (March to October) was in force in 1917 and 1918 and again from 1942 to 1945 (all the year round and known as **War Time**). In 1966 the Uniform Time Act re-introduced Summer Time (from the last Sunday in April until the last Sunday in October) while allowing individual states the right of option. In the years following World War II a number of other countries have adopted some form of Summer Time.

go ahead, make my day A catchphrase meaning 'go ahead if you dare', with the implication that the outcome will benefit me not you. It was used by US President Reagan in March 1985 when speaking to a business conference about tax increases that he was not willing to condone. He was quoting from a 1983 Clint Eastwood film *Sudden Impact*, in which 'Dirty Harry' (played by Eastwood) uses it twice, both times while pointing a gun at another armed gunman.

Have a nice day A US catchphrase widely used as a greeting or valediction, especially by sales staff in shops, restaurants, and garages. It originated in 1956 in California as 'Have a happy day' when the Los Angeles advertising agency, Carson Roberts, used it as a greeting and as a slogan on all their promotional products. In the 1970s it became 'Have a nice day'. It is also used, rather self-consciously, in the UK, especially by those who wish to let it be known that they are frequent travellers to America.

> . . . the Americanization of western culture: *Dallas* and Coca-Cola and 'Have a nice day!'
>
> MARK LAWSON, *The Independent* Magazine, 5 January 1991.

Daytona Beach A city and popular beach resort on the NE Florida coast. It was named in 1876 after local landowner Mathias Day of Ohio. The hard sandy beach stretches for 37 km, and the surface has attracted motor-sport enthusiasts since 1903, including the British land-speed record holder, Sir Malcolm Campbell (1885–1948). Motor sport is also found at the Daytona International Speedway, a 4-km race track used for motorcycle, stock-car, and sports-car events.

Dayton anti-Darwinist trial The test case brought in 1925 by evolutionists to challenge the anti-evolutionist campaign of religious fundamentalists then gaining momentum in many southern US states (*see* FUNDAMENTALISM). In Tennessee, such fundamentalist opinions were embodied in an Anti-Evolution Law, passed in March 1925. A biology teacher at Dayton high school, John T. Scopes, was arrested for using the standard high school text, which incorporated Darwinian theory. His arrest was contrived by a friend and anti-fundamentalist, George Rappelyea. Scopes was defended by the illustrious attorney, Clarence Darrow (1857–1938); the prosecution's case was put by William Jennings Bryan (1860–1925), leader of the fundamentalists. Darrow vehemently argued the case against religious interference in education and managed to humiliate Bryan during the course of the trial. Nevertheless, Scopes was found guilty and fined 100 dollars. On appeal the decision was reversed on a technicality. Moreover, one of the appeal judges ruled the Tennessee Anti-Evolution Law unconstitutional. Bryan died shortly after the initial trial and the tide of fundamentalism began to ebb, allowing a more liberal tradition to prevail.

dazzle. **dazzle gun** A weapon used by the Royal Navy against Argentinian pilots in the FALKLANDS CONFLICT in 1982 but not made publicly known until the late 1980s. It consists of a laser gun designed to dazzle pilots of enemy aircraft or other attackers.

dazzle ships In World War I, warships painted in zigzag patterns designed to confuse the enemy as to the vessel's size, speed, and course. A highly specialized application of CAMOUFLAGE techniques, the patterns were designed by leading contemporary artists and are now considered to have had significant value as art in their own right.

DBE *See* ORDER OF THE BRITISH EMPIRE.

DC aircraft *See* DOUGLAS AIRCRAFT.

DDT DichloroDiphenylTrichloroethane. A highly toxic synthetic insecticide. First made in 1874, it was first used as an insecticide in 1939 by the Swiss chemist Paul Hermann Muller. Extensive use was made of it during World War II against lice, fleas, and mosquitoes, as well as crop pests. Unfortunately many insect species become immune to the compound, which builds up in their bodies and then contaminates animals, such as birds and mammals, higher up in the food chain. As a result, in 1972 severe restrictions were imposed on its use in America, and many other countries subsequently banned it.

de. **de-dyke** British lesbian slang of the 1980s meaning to remove or hide the traces of a lesbian lifestyle from a house or flat, usually before a parental visit. *See also* DYKE.

de facto Australian slang of the 1970s for a live-in partner with whom one has an enduring relationship but to whom one is not married. Although, in the UK, 20% of women in the age range 18–49 in the year 1988 were cohabiting in this way, there is no widely accepted word to describe either of the partners to the relationship. In casual contexts, 'my partner' is used more formally 'my common-law spouse' is heard, either in a legal context or as a joke.

de-frosted US slang meaning worked up, the opposite of cool and unflustered.

De Havilland Aircraft Company The aircraft manufacturing company founded in the UK in 1920 by Geoffrey de Havilland (1882–1965). One of the earliest models to achieve fame was the de Havilland Moth, first produced in 1925. One was piloted by Amy Johnson (1903–41) in 1930 on a daring solo flight from the UK to Australia (*see* QUEEN OF THE AIR). During the 1930s the de Havilland Tiger Moth was adopted by the RAF as their principal trainer, while the all-wooden MOSQUITO bomber, capable of 400 m.p.h., was one of the fastest planes to fight in World War II. However, perhaps the company's greatest contribution to aviation history is the COMET airliner, the world's first jet-propelled airliner. De Havilland's companies were taken over by Hawker Siddeley in 1959.

de-Maoization *See* DE-STALINIZATION.

de-Stalinization The reversal of the policies and reputation of the Soviet leader Joseph Stalin (1879–1953) following his death. A campaign to discredit Stalin's memory was started by his successor, Nikita Khrushchev (1894–1971), in a bitter speech at a closed session of the 20th Party Congress in March 1956. Here he denounced Stalin as a despot and brutal mass-murderer interested only in "the glorification of his own person". It has been said that Khrushchev's speech was interrupted by a shout from the audience of "Why didn't you stop him?". Khrushchev glared at the delegates and shouted "Who said that!". Nobody spoke, and Khrushchev continued, "Now you know why!". The term 'de-Stalinization' has been adapted to other cases of discrediting the influence of powerful people after their death or loss of power; similar terms have been coined, for instance **de-Maoization** (or **de-Maoification**) for the reversal of the ideas of the Chinese leader Mao Tse-tung (1893–1976) following his death; and **de-Thatcherization** following the resignation of the British prime minister Margaret Thatcher in 1990.

de Stijl (Dut. the style) A school of Dutch artists and architects dating from 1917 and partly founded by the painter Piet Mondrian (1872–1944). It was influenced by neoplasticism, stressing the use of horizontal and vertical lines and of white, black, grey, and primary colours.

De Wet Rebellion or **Rebellion of 1914** A rebellion among the Boers of South Africa, led in 1914 by General C. R. de Wet and C. R. Beyers, in protest at the decision of the newly formed South African government to support the UK at the outbreak of World War I. The rebellion, badly coordinated and lacking appreciable popular support, was quickly suppressed by Boer forces led by General L. Botha and Jan Smuts. De Wet was captured, while Beyers drowned crossing the Uaal River. By the end of 1914, the rebellion was over.

dead. dead beat Completely exhausted, absolutely 'whacked', like a dead man with no fight left in him. A **deadbeat** is a down-and-out. In America it denotes a sponger, one who deliberately avoids settling his debts.

dead but won't lie down Catchphrase used since around 1910 in statements such as 'he's dead but he won't lie down', meaning that someone, through stupidity or courage, does not know when to give up.

dead-cat bounce An expression that originated on the New York Stock Exchange to indicate a temporary recovery in prices (after a substantial fall) caused by speculators buying in stock they have sold at a higher level. It does not imply a sustained upward trend in the market and the fall may well continue when these buyers have covered their purchases.

deadhead (1) Slang for a very boring or dull person. *See also* AIRHEAD. (2) US slang for a scrounger or someone who avoids paying, for example someone who fails to buy a ticket on a train. It is derived from the phrase 'a dead head of cattle'. (3) A fan of the US rock group 'The Grateful Dead' whose long career started in the late 1960s. The group are known to their devoted fans as 'The Dead'.

Dead Heart In Australia, the central barren desert region of the country.

dead-in-the-water Denoting a company or corporation that is making very little progress and is therefore ripe for a takeover bid. The allusion is to a dead fish, which is simply drifting in the water rather than swimming in a specific direction.

dead-letter box A box or other receptacle in which spies are supposed to deposit messages and other information to be picked up by other agents. The term has been popularized by writers of spy fiction. *See also* DROP.

dead man's handle A handle on the controller of an electric train, etc., so designed that it cut off the current and applied the brakes if the driver released his pressure as a result of sudden illness or some other cause. It was formerly applied to electric, diesel-electric, diesel-mechanical, and diesel-hydraulic trains but was renamed *driver's safety device*, a term with less distressing associations.

dead president US Black slang from the 1940s for any paper money bearing the head of a deceased US president.

Dead Sea Scrolls In 1947 a Bedouin goatherd, Muhammed the Wolf, made the first scroll discoveries in a cave at the NW end of the Dead Sea, since when 500 more have been found. Most scholars accept them as originating from the monastery of the Jewish sect of the Essenes at Qumran. There is still much controversy over their interpretation but these manuscripts (dating from the period 150 BC to 70 AD) have added considerably to the understanding of Old Testament textual criticism and the background of the New Testament.

dead soul An expression that owes its origin to the title of the Russian author Nikolai Gogol's novel *Dead Souls* (1842). In this book a swindler, Chichikov, buys serfs who are in fact dead but officially still alive, as their names still appear in the tax register. The expression was revived in the West in 1989 to describe a person who retains a position in an organization, even though the duties relating to that position are no longer being carried out by that person. The expression re-emerged when 110 members of the Central Committee of the Communist Party of the Soviet Union were removed from office by President Gorbachev, whose plans for PERESTROIKA they were obstructing.

dead thing US Black slang used to denigrate any idea or thing of White origin.

drop dead *See under* DROP.

dear. Dear John letter A letter or note from a wife, girlfriend, or female partner indicating that the relationship with the recipient is over. The expression originated during World War II, the recipients of Dear John letters often being members of the armed forces whose female partners at home had formed a new relationship as they were unwilling to tolerate the long separation that overseas service entailed.

dear money or **tight money** A monetary policy in which interest rates on loans are high. *See also* CHEAP MONEY.

death. death duty *See* INHERITANCE TAX.

Death Row US name for the cells of a prison in which condemned prisoners are held until their execution. Because of the protracted nature of US legal processes, prisoners can spend many years waiting for the sentence to be carried out. During the 1960s and 1970s only a few executions actually took place; most death sentences were automatically commuted to life imprisonment. However, under the more conservative political climate in the 1980s, executions took place in many US states on a regular basis.

death seat Slang for the seat next to the driver in a car, so called because it is the most vulnerable position in an accident.

death squad A group of people organized, either unofficially or officially, to commit murder. The term was originally applied in the 1970s to unofficial vigilante groups in certain Latin American countries, who worked to assassinate politicians and others who opposed the current military regime. More generally, it has been applied to any group organized for assassination or terrorism.

death star or **throwing star** A weapon consisting of a small thin metal disc cut into the shape of a star and having sharp-edged points. Designed to be thrown, it became popular in the UK in the late 1980s as one of the weapons used in street fights by football hooligans and others. The death star is one of a range of weapons popularized by martial arts enthusiasts, who use a less dangerous rubber version.

death-valley curve The ominous decline in the curve on a graph that records the use of a new company's capital. With high start-up expenses and small income from sales, the death-valley curve is likely to frighten off new investors and sources of venture capital. The decline should be halted as sales reach predicted levels and start-up expenses fall.

debrief To question a member of the armed forces, spy, astronaut, etc., after a tour of duty or mission has been completed in order to obtain the maximum information from him or her as soon as possible, *i.e.* before other influences can colour the experience. It is the opposite of the briefing before the duty or mission begins.

deb's delight British slang of the 1960s for an upper-class young man, noted more for his inherited wealth than his intelligence, who nevertheless might be chosen as a suitable escort, or even a marriage partner, by a debutante's parents. It was often used disparagingly by debs themselves.

> The debs had names such as Charlotte, Eleanor, Sophie, Annabel, Samantha, Astrid, and Jokey. Their escorts – the deb's delights – were called Patrick, Hugo, and Alexander.
>
> *The Independent*, 10 April 1991.

decaffeinated Denoting coffee and some other drinks that have had their caffeine content removed in response to consumer demand for natural beverages free from potentially harmful stimulants. Decaffeinated coffee, colloquially known as **decaf**, is now widely available in supermarkets, restaurants, and other outlets. There is some concern, however, about the health risks from the solvents, such as methylene chloride, used to dissolve out the caffeine. Traces of this solvent remaining in the product can make decaffeinated coffee more of a health hazard than the natural drink.

decathlon An athletic contest in the modern OLYMPIC GAMES consisting of ten events: 100 metres sprint, long jump, putting the shot, high jump, 400 metres sprint, 110 metres hurdles, discus, pole vault, throwing the javelin, and 1500 metres run. *See also* PENTATHLON.

deccie or **deccy** A derogatory slang name for someone who is constantly redecorating his or her house and who moves house frequently in order to start another round of interior decorating. The term originated in the 1980s when much GENTRIFICATION of old property was taking place. This form of word, ending in *-ie* or *-y*, was very popular at the time, having been formed by analogy with YUPPIE (or yuppy) and DINKIE (or dinky).

decimal currency The currency introduced in the UK on 15 February 1971, the new pound consisting of 100 pence. The new coins were the seven-sided 50p piece, the 10p piece (the same size as the former florin), the 5p piece (the same size as the former shilling, though later reduced), the 2p piece, the 1p piece, and the ½p piece (subsequently dropped). A 20p piece and a pound coin were added in the 1980s. The first three coins and the 20p coin are silver in colour, while the pound coin is gold-coloured and the remainder copper-coloured. The introduction of a decimal currency was first mooted by the Tory MP, John Croker, in 1816. The idea was again put forward in parliament in 1824, 1847, 1853, and 1855.

> During the last two years he had devoted himself to decimal coinage with a zeal only second to that displayed by Plantagenet Palliser . . .
>
> ANTHONY TROLLOPE: *Phineas Redux* (1874), Vol i, ch. xxxii.

decision tree A diagram sometimes used in the analysis of a financial situation, especially in making investments. The diagram is used to illustrate the possible courses of action that flow from a decision; the possible courses are represented by branches at different levels arising from a series of decisions taken subsequent to the initial decision.

deck-access Denoting a block of flats in which there is a continuous inset balcony on each floor onto which the front doors of the individual flats open.

decompression chamber A room or space in which the air pressure can be varied at a controlled rate to enable people, such as divers, who have been exposed to abnormal atmospheric pressure to be returned to normal pressure slowly, in order to avoid **decompression sickness**.

Dedalus, Stephen The eponymous hero of James Joyce's novel *Portrait of the Artist as a Young Man* (1914–15), who also appears in Joyce's *Ulysses* (1922). The earlier book, which is mainly autobiographical, relates the story of Stephen's upbringing and development in Dublin, through school and adolescence, to his student days at Trinity College. Exposed to the pressures of Irish nationalism and Catholic dogma, and afflicted by poor eyesight, Stephen struggles to retain his individuality and to create a sense of personal destiny as poet and patriot. At the end of the book he resolves to leave Dublin for Paris:

> I go to encounter for the millionth time the reality of experience, and to forge in the smithy of my soul the uncreated conscience of my race.

In *Ulysses* Dedalus is reincarnated as the young poet adrift, like Bloom, in Dublin on one particular day – 16 June 1904. But, unlike his mythological Greek namesake, Daedalus, who made himself a pair of wings, Stephen Dedalus cannot fly away from the futility and loneliness of a mortal existence.

deece US Black slang from the 1940s for a dime.

deelybobber or **deely bopper** US slang for the set of imitation antennae worn on the head by children. A brief craze in 1975, deelybobbers caught on elsewhere later.

deep. **deep cover** The cover story of a spy, who sustains his or her role in an enemy country for such a long time and so intensely that the details of the invented character of the espionage agent virtually take over from those of the real character.

deepfreeze A type of refrigerator in which food, etc., can be stored for long periods at below freezing. Most deepfreezes operate at −15°C to −20°C, these same temperatures are also achieved in the deepfreeze compartments of an ordinary domestic refrigerator. Not all foods are suitable for deepfreezing but many can be maintained for three months, while raw beef and fresh fruit and vegetables can be kept for up to one year. *See also* BIRDS EYE.

deep-sea diver British rhyming slang for a fiver, a £5 note. It was mainly used in the mid-1970s.

deep sin US Black slang from the 1940s for a grave.

deep-six US slang meaning to bury or dispose of, *i.e.* to kill. It has been used since 1950s and is derived from the underworld euphemism **deep six**, for a grave, which is based on the minimum depth for a grave and the minimum depth of water for burials at sea.

deep sugar US Black slang for 'romantic' talk, first heard in the 1940s.

Deep Thought A character in the humorous sci-fi novel *The Hitch Hiker's Guide to the Galaxy* (1979) by Douglas Adams. Deep Thought is an extraordinarily intelligent supercomputer which, when asked to provide the Ultimate Answer to the meaning of Life, the Universe, and Everything, ponders for seven and half million years – and comes up with the answer of 42.

Deep Throat Deep Throat was the code name of the top-secret information source within the administration of President Richard Nixon, used by *Washington Post* reporters Carl Bernstein and Bob Woodward during their investigation into the WATERGATE AFFAIR (1972–74). The journalists refused to reveal the identity of this source although some commentators have suggested possible candidates. The codename was taken from the title of an explicit pornographic film (1974), starring Linda Lovelace. In interviews later, she claimed to have developed a method for controlling the gagging reflex in fellatio, which accounts for her spectacular performance.

def British slang of the late 1980s denoting extreme approval; excellent. It is a shortening of 'definitive' and was originally part of HIP-HOP jargon. In 1988, BBC2 started a TV series for young people called **DEF II**.

Defense Intelligence Agency (DIA) The organization created in 1961 to coordinate all gathering and analysis of US military intelligence. It largely took over and combined the previously separate intelligence branches of the US Army, Navy, and Air Force. The DIA's director is responsible for supplying the Defense Secretary and Joint Chiefs of Staff with military intelligence information.

defensive medicine The practice by doctors of taking extreme precautions to cover themselves against possible accusations of negligence and to avoid being sued by patients or relatives of patients for supposed malpractice. Defensive medicine involves a barrage of diagnostic tests, many of which are totally unnecessary, and routine referrals to a consultant or other doctor for a specialist or second opinion when these are not needed. The tests can in fact be harmful to patients and both these and second opinions are extremely expensive and time-consuming. Originally, defensive medicine was restricted to America but from the 1980s some doctors in the UK also began to practise it in the light of an increase in negligence and malpractice suits brought against them.

Dehra Dun Academy The military academy of the Indian army, established in 1932 at Dehra Dun, a city in NW Uttar Pradesh. From 1949 it also catered for airforce and naval officer cadets, but in 1955 all basic officer cadet training was transferred to the new National Defence Academy at Khadakvasala, near Poona. Thereafter Dehra Dun provided advanced training for newly qualified officers.

Delaney amendment In America, an amendment to the Food, Drug, and Cosmetic Act prohibiting the use of substances that cause cancer. The amendment, proposed in 1970 by the US Congressman James J. Delaney (1901–), stated that "no additive shall be deemed to be safe if it is found, after tests which are appropriate for the evaluation of food additives, to induce cancer in man and animals". The amendment became extremely controversial in the 1970s because the US Food and Drug Administration interpreted it in a strict way, irrespective of the dose involved. For example, in 1970 they banned the use of **cyclamates**, artificial sweetening agents widely used in the food industry, on evidence that massive doses caused bladder tumours in rats. In 1977, they invoked the Delaney amendment to ban the sweetener SACCHARIN.

delayed drop A descent from an aircraft by parachute in which the opening of the parachute is delayed, usually for a predetermined period, to enable the parachutist to take part in SKY DIVING.

Delgado murder The violent death of Humberto Delgado, former leader of the Portuguese opposition, whose battered body was discovered on 24 April 1965 near Badajoz, on the Spanish side of the Portuguese border. His wounds suggested that he had been clubbed to death. Delgado had been defeated in the 1958 presidential election, after which he found political asylum in Brazil. However, he remained a focus of political opposition to the Salazar dictatorship and his death took place amid growing political unrest in Portugal. He was last seen alive in Badajoz in February 1965. No perpetrator of the murder has ever been identified.

Delhi Pact Either of two separate pacts signed in Delhi that figure in modern Indian history. The first, signed in 1931 and also called the Gandhi–Irwin pact, was an agreement between the leader of the Congress Party, MAHATMA Gandhi, and Lord Irwin, viceroy of India. The pact, addressing some of Congress's grievances against the British, marked a truce in the Congress campaign of civil disobedience. It also established Congress as the principal conduit of Indian opinion in the Round Table constitutional conference. The second Delhi pact was signed in April 1950 between the Indian prime minister, Jawaharlal Nehru, and his Pakistan opposite number, Liaqat Ali Khan. The pact ensured the rights of Muslim and Hindu minorities in their respective countries; it was prompted by a massive two-way migration across the East Pakistan–Indian border following partition and fears that religious minorities in both countries would suffer persecution.

deli Short for delicatessen.

delta wing An aircraft wing in the form of a triangle with its apex pointing in the direction of motion, which facilitates passage through the sound barrier. Experiments with delta-wing designs, also known as sweptback wings, were carried out by the Germans during the 1940s; after the war this knowledge passed to the Allies. By the early 1950s the Americans had introduced the first supersonic fighter aircraft based on the delta-wing design, the F-102. British models, such as the Hawker Hunter and the Vulcan bomber, followed later. Because of its benefits at supersonic speed, narrow delta wings were chosen for CONCORDE, which was designed to cruise at Mach 2; the American SPACE SHUTTLE also uses a similar design.

deltiology The pastime of collecting picture postcards. Picture postcards became popular early in the 20th century, especially in the form of greetings cards sent by people on holiday to their friends and relations. As the cards became more diverse, some having photographs on one side depicting local scenery and some containing cartoons with faintly risqué jokes, so the hobby of collecting them began to grow. The word is formed from Greek *deltion*, a diminutive of *deltos*, a writing tablet, and the suffix *-ology*, as in biology.

demand-pull inflation *See* INFLATION.

dementoid US high-school slang meaning crazy or a crazy person. It is usually used contemptuously.

demi-veg Short for demi-vegetarian, a diet in which the major components are vegetarian but, unlike a completely vegetarian diet, it permits the consumption of poultry and fish. Such a regime rules out the eating of red meat, which some medical experts regard as being injurious to health. 'Demi-veg' is used to describe the person eating such a diet as well as the diet itself.

demo (1) Slang for a street demonstration. (2) Slang for a demonstration tape recording or record that would-be pop musicians send in to recording companies or DISC JOCKEYS, hoping to get their work known. (3) Slang for a demolition job, either in the sense of knocking a building down or in the figurative sense of denigrating someone behind his or her back.

Demochristian An informal name for a member of any of a number of European political parties that have the name 'Christian Democrat Party'.

demographics The statistical study of human populations, including their size and composition by age, sex, and occupation; it also includes such sociological features as geographical distribution and migration, average family size, etc. The statistical data is derived mainly from censuses and records of births, deaths, and marriages.

demographic timebomb An expression coined at the end of the 1980s to describe an anticipated shortfall of potential workers as a result of an earlier drop in the national birth rate. The assumption is that, in the absence of enough young people to fill the jobs available, others, such as retired people or women who had not previously worked, would be required to work. The phrase was used despite the high unemployment rate current at the time.

demon US Black slang from the 1940s for a dime.

demonstration model A consumer product, such as a car or washing machine, that has been used in a showroom of a retail outlet to demonstrate the model to potential buyers. When the model being demonstrated is changed, or the demonstration model begins to show signs of use, it may be offered for sale at a discount to the normal price.

denim Coloured twilled cotton material used for overalls and especially jeans. A contraction of *serge de Nîmes*, originally made at Nîmes in the south of France. The garments themselves are known as 'denims'. *See also* GRANITE-WASH.

Denning report The report of an enquiry into the security aspects of the PROFUMO AFFAIR, conducted by the Master of the Rolls, Lord Denning (1899–). He concluded that the liaison between the UK's former war minister, John Profumo, and the call girl, Christine Keeler, had posed no threat to national security in spite of Keeler's association with a Soviet naval attaché. Denning also found no evidence to support rumours about the possible involvement of other ministers. However, Denning's criticisms of the existing security arrangements prompted the prime minister, Alec Douglas-Home, to establish a standing committee on security.

Denver boot A wheel clamp; a metal clamp attached by the police, or a private firm acting for the police, to one wheel of an illegally parked car to prevent it from being driven away until the driver has paid a substantial fee to have it unlocked, plus a statutory fine. It takes its name from Denver, Colorado, where the device was first used. In the streets of New York and London (from 1983) its introduction greatly reduced illegal parking.

Depression *See* GREAT DEPRESSION.

depth charge A drum packed with explosives, which can be timed to detonate at a pre-set depth, used by surface vessels to destroy submerged submarines. Depth charges are usually launched in groups to cover a pattern and were used with considerable success against diesel-engined submarines during World War II. However, they are not so effective against nuclear submarines and are little used today.

Derbyite In World War I, a soldier enlisted under the Derby Scheme of 1915. The Earl of Derby was Director of Recruiting and sought to promote a scheme of voluntary enlistment by age groups. The response was quite inadequate and conscription was instituted in May 1916.

deregulation The removal of government control on the flow of capital between countries and the operation of international markets. In the post-war years it was fashionable to impose exchange controls and other restrictions. Most economists now argue against the imposition of those restrictions, except in certain circumstances, such as the involvement of a monopoly.

DERL Derived Emergency Reference Level. The point at which action must be taken to counteract a potentially dangerous rise in radiation levels. The reference level is calculated on the basis of the most sensitive members of the public, usually children below one year of age.

derry British slang for a derelict building. It is used by tramps looking for shelter, by homeless people seeking a place in which to squat, or by people looking for derelict country properties to renovate.

derv Diesel-Engined Road Vehicles. A type of diesel oil used in lorries, etc.

deselect A euphemism meaning to exclude from participation or availability. It was first used in the UK in the early 1980s in the context of Labour party politics. Sitting MPs who lost the confidence of their constituency parties were faced with potential deselection, *i.e.* having their candidature rescinded before the next general election. The verb was later applied to others in a similar situation, such as local-government councillors. It has now acquired much more general application; for example, 'deselected' library books are those removed from public circulation.

desert. Desert Fox Nickname of Field Marshal Erwin Rommel (1891–1944), so called because of his intuitive strategy as commander of the German AFRIKA KORPS in World War II. One of Hitler's most popular generals, he also enjoyed the respect of many Allied soldiers. After the success of the Allied landings in France in 1944, he became convinced that Germany would be defeated. After Hitler refused to listen to his entreaties to end the war, he was implicated in the July 1944 bomb plot (*see* STAUFFENBERG PLOT) against Hitler, although he was not involved in the assassination attempt itself, preferring that Hitler should be brought to trial. In October 1944, while at home recovering from a wound received in an air raid, he was visited by two fellow generals, who gave him a choice between a public trial and suicide. He chose the latter and was given a hero's state funeral.

desertification The transformation of fertile land into desert or semi-arid land through soil erosion, over-intensive farming, poor soil management, or desert expansion. The constant expansion of the Sahara, for example, has desertified large areas of North Africa in the last 50 years. However, a policy of reforestation and such projects as spraying the land with synthetic water-holding resins to retain moisture and promote plant growth, promise to help restore the desert to agricultural use.

Desert Island Discs A BBC radio programme, which claims the title of the longest-running record programme in the world. It was first broadcast on 29 January 1942, presented by its deviser Roy Plomley. Each celebrity 'guest' to be cast away on the mythical desert island is invited to select eight records, a book, and a luxury item to take there. When Plomley died in 1985 he was succeeded as presenter by Michael Parkinson and subsequently by Sue Lawley; the only person to be 'cast away' to the island four times was the comedian Arthur Askey. *See also* AMOS 'N' ANDY; ARCHERS, THE; BLUE PETER; CORONATION STREET; SOOTY.

Desert Rats The name associated with the 7th Armoured Division of the British Army, whose divisional sign was the desert rat (jerboa), which was adopted during its 'scurrying and biting' tactics in Libya in World War II. The nickname was inspired by the pet jerboa of a regimental signaller; the jerboa badge was originally sketched by the divisional commander's wife. The division served throughout the North Africa campaign, and in NW Europe from Normandy to Berlin. The Division's descendants returned to the desert in 1990 as part of the British contingent sent to Saudi Arabia in response to the Iraqi invasion of Kuwait.

Desert Storm The military codename for the attack on Iraq, which began on 17 January 1991, by the Allies led by America and the UK, in response to Saddam Hussein's invasion and rape of Kuwait (August 1990). In order to protect the other Gulf States and Saudi Arabia, to force Hussein to leave Kuwait, and to achieve supremacy over the Iraqi war machine (the fourth largest in the world), a massive multinational force was built up in Saudi Arabia under the codename **Desert Shield**. With armed intervention sanctioned by the UN, Saddam Hussein's rebuttal of all attempts at negotiation, and the failure of five months of sanctions to make an appreciable impact, the Allies had little alternative to unleashing its forces (*see* GULF WAR). As a way of showing support for the forces in the Gulf, groups of women in SE England banded together to send parcels of Dundee cakes to the Gulf under the operational name 'Dessert Storm'.

designer A word that came into use in the 1980s to describe goods sold under the label or logo of a specific designer. Although such goods are frequently not very different from others of their kind sold on the mass market, they are considerably more expensive. First applied to wearing apparel, especially jeans, the word spread to other goods, such as bags and other items of luggage. Eventually so many things were so designated that the word became virtually meaningless.

designer drug An illegal drug produced by a chemist rather than made from a natural substance. It implies that the chemist has devised a formula to make the drug as potent as the illegal drug but slightly different so that he and the users avoid prosecution.

designer socialism A derogatory term for the UK Labour Party's attempts to present a modern nondoctrinaire image in the late 1980s and 1990s. This has involved both a retreat from unpopular leftwing policies and a new emphasis on PR, media skills, and visual presentation. The latter is usually put down to the influence of Peter Mandelson (1953–), the party's director of campaigns and communications from 1985 to 1990. Old-style socialists bemoan it as the triumph of image over substance.

designer stubble A man's one- or two-day's growth of beard that has intentionally been left unshaved to create a relaxed unsmart image. It goes with an unbuttoned shirt collar, a tie knotted over the chest, and jeans.

designer water An ironic description of bottled water. For many years, the idea that the British should actually buy water in bottles in their own country would have seemed ludicrous. It was the sort of thing that they felt obliged to do when venturing abroad: foreign tap water was regarded as unclean, unwholesome, and dangerous. In the 1980s, there was a change in attitude and home sales of bottled water increased dramatically for both carbonated and still water. There were a number of reasons for this. Perhaps the most significant was a highly successful advertising campaign for the French product **Perrier water**. This was helped by the deteriorating quality of British tap water and by a general increase in the public's awareness of health. Drinking bottled water rather than alcohol is now often regarded as prudent, especially by drivers. Drinking bottled water instead of tap water is expensive but chic, hence the 'designer' label.

desist, refrain, and cease Catchphrase meaning 'stop', popularized in the early 1910s by the British music-hall comedian George Robey (George Edward Wade; 1869–1954), the self-styled PRIME MINISTER OF MIRTH. It is now rarely heard.

desk. desk jockey A facetious and often derogatory description of an office worker. The expression was coined by analogy with DISC JOCKEY.

desk piano US Black slang from the 1940s for a typewriter.

desktop publishing (DTP) The use of a desktop microcomputer with page make-up software and a laser printer to produce professional-quality documents combining both text and graphics. The first page-layout software program, Aldus PageMaker, was released for the Apple Macintosh computer in 1985; this software and hardware combination remains the standard by which other DTP systems are judged. Because of the substantial savings in time and labour resulting from using DTP, similar technology is now used at the highest level to produce books, magazines, and newspapers.

Desmond British student slang of the 1980s for a lower second class degree, *i.e.* a 2/2. It is a play on the name of the South African archbishop, Desmond Tutu. *See also* DOUGLAS; PATTIE; TAIWAN.

Desperation, pacification, expectation, acclamation, realization – it's Fry's A British advertising slogan for Fry's chocolate used in the years after World War I. The poster showed the faces of five boys, each featuring one of these five different expressions in anticipation of the forthcoming sensations offered by a mouthful of Fry's chocolate.

des res Short for desirable residence. Originally estate agents' jargon used in advertisements, it passed into common usage in the late 1980s to refer to a property with many attractive features, together with the phrase 'all mod cons' (meaning the property includes all the usual modern conveniences).

Destour The Tunisian Liberal Constitutional Party: a nationalist political party formed in 1920 to press for Tunisian independence from French colonial rule and for reinstatement of the suspended Tunisian constitution (*dustūr*). After organizing strikes and boycotts in the early 1930s, Destour was banned by the French authorities in 1933. A breakaway faction, **Néo-Destour**, emerged soon after, and eventually eclipsed its progenitor, in spite of several attempts to revive Destour in the 1940s and 1950s. Under Habib Bourguiba, Néo-Destour achieved independence for Tunisia in 1956.

detente The relaxing or easing of tension between nations. The most ambitious efforts at superpower detente in the COLD WAR period after 1945 occurred during the 1970s, with the Nixon–Brezhnev meetings and US rapprochement with China. The early 1980s, however, saw a return to hardline Cold-War attitudes. The advent of the Gorbachev era in the late 1980s, the crumbling of European communist regimes, and the reunification of Germany in 1990 finally enabled the Cold War to come to an end and a new age of international disarmament and cooperation to begin.

detention centre An institution for the short-term detention of young male offenders aged between 14 and 20. Custodial sentences are usually for between 21 days and four months. These centres operate a regime of rigid discipline, hard work, and physical exercise, in accordance with the government's 'short sharp shock' policy, announced by William Whitelaw at the 1979 Conservative Party conference. However, statistics for those committing subsequent offences after release have failed to indicate that this tougher regime has had a deterrent effect in the decade since its introduction.

detox Slang for detoxification after becoming addicted to illegal drugs or alcohol. Originally a medical worker's term, it is now used by the patients themselves.

detoxification centre A clinic to which alcoholics and drug addicts go to receive professional help to reduce or eliminate their dependency by means of medical treatment, counselling, and therapy. The best-known detoxification centre is the Betty Ford Clinic (named after President Ford's wife) in America, an institution that numerous Hollywood stars and famous international figures have visited to receive treatment for various forms of addiction. There are many similar, but less glamorous, centres throughout the western world.

deuce US slang for a two-dollar bill.

deuce o' dims and darks on the cutback US Black slang from the 1940s meaning two days ago.

deuce of benders US Black slang from the 1940s for knees.

deuce of haircuts US Black slang from the 1940s for two weeks.

deuce of nods on the backbeat US Black slang from the 1940s meaning two nights ago.

Deutschmark The German unit of currency, which is divided into 100 pfennigs. The Deutschmark was introduced on 21 June 1948 as a replacement for the REICHSMARK. However, the new currency was forbidden to circulate in the Soviet-controlled eastern zone. This led to two different German currencies: the West German Deutschmark, or DM (West), and the Deutschmark (Ost), or Ostmark, in East Germany. With unification of East and West Germany in 1990, the DM (West) became the single currency of the united Germany.

Deutschland Either of two classes of German warship built in the 20th century. The first comprised five vessels built between 1903 and 1908, starting with the *Deutschland* itself, which was completed in 1906. Others were the *Hanover* (1904–07), *Pommern* (1904–07), *Schlesien* (1904–08), and *Schleswig-Holstein* (1905–08). The second Deutschland series, known as the Deutschland-Lützow class, comprised three armoured heavy cruisers built between 1929 and 1936. The *Deutschland* was launched in 1931, but renamed the *Lützow* in 1939. A bombing raid on the *Deutschland* in Ibiza harbour in 1937, resulting in the deaths of 23 men, gave Hitler the excuse he required to step up German involvement in the SPANISH CIVIL WAR. Others in the trio were the *Admiral Scheer* and *Admiral Graf Spee*. All three were built using a welded steel construction method, instead of the traditional reveting, and all three were sunk by the Allies during World War II.

deux-chevaux or **2 CV** (Fr. two horses) A small French Citroen car with a two-horsepower engine. Originally designed in the 1950s to provide French farmers with a practical and inexpensive car, it became a cult car in the UK and elsewhere in the 1960s. The original advertising claimed that the car would accommodate a bale of hay and enable the driver to hold a glass of champagne without spilling any, while driving across a field.

developing countries The countries with insufficient agricultural and industrial productive capacity to generate the savings required to sustain investment and economic growth. They are also called underdeveloped countries, THIRD WORLD countries, or less-developed countries (LDCs). These countries, which make up 70% of the world's population, include most of Africa, Asia, Central and Latin America, and the Caribbean. Common features include dependence on the export of primary products, widespread poverty and disease, illiteracy, and high birth rates. It was once thought that with economic aid from the industrialized nations, developing countries could reach the level of industrialization needed for 'take-off' into self-sustained economic growth. However, the viability of this western model in the Third World has been increasingly questioned by economists and sociologists; no real consensus exists as to the most beneficial form that either the aid itself or the means of distributing it should take. Meanwhile, unfavourable terms of trade, international protectionism, and enormous hungry populations that have failed to accept western methods of family planning (and in Catholic countries have been encouraged by the Church not to do so), have left many developing countries worse off in the 1990s than they have ever been.

devil. Devil's Island (Fr. *Isle du Diable*) The smallest of the Isles du Salut (Safety Islands) off the coast of French Guiana. Remote and desolate, it was used by the French first as a leper colony and then a penal colony (1895–1938). The island's most famous prisoner was Alfred Dreyfuss (1859–1935), who was imprisoned there for five years (1894–99) having been unjustly convicted of treason. *See* DREYFUSARD.

A graphic description of the appalling conditions on the island and the brutal treatment meted out to the unfortunates sent there is contained in *Papillon* (1973), the autobiographical best-seller by Henri Charrière, which was made into a film starring Dustin Hoffman and Steve McQueen. The island is now a popular winter tourist resort.

Devil's Triangle *See* BERMUDA TRIANGLE.

devolution The proposed transfer of legislative powers from central government to regional assemblies in Scotland and Wales. Pressure for devolution reached its peak during the 1970s, when the Scottish National Party gained over 30% of the vote of the Scottish electorate and 11 parliamentary seats in the October 1974 election. The Labour Party then drew up proposals for a Scottish legislative assembly with devolved powers, which, while falling short of Nationalist demands for complete independence, satisfied those Scots who supported a measure of independence without a complete break from the UK. In a referendum in March 1979, however, only a third voted in favour of the proposal, short of the 40% of the electorate required for the implementation of the devolution proposal. Thereafter the SNP's popularity declined; although it remains a force in Scottish politics, it has never regained the level of support it enjoyed in the mid-1970s. Unlike the SNP, the Welsh Nationalist Party (Plaid Cymru) is more interested in preserving Welsh culture and language than achieving independence. They did, however, campaign for a devolution proposal; only 12% of Welsh voters opted for the regional assembly in the 1979 referendum.

DEW line Distant Early Warning Line. A network of radar stations, mostly in the Arctic, intended to give America early warning of an aircraft or missile attack.

dex Slang for a pill or capsule containing the amphetamine Dexedrine; a pep pill. It was abused in the 1950s and 1960s, especially by the mods (*see* MODS AND ROCKERS) of the 1960s. The pills were also known as 'Dexy's Midnight Runners', which was also the name of a rock group in the late 1970s.

DGBE *See* ORDER OF THE BRITISH EMPIRE.

DHSS Department of Health and Social Security. The British government department that was responsible for the National Health Service and all the social security services until 1988, when it was split into the **Department of Health** (DH) and a separate **Department of Social Security** (DSS). When it was one single department it was responsible for all aspects of the WELFARE STATE and was the largest employer in Europe.

DIA *See* DEFENSE INTELLIGENCE AGENCY.

diamanté A fabric covered with artificial jewels or sequins to give it a glittering effect. The word derives from the French *diamanter*, to cover with diamonds.

diamond. a diamond is forever A slogan created in 1939 by B. J. Kidd of the N. W. Ayer Agency, Chicago for the South African-based De Beers Consolidated Mines, who mine diamonds and to a large extent control the diamond market. The advertisement was an attempt to increase the sales of diamond engagement rings. Sounding so much like an ancient proverb, it has become part of the language. Ian Fleming used a variation of it for one of his James Bond novels, *Diamonds are Forever* (1956), which was made into a film in 1971, starring Sean Connery.

diathermy (Gr. *dia*, through; *thermē*, heat) The production of heat in the human body by means of a high-frequency current passed between electrodes placed on the skin. The heat produced can be used to treat deep-seated arthritic or rheumatic pain.

diathermy knife An instrument used in surgery to make almost bloodless incisions. The knife used to make the incision is one electrode, the other being a pad applied to the patient's skin. As the knife is used the small blood vessels are sealed off, because the current causes the blood to coagulate.

dibbler A small Australian marsupial, *Antechius apicalis*. The dibbler is brown, about 8 inches long, and has a long snout. It had been thought to be extinct since the 1800s, but was rediscovered in 1967.

dick (1) Slang for a detective. (2) Slang for a penis.

dickless Tracey Australian slang for a policewoman. It is derived from a play on the name of the popular US comic-strip detective, Dick Tracey, in which 'dick' means either a detective or a penis.

Dictaphone Tradename for a dictating machine; a tape recorder used to record dictation for subsequent typing. The original models used wax cylinders as the storage medium.

die. died of wounds A phrase used by British soldiers during World War I, applied to anyone who was missing or killed in action.

Diehards Nickname given to Tory rebels who, in 1911, rejected the advice of their party leader, A. J. Balfour, and pledged to 'die fighting' the constitutional changes proposed in Lloyd George's Parliament Bill. Essentially, these changes limited the power of veto exercised by the House of Lords over bills passed by the Commons. The Diehards' revolt caused Balfour to resign the Tory leadership in November 1911.

die-in A type of public demonstration in which people lie on the floor pretending to be dead, to draw attention to the dangers of nuclear or chemical warfare. The idea was an extension of the 1960s SIT-IN.

Dien Bien Phu A large village in North Vietnam in an upland valley close to the Laos border. It was the site of the ignominious defeat of French forces by the Vietminh (Vietnamese nationalists) in May 1954, which ended French colonial rule in Vietnam. The French had chosen Dien Bien Phu in November 1953 as a land-air base from which to conduct offensive operations against Vietminh forces. By December, however, the Vietminh commander, General Vo Nguyen Giap, had surrounded the French garrison with over 40,000 men and heavy artillery sited in the mountains overlooking the base. The final battle began on 12 March 1954; the base was eventually taken on 7 May, the day before the opening of the international peace conference at Geneva. Although Eisenhower wisely refused French appeals for US military support during the siege and battle of Dien Bien Phu, the lessons of the French defeat were unfortunately ignored by later US presidents. Two decades later, the Americans themselves were forced to withdraw in similar humiliating circumstances, after the fall of Saigon to the Vietcong in April 1975 (*see* VIETNAM WAR).

Dieppe raid An Allied assault on the German-occupied French Channel port of Dieppe that took place on 19 August 1942. The Allied force comprised 5000 Canadian and 1000 British troops, plus some US Rangers and Free French forces. The landing, codenamed Operation Jubilee, proved very costly, with over 1000 Allied troops killed and some 2000 taken prisoner. However, nearly 50 German aircraft were destroyed in the raid and Allied commanders learned valuable lessons in assault strategy. After the war, Lord Mountbatten reflected that the Dieppe Raid "gave the Allies the priceless secret of victory".

diesel or **diesel dyke** Slang for a lesbian, especially one who is large, aggressive, and masculine. It reflects the rugged appearance of diesel engines and perhaps also the working clothes worn by the men who make or repair them, which are also worn by some lesbians. Originally heard in America, the word has been used in the UK since the 1980s, pejoratively by men but neutrally by one lesbian of another. *See also* DYKE.

diet pill or **slimming pill** Any of various drugs used to help reduce weight. Diet pills work in various ways: some (*e.g.* amphetamines) suppress the appetite, some speed up metabolism, others (*e.g.* diuretics) cause fluid loss, etc. They are generally regarded as harmful (unless prescribed by a doctor) and are of little use for long-term weight reduction without dieting. The best way to reduce weight is to eat less of the fatty and sugary foods – or to eat less of everything; compulsive overeating (*see* BULIMIA) may require psychological help.

different. And now for something completely different A British catchphrase from MONTY PYTHON'S FLYING CIRCUS, a zany TV programme of the 1960s and 1970s, which had its own cult following. The phrase was also used as the title of the same comedy team's first feature-length film in 1971. In the TV show the line was said by John Cleese wearing evening dress, like an early BBC announcer, and seated at a table behind a microphone in totally incongruous surroundings. It was previously used on magazine programmes as a useful link phrase between unrelated items, but Monty Python made this no longer possible.

dig Slang from the 1930s meaning to understand. Its origin is uncertain but a likely explanation is that it derives from the African *degu*, to understand. This sense lost its voguishness during World War II, but the word emerged in the late 1950s and 1960s as HIPPIE jargon, meaning to like or approve of. In the 1930s 'I don't dig him' would have meant 'I don't understand him'. In the 1960s 'I dig him' would have been said by a girl to mean that she found 'him' sexually attractive. The shift of meaning is unexplained. In either of these contexts the word now sounds dated.

dig for victory A campaign run by the British Ministry of Agriculture during World War II urging garden and allotment owners to grow food to help the war effort. The campaign featured a propaganda barrage – over ten million leaflets were distributed in 1942 alone. By 1944, 25% of fresh eggs were supplied by domestic hen keepers; there was also a pig-keeping craze, with over 6900 Pig Clubs in existence by the end of the war.

digger An Australian. The name was in use before 1850, consequent upon the discovery of gold, and was applied to ANZAC troops fighting in Flanders in World War I and again in World War II.

diggers In America, the name given to HIPPIES who help others, especially fellow hippies. The name was derived from its use by a small group of extreme English radicals and social revolutionaries under Gerrard Winstanley (*c.* 1609–60) who began to dig the common at St George's Hill, Surrey in 1649. Their aim was to give back the land to the common people, but they were soon suppressed by the Cromwellian army leaders.

digital In the 1970s 'digital' was used to describe watches and clocks (*see* DIGITAL CLOCK) in which the time is indicated by a set of digits rather than by hands moving round a dial. Digital was subsequently used of any recording instrument (*e.g.* a digital voltmeter) or machine (*e.g.* a digital computer) that used digits to represent quantities. This connection with computers, nearly all of which are now digital in that they manipulate discrete (rather than continuous) quantities, led to the general sense 'relating to computers or computerization'.

digital clock A watch or clock featuring a readout in figures (usually the 24-hour system) as opposed to the revolving hands of a normal (analogue) clock. Early forms of digital clocks used light-emitting diode (LED) displays but these were superseded by superior liquid crystal displays (LCD). Digital read-outs are now widely used in many measuring instruments.

digital mapping A method of map making in which the points and lines that make up the map are fed into a computer in digital form and stored on magnetic tape or disk. Subsequently the map, or a selected part of it, can be displayed on a screen or printed out, to any scale or in a variety of forms of projection. Changes can also be made without needing to redraw the map. In 1973 the UK Ordnance Survey began converting its maps to the digital form.

digital recording A method of recording sound either on digital audio tape or COMPACT DISCS, in which the music signal is sampled up to 30,000 times per second and the characteristics of the signal are represented by digits, in the same way as all forms of information that are handled by a computer in digital form. The digits are then transmitted or recorded and reconstituted as sound in the receiver or player. This process removes all chances of distortion or interference. *See also* HI-FI.

Diktat (Ger. something dictated, from Lat. *dictatum*) Hitler gave the word ominous weight by bitterly referring to the VERSAILLES TREATY as the Versailles *Diktat*. He is reported to have told the UK's ambassador: "Everything that comes under the Treaty of Versailles I regard as extortion".

dill A fool. US and Australian slang of the 1950s, heard in school playgrounds in the UK since the 1970s. The derivation is uncertain, but it is possibly a shortening of dill pickle cucumber.

Dillinger era *See* PUBLIC ENEMY NO. 1.

dim US Black slang for night.

dims and brights US Black slang for days and nights.

dimensions *See* FOURTH DIMENSION.

dingbat (1) Australian slang for a crazy or foolish person. It is derived from the expression **dingbats**, meaning a fit of nervousness, irritation, or irrationality. This sense is occasionally used in the UK. (2) US slang for an object the name of which has been forgotten or never known. The origin of this sense is unknown.

dingo baby case The disappearance of nine-week-old baby Azaria Chamberlain at Ayers Rock, central Austrialia, which led to what is now believed to have been one of the worst miscarriages of justice in the 20th century. When the baby vanished from her parents' tent at the popular tourist site immediate suspicion fell upon the dingo population of the area – several other campers reporting that their children had been threatened in such a way not long before. However, various odd details of the case coupled with general disbelief that a dingo would be capable of carrying off a sleeping infant, led to the suggestion that the baby's parents – especially the mother, 'Lindy' Chamberlain – were to blame. Blood-stained clothing was found but forensic tests failed to provide clear evidence to support the dingo theory. Moreover the Chamberlains were devout Seventh-Day Adventists; this led to rumours that the baby had been sacrificed in some awful religious ceremony. An inquest and then trial of the mother followed, the prosecution's case resting on a series of circumstantial but damaging items of forensic evidence (including the discovery of blood in the couple's car). The jury ignored the doubts that surrounded the chief elements of the prosecution's argument and the lack of any motive for the killing and found Lindy Chamberlain guilty. She was sentenced to hard labour for life, despite being pregnant. An appeal was dismissed in 1983 but the support of a lobby of scientists and massive public concern resulted in the case being reopened in February 1986. Lindy Chamberlain was finally released and later pardoned. The couple's story was filmed as *A Cry in the the Dark* (1989), with Meryl Streep in the leading role.

dink Slang term used by GIS in the VIETNAM WAR for a Vietnamese. *See also* GOOK.

dinkie or **Dinky** Acronym for Double Income No Kids. It refers to a couple with well-paid jobs and no family to support. It was one of a variety of neoligisms coined in New York during the early 1980s and subsequently used in the UK to describe various social subgroups and relationships. *See also* YUPPIE.

dinkum Australian slang for genuine, sincere, honest. The word probably derives from English country dialect. Also applied especially to the second shipment of ANZACS sent abroad in World War I. The third shipment were called 'Superdinkums'. A 'dinkum-Aussie' is a native-born Australian.

Dior A French fashion house founded by the designer Christian Dior (1905–57). In 1947 he introduced his **New Look**, which used fitted bodices and long full skirts, a departure that marked a change from wartime utility to post-war femininity. Later influential styles were the **A-line** and the **H-line**, so called because of their shape.

dioxin A highly poisonous chemical present in some herbicides as an impurity. The substance is extremely persistent, taking years to disappear, and minute quanities cause serious blistering of the skin. Dioxin is also thought to cause cancer, birth deformities, and other conditions. Serious dioxin contamination occurred in July 1976 in the region around Seveso near Milan following an explosion at a weedkiller factory.

dip US Black slang for a hat.

dipstick The word first made an appearance in the late 1920s meaning a rod inserted into a container in order to record the level of the liquid within it. In this sense it most commonly refers to the rod used to indicate the level of oil in the sump of an engine. It later took on a figurative meaning in relation to testing the popularity of such things as foodstuffs and television programmes. It also became, for obvious reasons, a slang euphemism for penis, later becoming one of the many slang words for a fool or idiot, for less obvious reasons.

dirt. dirt-track racing Motor-cycle racing on a track of cinders or similar material; introduced into the UK from Australia in 1928.

dirty dancing A form of dancing performed to pop music, which involves gyratory hip-to-hip contact with one's partner. Dirty dancing was popularized by the film (1987) of the same name directed by Emile Ardolino.

dirty old man A lecherous man of any age whose practices may include exposing his genitals in public to women or children and being excessively interested in pornographic magazines or films. The expression is sometimes embellished as 'a dirty old man in a raincoat': the raincoat is regarded as an anonymous garment that does not draw attention to its wearer; it may also have slit pockets to enable the wearer to masturbate during pornographic films or striptease acts. *See also* FLASHER.

dirty pool A US expression indicating an activity or organization that is dishonourable or lacking in morality.

dirty tricks Any deceitful or subversive activity, especially those allegedly carried out by a government or other large organisation, which may even be accused of having a 'dirty tricks department'.

dirty work at the crossroads In general, any nefarious or questionable activity. More specifically, the phrase is often applied to illicit sexual liaisons. It probably comes from the activities of highwaymen, who were often supposed to operate at crossroads.

Disarmament. Disarmament Commission A body created by the UNITED NATIONS in 1952 by merging the Atomic Energy Commission and Conventional Armaments Commission. It was given the task of preparing proposals for the "regulation, limitation and balanced reduction of all armed forces and all armaments in a coordinated, comprehensive programme". A new Disarmament Commission, comprising all UN members, was established as a result of the First Special Session on Disarmament, held in 1978. (The original Commission had not met since 1965.)

Disarmament Conference The *World Disarmament Conference*, a conference of 60 nations held in Geneva in the years 1932–34. The first session (February–July 1932) was marked by disparate approaches to the issue of disarmament, especially from France, Germany, and America. At the second session (February–October 1933), a British proposal to cut European troops by nearly 500,000 was opposed by Germany. The impasse proved insurmountable and after a brief session in 1934 the Conference broke up without agreement.

disaster film or **movie** A type of film that has been popular since Hollywood's earliest years, with such examples as *Tidal Wave* and *San Francisco* in the 1930s, *Titanic* in the 1950s, and *Krakatoa East of Java* in the 1960s. But the 1970s was the decade of the disaster movie, with such spectacular star-studded examples as *The Poseidon Adventure* (1972), *Airport '75* (1974) and *Towering Inferno* (1974);

these and numerous others attracted huge audiences to the cinemas. The plots mostly featured a collection of two-dimensional characters gathered together underwater, in the clouds, or within lethal distance of an erupting volcano, mouthing cliches at each other while being exposed to, and usually surviving, cataclysmic explosions, floodings, or conflagrations. The same decade also spawned a number of amusing spoofs of the genre, such as *The Big Bus* (1976) and *Airplane* (1980).

disc jockey (DJ) A person who introduces and plays pop records on the radio and in clubs. Radio DJs also provide a patter of lighthearted banter, which is intended to keep the listener company, and sometimes preside over phone-ins, competitions, etc. Disc jockeys became increasingly popular during the 1950s in America and the 1960s in the UK. However, record programmes with an introducer are almost as old as broadcasting. The BBC's Christopher Stone (1882–1965) ran a very popular record programme for many years in the 1930s.

disclosing agent A dye that is absorbed by plaque on the teeth and is used, usually in tablet form, to disclose areas of the teeth that have not been cleaned properly.

disco A nightclub in which people gather to dance to recorded pop music, which is often accompanied by elaborate computer-controlled lighting effects and laser shows. Disco was also a form of dance music, and a style of dancing, popular in the 1970s. The word *discotheque* (after *bibliotheque*) originated in France in the 1950s, and was adopted in its shortened form in the UK in the 1960s.

Discontent, Winter of A reference to Shakespeare (*Richard III* I, i) used by the popular press to describe the winter of 1978–79, when the Labour government under James Callaghan faced a wave of industrial unrest provoked by the frustration of workers after three years of government-imposed pay restraint. Strikes by dustmen, hospital porters, road-haulage and oil-tanker drivers, and Liverpool grave diggers provoked much dissatisfaction among the electorate with Labour's handling of the unions. This discontent effectively lost Labour the 1979 election, which ushered in 11 years of THATCHERISM.

discover. Discoverer A series of unmanned space SATELLITES launched by America from 1959. Discoverer 13, launched on 10 August 1960, carried the first capsule to be successfully recovered from orbit.

Discovery The ship that carried Robert Falcon Scott (1868–1912) on his first voyage of scientific exploration to the Antarctic in 1901–04. By all accounts the *Discovery* was poorly suited to Antarctic exploration. Launched in Dundee on 21 March 1901, she was probably the last big wooden sailing ship built in the UK. She had three masts, which were too short and badly positioned, and was under-rigged. The sails were supplemented by auxiliary steam engines but she did not have enough coal capacity to make long distances under steam. The person responsible for this poor design was Admiralty constructor, W. E. Smith, who also designed the Royal yacht, *Victoria and Albert*, which nearly turned turtle when launched.

Disgusted, Tunbridge Wells A British catchphrase that is meant to represent a typical signature on a letter of protest to the press, by someone who is unwilling to use his or her real name. It also plays on the image of Tunbridge Wells, a town in Kent, as a bastion of solid reactionary Conservative views. The origin of the phrase is uncertain. Some suggest Richard Murdoch, who had links with the town, used it in his radio show *Much Binding in the Marsh* of the late 1940s and early 1950s. It has always been used to convey an air of mock pomposity, as in the following caption beneath a photograph of actual protesters in the town of Tunbridge Wells:

> Disgusted of Tunbridge Wells came out to demonstrate against the poll tax yesterday . . .
>
> *The Independent*, 11 March 1990.

Tunbridge Wells is not alone in having been selected to represent some characteristic of the English. *See* NEASDEN; WIGAN.

dish (1) A very attractive woman or man. Originally this slang expression was more widely used of women by men; it has been heard in America and the UK since the 1930s and is an example of a euphemism for food being used to describe a desirable woman (*see also* CHEESECAKE). In an age of feminism, however, it is now considered rather insulting by most women. Consequently, since the 1960s, it has been more usually applied to men by women. (2) US slang for gossip. It is taken from the expression to **dish the dirt**, meaning to pass on all the gossip.

dish aerial A saucer-shaped dish, about one metre in diameter, used to receive television signals beamed from orbiting COMMUNICATIONS SATELLITES owned by broadcasters, such as British Sky Broadcasting. The dishes have to be placed on the outside of a building in correct alignment with the satellite, which is in geostationary orbit. Dish aerials of much greater diameter are also used for transmitting and receiving radio waves and microwaves in radio telescopes and radar installations. For example, the steerable radio telescope at Jodrell Bank, owned by Manchester University, has a 250 ft (76.2 metre) diameter dish.

disinformation Misleading or inaccurate information deliberately leaked or given to the media by official sources, such as government departments, to draw attention away from the true information. It was originally used of such information disseminated in the Soviet Union but has now spread worldwide.

disk. disk drive The part of a computer system that rotates a magnetic disk and enables data to be written on the disk and read from it.

diskette *See* FLOPPY DISK.

Disney. Disneyfication A pejorative description of the way in which historically interesting places, events, or people can be trivialized for commercial purposes. It derives from the name of Walt Disney (1901–66), the renowned US maker of 20th-century cartoon films; Disneyfication, however, refers not only to Disney's films and the characters he created in them, but also to the DISNEYLAND theme parks, which feature these characters and others in a wide variety of historical settings.

Disneyland One of the world's most famous amusement parks, opened in Anaheim, California, in 1955. Disneyland incorporates all the fantasy elements of the cartoon world created by Walt Disney. Other Disney parks are Walt Disney World, Orlando, Florida (1971) and its companion the Experimental Prototype Community of Tomorrow (EPCOT) Center (1982), Lake Buenavista, Florida. Another Disneyland was opened in Tokyo in 1983 and the most recent will open near Paris in 1992.

Disneyland daddy A US expression used to describe a father who is divorced or separated from his wife and does not have custody of the children of the marriage. He sees his children only at weekends or at less frequent intervals and therefore tends to give them more expensive treats than he otherwise would. A visit to DISNEYLAND is considered by some children to be the ultimate in treats.

Displaced Person *See* DP.

disposition. Not suitable for those of a nervous disposition A warning phrase that preceded certain programmes on British television in the 1950s, which probably acted more as an enticement to watch than as a disincentive.

diss Slang of the late 1980s meaning to snub or put down. It is a HIP-HOP jargon abbreviation of dismiss or disapprove, which became popular with teenagers in America. Many words in hip-hop jargon are formed in this way.

Distinguished Flying Cross (DFC) British decoration instituted in 1918 for officers and warrant officers in the RAF for acts of gallantry or bravery in action against the enemy.

District, the Storyville, the area of New Orleans that witnessed the beginnings of JAZZ in the years 1910–17.

ditsy or **ditzy** US slang for silly or frivolous. It is probably a corruption of 'dizzy' and is usually applied to females; it has been in use since the 1970s.

dittybop US Black slang for a pretentious young man or woman who aims to persuade others that he or she is more HEP than he or she really is.

div British prison jargon for a stupid or odd person, someone who doesn't fit in. It is a shortened form of 'divvy', which is thought to be a corruption of deviant. It has been used since the 1980s.

dive. deep-sea diver *See under* DEEP.

dive bomber An aircraft designed for precision bombing of individual surface targets by diving at them at a steep angle. The most famous dive bomber was the JU87b 'Stuka', used by the Germans in the *Blitzkrieg* (*see* BLITZ) against Poland at the outset of World War II. Dive bombers were also used by British, US, and Japanese air forces during the conflict. The most successful attack by a British force was the sinking of the German light cruiser *Königsberg* by the Fleet Air Arm in Bergen Fjord, in April 1940. Dive bombers also played a major role during the German siege of Malta, in the Japanese attack on PEARL HARBOR and in the Pacific theatre 1942–45. After the war, the theory and practice of dive bombing was superseded by high-level blanket bombing, as used by the Americans against large-scale targets in Korea and Vietnam.

dive bombing (1) British slang for covering a building or train with graffiti using spray paints. A graffiti artists' term, it has been in use since the 1970s. (2) British slang used by tramps in the 1980s for collecting cigarette ends from the street and smoking them.

don't forget the diver A British catchphrase that first appeared in 1940 in the popular radio programme ITMA, which ran from 1939 to 1949, starring Tommy Handley. It was spoken by Horace Percival as the Diver, and is said to have originated with a memory that Handley had of a man who used to dive off the pier at New Brighton, asking for money from onlookers with this phrase. It soon became a phrase of wartime public-house bonhomie.

Dix, Dorothy *See* DOROTHY DIX.

Dixie Short for **Dixieland**. A style of JAZZ characterized by White musicians using a combination of trombone, clarinet, and trumpet, that developed in New Orleans. It was named after the Original Dixieland Jazz Band (known as the ODJB), which was founded in 1912.

Dixiecrats A breakaway faction of the US Democratic Party, also known as States' Rights Democrats, formed to oppose the civil-rights policies of Truman in the 1948 presidential election. Support was concentrated in the traditionally conservative Southern states, hence the nickname 'Dixiecrats'. Governor Strom Thurmond of South Carolina was nominated as their presidential candidate, with Governor Fielding Wright of Mississippi as his running mate. Despite limited success in some of their heartland states, the Dixiecrats failed in their aim of denying the main contenders outright victory in the electoral college. Thurmond's share of the Southern vote was 22.5%, compared to Truman's 50.1%.

Dixie Dean Nickname of William R. Dean (1907–80), British footballer who was a famous centre forward in the 1920s and 1930s. He holds the record for the maximum number of goals scored in an English league season (60 goals in 39 games for Everton football club).

DIY *See* DO-IT-YOURSELF.

Dizzy Nickname of the Black US JAZZ trumpeter John Birks Gillespie (1917–). In the 1940s, with Charlie (BIRD) Parker, he revolted against the trend swing was taking and introduced BOP, using a smaller band.

DJ *See* DISC JOCKEY.

DM's British slang abbreviation for DOC MARTENS.

DMT Dimethyl triptamine. A synthetic hallucinogenic drug developed in the 1970s. The effects lasted only one hour, as oppsed to the four to eight hours experienced by users of LSD.

DMZ Abbreviation for demilitarized zone.

DNA Deoxyribonucleic acid. The complex molecule that constitutes the genetic material of living organisms. Each molecule comprises two helically coiled strands, cross-linked by bonds rather like the rungs of a ladder. Individual genes correspond to specific segments of the molecule, which forms the key component of chromosomes. The **double helix** structure of DNA was discovered by the molecular biologists James Watson (1928–) and Francis Crick (1916–) in 1953, working at the Cavendish Laboratory in Cambridge. Their model for DNA solved the mystery of the way in which living cells faithfully replicate their genes and hence how genetic information is passed on to successive generations of organisms. It has proved to be one of the most significant scientific discoveries of the 20th century.

do. can I do you now, sir? *See* ITMA.

do it A euphemism for having sexual intercourse. Because 'do it' has several other common nonsexual meanings, the sexual version often takes the form of a double entrendre. It was used by Cole Porter (1892–1964) in a song 'Let's do it' (1928) which began:

> Birds do it, bees do it,
> Even sentimental fleas do it,
> Let's do it,
> Let's fall in love.

do it now! Originally, a humorous exhortation, the phrase has become a serious slogan for efficient businessmen, etc.

do-it-yourself or **DIY** A post-World War II phrase applied primarily to the efforts of the amateur house-repairer, improver, and decorator, etc., but also more widely applied to many forms of self-help. A 'do-it-yourself' shop is one that caters for the growing needs of the amateur decorator, furniture repairer, etc.

don't just stand there, do something! An exhortation that became a catchphrase around the 1940s, usually used humorously. The SAMARITANS, a voluntary organization that helps the suicidal and despairing by listening to them at length, sometimes inverts the exhortation to 'don't just do something, stand there'.

do up US slang meaning to prepare for an intravenous injection of drugs by applying a tourniquet around the arm or leg.

doc. **Doc Martens** or **DM's** Tradename for heavy-duty lace-up shoes or boots with thick resistant soles and strong yellow stitching. Worn originally by workmen, they became fashionable as part of the SKINHEAD uniform dress in the late 1960s. In the 1980s they became fashionable again, being worn by certain groups of young people, both male and female.

What's up, Doc? The catchphrase used by the famous US cartoon character BUGS BUNNY; it was always said to Dr Elmer Fudd, whose sole purpose in life was to find a way of doing away with Bugs. The phrase was used as the title for a film in 1972, starring Ryan O'Neal and Barbra Streisand.

dock. **dock asthma** British police and criminal jargon for the theatrical gasps of surprise or disbelief affected by prisoners in the dock. It has been in use since the 1950s.

Dockers' KC A nickname gained by Ernest Bevin (1881–1951) for his successful championing of the dockers' case before the Commission of Inquiry of 1920. Many of his union's demands were met.

docking The connecting together of two orbiting spacecraft. In July 1975, there was a symbolic joint spaceflight in which a Soviet SOYUZ spacecraft docked with a US Apollo spacecraft. The astronauts moved between the two craft and carried out joint experiments.

docknie or **dockny** A word formed from 'dockland' by analogy with Cockney. It describes a person who lives in London's former dockland, which, since the demise of London as a port, has been redeveloped and gentrified (*see* GENTRIFICATION). As the original Cockney inhabitants can no longer afford to live there, 'docknie' is frequently used derogatorily. *See also* DECCIE; DINKIE; YUPPIE.

doctor. **Doctor Feelgood** A US expression for a person or a doctor who prescribes drugs to be used illegally for pleasure rather than as a remedy. The name was used by a popular rock group of the 1970s.

Doctor's mandate The virtual free hand sought from the British electorate by Ramsay MacDonald's National Government in the general election of October 1931. Such a 'Doctor's mandate' was deemed necessary in order to treat successfully the ailing British economy. In August, MacDonald had reached agreement with the Conservative and Liberal leaders on forming a National Government but paid the price of rejection by his own Labour Party. MacDonald stood as a National Labour Party candidate and convincingly won both his own seat and the election; the National Government was returned with 554 of the 610 seats. Labour was reduced to a rump of 52 seats.

Doctors' Plot An alleged conspiracy by a group of leading Soviet doctors to murder prominent political and military figures in Stalin's government. The nine doctors were arrested in January 1953 and charged with poisoning a former Leningrad party leader, Andrei Zhdanov, and with acting as US intelligence agents. Fears of an anti-Jewish purge were raised because six of the accused were Jews. However, following Stalin's death on 5 March, their planned trial never took place and charges against them were dropped. Certain police officers were subsequently executed for fabricating evidence against the doctors. In 1956 Khrushchev claimed that Stalin had indeed intended the doctors' trial to be a pretext for an antisemitic purge.

docudrama A film or television programme based on true events, presented in dramatized form. This format has been criticized for distorting historical fact but its defenders claim that docudramas are educational and thought-provoking while providing entertainment.

documentary film A film devised and produced for the purpose of giving a realistic and accurate picture of some aspect of everyday life or work. The term dates from 1929, although the first major work of the kind, Robert Flaherty's *Nanook of the North* (1920), was filmed as early as 1920.

dog. **dogface** US slang for a soldier. It has been in use since World War II and possibly reflects the 'hang dog' expression of enlisted men.

dogfight Close aerial combat between military aircraft. The dogfight originated during World War I with the invention of a synchronized system for firing forward-facing machine guns through a propeller's arc, without blowing it to pieces (although some pilots had previously used handguns to take potshots at one another). The system was first used by German Fokker E IIIs and was quickly copied by the British and French. The Germans also developed the classic aerial combat strategy, which is still used by the latest supersonic fighter aircraft. This involves the dive out of the sun at the enemy plane, followed by the turn over the vertical and another dive from the opposite direction. The first dogfights also produced the first air aces, different nations adopting different criteria for what constituted a legitimate kill, and how many kills were required for a pilot to qualify as an ace. During World War I, the best known ace was the German Manfred Von Richthofen (1892–1918), known as the RED BARON, who claimed to have shot down 80 enemy planes before being killed in action. In World War II, Douglas Bader (1910–82), the legless ace, became a British national hero. He was finally shot down and imprisoned by the Germans, who were only able to prevent his escape by depriving him of his artificial legs.

dogfood A US drug user's name for a dark-coloured refined heroin. It was much used in the 1950s.

doggy bag A bag in which the leftovers from a restaurant meal are put so that the diner can take them home to feed to his or her dog.

doghouse Slang for a double bass, heard in JAZZ circles since the 1940s.

dog's breakfast British slang for a mess: something that has been put together in a sloppy manner or something that has been bungled. *See also* DOG'S DINNER.

dog's breath British and US slang for a person who is heartily disliked. A term of abuse current in the 1980s.

dog's dinner (1) British slang for a mess. A synonym for **dog's breakfast**, but not as commonly used. (2) A slang phrase often used in such expressions as **done up like a dog's dinner**, meaning over-dressed in a vulgar attempt at chic. The expression dates from the 1920s.

dog-tags Identity discs of members of the US armed forces (World War II), from their similarity to the tags attached to a dog's collar to give its name and the address of its owners.

dog time An inferior JAZZ number.

Dogger Bank. Battle of Dogger Bank A naval action during World War I (January 1915) in which German vessels under Admiral Hipper confronted a British squadron led by Admiral Beatty off the East Anglian coast. The Germans, comprising three battle cruisers and a heavy cruiser, were intercepted and chased by five British battle cruisers. British guns crippled and sank the heavy cruiser *Blücher* on the Dogger Bank, but a combination of tactical errors and poor ship-to-ship communication in the British fleet enabled the remaining German vessels to escape.

Dogger Bank incident The tragic and startling attack by ships of the Russian Baltic fleet on Hull trawlers off the Dogger Bank in October 1904. Two of the British vessels were sunk, with the loss of their captains. Apparently, the Russians, en route to fight Japan, mistook the fishing boats for Japanese torpedo boats. After an international inquiry in Paris, the Russians agreed to pay Britain £65,000 in compensation for the attack.

Dolby System Tradename of a noise-reduction system used in hi-fi cassette tape and video recorders to reduce tape hiss when playing back recorded music. It is named after R. Dolby (1933–), its US inventor.

dole-bludger Australian slang for someone who claims unemployment benefit (dole) without being entitled to it. This phrase is sometimes used in a more general sense to mean a lazy and unreliable person.

Dolittle, Dr The amiable and eccentric vet, who was able to converse with animals. He became familiar throughout the world in the stories of the English-born US children's author Hugh Lofting (1886–1947). Dolittle, with his many friends in the animal kingdom, including the duck Dab-Dab and his parrot Polynesia, first appeared in letters sent from Lofting to his children while he was fighting on the WESTERN FRONT in World War I. The first Dolittle book was published in 1920, with a new book appearing annually until 1927. An attempt by Lofting to dispose of Dolittle by sending him to the Moon in a story of 1928 resulted in such a storm of protest that he was obliged to bring him back in 1933. A film version, *Dr Dolittle* (1967), starred Rex Harrison (*see* SEXY REXY) in the name part.

doll (1) Slang for a woman that originated in America but was widely used in the UK in the 1950s. Although probably not coined by the New York writer Damon Runyon, it appeared in the title of his collection of short stories *Guys and Dolls* in 1933. It later was used as the title of a Runyonesque musical show in 1950, which became a film in 1955 starring Frank Sinatra and Marlon Brando. The term became popular again in the 1970s, when it was also used of men by women. Feminists see it as having a patronizing and proprietorial flavour. (2) US slang for a pill containing either barbiturates or amphetamines, especially as used by middle-class abusers of prescribed drugs. It is thought to have been invented by the US writer Jacqueline Susann, who used it in a pun in the title of her novel *The Valley of the Dolls* (1965). It is thought to be derived from the idea of a doll as a source of comfort.

doll city A US teenage slang expression used to describe a beautiful person, either male or female, implying doll-like perfection and passivity; or a beautiful place or idea. It can also be used as an exclamation of approval.

dollar. dollar diplomacy Governmental support and furtherance of commercial interests abroad for both political and economic ends. The phrase, popular with critics of US policy, stems from the Taft administration (1909–13), which fostered such policies in the Far East and Latin America. Their intention was to control as well as to promote enterprise abroad by substituting dollars for bullets and lending "all proper support to every legitimate and beneficial American enterprise abroad".

dollar shop A shop in the Soviet Union or another communist country in which goods may be purchased for US dollars, or other hard foreign currency, rather than for roubles or the local currency. Such shops supply luxury goods and other items not readily obtainable in the ordinary local shops.

dolphinarium An aquarium or pool in which dolphins are kept, typically one in which the dolphins have been trained to perform tricks for public entertainment.

dome US Black slang from the1940s for the head.

domie US Black slang from the 1930s for home.

dominatrix A Latin word meaning either a female ruler or a mistress. In the late 1980s it became associated with the concept of a woman as the provider of sexual gratification in a dominant or disciplinarian role.

Dominici murder The murder of the British nutritionist Sir Jack Drummond, his wife Anne, and their ten-year-old daughter on 4 August 1952 while camping in the French Alps at Digne. A 77-year-old farmer, Gaston Dominici, was found guilty of the crime two years later, but reprieved in 1957. The mystery was never solved.

dominion status A self-governing status formerly used to describe certain countries within the British Commonwealth. The term 'dominion' was applied after 1919 to Canada, Newfoundland, Australia, New Zealand, and South Africa, and their status was defined in 1926 as "autonomous communities within the British Empire, equal in status...united by a common allegiance to the Crown". Subsequently, any such country was referred to as a 'dominion'. The term is now largely defunct.

domino. domino operation A surgical operation developed in the late 1980s in which the heart and lungs from a deceased person are transplanted into the body of a patient whose lungs are in need of replacement but whose heart is sound. This patient's heart is then transplanted into another patient whose lungs are healthy but whose heart is in need of replacement. The reason for this procedure is that it has been found that transplanting the lungs alone is less successful than transplanting heart and lungs together; the domino operation is also economical with transplant organs, which are often in short supply. First performed at Harefield Hospital, W London, the operation is thought to owe its name to the fact that the face of a domino piece is divided into two equal parts, rather than to any connection with the domino effect (*see* DOMINO THEORY).

domino theory The theory prevalent in US foreign policy during the COLD WAR, which justified US intervention in SE Asia to contain the spread of Communism. President Eisenhower explained the theory in a press conference on 7 April 1954: "You have a row of dominoes set up, you knock over the first one, and what will happen to the last one is that it will go over very quickly". The theory was embraced as a moral imperative by subsequent US administrations, in the belief that if Indochina went communist, then so would Burma, Thailand, and Malaya, followed by all the other countries of SE Asia. The communists could then pose a dangerous threat to Australia and New Zealand and thereafter to the remainder of the free world. The domino theory led directly to the US involvement in Vietnam (*see* VIETNAM WAR). The effect in which a row of dominoes collapses if one falls is used in other contexts, and is often known as the **domino effect**.

Donald Duck British and Australian rhyming slang for fuck, often abbreviated as in: 'shall we have a Donald?' It derives, of course, from the Disney cartoon character, an irascible duck who was first seen in *The Wise Little Hen* (1934).

Donington Park A motor racing circuit near Castle Donington, Derby. It was originally opened in 1931 for motor cycles and saw its first car racing event in 1933, which was organized by the Derby and District Motor Club. One of the first closed road ciruits in the UK, Donington track ran for 2¼ miles through wooded parkland of the former seat of Lord Hastings. During World War II Donington was used as an army vehicle depot and the circuit fell into disuse. It was not until 1977 that Donington reopened for motor cycling and automobile events, on a 3.15 km track. It is now a venue for saloon, sports car, and formula racing events, including Formula 3 and Formula 3000. Donington also hosts the British Motor Cycle Grand Prix.

donkey British slang for a slow or clumsy person. It is often used by football fans, who make braying noises at a player, particularly one from the opposing team, who misses a ball or plays badly.

Donovan Report The report of the Royal Commission on Trade Unions and Employers' Associations, chaired by Lord Donovan and published in 1968. The Report focused on ways of reducing the high incidence of unofficial strikes in British industry and recommended moving towards local plant agreements in place of national agreements between unions and employers. Donovan also advocated setting up an independent Industrial Relations Commission to investigate problem areas of industry and the establishment of Labour Tribunals to examine grievances held by individuals against either employers or unions. The report was criticized by some for rejecting legally enforceable collective agreements and criminal sanctions to curb unofficial strikes and picketing.

don't know A person who is undecided about a particular issue, especially someone who refuses to give a definite answer either way in an OPINION POLL. See also FLOATING VOTER.

doodle To play JAZZ in a spontaneous informal manner.

doodlebug *See* BUZZ BOMB.

doofer (1) Slang for a thing, usually when the object's name has been temporarily forgotten, as in 'pass that doofer over'. It is also used for a miscellaneous collection of odd bits and pieces. (2) Slang for a half-smoked cigarette, the other half of which will 'do for' later. This usage dates from World War II but is still heard.

doojie US drug-users' slang for heroin. It dates from the 1950s. Its origin is unknown.

Doolittle raid A US bombing raid on Tokyo and other Japanese cities by planes from the carrier USS *Hornet*, which took place on 18 April 1942. It was led by the US test pilot Colonel James H. 'Jimmy' Doolittle. He led his force of 16 bombers over 800 miles across the Pacific to their targets. Being unable to return over such a distance, the planes flew on into China. Two crashed in Japanese-controlled territory. Doolittle was awarded the Congressional Medal of Honour for his exploit.

doom-and-gloom merchant A person who seems to enjoy bad news and can be counted on to put the worst possible interpretation on any situation. 'Merchant' in this context is any person, not one associated with buying and selling.

Doomsday. Doomsday Clock An image of a clock contained in each issue of the Bulletin of Atomic Scientists (founded 1945) that points to the time remaining before the nuclear holocaust. In 1945 the time was set to 11.52, at the height of the COLD WAR it was moved to 11.58, but in the light of recent events in the Soviet Union and E Europe, it has been put back to 11.50.

Doomsday machine A hypothetical nuclear weapon designed to destroy all human life when triggered by a nuclear attack. The idea behind the Doomsday machine is that if nuclear weapons act as a deterrent then the ultimate deterrent would be automatic destruction of everybody. The concept was first put foward by the US mathematician and 'futurologist' Herman Kahn (1922–).

doorstep Journalists' slang for their unpopular and unprincipled habit of waiting outside the private house of someone in the news, in order to obtain a doorstep interview the moment the person steps outside.

Doorn The village near Utrecht in the Netherlands that was home for the exiled German Kaiser, William II, from November 1919 until his death in 1941.

doo-wop US slang for a type of male harmony singing popular in large US cities in the 1950s among Blacks and Italians. The name, which was only coined in the 1960s, after the popularity of the style had declined, is derived from the 'doo-da' of negro songs and the derogatory 'wop' for an Italian; it also reflects some of the nonsense sounds used in the singing.

dope (1) In the 20th century this word has become very familiar in its sense of an illegal drug, both as a noun and verb. This presumably derives from its 19th-century meaning, an additive used to improve the properties of something, which in turn comes from the Dutch *doop*, sauce. (2) A fool, stupid person. This later meaning probably derives from the illegal drug sense, in that someone given dope would be likely to behave in a stupid way. (3) Detailed information, as in 'give me the dope on this new invention'. This sense is of US origin, but unknown derivation.

Doppler shift *See* REDSHIFT.

Dora The popular name of the Defence of the Realm Acts (DORA), which imposed many temporary restrictions on individual freedoms during wartime. Their application to munitions factories and the drink trade caused particular irritation. It passed into common speech after being used in the law courts by Mr Justice Scrutton. In numerous newspaper cartoons *Dora* was portrayed as a long-nosed elderly female, the personification of restriction.

dormitory town A small town within commuting distance of a larger town, the majority of the residents of which work in the larger town. Because property is so expensive in the large cities of Europe and America, many people live in dormitory towns, where houses and flats are cheaper. In addition, many commuters regard their home towns as havens from the crowds, noise, and pollution of the cities.

Dormobile Tradename for a type of small van equipped with living accommodation; a type of camper.

Dorothy Dix or **Dorothy Dixer** In Australia, a planted question in parliament that has been pre-arranged so that the minister can make a political point from the answer. It is named after a newspaper AGONY COLUMN 'Dear Dorothy Dix'.

dosh British slang for money. Originally a working-class term from the 1950s, its use was revived in the late 1980s with similar words, such as 'bread' and 'spondulicks', by ALTERNATIVE comedians whose material frequently dealt with the current obsession with money and who therefore needed a wide range of euphemisms. This sense is thought to derive from the African colonial term 'dash' meaning a tip; it could also be derived from 'doss' meaning the price of a doss, somewhere to sleep overnight.

Dossena forgeries A series of paintings and sculptures, which were accepted as genuine old masters by the artistic establishment in the 1920s but were proved to be forgeries, actually by the Italian restorer Alceo Dossena. Unlike many other art forgers, Dossena was equally adept at faking the work of several artists. He was so scrupulous in using old materials and so skilled in imitating the styles of the old masters that it was only the sheer number of these 'newly discovered' masterpieces that finally gave him away. Even after he was unmasked several leading museums refused to withdraw his works, so convinced were they of their authenticity: indeed some of his works are thought still to remain on display.

double. double agent A spy who works for two opposing countries simultaneously. The most famous British double agents were Kim 'Harold' Philby (1912–88), Guy Burgess (1911–63), Donald Maclean (1913–83), and Anthony Blunt (1907–83). (*See* BURGESS AND MACLEAN.) All were recruited by Soviet intelligence in the 1930s, and later joined the British foreign and intelligence services. It was Philby and Blunt who warned Burgess and Maclean to flee to Moscow in 1951; Philby himself remained unexposed until

1963 and Blunt until 1979. *See also* BLAKE CASE.

double-bagged US teenage slang of the 1970s for a totally dreadful or hopelessly ugly person. It reflects the idea that the sight is so awful that the person concerned ought to wear two bags over his or her head; or perhaps only one, the other one being for the onlooker! 'Double-bagged' originated in baseball jargon, to describe a type of hit that enables the player to advance two bases (or bags).

double-blue British drug-users' slang of the 1960s for a blue pill containing amphetamines or barbiturates. They were very popular with the mods (*see* MODS AND ROCKERS).

double exposure A photographic film that has been exposed twice and therefore contains two superimposed images. The technique is used extensively in trick photography.

double helix *See* DNA.

Double Summer Time *See* DAYLIGHT SAVING.

doublethink A term used by George Orwell in his *Nineteen Eighty-four* (1949) to describe what unscrupulous propagandists achieved by NEWSPEAK, a kind of doubletalk. It denoted the mental ability to hold and accept simultaneously two entirely conflicting views or beliefs.

double your pleasure, double your fun An advertising slogan used from 1959 in America for Wrigley's doublemint chewing gum. However, in the UK a TV quiz show called *Double Your Money*, which started in 1955, had a signature tune that included the line "Double your money, double your fun".

dough *See* BREAD.

doughboy Colloquial name for a US soldier in World War I. The nickname was derived ultimately from a dough cake baked for sailors, but from the late 1840s the name came to be given to US soldiers until World War II, when GI generally took its place. The common explanation is that the large brass buttons of the soldier's uniform resembled the dough cake.

doughnutting A practice in which members of the British House of Commons form a close group or doughnut-like ring around a fellow MP, who has been chosen to address a session of parliament while it is being televised. This creates the impression that the chamber of the House is crowded, when in fact it might be very sparsely populated. The habit of doughnutting originated in November 1989, when the television cameras were first allowed to record the proceedings of the House of Commons.

Douglas British student slang of the 1980s for a third class honours degree; a third. It is a play on the name of the Conservative politician Douglas Hurd. 'Richard' is a synonym, *i.e.* from Richard III. *See also* DESMOND; PATTIE; TAIWAN.

Douglas aircraft Any of the large range of aircraft built by the Douglas Aircraft Company, which was founded by Donald Douglas (1892–1981) in 1921. Douglas started to build planes for the military; in 1924 two of his Douglas World Cruiser biplanes successfully completed a round-the-world flight. The long series of **DC** (Douglas Commerical) models began in 1932 with the prototype DC-1, followed by its production version, the DC-2. Successive DC models were at the forefront of aviation development; the DC-3 (*see* DAKOTA) was the first sleeper-transport, while the DC-4, first built in 1938 by the merged Douglas and Northrop companies, was the world's biggest air transport. During World War II military versions of both the DC-3 (C-47) and DC-4 (C-54) saw active service. In addition Douglas also built several completely new military craft, such as the A-20 Havoc light bomber (1939) and the SBD (Dauntless) naval dive bomber. The Douglas Company built nearly 30,000 aircraft during the war. In 1951 the Douglas F4D Skyray DELTA WING fighter established a new world record speed of 1211 k.p.h. (753 m.p.h.). Postwar commercial airliner development continued with the DC-6 (1947) and DC-7 (1953). The DC-8, which first flew in 1958, ranked with Boeing's 707 as one of the world's most popular long-haul jet transports. A short-range twin-jet DC-9 entered service in 1965, and the DC-10 airbus came on the scene in 1970, three years after the Douglas Company merged to become the McDonnell Douglas Corporation.

Dounreay The site, near Thurso in Caithness, of the UK's first fast-breeder reactor (*see* NUCLEAR REACTOR), and now the country's leading centre for fast-reactor research. Operation of the first experimental fast reactor at Dounreay started in 1955, while the large-scale prototype fast reactor came on stream in 1974. This is capable of contributing 250 megawatts of electricity to the Scottish grid. Dounreay also has its own fuel reprocessing facility, enabling plutonium and uranium to be separated from spent fuel assemblies. The plutonium is reused as fuel for the fast reactor.

dove A person who is opposed to war and favours negotiation and accommodation with the opposition, rather than military action. The term was first used during the VIETNAM WAR. People who take the opposite view are known as **hawks**. *See also* DAWK.

Dow Jones Industrial Average An index of prices on the New York Stock Exchange issued by the financial advisors Dow Jones Co. It is based on 30 consistent securities, with a base value of 100 in 1928. In the GREAT DEPRESSION it fell to a value of 41 and now stands at well over 2000. *See also* FOOTSIE.

down US Black slang from the 1940s for good, marvellous.

downcycle A downward movement of the economy or business activity, as part of a cyclic process.

downer (1) Drug-users' slang for a tranquillizing drug, especially a barbiturate. It is the opposite of an 'upper', or stimulant. (2) Slang for a depressing or very boring experience or person. It was originally part of US HEP jargon of the 1950s but became widely used in all English-speaking countries in the 1960s. It now sounds rather dated in the UK, but the phrase 'on a downer' for a depressed period is still widely used.

down in the forest something stirred A British catchphase meaning that at last something has happened. It comes from the 1915 song 'down in the forest' with music by Sir Landon Ronald and words by H. Simpson. The song goes on to reveal that it was only a little bird that stirred. It seems possible that there is sexual innuendo in the catchphrase unintended in the original.

download To transfer data onto a COMPUTER.

down-market *See* MIDDLE-MARKET.

downside A 1980s vogue word meaning the disadvantageous or negative aspect of something. Originally, the term was restricted to business jargon, meaning the potential loss that would be sustained if a financial investment did not do well. It was very often used in the negative sense, as in 'these shares have little downside potential', meaning that they would be unlikely to fall in price.

downtime The period during which a machine, particularly a computer, is inoperative, for example when it is undergoing overhaul or repairs. In common with many other technical and computing terms, 'downtime' has entered the general language and can be applied to any non-productive period. It is now quite common to refer to the annual closure of a factory during the holiday period as downtime.

down-town The business district of a US city, so called from New York, where financial houses are concentrated on the southern tip of Manhattan Island; the lower part of a town.

DP Displaced Person, a refugee. Any person forced to leave their own country because of persecution, famine, war, pestilence, etc. 'Displaced person' was used widely to refer to the vast number of people, especially in Europe, who at the end of World War II found themselves in a country other than their own, with no legal status to be there. It included survivors of the German CONCENTRATION CAMPS, people who had been deported, interned, become forced labour, etc. Perhaps the term was used to distinguish this army of people from the pre-war 'refugees' from Nazi Germany and Austria, mostly Jews and intellectuals who found Hitler and his associates unacceptable. By the end of the war most of these refugees were established in their new homes. Since the 1950s the word 'refugee' has been widely used again and now has a particular legal status under international law; it is defined by the UNITED NATIONS as "a person who, owing to a well-founded fear of persecution for reasons of race, religion, nationality, membership of a particular social group or political opinion, is outside the country of his nationality and is unable or, owing to such fear, unwilling to avail himself of the protection of that country". The rights and duties of refugees have been detailed in two international treaties; in 1950 the post of UN High Commissioner for Refugees was created, to safeguard these rights. Chief among the rights of refugees is the principle of *non-refoulement*, which prohibits forcible repatriation of a refugee to a country in which he or she has reason to fear persecution.

drag (1) A single inhalation of a cigarette or joint. This 20th-century slang meaning is clearly derived from the early meaning, to pull or draw. (2) A boring task or person. A teenager's colloquialism of the 1960s. (3) The wearing of women's clothes by a man. In such circumstances the man is said to be **in drag**, and a performer who dresses up in this way is known as a **drag artist**. (4) In US slang, power or influence. For example, a person may be described as 'having drag with the president'. (5) US slang for a street or thoroughfare.

draggin' wagon (1) US slang for a tow truck. (2) US high-school slang of the 1970s for a vehicle used on a date to impress and transport a member of the opposite sex. Also called a **pussy wagon**.

dragon A newly industrialized country. Often abbreviated to **NICs**, these countries include Taiwan and South Korea in SE Asia. The epithet dragon, or little dragon, is applied to them to reflect the fierceness of the competition they offer to the industrial world, especially to Japan, because it is in light industry and electronics that they excel. Hitherto their economies were based on agriculture and thus posed no threat to the established industrial powers.

chase the dragon *See under* CHASE.

dragon lady Originally any intimidating woman, a US usage derived from such a character in 'Terry and the Pirates', a comic strip of the 1930s. Recently the expression has become more popular worldwide and has changed its meaning slightly to indicate a woman who wields great power, not because she herself holds a powerful office but because she is the wife of someone who does. The most famous recent example of a dragon lady was Imelda Marcos, wife of Ferdinand Marcos (1917–89) who ruled the Philippines until his overthrow by Cory Aquino.

dragon light A very powerful mobile torch used by police to dazzle, and therefore bring to a standstill, criminal suspects, especially those thought to be violent.

Dragoon *See* ANVIL.

drain. Drain London commuters' nickname for the underground train line between Waterloo and Bank stations, so called because of the dark tunnels and the fast-travelling, rather antiquated trains.

drainpipes British slang for the very tight trousers worn by TEDDY BOYS in the 1950s. They were later fashionable with the rockers (*see* MODS AND ROCKERS) in the 1960s and then with the PUNKS in the 1980s.

drain the lizard A euphemism for urinating (of males). It has been heard in the UK, America, and Australia and is popular with students and drinkers. It it thought to have originated in Australia.

Drake. Drake Brass Plate During his voyage of circumnavigation (1577–80), Sir Francis Drake anchored off the Californian coast in 1579 and set up a brass plate naming the territory New Albion and claiming it in the name of Queen Elizabeth I. In 1936 the plate was said to have been found near San Francisco and the inscription seemed to be reasonably authentic although some authorities expressed doubt. A replica was, in due course, presented to Queen Elizabeth II and kept in Buckland Abbey, Drake's Devonshire property, now a museum. In 1977 a reported analysis of the composition of the brass by the Lawrence Berkeley Institute of the University of California and the Research Laboratory for Archaeology at Oxford found that it was of the late 19th- or early 20th-century manufacture.

Drake's Drum A drum that belonged to Sir Francis Drake, which has been said to have sounded three times in the 20th century as a warning of national peril. Drake ordered that his drum be returned to his home, Buckland Abbey near Plymouth, as he lay on his deathbed, promising that if it was sounded in the future he would return to aid England in its hour of need. The tradition is that the drum is beaten by an unseen hand when a national crisis threatens. In 1914 it beat to herald the start of World War I. In 1918 it was heard beating a victory roll aboard the flagship the *Royal Oak* as the German fleet arrived at SCAPA FLOW to surrender at the end of the war: an exhaustive search of the ship failed to reveal the source of the noise. Finally, in World War II, it was heard to sound once more – this time to mark the evacuation of DUNKIRK in 1940.

drape US Black slang from the 1930s for a stylish man's suit.

draw (1) British slang dating from the 1950s for tobacco. It is derived from the act of inhaling and came originally from prison jargon. (2) British slang dating from the 1970s for smokable cannabis – an obvious extension of the previous meaning.

drawing board *See* BACK TO THE DRAWING BOARD.

Drbal's pyramid The 'discovery' by the Czech enginer Karel Drbal, in 1959, that under certain conditions small pyramids have the power to sharpen razor blades and preserve food. These supernatural properties of the pyramid were studied by

Drbal after he read of research by a French scientist, who suggested that the shape of the pyramids of ancient Egypt in some way contributed to the preservation of mummies placed within them. Drbal found that food placed in small pyramids could indeed be made to last longer than could be reasonably expected; he further found that razor blades lying on an east-west axis inside the pyramid were inexplicably sharpened. Speculation to account for these alleged phenomena persists; Drbal himself successfully patented his discovery and a factory in Czechoslovakia still does a lively trade in small pyramids for sharpening razor blades.

dread. dreadlocks A slang name for the hairstyle worn originally by male members of the Rastafarian religion of Jamaica, in which the hair is worn in long tight ringlets that are never cut or brushed. The style has now also been adopted by both Black and White young people, male and female, but has no religious significance. It is often shortened to **locks**.

Dreadnought The name given to the 17,900-ton turbine-engined big-gun battleship completed in 1906, the first of a famous class, which greatly influenced subsequent naval construction. The first ship of this name was in use in the reign of Queen Elizabeth I. The name was revived in 1963 for the UK's first nuclear submarine.

Dreadnought hoax A practical joke that made the Royal Navy a laughing stock in 1910. The hoax centred around the visit of a supposed party of princes from Abyssinia to HMS DREADNOUGHT, the pride of the navy's battle fleet, as it lay at anchor in Weymouth Bay. A telegram warned the ship's captain of the visit, allowing him just enough time to assemble the Royal Marine band and make all the arrangements suitable for a royal visit. The guests resplendent in flowing robes and heavy beards toured the ship, exclaiming "Bunga, bunga!" with enthusiasm at regular intervals. They refused all offers of food, however, on religious grounds. The hoax was subsequently revealed in the papers to have been the work of the well-known practical joker William Horace de Vere Cole. The 'princes' had included a well-known cricketer, the artist Duncan Grant, and the novelist Virginia Woolf; their disguise was the work of Sarah Bernhardt's make-up artist (who had warned them against eating anything because it might smudge their 'brown' skin).

dream. dream factory A film studio, or the motion-picture industry in general.

dream ticket A combination of two political candidates seeking office together in an election, which is regarded as ideal and therefore dreamlike. The hope is that together they would appeal to a greater section of the electorate than either of them would individually. Mostly associated with the US elections for president and vice-president, the term has also been used in the UK of the leader and deputy leader of the Labour party.

I have a dream The phrase spoken on several occasions by the Black civil rights leader Dr Martin Luther King (1929–68); it became one of the most-often repeated statements of the 1960s. King's dream of racial harmony was advanced but not realised in his own lifetime, which was brought to an early end on 4 April 1968 by a White assassin, James Earl Ray, who shot him dead on a motel balcony in Memphis, Tennessee. Various conspiracy theories to account for the killing have been suggested but none substantiated. *See also* CIVIL RIGHTS MOVEMENT.

> I have a dream that one day this nation will rise up, live out the true meaning of its creed: we hold these truths to be self-evident, that all men are created equal.
>
> Speech, Washington, 27 August 1963.

Dresden fire bombing A bombing attack starting on the night of 13–14 February 1945, on the city of Dresden in SE Germany. The attack began with 800 RAF Lancaster bombers dropping bombs and incendiaries shortly before midnight. It caused a 'fire-storm', in which hot air rising from burning buildings led to high winds, which further fanned the flames. The next day the 8th US Air Force mounted a daylight raid with over 400 B-17 bombers. On 15 February another attack was made with 200 bombers. On 2 March 400 bombers attacked and finally, on 17 April, 572 aircraft were involved. The result was the almost complete destruction of one of the most beautiful cities in Europe and the death of many people (estimates vary from 30,000 to 130,000). This systematic destruction of Dresden in the closing months of the war was justified strategically as a way of destroying a German centre of communications to aid the Soviet advance on the Eastern Front. Probably, it had little military effect and it has subsequently been criticized as an example of Air Chief Marshal Sir Arthur Harris' theory that bombing civilians can be advantageous in weakening a country's will to continue fighting. *See* BOMBER HARRIS.

Dreyfusard An advocate of the innocence of Capt. Alfred Dreyfus (1859–1935), a French artillery officer of Jewish descent who was convicted in 1894 on a charge of betraying military secrets to Germany and sent to DEVIL'S ISLAND. In 1898 Clemenceau and Zola took up his case and Zola wrote his famous open letter *J'accuse*. In 1899 Dreyfus was retried, again condemned, but shortly afterwards pardoned. In 1906 the proceedings were finally quashed and Dreyfus was awarded the Légion d'Honneur. The whole affair reflected the greatest discredit on the French military hierarchy of the time.

drink. Drinka Pinta Milka Day A British advertising slogan used by the National Milk Publicity Council of England and Wales in 1958 in a drive to persuade every man, woman, and child in the British Isles to drink at least one pint of milk every day. 'Pinta' has now become an accepted slang word for a pint of milk, or occasionally a pint of beer.

drink-driving *See* BREATHALYSER.

drive. drive-by Denoting a murder or injury inflicted by someone shooting at the victim from a moving car. The shooting is usually random and conducted by members of US gangs.

drive-in A cinema, fast-food restaurant, bank, or other venue to which access can be made by car.

driving licence An official document authorizing a person to drive a motor vehicle. In most countries the applicant must be physically fit and pass a driving test. In order to use a vehicle to learn to drive a provisional licence is granted, which becomes a full licence when the test has been passed.

drone (1) An upper-class young man of the inter-war years, wealthy but not very bright, such as the characters who appear in the novels of P. G. Wodehouse, especially those who were members of the DRONES' CLUB in London. This sense no doubt reflects the word's standard meaning, a male bee who does not work and whose only function is to mate with the queen. A drone can also mean a sponger or a scrounger in contemporary slang, especially one who latches on to another person and becomes dependent on them. This meaning is, in turn, reflected in the technical usage: an unmanned radio-controlled aircraft. (2) In the 1980s a boring person was often called a drone. Perhaps an association with a low monotonous sound, especially as used in the phrase **droning on**.

Drones' Club The gentlemen's club frequented by Bertie WOOSTER and his circle in the novels of P. G. Wodehouse. Situated in Dover Street, the Drones' Club was particularly favoured by young men of good connections but limited intellect. The uninterrupted round of social pleasure enjoyed at the club included such events as the Clothes Stakes, in which bets were placed on the attire worn by the next person to enter the bar, with Claude 'Mustard' Pott making the book:

> I am offering nine to four against Blue Serge, four to one Pin-striped Grey Tweed, ten to one Golf Coat and Plus Fours, a hundred to six Gymnasium Vest and Running Shoes, twenty to one Court Dress as worn at Buckingham Palace, nine to four the field.

drongo A colloquial expression, originating in Australia, meaning a stupid or totally useless person. It is derived from a racehorse of this name, which was notorious for its lack of success on the racetrack.

droop-nose Describing a type of aircraft design in which the nose cone of the aircraft can be pivoted downwards to give the pilot more visibility during landing. It is used on the Anglo-French supersonic airliner CONCORDE.

drop A place in which secret agents leave messages or other information to be picked up by other agents. It is one of a number of terms popularized, and perhaps invented, by writers of spy fiction.

drop dead A catchphrase that originated in America in the 1930s, but is now used in all English-speaking countries and by all types of people. It does not mean exactly what it says, but is an emphatic way of saying 'be quiet' or 'go away'.

drop-dead fee If individuals or firms wish to take over another company using borrowed money, they often arrange a drop-dead fee to be paid to the lender if the bid fails and the loan is not required. If the bid succeeds the borrower pays interest to the lender in the usual way; the purpose of the fee is to ensure that they only incur interest charges if the takeover succeeds.

dropout A person who abandons or withdraws from something, for instance a student who drops out of a university course. It became a vogue word in the late 1960s applied to people who rejected conventional society (*see* HIPPIE). The US advocate of psychedelic drugs, Timothy Leary, coined the slogan 'turn on, tune in, drop out'.

droppies British slang for self-employed people: an acronym for Disillusioned Relatively Ordinary Professionals Preferring Independent Employment Situations. It was fashionable to coin such terms in the 1980s. *See also* DINKIE; YUPPIE.

good to the last drop A US advertising slogan for Maxwell House coffee, which dates from 1907. The story goes that President Theodore Roosevelt was visiting Joel Cheek of the Maxwell House Company. Having accepted a cup of the company's product, he drank it down, smacked his lips, and proclaimed "Good to the last drop". With this recommendation the company had little option but to adopt it as their slogan.

druzhinnik In the Soviet Union an auxiliary policeman. The *druzhinniki* assist the official police in crowd control and similar duties. The name comes from *Narodnaya Druzhina*, meaning 'People's Patrol'.

dry. dried-barkers US Black slang from the 1940s for a fur coat.

dries *See* WETS.

dubbing The practice of adding a soundtrack to a film or video recording, or of changing or augmenting the sound. In particular, it is used for replacing the soundtrack of a film in one language by the soundtrack in another language.

Duce (Ital. leader) The title adopted by Benito Mussolini (1883–1945), the Fascist dictator of Italy from 1922 to 1943.

> The Duce is always right.
>
> Fascist slogan, 1922.

duck. Honey, I forgot to duck US President Ronald Reagan's reaction to his wounding in an assassination attempt in 1981, addressed to his wife Nancy as he lay recovering. His assailant, John W. Hinckley, was found to be mentally ill. The remark was not original; the president was quoting the US boxer Jack Dempsey (1895–1983), who said the same thing to his wife when he was defeated by Gene Tunney in the title fight for the World Heavyweight Championship on 23 September 1926.

If it looks like a duck, walks like a duck and quacks like a duck, it's a duck Infamous test proposed in the 1950s by the US union leader Walter Reuther to determine whether someone was a communist or not. *See* MCCARTHYISM.

duds US Black slang from the 1940s for clothes.

Dugway Proving Ground A US test site for biological and chemical weapons in Utah.

Duke (1) Nickname given to the US film actor John Wayne (1907–79). He acquired it as a child from the name he gave to his dog. (2) Nickname given to the US JAZZ composer and pianist Edward Kennedy Ellington (1899–1974). His 'Mood Indigo' was a worldwide success.

Duke of Edinburgh's Award An award scheme for young people aged between 14 and 25, originally launched in the UK as two separate awards (for boys and girls) in 1962; the awards were merged in 1969. The scheme is administered by schools, youth clubs, voluntary organizations, etc. It was devised to match the needs of people from different backgrounds, with the aim of fostering self-reliance, a sense of responsibility, and a spirit of voluntary service. It comprises five sections: community service, expeditions, hobbies and interests, design for living, and physical activity. Bronze, Silver, and Gold badges and certificates are awarded on completion of the various activities in each section. By 1988 over two million youngsters had taken part.

Duma State Deliberative Assembly: the Russian parliament established in the wake of the 1905 revolution. The proposed constitution of the first Duma was detailed by Tsar Nicholas II in his October Manifesto of 1905, as part of a wide-ranging declaration guaranteeing civil liberties and greater representation for the Russian people. However, before its first session started in May 1906, the Duma's powers had been curtailed: all its decisions could be vetoed by the tsar and the tsar could pass laws when it was not sitting. Moreover, ministers were ultimately answerable to the tsar, not the Duma. Nevertheless, the first Duma proved to be radically inclined and demanded land reforms inimical to the government. It was duly dissolved in July 1906. The second Duma, which convened in March 1907, lasted only until June. However, changes in the electoral system ensured a more conservative third and fourth Dumas (1907–12 and 1912–17), which generally supported the government. During World

War I opposition to the monarchy again swelled in the Duma; after the tsar was deposed in 1917, a Duma Provisional Committee formed the first provisional government.

Dumbarton Oaks Conference A conference held in August–October 1944 between representatives of the UK, America, the Soviet Union, and China to discuss plans for setting up an organization of world nations, subsequently realized as the UNITED NATIONS Organization. There was general agreement over the basic structures, such as the General Assembly, Security Council, and Secretariat. More contentious were the issues of membership – the Soviet Union wanted separate membership for all of its 16 republics – and the right of veto in the Security Council. These questions were reconsidered at the YALTA CONFERENCE in February 1945. The talks were named after the mansion in which they were held, in Georgetown, Washington D.C.

dumper Australian surfing term for a wave that breaks suddenly in shallow water and crashes down on the surfer.

dun. Old Dun Cow A derisive nickname given by the troops to the steamer *River Clyde* beached at GALLIPOLI in 1915 during World War I. It was probably a reference to the popular song containing the words "The Old Dun Cow she's done for now", the *Old Dun Cow* in question being a public house that had run dry.

Dungeness The coastal site in Kent of two nuclear generating stations. Dungeness A uses a Magnox reactor, and Dungeness B an advanced gas-cooled reactor. The Dungeness site is linked by cross-Channel cable to the French electricity grid, enabling power to be transferred between the two countries.

Dunkirk This once notorious haunt of pirates and privateers has acquired fresh associations since World War II. The name is now used figuratively to denote a forced military evacuation by sea to avoid disaster, a speedy and complete withdrawal, an entire abandonment of a position. The allusion is to the successful evacuation (26 May–4 June 1940) of the main British Expeditionary Force (*see* BEF), in the face of imminent disaster, by Vice-Admiral Ramsay's motley force of destroyers, yachts, and a collection of little ships manned by their private owners, with essential air cover from RAF Fighter Command. Some 338,226 Allied troops were rescued at Dunkirk and survived to fight on to bring the war to a victorious conclusion.

> The little ships, the unforgotten Homeric catalogue of *Mary Jane* and *Peggy IV*, of *Folkestone Belle*, *Boy Billy*, and *Ethel Maud*, of *Lady Haig* and *Skylark* . . . the little ships of England brought the Army home.
>
> PHILIP GUEDELLA, *Mr Churchill*.

> Our great-grandchildren, when they learn how we began this war by snatching glory out of defeat . . . may also learn how the little holiday steamers made an excursion to hell and came back glorious.
>
> J. B. PRIESTLEY, radio broadcast, 5 June 1940.

> This was their finest hour.
>
> WINSTON CHURCHILL, speech, 18 June 1940.

Dunsterforce The name given to the men sent to Baku in 1918 under the command of Maj-Gen L. C. Dunsterville (1865–1946), who had been a schoolfellow of Rudyard Kipling and was the hero of *Stalky and Co*. The purpose of this expedition was to prevent the Turks and Germans seizing the oil-wells and Dunsterforce adequately accomplished its object.

Durex A tradename for a CONDOM, owned by LRC International (formerly London Rubber Co.). The name was coined by LRC's former chairman, A. R. Reid, who also coined the brand names 'Gossamer' and 'Fetherlite'. The implication conveyed, presumably intentionally, by the name Durex is that the product is sufficiently durable to provide the service required of it.

dust. dustbin US Black slang from the 1940s for a grave.

Dust Bowl An area of land transformed into a semi-arid state through overgrazing, intensive farming, soil erosion, etc. Historically the term applies to a section of the Great Plains in America (between Kansas and Texas), which suffered a severe drought in the 1930s; as a result most of the top soil was blown away in huge black dust storms. Thousands of families from the region had to migrate west at the height of the Depression and ended up in migrant camps in California. These events were movingly and accurately described in John Steinbeck's novel *The Grapes of Wrath* (1939), of which a film was made in 1940 by John Ford, starring Henry Fonda. In the 1940s, with Federal Aid, the area was largely recovered as productive agricultural land by erecting windbreaks and replanting grassland.

dust head Slang for a user of the drug ANGEL DUST.

dusty (1) British upper-class slang of the late 1970s for an old person. It is less widely used than WRINKLIE or CRUMBLIE. According to *The Official Sloane Rangers' Handbook* by A. Barr and P. York, the ages go: wrinklie, crumblie, dusty. (2) British slang for a dustman. This abbreviation is not as commonly heard as postie for postman.

dusty butt US Black slang for an ugly prostitute, who therefore attracts no business.

Dutch *See* GIPPER.

Dutch disease A decline in the effectiveness of the industrial sector of a nation's economy resulting in balance-of-trade problems, as a result of the discovery of a new natural resource. It is named after the situation that arose in the Netherlands with the discovery of North Sea oil and gas. The new resource raised the parity of the nation's currency against those of its trading partners, which caused a drop in exports as manufactured goods became less competitive. Imports, which became cheaper, rose and the country's balance of trade was seriously disturbed. The same series of events troubled the British economy after the discovery of North Sea oil.

Dutch elm disease A fungal disease of elm trees, which withers the leaves and causes the tree's eventual death. The disease is most commonly spread by the European elm bark beetle, which carries the spores from infected to healthy trees. The disease reached almost epidemic proportions in the UK in the 1970s and 1980s when millions of trees had to be felled. First described in 1919 in the Netherlands, the fungus responsible, *Ceratocystus ulmi*, blocks the vessels that carry water to the leaves.

dyarchy or **diarchy** A system of government, literally 'dual government', introduced into India by its colonial British rulers in 1919. Government of the provinces was divided between executive councillors, appointed by the governor and in charge of 'reserved' portfolios (*e.g.* police, justice, etc.), and Indian ministers responsible to their elected legislative council and in charge of 'transferred' departments, such as public health, agriculture, and education. The system was criticized because spending control remained the prerogative of the 'reserved' arm. However, dyarchy marked the first hesitant concession towards Indian self-government; it was replaced by a more comprehensive system of provincial autonomy in 1935.

dying sayings *See* FAMOUS LAST WORDS.

dyke British slang for a lesbian. Originally used pejoratively by heterosexuals, the word conveyed the stereotypical image of the very masculine and aggressive lesbian. It is now used by gay women themselves. The derivation is unknown.

> Every twentieth page or so, she treats us to some coupling, unmetaphorical, squelchy even, with a tidy spicing of perversion and peppering of dykery.
> Review of a Judith Krantz novel, *The Independent*, 20 March 1991.

dynamite US drug users' slang, dating from the 1960s, for good-quality heroin. This is an extension of the colloquial use of the word for anything especially good or powerful. It is also used for a particularly powerful marijuana cigarette, a potent mixture of cocaine and heroin, or a mixture of heroin and marijuana.

dyslexia Inability to read, write, and spell correctly in otherwise normally intelligent people (known as 'dyslexics'). It is often due to an impaired ability to learn these skills and affected children require specialized education to overcome their problems. The condition is often incorrectly called *word blindness*, but this is a different problem in which a person cannot read because of an inability to recognize printed letters, symbols, and words although writing presents no difficulty.

E

E The drug ECSTASY. A fashionable abbreviation used from 1988. An **E-head** is someone addicted to ecstasy.

E-free Describing any foodstuff that is (or is alleged to be) free of additives, such as preservatives and colourings, which are identified by their **E numbers**. Under EC regulations, each recognized additive is assigned a number, prefixed by the letter E (for EUROPEAN COMMUNITY). These should be listed, with the other ingredients, on the packaging of the foodstuff. Some additives are thought to have undesirable side-effects.

E-mail *See* ELECTRONIC MAIL.

$E = mc^2$ The equation proposed by Albert Einstein (1879–1955) in his Special Theory of RELATIVITY in 1905. The best known of all scientific equations, and of immense theoretical interest to the scientific community, it linked an object's mass (m) multiplied by the square of the speed of light (c^2) with energy (E). The more sinister aspects of this simple equation were revealed in July 1945 when the first atom bomb was exploded (*see* NUCLEAR WEAPON).

E number *See* E-FREE; FOOD ADDITIVE.

each way Australian slang for bisexual. A humorous extension of the betting term.

eager beaver A US expression in World War II for an over-zealous recruit whose keenness was marked by volunteering on every possible occasion; it was subsequently applied in civilian life to similar enthusiasts, whose eagerness is reminiscent of the frantic dam-building activity of beavers.

eagle *See* KRUGERRAND.

Eagle Day In World War II, the day appointed for the launch of the German air attack on Britain. It fell on 13 August 1940 and, in German eyes, marked the beginning of the BATTLE OF BRITAIN.

Eagle's Nest The mountain lair of Adolf Hitler at **Berchtesgaden**, near Salzburg, on the Austrian border. Heavily fortified, the *Eagle's Nest* or *Berghof* was constructed 1829 m (6000 ft) up the mountain; Hitler received many important guests here. *See* STAUFFENBERG PLOT.

Eagle Squadron One of the most distinguished squadrons of the RAF in World War II, manned by US volunteers. Having destroyed 73 German aircraft, the pilots transferred to the US 8th Air Force when America entered the war following PEARL HARBOR.

Ealing comedy A genre of British cinema that enjoyed enormous popularity in the 1940s and 1950s. Lacking the financial resources available to the US film industry, the film-makers at the Ealing studios in west London produced low-budget stories based on strong plots and excellent standards of production. Under Michael Balcon the genre built up a huge following with such films as *Kind Hearts and Coronets*, *The Lavender Hill Mob*, *Whisky Galore*, and *The Titfield Thunderbolt*. The BBC now occupies the studios in which these films were made.

ear. **ear-basher** A mainly British and Australian slang word for someone who talks incessantly; a nag.

ear-man US slang for a musician who cannot read music but plays 'by ear'.

ear music US slang for improvised music.

ear'ole British slang for a tedious person. Mostly used by working-class schoolchildren in the 1970s. As a verb, it could mean to pin someone down in conversation, that is, to 'buttonhole', to scrounge, to nag, to talk endlessly, or to eavesdrop.

earl. **Earl's Court** An exhibition centre in London in which the annual Royal Tournament and major trade shows are held. The present structure was built in 1937 and was on its opening the largest reinforced concrete building in Europe, covering 12 acres. The name of the hall (and of the surrounding area) was derived from that of the courthouse of the Earls of Warwick and Holland, who were once the lords of the manor.

The whole process has ground to a halt with a 14th earl The words with which Harold Wilson denounced the 14th Earl of Home's succession as prime minister in 1963, interpreting it as a denial of "a century of democratic advance." The earl himself was quick to deliver his retort:

> As far as the 14th earl is concerned, I suppose Mr Wilson, when you come to think of it, is the 14th Mr Wilson.
>
> TV interview, 21 October 1963.

early. early beam or **early bright** US Black slang from the 1940s for 'in the morning'. Variants include **early black** ('in the evening').

Early Bird The first commercial communications satellite. Launched from America in 1965, it was designed to provide uninterrupted transmission by maintaining a stationary orbit, i.e. to rotate at the same angular speed as the earth so that its position above the earth's surface remained unchanged.

early to rise and early to bed makes a male healthy and wealthy and dead An oft-repeated reworking of an old proverb, this parody was originally coined by James Thurber in 'The Shrike and the Chipmunks' from *Fables for Our Time* (1938).

earner British slang for a situation, especially an illicit one, that will bring financial reward. Originally part of police and criminal jargon, the phrase 'a nice little earner' became fashionable nationwide in the 1980s popularized by the TV series *Minder*. *See also* 'ER INDOORS.

earth. But did thee feel the earth move? This memorable image referring to a particularly successful session of lovemaking has become a cliché and is now used ironically. It is of relatively recent coinage, however, being first aired in Ernest Hemingway's novel *For Whom the Bell Tolls* (1940).

earth art or **land art** An art movement of the 1960s and 1970s in which artists utilised natural materials, such as boulders and earth, often bulldozed to create the desired effect. Most of this work survives only in the form of photographs.

Earth Day A day of action chosen annually by various environmental pressure groups to focus attention on ecological matters. The first such days, usually in April, were announced in the early 1970s and have sometimes been expanded into **Earth Weeks.**

> By the time Earth Day dawned on April 22, ecoactivists of all ages were suffused with quasi-religious fervour.
>
> *Time*, 4 January 1971.

earwig British slang meaning to eavesdrop. An underworld expression.

earwigging A British slang term for haranguing based on the 19th-century use of the verb *to wig*, meaning to scold.

easing British police jargon for relaxing or taking time off unofficially.

east. east is east and west is west This widely used and somewhat pessimistic observation upon cultural relations first appeared as part of a poem, *The Ballad of East and West* (1910), by Rudyard Kipling. The full version reads:

> Oh, East is East, and West is West, and never the twain shall meet.

Now we can look the East End in the face Arguably the most famous royal quotation from World War II, this was Queen Elizabeth's reaction on viewing the damage caused by a German bomb that fell on Buckingham Palace in 1940. With her husband, George VI, she made several tours of the extensively bombed East End of London during the BLITZ.

Easter. Easter egg A US expression for a child born nine months after a summer romance.

Easter Rising A rebellion against the British government that took place in Dublin in April 1916. Led by the Irish Republican Brotherhood (IRB) under Patrick Pearse and James Connolly, a Citizen Army of 2000 men seized vital positions (including the Post Office) throughout Dublin and held off government troops for several days before eventual defeat. The centre of the city was badly damaged; most of the rebel leaders were executed.

Eastern. Eastern bloc *See* COMMUNIST BLOC.

Eastern Front The theatre of conflict on the Russian frontier in the two world wars. Operations on this front in World War I included heavy fighting on the border with Russia. In World War II the Eastern Front was centred on the German invasion (reaching as far as STALINGRAD) of the Soviet Union in 1941 and the subsequent retreat through East Europe to Germany itself. Although activities on the Western front have always attracted more attention from the media, fighting on the Eastern Front in both wars was often more costly and savage, with both sides suffering badly from the vicious eastern winter weather. Being sent to the Eastern Front was considered a punishment or demotion within German army circles.

Eastern Question The diplomatic problems arising from the disintegration of the Ottoman Empire in the 19th and 20th centuries, focusing on the struggle for control of the former Ottoman territories by the European powers. Throughout the 19th century recurring political instability within the Turkish domains in south-eastern Europe provoked a series of international crises including the Crimean War (1853–56) and the Balkan Crisis (1876–78) as Britain, France, Russia, Germany, and the Austro-Hungarian empire struggled to prevent one power from dominating the region. The situation was further complicated by emergent Balkan nationalism. The Eastern Question ended with the foundation of the modern Republic of Turkey in 1923.

easy An exclamatory cry, usually of triumph because the opponents are being easily defeated, heard on the terraces at British football matches since the 1960s. It is often extended to 'eezee' and repeated as a chant at all types of sporting events.

easy as you know how A phrase meaning something apparently difficult is actually very easy to perform, much used by members of the RAF in World War II.

easy-care Any garment that does not require special treatment in washing, drying, etc.

easy meat Either a gullible person, or something easily acquired. This has been a widely used phrase in the UK since the 1920s.

easy money *See* CHEAP MONEY.

easy-peasy British playground expression, meaning extremely easy, that has been common for many years and is still heard today throughout the country.

easy rider A BIKER. The term was made fashionable in 1969 when Peter Fonda starred in a film of the same name in which two drop-out bikers, seeking fulfilment, meet only death.

Easy Street A state of financial security, in which one is not obliged to work or do anything one does not want to. In 1917 Charlie Chaplin made a film of the same title, although Easy Street in this case was a poverty-stricken slum.

eat Slang expression dating from the 1960s meaning to perform cunnilingus. Variants include **eat pussy**.

eat dirt Originally a US expression, but now heard in the UK and Australia as well, meaning to humiliate oneself. Sometimes the expression is used as an exclamation of scorn. Variants include **eat shit.**

eat it A US euphemism for EAT DIRT.

eat my shorts! A US exclamation of scorn used by male students. Shorts is the US word for male underpants. In the late 1980s the phrase became particularly associated with the subversive CARTOON character Bart Simpson.

eat your heart out *See under* HEART.

you are what you eat A saying used by people who believe that a sensible diet leads automatically to good health. It gained in popularity as more and more people became concerned about fitness and diet in the 1970s and 1980s; it was the title of a US film first shown in the UK in 1969. This had more to do with the HIPPIE movement in America than diet but the title helped to popularize the phrase.

E-boat In World War II an abbreviation for 'Enemy War Motorboat', the British name for the German motor torpedo boat.

E-boat alley In World War II, the name given to the coastal convoy route, approximately off the Norfolk and Suffolk coast, which was the scene of much successful E-boat activity in the early years of the war.

EC *See* EUROPEAN COMMUNITY.

echo. Echo 1 The first communications satellite. It was launched from America in 1960 and relayed television and radio signals in an orbit 1000 miles above the earth.

echovirus Any of a group of viruses that multiply in the human intestinal tract and then migrate to the nervous system, where they cause various neurological symptoms. When first isolated in the mid-1950s, they were thought to produce pathological changes only in cell cultures and not to be associated with any disease, hence the name which is short for *enteric cytopathic* (cell-affecting) *human orphan* (i.e. unrelated to any disease) *virus*.

eckies British slang for expenses, mainly used by office workers.

eco-freak A somewhat disparaging term used to describe someone concerned with ECOLOGY and the environment that was first used in the UK and America in the 1970s when such concerns were considered rather eccentric. A variant name for such people is **econut.** *See also* GREEN.

ecology The study of the relationship between man and the environment, which has acquired a new relevance in the years since World War II when man began to appreciate the widespread damage occasioned by the indiscriminate use of pesticides, unmonitored waste disposal from industrial processes, vehicle exhaust fumes, etc. If unchecked, it has been argued, such abuses of the environment could lead to mankind committing **ecocide** (mass suicide) by rendering the world uninhabitable. Taken up by political parties throughout the western world, and indeed beyond, ecological arguments had become by 1990 an integral part of every political party's manifesto. *See also* ACID RAIN; GREENHOUSE EFFECT; OZONE LAYER.

economical with the truth The words used by the British Cabinet Secretary Sir Robert Armstrong in the course of a trial in the Supreme Court of New South Wales in which the British government was seeking to prevent publication of *Spycatcher* by Peter Wright (a damaging book about MI5). The phrase was universally interpreted as a newly minted euphemism for 'lying'. It had in fact been used in a similar form by a British diplomat in 1942 about the character of the former Czech president Edvard Beneš and before that by Arnold Bennett, Mark Twain, Edmund Burke, and Samuel Pepys.

economic refugee An emigrant from the Third World who moves to the developed countries of the West in the hope of improving his living standards.

Ecstasy (Gr. *ek* out; *stasis*, a standing). Literally, a condition in which one stands out of one's mind, or is 'beside oneself'. Because it implies a condition of unimpaired happiness, it is the street name of the stimulant drug 3,4-methylenedioxymethamphetamine, which emerged in America in the 1980s. As a hallucinogen, it is reminiscent of the ancient Greek diviners called **Ecstatici**, who used to give strange accounts of what they had seen while they were 'out of the body' (in a hallucinogenic trance). It was first manufactured in Germany in 1914. Those who use the drug are sometimes referred to as **Ecstatics**. Ecstasy itself is sometimes abbreviated to E. *See also* ACID HOUSE; EPSOM SALTS.

ecu An international currency unit adopted by the European Community in 1978. Derived from the initials of European Currency Unit, it had a distant antecedent in the *écu*, a silver coin used in medieval France. This in turn derived its name from the Latin *scutum* (shield), a shield being the symbol stamped on each coin.

Ecumenical Movement The movement towards re-unity among the various Christian Churches that has gathered strength in recent years, especially since the Second Vatican Council and the establishment of the World Council of Churches inaugurated at Amsterdam in 1948, which comprises most of the prominent Christian bodies.

edge. We stand today on the edge of a new frontier The words spoken by John F. Kennedy on receiving the nomination as presidential candidate for the Democratic party in 1960.

Edinburgh. Edinburgh Festival An internationally known festival of music and theatre that takes place annually in Edinburgh (in August). Founded in 1947 and lasting three weeks, it has developed its own 'fringe' tradition and has seen many notable performances by major artistes. *See* FRINGE THEATRE.

Edinburgh Festival Happening The sudden appearance of a naked woman on the stage during the EDINBURGH FESTIVAL of 1963, which did much to intensify interest in the shortlived craze for theatrical HAPPENINGS.

Edward. Edward the Caresser *See* BERTIE.

Edwardian (1) Belonging to the reign of King Edward VII (1901–10). (2) *See* TEDDY BOYS.

eek (1) face. A camp word from the London theatre of the 1950s, of obscure origin. (2) face paint; stage make-up. This meaning obviously derives from the first.

eel-ya-dah US JAZZ slang for various existential verbal jazz sounds used in BEBOP, originating in the 1940s.

Eeyore A character in the WINNIE-THE-POOH stories of A. A. Milne. Eeyore is a melancholy donkey who suffers a series of disasters, including the loss of his tail and falling into a river, with characteristic resignation. His name is occasionally applied to people who show similar traits. Eeyore's character was based on that of Sir Owen Seaman (1861–1936), who as editor of *Punch* was Milne's employer for eight years.

eff A British euphemism and abbreviation for fuck, sometimes also heard in Australia and America. It is mostly used in the phrases 'eff off', and 'effing and blinding' meaning to curse and swear.

Effie An award given annually to US advertising agencies. Derived from effective, such awards were first presented in 1970 for particularly striking advertising campaigns.

effort, St. Swithins! An exhortation popularized by Joyce Grenfell in one of her film roles. Picked up by public schools everywhere, it was used (usually ironically) as a rallying cry in innumerable school matches and other contests.

EFTPOS Electronic funds transfer at point of sale. A computer-based system that automatically debits the cost of goods or services to a customer's credit card or bank account. The check-out till at the point of sale has a computer and telephone link to the appropriate credit-card company or bank, which responds to the use of the customer's credit card, usually in conjunction with a PIN (personal identification number).

egg A British slang expression as in either a 'good egg' or a 'bad egg', meaning either a thoroughly nice chap or a definitely dubious character.

eggbeater An old and unsophisticated motor or motor vehicle; it is also used of helicopters in America and Canada.

egghead An intellectual. British slang from the 1910s that is still widely used. Scientists in particular are fancifully imagined to have large balding heads to accommodate their supposedly larger-than-normal brains.

go to work on an egg Slogan used as the main theme of an advertising campaign mounted by the British Egg Marketing Board in the 1960s to persuade people of the energy-giving power of eggs. The phrase caught the public fancy and was much quoted as a catchphrase. It has been ascribed to the novelist and playwright Fay Weldon, then a copy-writer with the Egg Marketing Board, although she herself does not lay claim to it. The slogan had fallen into disuse before the salmonella scare of the 1980s, partly due to the decline of the full ENGLISH BREAKFAST.

ego-trip A display or attitude of egotism, self-obsession, or self-importance. Trip, originally a US expression from the drug culture of the 1960s when it specifically meant to be under the influence of the drug LSD, is now widely used in the UK to mean any kind of obsession or particular interest.

Egyptian PT Army slang for sleeping. The term was adopted by British forces serving in the Middle East before World War II and referred to the widely held belief that all Arabs were irredeemably lazy: the phrase remained current for many years in both army and public-school slang.

Eichmann trial The trial in 1961 at which the notorious NAZI Adolf Eichmann was brought before an Israeli court. Eichmann was accused of involvement in the mass murder of thousands of Austrian Jews and was hanged in 1962 after being found guilty. He was brought to trial after being kidnapped by Israeli agents in Argentina, where he was in hiding. *See also* BUTCHER OF LYONS; FINAL SOLUTION; IVAN THE TERRIBLE; MOSSAD; WIESENTHAL CENTRE.

eight. eight millimetre A size of ciné film used by amateur film-makers. Sound was impossible with eight millimetre until the superior 'Super 8' gauge was developed.

eight to the bar The basic rhythm of the BOOGIE-WOOGIE style of jazz piano playing, developed in the 1930s.

eighty-eight (1) US slang for a piano, referring to the usual number of keys. (2) A piece of heavy but mobile German field artillery firing 88 millimetre shells, much used in World War II.

Ein Reich, Ein Volk, Ein Führer The slogan of the NAZI party, meaning 'One Realm, One People, One Leader'. It was first used at the Nuremberg rally in September 1934.

Eisenhower. Eisenhower Doctrine The promise (5 January 1957) by US President Dwight D. Eisenhower of economic or military aid to Middle Eastern countries under threat from communist aggression. Eisenhower's commitment was the product of America's determination to contain Soviet influence in the region during the COLD WAR period after World War II.

Eisenhower jacket A short belted military jacket (also called *battle-jacket*) as worn by General Eisenhower in World War II.

Eisenhower Platz or **Little America** Nickname of Grosvenor Square, London, during World War II, when all the buildings surrounding the square were occupied by American Military Headquarters.

A statue of Eisenhower now stands in the square.

ejaculatorium A room set aside at a SPERM BANK in which donors may produce semen.

E'knows He knows. A catchphrase that became popular in the first half of the 20th century. It was derived from a pun based on advertisements for *Eno's* antacid preparations for indigestion, first appearing *c.* 1905.

el. el primo (Sp. the first) The best. A US expression that is widely used in imitation of Hispanic speech.

el ropo A cigar, or a joint. Derived from the idea that rough tobacco and marijuana looks like, and smells like, burning rope.

élan vital (Fr. vital impetus). A metaphysical energy that drives the evolutionary process in all living things, as described by the French philosopher Henri Bergson (1859–1941) in his *Creative Evolution* (1907, translated 1911). The concept was developed in opposition to Darwin's evolutionary theories, which Bergson believed presented too mechanistic an account of the phenomena of evolution. *See* CREATIVE EVOLUTION.

elbow British slang meaning to dismiss someone, or reject something. It is sometimes used in the passive form 'to be elbowed', and sometimes in the phrase 'to give someone the elbow'.

elbow bender British slang for a heavy drinker, reflecting the image of someone constantly bending their elbow to lift a glass to their lips.

electric soup A strong alcoholic punch. A British middle-class expression of the same type as GIGGLE WATER.

electrification. Communism is Soviet power plus the electrification of the whole country A political slogan adopted in the Soviet Union in 1920. It was coined by Lenin with reference to the proposed electrification programme, but proved to be a gross oversimplification of what communism was actually capable of producing.

electronic. electronic mail (E-mail) Letters or other documents transmitted from one computer terminal to another.

electronic tagging A system for monitoring the movements of certain categories of convicted persons or persons on bail by attaching a low-powered radio transmitter to a bracelet worn on the wrist or ankle. The continuous signal emitted by the transmitter is picked up by a device attached to a telephone in the person's home, which sends a message to a controlling computer in a remote centre if the offender moves more than 75 metres from the telephone.

electronovision A system enabling films to be transferred from videotape to film, which was hailed on its introduction in 1965 as a breakthrough for the cinema industry. Two films were made by this method before it was discarded as artistically and financially unviable.

electroweak theory *See* FUNDAMENTAL FORCES; UNIFIED-FIELD THEORY.

elementary particle The fundamental constituents of which all the matter in the universe is constructed. Until J. J. Thomson (1856–1940) discovered the electron in 1897 it was assumed that matter was made from indivisible atoms. When Ernest Rutherford (1871–1937) discovered the atomic nucleus in 1906, it was thought that electrons orbited a central indestructible nucleus. By 1932, with James Chadwick's (1891–1974) discovery of the neutron, the atomic model consisted of a nucleus of protons and neutrons surrounded by sufficient negative electrons to balance the positive charge of the nucleus. Since the mid-1930s various models to account for the stability of the nucleus have been proposed, accepted, and superceded. In the current model, electromagnetic, strong, and weak forces are recognized as controlling the structure of matter (*see* FUNDAMENTAL FORCES). The electromagnetic force, mediated by photons, holds the electrons in orbits around the nucleus and determines the 'chemical' properties of atoms. This is described by the theory of quantum electrodynamics. The strong force, mediated by gluons between the constituents of hadrons (protons, neutrons, and pions) is described by quantum chromodynamics. Hadrons are not themselves fundamental particles but consist of QUARKS between which gluons are exchanged. Weak interactions controlling radioactive decay are mediated by photons, W, and Z particles, according to quantum flavourdynamics (also called the electroweak theory or the Glashow-Weinberg-Salaam theory). The ultimate objective of particle physics is to combine these elementary particles and fundamental forces into one unified theory.

eleven plus The name given to the much-abused selection tests formerly set to school-children at the age of eleven, or just over that age, and used in England and Wales as a means of judging their suitability for the various types of secondary education provided by the Education Act of 1944 (secondary modern, secondary technical, secondary grammar, etc.). It soon became a target for all those who, for reasons political and social as well as educational, were seeking to demolish the existing pattern of education in England in favour of comprehensive schools. When these objectives were achieved the examination largely disappeared with the majority of grammar schools, which were phased out in the 1960s and 1970s; in some areas it was replaced by a twelve plus examination.

Elginism The illicit removal of items of cultural value – especially antique fireplaces – from stately homes or other sites of historical interest. The word was first used in 1986 when a rash of such thefts was reported; it derived from Lord Elgin's controversial removal of friezes from the Parthenon in Athens to the British Museum in 1816 (at a time when occupying Turkish forces were using the Parthenon for target practice).

Ellis. Ellis hanging The execution of Ruth Ellis, the last woman to be hanged in the UK. She was sentenced to death for murdering her lover (who was having an affair with another woman) and was hanged at Holloway Prison on 13 July 1955. Her story provided the plot for the films *Yield to the Night* (1956) and *Dance with a Stranger* (1985).

Ellis Island An island in Upper New York Bay that served as the main immigration station for America from 1892 to 1943 and as a detention centre for illegal aliens until it was closed in 1954. Ellis Island is close to the Statue of Liberty, whose inscription ("Give me your tired, your poor, your huddled masses . . . Send these, the homeless, tempest-tost to me") must have had a hollow ring for many of those detained there: the centre was infamous for its impersonal procedures and the casual brutality of its staff. It is now part of the Statue of Liberty National Museum.

Elstree The site near Borehamwood, in outer London, of the famous British film studios. Elstree became a centre of film-making in the 1920s and provided settings for numerous classics of the cinema before being sold in the 1980s, when activity there was greatly reduced, although it continued to be used from time to time by top producers.

Elvis the Pelvis The nickname by which the popular US singer Elvis (Aaron) Presley (1935–77) became known in the 1950s. His suggestive hip movements on stage while performing such hits as 'Hound Dog' and 'Heartbreak Hotel' earned him his nickname, although many referred to him as 'the King of Rock 'n Roll' or simply 'the King'. By the 1990s, however, anything called 'Elvis' meant it was dead, or out of date. *See also* GRACELAND.

embuggerance A complicated problem. The word was apparently used in the engineering fraternity for some years before it came to wider notice during the FALKLANDS CONFLICT of 1984, when it was used by the Royal Engineers, who were faced with complicated logistical tasks.

Emden. Didn't you sink the Emden? An Australian catchphrase of World War I, used to deflate anyone indulging in excessive self-praise. The *Emden* was a German light cruiser that caused considerable damage to shipping and ports in the Pacific before it was eventually sunk by the Australian cruiser *Sydney* off the Cocos-Keeling Islands in November 1914.

emmet A tourist. A Cornish dialect word, meaning an ant, that is used disparagingly to describe the masses of summer tourists that flock to Cornwall each year. **Grockle** is another dialect word with the same meaning.

Emmy A US TV award granted annually in various categories to television programmes that have achieved a certain standard of excellence. The awards themselves are statuettes not dissimilar to the OSCARS awarded in the film industry. The name is derived from 'Immy', a shortened form of image orthicon tube.

empaquetage A work of art in which an object is wrapped in polythene, canvas, or some other packaging material. Objects treated in this controversial way have included boulders, islands, and entire buildings.

empire. Empire Day Instituted by the Earl of Meath in 1902, after the end of the South African War, as a way to encourage schoolchildren to be aware of their duties and responsibilities as citizens of the British Empire. The day set aside was 24 May, Queen Victoria's birthday. In 1916 it was given official recognition in the UK, and was replaced by **Commonwealth Day** (12 March) in December 1958.

Empire Free Trade An unsuccessful campaign (1929–31) to establish free trade throughout the British Empire. It was spearheaded by the press barons Lords Beaverbrook and Rothermere, who argued the case with crusading zeal in their newspapers and founded the United Empire Party in an attempt to gain a parliamentary platform. The campaign foundered on the reluctance of the Dominions to give free entry to British goods and finally collapsed with the onset of the GREAT DEPRESSION in the 1930s.

Empire State Building One of New York's best-known SKYSCRAPERS, built in Manhattan in 1930–32 by Shreve, Lamb, and Harmon at a cost of $41 million. The scene of the climax of the film *King Kong* (1933, remade 1976), in which the giant gorilla ascends the building and fights off attacking aircraft, the Empire State Building remained, at 381 m (1250 ft) high, the tallest in the world until the World Trade Center was completed in the same city in 1974. The building acquired its name by allusion to one of New York City's colloquial titles, the **Empire City** (acknowledging its wealth and importance).

How is the empire? The last words of George V, as he lay dying in 1936. Another version of his last words, in reply to his doctor's assurance that he would soon be well enough to visit Bognor Regis, was: "Bugger Bognor."

Empress of Emotion The nickname applied to the Austrian-Italian film star Elissa Landi (1904–48). A leading lady in the 1930s, she starred in such films as *The Sign of the Cross* (1932) and *The Count of Monte Cristo* (1934).

empty nest An expression used of a household when all the children have grown up and left home. The parents, who are left feeling bereft and directionless after all the years of taking care of the children, are known as **empty nesters**. The phrase has a particular financial relevance as these parents, who will usually have paid off their mortgage and have acquired some savings, may find themselves in possession of a substantially larger amount of disposable income than they have been accustomed to when there were more demands on their pocket.

EMS *See* EUROPEAN MONETARY SYSTEM.

emu. emu-bobber A worker employed to remove debris after an area of Australian bush has been cleared.

> We . . . went to Wingadee to work for a contractor at burning-off. This work is also known as 'stick-picking' or 'emu-bobbing'. A group of men bending to pick up the fallen timber, with heads down and tails up, look very much like a flock of emus.
>
> H. P. TRITTON: *Time Means Tucker.*

emu parade Australian army slang for an operation in which an area is cleaned up by EMU-BOBBERS.

enchilada *See* BIG ENCHILADA.

encounter group A group of people who gather together to share their feelings and anxieties. Participants in such sessions are encouraged to lose their inhibitions in order to develop their own self-awareness (**consciousness raising**).

> As encounters multiplied and perspective deepened, Jane found herself kicking pillows and hurling finger paint with the worst of them – and feeling, as a result, relieved of some fossil fears.
>
> BRAD DARRACH, 'Gropeshrink'.

end. end of the beginning The words with which Winston Churchill greeted news of the Allied victory in North Africa in November 1942. His words in full were: "This is not the end. It is not even the beginning of the end. But it is, perhaps, the end of the beginning."

endsville A US expression for the absolute worst. It was part of the BEATNIK jargon of the 1950s, already considered out of date by the 1960s. The suffix '-sville' was used in a similar way in numerous other contexts.

end to the beginnings of all wars The aim that President Franklin D. Roosevelt hoped would be fulfilled when World War II was over. Broadcast the day after his death in April 1945, his words in full were: "More than an end to war, we want an end to the beginnings of all wars."

endangered species A category of THREATENED SPECIES identified by the International Union for the Conservation of Nature and Natural Resources (IUCN). Populations of these species are at a critical level and are in immediate danger of extinction; the term also includes species that may already be extinct but have definitely been seen in the wild in the previous 50 years. Such species include:

orang-utan (*Pongo pygmaeus*)
mountain gorilla (*Gorilla gorilla*)
tiger (*Panthera tigris*)
European otter (*Lutra lutra lutra*)
black rhinoceros (*Diceros bicornis*)
Indian elephant (*Elephas maximus*)
wild yak (*Bos grunniens*)
Malayan tapir (*Tapirus bairdii*)
red wolf (*Canis rufus*)
blue whale (*Balaenoptera musculus*)
peregrine falcon (*Falco peregrinus*)
Californian condor (*Gymnogyps californianus*)
leatherback turtle (*Dermochelys coriacea*)
green turtle (*Chelonia mydas*)
Central Asian cobra (*Naja oxiana*)
Chinese alligator (*Alligator sinensis*)
common sturgeon (*Acipenser sturio*)
longhorn beetle (*Cerambyx cerdo*)
large copper butterfly (*Lycaena dispar*)

See also EXTINCT; VULNERABLE SPECIES.

endorse A South African term describing the removal of urban Black Africans to rural areas as part of the official policy of APARTHEID.

Endurance The ship in which Sir Ernest Shackleton travelled to the Antarctic in 1914. The expedition's problems began when the *Endurance* became locked fast in ice. For months the members of the team waited for the ship to free itself from the ice, but finally it sank. Living off penguin meat and seaweed, Shackleton and his fellow-explorers spent the next five months drifting on an ice floe. Two years after setting out on the voyage, they transferred to the three remaining ship's boats and landed on a bleak ice-covered island. The only hope was to reach South Georgia, 800 miles away across one of the worst stretches of ocean in the world. Undaunted, Shackleton and five volunteers set off in one of the boats, just 22 feet long. Over the next two weeks the six men were constantly soaked, subjected to intense cold, and frequently threatened with being washed overboard by huge waves. Remarkably, they survived, enabling the whole team to be rescued without a single loss of life.

> For scientific leadership give me Scott; for swift and efficient travel, Amundsen; but when you are in a hopeless position, when there seems no way out, get down on your knees and pray for Shackleton.
>
> Fellow-explorer of SHACKLETON's.

Enewetak *See* ENIWETOK.

Enfield Any of various rifles, including rifle-muskets used in the mid-19th century, which were originally manufactured at the royal small arms factory in the London borough of Enfield, England. In its final version it was used by British and US soldiers during World War I; the magazine held six cartridges, the barrel was 26 inches long, and the weapon's total length was 46 inches.

England. If I should die, think only this of me: That there's some corner of a foreign field that is forever England Perhaps one of the best-known quotations to emerge from World War I, this couplet comes from 'The Soldier' by Rupert Brooke (1887–1915). Brooke died of blood poisoning on a hospital ship in the Aegean, on his way to the DARDANELLES; his corner of a foreign field is on the island of Scyros.

Speak for England The resounding cry of an anguished Conservative backbencher on the eve of World War II. At 7.30 p.m. on 2 September 1939, Neville Chamberlain disappointed the House of Commons by telling them that further negotiations were in progress to persuade Hitler to withdraw his troops from Poland. What both sides of the House wanted was an ultimatum. As Chamberlain sat down to a dismayed silence, Arthur Greenwood, acting leader of the Labour Party (Attlee was ill), rose to speak. Leo Amery reflected the mood of everyone present when he shouted from the Conservative benches: "Speak for England, Arthur." Greenwood's "Every minute's delay now means the loss of life, imperilling our national interests . . . imperilling the very foundations of our national honour" was probably influential in persuading Chamberlain to send the ultimatum the next morning. The absence of a German reply to this ultimatum led Britain and France to declare war on Germany on 3 September.

Stately Homes of England The title of a lighthearted song by Noël Coward that subsequently became a cliché for the country's great houses. It is still used by the NATIONAL TRUST, and others.

> The stately homes of England
> How beautiful they stand,
> To prove the upper classes
> Have still the upper hand.
>
> NOËL COWARD, *Operette*.

English. English as she is spoke A catchphrase used to refer to the attempts of foreigners or illiterates to speak the English language.

English breakfast The large cooked morning meal beloved of Victorian England and still produced, with varying degrees of competence, at hotels throughout the UK as well as on trains, in gentlemen's clubs, and some private homes at weekends. Interpretations of the phrase range from the full repast starting with porridge and continuing with grilled kidneys, kippers, kedgeree, and other similar dishes to any menu including cooked food (usually bacon and egg). The US invention of breakfast cereal early in the 20th century and the later introduction of Swiss muesli have done much to undermine the institution, which has been further eroded by health warnings of the dangers of eating too much fatty food. Besides, with two wage earners and little or no domestic staff, very few homes have time to prepare such a lavish spread.

English culture A term describing sadomasochistic sexual practises in which whips, canes, and various instruments of torture are used.

English disease or **English sickness** A variety of complaints and malaises have been ascribed to the English. Since the time of Columbus the French have described syphilis as the English disease; the English response to this insulting insinuation was to call it the French disease. Later, after the industrial revolution, the damp climate combined with industrial smoke to create a high prevalence of bronchitis. On the continent and elsewhere, this also became known as the English disease. In the 20th century, air travel has meant that physical disease can no longer be confined to particular nations and therefore cannot be characterized in this way. Now more social ailments are described as English. They include class conflict, poor industrial relations, and economic stagnation. In the 1950s and 1960s, when trade union power was at its zenith, strikes were widely known as the English disease. More recently, especially in the 1980s, disgraceful behaviour at football matches, both at home and abroad, has been so described.

English spliff or **English joint** The US term for a marijuana cigarette that is rolled with tobacco.

to put on English (US) In billiards and in baseball, to apply spin to the ball, presumably an allusion to the practice of spinning the ball in cricket.

ENIAC Electronic Numerical Integrator And Calculator. *See* COMPUTER.

Eniwetok or **Enewetak** An atoll in the Republic of the Marshall Islands in the Pacific Ocean designated as a testing site for NUCLEAR WEAPONS shortly after World War II. Testing began in 1948; the first hydrogen bomb was exploded here in 1952, and there were further tests throughout the 1950s. In 1980 the tiny population (88) was allowed to return until evidence of lingering contamination resulted in their re-evacuation.

enjoy! An exclamation inviting people to sample and enjoy food, later extended to books and other commodities. The construction is Yiddish in origin and the phrase came to the UK from America. In America, the Yiddish *enjoy* is an intransitive verb and the imperative is usually duplicated as *enjoy, enjoy*. This was the title of a book by Harry Cohen, published in 1960. When the phrase was brought to the attention of advertisers they used it in various slogans.

Enola Gay The name of the US bomber that dropped the ATOM BOMB on HIROSHIMA on 6 August 1945. A SUPERFORTRESS, the aircraft was named in honour of the mother of the pilot, Colonel Paul W. Tibbets. The force of the explosion hit the *Enola Gay* with all the power of a near-miss by flak, although the aircraft was by then 10 miles away from the point of impact. More than 75,000 people died. Many years later members of the Enola Gay's crew visited Hiroshima once more to see the rebuilt city. A Peace Memorial Park commemorates those who died. 'Enola Gay' is also a character in the novel *London Fields* (1989) by Martin Amis.

enosis (Gr. union) The political union of Greece and Cyprus, pursued by Greek Cypriots in the 1950s. *See* EOKA.

Ensa concerts In World War II, concerts provided for the British fighting forces on active service by the Entertainments National Service Association (ENSA). Many famous figures in the entertainment and musical world took part, greatly helping to boost morale. By the time of the last ENSA show in 1946, 2½ million performances had been given. The US equivalent was **USO** (United Service Organizations).

Entente Cordiale (Fr.) A cordial understanding between nations; not amounting to an alliance but something more than a *rapprochement*. The term is particularly applied to the Anglo-French Entente of 1904, for which King Edward VII's visit to Paris in 1903 was a valuable preliminary.

enterprise culture *See* THATCHERISM.

EOKA (Gr. *Ethniki Organosis Kipriakou Agonos*) The National Organization of Cypriot Struggle, founded in 1955 to pursue the political goal of ENOSIS. Led by Georgios Grivas, and supported by Archbishop Makarios, it conducted a guerrilla campaign against the occupying British forces. It disbanded on independence in 1959 but was reformed in 1971.

EP Extended Play. A gramophone record that is 7 inches (18 cm) in diameter but plays for longer than the more common SINGLE. It is also known as a **maxisingle**.

epic theatre A theatrical genre that emerged in Germany in the 1920s. Derived from the theories of Aristotle, it was developed by Bertolt Brecht (1898–1956) among others; it argued for more politically relevant drama. *See also* A-EFFECT; BERLINER ENSEMBLE.

epitaph Strictly, an inscription on a tomb, but usually it refers to any brief verses or apt commemoration of the departed. Some noted examples from the 20th century (some in jest) include:

> Hereabouts died a very gallant gentleman, Captain L. E. G. Oates of the Inniskilling Dragoons. In March 1912, returning from the Pole, he walked willingly to his death in a blizzard, to try and save his comrades, beset by hardships.
>
> E. L. ATKINSON.

> I've played everything but the harp.
>
> LIONEL BARRYMORE's suggested epitaph on himself.

> Over my dead body!
>
> GEORGE S. KAUFMAN's suggested epitaph on himself.

> Beneath this slab
> John Brown is stowed.
> He watched the ads
> And not the road.
>
> OGDEN NASH, *Lather as You Go.*

> He lies below, correct in cypress wood,
> And entertains the most exclusive worms.
>
> DOROTHY PARKER, *Epitaph for a Very Rich Man.*

EPOS *See* BAR CODE.

Epsom salts A British ACID HOUSE name for the drug ECSTASY used from 1989. Epsom salts are actually hydrated magnesium sulphate, a traditional remedy for indigestion and constipation.

EPT Excess Profits Tax. A tax imposed in the UK during World War II. Between 1940 and 1945 any profit a company made above its pre-war profit level was payable in full to the government; 20% of it was returned when peace was restored.

equal. All animals are created equal but some are more equal than others A political slogan created by George Orwell in his novel *Animal Farm* (1945). Although ironically reflecting contemporary Stalinist doctrine, Orwell was guying a statement from the Declaration of American Independence (1776) that "All men are created equal". *See also* I HAVE A DREAM *under* DREAM.

Equal Opportunities Commission *See* FEMINISM.

equal opportunity A phrase used in the business world, indicating that employees are taken on regardless of their colour, sex, or age.

equal time *See* FAIRNESS DOCTRINE.

Equal Rights Amendment (ERA) A proposed amendment to the US constitution that was first pressed in 1923 but failed to be ratified in 1982. Under its terms women would receive explicit constitutional protection from sex discrimination. Its opponents argued that the amendment was inappropriate because it ignored the biological and psychological differences between the sexes, that it would harm the institutions of marriage and the family, and there was protection already under the 5th and 14th Amendments.

equalizer A euphemism for a revolver. The word, derived from the view that in death all men are equal, became common currency in America in the years before World War II. Its usage has since spread to both sides of the Atlantic, largely through its adoption in crime thrillers and screenplays.

equipment (1) A euphemism for the male genitals. (2) A rarely used euphemism for a woman's breasts.

Equity The actors' trade union, founded in the UK in 1929 to regulate the employment of professional actors in the theatre, radio, film, and television. The strict rules surrounding Equity membership have made the 'Equity card' much sought-after. The CATCH-22 of the theatre is that in order to be given a first part an aspiring actor needs an Equity card, but in order to achieve an Equity card, the aspiring actor has to show that he has had previous professional engagements. The US version was founded in 1913 and the Canadian trade union followed in 1955.

'erbert British slang for a cheeky, snotty little boy, or stupid person. Originally a London working-class term for any unnamed man or boy, Herbert was a common working-class name during the Edwardian period.

Eric (1) A former British schoolboy abbreviation for an erection. It is not thought to owe its derivation to F. W. Farrar's novel of school life at Harrow, *Eric, or Little by Little*. (2) A former schoolboy expression for a stupid man or fool that was possibly derived from *oik*.

'er indoors A catchphrase popularized by the ITV series, *Minder*, which was first screened in 1979. The expression was used by the chief character Arthur Daley (played by George Cole) when referring to his wife. The implication is that, although the wife is indoors and therefore unseen, she wields a considerable amount of power. *See also* EARNER; FLASH HARRY.

erk Originally 'airk', an RAF nickname of World War I given to aircraftmen and mechanics. It later became 'erk' and is applied to beginners, juniors, and underlings generally.

ERM Exchange Rate Mechanism. *See* EUROPEAN MONETARY SYSTEM.

ERNIE Electronic Random Number Indicating Equipment, the electronic equipment used to select winners in the premium bonds issued by the Department of National Savings of the UK government. Premium bonds were first issued in 1956 and play on the British public's love of gambling. The prize fund of 6.5% of the bond money received is distributed to bond holders selected weekly and monthly by ERNIE; bond holders receive no interest.

ersatz (Ger. *ersetzen* to substitute) An artificial substitute for something that is no longer available. The word was much used in Germany after World War I, when the country's economic collapse led to the widespread introduction of such goods; it was applied especially to coffee made from acorns. The word was subsequently adopted by most countries (including the UK) during World War II, particularly during rationing.

Erté The pseudonym adopted by the French artist and fashion designer Romain de Tirtoff (1892–1990). He derived it from the French pronunciation of the first letters of his Christian name and surname.

ERTS Earth Resources Technology Satellite. *See* LANDSAT.

esky An Australian trademark for a portable drinks cooler. It is the abbreviated form of *eskimo*.

ESP Extra-sensory perception, a modern phrase for the supposed ability of some people to acquire accurate knowledge of the outside world independently of the five senses. The subject of much serious scientific research throughout the century, the term covers such activities as telepathy (mind-to-mind communication), clairvoyance (knowledge of remote objects, events, or persons), precognition (foretelling the future), and retrocognition (personal knowledge of the past). Celebrated instances of alleged ESP in recent years have included the spoonbending demonstrations of Uri GELLER and the regression of subjects into past lives under hypnosis by Arnall Bloxham (1896–1976) in the 1970s (*see* BLOXHAM TAPES). The US psychologist J. B. Rhine (1895–1980) used special packs of cards to produce statistical evidence in favour of ESP, but the conclusion is not universally accepted.

Essex Man A wealthy but poorly educated male, who typically lives in Essex, supports right-wing Thatcherite politics, shows conspicuous bad taste, and has few, if any cultural interests. The implication is that Essex man is a throw-back to a less civilized form of hominid. *See also* LOADSAMONEY.

> ... the human species known as 'Essex man': father with extensive collection of gold rings, bracelets and neck chains; wife probably aged 50 but dressed as if she was 20; sullen adolescent son in unlaced trainers, with baseball cap on back to front, lugging around a ghetto-blaster.
>
> *The Independent*, 19 January 1991.

Establishment, The (1) A term long used to denote the established Church of England. The subject of much discussion in the 19th century, the link between Church and State has been a subject of increasing controversy in the 20th century. Those who support the link are termed Establishmentarians. Those who argue for its abolition are thus disestablishmentarians, while those who range themselves against the disestablishmentarians are therefore adherents of antidisestablishmentarianism. (2) Since the 1950s it has been used to designate the influential hierarchy or inner circle in any particular sphere of the community (especially the government or civil service), or of the community in general.

It is often used pejoratively to indicate reaction, privilege, and lack of imagination.

> They were in fact appointed, of course, because they had been trained to think in the way that what is now called "the establishment" thinks and it was clear that they did not dissent from this manner of thinking.
>
> S. G. EVANS: *The Social Hope of the Christian Church*, ch. vi (1965).

estate. estate duty *See* INHERITANCE TAX.

The Fifth Estate The British Broadcasting Corporation has jocularly been so called. The other four estates are the Lords Spiritual, the Lords Temporal, the Commons, and the press. *See also* AUNTIE; BBC; BEEB.

ET Extra-Terrestrial. Stephen Spielberg's film (1982) with this title had as its central character a lovable space creature itself named ET. The film did much to increase the popularity of films dealing with space travel and creatures from other planets. Most children wept copiously when ET finally abandoned his earth friends to return to his native planet, although one critic was driven to comment that he found it hard to be emotional about a collection of Hoover parts.

ethnic A pejorative slang term for an immigrant, used in Australia and elsewhere since the 1970s. In the UK, and other multicultural societies, it is now used to refer to minority groups without any pejorative overtones.

Eton crop A short boyish hairstyle, fairly popular among English women in the 1920s, called after the famous school for boys at Eton.

Eureka project An international science initiative launched between the European nations in the 1980s in an attempt to pool resources on projects of mutual interest. Its name refers to Archimedes' shout of 'Eureka!' (lit. I have found it) on discovering, while taking a bath, how he might test the purity of a gold crown by employing the law of displacement. As Vitruvius says:

> When the idea flashed across his mind, the philosopher jumped out of the bath exclaiming, "Heureka! heureka!" and, without waiting to dress himself, ran home to try the experiment.

eurhythmics (Gr. proportion, Lat. rhythm) A system of exercise for health and fitness through energetic dance routines, which became popular in the 1980s. At the **Dalcroze Institute of Eurhythmics**, founded in 1910 by the Swiss composer Emile Jacques-Dalcroze, children were encouraged to respond to music through dancing.

euro-. euro-ad An advertisement designed so that it will be relevant in all European countries. Recent products, such as cars and electric shavers, are usually suitable for multinational advertisements. On the other hand, more traditional products, such as food, are not.

eurocheque A cheque drawn on a European bank, which can be cashed at any bank displaying the sign of the EUROPEAN COMMUNITY or used to pay for goods or services at outlets displaying this sign.

Eurocrat A high-ranking civil servant working for the EUROPEAN COMMUNITY. *See also* GLOBOCRAT.

eurocurrency Any currency held in a European country other than that which issued it. For example, dollars and yen deposited in a European bank are **eurodollars** and **euroyen**, respectively. *See also* ECU.

Europort Any port for ocean-going vessels in Europe. The primary Europort is Rotterdam.

eurotrash The European JET SET, an expression used in society circles and journalism. A version of the original Black expression 'white trash', meaning wealthy racist white people.

Eurotunnel *See* CHANNEL TUNNEL.

Europe. l'Europe des patries The most frequently cited version of a phrase used by General de Gaulle to define his vision of the final goal of the European Economic Community. The phrase, first used in connection with the Fouchet plan (1961) for closer political cooperation, was meant to distinguish de Gaulle's ideal of a loose organization of sovereign states from more ambitious schemes for European government. Although it became current in this form, de Gaulle insisted that he had actually used the words "L'Europe des etats".

The lamps are going out all over Europe The melancholy observation made by the British statesman Sir Edward Grey (later Viscount Grey of Fallodon; 1862–1933) just before the outbreak of World War I. His further remark "we shall not see them lit again in our lifetime" was, arguably, a little too apocalyptic. *See also* BELLE EPOQUE.

European. European Community (EC) An organization of European states created in 1967 when the European Atomic

Energy Community (founded by the Treaty of Rome in 1958) and the European Coal and Steel Community (founded in 1952) merged with the European Economic Community (founded by the Treaty of Rome in 1957). The original members were Belgium, France, Italy, Luxembourg, the Netherlands, and West Germany (which became the reunified Germany in 1990). Denmark, the Republic of Ireland, and the UK joined in 1973. Greece joined in 1981 and Spain and Portugal joined in 1986. In 1985 Greenland left on obtaining home rule from Denmark.

It was decided that barriers to the free movement of labour, services, and capital between members would be completely removed by 1992. Other economic measures (*see* EUROPEAN MONETARY SYSTEM) are already working and complete economic union, with a single currency and a central European bank, is envisaged but not supported by all members. Further political measures, including a declaration of the rights of workers within the EC, the so-called **Social Charter**, are also being discussed.

European Monetary System (EMS) The system for stabilizing European currencies in the short term and for establishing a single currency unit for the whole of Europe in the long term. The length of the short term and even the ultimate goal of a single currency are hotly debated political issues. In the meantime, the stabilization of the existing currencies is achieved by two measures: the **Exchange Rate Mechanism** (ERM) and a balance of payments support mechanism organized by the **European Monetary Cooperation Fund.** In the ERM, participating governments commit themselves to maintaining the value of their currencies within agreed limits (4.5% in the narrow band and 12% in the broad band). The ERM, which Britain joined in October 1990, values each currency in ECUs and a parity grid gives exchange values in ecus for each pair of currencies. If the market rate differs from the parity rate by more than the permitted percentage the relevant government has to take action to correct the disparity.

Evans. Evans of the Broke Sir Edward Ratcliffe Garth Russell Evans (1881–1957), British admiral, explorer, and author. His nickname derives from his World War I exploit of sinking six German destroyers while commanding HMS *Broke* (pronounced 'brook': the ship was named after an earlier English naval hero, Sir Philip Broke). This was only one incident in a colourful career: in 1909 Evans was second in command of Scott's first expedition to the Antarctic.

Evans the Leak The nickname given to Harold Evans, public relations advisor to Harold Macmillan. It referred to both his Welsh background and his job.

eve The stimulant drug MDEA, so named because it is related to ECSTASY (MDMA); Ecstasy is sometimes known as **adam**, from an anagram of MDMA; the jump to **eve** for the related drug is not hard to understand.

événement (Fr. event) The *événements* of 1968 were a series of violent left-wing protests, led largely by students, in the streets of Paris. They precipitated the fall of Charles de Gaulle.

> During the événements of May and June, 1968, the red flag of communism and the black flag of anarchism fluttered side by side on the occupied Théâtre de l'Odéon.

evenin' all A catchphrase popularized by the BBC TV series 'Dixon of Dock Green' (1955–76), the hero of which was PC George Dixon, played by Jack Warner. His characteristic opening greeting 'evenin' all' was accompanied by a sketchy salute and was much copied by enthusiastic viewers of the programme. Somewhat ironically, the classic TV series was born out of the film *The Blue Lamp* (1950) in which Dixon is shot dead by the young Dirk Bogarde. Just how he recovered from this misfortune to enjoy such a long ensuing career in the police force has never been explained.

event horizon *See* BLACK HOLE.

eventide home A euphemism for an old people's home.

> The House of Lords is a perfect eventide home.
>
> MARY STOCKS.

Everest syndrome An expression used to indicate that people tend to undertake challenging enterprises, such as climbing mountains, rowing the Atlantic, tight-rope walking across the Niagara Falls, undertaking esoteric scientific research, etc., simply because the object of the challenge exists rather than for any more worthwhile reason. George Mallory is said to have wished to climb Everest "because it is there." Everest was finally conquered on 29 May 1953 by Sir Edmund Hillary and

Sherpa Tenzing Norgay; news of the climb reached the UK during celebrations of the coronation of Elizabeth II, doubling its impact.

> We done the bugger!
>
> TENZING NORGAY, 29 May 1953.

Ever Readies Nickname of the Territorial Army Volunteer Reserve, a former (1922–67) division of the Territorial Army. The Ever Readies were called upon to supply trained and equipped men on the outbreak of war or in other sudden emergencies overseas. The name is also a tradename for a brand of battery made by Berec (formerly the British Ever Ready Electrical Company), founded in 1906.

everybody. everybody out A catchphrase associated with trade-union leaders when calling their members out on strike. When the British trade-union movement was at its most powerful in the 1950s and 1960s the leaders acquired a reputation for calling strikes frequently for very little reason. "Everybody out" was the supposed automatic response to any dispute with management. It was popularized by a TV series called 'The Rag Trade' in which Paddy, the shop steward (played by Miriam Karlin), shouted the phrase at the least provocation. *See also* I'M ALRIGHT JACK *under* JACK.

everybody's doing it A popular phrase of the period immediately preceding World War I, taken from the song 'Everybody's Doing It Now' by Irving Berlin. The 'it' in question was the **turkey trot**, a lively dance performed to RAGTIME music.

every day and in every way I am getting better and better *See* COUÉISM.

Evian agreement The treaty under which France granted Algeria independence in 1962, named after Evian (the French town in which independence talks began in 1961).

evil US slang for very good, impressive. A rarer version of the expressions 'bad' or 'wicked' originally used by Black US musicians and now widely used by teenagers of all social groups in the UK and Australia.

Evita The popular nickname by which María Eva de Perón (1919–52) became known to the adoring Argentine public. Evita's charitable work, beauty, and early death all contributed to the popular myth surrounding her name; in 1978 her life became the subject of the successful stage musical *Evita* by Andrew Lloyd Webber and Tim Rice.

> If a woman like Eva Perón with no ideals can get that far, think how far I can go with all the ideals that I have.
>
> MARGARET THATCHER (1980).

ex Colloquialism for a former lover or former spouse.

exes British slang for expenses. A variant of ECKIES.

ex tenebris lux (Lat. out of darkness, light) The motto of HMS *Glow-worm*, the Royal Navy ship that in 1940 succeeded in ramming and badly damaging the German heavy cruiser *Admiral Hipper*. The *Glow-worm* exploded and sank after the impact.

excrementum bellum vincit (Lat.) Army catchphrase from World War II; roughly translated as 'bullshit conquers all'.

excuse. excuse my dust An apology uttered by early motorists to other road-users for any dust their vehicles threw up in passing.

excuse my pig Humorous apology offered when one's companion disgraces himself by his poor behaviour when in public.

exercise. exercise is bunk The US car manufacturer Henry Ford's refutation in 1920 of the contemporary fashion for exercising to keep healthy, since quoted by COUCH POTATOES everywhere. Ford justified his belief with the further comment:

> If you are healthy, you don't need it: if you are sick, you shouldn't take it.

See also HISTORY IS BUNK.

exercise the ferret Australian slang meaning to have sex. A MACHO male expression that likens the penis to the aggressive animal the ferret.

Existentialism A philosophical attitude, owing much to the writings of Søren Kierkegaard (1813–55), that developed in Germany after World War I and somewhat later in France and Italy. Atheistic existentialism was popularized in France by Jean-Paul Sartre (1905–80) and Albert Camus (1913–60) during World War II. Existentialists emphasize the freedom and importance of individual 'existence' and personality, and show a distrust of philosophical idealism. Much of their writing is characterized by disillusionment. The term is the translation of the German *Existenz-philosophie*.

exit poll *See* OPINION POLL.

Exocet An anti-ship missile developed by the French and used with great effect by the Argentinian air force in the FALKLANDS CONFLICT. The most notable British casualty to this missile was HMS *Sheffield*, which was sunk. Hence, to 'Exocet' a project is to cause it to be brought to a complete standstill.

expanded cinema A type of film show in which live actors and musicians interact with the film being projected as part of a multi-media performance.

expanding universe The generally accepted cosmological theory that the universe is expanding. *See* BIG BANG.

expense A new-born baby – a euphemism first heard in the 1940s, in US Black slang.

expletive deleted A phrase widely used in the 1970s in substitution for an obscenity or blasphemous comment, especially in printed documents. It entered popular use after the publication of transcripts of recorded exchanges relating to the WATERGATE scandal of 1974. In these the words "expletive deleted" or similar phrases were employed so frequently that it was inevitable that they should win wider currency.

explosion A loud passage in JAZZ music.

extended family *See* NUCLEAR FAMILY.

exterminate, exterminate A catchphrase popularized by the British science fiction TV series 'Dr Who'. It was the characteristic cry of the **Daleks**, mobile metallic extraterrestrial beings equipped with ray guns. 'Dr Who' has long been a great favourite with children, many of whom have enjoyed being scared by the series, and the Daleks were the most popular of the aliens. "Exterminate exterminate" was often heard in children's games in the days of the Daleks. The series enjoyed similar success when shown in America, where a thriving fan club was founded.

extinct A species of animal or plant defined by the International Union for the Conservation of Nature and Natural Resources (IUCN) as not having been definitely located in the wild in the previous 50 years. Animal species that have become extinct in the 20th century include:

broad-faced potoroo (*Potorous platyops*)
desert bandicoot (*Perameles eremiana*)
thylacine (*Thylacinus cynocephalus*)
Palau flying fox (*Pteropus pilosus*)
Falkland Island wolf (*Dusicyon australis*)
Mexican grizzly bear (*Ursus arctos nelsoni*)
Syrian wild ass (*Equus hemionus hemippus*)
glaucous macaw (*Anodorhynchus glaucus*)
silver trout (*Salvelinus agassizi*)
Texas tailed blue butterfly (*Everes comyntas texanus*)

See also ENDANGERED SPECIES; THREATENED SPECIES; VULNERABLE SPECIES.

extra two inches The phrase 'the extra two inches you're supposed to get after you're forty' was a well-known army myth of World War II. It implied that the sexual disappointments of one's early adulthood would be compensated for in later life by a natural phallic extension of two inches.

eye. eye! eye! British criminal slang instructing a companion to keep a good look-out for police, etc. It was first heard around 1920.

eyeball To stare at, often provokingly or threateningly. Mostly used by young people and the police in the UK and Australia in the 1970s, it is thought to have originated in the Black jargon of the 1940s in America.

eyeball to eyeball Person to person contact; usually with the suggestion that the contact is confrontational. The phrase has been much used in America in diplomatic negotiations since the CUBAN MISSILE CRISIS of 1962.

eyefuck An aggressive expression meaning to stare lustfully. *See also* MINDFUCK.

eye in the sky Electronic surveillance from the air. Sophisticated cameras in aircraft and satellites are reputed to be able to read a car registration plate from a distance of many miles.

eye it – try it – buy it US trade slogan first adopted by salesmen of Chevrolet cars (*see* CHEVY) and heard frequently in the 1950s and 1960s.

eyelyser A device for estimating the amount of alcohol in the blood by measuring the percentage of alcohol in the vapour given off by the eyes. The word is a coinage from *eye* and *breathalyser*. The device, developed in Canada by the Addiction Research Foundation, involves placing a funnel over the eyeball for 15 seconds and using a gas sensor to analyse the vapour. The main advantage claimed for the method is that it can be used on people who are unconscious.

eyeopener A US expression for the first drink or fix of drugs of the day, sometimes used as a euphemism for LEG-OPENER.

eyes and ears of the world The motto of British Gaumont News, which became a more widespread catchphrase after World War II.

eyetie An Italian. A popular expression based on a mispronunciation of the word *Italian*, dating from World War I and used in the UK and America. It is a more friendly and less racist term than 'wop'. *See also* DIGGER; FRITZ; SPICK.

F

F. F 111 (F one-eleven) A long-range bomber with SWING-WINGS, introduced in the 1960s and used by both the US Air Force and the US Navy. The cockpit of the plane can be ejected to become a survival capsule on land or sea. The design for the F 111 served as an almost exact model for the Sukhoi Su-24, its counterpart in the Soviet Union. The F 111's most publicized operation in recent years was the bombing of Libya in April 1986, when Margaret Thatcher allowed President Reagan to use British bases at Lakenheath and Upper Heyford for the bombing mission.

F_1 hybrids Plants, especially crop plants (*e.g.* brassicas or maize), that have been grown from seed obtained by crossing two plants of dissimilar genetic make-up that have been specially selected for their desirable qualities. The offspring from this cross combine the qualities of both parental lines and, in addition, show the more vigorous growth and greater yield that is characteristic of hybrid plants. 'F_1' denotes the first *F*ilial generation, *i.e.* the generation produced by crossing the two selected parental lines; the **F_2 generation** (second filial generation) would consist of the plants produced by self- or cross-fertilization of the F_1 hybrids.

f-word A euphemism for the four-letter taboo word describing sexual intercourse (fuck). It originated in the 1980s in America and gave rise to a number of similar constructions used by people trying to avoid taboo expressions, for example, 'the T-word' (for Margaret Thatcher).

FAB *See* FUEL AIR BOMB.

Fab Four *See* BEATLES.

Fabergé The near legendary firm of goldsmiths made famous under Peter Carl Fabergé (1846–1920). The company was founded by Fabergé's father in 1842 but it was the son who established the firm's name for *objets d'art* in gold, silver, enamel, and precious stones. Among the valuable items produced by Fabergé was a series of ingenious Easter eggs made for the Russian Tsars. The firm went out of operation after the OCTOBER REVOLUTION of 1917. Fabergé died in exile in Lausanne.

face (1) British slang for someone who stands out in the crowd, a stylish trendsetter. A fashionable word with the mods (*see* MODS AND ROCKERS) of 1963 and 1964, it was also used in America. It probably derives from the idea of a famous face being instantly recognizable or from the fact that the picture cards in a pack are the ones with the highest values. (2) British street slang of the 1980s for nerve or brazenness.

facedown *See* FACE-OFF.

faceless man A person who is not known to the public, but who wields power behind the scenes. It is usually used in the plural; for example, one criticism of the Australian Labor Party was that it was run by a non-Parliamentary Federal Executive consisting of '36 faceless men'. *See also* MEN IN GREY SUITS.

face-off or **facedown** A confrontation between individuals, organizations, countries, etc., in which each tries to make the other back down. Originally a US term, the analogy between the conflict and the idea of two people staring at each other is extended in such phrases as 'eyeball-to-eyeball confrontation' and in the question of who blinks first.

fact. faction A blend of fact and fiction in a novel, film, play, etc. For instance, a faction novel might contain actual people as characters and give a fictional account of real historical events. Incidents presented as if they were facts are sometimes called **factoids**.

Theatre of Fact or **Documentary Theatre** A theatrical genre in which plays are accurately based on historical fact. Having its roots in classical theatre, it became a recognizable theatrical form in the 1950s and 1960s, notably in the plays of Rolf Hochhuth (1931–), *e.g. The Representative* (1963) and *Soldiers* (1967), and Peter Weiss (1916–82), *e.g. The Investiga-*

tion (1965) and *Trotsky in Exile* (1970). *See also* DOCUDRAMA.

fade (1) US slang meaning to leave or go away. It was part of BEATNIK jargon in the 1950s, and was revived by adolescents in the 1980s. (2) US slang from the world of gambling, especially used in the dice game craps, meaning to meet a bet.

faff or **faff around** British slang meaning to dither about in a disorganized way. It is usually said with an air of exasperation.

fag (1) Slang for a cigarette. (2) A male homosexual; short for **faggot**.

fag hag Slang for a woman who consorts with gay men. Originally a US expression from the 1960s, it is now also heard in the UK and Australia. It has lost its earlier pejorative overtones and may even be used by the woman herself.

fag tag US college-student slang for the loop at the top of the back pleat of the traditional US Oxford shirt. The loop (the tag) is facetiously regarded as being in some way helpful during a gay sexual encounter – something to hold onto, perhaps.

fail-safe Of a system or mechanism, designed to return to normal functioning in the event of human error or mechanical failure. At the height of the COLD WAR in the 1950s, the US Air Force introduced a fail-safe limit beyond which US bombers could not fly without specific orders; it was intended to prevent nuclear conflict by mistake or as a result of the actions of a madman. The threat of nuclear annihilation through human error or derangement is also countered by the so-called 'two-man system' ('four-man' in the Soviet Union), in which personnel guarding, handling, or in charge of firing nuclear weapons operate in tandem. A more mundane, but no less vital, example of a fail-safe system is the DEAD MAN'S HANDLE, a safety switch that must remain depressed by train drivers to prevent the automatic application of the brakes.

fair. **Fair Deal** A post-war programme of social and economic reform put forward by Harry S. Truman during his presidency (1945–53) of America. Only a few of the recommendations, including increased retirement benefits and slum clearance, passed Congress.

fairness doctrine In America, the principle, applied by the Federal Communications Commission, that radio and TV broadcasting stations should give reasonable coverage of opposing viewpoints on controversial issues. For example, the principle of **equal time** is that two politicians, say, in an election should have equal opportunities to air their views. In the UK, the broadcasting authorities apply the equal-time principle to the main political parties.

fairy Widely used slang for a male homosexual. The US equivalent is **farley**.

Falaise A small town in Calvados, NW France. A crucial battle was fought here in August 1944, when a large contingent of the German army was almost encircled by Allied forces S of Caen. However, a number of them managed to escape through the so-called 'Falaise Gap', before it was closed. The town was virtually destroyed.

Falange (Sp. phalanx) At first a right-wing party in Spain formed in 1932 by José Antonio Primo de Rivera (son of the general Miguel Primo de Rivera, dictator of Spain 1923–30) to uphold his father's memory against republican criticism, and later adopted by General Franco as the one official party in the state. Essentially representing a combination of European FASCISM and Spanish nationalism, it was used to counterbalance royalist, army, and Church influence and in 1937 forced the CARLISTS to join with it. The latter group re-emerged after 1957. The Falange (latterly known as the National Movement) lost its unique position after the CAUDILLO's death in 1975, and was formally disbanded in 1977.

Falashas An Ethiopian tribe that practises a form of biblical Judaism. In this century many Falashas have adopted modern Judaism and some have emigrated to Israel. Israel accepts Falashas as Jews, in terms of its immigration laws, and in 1985 organized a secret airlift (known as Operation Moses) of some 7000 Falashas to Israel to escape the devastating Ethiopian famine. In 1991, during the final stages of the Ethiopian civil war, a further 15,000 Falashas were airlifted (Operation Solomon) to Israel in a few days by a fleet of airliners (some of which had been stripped of their seats to enable 1000 passengers to sit on mattresses on the cabin floor). This left behind tens of thousands of **Feres Mora**, Falashas who, having converted to Christianity, no longer qualify as Israeli immigrants under a 1962 Israeli supreme court ruling. Raramin Elazzar, head of

Israel Radio's Amharic (Ethiopian Language) Service, pleading for their admission on the grounds that many of their relatives are now in Israel, commented quizzically:

> They are not converted Jews, they are Jews who left Judaism.

Falcon, the A character inspired by the novelist Michael Arlen (1895–1956), a suave detective with a comic but muscular servant, Goldie. The Falcon appeared in some 16 second-feature films in the 1940s. Originally played by George Sanders, the Falcon was shot in *The Falcon's Brother* (1942) to enable Sanders to retire. The Falcon's brother thereafter became the detective, played by Sanders' real-life brother, John Conway. In nearly all the films Goldie was played by Edward Brophy.

Falklands. Battle of the Falkland Islands A naval battle of World War I, fought in December 1914, in which the Germans were decisively defeated by the British, Germany losing several ships, including the *Scharnhörst* and *Gneisenau*. It was in revenge for the battle off the Chilean port of **Coronel**, fought in the previous month, in which the British lost the cruisers *Monmouth* and *Good Hope*.

Falklands Conflict The war between the UK and Argentina for possession of the Falkland Islands in 1982. The bleak South Atlantic islands have been a Crown Colony since 1828, but despite the opposition of the majority of the 1800 inhabitants, Argentina has consistently asserted its claim to what it calls the Islas Malvinas. In April 1982, after British defence cuts led to the withdrawal of the only remaining Royal Navy frigate stationed at Port Stanley, Argentina launched an invasion of the islands. Much to the Argentine's surprise, the British immediately declared a 200-mile exclusion zone around the island and dispatched a strong military task force, which restored British sovereignty in June 1982, when Argentina was forced to surrender. This bravura military episode was regarded with pride by many British people and certainly enhanced the UK's status in the world. It also made a heroine of Margaret Thatcher, who was responsible for the promptness of the response (*see* FALKLANDS FACTOR). Others, however, questioned the economic and human costs (1000 lives lost in the conflict) involved in defending such an inhospitable and geographically remote territory, which has little strategic or economic value. Argentina's president, General Leopoldo Galtieri, resigned after the surrender and – with members of his junta – was tried and imprisoned.

Falklands factor The boost in the electoral fortunes of the previously flagging Conservative Party after the success of British forces during the FALKLANDS CONFLICT in 1982. The Falklands factor significantly contributed to the Conservative victory in the 1983 general election, despite the government's poor economic record. It certainly revived support for Margaret Thatcher, who thereafter commanded worldwide respect as a resourceful and forceful leader. The term has now passed into general usage to decribe any unpredictable event that increases the popularity of a political party.

fall. Did she fall or was she pushed? Originally a reference to a young woman who has lost her virginity. In 1908 the phrase was applied in a new context in newspaper articles about the death of Violet Charlesworth, whose body was found at the foot of Beachy Head. Thorne Smith wrote a comic novel with the title *Did She Fall?* in 1936.

fall guy Originally a term that came into use with the popularity of professional wrestling at the turn of the century. As soon as wrestling became a spectator sport, contests, not surprisingly, started to be rigged. The winner was decided beforehand; the loser was the fall guy, the contestant who agreed to take the falls. In fact, the wrestling fall guy may have been more prudent than unfortunate; perhaps having thought little of his chances of winning the purse, he preferred to settle for the smaller but surer fall guy's fee. His agreement with the winner may also have included a promise that no lasting damage would be inflicted on him in the ring. In modern usage, however, the fall guy is the one who takes the blame for some catastrophe, which may not have been of his own making. Either he may have volunteered to be the fall guy or been framed to become one.

fall-out Radioactive dust resulting from atomic and nuclear explosions. Figuratively, the effect of an action which extends beyond the intended range.

It fell off the back of a lorry Said of something picked up or acquired fortuitously or by somewhat questionable means.

family In America, a criminal organization that is a subdivision of the MAFIA. Although families are known by name – for example, the 'Luchese family' – the members are not necessarily related. *See also* GODFATHER; MOB.

family ganging In America, the practice of giving unnecessary medical treatment to members of a family who accompany the actual patient. It is a way in which doctors increase their fees from the US MEDICAID scheme. *See also* PING-PONGING.

family hour In America, the period during the early evening up to about 9 p.m. when television programmes suitable for viewing by both parents and children are shown. In the UK there is a similar policy of no sex or excessive violence before 9 p.m. (the '9 p.m. watershed'), based on the idea that children go to bed at this time. *See also* GODSLOT.

family jewels Shameful secrets that an organization, company, political party, etc., keeps hidden. The term was first used in this sense in the late 1970s, referring to a leaked list of DIRTY TRICKS and other illicit activities indulged in by the US CIA.

family planning See BIRTH CONTROL.

family saviors Facetious term used to describe adherents to the New Right in US political life, formed largely of proselytizing fundamentalist Christians, who lobby for the defence of traditional family values. According to the journalist Andrew Kopkind, who carried out research among the BORN-AGAIN CHRISTIAN community in Illinois, family saviors support "the death penalty, Laetrile, nuclear power, local police, Panama Canal, saccharin, FBI, CIA, defense budget, public prayer, and real-estate growth".

> Fiercely, these zealots condemn promiscuity, adultery, homosexuality, masturbation, long hair and flouride.
>
> GORE VIDAL: Sex is Politics (1979).

famous last words The following are examples of well-known final observations by some of the great figures of the 20th century:

BEHAN, BRENDAN (*playwright*; on having his pulse taken by a nursing nun): Bless you, Sister. May all your sons be bishops!

CHURCHILL, SIR WINSTON (*statesman*): Oh, I am so bored with it all.

COOPER, DAME GLADYS (*actress*; on looking into her mirror): If this is what virus pneumonia does to one, I really don't think I shall bother to have it again.

COWARD, SIR NOEL (*playwright*): Good night, my darlings, I'll see you in the morning.

DREISER, THEODORE (*novelist*; his intended last words): Shakespeare, I come!

DUNCAN, ISADORA (*dancer*): Adieu my friends, I go on to glory!

FAIRBANKS SNR, DOUGLAS (*actor*): I've never felt better!

FERRIER, KATHLEEN (*contralto*): Now I'll have *eine kleine Pause*.

HEATH, NEVILLE (*murderer*; on being offered a drink before his execution in 1946): You might make that a double.

HENRY, O (*William Sidney Porter, short-story writer*; quoting a popular song): Turn up the lights, I don't want to go home in the dark.

IBSEN, HENRIK (*playwright*; on being told by the nurse that he was feeling better): On the contrary!

JAMES, HENRY (*novelist*): So it has come at last, the distinguished thing.

JOYCE, JAMES (*novelist*): Does anybody understand?

MAHLER, GUSTAV (*composer*): Mozart.

OATES, CAPT. LAWRENCE (*explorer*; on leaving the tent occupied by fellow-members of the ill-fated Antarctic expedition led by Scott in 1912, fearing that his lameness would hinder the team's chances of survival): I am just going outside and may be some time.

RHODES, CECIL JOHN (*statesman*): So little done, so much to do.

RUNYON, DAMON (*writer*): You can keep the things of bronze and stone and give me one man to remember me just once a year.

SANDERS, GEORGE (*actor*; his suicide note): Dear World, I am leaving you because I am bored. I am leaving you with your worries. Good luck.

SAROYAN, WILLIAM (*playwright*): Everybody has got to die, but I have always believed an exception would be made in my case. Now what?

SMITH, LOGAN PEARSALL (*writer*): Thank heavens the sun has gone in and I don't have to go out and enjoy it.

SPENCER, STANLEY (*artist*; to the nurse who had just injected him): Beautifully done.

STRACHEY, LYTTON (*writer*): If this is dying, I don't think much of it.

THOMAS, DYLAN (*poet*): I've had eighteen straight whiskies. I think that's the record.

THURBER, JAMES (*humorist*): God bless . . . God damn.

TOLSTOY, LEO (*novelist*; refusing to see a priest): Even in the valley of the shadow of death, two and two do not make six.

VICTORIA (*Queen*; referring to the war in South Africa then in progress): Oh, that peace may come.

WILDE, OSCAR (*dramatist*; contemplating the room in Paris in which he lay): Either that wall paper goes, or I do.

See also CAVELL MEMORIAL; EMPIRE, HOW IS THE; SCOTT OF THE ANTARTIC.

fan Used from about 1900 for an ardent admirer or devotee (an abbreviation of fanatic). Admiring letters written to the object of such admiration are known as **fan mail**.

fan club (1) A club consisting of the admirers of a famous person, especially a pop star or film star. (2) In business jargon, a number of individuals who, independently of each other, and without collusion, decide to purchase a significant number of shares in a company. A fan club is legal, whereas the related **concert party** is an illegal combination of two or more persons who buy or sell shares in a company to influence its market value. Members of a concert party usually contrive to appear unconnected with other members; however, once their connection becomes established, the 1981 Companies Act lays down that the shares owned by all the members must be treated as if they are owned by one person, from the point of view of disclosing interests in a company's shareholding.

fanzine A neologism created from 'fan' and 'magazine' for a cheap magazine or newsletter produced by amateur followers of a particular sport, hobby, television programme, etc. The term was originally exclusively used for publications for SCI-FI enthusiasts in America in the 1940s.

fantasy British slang for an extremely potent hallucinogenic drug invented in the UK in 1989; it is a mixture of ECSTASY and LSD or mescaline.

FANY First Aid Nursing Yeomanry. An organization of women formed in 1907. It provided amateur nursing, ambulance drivers, and other driving services in World War I. In World War II FANYs provided drivers for military cars. An elite women's service with an elegant khaki uniform, it was said of it that a girl had to be a debutante to be accepted. After World War II it was amalgamated with the Women's Transport Service but is still referred to as the FANY; today its main function is in helping to maintain communications in civil and military emergencies.

FAO Food and Agricultural Organization. A specialized agency of the UNITED NATIONS, formed in 1945 to coordinate international efforts in raising food production and nutrition levels, especially in the developing countries. It also organizes work to improve forest management, carries out research, and provides educational services. Its headquarters are in Rome.

farley *See* FAIRY.

farm. buy the farm *See* BUY.

farmers British rhyming slang for piles (haemorrhoids), from the name Farmer Giles, a common personification of a country farmer.

far-out A HIPPIE slang expression of extreme approval for something remarkable. It originated in America in the late 1960s but became widely used in the UK. Within 10 years it sounded very dated.

fascines Bundles of faggots used to build up military defences or to fill ditches for impeding attack. They were much used in World War I for road foundations and for horse standings and also used to impede attack in World War II. *See also* FASCISM.

Fascism Originally an Italian political movement taking its name from the old Roman *fasces* (the bound bundles of rods used as a symbol of the authority of magistrates in ancient Rome). It was founded in 1919 by Benito Mussolini (1883–1945) who took advantage of the discontent in Italy after World War I to form a totalitarian nationalist party against left-wing radicalism and socialism. In 1922 the Fascists marched on Rome and demanded power, and King Victor Emmanuel III made Mussolini prime minister. He styled himself DUCE (leader) and made himself dictator in 1925, suppressing all other political parties the following year. The Fascists controlled Italy until 1943.

The term 'fascism', soon came to be applied to similar totalitarian movements in other countries. Ruthlessness, inhumanity, and dishonest and disreputable practices were notable characteristics of its adherents. *See* HITLERISM; NAZI.

> Benito Mussolini provided Italy with a new theme of government which, while it claimed to save the Italian people from Communism, raised himself to dictatorial power. As Fascism sprang from Communism, so Nazism developed from Fascism.
>
> WINSTON CHURCHILL: *The Gathering Storm*, ch. i.

fashion victim Someone who is so obsessed with the idea of being fashionable that their clothes are dictated by trend rather than suitability or taste. Their only standard is that it be the most up-to-the-minute style.

> One week he's in polka dots, the next week he's in stripes,

Cos he's a dedicated follower of fashion.
RAY DAVIES: *Dedicated Follower of Fashion.*

fast. fastback A car with a sloping rear, which forms a continuous line from roof to tail and into which the rear-view window is set.

fast breeder A type of nuclear reactor that uses fast (*i.e.* high-energy) neutrons and produces fissionable plutonium as a by-product. *See* NUCLEAR REACTOR.

fast food Food that can be prepared and served very quickly, such as hamburgers, french fries, pizzas, kebabs, etc. In the UK, fast food was once confined to fish 'n' chips or jellied eels from a market stall. Today US-style fast-food outlets have become a dominating feature of the UK's urban landscape; they are also to be found in the high streets of many other countries. A large amount of fast food is also JUNK FOOD. Apart from the fast-food outlets outside the home, there is now a vast range of food available for working housewives, old people, etc., who do not have the time, facilities, or inclination to cook a meal. This may consist of deep-frozen food or COOK-CHILL foods. *See also* HEALTH FOOD; WHOLEFOOD.

faster than a speeding bullet *See* SUPERMAN.

fast one (1) US slang from the 1970s for Ritalin, a brand of amphetamine. (2) British slang used in the phrase **pull a fast one**, meaning to try and get away with an unscrupulous act.

living life in the fast lane A cliché beloved of tabloid journalists when describing people whose lifestyle involves high living with an element of danger and excitement. It refers, of course, to the fast lane of a motorway in which the most powerful cars are to be found.

Fastnet A rock and lightship off Cape Clear, SW Ireland. The **Fastnet Race**, from Ryde, Isle of Wight, to the Fastnet Rock, is one of the five races contributing to the ADMIRAL'S CUP. In the Fastnet race of 1979, 18 yachtsmen died in severe storms; 25 of the 330 yachts competing were sunk or disabled.

fat. fat cat Slang for a smug, wealthy, and privileged person who flaunts his or her lifestyle even though it has been attained by exploitation or connections, rather than merit. The term is thought to have been first used of those who did well financially from World War I; it is usually said of businessmen and politicians.

fat farm A HEALTH FARM or resort to which people go to lose weight. The term is mostly used by thin people.

Fats (1) Nickname of the talented Black US JAZZ pianist, composer, and entertainer, Thomas 'Fats' Waller (1904–43). His own compositions, which he recorded many times and in many versions, include 'Honeysuckle Rose' (1928) and 'Ain't Misbehavin' (1929). As a nightclub entertainer he could be extremely funny; perhaps this talent, and the great demand it created, detracted from full appreciation of his technical ability on the piano. A great fat man (hence his name), he has left a legacy of sparkling recorded jazz music. (2) Nickname of another fat Black US jazz musician, Antoine 'Fats' Domino (1928–), a singer, pianist, and songwriter of the ROCK 'N' ROLL era. His rhythm-and-blues songs include 'Blueberry Hill' (1959).

fatso Slang for a fat person. This unkind term originated in America but has become widely used in the UK since the 1960s. *See also* FATTY.

fat transfer An experimental surgical operation in which fatty tissue is withdrawn from the thighs, buttocks, and similar fleshy areas by vacuum suction and injected beneath the skin of the face. The aim of this cosmetic technique is to pad out the facial tissues and thus reduce wrinkling, but there is no way of ensuring that the transplanted tissue remains in position and does not become absorbed.

Fatty Nickname of Roscoe 'Fatty' Arbuckle (1887–1933), a star of comedy films. A man of considerable size, he is interesting not so much for his films as for the way in which **Fatty Arbuckle** has entered the language as an epithet to describe any fat man and for the Hays Code (*see* HAYS OFFICE), a film censorship code that emerged in Hollywood in the 1920s after a case of indecent assault and manslaughter had been brought against Fatty Arbuckle. He was accused of seducing and raping a starlet, who subsequently died of complications from the assault. Although Arbuckle was eventually acquitted of the charges, his film career came to an end and even the films he had previously made were banned. No studio would employ him under his own name, although he subsequently tried, unsuccessfully, to make a comeback as a director under the name 'William B. Goodrich'.

father. Fatha Nickname of Earl (Kenneth) 'Fatha' Hines (1905–83), Black US

JAZZ pianist and band leader. Trained as a concert pianist, he played with several bands before forming his own (1929–48). He then joined Louis Armstrong's 'All Stars' (1948–51).

Father Brown A fictional detective and East Anglian Roman Catholic priest, created by G. K. Chesterton (1874–1936). Reflecting the author's own opinion, Father Brown regarded criminal activity as a sin and relied on his intuition to solve the crimes he was investigating. Chesterton himself became a Catholic convert in 1922. His first Father Brown story was published in 1911 as *The Innocence of Father Brown*.

Father's Day The day set aside for fathers to receive cards and gifts from their children, in imitation of the more traditional MOTHER'S DAY. Father's Day was devised in 1910, in Spokane, Washington but remains unrecognized in most families on both sides of the Atlantic.

fatwa A word that is neither English nor 20th-century, although it was widely used in English during the **Rushdie affair** of the late 1980s. An Arabic word for an edict issued by a Muslim religious leader, it became familiar to a startled non-Islamic world in February 1989, when Ayatollah Khomeini (1902–89) issued a *fatwa* offering a cash reward for any Muslim who succeeded in assassinating the British author of Indian Muslim origin, Salman Rushdie (1947–). Rushdie was the author, and Viking Penguin the publishers, of a novel, *The Satanic Verses* (1988), in which a character identified by many Muslims as the prophet Muhammed was treated in a manner that they regarded as disrespectful.

> The author of *The Satanic Verses* book, which is against Islam, the Prophet and the Koran, and all those involved in its publication who were aware of its content, are sentenced to death. I ask all Muslims to execute them wherever they find them.
>
> AYATOLLAH KHOMEINI, speech 14 February 1989.

The incident flared into a diplomatic and political cause célèbre as a result of the *fatwa*, with fundamentalist Muslims in Tehran, Bradford, and elsewhere burning copies of the book in the streets and calling for the death of the author, who by then had gone into hiding, a much richer but much sadder man. Diplomatic relationships were broken off and the literary world protested that no such violent acts of religious intolerance had been seen since the Roman Catholic Church burnt and tortured its dissidents in the middle ages. The British government made strong but circumspect protests, unwilling to endanger its Iranian oil interests or adversely influence the Iranian support it hoped to gain in obtaining the release of the Archbishop of Canterbury's special envoy, Terry Waite, who had earlier been a victim of Middle Eastern hostage taking. With Viking Penguin books banned in all Muslim countries, the affair dragged on until Christmas Eve 1990, when Rushdie announced, to the dismay of his supporters, that after a meeting with Islamic scholars, he had become a Muslim.

> I used to describe myself as a person with a God-shaped hole inside . . . I don't pretend to fully understand what has happened. I don't think I am a good Muslim. But now I am happy and quite pleased to be able to say that I am inside the fold.

In this announcement he cancelled the plan for a paperback edition of the book but refused to agree that the cancellation amounted to a disavowal of the book: "The binding of a book is not a moral principle", he said while refusing to withdraw the hardback edition. World reactions to Rushdie's surprise conversion were mixed. On the following day, Ayatollah Khamenei, Khomeini's successor as Iran's spiritual leader, renewed the *fatwa*. An Iranian newspaper reporting this event said it hoped that Rushdie would now visit a Muslim country because that would make it easier to kill him without embarrassing the British government. On 30 December 1990, Rushdie's conversion was welcomed in Cairo: in a formal blessing, Grand Sheikh Gad el-Haq Ali Gad el-Haq, supreme theological authority of all Sunni Muslims, forgave him any past sins, while President Mubarak of Egypt invited him, perhaps rather ominously, to visit Egypt to meet the Grand Sheikh. Arnold Wesker, the dramatist and a leading member of the Rushdie defence committee, found the whole affair 'incredibly depressing':

> It seems the religious terrorists have won...it seems to me that there is a new madness in the world and it calls itself Islamic fundamentalism.

fauvism The name given to the work of a group of young French artists of the first decade of the 20th century, whose leader was Henri Matisse, and which included Derain, Braque, Vlaminck, Dufy, Marquet, Friez, and Rouault. There was a corresponding German movement known as DIE BRÜCKE (The Bridge). The French school derives from the influence of Van

Gogh and its work was characterized by the imaginative use of brilliant colour, decorative simplicity, vitality, and gaiety. The name *fauves* (wild beasts) arose from a remark of the critic Vauxcelles at an exhibition of their work in 1905, *Donatello au milieu des fauves*, occasioned by the sight of their spectacularly coloured pictures. *See also* CUBISM; DADAISM; FUTURISM; SURREALISM; SYNCHRONISM; VORTICISM.

Fawlty Towers A fictional West-of-England private hotel that featured in the British TV series of this name in the late 1970s. Run with manic incompetence by Basil Fawlty (John Cleese) and his nagging wife Sybil (Prunella Scales), the hotel managed to demolish a fresh set of pompous middle-class guests in every episode. The Fawltys and their Spanish waiter Manuel (Andrew Sachs) – a buffoon whose incomprehensible use of English was matched only by his inability to understand it ('qué?' – Spanish for 'what?' – he asks, every time he is addressed) – have entered British 20th-century folklore as archetypes of humour. The series was not very successful abroad; in Spain, Manuel was rewritten as an Italian waiter. The actual house in Buckinghamshire used in the series for the hotel burnt down in 1991.

fax Facsimile Transmission. The sending of printed text and images through the telephone network or other communication link. The document to be faxed is scanned and converted into digital code by a fax machine at one end and then transmitted by a phone line or other link to the receiving fax machine, which reconstitutes the data to produce a printed copy of the original. The fax machine was once a cumbersome and expensive piece of technology, used by such organizations as police forces, who needed to transmit and disseminate text and images (*e.g.* mug shots) quickly and easily. By the early 1980s, however, small low-cost fax machines became widely available and have now become as commonplace in offices as photocopiers and word processors. They have largely replaced the TELEX for many purposes, although it is easier to have a two-way conversation on the telex.

fax-napping The crime of stealing someone's FILOFAX and demanding a 'ransom' for its return. Coined by analogy with 'kidnapping', it is also called **filonapping** or simply **filofaxing**. The loss of a Filofax is a serious matter to its owner, causing complete breakdown of both social and business activities.

fax shot *See* JUNK MAIL.

FBI Federal Bureau of Investigation. An agency of the US Department of Justice established in 1908 to investigate breaches of federal law, especially those related to security. It developed considerable autonomy under the directorship (1924–72) of J. Edgar Hoover, during which it did much to control organized crime in the 1930s and to implement MCCARTHYISM in the 1950s.

FDR Franklin Delano Roosevelt (1882–1945). The only US president (1933–45) to be elected three times; he died in office. His NEW DEAL programmes helped America to recover from the GREAT DEPRESSION. In World War II he introduced LEND-LEASE aid to the Allies and, after the Japanese attack on PEARL HARBOR, led America into the war. He was widely known by his initials. Paralysed from the waist down by poliomyelitis from 1921, he was filmed in newsreels in contrived sedentary poses to disguise his disability. *See also* FIRESIDE CHATS; HOUDINI IN THE WHITE HOUSE.

feasibility study An initial pilot investigation to determine whether some plan, project, etc., is desirable or practical.

feather. featherbed To give favourable treatment to a particular group of people, especially financially. The verb is often used in connection with companies giving large wage settlements to certain trade unions or to governments favouring certain sections of the community with subsidies. The allusion is to the luxury of sleeping on a feather bed.

feather one's propeller In flying, to rotate the aeroplane's propeller blades, when the engine is stopped, to an angle at which they produce minimum drag. In boats, to perform a similar operation to lessen water resistance on the screw.

feature film A fictional film produced to provide entertainment. It will normally run for at least 34 minutes (anything less is called a 'short'), but most feature films run for 90 minutes or more. Feature films usually have at least one well-known actor and provide the main item of a cinema programme, often supported by one or more shorts. Formerly, it was usual for most suburban and provincial cinemas to show two feature-length films, the **main feature** and a low-budget production designed to be a supporting feature or a **B-feature**.

February Revolution Part of the Russian Revolution that started in February 1917 with riots in Petrograd, in protest against food and fuel shortages and what was seen to be military incompetence in World War I. It led to the abdication of Tsar Nicholas II and the formation of a provisional government led by Prince Lvov. The February Revolution was the precursor to the OCTOBER REVOLUTION of the same year, which saw the BOLSHEVIKS, with Lenin as their leader, finally installed as the new government of Russia.

> Revolution is not the uprising against pre-existing order, but the setting up of a new order contradictory to the traditional one.
>
> JOSE ORTEGA Y GASSET: *The Revolt of the Masses.*

Fed Slang for the Federal Reserve System, the banking system of America that acts as its central bank. 'The Fed' consists of 12 Federal Reserve Districts, in each of which a Federal Reserve Bank acts as the lender of last resort. The whole system is controlled by the Federal Reserve Board in Washington.

Feds US slang name, mainly used by criminals, for agents of the FBI (Federal Bureau of Investigation), which was prominent in the 1930s campaign against organized crime and also in the anticommunist smear campaigns of the McCarthy era in the 1950s (*see* MCCARTHYISM). In the UK, the police are sometimes inaccurately called 'the Feds'.

Feebie A member of the US Federal Bureau of Investigation (the FBI). It is a somewhat derisive term that was used by other government officers in the 1960s and 1970s. A play on the initials FBI, it has connotations of 'feeble'.

feed In JAZZ slang, the playing of chords as backing for a soloist.

feedback Originally used in electronics, the use of part of the output signal from an electronic device to modify the performance of the device. In 'positive feedback' the signal augments the output (as in an amplifier); in 'negative feedback' it reduces it. Feedback is the unwanted effect that causes a whistling noise in a loudspeaker as a result of the output from the loudspeaker being picked up by a microphone connected to the same amplifier. The concept of self-modification of a system has been applied in other fields; for example, the effect of a product in a biological reaction on other stages in the reaction (*see also* BIOFEEDBACK). More generally, feedback is any sort of information given in response to an action, question, etc., especially one that modifies an action or policy.

feederliner An airline of moderate size designed to link small domestic airports with a main airport.

feelie An artistic medium in which the 'spectator' has physical contact with the work as part of his or her appreciation of it. An example would be a sculpture that the public was encouraged to touch as well as look at. The term 'feelie' was used first by the British author Aldous Huxley (1894–1964) in his futuristic novel BRAVE NEW WORLD (1932) for a type of film entertainment in which the viewer could actually experience the emotions and physical feelings of the people shown on the screen.

Felix the Cat Hero of early animated film cartoons who first appeared in 1921 in a production by Pat Sullivan. Throughout his many adventures **Felix kept on walking** and thus originated the once-familiar catchphrase.

fellow-traveller A person in sympathy with a political party but not a member of that party; usually restricted to Communist sympathizers. The term (Russ. *poputchik*) was coined by Leon Trotsky.

> He is but one of a reputed short list of seven fellow-travellers under threat of expulsion.
>
> *Time and Tide*, 1 May 1948, on the Labour Party's expulsion of one of its members.

felt-tip pen or **fibre-tip pen** A type of pen, introduced in the 1950s, in which the writing point is made of compressed fibre, through which the ink soaks. *See also* BIRO.

female chauvinist pig A strident feminist, the reverse of a MALE CHAUVINIST PIG. Female chauvinist pigs regard all women as inately superior to men in all respects, men being useful only as studs.

feminism The social beliefs that women should have an equal role to that of men in society. In the UK in the 20th century this began with the activities of the SUFFRAGETTES, who campaigned for voting rights for women. In 1903 Emmeline Pankhurst (1858–1928) and her daughters formed the Women's Social and Political Union (WSPU), which finally achieved votes for women in 1918. However, the educational and property qualifications attaching to women's suffrage were not removed for 10 years, when men and women became political equals. During this century, too, equal educational opportunities have been a priority, with many of the exclusively male educational establishments now admitting women. Post-World-War-II feminism has largely been expressed by consciousness-raising groups in America in the 1960s and the formation of the Women's Liberation Workshop (known as **Women's Lib**) in London in 1969. This organization has worked for, and largely achieved, equal education and job opportunities for women and equal pay for women. In the UK the Equal Pay Act (1970) ensures that women are paid the same rate as men for a particular job. The Sex Discrimation Act (1975), which included setting up the Equal Opportunities Commission, promotes equality of opportunity between men and women. In a country in which, in the 1980s, both the head of state and the prime minister were women, feminism was considered by some to have achieved its principal aims (*see also* GENDER GAP; ORDINATION OF WOMEN). However, many of the aims of Women's Lib have not yet been achieved; these include free contraception, abortion on demand, and 24-hour nurseries for working mothers. *See also* SEXUAL POLITICS.

fender-bender A car accident in which the car is damaged ('fender' being the US term for the wing of a car). A fender-bender is also a driver who tends to have accidents. *See also* GENDER-BENDER.

Ferdinand the Bull A character in a children's book by Munro Leaf who was more interested in smelling flowers than in tossing matadors. The antithesis of a macho bull, he was popularized in a Walt Disney cartoon film of 1939.

Feres Mora *See* FALASHAS.

ferry pilot A World War II term for a pilot flying new aircraft from the factory to the air station.

fertility drug Colloquial name for a hormonal preparation administered to women who are unable to conceive because their ovaries fail to produce egg cells. Available since the 1960s, such drugs, which include clomiphene, act either by stimulating the pituitary gland to release hormones that, in turn, cause the ovary to produce egg cells, or they act directly by stimulating the ovary itself. Fertility drugs may cause the simultaneous release of several egg cells, resulting in multiple births; similar drugs are used to stimulate the ovary in the technique of *in vitro* fertilization (*see* IVF).

festival. Festival Gardens The gardens in Battersea Park in London, laid out by Osbert Lancaster and John Piper for the FESTIVAL OF BRITAIN in 1951. A pleasure garden in the style of the 18th-century Vauxhall Gardens, it had bowered walks, a grotto, and many decorative fountains.

Festival of Britain An event organized in 1951 to mark the centenary of the Great Exhibition, a display of British industrial supremacy mounted in Crystal Palace (which was built especially for the occasion) in 1851. As well as commemorating the Great Exhibition, the Festival of Britain was designed to boost morale after the austerities of World War II and to demonstrate the UK's post-war developments in science, technology, architecture, and the arts. Exhibitions were held throughout the country, the main site being the SOUTH BANK of the Thames in London, where the FESTIVAL GARDENS and the ROYAL FESTIVAL HALL were built as part of the event.

Festung Europa (Ger. Fortress Europe) Hitler's dream of Europe under German domination, so fortified that it would become impregnable against interference from the rest of the world.

fetus. fetal alcohol syndrome A condition affecting newborn babies whose mothers have consumed excessive amounts of alcohol during pregnancy. Affected babies suffer from various defects, including mental retardation and abnormally small head size, caused by the toxic effects of the alcohol, which is carried in the mother's bloodstream across the placenta and impairs normal development in the fetus. The syndrome was first recognized in the 1970s; even moderate drinking during pregnancy can adversely affect the fetus, and women should be aware of this danger.

fetoscope A medical instrument employing FIBRE OPTICS used to observe an unborn baby in the womb. Inserted into the abdomen of a pregnant woman, it enables the fetus to be examined for the presence of any visible abnormalities and also allows samples of fetal blood to be withdrawn through a hollow needle passed through the instrument. Analysis of this blood enables the prenatal diagnosis of such disorders as haemophilia and Duchenne muscular dystrophy. Inspection of the fetus using this instrument is called *fetoscopy*.

Few, the The RAF pilots of the BATTLE OF BRITAIN, so called from prime minister Winston Churchill's memorable tribute in the House of Commons (20 August 1940):

> Never in the field of human conflict was so much owed by so many to so few.

Feynman diagram A type of diagram used in particle physics to show how charged particles interact by the exchange of virtual photons (a branch of physics known as QUANTUM ELECTRODYNAMICS). They were invented by the US physicist Richard Feynman (1918–88).

FFI *Forces françaises de l'intérieur* (French Forces of the Interior). The grouping together in February 1944 of the various forces fighting for liberation after the fall of France in 1940. It included partisans, francs-tireurs, MAQUIS, and others, and was subsequently merged with the army (November 1944). *See also* FIGHTING FRENCH.

FFL *Forces françaises libres* (Free French forces). French forces organized by General de Gaulle after the German occupation of France (from June 1940) to continue the struggle in cooperation with the Allies. Later called the FIGHTING FRENCH.

Fianna Fáil The Irish Gaelic for Warriors of Ireland (from *fianna* warriors and *Fáil* of Ireland). The Irish Republican Party founded by the Irish nationalist, Eamon de Valera, in 1926 in opposition to the treaty of 1921, which brought about the Irish Free State. It aims at the establishment of a united, independent, and self-supporting Ireland. Apart from three breaks from office during 1948–51, 1973–77, and 1982–87 it has been the governing party in the Republic of Ireland since 1932. Fianna Fáil has also paid particular attention to the revival of the Irish language. *See also* FINE GAEL.

fibre. fibreglass Glass spun into a fibrous form, which can be used in many different manufacturing processes, ranging from fireproof textiles to aircraft parts.

fibre optics The use of flexible glass or transparent plastic fibres to transmit light (or, in some cases, ultraviolet or infrared radiation) around curves. Optical fibres are designed to work by internal reflection of the light, which travels through the filament, or bunch of filaments, with very little loss of intensity. Fibre optics is a method of examining otherwise inaccessible sites, as in medical examinations (*see* FETOSCOPE). The fibres can also be used to transmit pulsed light as a highly efficient method of transmitting data.

fibre-tip pen *See* FELT-TIP PEN.

fiche Short for MICROFICHE.

fiddle-cases US Black slang for shoes, presumably from the similarity in shape.

Fidelism or **Fidelismo** *See* CASTROISM.

FIDO (1) Fog Investigation and Dispersal Operation. The code name for a system used in World War II to clear fog from the runways of RAF airfields. It consisted of burning jets of petrol in specially designed burners. (2) Film Industry Defence Organization. A body, formed in 1959, by British renters and exhibitors to prevent old FEATURE FILMS from being sold to television companies. It collapsed in 1964.

FIFA Fédération Internationale de Football Association. The governing body that runs international football and organizes the WORLD CUP.

fifth. Fifth Beatle George Martin (1926–), producer for the EMI Parlaphone label, who recognized the talent of the BEATLES in 1962, after they had been turned down by various other major record companies. He played keyboards for a while and helped as an arranger, working closely with Lennon and McCartney in the early years of their song-writing partnership. Martin also exhibited considerable technical skills as a producer, using innovative and (for then) complex four-track recording techniques on such albums as *Sgt Pepper's Lonely Hearts Club Band* (1967), which allowed the Beatles to remain a vital force in the British pop-music scene for so long.

fifth column Traitors; those within a country who are working for the enemy, often by infiltrating into key positions, and seeking to undermine the body politic from within. The origin of the phrase is attributed to General Mola, who, in the SPANISH CIVIL WAR (1936–39), said that he had four columns encircling Madrid, and a fifth column working for him in the city.

fifth-generation computer An advanced type of COMPUTER, under development during the 1980s and 1990s, which deviates radically from the Von Neumann architecture common to previous computer generations. Instead of sequential processing, the new breed will use multiple parallel processors packed onto a single chip or small chip sets, made possible by Very Large Scale Integration (VLSI) production methods. These super-fast computers will be connected to, and communicate with, each other in large networks, and will have an ARTIFICIAL INTELLIGENCE (AI) capability, using 'expert' systems with vast databases of information on specialized subjects; communication to users will be in a friendly and intelligent manner, using sound, graphics, voice recognition, and speech synthesis. These machines will also feature very high-level programming languages enabling users to specify computational problems without recourse to complex notation.

fifth man *See* BURGESS AND MACLEAN.

Fifth Republic The name given to the period of French history that began in 1958, when de Gaulle was recalled from retirement to become president again.

plead the fifth amendment To refuse to comment or act on the grounds that to do so would be embarrassing or damaging to oneself. The phrase is usually used humorously but comes from the right of US citizens to decline to give evidence against themselves, which is enshrined in the fifth amendment to the Constitution.

fight. Fighter Command The part of the RAF that controlled its force of fighter aircraft. It was formed in 1936 under Hugh Dowding (1882–1970), with headquarters in NW London at Stanmore. It was Dowding who led Fighter Command's 55 squadrons during the BATTLE OF BRITAIN, and Dowding who refused to allow his main force to be distracted for other skirmishes. His resoluteness defeated the German Luftwaffe and saved the UK from invasion. Fighter Command and BOMBER COMMAND were amalgamated in 1968 to form STRIKE COMMAND.

Fighting French or **La France Combatante** All those Frenchmen at home and abroad who combined with the Allied nations in their war against the AXIS powers after the fall of France (in June 1940). General de Gaulle and others escaped to England and he formed them into 'The Free French' with the Cross of Lorraine as their emblem. The name was later changed to 'The Fighting French' (14 July 1942). One of their most noted feats was the march of General Leclerc's column across the Sahara, from Lake Chad, to join the British 8th Army in Libya. These men were honoured by being the first formation to enter Paris on 23 August 1944. The Fighting French supported the Allies in Africa, Italy, and elsewhere and made a valuable contribution to the liberation of France, in conjunction with the FFI.

film noir (Fr. dark film) Any of the US crime and gangster films of the 1940s and 1950s. The term was coined by French critics in 1946, after viewing Hollywood output since 1940 for the first time. They detected a new mood of cynicism and despair in depicting US society, with many films concentrating on corruption and brutality as epitomized by the classic *Double Indemnity* (1944), directed by Billy Wilder – a sordid tale of lust, greed, and murder. In addition to the brooding subject-matter, the film noir is characterized by dim lighting and genuine (as opposed to studio) night shots, emphasizing contrasts between light and dark in the framing of each scene. The style is reminiscent of German Expressionism, which is understandable, as many of the directors responsible, such as Billy Wilder, Fritz Lang, Otto Preminger, and Max Ophüls, were émigrés who began their film careers in Europe during the 1930s.

Filofax Tradename for the best-selling and most prestigious brand of **personal organizer**, a portable loose-leaf ring-binder filing system using different coloured papers for recording appointments, names and addresses, useful information, etc. Possession of a bulging leather-clad Filofax became synonymous with YUPPIE lifestyle during the 1980s, together with the GTI (*see* GT), DES RES, and a highly paid City job.

filofaxing or **filonapping** *See* FAX-NAPPING.

filth or **the filth** British slang for the police, especially plainclothes policemen. A pejorative term widely used since the 1960s, especially by those who have reason to be apprehensive of their activities. *See also* PIG.

final. Final Solution (Ger. *Entlösung*) The euphemism used at the NAZI conference at Wannsee, in 1942, for the grotesque German plan to exterminate all European Jews. The schedules were laid down by the conference and the logistics were left to Adolf Eichmann (*see* EICHMANN TRIAL). That the final solution was to be a mass extermination was not generally known in 1942, but by the time that Eichmann had organized the identification, arrest, and transportation of European Jews into death camps, there could not have been many Germans unaware of what was meant by it. *See also* HOLOCAUST.

final thrill US Black euphemism from the 1940s for death.

Financial Times *See* FOOTSIE.

Fine Gael The Irish Gaelic for Tribe of the Gaels (from *fine* tribe, race and *Gael* of the Gaels. The Irish political party founded by William T. Cosgrave and other members of the DÁIL ÉIREANN, who were in support of the treaty of 1921 that brought about the Irish Free State. It is traditionally considered to be the more conservative party seeking accommodation and reconciliation with the UK. However, during the Fine Gael–Labour coalition government of 1948, a republic was declared and Ireland withdrew from the Commonwealth. The Fine Gael party, led by Garrett Fitzgerald, attempted to solve the Northern Ireland dispute by participating in the Anglo-Irish agreement of 1985 and trying to remove some of the more overtly Catholic features of the constitution to make the Republic more attractive to Northern Protestants.

finger. fingerprint An impression taken in ink of the whorls of lines on the finger. In no two persons are they identical, and they never change throughout life, hence their great value as a means of indentification. From ancient times they were used for certifying documents by the Chinese and Japanese. Sir Francis Galton's *Finger Prints* (1892) and *Finger Print Directories* (1895) drew attention to their usefulness for identifying criminals. Sir Edward Henry, Commissioner of the Metropolitan Police (1903–18), devised a system for classifying impressions which was widely adopted. The FBI uses his method.

fingers British slang for a pickpocket, *i.e.* someone who is light-fingered. It has been in use, especially among the police and criminals, since the 1950s.

It's fingerlickin' good An advertising slogan used in the 1970s and possibly earlier for Kentucky Fried Chicken. Many songs also used the expression in the 1960s and 1970s, for example, Lonnie Smith's 1968 album *Fingerlickin' Good Soul Organ*. It is possible that the phrase was an earlier example of US Black musicians' jargon.

Fings Ain't Wot They Used t'Be Cockney version of 'things aren't what they used to be', used as the title of a musical by Frank Norman with lyrics by Lionel Bart. Put on in 1959 by Joan Littlewood (1914– ; *see* THEATRE WORKSHOP) at the Theatre Royal, Stratford, in E London, it was sufficiently successful for the title to become a popular catchphrase.

fire. Fiery Fred Nickname of Fred Trueman (1931–), British cricketer who played for Yorkshire and England. He acquired his name from a combination of his fast bowling and his somewhat abrasive temperament.

firebase A military base set up to be a point from which artillery and gunfire can be used against the enemy. The term was applied to certain bases during the VIETNAM WAR.

fire-break In the escalation of a military conflict, a check between the use of conventional weapons and the use of nuclear weapons. The term, used in military jargon since the 1960s, was derived by analogy with the strip of land cleared between trees to check the spread of a forest fire.

Fireside Chats The name adopted by President F. D. Roosevelt (*see* FDR) for his broadcasts to the US people on topics of national interest and importance. They began in 1933 and became customary during his administration.

firestorm A violent storm that can be caused by the explosion of a nuclear weapon or incendiary bomb. Hot air rising from the fireball causes strong winds to rush in, producing further damage and fanning the flames. Firestorms occurred at HIROSHIMA and NAGASAKI as a result of nuclear bombs and in the DRESDEN FIRE BOMBING.

firewatchers A force of volunteers who, during German air raids on the UK in World War II, kept watch for incendiary bombs. Very often stationed on the roofs of large buildings and equipped with only a stirrup pump, a bucket of water, and a bucket of sand, they saved many buildings from destruction.

Great balls of fire The chorus phrase from the Jerry Lee Lewis hit song of 1957, written by Jack Hammer and Otis Blackwell. It was used as an exclamation of surprise in the 1939 film *Gone with the Wind* and would therefore appear to be of southern US origin.

first. First Aid Nursing Yeomanry *See* FANY.

first base US young person's slang for kissing. Taken from baseball jargon, the analogy is that kissing is the first stage in a romantic encounter, just as first base is the first stage on the way to scoring a run in the ball game.

First Gentleman of the Screen Nickname of George Arliss (1868–1946), a distinguished British actor, who entered the film world in middle age and unexpectedly became a star on both sides of the Atlantic. He earned his nickname from the number of films in which he was cast as a king or rajah, or at least a nobleman or millionaire.

First Lady of the Screen Nickname of Norma Shearer (1900–83), a Canadian-born actress who made the big time in Hollywood. Her many films of the 1920s and 1930s ranged from the silent *Flapper* (1920) to *Escape* (1940), a not inconsiderable war film. She earned her nickname by being one of MGM's most coverted properties and perhaps for her role in *Marie Antoinette* (1938).

first light In the armed forces 'first light' denotes the earliest time (roughly dawn) at which light is sufficient for movement of ships, or for military operations to begin. Similarly **last light** is the latest time when such movements can take place. The expression became current in World War II.

first strike An initial attack by a combatant in a military action. The term is part of the jargon of nuclear strategy. First-strike weapons are usually unprotected and designed, as their name implies, to be used first, to destroy the enemy's planes, missiles, etc. **Second-strike** weapons are kept in reserve and protected (*e.g.* in missile 'silos'). They are held back in case the enemy makes a surprise attack to 'take out' the first-strike weapons. Military analysts are much concerned with relative first- and second-strike capabilities. *See also* PRE-EMPTIVE STRIKE.

First World *See* THIRD WORLD.

the first seven years are the hardest A cliché usually said with the wisdom of experience about a marriage or a new job. The implication is that if you can get through the early stages things will improve as time goes on. It probably derives from World War I, "Cheer up – the first seven years are the worst", with reference to the length of regular service in the army.

Fisher Act The 1918 Education Act named after the historian Herbert Albert Laurens Fisher (1865–1940) who, as President of the Board of Education and a Liberal MP, was responsible for it. The Act forced pupils to remain in full-time education until aged 14, abolished all elementary school fees, and introduced nursery schools. It was not implemented until after the end of World War I.

fishing expedition (1) British slang from the colonial era for the trip to India, or other outposts of the Empire, made by upper-class single women in search of husbands among the army or naval officers stationed there. The members of the expedition itself were known as the **fishing fleet**. (2) British slang taken from the language of espionage for the practice of gathering information while giving the impression of doing something else. It is also used by business corporations who advertise for and interview prospective employees, not with a view to employing them but to gather any information they can about their rivals' plans.

fission bomb *See* NUCLEAR WEAPON.

fit up British police and underworld slang meaning to invent or plant evidence of criminal activity in order to gain a false conviction. The expression is now widely known through TV crime series and, more recently, through reports in the press of examples of such police activity. Mainly used as a verb, the expression also functions as a noun, **fit-up**, as in 'he got five years, but everyone in the court, except the judge, knew it was a fit-up'.

five. **five-bob deal** Obsolete slang from the 1960s for the small quantity of cannabis that could be bought for five shillings, the smallest quantity available for sale. Since decimalization, the impact of inflation, and better policing of illegal drugs the phrase is only of nostalgic interest.

five-mile-high club A notional club open to those who claim to have made love on an airliner cruising at an altitude of five miles (25,000 feet), although it is not clear what proof is required either for the act having taken place or the altitude. There is also said to be a **125 club**, for those who have managed the feat on a British Rail Inter-City 125 train.

Five-Year Plans In the Soviet Union, plans for developing the whole of the nation's economy in a coordinated effort by a five-year programme. The first Five-Year Plan was launched by Stalin in 1928 with the aims of making the Soviet Union self-supporting, mechanizing agriculture, promoting literacy, etc. Further Five-Year Plans followed and the example was copied by other countries.

take five Phrase meaning to take a break or to suspend some action or simply to relax. It originates in the call of the director of a film or play, meaning to take a five-minute break. It was popularized by the composition 'Take Five' by the US modern JAZZ pianist and composer Dave Brubeck (1920–).

fix Slang for an intravenous injection of a narcotic drug. This sense orginated in America and in the 1960s became widespread throughout the English-speaking world.

fizzical culturist US Black slang from the 1940s for a bartender.

flag. black flag In World War II, submarines, on returning to base, sometimes hoisted a black flag to indicate a 'kill'. In motor-racing, the showing of a black flag signals to a driver that he must quit the race, usually for some serious infringement of motor-racing rules.

flag of convenience A foreign flag under which a vessel is registered, usually to lessen taxation and manning costs. The practice became commonplace after World War II. Liberia, Honduras, and Panama are the most widely used flags of convenience and Liberia has the largest merchant fleet in the world.

red flag A red flag is generally used to indicate danger or as a stop signal. It is also the symbol of international socialism and *The Red Flag* is a socialist anthem still used, somewhat incongruously, by the British LABOUR PARTY.

> Then raise the scarlet standard high,
> Beneath its shade we'll live and die
> Though cowards flinch and traitors sneer
> We'll keep the Red Flag flying here.
>
> JAMES CONNELL: *The Red Flag*.

run it up the flagpole To put forward an idea, plan, etc., tentatively to gauge the reaction to it. The full form is 'run it up the flagpole and see if anyone salutes'.

flak An acronym for *Flugabwehrkanone* or *Fliegerabwehrkanone*, the German name in World War II for anti-aircraft guns. Originally used in English to describe the bursting of shells of anti-aircraft guns, as in 'our bombers passed through a heavy barrage of flak over the target area', it later became a colloquialism for any criticism or hostility. It is widely used in this sense, especially in politics, with individual politicians always keen to avoid 'taking the flak' for an unpopular decision.

flak jacket A military jacket having thin metal plates sewn into the lining, used to protect the wearer against bullets or shrapnel.

flake (1) US slang for an eccentric and unreliable person. It was formed from the adjective FLAKY. (2) Australian slang for shark meat. (3) US slang for cocaine. Good-quality cocaine is often sold in flake form. (4) US police slang for an arrest made to satisfy public opinion rather than on substantial evidence.

flaky US slang for eccentric, unreliable, or unstable. It was not well known in the UK until President Reagan used it of Colonel Gaddafi in January 1986. The word was first used in America in this sense in the 1960s and is possibly derived from the sense of flaky meaning crumbling.

> She did indeed have a very flaky image – she claimed that she drank her own urine.
>
> *The Independent on Sunday*, 27 January 1991.

flame. flame-thrower A weapon that ejects a stream of burning fluid either from a hand-held device with an accompanying back pack or from a device mounted on a tank. Modern flame throwers were first developed by the Germans in the early years of this century and were first used by them in 1915 in World War I. By World War II they were in use by all sides; the portable type burned oil and had a range of some 41 metres (135 ft), burning for 10 seconds. The tank-mounted units had a range of 90 metres (300 ft) and carried enough fuel for a one-minute continuous blast. A sinister development of flame throwing was the invention of **napalm**, used by British and US troops towards the end of World War II and later in Korea and Vietnam. This consists of a mixture of the aluminium salts of *na*pathenic and *palm*itic acids used to thicken petrol. It carries further than petrol alone, burns at a higher temperature, and clings like a jelly to anything it touches, including enemy soldiers. Napalm is also used in incendiary bombs.

flaming (1) An intensifier used as a euphemism for 'fucking'. It now sounds rather dated in the UK but is still heard in Australia. Among older people in N England such mild oaths as 'flaming heck' are common; however, in this case the reference is to 'flaming hell'. (2) US slang meaning overt, especially of a homosexual. (3) A noun sense from the late 1980s for using computer networks to send obscene messages or to carry on obscene conversations.

Flanders poppies The name given to the red artificial poppies sold for REMEMBRANCE DAY to benefit ex-service men. The connection with poppies comes from a poem by John McCrae, which appeared in *Punch*, 8 December 1915:

If ye break faith with us who die
We shall not sleep, though poppies grow
In Flanders fields.

flap. flapper In the early years of the 20th century a term applied to a girl in her teens, now called a teenager, from her plaited pigtail tied at the end with a large bow. When stepping along the pigtail flapped her back. Subsequently her hair was 'put up' in a 'bun' or other hairstyle. By the 1920s the name was commonly applied to a young woman, or 'bright young thing'.

Flapper Vote An irreverent name for the vote granted to women of 21 by the Equal Franchise Act of 1928, sponsored by Baldwin's Conservative government. *See* FLAPPER.

flash. flashback An interruption in the narrative of a novel or film, involving a transition to an earlier scene or events pertinent to the present situation. Always widely used in films, flashbacks introduced by a leading character became extremely popular in the 1930s and 1940s. In her review of *Ruthless* (1948), a labyrinthine melodrama featuring Zachary Scott, the British film critic, C. A. Lejeune, wrote:

Beginning pictures at the end
Is, I'm afraid a modern trend.
But I'd find *Ruthless* much more winning
If it could end at the beginning.

flasher Slang for a man who exposes his genitals in public places, usually in the presence of young women or young girls. A deviant form of sexual gratification, flashing appears to be a compulsive act, which the flasher deeply regrets after he has done it. Flashers rarely have normal sexual relations and are very rarely violent. *See also* DIRTY OLD MAN.

Flash Gordon US SCI-FI hero who first appeared in a 13-part King Features newspaper comic strip in the 1930s. In 1936 he appeared in *Flash Gordon*, the first of a three-part film series, in which Flash (actor Larry 'Buster' Crabbe; *see* KING OF THE SERIALS), his companion Dr Zarkov, and sweetheart Dale Arden blast off to rescue the Earth from collision with the Planet Mongo, ruled by the evil Ming the Merciless. The two sequels, *Flash Gordon's Trip to Mars* (1938) and *Flash Gordon Conquers the Universe* (1940), were in a similar vein. A faintly pornographic spoof version, *Flesh Gordon*, appeared in 1974. In 1980 *Flash Gordon* itself was remade with Sam J. Jones and Topol in the cast. Some thought it lacked the kitsch charm of the original version.

Flash Harry Nickname of Sir Malcolm Sargent (1895–1967), British conductor of the BBC Symphony Orchestra (1950–57) and chief conductor of the London Promenade Concerts (1957–67). Widely travelled and always immaculately dressed, an apparently fresh flower always in his buttonhole, Sargent was the epitomy of a debonair man of the world: his nickname fitted him as well as his perfectly tailored suits. However, the term is also used of a person who dresses flashily and inelegantly – especially a new-money entrepreneur who has come up too quickly to notice how his old-money contemporaries have learnt the knack of wearing expensive clothes unobtrusively. Malcolm Sargent earned his nickname not because he was NAFF, but because most of his peers in the world of concert-giving musicians wore what looked hired tail coats, while Sargent's fitted perfectly. *See also* WIDE BOY.

flat top (1) A World War II name for an aircraft carrier. (2) A style of haircut that originated in America in the 1950s and has moved in and out of fashion periodically ever since. The hair is cut and shaped so that it forms a perfectly level plateau from the crown to the forehead. Some stylists use a spirit level to ensure accuracy.

flaunt. When you've got it, flaunt it An advertising slogan used in 1969 by the US airline Braniff. The poster showed pictures of famous extrovert people. The sentence had appeared earlier in the 1967 Mel Brooks comedy film *The Producers*, which may have been the original source.

flavour A property of QUARKS used in particle physics. Quarks come in six flavours: up, down, strange, charmed, top, and bottom.

flavour of the month A phrase originally used in America in an attempt to persuade people to try a different flavour of icecream each month. It has come to be used with reference to any ephemeral favourite person, thing, theme, etc.

fleas and itches or **fleas and itchers** Australian rhyming slang for the pictures, *i.e.* the cinema. Derived from the earlier **fleapit** for cinema, the expression was popular in the 1950s but is now obsolete.

Flèche d'Or *See* GOLDEN ARROW.

fleet. the fleet's lit up A British catchphrase that originated in what can only be described as every broadcaster's nightmare. The broadcast made on 20 May 1937 was by Commander Tommy Woodrooffe (1899–1978), a leading BBC commentator, and was meant to be a 15-minute description of the illumination of the fleet after the Coronation Naval Review at Spithead. Unfortunately Woodrooffe dried up and all he could manage was a few repetitive sentences basically consisting of "the fleet's lit up" before he was mercifully faded out. The phrase probably caught on because of the slang meaning of 'lit up', *i.e.* drunk. Many of those listening must have presumed that this was the problem with the broadcaster.

flesh-pressing Also referred to as 'pressing the flesh', the practice of politicians of shaking hands with as many people as possible in election campaigns.

flexitime A system allowing flexibility in the time at which an employee starts and finishes work, usually operated in conjunction with a core time, an agreed minimum number of hours for which each employee has contracted to work each week. Flexitime is widely operated in both the public and private sectors, largely to ease rush-hour traffic problems and to enable employees to travel to work in greater comfort. It is also useful for women with young families. Research has indicated that the system increases productivity by encouraging the more efficient use of an employee's time.

flick Slang for a film. It presumably derives from the pre-cinema wad of drawings or photographs that, when flicked through, creates the illusion of movement. The 'flick' is the film, the 'flicks' is the cinema. Both words were extremely widely used in the heyday of the cinema, as in 'Saw a super flick last night' and 'Shall we go to the flicks?' but now that the cinema habit is much less frequent, the words are less common. *See also* SKIN FLICK.

flick knife A type of knife with a spring-loaded retractable blade operated by a button. It has earned itself a reputation for being the preferred weapon of the street lout and mugger. It can be carried inconspicuously and used to inflict cruel wounds.

flight. flight deck The compartment of a passenger aircraft in which the pilots, navigator, radio operator, and engineer sit. Access to the flight deck is usually prohibited during flight, except to members of the crew.

flight recorder An electronic device carried by a passenger aircraft to collect and store information regarding the aircraft's performance in flight and the voices of the pilot and crew. In the event of a crash or malfunction the flight recorder can provide valuable information regarding the cause of the trouble. If the plane has crashed and killed the crew, the flight recorder may provide the only evidence of the cause. It is therefore housed in a strong metal box and is usually painted orange to make it easy to find (in spite of being known colloquially as a **black box**).

flight simulator A computer-controlled ground-based training capsule, which reproduces the conditions of the FLIGHT DECK of an aircraft or space vehicle. Flight simulators allow students to familiarize themselves with the hardware before potentially hazardous and expensive in-flight training. The first flight simulators appeared shortly after the Wright Brothers' invention of powered flight; in 1929 aviator Edwin A. Link produced the Link Trainer with cockpit instruments and controls, which reproduced all the movements of a proper aircraft; it was used extensively until the end of World War II. In accordance with advances in aircraft design and technology, modern simulators are even more realistic and complex, allowing every aspect of an aircraft's or spacecraft's performance to be reproduced in minute details. Flight simulation software can also be run as a game on microcomputers; the best-known program is produced by Microsoft, who have claimed that devotees could fly solo in a real aircraft after mastering the screen simulation.

flimsy A journalist's term for newspaper copy, arising from the thin paper (formerly often used with a sheet of carbon paper to take a copy) on which reporters and others wrote up their matter for the press.

The white £5 Bank of England note, which ceased to be legal tender in March 1961, was known as a *flimsy*. In the Royal Navy the name is also given to the brief certificate of conduct issued to an officer by his captain on the termination of his appointment to a ship or establishment; the name again derives from the thin-quality paper.

flip. flip-flop A component of an electronic circuit that can have two possible stable states (hence the alternative name **bistable**), and can 'flip' from one state to the other as a result of a suitable input signal. Flip-flops are an essential part of the electronic circuitry of digital computers, the two states of the elements of representing BITS.

flip-flops Open sandals consisting of a rubber or plastic sole with loops on the front through which the toes go. They date from the 1960s and are so called because of the flip-flopping movement of the sole while the wearer is walking.

flip out Slang meaning to lose control through anger or pleasure, probably under the influence of illegal drugs, or to become temporarily deranged as a result of stress. Originally derived from **flip one's lid**, a US phrase of the 1950s from BEAT jargon, 'flip out' was used by the HIPPIES of the 1960s to describe the state of temporary instability induced by an LSD trip. More recently it has been used of any over-emotional state; it is sometimes shortened to **flip**, as in the expression 'when I turned off the tape, he flipped'.

flip side *See* B SIDE.

FLN Front de Libération Nationale. The Algerian nationalist group that fought the war of independence (1952–62) against France. Formed in 1954 as a terrorist organization, it set up a provisional government in Tunis. In 1962 de Gaulle conceded independence to Algeria after referenda in both France and Algeria, when the FLN under Ben Bella (1916–) became the sole political party; multi-party government was not restored until 1989.

float. floating Slang word for experiencing a state of euphoria, especially one induced by illegal drugs. Common in the late 1950s and the 1960s, it is now rarely heard.

floating voter A person who has no deep allegiance to any of the main political parties and who can be persuaded to vote for any party by the force of their arguments. *See also* DON'T KNOW.

flob British schoolchildren's slang meaning spit, a synonym for gob, and probably derived from the sound of that activity.

floor manager (1) The stage manager of a television programme or studio. (2) The person who is in charge of one floor of a large retail store.

flop. floppy disk A flexible plastic disk coated with magnetic material and used for storing data in small computer systems. There are two common sizes: 5¼-inch diameter and 3½-inch diameter. The former has a flexible jacket and is protected by a paper envelope when not in use. The 3½-inch disk has a rigid plastic cover. Floppy disks are sometimes called **diskettes**. *See also* HARD DISK.

FLOPS Floating-point operations per second. A measure of the speed with which a digital computer can operate. A floating-point operation is an arithmetic operation (*i.e.* a multiplication, division, addition, or subtraction) between two numbers – the 'floating' implies that the position of the decimal point may change.

flotsam and jetsam Properly, wreckage and other goods found in the sea. Flotsam consists of goods found floating on the sea (O. Fr. *floter*, to float); jetsam are things thrown overboard (Fr. *jeter*, to throw out). The term is now also applied to wreckage found on the shore. *Lagan*, a word of uncertain origin, applies to goods thrown overboard but tied to a float for later recovery.

> The house bore sufficient witness to the ravages of the ocean, and to the exercise of those rights which the lawyers term Flotsome and Jetsome.
>
> SIR WALTER SCOTT: *The Pirate*, ch. xii.

Flotsam and Jetsam were also the names adopted by two popular entertainers of variety stage and broadcasting fame. B. C. Hilliam (1890–1968), British composer and pianist, took the name *Flotsam* and his partner, the Australian bass singer Malcolm McEachern (1884–1945), that of *Jetsam*.

flower. flower people Supporters of a brightly clad cult of the mid-1960s who advocated 'universal love' as a substitute for materialism. **Flower power**, their guiding philosophy, was summed up in the slogan 'make love not war'. The association with flowers is that flowers represent a peaceful and beautiful aspect of nature. *See* HIPPIE.

Say it with flowers An advertising slogan coined in 1917 by a Major Patrick O'Keefe for the National Publicity Committee of the Society of American Florists. It has been used in several songs since then.

fluff A British euphemism for fuck, usually used as the intensifier **fluffing**, or in the expression **fluff off**, as said by Prince Philip to journalists in October 1987. *See also* FOUR-LETTER ANNIE.

bit of fluff British slang for an attractive but unintelligent young woman. It is a derogatory expression used by men from the early 1900s.

fluff your duff British slang meaning masturbate (of a male).

fluoroplastic Any of a number of synthetic plastics derived from hydrocarbons by including fluorine. Fluoroplastics tend to be stable substances; Teflon (*see* PTFE) is a common example.

fly Slang from the 1900s for someone who is 'fast' or brash.

fly a kite (1) A British slang expression meaning knowingly to write a worthless cheque. It derives from an earlier City use, meaning to discount a bill at a bank knowing that the person on whom it is drawn will not honour it. It is now also used in the wider sense of presenting a doubtful plan for approval. (2) British slang meaning to write a begging letter asking for money. (3) British slang meaning to smuggle items into or out of prison. The items are usually drugs on the inward journey and letters on the way out.

fly blind To pilot an aircraft solely by means of instruments; the opposite of visual navigation.

flychick A lively party-loving young female.

fly-drive A holiday package-deal offered by travel agents and tour operators, which includes the cost of the return flight to a foreign airport and the provision of a hired car in the price of a holiday. This normally works out cheaper than arranging the holiday and car hire separately. In some of these packages it is not necessary to return the car to the original airport. Arrangements can be made to drop the car off at another airport, from which the flight home can be arranged.

flying bedstead Nickname of the experimental wingless and rotorless vertical take-off jet aircraft demonstrated in the UK in 1954. Built by Rolls-Royce, the name was inspired by its appearance.

flying boat A large seaplane with a boat-shaped hull for buoyancy. Flying boats were developed between the two world wars for both civil and military applications. The most famous of all flying boats is millionaire Howard Hughes's folly, the H4 *Hercules* (the *Spruce Goose*), the largest aeroplane ever flown, with the world's largest wing span and seating for 700 passengers. It was flown only once, for a distance of about one mile at a height of 80 feet over Los Angeles Harbor, California, in November 1947. It is now a tourist attraction.

flying doctor An airborne medical service to provide emergency aid to geographically remote communities lacking adequate health facilities. The **Royal Flying Doctor Service of Australia**, set up in 1928, both transports doctors to remote areas and has also set up a radio long-range consultation service. Similar services are run in Canada, Africa, and elsewhere.

Flying Duchess Mary du Caurroy Russell, Duchess of Bedford (1865–1937). After making record-breaking return flights to India (1929) and South Africa (1930) with Captain Barnard, she obtained an 'A' pilot's licence in 1933 and disappeared on a solo flight over the North Sea in March 1937.

Flying Fortress The name by which the US bomber, the Boeing B-17, was known during World War II. It owed its name to the fact that it was exceptionally heavily armed.

Flying Officer X Pen name of H. E. Bates (1905–74), the British novelist best known for *The Darling Buds of May* (1958). A solicitor's clerk and provincial journalist, he joined the RAF in World War II, writing many short stories about life in the service under this pen name.

flying picket An industrial picket that can be moved quickly between different locations to reinforce local pickets. The use of flying pickets was a feature of the industrial strife during the UK's Winter of DISCONTENT (1978–79). Their use can be construed as illegal under Section 15 of the Labour Relations Act (1974), which stipulates that pickets should be peaceful and be from their own place of work. As a result employers can take out injunctions or extract damages under civil law to prevent flying picketing.

flying saucers On 24 June 1947 a US pilot saw a group of strange objects in the sky, which he described as moving "like saucers skipping across the water". From this report journalists coined the phrase flying saucers for these objects, which they suggested could be reconnaissance craft from outer space. Captain Ruppelt, the USAF intelligence officer responsible for the investigation of the flying saucer phenomenon, gave them the name UFOs (unidentified flying objects). A few cranks believe that various governments have engaged in a conspiracy to prevent the public from knowing the 'truth' about flying saucers, in order to avoid panic reactions. In 1978 Steven Spielberg directed a film, *Close Encounters of the Third Kind* (*see* CLOSE ENCOUNTER), based on an alleged landing of a UFO, which has been covered up by the US government. Flying saucers and UFOs continue to populate a vast range of science-fiction literature, but no evidence has ever been produced to confirm the existence of such an object, let alone any occupants. Sightings of UFOs have been reported from all parts of the world since the term was first coined. *See also* CROP CIRCLES.

Flying Scotsman The steam train service run by the London and North-Eastern Railway between London (King's Cross) and Edinburgh. The record for the service was 5 hours 55 minutes.

Flying Tigers The nickname of a volunteer group of US airmen who supported China against Japanese aggression. Formed in August 1941, under Major-General C. L. Chennault, some months before America's entry into the war, they fought with distinction until merged with the 23rd Fighter Squadron of the USAAF in July 1942.

Flynn. in like Flynn A phrase meaning that the person concerned does not miss a chance to seduce a woman. It is also used in a more general sense to mean that the person is quick to take advantage of anything on offer. Flynn is the Australian-born film star, Errol Flynn (1909–59), who was one of Hollywood's most swashbuckling screen lovers. The phrase was particularly popular with the armed forces during World War II. Flynn himself was not flattered by it, despite his own partiality for boasting about his conquests.

Flyte, Sebastian The aristocratic central character of Evelyn Waugh's novel *Brideshead Revisited* (1945). He was based upon Hugh Lygon (1904–36), a fellow undergraduate of Waugh's at Oxford and the second son of the Earl of Beauchamp. Waugh paid several visits to the Beauchamp seat at Great Malvern, Worcestershire, and various features of this house (Madresfield Court) are accurately described in the fictional **Brideshead** (although Castle Howard in Yorkshire was used as the location in the celebrated BBC TV adaption of the novel in the 1980).

FM Frequency Modulation. A form of radio transmission in which the frequency of the carrier wave is varied within a narrow bandwidth of the reference frequency by the audio frequency information that is to be broadcast. It provides a better signal-to-noise ratio than **AM** (Amplitude Modulation), in which it is the amplitude of the carrier wave that is varied. FM is used in VHF (very high frequency) radio broadcasts, using a frequency of the order of 100 megahertz.

FMS Federated Malay States. The British protectorate consisting of Selangar, Negri Sembilan, Perak, and Panang established in 1909 after British trade interest in the area increased as a result of the opening of the Suez Canal. The capital of FMS was Kuala Lumpur. Occupied by the Japanese during Word War II, it became the Federation of Malay in 1948, achieving independence in 1957 and becoming part of the Federal State of Malaysia in 1963.

FN Fabrique Nationale (d'Armes de Guerre). The Belgian armaments firm that produced the **FN30** rifle, used by the British Army from 1954.

FOBS Fractional Orbital Bombardment System. A method of delivering a nuclear bomb by a rocket travelling in a low (100-mile-high) partial orbit, which does not contravene the Outer Space Treaty (1966) prohibiting the launching of nuclear warheads into a complete orbit around the Earth. The FOBS method enables a nuclear warhead to be delivered using a retro-rocket to slow the missile at a predetermined point, causing it to drop out of orbit onto the target. This can cut the defender's radar warning time to about 3 minutes, seriously prejudicing a ballistic missile defence system. However, FOBS weapons are not sufficiently accurate to be targeted onto missile silos and were abandoned by America in 1967.

Fog Nickname of Capt. Mark Phillips (1948–), husband of the Princess Royal (*see* FOUR-LETTER ANNIE). A rather unkind epithet, probably invented at Sandhurst and taken up by *Private Eye*, for a man described as "thick and wet".

Fokker One of a number of World War I aircraft designed by Anton Hermann Gerard Fokker (1890–1939), a Dutch-born aircraft designer who opened a factory in Germany in 1912. The Fokker was the first aircraft to have a machine gun that fired through the propeller, using a synchronizing method invented by Fokker. This gave the German Air Force a temporary advantage on the Western Front in Word War I.

folk. folk rock or **progressive rock** Music with folk-orientated lyrics and pop accompaniment. In the UK the style was virtually invented by Fairport Convention (formed 1966), who performed traditional folk songs with a lively electronic backing; they were followed by other successful bands, such as Steeleye Span (1969), Jethro Tull (1968), and Lindisfarne (late 1960s). America produced one of the greatest folk-rock artists of all in Bob Dylan (1941–), whose change from acoustic to electric accompaniment on his World Tour in 1966 brought boos and cat calls from traditional folk fans.

> Folk music is a bunch of fat people.
>
> BOB DYLAN.

That's all folks! The catchphrase that appears written across the screen at the end of the *Merry Melodies* cartoon series by Warner Bros. It was first used in 1930. Mel Blanc (1908–89), who had done so many of the voices for the cartoon characters, chose it as his own epitaph.

Follow that car! A line used in so many films that it has become a cliché. It is said when the hero or a policeman leaps into a taxi and orders the driver to chase after the villain's car.

food. food additive Any natural or synthetic substance added by manufacturers to food products and including flavourings, preservatives, colouring agents, antioxidants, emulsifiers, stabilizers, thickeners, artificial sweeteners, flavour enhancers, etc. Increasing consumer demand for convenience foods since the 1960s has led to a great increase in food processing and the need for additives. However, despite the benefits of additives as preservatives, etc. there has been increasing concern about the possible long-term effects on health of these products. Some are thought to produce toxic, carcinogenic, or allergic effects. For example, studies indicate that tartrazine (E102) can trigger allergies and cause hyperactivity in children. The Food Labelling Regulations (1984) of the European Community introduced **E numbers** to identify approved substances. Since 1986 all foods must carry a full list of additives on the package either by stating their E number or by giving the additive's full name if it does not have an E number. At present there are around 3800 additives in use.

foodaholic Someone who over-indulges in eating. *See also* BULIMIA.

Food and Agricultural Organization *See* FAO.

foodie A name given by Peter York (who coined the term SLOANE RANGER) to a person whose life appears to have been dominated by the buying and preparation of food, especially expensive delicacies and exotic dishes. Its appearance in the late 1980s reflects the mushrooming of high-class delicatessens, kitchenware shops, and restaurants producing food cooked in the latest styles.

food processor An electric domestic appliance that takes the effort out of everyday cooking tasks, such as chopping, slicing, grating, liquidizing, creaming, blending, and beating. It usually consists of a bowl on a motor housing with various blades and cutting disks for different tasks. Food processors are particularly useful for making soups, purées, pastry, and baby foods.

foot. foot-and-mouth disease An infectious viral disease of cattle, sheep, goats, and pigs, which causes fever, blisters on the mouth and feet, abortions, and deterioration of milk yields. Foot-and-mouth disease is a notifiable disease in many countries; infected animals are usually slaughtered and movements of herds are restricted.

footprint (1) The area over which the signal from a communications satellite can be received. (2) In computing, the physical space taken up by a computer device.

Footsie The familiar name by which the **Financial Times Stock Exchange 100 Index**, or FTSE 100 Index, is known in the City of London and in commercial markets throughout the world. Starting with a value of 1000 in 1984, Footsie is based on the day-to-day price of 100 chosen securities and is regarded as giving the best indication of daily movement in price on the London Stock Exchange (properly known as the International Stock Exchange of the UK and Republic of Ireland Ltd). Footsie is published daily (except Sunday and Monday) in the *Financial Times*, the London commercial journal (traditionally printed on pink paper). The FT, the initials by which this paper is widely known, also has other indexes: the **Financial Times Ordinary Share Index**, representing the movements of 30 leading industrial shares, and the **Financial Times Actuaries Share Indexes**, of which there are 54, giving weighted arithmetic averages for various sectors of the market. Divided into separate industries, it is much used by portfolio managers and other large investors. The equivalent indicator of price movements on the New York Stock Exchange is the DOW JONES INDUSTRIAL AVERAGE.

football hooliganism Uncontrolled violence by sections of the crowd at footbal matches. British fans earned an unenviable reputation in the 1980s for their unruly behaviour, which culminated in the death of 39 mainly Italian supporters at the 1985 European Cup Final (Liverpool vs Juventus of Turin) at the Heysels Stadium in Brussels. Subsequently English football league clubs were banned from taking part in European competitions until the 1990–91 season, when all but Liverpool were readmitted. The causes of hooliganism at football grounds are usually overcrowding, drunkeness (*see* LAGER LOUTS), unreasonable hostility towards rival supporters, and the uncontrolled aggression that can emerge from badly controlled crowds. Measures to curb football hooliganism include segregation of rival fans, banning of alcohol in and around grounds, abolition of terraces on which supporters stand in favour of all-seater stadiums, the use of closed-circuit TV, the issue of identification cards, and better policing. At one point such behaviour was so closely identified with the UK that it was called the ENGLISH DISEASE.

footling British slang meaning trivial or unimportant. It is derived from the nearly obsolete verb 'footle' meaning to idle, to indulge in futile activities. It is widely used.

force. Forces' Sweetheart The nickname of the British singer Vera Lynn (1917–) used by British forces serving overseas during World War II. With her repertoire of sentimental songs, such as 'We'll Meet Again' (1944), she came to symbolize many of the qualities, freedoms, and loyalties that motivated the British people in their determination to destroy Nazi Germany. She gave her first public performance in 1924, broadcast with the Joe Loss Band for a period, and eventually became a solo star in 1940. Voted the UK's most popular singer in a *Daily Express* competition in 1939, she had her own radio show, 'Sincerely Yours' from 1941 to 1947. She was made a Dame in 1975.

May the force be with you! A catchphrase used as a valediction, almost as a blessing, in the US film *Star Wars* (1977) and its sequals. The Force is the lifeforce of the Universe, the power of good; it is therefore almost equivalent to saying "May God go with you". It has been used since as an advertising slogan in a recruitment drive by the Cornish Police in the UK and by President Reagan, always ready to quote from Hollywood, in America. In a speech about his STAR WARS weapons programme after the film, he said, "The force is with us".

Ford's Peace Ship The ship on which the car manufacturer, Henry Ford (1863–1947), sailed to Europe from America with a number of similarly minded prominent pacifists in 1915. The intention of this unsuccessful mission was to bring World War I to an end by negotiation.

forest. Forest Hills A residential area on Long Island, New York City, noted for its West Side Tennis Club and the tennis tournaments held there.

Forestry Commission The UK government organization that controls forestry, advising the Minister of Agriculture, Fisheries and Food and the Secretaries of State for Wales and for Scotland on matters relating to forestry. It conducts forestry research, administers grant-aided schemes for private woodlands, and is responsible for providing timber for industry, achieving a reasonable balance between the needs of industry and conservation. Situated in Edinburgh, it was established in 1919.

forfaiting The financial service that has grown up in recent years of discounting, without recourse, a promissory note, letter of credit, bill of exchange, etc., received from an overseas buyer. This enables an exporter to receive his money immediately, without waiting for the payment to become due. The word is derived from the French *forfaire*, to forfeit or surrender.

forgeries *See* DOSSENA FORGERIES; DRAKE BRASS PLATE; HITLER DIARIES; KEATING PICTURES; PILTDOWN SKULL; TURIN SHROUD; VAN MEEGEREN FORGERIES; VINLAND MAP; WISE FORGERIES; ZINOVIEV LETTER.

forgotten. Forgotten Army The British troops serving in Burma towards the end of World War II. Following the defeat of Germany and VE DAY, the public at home felt that the war was over. Nor surprisingly the troops in the Far East felt neglected. Lord Louis Mountbatten (1900–79), who was supreme Allied commander in SE Asia (1943–45), reassured his men with the words:

> You are not the Forgotten Army – nobody's even heard of you!

Forgotten Man A phrase derived from W. G. Summer (1840–1910), the US sociologist, to describe the decent, hardworking, ordinary citizen. It was later popularized by F. D. Roosevelt (*see* FDR) in 1932 during the presidential election campaign, although he actually used the expression before his nomination. He advocated a NEW DEAL and appealed to the "forgotten man at the bottom of the economic pyramid".

form British police and criminal underworld jargon for a criminal record. It is based on the horse-racing term for a horse's record of achievement, which is most frequently used as **studying form**, meaning to study a horse's record in previous races before placing a bet.

Former Naval Person A codename by which Winston Churchill referred to himself in messages to President Roosevelt during Word War II. It refers, of course, to the post of First Lord of the Admiralty, which he held (1911–15) in World War I and again (1939–40) in World War II.

Formica A tradename for a plastic laminate, widely used on table tops, counters, etc. The name was invented and registered by two US scientists, Herb Faber and Don O'Connor, who devised it as an insulating material as a substitute 'for mica'. They founded the Formica Corporation, which was subsequently taken over by the Cyanamid Co. Although the company has fought hard in the courts to protect its tradename, 'formica' is frequently loosely used as a generic name for almost any table top with a plastic appearance. Unless and until Cyanamid lose the protection given to them by the registration of this product as a tradename, it is illegal to use the word Formica to describe any other product.

Forsyte Saga The trilogy of novels by John Galsworthy (1867–1933), comprising *The Man of Property* (1906), *In Chancery* (1920), and *To Let* (1921). The trilogy traces the decline of four generations of the affluent Forsyte family, headed by Soames, a successful solicitor. The *Forsyte Saga* has reached a wide audience in book form since its publication in 1922, but the television serial, starting in 1967, familiarized most British and US families with the love affairs and acquisitive habits of Galsworthy's fictional characters.

fort. Fort Belvedere A large castellated house near Sunningdale in Berkshire (England) that became the home of the Prince of Wales from 1929 until his abdication as Edward VIII in 1936. *See* ABDICATION CRISIS.

Fort Detrick The site in Maryland of a US army microbiological research station. It investigates the use of the vectors that carry the diseases of man and domestic animals as a weapon of war.

Fort Hare A university college for the Xhosa people of the Republic of Transkei in South Africa. It is the oldest college for Black Africans in South Africa, having been founded in 1916.

Fort Knox A US military base in N Kentucky established in 1917. In the bombproof vaults within the Fort, the US gold reserves are held. Said to be worth between 10 and 20 billion US dollars, the reserves are not surprisingly guarded by elaborate security measures. In the film *Goldfinger* (1964), based on the Ian Fleming novel, international gold smugglers are only foiled in their attempt to rob Fort Knox by the intrepid and highly unlikely activities of James BOND, played by Sean Connery. Fort Knox's legendary security has led to the use of the phrase **as safe as Fort Knox**.

FORTRAN Formula Translation. A high-level computer-programming language developed by IBM in the early 1950s. It is mainly used for mathematical and scientific application. Fortran exists in a number of different versions; it was the first program that allowed general users to communicate effectively with a computer system.

forty. Life begins at forty A catchphrase taken from the title of a book by the US professor William B. Pitkin (1878–1953), which was published in 1932. The book dealt with the new-found leisure time that many people have after forty and aimed to encourage them to enjoy the second half of their lives, especially by embarking on new projects. A song with this title was written by Jack Yellen and Ted Shapiro; a rumbustious recording of it in 1937 by Sophie Tucker, who was by then 53, became a great hit.

forward. One step forward, two steps back A catchphrase reflecting the nature of progress. It was used by Lenin as the title of his book about the state of the Communist Party in 1904.

Fougasse Pen name of Kenneth Bird, the cartoonist and editor of *Punch*, in which many of his cartoons appeared. He is also remembered for his World War II cartoon posters containing warnings about careless talk. *Fougasse* is the French word for a small landmine.

four. 4711 (Four Seven Eleven) A tradename for an eau de Cologne (a fragrant liquid first made in the German city of Cologne in 1709). The name arose in 1792 when a Cologne banker, Ferdinand Muhlens, gave refuge to a monk. The monk, in gratitude, gave Muhlens a slip of paper on which were written the figures 4-7-11, which he alleged constituted a secret formula for making a cologne. The numbers were later adopted by Muhlens as a tradename, although they could not be registered in Germany until 1915, because numbers could not previously be registered in names. The name achieved international registration in 1923.

four-colour problem A problem in mathematical topology concerning the minimum number of colours required to colour a map so that adjacent regions have different colours. Adjacent regions are ones that have a common line boundary. It has long been known that on a flat surface or on a sphere only four colours are required to distinguish different regions. However, this was not proved mathematically until 1976 (by Appel and Haken).

four corners of the Earth Generally speaking, the uttermost ends of the Earth, the remotest parts of the world. In 1965 members of the John Hopkins Applied Physics Laboratory named the four corners of the Earth as being in Ireland, SE of the Cape of Good Hope, W of the Peruvian coast, and between New Guinea and Japan. Each of these 'corners' (of several thousand square miles in area) is some 120 ft above the geodetic mean and the gravitational pull is measurably greater at these locations.

Four Freedoms These were defined by President F. D. Roosevelt in his message to Congress, 6 January 1941, as the freedom of speech and expression, the freedom of worship, the freedom from fear, and the freedom from want. They were to be the aims of America and ultimately the world. The occasion was his proposal to make America "the arsenal of democracy" and to extend LEND-LEASE to the UK.

Four-letter Annie Nickname of the Princess Royal in her younger days. A hardworking intelligent woman, she had reason to feel hounded by elements of the press. She was reported, on one occasion, to have told unwanted members of the press corps to 'naff off' (some said she used a stronger four-letter epithet). In 1982 the *Daily Mirror* ran a headline 'Naff off, Anne'.

four-minute men In America during World War I, the name given to members of a volunteer organization, some 75,000 strong, who, in 1917–18, set out to promote the sale of Liberty Loan Bonds and stir up support for the war in Europe. They gave talks of four minutes duration to church congregations, cinema audiences, lodges, etc.

four-minute mile The running of a mile in four minutes was for many years the hoped-for achievement of first-class athletes. The rigorous training and timed pacing of P. J. Nurmi (Finland) achieved a time of 4 mins. 10.4 secs. in 1924 but R. G. Bannister (1929–) was the first man to reach the goal in 1954. He achieved a sub-four-minute mile at Oxford in 1954 (3 mins. 59.4 secs.) after constant and carefully planned efforts. In July 1979 Sebastian Coe achieved a new world record of 3 mins. 49 secs. only to be beaten almost immediately by Steve Ovett, who reduced his time by one-fifth of a second. In 1981 Coe ran the mile in 3 mins. 47.33 secs; in 1985 Steve Cram reduced the record for the mile to 3 mins. 46.32 secs.

> The four-minute mile had become rather like an Everest – a challenge to the human spirit.
>
> R. BANNISTER: *First Four Minutes*, ch. xiii.

four-on-the-floor Slang expression for flat out speed. It comes from hot rodder's (*see* HOT ROD) jargon for a four-speed gear system in top gear, and was used by young people in the 1980s.

Four Square Gospel A fundamentalist Christian sect founded in Belfast in 1925 by George Jeffreys. It amalgamated with the Elim group to form the *Elim Four Square Gospel Alliance*. They believe in baptism by total immersion, the Second Coming of Christ, and healing by anointing with holy oil.

fourth dimension As a mathematical concept, a hypothetical dimension, whose relation to the recognized three of length, breadth, and thickness is analogous to their relation with each other. Albert Einstein in 1921 introduced time as the fourth dimension in his theory of RELATIVITY. The expression is also sometimes used to describe something beyond the limits of normal experience.

fourth-generation computer Those computers developed during the mid-1970s using large-scale integration technology. The first generation of computers, developed in the early 1950s, used vacuum tube technology; the second, in the late 1950s, solid-state components; and the third, in the mid-1960s, integrated circuits. Fourth generation machines will soon be followed by FIFTH-GENERATION COMPUTERS, due to come into operation in the 1990s.

fourth man A suspected fourth Soviet agent involved in the defection of BURGESS AND MACLEAN. It was later revealed that the fourth man was Anthony Blunt.

Fourth Republic The French Republic established in 1946 that replaced the provisional governments that followed the collapse of the VICHY regime after D DAY. Essentially a continuation of the Third Republic (1870–1940), it gave way to the FIFTH REPUBLIC in 1958.

Old Fourlegs Nickname for the coelacanth, a species of fish held to be extinct for millions of years until a specimen was caught in 1938 off East London, South Africa. Another was caught off the Comoro Islands, north of Madagascar, in 1952 and subsequently numerous others were found. The lobate fins, which could be used more or less as limbs, give rise to the name.

> My surprise would have been little greater if I had seen a dinosaur walking down the street.
>
> J. L. B. SMITH, British organic chemist who identified the first specimen.

Fourteen points The 14 conditions laid down by President Woodrow Wilson (1856–1924) as those on which the Allies were prepared to make peace with Germany on the conclusion of World War I. He outlined them in a speech to Congress on 8 January 1918 and they were eventually accepted as the basis for the peace. They included the evacuation by Germany of all Allied territory, the restoration of an independent Poland, freedom of the seas, reduction of armaments, and OPEN DIPLOMACY.

fox. foxhole A small slit trench for one or more men.

Foxhunter An outstanding showjumping horse owned by Lt-Col. Llewellyn (1911–). He won the King George V Cup three times in the 1950s and Llewellyn and Foxhunter were part of the British team that won the Olympic Gold Medal in Helsinki in 1952. Foxhunter died in 1959 at the age of 18.

foxtrot A ballroom dance originating in America, popular from the 1920s until the 1950s. It combines slow walking steps with quick running steps in 4/4 time.

foxy In US Black slang, a sexy young woman. The term was popularized by its frequent use by the boxer Muhammad Ali.

There are no atheists in foxholes *See* ATHEISTS.

fractal A class of mathematical curves or surfaces that are self-generating. The idea of fractals was developed by the Polish-born US mathematician Benoit Mandelbrot in 1975. A simple example is the **snowflake curve**, which can be generated by taking an equilateral triangle and dividing each side into three equal parts. The middle secton of each side is removed and replaced by two sides of a new equilateral triangle, to produce a new star-shaped curve with six points and 12 sides. The same process is then applied to each of these sides, and the process is continuously repeated. The result is a changing snowflake-shaped figure. Fractals are described as 'self-similar' figures; each is generated from the preceding one by a fixed set of rules. The name 'fractal' comes from the fact that they have a fractional dimension between that of a one-dimensional line and a two-dimensional surface. **Fractal geometry** is the study of such figures. It is used in producing designs in computer graphics and in certain branches of science.

frail In US Black slang from the 1940s, a thin young woman.

frame Slang for falsely accusing someone of a crime that they did not commit, substantiating it with contrived evidence. It is derived from the obvious image of the frame fitting around a ready-made picture. The noun form, **frame-up**, was originally an Americanism from the early years of this century and is said to derive from the framed photographs of known criminals held by law-enforcement officers.

Franglais An informal version of French, containing a large number of English words, treated largely as a joke language. Miles Kington wrote several books featuring Franglais.

Frank, Anne A German girl of Jewish descent who, during World War II, kept a diary (1942–43) while in hiding with her family in an attic in Amsterdam. This moving account of an adolescent's view of a clandestine existence dominated by the German occupation of the Netherlands was published in 1947 and subsequently made into a play and a film (1959), both called *The Diary of Anne Frank*. Shortly before the end of the war the family was betrayed to the Germans and sent to AUSCHWITZ (*see* WIESENTHAL CENTRE); Anne was subsequently transferred with her sister to Bergen-Belsen, where both died of typhus. Their father, Otto Frank, survived the war and was responsible for the publication of Anne's diary. The house in which the family hid has been preserved as a memorial.

> In spite of everything I still believe that people are really good at heart.
>
> ANNE FRANK: *Diary.*

Franks Report A report by a Commission of Inquiry into Oxford University (1964–66) headed by Lord Franks (1905–), Provost of Worcester College, Oxford. The report recommended increasing the size of the university by 30%, doubling the number of postgraduates, diminishing the autonomy of the colleges, and paying more attention to science and technology.

fraternize A British forces euphemism for having sex with the civilians in a militarily occupied country. In a more general sense it means to be friendly with an enemy or someone who sympathizes with one's enemies.

Fraud Squad The name of the section of the police at Scotland Yard that deals with investigation concerning commercial frauds.

frazzled British slang meaning exhausted.

freak (1) Slang used of someone exhibiting a form of deviant behaviour, often of a sexual nature. (2) Slang for a HIPPIE, a member of the alternative social group that flourished in the 1960s and 1970s; hippies, both male and female, wore their hair long and dressed in exotic, if rather tattered, clothes. In this sense, the word was used pejoratively by those outside the group but was quickly adopted by the hippies themselves, who rarely referred to themselves as hippies. (3) As a suffix, an enthusiast or fan: used, slightly derogatorily, by people outside the particular persuasion. An **eco-freak**, for example, has an over-enthusiastic interest in ecology and a **health freak** is unnaturally interested in ALTERNATIVE health remedies and foods. *See also* JESUS FREAK. (4) Short for FREAK OUT.

freak lips In JAZZ slang from the 1920s, a wind instrument player who is able to sustain high notes for a long time.

freak out Slang for to lose control and behave in a wild or disturbed way. It was first used by US HIPPIES in the 1960s to describe the behaviour caused by the effects of such hallucinogenic drugs as LSD, but was soon used more generally to describe any loss of control, whatever the cause. To **freak someone out** means to upset someone to such an extent that they freak out.

Fred. Fred Karno's army *See* KARNO.

Fred's British upper-class joke name for Fortnum and Mason's, the exclusive shop in London's Piccadilly.

free. freebasing Drug users' slang for the method of taking cocaine by mixing it with various solvents to make it into a substance that can then be smoked.

freebee Slang for any free gift or treat.

free enterprise or **free market economy** An economic system in which commercial organizations compete freely in order to make a profit and the laws of supply and demand regulate prices, wages, etc., unfettered by government regulations.

free fall (1) The descent of a body falling through space in which the only force acting on it is gravitational. The **acceleration of free fall** is the acceleration that results from the action of this force. The value of this acceleration has a standard value within the Earth's gravitational field of 9.806,65 $\mathrm{m\,s^{-2}}$, although the actual value varies slightly with locality. (2) The part of a parachute descent during which the parachutist falls through the air unimpeded by an open parachute. To end the free fall the parachutist pulls the rip cord and thereafter descends slowly to Earth.

Free French *See* FIGHTING FRENCH.

free love The practice of engaging in sexual relationships with whoever one finds attractive at the time. A person who practises free love is not bound by ties of fidelity to one partner, either within a legal marriage or outside it. In the 20th century, the gradual erosion of religious beliefs and the sacramental view of marriage, coupled with widespread use of efficient methods of BIRTH CONTROL, led to a situation in which free love seemed to be an acceptable alternative to marital fidelity, in that there were no obvious ethical reasons for the community to discourage it. This philosophy is especially associated with the 'swinging sixties'.

In the 1980s, the concept of free love received a setback in the form of the sexually transmitted disease AIDS, and the threat that it will assume epidemic proportions if sexual promiscuity continues. *See* FAMILY SAVIORS; NEW MORALITY.

free lunch Economists' jargon for an apparently free benefit that has to be paid for in the end. It derives from a City tavern that offered free lunches; anyone attempting to make use of the offer without buying a drink was thrown out.

free market economy *See* FREE ENTERPRISE.

Free Staters In the Irish Civil War (1922–23), supporters of the provisional government of the Irish Free State set up according to the Anglo-Irish Treaty of 1921. The Free Staters, led by Michael Collins (1890–1922), were opposed by the Republicans under De Valera, who repudiated the Treaty because it left Northern Ireland outside the Irish state and demanded an oath of allegiance to the British crown. Collins was assassinated in 1922 but the severe measures taken by the Free State government forced the Republicans to abandon the armed struggle in 1923.

free verse A breakaway from the regular classical metres, which dominated European and English poetry from the later mediæval period, and the substitution of ordinary speech rhythms and little or loose rhyme-patterns, in place of regular stanza forms. Milton experimented with irregular forms and much of Browning's poetry breaks away from the older tradition. From the early 20th century, free verse came into its own through the influence of Ezra Pound, T. S. Eliot, and others. There was a similar trend in France towards *vers libre*.

Free World Before 1990 this was a term used to describe all the non-communist countries of the world. Since the collapse of communism in E Europe, the term has little significance.

Freedom from Hunger Campaign A campaign organized by the UN special agency, the Food and Agricultural Organization (*see* FAO), in 1960. Originally intended as a five-year rededication of FAO's determination to eliminate hunger and malnutrition from the world, it was later extended for a second five-year period. It achieved a considerable success in publicizing the horrific problems of hunger, resulting from primitive agricultural methods in the THIRD WORLD.

Freeman, Hardy, and Willis The name of a British chain of shoe shops. Freeman, Hardy, and Willis are also used by members of the Royal Navy as nicknames for the three medals: 1914–15 Star, General Service Medal, and the Victory Medal, awarded to servicemen who served throughout World War I. *See also* PIP, SQUEAK, AND WILFRED.

freeze bank A term of US origin for a refrigerated stock of perishable organic substances, such as human blood and bone, kept in large modern hospitals for surgical use. *See also* SPERM BANK.

Freightliner A door-to-door container service provided by British Rail. The containers, owned by BR, are delivered to the sender of the goods, who fills the container himself. The container is delivered anywhere in the UK by a road-rail-road service direct to the consignee.

Freikorps (1) A post-World War I manifestation of German militarism and right-wing thuggery. First appearing in December 1918, after Germany's defeat, and consisting of ex-soldiers (men and officers), unemployed youths, and others, by 1919 there were some 65 groups spread throughout Germany. They were used subversively by the government to beat up left-wing agitators and once they had acquired a taste for this sort of bullying violence, soon chose their own targets for plundering and vandalism. Ernst Röhm, a Freikorps commander, became head of the Nazi BROWNSHIRTS and many of the groups were later absorbed by the Nazi party. *See also* KAPP PUTSCH. (2) In post-World War II Germany a neo-Nazi group appeared in West Germany, calling themselves **Freikorps Deutchland**. They were banned in 1953.

Frelimo Front for the Liberation of Mozambique. The Mozambique Marxist ruling party founded in 1962 by Eduardo Mondlane (1920–69). The Front fought a successful ten-year War of Independence (1964–74) against Portuguese rule, which ended with a military coup against the Portuguese government. This led directly to the granting of independence to Portugal's African colonies, including Mozambique, in June 1975.

French (1) Slang for performing cunnilingus or fellatio, based on the Anglo-Saxon belief that all such sexual activities are foreign, dirty, and undesirable and therefore ascribable only to Gallic appetites, which are known to be depraved. (2) Short for FRENCH KISS, used as a verb.

excuse my French An expression used after swearing, pretending that the swear word just used was really in a foreign language.

French blue Drug users' slang for a blue amphetamine tablet, the pep pill Drinamyl. The 'French' either represents the country of manufacture or is used simply to differentiate this pill from other BLUES.

French Community (Fr. La Communauté) An association of former French colonies formed in 1958 by the constitution of the FIFTH REPUBLIC, when de Gaulle was called back to become president of France. It replaced the earlier French Union, which was itself the replacement of the French Colonial Empire. By 1970 the Community had ceased to exist.

French kiss An open-mouthed kiss during which the tongues of the participants make contact. This expression has been used since the 1920s both in the UK and America; it reflects an Anglo-Saxon conviction in Gallic passion.

Freon Tradename for a group of chlorofluorocarbons (*see* CFC).

fresh US teenage slang used to indicate extreme approval. It dates from the late 1980s.

freshwater trout US Black slang of the 1940s for an attractive young female.

Freudian slip An error of speech or in writing or an act of omission that is motivated by an unconscious desire. In his *Psychopathology of Everyday Life* (1914), Freud tried to show that many such slips are so motivated. For example, the nervous and inexperienced chairman of a meeting who rises to his feet at its start and says: "I would like to welcome everyone here and now declare the meeting closed", is clearly wishing that the whole thing was over. Likewise, the flustered hostess who, glancing at a guest who is making signs of leaving, says "Oh, please can't you go – don't stay", is expressing a desire to break up the party and get to bed. However, it is clear that most everyday blunders do not fall into this category and are entirely without sinister motivation. It is only the highly improbable errors, and those that are likely to have long-lasting effects, that express an unconscious wish and are therefore worth investigating in psychoanalysis.

Friday. Black Friday *See* BLACK.

Red Friday *See* RED.

Friedmanism The economic theory associated with the US economist Milton Friedman (1912–). Friedman's ideas contradicted those of Maynard Keynes (*see* KEYNESIANISM), stressing regulation of the money supply and the encouragement of a free-market economy. Friedmanism was influential in determining British government policy in the early years of Margaret Thatcher's government (*see* THATCHERISM).

friend. -friendly Good for the person or thing specified. For example, USER-FRIENDLY implies that a device, such as a computer, is organized in such a way that it is easy to use. **Ozone-friendly** is often used to describe something, such as an aerosol can in which the propellant is not a CFC, that does not cause damage to the ozone layer. **Environment-friendly** is used more widely to describe a politician, policy, substance, or device that is kind to the environment. A returnable glass bottle with a deposit on it, for example, is considered more environment-friendly than a throw-away can. In the run-up to an election many politicians try to give the impression that they are environment-friendly, with strong opinions on pollution, avoiding damage to the environment, etc.

friendly fire Gun shots, rockets, bombs, etc., that accidentally kill members of one's own side, especially in battle. The expression was used, for instance, in the

GULF WAR of 1991 by the Americans to describe the killing of nine British servicemen by the crew of an antitank aircraft, who mistook the British personnel carrier for an Iraqi vehicle. While it is something of a euphemism to describe the fire that kills a person as friendly, the expression is intended to convey the idea that the servicemen operating the weapon are friends, who have made a tragic mistake.

Friends of the Earth An organization founded in the UK in 1971, with some 250 local groups, to campaign for the protection of the environment. It now has branches in a number of other countries. Protests and propaganda are furthered by public meetings, demonstrations, etc. They are active against all forms of pollution (especially nuclear power), developments which ruin the countryside, and the destruction of wildlife. *See also* GREENPEACE.

frighteners. put the frighteners on Slang for intimidating someone to make them comply with one's wishes or to make them tell one something one wants to know. The expression is mostly used in the underworld or by the police.

fringe. fringe benefits Concessions and benefits given to employees, or extra 'perks' that go with a job or appointment, such as medical insurance, use of a car, pensions, etc.

> The main "fringe benefit" is a Government chauffeur-driven car.
>
> *Daily Telegraph*, 11 February 1975.

fringe medicine *See* ALTERNATIVE MEDICINE.

fringe theatre A form of theatre that explores beyond the bounds of traditional drama; it is the British equivalent of the US 'off-off-Broadway' theatre. The term probably derives from the growth of unconventional theatrical productions on the 'fringe' of the EDINBURGH FESTIVAL during the 1950s. In 1960 the Cambridge Footlights team, including Jonathan Miller and Alan Bennett, appeared at the Edinburgh Festival in the satirical revue BEYOND THE FRINGE, indicating that by then the limits set by the fringe had already been surpassed. Fringe productions often tackle political and experimental themes, attracting younger audiences in small informal venues temporarily established in such places as arts and community centres, colleges, and church halls.

Frisbee A light plastic disc, about 8 inches in diameter, which is thrown into the air with a flick of the wrist. It was first produced in California in 1957 by the Wham-O-Production Company but was based on an idea by Yale University students, who discovered the aerodynamic properties of pie plates produced by the Frisbie Pie Company of Bridgeport, Connecticut. The Frisbee is sold as a toy in the UK but on the W coast of America Frisbee throwing has reached the combined status of sport and art form.

frisking the whiskers JAZZ slang from the 1940s for a warm-up session prior to a performance.

Fritz In World War I, the men in the trenches commonly called any German in the enemy lines *Fritz*. Fritz is the traditional German shortening for the name of Friedrich (Frederick the Great of Prussia, for instance, was called *Old Fritz*). *See also* TOMMY.

frog. frogmen In World War II, strong swimmers dressed in rubber suits with paddles on their feet resembling the feet of frogs, who operated in enemy harbours by night attaching explosives to shipping, etc. Frogmen now work in salvage operations, etc.

frogspawn British schoolchildren's slang for tapioca or sago pudding. This name reflects the extremely unappetizing appearance of the dish, which is often served for school lunches.

frolic pad In US slang of the 1940s, a venue for dancing.

frug A dance, introduced in the mid-1960s and often seen at DISCOS, involving little movement of the feet with rhythmic gyrations of the body. In the 1980s 'frug' was re-introduced as a verb meaning to dance uninhibitedly to disco-type music.

fruit. fruitcake (1) 1960s slang for an eccentric person, often used in the phrase **nutty as a fruitcake**, which covers the whole range from slightly odd to raving lunacy.

> Nobody interrupted. We all sat like dummies on an Underground train while the fruitcake in the corner raved on.
>
> *The Independent*, 29 January 1991.

(2) US pejorative slang for a male homosexual. An extension of 'fruit', it has been in use for most of this century.

fruit machine A mechanical or electronic gambling machine, operated by a lever or button, which pays out cash for lining up images of the same type of fruit, or combination of fruit, on a series of revolving cylinders when they come to rest. The machines, which were originally simple, have become more and more complicated as various refinements have been added. Fruit machines are found in pubs, amusement arcades, etc. *See also* PAC-MAN DEFENCE; SPACE INVADERS.

Fruity Metcalfe Nickname of Capt. Edward Metcalfe, who was an equerry to the Prince of Wales before the ABDICATION CRISIS. King George V had a low opinion of Metcalfe and tried unsuccessfully to dissuade his son from making use of his services.

fry (1) US slang meaning to be killed in the electric chair. (2) US slang meaning to punish someone. It is widely used by students or recruits to the armed services.

FT *Financial Times*. *See* FOOTSIE.

FTA Fuck the Army, or, sometimes, less offensively, Free the Army. A slogan coined in the US army in the 1960s. It is often seen as graffiti. Jane Fonda used the initials *FTA* in 1972 as the title of her anti-war film about Vietnam. Variations also abound: examples include FTP (fuck the Pope) and FTQ (fuck the Queen), both of which were seen in Northern Ireland in the early 1970s.

Fuchs spy case The case of Klaus Fuchs (1911–88), a German-born British physicist, who worked on the atomic bomb during World War II in both the UK and America. In 1950 he was tried for, and confessed to, having passed atomic secrets to Soviet agents since 1943. His motives were purely idealistic, having himself been a communist. He was sentenced to 14 years imprisonment, but was released in 1959, when he emigrated to East Germany. He remained there until his death. *See* ROSENBERG SPY CASE.

fuel air bomb (FAB) a type of bomb giving high explosive power over a wide area. The fuel air bomb acts in two stages: first an explosion spreads a large cloud of gas over the target; secondly, this is detonated to cause widespread destruction. Fuel air bombs are conventional weapons that have a power equivalent to that of small nuclear weapons. They were first used by US forces during the GULF WAR (1991) to clear minefields in Kuwait and S Iraq.

Führer (Ger. leader) The title assumed by Adolf Hitler (1889–1945) when he acceded to supreme power in Germany on the death of Hindenburg in 1934.

Fu Manchu A sinister Chinaman created by the British novelist Sax Rohmer (Arthur Sarsfield Ward; 1883–1959). *Dr Fu Manchu* (1913), the first of a series of novels, was a great success, encouraging the author to create more of the same. The last of the series, *Emperor Fu Manchu* (1959), was written while Rohmer was living in America. Reflecting the witch-hunt then just ending (*see* MCCARTHYISM), in the last book Fu had been transformed from an inscrutable villain into a dedicated anti-communist. Fu Manchu was also an early stalwart of the cinema: in the 1920s he was played by the British actor Harry Agar Lyons and in Hollywood by the Swedish actor Warner Oland (who later played the Chinese detective CHARLIE CHAN). In the 1940s Boris Karloff took over the role and in the 1960s Christopher Lee appeared in another British series. In all of them Fu Manchu was depicted as he had been described by Rohmer, with a thin rounded moustache hanging down on either side of the mouth. This became known as a **Fu-Manchu moustache**.

fun. **funny farm** Slang for a mental hospital.

funny peculiar or funny ha-ha? A catchphrase used to distinguish between two senses of the word funny; odd or peculiar (*e.g.* a funny way to behave) and amusing (a funny joke). It has appeared as a line in several plays, the first probably being the *Housemaster* (1938) by Ian Hay Beith.

Getting there is half the fun A slogan that has most recently been used as promotion for the 1980 film starring Peter Sellers called *Being There*: "Getting there is half the fun. Being there is all of it". It is a paraphrase of the sentiments expressed by Robert Louis Stevenson in *Virginibus Puerisque*, "To travel hopefully is a better thing than to arrive".

functionalism (1) In architecture, a genre in which the central motivation of the architect should be to create buildings that fulfil the functions to which they will be put; aesthetic considerations should not be allowed to influence the design to the detriment of function. Developed originally in the 1890s by Louis Sullivan (1856–1924), who coined the maxim, 'form must follow function', the theory of functionalism found its most influential proponent in LE CORBUSIER, although the style lost some ground after 1930. (2) In sociology, a perspective in which the various components of society are considered to be parallel to the workings of the different organs in a living body. The theory was devised by Emile Durkheim and subsequently developed by Talcott Parsons after World War II.

fundamental. fundamental forces The four different types of force that can exist between bodies that are not in contact. These forces (or **interactions**, as they are sometimes called) account for the way the universe is held together and for every physical event that occurs in it. The weakest of these forces is the **gravitational force**; this is 10^{40} times weaker than the electromagnetic force and acts between all bodies that have mass. The force is always attractive and although negligible on the atomic scale it is the force that holds the galaxies, stars, planets, etc., together. The **weak (nuclear) force**, 10^{10} times weaker than the electromagnetic force, occurs within certain sub-atomic particles. The **electromagnetic force** occurs between all electrically charged bodies and can be either attractive or repulsive. It controls atomic structure, chemical reactions, and all electric and magnetic phenomena. The **strong (nuclear) force**, 100 times stronger than the electromagnetic force, is the force that holds the atomic nucleus together. It acts only at very short distances (in the range 10^{15} metres).

The aim of physics is to unify these four fundamental forces into one theory, with one set of equations. This has not yet been achieved although the **electroweak theory** has successfully unified the electromagnetic and the weak forces. The elucidation of these fundamental forces has been one of the supreme achievements of 20th-century science.

fundamentalism The maintenance of traditional protestant Christian beliefs based upon a literal acceptance of the scriptures as fundamentals. Fundamentalism as a religious movement arose in America about 1919 among various denominations. What was new was not so much its ideas and attitudes, but its widespread extent and the zeal of its supporters. It opposed all theories of evolution and anthropology, holding that God transcends all laws of nature and that he manifests himself by exceptional and extraordinary activities, belief in the literal meaning of the Scriptures being an essential tenet. In 1925, John T. Scopes, a science teacher of Dayton, Tennessee, was convicted of violating the state laws by teaching evolution, an incident arousing interest and controversy far beyond the religious circles of America (*see* DAYTON ANTI-DARWINIST TRIAL).

Fundamentalism has also been a feature of other religions in the 20th century, often emerging as a means of holding together a religion that is in danger of crumbling into the sands of secularism. In particular, Muslim fundamentalism has been a source of considerable controversy in recent years (*see* FATWA). In general, religious fundamentalism has to be accepted by its advocates as an act of faith rather than reason and imposed on waverers by edict rather than by argument. Scriptural truths, and any fundamentalist system of theology based on them, are, by their alleged God-given nature, true for all time. Scientific truth, based on reproducible evidence, changes and evolves as the evidence is interpreted at deeper and more generalized levels. The divergence between religious fundamentalism and scientific understanding therefore tends to become wider and wider. *See also* MODERNISM; MORAL MAJORITY.

fund raiser A person employed by a charity to raise the money required to keep the charity alive. In the 19th century, as charities grew, the founders of charities and members of their immediate circle raised the funds required. However, in the 20th century, as charities became larger, resources became more expensive, and charitable trusts founded by rich men became more numerous, professional fund raisers appeared. Now every sizable charity employs a professional fund raiser.

Funf The name of a telephone character who appeared in the first series of the radio programme 'It's That Man Again', which later became ITMA. Funf, a corruption of *fünf*, the German word for five, was a half-baked German spy with a muffled guttural accent (obtained by having the actor Jack Train speak into a tumbler) – his catchphrase, **this is Funf speaking**, immediately caught on as an echo of the country's preoccupation with real German spies at the beginning of the war. Many telephone conversations of the period began with this joke introduction.

funky music Urban Black music, especially DISCO or SOUL, characterized by strong rhythm and heavy bass, combining elements of African, JAZZ, blues, and ROCK. The origin of the word funky is obscure, but it became a Black American term of approval in the mid-20th century. A 'funky guy' was much the same as the earlier 'cool guy', a person of whom one approved.

furphy In World War I containers for sanitary purposes were supplied to Australian military camps by the firm of Furphy and Co., whose name appeared on all their products. Hence a 'furphy' was a latrine rumour or a report of doubtful reliability.

fusion The form of nuclear reaction in which atomic nuclei of low atomic number fuse together to form a heavier nucleus, with the release of a considerable amount of energy. For example, when two deuterium nuclei (heavy hydrogen nuclei) fuse to form a tritium nucleus (the heaviest isotope of hydrogen) 10^{13} joules of energy are released. Before two such positively charged nuclei can fuse, however, the repulsive electromagnetic forces between them have to be overcome. This can be achieved if the reacting nuclei have very high kinetic energies, which implies a temperature of around 10^6 kelvins. *See also* COLD FUSION; NUCLEAR WEAPON.

futon A Japanese soft cotton mattress used as a bed; a simple and unobtrusive design, which can be folded to make seating or easily stored when not in use. The word itself is Japanese.

future. futurism An art movement that originated in Turin in 1909 under the influence of E. F. T. Marinetti. Its adherents sought to introduce into paintings a 'poetry of motion' whereby, for example, the painted gesture should become actually 'a dynamic condition'. The Futurists tried to indicate not only the state of mind of the painter but also that of the figures in the picture. It was another movement to shake off the influence of the past. The original Futurists included Marinetti, Boccioni, Carra, Russolo, and Severini, and they first exhibited at Paris in 1912. *See also* CUBISM; DADAISM; FAUVISM; ORPHISM; SURREALISM; SYNCHRONISM; VORTICISM.

I have seen the future and it works Famous catchphrase widely applied since its first coinage by the US reformer and journalist Lincoln Steffens (1879–1955), inspired by a recent visit to the Soviet Union and his meeting (1919) with Lenin.

Your future is in your hands A slogan from the Conservative Party campaign under the leadership of Winston Churchill in the 1950 General Election. It turned out to be a winner because although the Labour party won a small majority in 1950, the majority was too small to be workable and the Conservatives were returned to power in 1951, with Churchill as prime minister.

fuzz Slang for the police or a policeman. It originated in America in the late 1920s; the exact etymology is uncertain but in his *American Tramp and Underworld Slang* (1931) G. Irwin says: "a detective; a prison guard or turnkey. Here it is likely that 'fuzz' was originally 'fuss', one hard to please or over-particular". Not very likely, but in the absence of anything more convincing, it will have to do. Surprisingly, the use of the word fuzz did not appear in the UK until well after World War II, in the 1950s, probably in the wake of US crime TV programmes and films.

Fylingdales A moor to the south of Whitby in Yorkshire upon which the British station of the US Ballistic Missile Early Warning System (BMEWS) is built. It is a giant radar installation, a companion to those at Clear in Alaska and Thule in Greenland, that has continually monitored the sky in the general direction of the Soviet Union since 1963.

G

G or **Gee** (1) Informal abbreviation for gram, usually used with reference to a quantity of an illegal drug, especially cocaine, that is sold in gram units. (2) Abbreviation for grand, a slang word for 1000. Usually applied to money, in America it is used of $1000 and in the UK of £1000. This usage has largely been replaced by K, an abbreviation for kilo. It is now more usual to say that something costs 50K than 50G. (3) A cinema certification in America for films that can be shown generally. *See* PG; R.

G3 *See* GROUP OF THREE.

G5 *See* GROUP OF FIVE.

G7 *See* GROUP OF SEVEN.

G10 *See* GROUP OF TEN.

G77 *See* GROUP OF SEVENTY-SEVEN.

G-man US slang for a federal policeman, *i.e.* an officer of the FBI. G stands in this case for government.

G-string A very small triangular piece of cloth attached to the body by a string around the waist and between the buttocks; it is designed to cover the genitals of striptease artistes, go-go dancers, etc. The term was originally used for the strip of cloth tied round the waist and between the legs of male warriors, such as North American Indians. It is thought that the G-string is so called because it is the lowest string of a violin and possibly also as a result of a play on words with the title of the Air from Bach's Suite No. 3 in D, known in one particular arrangement as the 'Air on a G-string'.

G suit or **anti-G suit** A special tunic worn by jet pilots and astronauts that helps counteract the effects of high acceleration, named after the symbol, *g*, for the acceleration of free fall (formerly called the acceleration due to gravity). Built into the suit are air pockets that automatically inflate under high acceleration. These then press against the abdomen and thighs to lessen pooling of blood in the extremities and maintain an adequate supply of blood to the brain, so reducing the risk of blackouts.

gaff (1) British slang for a house, home, or place as in 'nice gaff you've got here'. In the 19th century gaff meant fairground but since the 1920s the usage has expanded to mean any place. It was popularized in the 1950s by the TEDDY BOYS and is still heard colloquially.

> But later in the day, the governor found me and apologised. That one thing completely changed my attitude to the gaff and to him.
>
> *The Independent*, 11 February 1991.

(2) British slang meaning to cheat, a meaning derived from the fact that cheating was regarded as a regular feature of fairground practice.

gag. gag-man One who is employed to supply jokes for films, radio programmes, etc.

gag me with a spoon! US slang exclamation of extreme surprise or feigned disgust.

gaga (1) Slang for senile, mentally unstable. Derived from the French nursery version of *grandpére*, grandfather, it became part of upper-class English speech in the 1920s. An alternative derivation is that the word is a corruption of *Gaugin*, the impressionist painter, who was known to be mentally disturbed. (2) Emotionally unstable in a non-clinical sense. An extension of the previous meaning, it can be used of people of any age, as in 'she is completely gaga about her new boyfriend'.

gage US slang for cheap whisky. This now obsolete usage is derived from the US name for a quart-sized container, which gave rise to **gaged**, meaning drunk. (2) Slang for a pipe or a pipeful of tobacco. (3) US and Jamaican slang for hashish or marijuana. This word was used in the 1960s as part of underworld and BEATNIK jargon. It is rarely heard now and is considered dated. This is another example of the way in which a word for one intoxicating substance can be transferred to another. *See also* STONED.

Gaiety Girl A member of the chorus of the Old Gaiety Theatre in the Strand, London, which became a popular feature of the musical comedies staged at the theatre in late Victorian and early EDWARDIAN times. Such productions as *The Shop Girl* (1894) and *The Circus Girl* (1896) were designed to give full reign to the singing and dancing talents of the chorus, as well as to display their good looks. Several of the Gaiety Girls, many of whom were of humble origins, married into the peerage. The New Gaiety Theatre replaced the Old Gaiety in 1903 when the latter was demolished to allow widening of the Strand; the tradition of musical comedies continued, however. *See also* GIBSON GIRL.

Gaillard Cut The SE section (formerly the Culebra Cut) of the PANAMA CANAL that was cut through the Culebra Mountain and extends for about 13 km (8 miles). It is named after David Du Bose Gaillard (1859–1913), the US Army engineer who supervised this section of the construction work.

gain sharing A form of profit-sharing among employees closely linked to work performance. Under this scheme employees benefit from any savings or cost-cutting for which they are responsible.

galah Australian slang for a silly person, a fool. The galah is a type of Australian cockatoo that is known for its habit of gathering in groups and chattering.

galah session In Australia, a period during which the FLYING DOCTOR radio network is thrown open for public use. It is so called because the chatter of the airwaves between radio users is likened to the noise of a flock of cockatoos (*see* GALAH).

Galaxy The C-5A/B Galaxy. A heavy transport aircraft used by the US Air Force for airlifting troops, vehicles, and equipment. Manufactured by Lockheed, the C-5 Galaxy is one of the world's largest aircraft. The C-5A first entered service in 1969; it has a wingspan of 68 m and is powered by four turbofan engines giving it a maximum payload of 132 tonnes. The upgraded C-5B version was introduced in the late 1980s.

Galbraithian Relating to the economic and social theories of the US economist Kenneth Galbraith (1908–). The term is also applied to a supporter of these theories. Galbraith, an economist in the tradition of KEYNESIANISM, was influential in the 1950s and 1960s and was noted for his book *The Affluent Society* (1958); he also coined the slogan "Private opulence and public squalor".

Gallipoli A peninsula in the DARDANELLES, which in 1915 became the scene of a disastrous Allied offensive against the Turks during World War I. Initially the campaign involved naval forces, but subsequently a large contingent of Australian and New Zealand forces (*see* ANZAC) were sent, as well as British and French troops. Allied commanders failed to order a rapid advance from the beachheads at Suvla Bay, Ari Burnu, and Cape Helles and, despite heroism from the troops themselves, the Allied forces subsequently failed to breach the Turkish lines. The final evacuation after 10 months was better managed. Allied troops were taken out by ship at night and small forces were landed during the day, convincing the Turks that the Allies were continuing to reinforce their position – not a single life was lost in the evacuation. In all, though, 25,000 Allied troops died, with 13,000 missing.

Gallup Poll The best known of the OPINION POLLS, instituted by Dr George Gallup (1901–84) of the American Institute of Public Opinion in 1935. Trained interviewers interrogate a carefully selected but small cross section of the population. For the British parliamentary election of 1945, out of 25 million voters, 1809 were interviewed, but the Gallup Poll forecast was within 1 per cent; however the forecast was wrong for the US presidential election of 1948. The LABOUR PARTY victory was forecast for the British parliamentary election in 1964 and 1966. It is held that such polls in themselves influence the result; for example, if a poll indicates that a particular party is in the lead, this may influence some voters to vote for it (because they want to be on the winning side). On the other hand, it may persuade some voters, who otherwise would not have bothered to vote, to vote against it. Straw polls and market research surveys were the forerunners of the Gallup Poll.

game. **gameplan** A term, originating in American football, meaning a series of tactics adopted in order to ensure the achievement of an objective. It is now used, on both sides of the Atlantic, to refer to a plan for a series of tactics, such as a career plan involving a number of job changes.

gamesmanship A term popularized by Stephen Potter (1900–70), whose book *The Theory and Practice of Gamesmanship* (1947) defines the meaning in its subtitle: 'The Art of Winning Games without actually Cheating'. *See also* LIFEMANSHIP; ONE-UPMANSHIP.

game theory A branch of mathematics that analyses the optimum strategy to adopt in a given situation. The theory was first introduced by the French mathematician Emile Borel (1871–1956) in 1921 and was developed by the Hungarian-born US mathematician John von Neumann (1903–57) and the German-born US economist Oskar Morganstern (1907–) in their book *The Theory of Games and Economic Behaviour* (1944). Here, they argued that the type of applied mathematics used in engineering and the physical sciences was not suitable for analysing economic activity. In the physical sciences, the subject under investigation is disinterested in the result; in economics, the individuals, companies, countries, etc., can take into account and anticipate the behaviour of other participants in the system. Consequently, economics is more like a game in which the players attempt to get the best possible result for themselves (*i.e.* to maximize their gain, or 'payoff', and to minimize their loss). Game theory (which is also known as the **theory of games**) is a formal mathematical way of analysing what the 'best' result might be. Although originally developed as a way of looking at economics, game theory has been applied in many other fields. During World War II it was used successfully to determine strategy in submarine warfare; it has subsequently been applied in politics, social science, business, biology, etc.

Games are classified in various ways. One distinction is the number of people (or parties) involved. For example, patience and solitaire are examples of 'one-person games' in which the participant is playing against chance. 'Two-person games' have two conflicting participants and '*n*-person games' have three or more protagonists. Another aspect of game theory is the overall result. A 'zero-sum game' is one in which the overall payoff is constant; one person's loss is another's gain. In a 'nonzero-sum game' all the participants may gain. Another classification is into 'cooperative' and 'noncooperative' games. Poker, for example, is an *n*-person zero-sum noncooperative game. Essential features of the mathematical analysis of games are that the participants should be regarded as acting rationally and, in most cases, that chance or incomplete information may affect the result.

gang. **gang-bang** Slang for an act of group sex, usually involving one woman and a number of men. 'Bang' is an example of a violent slang euphemism for copulate. A gang-bang normally is an instance of multiple rape in which the woman is forced to take part against her will.

gangbusters US schoolchildren's slang to describe something excellent, or highly approved of. It is a shortening of the phrase 'like gangbusters' meaning very energetically. Gangbusters were the law men who fought against the underworld mobs in America in the 1930s, especially as portrayed in fiction.

Gang of Four (1) Leaders of a Chinese radical group who unsuccessfully attempted to seize control after the death of Mao Tse-tung in 1976. The gang consisted of Jiang Qing (Mao's widow and third wife), Zhang Chungao, Wang Hungwen, and Yao Wenyuan. (2) In the UK, the name given to the four MPs who left the LABOUR PARTY in 1981 to form the Social Democratic Party (SDP), namely Roy Jenkins (leader until 1983), David Owen, Shirley Williams, and William Rodgers. Owen became leader in 1983 and was succeeded by Robert Maclennan in 1987 (*see* SOCIAL AND LIBERAL DEMOCRATIC PARTY).

ganja Slang for marijuana. Derived originally from the Sanskrit *gañja*, via Hindi *gājā*, ganja is now widely used by Black West Indians and young White users in the UK.

gannet British slang for a greedy person who gobbles his food. It is a reference to the large sea bird of the same name, which eats fish whole.

Gannex Tradename for a type of clothing manufactured by the Kagan Corporation, which was set up in the 1950s. It is particularly noted for a type of light-coloured trench coat with distinctive lapels (the 'Gannex mac') favoured by Harold Wilson during his premiership. The founder of the company, Joseph Kagan, was elevated to the peerage in Wilson's resignation honours list in 1976 (*see* LAVENDER LIST).

ganny British drug users' slang abbreviation for Afghani cannabis. The word has been in use since the 1980s.

gaper's block US slang for a traffic hold-up caused by car drivers stopping or slowing down to 'gape' at a road accident, fire, or other traffic incident. Frequently gapers prevent emergency rescue vehicles, such as ambulances and fire-engines, from reaching the scene of an accident rapidly.

garage. garage band An amateur rock or pop group that rehearses in a garage or similar makeshift premises.

garage sale A sale of second-hand objects held by a householder, typically in the garage to get rid of unwanted articles. The idea originated in America, where it is also called a **yard sale**. *See also* CAR-BOOT SALE.

Garand rifle Otherwise known as the M1 semi-automatic rifle, the standard-issue rifle of the US military from 1942. It was in use up to and during the KOREAN WAR. It was named after US small arms engineer, John C. Garand, who worked at the Springfield Armory, the national armoury of the US Army. During World War II Garand adapted his M1 rifle for selective fire, producing the T20 in 1944. Production of the M1 was resumed for the Korean War, to supply UN forces; it was superseded by the M14 rifle in 1957.

garbage. garbage in, garbage out or **gigo** An expression that originated as computer jargon meaning that what you get out of a system is dependent on the quality of what you put into it. Its usage is now somewhat more generalized and can be applied to almost any kind of system.

garbageology A blend of 'garbage' and 'archaeology'; the idea that is it possible to learn about the culture and life styles of people by studying what they have thrown away.

garbo Australian slang for a dustman, the man who collects the garbage. This is another example of an Australian word ending in *-o*. *See also* DRONGO.

garbology A grandiose US name for the study of waste disposal, rubbish or waste being commonly known as garbage in America. It has also become common in the UK to apply rather grandiose terms to activities associated with menial duties. For example, dustmen became known as 'cleansing operatives' and rat catchers as 'rodent officers'.

garbonzas US slang for breasts. A term, like BAZUMAS and GAZUNGAS, that is used by men. It is very similar to the Spanish word *garbanzos*, chick peas, although the connection, if any, is unclear.

garden. Garden City A name given to both Norwich and Chicago; also, as a general name, to model townships specially planned to provide attractive layouts for housing and industry with a surrounding rural belt and adequate open spaces. The term was first used by an American, A. T. Stewart, in 1869, and applied to an estate development on Long Island. The garden city movement in England was due to the social ideals of Sir Ebenezer Howard (1850–1928) set out in his book *To-morrow* (1898). His first garden city was founded at Letchworth, Hertfordshire, in 1903 and his second at Welwyn (1919–29). *See also* GREEN BELT; NEW TOWNS.

Garden Suburb (1) A model suburb (*e.g.* Hampstead Garden Suburb) with many characteristics of a GARDEN CITY. (2) The nickname applied to Lloyd George's personal secretariat, of which he made increasing use after he became head of the War Cabinet (December 1916), to help him in effecting his policies. The name derives from the fact that they were accommodated in huts in St James's Park. The 'Garden Suburb' was dispersed when Bonar Law assumed the premiership in 1922.

Garlic Wall The satirical name applied by Gibraltarians to the Spanish barrier that closed the frontier to La Línea in 1969 as a consequence of Spain's claim to the Rock. Gibraltar was ceded to Great Britain by the Treaty of Utrecht, 1713. Spain reopened the frontier at La Línea in 1985.

garryowen In Rugby Union, a high kick forwards in support of a charge (also known as an **up-and-under**). The word is derived from Garryowen RFC, a Limerick club founded in 1884, which has a reputation for excellent forward play. Garryowen won the Munster premier trophy more often than any other club and has provided over 30 internationals for Ireland.

gas (1) Slang for something very exciting or enjoyable, as in the exclamation 'what a gas!'. HIPPIE jargon of the 1960s and 1970s, it is thought to have originated in America in the 1950s as a Black slang expression of approval for the stimulating effects of taking nitrous oxide (laughing gas). (2) Slang for a chat, from the idea of breath being a gas.

gas guzzler US slang for a car that consumes large quantities of petrol; it is therefore uneconomical and not environmentally friendly. It was first applied to the very large US cars, gas being the US word for petrol. The expression is now also heard in the UK, where such a car might also be called 'juicy'.

gas pipe US slang for a trombone, used in the 1940s in JAZZ circles.

gash (1) British slang meaning spare, surplus to requirements. Now rarely heard, it was common among members of the forces in the 1950s. (2) British slang meaning attractive, possibly an extension of the previous meaning implying that an unattached woman is attractive. This is now rarely used, but was common until the 1960s. (3) British slang meaning broken, useless. This meaning is still heard from technicians and workmen, as in 'this computer is gash'. (4) A slang word for a woman, especially one viewed in a sexual way. This is obviously an extension of the sense used by men as a vulgar name for the vagina. In this sense it is sometimes used in the form **a bit of gash**. There is probably a connection here with the adjectival sense used in (2) above. In the 1980s gash was also used as a synonym for girlfriend among young RAP music fans.

gasper British slang from World War I for a cigarette. The word reflects the fact that cigarettes make one short of breath, or gasp, something that was not taken very seriously before the anti-smoking campaign of the early 1970s and the connection between smoking, cancer, and heart disease became clear.

Gastarbeiter (Ger. guest worker) An immigrant worker in Germany (West Germany until 1990) from Turkey, Yugoslavia, etc., allowed into the country to alleviate the labour shortage.

gat US slang for a pistol, heard in the early 1900s. It is an abbreviation of Gatling gun, the crank-operated prototype of the modern machine gun, invented by Richard Jordan Gatling (1818–1903). In the 1950s 'Gat' was the tradename of a British air pistol.

gate A JAZZ musician, or any person of whom one should approve. The term was made popular in the 1920s by the jazz trumpeter Louis Armstrong (1900–71).

Gatsby Jay Gatsby, a character in a novel by the US writer F. Scott Fitzgerald (1896–1940), *The Great Gatsby* (1925). The character was, it is thought, inspired by one of Fitzgerald's neighbours on Long Island, New York, the bootlegger Max Gerlack, and partly by a New York socialite and fraudster Edward M. Fuller. Fitzgerald said that Gatsby was based on someone he knew, but then grew into himself. The story has been filmed three times: the silent version in 1926 starred Warner Baxter, a 1949 Paramount film starred Alan Ladd, and a lavish 1974 production had Robert Redford in the name part. Of the last version the English film critic Michael Billington said:

> Profoundly unfilmable: a poetic and ultimately pessimistic comment on the American dream is transformed by cinematic realism into pure prose.

GATT General Agreement on Tariffs and Trade. A treaty signed by over 90 nations to regulate trade barriers and encourage free trade. The original agreement, signed by 23 nations, came into force on 1 January 1948 following talks in Geneva the previous year. A proposed UN International Trade Organization never came into being, leaving GATT as the principal regulatory framework. Fundamental principles of GATT include non-discrimination among the signatories ('most-favoured-nation' clause); the limitation of protective measures to customs tariffs rather than import quotas or embargoes; and support for movement towards reducing and eliminating tariffs by multilateral agreements. The GATT secretariat is based in Geneva, where it also operates the International Trade Centre, in conjunction with UNCTAD, to support trade promotion by developing countries. A Council of Representatives convenes every 4–6 weeks to deal with routine business, while Ministerial Sessions are held less frequently to consider major developments in international trade.

gauchist or **gauchiste** In France, a left-wing political radical. From the French *gauche*, left.

Gauleiter (Ger. district leader) The head (*Leiter*) of a *Gau*, one of the administrative territories into which Germany was divided under the THIRD REICH. The *Gauleiter* (sometimes called the *Gaufuehrer*) was a high-ranking official, often appointed directly by Hitler; he was responsible for all economic and political activities in the area, as well as civil defence and sometimes policing. The bureaucracy was known as the *Gauleitung*.

Gaumont Tradename for a British chain of cinemas. The company originated in France and was named after the inventor Léon Gaumont, who developed (1901) a method of synchronizing film with sound. The company Gaumont-British was founded in 1909 and acquired by The Rank Organization in 1942.

gay Light-hearted, merry, in high good spirits; also bright looking, as 'she wore a gay-coloured dress'.

> Belinda smiled and all the world was gay.
> ALEXANDER POPE: *The Rape of the Lock*, II, 52

As time went by, however, 'gay' also acquired the sense of given to pleasure and hence dissipated, as in 'he's a bit of a gay dog' and **gay house** (formerly a once common name for a brothel). In current slang, the word is applied to homosexuals. This once straightforward word has now become so identified with homosexuality that to use it in one of its previous senses is to risk titters from one's companions.

gay deceiver Slang for a brassière lined with sponge-like plastic padding.

Gay Liberation or **Gay Lib** The campaign by lesbians and homosexual men to fight discrimination, especially in the areas of employment, criminal law, and custody rights. The symbolic beginning of the movement was on 28 June 1969 when the clientele of gay bars on Christopher Street, New York, rioted against police raids. These events triggered the appearance of the Gay Liberation Front (GLF) in America and subsequently of similar organizations in other countries, including the UK.

gayola Money extorted as blackmail from people, especially homosexuals, who wish to keep their sexual proclivities secret. It is formed from a combination of GAY (a homosexual) and PAYOLA.

Gaza Strip A disputed belt of land on the Mediterranean coast between Egypt and Israel; it includes the city of Gaza. The Strip itself, some 42 km long and 6–10 km wide, was created in 1948 when Gaza and its surroundings were taken by Egypt following the UN proposals for the division of Palestine. It remained under Egyptian control until 1956, when it was briefly held by Israel. Israel again wrested control from Egypt in the 1967 SIX-DAY WAR, since when it has remained in Israeli hands. An uprising (*see* INTIFADA) by Palestinians living in the Gaza Strip and West Bank started in 1987, resulting in increased military confrontation with the Israeli occupiers and diminished prospects for peace.

Gazelle Boy In 1961, Jean-Claude Armen, travelling by camel through the Spanish Sahara in W Africa, was told by nomad tribesmen of the whereabouts of a young boy living with a herd of gazelles. In due time he sighted the boy and eventually attracted him to close quarters by playing a Berber flute. The boy fed on the same plants as the animals, sometimes eating worms and lizards. On a subsequent expedition in 1963, this time in a jeep, the speed of the boy when galloping with the herd was established at over 30 m.p.h.

gazump A word of unknown origin that entered the language after World War II when house prices were rising sharply. A buyer is gazumped if the seller of a house verbally agrees to sell it to him at a certain price and then accepts a higher offer from someone else. The practice is not illegal, as in England and Wales verbal contracts for the sale of land are invariably made subject to contract and subject to survey. Once contracts have been exchanged, however, the sale is binding and any attempt to gazump the buyer then would be actionable. As rising prices imply a seller's market, it is the seller who benefits from gazumping: the buyer may lose the cost of his survey and legal fees and has no recourse to claim them from the seller. In a market in which prices are falling, the opposite may occur; just before signing the contract the buyer may reduce his offer for the property, aware that the seller is anxious to sell, may have incurred legal expenses, and may also be in the process of buying another property. This became known as **gazundering** in the 1980s when the practice started. In order to prevent these two dishonest practices the authorities concerned are seeking ways of making verbal contracts binding or of shortening the time that elapses between the acceptance of an offer and the issuing of a binding written contract.

gazungas A male slang euphemism for breasts. *See also* GARBONZAS.

Gazza Nickname of Paul Gascoigne, British footballer with Tottenham Hotspur and England. He became a household name in 1990 following England's success in the World Cup and achieved a certain notoriety by bursting into tears when booked by the referee in the semi-final against West Germany – a decision that would have barred him from the final had England won. He subsequently launched a modest career as a popstar on the strength of his fame.

GCE General Certificate of Education. A secondary education certificate that was introduced in 1951 to replace the School and Higher School Certificate Examinations. There were two levels: O-level (ordinary level), taken usually at age 16 after a three- or five-year course, and A-level (advanced level), taken at 18 after an additional two-year course. The syllabuses and examinations were set by various national and regional examination boards. GCE O-level and CSE were both superseded by GCSE in 1988. A-levels continued to be taken by those in full-time education for two years after sitting GCSE exams. As an alternative to, and to complement, A-levels, Advanced Supplementary level (AS-level) exams were introduced in 1989. They are intended to broaden the course of A-level students and require half the teaching time of the corresponding A-level, but are also spread over a two-year period.

GCSE General Certificate of Secondary Education. A certificate of education for 16–19 year-olds, which replaced GCE O levels and the CSE from 1988. The GCSE is designed to allow pupils of different abilities to be regularly assessed and graded within each subject according to a variety of criteria (not only by their examination performance). These criteria include cognitive development and the acquisition and demonstration of practical, creative, and social skills, enabling the majority of pupils to attain some degree of achievement during their school years.

gear (1) Clothing, equipment, etc., as, for example, **sports gear** (O.E. *gearwe*, dress). (2) Slang for illegal drugs.

Geddes axe The drastic cuts in public expenditure, especially on the army, navy, and education, recommended by the Geddes Committee in 1922.

Gee (1) Codename for a radio navigation system, originally known as TR 1335, used by British bombers during World War II. Signals from three widely spaced transmitters – one 'master' and two 'slaves' – were received by the bomber. The navigator used a cathode-ray tube to display the path difference between each slave signal and the master signal, and with a special grid map could pinpoint the position of the bomber. The system was introduced operationally in 1941 but had a limited range of only 400 miles. (2) *See* G.

geek (1) US slang for a freak, a weirdo, a crazy person, mostly used by schoolchildren and young people. An extension of the fairground sense of the word, meaning someone who bites off the heads of live chickens as a side-show attraction. It is possibly derived from the Scottish *geck*, fool. (2) US slang of the 1980s meaning to search desperately for any particles of the drug CRACK that might have been dropped. *See* GEEK ROCK.

geek rock US slang of the 1980s for the drug CRACK. A GEEK is a crazy person and 'rock' is any narcotic in granule form.

geep An animal, produced by GENETIC ENGINEERING at Cambridge in 1984, that is a cross between a sheep and a goat; it has a sheep-like coat and goat-like horns. Such crosses cannot reproduce themselves. *See also* BEEFALO.

gefilte fish A Jewish delicacy consisting of a fish cake made of a variety of chopped fish, mixed with matzo meal, eggs, onions, pepper, and salt. It can be eaten hot or cold. Widely available in Jewish delicatessen stores, especially in New York, the dish has in the 20th century come to be regarded as the epitome of Jewish cuisine.

> I am sitting in Mindy's restaurant putting on the gefilte fish.
>
> DAMON RUNYON: *Guys and Dolls* (1932).

Gehazi *See* MARCONI AFFAIR.

Geiger counter or **Geiger-Müller counter** A scientific instrument used to detect ionizing radiation (especially as produced by radioactive substances). It is named after the German physicist Hans Geiger (1882–1945), who invented it in 1913. It was developed in the 1920s by W. Müller, also a German physicist. It is usually known in technical circles as a 'G-M counter'.

Geller, Uri Israeli psychic performer who became world famous in the 1970s. Born in Tel Aviv in 1946, he attracted considerable publicity with his apparent ability to influence the physical world by telepathic means. In front of incredulous audiences, including huge numbers watching on television, he bent cutlery, stopped watches, drove a car blindfolded, and controlled the movements of a cable car, amongst other feats. He has agreed to participation in many scientific investigations but none have provided conclusive evidence for or against the powers he claims.

gelt The Yiddish word for money (from the Ger. *geld*, money), widely used in US slang, especially in New York.

Gemini A series of US space missions launched in the 1960s to test various manoeuvres and explore the capabilities of men under space conditions in preparation for the APOLLO MOON PROGRAMME. Each manned Gemini mission carried a two-man crew, starting with Gemini 3 in March 1965. In June, from Gemini 4, Ed White performed the first **space walk** (extravehicular activity or EVA) by a US astronaut. Geminis 5 and 7, launched in August and December 1965, both set new records for the duration of a manned space mission. Gemini 6, also launched in December, successfully achieved a rendezvous with Gemini 7, while Gemini 8 docked with an unmanned spacecraft in March 1966. Four further Gemini missions were launched, the series ending with Gemini 12, launched in November 1966, during which mission Buzz Aldrin made a record EVA of over 5½ hours duration. The success of the Gemini programme paved the way for an eventual moon landing by Apollo 11.

gen World War II RAF slang for information or the true facts. Several possible derivations have been suggested; it may be a shortened form of *gen*uine or of intelli*gen*ce, or it may be short for *gen*eral as used in the military phrase 'for the general information of all ranks'. It also appears in the verb **gen up**, as in the phrase 'I'm genned up on the project'.

gender. gender-bender Slang name from the mid-1980s for a transvestite or for someone who is transexual.

> Gender-bender Brenda standing for Liberals.
> Headline, *The Sun*, 19 April 1991.

gender gap A variation between the political, social, and cultural views and values held by males and females and between their levels of attainment in a whole range of occupations. This has been monitored, for example, in the different voting patterns of the sexes in America. In this study, women appeared to be more concerned with social and environmental issues and less with foreign affairs. The traditional explanation for this phenomenon links it to the fact that women are biologically equipped to carry and give birth to babies; the equivalent of the nest and its environment is therefore their paramount concern. Defending the family's territory, often providing for its defence, etc., is (the argument runs) the customary preoccupation of the male. Men and women are biologically different; their emotional responses are mediated by different hormones. The gender gap is therefore predictable – indeed conventional family life is based on it. However, because men and women are intellectually roughly on a par, women are able to perform as well as, and sometimes better than, men at many of the tasks usually regarded (by men) as male preserves. It is true that on average men do have heavier brains than women, but the difference (if any) that this is likely to make to average intellectual performance is small enough to be swamped by individual variation. In this century it has been discovered that, in spite of the gender gap, women make equally good doctors, stockbrokers, solicitors, barristers, scientists, engineers, computer programmers and analysts, etc. *See also* FEMINISM; ORDINATION OF WOMEN; SEXUAL POLITICS.

general. General Assembly One of the six principal organs of the UNITED NATIONS,and the forum in which every UN member has equal influence by virtue of their single vote. The Assembly may consider any matter embraced by the UN Charter, and make recommendations to member states or the Security Council. Any issues may be discussed, including peace and security, environmental matters, and economic and social questions. The ten non-permanent members of the Security Council are elected by the Assembly, as are members of the Economic and Social Council. Decisions on important questions require a two-thirds majority; less momentous resolutions need only a simple majority. Regular sessions, lasting three months, are held annually in New York, beginning on the third Tuesday in September. Special sessions may be called at the behest of the Security Council or a majority of member states. Main committees and special committees consider specific issues in detail and report to the Assembly.

General Strike The national strike among vital sectors of the UK's workforce called by the Trades Union Congress (TUC) in 1926 in support of the miners' dispute with the colliery owners. A lock-out of the miners on 30 April was the culmination of a long and bitter fight against threatened wage cuts and longer hours, summarized by their slogan 'Not a penny off the pay, not a minute on the day'. The strike, officially declared from midnight on 3 May, affected transport and railway workers, the iron and steel industry, building, gas, electricity, printing, and other key areas. The government, headed by Stanley Baldwin, enacted a state of emergency and introduced a range of measures to counter the effects of the strike. The country was divided into areas under the control of Civil Commissioners and troops were deployed in likely trouble spots. From the outset the TUC had promised to maintain vital food supplies, but many additional services were run by students and volunteers drawn from the middle and upper classes. With national newspapers suspended by the strike, the government produced its own *British Gazette*, belligerently edited by the then chancellor of the exchequer, Winston Churchill; he dubbed strikers "the enemy" and called for their "unconditional surrender". The TUC countered with its own publication, the *British Worker*.

Government measures quickly reduced the effectiveness of the strike, which was unconditionally called off by the TUC on 12 May. The miners' lockout lasted another six months, when hunger forced them to accept their employers' terms. In 1927 the Trades Disputes Act was amended to outlaw any strike "designed or calculated to coerce the government". Although never invoked, it was repealed by the LABOUR government in 1945.

General Synod The highest governing body in the Church of England. The General Synod was introduced in 1969 to improve ecclesiastical government and admit greater lay involvement. The General Synod replaced the dual government of Convocations and the Church Assembly, and comprises members of the Upper Houses of the Convocations of Canterbury and York, a House of Clergy, and House of Laity of not more than 250 elected members. It meets at least twice each year and determines issues of doctrine, church services, and the administration of the Sacraments.

general theory (1) *See* RELATIVITY. (2) A theory in economics relating consumption, investment, and the behaviour of the money markets to employment levels. It was put forward in 1936 by J. M. Keynes (1883–1946) and has had a profound effect on the development of economics. *See* KEYNESIANISM.

generalissimo The supreme commander, especially of a force drawn from two or more nations, or of a combined military and naval force; the equivalent of *Tagus* among the ancient Thessalians, *Brennus* among the ancient Gauls, and *Pendragon* among the ancient Welsh or Celts. The title is said to have been coined by Cardinal Richelieu on taking supreme command of the French armies in Italy, in 1629.

In modern times the title has beeen applied to Marshal Foch (1851–1929), who commanded the Allied forces in France in 1918; to Joseph Stalin (1879–1953), who was made generalissimo of the Soviet forces in 1943; to General Franco (1892–1975), who proclaimed himself generalissimo of the Spanish army in 1939; and to Marshal Chiang Kai-shek (1888–1975), leader of the GUOMINDANG, who was in power in China from 1927 to 1949.

generation gap The difference in attitudes, social values, lifestyle, etc., between one generation and the next, typically between parents and their adolescent children. The generation gap is not primarily a 20th-century phenomenon. As Shakespeare pointed out:

> Crabbed age and youth cannot live together;
> Youth is full of pleasure, age is full of care;
> Youth like summer morn, age like winter weather;
> Youth like summer brave, age like winter bare.
>
> *The Passionate Pilgrim*, XII.

Nevertheless, interest in the difference between generations has been a particular feature of social life from the mid-20th century, when Western youth sought to assert its own identity. The problem was spelled out by George Orwell:

> Each generation imagines itself to be more intelligent than the one that went before it, and wiser than the one that comes after it.
>
> Book review.

generic A product that is sold under its own name rather than a brand name of a particular manufacturer. For example Panadol is a tradename for a particular brand of the drug paracetamol. Paracetamol, the generic, can be sold more cheaply than the branded product because it can be packaged more simply and does not have to bear the cost of brand advertising.

generic advertising Advertising a type of product, such as wool or milk, rather than a branded product. This is usually undertaken by a group of manufacturers or producers for the benefit of all of them.

generic name The name of a branded product that has been so extensively advertised and in use for so long that it has become part of the language. HOOVER is a prime example. This is now used without an initial capital letter to refer to any brand of vacuum cleaner. Similarly BIRO and WALKMAN are now used for any brands of ball-point pen and personal tape player respectively.

gene therapy A medical application of GENETIC ENGINEERING, still in the experimental stage, that seeks to replace defective human genes by normal ones. The ultimate aim is the prevention of inherited diseases, such as haemophilia, by replacing the faulty genes that cause them.

genetic. genetic code The means by which genetic information for constructing proteins (the bases of living matter) is stored in the molecular structure of DNA. It is this code, carried in the chromosomes of the nuclei of living cells, that determines the genetic characteristic of each individual. The basic unit of the code (called a *codon*) consists of a group of three particular chemicals (called bases); it is the sequence of these codons that forms the genetic code. There are four bases present in DNA, therefore 64 codons are possible from a combination of these bases. Proteins are made up of chains of chemicals called amino acids, each of which is specified by a particular codon; different proteins have different sequences of amino acids in their chains. As the sequence of codons determines the sequence of amino acids in the protein, the genetic code directs which paricular proteins are produced. *See also* MESSENGER RNA.

genetic counselling Guidance given to patients in whose families there is a history of inherited disorders, such as cystic fibrosis, muscular dystrophy, and Huntington's chorea. It includes discussing the possibilities that the patient may develop the disease, the likelihood of the children of such patients being affected, and any means of prevention and management of the disease.

genetic engineering A late 20th-century development of genetics that allows alteration of the genetic make-up of an organism. It typically involves inserting desirable genes from one species into the DNA of another species (usually a bacterium) via an agent called a 'cloning vector'. Multiple copies of the gene (**gene clones**) are formed when the bacterium replicates itself. In this way, human genes that control the synthesis of useful substances, such as hormones (*e.g.* insulin), enzymes, and antibodies, can be cloned in bacterial hosts to enable large quantities of such substances to be produced. Genetic engineering can similarly be applied to economically important plants to improve crop yield, disease resistance, etc. *See also* TRANSGENIC.

genetic fingerprinting The analysis of characteristic patterns in DNA to identify one individual from another; it constitutes the most significant advance in crime detection since the FINGERPRINT. The method was invented by Professor Alex Jeffreys at Lancaster University, and relies upon the uniqueness of each person's genetic make-up as determined by the DNA molecule in each living cell. These DNA variations can be identified from small samples of blood, tissue, hair root, or semen and then photographed for purposes of comparison. This virtually infallible technique is now used extensively in criminal investigations, in verification of paternity, and in immigration screening to confirm blood relationships. National and international databases of genetic fingerprints are now being established, while research continues to investigate new applications for the technique.

genetic mother The woman who produces the egg cell from which a baby develops; the term is used in cases of assisted reproduction, in which the egg cell, after *in vitro* fertilization (*see* IVF), is implanted into another woman's womb. The woman who gives birth to the baby is then known as the **birth mother**. Such differentiating terms became necessary in the late 20th century with the success of research and development into problems of infertility. *See also* SURROGATE MOTHERHOOD.

Geneva A synonym for the LEAGUE OF NATIONS, the headquarters of which were situated there.

Geneva Agreements The settlement signed in Geneva in 1954 between the warring parties in Indochina, which was intended to end conflict between French and VIET MINH forces in Vietnam and to ensure the evacuation of communist troops and guerrillas from Laos and Cambodia. After difficult negotiations, which also involved representatives of America, the Soviet Union, the UK, and China, the agreements were signed in the early hours of 21 July, on the 'midnight or never' deadline set by the French. Chief among the provisions agreed was the establishment of a ceasefire line along the **17th Parallel**, dividing the country into the North under Viet Minh control and the South under Emperor Bao Dai, supported by the French. A timetable was drawn up for the relocation of troops and the holding of free elections in Laos, Cambodia, and all Vietnam. The agreements stressed that the ceasefire line "should not in any way be interpreted as constituting a political or territorial boundary". However, neither the major powers nor the South Vietnamese regime signed the agreements and this crucial flaw left the way open for America to pursue its own policy of bolstering a separate anti-communist state south of the 17th parallel. The free elections for all of Vietnam, envisaged in the Agreements, never took place, and America was destined for protracted and costly involvement in that country's affairs (*see* VIETNAM WAR).

Geneva Protocol Protocol for the Pacific Settlement of International Disputes. A procedure for resolving international conflict proposed to the LEAGUE OF NATIONS in 1924 jointly by the British prime minister, Ramsay MacDonald, and the French premier, Édouard Herriot. Essentially, all disputes were to be settled by compulsory arbitration by the League's Permanent Court of International Justice or by other League bodies. The Protocol received the unanimous endorsement of the League Assembly on 2 October. Shortly after, however, MacDonald's Labour government fell in a general election and was replaced by a Conservative administration under Stanley Baldwin; the new government reversed the UK's position on the Protocol, causing its eventual demise.

Genghis Khan. somewhere to the right of Genghis Khan A phrase used to describe a person whose politics are extremely right wing. Genghis Khan (*c.*1162–1227) was the founder of the Mongol empire, a ruthless leader whose hordes ravaged, raped, and pillaged their way across central Asia.

genocide A word invented by Professor Raphael Lemkin, of Duke University, and used in the drafting of the official indictment of war criminals in 1945. It is a combination of Gr. *genos*, race; and Lat. *cœdere*, to kill. It is defined as acts intended to destroy, in whole or in part, national, ethical, racial, or religious groups, and in 1948 was declared by the United Nations GENERAL ASSEMBLY to be a crime in international law. *See* HOLOCAUST.

Gentleman's Agreement An informal understanding reached in 1907 between America and Japan, restricting the flow of Japanese emigrants to America. Prior to this agreement, the influx of unskilled Japanese had created racial tension and incipient racial discrimination, particularly in California.

gentrification The upgrading of town houses and flats, especially those situated in areas traditionally occupied by poorer families. Typically, it occurs in terraced houses originally built for workers and usually consists of knocking two ground-floor rooms together and adding modern kitchens and bathrooms, or radically improving existing ones. The word came into use in the 1970s, by which time the practice was well established. In London, for example, whole areas, such as Islington, have been gentrified.

geodesic dome A dome-shaped structure of metal, wood, or plastic based on octahedrons or tetrahedrons, devised by the US architect Richard Buckminster Fuller (1895–1983) in the 1950s to span large areas. The best known such dome, and the one that drew attention to its versatility was that which enclosed the US Pavilion at the World Fair in Montreal (1967). The largest has a diameter of 117 metres (384 ft) and was the repair shop of the Union Tank Car Co., in Baton Rouge, Louisiana.

geopolitics The name given to the German theories of applied political geography developed by Karl Haushofer in the 1920s and earlier by F. Ratzel, whose pupil Kjellen coined the term. Sir Halford Mackinder (1861–1947) and others formulated similar theories. These teachings were used by the NAZIS to support their demand for LEBENSRAUM.

George Nickname for the automatic pilot in an aircraft. It is possibly derived from the use of 'George', since World War I, as forces' slang for an airman, rather like 'TOMMY' is used for a soldier. Hence the invisible pilot comes to be represented as George – "Let George do it!"

George Cross and Medal The George Cross is second only to the Victoria Cross. It consists of a plain silver cross with a medallion showing St George and the Dragon in the centre. The words "For Gallantry" appear round the medallion, and in the angle of each limb of the cross is the royal cipher. It hangs from a dark blue ribbon. The George Cross was founded in 1940 for acts of conspicuous heroism, primarily by civilians. It is named after King George VI, the ruling monarch. It is only awarded to service personnel for acts of heroism not covered by existing military honours.

The George Medal (red ribbon with five narrow blue stripes) is awarded for similar but somewhat less outstanding acts of bravery.

George Cross Island The Island of Malta, which was awarded the GEORGE CROSS by King George VI in April 1942, in recognition of the steadfastness and fortitude of its people while under siege in World War II. It had suffered constant aerial attacks from Italian and German bombers.

George Raft British rhyming slang for a draught (of cold air). George Raft (1895–1980) was a well-known US film star who specialized in gangster parts, having himself been a nightclub gigolo with underworld connections.

Georgian poets A disparate group of poets associated by virtue of publication of their works in the anthology *Georgian Poetry*; the epithet is often extended to include any poets active in the period 1912 to 1922, during which the five volumes of the anthology appeared. *Georgian Poetry* was edited by Sir Edward Marsh, a scholar and patron of English poetry; preparation of the first volume coincided with the accession of George V (1910), hence 'Georgian'. Beyond that, Marsh had a vague notion of some new poetic movement emerging to replace Edwardianism; he had in mind the works of Rupert Brooke, W. H. Davies, D. H. Lawrence, Walter de la Mare, John Masefield, and others, all of whom featured in the first volume. However, the idea of 'Georgianism' as a coherent movement is not tenable; for instance, the later volumes contained works by such contrasting poets as Siegfried Sassoon and the traditionalist J. C. Squire. Indeed, Graves, Sassoon, Blunden, and others resented being labelled 'Georgian'; eventually the term came to acquire a pejorative sense.

geothermal energy Subterranean heat energy that makes its way to the Earth's surface in the form of steam or hot water. It is harnessed directly, or by means of heat exchangers, to drive turbines to generate electricity. This form of inexhaustible natural energy is exploited in various areas in the world, particularly North and South America, Iceland, and New Zealand, where there are large numbers of geysers and thermal springs. The oldest geothermal installation is at Lardello in Tuscany, Italy, which began to exploit local steam geysers in 1818 and still supplies a series of power stations.

Gerbil An acronym for the Great Education Reform Bill — a controversial education bill introduced in the UK by the Secretary of State for Education, Kenneth Baker, in 1988. Among its aims were the creation of a NATIONAL CURRICULUM and transference of the financial management of state schools from the local authorities to the schools themselves.

Gestalt A movement in psychology, which takes its name from the German word *Gestalt*, which approximates in English to 'form' or 'shape'. Essentially it considers psychological phenomena as wholes, rather than as combinations of separate components, each to be analysed individually. The movement emerged around the turn of the century, but it was Max Wertheimer who first set out the principles of Gestalt in 1912. Working with Kurt Koffka and Wolfgang Köhler at Frankfurt University, Wertheimer described certain phenomena of visual perception indicating that the neural organization and perceptual experience elicited by any set of stimuli are together created as a *Gestalt* or 'whole', and cannot be analysed as the summation of sensory elements. Wholes are thus configurations (*Gestalten*) of different parts, with each part defined by its role in the configuration. But as the beauty of a melody cannot be perceived by analysing the individual notes, analysis of the components individually cannot reveal the nature of the Gestalt. Starting from this view of mental processes as dynamic wholes, the concepts of Gestalt were applied to other areas of psychology, including animal behaviour, child development and education, thinking, learning, and memory. Indeed, Gestalt principles have penetrated to many other intellectual fields during the 20th century, notably sociology, politics, aesthetics, and economics. The Gestalt approach to psychotherapy seeks to restore a wholeness to the individual's inner world and relationship to his or her surroundings, drawing on other psychoanalytical techniques as appropriate.

Gestapo Shortened from the Ger. *Geheime Staatspolizei*, secret state police, which acquired such sinister fame in NAZI Germany after 1933. It was formed by Goering and later controlled by Himmler and was responsible for terrorizing both the Germans and the peoples of occupied territories. It was declared a criminal organization by the Nuremberg Tribunal in 1946.

get. **getaway** A short holiday or break spent away from home.

get away from it all A cliché, much used in travel journalism, meaning to go away to a quiet place for a holiday and a rest.

get down US slang meaning to get on with it, get down to business. It is often heard as an exhortation to a group of musicians who are improvising or to disco dancers. In the early 1970s it became a catchphrase among young people, meaning to communicate openly, to bare one's soul.

get into bed with (1) Slang euphemism for having sexual intercourse with. (2) Business slang meaning to work closely with, or to merge with. This sense has been widely used since the late 1970s.

get it on US slang euphemism for having sex with. The expression was first used in the 1960s and is also still widespread in the UK.

get it together *See* GET ONE'S ACT TOGETHER; TOGETHER.

get off or **get off on** Slang meaning to receive stimulation or inspiration from. Originally the phrase meant to achieve orgasm, indeed 'get off' is still teenage slang, meaning to choose a partner at a dance or party and then indulge in petting; it was then adopted by drug users in the early 1970s, as in 'I really got off on the acid yesterday'. The expression was subsequently used more generally to describe any peak of experience, be it drug-induced, sexual, or inspired by music.

get one's act together Slang meaning to get oneself organized. It is similar in meaning to 'get it together' (see TOGETHER) and is widely used in both the UK and America.

getting any? A friendly greeting, usually between men, meaning 'getting any sex at the moment?' It originated in Services slang during World War II.

getting there is half the fun *See under* FUN.

Ghan, The In Australia, a weekly train from Adelaide to Alice Springs. The construction of a railway line from Adelaide to the northern coast was begun in 1877 but got no further that Oodnadatta (472 km from Alice Springs). For about 40 years camel trains conducted by Afghans carried goods and passengers from Oodnadatta to Alice. When the railway reached Alice in 1929 the train came to be known as 'The Ghan', presumably because it replaced the Afghan camel train.

ghettoblaster Slang for a portable stereo cassette player, especially one that is playing loudly while it is being carried. It is particularly associated with loud Black music, *e.g.* REGGAE, hence 'ghetto'. These machines were popular before the advent of the personal stereo system (*see* WALKMAN), but the name has stuck for any twin-speaker cassette player which may also be known as a BOOGIE BOX or a BRIXTON BRIEFCASE.

ghost US slang for a person who is listed as being present at work although he is not. It is also used to refer to schoolchildren who are skipping school but who appear in the register as being present. In both circumstances illicit arrangements are made by someone who is present to cover the absence of the truant.

ghost note A soft, almost inaudible, note played in a series of louder notes in a JAZZ composition.

GI Nickname for a member of the US Army, also used as an adjective to describe army kit, duties, standards, etc. – as in 'GI blankets', 'GI haircut', and as a verb – as in 'you'd better GI your whole goddam' kit, private'. The term was originally used by US Army clerks to mean galvanized iron, as in 'GI can' (at the time of World War I 'GI can' was also the nickname for a German shell, owing to a physical similarity between the two objects). The meaning of GI later changed to 'general issue' or 'government issue', which is the modern meaning. During World War II, US army servicemen were affectionately known, especially to the British, as **GI JOES** (*see also* JOE).

GI bride A woman of non-US nationality who marries a US serviceman while he is on a foreign tour of duty. During World War II about 80,000 British women became GI brides and emigrated to America after the war.

GI Jane Nickname given in the 1980s to US army servicewomen who were eligible for all army roles except front-line combat ('jane' is US slang for a woman).

Gibson Girl A type of elegant female beauty characteristic of the turn-of-the-century period depicted by Charles Dana Gibson (1867–1944) in several series of black-and-white drawings beginning in 1896. His delineations of the ideal girl enjoyed an enormous vogue and the series entitled *The Adventures of Mr. Pipp*, which appeared in *Collier's Weekly* (1899), formed the basis of a successful play. The Gibson

Girl was portrayed in various poses and occupations, her individuality accentuated by the sweeping skirts and large hats of the period. She was based on Gibson's wife Irene (neé Langhorne) and her sisters, among whom was Nancy, Viscountess Astor. *See also* GAIETY GIRL.

gig (1) Slang for a musical performance, particularly of rock music. Originally used by US JAZZ musicians in the 1930s, the term was adopted by the rock musicians of the 1960s. Its origin is unknown.

> The gigs became almost a secondary thing to getting to the nearest jam, just getting together with whoever was in town and playing for the pure love of it.
>
> JIM CAPALDI, *The Independent*, 17 January 1991.

(2) A slang word for any event of interest. This is an extension of the first meaning and was part of the HIPPIE jargon of the 1960s and 1970s. It now sounds very dated. 'That's not my gig' means I'm not interested in that.

giggle. gigglestick (1) Slang for a joint, a marijuana cigarette. This name reflects a typical effect of such a cigarette and was used by middle-class drug users (rather than heavy drug abusers) in the 1970s. (2) Rhyming slang for prick, penis. It is also a pun on the swizzlestick used to stir GIGGLEWATER.

gigglewater Slang for champagne or sometimes alcoholic spirits, so called because of the effect it can have. *See also* ELECTRIC SOUP.

gigo *See* GARBAGE IN, GARBAGE OUT.

gimmick The first use of this word in US slang was to describe some device by which a conjurer or fairground showman worked his trick. In later usage it applied to some distinctive quirk or trick associated with a film or radio star. Its meaning has now extended to include anything designed to attract attention, publicity, or trade. Its origin is unknown.

ginger British rhyming slang for a male homosexual, from gingerbeer, a queer. This expression dates from the 1930s and is now rarely heard.

Giovinezza, La The official anthem of Italy's Fascist Party. It was written by Giuseppe Blanc in 1909 and originally entitled *Commiato* (Farewell), in which form it was adopted by Turin University. In 1926 Blanc reissued the song with words by Salvatore Gotta, under the title *Giovinezza*. This followed a legal battle to stop the circulation of a plagiarized version of his original, published in 1918 by Marcello Manni.

Gipper Nickname for the US footballer George Gipp and also for Ronald Reagan. *See* GREAT COMMUNICATOR.

Gipsy Moth IV The 53-ft yacht in which Sir Francis Chichester (1901–72) made his solo voyage around the world in 1966–67. Chichester took the name of his boats from the Gipsy Moth biplane in which he made a solo flight from the UK to Australia in 1929. The yacht was designed specially for fast solo ocean racing. Both the yacht and her owner featured on a commemorative 1s 9d stamp issued in August 1967, the first British stamp to celebrate a living person other than the sovereign.

girl. girlcott A feminist reworking of 'boycott', which was used seriously as well as humorously in the 1980s to mean a ban, agreed among a number of girls or women, on something.

Girl Guides The feminine counterpart to BOY SCOUTS, organized in 1910 by General Baden-Powell and his sister Miss Agnes Baden-Powell. Their training and organization is essentially the same as the Scouts and is based on similar promises and laws. The three sections of the movement were called Brownies, Guides, and Rangers, but the names and groupings have now been modified to Brownie Guides (7–11 years); Guides (10–16 years); Ranger Guides (14–19 years). *See also* QUEEN'S GUIDE.

In America, where they were formed in 1921, they are called **Girl Scouts.**

Girl in the Red Velvet Swing The nickname of Evelyn Nesbit (1885–1967), a US dancer, GIBSON GIRL, and actress. A notorious beauty, she married an excitable industrialist, Harry K. Thaw, who accused Stanford White (1853–1906), a partner in the largest and most prestigious firm of US architects, McKim, Mead, and White, of having an affair with his wife. The argument flared into one of the most widely discussed dramas of 1906, when Thaw shot and killed White. The 1955 film, *The Girl in the Red Velvet Swing*, featuring Joan Collins as Miss Nesbit, was described by one critic as "a longwinded piece of lush sensationalism".

what's a nice girl like you doing in a place like this? A cliché now so overused as a chat-up line that no-one would seriously think of using it except as a joke. It is similar, in that sense, to 'Do you come here often?' Both were well-used lines in films by the 1950s and probably originated in Hollywood in the 1930s.

giro A system for transferring money to people who do not have bank accounts; it originated in Austria in 1883. The word derives ultimately from Greek *guros*, circuit. In 1968 the British Post Office set up the National Girobank, now called **Girobank plc**. This organization is used by the Department of Social Security to pay unemployment or family support benefits. For this reason a payment of these benefits is often known as a giro. Being **on the giro** means being on the dole (receiving unemployment benefit).

The **Bank Giro** is a giro system used by banks in the UK to enable customers to make payment from their accounts to anyone, whether or not they have a bank account. This is independent of Girobank.

gismo or **gizmo** Slang for a thing, object, mechanical item, often used when the correct name has been temporarily forgotten. Originally a US forces word, it has been used in the UK since the 1960s.

give. Give 'em Hell Harry One of the many names by which President Harry S. Truman (1884–1972) was known. He was also called **High-Tax Harry**. Truman goes down in history as the man who ordered the first atomic weapon to be used in war and the man who, lacking a second name, assumed the initial S (which doesn't stand for anything). He earned the epithet **Give 'em Hell Harry** during his campaign for re-election, when he told his running mate, Alben Barkly, "I'm going to fight hard. I'm going to give 'em hell". He served a second term!

give head US vulgar slang of the 1950s and 1960s meaning to perform fellatio. It can also mean to copulate (of a male) and has occasionally been used of cunnilingus.

gi'z a job, I could do that A catchphrase taken from the 1982 TV series *The Boys from the Blackstuff* by Alan Bleasdale. The line was spoken by the character Yosser Hughes in his search for a job in Liverpool, an area of high unemployment; it gained popularity nationwide as a catchphrase at a time when unemployment was rising.

glad pad US slang for a dance hall, bar, etc., used in the 1940s.

glam Greying, Leisured, Affluent, Married. One of many voguish acronyms popular in the 1980s, coined by analogy with YUPPIE. Glams were held to be the most important socio-economic group as a result of their economic stability and spending power. *See also* EMPTY NEST.

glam rock A genre of popular music of the 1970s. Performers of glam rock, who wore colourful – even sequined – clothes and PLATFORM SOLES, included Marc Bolan, David Bowie, Gary Glitter, and Alvin Stardust.

Glasgow kiss British slang for a headbutt. Glasgow has a reputation for being a violent place. Another euphemism for a headbutt is a **Gorbals kiss**, the Gorbals being reputedly the most violent part of Glasgow (largely rebuilt in the 1980s).

glasnost (Russ. openness) Mikhail Gorbachev became General Secretary of the Soviet Communist party in 1985 and in 1986 he introduced a policy of *glasnost* (in conjunction with PERESTROIKA) relaxing repression on human rights, but within the framework of socialism. The intention is to give more freedom in social and cultural affairs. The adoption of *glasnost* and *perestroika* policies stimulated nationalism in satellite states of the Soviet Union and ultimately threatened Gorbachev's political standing.

> Mr Gorbachev has said Moscow no longer claims a monopoly on the right path to Communism but he has been at pains to stress the international benefits of a bit of *glasnost*.
>
> *Sunday Telegraph* (17 July 1988).

glass shot A device used by film makers in their fabrication of dream worlds. It consists of a glass slide on which part of a background, such as a town, castle, seascape, etc., is painted; it is held in front of the camera in such a way that it blends with the action. A glass shot can save enormous amounts of money.

GLC Greater London Council. Part of the two-tier administrative structure devised in 1963 to govern London – the GLC (replacing the London County Council) formed one tier, while the 32 London borough councils formed the second tier. The GLC, however, was abolished in 1986 by the Conservative government (together with the six metropolitan county authorities) as promised in their 1983 election manifesto. The GLC's London-wide responsibilities for strategic planning, transport, housing, and other services were transferred back to the local borough councils, in an attempt to control local authority spending and rate increases. The abolition went ahead despite a popular campaign within the capital, mounted by the leader of the GLC, Ken Livingstone (*see* RED KEN).

The building in which the GLC was housed (known as COUNTY HALL) was designed by Ralph Knott on a prestigious site on the SOUTH BANK of the river immediately to the E of Westminster Bridge. The main building was available for the London County Council in 1933 but the whole structure was not completed until 1963, when it became the home of the GLC. Since the abolition of the GLC the building has remained unused, plans for a hotel in part of it proving unworkable.

Gleichschaltung (Ger. co-ordination) The NAZI policy of integrating all aspects of German social economic life into their movement. For example, all trade unions were merged into a single body, the German Labour Front (*Deutsche Arbeitsfront*) in 1933. Various other fronts were created as part of this policy, including a German Milk Front and German Shoe Front.

glide path The line of an aircraft's descent to land. Few aircraft actually glide on their final approach to land, as it is safer to fly under power, which allows greater control over the aircraft. The pilot can assess whether he is flying on the correct glide path using simple radio beacons, checked against the aircraft altitude, or more elaborate instruments, such as the Instrument Landing System (ILS) using a pair of radio beams arranged across the glide path to register deviations on the cockpit ILS indicator. The ILS is essential when landing by instruments only. In modern aircraft the ILS is being replaced by an even more accurate system, the Microwave Landing System (MLS).

glitch Slang for a technical hitch, a mechanical problem, especially with a computer. A technical term of the late 1960s from the aerospace industry, it probably derived from a Yiddish word based on the German *glitschen*, to slip. It also has obvious echoes of the word 'hitch'. In New York Yiddish, a glitch is a risky undertaking or a shady deal.

glitter. glitterati A word coined in the 1980s by analogy with *literati*, a collective word for writers, scholars, and people interested in literature. 'Glitterati' is often used derogatorily to denote famous or fashionable people; the *glitter* part of the word suggesting that their fame and glamour are flashy and superficial.

glitter rock *See* GLAM ROCK.

glitz Slang for showbiz-style glamour, tacky sophistication. It is a combination of 'glamour' and 'ritzy'. A word much used by journalists in the 1980s to describe the style aspired to by aficionados of the US TV soap *Dallas*. The sound of the word itself reflects the hard-edged superficiality implied.

globe. global product A product or service marketed throughout the world with the same brand name. COCA-COLA and MCDONALD'S are typical examples. This practice is clearly an advantage from the point of view of advertising, although it cannot be used for all products. For example the Vauxhall Nova sold well in most European countries except Spain. The reason, it was discovered, is that in Spanish *nova* means 'no-go'.

global village A term coined by the Canadian writer, Marshall McLuhan (1911–81), in the late 1960s to denote the world looked upon as a relatively small community within which modern communication technology makes it possible for information of all kinds to be transmitted rapidly and easily. Air travel has also made most parts of the world accessible.

global warming *See* GREENHOUSE EFFECT.

globocrat A high-ranking official of an international organization, such as the World Health Organization or the United Nations. The term is especially applied to someone who travels the world in the course of his or her job; it is a blend of 'global' and 'bureaucrat'. *See also* EUROCRAT.

Gloster Meteor The first jet fighter to enter service with the RAF, in July 1944, and the only operational jet among Allied forces during World War II. Manufactured by the Gloster Aircraft Co., the twin-engined Meteor made its maiden flight on 5 March 1943. The Meteor F-3 was the mainstay RAF fighter in the late 1940s, followed by the Meteor F-8, introduced in 1950. Other variants included the T-7 trainer and the Armstrong-Whitworth Meteor night fighter. A world record speed of 975.67 k.p.h. (606.38 m.p.h.) was set by Group Captain H. J. Wilson piloting a Meteor F-4 in November 1945.

glue sniffing The practice, indulged in by young people in the 1970s, of inhaling the fumes from synthetic adhesives, cleaning fluids, aerosols, etc., to produce hallucinatory or other intoxicating effects. It is extremely dangerous because of the side effects caused. The more formal name is **solvent abuse**.

Glyndebourne The country estate near Lewes, in Sussex, in which John Christie (1882–1962) opened the Glyndebourne Festival Theatre in 1934 for operatic and musical performances, which became an annual event. Glyndebourne opera remains a centre of operatic excellence, attracting world-class singers during its summer seasons. Christie founded it for his wife, the opera singer Audrey Mildmay (1900–53).

GMT *See* GREENWICH MEAN TIME.

gnarly or **narly** (1) US slang for something wonderful. (2) US slang meaning the exact opposite, *i.e.* awful. In this sense it has also been used in the UK.

Gnomes of Zürich An uncomplimentary name given to those financiers of Zürich controlling international monetary funds. The phrase became popular after its use in November 1964 by George Brown (then the Labour Minister of Economic Affairs) at the time of a sterling crisis.

> What most infuriated George Brown, and Labour MPs such as John Mendelson and Ian Mikardo...was that the men they disparaged as the "gnomes of Zürich" were really giants.
>
> T. R. FEHRENBACH: *The Gnomes of Zurich.*

go. go down (1) US slang for to happen, from Black street jargon that has been widely used since the late 1960s. 'What's going down, man?' means 'What's happening?'. (2) Slang meaning to be sent to prison. 'Will he go down for that?' means 'Will he be sent to prison?'. This meaning is probably derived from the descent from the dock in the court room to the cells below.

go down on To perform fellatio or cunnilingus on.

go for it! An exhortation that became popular in the 1980s in everyday speech, first in America and then in the UK. President Reagan used it in "America, go for it!" in 1985 on tax reform; British Airways used it in "Go for it America", an advertising slogan in 1986 to entice more Americans to visit Europe.

go-go Relating to a lively style of music and dancing associated with DISCOS or nightclubs in the 1960s. A **go-go dancer** is a young man or woman employed to dance at such establishments. The term 'go-go' has been extended to describe anything lively, energetic, up-to-date, enterprising, or otherwise admirable. For example, 'go-go funds' are unit trusts or other investments expected to give high financial returns.

go-kart A small one-man racing vehicle propelled by a light engine. In the late middle ages a *go-cart* was a device for training toddlers to walk, which at the same time combined some of the features of a playpen. They were introduced into England in the early 17th century. They consisted of a small framework on wheels or rollers splayed out at the base so that they could not be overturned. The top was usually in the form of a tray for containing toys with a circular opening in which the child could stand upright, and be held secure at waist height. Similar devices sold under a variety of tradenames, have also been available in the 20th century.

go, man, go! A catchphrase originating in US JAZZ clubs of the 1940s and used by the audience as an exhortation to musicians. As far back as the jazz band era of the 1920s and 1930s, to 'go' meant to 'really swing', but the catchphrase 'go, man, go' is associated more with the driving rhythms of BEBOP jazz, introduced in the 1940s. It has been borrowed or adapted by many songwriters and others, including Carl Perkins in his 1956 rock and roll standard, *Blue Suede Shoes*:

> Well it's one for the money, two for the show, three to get ready, now go cat go! But don't you step on my blue suede shoes.

Perhaps the most famous adaptation of the phrase is "Go, baby, go!" first used by the excited US broadcaster Walter Cronkite, at the launch of the rocket Apollo XI in 1969. Thereafter, it became a stock phrase at such events.

go, no go A phrase originating in US astronautical jargon of the 1970s to denote the last stage of a space project at which the decision can be made to proceed with it or abort it. The expression later spread into the more general language meaning the point in any project or situation just before one commits oneself irrevocably to proceeding with it.

go slow The deliberate slowing down of work or production by employees engaged in an industrial dispute. In Canada and America the term is **slowdown**. *See also* INDUSTRIAL ACTION.

go the full distance Police and criminal underworld euphemism for to be arrested, tried, and sent to prison. The expression comes from boxing jargon, meaning to fight to the end of the contest.

go to it! A British wartime slogan, dating from 1940, exhorting people to offer themselves as a voluntary labour force in a time of need.

when the going gets tough, the tough get going A slogan said to have been coined, or first used, by Joseph P. Kennedy (1888–1969), the father of President John F. Kennedy. It is an exhortation to act aggressively. It was used as a slogan for the film *The Jewel of the Nile* in 1985; a hit song sung by the stars of the film (with Billy Ocean) followed in 1986.

goalpost. move the goalposts A colloquial expression derived from football, meaning to change the conditions or rules attaching to some activity after it has already started. The implication is that to do so involves an attempt to gain some dishonest or unfair advantage.

goat hair US slang for bootleg liquor.

gobble. gobbledygook A term coined in 1944 by a US congressman, Maury Maverick, to denote the kind of long-winded, jargonistic, and virtually unintelligible language frequently used by bureaucrats and others instead of plain English. The word has its origins in the behaviour of turkeys, who strut about and *gobble*.

gobbling rods Army slang of the GULF WAR of 1991 for a soldier's knife, fork, and spoon.

gobsmacked British slang for dumbstruck, or completely amazed, gaping in disbelief. Originally a Liverpudlian expression (where 'gob' means mouth), it was taken up more widely in the late 1980s. In 1991 it was used by Chris Patten, the chairman of the Conservative Party, when told of a Labour Party comment on the Health Service. Its use by a senior member of the government provoked much press comment.

god. godfather The head of a MAFIA family, also called a **don** (ultimately from the Latin *dominus*, Lord). The name was popularized by the best-selling novel *The Godfather* (1969) by Mario Puzo, which was later (1972) made into a popular film, which had several sequels. The word has since been applied to the head of any criminal organization and, further, to any autocratic leader.

godfather offer An offer made in a takeover bid for a company that is so high that, in spite of discouragement by the management of the target company, shareholders cannot resist accepting it.

Godslot A regular period of time set aside in radio or TV schedules for a religious programme. *See also* FAMILY HOUR.

God squad British slang originating in the 1950s for zealous members of religious organizations, especially those that do house-to-house visits attempting to convert people.

Gödel's proof A proof in mathematical logic that a formal system of reasoning based on axioms, such as arithmetic, always contains statements that can neither be proved nor disproved. It was shown to be true in 1931 by the US mathematician Kurt Gödel (1906–78) and is known as **Gödel's first incompleteness theorem**. A further theorem, **Gödel's second incompleteness theorem**, states that it is impossible to prove the self-consistency of any formal logical system by using the formalization of the system itself. Gödel's proof effectively ended attempts by mathematicians to develop the whole of pure mathematics from a few basic logical axioms.

Godzilla A mythical Japanese prehistoric monster brought back to life by H-bomb tests. Clearly based on a man concealed in a rubber suit, Godzilla has featured in a large number of frankly inferior Japanese films, ranging from a rather horrific debut in *Godzilla* (1954) to what one may hope will be a permanent disappearance in *Space Godzilla* (1979).

gofer Slang for a messenger or a junior assistant. Someone whose job it is to 'go for' this and 'go for' that. It is also a pun on the small North American burrowing rodent, the gopher. The term originated in the US film industry but is now used in all English-speaking countries.

gogglebox British slang for a TV set. Coined in the 1950s, it was used pejoratively at first, 'goggle' implying mindless watching. It is now used quite neutrally.

Golan Heights A hilly area on the border between Syria and Israel, designated as a demilitarized buffer zone between the two countries in 1949; it was bitterly contested in subsequent Arab-Israeli conflicts (1956, 1967, and 1973). During the 1950s and 1960s Israeli settlements spread eastwards through the territory, which provoked constant armed clashes with Syria. In the 1967 War, over 100,000 Syrians fled when the Israeli army stormed the Heights. The Syrians succeeded in regaining some of the territory during the October 1973 War, with the remaining territory designated as a UN buffer zone by the Separation of Forces agreement of May 1974. However, this territory was annexed by Israel in 1982, in contravention of UN Resolution 242. Some commentators think that while Israel remains in occupation of the area, a lasting Middle East peace settlement will be difficult to conclude. However, from the Israeli point of view, it would be both tactically and strategically dangerous if the Syrians were allowed to occupy the high ground again as before 1967 Syrian artillery made great use of the region to bombard the upper Jordan and Hula valleys.

Gold Allied codename given to a beach NW of Bayeux, which was one of the landing sites for British and Canadian forces on D DAY. *See also* JUNO; OMAHA; SWORD; UTAH.

gold-bricking In World War II, a synonym for idling, shirking, or getting a comrade to do one's job. It was derived form *gold brick*, a US phrase descriptive of any form of swindling. It originated in the gold-rush days when a cheat would sell his dupe an alleged (or even a real) gold brick, in the latter case substituting a sham one before making his get-away.

gold card A credit card that confers on those who hold it certain advantages and privileges not available to those in possession of ordinary credit cards. These privileges include generous overdraft facilities, but not advantageous rates of interest. The credit card companies are therefore likely to be the greatest beneficiaries from gold cards, because they are only awarded to those who have high regular incomes. For this reason the gold card has come to have a great snob value. In view of the cachet attached to it, the use of the term has extended beyond the credit card and became associated, for example, with travel facilities, sales offers, etc., when these are held to be of a superior nature.

Golden Arrow A fast train service between London and Paris. It ran from Victoria in London and – across the Channel – was known as the **Flêche d'Or**. It ceased to run in the late 1960s, by which time most of the traffic between the two capitals was carried by air. It could be that the advent of the CHANNEL TUNNEL will again make a fast train service attractive.

Golden Foghorn Nickname of Ethel Merman (1908–84), US entertainer with star quality, known for her ability to be heard in the next block. Her autobiography, *Who Could Ask for Anything More?* (1955), was titled *Don't Call Me Madam* in the UK, a reference to the 1953 film *Call Me Madam*, in which she played a Washington hostess who became US ambassador to Lichtenberg.

Golden Gate Bridge The suspension bridge, opened in 1937, that spans the Golden Gate waterway in San Francisco, California. The centre span stretches for 1280 m (4200 ft), for many years one of the world's longest single spans. Its orange-red towers and graceful lines have become a much-admired symbol of the city it serves. The bridge was designed to withstand 160 k.p.h. (100 m.p.h.) wind gusts, and swing up to 8.2 m (27 ft). The midway point, 79.2 m (260 ft) above water, is a favourite spot for suicides.

golden handcuffs A large financial incentive paid to an employee, especially by a stockbroker, market maker, investment trust, etc., to persuade him or her not to be attracted away by an offer from a competitor. *See also* GOLDEN HELLO.

golden handshake A phrase applied to the often considerable terminal payments made to individuals, especially business executives, whose services are prematurely dispensed with. It has also been applied to the final grants made to colonial dependencies on attaining their independence. The phrase was coined by Frederick Ellis (d. 1979), City Editor of the *Daily Express*:

> This year promises to be an expensive one for the British taxpayer in "golden handshakes".
>
> *The Times* (4 June 1964).

golden hello A large financial incentive paid to a new employee, especially by a stockbroker, market maker, investment trust, etc., to attract him or her from a competitor. *See also* GOLDEN HANDCUFFS.

Golden Miller One of the most famous steeplechasers in the history of British racing, renowned for winning both the Cheltenham Gold Cup and the Aintree Grand National in the same year (1934). Owned by the Honourable Dorothy Paget, the gelding accumulated an impressive tally of results, including five consecutive wins in the Cheltenham Gold Cup (1932–36). He was ridden to his Aintree victory by Gerry Wilson, in record time.

golden oldie A pop-music name, coined in the 1960s, for an old record, song, or piece of music that is either still popular or has been revived. Older people, particularly those who join in the pursuits of the young, are themselves sometimes facetiously called 'golden oldies'.

golden palm *See* PALME D'OR.

golden parachute A clause written into a contract of employment of a director or senior executive of a company that provides for large financial benefits if the executive is sacked or decides to leave as a result of a change in the ownership of the company.

Golden Rose The premier award of the annual competition for television light entertainment programmes held in Montreux, Switzerland. It is organized by the Swiss Broadcasting Corporation in conjunction with the European Broadcasting Union and the City of Montreux. Besides the Golden Rose, a Silver Rose and a Bronze Rose are awarded to the second- and third-placed entrants. Past British winners include *Frost Over England* (BBC, 1967); *Marty: The Best of the Comedy Machine* (ATV, 1972); *The Muppet Show* (ATV, 1977); *Dizzy Feet* (Central, 1982); *The Paul Daniels Magic Show* (BBC, 1985); and *Nigel Kennedy: Four Seasons* (Zenith North and Picture Music International, 1990).

Golden Triangle A roughly triangular area of SE Asia comprising parts of China, Burma, Thailand, and Laos where opium poppies are grown. It is the source of most of the world's raw opium.

Goldfine affair A US political scandal of 1958 in which a presidential assistant in the Eisenhower administration, Sherman Adams, allegedly exerted political influence in favour of his friend, the Boston industrialist Bernard Goldfine. Adams admitted receiving gifts from Goldfine, but denied putting pressure on federal agencies investigating Goldfine's affairs. In the face of mounting pressure, both from his own Republican Party and from the Democrats, Adams resigned in September. The scandal was a contributory factor in the Democrats' landslide victory in the national and state elections held two months later.

Goldfinger The eponymous villain of the 1959 thriller by British writer Ian Fleming. Goldfinger is a gold smuggler and banker for the dreaded criminal organization SMERSH, but his plan to rob America's FORT KNOX of its gold is thwarted by British agent James BOND, 007. In the 1964 film, Goldfinger was played by the German actor, Gert Frobe, in one of the more convincing screen impersonations of Fleming's villains.

Goldfish Club A notional 'club' for RAF pilots who were forced down in the sea during World War II. The **Goldfish Gang** was naval slang of the same period for the Fleet Air Arm.

Goldie A golden eagle that captured British newspaper headlines in 1965 after it escaped from London Zoo. The seven-year old eagle spent nearly two weeks in the trees of Regent's Park, attracting many sightseers, before he was finally recaptured.

Gold Standard A currency system based upon keeping the monetary unit at the value of a fixed weight of gold. Great Britain adopted the Gold Standard from 1821 but suspended gold payments in 1914, returned to the Gold Standard in 1925, and abandoned it in 1931 during the slump (*see* GREAT DEPRESSION). Most countries of the world were on the Gold Standard from 1894 to 1914. Gold became the monetary standard of America by the Coinage Act of 1873 but the Gold Standard was abandoned in 1933.

Goldwater caper The phrase coined to describe the 1964 US presidential election campaign of Barry Goldwater, the Republican candidate. Goldwater's extremist right-wing platform was aimed at conservative voters in the South and Mid-West and alienated traditionally more liberal Republicans in the northern industrial centres. Goldwater was heavily defeated by Lyndon B. Johnson, split his own party, and came to be regarded by Republicans as an unmitigated disaster.

the golden eagle lays its eggs British slang, dating from World War II and meaning 'it's pay day'. It derives from US forces slang for payday, current before and during the same war: 'the day the eagle shits' or 'the day the eagle screams'. This alludes to the eagle emblem appearing on banknotes and coins, and also the eagle symbolizing the serviceman's employer, *i.e.* the US government. Payday was also known simply as 'eagle day'. British forces adapted the phrase, substituting the native species of bird.

Goldwynisms Malapropisms coined by Samuel Goldwyn (1882–1974), the US film producer, who emigrated from Poland in 1895. Originally calling himself Sam Goldfish (his Polish name was unpronounceable), he obtained his first job in America as an apprentice glovemaker. By 1924 his own film production company had merged with others to form Hollywood's legendary **MGM** (Metro-Goldwyn-

Mayer). A non-native English speaker, he made eccentric use of his second language, perhaps not quite as naively as he pretended. "Gentlemen, kindly include me out", "Anyone who goes to a psychiatrist should have his head examined", "A verbal contract isn't worth the paper it's written on", "We have all passed a lot of water since then", "In two words IMPOSSIBLE", and "Directors are always biting the hand that lays the golden egg" are some of the fractured idioms attributed to him. An intuitive salesman, he insisted that films should be acceptable to the whole family:

> Motion pictures should never embarrass a man when he brings his wife to the theatre.

and

> I seriously object to seeing on the screen what belongs in the bedroom.

These were not the utterances of a prude but of someone who understood how to fill cinemas. Goldwyn appears to have been a mixture of shrewdness and absurdity. For example, he had been told that Radclyffe Hall's *The Well of Loneliness* was a controversial novel that would make a good film; he gave instructions that he wanted to buy the film rights. "But you can't make that into a film", said his rights man, "It's about lesbians". "That's not a problem ", replied Goldwyn. "Where he's got lesbians we'll use Austrians". Goldwyn's showmanship was legendary:

> What we want is a story that starts with an earthquake and works its way up to a climax . . .

Was it subtlety or absurdity when he told the assembled press at the release of *The Best Years Of Our Lives* (1946):

> I don't care if it doesn't make a nickel, I just want every man, woman, and child in America to see it.

Lindsay Anderson said of him in 1974:

> Goldwyn is blessed with that divine confidence in the rightness (moral, aesthetic, commercial) of his own intuition – and that I suppose is the chief reason for his success.

gollum Slang from the jargon associated with the game of FRISBEE that means a wild throw, *i.e.* one that is difficult to catch. Gollum is a rather troublesome character in J. R. R. Tolkein's books *The Hobbit* and *The Lord of the Rings*. *See* HOBBIT; LORD OF THE RINGS; MIDDLE-EARTH.

Gondwanaland *See* PANGAEA.

gone Slang for being in a euphoric or exhilarated state induced by drugs or alcohol; drunk or stoned. Used in the 1940s, it was later part of BEATNIK and HIPPIE jargon.

gone to Lyonch An advertising slogan used by the catering firm J. Lyons & Co. A combination of 'gone to lunch' and 'Lyons', it was a catchphrase of the 1930s.

gone with the wind A phrase, meaning vanished without trace, that first appeared in a poem by Ernest Dowson (1867–1900), one of the Decadent English poets of the 1890s. Falling hopelessly in love with a 12-year-old Polish girl, Adelaide Foltinowicz, a waitress in her parents' Soho restaurant, he indulged in a fairly rumbustious round of wine and women after she had turned him down. She inspired his best-known poem, 'Num Sum Qualis Eram', better known as 'Cynara', which contains two famous lines:

> I have forgot much, Cynara! Gone with the wind.

and

> I have been faithful to thee, Cynara, in my fashion.

The latter has entered the language as a cynical joke, while the former blossomed into quite another sort of fame with the publication of Margaret Mitchell's epic *Gone With the Wind* in 1936. America's most widely read novel, it is a romance of the Civil War, set in Georgia. The book is so well known in America that its chief characters, Scarlett O'HARA, Rhett Butler, and Ashley Wilkes, have entered US folklore. MGM's film (1939) of the same name starring Vivien Leigh, Clark Gable, and Leslie Howard, was – and still remains – one of Hollywood's greatest money makers, in spite of Irving Thalberg's remark to his partner Louis B. Mayer:

> Forget it, Louis, no Civil War picture ever made a nickel.

gong. to be gonged To be signalled to stop by motorized police for some breach of the traffic laws. A colloquial usage from the loud electric bell formerly used to attract the offender's attention.

gonk British slang for a stupid person. A contemptuous term used in the 1960s, when Gonk was a tradename for a fat ugly egg-shaped doll, which was something of a fad at the time. 'Gonk' is army slang for sleep, from 'conk out', to fall asleep.

gonov (From Hebrew *ganov*, thief) A Yiddish word for a crook, especially a business man who is dishonest, or one who overcharges. It was used in the UK as an underworld word for a thief or pickpocket in the 19th century, even by Dickens, but has become widely used in New York during this century for any kind of dishonest person.

gonzo US slang for wild, eccentric, or bizzare. The word comes from the Italian meaning simpleton. It first appeared in English in the phrase **gonzo journalism** in a book by Hunter S. Thomson called *Fear and Loathing in Las Vegas* (1972) and was popularized as the name of a strange character in the TV puppet series *The* MUPPETS.

good. a good time was had by all A phrase widely employed in a literal or ironic sense during the 20th century and used by the poet Stevie Smith (1902–71) as the title of her first anthology of verse, published in 1937.

good field, no hit A baseball phrase meaning a player who is a good fielder but no good at batting. It derives from a telegram sent in 1924 by a baseball coach, Miguel Gonzales, describing the Brooklyn Dodgers' player Moe Berg in these words. It was subsequently used for anyone proficient in one area but inexpert in another.

good for General Motors A widely heard misquotation that usually takes the form, 'What's good for General Motors is good for America', an ironic reference to the influence of big businees on US political thought. In fact, what a US engineer, Charles E. Wilson (1890–1961), said in testimony before a Senate Armed Services Committee in January 1953, was:

> For many years I thought what was good for our country was good for General Motors, and vice versa.

good neighbour policy A US policy intended to allay fears of South American countries in the 1930s that America was bent on domination of the whole American continent. Its measures – withdrawal of forces, removal of trade barriers, and a common defence policy – were foreshadowed by President Franklin D. Roosevelt in 1933 in his first inaugural address:

> In the field of world policy; I would dedicate this nation to the policy of the good neighbor.

Good News Bible A new translation of the Bible published by the American Bible Society in 1976. The 'Good News' is from the word *gospel*, which comes from Old English *godspell*, from *god* meaning 'good' and *spell* meaning 'message'.

good night, children everywhere The catchphrase of Uncle Mac (Derek McCulloch) on the BBC radio programme *Children's Hour* during World War II. It was meant to include all the children who had been evacuated to the safety of the country. J. B. Priestley wrote a play with this title during the war, and Vera Lynn recorded a song with the same title in 1939.

Goodtime George George Melly (1926–), British JAZZ singer and writer. An expansive bon viveur usually seen in a broad-brimmed black trilby, Melly has made it clear that his omnivorous appetites, gastronomical, alcoholic, and sexual, know no bounds. He sings John Chilton's song, 'Goodtime George', with evident relish.

good to the last drop *See under* DROP.

if you can't be good, be careful! A catchphrase with sexual innuendos used as a valediction. It is heard mostly in the UK but is also used in America. It frequently has a little bit tagged on the end, such as 'if you can't be careful, have fun', or 'name it after me'.

you've never had it so good A phrase used by the prime minister Harold Macmillan (later 1st Earl of Stockton; 1894–1986) in a speech at Bedford, 20 July 1957. He said it as a warning that such prosperity would be difficult to maintain but it was taken out of context and used to damn him as a complacent man interested only in material comforts. As 'you never had it so good' the phrase was already well known in America; it was used by the Democrats in the presidential election of 1952.

goof (1) A stupid mistake or to make a stupid mistake. (2) A foolish person. (3) To **goof around** is to mess about. In all senses the word probably derives from the Old French *goffe*, clumsy.

gook US slang for a North Vietnamese, derived from the Filipino word *gugu* (spirit), heard during the VIETNAM WAR. *See also* DINK.

goon (1) Slang for a stupid person, or someone who plays the fool. A word that became popular in the 1950s in the UK with the rise to fame of the radio programme The GOON SHOW. The word itself derives partly from the English dialect word *gooney*, meaning fool, and partly from the name of the US cartoon character *Alice the Goon*, created by E. C. Segar (1894–1938). (2) US slang of the 1930s for a hired thug, usually of low intelligence, whose job it was to break up strikes or to intimidate people.

Goon Show An extremely popular British comedy radio show that was broadcast by the BBC from 1952 to 1960 with an extra show in 1972. It has been repeated frequently, having become something of a cult. The Goons were Peter Sellers, Harry Secombe, and Spike Milligan, and the early programmes also included Michael Bentine. The show consisted of a range of strange characters with peculiar voices involved in crazy little sequences that owed much to the music hall tradition. The programme gave rise to many catchphrases including: 'the dreaded lergy', 'it's all in the mind', and 'you dirty rotten swine, you'.

Goonhilly The downs on Cornwall's Lizard peninsula where the UK's first satellite earth station was opened in 1962. Now operated by British Telecom, the station's array of dish aerials transmits and receives telephone calls, facsimiles, television pictures, and other data to and from communications satellites in space. The plateau at Goonhilly was chosen to give a good 'view' of the early satellites, such as TELSTAR, and because of the firm foundation of bed rock underneath. It was the first European station to transmit colour TV signals and the first to transmit a live TV programme from Europe to America.

goose. Goose Green A settlement in the Falkland Islands, which in May 1982 was the scene of fierce fighting during the British assault on the Argentinian occupying forces. 17 British paratroopers, including their commanding officer, died there before victory was secured against the defenders, who outnumbered them three to one. The Argentinians lost 250 dead and 1200 were taken prisoner.

goose-step A military step in which the legs are moved from the hips, the knees being kept rigid, each leg being swung as high as possible. (It was introduced as a form of recruit drill in the British army but never became popular; it exists in a modified form in the slow march.) The goose-step (*Stechschritt*) was first introduced as a full-dress and processional march in the German army in the time of Frederick the Great. When the AXIS flourished it was adopted by the Italian army (*il passo romano*) but was soon ridiculed into desuetude. It continued to be used after World War II by armies of the EASTERN BLOC; East Germany dropped it shortly before the reunification of Germany in 1990.

Gorbals kiss *See* GLASGOW KISS.

Gorbymania or **Gorbasm** Public adulation of the Soviet leader Mikhail Gorbachov (1913– , president 1988–), especially in the West during his international visits in the late 1980s. His popularity was fostered by the Western press, which nicknamed him 'Gorby', and resulted from his policy of reform which brought the COLD WAR to an end. *See* GLASNOST; PERESTROIKA.

Gordon. Flash Gordon *See under* FLASH.

Gordon Bennett A mild expletive, equivalent to saying 'Oh God'; indeed 'Gawd and St Bennet' has been suggested as the derivation of the phrase. However, it seems more likely that the Gordon Bennett in question was an American, James Gordon Bennett (1841–1918), the editor-in-chief of the *New York Herald*, who was responsible for sending Henry Stanley to find David Livingstone in Africa (he was the son of the paper's founder who had the same name). The son also gave his name to a motor race held in France in the early 1900s, where he resided as a exile after a scandal in America. He lived in flamboyant style and is described in the *Dictionary of American Biography* as "one of the most picturesque figures of two continents". There is a street named Avenue Gordon-Bennett in Paris. Clearly this extrovert and extravagant man's name was well known; it is therefore not unlikely that the similarity in sound between 'Gordon' and 'Oh Gawd' became a convenient circumlocution in an age in which blasphemy, however mild, was socially unacceptable.

Gordonstoun School A UK public school founded in 1934 at Gordonstoun House on the Moray Firth near Elgin, Morayshire. Its founder was a refugee from NAZI Germany, educationalist Kurt Hahn (1886–1974), who regarded education as a process of all-round character development, with emphasis on exploring an individual's physical and spiritual resources as well as academic pursuits. As Gordonstoun's headmaster until his retirement in 1953, Hahn encouraged pupils to pit their wits against mountain, loch, and sea in the belief that "there is always more to us than we think". Hahn's ideas were inspirational to the OUTWARD BOUND TRUST, which started in 1945. Gordonstoun first admitted girls in 1972, and they now account for almost half the intake to the school, which has some 475 pupils in total. Fees are on a sliding scale according to parents' means – another of Hahn's principles – and the school offers a large number of scholarships and bursaries. Illustrious former pupils include the Duke of Edinburgh and the Prince of Wales.

gorilla Slang term for a sum of £1000. It was coined in the 1980s by analogy with 'monkey', racing slang for £500 dating from the 19th century – gorillas being larger than monkeys.

Gormenghast The title of a novel by Mervyn Peake (1911–68) published in 1950, the middle book of a trilogy, coming between *Titus Groan* (1946) and *Titus Alone* (1959). The trilogy is an elaborately detailed gothic fantasy, evoking an enclosed world peopled with fantastical characters, the central figure being Titus, 77th Earl of Groan, owner of Gormenghast castle. The books received relatively little critical notice or popular success until the 1960s and 1970s, when a vogue for lengthy fantasy works brought them considerable popular appeal, especially among students.

Gosplan Acronym for *Gosudarstvenny Planovyy Komitet*, the State Planning Committee of the Soviet Union, established in 1921. In 1927 it was given the job of formulating the first of the FIVE-YEAR PLANS for Soviet economic development. This was delivered in 1929, after Stalin had purged Gosplan of its more cautious members in order to obtain a more optimistic projection. The committee continued to function at the apex of the Soviet economic planning system, its strictures affecting all reaches of Soviet industry and its decisions being implemented through industry ministries.

gotcha! The jingoist headline in the earliest editions of the *Sun* newspaper of 4 May 1982, celebrating the sinking of the Argentine cruiser *General Belgrano* by the British submarine HMS *Conqueror* during the FALKLANDS CONFLICT. Of a crew of 1093, 323 were killed. On the same day, the Argentinians managed to destroy HMS *Sheffield*, which somewhat dampened the war fever of the British tabloid press.

goth British slang of the late 1980s for a young person, of either sex, belonging to a particular sub-cult identified by their taste for heavy rock music and black clothes. They also frequently dye their hair black. Both sexes wear large pieces of silver jewellery; the girls use cosmetics to make their faces very pale, their eyes very black, and their lips very dark. The word is a shortened form of 'Gothic' and reflects their gloomy melodramatic appearance.

Gotha Any of several German military aircraft of World War I built by Gothaer Waggonfabrik, notably the Gotha IV and V long-range bombers, which carried out daylight bombing raids on London in 1917. The Gotha G I, a twin-engined bomber originated by Oskar Ursinus, began production in 1915, but was succeeded by the more powerful G II and G III models in 1916. These carried a three-man crew, defensive guns fore and aft, and a payload of 14 10-kg bombs. The G IV, which appeared in 1917, had a fuselage with a wooden rather than a cloth skin, and a gallery along the fuselage connecting the rear gunner's position to the cockpit. On 25 May 1917 a squadron of 16 G IVs left Belgium for a bombing mission over London. As darkness fell they missed their target and instead released their bombs over Shornecliffe Camp in Essex, causing 100 casualties among Canadian troops stationed there. The first successful raid on London took place on 13 June 1917, when the Gothas' bombs killed 104 people in the vicinity of Liverpool Street Station. Successful air defences soon forced the Gothas to fly at night and, in the face of heavy losses, their raids ceased in May 1918.

gouch out British drug abusers' slang, meaning to mess up an injection or fix, by missing the vein.

government. government health warning A phrase used as a general warning, suggesting that the person, time, or activity concerned should be avoided. The phrase was used originally in 1971 in the UK on cigarette packets. "Danger. H. M. Government health department's warning: cigarettes can seriously damage your health". A similar notice had appeared on cigarette packets in America in 1965. Both were originally worded more mildly but the wording was later strengthened when the links between cancer and smoking became irrefutable.

government-inspected meat US slang used in homosexual circles for a soldier, sailor, or airman regarded as a sexual object.

goy (From Hebrew *goy*, people) A Yiddish word for a non-Jew, a gentile. It is often, but not always, used pejoratively. The plural is *goyim* and the related adjective is *goyisher*.

GPU *Gosudarstvennoye Politicheskoye Upravlenye* (State Political Administration). The Soviet state security organization, created out of the existing Bolshevik secret police, the CHEKA, in 1922. Its function was to identify 'counter-revolutionaries' and monitor their activities. It was renamed **OGPU** (*Obedinennoye Gosudarstvennoye Politicheskoye Upravlenye*; United State Political Administration) in 1924 and became absorbed into the newly formed NKVD in 1934. *See also* KGB.

grabby Describing something, especially a film, show, or other performance, that is striking and seizes (*i.e.* 'grabs') the attention of the audience. It is an extension of the sense of 'grabby' meaning grasping.

Graceland The two-storey mansion in Memphis, Tennessee, which was the home of singer Elvis Presley from 1957–1977. The house is now open to the public as a tourist attraction at $5 a head, and averages about 2500 visitors every day. The tour includes visits to the singer's living room, music room, TV room, pool room, trophy room, jungle den, and automobile collection. There is a myth that Elvis Presley is still alive and that his death was faked. Like most myths, there is no evidence to support it, yet sightings of the unfortunate singer continue to be reported by some of his more impressionable fans. In fact, there seems to be little doubt that a grossly overweight Presley died of heart failure brought on by drug dependence.

Graf. Graf Spee A German battlecruiser of the Mackensen class launched in 1917 but never completed for lack of resources. It was broken up in 1921–22. It should not be confused with the German battleship ADMIRAL GRAF SPEE, which saw action in World War II.

Graf Zeppelin One of the most famous airships of all time, the German LZ 127 Graf Zeppelin, launched at Friedrichshaven in 1928 (*see also* ZEPPELIN). This immense dirigible, 236.5 m (776 ft) long and roughly 30 m (100 ft) in diameter, was powered by five outboard engines and capable of cruising at 113 k.p.h. (70 m.p.h.) with a range of over 9650 km (6000 miles). Its maiden transatlantic crossing on 11 October 1928 was the first of 144 Atlantic crossings. The gondola suspended below the hydrogen-filled envelope contained accommodation for 20 passengers and included sleeping cabins, a lounge/dining room, and a galley. In 1929 the Graf made a round-the-world flight, travelling 31,000 miles in over 12 days, while in 1931 it was used for an aerial survey of the Arctic. During the 1930s passengers paid less than $1000 for the transatlantic round trip in the Graf, lured by the luxury and elegance of airship travel. The Graf was retired from service in 1937, and was stored in its hangar until 1940, when Goering ordered its destruction to provide valuable war materials. The name 'Graf Zeppelin' was also given to the LZ 130, an airship structurally identical to the ill-fated HINDENBURG and launched in 1938. This never saw regular service and was scrapped, with its more illustrious forebear, in 1940.

Grammy An award (a replica of a gold-plated gramophone record) presented annually by the US National Academy of Recording Arts and Sciences for particular achievement in the record industry.

Gran Chaco *See* CHACO WAR.

grand. Grand Design The title of a book, written by Joseph Kraft and published in 1962, that set out the Kennedy administration's view of a unified W Europe acting in economic and military alliance with America. This vision was rudely shaken by a speech made by de Gaulle early in 1963 when he made clear his anti-Americanism and his opposition to the UK's entry to the EEC.

Grand Prix (Fr. great prize) Name given to the various formula motor races in the annual season to decide the Driver's World Championship, usually applied to races for Formula One cars, the most powerful of several racing classes.

Grand Slam The nickname for the heaviest conventional bomb ever used, dropped by the RAF during World War II. Measuring 7.74 m in length and weighing 9975 kg (22,000 lb), Grand Slam was carried by a specially modified Lancaster bomber of RAF Bomber Command 617 Squadron on 14 March 1945 (*see* DAMBUSTERS). Dropped from about 3660 m (12,000 ft), it scored a direct hit on its target, the Bielefield Railway Viaduct, Germany.

grand unified theory (GUT) *See* UNIFIED-FIELD THEORY.

Grandma Moses Anna Mary Robertson Moses (1860–1961). A US primitive painter well known for her nostalgic depictions of rural life. Grandma Moses was born in Greenwich, New York State. From the age of 12 she worked on farms around her birthplace; in 1887 she married a dairy farmer and moved to Virginia. She began painting as a hobby, and after her husband's death in 1927, turned to embroidered pictures, although arthritis later restricted her to painting. Her talents were introduced to a wider audience thanks to New Yort art collector Louis Caldor, who noticed some of her works in a drugstore in Hoosick Falls, NY, in 1938. During the 1940s, by now well into her 80s, Moses painted some of her most memorable works, such as *Catching The Thanksgiving Turkey* and *Out For The Christmas Trees*. At 91 she began painting on ceramic tiles, a new medium for her, and her final paintings, *White Birches* and *Rainbow*, were done in her 101st year. She was regarded with great affection by fellow Americans; her 100th birthday, 7 September 1960, was proclaimed 'Grandma Moses Day' by New York's governor.

granite-wash A term used of cloth, especially blue denim, that has a pale streaking appearance. This effect is deliberately created to make articles made of the cloth look fashionably faded and worn, as though they had been washed against rough stones.

granny. granny bond A colloquial name for a British index-linked savings bond that was formerly only available to savers who were over retirement age.

granny farm A derogatory term for an old people's home, particularly one that charges very high rates but provides poor care and services. The term became popular in the second half of the 1980s when many unscrupulous people were taking advantage of the rapidly growing numbers of elderly people in need of care, especially those who could not be cared for by their families. 'Granny' was used because women tend to outlive men of the same age and represent a greater proportion of residents of old people's homes. *See also* EVENTIDE HOME; GRANNY FLAT.

granny flat A self-contained flat in, or built onto, a house that is suitable for an elderly parent. It often provides a successful arrangement, with the elderly parent achieving a measure of independence within easy reach of their relatives should help be required, at the same time being available for baby-sitting, etc.

Grantchester This village, of ancient origin, two miles south of Cambridge, has a fine old church with many interesting features but it owes its fame to its associations with Rupert Brooke (1887–1915), who lived at the Old Vicarage. An extremely romantic figure, whose World War I poetry made him a national hero, he died before seeing active service in the war (*see under* ENGLAND).

> But Grantchester! ah, Grantchester,
> There's peace and holy quiet there.
>
> RUPERT BROOKE: *The Old Vicarage, Grantchester.*

grape. Beulah, peel me a grape A catchphrase that is a quotation from the 1933 US film, *I'm No Angel*, starring Mae West. The line, delivered by Mae West to her Black maid with an air of detachment after her lover had left her, is intended to indicate her emotional self-sufficiency; it is often quoted for this reason.

grass (1) Slang for the dried leaves and flowers of the cannabis plant or hemp. *See also* HASH; POT. (2) In criminal slang, to inform, which may derive from rhyming slang 'grasshopper' for copper. A **supergrass** is one who informs on a number of his associates.

grasshopper US slang for a person who smokes grass (*i.e.* marijuana).

graveyard shift In World War II, the name given by shift workers in munitions factories, etc., to the shift covering the midnight hours.

gravlax or **gravadlax** Dry-cured marinated salmon, a Scandinavian delicacy that is now widely available. The name comes from the Norwegian *grav*, to bury in a grave (because it is left to ferment in the marinade), and *laks* (or Swedish *lax*), salmon. *See also* LOX.

gravy Slang for money, especially unexpected extra money obtained with little or no effort. *See also* GRAVY TRAIN.

gravy train A source of easy money that does not involve too much work. The expression is believed to have its origins in US railroad slang of the early 20th century, originally referring to an easy railroad run that required very little work on the part of the train's crew. *See also* GRAVY.

graze British slang from the late 1980s, meaning to consume snacks continuously, but in small quantities.

> I responded to an invitation to a 'light lunch' in a private house to find the excellent food – we grazed on the hoof as we talked – was served by a butler and three uniformed maids.
>
> MRS D. MAY, correspondent in *The Times* (28 December 1990).

grease (1) Slang for money. Originally from the early 20th century criminal underworld, it was revived by the BEATNIKS in the 1950s and early 1960s. Grease in this sense reflects the idea of a substance that makes things run more smoothly. (2) Slang meaning to bribe with money. Again it refers to something with which to oil the wheels, as in the expression 'to grease the palms'. (3) US slang from the 1970s meaning to kill, usually by shooting. This sense reflects the rather unpleasant idea of reducing someone to nothing more than a pile of blubber. 'Crease' has also been suggested as an alternative derivation. This is also a US euphemism meaning to kill, reflecting the idea of the victim crumpling up when shot.

greaser (1) British slang for a rocker (*see* MODS AND ROCKERS); a motorcycle rider who is usually dressed in greasy black leathers with greasy hair and a generally untidy appearance. This was the contemptuous term used by the mods of their enemies, the rockers, in the early 1960s. (2) US offensive slang for someone of Hispanic or Mediterranean descent. This is a reference to the oily complexion they are supposed to have. (3) US slang for a young thug; a reference to his leather jacket and slicked-back hair.

greasy spoon (1) Slang for a cheap café where most, if not all, of the food is fried in animal fat, making the atmosphere and the cutlery greasy. This expression originated in America in the 1930s but is now also widely used in the UK. (2) In America, a restaurant serving oily food, especially a SOUL FOOD restaurant.

great. Great Beast Nickname for the satanist Aleister Crowley (*see* BEAST 666).

Great Communicator Nickname for the US statesman Ronald Reagan (1911– ; president 1981–89); it originated with the skill he used on television to communicate with the US public. A former Hollywood film actor, Reagan was also known as **the Gipper** after a part he played in 1940 in the film *Knute Rockne – All American*. The film is based on the life of an American footballer, George Gipp (1895–1920), who played for Notre Dame and died of pneumonia at the height of his brilliant career. On his deathbed he told the team's coach, Knute Rockne:

> Someday, when things look real tough for Notre Dame, ask the boys to go out there and win one for the Gipper.

Rockne used Gipp's deathbed request in 1928 as an exhortation before the game with Army, which Notre Dame won 12–6. The next day the *New York Daily News* headlined its report with 'Gipp's Ghost Beats Army' and the phrase 'win one for the Gipper' entered the American language.

A less flattering epithet applied to Reagan was the **Great Rondini**, alluding to the US escape artist Harry Houdini and to Ron's talent for extricating himself from difficult political situations. In his autobiography, Reagan wrote that his family nickname was **Dutch,** from his father's comment after his birth:

> For such a little bit of a fat Dutchman, he makes a hell of a lot of noise . . .

Great Depression The world economic crisis of the period 1929–35, triggered by the collapse of the US stock market in 1929 (the **Great Crash**). The financial collapse ended the post-war economic boom of the 1920s, and plunged America and the other industrialized nations into an era of business failures, mass unemployment, poverty, and hardship. In America, President Franklin Roosevelt's NEW DEAL reforms helped alleviate some of the worst economic and social effects of the depression. In Germany the economic crisis precipitated the fall of the WEIMAR REPUBLIC and the rise of Hitler. Worldwide recovery did not occur until World War II began.

Greater East Asia Co-Prosperity Sphere Japan's plan for a new political and economic order in SE Asia, drawn up in 1941. It envisaged concentrating industry in Japan, N China, and Manchuria, with other countries in the region supplying raw materials and forming part of the consumer market. By a combination of military conquests and political alliances the plan was embarked upon, but ultimately collapsed with Japan's defeat in World War II. It did, however, serve to fragment colonialism in the region and foster independence aspirations among such nations as Burma, Indonesia, and Netherlands East Indies.

Greater London Council *See* GLC.

Great Leap Forward A radical economic and social reorganization in China, introduced in 1958, that was intended to transform the country into an industrialized society in the shortest possible time. The policy, which owed much to romantic Maoist notions of inspiring the peasants and harnessing their latent skills, sought to bypass the usual lengthy process of developing heavy industry and concentrate instead on labour-intensive small-scale industries and agriculture based on communes. Traditional customs and living patterns rapidly gave way to the new commune system throughout the country, but at the cost of major economic disruption. This was compounded by bad harvests and the withdrawal of Soviet technical advisers. By early 1960 the Great Leap Forward was being modified and the elements of individual incentive and land ownership reintroduced. The policy's failure continued to haunt the Chinese leadership: supporters blamed the problems on poor implementation by overzealous cadres plus bureaucratic ineptitude; opponents argued for a more conventional approach to industrialization.

Great Profile Nickname for the US film actor John Barrymore (1882–1942).

Great Rondini Nickname for Ronald Reagan. *See* GREAT COMMUNICATOR.

Great Society The catchphrase used by US president Lyndon B. Johnson to describe his vision of US society, first outlined in a speech to the University of Michigan on 22 May 1964:

> The Great Society rests on abundance and liberty for all. It demands an end to poverty and racial injustice, to which we are totally committed in our time.

Johnson borrowed the phrase from the title of a 1914 book by economist Graham Wallas. In the 1964 presidential elections, the Johnson platform contained policies consistent with such social objectives, such as anti-poverty programmes, expanded social security schemes, and legislation to strengthen voting rights. He was returned in a landslide Democrat victory.

Great Train Robbery A robbery by a well-organized gang that took place in the early hours of the morning of 8 August 1963, at Cheddington in Buckinghamshire, on the main line from London to N England. The gang stopped a mail train by changing a signal and escaped with mailbags containing over two and a half million pounds in cash. During the raid, the train driver, Jack Mills, suffered severe head injuries, which brought his career as a train driver to an end. At the time, the crime was the largest in British history. The media called it 'The Great Train Robbery', perhaps after the 1903 silent film of the same name. Most members of the gang were arrested and received long prison sentences, although one of them, Ronald Biggs, escaped from prison to Brazil, where he managed to avoid extradition. Of those that served their sentences, one, Charlie Wilson, died in suspicious circumstances in his villa in Marbella (Spain) and another, Buster Edwards, now sells flowers in Waterloo Station in London.

If the robbers had dealt less viciously with the train driver, their audacity and apparent success might have attracted greater public sympathy. As it is, although they have entered the mythology of the underworld, most people regard them as having got what they deserved.

Great War The war of 1914–18 was so called until that of 1939–45, when the term World War I largely replaced it, the latter becoming World War II. Popular opinion of the time said that World War I would be the last major war – the 'war to end wars'. David Lloyd George was nearer the mark when he commented in 1916: "This war, like the next war, is a war to end war".

Great White Way A once popular name for Broadway, the theatre district of New York City. It was inspired by the profusion of brilliant electric lighting in the area.

I am the greatest The catchphrase frequently used by the US heavy-weight boxer MUHAMMAD ALI (Cassius Clay; 1942–), who became world champion in 1964. He apparently took to using the phrase after he had seen a wrestler named Gorgeous George promoting himself thus to great effect.

the greatest thing since sliced bread A phrase used to describe something or someone considered to be a great boon, as sliced bread is presumed to be in the age of convenience foods. It is often used ironically – sliced bread is not really one of the 20th century's greatest inventions.

Greek. The Greeks Had a Word For It The title of a play by US poet and playwright Zoë Akins, first produced in 1929. The phrase was originally part of the dialogue but was retained only as the title of the final version. The word alluded to ἑτερο (*hetero*, other, different), describing certain characters in the play with rather outlandish personalities; it is not a reference to their sexual proclivities. The phrase became popular in the 1930s, spreading more or less simultaneously across the Atlantic, being used to mean anything unusual or unconventional.

green Describing those who are actively concerned with conserving the environment, preventing pollution, and avoiding ecological destruction; the word is also applied to issues, attitudes, etc., connected with protection of the environment. Originally regarded as eccentric or freakish, green politics spread widely in the 1980s with several countries in Europe having Green parties (whose members became known as **Greens**) and ultimately politicians of all parties claiming 'green' credentials.

green and blacks Drug abusers' slang of the 1960s and 1970s for the tranquillizer Librium in capsule form. The capsules were half green and half black.

green audit *See* GREEN LABELLING.

green belt A stretch of country around a large urban area that has been scheduled for comparative preservation and in which building development is restricted.

Green Berets The nickname for the US Army's Special Forces, a unit trained as specialists in unconventional warfare, such as guerrilla and undercover techniques. Named after their distinctive headgear, the Green Berets were formed in 1957 with the establishment of the Special Warfare School at Fort Bragg. Their strength was greatly increased during the 1960s in response to America's involvement in Indochina, where they were sent to advise anticommunist forces in counterinsurgency tactics and psychological warfare. Since then the Green Berets have been deployed in various parts of the world, notably Central America. Wearers of the Green Beret are trained not only in warfare but in languages, medicine, sanitation, communications, and other skills essential for liaising with indigenous forces. 'Green Berets' is also the nickname for the UK's Royal Marines, from whom most British commando units are drawn.

green card (1) In the UK, a green-coloured document issued by insurance companies to extend motor insurance to foreign countries. (2) In America, a green-coloured work permit allowing Mexican and other foreign nationals across the Mexican border to do temporary work.

Green Cross Code A road safety code for children introduced by the UK Department of Transport during the 1970s. It is part of the Highway Code, which is aimed at all road users, whether on foot or in a vehicle. The Green Cross Code is valid for all pedestrians but is particularly relevant for children; it comprises 25 points describing the correct procedure for using various types of road crossing, getting on and off buses, etc.

Green Goddess (1) Nickname for a green-coloured military fire tender first used in World War II. Green Goddesses have made subsequent appearances on British roads during Fire Service strikes. (2) A cocktail containing crème de menthe.

greenhouse effect An effect that occurs in the Earth's atmosphere as a result of which some of the energy of the Sun's radiation is retained by the Earth as heat, causing the temperature of the planet to rise (**global warming**). Light and ultraviolet radiation from the sun is transmitted through the Earth's atmosphere, absorbed by its surface, and re-radiated back into the atmosphere as infrared radiation. Some of this infrared radiation passes through the atmosphere back into space but some of it is absorbed by atmospheric gases, especially carbon dioxide (CO_2). The amount of the Sun's energy that is absorbed by the Earth's atmosphere in this way is directly related to the quantity of CO_2 in the atmosphere. Before the Industrial Revolution there were some 275 parts per million of CO_2 in the atmosphere; this has now increased to 350 p.p.m., causing a rise of about 1° in the average temperature of the Earth in the last 130 years. The increase in CO_2 in the atmosphere has two main causes, the burning of fossil fuels (about 25×10^{12} kilograms of CO_2 are produced every year by burning coal, oil, and natural gas) and burning of wood in the process of deforestation (about 9×10^{12} kg/yr of CO_2). Together these two causes account for 55% of global warming. The balance is provided by other so-called **greenhouse gases**, such as methane, oxides of nitrogen, etc., that are pumped into the atmosphere. The phenomenon, which is of great concern to scientists and environmentalists throughout the world, takes its name from the horticultural greenhouses in which a similar effect occurs. *See also* OZONE LAYER.

greening Concern about pollution and the destruction of the environment as well as attempts to prevent these things from happening.

green labelling The practice by manufacturers of labelling their products to persuade the buyer that the product will not damage the environment or that environmental damage does not result from its manufacture. Examples of green labelling are the designations of aerosols as 'ozone-friendly' (*see* -FRIENDLY), the marking of packages as 'recycled paper' (*see* RECYCLING), and declarations that tinned tuna fish has been produced without endangering dolphins. Green labelling arose during the late 1980s out of a general increase in concern about GREEN issues. Manufacturers and marketing people were quick to see that the protection of the environment could be a useful angle for selling their products. Environmental pressure groups have set up so-called **green audits** to investigate the validity of such claims.

greenlight To give the go-ahead to a project, enterprise, etc. The term originated in the film industry.

green lung A park or other green area in a large city. The 'lung' refers to the production of oxygen by plants.

greenmail The somewhat dubious practice of buying a large number of shares in a company on the open market and then selling them back to the company at a profit in return for a promise not to make a takeover bid for the company.

green money *See* CAP.

green monkey disease *See* MARBURG DISEASE.

Greenpeace A movement originating in Canada in 1971, aiming to persuade governments to change industrial activities that threaten natural resources and the environment. It supports direct non-violent action and has gained wide attention by its efforts to protect whales and to prevent the killing of young seals. When acting against French nuclear tests in the South Pacific in 1985 their ship, *Rainbow Warrior*, was sunk by a French saboteur. *See also* FRIENDS OF THE EARTH.

green pound *See* CAP.

greenroader A person who makes a hobby of driving cars or motorcycles along **green roads**. These are country roads and tracks that have not been metalled although at some time in the past they have been open to vehicles other than bicycles. The greenroaders can thus claim a precedent and drive along such roads, frequently at high speeds, even though they are now only used by walkers or cyclists.

Green Shield stamps *See* TRADING STAMPS.

Greenshirt A supporter of the Social Credit Movement established in the UK by Major Douglas in the 1920s, and so named from the green uniform shirt adopted.

green stuff Slang for paper money. In America all bank notes are green. In the UK, £1 bank notes used to be green; when they were phased out in the 1980s in favour of £1 coins, the expression ceased to be appropriate.

green-wellie brigade British slang of the 1980s for upper-middle-class people who spend weekends in their second homes in the country, dressed in green Wellington boots and BARBOUR jackets in an attempt to look like country people.

Greenham Common The site of a US Air Force base near Newbury, England, designated in 1981 as one of the sites for American Cruise missiles, which were installed in 1983. In September 1981 women anti-nuclear protesters set up a permanent Peace Camp outside the base; in the following years they maintained a constant vigil, harassing military convoys and breaching the perimeter fencing of the base in order to maintain public awareness of the threat from nuclear weapons. Many of the women were arrested and jailed, but the missiles were deployed on schedule in 1983. The camp remained in spite of declining public support for the CND after the mid-1980s. The cruise missiles were eventually removed in 1988–89 in accordance with the superpower arms-reduction talks in the mid-1980s; the closure of the base was announced in 1990.

Greenwich Mean Time (GMT) The time at Greenwich, London, through which the 0° meridian passes. From 1884 until 1986 the standard times of different areas of the world were calculated using this meridian as the basis, every 15° of longitude representing one hour of time in advance or behind it. In 1986 this was replaced by **Coordinated Universal Time** (UTC), which is based on International Atomic Time and, unlike GMT, is independent of the place of observation.

gregory British rhyming slang from the late 1980s for a cheque; it refers to the US film star, Gregory Peck (1916–).

grem or **gremmie** Australian slang for an inexperienced surfer. It is also British and Australian slang for an inexperienced skateboarder, first heard in the UK in the late 1970s. Both senses probably derive from GREMLIN.

gremlin One of a tribe of imaginary gnomes or goblins humorously blamed by the RAF in World War II for everything that went wrong in an aircraft or an operation. The name was probably coined at the end of World War I or in the 1920s and was apparently in use on RAF stations in India and the Middle East in the 1930s. This sense is first traced in print to *The Aeroplane* (10 April 1929). A common explanation is that a gremlin was the goblin that came out of Fremlin's beer bottle (Fremlin being a brewer in Kent), although there are numerous other stories. In the film *Gremlins* (1984), small furry creatures called mogwais wreak havoc on everyone who comes into contact with them.

Gretna Green rail disaster or **Quintinshill disaster** The UK's worst railway disaster, which happened on 22 May 1915 and resulted in 227 deaths. A southbound troop train, carrying members of 1/7 Royal Scots, collided with a stationary local train at Quintinshill near Gretna Green. 53 seconds later a northbound express ploughed into the wreckage, which promptly caught fire. Two other trains were also involved. The troop train was almost completely destroyed, its 194-m length being telescoped to 61 m in the first collision. Of the dead, 214 were passengers on the troop train. Two signalmen and the fireman of the local train were convicted of manslaughter.

grey (1) British colloquialism for a very conventional and conformist person: used in the 1960s, with slightly contemptuous overtones, by the more conventional people, who were abandoning their grey suits for more colourful clothes. A later synonym of the 1970s would be STRAIGHT. Used adjectivally, 'grey' had a new lease of life in 1990, with the election of the relatively obscure John Major to replace Margaret Thatcher as prime minister (*see also* MEN IN GREY SUITS).

> John Major confirmed yesterday that he is a grey man...
>
> COLIN BROWN: *The Independent* (8 December 1990).

> The Conservative Party happily reunited...to sing the praises of John Major, the grey man with glasses.
>
> *The Independent Magazine* (8 December 1990).

(2) US Black slang for a white man, usually used pejoratively.

grey knight *See* WHITE KNIGHT.

grey market In World War II, a transaction regarded as a lesser breach of the rationing regulations than one on the BLACK MARKET.

Grey Panthers Humorous name for members of a pressure group organized to promote the rights of retired and elderly people. The name alludes to the GREY POPULATION and was formed by analogy with BLACK PANTHERS.

grey population A population with an increasingly high proportion of elderly people compared to that of young people. Grey populations are caused by successive falls in birth rates and higher expectation of life owing to improved medical care and nutrition. Grey populations are obviously so described because elderly people tend to have grey hair.

Old Grey Whistle Test In TIN-PAN ALLEY, songwriters used to play their compositions to the 'old greys', the elderly doorkeepers and other workers in the offices of the music publishers. If the 'old greys' were still whistling the tunes after a week or so, then they were likely to be worth publishing. It subsequently became the title of a popular rock music programme on BBC television.

gridlock A major traffic jam in which all the vehicles involved come to a complete halt. Figuratively, it has been extended to mean a total stoppage or breakdown of any system, organization, etc., such as that caused in an industry by a national strike.

grifter US slang from the early years of the 20th century for a dishonest person, a gambler, a petty crook. The word is a combination of 'graft' in the sense of dishonest financial activities and 'drifter', with its implication of unreliability.

Grim Grom Nickname for the Soviet diplomat Andrei Gromyko (1909–90; foreign secretary 1957–85). He was noted for his grim expressionless approach to diplomacy.

grocer. the Grocer Nickname for Edward Heath. *See* IRON LADY.

the Grocer's Daughter Nickname for Margaret Thatcher. *See* IRON LADY.

grockle British slang for a tourist, an unwelcome visitor. Originally a Devonian word, it has now spread to all parts of the UK. *See also* EMMET.

grody US teenage slang version of GROTTY, meaning awful or distasteful.

groovy or **in the groove** To be in the right mood, to be doing something successfully, to be up to the current style or 'with it'; it derives from the accurate reproduction of music by a needle set in the groove of a gramophone record or disc. Widely heard in the 1960s and 1970s, but later only used sardonically.

Grosvenor Squares British rhyming slang for flares, *i.e.* bell-bottom trousers. A contemptuous term of the late 1970s, when this style of trousers was no longer fashionable and considered ludicrous. Another rhyming slang name for flares is **Lionel Blairs**, after the British dancer and entertainer.

grotty British slang for awful, revolting, distasteful. A shortened form of 'grotesque' (or its Italian equivalent *grotteschi*) favoured by Liverpudlians, first heard in the 1960s. In the era of the MERSEY SOUND, it became widely popular among young people. It has given rise to the back-formation **grot** for squalor or filth. *See also* GRODY.

ground. **ground control** The teams of scientists, engineers, and technicians and their radar and computer systems, who monitor the takeoff and landing of an aircraft or space vehicle, and observe and maintain contact with the crew throughout the flight or mission.

grounded US and Australian slang used by teenagers for being forced to stay at home as a punishment. It is taken from pilots' terminology, denoting a plane or a pilot that is prevented from flying.

Groundnut Scheme Figuratively, an expensive failure or ill-considered enterprise; from a hastily organized and badly planned British government scheme (1947) to clear large areas of hitherto unprofitable land in Africa to grow groundnuts. The venture was abandoned three years later at considerable cost to the taxpayer.

ground zero The area on the ground directly beneath an exploding nuclear weapon. Also called the HYPOCENTRE.

group. **Group Areas Act** Legislation introduced in 1950 by South Africa's ruling National Party in which certain residential and business areas were designated exclusively for particular racial groups. This was part of the minority White government's increasingly systematic enforcement of APARTHEID, and had the effect of expelling African, Coloured, and Asian citizens from many suburbs and causing expropriation of their property. For the White population the Act served to consolidate their economic and political power. At the beginning of 1990, president F. W. de Klerk promised to repeal or radically reform the Group Areas Act as part of his government's relaxation of apartheid.

group-grope Slang from the early 1960s for a group petting session. It was later used euphemistically as a synonym for GANG-BANG. In the 1980s it has been used contemptuously to describe GROUP THERAPY sessions.

groupie or **bandmoll** Slang for a girl who follows a rock group or a rock star around and makes herself sexually available to them. The word groupie originated in the 1960s when the practice began; it is usually used pejoratively. By the 1980s it had come to be used in a more general sense, as any admirer or a fan, *e.g.* a **political groupie**.

Group of Five (G5) The countries France, West Germany, Japan, the UK, and America that agreed to stabilize their exchange rates by mutual agreement. This grouping preceded the European Monetary System.

Group of Seven (G7) The group of seven countries that evolved from the first economic summit, held in 1976. They were the main industrial nations outside the communist bloc, *i.e.* Canada, France, West Germany, Italy, Japan, the UK, and America. Originally a purely economic grouping, their agenda later extended to some political issues.

Group of Seventy-Seven (G77) A grouping consisting of the developing countries of the world.

Group of Ten (G10) Also known as the **Paris Club**, this group of ten prosperous nations agreed at a meeting in Paris in 1962 to lend money to the International Monetary Fund (*see* IMF) and inaugurated the concept of special drawing rights, as a standard unit of account. They were Belgium, Canada, France, Italy, Japan, Netherlands, Sweden, West Germany, the UK, and America.

Group of Three (G3) The three most powerful western economies: Germany, Japan, and America.

group therapy A form of psychotherapy that has been widely used since World War II, when the treatment of psychological problems by therapists, psychiatrists, and psychoanalysts became popular but extremely expensive. In group therapy a number of patients meet together, usually in the presence of a therapist, to discuss their problems with a view to increasing their psychiatric or psychoanalytic insight, sometimes by acting out distressing events in their past. Such a group can also provide an opportunity for learning social skills or offering support to the members in overcoming a common addiction, obsession, etc.

growl A crude low-pitched growling sound produced on the trumpet in JAZZ.

GRU *Glavnoye Razvedyvatelnoye Upravleniye* (Central Intelligence Office). The principal intelligence organization of the Soviet Army; the military equivalent of the KGB.

grumpie One of the many words coined in the mid-1980s by analogy with YUPPIE. It refers to an older person who does not look favourably on the frivolities of the young and upwardly mobile, who staunchly defends the status quo, and who expresses these views in a manner that assumes that they are unquestionable.

GT Gran Turismo or Grand Touring. A description used in motoring and motor sport, originally applied to a closed coupé of sporting performance, as might be preferred for a lengthy motor tour of the Continent. In the 1960s there was a specific championship for GT cars, defined as distinct from 'sports cars' in international motor-sport regulations. Among the most successful models on the track, and arguably paradigms of the GT car, were the Ferrari 250 GT and GTO. In recent years the epithet 'GT' has been applied indiscriminately by car manufacturers to any model having modestly uprated performance or appointment, and has thus been debased in the eyes of motoring purists. Since the introduction of fuel injection to replace the carburettor, the GT is often known at **GTI**, Gran Turismo Injection.

Guadalcanal, Battle of A key military engagement of World War II and a turning point in the battle for supremacy of the Pacific. It began in August 1942 when US forces seized Henderson Field, a large airfield on the island of Guadalcanal in the Solomon Islands, then under Japanese occupation. In the face of fierce Japanese opposition, the Americans gradually advanced over the island, while at sea the opposing navies fought air and naval battles to prevent reinforcements reaching the island. However, by early 1943 Japanese resistance had crumbled, and on 9 February their last forces were evacuated. The battle for the island had cost the lives of over 9000 Japanese and 2000 US servicemen.

Guardian Angels A group of unpaid self-appointed vigilantes, founded in New York in 1979 by Curtis Sliwa to police the crime-ridden subway system. There are over 5000 members in America, 20% of them women, all trained in the art of self-defence. They are easily identified by their distinctive red berets. The move by Sliwa, in 1989, to train a British chapter of the Angels to police the London Underground met with coolness from Scotland Yard, who promptly announced the formation of their own community volunteer force, the Blue Angels. In America, police cooperation with the Angels has caused crime on the subway to decrease, although it has been argued that this is due largely to the extra police drafted in after the publicity arising from police failure to combat subway crime.

Guernica A town near Bilbao in N Spain, for centuries the symbolic centre of Basque nationalism and, until 1876, the seat of the provincial parliament. Traditionally, the town's male population met under the famous oak known as the Tree of Guernica, where representatives of the king swore to uphold Basque privileges. On 26 April 1937 the town was destroyed by German bombers sent by Hitler to assist Franco's Fascists fighting in the SPANISH CIVIL WAR. The town suffered repeated and indiscriminate bombing and incendiary attacks, and civilian survivors were mercilessly strafed by the Germans. Field Marshal Goering admitted that the German objective was to test the effectiveness of saturation bombing. The resulting carnage shocked the world. Pablo Picasso commemorated the event in his famous large-scale work, *Guernica*, completed two months after the attack.

guerrilla war Irregular warfare carried on by small groups acting independently; especially by patriots when their country is being invaded. From Span. *guerrilla*, diminutive of *guerra*, war. The word was first used with reference to the Spanish and Portuguese action against the French in the Peninsular War (1808–14). However, in the 20th century guerrilla warfare has been employed by many movements for national liberation. *See* FFI.

guesstimate An estimate based partly on guesswork and partly on calculation. It is formed from 'guess' and 'estimate'.

guest beer A brand of draught beer available, usually for a temporary period, in a pub or bar in addition to the brand normally sold. Landlords of tied public houses are obliged, under their tenancy agreement, to sell the beer produced by the brewery that owns the pub. They may also 'put on' guest beers. Often these are REAL ALES produced by small independent breweries.

Guggenheim Museum The museum on New York's Fifth Avenue that houses the art collection of the US industrialist Solomon R. Guggenheim (1861–1949). The building was designed by US architect Frank Lloyd Wright and has always aroused excitement and controversy. The main exhibition space is a circular structure, within which a concrete ramp gently spirals upwards and outwards around the domed central void. The paintings hang away from the inclined and curving exterior walls. From its opening in 1959, the building has been widely admired for its brilliant harmony of material and form but criticized as a gallery space. Wright himself described his building as "the liberation of painting by architecture".

Gugnunks *See* PIP, SQUEAK, AND WILFRED.

guide. guided missile A missile that can be fired in the general direction of a target and then alter its flight path after its launch, either by means of remote control or its own internal equipment. A wide range of missile guidance systems now exists. Long-range missiles, such as ICBMs, use a form of inertial guidance in which they are aimed at a pre-programmed map reference and make in-flight computer-controlled changes of direction to reach their target. Middle- and short-range weapons, such as air-to-air, air-to-surface, and anti-tank missiles, are either steered by the operator using fine wires connected to the missile or 'ride' radar or laser beams that lock onto the target. Other guided missiles direct themselves to the target by homing onto its heat, sound, or radar emissions.

guide dog A dog specially trained to act as a guide, companion, and protector to its blind owner. Dogs were systematically trained in this role in Germany during World War I to aid blind war veterans. The most common breeds used are the German shepherd, labradors, and golden retrievers. In the UK, the first guide dogs were trained in 1931; the Guide Dogs for the Blind Association was established three years later and remains the only organization that trains dogs (and their owners) in the UK.

Guides *See* GIRL GUIDES.

Guildford Four The four individuals (Gerard Conlon, Paddy Armstrong, Paul Hill, and Carole Richardson) who were falsely convicted of the 1974 IRA bombing of a Guildford public house. They were released in October 1989 after 15 years in prison. This miscarriage of justice, one of the most scandalous in British legal history, became the subject of a judicial inquiry. It is clear that in this case (*see also* BIRMINGHAM SIX) the police extracted fake confessions from the defendants under duress and that the crown prosecution and police withheld forensic and alibi evidence from the defence (both at the time of the trial and subsequently). Had this evidence been available there is little doubt that it would have established the innocence of the defendants and led to their acquittal or, later, release on appeal. While the damage to the reputation of the British police may eventually be repaired by the appropriate purgings, it is unlikely that the legal establishment will ever live down the complacency and ill-judged reactions of senior legal figures to this episode, which exposed the frailty of a system of justice that was formerly the envy of the world.

> The lies took police three weeks to concoct in 1974, the truth took half an hour to spell out in court fifteen years later.
>
> *The Independent*, 20 October 1989.

Guild Socialism A movement, prominent in the early 20th century, that sought to reorganize industry under the control of workers' guilds. Its ideological impetus came from A. J. Penty's *The Restoration of the Gild System* (1906). His arguments for revitalizing the guilds of medieval times were taken up by A. R. Orage and S. G. Hobson, who developed them into a comprehensive system of modern guilds based on existing trade unions and incorporating elements of syndicalism and other contemporary ideas. Orage and Hobson envisaged workers' control of each industry through a guild chartered by the state. They argued that this would avoid the unwieldy bureaucracy associated with centralized control of industry in a socialist state.

The movement became influential before and during World War I; in 1915 the National Guilds League was formed to promulgate Guild Socialism. Support grew in many industries, including coalmining, railways, and the Post Office. However, by 1917 the trade unions were becoming increasingly politicized, and attention was diverted from shop-floor restructuring to wider issues. Moreover, after the war, the government frustrated moves towards meaningful worker participation in management, and splits appeared in the movement's leadership. The National Building Guild operated successfully for a while, building low-cost houses on contract to the government as part of the Addison housing scheme of 1919. But this too failed after government support was withdrawn, succumbing to the deepening economic depression in 1922. The National Guilds League was wound up in 1925. In spite of these failures, the aims of Guild Socialism were assimilated into socialist ideology and survive to this day.

Guinea Pig Club A group of RAF aircrew members who suffered serious burns during World War II and were treated by the New Zealand surgeon Sir Archibald McIndoe (1900–60), who used pioneering techniques of plastic surgery involving skin grafts (hence the name 'guinea pig').

Guinness is good for you The advertising slogan for Guinness stout that was first used in 1929. It accurately reflects what everyone hopes to be true and is probably so memorable for that reason.

gulag Glavnoye Upravleniye Ispravitelno-Trudovykh Lagerey. Chief Administration of Corrective Labour Camps, the section of the KGB, the Soviet Union's secret police department, in charge of forced labour camps for dissidents and others. The word came into the English language from the novel *The Gulag Archipelago* (1974–78) by Alexander Solzhenitsyn (1918–).

Gulf War (1) The conflict between Iran and Iraq that followed upon Iraq's invasion of W Iran in 1980. By the time the war ended in 1988, the region had witnessed the deaths of hundreds of thousands of combatants, toxic gas attacks by Iraq, and Iranian rocket attacks on Iraqi cities. The war ended without appreciable benefit to either side. (2) The conflict between Iraq and an alliance of UN powers, led by America, that was precipitated by Iraq's invasion of Kuwait on 2 August 1990 (*see also* HUMAN SHIELD). Under Saddam Hussein (*see* BUTCHER OF BAGHDAD), the Iraqis refused UN demands for their withdrawal and subsequently (17 January 1991) they came under attack from allied aircraft. By the time that the allied ground forces had moved into Kuwait and S Iraq on 24 February 1991, the Iraqis were unable to offer more than token resistance and Kuwait was liberated, although not before extensive damage was done to Kuwait City and the country's oilfields. Saddam Hussein, however, succeeded in maintaining his authority within Iraq and subsequently pursued a vindictive policy against rebellious Kurds in the N of the country, leading to further Western involvement in the area.

gum. gumball US drug abusers' slang from the 1980s for highly refined heroin.

gumballs US slang for the flashing lights on the roof of a police car, so called because they resemble brightly coloured balls of bubble gum.

gumboot A derogatory African name for a CONDOM, obviously so-called from the similarity of a condom, when in place, to a Wellington boot.

gumshoe Early 20th-century US slang for a private detective or plain-clothes policeman, so called because of the rubber-soled shoes said to be worn by such a policeman to allow him to creep up on a suspect. They are the opposite of the heavy and noisy boots worn by policemen on the beat. A film of this name starring Albert Finney was made in 1971. The word is also used as a verb, meaning to move about stealthily.

gun. give it the gun In RFC slang in World War I, also used by the RAF in World War II, to open the throttle of an aeroplane suddenly and hard. Sometimes also used of cars.

guns before butter A slogan attributed to Nazi propagandist Joseph Goebbels during World War II, although it probably dates from 1936, when very similar phraseology was employed in speeches by both Goebbels and Herman Goering. In a speech in Berlin in January 1936 Goebbels said:

> We can do without butter but, despite our love of peace, not without arms. One cannot shoot with butter, but with guns.

The theme was continued by Goering in a broadcast later in the year:

> I must speak clearly. There are those in international life who are hard of hearing. They listen only if the guns go off. We have no butter, my good people, but I ask you, would you rather have butter or guns? Should we import lard or metal ores? Let me tell it to you straight – preparedness makes us powerful. Butter merely makes us fat!

This is popularly known as Goering's 'guns-or-butter' speech.

guns, gas and gaiters A naval catchphrase said to have originated at the Royal Navy's Gunnery School, Whale Island, to describe its disciplined regime. 'Guns' is slang for Gunnery Officer, while 'gas and gaiters' is a variant of 'gate and gaiters', referring to a loudmouth ('gate') and the gaiters worn by ratings and instructors alike. It was current by the 1920s.

gunsel (1) US slang for a youth (from the Yiddish *genzel*, a young goose). In this sense, the word seems to have two particular uses, one to describe a young boy who accompanies an older tramp on the road; the other is a passive young male homosexual. (2) By extension, a gunsel is also an informer, or petty criminal and, because of its association with the word 'gun', a gunman.

gunship British slang from the 1980s for an unmarked police car. The earlier name for an ordinary car containing policemen, usually used to catch speeders, was **Q-ship** or **Q-car**, from the World War II usage of Q-ship, for a merchant ship with concealed guns. The aggressive implications of the change to gunship are typical of the era in which the relationship between the public and the police force deteriorated.

Guomindang or **Kuomintang** The National People's Party, a Chinese political party formed by Sun Yat-sen in 1905 which, after his death in 1925, passed under the control of General Chiang Kai-shek. The Guomindang was in power in China when it was driven out by the Communist Party under Mao Tse-tung. The Nationalists still maintain themselves in Taiwan.

guppie Slang for a YUPPIE who is GREEN, an environmentally aware young urban professional.

gutbucket An earthy style of JAZZ blues. Originally played in low drinking houses in America, it is named after the small drip buckets that were placed under the liquor barrels to catch the leakages.

gutter press The section of the British TABLOID press that makes use of sensationalist and intrusive journalism to boost its circulation. The gutter press is characterized by an obsession with the private lives of public figures, especially pop musicians and TV celebrities. The techniques of gutter journalism include relentless surveillance of their victims, offers of large sums of money (*see* CHEQUE-BOOK JOURNALISM) to obtain information about their targets, and even the fabrication of stories. Attempts to monitor and punish such abuses by means of the Press Council have proved ineffective. There is now a growing lobby in favour of legislation to protect privacy, although many fear that such a measure would inhibit legitimate investigative journalism.

> Journalists belong in the gutter because that is where ruling classes throw their guilty secrets.
>
> GERALD PRIESTLAND (broadcaster and writer, especially on religious subjects), 22 May 1988.

Guy the Gorilla Nickname for the British cricketer Ian Botham, who played for Somerset (1973–86) and Worcestershire (1987–). A noted all-rounder, he captained the England side (1980–81). The name comes from that of an actual gorilla, Guy, at London Zoo.

GWR Great Western Railway, or, in the eyes of its devotees, God's Wonderful Railway. Originally designed by Brunel in the 1830s, the GWR, extending over 1000 miles (1600 km), enjoyed its golden period at the turn of the century, when many of the most famous British steam locomotives ran on its broad (7 ft) gauge track. The GWR was reorganized as one of the four great railway conglomerates after World War I and vanished as a separate entity in 1947, when it was merged into British Railways. *See also* LMS; LNER; SR.

gynopathy A condition observed in men who feel threatened by women, particularly in a work-force. It is derived from the Greek words *guné*, woman, and *pathos*, feeling.

H

H (1) Drug abusers' slang for heroin, common in the 1970s. (2) A film certification category denoting horror films. Introduced by the British Board of Film Censors in 1932, it was merely an advisory label to warn parents of films that might be disturbing to children. In 1951 it was superseded by the 'X' category, denoting films for showing only to persons over 16.

H-block The section of the MAZE PRISON in Northern Ireland in which convicted IRA terrorists are housed.

H-bomb *See* NUCLEAR WEAPON.

H-line *See* DIOR.

Habakkuk An ambitious scheme to use iceberges as mid-Atlantic airstrips as a counter to the U-BOAT threat during World War II. The idea, conceived by the British aviator Geoffrey Pyke in 1942, was to enable aircraft to extend their range by refuelling on giant 'artificial' icebergs, complete with workshops, hangars, and living quarters. Secret work on prototypes began in Canada, where it was found that the addition of wood pulp would greatly increase the strength of the ice. However, when it became apparent that such a base would cost as much as a conventional aircraft carrier, the project was abandoned. The scheme was called Habakkak after an Old Testament prophet, who said:

> For I will work a work in your days, which ye will not believe, though it be told you.

hacker (1) Slang for a computer enthusiast who uses a personal computer to break into the computing system of a company, bank, or government department in order to obtain information, money, etc. In this context a hacker conjures up the image of someone cutting their way through the computer jungle; it became widely used when the practice was publicized in the press. It was reported that someone had even managed to hack into Prince Philip's personal computer. (2) British slang for a taxi driver. This derives from 'Hackney cab', the official name still used for London taxis. This name was kept on when the horse-drawn vehicle for hire became motorized at the beginning of the 20th century, even though the hackney was actually the horse that drew the carriage. (3) Slang for someone who clumsily chops at things rather than handling them competently. It is not always used literally.

had. to have had it A colloquial expression widely popularized during World War II and possibly of Australian origin. It is applied to that which is 'finished with' or 'done for'. Thus a man seriously wounded was said to have had it. At Roman gladiatorial combats the spectators cried *hoc habet* or *habet* (he has it, he is hit) when a gladiator was wounded or received his death-wound. It is also applied to one who has missed his chance or opportunity.

You've never had it so good *See under* GOOD.

Hadow Reports Any of several reports by the Consultative Committee to the Board of Education, chaired from 1920 to 1934 by Sir Henry Hadow (1859–1937), in particular the 1927 report *The Education of the Adolescent*. This introduced the terms 'primary' and 'secondary' for education before and after the age of 11 or 12, and advocated the establishment of separate schools for secondary education. Other influential reports by his committee included *The Primary School* (1931) and *Infant and Nursery Schools* (1933).

Haganah (Heb. defence) The Jewish defence force that operated from 1920 until the declaration of the State of Israel in 1948 to defend Jewish settlements in Palestine. It was the successor to Ha-Shomer (1909–20), and generally adopted a moderate policy, eschewing the terrorist tactics of the STERN GANG and IRGUN ZVAI LEUMI. A commando offshoot, Palmach, was formed in 1941. Under the British mandate, Haganah was proscribed, resulting in clashes with the British as well as Palestinians, especially in the run-up to thc partition of Palestine after World War II. With the granting of Israeli autonomy,

Haganah formed the basis of the country's armed forces.

Hague Conference or **Second Hague Convention** An international peace conference held in The Hague, Netherlands, in 1907 and attended by 44 nations. It was convened at the request of US President Theodore Roosevelt in an attempt to build on the conventions adopted by the First Hague Conference, held in 1899, which had created a Permanent Court of Arbitration for international disputes. In the event, the achievements of the 1907 Conference were modest, although the principle of compulsory arbitration was accepted, and conventions were adopted on such issues as the rights and duties of neutral powers and the status of merchant shipping in a conflict. A third conference planned for 1915 never took place because by then World War I had broken out.

ha-ha A British slang euphemism for hashish or marijuana. It is probably a pun based both on a shortened form of hashish and 'ha-ha' meaning laughter, because of the light-hearted mood induced by the drug.

Haig. Don't be vague – ask for Haig The advertising slogan for Haig whisky since about 1936. The phrase had appeared in several different forms: 'Don't be vague, order Haig' and 'Why be vague? Ask for Haig', but this is the one that stuck.

hairy (1) Slang for frightening or dangerous. It was first heard as student slang in the early years of this century, when it meant difficult. It later took its present meaning from army slang. It probably derives from the idea that something frightening makes one's hair stand on end; however, the idea of a frightening hairy monster has also been suggested as a derivation. There is also a possible connection with the word 'scary'. (2) British slang of the early 1960s for a long-haired bearded male. It was typically used disparagingly of poets and intellectuals. It is still heard occasionally.

Haldane mission The diplomatic mission to Berlin, undertaken by the UK's war secretary, Viscount Haldane, in February 1912, in a bid to persuade the German government to reduce its programme of warship construction. No agreement was reached, prompting the First Lord of the Admiralty, Winston Churchill, to call for increased British military spending.

Hale's tours A clever idea from the early days of cinema. The ex-chief of the Kansas City Fire Department, George C. Hale, produced it for the St Louis Exposition of 1902. He shot a film from the observation car at the rear end of a moving train, then projected the film onto a screen at the end of a small narrow theatre decorated like an observation car. The illusion was enhanced by arrangements to make the theatre rock slightly, with the sound of train whistles and clanging bells as an accompaniment to the screening. The idea was sufficiently popular for Hale to take it on tour for several years throughout America.

half. half-care Partial care provided for elderly people, as in SHELTERED ACCOMMODATION.

half-life As a scientific term, the time taken for half the atoms of a particular radioactive substance to disintegrate. This time may vary from a fraction of a second to millions of years according to the given substance. A knowledge of this process has enabled archaeologists and geologists, etc., to date materials with considerable accuracy. *See* CARBON DATING.

half-timer One engaged in some occupation for only half the usual time; the term formerly applied to a child attending school for half time and working the rest of the day. This practice was terminated by the Education Act of 1918.

half-tone block A typographic printing-block for illustrations, produced by photographing on to a prepared plate through a screen or grating, which breaks up the picture to be reproduced into small dots of varying intensity, thus giving the lights and shades, or tones.

Halifax bomber A four-engined bomber built by Handley Page and used by the RAF during World War II. The Halifax Mark 1, fitted with Rolls Royce Merlin engines, made its first operational flight in March 1941. It was followed by more powerful versions equipped with Bristol Hercules engines. The planes had gun turrets situated aft and in the tail, combined with a machine gun in the nose. The Mark II was capable of carrying up to 6000 kg (13,000 lb) of bombs. Wartime variants included paratroop and glider-tug versions; after the war modified versions of the Halifax, called Haltons, were used for civilian transport.

Halley's comet The brightest of the comets with known periodicity, named after Edmund Halley (1656–1743), the astronomer royal who first described the elliptical orbit of comets around the Sun. Halley observed this comet in 1682 and accurately predicted its return in 1759. Halley's comet passes close to the Earth roughly every 76 years. The first definite sighting was made by Chinese astronomers in 1059–58 BC. In the 20th century it has passed close to the Earth in 1910 and 1986. In the latter passage five spacecraft were launched to investigate it: two from Japan, two Soviet craft, and Giotto – the European Space Agency probe. These missions revealed a black peanut-shaped nucleus approximately 15 km long and 10 km across, giving off 25 tons of gas and 5 tons of dust every second. At its present rate of material loss, it is estimated that Halley's comet will survive for less than another 100,000 years.

Hallstein doctrine The policy, adopted by the Federal Republic of Germany in December 1955, that made recognition of East Germany (German Democratic Republic) by another state a hostile act against the Federal Republic. It was named after the West German State Secretary of the Foreign Office, Dr Walter Hallstein, but was actually devised by Wilhelm Grewe, West Germany's ambassador to America. The doctrine was part of the Adenauer government's strategy to promulgate the view that East Germany was not a legally constituted state and that German reunification was imperative. Because of the doctrine many countries were dissuaded from establishing diplomatic relations with East Germany, particularly by the threat of losing West German economic assistance.

halon A type of chemical compound made from hydrocarbons by replacing some of the hydrogen atoms by bromine atoms and additional chlorine and fluorine atoms. Halons are extensively used in fire extinguishers. Like chlorofluorocarbons (*see* CFC) they have been implicated in depletion of the OZONE LAYER.

ham (1) Slang for a licensed amateur radio operator. The word is an aspirated form of the first syllable 'amateur'. (2) Theatrical slang for a bad actor or actress who overdoes all his gestures and gives a wildly histrionic performance rather than a convincing one. Various etymologies have been suggested for this sense, which first appeared in the 19th century. It is possibly, as in (1) above, derived from the word 'amateur'. The second possibility is that it is derived from 'ham fat', the substance used to remove grease paint – thus a 'ham fatter' was an actor. A third possibility is that it is derived from the name of Hamish McCullough (1835–85), an actor who toured the Mid-West of America with his theatre company, called Ham's Actors, who apparently put on the most dreadful productions. In the 20th century the word often appears in such phrases as 'hamming it up' and adjectivally as 'hammy'.

hammer A radio HAM.

Hammer and Sickle Since 1923, the emblem of the Soviet Union, symbolic of productive work in the factory and on the land.

Hammer horror A series of low-budget British horror films produced from the late 1950s onwards by Hammer Films, a small independent company. Hammer had been making films at its Thameside studios for the US B-movie market since the late 1940s. In 1955 it bought the film rights to a popular sci-fi TV series, which resulted in the release of *The Quatermass Experiment* (1955). This success was soon followed by *X The Unknown* (1957) and *Quatermass 2* (1957), which proved equally popular. Over the next 15 years Hammer specialized in making gruesome and sometimes titillating remakes of original Hollywood monster movies, featuring Frankenstein, Dracula, and the Mummy, the first of which was *The Curse of Frankenstein* (1956).

Mike Hammer The tough investigator who features in many of the crime thrillers written by US author Mickey Spillane (Frank Morrison Spillane; 1918–). Hammer, an ex-cop and war veteran, made his first appearance in *I, The Jury* (1947); in subsequent novels he established his reputation as a highly unorthodox agent of 'justice', combining the roles of judge and executioner with scant regard for legal niceties. The books have proved immensely popular and have spawned a television series. However, Hammer's predilection for sex and violence have brought criticism for the character's creator, the outspokenly conservative Spillane.

Hampshire, HMS The British cruiser that was sunk by a mine off the Orkney Islands in June 1916, while carrying the British Secretary for War, Lord Kitchener, to Russia. It went down with the loss of all on board. Curiously, many years earlier, Kitchener's death by drowning had been foretold by a gipsy – a prophecy in which Kitchener himself believed.

Hampstead set A name given in the 1950s to a group of close friends of the Labour Party leader, Hugh Gaitskell (1906–63), some of whom, like Gaitskell himself, were Oxford-educated middle-class intellectuals living in Hampstead. Members of the set included Anthony Crosland, Roy Jenkins, Douglas Jay, Denis Healey, and Frank Pakenham (later Lord Longford; *see* HOLY FOOL). They were accused by some of exercising undue influence over Party affairs, while others criticized Gaitskell for ill-judged favouritism.

hand. handbag British slang verb meaning (of a woman) to attack or obstruct. It has also frequently been used as a nickname for the former Tory prime minister, Margaret Thatcher, especially as a handbag was one of her props that was made much of by cartoonists. Neil Kinnock, the Labour leader, referred to John Major, her successor, as "son of handbag".

> Handbag Finds Launch Pad
>
> *The Independent* (7 January 1991), headline of an article about Mrs Thatcher's new post as honorary president of the Bruges Group.

Handcuff King The nickname of Harry HOUDINI (1874–1926), entertainer and escapist, especially from handcuffs.

Hand of God Phrase used by the Argentinian footballer Diego Maradona (1960–) following an incident in the 1986 WORLD CUP. Argentina met England in the quarter finals of the competition and the confrontation caused considerable interest because it was the first time the two nations had competed since the FALKLANDS CONFLICT. Maradona, who at the time was regarded as one of the world's best footballers, scored two goals. The second was a brilliant solo performance, in which he took the ball through the English defence before scoring. The first was less impressive: Maradona had apparently headed the ball into the net but slow-motion replays showed that, unseen by the referee, he had knocked it in with his hand. As a result, England were knocked out of the competition. Challenged later, Maradona, unrepentant, said:

> It was a little the hand of God and a little the hand of Diego.

Possibly Maradona was trying a pun on his name ('little God'). The humour was lost on most English football fans.

hand-out Originally something handed out or given away, such as oranges and buns at a children's party or gifts of food and clothing to tramps. It is now more commonly used to designate (1) free advertising material, brochures, etc., given to potential customers, (2) a press release by a news service, and (3) a prepared statement to the Press by a government, official body, publicity agent, etc.

hands-off An adjectival form of an earlier interjection indicating a lack of involvement in a particular situation or the distancing of oneself from matters that may be thought to be under one's control. This usage became popular in the 1980s, as in 'a hands-off policy towards industry'. *See also* HANDS-ON.

hands-on An adjective indicating active personal involvement in situations or affairs. Specifically the term refers to the use of practical, rather than theoretical, experience. It is often used in the field of computers, as in 'hands-on training'. *See also* HANDS-OFF.

Handy Man The popular name for *Homo habilis*, the species of prehistoric man thought to be the earliest member of our own genus, *Homo*. Discovery of *H. habilis* was announced in April 1964 by Louis Leakey, Phillip Tobias, and John Napier, based on the evidence of remains unearthed in the OLDUVAI GORGE, Tanzania. The Latin specific name, *habilis*, was proposed by Raymond Dart; it means handy, skilful. The species is thought to have lived in E Africa between about 2 and 1.5 million years ago. Adults were only 5 ft tall but possessed a markedly larger brain than their australopithecine ancestors. There is evidence that Handy Man built simple shelters and made rudimentary tools.

handle. dead man's handle *See under* DEAD.

Handley Page bomber The largest British bomber to fly operationally during World War I. The Handley Page 0/100, designed by Frederick Handley Page (1885–1962), entered service in 1916 with the Royal Naval Air Service. It was a twin-engined biplane with a wingspan of 30.48 m (100 ft) and a length of 19.15 m (62 ft 10 in.); top speed was 115.87 k.p.h. (72 m.p.h.). At first the bomber was used for attacks on the coast of mainland Europe but by 1917 operations had been extended to include night attacks over German-occupied France and Belgium. A more powerful version of the 0/100, the 0/400, entered service with the RAF in 1918. This had a maximum speed of 156.9 k.p.h. (97.5 m.p.h.) and was capable of carrying 750-kg bombs. After the war, many 0/400 bombers were converted for civilian use.

Handsomest Man in the World The nickname, probably a promotional tag, of the US stage and film actor Francis X. Bushman (1883–1966), the star of many silent films. His film career began in 1911, his good looks and powerful well-built physique quickly bringing him popular acclaim as a romantic lead and earning him his nickname. His films included *Romeo and Juliet* (1915) and *Ben Hur* (1925), in which he played the role of Messala.

hang. **hang five** US surfing slang from the 1960s meaning to ride a surfboard fast with the toes of one foot hooked over the front of the board. To **hang ten** means to ride a surfboard with the toes of both feet hooked over the front of the board. Both phrases are still used, the second one often in the more general sense of going dangerously fast.

hang-gliding Unpowered flight by a sailplane using air currents to maintain height and prolong the flight time. Once the province of the adventurous, it is now an increasingly popular international sport. The first generation of gliders was based on a design perfected in 1948 by the US NASA engineer Professor Francis Rogallo, using a flexible wire-frame wing covered in a silicon material. In the 1960s Bill Moyes, an Australian engineer, experimented with a more efficient DELTA WING design; in 1969 he made his celebrated flight with colleague Bill Bennett over the Statue of Liberty. There are now various designs of glider, although all make use of a light aluminium frame bearing a terylene sail, under which the pilot is strapped in a harness, usually in the prone position. The best area for flying is California, which has plenty of mountainous terrain, cliffs for take-off, and warm-air currents. *See also* PARAGLIDING.

hanging on the (old) barbed wire *See* MONS.

hang in there A catchphrase originating in America, probably in the 1950s, meaning hang on or stay with it, *i.e.* an entreaty to persevere with an undertaking or persist with a point of view. It was adopted by the HIPPIE generation in the 1960s, and was still current at the beginning of the 1990s.

hang loose A British slang expression originating in the 1960s with the HIPPIE movement, meaning to be totally relaxed and unconcerned. In common with much of the slang of the period, it has now become dated.

hang the Kaiser! A catchphrase used by British soldiers during World War I as an expression of their weariness with the whole wretched enterprise; it was said half in jest, half seriously.

hang-up Slang for an obsession, a preoccupation, or something that is persistently annoying, as in the retort 'That's your hang-up'. The term originated in HIPPIE jargon of the 1960s and is now widely used.

Hannah In World War II, a nickname give to a Wren serving with the Royal Marines, after Hannah Snell (1723–92), who joined the marines posing as a man and took part in the attack on Pondicherry. It is said that she ultimately opened a public-house in Wapping, but retained her male attire.

Hannay, Richard Typically British hero of a number of adventure novels by the Scottish writer John Buchan (Baron Tweedsmuir; 1875–1940). Buchan was Director of Information during World War I and became Governor General of Canada in 1935. He first introduced Hannay in his best-known novel, *The Thirty-Nine Steps* (1915). Three film versions of the book have been made, the best being the early (1935) adaptation directed by Alfred Hitchcock and starring Robert Donat as Hannay. Possibly the character of Hannay was based on that of William Ironside (later Lord Ironside of Archangel; 1880–1959), whom Buchan met in South Africa. Ironside was an intelligence officer who was fluent in 14 languages (and, it has been said, made sense in none of them!).

happening (1) US teenage slang of the 1970s meaning exciting, the thing of the moment. It is thought to derive from the HIPPIE expression 'It's all happening', meaning that life was exciting and exhilarating. (2) An artistic or musical event, usually involving considerable audience participation. In the theatre, happenings were apparently spontaneous dramatic performances designed to challenge an audience's perception of the nature of theatre itself (*see also* EDINBURGH FESTIVAL HAPPENING). Both the word and the concept are now dated and would only be used facetiously or contemptuously in the UK.

happy. are you happy in your work? An ironic question addressed to someone performing an obviously onerous or unpleasant task, or one equally clearly not to their liking. Originally a services phrase dating from World War II, it was later widely used. The Royal Navy variant was 'are you happy in the Service?'

bomb happy A World War II expression to describe one in a state of near hysteria induced by bombing, which often took the form of wild elation of the spirits.

Don't worry, be happy This song title could be said to be the catchphrase of George Bush's successful presidential election campaign of 1988. It won a Grammy award that year for the singer Bobby Mcferrin and became the president's unofficial theme song.

Happiness is . . . This phrase attempting to define happiness became a huge moneyspinner for the US creator of the *Peanuts* cartoon strip, Charles M. Schultz (1922–), starring the boy CHARLIE BROWN and his dog Snoopy. He was not the first; for centuries people had been trying to encapsulate the essence of happiness. Rousseau (1712–1778) said:

> Happiness: a good bank account, a good cook, a good digestion.

Archbishop Whately of Dublin (1787–1863) wrote:

> Happiness is no laughing matter.

The illusive nature of happiness was noted by Anna Pavlova (1881–1931):

> Happiness is like a butterfly which appears and delights us for one brief moment, but soon flits away.

and by Bertrand Russell (1872–1970):

> Happiness is not best achieved by those who seek it directly.

But Schultz hit on a winning formula by leaving the phrase open for anything or anyone to be included or excluded as the mood changed. The first, in 1957, was 'Happiness is . . . a warm puppy', featuring Charlie Brown and Snoopy. A best-selling book appeared in 1962. The slogans appeared on mugs, T-shirts, and posters. It was then adopted by various companies as an advertising slogan, one of the most memorable of which was 'Happiness is a mild cigar called Hamlet'. Having seen the caption to a photograph on a shooting magazine, John Lennon wrote, and the Beatles recorded, a song called 'Happiness is a warm gun'. The possibilities are endless.

Happy The nickname of Margaretta Rockefeller, a leading lady of US society and widow of Nelson Rockefeller, governor of New York (1959–74) and US vice-president (1974–77) in Gerald Ford's administration. According to the story reported in the *New York Times*, the name was given to the infant Margaretta by her French nursemaid in 1927. Bouncing the baby on her knee on hearing the news that Charles Lindbergh had achieved the first nonstop flight from New York to Paris, she was delighted to note that the baby responded with happy gurgles and smiles.

happy clappies Derogatory name for adherents of the modern evangelical movement, who support the incorporation of gospel-style music and informality in church services, with participation from the congregation and bursts of spontaneous applause.

happy days are here again A catchphrase that originated as the title of a song written by US composer Milton Ager with lyrics by Jack Yellen, published in 1930. The phrase was subsequently adopted for the presidential campaign of Franklin D. Roosevelt (*see* FDR) and soon became a familiar idiom on both sides of the Atlantic.

happy dust Drug users' slang for any narcotic in powder form, especially cocaine or ANGEL DUST.

happy hour A promotional ploy used by certain British pubs and bars to attract customers by offering half-price drinks for a limited period (usually an hour but it can be longer) at a certain time of the day, usually in the early evening. The concept was first introduced around 1961. In cricket, the 'happy hour' is the final hour of play in a limited-overs match, when batsmen take more chances than they would do at an earlier stage of the game.

trigger happy Over ready to shoot: a term originating in World War II. Now applied metaphorically to any kind of reckless overeagerness: "trigger-happy journalists rushed into print before the true facts emerged".

hard. hardball or **play hardball** US slang meaning to behave in a tough or MACHO way. The image is from baseball, in which professionals play with a hard ball, while some amateurs and children use a soft ball (this game is often called 'softball'). The phrase is now widely used in the business, political, and sporting worlds.

hard copy The output of a computer (such as text or graphics) on paper, as opposed to being displayed on the screen. Hard copy output to a dot matrix printer or laser printer is permanent, whereas screen output only exists for as long as the computer is switched on.

hardcore (1) An adjective used to describe someone who is irredeemably committed to an activity or belief, *e.g.* a **hardcore criminal** will do anything to anyone and is never likely to reform, while a **hardcore communist** will remain a party member no matter what happens, It is also used to describe pornography that depicts sexual activities without any restraint, including violence and acts with children. (2) A style of US pop music that developed out of PUNK in the 1980s and spread to the UK in about the middle of the decade. Anarchic, loud, and aggressive, it did not last long. *See also* THRASH.

hard disk A magnetic disk in a hermetically sealed unit, which can be mounted either in a computer or in a separate unit outside the computer with its own housing and power supply. Removable hard disks are available, which can be switched between computers. The magnetic storage medium in a hard disk is a rigid platter, which is more robust than the FLOPPY DISK and can store and retrieve much larger amounts of data at a much faster rate. A hard disk is essential for most modern microcomputing applications, floppy disks being reserved for transferring data between machines and for data back-up in case of hard disk failure.

hard dog US police slang of the 1980s for a dog owned by a criminal and trained to attack. Hard dogs are kept especially by drug dealers, to protect themselves and their property.

hard drug A drug, such as heroin or morphine, that is both physically and psychologically addictive and seriously detrimental to the health of the user. The description 'hard' has been used of such drugs since the early 1970s; they are contrasted with 'soft' drugs, such as marijuana and some amphetamines, whose effects on health are generally considered less damaging. However, it seems that most hard-drug users began their addiction with soft drugs, although, of course, not all users of soft drugs end up as hard-drug addicts. Because the price of addiction to hard drugs is so high (some recover from it but many do not), and the passage from soft to hard drugs is so well trodden, the use of soft drugs is no longer regarded as sympathetically as it was in the 1960s.

hard hat US slang for a building worker who espouses right-wing political views. The term was first heard in the late 1960s when hard hats joined demonstrations against the anti-VIETNAM WAR demonstrators. The term derives, of course, from the safety helmet, called a hard hat, worn by building workers.

Hard John US Black slang for an FBI agent, used quite persistently through the 1940s and 1950s.

hard landing or **crash landing** A landing by a rocket or spacecraft in which the vehicle is destroyed on impact.

hard rock *See* ROCK.

hard sell The aggressive marketing of a commodity or service. Salespersons using the technique tend to use aggressive and forceful persuasion, neglect the consumer's actual requirements, and make dishonest or exaggerated claims for the product. The practice is widely used by holiday timeshare companies who, with the bait of quite expensive gifts, lure people into their premises, where they are often subjected to persistent pressure to buy a share in a property, which most can ill afford. *See also* SOFT SELL.

hard shoulder The raised roughly surfaced strip running along the edge of a motorway, which is used for emergency stops. It is illegal to use – or stop on – the hard shoulder for any reason that is not an emergency.

hardware A long established term for ironmongery – kettles, pots and pans, cutlery, tools, etc., sold in hardware stores. Currently the word usually denotes the equipment used in a COMPUTER system (*see also* SOFTWARE). It is also used in military circles to refer to various items of weaponry.

Hardy family An insufferable fictional family that featured in some 15 Hollywood films between 1936 and 1946. Made by MGM on modest budgets, the films were financially extremely successful and won a special Academy Award (1942) for furthering the American way of life. The hero of the family, the son Andy Hardy, played by the bouncy Mickey Rooney, was every American's idea of the boy next door. His girlfriends, typifying the girl next door but one, included several starlets who later became Hollywood greats – Judy Garland, Lana Turner,

Kathryn Grayson, and Esther Williams, among them. The pater familias, a small-town judge with a fund of patronizing small-town wisdom, was first played by Lionel Barrymore but subsequently by Lewis Stone. The mother, in whose mouth ice would not melt, was played endearingly, if not convincingly, by Fay Holden. A post-war revival of the family in *Andy Hardy Comes Home* (1958) demonstrated that the whole schmaltzy circus belonged to another era.

Hare Krishna A religious movement, formally known as the International Society for Krishna Consciousness (ISKCON), founded in America in 1966 by A. C. Bhaktivedanta (religious title Swami Prabhupāda; 1896–1977) and dedicated to the worship of the Hindu deity Krishna, an incarnation of the god Vishnu. The name comes from the title of a mantra (Hindi *Hare*, god, lord) chanted by believers as part of their daily ritual. Members of the sect live in communes, are vegetarian, and observe strict moral taboos against the use of intoxicants, sex outside marriage, and gambling. They adopt Hindu dress and customs and are a familiar sight in cities in Europe and America in their yellow robes, the men usually with shaven heads, soliciting funds and food. *See also* HONKERS.

Harlem toothpick US Black slang for a pocket flick-knife. As a switch-blade knife it features in 'Mac the knife', a well-known song by Kurt Weill (1900–50) from his *Threepenny Opera* (1928).

Harlot's Romp *See* QUEEN CHARLOTTE'S BALL.

harpic British slang used by young people in the 1960s, meaning mad or crazy. It derives from the advertisement for Harpic, the tradename for a lavatory cleaner, which claims to be able to clean 'round the bend'.

harpoon (1) Drug-abusers' slang for a hypodermic syringe used for injecting drugs. (2) Slang for a harmonica, another version of **harp**, which is widely used in pop-music circles for a harmonica.

Harrier jump jet The first operational short take-off and vertical landing (STOVL) fixed-wing fighter aircraft, developed by Hawker Siddeley in the 1960s. The Harrier made its maiden flight in 1966 and entered service with the RAF in 1969. The plane is powered by a single Rolls Royce Pegasus turbofan engine with vectored thrust, giving it a maximum forward speed of 1184 k.p.h. (736 m.p.h.). Jet nozzles at the wing tips, nose, and tail enable the plane to manoeuvre while hovering. Initially, vertical take-off was the objective, but a short take-off was subsequently found to be preferable because it enabled the plane to carry a greater payload. The wingspan of only 8.3 m (27.25 ft) and length of 14.1 m (46.25 ft) mean that the Harrier can operate from confined areas, giving it great versatility in supporting ground troops and other operational roles. In America, the Harrier has been modified by McDonnell Douglas as the AV-8B, for use by the US Marine Corps. This was introduced in 1985. A similar plane, the Harrier GR5, has been used by the RAF as the successor to their original Harriers. The Sea Harrier is the version flown by the Royal Navy. *See also* FLYING BEDSTEAD.

Harrow rail disaster One of the UK's worst railway accidents, second only to the GRETNA GREEN RAIL DISASTER in terms of casualties. It occurred at 08.18 on 8 October 1952 in Harrow station, NW London. An express sleeper travelling from Perth to Euston overran signals at Harrow and ploughed into a stationary local train waiting in the station. Immediately afterwards a northbound express from Euston collided with the wreckage causing a terrible pile-up in the station, then crowded with rush-hour commuters. 112 people were killed and over 150 injured. The reasons for the crash remain unknown; the driver of the southbound express was killed. However, it is thought that patchy fog may have affected the driver's view of the signals.

harry (1) British drug-abusers' slang from the 1960s for heroin. Cocaine was personified as CHARLIE. *See also* HENRY. (2) *See* HONKERS.

Harry Tate's Navy A good-humoured sobriquet applied to the Royal Naval Volunteer Reserve from about the time of World War I or a little earlier. The allusion is to the famous music hall artist Harry Tate (Ronald Macdonald Hutchinson; 1872–1940), perhaps best known for his motoring sketches. The term 'Harry Tate' came to signify anything that was disorganized or chaotic. *See also* KARNO; WAVY NAVY.

Hartmannsweilerkopf A mountain peak in the Vosges, near Steinbach in Alsace. During World War I it was the scene of fierce fighting between French and German forces for control of its strategic heights. In March 1915 the French wrested the heavily fortified summit from the Germans, who recaptured it briefly in April only to be driven out once more by the French. The heavy losses sustained on both sides gave a lasting and bloody fame to the name of the peak.

Harvey Smith A British colloquial term for a V-sign given as a gesture of contempt or abuse. The name comes from the Yorkshire-born showjumper Harvey Smith (1938–), who is known for his outspoken and blunt manner. At a show-jumping contest at Hickstead in 1971, in a moment captured by the television cameras, he made this sign. Although apparently directed disapprovingly at Douglas Bunn, Hickstead's owner, Smith maintains that it was a V FOR VICTORY salute (as popularized by Winston Churchill during World War II). The essential difference between the two gestures is that in the Churchillian salute the palm faces outwards, whereas it faces inwards when 'flicking a Harvey Smith'.

Harwell The UK's main nuclear research laboratory, located near Didcot in Oxfordshire and operated by the United Kingdom Atomic Energy Authority. Harwell performs experimental work on many aspects of nuclear technology, including nuclear-waste disposal, besides basic research into nuclear physics and nuclear applications in science, medicine, and industry. Scientists at Harwell are also engaged in many other fields, including toxicology, radiological protection, and the study of various types of pollution. The laboratory has a range of particle accelerators and three experimental reactors – Gleep, Dido, and Pluto.

hash Slang abbreviation of hashish, the resin form of the drug cannabis as obtained from Morocco, the Lebanon, or the Indian subcontinent. In the 1960s and 1970s this was the most widely available form of the drug in the UK. The term hash now sounds dated and has been replaced by such words as DOPE or 'blow'. *See* POT.

Hashbury The nickname of the district of San Francisco, Haight-Ashbury, in which the HIPPIE cult began in the mid-1960s. It involves a play on the word HASH, the smoking of which was central to the hippie lifestyle.

hashing A boisterous version of the popular game 'hare and hounds', in which a trail, usually of paper, is laid by the 'hare' for the 'hounds' to follow. The word is said to have come from Hash House, the name of a restaurant in Kuala Lumpur, which marked the end-point of the traditional hashing game, usually played by expatriate British. In this 'colonial' version, the chase is invariably followed by riotous partying.

hat. keep it under your hat A slogan from World War II reminding people of the need for national security. The US version was 'Keep it under your stetson'. *See also* KEEP IT DARK.

hatchback A car with a sloping back, which opens upwards giving access to the interior of the car; it provides a large luggage area, replacing the conventional boot. The term, which was first introduced in America in 1970, is also used of the back itself, which in effect provides an extra door to the vehicle. The practicality of such vehicles, often called 'five-door cars', has made them very popular thoughout the world.

hate. the man you love to hate *See under* MAN.

hatikvah (Heb., hope) A Jewish song with words by Naftali Imber (1856–1909) and music by Samuel Cohen. It was used as a rallying song by the Zionist movement from 1907 and became the national anthem of Israel in 1948, after a minor change in wording. *See* ZIONISM.

Havana Conference A conference of American states held in Havana in 1940 to consider various issues arising from World War II. The participants agreed on the 'No Transfer' principle in which control over colonies in the Americas could not be transferred between non-American states.

have. Have a nice day *See under* DAY.

Have a go The title of a popular travelling radio quiz show of the 1940s and 1950s hosted by Wilfred Pickles (1904–78) and his wife Mabel. The format was jokey and familiar, the accents north country, and the questions easy, the successful contestants being awarded small money prizes. If the question was answered correctly Pickles called out "Give her the money, Barney". Barney was the producer who doled out the prizes.

The phrase 'Have a go' was also used in a different context in 1964 by the Assistant Commissioner of Scotland Yard, Sir Ranulph Bacon. He advised members of the general public to 'have a go' (intervene) if they witnessed an armed robbery. Understandably this prompted a public outcry and was deemed foolhardy, but the phrase is still used in this sense.

> Have-a-go heroes who helped police track down an apparently armed post office raider received cash awards and bravery certificates yesterday in Carmarthen.
>
> *Carmarthen Journal* (9 January 1991).

Hawaii British slang for £50, based on the title of a US TV crime series *Hawaii Five-O*, which was popular in the 1970s.

Haw-Haw *See* LORD HAW-HAW.

hawk *See* DOVE.

hay US slang of the 1950s for marijuana. It now sounds dated and is rarely used.
and that ain't hay A US cliché, usually applied to money; it means, 'don't turn your nose up at that, it's not to be ignored'. It was used as the title of an Abbot and Costello film in 1943.

Hays Office The popular name for the Motion Picture Association of America (MPAA), founded in 1922 as the Motion Picture Producers and Distributors of America (MPPDA) under the directorship of the lawyer and political organizer Will H. Hays (1879–1954). The organization was formed by the principal Hollywood studios to impose self-censorship over their movies, in response to growing public indignation at sexual boldness on the screen and the unsuitable behaviour off screen of some film stars, notably FATTY Arbuckle. One of Hays' first moves was to insert morality clauses into players' contracts, enabling them to be dismissed for transgressions in their private lives. The Hays Office registered and collated complaints from the various local censorship boards and forwarded them to the studios. In 1930 a Production Code (the **Hays Code**) was issued detailing what could and could not be shown on the screen. For example:

> Excessive and lustful kissing, lustful embracing, suggestive postures and gestures, are not to be shown.
> Miscegenation (sex relationships between Black and White races) is forbidden.

This code was not implemented until 1934, when it became a constant source of friction between film producers and the Hays Office. Although it caused many tame and bowdlerized films to be produced, it had the effect of holding at bay calls for government censorship. Perhaps one of the most famous concessions made by Hays was to pass the last word in Rhett Butler's line in *Gone With The Wind* (1939), addressed to Scarlet O'Hara: "Frankly, my dear, I don't give a damn". In time fewer and fewer people did give a damn, and the Code was scrapped in 1966.

hazard lights The yellow lamps at the back and front of a car that flash simultaneously as a warning to other motorists to keep clear. They are switched on if the car has temporarily broken down on the road.

Hazchem A system of labelling road tankers and other containers of chemicals with special codes and symbols so that, in the event of an accident, the emergency services know what type of chemical is involved and how to treat it. The word is short for 'hazardous chemical'.

H.C.E. The initials of the Dublin publican, H(umphrey) C(himpden) Earwicker, whose dreams of a single night are described in James Joyce's *Finnegans Wake*. In this perplexing and, to many, incomprehensible novel, the initials stand not only for Earwicker himself, but are punningly alluded to by a host of phrases throughout the text, for example 'Here Comes Everybody', 'Heinz cans everywhere', 'Haroun Childeric Eggeberth', and 'How Copenhagen ended'. Earwicker's wife, Anna, is similarly referred to as A.L.P. – Anna Livia Plurabelle.

HD The pseudonym of the US poet and novelist Hilda Doolittle (1886–1961). Originally from Bethlehem, Pennsylvania, she moved to Europe in 1911 and became a member of the Imagist movement (*see* IMAGISM) with her friend Ezra Pound. Her interest in classical Greek culture and mythology is reflected in her poems, including *Hymen* (1921), *Heliodora and other Poems* (1924), and *Helen in Egypt* (1961). Among her novels are *Palimpsest* (1926), *The Hedgehog* (1936), and *Bid Me to Live* (1960).

head Slang for an anti-establishment cannabis smoker. The word was adopted in the late 1960s by the HIPPIES from the jargon of Black musicians and became the word they used to describe themselves; it was interchangeable with FREAK. It then became used in such expressions as HEAD SHOP and as a suffix in such words as **acidhead**, for someone who takes LSD; **snowhead**, for someone who takes cocaine; and **pothead**, a user of POT.

headbanger (1) Slang for a young person, usually male, who is a fan of heavy ROCK music. Headbangers do not dance to the music but violently shake their heads to the beat. This practice, which was considered somewhat hazardous by the medical profession, was popular in the 1970s. (2) Slang for a crazy or stupid person, especially someone who acts in an extreme way or adheres rigidly to extreme views.

head case Slang for a zany person rather than one who is clinically insane. The term was first used in America but has been heard in the UK since the 1980s. It can be used either contemptuously or affectionately.

headhunt To seek out a person already in employment and offer him or her a post, usually at a higher level, in a company involved in the same type of business. The headhunting is usually carried out by a recruitment agency, known colloquially as **headhunters**, who are hired to find the best person for a particular job, rather than simply to select from candidates who have answered a vacancy advertisement.

head shop A shop selling articles of psychedelia, such as incense sticks and hashish pipes. These shops, also known as *psychedelicatessens*, began to appear in California in the late 1960s HIPPIE era.

headshrink or **headshrinker** US slang for a psychoanalyst or a psychiatrist. Now invariably shortened to **shrink** and used widely on both sides of the Atlantic, it is often disparaging.

head trip Slang for a period of self-absorption or a self-obsessed thought-pattern that borders on the neurotic. This expression was first heard as US HIPPIE jargon but its use spread to the UK, where it is still used occasionally. The trip does not necessarily refer to a drug-induced state but rather to a profound experience that is going on in one's own head.

healie-feelie An informal, and often derogatory, term for someone who believes in healing or therapy by means of handling mineral crystals, such as quartz or tourmaline. Crystal therapy is becoming known in the UK as ALTERNATIVE MEDICINE generally becomes recognized.

health. **health farm** An establishment, usually a luxuriously appointed residential complex in the countryside, equipped with specially trained staff, saunas, swimming pools, and all the latest exercise equipment. Clients pursue a strict regime of diet and exercise to help them lose weight and restore their minds and bodies to fitness.

health food Food that is alleged to be 'better' for people, *i.e.* it prevents disease and promotes physical well-being. Ideas of what is a healthy diet have changed thoughout the century. It has been claimed that the healthiest diet for the British people was that available during World War II, when food rationing was in operation. After the war, people were told that dairy products were good for them, and that they should drink more milk and eat more eggs. These are now not considered healthy foods because of the saturated fats (*see* POLYUNSATURATE) they contain. In general, health food faddists now seek nourishment that is low in calories, high in nutritional value, contains little fat (especially saturated animal fat), and makes little or no use of artificial colouring or preservatives (*see* FOOD ADDITIVES). **Health-food shops**, which appeared in the UK in the 1960s, tend to concentrate on WHOLEFOOD, vitamin pills, and a miscellaneous collection of herbalist remedies. The idea of health foods has even been incorporated into French haute cuisine in cuisine minceur (*see* NOUVELLE CUISINE). In fact, interest in health food is part of a general concern with 'healthy living' in which regular exercise, jogging, etc., play an important part. It can be contrasted with junk food (*see* FAST FOOD) and, although very worthy, it is not to everyone's taste. For example:

> Some breakfast-food manufacturer hit upon the simple notion of emptying out the leavings of cart-horse nosebags, adding a few other things like unconsumed portions of chicken layer's mash and the sweepings of racing stables, packing the mixture into little bags, and selling them in health-food shops.
>
> FRANK MUIR, *Upon My Word!*

hear. **Can you hear me, mother?** This is reputed to be the first line from a radio show to become a catchphrase. In fact, it came about by accident. The comedian Sandy Powell (1900–82) was performing a sketch for the BBC in 1932 or 1933 in which he was supposed to be broadcasting from the North Pole and trying to get in touch with his mother. The first time he used this line, he dropped his script. While he retrieved it he repeated the line several times. The following week, at a live show, the line was expected by the audience, who joined in with great gusto when he repeated it.

You ain't heard nothin' yet! *See* TALKIES.

heart. A heartbeat away from the presidency A well-known expression to describe the position of the US vice-president. Used since the 1950s, it is probably meant to focus the voters' attention on the candidate's potential. A book by Jules Witcover about Spiro Agnew's resignation was called *A Heartbeat Away*. When Bush won the presidential election with Dan Quayle as his vice-president, there was a story going round Washington that Quayle was accompanied wherever he went by two armed CIA men – with orders to shoot Quayle if anything happened to Bush.

Eat your heart out! A phrase usually addressed by a lesser-known performer to a superstar, as if to say 'I can do as well as you can, mate', or 'It's time to watch out, you have a rival'. It is always said humorously and usually raises a laugh from the audience. This phrase became popular in the 1950s and 1960s in showbusiness.

Heartbreak Ridge The site of one of the bloodiest battles of the KOREAN WAR, also known as Height 1211. It is located in hilly country, W of the Hwachon Reservoir and near the 38TH PARALLEL. The worst fighting occurred in October 1951, when troops of the US 2nd Marine Division fought to push the enemy northwards following the collapse of truce negotiations. The Americans secured the ridge on 15th October, against fierce opposition from North Korean defenders.

hearts and minds A slogan associated with the disastrous involvement of US forces in the VIETNAM WAR. The administration's failure to capture 'the hearts and minds of America' and convince the US public of the reasons for US involvement was a major factor in the eventual withdrawal. Previously the phrase was linked with President Theodore Roosevelt, who in conversation with Douglas MacArthur, summed up his attributes as leader of the US nation in terms of his ability to "put into words what is in their hearts and minds but not in their mouths".

In your heart you know I'm (or **he's**) **right** The slogan used by (or about) Barry Goldwater in his unsuccessful presidential election campaign in 1964 against President Lyndon Johnson. The slogan has been frequently parodied; for example, 'You know in your heart he's right – far right'.

The Immaculate Heart of Mary In the Roman Catholic Church, devotion to the heart of Mary is a special form of devotion to Our Lady, which began in the 17th century. In 1947 Pius XII recognized 22 August as the Feast of the Immaculate Heart of Mary.

heat or **the heat** (1) Slang for the police. The term originated in US Black street jargon and was later adopted by the HIPPIES, before becoming more widely used. The image is that of an oppressive force. (2) British slang for a police investigation after a crime has been committed, as in the phrase 'the heat is on'. (3) Slang for a hand gun, an abbreviation of HEATER.

heater US slang for a handgun, first heard in the 1930s. It became well known through films and books about the underworld.

heat death The end that befalls a thermodynamically closed system that has attained its maximum total entropy. A thermodynamic concept, it has been applied to the universe as a whole, on the assumptions that the universe is subject to the second law of thermodynamics, which states that entropy either remains constant or increases in an isolated system, and that the universe is, in fact, an isolated system. At present there are many hot stars cooling in space, but eventually this energy flow will cease and the universe will attain thermodynamic equilibrium. All change and fluctuation will then cease and the universe will be cold, still, and timeless. There is some evidence, however, that the universe is expanding and contracting, in which case its eventual heat death will be followed by a rebirth. The concept of the heat death of the universe is highly speculative.

If you can't stand the heat, get out of the kitchen A saying that is usually attributed to US President Harry S. Truman, but he himself gave Major-General Harry Vaughan as the original source. Truman used it in 1952 when he announced that he would not be standing again for the presidency.

Heath Robinson or **Heath Robinsonian** A phrase commonly applied to complicated, ingenious, and fantastic contraptions of machinery, etc., after W. Heath Robinson (1872–1944). His amusing drawings of such absurdities in *Punch* and elsewhere were distinctive of their kind.

Heaviside layer or **Heaviside-Kennelly layer** or **E-layer** A belt in the Earth's atmosphere that contains ionized gases that act as a reflector for radio signals transmitted from Earth. It is named after the British physicist Oliver Heaviside (1850–1925). His studies of radio waves prompted him in 1902 to propose the existence of such a component in the atmosphere. A similar proposal was made independently by the US engineer Arthur Edwin Kennelly (1861–1939) at the same time, hence the alternative name.

heavy (1) Slang from the HIPPIE and youth culture of the late 1960s and early 1970s for serious, important, or meaningful, *e.g.* a heavy date. Its meaning has since progressed to aggressive, threatening, or antagonistic. (2) Since the late 1960s, surfing slang for an extremely large wave.

heaviest men Jon Brower Minnoch (1941–83) of Washington State was the heaviest recorded man. His greatest weight was 99 st. 1 lb. The heaviest recorded Briton was Peter Yarnall (1950–84) who reached 58 st. When he died firemen had to knock down his bedroom wall to remove his body. Previous claimants to the title included:

William Campbell (1856–78), born at Glasgow, the heaviest man recorded in the UK. He attained 53 st. 8 lb.

Daniel Lambert (1770–1809) of Leicester, the previous record-holder at 53 st. 11 lb. He was a keeper at Leicester gaol.

There are others said to have been heavier, but their weights are not verified.

heavy hitter A colloquial expression for a person with a great deal of power, authority, or effectivess. It is usually applied to someone in the world of commerce or politics.

heavy metal A form of ROCK music, popular during the 1970s and 1980s, basic in form and characterized by shrill guitar solos, repetitive rhythms, and high sound levels.

heavy water Deuterium oxide, *i.e.* water in which some or all of the hydrogen has been replaced by deuterium; either HDO or D_2O. Heavy water is used as a moderator to slow down the neutrons in a nuclear reator. The German attempts to secure large supplies of heavy water from an industrial plant in Norway in the early 1940s convinced the Allies that the Nazis were developing an atomic weapon. The belief spurred the Anglo-American determination to build, and eventually use, the first atomic weapons.

hedge. hedgehopper British slang coined during World War I for an air-force recruit; it is still used by new airmen of themselves. It is derived from the practice of flying close to the ground while still inexperienced.

Hedgers and Ditchers In 1911, during the struggle against the parliament bill proposing to curtail the powers of the House of Lords, the Conservative majority in the Lords was split. The 'Hedgers' under Lord Landsdowne were prepared to acquiesce rather than risk the creation of enough Liberal peers to ensure the bill's passage. The 'Ditchers' led by Lord Halsbury were prepared to die in the last ditch rather than yield. The Hedgers (the 'Judas group') prevailed and the bill passed, thus formally ending the power of the Lords over money bills and limiting that over other legislation to two years. *See* BALFOUR'S POODLE.

heebie-jeebies (1) Slang for a state of apprehension and fearfulnees. It was coined by the US cartoonist W. De Beck (1890–1942). It is now used in all English-speaking countries. (2) Slang for Jews. An elaboration of 'hebe', from Hebrew, it is less offensive that 'yid', but is still a racist term.

Heidelberg man A form of prehistoric man known from a fossilized lower jaw discovered in 1907 at Mauer, near Heidelberg, Germany. The thick-boned chinless mandible, about 500,000 years old, suggests that the owner had a broad projecting face, similar to *Homo erectus* ('upright man'). However, other features, such as the evenly proportioned teeth, are more characteristic of modern man (*Homo sapiens*). Heidelberg man was thus probably a type transitional between the two species.

heightism Discrimination on the grounds of height. This can be practised against those who are considered too tall and too short by conventional standards; it is usually women who are labelled too short. The word was coined by analogy with other discriminative words, such as SEXISM and AGEISM.

hei jen In China in the 1960s, young people who absconded from rural areas and went to live illegally in the city with no fixed abode. The word in Chinese means 'black people'.

Heimwehr Home Defence Force: an Austrian paramilitary movement, consisting of several distinct regional forces, that was founded after World War I, partly to repel border incursions by Yugoslavs and Hungarians. The groups had strong conservative or Fascist tendencies, and gained support mainly from rural areas. During the 1920s and early 1930s the Heimwehr was increasingly courted by politicians of the right to act as a counterforce to socialist movements in Vienna and other cities. The Heimwehr leadership forged ties with Mussolini in 1930, and in 1932 the right-wing Christian Social Party gave the Heimwehr leader, Fey, the post of national security chief in return for Heimwehr support. Although it helped in suppressing the Austrian socialists in 1934, the Heimwehr found its power draining away to the NAZIS. It was dissolved by the government in 1936.

Heineken refreshes the parts other beers cannot reach The advertising slogan for Heineken lager that was written by Terry Lovelock for the Collett, Dickenson, Pearce Agency in 1974. Considered to be one of the best advertisements ever written, the slogan was still used 20 years later. Since it first appeared there have been a variety of amusing characters, both on TV and on hoardings, experiencing the remarkable effects of the lager. These include a policeman's feet, Frankenstein's monster, and Concorde's nose. It is so widely known that it has been frequently parodied in such diverse contexts as graffiti and political speeches. Margaret Thatcher referred, in one of her rare jokes, at the 1980 Tory Party Conference to her then foreign secretary, Lord Carrington, as "the peer that reaches those foreign parts other peers cannot reach".

Heinkel bomber Any of several aircraft manufactured in Germany by Heinkel Flugzeugwerke, especially the He 111, the Luftwaffe's main medium-range bomber during World War II. The He 111 was a twin-engined development of the He 70 single-engined airliner. It first flew in 1935, and from 1936 was introduced into the Luftwaffe. The plane soon saw active service on the Nationalist side in the SPANISH CIVIL WAR. More streamlined versions, the He 111P and 111H, had been developed by 1939; these had a wingspan of 22.6 m (74 ft 1 in.) and a length of 16.39 m (53 ft 9 in.). Many of these planes flew bombing missions over Britain during World War II, and losses were heavy during the BATTLE OF BRITAIN.

Heisenberg's Uncertainty Principle or **Indeterminacy Principle** This states that one cannot measure precisely and simultaneously both the position and velocity of an object. It was formulated by the German physicist Werner Heisenberg (1901–76) and published in 1927. In practical terms the uncertainties involved are so small that they are significant only when considering atoms and sub-atomic particles. These uncertainties arise from the wavelike properties of such particles, *i.e.* they behave as both particles and waves. Position can only be determined accurately when the wave shows greatest undulation; but at this instant the wavelength is ill-defined, creating uncertainty in velocity measurement. The converse is true of precise velocity measurement. Heisenberg's principle also applies to other related pairs of physical variables, such as momentum and position, energy and time. Moreover, it has implications not only for quantum mechanics and particle physics but also for philosophy, especially arguments about cause and effect. If Heisenberg is correct, the identity of a particle can only be expressed in terms of probability and therefore its destiny cannot be stated with certainty. If one is unable to identify positively a particle and unable to be sure what will become of it in the future, one cannot say whether or not it is obeying the law of cause and effect. The breakdown of this law at the level of particles thus casts doubt on a principle that has been intuitively accepted for thousands of years – that every effect must have a cause.

heist US slang for a robbery, usually an armed robbery. First used in the early years of the 20th century, it probably derives from 'hoist', meaning to lift. Lifting is itself a euphemism for stealing.

heli-. helipad A place for helicopters to land and take off. The word, a combination of 'helicopter' and 'pad' (a flat surface for vertical takeoff and landing), was coined in 1960. The earlier word, ***heliport***, is also used.

heli-skiing A form of skiing in which the skiers are transported to the top of the slopes by helicopter. Usually these slopes are remote from the usual tourist ski areas and certain to have copious snowfalls. Heli-skiing first became popular in Canada but has spread to the European ski slopes.

Heligoland Bight, Battle of The first naval battle of World War I, fought between the Royal Navy's Harwich Force, led by Commodore Reginald Tyrwhitt, and German vessels patrolling the waters of Heligoland Bight in the S North Sea. The intention was to lure into battle the larger German battleships anchored in nearby ports. In spite of near calamitous confusion among the British, caused by poor communications and bad visibility, several enemy ships were engaged resulting in the loss of three German light cruisers and a torpedo boat. Tyrwhitt's own cruiser, *Arethusa*, was severely crippled, and three British destroyers were damaged. The action, in August 1914, impressed the UK's naval supremacy on the Germans at the outset of the war, and prompted the Kaiser to instruct his fleet to "hold itself back and avoid actions which can lead to greater losses".

hell. Hell is other people A much-quoted remark by the French existentialist philosopher and writer Jean-Paul Sartre (1905–80) in *Huis-clos* (1944). T. S. Eliot (1888–1965) did not agree:

> Hell is oneself
> Hell is alone, the other figures in it
> Merely projections. There is nothing to escape from
> And nothing to escape to. One is always alone.
> *The Cocktail Party.*

Hell's Angels Members of a group of unruly and often trouble-making motorcyclists originating in California in the 1950s. Usually wearing leather jackets, their symbol is a winged death's head.

In due course Hell's Angels appeared in the UK and Europe among devotees of the motorcycle, united by a taste for a rootless existence on the fringe of society. Often tattooed and badge-bestrewn, they still have a somewhat dubious image, although members have claimed that 'angels' support one another and have even organized charitable fundraising efforts.

hell's a-poppin A US catchphrase of the 1930s onwards describing a manifestation of immense exuberance or energy. The phrase might have been used to describe a band playing with abandon or a very lively nightclub. The phrase was adapted as the title of the 1942 comedy film, *Hellzapoppin*, written by Nat Perrin and directed by H. C. Potter.

Hell's Corner The triangle of airspace above Kent with its apex above Dover; it was so called in World War II as it was here that much of the fiercest air combat took place during the BATTLE OF BRITAIN, 1940.

hello. hello! hello! hello! The suspicious greeting uttered by the traditional, and probably mythical, British bobby. It has been much used by comedians since the 1940s to caricature a member of the uniformed constabulary. In the classic pose, the phrase is delivered in grave tones, with the constable thrusting out the flaps of his tunic pockets with his thumbs, while simultaneously flexing his knees. This caricature was parodied to perfection in the 1970s' BBC television series MONTY PYTHON'S FLYING CIRCUS.

Hello playmates! One of several catchphrases used by British comedian Arthur Askey (1900–82), originally associated with his appearances on the BBC radio show 'Band Wagon' (first broadcast January 1938). The catchphrase was widely mimicked by others throughout Askey's long career, especially in the 1940s and 1950s.

help. helping the police with their inquiries A well-known police euphemism that actually means that the police are holding a suspect and rigorously questioning him. In the light of the GUILDFORD FOUR debacle, the phrase has taken on a sinister note that the police will have to work hard to dispel.

helpline A telephone line set up by special organizations to provide information, support, or counselling to groups such as the suicidal (*see* SAMARITANS), AIDS patients (*see* TERRENCE HIGGINS TRUST), CHILD ABUSE victims, etc.

henry (1) British slang from the 1970s for heroin. *See also* HARRY. (2) British drug-users' and -dealers' slang from the 1980s for an eighth of an ounce of cannabis, based on the name of Henry VIII. *See also* HOORAY HENRY; LOUIE.

hep or **hip** US slang meaning alive to, aware of, wise to. It is probably from the West African Wolof word *hipi*, meaning to open one's eyes. *See* HIPPIE.

hep-cat One who is fond of and moved by fast and noisy music. In Wolof, a *hipi-kat* is one who has opened his eyes. *See* CAT.

Herald of Free Enterprise The Townsend Thorensen roll-on roll-off (roro) car ferry that capsized off the Belgian port of Zeebrugge on 6 March 1987 with the loss of 188 lives. The ferry had embarked on a routine crossing to Dover but, due to negligence on the part of the crew, the bow doors had been left open and the ship turned turtle within a mile of the harbour. Despite the high death toll, the loss of life could have been far greater if the ferry had not settled upside down on a sandbank, which allowed many of the passengers to escape.

herb Caribbean slang for marijuana, usually pronounced in the US way, 'erb'. It was used by RASTAFARIANS and in Black music during the 1970s and has since been adopted by White users as an alternative to GRASS.

Herbert Divorce Act The Matrimonial Causes Act 1937: a divorce reform act introduced to parliament as a Private Member's Bill by Sir A. P. Herbert (1890–1971), the humorist and writer who had been elected to the Commons in 1935 as an Independent MP. The Act extended the grounds for divorce to include desertion (of more than three years duration), insanity (of over five years duration), and cruelty. It also rectified discriminatory anomalies regarding adultery, and made it possible for a wife to divorce her husband for rape, sodomy, or bestiality.

here. Here's Johnny The phrase that has been used since 1961 on US TV to introduce the chat show host Johnny Carson on the NBC's programme *Tonight*. His appearance was preceded by a drum roll and the 'here's' spun out to 'heeere's', the voice tone rising dramatically. A similar effect was used to introduce Simon Dee in his chat show on British TV in the mid-1960s.

here's looking at you, kid The line from the film *Casablanca* (1942), starring Ingrid Bergman and Humphrey Bogart, that became the latter's catchphrase. It was based on a well-established US toast. Unlike the other catchphrase from this film, PLAY IT AGAIN, SAM, Bogart actually said it.

here we go, here we go, here we go The British football fans' chant, usually sung to the tune of 'Stars and Stripes for Ever'. The fans start chanting this when their team is doing well. In 1985 Everton made it into a record, adapted and arranged by Tony Hiller and Harold Spiro. It is also used provocatively by fans outside the ground and by extension in any situation in which a large crowd (*e.g.* striking miners) finds itself in a confrontational situation.

Herero A Bantu-speaking tribe native to parts of what is now Namibia and Botswana. They are traditionally herders of cattle, sheep, and goats, organized into self-governing groups comprising extended families, with an elaborate clan system. In the late 19th century and early 20th century the Herero came into conflict with the German settlers of South West Africa, who were expropriating their land and livestock. This culminated in a full-scale rising in 1904, led by the Herero chief, Samuel Maherero. The German forces, led by General von Trotha, implemented a policy of systematic genocide against the poorly armed tribespeople; two-thirds of Herero men, women, and children were butchered, often in a sadistic fashion. The survivors fled to neighbouring British territory or into the Kalahari Desert.

heritage. heritage coast A stretch of coastline in the British Isles that is considered to be of great natural beauty and is therefore protected from development; heritage coasts are managed by the Countryside Commission. The idea of conserving stretches of coastline arose in the 1970s. Heritage coasts often coincide with NATIONAL PARKS.

heritage industry A derogatory term for those economic activities that depend upon and perpetuate a nostalgic view of the nation's past. It is applied principally to tourism, but is also used to indict such phenomenon as BBC costume drama, the trade in reproduction furniture, and the use of nostalgic imagery in advertising. It is applied with some bitterness to the re-creation of bygone customs or working practices (*see* INDUSTRIAL TOURISM) to provide a tourist attraction. Opponents of 'heritization' argue that it promotes an ERSATZ version of history, harmful to our understanding of both the past and the present. The term was popular with left-wing cultural commentators in the 1980s and provided the title of a book by Robert Hewison in 1987. *See also* DISNEYFICATION.

> There used to be coal mines in South Wales; now there's Heritage. The only working miners in the Rhondda Valley have moulded bodies and glass eyes . . . an organization called Heritage Projects is making glass-fibre miners for an organization called the Rhondda Heritage Park.
>
> *The Independent*, 26 January 1991.

hero Hazards of Electromagnetic Radiation to Ordnance. This acronym refers to the risk that electromagnetic radiation will accidentally ignite the fuse of the warhead of a missile, causing it to explode.

a country fit for heroes A phrase popularized by the Liberal statesman David Lloyd George (1863–1945) in a speech on 24 November 1918, following World War I. Although often misquoted as 'a country fit for heroes', what he actually said was:

What is our task? To make Britain a fit country for heroes to live in.

The reality was rather different, as suggested by Kensal Green's couplet about Lloyd George:

Count not his broken promises as a crime
He MEANT them, HOW he meant them – at the time.

These sentiments are echoed by G. K. Chesterton in his verse 'A Land Fit for Heroes', with the ironic subtitle 'Refutation of the Only Too Prevalent Slander that Parliamentary Leaders are Indifferent to the Strict Fulfilment of their Promises and the Preservation of their Reputation for Veracity':

They said (when they had dined at Ciro's)
The land would soon be fit for heroes;
And now they've managed to ensure it,
For only heroes could endure it.

heroin An addictive drug (chemical name diacetylmorphine) with harmful side-effects that became widely used in Western societies during the HIPPIE era. First developed from morphine in 1898 for use as a narcotic analgesic, it was subsequently banned in many countries after its undesirable addictive and physically damaging properties became known. It can be injected, sniffed, or inhaled and causes a shortlived sensation of euphoria followed by sleep; it can lead to severe withdrawal symptoms. The injection of pure heroin can kill as well as put addicts at risk from hepatitis, AIDS, and other infections. The high expense of the drug has been blamed for a major proportion of criminal activity in the West as addicts seek to find means to buy it. The first heroin addicts were diagnosed in the West in the early years of the century; by the end of the century the problems associated with heroin were being felt throughout the world despite severe legal penalties for use or possession of heroin and international efforts to prevent trafficking in drugs.

heroin baby A baby born to a heroin addict. Heroin babies are usually born prematurely and with a dependence on the drug.

Herrenvolk A German word meaning broadly master race. In NAZI usage it implied the superiority of the German peoples.

Herries Chronicle A sequence of novels written by the British author Hugh Walpole (1884–1941) recounting the fortunes of the Herries family of Cumberland. The original quartet of works deals with the period 1730–1932; it comprises *Rogue Herries* (1930), *Judith Paris* (1931), *The Fortress* (1932), and *Vanessa* (1933). Walpole later extended the saga with *The Bright Pavilions* (1940) and *Katherine Christian*, on which he was working at the time of his death. This was published posthumously in 1943.

Herriot, James The pseudonym of James Alfred Wright (1916–), who was born, and trained as a veterinary surgeon, in Glasgow and began practising in N Yorkshire in 1940. The first of his many entertaining stories, based on his professional experiences in the Yorkshire Dales, appeared in 1970. These were used as the basis of a popular TV series, *All Creatures Great and Small*, in the 1980s.

Hershey Bar The tradename for a US chocolate bar, which, in World War II, was only available to the troops. General L. B. Hershey was director of the Selective Service System, 1941–46. Hence in US army slang the term was applied to the narrow gold bar worn by troops on the left sleeve to indicate that they had done six months' overseas service.

HGV Heavy Goods Vehicle. An articulated or fixed-chassis lorry used for road haulage. An HGV licence is issued in addition to the normal car licence and is graded according to the type of vehicle in which the HGV test was taken. A Class 3 licence covers two-axle rigid straight trucks; a Class 2 covers three- and four-axle straight trucks; and a Class 1 licence (the most coveted) covers articulated vehicles of any size or gross weight.

hi-. Hi-de-hi! The title of a long-running BBC TV comedy programme, first broadcast in 1980, that was set in a 1950s holiday camp. The phrase echoes the line from the Butlins' holiday camp song 'Hi-de-hi! Ho-de-ho!', a nonsense-word chorus intended to express the euphoria of being at Butlins but little else. The line had been used previously by the BBC broadcaster Christopher Stone as his catchphrase in 1937 on Radio Normandy. Another story concerns an army officer who trained his troops to answer 'Ho-de-ho' to his call of 'Hi-de-hi'; he was court-martialled.

hi-fi The reproduction of speech or music with little distortion; also equipment that faithfully reproduces sound. The term, an abbreviation of *high-fidelity*, was first used in the late 1940s. The reproduction of music in the home has passed through a number of stages, requiring the user to buy new equipment and a new collection of recorded works several times during his lifetime. Recording of music began with the phonograph (invented 1877), using wax cylinders, and progressed rapidly to the gramophone (1888), using shellac records. Electrified gramophones appeared in the 1930s; called radiograms and record players, they continued to use shellac records rotating at 78 r.p.m. until the late 1940s, when vinyl discs were introduced, using rotation speeds of 45 and 33⅓ r.p.m. It was the vinyl 33⅓ r.p.m. discs (so called long-playing or LPs) that were first called hi-fi recordings. They were advertised as giving distortion-free reproduction between frequencies of 80 and 12,000 hertz. Since then vinyl discs have had to compete with magnetic tape cassettes, the latest of which use the DOLBY SYSTEM. In turn, current hi-fi systems have abandoned cassettes and tape recorders in favour of COMPACT DISCS using DIGITAL RECORDING and laser-driven compact-disc players. Thus a music enthusiast in his sixties is likely to have his favourite music recorded in four separate collections: shellac 78s, vinyl LPs, cassettes, and compact discs, all requiring different equipment. In the not too distant future, the hi-fi enthusiast is likely to have to re-equip with digital audio tape, a new breed of magnetic tape using digital recording.

hiba kusha (Jap. explosion-affected group) A person or people who survived the atom bombs dropped on HIROSHIMA and NAGASAKI by America in 1945. It came into English usage around 1970.

hide. hide-and-seek British rhyming slang for a boutique. It was coined in the swinging sixties when boutiques became fashionable.

hideaways US Black slang for pockets in one's clothes.

You can run, but you can't hide A phrase associated with the US boxer Joe Louis (1914–81); although he probably didn't invent it, he used it as part of his bravado speech before his World Heavyweight Championship bout in 1946 against the nimble Billy Conn. Louis won. President Reagan used the phrase in 1985 as a warning to all international terrorists following the hijacking of a TWA airliner to Beirut.

Higgins, Professor The phonetics expert in Shaw's *Pygmalion*, who tutors the Cockney flower-seller, Eliza Doolittle, in order that she may be passed off as a duchess. The play ends with Eliza at odds with Higgins, who persists in seeing her as an experimental subject, rather than a human being. However, for the 1938 film version, directed by Anthony Asquith and Leslie Howard, Shaw approved the scripted 'happy ending', with a reconciliation between the Professor and 'Liza (played by Leslie Howard and Wendy Hiller, respectively). This modified plot was adapted for the musical version, *My Fair Lady* (1956), which was filmed in 1964, with Higgins played by Rex Harrison. Shaw is said to have based the Higgins character on the distinguished Oxford phonetician, Henry Sweet (1845–1912).

high Slang for a state of intoxication induced by drugs or alcohol. It has been widely used to mean specifically under the influence of drugs since the 1960s, whereas to earlier generations it meant drunk.

for the high jump British slang meaning in deep trouble, usually implying dismissal or that a serious punishment will be exacted. It originally meant that someone was to be executed by hanging, the former British judicial method in which the person to be executed stood on a platform with a rope round his (or her) neck: when the executioner pulled a lever the platform fell away and the person was left hanging (*see* DANCING IN THE AIR). The height of the 'jump' and length of rope was assessed for individual cases by the hangman. If he miscalculated, either the body was decapitated or the unfortunate victim had to be finished off by the doctor.

high-brow A learned person, an intellectual. The term originated in America about 1911 and is also used to denote cultural, artistic, and intellectual matters above one's head. Derivatives are **low-brow** and **middle-brow**.

High ho, Silver A catchphrase given to a grateful world by the US radio serial of the 1930s and 1940s, *The* LONE RANGER. The phrase was uttered by the show's eponymous masked hero as a means of spurring on his grey steed, Silver. The show later transferred to the small screen, which is how British audiences came to know the phrase in the 1960s.

high-involvement product A product on which a purchaser spends a considerable amount of time and thought before deciding to buy it. Cars, houses, TVs, video recorders, etc., are the typical high-cost items that fall into this category. Advertisements for such products will tend to be informative, providing the potential buyer with the kind of technical information required to make an informed judgment between it and its competitors.

Low-involvement products, on the other hand, involve the consumer in little deliberation. Such products are cheap and advertisers strive to make their advertisments interesting or funny in order to develop a brand loyalty, because they know that their product is unlikely to be better (or worse) than its competitors.

high-level language A computer programming language that uses a notation closer to human language or mathematical symbols than a machine code. High-level languages, such as FORTRAN and BASIC, are easy to use but slower to execute and more restricted than LOW-LEVEL LANGUAGES. As low-level languages are closer to the computer processor instructions, they are faster and more versatile but more difficult to use.

high rise An office or residential building with a large number of floors. The high rise, or tower block, came into vogue during the late 1950s and 1960s following the example of the Modernist architect, Le Corbusier (1887–1965). The idea of modern, hygenic, and streamlined space-saving buildings using cheap modern concrete materials proved particularly appealing to post-war local councils faced with restricted housing budgets. The first of the high-rise estates, Alton West in Roehampton, was erected by the London County Council in 1958. Hundreds of similar sprawling estates, some with slimmer and taller tower blocks, were erected in the next 20 years all over the UK. They were not, however, popular with the people housed in them. Perched high above the ground in cramped flats, young mothers longed for their own houses and back gardens in which the children could play and babies could sleep in their prams. In addition, shoddy workmanship and flawed design, such as poor waterproofing and dangerous lifts, together with lack of supervision and recreation facilities, turned many of these estates into brutal, damp, and vandalized areas, plagued by crime and vermin; the architects and town planners of the period have much to answer for.

high tech A style of domestic decor, popular in the 1970s, which favoured high-quality industrial furniture and fittings, such as metal factory shelves and tubular steel shelving, to imitate the hard metallic surfaces and textures of the industrial and technological environment. 'High-tech' is also used to describe a style of modern architecture, which regards architectural design as a branch of industrial technology. A recent classic example of the high-tech glass and metal style is the new Lloyds Building (1986) in London, designed by Richard Rogers (1933–). More generally, 'high-tech' is applied to any process, product, etc., using sophisticated electronic equipment or techniques.

Highway Code A code issued by the Department of Transport for road users, both pedestrians and those using vehicles (including lorries, cars, motorcycles, and bicycles). The code contains detailed instructions on road and motorway use, and knowledge of the code is essential to pass a driving test. *See also* GREEN CROSS CODE.

pile it high, sell it cheap The guiding principle adopted by Sir John Cohen (1898–1979) as his slogan when building up his commercial empire based on Tesco supermarkets.

Royal Highness In the UK this title is now confined (since 1917) to the sovereign and his or her consort, to the children of the sovereign, to grandchildren in the male line, and the eldest son of the eldest son of the Prince of Wales. It was formerly granted to a somewhat wider group of relations.

hijack Illegally to take possession of a vehicle and its contents, whether goods or passengers, usually by means of force or threats of force. Hijacking can apply either to lorries, etc., or to planes, for which the word **sky-jack** can also be used. A hijack has its origins in the command given by robbers raiding lorries transporting illicit alcohol in America during Prohibition: "Stick 'em up high, Jack". In the late 20th century, however, hijacking has applied to the act by terrorists of taking over control of a passenger aircraft in flight, ordering the pilot at gunpoint to fly to a new destination where political or ransom demands are made using the passengers as hostages.

Hill 60 (1) A small hill SE of Ypres, Belgium, that figured in fighting on the WESTERN FRONT during World War I. It was so named because of its height – 60 metres. In April 1915 British forces mined and destroyed German positions and captured the hill. There followed a fierce but unsuccessful counterattack by the Germans, whereupon both sides announced possession of Hill 60. The propaganda value of holding the hill thus came to outweigh its strategic importance; as the British still held the hill, the Germans were forced to launch a determined attack to give substance to their false claim. On 5 May as a result of a combination of gas and heavy shelling, the British retreated. Although by now partly demolished by sheer weight of explosives, Hill 60 continued to be fought over until the Allied breakthrough of 1917. (2) A quite different Hill 60 featured in the GALLIPOLI campaign, again during World War I. It is one of the foothills of the Sari Bair range on the Gallipoli peninsula.

Hillsborough disaster The UK's worst sports tragedy, in which 95 spectators died at the Hillsborough football ground, Sheffield, on 15 April 1989. The disaster occurred shortly after the start of the FA Cup semi-final between Liverpool and Nottingham Forest. Several hundred Liverpool fans arriving late caused severe congestion in the approaches to the Leppings Lane end of the ground, causing the police to open the turnstiles into the ground in an attempt to relieve the crush outside. However, the fans surged onto already crowded terraces, so that spectators at the front were crushed against the perimeter fencing, unable to escape onto the pitch. Besides the fatalities, some 400 fans were treated in hospital for their injuries. The official inquiry into the disaster, conducted by Lord Justice Taylor, placed the blame on inadequate policing of the crowd coupled with design flaws in the stadium. Taylor's recommendations prompted an urgent overhaul of football ground safety in the UK.

Hindenburg The German airship whose tragic demise in 1937 marked the end of an era in aviation. She was built by the makers of the highly successful GRAF ZEPPELIN I for regular service across the North Atlantic, and measured 245 m (804 ft) in length with a gas capacity of 196,000 m^3 (7,000,000 cu ft). When completed in 1936 this made her the largest airship ever built, although the record was soon to be taken by her sister ship, *Graf Zeppelin II*, with a slightly larger gas volume. The Hindenburg's scheduled transatlantic service began in 1936, between Friedrichshafen, Germany, and Lakehurst, New Jersey. On 6 May 1937, while coming in to land at Lakehurst, hydrogen gas in the airship's tail section caught fire. The flames quickly spread and the airship collapsed to the ground in a mass of burning wreckage, killing 35 of the 97 passengers and crew on board. The exact cause of the fire was never established, but the accident, combined with the growing prospect of war, effectively put paid to airship travel, and her sister ship never entered commercial service.

Hindenburg Line The line that formed part of the WESTERN FRONT during World War I and was under the authority of the German commander, von Hindenburg (1849–1934). It was a defensive line stretching some 90 miles SE from Arras to Soissons and comprised sentry posts, trench systems, dugouts, and other features forming a zone in places up to 7300 m (8000 yd) wide. Around 65,000 people were employed in its construction, between October 1916 and March 1917, including 50,000 Russian prisoners-of-war. In March 1917 the Germans started a strategic withdrawal from the existing front to the Hindenburg Line, in some places retreating a distance of over 40 km. The move enabled consolidation of both German men and materials and considerably strengthened their defensive capability. Only in September 1918 were the German forces finally ousted from large sections of the line.

hip *See* HEP.

hip-hop A form of music and dancing originated by Black youths in New York. It became popular in the UK in the 1980s. It consists of RAP accompanied by rhythmical jerky dancing, such as BODY-POPPING.

hip-huggers Trousers or jeans that fit closely round, and hang from, the hips rather than the waist. Hip-huggers, also known, especially in the UK, as **hipsters**, were fashionable dress in the late 1960s and early 1970s, with bellbottoms, epaulettes on jackets, and Indian clothing and jewellery.

hippie or **hippy** In the late 1960s, a young person who rejected conventional society in favour of an unstructured lifestyle based on communal living, free love, and experimentation with PSYCHEDELIC drugs. Hippies wore fantastic multi-coloured clothes, often set off with flowers and bells, and preached a pacific anarchistic philosophy; many were interested in ecology and eastern religions. The movement began in San Francisco in 1966–67 and soon spread throughout Europe and America. In the UK, social security payments enabled disaffected young people to drop out of conventional life, although a few from wealthy middle-class families had private means and a few attempted to make a living from the land.

In the 1980s the term was applied by the British tabloid press to the new phenomenon of young people, mostly unemployed and homeless, travelling around the country in convoys of ramshackle vehicles. These new-age travellers (*see* NEW AGE), as they preferred to be called, became particularly known for their attempts to occupy Stonehenge at the time of the Summer Solstice (21 June). *See* BEATNIK; DROPOUT; HELL'S ANGELS.

hipster *See* HIP-HUGGERS.

Hiroshima A Japanese city and military base, the target of the first ATOM BOMB dropped in warfare (6 August 1945). Over 160,000 people were killed or injured and far more rendered homeless. The flash of the explosion was seen 170 miles away and a mushroom-shaped column of black smoke rose over the city to a height of 40,000 feet (*see* MUSHROOM CLOUD). Hiroshima remains a solemn portent of the fate over-shadowing mankind in the event of a nuclear war. *See also* ENOLA GAY; HIBAKUSHA.

His Master's Voice A phrase familiar to record buyers in America and Europe as the tradename of the Gramophone Company, now part of EMI. It was originally the title of a painting by Francis Barraud (1856–1924), showing the artist's terrier cross, Nipper, looking curiously at the black horn of a wax cylinder phonograph player from which the sound of 'his master's voice' is emerging. The record company agreed to purchase the work in 1899 but stipulated that the picture be altered to show a brass horn and a more up-to-date gramophone; close examination of the picture reveals the faint outline of the older model still visible. Nipper had died in 1897 but the deal involving Barraud's picture ensured that his image lived on to become the most frequently reproduced dog of all time. Nipper was first used on an advertisement in 1900 in America, and from 1902 the US Victor company incorporated his image on its record labels. In the UK, Nipper appeared on records from 1909, and the phrase 'His Master's Voice' became part of the logo in 1910. Nipper also appeared in an advertisement for Reid's Stout, sniffing at a glass of beer; the caption ran "What is it that master likes so much?"

Hiss affair The sensation caused in 1948 by allegations that a US State Department official, Alger Hiss (1904–), was a former Communist spy. The accusation was made by Whittaker Chambers, one-time Communist Party member and a former editor on *Time* magazine, before the House Committee for Un-American Activities (*see* MCCARTHYISM). Hiss strenuously denied Chambers' allegations, and in August brought a suit for slander against him. When challenged for evidence to support his accusations, Chambers produced copies of State Department papers that he claimed had been supplied by Hiss. Chambers even led investigators to his Maryland farm, where he produced three rolls of microfilm hidden in a pumpkin – the infamous 'pumpkin papers'. Hiss was indicted and appeared before a grand jury in 1949 on charges of perjury – for his previous denials of passing papers to Chambers. This first trial resulted in a hung jury, but at a re-trial in 1950 Hiss was convicted and sentenced to five years imprisonment. He was released in 1954. Many believed that Hiss fell victim to the anti-communist hysteria then widespread in America; others were convinced of Hiss's guilt. The affair certainly boosted the career of Richard M. Nixon, then a junior member of the Un-American Activities Committee, who was instrumental in constructing the case against Hiss.

history is bunk A phrase normally attributed to the US car manufacturer Henry Ford (1863–1947). Ford's opinion, however, was actually less definite:

> History is more or less bunk.

He went on to say:

> It's tradition. We don't want tradition. We want to live in the present and the only history that is worth a tinker's damn is the history we make today.
>
> *Chicago Tribune*, 25 May 1916.

hit (1) Slang for one puff on a marijuana cigarette or a pipe, or a single dose of an illegal drug. In the sense of one dose of something exotic, the meaning has been extended to include delicious items of food that would not be eaten in large quantities. (2) Slang for an assassination. Originally from US underworld jargon, it is now widely used both as a noun and a verb. (3) British rhyming slang for drunk, from 'hit and missed', *i.e.* pissed. (4) Slang for to borrow, or beg, *e.g.* 'He hit me for another fiver'.

hit-and-run An accident involving a motor vehicle, in which the driver has neither stopped after the accident to help the victim nor informed the police. Hit-and-run drivers hope to escape the consequences of the accident but if they are caught they are dealt with very severely by the courts.

hit list A list of people targeted for some form of violence, such as murder. Several hit lists have been discovered in premises occupied by IRA terrorists.

hitman Slang for a hired killer. Originally US underworld jargon, it is now widely used in the UK.

hit the ground running A phrase meaning to start a new enterprise, or get involved in something new, and immediately be able to operate at full strength. It probably derives from the image of such MACHO activities as parachuting and being able to run off immediately one touches the ground, rather than being disorientated by the fall, and from the rapid disembarking of troops from helicopters (as practised in the VIETNAM WAR).

hitting on all six Doing well, giving a fine performance. A motor-car engine when running well is described as having the pistons in all six cylinders hitting (firing) perfectly.

hitch-hike To travel from place to place by standing at the roadside asking for lifts from passing vehicles. The hitch-hiker indicates that he wants a lift by passing his hand across his chest with the thumb extended in the direction in which he wishes to travel. For this reason, hitch-hiking is often called 'thumbing a lift'.

Hitler. Heil Hitler (Hail Hitler) The familiar salutation to the FÜHRER, often used derisively of one adopting dictatorial methods or attempting dictatorial policies. It is accompanied by the NAZI salute, in which the right arm is raised outstretched diagonally to the body and the heels are clicked. The salutation is a caricature of the German militarism and brutality of the Nazi period.

Hitler Diaries In April 1983 *The Sunday Times* reported the discovery of 60 volumes of Hitler's diaries which had been acquired by the Hamburg colour magazine *Stern* for £2,460,000 and delivered to them by their reporter Gert Heidemann. They were said to have been salvaged from an aircraft wrecked in 1945 and found in a hayloft. Professor Hugh Trevor-Roper (Lord Dacre) had vouched for their authenticity and *The Sunday Times* (after paying *Stern* for publication rights) obtained two volumes (1932 and 1935) for testing. Dr Julius Grant, a chemical expert, proved that the paper in the diaries was not in use until after World War II. Two weeks after their alleged discovery the Bonn government also declared them to be forgeries. Heidemann revealed that he had obtained them from a Stuttgart dealer in military relics, Konrad Fischer, whose real name was Kujau; he later confessed to the forgery. Both were imprisoned in May 1983, brought to trial in August 1984, and sentenced in July 1985. Kujau was jailed for 4 years 6 months for forgery and Heidemann for 4 years 8 months for fraud. *The Sunday Times* emerged from the whole episode looking rather foolish; newspapers are now extremely cautious about announcing scoops before they have proved them to be valid.

Hitlerism The doctrine and practice of the NAZI regime of Adolf Hitler (1889–1945), who became German Chancellor in 1933 and ruled Germany until his suicide. His brutal, aggressive, and expansionist policies led directly to World War II in which over 20 million people were killed. Pursuing totally spurious and absurd racial theories, he was also responsible for the HOLOCAUST, in which six million Jews were murdered on his orders.

Hitlerjunge Quex (Ger. Hitler Youth Quex) The title of a NAZI propaganda film produced in 1933 under the auspices of Dr Paul Joseph Goebbels, the German Minister for Public Enlightenment and Propaganda. The plot concerned the real-life case of Herbert Norkus, a member of the Hitler Youth but the son of a communist family, who was allegedly murdered by communists. It was a box-office flop, like the two other Goebbels-inspired movies of the same year – *SA-Mann Brand*, about Nazi stormtroopers, and *Hans Westmar*, based on the life of the Nazi 'martyr', Horst Wessel (*see* HORST WESSEL LIED).

Hitler-Stalin pact A pact of non-aggression between Germany and the Soviet Union signed in Moscow on 23 August 1939 by Germany's foreign minister, von Ribbentrop, and the Soviet Commissar for foreign affairs, Molotov (it is also known as the **Ribbentrop-Molotov pact**). The two countries agreed not to support any third party that launched an attack on the other signatory, and to consult with each other on matters of mutual interest. More significant, however, was a secret protocol that effectively partitioned Europe into German and Soviet spheres. The pact was greeted triumphantly by Hitler but viewed with dismay by the UK and the other Western democracies. Hitler and Stalin had managed to swallow their long-standing rancour towards each other to win significant strategic gains: Stalin was given the defensive buffer he badly needed, while Hitler saw the final obstacle to a German invasion of Poland removed. German tanks crossed the Polish border on 1 September, and by the end of the month all of Poland was divided between the German and Soviet armies, according to the terms of the pact. The Allies were by now at war with Germany.

Hitler Youth (Ger. Hitler Jugend) The principal male youth organization of NAZI Germany. It was established in 1933, like the equivalent organization for girls – the League of German Girls (*Bund Deutscher Mädel*), and encompassed all existing youth clubs in the country. In 1935 Baldur von Schirach was appointed Reich Youth Leader, and the following year all youth organizations other than Hitler Youth were banned. The Hitler Youth embodied the vehement anti-intellectualism of the Führer, who wanted its youngsters to be "swift as the greyhound, tough as leather, and hard as Krupp steel". Boys were admitted to the Hitler Youth at the age of 14, normally after three or more years in the junior division, the Deutsches Jungvolk (German Young People). At 18 members graduated to the National Socialist Party, and so into the adult echelons of Nazism, having by then been indoctrinated in Hitler's demented philosophy.

HIV Human Immuno-Deficiency Virus. The virus that causes AIDS. If someone is diagnosed as HIV-positive, he or she shows traces of the virus in their system but can remain free of AIDS symptoms indefinitely. However, research into the precise links between HIV infection and full-blown AIDS, and into whether the virus can remain dormant indefinitely, is as yet inconclusive.

Hoare-Laval pact Secret proposals for ending the conflict caused by the Italian invasion of Abyssinia (Ethiopia) in 1935, formulated in early December of that year by the British foreign minister, Samuel Hoare, and his French opposite number, Pierre Laval. The proposals granted substantial territorial concessions to Italy, plus a zone of exclusive economic interest; the LEAGUE OF NATIONS would protect Abyssinian sovereignty over remaining areas. The pact was leaked to the press on 9 December causing a storm of public protest against this apparent appeasement of Italian aggression. By 18 December the British government had been forced to repudiate the pact, and Hoare resigned, to be succeeded by Anthony Eden. Unhindered, Italy proceeded to complete her conquest of Abyssinia.

Hobbit A member of a benevolent hospitable burrow people, two to four feet high and fond of bright colours, the creation of Professor J. R. R. Tolkein. They are featured in his works *The Hobbit* (1937) and *The Lord of the Rings* (1954–55).

hobble skirts A women's fashion of skirts, so tight around the ankles that the wearer was impeded in walking (much as a horse is hobbled), that was at its height in 1912; it was gone by 1914.

hobo In US usage, a migratory worker who likes to travel, in contrast to a tramp, who travels without working, and a bum, who neither travels nor works. It derives probably from *hoe-boy*, a migratory farm worker.

Ho Chi Minh Trail A network of routes running S from what was formerly North Vietnam, through E Laos into Cambodia and S Vietnam. It is named after North Vietnam's president (1954–69) and leader of the independence struggle, Ho Chi Minh (1890–1969). Parts of the trail date back to the 1940s and 1950s, when the Vietnamese were fighting for independence from the French. During the VIETNAM WAR of the 1960s and 1970s it was greatly expanded to supply the Communist National Liberation Front (VIET CONG) with men and materials for their campaign in South Vietnam and neighbouring countries. The trail comprises a mixture of footpaths, tracks, and roads through the mountains and jungles, built and maintained largely by manual labour. Some stretches were suitable for trucks, but most parts were passable only by bullock cart, by bicycle, or on foot. Supplies could take up to six months to pass the full extent of the trail into South Vietnam. In spite of intensive US bombing, and efforts by the South Vietnamese army to cut Viet Cong supply lines, the North

Vietnamese army and NLF kept the trail open throughout the war. This proved to be a crucial factor in their ultimate victory.

The **Sihanouk Trail**, named after the Cambodian leader, Prince Norodim Sihanouk, branched off the Ho Chi Minh Trail in S Laos to provide a route into NE Cambodia.

Hockey Stick The Hollywood nickname of the British film star Julie Andrews (1935–). Many Hollywood Americans regard such beautiful and cool English girls as a product of the JOLLY HOCKEY STICKS! tradition of private schools. Indeed, Moss Hart, the US playwright and producer said of her:

> She has that wonderful British strength that makes you wonder why they lost India.

This reputation, largely earned in her two governess roles (in *Mary Poppins* and *The Sound of Music*), made her a great deal of money, brought her worldwide stardom, and endeared her to several generations of children. It did not, however, please Julie Andrews herself. In 1966 she said:

> I don't want to be thought of as wholesome.

She was also in the habit of wearing a badge saying: 'Mary Poppins is a junkie'.

hog (1) US slang for a motorcyle, especially a Harley Davidson. It was first used by the HELL'S ANGELS in America, but later became well known in the UK and Australia. *See also* CHOPPER. (2) US slang for an aggressive and angry woman. (3) Slang for the illegal drug PCP (*see* ANGEL DUST), which was originally developed as an animal tranquillizer and tested on pigs.

hokey cokey A light-hearted dance, popular during the 1940s, based on the song and tune of this name.

Holcomb murders The murder in 1959 of four members of a farming family at Holcomb, Kansas. Two ex-convicts were later arrested and convicted of the brutal crime. The case occupied the attentions of US novelist Truman Capote, who used it as the basis of his book *In Cold Blood* (1966). This he described as 'a nonfiction novel': "a new art form . . . that employed all the techniques of fictional art but was nevertheless immediately factual." Serialized in *The New Yorker* magazine prior to publication, the novel attracted great attention, and no little acclaim, from critics and public alike, and became a bestseller. The British critic, Kenneth Tynan, accused Capote of being less than strenuous in his efforts to win a reprieve for the convicted men and it was undeniable that their execution helped generate interest in Capote's book. Capote retorted that the appeals procedure had been exhausted.

holding US drug-users' slang for carrying illegal drugs, either for resale or for personal use. The British equivalent is 'carrying'.

holding pattern A repetitive circuit flown by an aircraft while waiting permission to land at an airport. The term has been extended to other states of delay or deferment.

hole. a better 'ole *See under* BETTER.

foxhole *See under* FOX.

holistic medicine A form of ALTERNATIVE MEDICINE that aims to treat the patient as a whole unit, rather than applying remedies to specific areas of the body or mind. The word 'holistic' was invented by Jan Smuts, prime minister of South Africa, in the mid-1920s to describe his philosophical theory of **holism**. However, the medical movement in the UK arose much later in the 20th century, as part of a minority interest in homeopathy and other non-scientific therapies.

Hollywood A suburb of Los Angeles, California (also called **Tinsel Town** or **Sodom-by-the-sea**), famous as the centre of the US film-making industry from its foundation in 1911. The **Golden Age of Hollywood** comprised the years of the studio system, 1930–49, when a handful of powerful producers dominated the US motion-picture output and the world mass-market entertainment business. By the mid-1950s, a combination of factors, including the rise of television, MCCARTHYISM, and the advent of the actor-producer conspired to end the hegemony of the Hollywood 'dream factory', although it remains a byword for showbiz glitz and glamour.

> A place where they pay you $50,000 for a kiss and 50 cents for your soul.
>
> MARILYN MONROE.

Hollywood Bowl An open-air auditorium in the Hollywood area of Los Angeles, noted for its summer season of concerts given by the Los Angeles Philharmonic Orchestra. The concert platform, designed by the US architect Frank Lloyd Wright, is a fairy-tale shell-like structure, 30 m (100 ft) wide, located at the base of a natural amphitheatre capable of seating

17,500 people. The Bowl's first concert was held in 1921. Today, pop, jazz, and rock events are held in addition to the light classical performances. Los Angelinos traditionally bring picnics to consume before, and often also during, the concerts.

Hollywood Ten The group of ten US screenwriters, film producers, and directors who refused to confirm or deny their affiliation to the Communist Party during the investigations of the House of Un-American Activities Committee in 1947 (*see* MCCARTHYISM): Alvah Bessie, Herbert Biberman, Lester Cole, Edward Dmytryk, Ring Lardner Jnr., John Howard Lawson, Albert Maltz, Sam Ornitz, Adrian Scott, and Dalton Trumbo. All were subsequently imprisoned for a short time for contempt of court and on their release were blacklisted and unable to work in Hollywood for several years. Many did not return to the film industry.

HOLMES A large computer maintained by the British Home Office for the investigation of crime. The acronym is for 'Home Office Large Major Enquiry System', and was coined in honour of Conan Doyle's detective SHERLOCK HOLMES.

Sherlock Holmes The most famous figure in detective fiction, the creation of Arthur Conan Doyle (1859–1930). His solutions of crime and mysteries were related in a series of 60 stories that appeared in the *Strand Magazine* between 1891 and 1927. The character was based on Dr Joseph Bell of the Edinburgh Infirmary, whose methods of deduction suggested a system that Holmes developed into a science – the observation of the minutest details and apparently insignificant circumstances scientifically interpreted. Dr Watson, Holmes's friend and assistant, was a skit on Doyle himself and Baker Street, in which he lived at a fictional number 221B, acquired lasting fame through his writings. Letters still arrive at the real address (now occupied by a building society) asking for the detective's help: they are answered with the information that Holmes has now retired to take up bee-keeping in the country. Conan Doyle himself grew so tired of his creation that he attempted to kill him off by having him plummet over the Riechenbach Falls with his arch-enemy Moriarty. The public outcry was such that Doyle was obliged to resurrect him in a further series of stories. *See also* BAKER STREET IRREGULARS; HOLMES.

> 'Excellent!' I cried. 'Elementary,' said he.
> *The Crooked Man.*

holo-. holocaust The word originally referred to a sacrifice to the Greek gods in which the victim was burnt whole. It is derived from the Greek words *holos*, whole, and *kaustos*, burnt. It later came to mean slaughter or destruction on an immense scale. In the 20th century it is used specifically of the extermination of six million European Jews by the Germans under Hitler in the period 1940–45. **Holocaust Day** is observed in Israel on Nisan 27 (April 19 or 20). *See also* CONCENTRATION CAMP; EICHMANN TRIAL; FINAL SOLUTION; WIESENTHAL CENTRE.

hologram (*holo-*, whole; *-gram*, record) A permanent record on a photographic film or plate of a three-dimensional image created by the interference pattern formed by the two intersecting light beams from a split laser light source. When the developed film or plate is illuminated by laser light or, after further treatment, by ordinary white light, the 3-D image is reconstructed from the interference pattern recorded on the photographic emulsion. **Reflective holograms** that can be viewed in daylight or artificial light now appear on credit cards as a safeguard against counterfeiting.

Holography, the technique of producing 3-D images using a coherent beam of light or other radiation, was developed in 1947 by the Hungarian-born scientist Dennis Gabor (1900–79), but was largely ignored until after the construction of the laser in 1960. Among its uses are the detection of defects in industrial apparatus and the production of 3-D reference models for use in building, engineering, etc.

holon A distinct entity or structure that is also part of a larger entity or structure. The term (from Greek *hólos*, whole) was coined by the writer Arthur Koestler (1905–83) in his book *The Roots of Coincidence* (1972). Here he put forward the theory that some paranormal phenomena, such as telepathy, might be explained by the fact that people are holons (in the sense of being integrated into some larger whole).

Holt drowning The mysterious death of the Australian prime minister Harold Holt on 17 December 1967, which subsequently gave rise to intense speculation as to his fate. The prime minister was a keen swimmer and on the day of his death had chosen to swim off Cheviot Beach in Victoria, on a coastline known to be hazardous to bathers. The sea 'churned up' around the prime minister and he disappeared; no body was ever found. The prime minister's death caused political turmoil. Speculators ventured a suicide theory, but the most remarkable theory came 15 years later, in Anthony Grey's book *The Prime Minister Was a Spy*. According to Grey, Holt had swum out to a Chinese submarine and been spirited away to Red China, having completed his nefarious activities on behalf of Mao's regime. Grey's theory was based on Holt's evident desire to accommodate Chinese wishes at various points during his career; it also hinted that the Australian secret service knew more about Holt's disappearance than was generally supposed.

Holy. Holy Fool The nickname given by the British tabloid press to Frank Pakenham, 7th Earl of Longford (1905–), noted for his strong Roman Catholic beliefs, which underlie his vigorous crusading for moral causes. On some occasions his obviously good intentions have been made to look rather foolish, for example his befriending of Myra Hindley (*see* MOORS MURDERS). *See* LORD PORN.

Holy Joe Forces slang for a chaplain. Used in the US Navy since the turn of the century, it was common throughout the services, especially the US forces, during World War II, whence it spread into civilian use.

Holy Loch A loch in Scotland W of the Firth of Clyde. In 1961 it became the British base for US POLARIS nuclear submarines; the closure of the base was announced in 1991.

Homburg A soft felt hat popularized by Edward VII. Such hats were originally made at Homburg in Prussia where the king 'took the waters'.

home. every home should have one Originally, a slogan used in advertising in the 1920s. The phrase is now used humorously as a general recommendation for anything.

home banking A banking facility by which a bank's clients have access to their accounts through a computer terminal in their homes. This enables them to perform routine transactions, such as paying bills, ordering chequebooks, etc., without visiting the bank.

homeboy US street slang, heard particularly in Los Angeles, for a member of a neighbourhood gang experienced enough to guard the territory. The word originally meant a responsible citizen, a good neighbour.

Home Guard In the UK, the force of volunteers raised early in World War II and trained for defence against the threat of invasion. Originally known as the LDV (Local Defence Volunteers), it was renamed the Home Guard at Winston Churchill's suggestion. It featured in the postwar TV series DAD'S ARMY. Although the Home Guard never saw action, it relieved the wartime army of many duties.

homeland *See* BANTUSTAN.

Home Rule The name given by Isaac Butt, its first leader, to the movement for securing governmental independence for Ireland under the British crown, after failures of earlier movements to secure the repeal of the Act of Union of 1800. **The Home Government Association** was founded in 1870 (renamed the **Home Rule Association** in 1873) and when C. S. Parnell became leader in 1879 its policy of obstruction in parliament became a growing bugbear to English governments. A **Home Rule Bill** was eventually passed in 1914 but its implementation was postponed by the advent of World War I. The EASTER RISING in 1916, the activities of Sinn Féin, and resistance in Ulster led to the establishment of the Irish Free State in 1921, but Northern Ireland continues to be represented in the British Parliament.

homeys or **homies** Slang for YUPPIES who have settled down to a houseproud and home-orientated existence. It was first heard in the late 1980s.

honcho US slang for the boss, the top man. It is often used in the phrase the **head honcho**. Although it sounds as if it is derived from Spanish, it comes from the Japanese word *hancho*, meaning squad leader. It was adopted by US soldiers during the KOREAN WAR, but is now used of businessmen rather than the military.

Honey Fitz A nickname of J. F. Fitzgerald (1863–1950), US public official and grandfather of president John F. Kennedy. A Democratic congressman from 1895 to 1901, he was elected mayor of Boston in 1905 and 1910. The nickname 'Honey' came from both his charm and his fine singing voice.

honk (1) Slang for a bad smell. It is related to the Liverpudlian dialect word 'ronk' and is widely heard in both Australia and the UK. It is also used as a verb, meaning to stink. (2) Slang for a wildly drunken and uproarious party. This usage, popular in the UK in the 1950s, is probably derived from **honkers** and **honking**, meaning drunk. As a verb, to honk means to drink excessively and, by extension, to vomit. (3) Prostitutes' jargon for feeling a man's genitals.

honkers or **honking** British slang for drunk, but not necessarily to the point of vomiting. *See also* HONK.

Honkers British slang for Hong Kong. It was much used by members of the armed forces serving in the Far East and by upper-class young people who worked there. The suffix *-ers* is typical of British army and public school slang, *e.g.* preggers (pregnant), starkers (naked), brekkers (breakfast). The forename *Harry* is often mysteriously used with these *-ers* words, especially in service jargon, *e.g.* Harry flatters (a flat sea), Harry flakers (flaked out, exhausted), and Harry pinkers (a pink gin). The identity of Harry is interesting. It probably comes from British servicemen who served in India during the Raj, whose pidgin Hindi (or Urdu) included the word *Hare*, meaning God, or the highest (*see* HARE KRISHNA).

honky US Black pejorative slang for a White person. The derivation is obscure but it may be related to the noise that pigs make – the typical pig being pink-skinned. It could also be related to the large noses White people have compared to Blacks, **honker** being the US slang for nose.

honky-tonk A disreputable night club or low roadhouse. A place of cheap entertainment. A *honky-tonk piano* is one from which the felts of the hammers have been removed, thus making the instrument more percussive and giving it a noticeably different tone quality. They are also usually out-of-tune. Such pianos are still used for playing RAGTIME and popular melodies in public houses.

Hons, The The name given by Jessica MITFORD (1917–) and her sister Deborah, daughters of the eccentric Lord Redesdale, to their self-styled 'society', as described in Jessica Mitford's account of their childhood, *Hons and Rebels* (1960). The two sisters were the society's only members, and conducted proceedings in 'Honnish', "a sort of mixture of North of England and American accents". The principal activity of the Hons was apparently the persecution of their brother, Tom – a 'Counter-Hon'.

hooch US slang for illicitly distilled alcohol. The name derives from Hootchinoo, an Amerindian tribe that distilled a type of liquor.

hood or **hoodlum** US slang, dating from the beginning of the 20th century, for a petty crook. The abbreviated version, hood, became widely used in the 1940s. The derivation of hoodlum is obscure, but it is possibly related to the S German dialect word *Haderlump*, meaning a good-for-nothing person. Another possibility is that it is a version of the phrase 'huddle 'em', that was said to be the war cry of street muggers.

HMS Hood A British battle cruiser sunk by the German battleship BISMARCK off the Greenland coast on 24 May 1941. A shell fired by the German guns entered the main magazine of the *Hood*, causing a catastrophic explosion. The British ship, the world's largest vessel in its class, sank in four minutes with the loss of all but three of her 1416-strong crew.

hoolivan A police van equipped with roof-mounted video cameras to monitor the behaviour of crowds, particularly football crowds. A combination of 'hooligan' and 'van', the word reflects the reputation that footballs crowds have for behaving like hooligans.

Hooray Henry British pejorative slang of the 1970s and 1980s for an empty-headed upper-class young man noted for his loud, ineffectual, and sometimes arrogant behaviour. The term has more recently been shortened to 'Hooray'. Viscount Linley won a libel case against the *Today* newspaper, in which he had been labelled a Hooray, in March 1990.

hoosegow One of many US slang names for jail. It is derived, through Mexican, from the Spanish word *juzgado*, a law court.

hootchie-cootchie US Black slang from the early years of the 20th century for sexually evocative dancing. It is best known since the 1960s from the song 'Hootchie-cootchie Man' by the US blues singer, Muddy Waters (1915–83). A **hootchie-cootchie man** is a lover.

Hoover The tradename of a firm of vacuum-cleaner makers which has come to be used as a noun and a verb relating to vacuum cleaners and vacuum cleaning in general. The first vacuum cleaner made by Hoover was sold in 1908 for $70; they first came on sale in the UK four years later. The original inventor of the machine, however, was one J. Murray Spangler, a caretaker in an Ohio department store, who sold his rights in the invention to William Henry Hoover (1849–1932). To **hoover** or **hoover up** is also slang for devouring greedily in the manner of a vacuum cleaner.

Hoover apron A US slang name for a dress with a reversible double front. When one side became dirty, the other side could be turned out. It was popular in America during World War I when Herbert Hoover (1874–1964) was Food Administrator.

Hoover Dam The dam across the Colorado River on the Nevada–Arizona border, formerly known as the **Boulder Dam** or Black Dam. Construction of the Boulder Dam, in Black Canyon, started in 1931. Up to 5000 workers were employed on the project, and some 30 million cubic metres (40 million cu yds) of concrete used in building the horseshoe-shaped dam. This stands 221.3 m (726 ft) high and measures 379 m (1244 ft) across. The base, 201 m (660 ft) thick, narrows to 13.7 m (45 ft) at the crest, along which runs a two-lane highway. At the base of the dam are housed 17 electricity-generating turbines. The dam was completed in 1935, and in 1947 was renamed in honour of Herbert Hoover, who was Secretary of Commerce (1921–28) when the project was being planned. Upstream of the dam is Lake Mead, 110 miles long.

hooverers Fishermen and fishing vessels that take up enormous numbers of fish using drift nets covering large areas of the sea. The name, used disparagingly, describes the manner in which the contents of the nets are sucked up from the sea, as if by a giant vacuum cleaner; it comes from the tradename HOOVER. In the 1970s this method of fishing in European waters threatened the survival of the herring fishing industry. Environmentally it is frowned on because of the indiscriminate way in which fish of all types and sizes are caught with those that are actually wanted.

Hoover moratorium The concession made by US president Herbert Hoover in June 1931 allowing European nations to suspend repayment of intergovernmental war debts for one year, in order to help ease their plight during the GREAT DEPRESSION. The policy was implemented from 1 July 1931.

horizontal dancing US slang, popular with students in the 1980s, for sexual intercourse. 'Horizontal jogging' has also been heard.

horlicks British slang from the 1980s for a complete mess, named after the tradename for the malted milk drink but probably more closely related to the fact that the word sounds like, and is more socially acceptable than, 'bollocks'.

Hornblower, Horatio The seafarer whose adventures in the Royal Navy during the Napoleonic Wars are described in the series of 11 novels by C. S. Forester (1899–1966). Hornblower makes his debut in *The Happy Return* (1937) and various episodes in his navy life are recounted in subsequent novels. For instance, in *Mr. Midshipman Hornblower* (1950) the 17-year-old Horatio is seen at the outset of his career. Others in the series include *Lord Hornblower* (1948), *Lieutenant Hornblower* (1954), and *Hornblower in the West Indies* (1958). Forester also wrote *The Hornblower Companion* (1964), which provides more general information about the characters and places encountered in the books.

horse (1) A drug-user's slang name for heroin, popular in the 1950s but dated by the time the real drug problem affected the UK in the 1970s, when heroin was widely known as 'H' or 'smack'. It has been suggested that the derivation of the word has nothing to do with the animal but derives from the Greek word *heros*, hero, from which heroin itself is thought to be derived. The grounds for the association are that the inadequate user hopes to feel like a hero while under its influence. (2) Rare British rhyming slang for gonorrhoea, from 'horse and trap', clap, the street name for this disease. The same rhyme also gives crap, to defecate. Thus **to horse** is to defecate. (3) US prison slang for a corrupt prison warden who carries illegal items in and out of prison. This usage probably derives from the idea of the Trojan horse.

Get a horse! A jibe, current in the early 1900s, said to have been directed at pioneer US motorists when their automobiles, novel and frequently unreliable, failed them. A variant was 'Hire a horse!'

horse feathers One of the many colloquial terms for rubbish or nonsense. It was coined by the US comic-strip artist, Billy de Beck, in the 1920s to mean something of little consquence. **Horse shit** is now more frequent. *Horse Feathers* (1932) was a film made by the MARX BROTHERS.

horses sweat, men perspire, (and) ladies only glow A genteel adage used to rebuke anyone, lady or gentleman, who says they are sweating. With the advent of sexual equality, the phrase has fallen from serious use and now elicits, at best, mild amusement, at worst – scorn.

Horst Wessel Lied Horst Wessel Song: the official marching song of the German NAZI Party. It was written by a young student and Nazi stormtrooper, Horst Wessel, and adopted by the Nazis following Wessel's murder in 1930, supposedly at the hands of the Communists. The lyrics incorporate many odious sentiments dear to the Nazis; indeed, Wessel was elevated to the status of martyr by Nazi propagandist, Dr Paul Joseph Goebbels. The first verse translates as:

> Hold high the banner! Close the hard ranks serried!
> SA marches on with sturdy stride.
> Comrades, by Red Front and Reaction killed, are buried,
> But march with us in image at our side.

The tune was taken from a traditional fishermen's song.

hospice movement A movement that provides specialist care, relief from pain, and emotional support for the terminally ill and their families. The first hospice in this sense, the Dames de Calvaire, was established by Mme Jeanne Carnier in Lyon, France in 1842. The first hospices in the UK were established in the late 19th and early 20th centuries by the Irish Sisters of Charity, who had set up their first home for the sick in Dublin in 1879. The movement had a renaissance in the 1960s with the foundation of St Christopher's Hospice in 1967 by Dame Cicely Saunders (1918–), upon which most modern hospices are modelled. There are now over 400 different hospice services in Britain and Ireland, which include special NHS-funded units, independent hospices, hospital support teams, voluntary home care services, and the homes run by the Cancer Relief Macmillan Fund and Sue Ryder Foundation.

hot. hot and strong A catchphrase said to have originated in Australia in the 1940s; it is used in such phrases as 'I like my women hot and strong', *i.e.* highly stimulating sexually. The allusion is to coffee, usually preferred 'hot and strong' (and possibly 'black').

hot dog A frankfurter sausage, heated and served in a split oblong bread roll, often with onions and ketchup or other relishes. It originated in America but its popularity spread to the UK and the rest of Europe, with the rise of the FAST FOOD industry. The invention of the hot dog has been ascribed to Harry Stevens, caterer to the New York sports stadium in 1900, but the name is thought to have been coined by a US sports cartoonist, T. A. Dorgan.

hot-dog (1) US slang meaning to show off, or to perform very well, especially in skiing or surfing. (2) Also **hot-dogger**. US slang for a high achiever, or a successful person, sometimes said with a tinge of envy. It is possibly a combination of 'top dog' meaning the best and 'hot' meaning especially good.

Hot Gospellers An old nickname for Puritans, now frequently applied to the more energetic and colourful evangelists and revivalists.

hot-housing An educational system involving intensive methods of teaching young children, allowing little or no time for leisure, in order to achieve levels of exceptional intelligence and high attainment.

hot jazz The term used for JAZZ music when the tone is less pure than in COOL JAZZ, and when vibrato is prominently employed.

hot line A direct exclusive telephone line between two important points, only to be used in times of crisis. It was used particularly of the private line between the US White House and the Soviet Kremlin in the early 1960s, but has since extended its meaning to cover any urgent telephone line, for example in accident services, commerce, or the commercial markets.

hot mooner A person who adheres to the *Hot Moon theory*, which proposes that the moon has or had a molten core, whose volcanic activity produced the lunar craters. In opposition to the hot mooners are the **cold mooners** ('hot' and 'cold' referring to the temperature of the moon's core), who believe that the craters were formed by meteorite bombardment rather than thermal or volcanic activity. Both terms were coined *c.* 1969. Hot mooners are also called **vulcanists**.

hot pants (1) Slang meaning eager for sex, usually applied to women. (2) Provocatively short shorts, which were fashionable for women in the early 1970s.

hot rod An old car stripped and tuned for speed, and, by transference, the owner of such a vehicle or other unruly youth.

hot shot US underworld slang for a deliberately fatal dose of an illegal narcotic, usually heroin. It is administered, as a method of murder, either by giving a huge overdose of the drug or by adulterating it with another substance.

hot-wire Slang meaning to start a car without using the ignition key or switch, by altering the wiring. 'Hot' probably reflects both the slang meaning, stolen, and the heat generated by the joining of the wires to make a spark. Hot-wiring is a popular method of stealing unlocked cars.

Houdini, Harry The stage name of Erik Weiz (1874–1926), the world's most celebrated illusionist and escapologist. Born in Budapest of Jewish parents, who emigrated to New York, he began his career as a magician in 1890 but world fame began with his appearance at London in 1900. No lock could hold him, even that of the condemned cell at Washington gaol. He escaped from handcuffs, ropes, safes, etc., and was deservedly called 'the Great Houdini'. He died from a punch in the stomach, delivered before he had tensed his muscles.

Houdini in the White House Franklin D. Roosevelt (1882–1945), 32nd US president (1933–45). He acquired this nickname – one of many – because of his ability while president to find a way out of difficult situations. *See* FDR.

Houdini of American Politics One of the nicknames of Richard Milhous Nixon (1913–), 37th US president (1969–74), noted for his ability to evade or extricate himself from awkward situations. This ability failed him during the WATERGATE scandal. *See* TRICKY DICKY.

hour. their finest hour The famous phrase from Winston Churchill's speech (18 June 1940) given at the time when the collapse of France was imminent and the BATTLE OF BRITAIN was about to begin.

> Let us therefore brace ourselves to our duties, and to bear ourselves that, if the British Empire and its Commonwealth last for a thousand years, men will say: "This was their finest hour".

house Slang for a style of disco music that became popular in the late 1980s. The name itself comes from the Warehouse Club in Chicago, where the style first started. The sound is heavily electronic with a strong beat and a RAP overlay. *See also* ACID HOUSE.

househusband *See under* HUSBAND.

house sitting The practice of living in someone else's house while they are away, in order to take care of it, tend the garden, feed the pets, etc.

hover. hovercraft Any vehicle that travels supported on a cushion of air relatively close to the surface. Hovercraft are thus distinct from both conventional surface craft, such as boats and wheeled vehicles, and aircraft, which employ aerodynamic lift to support themselves in the air. Their great advantage is their ability to move over any reasonably flat surface, land or water. The world's first working hovercraft was the SR.N1 (Saunders-Roe N1), invented by the British engineer Sir Christopher Cockerell (1910–). This was launched in 1959 after a development programme financed by the UK's ministry of defence. Hovercraft design essentially involves a central air inlet and fan, which forces air outwards and downwards through jets around the periphery of the underside, creating the supporting air cushion. Forward thrust is provided by jets from the fan or by separate vertical propellors. An alternative arrangement underneath is the plenum chamber, in effect an entirely open bottom, which is fitted with a peripheral flexible skirt to contain the air cushion. The prototype SR.N1 was capable of carrying three people at speeds of up to 25 knots. By 1963 the payload capacity had been increased to 7 tons and the maximum speed to 50 knots. Interest in the new machines was by now spreading to other countries. However, development in the 1960s was hampered by several design hurdles, notably the high frictional wear of the skirts and the susceptibility of gas-turbine engines to saltwater-induced corrosion. By the 1970s, with these problems largely overcome, the hovercraft had created various roles for itself, including short-haul ferry, survey vehicle, and amphibious troop carrier. The largest hovercraft yet built is the SR.N4 Mk III, weighing 305 tonnes and measuring 56.38 m in length. It operates on a scheduled cross-Channel ferry service carrying up to 418 passengers and 60 cars. However, the new generation of cross-Channel ferries will be catamarans, which turn out to be more efficient than hovercraft. The hovercraft principle, therefore, is only likely to be made use of in special situations (especially military). *See also* HOVERTRAIN.

hovertrain A train that rides along a concrete track on a cushion of high-pressure air produced by powerful fans. The idea of frictionless travel by train or monorail using air-cushion suspension was first postulated in 1969, following the successful introduction of the HOVERCRAFT into public service. The first successful hovertrain was introduced in France in the 1970s between Orléans and Paris. In the UK, research has also been taking place into the use of a magnetic suspension system (*see* MAGLEV) with propulsion using a linear induction motor, although no commercially viable system has yet been developed.

How to win friends and influence people A catchphrase that originated in America as the title of a book on business psychology, written by Dale Carnegie (1888–1955) and published in 1936. Since then the phrase has appeared in a number of variants. In a now forgotten 1955 movie, written and directed by Nunnally Johnson, it was adapted as *How To Be Very Very Popular*.

HRT Hormone Replacement Therapy. The administration of small doses of oestrogenic hormones (the main female hormones) to correct hormonal imbalance in menopausal women. HRT is effective in relieving physical symptoms of the menopause, such as hot flushes and vaginal dryness; its usefulness in treating the psychological symptoms, such as irritability and fatigue, is less evident. HRT has also proved valuable in preventing osteoporosis, a brittle bone condition that is common in women over 50. There is, however, some medical concern over certain adverse side effects, which include such minor problems as nausea and water retention and the more serious cancer of the endometrium.

H_2S Codename given to a secret navigational device developed for use in Allied bombers when operating against German U-BOATS. Fearing that the enemy would hear about the new system, the British authorities enlisted the aid of one of the country's best-known practical jokers, Professor Reginald Jones of Aberdeen University. Jones relished the opportunity for a good hoax and accordingly arranged for the Germans to learn of a newly developed infra-red beam being used to detect their U-boats. With great haste the Germans set about painting the entire U-boat fleet with special paint to deflect the rays. Of H_2S they knew nothing: the infra-red beams were, of course, a figment of Jones's imagination. H_2S is also, of course, the chemical formula for the gas hydrogen sulphide.

Hubble's law The principle in astronomy that the velocity with which distant galaxies are moving away is directly proportional to their distance; *i.e.* the more distant the galaxy, the faster it is moving. The law was discovered in 1927 by the US astronomer Erwin Hubble (1889–1953) as a result of measurements of the red shifts of galaxies. It is regarded as direct evidence that the universe is expanding (*see* BIG BANG). The constant relating the velocity to the distance is the **Hubble constant** and the reciprocal of this, the **Hubble time**, is a measure of the age of the universe, currently estimated at between 10 and 20 billion years. In 1990 the **Hubble space telescope** was named in his honour.

Hughie A 20th-century Australian euphemism for God, especially in contexts that have to do with the control of the weather. **Send her down, Hughie** is a common outback exhortation to the Almighty Rainmaker.

> 'Don't worry about the money. Hughie looks after that, my boy'. The Corporal was diverted. 'Who's this Hughie?' he said . . . 'Ah', Gell said, affecting a gravity which was not altogether false. 'You don't say "God", you see, because nobody believes in God but everybody believes in Hughie. I dunno – it's just a thing you hear the boys say.'
>
> SEAFORTH MACKENZIE: *Dead Men Rising* (1951).

Huks, The Nickname for the Hukbalahap (Hukbo nang Bayon Laban sa Hapon: People's Army Against Japan), a communist-led Philippines guerrilla force that came close to toppling the Manila government in the late 1940s and early 1950s. The Huks were formed in 1942 in central Luzon to fight the Japanese occupiers, although the movement's origins lie in the communist-inspired peasants' struggle against the wealthy landowners of Luzon in the 1930s. By the end of World War II, the Huks controlled much of Luzon. In the 1946 election the Huk leader, Luis Taruc, won a Congressional seat, but was barred from taking office. This prompted open rebellion by the Huks, who gained in popular support. But in 1950 the government captured most of the country's leading communists in a swoop on their

Manila headquarters, and won renewed military backing from America. Even more significant in the Huks' downfall was the election in 1953 of President Ramon Magsaysay, who greatly restored popular support for the government. The nadir came with Taruc's surrender in 1954. Even so, the outlawed Huks survived through the 1950s and 1960s, reorganized as the People's Liberation Army (Hukbong Magpapalaya nang Bayan). In 1970 it was renamed the New People's Army (Bagong Hukbo nang Bayan).

Hula-Hoop A light plastic hoop that is spun around the waist by swinging the hips, used by children for recreation and by adults for exercise. It was invented in 1958 by Richard P. Knerr and Arthur K. Melvin of the Wham O Manufacturing Company, San Gabriel, California, the same company that was responsible for the FRISBEE. It became an instant craze and earned its inventors a considerable fortune.

Hulot, Monsieur The eccentric accident-prone character who appears in the films of French director Jacques Tati (1908–82). Hulot, played by Tati himself, is a gangling pipe-smoking bachelor whose tangles with the modern machine age provide a number of very funny film sequences. In *Monsieur Hulot's Holiday* (1953) he causes havoc in a quiet seaside resort. The subsequent films – *Mon Oncle* (1958), *Playtime* (1968), and *Trafic* (1971) – have an element of social satire, with Hulot often playing a peripheral role.

human. All human life is there A slogan used to promote the *News of the World* newspaper in 1958–59. It came originally from the US writer Henry James: "Cats and monkeys, monkeys and cats – all human life is there." ('Madonna of the Future', 1879).

Humanae Vitae 'Of Human Life': the encyclical issued by Pope Paul VI on 29 July 1968, in which he reaffirmed the Vatican's total opposition to all artificial forms of BIRTH CONTROL and to abortion. In addition he urged restraint in the use of the rhythm method of contraception, declaring that "each and every marriage act must remain open to the transmission of life". The encyclical caused dismay to some liberal Catholics, who had been hoping for some relaxation of the long-established dogma. The Vatican's solution to poverty and misery caused by world overpopulation remains one based on economic and social reform, rather than biological intervention. For some non-Catholics the Pope's continued opposition to birth control is seen as a cynical knee-jerk reaction to the reduction it would cause in the world's Catholic population.

Human Fly The stage name of the US performer George Gibson Polley, who became famous throughout America for climbing SKYSCRAPERS. His first serious climb was the result of a bet in Chicago in 1910: his ascent of a lofty department store attracted such a large crowd that Polley realized he had stumbled on an entirely new form of street entertainment. Subsequently be shinned up the 500-foot Customs House in Boston, a flagpole on Rhode Island, the Woolworth Building in New York (then the tallest building in the world) and numerous department stores – for generous publicity fees. In all, before his death from a brain tumour at the age of 29, he climbed over 2000 buildings without ever falling – although his 'act' did include a deliberate slip from one ledge to another, to thrill the crowds below.

human interest The quality of a newspaper story or television news item that focuses on the experiences of a particular person, group, or family and is presented in such a way that it evokes an emotional response in the reader or viewer – usually either sympathy with others' misfortunes or envy at their success.

human shield The policy adopted by Saddam Hussein in the GULF WAR of posting foreign hostages (and subsequently captured aircrew) at various strategic installations in the hope that this would deter Allied attacks. Iraq's use of such a policy was widely condemned as contrary to the Geneva Conventions and Allied commanders denied that they would be influenced by such tactics.

Hundred Flowers policy The short-lived period of liberalization in China instituted by chairman Mao Tse-tung in 1957. The policy was set out in a speech given by Mao to the Supreme State conference in Peking on 27 February:

> The policy of letting a hundred flowers blossom and a hundred schools of thought contend is the policy for promoting the flourishing of the arts and the progress of science.

Mindful of the recent HUNGARIAN RISING and of Khrushchev's denunciation of Stalin in February 1956, Mao was endeavouring to resolve the 'contradictions' becoming increasingly apparent within the

Chinese communist state. Critics of the regime saw the speech as a green light and a barrage of complaint was directed at the Peking regime, especially from liberals and anti-communists. Communist Party bosses were alarmed and on 8 June a policy change was signalled by the publication of an amended version of Mao's speech. This was followed in July by a crackdown on the more outspoken critics. *See also* CULTURAL REVOLUTION.

Hungarian Rising The popular revolt against the Soviet-backed communist regime in Hungary that cost thousands of lives in the autumn of 1956. The rising started on 23 October when police tried to break up a student demonstration in Budapest calling for the reinstatement of Imre Nagy, the reformist leader who had been ousted in April 1955 by the hard-line Stalinist, Mátyás Rákosi. Rákosi's policy of limited liberalization while strengthening ties with the Soviet Union became increasingly untenable in the face of mounting pressure for radical reforms. This was intensified by the successful Poznán Revolt in Poland on 28 June, and on 18 July Rákosi was forced to resign. Pro-Moscow communists struggled to contain the situation, but the students provided the spark that set off widespread anti-Soviet protest.

In Budapest, Soviet flags were burned and Stalin's statue destroyed. The uprising was supported by Hungary's own police and army, while members of the notorious secret police (AVO) were hunted down. Imre Nagy was installed as prime minister on 24 October and promised the withdrawal of Soviet troops. But fighting was intense, especially in E Hungary, and by 30 October some 10,000 lives had been lost. Nagy attempted to negotiate with the Soviets, but the arrival of Soviet reinforcements in early November prompted Nagy to announce that Hungary had quit the WARSAW PACT and was now a neutral country. He appealed for United Nations intervention, but no outside assistance was forthcoming.

The Soviet counter-strike began on 4 November with the bombing and military takeover of Budapest. By 12 November most of the country was under Soviet control, and Hungary had a puppet government led by János Kádár. An estimated 155,000 Hungarians had fled across the border into Austria by the end of 1956. On 18 November Nagy was tricked into leaving his refuge in the Yugoslav embassy, taken to Romania, and shot. In spite of a continuing general strike, the Kádár government imposed its authority on the country, and the uprising was extinguished everywhere, except in the hearts and minds of the Hungarian people.

hunger. hunger march A march of the unemployed to call attention to their grievances, as that of 1932, the year in which Wal Hannington, the leader of the National Union of Unemployed Workers, led a march on London. The biggest of the marches organized by the NUWM was that against the MEANS TEST in 1936. *See* JARROW MARCH.

hunger strike The refusal of prisoners to take food in order to embarrass the authorities or to secure release; a notable tactic of the SUFFRAGETTES. It has also been used by convicted IRA terrorists held in British prisons. *See* CAT AND MOUSE ACT.

Hungerford massacre The events of 20 August 1987, during which 13 people were killed and 15 wounded by Michael Ryan in and around the Berkshire town of Hungerford. Ryan, a deranged firearms enthusiast, whose motives have never been fathomed, ended by turning his weapon on himself: his victims included his own mother. To many in the UK, the horror of these events was all the greater for their setting, a small sleepy town that seemed to epitomize rural England. *See also* SERIAL KILLER; SURVIVALIST.

hunky-dory Slang for perfectly OK. Originally an Americanism from the mid-19th century, it was first used in the UK in the 1920s. The origin is uncertain.

hunter-killer A nuclear-powered submarine designed to stalk enemy submarines and destroy them. The key to hunter-killer ASW (anti-submarine warfare) success is speed, quietness, and powerful detection capabilities. The US Navy employs nuclear hunter-killers with torpedo tubes in the stern, which leaves the bow free for carrying sophisticated underwater listening devices, such as active sonar and passive hydrophones.

Huntley British rhyming slang of the 1980s for karma (fate), from Huntley and Palmer, the well-known British biscuit company. This is a rather unique blend of the old rhyming slang tradition and a recently adopted 'new age' concept.

Hurricane The RAF's main fighter plane during the first years of World War II, and, with the SPITFIRE, staunch defender of the skies during the BATTLE OF BRITAIN. Made by Hawker (from 1935 part of Hawker Siddeley), the Hurricane made its maiden flight in 1935 and two years later entered service with the RAF – its first monoplane fighter. The Mark I Hurricane had a wingspan of 12.19 m (40 ft) and was 9.57 m (31.42 ft) long. The single Rolls-Royce Merlin engine gave it a top speed of 521 k.p.h. (324 m.p.h.). Armament consisted of eight wing-mounted machine guns. By 1941 the Hurricane, outpaced by Germany's Messerschmitt 109 fighter, had switched roles to night fighter and fighter-bomber; versions were equipped with 12 machine-guns, cannons, or anti-tank guns, as well as bombs. The Sea Hurricane was a modified version launched by catapult from a ship or carrier. Although the Spitfire is usually thought of as the principal aircraft in the Battle of Britain, there were, in fact, twice as many Hurricanes as Spitfires in the battle and they shot down more German aircraft.

husband. housekusband A married man who stays at home and undertakes the housekeeping duties traditionally the province of the wife. These may include care of small children. An analogue of 'housewife', the word was first used in America from 1970, but has since become common in the UK. Increasingly, traditional roles have become less entrenched, as working wives have built successful careers, which can make them the main income earners. *See* NEW MAN.

My husband and I The Queen's memorable phrase with which for many years in the 1950s and 1960s she began her Christmas message. For some reason, probably to do with her delivery, it became a joke much used by the satirical TV puppet programme *Spitting Image*. In 1988 the phrase was used as the title of an ITV comedy programme, starring Mollie Sugden. The Queen herself was clearly aware of the joke; in her speech at the Guildhall on the occasion of her silver wedding anniversary (1972), she began:

> I think that everyone will concede that – today of all days – I should begin by saying, 'My husband and I'.

hush-hush A term that came into use in World War I to describe very secret operations, designs, or inventions; from the exclamation 'hush' enjoining silence. *See also* TOP SECRET.

Husky Codename for the Allied invasion of Sicily during World War II. Forces of the US 7th Army and British 8th Army began the seaborne invasion on 10 July 1943, surprising the island's Italian and German defenders. By 17 August, the last AXIS troops had withdrawn to mainland Italy, and Sicily was under Allied control.

hustler (1) US slang for a prostitute of either sex. The noun is rarely used in the UK, although the verb, to hustle, meaning to solicit, is. (2) Slang for an insistent and demanding person.

> In trying to analyse the psychology of why some banks lend even more money to "hustlers", Mr Sampson goes too far. True, some bankers . . . may want to meet flamboyant entrepreneurs.
>
> MS S. M. KENNEDY, correspondent in the *Independent Magazine* (12 January 1991).

hutzpah *See* CHUTZPAH.

hydro-. hydroelectric power Electricity generated by water pressure, which accounts for about 7% of the world's energy supply. A typical hydroelectric power plant (HEP) uses water stored in a high-level reservoir (usually created by damming a river), which falls through pipes to drive water turbines coupled to electricity generators at a lower level. In pumped HEP schemes, at times of low electricity demand, the turbines are reversed and used to pump water back up to the reservoir to ensure high water pressure during peak operation. The feasibility of hydroelectric power depends on the availability of suitable sites with the required fall of water. Unfortunately in the UK not many such sites are available and only some 0·7% of the UK's energy is provided by hydroelectric power stations.

hydrofoil A light vessel that has two or more pairs of fixed vanes (foils) attached to the hull, which produce lift (similar to wings of an aircraft) and raise the hull from the water to reduce friction and increase speed. The first successful hydrofoil to 'fly' with its hull clear of the water was invented by Professor Enrico Forlanini of Milan, whose experimental craft reached a speed of 38 knots on Lake Maggiore in 1906. Early designs were handicapped by poor rough water performance and unsatisfactory engines, but in the following decades the Germans and the Americans refined foil designs and introduced lighter and more powerful engines to develop commercial and military hydrofoil craft. In the 1960s water jet propulsion was introduced by Boeing, whose passenger-carrying JETFOIL fleet now operates on sea and inland waterways at suitable sites throughout the world.

hydrogen bomb *See* NUCLEAR WEAPON.

hydronaut A person who operates in deep submersible vessels for purposes of underwater exploration, salvage of submerged vessels, laying of cables and pipelines, etc.

hydrophonics A system of cultivating plants by stimulating their growth with music or other sound. It was used in the late 1980s by the Japanese, who also investigated the effect of magnetism. The term was probably coined by analogy with HYDROPONICS. The idea that the growth of plants can be affected by music or verbal encouragement has no scientific basis but is surprisingly widely held. In 1986, Prince Charles attracted good-natured ridicule for his remark in a TV interview:

> To get the best results, you must talk to your vegetables.

hydroplaning *See* AQUAPLANING.

hydroponics A technique for cultivating plants without soil, using an inert medium, such as sand or gravel, through which a nutrient solution is circulated. (Originally the plants' roots were immersed in water to which fertilizer was added, hence the prefix *hydro-*, from Gr. *hudōr*, water.) It is useful in arid regions but only commercially viable for flowers and special vegetables. *See also* HYDROPHONICS.

hype (1) Slang for exaggerated publicity or marketing for a product or person, typically a celebrity, as in the phrase **media hype**. The implication is that it is totally deceptive. As a verb, to hype is to market someone or something in a totally exaggerated and deceptive way. It has a specific sense in the pop music business in which it means to put out large quantities of a particular record in order to boost the sales figures and thus push the record up the charts. The origins of the word are uncertain, but it seems probable that it derives from 'hyperbole' or 'hyperbolize', in which the Greek prefix *hyper-* means above or abnormally high.

> There is no reason in particular why anyone should get overexcited about the 200th anniversary of Mozart's death. But a lot of people are hoping to cash in by building up a big "hype".
>
> *Independent Magazine*, 12 January 1991.

(2) Slang meaning to over-excite. It is often used in the phrase **hyped up**. This usage is probably derived from 'hyperactive', in which the prefix *hyper-* means abnormally high, as in *hypertension* (high blood pressure). (2) Also **hypo**. Slang abbreviation for a hypodermic needle, as used for injecting illegal drugs.

hyper-. hyperinflation *See* INFLATION.

hypermarket A very large SELF SERVICE store selling a wide range of goods in addition to food. The word is a translation of the French *hypermarché*, such stores being more common in France than in the UK. The first hypermarket in the UK opened in the early 1970s. Known also as **superstores**, built typically on the outskirts of towns and with their own extensive car parks and often service stations, they offer the customer the facility of one-stop shopping without the traffic congestion of town centres. Since their introduction, the concept of out-of-town shopping has flourished in the UK, with many large furnishing and DO-IT-YOURSELF retail outlets sharing car parks with the superstores.

hypersonic Having a speed at least five times that of sound. Only missiles and space re-entry vehicles, such as the US SPACE SHUTTLE, reach such speeds.

hypo-. hypoallergenic A description of cosmetics and other products that come into contact with the skin, indicating to the consumer that their use is not likely to cause an allergic reaction.

hypocentre The area directly beneath the explosion of a nuclear weapon, also called GROUND ZERO. The term was originally used to describe the central point from which an earthquake spreads.

I

IA *See* INFORMATION ANXIETY.

IBM International Business Machines. The world's largest computer manufacturer (its earnings were $6 billion in 1988), which has its headquarters in Armonk, New York State. IBM was incorporated in 1911 as the Computer-Tabulating-Recording Company and adopted the name IBM in 1924. In the 1920s it dominated the market in time clocks and punch-card tabulators and in the 1930s it developed the electric typewriter. In 1951 IBM began to manufacture computers – quickly cornering the world market because of its massive R & D budget. In 1981 IBM introduced the Personal Computer (PC), a desktop micro, which became the industry standard.

ICBM Intercontinental Ballistic Missile. ICBMs are defined as those missiles with a range in excess of 5500 km, *i.e.* capable of reaching the Soviet Union when fired from America and vice versa. The basic principles of ballistic missile design were perfected by German rocket scientists during the 1940s and first put to practical use in the V2 rocket used in an attempt to terrorize London during the latter stages of World War II. Both America and Soviet Union then employed captured German scientists on their own missile programmes and have developed more sophisticated, accurate, and deadly systems. The latest ICBMs, such as the US Minuteman III and the Soviet SS-18 and SS-19, have three stages: the booster for take-off, the second-stage delivery rocket, and the unpowered re-entry vehicle, which since 1968 takes the form of **MIRVS** (multiple re-entry vehicles), carrying multiple warheads, each capable of being independently targeted.

ice (1) Slang for diamonds. This word is widely used in all English-speaking countries. (2) Slang for powdered methamphetamine, a highly addictive illegal stimulant drug. When smoked it produces a powerful and unpredictable effect on the nervous system – intensely euphoric or deeply distressing. The drug, which first appeared in Hawaii in 1989 and use of which has become epidemic in many parts of America, is particularly feared by drug enforcement agencies because it is very easy to manufacture from legally available materials. The name 'ice' refers to the translucent crystals from which the powder is produced and may have been coined by analogy with SNOW. (3) US slang for a bribe that is supposedly derived from the initial letters of 'Incidental Campaign Expenses'. (4) US underworld slang meaning to kill. It is a shortening of 'to put someone on ice' (a reference to the refrigeration of corpses in mortuaries). The word has become part of everyday speech by way of popular TV crime series and films. Putting a project 'on ice' means that no progress will be made on it for an indefinite period.

Iceberg Nickname of the US film actress Grace Kelly (1929–82). It is perhaps a reflection of her cool beauty or her aloof film persona. It was a combination of these attributes that made her a star, playing opposite Hollywood's leading men in such films as *High Noon* (1952), *The Country Girl* (1955), and *High Society* (1956). At the height of her career, however, she retired from the cinema to marry Prince Rainier III of Monaco (1956) in what was publicized as a fairytale romance. She fulfilled her royal duties in Monaco with great dignity, despite the attention paid by the press to the various romances of her children. The fairytale ended abruptly in a car accident on the winding roads above Monte Carlo.

> Writing about her is like trying to wrap up 115 pounds of smoke.
>
> PETE MARTIN.

ice cream (1) British slang from the 1950s for a man. It is derived from the rhyming slang 'ice-cream freezer' for geezer (meaning 'fellow' and probably derived by British soldiers in the Napoleonic Wars from the Spanish *giza*, man). It is now obsolete. (2) British Black and Asian schoolchildren's derogatory slang for a White person; presumably a reference to their white skin. (3) US slang for any illegal drug in crystalline form. This is also a reference to its pale colour.

ice creamer (1) British derogatory slang for an Italian. It derives from the occupation of many Italian immigrants, in the early part of this century, who opened small ice-cream businesses. (2) US slang from the 1950s for a drug user, rather than a drug addict. This term is used contemptuously by drug addicts, presumably because, like the drugs, ice cream is for them an occasional treat rather than a necessity of everyday life.

iceman (1) US slang for a jewel thief; it is based on ICE, meaning diamonds. (2) US slang for a hired assassin; it is based on the use of ICE as a verb, meaning to kill. In Eugene O'Neill's tragedy *The Iceman Cometh* (1946) a group of disillusioned drinkers anticipate the arrival of the man who delivers ice to the saloon in which they meet and who comes to represent death itself.

ice palace US slang for a jewellery shop. Originating in the Black community, it derives from ICE, slang for diamonds.

ICI Imperial Chemical Industries. The largest UK manufacturer of alkalis, paints, plastics, dyestuffs, and numerous other products. It was formed in 1926 by the merger of the four largest chemical firms of the day: Brunner, Mond & Co. Ltd, Nobel Industries Ltd, the United Alkali Co. Ltd, and the British Dyestuffs Corporation Ltd. The merger was a direct response to the formation of the I. G. Farben chemical combine in Germany in 1925, in order to ensure that the UK, which pioneered the chemical industry during the Industrial Revolution, retained a leading role in international heavy chemical production. In 1991 Lord Hanson, a powerful City entrepreneur, acquired 2.8% of the voting shares on the open market. This was widely regarded as a precursor to a takeover bid for the whole company, probably with a view to UNBUNDLING the conglomerate.

icon A pictorial representation that appears on the screen of some computers to enable the service it represents to be activated by means of a screen cursor. It saves having to tap the instruction on the keyboard.

ICU *See* INTENSIVE CARE UNIT.

ID Short for identity or identification, as in ID card.

Identikit A method of identifying criminals from composite photographs based on an assemblage of individual features selected by witnesses from a wide variety of drawings. The method was developed by Hugh C. McDonald (1913–) and first used at Los Angeles in 1959. PHOTOFIT is an updated version using photographs and **E-fit** employs computer graphics to the same end. *See also* GENETIC FINGERPRINTING.

idiot. idiot box Slang from the 1960s for a TV set. Reflecting the idea that too much television stunts the brain, it is no longer widely used. The TV is still widely referred to as 'the box', but this is likely to be a shortening of the more widely used GOGGLEBOX.

idiot dancing British slang dating from the late 1960s and 1970s for a style of wild, abandoned, but solitary dancing seen at rock concerts and festivals. Surprisingly, it does not take up much space because all the movement is in the top half of the body and the head. The disparaging nature of the name reflects the idea that many people found the spectacle both ridiculous and irritating, as to have one's view of the stage obscured by such a dancer was extremely frustrating. Idiot dancing still takes place, but the late 1970s saw the arrival of HEADBANGERS, who adopted a more aggressive style of solitary dancing to match the more aggressive music.

Idlewild New York City airport, built on the site of Idlewild Beach golf course beside Jamaica Bay in Queens, 24 km (15 miles) from Manhattan. The new airport was opened on 1 July 1948 as the New York International, although it was still popularly called Idlewild until 24 December 1963, when it was renamed **John F. Kennedy International** (or **JFK** for short).

iffy British slang dating from the 1960s for suspicious, of doubtful origin; it can also mean stolen or criminal, depending on whether it is being applied to a person or to an item. It became more widely used in the 1970s and its use has spread to America.

IJsselmeer A shallow freshwater lake in the Netherlands, which was formed in 1932 by the construction of a dam, designed by the engineer Cornelis Lely, to divide the former Zuider See from the North Sea. The project created a valuable source of fresh water for the region; it also created four polders, large areas of fertile land reclaimed from the lake by a system of dykes, which are used for agriculture, housing, and recreational facilities. Parts of the reclaimed land were flooded once more during World War II and had to be redrained after hostilities ended. Even before that their strategic value had been recognized by Queen Wilhelmina (1880–1962) for one; in reply to a threat from the German Kaiser Wilhelm II that the Dutch would be unable to resist his seven-foot tall Guardsmen if they invaded, she commented: "And when we open our dykes, the waters are ten feet deep".

Ike Nickname of General (later President) Dwight D. Eisenhower (1890–1969). Despite graduating well down in the 1915 class at West Point and enjoying an undistinguished military career between the wars, Eisenhower advanced rapidly after the outbreak of World War II due to his strategic knowledge, organizational skills, diplomacy, and amiability. In 1942 he was given the command of the Anglo-American amphibious landings in North Africa and subsequently commanded the Allied forces in Italy in 1943. In 1944 he was appointed Supreme Commander of Operation OVERLORD, the Allied invasion of Europe. His war record ensured the success of his presidential candidacy in the 1952 election; despite the recurring crises during his two terms of office as a result of COLD WAR tensions, his presidency is remembered as a period of relative peace and prosperity.

I like Ike The campaign slogan of Dwight D. (Ike) Eisenhower, used to great effect as part of his successful presidential election campaigns in 1952 and 1956. During the late 1950s and early 1960s it was used to describe any inexplicable liking for something; it subsequently fell into disuse.

illywhacker Australian term, originating in the 1940s, for a professional trickster selling cheap goods, patent medicines, etc., especially at fairs and country shows. *Illywhacker* (1985) was a novel written by the Australian writer Peter Carey.

Ilyushin Various types of Soviet civil and military aircraft produced under the auspices of Sergei Ilyushin (1894–1977), the Soviet aircraft designer. As head of the Scientific Research Committee, he directed the formulation of the requirements for new types of military aircraft for the Red Air Force (1926–33); subsequently he became head of the Central Design Bureau (1933–70). He created the Il-2 Stormovik bomber, one of the most effective of World War II, as well as various civil aircraft, such as the Il-12 twin-engined passenger aircraft (1946) and the Il-86 airbus (1976).

image. imaging A method of relieving stress that originated in America in the late 1980s. The aim is to encourage the patient consciously to conjure up mental images of pleasant and enjoyable things or situations. Stress was recognized in the 1980s as a contributing factor in many illnesses and many techniques, such as relaxation and meditation, are used to relieve the condition. The deliberate attempt to summon up mental images of beautiful things is not new. For example, the poet Wordsworth indulged in this habit. However, it is an innovation in modern stress-therapy techniques.

Imagism A school of poetry founded by Ezra Pound (1885–1972), derived from the ideas of the philosopher T. E. Hulme (1883–1917). The Imagist poets were in revolt against excessive romanticism, proclaiming that poetry should use the language of common speech, create new rhythms, be uninhibited in choice of subject, and present an image.

IMF International Monetary Fund. An organization established by the BRETTON WOODS CONFERENCE (1944) as a specialized agency of the United Nations. The main aim of the organization is to promote international trade by easing international liquidity problems and stabilizing exchange rates. Funds are made available to countries experiencing short-term balance of payments difficulties. Deposits of gold or domestic currencies are made by member countries, who can then borrow automatically up to the amount of their **reserve tranche**, which was until 1978 paid in gold and known as the **gold tranche**. In 1970 Special Drawing Rights (SDRs) were introduced to allow members to borrow in convertible currency from other member countries, and SDRs became the IMF's unit of account. Since 1978 the reserve tranche has been paid in SDRs.

Immelmann turn An aerobatic manoeuvre invented in World War I by the German Air Force pilot Max Immelmann, who was shot down in 1916. His celebrated 'turn' was a refinement of the classic aerial combat manoeuvre – a hawklike dive out of the sun at an enemy target – to which Immelmann added a climb with a half loop and half roll at the top to enable the attacker to gain height and dive from the reverse direction.

Imperial. Imperial Conferences The name given to the conferences held in London between the prime ministers of the various dominions of the British Empire between 1907 and 1946 inclusive. These conferences had their origin in the first Colonial Conference, which met in 1887 on the occasion of Queen Victoria's Jubilee. Since 1948, **Commonwealth Conferences** have replaced the Imperial Conferences.

Imperial Preference A system for encouraging trade with countries within the British Empire by applying favourable rates of customs duties to goods imported from these countries; in some cases import controls were imposed on goods from outside the Empire. The system was negotiated at the Imperial Economic Conference in Ottawa (1932) and after 1948 also applied to trade with Commonwealth countries, when it became known as **Commonwealth Preference.** The system was gradually dismantled as a result of the anti-protectionist conditions imposed by the General Agreement on Tariff and Trade (*see* GATT) in 1947 and by British entry into the EEC in 1973. It was finally abandoned completely in 1977.

implosion A sudden violent collapsing inwards as a result of external pressure. A light bulb, for example, will implode if broken because of the low pressure of gas inside it. The term has been extended to a technique in psychotherapy for treating phobias. This consists of suddenly confronting the patient with the cause of the fear; for example, a patient with agoraphobia is left in the middle of a large field to come to terms with his situation.

impossible art *See* CONCEPTUAL ART.

impro or **improv** An actor's or comedian's shorthand for improvisation. Once used mainly as a rehearsal technique or (more rarely) as a means of generating naturalistic dialogue, improvisation has recently enjoyed a vogue among stand-up comedians. The performer usually asks the audience to suggest characters, situations, props, and literary styles that might be used as the basis for an improvisation: a typical outcome might be a dialogue in the manner of Noël Coward between Benito Mussolini and Barbara Windsor, involving a woodlouse and a propelling pencil. Although the aim is anarchic spontaneity, the results may just as easily be laboriously unfunny. As a result impro has itself become an object of parody and ridicule for some young comedians. *See also* HAPPENING.

impulse buying The purchase of goods on the spur of the moment, without forethought. Because impulse buying is encouraged by the prominence given to goods by retailers, manufacturers often provide point-of-sale display units to enhance their sales.

imshi Slang exclamation from the Arabic meaning go away. It became part of army slang when the British troops were in Egypt during World War I.

in British slang for fashionable, trendy. This was the word of the 1960s, but by the 1970s for someone to call something 'in' only demonstrated how out of date they were.

in-flight Referring to goods and services provided during the course of a flight. For example, **in-flight entertainment** usually refers to a film show or music provided through individual headphones with a choice of several channels.

in vitro fertilization *See* IVF.

incidental music Background music used for a film, television programme, etc. In some cases the music may have been written exclusively for the film or programme; in others a well-established piece of music may be used as a background.

Examples of the latter include the use of Rachmaninov's second piano concerto in David Lean's *Brief Encounter* (1945) and Beethoven's violin concerto in Selznick's *Escape to Happiness* (1939; *Intermezzo* in America). In both cases the music provided a muted background for much of the film, the strongly lyrical passages in the concertos being used to heighten the most evocative moments in the love stories. A different example of incidental music was provided by the stylish way in which Scott Joplin's rags, especially 'The Entertainer', were used in *The Sting* (1975). In this case the rags experienced an enormous leap in popularity, purely as a result of being revived in the film.

Music written specially for a film or programme may either be innocuous, intended to enhance the mood of the action without being obtrusive, or it may provide a new dimension of its own. The zither music of Anton Karas (1906–85) in Carol Reed's *The Third Man* (1949) became almost as well known as the film itself. Another example is *Chariots of Fire* (1981), in which Vangelis' highly appropriate incidental music took off to a life of its own. In some cases the incidental music may prove more enduring than the film. The wartime *Dangerous Moonlight* (1941), for example, is now largely forgotten, but Addinsell's 'Warsaw Concerto' is still familiar to most people. *See also* MUZAK.

include me out *See* GOLDWYNISMS.

income support A form of social security payment, introduced in the UK in 1988; it is payable to the unemployed or people on low incomes, such as part-time workers. It replaced the former social security payment known as supplementary benefit and was part of a controversial series of changes in social-security legislation.

Indianapolis 500 US Grand Prix 500-mile motor race run annually in May at the Indianapolis Motor Speedway, Indiana. It was first run in 1911 and is now the fastest and most dangerous race of its kind in the world, with cars reaching speeds of up to 200 m.p.h. (321.8 k.p.h) on the 2.25-mile (3.6-km) circuit. With prize money in excess of $1.5 million, the **Indy**, as it is called, tempts numerous entrants; it is also very popular with spectators, attracting crowds of up to 300,000 annually.

indie British slang for a small independent record company, as opposed to the large recording giants. Many such small companies were formed during the mid-1970s to satisfy the demand for non-establishment pop music, especially for punk and Black ethnic music. The word had been used previously in America, for the films produced by small independent film companies.

Indochina War The struggle of the VIET MINH (Vietnamese nationalist and communist guerrillas) against French colonial rule 1945–54. The Viet Minh, led by Ho Chi Minh and supported by the Americans, had fought valiantly against the Japanese occupation of the region after 1940. With the collapse of the Japanese in 1945, Ho Chi Minh declared Vietnam independent but the French, with British assistance, re-established their dominion, precipitating the war. This culminated in the ignominious French defeat at DIEN BIEN PHU and the international Geneva Conference (April–July 1954), which agreed the partition of Vietnam into North and South along the **17th parallel** (*see* GENEVA AGREEMENTS).

industrial. industrial action Action by a workforce, usually organized in a trade union, in support of a pay claim or other demands concerned with terms and conditions of employment. The most serious industrial action, and the weapon of last resort, is the strike; other less drastic measures include an overtime ban, a go slow (a deliberate slackening in the work rate), and a work-to-rule (strict adherence to the rule book governing working practices, which results in a similar decrease in the work rate).

industrial espionage The practice of spying on one's competitors to discover their trade secrets. This is achieved by planting employees in their workforce, bribing existing members of their workforce, or making illegal use of telephone- or computer-tapping devices. The information sought usually refers to the competitor's plans for research, launching of new products, or advertising campaigns; or it may involve the competitor's manufacturing techniques, pricing policy, takeover plans, etc.

industrial medicine The health care provided for a workforce by the management. There are usually three facets: the first-aid and nursing care provided to cope with accidents, illness at work, etc.; the prevention of accidents, work-related diseases (*e.g.* those caused by noxious fumes or dusts), and the minimization of the factors causing stress; and a regular service of physical check-ups, especially for senior members of staff.

industrial tourism A recent development in the tourist trade, in which factories, workshops, and other industrial sites market themselves as attractions for sightseers. For the companies involved the revenue generated is usually much less important than the public relations opportunity. In the UK, the best-known example is British Nuclear Fuels' promotion of the SELLAFIELD nuclear power station as a holiday attraction – an all-too-obvious attempt to erase the sinister reputation the plant had acquired when it was called Windscale. The concept of industrial tourism seems to have developed in parallel with that other phenomenon of the 1980s – the repackaging of newly defunct coal mines, cotton mills, etc., as heritage centres (*see* HERITAGE INDUSTRY).

Industrial Workers of the World *See* WOBBLIES.

Indy (1) Short for INDIANAPOLIS 500. (2) A supplement of *The Independent* newspaper. *The Indy* is issued on a Thursday and aimed at younger readers.

inertia. inertial guidance The control of the flight path of a rocket or missile by internal instruments, as opposed to some form of external remote control. Most intermediate- and long-range missiles use inertial guidance, navigating themselves to a predetermined target (*e.g.* a map reference) by means of sophisticated internal sensing instruments and electronics, including gyroscopes, accelerometers, and gravitational computers.

inertia selling The illegal practice of sending unsolicited goods through the post and invoicing the recipient if the goods are not returned within a specified time. The practice became increasingly common during the 1960s, but is now controlled under the provisions of the Unsolicited Good and Services Acts (1971; 1975).

inferiority complex Originally a psychiatric term, made popular by the psychiatrist Alfred Adler (1870–1937), denoting unrealistic or unreasonable feelings of inadequacy brought on by actual or imagined inferiority in life. Adler's work concentrated on this area of behaviour because he believed that Freud had overemphasized the sexual element. Sufferers from this psychiatric condition may sometimes compensate for their feelings of insecurity by exhibiting markedly aggressive behavioural tendencies. The term inferiority complex has become popular in the general language, not to denote a mental or personality disorder but to describe extreme feelings of inadequacy or insecurity, temporary or permanent, aroused in the presence of certain people or situations.

inflation A continuing increase in the level of prices, which can be caused by an excessive demand for goods (**demand-pull inflation**), increased selling prices without an increase in demand (**cost-push inflation**), or an increase in the money supply (**monetary inflation**). The opposite process is **deflation**, in which both output and employment fall. In 19th-century Europe, periods of inflation and deflation alternated regularly but it was not until more recent times that the fundamental influence of such movements was recognized. In the 20th century the rapid inflation following World War I was followed by the protracted deflation of the GREAT DEPRESSION. This was succeeded by a continuous period of inflation after World War II, which rose to over 20% per annum in the mid-1970s; the control of inflation has been a principal preoccupation for national governments ever since. **Hyperinflation** is extremely high inflation, of the order of 50% or more each month. This usually causes social disorder. When the inflation rate is high consumers make strenuous efforts to convert their currency to material goods, as their notes can lose their value literally overnight. The German experience of this phenomenon, which meant that a suitcase of notes was needed to buy even a loaf of bread, made the control of inflation a top priority for most governments.

information. infomercial A compound of *inf*ormation and com*mercial* to describe a short television film produced by a company to advertise its goods or services. In general, such films are longer than the usual television advertisements or 'commercial breaks'.

infopreneurial Denoting electronic industrial equipment for the distribution of information. A combination word, made up from *info*rmation and entre*preneurial*, it is often used in the form **infopreneurial industry**, to describe the design, manufacture, and sale of such equipment.

information anxiety (IA) Feelings of panic or despair brought on by a surfeit of unassimilable information pumped out by the media. These may include a sense of inadequacy at one's failure to grasp matters, such as the teachings of Islam or Gorbachov versus Yeltsin, that have acquired a spurious familiarity as a result of constant media exposure. The phrase, coined by the US writer Richard Wurman, points to the paradox that advances in technology and the proliferation of channels of communication may leave people feeling less able to make sense of the world around them than ever before.

information pollution A large amount of information on a particular subject, especially unnecessary or redundant information, put out by the media. For instance, during the second Gulf War of 1991, television companies in the UK and America had very little 'hard news', but expended vast amounts of air time in analysis by political and military pundits.

information technology The distribution of information using electronic means, especially those involving computers. Networks of computers can be used to send ELECTRONIC MAIL and are used in electronic transfer of funds between banks. Many other examples of information technology exist.

infotainment A compound of *info*rmation and enter*tainment* used to describe media items of programmes, either news or documentary, that aim to provide information or knowledge about a certain subject by entertaining as well as instructing the receivers of the programme. The hope is that people who would not normally be interested in 'hard news' or documentaries could become better informed through the blander medium of infotainment.

infrastructure The goods and services, including roads, railways, airports, public utilities, and appropriate educational facilities, that a community in the Western world expects its national government to provide and, at least partially, pay for out of taxation.

inheritance tax There has been a tax in the UK on property, which becomes payable on the owner's death, for all of the 20th century. Introduced in 1894 as **estate duty** at a modest maximum rate of 8%, the tax was immediately and vehemently opposed by landowners. It was also a major factor in the unprecedented rejection of Lloyd George's 1909 budget by the House of Lords (*see* PEOPLE'S BUDGET). For the first half of the century the impact of the tax varied, but it gradually became more and more effective, both as a source of revenue for the exchequer and as a means of breaking down class barriers by restricting inherited wealth. By the time of the post-war Labour government under Clement Attlee, it was causing many large estates to be broken up on the death of their owners. In 1950, for example, the estate of the Duke of Devonshire attracted a duty of £5 million. However, the more intelligent of the landed gentry were finding legal ways round the tax, especially by making gifts of their property to their heirs while they were still alive and by putting their property into complicated trusts. For many, estate duty came to be regarded as a voluntary tax.

This situation ended with estate duty itself, when, in March 1975, **capital transfer tax** was introduced. The impact of this tax was not limited to the value of an estate at the time of its owner's death, but applied to many of the gifts the owner had made during his or her lifetime. In March 1986 substantial changes were made to capital transfer tax and thereafter it became known as **inheritance tax**. This tax now combines many features of the former estate duty with those of the capital transfer tax. Broadly, in 1990, no tax was payable on inheritances of less than £128,000, but a single 40% tax rate applied to inheritances in excess of this figure. Life-time gifts within a seven-year period before death are taxed on a sliding scale.

injury time Extra time added to the playing time of certain games (at the discretion of the referee), most notably Association Football and Rugby, to compensate for stoppages during the game to treat players' injuries. The phrase is occasionally heard in relation to other matters, such as wage negotiations.

Inkatha (Inkatha Yenkululeko Yesizwe – National Cultural Liberation Movement) A Zulu political movement, led by Chief Mangosouthu Gatsha Buthelezi (1928–), which was originally founded in 1928 mainly as a cultural organization; it was revived by Buthelezi in the 1970s as a political movement. Although opposing APARTHEID, Inkatha pursues a less radical approach to South African politics than the African National Congress (*see* ANC), opposing sanctions and foreign disinvestment, and favouring some form of power sharing as opposed to outright Black majority rule. The political differences between Inkatha and the ANC have frequently erupted into sporadic armed conflict between their supporters in the townships, especially since the ban on the ANC was lifted in 1989. However, a meeting between Buthelezi and Nelson Mandela of the ANC, early in 1991, seemed to set the scene for a more peaceful solution to the differences between them. Inkatha is the Zulu word for the grass coil Zulu women use to carry loads on their heads; its strength depends on the weaving together of many strands.

Inklings A literary circle run by C. S. Lewis (1893–1963) at Oxford University from the 1930s to the 1960s; its members included J. R. R. Tolkein (1892–1973) and Charles Williams (1886–1945). The Inklings was originally a literary club founded in 1931 by an undergraduate at University College; Lewis and his friends occasionally attended these meetings and when the club folded, Lewis decided to continue the meetings on an informal basis. Thereafter he and his small group of friends met regularly at a local pub or in Lewis's rooms, to talk and read aloud from their original literary works.

inner city The densely populated central part of a city. Since the 1960s the term has been associated with areas of urban squalor characterized by abandoned industrial sites, substandard housing, and social deprivation. Inner cities have also earned a reputation for vandalism, crime, and racial tension. In the UK following World War II, slum clearance outpaced housebuilding programmes, creating overcrowding in high-density estates and tower blocks. Rigid rules covering the segregation of residential from industrial and commercial zones combined with rules prohibiting expansion of existing industrial sites in city centres led to the closure of many smaller firms and the relocation of others to new towns and greenfield sites. As jobs disappeared, people with skills and resources moved out to the suburbs, leaving the inner cities inhabited largely by the unemployed (some of whom were unemployable) and disadvantaged. With sources of investment and affluence removed, the areas rapidly decayed. The problems were first recognized in the late 1960s, but little was done until a decade later when the urgency of rehabilitating these areas became a national priority. Planning policy in the UK now supports redevelopment schemes designed to enhance the status of the inner cities and encourage industry to move back. Educational facilities in inner cities have also been improved.

inside. **inside job** A crime, such as a burglary, committed by someone, or with the aid of someone, working or living in the organization or premises concerned. An inside job is usually one perpetrated by someone trusted by the victim.

insider dealing A stock-exchange term used to describe the illegal practice of trading in stocks and shares to one's own advantage using confidential information to which one's job or position affords access. By this means profits can be made before the confidential information becomes public. The term arose in the 1960s, particularly with reference to company takeover bids. It took on a broader significance after the BIG BANG, when brokers and jobbers amalgamated. *See* CHINESE WALL.

Instamatic A tradename for a small fixed-focus camera made by the Eastman-Kodak company. It heralded a whole generation of cheap ready-for-use cameras.

instant. **instant camera** A type of camera that uses special film enabling developing and processing to take place inside the camera. Finished prints can be produced within a few seconds of taking the photograph. The first instant camera was the POLAROID (or Land) camera, invented by Edwin Land (1909–) in 1947. A colour process was developed in 1963.

instant karma Slang from the late 1960s and early 1970s for any illegal barbiturate drug. The name is a pun on calmer, the required effect of a barbiturate. The phrase 'instant karma' was also frequently used at this time, especially by HIPPIES, to describe the idea that divine retribution would immediately befall the perpetrator of an evil deed or unkind act. This was based on a slightly muddled interpretation of the word KARMA, a concept of personal destiny from Indian religious philosophy. During the 1960s an interest in Eastern religions developed in the West, especially among young people; however, much of the philosophy was poorly understood and used to support many of the ideas prevalent among such people.

instant zen Slang from the late 1960s for LSD or any hallucinogenic drug. The term was not widely used. It was based on the Zen Buddhist concept of meditation, regarded as the only path to enlightenment. LSD was also supposed to provide a path, albeit a short cut, to enlightenment.

integrated circuit A miniature electronic circuit, including transistors, resistors, and capacitors, contained within a semiconductor crystal. They range in complexity from a simple logic circuit to a highly complex system containing as many as a million transistors. Integrated circuits are widely used in computers, calculators, and most electronic equipment. Small (1–8 mm), light, reliable, and fast, they are made by introducing impurities into specified regions of a semiconductor crystal.

intelligent terminal A computer terminal that is itself capable of processing data without reference to the main computer of the system to which it is connected.

Intelsat International Consortium for Satellite Communications. The consortium, initially comprising 14 countries, was established in August 1964 with the aim of providing global communication facilities, including telephone, television and other communications, by means of a network of satellites in 24-hour synchronous orbit. Each country invested in the system in proportion to the use it expected to make of it; revenues were then shared in this proportion. Intelsat 1 (EARLY BIRD) was launched on 4 April 1965 and made transatlantic TV possible for the first time. By 1976, 23 satellites of progressively improved technological sophistication had been launched by NASA from Cape Canaveral. The latest Intelsats have been placed in orbit by the SPACE SHUTTLE.

intensive care unit (ICU) A hospital unit equipped with the facilities to provide constant medical care and monitoring for critically ill patients. Intensive care units were first set up in the 1960s to look after patients whose lives were at risk, as in cases of multiple trauma, coronary thrombosis, or some types of post-surgical care. An ICU is characterized by its specially trained nurses and its life-saving equipment, such as respirators and devices that continuously monitor the vital functions. Some hospitals also have specially equipped ambulances that can be sent out to deal with emergencies, such as heart attacks, in the patients' homes.

interactive fiction or **computer fiction** A HIGH TECH genre of fiction in which stories and novels are stored on computer and are provided with several sets of alternative plots and story-lines. This enables the users to make choices in order to create their own versions of the story, within the limits set by the computer programs.

Inter-City A fast rail service between British towns and cities. British Rail introduced its first 'Inter-City 125' High Speed Trains (HST) in 1976 on the London to Weston-Super-Mare and London to South Wales routes. The service was later extended to other lines, including the east coast route between London and Edinburgh. The distinctive wedge-shaped design of the HST used on these routes won a Design Council Award in 1978.

intercom A telephone communications system within a building, aircraft, etc. The word is a shortening of *inter*nal *com*munications.

interesting. Very interesting . . . but stupid A well-known catchphrase from the popular US TV show of the late 1960s and early 1970s *Rowan and Martin's Laugh-In*. This show, which became extremely popular in the UK, consisted of sketches linked by zany characters, each with their own catchphrase. One such was Arte Johnson, wearing glasses and dressed as a Nazi soldier who spoke the line slowly with a long pause and a very strong German accent.

interferon Any of a group of proteins produced by certain body cells, such as white blood cells and fibroblasts, that act to inhibit the reproduction of invading viruses. They can also enhance the tumour-destroying capability of the body's immune system. Interferons were discovered in 1957 by Alick Isaacs and Jean Lindemann at the National Institute of Medical Research, Mill Hill, in London. Since then much attention has focused on their potential as therapeutic agents in the treatment of virus infections and cancer. Progress was hampered by the minute amounts obtainable from the blood; it was only in the 1980s, when interferons could be produced in much larger quantities using GENETIC ENGINEERING techniques, that the clinical value of these proteins could be assessed. They have proved effective in combating certain viruses, *e.g.* herpesviruses, but can produce severe side-effects. Interferons may have a role in treating AIDS; they have shown activity against both the AIDS virus, HIV, and the tumours that develop during the later stages, such as Kaposi's sarcoma.

Interlingua or **Latino Sine Flexione** A simplified form of Latin in which there are no inflections, developed, like Esperanto, for use as an artificial international language. It was originally formulated in 1903 by the Italian mathematician, Giuseppe Peano, and then revived and reformulated in the 1950s by the linguist Alexander Gode, for use by the international scientific community. Abstracts and summaries are published in Interlingua by several international scientific journals although its use has not spread beyond a minority of dedicated enthusiasts.

International. **International Brigades** Brigades of foreign volunteers, including Europeans and Americans, who fought for the Republicans against General Franco in the Spanish Civil War (1936–39). Recruitment was largely organized by the Communist Party (although not all volunteers were Communists) and the membership included intellectuals and writers, adventurers, the unemployed, and ordinary workers. The seven brigades, divided by nationality, were involved in the defence of Madrid in November 1936 and subsequently reinforced Republican forces in the defence of the Jarama Valley and Guadalajara in the spring of 1937. In 1938 the brigades suffered heavy losses during fighting in the Ebro valley. Members of the brigade who came from the UK included the novelist George Orwell and the poet W. H. Auden.

International Monetary Fund *See* IMF.

Internationals The name usually applied to the international federations of Socialist and Communist parties, the first of which was set up under the auspices of Karl Marx in 1864 as the International Working Men's Association, lasting till 1872. The Internationale was adopted as its anthem. The Second, or Social-Democratic, International was formed in 1889 and the Third, or Communist, International was set up by Lenin in 1919 and lasted until 1941. The abortive Trotskyite Fourth International dates from 1936.

International Style An architectural movement, which began in central Europe soon after World War I and spread throughout Europe and America during the late 1920s. The style favoured orthogonal cubic forms shorn of ornamentation, open internal spaces, and the use of such modern materials as sheet glass, steel, stucco, and concrete. The movement was intended to represent an anti-eclectic, anti-bourgeois, and utilitarian fusion of art and new building technology. Its best known European exponents were the German architects Walter Gropius (1883–1969, founder of the Bauhaus movement), Mies Van der Rohe (1886–1969), and the French architectural visionary LE CORBUSIER (1887–1965). Their ideals were enthusiastically promoted in America by Philip Johnson (1906–89), who, together with the US architectural historian Henry-Russell Hitchcock, coined the term 'International Style' in the title of a catalogue for an exhibition of the latest trends in European architecture at the Museum of Modern Art in New York in 1932.

Interpol International Criminal Police Commission. The organization that coordinates the police forces of over 125 countries in the fight against international crime, such as drug smuggling and counterfeiting. It was set up in Vienna in 1923 but was reformed and relocated in new headquarters in Paris in 1946. French police officials staff the General Secretariat, which administers its day-to-day functions; affiliated police forces communicate through domestic clearing houses and criminals are apprehended by means of extradition.

intifada (Arab. uprising) The revolt by the Palestinian inhabitants of Israel that began in 1987. It later extended its meaning into the general language to denote any uprising, with or without Middle-Eastern connections.

Invar An alloy of iron, nickel, and carbon that has a low coefficient of expansion and is used in the manufacture of balance springs for clocks and watches, electronic components, precision instruments, and jet engines. Short for 'invariable', it was invented by the Swiss metallurgist Charles Édouard Guillaume in the early years of the 20th century to help eliminate the adverse effects of temperature variations on timekeeping mechanisms.

Invergordon Mutiny A mutiny in the Royal Navy's Atlantic Fleet at the naval base in the Cromarty Firth, Scotland, on 15 September 1931. Ratings, led by Able Seaman Len Wincott, refused to prepare ships for sea in protest at cuts in pay ordered by the National Government, which had been announced over the radio in advance of official notification. The Board of Admiralty averted further embarrassment to the navy by agreeing to limit the cuts to below 10%. However, the incident accelerated the gathering financial crisis that led to the UK's abandonment of the Gold Standard on 21 September 1931.

investigative journalism Reporting by newspaper or television journalists involving investigation of corruption, crime, governmental inefficiency, etc. In countries with a free press this is regarded as a valuable contribution that the media can make to the quality of a social system and as a safeguard against complacency or abuse of the system. While it is not always popular with governments, to restrict it, in a democracy, would be electorally unacceptable. Investigative journalism does not exist in totalitarian countries.

IRA Irish Republican Army. A guerrilla force largely reorganized by Michael Collins from the former Irish Volunteers, which confronted the Royal Irish Constabulary and the BLACK AND TANS from 1919 to 1923. After the civil war, extremists kept it in being as a secret organization and although proscribed in 1936 it continued to make occasional raids into Ulster and commit bomb outrages in mainland Britain, its aim now being to establish a united Irish Republic. After a period of quiescence, violence steadily increased from the mid-1950s. Since 1969 its many senseless acts of terrorism in Ulster, England, and elsewhere have made a settlement of the Ulster problem increasingly difficult. IRA terrorists were responsible for (among other acts of violence) the murder of Lord Mountbatten in 1979, the attempted assassination of Margaret Thatcher in 1984, the Remembrance Day bombing in Enniskillen (1987), attacks on British military bases in Germany and England (1989), and an unsuccessful mortar bomb raid on the British cabinet in 10 Downing Street (1991). Funds for the IRA are raised in America by **NORAID**.

Irangate Following WATERGATE, the suffix -*gate* became an indicator of political scandal involving corruption and secret transactions. 'Irangate' was used to describe a plan devised in 1986 by Oliver North and other members of the US administration to supply arms to Iran and use the profits to give military aid to the right-wing CONTRA rebels in Nicaragua, after the US Congress had voted against giving this aid.

IRBM Intermediate Range Ballistic Missile. A medium-range ballistic weapon, such as the US Tomahawk cruise missile and Pershing II, or the Soviet SS-20, SS-4, and SS-5, which normally has three warheads and a range of between 1000 km and 5500 km. These IRBMs were extensively deployed in Europe by both America and the Soviet Union during the late 1970s and early 1980s (*see* GREENHAM COMMON), but were later removed in accordance with the provisions of the US–Soviet INF (Intermediate Nuclear Forces) Treaty of 8 December 1987. The modified Soviet SCUD missiles fired by Iraq at targets in Israel and Saudi Arabia during the GULF WAR of 1991 are sometimes classed as IRBMs.

Irgun Zvai Leumi (Heb. National Military Society) A Jewish terrorist organization founded in 1931; it was active in Palestine 1946–48. Its most notorious act, led by Yisrael Levy (1926–90), was the bombing of the King David Hotel in Jerusalem on 22 July 1946, destroying the quarters of the British administration with the loss of 91 lives. It claimed responsibility for over 200 acts of terrorism against the British and Arabs before being disbanded in 1948, when members took an oath of loyalty to the newly founded Israeli state.

Iris Acronym for *infrared intruder system*. An alarm system in which an alarm is set off when a beam of infrared radiation is broken by an intruder.

Irish. **Irish confetti** A euphemism for stones, rocks, or other such missiles thrown at riots.

Irish crown jewels theft The disappearance of the Irish crown regalia from the safe of Dublin Castle's Bedford Tower in July 1907. The theft caused a major scandal. Edward VII himself demanded the resignation of the four men responsible for the safekeeping of the jewels and a commission of inquiry was hastily set up to investigate. Lengthy recriminations ensued but were never resolved and the thief's identity was never discovered. The jewels themselves have never reappeared.

Irish Free State The 26 counties of southern Ireland that were granted dominion status within the Empire under the provisions of the Anglo-Irish Treaty of 6 December 1921. Its first president, W. T. Cosgrave (1880–1965), was replaced in 1932 by Éamon de Valera (1882–1975), founder of the Fianna Fáil party. In 1937 the Irish Free State was renamed Eire. It remained a member of the Commonwealth until 1949, when it became known officially as the Republic of Ireland.

Irish National Volunteers An irregular force raised by the Irish Republican Brotherhood (IRB) in November 1913 to counteract the Ulster Volunteers. The movement had attracted over 150,000 recruits by June 1914 but the organization soon afterwards split into two factions; the majority (the National Volunteers) following the moderate nationalist leadership of John Redmond and the rump (the Irish Volunteers) joining Eoin MacNeil, who was more directly influenced by the radical separatists within the IRB. By the end of World War I, however, the anti-war anti-conscription Irish Volunteers had flourished at the expense of the moderates, who dwindled into insignificance. By 1919 the Irish Volunteers had evolved into the radical Irish Republican Army (*see* IRA).

iron. **Iron Butterfly** The Hollywood nickname for Jeanette Macdonald (?1901–65), US singer and film star of the 1930s. She began her career on Broadway as a chorus girl, progressing to leading roles in several musicals of the 1920s. In her first films she was cast with Maurice Chevalier before going on to partner Nelson Eddy (1901–67) in a famous series of screen operettas, such as *Rose Marie* (1936) and *Maytime* (1937). The pair were sometimes known as the **Singing Capon** and the Iron Butterfly, especially by those who were jealous of their popularity. The taste for their particular brand of shrill romantic duets with their operatic pretensions did not survive the war, however. The nickname Iron Butterfly has also been used occasionally of Julie Andrews (*see* HOCKEY STICK).

Iron Cross A Prussian military decoration (an iron Maltese cross, edged with silver), instituted by Frederick William III in 1813 during the struggle against Napoleon. Remodelled by William I in 1870 with three grades, in civil and military divisions, the Iron Cross was awarded to some 3,000,000 servicemen in World War I.

Iron Curtain The notional barrier created by the Soviet Union and other satellites along a line running from Stettin (Szczecin) to Trieste. The communist countries east of this line cut themselves off from Western Europe after World War II. The phrase was popularized by Sir Winston Churchill in his Fulton Speech (5 March 1946) but it was used previously in Germany by Count Schwerin von Krosigk on 2 May 1945 and by Lord Conesford in February of that year. It has an earlier antecedent; Ethel Snowden used it in 1920 with reference to BOLSHEVIK Russia, Lord D'Abernon used it in 1925 with regard to the proposed Locarno Treaties, and the Queen of the Belgians, in 1914, spoke of a "bloody iron curtain" between her and the Germans. The phrase occurs in the Earl of Munster's journal as far back as 1817. The demolition of the BERLIN WALL following radical political reforms in East Germany in 1989 signalled the end of the Iron Curtain as an effective barrier between East and West.

> From Stettin on the Baltic to Trieste on the Adriatic, an iron curtain has descended across Europe.
> SIR WINSTON CHURCHILL.

Iron Guard The title adopted by the Romanian Fascist party of the 1930s. *See* FASCISM.

Iron Lady The name bestowed upon Margaret Thatcher (1925– ; prime minister 1979–90), when she was leader of the Opposition in the House of Commons, by the Soviet Defence Ministry newspaper *Red Star* (24 January 1976). After her speech warning the Commons of the increasing Soviet threat to the West, the Red Star accused the "Iron Lady" of trying to revive the COLD WAR, referring to her "viciously anti-Soviet speech", and to "the peace-loving policy of the Soviet Union". Although the Russian coinage Iron Lady was probably based on an analogy to Stalin as the MAN OF STEEL, the British press were quick to retranslate the Russian as **Iron Maiden**, an allusion to the medieval instrument of torture. During that period caricatures appeared in which the spiked iron person-sized torture devices had Thatcher faces. In a similar vein Mrs Thatcher was characterized as the **Cold War Witch**. Mrs Thatcher attracted a large number of nicknames during her career. The Conservative minister Norman St John Stevas referred to her as **the Blessed Margaret** and **the Leaderene**; her husband, Denis Thatcher, is reputed to call her **the Boss**. Other nicknames include **the Milk Snatcher**, referring to her decision to stop free school milk when she was education secretary and its convenience in the rhyming catcall 'Thatcher, Thatcher – Milk Snatcher'. **The Grocer's Daughter** refers to the grocer's shop in Grantham run by her father. It also has echoes of the nickname of her predecessor, Edward Heath (1916– ; prime minister 1970–74), who was dubbed **the Grocer** by the magazine *Private Eye*, possibly because of his preoccupation with the price of groceries during negotiations to join the European Community (1973). Other Thatcher nicknames refer to her uncompromising and autocratic style: **Attila the Hen** and **TINA** (the latter from her habit of using the phrase 'There Is No Alternative!').

iron lung A rigid chamber fitted over the top part of a person's body to provide prolonged artificial respiration to patients with respiratory problems by means of mechanical pumps, which force the air in and out of the patient's lungs. The apparatus has been in use since the early 1930s but has now been largely replaced by more modern methods.

Iron Maiden Nickname for Margaret Thatcher. *See* IRON LADY.

iron rations Emergency rations, especially as provided in the army; usually tinned food, particularly bully beef and biscuits. Also, in World War I a popular name for hot shell-fire.

pump iron To lift weights for exercise or bodybuilding. The phrase was popularized by the film *Pumping Iron* (1970).

Irving US slang for a dull and boring man. This name supposedly epitomizes such a person. BRIAN is the British equivalent.

Irvin suit The flying suit worn by the RAF during World War II, which was designed by Leslie Irvin and manufactured at his factory in Letchworth.

ISBN International Standard Book Number. An internationally agreed system of numbering and registering editions of books. Every book in the world carries an ISBN number on its copyright page.

iso-. isometrics A system of physical exercises to develop muscular strength; it involves brief contractions of the muscle or muscle group against the fixed resistance of an immovable object or the equal force of opposing muscles acting in the same way. Isometrics is based on the principle of isometric, or static, contraction in which tension is developed in the muscle without change in the length of the muscle fibres (the prefix *iso-* means 'the same'). The static strength and rigidity developed by isometric exercises is required in many sports, such as gymnastics, weightlifting, and wrestling. This type of training became very popular, especially in America, in the 1960s and 1970s following reports of the significant increases in strength that could be achieved by making use of it.

isomoodic Describing music that matches (rather than alters) the mood of the person (the prefix *iso-* means 'the same'); such music is used as an introduction to music therapy. Listening to this music is regarded as the first step in improving one's state of mind through musical suggestion. The similarity of this word to such recognized scientific terms as isobar, isomer, isotope, etc., is presumably intended to bestow the appearance of scientific rigour on the practice.

Isonzo A river, formerly in Italy (now in Yugoslavia and called the Soca), that was scene of a series of fierce battles between Italian and Austrian forces between 23 June 1915 and 12 November 1917. The Italian strategy aimed at the capture of Trieste and then an advance on to Vienna, but the Austrian defences withstood all Italian attempts to break through, and in the final battle, 24 October–12 November 1917 (known as the 12th Battle of Isonzo of CAPORETTO), the Germans aided the Austrians in inflicting a catastrophic defeat on the Italians, who lost 305,000 men, of whom 275,000 were captured.

I-Spy A series of children's educational game books, which became enormously successful in the UK after their first appearance in the 1950s. The books gave children a list of items on a particular subject (such as history) to seek out; their rewards for finding a certain number of them were badges and an 'Order of Merit' making the participant a 'Redskin of the I-Spy Tribe'. The awards were bestowed by 'Big Chief I-Spy', in reality Charles Warrell (1889–) who created the books and ran the whole enterprise until it ended in 1986. The Michelin company announced plans to relaunch the I-Spy books in 1991.

> I invented the name Big Chief I-Spy. I travelled the country holding I-Spy pow-wows – enormous gatherings. One of the last was 'I-Spy the city of Bath'. About 5,000 children and adults turned up.
>
> CHARLES WARRELL, 1990.

Is you is or is you ain't? A phrase taken from the title of the 1944 song *Is You Is or Is You Ain't My Baby?*, written by Louis Jordan and Billy Austin and meaning *are* you, or *aren't* you my girl? The phrase enjoyed a revival in the late 1980s and early 1990s, thanks largely to a series of television commercials for a leading credit card. These featured a frustrated cardholder imploring a restaurateur to accept his Access card with the line "Does you do or does you don't take Access?"

It A humorous synonym for sex appeal, popularized by the novelist Elinor Glyn in *It* (1927), though Kipling had used the word earlier in the same sense in his story *Mrs Bathurst* (*Traffics and Discoveries* 1904).

It Girl One of the most famous Hollywood nicknames; it was given to Clara Bow (1905–65), a leading actress of the silent films of the 1920s, who was hailed as the sexiest woman in films. She acquired the title after appearing in *It*

(1927), the film based on Elinor Glyn's story (*see* IT), in which she portrayed a vivacious pouting flapper. Red-haired and exuberant, Clara Bow epitomized the JAZZ AGE, hence another of her nicknames, the 'Jazz Baby'. Although typecast as a flapper, she was capable of portraying much deeper characters. In the 1930s she suffered a series of breakdowns, which ruined her career.

to be with it A much-used mid-20th century phrase meaning to be completely in with current trends, fashions, music, etc., especially of the kind popular with certain sections of the young.

Italian Alp One of the nicknames of the Italian heavyweight boxer Primo Carnera (1906–67); he was also known as the 'Ambling Alp' on account of his size (almost 6 ft 6 in tall and weighing 19 stone). He was discovered while employed as a circus wrestler and strongman. Having taken up boxing professionally in 1928, he became world heavyweight champion in June 1933, when he knocked out Jack Sharkey in the sixth round. He held the title for only one year, however, being floored 11 times in as many rounds by Max Baer in 1934. He later went on to become a professional wrestler and appeared in several films.

ITMA It's That Man Again. A popular British radio series, which did much to brighten up the dreariness of the BLACK-OUT years of World War II. It was devised by the comedian Tommy Handley (1896–1949), the script being written by Ted Kavanagh. It ran from 1939 until Handley's death in 1949. Mrs Mopp and FUNF were among the characters in this hilarious weekly skit on English life. The show introduced many popular catchphrases, including Mrs Mopp's "Can I do you now, sir?"

Ivan Slang for a Russian person. It is based on the belief that Ivan is the most common Russian forename, much as a German is supposed to be called Fritz and an Irishman Paddy.

Ivan the Terrible Ivan IV of Russia (1530–84), infamous for his cruelties, but a man of great energy. He first adopted the title of Tsar (1547).

In the 20th century the name was also given to a NAZI guard at the Treblinka CONCENTRATION CAMP who was responsible for numerous atrocities against prisoners. Identified as John Demjanjuk (formerly Ivan Grozny), a retired Ukrainian car worker living in Cleveland, Ohio, he was extradited to Israel in 1986 and sentenced to death.

IVF In Vitro Fertilization. The technique in which an egg is fertilized with sperm outside the body of the female. The description *in vitro* (literally 'in glass') is not strictly accurate since the process is generally performed in a metal dish. The IVF technique for humans was pioneered in the UK by gynaecologist Patrick Steptoe and physiologist Robert Edwards, in order to help women with certain types of infertility, particularly blocked or damaged Fallopian tubes. The world's first IVF baby (**test-tube baby**) was Louise Brown, born in 1978 at Oldham General Hospital, since when IVF has benefitted thousands of women throughout the world. An egg is removed from the woman's ovary using a long hollow tube inserted through the abdominal wall. The egg is then introduced into a suspension of the husband's sperm under sterile conditions. When fertilization has taken place and the embryo has undergone several divisions of its cells (about 40 hours old), it is inserted in the womb through the vagina, and allowed to implant in the wall of the womb. Often, two fertilized eggs are implanted to increase the chances of success. Failure to implant and subsequent spontaneous abortion are both common, enabling only a minority of women to be successfully treated by the technique.

In the UK, IVF and such related techniques as embryo freezing and storage, womb leasing, and embryo donation, are regulated by the Human Fertilisation and Embryology Act (1990). This set up a special authority to oversee all work in this field and to issue licences to medical practitioners and researchers. In America legislation varies from state to state. Another major application of IVF has been in farm livestock breeding programmes. *See also* AI.

ivy. Ivy League A group of old-established northeastern US colleges and universities that has acquired a reputation for academic achievement and social prestige: so-called because many of the stately college buildings were ivy-clad. The term was first used in the 1930s by sports writers; the Ivy League colleges and universities usually include Yale, Harvard, Princeton, Columbia, Dartmouth, Cornell, Pennsylvania, and Brown. **Ivy Leaguers** are students or graduates of these establishments, the use of the term now usually being confined to contexts in which their well-spoken voices and snobbishness are being emphasized. The Ivy League in America is roughly equivalent to OXBRIDGE in the UK.

> The jerk had one of those very phoney, Ivy League voices, one of those very tired, snobby voices.
> J. D. SALINGER: *Catcher in the Rye* (1951).

Operation Ivy Codename for the testing of the first hydrogen bomb by the Americans on ENIWETOK.

Iwo Jima A small volcanic island in the Pacific Ocean, about 600 miles SE of the Japanese mainland. During the closing stages of World War II it was bitterly fought over as a strategic stepping stone in the Allied advance on Japan. The Americans were determined to stop the Japanese from using it as a base for their fighters intercepting US B-29 Superfortresses en route from the Marianas to bomb the Japanese mainland. After a naval and air bombardment of Japanese defences, US marines went ashore on 19 February 1945. On 23 February the US flag was raised on Mount Suribachi, the island's highest point. A second flag-raising, performed on the same day, was photographed by pressman Joe Rosenthal and transmitted to America, where it quickly assumed enormous symbolic significance. There is now a statue of this flag-raising incident in Washington DC. Meanwhile, the stubborn Japanese resistance on the island was gradually overcome but with heavy casualties on both sides. The marines finally secured the island at the end of March. Over 6800 marines and nearly all 22,000 Japanese defenders were killed.

Izvestia (Russ. news) The official national newspaper of the Soviet government. It was established in Petrograd in 1917 as an organ of the Revolution, then transferred to Moscow in 1918. By 1932 it enjoyed a circulation of over 1.5 million. It represents the government's views, especially on foreign policy and international relations, reproduces official documents at length, and is intended to educate and inform the public in the light of official policy.

J

J Abbreviation for a JOINT, a marijuana cigarette. This has been used since the mid-1960s, both in the UK and America.

J. Arthur British rhyming slang meaning to masturbate, from J. Arthur Rank, to wank. J. Arthur Rank (1888–1972) was an industrialist and film mogul. The term was used in this sense in the 1960s, although in the 1940s it had been used to mean a bank. *See* RANK ORGANIZATION.

Who shot J. R.? An advertising slogan from the early 1980s used between the end of the first series of the popular US SOAP OPERA *Dallas* and the beginning of the second. The villain of the story, oil magnate J. R. Ewing (played by Larry Hagman), was shot in the final episode of the first series. In order to maintain the high level of interest in the show on both sides of the Atlantic, the slogan was widely advertised; when the second series began the viewing ratings were gratifyingly high. The shot, fired it transpired by an abandoned lover, was not fatal and J. R. was spared to perpetrate yet more evil deeds. *See* CLIFF-HANGER.

jack (1) British slang for alone, from the rhyming slang 'Jack Jones', alone. It is usually used in the phrase **on one's jack**. (2) Prison slang from the 1960s for heroin, or a single dose or a single injection of a narcotic, particularly a tablet of prescribed heroin or a heroin substitute (such as methadone) that is given to addicts. This is derived both from the use of JACK UP, meaning to inject oneself, and from the rhyming slang JACK AND JILL, for pill. (3) US slang for money. This term is also used in the UK and Australia. (4) Tramps' and dossers' slang for methylated spirits. (5) British slang for buttocks or anus. (6) British slang for a penis. This sense is obviously influenced by the US **jack off**, meaning to masturbate. It also reflects the old rhyming slang 'Jack in the box', pox. (7) Australian slang for fed up. This is probably related to the US **jacked off**, meaning angry.

I'm alright Jack A catchphrase indicating that as the self-interests of the speaker have been satisfied he has no intention of spending any effort considering the plight of others. The use of the name Jack implies a nautical origin. In some nautical contexts the whiff of the ocean is even more conspicuous: **Pull up the ladder, Jack, I'm inboard**, is its full naval form.

Perhaps the catchphrase reached its widest public through the Boulting Brothers film *I'm Alright Jack* (1959), in which Peter Sellers played a communist shop steward and Ian Carmichael a naive young graduate who precipitates a strike by starting his industrial career at the bottom. John Boulting's swipe at the idiocies of British labour relations in the 1950s was fairly close to the mark. Sellers' operatic performance, no doubt intended to caricature the antics of union leaders, appeared slightly underplayed by the end of the 1960s.

> It's 'Damn you, Jack – I'm all right!' with you chaps.
>
> DAVID BONE: *The Brassbounder* (1910).

Jack and Jill British drug abusers' rhyming slang from the 1960s for a pill, particularly one containing an illegal drug.

jackboot A large leather boot extending over the knee, originally worn as protective armour by troopers in the 17th and 18th centuries and still part of the uniform of the Household Cavalry. It was later adopted as part of the uniform of various military organizations, notably the NAZI stormtroopers. Because of the military associations, the jackboot came to be used figuratively in such phrases as **under the jackboot**, to denote the repressive totalitarian rule exerted by militaristic or Fascist regimes. Since the 1960s the word has been widely used to mean any authoritarian or bullying measures as well as someone who employs these tactics.

jack it in To give up, leave, abandon something prematurely.

There were only fifteen of us on the hunger strike, I suppose the others must have got hungry, anyway, they jacked it in.

F. NORMAN: *Bang to Rights* (1948).

jack up (1) Slang for to inject oneself with heroin or any other illegal narcotic. (2) British police and criminal underworld slang meaning to put together or to organize a plan. It is thought to be derived from jacking up a car, the preparatory stage to doing any actual work on it.

Jolly Jack *See under* JOLLY.

Jackal, The A journalists' nickname for Carlos Martinez (1949–), a Venezuelan known to have worked as an assassin on behalf of various terrorist organizations. The name comes from Frederick Forsyth's novel, *The Day of the Jackal* (1970), in which a professional assassin, codenamed 'The Jackal', is hired by a group of veterans of the Algerian war to kill President de Gaulle.

They really are bad shots.

CHARLES DE GAULLE; on narrowly surviving an attempted assassination in 1962.

Jackie O. Jacqueline Onassis (1929–), famous for her marriages to US president John F. Kennedy (1917–63) and the Greek shipping magnate Aristotle Socrates Onassis (1906–75). Later to become one of the world's most photographed women, she was herself a press photographer before marrying Kennedy in 1953. As first lady, her youth, beauty, and sense of style contributed greatly to the image of Kennedy's White House (*see* CAMELOT); indeed, her activities became a staple of gossip columns and society journalism. When she accompanied the President on a visit to Paris in 1962 she so charmed everyone, including General de Gaulle, that when Kennedy held a press conference, he said:

I do not think it is altogether inappropriate to introduce myself to this audience. I am the man who accompanied Jacqueline Kennedy to Paris, and I have enjoyed it.

The events of 22 November 1963, when she rode beside her husband in the Dallas motorcade (*see* OSWALD, LEE HARVEY), made her the world's most celebrated widow. However, it was not long before the question of her remarriage was frequently being mooted in the press. In 1968 she married the 62-year-old Onassis, whose fabulous wealth, friendships with the famous, and stormy relationship with Maria Callas had made him a celebrity in his own right. The marriage took place on the groom's private island of Scorpios. After being widowed for the second time, Jackie O. returned to New York and a career in publishing.

Jacuzzi Tradename for a hot whirlpool bath, installed in leisure centres and some private homes as an aid to relaxation. It was developed and marketed by Roy Jacuzzi from a pump invented by his brother Candido Jacuzzi and became internationally popular from the 1970s.

jag (1) Slang for a binge, a bout of drug-taking, drinking, or any other self-indulgent activity.

Ronnie Kray was then on a religious jag and offering only fruit juice and gramophone recordings of the Lord's Prayer.

The Independent, 2 February 1991.

(2) Slang for intoxication from drugs, particularly inhalants, such as glue. (3) Slang for to inject oneself. This is closely related to 'jab'.

jalopy or **jallopy** Slang for a dilapidated old car. Particularly popular in the 1950s, the term was first used in America in the 1930s. It has also been used to refer to an old aeroplane. The derivation is unknown.

jam (1) Slang for an improvised music or RAP session. It is a shortened version of **jam session**. It is also used as a verb in this sense, meaning to improvise. This was originally used of groups of JAZZ musicians and later by blues and ROCK musicians. In recent years the use of the term has been extended to include the practice of improvising rap chants.

The gigs became almost a secondary thing to getting to the nearest jam, just getting together with whoever was in town and playing for the pure love of it.

JIM CAPALDI, rock musician, in *The Independent*, 17 January 1991.

(2) US slang for a wild party. This usage reflects the idea of people being crowded into a room. (3) Slang for an act of sexual intercourse, or a sexual partner, or the vagina. These sexual senses reflect both the close proximity of entwined bodies and jam, the conserve, as something sweet and desirable. Jam, in this sense, can also be used as a verb. (4) Slang for an illegal drug, particularly cocaine. This usage again reflects the idea of jam as something sweet.

all jam and Jerusalem Derisive catchphrase aimed, since about 1925, at the Women's Institute organizations in the UK. The popular conception of the 'WI' is that its activities revolve around the making of jam and the singing of Blake's

'Jerusalem' at each meeting – an increasingly inaccurate view.

jam jar British rhyming slang for a car, in use since the 1920s, mainly in London.

jamboree bags British vulgar slang for female breasts. In the 1950s a jamboree bag was a small lucky-dip bag containing sweets and a toy. This new slang sense is heard mostly among men old enough to remember these childhood delights.

jane (1) British slang for a female prostitute. It is derived both from the rhyming slang Jane Shore, whore, who was a mistress of King Edward IV, and from the fact that Jane is the female form of John – the slang name for a prostitute's customer. In America, where the word is also used, the derivation is thought to have been influenced by the Hungarian word *jany*, a girl. (2) Slang for a women's lavatory. This is a feminist's version of John, a widely used Americanism for a men's lavatory.

Jane A nubile comic strip character, created by Norman Pett, who first appeared in *The Daily Mirror* in 1932 and soon became a national institution. The strip continued until 1959, Don Freeman taking over the writing in 1938 and Mike Hubbard the drawings from 1949. In 1942 Jane emerged from her bath in the nude for the first time. On the same day the 8th Army in North Africa advanced six miles. Robert Maxwell, who was in North Africa at the time, reintroduced Jane when he bought the paper in 1985. The new strip ended on 1 September 1990.

Jane Q. Citizen or **Jane Q. Public** US slang for the average woman. *See* JOHN Q. CITIZEN.

jankers British forces' slang for a military punishment. It was widely used during the 1950s when military service was still compulsory but was originally coined during World War I. The derivation is uncertain, but the word is possibly related to an obsolete meaning of jangle, to complain.

jansky A unit of measurement of flux density used in RADIOASTRONOMY. It is equal to 10^{-26} W m^{-2} Hz^{-1}. It is named after Karl G. Jansky (1905–50), a US radio engineer who developed the first radio telescope (by accident) in 1932. He was employed by Bell Telephone Laboratories to investigate spurious signals, which were interfering with telephone communications; with his homemade receiver he realized that the whistles he was hearing came from the radio emissions of celestial bodies. This became known as **Jansky noise**.

JAP *See* JEWISH AMERICAN PRINCESS.

Japs. Send us more Japs! Widely publicized quotation by Lt.-Colonel James P. S. Devereux (1903–) during the Battle of Wake Island (1941). It was allegedly the text of a defiant message sent by Devereux shortly before US forces surrendered to the Japanese and was enthusiastically taken up by the US press. However, when Devereux returned home after four years in a Japanese prisoner-of-war camp, he was totally ignorant of the whole thing:

> I did not send any such message. As far as I know, it wasn't sent at all. None of us was that much of a damn fool. We already had more Japs than we could handle.

Jarrow march or **Jarrow Crusade** A protest march from Jarrow in NE England to London in October 1936 by a selection of local workers made redundant by the closure of Palmer's Shipyard on the River Tyne. The march was organized by the Jarrow town council and led by the local Labour MP, Ellen Wilkinson ('Red Ellen'), who, after 26 days on the road, presented a petition in the House of Commons to elicit government aid to alleviate the suffering caused by mass unemployment in the northeast and other regions of the UK. The marchers attracted enormous public sympathy and the march became one of the most famous incidents in industrial folklore.

Jar Wars A campaign set up by the Reagan administration in America in 1986 to try to prevent illegal drug taking and drug dealing. The campaign was so called, by analogy with the title of the space adventure film *Star Wars* (1977), because all government personnel were required to supply samples of urine to be tested for the presence of drugs. These specimens were usually taken in jars or bottles.

jaw. jaw-jaw A lengthy or long-winded discussion. It can also be used as a verb, meaning to discuss. It was first used, both as verb and noun, as early as 1748 in Smollett's *Roderick Random*. The *OED* gives an isolated example from 1831 of *jaw-jaw* used as a verb, but the term gained wide currency only from the late 1950s, following Harold Macmillan's speech in Canberra on 30 January 1958, in which he coined the ugly but true aphorism:

Jaw-jaw is better than war-war.

These words echoed those of Winston Churchill, spoken four years earlier at a lunch at the White House in Washington on 26 June 1954. Here he was reported to have said:

Talking jaw to jaw is better than going to war.

Jaws A financially successful 1975 horror movie directed by Steven Spielberg about a great white shark that terrorizes a small seaside resort on Cape Cod in America. Based on the bestseller by Peter Benchley, it features Robert Shaw as the veteran shark hunter and sparked off an era of 'shark mania'. Its well-known INCIDENTAL MUSIC is by John Williams. The success of *Jaws* encouraged a spate of highly derivative sequels designed especially for the POPCORN MARKET. It did little, however, for the reputation of the shark, leading several conservation groups to point out that shark attacks are rarer than the film suggests and that certain species of shark are declining alarmingly in numbers as a result of persecution by hunters. The shark in the film itself was mechanical, built at a cost of millions of dollars. The film's sequels were released with the slogan 'Just when you thought it was safe to go back in the water', which acquired the status of an international catchphrase.

Jaycee (initials of Junior Chamber) A term common in North America, Australia, and New Zealand for a member of a junior chamber of commerce.

jay-walker A pedestrian who crosses roads carelessly, paying no attention to pedestrian crossings or traffic regulations. Originating in America around the time of World War I, the term owes its derivation to the US word 'jay', a simpleton or rustic, one who is not sufficiently sophisticated to cope with town or city traffic.

jazz A type of popular music originating in the folk-music of the US Blacks of the cotton fields. It first developed in New Orleans and by 1914 reached Chicago, where it gained its name. It was influenced by the BLUES, RAGTIME, and popular European music; its main characteristics are syncopation, a strong rhythmic beat, and improvisation on a melodic theme by trumpet, clarinet, and trombone. Its impact grew steadily and it has had many notable exponents. The name has been somewhat loosely appropriated by popular dance orchestras playing in the jazz idiom. The word jazz, originally jass, was a New Orleans word for sexual intercourse. The connection between the music and the sexual activity is that jazz emerged in the brothels of Storyville in New Orleans, where musicians were employed to entertain, and perhaps to stimulate, the clientele waiting their turn to enjoy what they had come for. *See also* BOOGIE-WOOGIE; SWING.

a load of jazz A load of nonsense, a lot of codswallop.

Jazz Age An epithet for the 1920s in America, popularized by the writer F. Scott Fitzgerald (1896–1940). His own hedonistic lifestyle and the excesses of the age featured in his *Tales of the Jazz Age* (1922). Jazz music, wild parties, the SPEAK-EASY and the CHARLESTON, bobbed hair and short skirts, and greater sexual freedom represented a rebellion against the repressive social mores that had governed the pre-war generation.

A new generation grown to find all Gods dead, all wars fought, all faiths in man shaken.

F. SCOTT FITZGERALD.

jazz ballet bottom A colloquial medical term used to describe an abscess between the cheeks of the buttocks. This condition is common among people performing jazz ballet exercises, many of which require the performers to sit on the floor for long periods.

jazz rock Jazz-influenced ROCK music that employs some of the instruments (such as woodwind and brass), sounds, and techniques (such as improvisation) associated with jazz while retaining the heavy beat and rhythm of rock. It enjoyed some commercial popularity in the second half of the 1960s and early 1970s, when many rock musicians were experimenting with a variety of musical influences: rock music was then divided into such categories as folk rock, progressive rock, jazz rock, etc. Well-known exponents of jazz rock in the 1960s included the groups Soft Machine and Chicago.

JCB A tradename for a multipurpose earthmoving machine, commonly used on building sites, which has a hydraulically operated shovel at the front and an excavator arm (backhoe) at the rear. The excavator is normally operated by a second set of controls situated behind the driver; most models have two sets of seats, one for driving and operating the shovel and another for the excavator. It is named after Joseph Cyril Bamford (1916–), its British manufacturer, whose company pioneered the development of hydraulically operated wheeled loaders and backhoe machines in the late 1940s and early 1950s.

Jebru, Mythical Isle of A phrase used by the US army in World War II. GIs would claim they were being sent there, *i.e.* 'destination unknown'.

Jeep A small all-purpose car first developed in America during World War II and known as a GP, *i.e.* General Purpose (vehicle), hence the name. Its four-wheel drive and high and low gearboxes gave it astonishing cross-country performance. The experimental models were also called Beeps, Peeps, and Blitz Buggies. However, it was as a Jeep that it was known throughout the world from 1941 onwards. Another possible derivation of the name was the pet, Eugene the Jeep, of the Popeye cartoon strips of the 1930s, which was said to be able to do 'almost everything' and made a 'jeep' noise (*see under* SPINACH).

Jeeves The intelligent and resourceful valet of the brainless Bertie Wooster in the comic tales and novels of P. G. Wodehouse (1881–1975). Reginald Jeeves first appeared with Wooster in a collection of stories called *The Man with Two Left Feet* (1917) and subsequently featured in a series that began with *My Man Jeeves* (1919). The first Jeeves novel was *Thank You, Mr Jeeves* (1934). It is thought that he may have been based loosely upon Wodehouse's own butler, Eugene Robinson; his name was borrowed from a noted cricketer, Percy Jeeves, who was killed in action in 1916. The character was portrayed on the big screen by Arthur Treacher in two 1930s films and by Dennis Price and Stephen Fry in two television series (1960s and 1990s respectively); he also inspired a stage musical, *Jeeves* (1975), adapted by Alan Ayckbourn with music by Andrew Lloyd Webber. *See also* DRONES' CLUB; BLANDINGS, EMPRESS OF; PLUM.

Jeffrey *See* ARCHER.

Jehovah's Witnesses The name given in 1931 to the religious movement founded in 1872 by Charles Taze Russell in Philadelphia, and formerly known as the International Bible Students. It does not ascribe divinity to Jesus Christ, regarding him instead as the perfect man and agent of God. Recognition of Jehovah as their sole authority led the Witnesses to refuse to salute a national flag or to do military service. The periodical *The Watch Tower* is their main publication.

jelly British underworld slang for the safebreaker's explosive, gelignite. It originated in the 1950s and is clearly a shortening of the pronunciation of gelignite; it is also influenced by the jelly-like appearance of the explosive.

jelly beans US drug users' slang from the 1950s for amphetamine tablets. The name reflects their use as a recreational treat reminiscent of the children's sweets of the same name. US president Ronald Reagan was reported to be very fond of them. *See also* JOLLY BEANS.

jellies British slang for the cheap clear plastic sandals, usually made in bright colours, that are worn by children and some adults, especially on the beach.

jelly bomb British soldiers' slang for a crude incendiary device containing a highly flammable substance, usually petrol, that ignites on impact or by means of a fuse (*see also* MOLOTOV COCKTAIL). 'Jelly' in this context refers to the glutinous state of the liquid contained in the bomb rather than to the slang name for gelignite.

Jelly Roll Nickname of Ferdinand Lemott Morton (1890–1941), flamboyant JAZZ pianist, composer, and self-styled 'Originator of Jazz Stomps and Blues'. He began his musical career playing the piano in the Storyville brothels of New Orleans in 1906; after spells as a pimp, boxing promoter, and gambling-hall manager he moved to Chicago in 1923. Here he achieved his greatest success recording the 'Red Hot Peppers' sessions for Victor records, which included many well-known songs, such as 'Sidewalk Blues'. In 1928 he moved to New York; however, the early 1930s saw the beginning of the big-band era, which eclipsed Morton's small-band New Orleans jazz style. He spent the rest of his career in ill-health and obscurity.

Jemima Puddle-duck The title of a children's book (1908) featuring a duck so named, written and illustrated by Beatrix Potter (1866–1943). The story of Jemima and her narrow escape from the designs of "the gentleman with sandy whiskers", whom she fails to recognize as a fox, has become a perennial children's favourite and the focus of an enormous trade in children's toys and furnishings. *See also* PETER RABBIT.

Jenkins, Nick The upper-class narrator of *A Dance to the Music of Time*, the 12-volume novel sequence by Anthony Powell (1905–) that begins with *A Question of Upbringing* (1951) and ends with *Hearing Secret Harmonies* (1975).

Jensenism The school of thought that believes human intelligence to be largely determined by hereditary factors, as opposed to environmental factors. It is associated with the US educational psychologist Arthur R. Jensen (1923–).

jerk Slang for a stupid person, usually male. It is probably derived from the verb to **jerk off**, meaning to masturbate.

Jerry Since World War I a nickname for a German, or Germans collectively.

jerrican A 4½-gallon petrol or water container that would stand rough handling and stack easily, developed by the Germans for the AFRICA KORPS in World War II. Copied by the British in Libya, it became the standard container for fuel replenishment throughout the Allied armies. The name is an allusion to its origin. *See* JERRY.

Jersey Lily Emily Charlotte Le Breton (1852–1929), known as Lillie Langtry, was so nicknamed after her debut on the professional stage in 1881. A famous EDWARDIAN beauty and one-time intimate of the Prince of Wales (later Edward VII), she was the wife of Edward Langtry and daughter of W. C. Le Breton, Dean of Jersey. She was the first British society hostess to become an actress. After Langtry's death she married Sir Hugo Gerald de Bathe in 1899.

Jerusalem Bible An English translation (1966) of *La Bible de Jérusalem*, a French version of the Bible made by members of the Dominican École Biblique in Jerusalem and published in France (1948–54). The English text follows the French translation but reference was made to the original languages, and the notes to the original French version were revised.

jessie British contemptuous slang for a weak or effeminate man. Originally a Scottish and N English term, it has become more widely heard in the UK since it was used by the Scottish comedian Billy Connolly. The derivation is uncertain.

Jesus. Jesus boots British slang for a type of thonged sandal worn by BEATNIKS in the late 1950s and early 1960s. The term was used disparagingly by the more sharply dressed fashion-conscious mods (*see* MODS AND ROCKERS), who wore elastic-sided Chelsea boots. **Jesus sandals**, as worn by HIPPIES, are similar. The allusion is to the footwear often seen on the feet of the crucified Christ in early paintings.

Jesus freak Disparaging name for a BORN-AGAIN CHRISTIAN, or a member of an evangelical Christian group. In the late 1970s FREAK was used as a suffix, meaning a fan or enthusiast.

Jesus wept Originally a quotation from the Bible, from John 11:35, which describes how Jesus was moved to tears when he went to the house of Mary and Martha and heard of the death of their brother Lazarus, whom he then raised from the dead. However, the phrase has come to be used as an oath or an interjection of extreme agitation or annoyance. During a Royal visit to West Germany in May 1965, which was being reported for TV by Richard Dimbleby, the broadcast was beset by problems. Dimbleby, thinking that the microphone had already been switched off, was clearly heard to say "Jesus wept" as some unseen calamity befell the TV team.

jet. jetfoil A HYDROFOIL powered by jet engines.

jet lag The physical and psychological symptoms experienced when the normal biological rhythms are disrupted by air travel involving crossing time zones. Jet lag occurs when the normal 24-hour cycle of fluctuations in hormone levels, body temperature, pulse rate, etc. (*see* BIORHYTHM) is disrupted by clock changes. This can affect waking and sleeping patterns, activity levels, and mood. Several days may be needed for the body to reestablish its normal rhythms; pulse rate, for example, taking up to eight days to normalize after an eight-hour shift in time zones. Crossing from west to east causes greater disruption of the biological rhythms than travel in the opposite direction. Apart from general fatigue, the effects are not apparent following a long flight from north to south as no time zones are crossed. The term was coined in the 1960s when airliners became jet-propelled.

Jet Propulsion Laboratory (JPL) The headquarters of the US space programme for unmanned spacecraft, situated near Pasadena, California. The JPL is a subsidiary of NASA, run under contract by the California Institute of Technology; it consists of a large complex of buildings, including a Space Flight Operations Facility, which is the command and control centre, and a separate science laboratory for analysing the photographs and other data received from such craft as the PIONEER (1958–78) and VOYAGER space probes (1977).

jet set Affluent socialites who can afford to fly around the world from one fashionable resort to another (*see also* EUROTRASH). Although the phrase was coined after all airliners became jet-propelled, the *Sunday Telegraph* (3 February 1980) managed a feeble jet-set joke:

> The Royal Family can hardly be said to belong to the Jet Set – all the aircraft in the Queen's Flight are prop-driven (and 15 years old).

jet ski A small powered water vehicle with a flat keel shaped like a water ski. People taking part in the sport of jet skiing can stand, sit, or kneel on the ski. The sport became popular in the 1980s but constituted a hazard to swimmers.

Jew. Jewish Agency An organization created in 1929 by Chaim Weizmann to encourage Jewish settlement in Israel. Under Weizmann's conciliatory leadership during the 1930s, the agency played a variety of roles: raising funds for the Jewish National Home in Palestine, overseeing Jewish immigration, helping to resolve the resulting conflicts with Palestinian Arabs, establishing the Youth Aliyah programme to help resettle orphaned Jewish children fleeing from the NAZIS, and representing Jewish interests at the LEAGUE OF NATIONS. Under the subsequent leadership (1935–48) of David Ben Gurion, the agency gradually abandoned its ancillary roles and became an uncompromising instrument of militant Zionism. In 1951 it became officially identified with the World Zionist Organization.

Jewish American Princess (JAP) US slang for a rich young Jewish girl, especially one who is spoilt by her parents. Originally used affectionately by Jews themselves, in the 1980s it became a derogatory term with both racist and sexist overtones. 'Princess' has always been a term of endearment, albeit a rather sexist one, much used by indulgent fathers. The acronym is pronounced in the same way as the slang name for a Japanese.

> Nor does she feel Jewish: 'My mission is to wipe out all Jewish American Princesses', she grins.
>
> *Daily Telegraph*, referring to US comedienne Ruby Wax, 19 January 1991.

Jew Süss Josef Süss Oppenheimer, the central character in the bestselling novel of this title by the German author Leon Feuchtwanger (1884–1958). The story, a satire about a Jew who rises from the ghetto to a position of power in 17th-century Württemberg only to discover that he is a Gentile, has been filmed several times. A notorious German film *Jud Süss* (1940), directed by Veit Harlan, was used as antisemitic NAZI propaganda to prepare the Germans for acceptance of the FINAL SOLUTION. Goebbels himself revised the script, and the actor Ferdinand Marian, who played the title role, is said to have later committed suicide as a result of his feelings of guilt for having taken part in the film.

You don't have to be Jewish . . . A US advertising slogan used in 1967 for rye bread. The rest of the slogan is '. . . to love Levy's real Jewish rye.' The accompanying picture showed such people as Eskimos and Chinese enjoying the bread, to emphasize the point. The phrase probably originated in the title of the Broadway show of Jewish humour *You don't have to be Jewish . . .* . As with other catchphrases that use an ellipsis, the temptation to add a facetious ending is great. On a more sombre note, the form of the catchphrase has been echoed in a publicity slogan used by the SAMARITANS in the UK, 'You don't have to be suicidal to call the Samaritans'.

jewel. Jewel of the Ghetto The nickname of Ruby Goldstein, a US boxer of the early 1900s, who later became America's premier boxing referee, officiating in seven world heavyweight title fights. The Ghetto of the nickname refers to his origins in New York City on Manhattan's Lower East side.

the jewel in the crown A cliché, the popularity of which in recent years probably stems from its use as the title of the 1984 TV series of Paul Scott's 'Raj Quartet', the first book of which also bears this title. The jewel referred to here, of course, was India – in the crown of Queen Victoria. The exact origins of the phrase are obscure, although a painting called 'The Jewel in her Crown', depicting the Queen receiving a large jewel (representing India) from an Indian prince, is mentioned in Paul Scott's novel. The phrase has been in use for most of this century in relation to the British colonies, and probably earlier. It is also sometimes used facetiously with respect to a good deed, which might be described as adding a jewel to the crown that a person will wear in heaven.

JFK *See* IDLEWILD.

jiffed British army slang from the GULF WAR of 1991, meaning that someone has been given an unpopular task by his officers. The derivation is unclear. *See also* SPAMMED.

Jiffy Bag A tradename for a padded envelope for sending fragile objects by post, available in a variety of different sizes. It was so called because it could be used quickly and easily – 'in a jiffy'.

Jilleroo Nickname given to Australian landgirls in World War II. It was formed by association with Jackaroo, a name used in Australia in the first half of the 19th century to describe a young Englishman newly arrived to learn farming, derived, according to some, from the Queensland *tchareroo*, the shrike, noted for its garrulity. Others derive it from *Jack Carew*; *Jack* and *Kangaroo*; etc. Later the name was applied simply to station hands.

jillion US slang for a vast number, bigger than a billion and synonymous with trillion and zillion.

Jim. I'm worried about Jim The catchphrase used by imitators to sum up the essence of the long-running BBC radio saga *Mrs Dale's Diary* (1948–69). Jim was Mrs Dale's doctor husband, about whom she seemed to be continually anxious.

jimmy (1) British slang for urination. It is a shortened version of the rhyming slang jimmy riddle, piddle. (2) Drug abusers' slang for an injection of heroin.

Sunny Jim A name often patronizingly applied to men, whatever their name, or to naughty small boys. It comes from the advertising slogan created in the early years of the century by two US women, Miss Ficken and Minnie Maud Hanff, for Force breakfast cereal. The slogan, which was accompanied by a cartoon drawing, went:

> High over the fence leaps Sunny Jim
> Force is the food that raises him.

The nickname was often used by the media for the British Labour prime minister (1976–79) James Callaghan, later Lord Callaghan (1912–).

Jiminy Peanuts *See* PRESIDENT PEANUTS.

jinkai senjitsu (Jap.) The tactic of flooding an area with personnel or urging large numbers of people into action. The practice first came to Western notice in the early 1970s in the field of business and marketing; the Japanese interest in opening up markets in North America resulted in waves of researchers and trade delegates being sent to investigate the potential of the market.

jitterbug An energetic and acrobatic dance that originated in America in the 1930s and was spread worldwide by US troops during World War II. Performed to music with a syncopated rhythm, it includes elements from several other dances, notably the JIVE and the LINDY HOP.

jive (1) A fast style of JAZZ, more or less synonymous with SWING. **Jiving** was a 1940s word for dancing to this music. The JITTERBUG is a form of jive. (2) A slang form of American English used by Black JAZZ musicians in Harlem in the 1930s. Also known as **jive talk**, it was imitated by US teenagers in the 1950s and became the basis for BEATNIK, and later HIPPIE, slang. (3) Empty or misleading talk and by extension anything worthless or unacceptable. (4) Marijuana or a cigarette containing it.

Jix The nickname of Sir William Joynson-Hicks, first Viscount Brentford (1865–1932). He was Home Secretary (1924–29); a noted puritan, he was prominent in defeating the adoption of the Revised Prayer Book of 1928.

> We mean to tread the Primrose Path,
> In spite of Mr. Joynson-Hicks.
> We're People of the Aftermath
> We're girls of 1926.
>
> JACQUES REVAL: *Mother's advice on Father's fears* (*The Woman of 1926*).

job. job centre A UK government employment agency. Formerly called **employment exchanges** and before that **labour exchanges**, they used to be involved also in registering out-of-work people for the unemployment benefit (dole). Now, however, job centres seek to find jobs for applicants, assist employers in finding suitable employees, provide training for trades in which a shortage of skilled workers exists, and offer occupational advice on retraining.

jobs for the boys A catchphrase reflecting nepotism, especially in government; it dates back to the 1930s or earlier. An incoming political party tends to reward its supporters with the best jobs in its administration, thus giving commentators an opportunity to make use of this phrase.

jobsharing A system in which one full-time job is shared by two or more part-time employees.

jobsworth A petty (often uniformed) official, such as a car-park attendant or commissionaire, who unreasonably refuses to cooperate beyond the limits of his or her responsibilities by invoking the phrase "It's more than my job's worth to . . . ". The term was first used in the British rock-music press during the 1970s, referring to bouncers in clubs who refused journalists access to rock musicians. It has now passed into more general usage.

Jock US, Canadian, and Australian slang of the late 1980s for a young sporting male, a keen football player, a redneck, and one who usually exhibits right-wing jingoistic political views.

> The majority of us, who are not jocks, should come out and show our disgust, our dread, our grief.
>
> GERMAINE GREER, expressing her views on the Gulf War in the *Independent Magazine*, 2 February 1991.

Jodrell Bank Site of the Nuffield Radio Astronomy Laboratories in Cheshire, which is owned by Manchester University. It contains a large steerable radio telescope, 75 mm (250 ft) in diameter, the first to be in operation. It was designed by Sir Bernard Lovell (1913–) and built in 1957.

Joe US slang for the man in the street and as a form of address for someone whose name is unknown. *See also* GI; JOE BLOGGS; JOE PUBLIC.

Joe Bananas A corruption of Joseph Bonano (1905–), former boss of the Castellamarese crime family in New York, one of the big five of the city's MAFIA gangs (the others being Gambino, Genovese, Colombo, and Lucchese). Arriving in New York from the Sicilian town of Castellamare del Golfo in 1925, he soon became the youngest *don* in America in the aftermath of the so-called Castellamarese War. He retired in 1968 after a period of bloody feuding, known as the Bonano War, with rivals in the Mafia commission (the organized crime's regulatory body). He was jailed in the mid-1980s for refusing to answer questions before a Grand Jury about Mafia operations alluded to in his autobiography *A Man of Honour* (1983). Released in November 1986 for health reasons, he is the only survivor of the five original 1930s New York bosses.

Joe Bloggs An average man assumed to be a typical member of the population; *i.e.* 'the man in the street' or 'the man on the CLAPHAM OMNIBUS'. The name is regarded as comic and perhaps slightly disparaging. Joe Bloggs has equivalents in North America and Australia, both known as **Joe Blow**.

Joe Palooka A simple-minded boxer, the popular hero of a US comic strip created by Ham Fisher in 1928. The character first appeared on film in *Palooka* (1934), with Stuart Erwin playing the boxer and Jimmie Durante his trainer, Knobby Walsh. A decade later Monogram produced a series of short films starring Joe Kirkwood.

Joe Public Slang for the general public. The use of JOE as a term for an ordinary person was originally an Americanism that spread across the Atlantic (as in Joe Bloggs) after World War II. It is sometimes, but not always, derogatory.

jog. jogger's nipple A painful inflammation of the nipple caused by chafing on clothing. The condition affects both men and women. Formerly confined to professional marathon runners, it became a common problem among fun runners and joggers in the 1980s.

jogging Running at a slow steady pace, typically over a moderate distance, as a recreation or a means of improving physical condition. Jogging became popular in America in the late 1960s, particularly among those with a sedentary lifestyle. Its popularity increased and spread to other countries with growing public awareness of the importance of physical health, especially in relation to the prevention of heart disease. There can be little doubt that the pursuit of physical fitness by jogging has done a great deal to decrease the likelihood of early heart attacks among YUPPIES and others. Some older enthusiasts, however, may well have run themselves into an early grave.

John. Here's Johnny *See under* HERE.

John Birch Society An ultraconservative US secret society founded on 9 December 1958 by Robert H. W. Welch Jr (1899–1985), a retired Boston sweet manufacturer, to combat communism and other potential threats to the American way of life. It was named in honour of John Birch, a Baptist missionary and US Army intelligence officer killed by Chinese Communists in August 1945. Welch regarded John Birch as the first US victim of the COLD WAR against international communism.

John Q. Citizen or **John Q. Public** US slang for the average man. The 'Q' is an invention to cater for the American habit of including the initial of the middle name in the formal name by which a person wishes to be known. It is said that Harry S. Truman, having no middle name, invented the initial 'S' to comply with the usual practice. The female equivalent is JANE Q. CITIZEN.

join. If you can't beat 'em, join 'em *See under* BEAT.

joiner A type of photographic collage invented in 1982 by the British artist David Hockney (1937–), who also coined the name. A scene is photographed repeatedly from a number of different angles and over a period of time: the prints are then 'joined' together to form a composite design. Enthusiasts for the technique compare it to the cubist revolution in painting (*see* CUBISM), claiming that it introduces a dimension of time, change, and movement that is absent from conventional photography.

Join the army and see the world An army recruiting slogan from the 1940s, since then used ironically by soldiers to describe any humdrum posting, especially one near to home. A sharper variant, especially in anticipation of military action, is 'Join the army and see the next world', while the pacifists of the 1960s preferred 'Join the army and see the world, meet interesting people – and kill them'.

joint (1) Slang for a marijuana cigarette or a cigarette containing a mixture of tobacco and hashish. Joint became the accepted name for such a cigarette in the 1960s in both the UK and in America, replacing reefer, which had been current in the 1950s. A joint can either be an American-style unadulterated marijuana (or grass) cigarette, usually rolled in one cigarette paper, or the more elaborate three-cigarette-paper English-style cigarette, containing a mixture of hashish and tobacco. The latter is also called a **spliff**. Among friends, both types of joint are smoked communally, being passed from one to the other. *See also* JOLLY. (2) US slang for a penis, reflecting the image of a piece of meat. To **unlimber the joint** is to urinate.

joint custody An agreement between two partners in a divorce or separation to take joint responsibility for the children involved and to share joint access.

the joint is jumping A US phrase of the 1930s used to describe a party or club in which people were dancing to or enjoying exuberant fast-tempo JAZZ. The phrase was immortalized by FATS Waller in his 1937 recording *The Joint Is Jumpin'*, which he wrote in conjunction with Andy Rozaf and J. C. Johnson. His vivid and exhilarating piano playing provides a fitting background to the amusing words describing the riotous atmosphere typical of Harlem RENT PARTIES of the 1920s and 1930s:

> Check your weapons at the door
> Be sure to pay your quarter
> Drag your body on the floor
> Grab anybody's daughter
> The roof is rockin'
> The neighbors are knockin'
> We're all bums when the wagon comes
> I'll say the joint is jumpin'.

jolly (1) British middle-class drug-users' slang from the 1970s and 1980s for a JOINT, a marijuana cigarette. It is inspired by the similarity in the sound of the two words as well as by the effects of the drug. 'Jolly' has always been a popular word among a certain type of hearty middle-class person. (2) Acronym for Jet-setting Oldster with Lots of Loot: a wealthy senior citizen. One of the more contrived products of the journalistic craze for acronyms based on lifestyles, it followed the success of the term YUPPIE in the 1980s.

jolly beans British drug users' slang for amphetamine pills. This is the British version of the US JELLY BEANS, reflecting the effect of taking them as well as their resemblance to sweets.

jolly hockey sticks! A catchphrase originally associated with English girls' public schools. It is used by the pupils and others to epitomize the regime of mandatory games, particularly hockey, which these institutions used to enforce in imitation of the boys' public schools – also, mockingly, to deride the mistresses whose job it was to organize these activities.

The jolly-hockey-sticks mistress was caricatured inexhaustibly by Joyce Grenfell (1910–74) in many films, including *The Happiest Days of Your Life* (1949), made by Frank Launder. One critic commented about this film, in which a girls' school was mistakenly billeted on a boys' school:

> Launder couldn't have knocked another laugh out of the situation if he'd used a hockey stick.
> *Sunday Express.*

Joyce Grenfell went on to embellish this image in her many ST TRINIAN'S films of the 1950s. *See also* HOCKEY STICK.

Jolly Jack The nickname of J. B. Priestley (1894–1984), British writer, literary critic, and wartime broadcaster. Although his work includes comedy (the novel *Laburnum Grove*; 1933 and the play *When We Are Married*; 1938), the description 'jolly' is generally considered to be an ironic reference to his well-known tendency for expressing dissatisfaction.

Jonah word A word, such as 'mother', that a chronic stutterer finds difficult to utter. The term comes from Jonah in the Bible who, as far as one knows, did not stutter – the allusion is to bad luck.

Jones. Jones Family A series of Twentieth Century Fox B-MOVIES about the comic exploits of a supposedly typical US small-town family, which began with *Every Saturday Night* (1936) and was followed by 16 other films. The series attempted, unsuccessfully, to emulate the more sentimental HARDY FAMILY films.

Jonestown massacre The enforced mass suicide in Guyana in 1978 of followers of Jim Jones (1933–78), charismatic leader of the People's Temple Sect. The sect was founded by Jones in San Francisco but in 1977 moved to an agricultural commune in Guyana, christened Jonestown. On 14 November 1978, prompted by persistent allegations of mistreatment of sect members, the commune was visited by a US congressman, Leo Ryan, together with newsmen and a group of concerned relatives. Ryan was shot on Jones's orders, together with four other members of his party. On 18 November Jones ordered the mass suicide of all members of the sect. According to official figures, 914 people died, including 240 children, by voluntarily drinking soda pop laced with cyanide.

jordim (Heb. those who descend) Israeli citizens who leave Israel and emigrate to another country. *See also* CHOZRIM.

Josephson effects Two effects in physics concerning the behaviour of superconductors (*see* SUPERCONDUCTIVITY). The British physicist Brian Josephson (1940–) showed theoretically in 1962 that if two superconductors were separated by a thin insulating layer a current can flow across the junction in the absence of an applied voltage. Moreover, if a small voltage is applied across the junction, an alternating current flows with a frequency inversely proportional to the applied voltage. The effects were later verified by experiment and the combination of superconductors and insulator is known as a **Josephson junction**. Two Josephson junctions can be connected together to form a **SQUID** (superconducting quantum interference device), which is used for measuring weak magnetic fields to a high degree of accuracy. The junctions also have applications as extremely fast switching devices in computers.

journey. Is your journey really necessary? A slogan from World War II, aimed at discouraging civilian travel to save fuel. The campaign was promoted by posters. Whether or not these posters were effective is hard to say. More of a disincentive was that public transport was infrequent and overcrowded and petrol was severely rationed.

joy. joy bang *See* JOY POP.

joy-firing The practice of discharging live ammunition into the air as a welcome or to express delight at good news or a mood of exhilaration. This wasteful (and dangerous) custom seems to be particularly prevalent among Arab soldiery. It was commented upon by T. E. Lawrence (who coined the term – presumably by analogy with joy-riding) and has been recently revived by western reporters. Distressed and angry Arabs have also been known to discharge their guns into the air, although it would be inappropriate to describe this as joy-firing. In the GULF WAR of 1991, following the US bombing of a civilian shelter, which caused the deaths of several hundred civilians, Iraqi soldiers were seen on TV programmes discharging many rounds of ammunition to express their frustration and rage.

joy pop (1) US drug users' slang meaning to inject a narcotic occasionally and for pleasure rather than habitually as an addict. This term is more widely used than the synonymous **joy bang**. (2) Drug users' slang meaning to inject a drug (usually heroin). This is more commonly known as 'skin popping'.

joy-ride A ride for pleasure in a car or other vehicle, especially in a stolen vehicle. The term is also used as a verb.

joy smoke US teenage slang of the 1980s for marijuana.

joystick The control column of an aeroplane or glider, which is linked to the elevators and ailerons to control them.

jubbies British teenage slang for female breasts, probably closely related to 'bubbies', which also means breasts.

jubbly British slang for money, often used in the phrase **lovely jubbly**. Jubbly was originally the tradename for an orange drink, popular in the 1950s and 1960s, which was advertised using the slogan 'lovely jubbly'. The phrase became widely used in the 1980s with the popularity of the BBC comedy series *Only Fools and Horses*, being a favourite catchphrase of Del Boy (David Jason). 'Dash', 'spondulicks', and 'lolly' are other words for money that share similar origins.

Judges' Rules Rules concerning the questioning of suspects by the police and the taking of statements. First formulated in 1912 and revised in 1918, they were reformulated in 1964 by a committee of judges and approved by a meeting of all judges of the Queen's Bench.

Juggernaut or **Jagganath** A Hindu god, 'Lord of the World', having his temple at Puri in Orissa. It is a cult-title of Vishnu; the pyramidal temple was erected in the 12th century and held the Golden Tooth of Buddha. The chief festival is the car festival when Jagganath is dragged in his car (35 feet square and 45 feet high) over the sand to another temple. The car has 16 wheels, each seven feet in diameter. The belief that fanatical pilgrims cast themselves under the wheels of the car to be crushed to death on the last day of the festival is largely without foundation. However, it has led to the phrase the **car of the juggernaut**, used to denote customs, institutions, etc., beneath which people are ruthlessly and unnecessarily crushed. 'Juggernaut' is thus also applied to any wheeled 'monster' – most recently, in the UK, to the giant articulated lorries increasingly prevalent since the UK's entry into the EC.

juke box An automatic musical box or record-player that plays selected pieces when coins are inserted. Such machines reached new levels of sophistication in the 1950s, incorporating brightly flashing lights, and were later much-valued by collectors.

July Plot *See* STAUFFENBERG PLOT.

jumble sale The sale of miscellaneous, usually second-hand, articles to raise money for charity or other good causes. Jumble sales often take place in local church halls or community centres at weekends.

jumbo (Swahili *jumbe*, chief) (1) Slang for a large slow-witted person. It was taken from the popular name for an elephant, a tradition established after the name was given to a famous elephant exhibited by the circus owner P. T. Barnum. This usage also echoes the slang word **dumbo** meaning a stupid person. *Dumbo* was also a 1941 Walt Disney film about a baby elephant. (2) British slang for the bottom, the buttocks. (3) US drug abusers' slang for the drug CRACK. (4) British rhyming slang for a drunk, from 'jumbo's trunk'.

Jumbo jet The nickname of the Boeing 747 airliner, the world's first wide-bodied commercial transport aircraft, introduced into service on 22 January 1970 by Pan American Airways on their New York–London route. The latest models are 71 m (233 ft) long, have a wing span of 60 m (196 ft), and can carry over 400 passengers.

jump. jump seat A folding seat in some aircraft used for an extra crew member. Also a folding seat in a motor vehicle.

jump start (1) A method of starting a car by pushing it or rolling it downhill and then engaging the gears while it is moving in order to turn the engine. (2) A method of starting a car using **jump leads** to connect the car's own battery to another battery, especially one in another vehicle.

jump suit An all-in-one garment consisting of trousers and a top, often with a zippered front fastening. Children's one-piece jump suits date back to the early 19th century, when they were used in the transition between the dress and trousered suit for young boys.

jump the gun To act prematurely. The phrase is derived from athletics, in which contestants who cross the starting line before the pistol has been fired by the starter are said to have jumped the gun. It dates from around the mid-20th century.

jungle. Jungle Jim US comic-strip hero created by Alex Raymond in the 1930s. The character also appeared in a film serial, *Jungle Jim* (1937), and was later played by Johnny Weissmuller in a series of 16 low-budget films (1948–55) in which he was described as 'Tarzan with clothes'.

jungle juice Slang for potent, but poor-quality, alcohol. Originally a slang name for African rum, the term was used by the armed forces during World War II for any home-made alcoholic brew.

junk. junk bond A high-yielding bond that offers low security. Such bonds were popular in Wall Street from the late

1970s; they are often specifically bonds issued to raise the capital required to finance the take-over of a firm.

junk fax *See* JUNK MAIL.

junk food Food such as hamburgers, hot dogs, french fries (chips), potato crisps, and fizzy drinks, which are high in calories and FOOD ADDITIVES (such as artificial flavourings and colourings) but of little nutritional value. Junk food is often eaten in addition or in preference to regular meals, especially by children. Much FAST FOOD is also junk food.

junkie or **junky** Slang for a drug addict, a habitual drug abuser, especially one who injects heroin or morphine. It is derived from **junk**, which comes from the 15th-century Middle English *jonke*, meaning useless old rope, hemp; hence drugs in general. In 19th-century America the word was used specifically in underworld circles for opium. It was first used of heroin in the early 1900s and has remained in wide use for any addictive narcotic. 'Junk' and 'junkie' also carry with them the inferred sense of dereliction and uselessness that surrounds those unfortunate people who are addicted to heroin.

junk mail Unsolicited material sent through the post for advertising purposes, so called because most of it ends up in the dustbin. The volume of this type of advertising increased during the 1970s when organizations gained access to computerized mailing lists giving the names and addresses of individuals and companies. This enabled direct-mail selling by organized **mailshots** to develop. Further technological developments in the 1980s led to the **fax shot** and **junk fax** (by analogy with 'mailshot' and 'junk mail'). **Cold faxing** is the practice of sending unsolicited faxes (by analogy with COLD CALLING). Junk faxes are even more intrusive items than junk mail; they use the recipient's toner (ink) and paper and may delay transmission of legitimate faxes.

Junkers bombers A series of military aircraft, including heavy bombers and the JU-87 STUKA divebomber, produced at the Dessau factory established by Professor Hugo Junkers (1859–1935) in 1920. Junkers JU-52 bomber-transport aircraft formed part of the Condor Legion, which aided General Franco during the Spanish Civil War (1936–39); the JU-87 divebomber and JU-88 heavy bomber were leading Luftwaffe aircraft in World War II.

Juno Allied codename given to a beach NW of Caen, which was one of the main landing sites for British and Canadian forces on D DAY. *See also* GOLD; OMAHA; SWORD; UTAH.

Juno space mission An Anglo-Soviet space mission that put the first Briton into space in May 1991. 13,000 applicants were considered before the confectionery technologist Helen Sharman (1964–) was selected for the pioneering role.

Jupiter-C A four-stage rocket, which put the first US satellite, Explorer 1, into orbit on 31 January 1958. The Jupiter-C was a version of the Redstone, a rocket developed by the captured German rocket scientist, Dr Wernher von Braun, at the Army Ballistic Missile Agency. It was based on his V-2 rocket, which was used by the Germans against London during World War II.

Juppie A Japanese YUPPIE.

Just So Stories A book (1902) for children by Rudyard Kipling (1865–1936), comprising 10 imaginative animal fables, such as 'How the Leopard got his Spots', two whimsical stories about the origins of the alphabet and written letters, and various poems, with illustrations by Kipling himself. It has remained a children's classic throughout the 20th century.

Jutland, Battle of A World War I naval battle between the UK and Germany off the west coast of Jutland on 31 May 1916 – the last great encounter with massed naval forces coming into direct contact. The British Grand Fleet, commanded by Sir John R. Jellicoe, and a battle cruiser squadron under Earl Beatty lost three battle cruisers, three cruisers, and eight destroyers, suffering 6784 casualties; the German High Seas Fleet, under Vice Admiral Reinhard Scheer, lost one old battleship, one battle cruiser, four light cruisers, five destroyers, and 3039 men. The Germans claimed victory, although the outcome was indecisive and the German fleet never re-emerged to engage the Grand Fleet during the remainder of the war.

> There's something wrong with our bloody ships today.
>
> EARL BEATTY to his flag captain during the battle.

K

K (1) A colloquial term for one thousand, derived from the prefix *kilo-*. In business and commercial contexts it means specifically £1000. Thus 30K would be £30,000. In computing it refers to a unit of 1024 words or BYTES but is also used loosely to refer to a unit of 1000 words or bytes. (2) Nickname of the British art historian Sir Kenneth Clark (1903–83). He was director of the National Gallery from 1935 to 1945 and chaired the Arts Council from 1953 to 1960; however, he was best known to the British public for his television lecture series *Civilisation*, broadcast in 1969, in which he examined human achievements in the arts. In 1969 he was also made a life peer, taking the title Lord Clark of Saltwood. The satirical magazine *Private Eye* dubbed him 'Lord Clark of Civilisation'.

K-boat A class of steam submarine developed by the Royal Navy during World War I. The idea was to produce a submarine capable of acting the role of a surface destroyer as part of a battle fleet. Weighing more than a conventional destroyer, they were incapable of executing a crash-dive, unlike the rival German U-BOAT, and were notoriously difficult to control. K-2 caught fire, K-3, K-6, and K-13 sank (the future George VI narrowly escaping from K-3), K-4 ran aground, K-5 disappeared without trace, and K-14 sprang leaks. Worse was to come, however. On 30 January 1918 a full-scale attempt was made to integrate K-boats into a major battle fleet manoeuvre in the Firth of Forth. A disastrous series of collisions ensued involving K-3, K-6, K-7, K-14, K-22, HMS Fearless, and HMS Invincible. The death toll of what became known as the 'Battle of May Island' brought the total of lives lost on the project to 270; the programme was rapidly brought to an end without a single K-boat ever seeing active service.

K-rations US army field rations, equivalent to one meal (3726 Calories). It was originally developed for paratroopers but became the standard ration for US frontline troops during World War II. There were three separate meals, which could be eaten either hot or cold, each in a waterproofed cardboard box: *Breakfast* consisted of a fruit bar, Nescafé, sugar, crackers, and a small tin of ham and eggs; *Dinner* and *Supper* each comprised one can of cheese or potted meat, crackers, orange or lemon powder, sugar, chocolate, and chewing gum.

K2 The world's second highest mountain peak (28,251 ft; 8611 m) after Everest, situated in the Karakoram Range in the Himalayas. It was discovered and measured in 1856 by Colonel T. G. Montgomery of the Survey of India and designated K2 because it was the second of the Karakoram peaks to be measured. The first successful ascent to the summit was achieved on 31 July 1954 by two members of an Italian expedition, Achille Compagnoni and Lino Lacedelli. The peak has claimed the lives of many leading climbers.

Kafkaesque Evoking the sinister and nightmarish world portrayed in the novels of Franz Kafka (1883–1924), the Czech-born German writer, especially *The Trial* (1925) and *The Castle* (1926). The turmoil in his own life is reflected in the fantasies of his fiction, in which individuals are isolated in an environment that is both incomprehensible and threatening. Most of his books were published after his death, and against his specific instructions, by his friend Max Brod.

> Someone must have slandered Joseph K., because one morning, without his having done anything wrong, he was arrested.
>
> FRANK KAFKA: *The Trial.*

Kaiser Bill Kaiser Wilhelm II (1859–1941), who ruled as emperor of Germany and king of Prussia from 1888 to 1918. Often ineffectual and vacillating in his policies, the Kaiser was frequently depicted in British newspapers, and especially by cartoonists, as a rather ludicrous and pompous militaristic figure. This nickname, by which he was known in

World War I, also served to diminish his status in the eyes of the British public.

Kalashnikov A Soviet automatic or semi-automatic assault rifle capable of firing 600 rounds per minute. Manufactured in China, North Korea, and many eastern European countries as well as in the Soviet Union, the Kalashnikov is used by EASTERN BLOC armies and by nationalist and guerrilla groups throughout the world. It was named after its inventor, Mikhail Timofeyevich Kalashnikov (1919–); it is also known as the AK-47 (Russ. *Automat Kalashnikov*, automatic Kalashnikov, 1947).

kalied (pronounced kay-lide) Drunk; the term is used extensively in the north of England and has gained some currency in the rest of the country through its use in the TV SOAP OPERA, *Coronation Street*. The origin is uncertain. One suggestion is that it comes from an old northern prefix 'kay' (or 'key') meaning left-handed; this has sometimes been used in the sense 'awry'. A more likely explanation is that it comes from 'kali' (rhymes with 'pie'), which is a plant – the saltwort (the name is from the Arabic *alkali*). In the early days of the chemical industry, saltwort and similar plants were calcined to produce a whitish powder rich in potash, also known as 'kali'. In parts of the north of England, children still use the word for lemon-flavoured sugar crystals – known in the rest of the country as 'sherbet'. Possibly, a person who is kalied has drunk too much kali. The word 'sherbet' is similarly used jokingly to mean an alcoholic drink.

kalimba A hand-held African musical instrument consisting of a hollow wooden box with a series of metal strips inserted along its length. These strips vibrate when plucked with the thumbs or fingers. The kalimba is a modern instrument derived from the mbira or the zanza, both tribal instruments. It is tuned to play western music and first attracted attention in the west in about 1952. The word *kalimba* is of Bantu origin.

kamerad (Ger. comrade) A word used by the Germans in World War I as an appeal for quarter. It is now used in English with the meaning 'I surrender'.

kamikaze A Japanese word meaning 'divine wind', in reference to the providential typhoon which once baulked a Mongol invasion. In World War II it was applied to the suicide aircraft attacks organized under Vice-Admiral Onishi in the Philippines between October 1944 and January 1945 (first at the Battle of Leyte Gulf). Some 5000 young pilots gave their lives when their bomb-loaded fighters crashed into their targets. 21 US ships were sunk in this way at Okinawa in 1945 as the result of 3000 such sorties. The word has since been applied to any military or terrorist attack in which the assailant risks almost certain death. It also found wider usage when the British police described drivers who speed on icy or foggy motorways as kamikaze drivers.

Kane, Citizen The eponymous central character in a 1941 film regarded by critics as one of the classics of the cinema, which was produced and directed by Orson Welles (1915–85) at the age of 26. Welles also portrayed Citizen Kane (newspaper tycoon Charles Foster Kane), a figure said to be based on the newspaper proprietor William Randolph Hearst. Scripted by Welles and Herman J. Mankiewicz, the film is filled with visual and audio invention, demonstrating throughout its 119 minutes the full potential of the cinematic medium. At the time, however, critics were not unanimous. The two leading British critics of the 1940s had sharply differing views:

> Probably the most exciting film that has come out of Hollywood for twenty-five years. I am not sure it isn't the most exciting film that has ever come out of anywhere.
>
> C. A. LEJEUNE in *The Observer*.

> A quite good film which tries to run the psychological essay in harness with the detective thriller, and doesn't quite succeed.
>
> JAMES AGATE in *The Sunday Times*.

kangaroo. kanga Slang for a pneumatic drill. A shortened form of 'kangaroo', the word reflects the leaping movement of the animal and also of the person operating the machine. It is sometimes pronounced 'can-go', to suggest that this very powerful machine has a life of its own. Originally an Australian usage, it is also heard in the UK.

kangaroo hop The jerky movement of a car when the engine is cold, particularly when being driven by an inexperienced driver who has not learnt how to manipulate the clutch correctly.

kangaroo valley Nickname for the Earls Court district of W London because many young Australians settled here in flats and bedsits when they came to work in London in the 1960s. The area still has a large Australian community and the name persists. Originally used by both the Australians and the locals, the nickname achieved wider fame after it was used in the cartoon *The Adventures of Barry Mckenzie* by Barry Humphries and Nicholas Garland, which appeared in the satirical magazine *Private Eye* in the 1970s.

KANU Kenya African National Union. Founded in 1960 as a pan-tribal national party, KANU was the successor to the Kenya African Union (KAU), established by Jomo Kenyatta (1891–1978) in 1944, which itself replaced the Kikuyu Central Association, banned by the British in 1940. Jomo Kenyatta (who had been interned by the British in April 1953) became the president of the new national party after his release in August 1961. KANU then went on to win the pre-independence elections of May 1963; Kenyatta was elected prime minister and formed a provisional government. After independence in December 1963, KANU continued to dominate the Kenyan government and legislature.

KAP *Cheng pao k'o* (Chinese Ministry for Public Security). A branch of the Chinese secret services responsible for counter-espionage and the control and monitoring of overseas Chinese.

Kaplan, Hyman A fictional immigrant to America who has difficulties with spoken English; a character created by the US humorist Leo Rosten (pen name Leonard Q. Ross) after his own experiences teaching English to immigrants. Kaplan first appeared in a series of sketches in the *New Yorker* magazine, which were then published in book form as *The Education of Hyman* (1937). This was followed by two sequels, *The Return of Hyman Kaplan* (1938) and *O Kaplan, My Kaplan* (1979).

Kaposi's sarcoma A previously rare form of malignant skin cancer, found mostly in Africans and elderly men in the S Mediterranean region, which is now common in AIDS sufferers. It is named after Moritz Kohn Kaposi (1837–1902), an Austrian dermatologist, who first described the purple skin lesions that characterize the disease.

Kapp Putsch An armed rising against the German government in March 1920 by the Erhardt FREIKORPS Brigade. The Brigade marched into Berlin in protest at the government's acceptance of the VERSAILLES TREATY, which required the Brigade's dissolution. The WEIMAR REPUBLIC was declared overthrown and a right-wing journalist, Wolfgang Kapp (1888–1922), proclaimed chancellor. However, a general strike by Berlin workers exposed the lack of public sympathy with the putsch and the regular army disassociated itself from the Freikorps. The putsch collapsed after five days and Kapp fled to Sweden.

kaput A term derived from the German *kaputt* (done for) now commonly used in English to describe something that is ruined or broken.

karaoke (Jap. empty orchestra) A pastime that originated in Japan and spread to other countries, including the UK, in the late 1980s. It involves singing well-known popular songs solo to the accompaniment of a specially prepared backing audio tape. Karaoke usually takes place in bars and nightclubs with the customers taking it in turns to perform. In Japan it became a regular feature of the semi-compulsory social evenings at which male employees curry favour with their employers. The need for an employee to attend such functions perhaps seven nights a week has led to government concern in recent years at the threat thus posed to family life and the already declining national birth rate, so much so that the state named certain days to be set aside for 'family activities'.

Karlmarxhof A block of workers' flats in Vienna designed by the chief architect of the city, Karl Ehn (1884–1957), in 1927–30. The building was commissioned by the socialist district council as part of a massive programme of public housing construction. The block later became famous as a socialist fortress during the bloody Civil War of 1934, when the socialists revolted against the administration of the Austrian chancellor Dolfuss.

karma (Sans. act) In Hinduism and Buddhism, the sum of an individual's actions, which determines the quality of his or her future life, especially after rebirth. The mystic associations of karma with its personal destiny, responsibility, and retributive justice became popular in the HIPPIE culture of the 1960s. In common speech, karma is also used to describe the aura or influence, good or bad, possessed by certain individuals.

Karno. Fred Karno's army The nickname of the new British army raised during the war of 1914–18, in allusion to the comedian and producer of stage burlesques, properly, Fred John Westcott (d. 1941). Fred Karno's company was a household name at the time from its merry and eccentric performances. The well-known army chorus, sung to the tune of 'The Church's one foundation', runs:

We are Fred Karno's army,
Fred Karno's infantry;
We cannot fight, we cannot shoot,
So what damn good are we?
But when we get to Berlin
The Kaiser he will say
Hoch, hoch, mein Gott
Vot a bloody fine lot,
Fred Karno's infantry.

There are, of course, variants and in World War II 'Old Hitler' was substituted for 'The Kaiser'. The name is also applied derisively to other nondescript bodies. *See also* HARRY TATE'S NAVY; MEREDITH.

Kashmir dispute The struggle between India and Pakistan for possession of the state of Kashmir, which erupted into armed conflict in October 1947 and lasted until March 1949. The dispute began shortly after the partition of India and Pakistan, when the Maharajah of Kashmir acceded to India without consulting the Muslim population, which formed 80% of the whole. Indian troops were flown into Kashmir to suppress the resulting Muslim uprising, which was supported by Pakistan. An undeclared war raged until a ceasefire was agreed in March 1949. In August 1965 border skirmishes along the ceasefire line again erupted into full-scale war, which ended in January 1966 with the disengagement and withdrawal of both armies from the disputed region.

Kate and Sidney British slang for steak and kidney pie or pudding, traditional dishes in British cuisine. It is still heard, although the dishes are less popular now than they were.

Kathleen Mavourneen Australian slang for an habitual criminal or for an indeterminate length of time. First heard in the early years of the century, it was derived from a popular song, the chorus of which went: 'It may be for years, it may be forever'. It was sometimes shortened to 'Kath'.

Katyn massacre The mass execution of 5000 Polish officers in April–May 1940 by Soviet Secret Service officers in a wood near Smolensk. The officers belonged to a Polish military force of 15,000 captured and imprisoned by the Soviets after their occupation of E Poland, under the terms of the 1939 Nonaggression Pact with Hitler. The mass graves were discovered by the Germans in April 1943, in the aftermath of their invasion of the Soviet Union (1941). Germany and the Soviets accused one another of the slaughter; in 1943 the Polish government-in-exile asked the Red Cross to investigate the atrocity. The Soviet government refused to cooperate, which led to the severance of diplomatic relations with the Polish government. The Soviet Union finally admitted responsibility for the massacre in 1989, although the whereabouts of the remaining 10,000 Polish officers remains a mystery.

KBE *See* ORDER OF THE BRITISH EMPIRE.

Keating pictures Tom Keating (1918–84), beginning as a picture restorer, produced about 2000 drawings and paintings and (supposedly in protest against art-dealing) sold them as originals by Constable, Gainsborough, Turner, Rembrandt, Palmer, and others. He admitted they were fakes in 1976; charges against him were dropped in 1979 due to ill-health. His paintings became highly valued collector's items in their own right.

keen US teenage slang word of the 1960s used to express approbation. It now sounds dated, although it is occasionally heard as an exclamation of enthusiasm.

keep. Keep Britain Tidy A slogan adopted by the Central Office of Information to promote an anti-litter campaign in 1952. It is still in use. It was originally coined by the Women's Institute in the 1930s.

keep fit Exercises designed to promote fitness among those who are normally inactive. Keep fit includes a variety of traditional activities, such as JOGGING and weight training, as well as various relatively new forms of exercise, such as AEROBICS and CALLANETICS. The passion for keep fit is a product of the health craze, which originally began in America in the 1970s and then spread throughout other western industrialized nations by the 1980s. The effectiveness of these measures continues to be debated.

keeping up with the Joneses The catchphrase that sums up 20th-century bourgeois materialism in terms of the unceasing struggle to match the apparent affluence of one's neighbours as measured by the consumer goods they possess, the holidays they take, or other lifestyle indicators. The probable origin of the phrase is the US strip cartoon of the same name, created and drawn by Arthur R. ('Pop') Momand and first published in several US newspapers in 1913. Momand based it on his own experiences of living far beyond his means in a prosperous neighbourhood and his realization that all his neighbours were playing the same game. His first idea for the title, 'Keeping up with the Smiths', was abandoned in favour of the more euphonious 'Keeping up with the Joneses'. The catchphrase had spread to the UK by World War II.

keep it dark *See* DARK.

keep it under your hat *See* HAT.

'Keep Left' group A group of left-wing Labour MPs critical of the policies of the foreign secretary, Ernest Bevin, in 1946–47. Launched in November 1946, the group's criticisms were expressed in a pamphlet, *Keep Left* (published by the *New Statesman* in April 1947), written by Richard Crossman, Michael Foot, and Ian Mikado and signed by 12 other Labour MPs, who met regularly in the House of Commons. They objected to Bevin's pro-NATO stance and advocated the creation of a 'Third Force', consisting of a European socialist alliance, based in the UK and France, to hold the middle-ground between America and the Soviet Union, end Britain's dependence on America, and heal the widening breach between East and West.

keep on truckin' Slang phrase meaning to keep going, to persevere, to keep struggling on cheerfully. It was very popular among the HIPPIES of the late 1960s and 1970s, epitomizing their easy-going attitude; first used in America, it quickly spread to the UK. There were a number of records in the late 1960s with this title and the underground newspaper *International Times* featured a 'keep on truckin'' cartoon strip, drawn by Robert Crumb (1943–). The main character of this strip appeared striding out with a determined loping walk, wearing his LOONS. This character, with the slogan beneath him, frequently appeared on the front of T-shirts. The phrase probably derives from TRUCKING, a dance step popular in the dance marathons of the 1930s. An alternative suggestion is that it comes from the practice by US tramps of riding or clinging on to the trucking hardware between the wheels of a train. This reflects the tenacity and perseverance suggested by the phrase.

keep the faith, baby! US slogan adopted by Black activists in the 1960s, urging fellow Blacks to carry on the struggle for Black civil rights regardless of all setbacks. It was popularized by the US Congressman Adam Clayton Powell when he was expelled from Congress.

keep your eye on the sparrow A US catchphrase apparently dating from the 1970s and meaning 'watch out!' – especially for the unexpected. It is an allusion to the unpredictable defecatory habits of sparrows (and birds in general), and the inconvenience this may cause to the hapless people below.

Keller, Helen (1880–1968) US writer and lecturer who became world-famous for triumphing over her physical disabilities. Deaf and blind from the age of 19 months, as a result of scarlet fever, she was also unable to talk and existed in almost total isolation from the world until the age of six, when her teacher Anne Sullivan found a way to communicate with her through touch. Keller subsequently learned to read (through Braille) and speak and obtained a university arts degree; throughout her life she campaigned tirelessly on behalf of the blind. Her career and fame have entered modern mythology as an inspiration for all who suffer some degree of physical disability.

> How reconcile this world of fact with the bright world of my imagining? My darkness has been filled with the light of intelligence, and behold, the outer day-light world was stumbling and groping in social blindness.
>
> HELEN KELLER: *The Cry for Justice.*

Kellogg Pact or **Kellogg-Briand Pact** Multilateral renunciation of war as an instrument of policy, suggested by the French foreign minister Aristide Briand to the US secretary of state Frank B. Kellogg and signed in Paris on 27 August 1928 by America, France, Germany, Italy, Japan, and other nations. This optimistic declaration was one of several international agreements during the 1920s aimed at securing disarmament and the settlement of disputes by peaceful means under the auspices of the LEAGUE OF NATIONS. It was, however, hedged with enough caveats to render it meaningless, as demonstrated by Japan's invasion of Manchuria in 1931.

Kelly's eye Bingo term for the number one, which is derived from early 20th-century British army slang.

kelper British slang for a Falkland Islander. The name was first used during the 1982 FALKLANDS CONFLICT. It derives from *kelp*, a seaweed gathered from the shore and used as a fertilizer and fuel by the islanders.

kemo sabe One of the phrases, often appearing as 'him, bad man, kemo sabe!', used by the LONE RANGER's faithful Indian companion Tonto, a man of few words. 'Kemo Sabe' means 'trusty scout' and was derived from the name of a boys' camp at Mullet Lake, Michigan, in 1911.

Ken Slang for a dull clean-living male. Ken was the male companion doll for the BARBIE DOLL.

Kennedy Round A multilateral conference on tariff reductions, suggested by US President John F. Kennedy, which took place under GATT (General Agreement on Tariffs and Trade), 1964–67. The negotiations were the sixth and most comprehensive of the GATT tariff reduction talks and secured average cuts of 35%.

Kenny polio treatment A method of treating poliomyelitis (infantile paralysis) by physical therapy, as opposed to immobilizing the patient by using casts and splints, devised by the Australian nurse Elizabeth Kenny (1886–1952). Kenny opened a clinic in the UK in 1937, but her unorthodox methods were opposed by the British medical establishment, and still are. She achieved much wider success in America, which she toured in 1940, and, with the support of the American Medical Association, opened the Sister Kenny Foundation (1942) in Minneapolis, Minnesota, to train nurses and physiotherapists for a chain of Kenny clinics. As well as textbooks on her method, she wrote two works of autobiography, *And They Shall Walk* (1943) and *My Battle and Victory* (1955).

Kenyapithecus A type of prehistoric ape dating from the early to mid Miocene Epoch, fossilized remains of which have been found in Africa. Certain features of its skull suggest similarities with the human face and jaws, causing it to be ranked as one of the earliest members of the family Hominidae, which also contains the modern great apes and extinct 'near men' as well as modern *Homo sapiens*. Fossils of *Kenyapithecus* were first discovered by the anthropologist Dr Louis Leakey in 1962 at a site called Fort Ternan in Kenya. Leakey named his hominid *Kenyapithecus wickeri*, after the owner of the site, Fred Wicker. It was shown to be some 14 million years old (mid Miocene). Leakey later claimed that another hominid-like ape, known as *Sivapithecus africanus*, was an ancester of his Fort Ternan hominid, and renamed it *Kenyapithecus africanus*. However, the precise relationships of these early hominids are still the subject of scientific debate.

kerb-crawling The practice of driving a car very slowly beside the pavement seeking to entice someone into the car; especially as used by a male motorist approaching and picking up a prostitute. This activity was prohibited by British law in 1990.

Kerensky government The second Provisional Government in Russia (July–November 1917) in which the moderate socialist Alexander Kerensky (1881–1970) replaced Prince Lvov (1861–1925) as prime minister. Kerensky attempted to continue the war against Germany but a series of disastrous defeats, BOLSHEVIK agitation, and the collapse of military discipline led to the OCTOBER REVOLUTION in which Lenin seized power.

Kermit British student slang from the early 1980s for a Frenchman. It is taken from the character Kermit the frog, who featured in the US television show the MUPPETS, which was also popular in the UK. A frog, of course, is the traditional slang name for a Frenchman.

Kettle, Ma and Pa A hillbilly couple, played by Marjorie Main (1890–1975) and Percy Kilbride (1888–1964), who first appeared in a film, *The Egg and I* (1947), based on the novel of the same name by Betty Macdonald. The Kettles and their numerous offspring went on to feature in a further nine cheap but popular film comedies, which continued until the late 1950s. The legacy of hayseed humour embodied by the Kettles was later revived in the popular US television series *The Beverley Hillbillies* (1962–71).

Kevin British contemptuous slang for a vulgar uncouth youth, or the epitome of a rough working-class male. It was first used in the 1970s by the middle classes, when Kevin was a particularly popular name among working-class people. It is the male equivalent of 'Sharon' or 'Tracey'.

> ...there was every chance their father would come steaming across the playground and chin the

teacher if he thought you were picking on his 'little Kevin'.

Teacher in a working-class area, *The Independent*, 7 January 1991.

kewpie doll US slang for an overdressed or over-made-up woman. In Australia the term is used as rhyming slang for moll, in the sense of prostitute. The name derives from the US tradename for a plump baby doll with a curl on top of its head, designed by Rose O'Neill early in the 20th century. 'Kewpie' derives from Cupid, the God of love, whom the doll was thought to resemble.

key. key grip The person in charge of the stagehands, called grips, who are responsible for moving and setting up the camera tracks, props, and scenery in a television or film studio. For these assorted tasks a strong grip for handling heavy props and cameras is essential.

keyholing a round tripper US Black slang from the 1940s, meaning to witness something interesting, as by peering through a keyhole. A 'round tripper' is slang for a home-run in baseball.

Keystone Comedies Mack Sennett's notable early film comedies made by the Keystone Comedy Company at Hollywood. The first of these slapstick burlesques appeared in 1913. Charlie Chaplin worked with this company between 1916 and 1918. One of the most popular features of the Keystone Comedies was the hectic chase sequence involving the **Keystone Kops**, a chaotic team of comedians (led by Ford Sterling) who executed daring comic stunts in numerous films, dressed in oversized police uniforms.

Keynesianism The economic doctrine based on the principles established by John Maynard Keynes (1883–1946) in *The General Theory of Employment, Interest and Money* (1936). Keynes proposed a method of solving the contemporary problem of mass unemployment by government spending to stimulate aggregate demand and employment. Keynesianism was adopted by many nations in the 1950s and 1960s but in the 1970s problems of inflation led to a reaction in favour of MONETARISM and the unrestricted free market mechanism.

KGB (Russ. *Komitet Gosudarstvennoi Bezopasnosti*; Soviet State Security Committee) The Soviet agency responsible for internal security, intelligence gathering, foreign operations, and border control. It was set up in 1954 after a shake-up in the Soviet secret intelligence services and has developed into the largest and most powerful secret service in the world. It is estimated that the KGB employes 90,000 officers, supported by 150,000 technicians and clerical staff, controls 250,000 border guards, and has 25,000 agents abroad. Its annual budget is between $6 and $12 billion.

KGBE *See* ORDER OF THE BRITISH EMPIRE.

khaki A Hindu word, meaning dusty, or dust-coloured, from *khak*, dust. Khaki uniform became general in the British army during the South African War of 1899–1902. It was first used by an irregular corps of guides raised by the British at Meerut during the Indian Mutiny known as the *Khaki Risala* (khaki squadron), nicknamed 'the Mudlarks'. It was subsequently adopted as an active service uniform by several regiments and in the Omdurman campaign, etc. *See also* CAMOUFLAGE.

Khaki Election The General Election of 1900 (18 September–24 October), in which the Conservatives sought to profit from the recent military victories in the South African War. It was promoted by Joseph Chamberlain and the Conservatives won, although the gain in seats was very slight. *See also* FALKLANDS FACTOR.

khazi British army slang from World War II for a latrine. It was derived from Arabic during the North African campaigns of 1940–43.

Khedive The title, meaning 'prince' or 'sovereign', by which the ruler of Egypt as viceroy of the Turkish Sultan was known from 1867 to 1914. In 1914, when Turkey joined the Central Powers, Khedive Abbas II was deposed by the British and Hussein Kamil was set up as Sultan. The title of King was adopted by Faud in 1922 when the British terminated their protectorate.

Khmer Rouge A communist movement in Cambodia that has been active since the early 1970s. The Khmer are the indigenous people of the country; 'Rouge' (French for red) indicates the political colour of the movement. French has been a widely spoken language in Cambodia since it was a French protectorate and, later, part of the Union of Indochina. In 1970, the ruling Prince Sihanouk (1923–) was deposed and a republic, called the **Khmer Republic**, was established under General Lon Nol (1913–85). For the next few years Lon Nol, supported by America, resisted a guerrilla war waged by the Khmer Rouge under Pol Pot (1925–). In 1974, the Khmer Rouge were victorious and in 1975 a new constitution was established, the country's name being changed to **Democratic Kampuchea**. There followed a number of years of reorganization, in which the country's social structure was radically changed, with townspeople being deprived of their property and driven to work in a cooperative agricultural economy. At the same time over three million of the country's dissenting, elderly, or sick citizens were murdered (see KILLING FIELDS). In 1979, the Vietnamese invaded Kampuchea and deposed the Khmer Rouge government. The world was shocked by photographs of piles of human skulls and reports of suffering comparable with that of the Nazi HOLOCAUST. Pol Pot was sentenced to death for genocide but escaped into the jungle. In 1988, following a peace conference, the Vietnamese began to withdraw, leaving the country, once again named Cambodia, under the control of a pro-Vietnamese government. Meanwhile the exiled factions, including the Khmer Rouge (controlled by Pol Pot from Thailand) and the supporters of Prince Sihanouk, had formed a coalition government in exile, the Coalition Government of Democratic Kampuchea (CGDK), which has western support and a seat at the UN. Fighting between government forces and CGDK guerrillas has continued. Both sides are considering the involvement of a UN peace-keeping force and the possibility of free elections.

khozraschot A word derived from the Russian phrase *khozyaistvenny raschot*, meaning 'self-supporting running'. Khozraschot, meaning economic accountability, was one of the aims of the Soviet leader, Mikhail Gorbachov, in his efforts to reconstruct and revitalize the economy (*see also* PERESTROIKA). It refers to the theory that commercial and industrial concerns should be responsible for their own financial state and should cease to rely heavily on subsidies from the government.

Kiaochow An area of China that became German territory from 1898 to 1914, after China's defeat in the Sino-Japanese War of 1894–95 prompted a bid for concessions by Russia, France, Germany, and the UK.

kibbutz A collective agricultural, or occasionally industrial, settlement in modern Israel. In 1899 Edmond de Rothschild and Maurice de Hirsch formed a Jewish Colonization Association to establish *kvutzoth*, later called kibbutzim, in Palestine. These communally run settlements, in which children are collectively reared, prospered throughout the 20th century, in spite of opposition, often violent, from Palestinian Arabs. After the declaration (1948) of the state of Israel, the kibbutzim became an essential part of the new country's ethos and an essential part of its defence system. However, as living standards in Israel have risen to those of the other western nations, the taxing and simple life of the kibbutz has become less attractive to young Israelis, many of whom have abandoned the unsophisticated rural life for the better schools and greater comfort of the cities. The word derives from the Hebrew *qibbutz*, a gathering.

kibitzer or **kibbitzer** US slang, from the Yiddish (from the German *Kiebitzen*, an onlooker), for someone who looks over the shoulder of a card player and offers unwanted advice. The kibitzer's activities are not restricted to cardplaying. Any onlooker of any activity, who imagines that he knows better than the participant what the next step or move should be, is a kibitzer. Kibitzers cannot expect to be popular nor are they regarded as a source of useful advice. If their opinions were sought they would not be kibitzers; if their recommendations were sound they would be consultants or advisers.

kick (1) Slang meaning to give up, usually to give up a drug habit. It was originally part of drug-abusers' jargon but is now more widely used. (2) US slang meaning to be successful or impressive. (3) Slang for a thrill, as in the Cole Porter song 'I get a kick out of you'. It is also used in this sense in the plural as in the phrase **just for kicks**, meaning just for the fun of it. This phrase may be used by young people to account for apparently meaningless aggressive behaviour. (4) Slang for a period of interest or a particular enthusiasm. It is a synonym for 'trip', which it predates. For example, a **health kick** is a period during which healthy eating seems important; it might now be called a 'health trip'. *See also* TRIP.

kickers US slang of the 1960s for shoes or boots. In the 1970s a French shoe company used it as a tradename for their fashionable sporty boots and shoes.

Kid, The A nickname of Warren Beatty (1937–), the US film actor and director, who is the kid brother of the actress Shirley Maclaine (1934–).

Kidbrooke The first British purpose-built urban comprehensive school, which was opened in Blackheath, London, by the London County Council in 1954. Kidbrooke School for Girls became the showpiece of the LCC's controversial comprehensive education policy in the mid-1950s, with parties of visitors from other local councils touring its five gymnasia, six science labs, and nine housecraft centres. *See also* COMPREHENSIVIZATION.

kidney machine A piece of medical equipment, properly known as a dialyser, that functions as an artificial kidney, cleansing the blood of impurities on the principle of dialysis (selective filtration) if a patient's own kidneys have failed, either partially or completely. The patient's blood is passed through tubes consisting of thin synthetic membranes immersed in a dialysing solution. Waste products pass through the membrane and are removed from the bloodstream, while blood cells and vital protein molecules, which are too large to pass through, are retained. The first kidney machine capable of partial haemodialysis was developed in the early 1940s by the Dutch physician W. J. Kolff; the first machine capable of totally replacing the kidney function was perfected by B. H. Scribner in the 1960s.

kidult A word formed from *kid* and *adult*, invented by Neil Postman, of New York University, to denote what he saw as the typical modern US child. The implication behind his theory was that children subjected to a modern US lifestyle, especially to the excessive influence of television with all its various kinds of information and advertising, grow up too fast and become adult-like in many respects too soon; the kidult remains, however, emotionally immature, will tend to neglect education in favour of television entertainment, and will grow up without culture and with too great a preoccupation with material possessions.

kike An offensive US name for a Jew, much in line with calling an Italian a wop, a German a kraut, or a Japanese a nip. The derivation of the name is interesting. Most reference books say it is a variant of *kiki*, a duplication of the common *-ki* ending of the names of many Jews from Slav countries. Leo Rosten, however, in his *Joys of Yiddish* (1968), has a more interesting, and perhaps more credible, explanation. He says that the word came from Ellis Island immigration officers who, faced with Jewish immigrants who were unable to write their names in the Roman alphabet, instructed them to sign their forms with a cross. Jews, for whom the cross is a symbol of a totally alien and barbaric form of execution, and moreover the symbol of the religion that has mercilessly persecuted them for some 2000 years, often prefer not to be associated with a cross. They used, instead, a circle as a means of identification. For the Jews a circle (Yiddish *kikel*) is a symbol of unending life. To the immigration officers, a person who asked to be allowed to make a *kikel* or a *kikeleh* (a little circle), soon became a kikee or simply a kike.

Kildare, Dr Fictional medical hero, based on a character in the novels of Max Brand, who first appeared on screen in the 1937 film *Interns Can't Take Money* and subsequently in a further 15 films made over the next 10 years. The young hospital intern was later resurrected in the popular US television series *Dr Kildare* (1961–66) and played by the apparently ageless US actor, Richard Chamberlain. The role of his gruff but wise patron, Dr Gillespie, was played by Raymond Massey.

kill. killer US Black teenage slang, originally from the 1940s, for something highly approved of. It was briefly popular in the UK with TEDDY BOYS in the 1950s, was revived in the 1960s and 1970s in America, and made an appearance again in the 1980s in both the UK and Australia as part of Black music jargon.

killer bee Originally a variety of African honeybee (*Apis mellifera adansonii*), noted for its high honey production and for its aggressive behaviour when disturbed, hence the alternative name **Mau Mau bee**. Imported into Brazil in 1956, the bees interbred with native bees, producing equally aggressive varieties. These have spread to other parts of South America and into the southern states of the USA.

killer cell A type of white blood cell (lymphocyte) that destroys cancer cells or cells infected with viruses. There are two kinds. The so-called 'natural killer cells' attack cancer cells, and patients with cancer usually have fewer of these cells in their bloodstreams than healthy people. The other type of killer cells are properly known as 'cytotoxic T cells'; these are capable of destroying cells in the body infected with viruses. Since the early 1980s much research has been directed towards elucidating the mechanisms by which killer cells act and developing similar cells, by means of GENETIC ENGINEERING, that could be used in combatting cancer and viral infections, notably AIDS.

killer satellite or **satellite killer** A military satellite equipped with sophisticated weapons, such as missiles and lasers, the purpose of which is to destroy other satellites and anything else within range, such as high-altitude aircraft and missiles. To date, no killer satellite has been deployed permanently, and research into and development of space laser weapons by both America and the Soviet Union is still in its early stages. However, analysts predict that relatively sophisticated killer or 'anti-satellite' satellites could be operational by the end of the century. *See also* STAR WARS.

Killing Fields The name given to the countryside around Pnomh Penh dotted with the mass graves of Cambodians killed by the KHMER ROUGE during the Pol Pot regime (1975–79). After the fall of Pnomh Penh the Khmers declared 'Year Zero', forced the entire population into agricultural labour camps, and embarked on a horrifying experiment, seeking to create a classless agrarian society through political indoctrination, economic reform, and the extermination of all professionals and intellectuals. In four years over one quarter of the population died through starvation, disease, overwork, or execution. These brutal and genocidal events were harrowingly told in *The Killing Fields* (1984), a film based on the true story of one man's struggle to survive this brutal regime.

Kilroy During World War II, the phrase 'Kilroy was here' was found written up wherever the Americans (particularly Air Transport Command) had been. Its origin is a matter of conjecture. One suggestion is that a certain shipyard inspector at Quincy, Massachusetts, chalked up the words on material he had inspected. *See also* CHAD.

Kim Nickname of Harold Philby (1912–1988), Soviet agent and a member of British intelligence, known almost universally as 'Kim' Philby. He began spying for the Soviet Union after leaving Cambridge in 1933, joined British military intelligence in 1940, and eventually defected to the Soviet Union in 1963, becoming a Soviet citizen. Born in the Punjab, he was given the nickname after the hero of Rudyard Kipling's novel *Kim* (1901). His name is linked with fellow Cantabrigians Anthony Blunt, Guy Burgess, and Donald Maclean who similarly became double agents (*see* BURGESS AND MACLEAN).

kindergarten. Milner's Kindergarten The nickname given to the notable group of young men gathered together by Sir Alfred (Viscount) Milner, High Commissioner for South Africa, for the work of reconstruction after the South African War (1899–1902). They were Robert Brand, Lionel Curtis, John Dove, Patrick Duncan, Richard Feetham, Lionel Hitchens, Philip Kerr, Douglas Malcolm, J. F. Perry, Geoffrey Robinson, and Hugh Wyndham. Among those associated with them were L. S. Amery, Basil Blackwood, John Buchan, and Basil Williams. They duly became advocates of closer imperial ties, both political and economic, and remained an important propagandist group for the imperial idea in the years before World War I. The name was probably invented by the lawyer, Sir William Marriott.

kinetic art Art involving movement or the impression of movement. This may be achieved by incorporating motor-driven components or mobile parts set in motion by air currents or water into the design. Alternatively the entire assemblage may undergo continuous change by means of fluids, optical effects, or electronic images. Kinetic art first appeared in 1961.

king. HMS King Alfred The name given to the shore establishment at Brighton in which RNVR officers were trained during World War II.

King and Country debate A famous debate that took place in the Oxford University Union on 9 February 1933 on the motion 'This House will under no circumstances fight for its King and Country'. The motion was passed by 275 to 153; although it was given little further thought by the students themselves, the vote was widely regarded as demonstrating the degeneracy of Oxford in particular and of Young England more generally. It caused a great deal of comment in the national press and disgusted certain contemporary politicians, such as Winston Churchill.

> There is no question but that the woozy-minded Communists, the practical jokers, and the sexual indeterminates of Oxford have scored a great success . . .
>
> *Daily Express.*

Six years later, when the country went to war against Germany, the young men from the universities were found to be flocking into the services. Despite the peace-time vote, some of the wartime warriors soon became Churchill's cherished FEW.

King Arthur Nickname of Arthur Scargill (1938–), the militant Yorkshire trade unionist; he was dubbed 'King Arthur' by the British press on account of the influence and power he has exerted as leader of the coal-mining community. Following his leadership of the Yorkshire miners' union (1973–81), he was elected president of the National Union of Mineworkers. His vociferous championing of the miners' cause led to frequent clashes with Margaret Thatcher's Conservative government in the 1980s, which were reported at length by the media. The miners' strike of 1984–85 eventually split the union.

King David Hotel bombing *See* IRGUN ZVAI LEUMI.

King Dick Richard John Seddon, Liberal prime minister of New Zealand (1893–1906), so called because his leadership appeared to some to partake of the nature of benevolent despotism.

Kingfish The nickname of Huey Pierce Long (1893–1935), the US politician who became governor of Louisiana (1928–31) and state senator (1930–35). Long was a demagogue whose populist appeal derived from a series of social and economic reforms aimed at relieving unemployment and improving standards of health and education, paid for by taxing large corporations. He built a powerful political machine to aid his campaigns for the governorship and hoped to win the presidency with his Share Our Wealth programme, aimed at overhauling the taxation system to facilitate a more equitable redistribution of wealth. He was assassinated on 8 September 1935 by Dr Carl Austin Weiss.

King Kong A towering ape-like monster used in the film (1933) of the same name. The atmosphere of the original film has survived surprisingly well, although a 1976 remake failed to achieve the same impact as its predecessor.

Kingledon The name bestowed on the Wimbledon international lawn-tennis championships by the *Daily Mirror* in 1972 in recognition of the prowess of the top-ranked US player, Billie Jean King (1943–), who won the ladies' singles championship for the fourth time in that year.

King of Calypso The nickname of the US singer Harry Belafonte (1927–), who spent five years of his childhood in Jamaica and became internationally famous as a calypso singer from the mid-1950s. His third LP, *Calypso*, was the first album to sell a million copies. His best known songs are the 'Banana Boat Song' (also known as 'Day-O') and 'Island in the Sun'.

King of Glam Rock Nickname of Gary Glitter (Paul Gadd; 1944–) who, as leader of the Glitter Band, dominated the glam- or glitter-rock era of the mid-1970s (*see* GLAM ROCK). The band, which played straightforward loud rock 'n' roll, brought colour and humour to the pop-music scene. Gary Glitter himself was a larger-than-life figure, strutting round the stage dressed outrageously in shoulder pads, leather, and lurex. Since the late 1970s he has made a series of farewell appearances, followed by the inevitable comebacks.

King of Hollywood The title conferred on the US film actor Clark Gable (1901–60), who starred in films for 30 years and became a Hollywood legend. Ruggedly handsome and with an air of self-assurance, he specialized in portraying MACHO heroes with charm. He was nicknamed 'King' in the 1930s, a decade in which he made some of his best-known films, including *It Happened One Night* (1934) and *Gone with the Wind* (1939). His final film, *The Misfits*, was released in 1961, shortly after his death from a heart attack.

King of Rock 'n' Roll *See* ELVIS THE PELVIS.

King of Swing Benny Goodman (1909–86), the band leader and virtuoso JAZZ clarinettist from Chicago. In 1934, at the age of 25, he was leading his own band and caused student riots in the Palomar Ballroom, Los Angeles, with teenagers jitterbugging in the aisles. In 1938 his band played at a Carnegie Hall concert, the first jazz gathering in a concert-hall setting. His band included such stars as the trumpeter Harry James and the drummer Gene Kruper, as well as (controversially for the period) such Black musicians as Lionel Hampton. He maintained his reputation throughout many jazz fashions, branched into classical music, toured Europe regularly for three decades, and was still playing to critical acclaim at the end of his life.

King of the Cowboys A title bestowed on two US stars of Hollywood cowboy films, Tom Mix and Roy Rogers (*see* SINGING COWBOY).

Tom Mix (1880–1940) was, by his own (disputed) account, a US marshall and war hero before turning to acting in 1909. His films, over 400 B-feature westerns, idealized the American West. In his private life he maintained the role of cowboy hero, invariably dressing in boots and a white suit.

King of the Serials Nickname of Buster Crabbe (Clarence Linden Crabbe; 1907–83), the US film star who won a gold medal for swimming in the 1932 Olympics, prior to his Hollywood career. Blond and athletic, he was ideally cast in the role of comic-strip hero, playing FLASH GORDON and BUCK ROGERS in several science fiction film serials in the 1930s. The film serial, a phenomenon which disappeared in the early 1950s, consisted of several 15- or 20-minute action-filled episodes, only one of which was shown each week (or whenever the cinema programme changed). As each episode typically ended with the hero in dire peril, the film serial ensured a regular cinema-going audience avid to discover how he would escape in the next episode.

King's English *See* RECEIVED PRONUNCIATION.

King's Medals Two medals instituted in the UK in 1945. The King's Medal for Courage in the Cause of Freedom and the King's Medal for Service in the Cause of Freedom were awarded to foreign citizens, the former being given to those who had offered British forces help in occupied territory.

King Street The London street (WC2) in which the Communist Party of Great Britain had its head office since its foundation in 1920. The term was also used as an epithet for the Party.

the King *See* ELVIS THE PELVIS.

kinky An adjective applied to a person with deviant sexual desires, often involving fetishism or sado-masochism. Kinky clothes are bizarre and provocative, often in a way that might arouse people who are kinky. Kinky is formed from the noun 'kink', which comes ultimately from the Middle Low German *kinke*, a twist or bend in a rope. In psychoanalysis a kink is a peculiar character trait, often one that relates to sexual needs. However, in 1960s slang 'kink' lost most of its sexual connotation and came to mean a rebel of almost any kind. **The Kinks** were a well-known pop group of the 1960s.

kinky boots British slang for knee- or thigh-high leather boots, highly desirable and fashionable items of clothing in the early 1960s. Worn with a MINISKIRT, they epitomized the SWINGING SIXTIES as the combination gave the outfit a hint of sexual deviancy. Kinky boots were worn by Diana Rigg in the cult TV programme *The Avengers*. She also recorded the song *Kinky Boots* in 1965 (rereleased in 1990).

Kinsey reports Two studies: *Sexual Behaviour in the Human Male* (1948) and *Sexual Behaviour in the Human Female* (1951), based on 18,500 personal interviews by Alfred C. Kinsey (1894–1956), Director of the Institute for Sex Research at Indiana University. The reports are notable as the first serious research on the subject, but the work has been criticized for sampling errors and the unreliability of personal communication. Nevertheless the works opened up the field of sexual response to scientific study and enabled many of the taboos that surround the subject to be broken. Basically, Kinsey asked his subjects to tell him in some detail what they did in their sexual encounters. Twenty years later MASTERS AND JOHNSON took the science of sexuality a stage further by establishing laboratory conditions to enable sexual reactions to be observed in terms of the specific physiological mechanisms that were involved under particular conditions of stimulation.

kipper Australian slang for an Englishman, dating from World War II. It originated from the popular idea of the typical English breakfast, which was thought to be based exclusively on kippers. The nickname also carried the implication that the English were two-faced and gutless, as a kipper is after smoking.

Kipps The hero of a semi-autobiographical comic novel of the same name (1905) by H. G. Wells (1866–1946). Kipps, a draper's assistant who inherits a fortune, fails in his attempt to join fashionable society; after losing his inheritance, he discovers true happiness in the quiet life. There is a silent film version of the novel (1921) and a later remake starring Michael Redgrave directed by Carol Reed (1941); a stage musical *Half a Sixpence* (1963), also based on the novel, was filmed with singer Tommy Steele in the leading role (1967).

Kirchner girls Mildly suggestive postcard pin-ups produced by the Austrian-born artist Raphaël Kirchner (1875–1917). Kirchner arrived in Paris in 1901 and achieved success (especially among combatants during World War I) with a series of pin-up photographs of partially clothed girls in coy poses.

Kirov murder The shooting of the popular Leningrad party chief Sergei Mironovich Kirov on 1 December 1934 by a deranged party member, Leonid Nickolaev. The murder was used as a pretext by STALIN (who helped bear Kirov's ashes to his grave) to justify the launch of a vicious purge of his opponents (1934–38) on the grounds that Kirov's murder had been part of a plot by counter-revolutionaries to assassinate the entire Soviet leadership. *See* LAW OF DECEMBER 1.

kiss. KISS Keep It Simple, Stupid! US computer acronym used as an instruction.

Kissagram A surprise greeting service provided for birthdays and other special occasions, in which a message, together with a kiss, is delivered by an attractive girl. Such services became increasingly popular during the 1980s; other types of popular greetings services available include **Stripagrams**, **Gorillagrams** (the messenger is dressed in a gorilla outfit), and **Tarzanagrams**.

kiss-and-tell Denoting intimate memoirs or stories sold to the more lurid tabloid newspapers by former friends, often former sexual partners, of people who are wealthy, famous, or hold important positions. These highly coloured and sexually explicit accounts are designed to demonstrate the weaknesses of the person written about. The commercial aspects of this form of journalism are emphasized by the fact that they are also known as **kiss-and-sell accounts.**

kissing tackle British slang for the mouth, used by teenagers and young people in the late 1980s.

kiss of death A phrase that derives from the kiss given to Christ in Gethsemane by Judas Iscariot before he betrayed him (Luke 23:48). In MAFIA circles a kiss from the boss is a sign that one's life will end shortly. The phrase is often used in political or business contexts, meaning that associating with a certain person may spell disaster. It is also sometimes used ironically as the opposite of the **kiss of life** – the life-saving method of mouth-to-mouth resuscitation.

kiss-off US Black slang from the 1940s, meaning to die.

Kitchener. Kitchener's Army The volunteer army raised by Field Marshal Horatio Herbert Kitchener, 1st Earl Kitchener of Khartoum (1850–1916), at the onset of World War I. Kitchener, recognizing the deficiencies of the regular army and the Territorials, saw the urgent need for a large well-equipped well-trained volunteer force. As secretary of state for war, he orchestrated a nationwide recruitment campaign through the press and the Parliamentary Recruiting Committee, which sponsored the poster campaign 'Your Country Needs You' (*see* COUNTRY). By 12 September 1914, 100,000 men had been recruited; the volunteers totalled three million before conscription was introduced in 1916 (*see also* CONTEMPTIBLES, OLD).

> We are in Kitchener's Army
> The ragtime A.S.C.:
> We cannot fight, we cannot shoot,
> What Bloody use are we?
>
> FRANK RICHARDS: *Old Soldiers Never Die* (1933).

Kitchener wants you An army catchphrase of World War I applied to anyone chosen for an unpleasant or onerous task. It was derived from the famous recruiting poster of the early war years, showing the stern features and pointing right arm of the war secretary, Lord Kitchener of Khartoum, above the slogan 'Your Country Needs You'.

kitchen sink A term used to describe a certain type of domestic drama of the late 1950s, depicting the reality of everyday life in working-class and lower middle-class households. The genre is exemplified by such plays as *Look Back in Anger* (1956) by John Osborne (*see* PORTER, JIMMY) and Shelagh Delaney's *A Taste of Honey* (1958). In part, these plays were an attack on the middle-class assumptions and values represented by the drawing-room comedies of Noël Coward and Terence Rattigan of the 1930s and 1940s. The term was first coined in a review of modern art in 1954.

kite (1) In lawyer's slang, a junior counsel who was allotted at an assize court to advocate the cause of a prisoner who was without other defence. (2) In RAF slang, any aircraft. (3) In Stock Exchange slang, an accommodation bill. (4) An invalid cheque.

Kitemark The trademark of the British Standards Institution, licensed to be used by manufacturers on products that conform to a British Standard.

kitsch Trashy, vulgar, or in bad taste (from the German *verkitschen*, to make cheap). An Elvis Presley table lamp, a lurid advertising poster, or a Hollywood Biblical epic could all be labelled kitsch. Traditionally, kitsch articles were mass-produced for mass consumption and were to be avoided by the aesthetically discerning. In the 1960s, however, the distinction between high and low art became obscured by POP ART, with its ironic elevation of the kitsch as a reaction to the snobbish and often phoney academicism of the established art world. As a result, some kitsch articles, now often called CAMP, have attained an even more phoney status as collectables, with a high market value.

> . . . the documentary *Pumping Iron* (1977) . . . that allowed him [Arnold Schwarznegger] to move bodybuilding from low camp to high kitsch and then big business.
>
> *The Independent*, 30 January 1991.

Kitty Hawk A town in North Carolina, USA, on the narrow dunes facing the Atlantic. It owes its fame to the WRIGHT BROTHERS, who made the first sustained powered flight here on 17 December 1903. To the south of the town at Kill Devil Hills is the Wright Brothers National Memorial (1927).

Kiwanis An organization founded in America in 1915 aiming to improve business ethics and provide leadership for raising the level of business and professional ideals. There are many Kiwanis clubs in America and Canada. The word is alleged to come from Amerindian, meaning to make oneself known.

kiwi A New Zealand bird incapable of flight. In flying circles the word is applied to a man of the ground staff of an aerodrome. It also denotes a New Zealander.

Klaxon The tradename for a type of loud mechanical horn formerly used on motor vehicles.

Kleenex The tradename for the world's first disposable paper hankies, produced in 1924 by the Kimberley-Clarke Company in Wisconsin, USA. The hankies were first called Celluwipes, then renamed Kleenex-'Kerchiefs, which was later shortened to Kleenex.

Kleinian Pertaining to the work and theories of the Austrian-born psychoanalyst Melanie Klein (1882–1960). A disciple of Sigmund Freud, she believed that complex emotional states, such as fear, anxiety, and grief, were present from early infancy and that psychoanalytic techniques could be applied successfully to very young children. She advocated the use of play as a means of allowing children to express their feelings and maintained that observing play with simple toys, drawing materials, sand, etc., provided an understanding of their behaviour and emotional needs. Although many of her theories are still controversial, the technique of 'play therapy', which she developed, is commonly used by therapists, for example in cases of suspected CHILD ABUSE or in dealing with disturbed children.

kludge US computer slang for an overcomplicated unclear system. The word was coined from a combination of 'sludge' and 'clumsy'.

klutz Slang for a fool. Originally from America, it is derived from the Yiddish *klots*, a lump, and is related to the English word 'clot', via the German *klotz*, lump. By the 1980s its usage had spread throughout the English-speaking world.

KMT Kuomintang. *See* GUOMINDANG.

knave British slang for an airline passenger who has, unknown to himself, had explosives planted in his luggage by terrorists. This method of terrorism was first practised in the late 1980s; the term was coined by security guards.

knee. kneecapping The process of damaging a person's kneecaps, typically by blasting them with a shotgun or drilling through them with an electric drill. It became notorious as a practice used by the IRA as a punishment for defectors.

knee jerk A reflex action, *i.e.* one that is automatic and requires no thought. It is derived from the patellar reflex (the involuntary jerk of the leg caused by tapping just below the knee). Becoming popular in America during the 1970s in common speech, it is often used in combination, *e.g.* a knee-jerk liberal is one whose liberal response to any situation is automatic rather than thought out.

knees-up A party, or any lively celebration, derived from the Cockney song *Knees-up, Mother Brown!* (1939), popular during World War II.

Knesset (Heb. Assembly) The Israeli parliament, a single chamber consisting of 120 members elected every four years by proportional representation. The first Knesset opened in Jerusalem on 16 February 1949 and elected Chaim Weizmann (1874–1952) as the first president of Israel.

Knickbein (Ger. bent leg) Codename of a simple radio aid used by the Germans early in World War II to guide bombers over the UK during night raids and in bad weather. It used two radio beams, which were picked up by receivers in the aircraft: one to track the target, the other to cross the first at the bomb release point. The transmitters were positioned along the coast of Holland and N France and could guide aircraft with reasonable accuracy over central and S England. Within two months of its discovery, however, the RAF had devised effective counter-measures.

knickers. get one's knickers in a twist British slang meaning to get agitated about something. It was first used in the 1950s to mean sexually excited rather than agitated. It is usually addressed to women in the negative form as a pacifying, if rather patronizing, remark. A recent masculine version is **get one's Y-fronts in a W**.

Knightsbridge The name given to a crossroads in the desert south of Tobruk, Libya, which was the scene of fierce tank battles during the Battle of the Gazala-Bir Hacheim Line between 28 May and 13 June 1942. The British Eighth Army under Auchinleck was forced to withdraw into Egypt, after which Rommel took Tobruk and advanced on to ALAMEIN.

knock. knocking off hen tracks on a roll top piano US Black slang from the 1930s, meaning to type a personal letter on a typewriter.

knock, knock! A catchphrase said to have been introduced to the UK by the music-hall comedian Wee Georgie Wood, who first used it in a radio programme in 1936. It was employed as a prefatory phrase in telling a joke, often of a risqué nature. However, by the 1960s the phrase had become part of a fairly rigid formula for a name play, of which the following is typical:

> Knock, knock!
> Who's there?
> Owl.
> Owl who?
> Owl you know unless you open the door?

knock for knock A practice adopted by British motor insurers in which they agree to pay the claims of their own policy owners, but not to counterclaim against other parties to an accident. In principle, if a motorist involved in an accident is the innocent party, his insurers could make a claim against the other party's insurers for the damage caused. In practice, the 'knock-for-knock agreement' enables insurance companies to avoid this expensive and time-consuming procedure on the grounds that, in the long run, such counterclaims tend to even out. This saving in administrative costs also benefits insured motorists by keeping down the cost of premiums. However, in individual cases some motorists may lose their NO-CLAIM BONUS, even though they were not to blame for an accident.

knocking copy *See* COMPARATIVE ADVERTISING.

Our Lady of Knock *See under* OUR.

knowledge, the British taxi-drivers' slang for the knowledge of the streets of London on which they are examined in order to become licensed taxi-drivers. Would-be taxi-drivers can be seen acquainting themselves with 'the knowledge', driving around London on mopeds following prearranged routes drawn out on a clipboard attached to the handlebars. This is known as being **on the knowledge**; the drivers themselves are called the **knowledge boys** irrespective of their age. These terms became more widely known through a 1983 TV play, *The Knowledge*, by Jack Rosenthal.

Kodak A tradename for a range of cameras and films invented by the eccentric American, George Eastman (1854–1932), the first of which appeared in 1888. This first Kodak camera was compact, light, and relatively cheap; it heralded the arrival of popular photography. The box-shaped device produced 100 round photos on paper stripping film. When all the photos had been taken, the camera was returned to the factory, which replaced the film, developed the pictures, and returned the camera and snaps to the owner within 10 days. Eastman has recorded his reasons for choosing the name Kodak:

> I chose it because I knew a trade name must be short, vigorous, incapable of being misspelled to an extent that will destroy its identity, and, in order to satisfy trademark laws, it must mean nothing. The letter K had been a favourite with me – it seemed a strong, incisive sort of letter. Therefore, the word I

wanted had to start with K. Then it became a question of trying out a great number of combinations of letters that made words starting and ending with K. The word *Kodak* is the result.

kode Slang for a code used by GAYS to communicate their sexual proclivities. The code includes modes of dress, key rings attached to belts, and certain coloured handkerchiefs in certain pockets, as well as the use of certain slang words, for example 'clone' and 'straight', in a specific way.

kogai A Japanese word to describe environmental pollution in Japan. From about 1970, reports of conferences held to discuss the problem of *kogai* began to appear in western newspapers. The term is widely applied to all types of environmental nuisance, including noise, water impurity, traffic congestion, obstruction of light, and air pollution.

Kolyma A region in NE Siberia, site of a complex of Soviet forced-labour camps administered by Dalstroy, the Far Eastern Construction Trust. The main camps serviced the Kolyma gold mines but there were also logging camps for women prisoners. In all, over two million died under a deliberately destructive regime, which provided a starvation diet, prohibited fur clothing, and enforced outside work 10 hours a day, unless temperatures fell below −50°C.

Labour is a matter of honour, valour and heroism.
Sign required by statute on all camp gates.

Komsomol All-Union Leninist Young Communist League, established in 1918 as a BOLSHEVIK youth organization for agitation and propaganda.

Kondratieff waves Long-term cycles in economic activity with a period of about 40 years, postulated by the Russian economist N. D. Kondratieff (1892–1931). According to the theory, for which there is little substantive evidence, the last trough in the cycle occurred during the GREAT DEPRESSION of the 1930s.

Kon-Tiki expedition The unique voyage made in 1947 by the Norwegian Thor Heyerdahl with five companions, who sailed a balsa raft from Callao in Peru to Tuamotu Island in the South Pacific. Their object was to support the theory that the Polynesian race reached the Pacific islands in this fashion and were descendants of the Incas of Peru. Their raft was called *Kon-Tiki* after the Inca sun-god.

kook US slang for an eccentric or crazy person. It is probably derived from 'cuckoo', a widely used word for crazy. Kook, however, is rarely heard in the UK, although it is used in Australia.

kopasetic US Black slang from the 1940s, meaning excellent.

Köpenick hoax An incident that took place in a Berlin suburb in 1906. An exconvict shoemaker, dressed in a Guardsman's uniform, commandeered a passing platoon of soldiers and arrested the Burgomaster, rifling his office in search of cash and a passport. He was brought to justice ten days later and identified as Wilhelm Voigt. The case, which made Prussian militarism a laughing stock, attracted wide publicity and the Kaiser was obliged to pardon the daring elderly hoaxer, who spent his remaining years in comfort on a pension given him by an admiring Berlin dowager. The episode provided the plot for the comic satire *Der Hauptmann von Köpenick* (1931) by the German dramatist and novelist Carlos Zuckmayer (1896–1977). It is now a standard work in the modern drama repertory.

Korean War (1950–53) The bitter, and ultimately inconclusive, conflict precipitated by the surprise invasion of democratic South Korea by communist North Korea on 25 June 1950. Korea had been temporarily divided across the 38th parallel by the allies in 1945, after which attempts by the UN to reunite the country failed. An international force was raised by the UN to combat the invasion, dominated by the Americans and led by General Douglas MacArthur, who masterminded the successful Inchon landings (September 1950) cutting the enemy supply lines. The UN forces then drove the communists back to the Yalu River, the boundary between North Korea and China. MacArthur was removed by President Truman in April 1951 for publicly advocating the bombing of China, which had invaded in support of the North in November 1950, pushing the UN forces back to the 38th parallel. Seoul, the southern capital, fell to the communists, but was recaptured in April 1951. Negotiations began as the fighting continued, until an armistice was finally signed at Panmunjon in 1953.

kosher A Yiddish word (from Hebrew *kasher*, proper) that came into use in the 19th century in English-speaking countries to describe food that complies with the Jewish dietary laws. Its use extended during the 19th and 20th centuries to describe restaurants and butchers selling this food and even to describe Jews themselves. Its wider sense, used to describe anything trustworthy, genuine, or above board, is essentially a 20th-century usage, which originated in New York, where so many Yiddish words entered the English language. From New York it crossed the Atlantic back to England, where it is now quite common to hear such questions as 'Is that antique kosher?' or such statements as 'You have no need to worry, he is absolutely kosher', meaning not that the person concerned is Jewish, but that he is honest, or is who he says he is. This is quite surprising, because in the mid-19th century Dickens had picked up an almost identical usage in London's East End, where 'kosher' was used to describe a deal that was fair. Very few Yiddish words commonly used by East End Jews, however, appear to have spread even a few miles west to become part of educated English speech. This usage of kosher, for example, simply did not exist in 20th-century English until it came back from America after World War II.

Kraft durch Freude (KdF; Ger. Strength through Joy) A popular NAZI scheme for cheap package holidays, which allowed thousands of working Germans to visit remote areas of the country, or take leisure cruises abroad, during the 1930s. The scheme, based on the Italian Fascist organization *Dopo Lavoro*, was initially financed from confiscated trade-union funds but later became big business, generating considerable income for the Nazis. KdF also organized sporting and other leisure activities, such as subsidized theatre visits and travelling cabaret shows. The scheme proved a valuable Nazi propaganda vehicle.

kraut Slang for a German. It originated in America and is now more widely used than the earlier 'hun' from World War I and 'jerry' from World War II. Kraut is shortened from *Sauerkraut*, a German national dish of pickled cabbage.

Kremlinology The science of Kremlin-watching by monitoring Soviet newspapers, TV, photographs, interviewing recent emigrants, etc., in an attempt to divine the internal workings of the Soviet political system. Kremlinology is practiced by academics, journalists, and foreign governments, who become adept at reading between the lines of official communiqués.

kreplach A Jewish form of ravioli, consisting of a square or triangular noodle containing chopped meat and cheese. It is usually served in soup, especially on the Jewish New Year's day (*Rosh Hoshanah*) and the day before the Day of Atonement (*Yom Kippur*). A Yiddish word that entered the English language in New York in the 20th century, it derives from the German *kreppel*, and is not far from the French *crêpe*, pancake.

Kretschmer's types Types of physique, which the German psychiatrist Ernst Kretschmer (1888–1964) believed could be correlated with certain mental disorders. In his work *Physique and Character* (1921), Kretschmer advanced the psychological theory that schizophrenia was more prevalent in tall and thin (*asthenic*) body types and that manic-depression is commoner in rotund (*pyknic*) builds. This association of body type with temperament goes back to the ancients although no convincing evidence of such a relationship has ever been confirmed.

Kreuger crash The bankruptcy in 1932 of the multinational corporation created by Ivar Kreuger (1880–1932), the Swedish 'match king'. During World War I Kreuger concentrated the Swedish match industry under his control; and after the war he embarked on a campaign to monopolize world match production. Backed by US investors, he made long-term loans to countries experiencing short-term balance of payments deficits in return for monopoly rights. With the onset of the GREAT DEPRESSION Kreuger's financial position collapsed and he shot himself in 1932, exposing the fraudulent and spurious nature of much of his empire's assets and profits.

Krishna. Jiddu Krishnamurti Hindu mystic (1895–1986) who attracted a huge following in the 1920s when he prophesied the Second Coming of Christ. In anticipation of the event, a massive amphitheatre was erected near Sydney Harbour, Australia, from which Krishnamurti predicted that the waiting crowd of 2000 would see Christ approaching across the Pacific Ocean. That he had not done so by 1929 led to a decline in enthusiasm for Krishnamurti's cult, the Order of the Star of the East (founded in 1911); the amphitheatre was subsequently demolished for housing. Krishnamurti himself, having been acknowledged as an incarnation of the messianic Buddha by the Theosophical Society, finally agreed that he was no such thing. He died in California, home of the Krishnamurti Foundation.

Krishna consciousness *See* HARE KRISHNA.

Kriss Kringle A US name for Santa Claus derived from the German *Christkindl* (little Christ child).

Kristallnacht (Ger. night of glass) The night of 9–10 November 1938 during which German mobs, led by the Nazi BROWN SHIRTS, roamed the streets of towns and cities all over Germany and Austria smashing the windows of shops and houses belonging to Jews (hence the name). The looting of Jewish property and the setting fire to synagogues was for many German and Austrian Jews the last straw in the humiliating persecution they had suffered at the hands of Hitler, his Nazi party, and the many ordinary Germans and Austrians who supported him. Those Jews who were able to, fled to the UK, America, Australia, and anywhere else that would accept them. Amongst this exodus were many of the European Jewish physicists who later became the key figures in the creation of the atom bomb.

Kroger affair The case of the Soviet spies Morris and Lona Cohen, alias Peter and Helen Kroger, who were both sentenced at the Old Bailey, London, on 18 March 1961 to 20 years' imprisonment for their involvement in the Portland Secrets Case (*see* LONSDALE AFFAIR). The Cohens, owners of a bookshop in the Strand, were associates of Gordon Lonsdale (Konon Molody Trofimovich), the Soviet 'mole' who had been receiving documents from Harry Houghton, a clerk at the top-secret Admiralty Underwater Weapons Establishment at Portland in Dorset. Special Branch officers discovered a radio transmitter in the Cohens' bungalow in the west London suburb of Ruislip, for communicating with Moscow Centre; they also found miniature cameras, a microdot reader, false passports, and large sums of cash. It transpired that they had been part of a Soviet spy network in America since the 1940s, had left America in 1951 using false Canadian passports, and had finally settled in the UK after travelling to Australia and Switzerland. Hugh Whitemore speculated upon the impact of the Krogers on their unsuspecting British friends in his play *A Pack of Lies* (1983).

Krondstadt mutiny A revolt against BOLSHEVIK rule by sailors at the Soviet naval base in the gulf of Finland in March 1921. The economic privations of the Civil War, including inadequate food distribution and harsh labour regulations, provoked widespread discontent with Bolshevik rule, which was manifested in a series of strikes by urban workers. The Krondstadt sailors established a Provisional Revolutionary Committee in support of the strikers and demanded an end to the Communist Party dictatorship, full power to the Soviets (local councils), the release of non-Bolshevik prisoners, and greater political freedoms. Although the mutiny was crushed by Trotsky and Marshal Mikhail Tukachevsky, it prompted Lenin to implement the milder NEW ECONOMIC POLICY soon afterwards.

krugerrand A South African gold coin introduced in 1967 and containing 1 troy ounce of gold. The coin was never intended as a currency unit but was designed as a way of enabling investors to hold gold in those countries in which there were restrictions on private hoarding. In the UK, an import licence has been necessary for krugerrands since 1975. The name comes from the standard South African monetary unit, the *rand* (from the gold-mining area at Witwatersrand), with the name of the Afrikaner statesman Paul Kruger (1825–1904). Krugerrands lost popularity as an investment in the late 1980s, partly for political reasons and partly because of competition from other coins, such as the **Britannia** and the **Eagle**. The Britannia, a range of four British gold coins, was introduced in 1987. They are sold in £10, £25, £50, and £100 denominations. The Eagle is a range of four US gold coins, introduced in 1986, sold in $5, $10, $25, and $50 denominations.

krypton An inert gas, discovered by Sir W. Ramsey in 1898, which occurs in minute quantities in the atmosphere and is used in fluorescent lights, high-speed photographic flash equipment, and lasers. Krypton is also the planetary home of the fictional comic-strip hero SUPERMAN and the source of the mysterious element 'kryptonite', a green crystalline substance that weakens his superhuman powers.

Ku Klux Klan (KKK) A US secret society founded at Pulaski, Tennessee, in 1866 at the close of the Civil War as a social club with a fanciful ritual and hooded white robes. The name is a corruption of the Greek *kuklos*, a circle. It soon developed into a society to overawe the newly emancipated Blacks; similar societies, such as the Knights of the White Camelia, the White League, the Pale Faces, and the Invisible Circle sprang up in 1867–68. Its terrorist activities led to laws against it in 1870 and 1871. Although it had been disbanded by the Grand Wizard in 1869, local activities continued for some time.

In 1915 a new organization, The Invisible Empire, Knights of the Ku Klux Klan, was founded by the Rev. William Simmonds, preacher, near Atlanta, Georgia. He adopted much of the ritual of the original, adding further puerile ceremonies, titles, nomenclature, etc., of his own. Klansmen held *Klonvocations* and their local *Klaverns* were ruled by an *Exalted Cyclops*, a *Klaliff*, etc. As well as anti-Black it was anti-Catholic, anti-Jewish, and xenophobic. Advocating Protestant supremacy for the native-born Whites, it grew rapidly from 1920 and gained considerable political control in the Southern states by unsavoury methods. By 1930 it had shrunk again to small proportions but a revival began before World War II and the Klan became noted for its Fascist sympathies. In 1944 it was again disbanded but continued locally and in 1965 a Congressional Committee was set up to investigate Klan activities.

kulak (Russ. fist) A prosperous Russian peasant who owned land and livestock and was capable of employing labour and leasing land. Kulaks were key figures in the traditional economic, social, and administrative structure of prerevolutionary Russian agriculture. Under Lenin, the position of the kulaks was gradually undermined although their economic and political value was exploited to maintain agricultural production along quasi-capitalist lines. However, the policy of rapid agricultural collectivization pursued by Stalin after 1929 aimed at the destruction of the kulaks as a class; by 1934 most of them had been deported to remote areas of the country, arrested or executed, and their property confiscated.

Kuomintang *See* GUOMINDANG.

kuru A fatal degenerative disease of the central nervous system whose symptoms include tremors, excitability, loss of muscular coordination and speech, and ultimately paralysis. It is caused by a virus allied to that which causes scrapie in sheep and bovine spongiform encephalopathy (BSE) in cattle (*see* MAD COW DISEASE). Identified in the 20th century, the disease occurs only among small groups of tribesmen in parts of New Guinea (*kuru* is a native name meaning trembling or shivering) and is probably transmitted by the practice of ritual cannibalism, which involves consuming the brains of dead relatives. As this practice has waned, outbreaks of kuru have rapidly declined.

Kut, Siege of The siege of a unit of the British army under Major General Charles V. F. Townshend in Kut-el-Amara at the confluence of the Tigris and Shatt-el-Hai rivers by the Turks in World War I, from 7 December 1915 to 29 April 1916. Townshend had been advancing up the Tigris towards Baghdad until the Turks inflicted heavy losses on his forces at the Battle of Ctesiphon (7–8 September); he withdrew his exhausted infantry to Kut (2 December), where he waited in vain for British reinforcements. On 29 April starvation forced the surrender of his 2070 British and 6000 Indian troops, must of whom died in captivity.

KVD Soviet Committee for Internal Affairs, the successor to the MVD (Ministry of Internal Affairs) in 1960.

kvetch US slang meaning to whine or complain. It is a Yiddish word meaning to press. A person who habitually whines or complains is also called a kvetch.

L

L-85 A fashion style dictated by the US government during World War II in order to save vital raw materials. Ruling L-85 laid down the styles allowed, which included narrow skirts, functional pockets only, and little in the way of frills or hems.

la. **LA** Los Angeles. A city in SW California on the edge of the Mojave Desert. Orginally founded by Spanish settlers in 1781 as El Pueblo de Nuestra Señora la Reina de los Angeles (Town of Our Lady the Queen of the Angels), LA is now America's third largest city, a vast 2082-square-mile urban sprawl crisscrossed by a repetitive grid of suburbs and convoluted freeways. Its three million citizens are plagued by chronic air and water pollution, traffic snarl-ups, and ethnic gang warfare; however, it is one of the world's most exciting cities – home to the faded grandeur of HOLLYWOOD, the affluence of BEVERLY HILLS and Rodeo Drive, the DISNEYLAND amusement park, and the even more exotic playground of Venice Beach.

La Guardia The airport for domestic flights in and out of New York City, named after Fiorello Henry La Guardia (1882–1947), US congressman and three times mayor of New York (1933–45), who had successfully campaigned for the airport's construction. La Guardia, nicknamed 'Little Flower' (Fiorello), was an energetic and colourful figure. A former translator for immigrants passing through ELLIS ISLAND, he became a mayor who opposed civic corruption and organized crime, promoted social welfare policies and public works, and is remembered as the most honest and best loved incumbent of New York's City Hall. As a politician he was a habitual dissenter, supporting such issues as women's suffrage, legal aid, and the rights of trade unions.

La Lollo Gina Lollobrigida (1927–), Italian film actress whose seductive beauty was made much use of by Hollywood from 1947, after which her international screen roles included a variety of temptresses – a trapeze artiste in *Trapeze* (1956), a glamour girl in an Italian village in *Buona Sera, Mrs Campbell* (1968), and a Munich bookseller's wife in *King, Queen, Knave* (1972).

La Tène A curvilinear decorative style derived from Iron-Age Celtic art. Such designs on pottery and metalwork in gold, silver, and bronze were found in the La Tène archaeological site on Lake Neuchâtel, Switzerland, in excavations between 1907 and 1917. La Tène art, which included interlaced patterns related to the Greek geometric style and stylized oriental animals, also existed in the UK and Ireland. La Tène has given its name to the second phase of the Celtic Iron Age in Europe (mid-5th century BC to the Roman conquest).

labour. **labour exchange** or **employment exchange** *See* JOB CENTRE.

Labour Party One of the major political parties of the UK, which aims to promote socialism. So called from 1906, it was first formed as the Labour Representation Committee in 1900 from such elements as the Independent Labour Party, the trade unions, and the Fabian Society. The first Labour government was that of Ramsay MacDonald in 1924; the second lasted from 1929 to 1931, when the party split over the cuts in unemployment benefit (*see* NATIONAL GOVERNMENTS). It was not returned to power again until 1945 and was replaced by the Conservatives in October 1951. It was again in office from 1964 to 1970 under Harold Wilson and from 1974 to 1979 under Wilson and subsequently James Callaghan. Michael Foot failed to heal party divisions as leader (1980–83) and was replaced by Neil Kinnock. Kinnock has attempted to rebuild the party's image as representing the broad middle class rather than the former working class alone; he has also curbed the influence of the left-wing extremists (*see* MILITANT). *See also* WELFARE STATE.

lad. laddish British slang used to describe rowdy and MACHO young males. This term, from the late 1970s, is generally used contemptuously by women or older men.

The Lad Nickname of the British comedian Tony Hancock (1924–68), who became a leading star during the 1950s in the radio programme *Hancock's Half Hour* (subsequently televised). As the lugubrious and ever-complaining tenant of 23 Railway Cuttings, East Cheam, he became a cult comedian with a huge following. Hancock once explained his comic persona: "You take your own weaknesses and exploit them."

His own weaknesses included irascibility towards his fellow-performers, who all eventually left the show, and to his long-suffering scriptwriters; his weaknesses also included an increasing reliance upon alcohol – in his last television shows he was obliged to have his lines written on slips of paper around the set. In 1968, on a tour of Australia he committed suicide in a Sydney hotel room, the quintessential example of the comic with an insupportable personal life.

Ladakh crisis The surprise Chinese invasion of the remote Ladakh region of E Kashmir in N India in October 1962, signalling a dangerous flare-up in the long-running Sino-Indian border conflict. Possession of the region, as with many other areas along the 2640-mile MCMAHON LINE (drawn up by Sir Henry McMahon in 1914 and never ratified by China), had been disputed by the two nations throughout the 1950s. On 20 October 1962 the Chinese inflicted a humiliating defeat upon the Indian Army, advancing effortlessly over the McMahon Line through the NE frontier, capturing the administrative centre of Bomdila, and threatening to sweep down the Assam Valley. On 21 November the Chinese declared a ceasefire and withdrew again, ending the crisis as suddenly as it had begun, although they retained 2500 square miles of Indian territory.

lady. Lady Bird The nickname of Claudia Johnson (1912–), widow of Lyndon Baines Johnson, 36th US president (*see* LBJ). The nickname was given to her as an infant by her nurse and taken up by family and friends and by Claudia herself. By a happy coincidence she married a man whose first-name initials, L. B., matched those of her assumed name, enabling her to continue using both the initials and name in her public life.

Lady Chatterley trial A famous test case in which Penguin Books were prosecuted under the Obscene Publications Act (1959) for publishing D. H. Lawrence's last novel, *Lady Chatterley's Lover*, in an unexpurgated edition. The book was published in Italy in a limited edition in 1928, but because of Lawrence's explicit description of sexual scenes and his use of four-letter words, it had never been published in the UK and America, other than in an expurgated version. At the six-day hearing, which opened at the Old Bailey on 20 October 1960 before Mr Justice Bryne, 36 defence witnesses – including the Bishop of Woolwich, E. M. Forster, Dame Rebecca West, and Richard Hoggart – provided evidence of the book's literary and artistic merits (a further 35 defence witnesses were not called). It was the first time that expert opinion of this kind had been admitted as defence against an obscenity charge in a British court. For the prosecution, Mr Mervyn Griffith-Jones took a somewhat paternalistic view, asking, "Is it a book you would wish your wife or your servant to read?" The jury's reply was an unanimous verdict of not guilty; the entire first impression (200,000 copies) sold out on the day of publication (10 November) and has since sold millions of copies.

> More to the point, would you allow your game-keeper to read it?
>
> Anonymous reaction to MERVYN GRIFFITH-JONES' question.

The Lady Chatterley trial proved to be a watershed in British publishing. Since this verdict was given, sex can be dealt with explicitly in books provided they do not contain material that tends to deprave or corrupt under the terms of the 1959 Act or the subsequent Act of 1964.

Lady Day The nickname of the US JAZZ singer Billie Holiday (1915–59). Her individual phrasing and the emotional intensity of her singing gained her the reputation of the greatest of all female jazz vocalists and the title 'First Lady of the Blues'. The nickname 'Lady Day' was given to her by the soloist Lester Young, who accompanied her on many recording sessions, and reflected the poise and dignity she possessed even in her later years when beset by drug problems.

Lady Macbeth strategy Business jargon describing the strategy adopted by one company in relation to another company, which is facing a hostile takeover bid from a rival. A company pursuing the Lady Macbeth strategy appears to act as a WHITE KNIGHT in support of the other firm in combatting the hostile takeover bid, then subsequently joins the aggressor.

Lady Macbeth syndrome *See* BACTERIOPHOBIA.

Relief of Ladysmith The rescue by forces led by General Sir Redvers Buller, on 28 February 1900, of General Sir George White and his Natal Defence Force from the beleaguered garrison of Ladysmith in NW Natal, which marked the turning point for British fortunes in the Boer War. The garrison had been under siege by General Piet Joubert and his 15,000-strong Boer army since 2 November 1899. The rescue saved Buller's military reputation, sullied by a string of defeats at the hands of the Boers in the preceding months, while General White's strategic blunder in allowing himself to be trapped in Ladysmith and encircled by Joubert's artillery cost him his health and reputation; he was invalided back to England shortly afterwards.

Lafayette. Lafayette squadron A squadron of US pilots, who served with the French air force in World War I prior to America's entry into the war.

Lafayette, we are here The words commonly attributed to US General John Pershing on his arrival in France in World War I. In fact they were said by US Colonel Charles E. Stanton (1859–1933) while representing Pershing at the grave of the Marquis de Lafayette in Picpus cemetery, Paris, on 4 July 1917, shortly after the American Expeditionary Force landed on French soil. Lafayette (1757–1834), an honorary American citizen, had been a friend of George Washington and fought on the site of the colonists against the British in the American War of Independence.

> Here and now, in the presence of the illustrious dead, we pledge our hearts and our honour in carrying this war to a successful issue. Lafayette, we are here.

lager louts Young hooligans who create disturbances, damage property, and commit violent assaults after drinking too much lager. The term first appeared in 1988 and is often associated with FOOTBALL HOOLIGANISM.

Lagonda One of the most famous marques in British motoring history, founded in 1904 by an American, Wilbur Gunn. The son of an engineer from Springfield, Ohio, Gunn came to the UK in 1897 to pursue an operatic career. Frustrated in this, he began making motorcycles in the greenhouse of his Staines home, naming them Lagonda – the Shawnee Indian for Bucks Creek, near his Ohio birthplace. The original two-wheelers were followed by a three-wheeled tricar, and in 1907 by the first four-wheeled Lagonda, a 20 hp four-cylinder model known as the 14/16. A 30 hp six-cylinder car came soon afterwards. In the 1920s the firm gave up its attempts to compete in the small-car mass-production market and turned to sports cars, launching the 2-litre 14/60 and 2.4-litre 16/65, which later became the Lagonda 3 litre. Another 3-litre model, the 16/80, was introduced in 1932, powered by a six-cylinder Crossley engine.

Lagonda managed to weather the economic slump of the 1930s but drastically slimmed its model range, leaving the 4½-litre M45 as its mainstay. Launched in 1933, the M45 won the LE MANS race two years later. The late 1930s saw the unveiling of several new Lagondas designed by one of the most illustrious names in motoring, W. O. Bentley. These included the LG45, the Rapide coupe, and the V12. Immediately after World War II the company was bought by David Brown and became part of Aston Martin. The Lagonda name lived on for a time in the Bentley-designed 2.5-litre Mark I, and in a new 3-litre model introduced in 1953. Production of Lagondas was discontinued in 1958, although the Lagonda badge has sporadically reappeared on certain Aston Martin models ever since.

laid back A term originating in America in the 1930s with reference to the playing of JAZZ. In this context it meant playing behind the main beat. However, in the 1970s it became part of the general language in all English-speaking countries, meaning relaxed and unhurried or easy-going.

Laingian Pertaining to the theories of the British psychiatrist R. D. Laing (1927–89) on the nature and origins of schizophrenia and psychotic behaviour. In his works *The Divided Self* (1960), *The Self and Others* (1961), *Sanity, Madness and the Family* (1965), and *The Politics of Experience* (1971) Laing suggested that mental illness may be a legitimate, even therapeutic, way of escaping from the alienating and constricting pressures to conform to which people are subjected in society, institutions, and even the family. As president of the Philadelphia Association (1964–82), he pursued the practical application of his radical 'anti-psychiatry', providing patients with social contexts within which they could live. Laing's explanations of psychosis remain controversial and perhaps his greatest legacy has been the stimulation of open debate, since the 1960s, on the causes and treatment of mental illness.

> Schizophrenic behaviour is a special strategy that a person invents in order to live in an unlivable situation.
>
> *The Politics of Experience.*

lair or **lare** Australian slang for a disreputable youth, a ne'er do well. Before World War II it was used to mean an overdressed young man. Although this sense is now rarely heard, the adjective **lairy** is still used in Australia and the UK to describe someone who is flashily or vulgarly dressed.

lake. Lake Success A village on Long Island in SE New York State, headquarters of the United Nations Security Council from 1946 to 1951. After the charter of the UN was signed at the San Francisco Conference in 1945 there was frenzied lobbying both by European capitals and US cities, all of which hoped to be chosen as the permanent home of the organization. New York was eventually accorded the honour, thanks mainly to John D. Rockefeller's donation of $8.5 million to purchase a site (Turtle Bay) on the East River for the new permanent headquarters. The headquarters building was not completed until 1952, and the UN held its first meeting in London early in 1946. It then occupied various temporary locations in New York, including the Waldorf Astoria Hotel, Hunter College in the Bronx, a disused skating rink at Flushing Meadow Park in Queens, and the Sperry Gyroscope Company Building at Lake Success.

Lake Wobegon effect An effect in which the standard of something or someone with which or with whom one is connected is grossly overestimated. The phrase refers to the title of a book, *Lake Wobegon Days* (1985), written by the US humorist Garrison Keillor (1942–). The stories in the book are set in the town of Wobegon, where all the inhabitants are depicted as being exceptional:

> . . . the women are strong, the men good looking and all the children above average.

Lalique glass A type of Art Nouveau glass designed and manufactured by the French jeweller and interior designer, René Lalique (1860–1945). Lalique was trained in London and Paris, and in his early career specialized in jewellery, textiles, and fans. His company sold designs to Cartier, made costume jewellery for the French actress, Sarah Bernhardt, and achieved some success with Art Nouveau brooches and combs at the Paris exhibition of 1900. After establishing a glass factory in 1910, Lalique mass-produced a wide range of moulded glassware, such as vases, statuettes, scent bottles, and desk accessories. These featured iced surfaces and pale opalescent hues, with elaborate relief patterns based on plant, animal, and sensuous female motifs.

lambada A late-1980s dance craze, in which a couple embrace tightly and gyrate their hips in a lubricious manner. It is thought to have originated amoung sailors and prostitutes in the shanty towns of Rio de Janeiro and was long considered unfit for respectable women. The music that accompanies this performance, also called lambada, is an infectious mixture of Latin American and Caribbean styles. In the 1980s it was taken up by North African musicians in Paris, and this modified form of lambada swept through European nightclubs in the summer of 1989. The name derives from a Portuguese word meaning the crack of a whip.

Lambaréné A village on an island in the Ogooué River in W Gabon, the site of the hospital built in 1913 by the German medical missionary, theologian, and musician Albert Schweitzer (1875–1965). Schweitzer was imprisoned by the French during World War I, but returned to Lambaréné in 1924, rebuilt the hospital, and founded a leper colony nearby. By 1963 the hospital had 350 patients; the leper colony treated 150 more people. The entire complex was staffed by 35 White doctors and nurses as well as African ancillary workers. Schweitzer, called the 'Saint of Lambaréné' by his admirers, died and was buried there in 1965. His writings on Bach and recordings of his recitals of Bach organ music are still highly regarded. This remarkable multitalented man was awarded the Nobel Peace Prize in 1952.

Lambeth Walk A thoroughfare in Lambeth leading from Black Prince Road to the Lambeth Road. It gave its name to an immensely popular Cockney dance featured by Lupino Lane (from 1937) in the musical show *Me And My Gal* at the Victoria Palace. Purporting to imitate the strutting walk of the typical Lambeth Cockney, it came to symbolize the spirit of defiance of Londoners during the BLITZ in World War II.

Any time you're Lambeth Way
Any evening, any day,
You'll find us all,
Doing the Lambeth Walk, Oi!

Lambretta A motor scooter manufactured by Innocenti from the 1950s at its factory in the Lambrate district of Milan. Together with the equally well-known **Vespa** motor scooter of the same period, it provided a more genteel alternative to the motorcycle, affording greater protection from the weather and enabling the rider to dispense with the more-or-less obligatory leathers and goggles of the motorcyclist. Most models were equipped with a 125 cc two-stroke engine, providing a stately average speed of about 45 m.p.h.; there were a few larger-engined versions.

lame brain Slang for slow-witted or stupid. A phrase that originated in America in the 1960s, it was heard in both the UK and Australia in the 1970s.

Lampton, Joe The ruthless self-seeking anti-hero of John Braine's novels *Room at the Top* (1957) and *Life at the Top* (1962). From a working-class home in a small Yorkshire town, Lampton achieves his ends by discarding his long-standing but impecunious mistress, Alice Aisgill, in order to marry Susan Brown, the daughter of a wealthy man. Both books were made into films, in which Laurence Harvey took the part of Joe Lampton: *Room at the Top* (1958; directed by Jack Clayton), *Life at the Top* (1965; directed by Ted Kotcheff). There followed a British television series entitled *Man at the Top* (1971–73) and a film of the same name (1973; directed by Mike Vardy) with Kenneth Haigh in the title role. Braine conceived the character of Lampton after seeing the body of a baby being removed from a house in Bradford into which a German bomber had crashed in 1941 and contemplating how the baby's life might have turned out. Years later the incident was recognized by Gareth Boyd, a public relations officer with a bus company, who it transpired had been that baby, having miraculously survived the destruction of his parents' home.

LAN Local Area Network. A group of computer terminals or word processors situated within a reasonably restricted area, such as the same office building, and linked both to each other and to such central facilities as a laser printer.

Lancaster bomber A British heavy long-range bomber, which was one of the most successful aircraft of World War II. The Avro 683 Lancaster, designed and built by A. V. Roe Ltd, was a four-engined bomber, which carried a heavier load of bigger bombs than any other aircraft in the European theatre of operations. It first went into service in April 1942 and eventually flew 156,000 sorties, dropping 608,612 tons of bombs. RAF 617 Squadron used Lancasters which had been specially modified to carry and release Barnes Wallis' 'bouncing bombs' used in the famous DAMBUSTERS raid against Germany in 1943.

land. land art *See* EARTH ART.

Land camera *See* POLAROID.

land girls Women recruited for farm work during the two World Wars to replace the men who were serving in the forces. In World War II they were organized as a Women's Land Army.

Land of Hope and Glory The UK was so portrayed in the heyday of imperialism in Elgar's famous melody with words by A. C. Benson. Sung by Dame Clara Butt in 1902, it was widely used at EMPIRE DAY celebrations and other occasions. The tune was taken from the first of the *Pomp and Circumstance* marches (1901). The words were originally used in Benson's *Coronation Ode* of 1902.

Land of Hope and Glory, Mother of the Free,
How shall we extol thee, who are born of thee?
Wider still and wider shall thy bounds be set;
God who made thee mighty, make thee mightier yet.

'Land of Hope and Glory' is traditionally sung by the whole audience at the last night of the proms (*see* PROM) in the Albert Hall. This annual outburst of overt jingoism is taken seriously by some but as a caricature by others. For most, the waving of Union Jacks, lusty singing, and high spirits is no more than youthful enthusiasm for a good tune stirringly orchestrated. In 1990, the conductor, Mark Elder, declared his intention of omitting 'Land of Hope and Glory' from the programme, because he thought jingoism was inappropriate with the GULF WAR imminent. The prospect of breaking with tradition in this way led to such an uproar that the

BBC decided to replace Mark Elder with Andrew Davis, who conducted the song with the customary panache.

Land Rover Any of a range of four-wheel-drive utility vehicles built by the British Rover Company and renowned all over the world for their rugged performance in all terrains. Design work on the Land Rover started in 1947 to provide the Rover Car Company with a stop-gap model to fill their post-war production vacuum. It was inspired by the US JEEP, which was proving popular with farmers after the war. The Land Rover was launched at the Amsterdam Motor Show in 1948, priced at £450. The engine and transmission, taken from Rover's saloon cars, were fitted to a sturdy box-section chassis. The body, with its simple flat panels, made few concessions to creature comfort: the early models had only a canvas cab roof, and a cab heater was not available until 1950.

The new model proved an instant success. In 1954 a 107-in long-wheelbase version was introduced to give greater load space and the power unit was upgraded; three years later came the first diesel-engined versions. Many variants had emerged by the mid-1950s, including a Station Wagon and Fire Engine, while the armed forces quickly appreciated the Land Rover's versatility. By 1958 production had topped 200,000 units, with over 70% going for export. Rover was taken over by British Leyland in 1967, but the company's plans for a luxurious up-market stable-mate for the Land Rover were unaffected, and the Range Rover was launched in 1970. During the 1970s and 1980s the Land Rover faced stiff competition from Japanese manufacturers, so that by the mid-1980s the Land Rover 90 and 110 series offered such options as turbocharged engines and stereo radio-cassette players – a far cry from the original spartan vehicles. In 1988 Land Rover was acquired by British Aerospace, as part of the Rover Group.

landsailing The sport of racing **land yachts**, wheeled vehicles equipped with sails. Landsailing is mostly done on sandy beaches.

Landsat A type of US orbital satellite used to obtain data about the Earth's resources. Originally called **ERTS** (Earth Resources Technology Satellite), it was introduced in 1968 and renamed Landsat (land satellite) in 1975. Landsats make cheap and accurate surveys of forestry, crop production, potential mineral resources, and fishing grounds.

Langtry, Lillie *See* JERSEY LILY.

language laboratory A room equipped with tape recorders and other audiovisual computer-controlled apparatus for learning a foreign language by listening and speaking. This method of providing foreign-language instruction first came into use in colleges and schools in the 1960s. It enables students to progress at a rate appropriate to their ability and makes efficient use of teaching resources.

Lansdowne letter A letter sent by the Irish peer Henry Charles Petty-Fitzmaurice (1845–1927), fifth Marquess of Lansdowne, to the *Daily Telegraph* on 29 November 1917. The letter outlined Lansdowne's views on the desirability of a compromise peace with Germany, which included offering various guarantees to Germany regarding its continuance as a political, territorial, and commercial power. Despite evidence that these views were shared by many MPs and even some members of the coalition government, the letter was violently repudiated by the government and the press as an act of disloyalty suggesting a weakening of allied resolve to defeat Germany. As a result Lansdowne was expelled from the Tory party.

Lao Dong The Vietnam Workers' Party, created by Ho Chi Minh in May 1951 to replace the Communist Party. The newly created Lao Dong absorbed the Lien Viet (National United Front), a nationalist and communist coalition, and became the ruling party of the Democratic Republic of Vietnam, which had been established in Hanoi on 2 September 1945 by Ho Chi Minh.

laptop A portable computer, usually weighing between 3 and 8 lbs and carried in a briefcase. It first appeared in 1984 and is used mostly for word processing in trains, hotels, etc.

Lari massacre The slaughter of 90 people, mostly Africans, by MAU MAU terrorists at Lari in Kenya on the night of the 24 March 1953. A British-appointed Kikuyu chief and his family had relinquished land designated as 'white' in return for land at Lari, NW of Nairobi; as a result, the displaced and disgruntled Lari cultivators had joined the Mau Mau. On the night in question the Mau Mau imprisoned the loyal Kikuyu intruders in their huts and burned them alive – those who tried to escape were hacked to pieces with machetes. Most of the men were absent, so those who died were almost exclusively women and children. The barbarity of the attack convinced the British authorities of the need to crush the Mau Mau with maximum force, an objective largely achieved in the two years following the massacre.

Lark Rise to Candleford An autobiographical trilogy (1945) by Flora Thompson (1876–1947) containing a detailed evocation of her rural childhood through the experiences of the character Laura. The work was originally published as *Lark Rise* (1939), *Over to Candleford* (1941), and *Candleford Green* (1943); it is an unsentimental portrait of a lost age of agricultural customs and rural culture.

Larry Informal name for the Laurence Olivier Awards presented by the Society of West End Theatre, in imitation of the OSCARS awarded in the cinema. 'Larry' was the nickname of the British actor-director Laurence Olivier (1907–89), used both by those in the acting profession who knew him well and – with stagey familiarity – by others who aspired to be on first-name terms with one of the finest British actors. In 1947 he was knighted and in 1970 he became the first actor to be made a life peer, largely for his work as director (1961–73) of the National Theatre company. The Olivier Theatre, part of the National Theatre, was named in his honour.

Lascaux caves A cave system near Montignac in the Dordogne, SW France, containing some of the most remarkable examples of prehistoric art ever found. The caves were discovered in 1940 by a group of boys after their dog disappeared through a hole, which turned out to be a hidden entrance to the grotto. The main cavern and a series of steep galleries off it contain vivid yellow, brown, red, and black paintings of various animals, including aurochs, red deer, oxen, horses, and stags' heads, which have been dated to the Upper Palaeolithic period (*c.* 18,000 BC). The dry atmosphere within the caves, together with a coating of calcite laid down over the centuries (which acted as a coat of varnish), had left the artwork in a remarkable state of preservation. However, when the caves were open to the public the humidity from tourists' breath and perspiration caused the paintings to deteriorate rapidly; since 1963 the caves have been closed to the public.

laser A device for producing an intense narrow beam of light (or infrared, ultraviolet, or other radiation). The first laser was made by the US physicist Theodore Maiman (1927–) in 1960. He used a rod of ruby with partially reflective surfaces at each end. In a ruby laser, intense pulses of light are applied from surrounding sources and these excite atoms within the material. These excited atoms decay with emission of light at a particular wavelength. The light is reflected backwards and forwards through the material and stimulates further emission. The result is a narrow beam of light with a single wavelength (monochromatic), with all the light waves in phase (coherent). The name was originally an acronym: 'light amplification by stimulated emission of radiation'. Maiman's idea came from an earlier device, the **maser** (microwave amplification by stimulated emission of radiation), which had been invented in 1955 by the US physicist Charles Townes (1915–) and, independently, by the Soviet physicists Nicolai Basov (1922–) and Aleksandr Prokhorov (1916–). The laser was originally called an 'optical maser'. Following Maiman's invention in 1960, a number of types of laser were developed using different materials and operating in different parts of the electromagnetic spectrum. Initially, the device was regarded as something of a scientific curiosity – 'a solution without a problem'. The possibility of applying laser technology to warfare meant that early research was highly secret, stimulating the popular image of the laser as *the* weapon of the future. Subsequently, a large and diverse number of applications were found: laser light shows, measuring and surveying devices, compact discs, computer printers (*see* LASER PRINTER), LASER SURGERY, and, as predicted, beam weapons (*see* LASER BOMB; STAR WARS).

laser bomb A type of bomb guided by a laser beam. An aircraft locks a laser beam onto its target; sophisticated bombs dropped by that aircraft – or accompanying aircraft – then follow the beam. First used in the VIETNAM WAR, they were highly effective during the GULF WAR of 1991 in destroying specific targets and minimizing civilian casualties (known in military jargon as 'collateral damage').

laser cane A type of walking stick for the blind that emits infrared laser radiation. The radiation is reflected by surrounding obstacles and detected by sensors in the cane; the signal is converted into an audible tone, which warns the user of the obstacle.

laser printer A type of printer used with computer systems. A laser beam is scanned across an electrically charged plate and discharges the plate in regions in which the image is required. Particles of pigment adhere to the discharged region; the process is similar to that in a photocopier. Laser printers can produce type similar to that of a typesetting machine and are extensively used in DESKTOP PUBLISHING systems.

laser surgery Surgical treatment using light from a laser. Since the late 1960s the advantages of using a laser beam, which can be focused precisely on a minute area of tissue, have revolutionized some areas of surgery. The main benefits have been in MICROSURGERY and ophthalmic surgery, where lasers have been used to make delicate incisions, selectively destroy damaged or tumorous tissue, seal bleeding blood vessels, and weld breaks in the retina, leaving surrounding tissue uninjured.

Lassa fever A contagious viral disease with a high mortality rate. It was first identified in 1969 in the Nigerian village of Lassa. Symptoms include a high fever, muscle aches, skin rash, mouth ulcers, haemorrhaging under the skin, and heart infection. The disease, thought to be transmitted to humans from mice and rats, occurs chiefly in rural areas of W Africa.

Lasseter's gold reef A seam of gold, reputed to be enormously rich, in the deserts of central Australia, which has so far eluded all searches. The seam, promising untold wealth to anyone who could find it, was said to have been discovered by a prospector called Harold Bell Lasseter in 1897. By 1911 he had raised sufficient funds for an expedition, but he and his companions were driven back by the harsh conditions. In 1930 he tried again. This time he refused to turn back, even when the heat had claimed all the members of his expedition except for two camels; his starved and dehydrated body was subsequently found in a cave. The search for his gold reef continues.

Lassie The doughty collie-dog heroine of Eric Knight's *Lassie Come Home* (1940), a novel for children, which provided the inspiration for a whole series of canine adventure films made by MGM in the 1940s, including *Lassie Come Home* (1943) and *The Courage of Lassie* (1946), both directed by Fred M. Wilcox, *Son of Lassie* (1945; directed by S. Sylvan Simon), and *The Sun Comes Up* (1949; directed by Richard Thorpe). The part of Lassie was actually played by a male dog called Pal; among his co-stars were Roddy McDowell, Elizabeth Taylor, and Jeanette MacDonald. There then followed *Lassie*, a popular and long-running US television series. Lassie has also featured as the heroine in an animated series, *Lassie's Rescue Rangers* (1973–75), and the television film *Lassie: The New Beginning* (1978; directed by Don Chaffey). Lassie returned to the big screen in the musical *The Magic of Lassie* (1978; directed by Chaffey).

last. Last Chance Trendy (LCT) A disparaging epithet applied to a person, particularly a middle-aged man, who attempts to conceal his age by dressing and behaving in a manner more appropriate to a younger person. In the 1970s and 1980s the hallmark of a Last Chance Trendy was hair carefully combed or styled to hide tell-tale bald patches.

last hurrah A final farewell appearance, more-or-less synonymous with 'swan song'. It derives from the US film *The Last Hurrah* (1958), in which a New England political leader (played by Spencer Tracy) undertakes the last campaign of his life.

last night of the Proms *See* PROM.

last of the big spenders An ironic jibe used to describe someone who is careful with money, or even downright mean. It is said to have originated in Australia in the late 1950s.

Last of the Red Hot Mommas The nickname of the vaudeville and cabaret singer Sophie Tucker (1884–1966), born somewhere in Russia as her parents were emigrating to America. Her nickname, derived from the song 'I'm the Last of the Red Hot Mommas', written by Jack Yellen, so suited her brash, often risqué, image and vigorous singing style that it was used in her billing from 1928 for the rest of her career. She was also known as 'Sophie Tuckshop', an allusion to her ample proportions.

last words *See* FAMOUS LAST WORDS.

Las Vegas The principal city of the US state of Nevada, a neon oasis set in the parched wasteland of the Mojave Desert. Famous for its luxury hotels and casinos, which line the 'Strip', it offers 24-hour year-round gambling and cabaret entertainment, often featuring some of the world's greatest show-business stars. Las Vegas means 'the Meadows' in Spanish, so-called from the artesian wells discovered here by the first Spanish settlers. Such a description, however, is no longer appropriate to this modern incarnation of glitzy vulgarity. The city owes its commercial success to the legalization of gambling by the Nevada state authorities in 1931, although it remained a shabby settlement with a few drab gambling halls, quick-wedding chapels, and legalized brothels until the first luxury casino, the Flamingo, was built with mob money in 1946. Since then it has steadily climbed up-market.

latchkey kid A young child whose parents are still at work when he or she returns home after school; the child must therefore carry the key of the house or flat. The problem of children remaining unattended and unsupervised at home began to be widely recognized in the 1960s as a serious side effect of the increasing numbers of working mothers and single-parent families.

lateral thinking An expression coined by the British physician Edward de Bono (1933–) in the mid-1960s to denote a way of thinking or of solving problems by the use of unorthodox or even apparently illogical means rather than by direct logical processes. The concept is explained in de Bono's *The Use of Lateral Thinking* (1967).

Lateran Treaty A treaty concluded between the Holy See and the Kingdom of Italy in 1929, establishing the Vatican City as a sovereign state, thus ending the 'Roman Question' begun in 1870 when the temporal power of the papacy was finally abrogated and Rome became the capital of the Italian Kingdom.

Laughing Murderer of Verdun *See* LITTLE WILLIE.

launch window A short period during which a spacecraft must be launched in order to accomplish its mission successfully. This is contingent on the astronomical conditions prevailing, in particular the relative position of the planets and their satellites, which enables the craft to travel on a path requiring the minimum input of energy. A suitable launch window for a flight from Earth to Venus occurs once every 19 months; one to Mars occurs once in 26 months.

launder. Launderette A self-service laundry (called a **Laundromat** in America) in which customers can wash and dry clothes and other items in coin-operated machines. Both versions are tradenames now loosely used for any such establishments. The social life of the launderette is a feature of many districts, especially the bed-sitter areas of London. Customers are obliged to wait for periods of up to half an hour while their laundry is being washed. Conversation with other customers is usually considered preferable to sitting in silence, watching one's clothes rotate, through the glass window of the washing machine.

laundering A colloquial expression originating in America to describe the process of passing money, which has been illegally obtained, through foreign banks or legitimate commercial enterprises so that it reappears in circulation in a context that makes it appear to have originated legitimately. The term became popular as a result of the WATERGATE inquiry in America (1973–74).

In 1991 the term was used in an official announcement of a new policy in Northern Ireland:

> . . . the Government introduced a new schedule and a new clause to the Bill [the Northern Ireland Emergency Provisions Bill] to create special investigators in Ulster with powers to combat the laundering of the proceeds from terrorist rackets, including money invested in legitimate business.
>
> *The Independent*, 6 February 1991.

Laurasia *See* PANGAEA.

Laurel and Hardy England's thin Arthur Stanley Jefferson (1890–1965) and America's chubby Oliver Norvell Hardy (1892–1957) were Hollywood's most successful comedy team. Stan and Ollie made 104 films between 1926 and 1951, receiving an OSCAR for *The Music Box* (1932), in which they suffered multiple disasters carrying a piano up a long flight of steps. Their humour ranged from subtlety to mayhem: in *Battle of the Century*, a record 3000 pies were thrown. Unlike many silent-film stars, they moved smoothly into sound, their screen chaos often ending with Hardy's exasperated complaint: "This is another fine mess you've gotten us into". Driving force of the team was film-editor

Laurel, who was awarded a special Oscar in 1960 for pioneering cinema comedy. Their characters had universal appeal: fans ranged from Winston Churchill to Joseph Stalin and in Germany they were known as 'Dick and Doof' (fat and dumb). Their films underwent a cult revival in the 1970s and remain popular on videos.

Lausanne Treaty A peace settlement signed on 24 July 1923 between Greece and the newly proclaimed Republic of Turkey, renegotiating the 1920 Treaty of Sèvres, which had been imposed on the Turks by the allied powers after the Ottoman defeat in World War I. In the Lausanne Treaty the Turks agreed to surrender the non-Turkish sections of the former Ottoman Empire; Greece returned Smyrna (Izmir) to Turkey, which also regained Thrace, Adrianople, and the Dodecanese; there was an enforced exchange of national minorities between Greece and Turkey; and the Bosphorous and Dardanelles were demilitarized and opened to international shipping.

Lavalier or **Lavaliere** A pendant worn on a chain around the neck, named after the Duchess of La Vallière, a mistress of Louis XIV who wore this type of jewellery. In the 1960s, the term was extended to a type of microphone hung round the neck of a broadcaster and, further, to a small microphone clipped to the broadcaster's clothing.

Lavender list The controversial resignation honours list drawn up to reward prominent LABOUR PARTY supporters by Harold Wilson in 1976. Among those honoured were the financier James Goldsmith (knighted); Sir Joseph Kagan (life peerage), whose company made the GANNEX raincoats that were Wilson's trademark; and such nonpolitical figures as the television impressionist Mike Yarwood (OBE), whose impersonations of Wilson were legendary. The final list had been amended and typed on lavender-coloured notepaper by Wilson's political secretary Marcia Williams (ennobled as Lady Falkender); apparently Wilson's original list had contained even more controversial figures.

law. Law Commission A UK regulatory body, established in 1965 to monitor the law on a continual basis with a view to its systematic development and reform. The commission has a permanent staff headed by five commissioners – two academics, two lawyers, and a judge – and considers the need for the codification of law, the elimination of anomalies, the repeal of obsolete enactments, and the general simplification and modernization of the law. Issues can be referred to the commission by the government and it is also empowered to investigate any question that may need reform. It produces reports, often accompanied by draft legislation, for the government to introduce into parliament.

Law of December 1 A decree issued in the Soviet Union on 1 December 1934 under the orders of Stalin after the murder of his aide, Sergei Kirov, at Smolny by a deranged gunman (*see* KIROV MURDER). The decree, unprecedented in peacetime, ordered that all investigators should speed up the preparation of cases against suspected terrorists (ten days was set as the maximum preparation period); that all pending death sentences should be carried out at once; and that future executions should be carried out immediately after sentencing, with no leave for appeal. By the end of the month the decree had spurred the arrest, summary trial, and execution of more than 100 suspected 'enemies of the people'. In the next four years a series of purges finally eliminated members of the Bolshevik Old Guard, such as Kamenev and Zinoviev, and thousands of other victims of Stalin's megalomania.

> To those who have served Russia faithfully Stalin has always been a loyal friend and generous colleague. He does not remove a man as Hitler does, nor does he kill by stealth as Mussolini.
>
> G. D. H. COLE, British socialist historian.

Lawrence of Arabia T. E. Lawrence (1888–1935), British soldier, writer, diplomat, and archaeologist, whose place in popular history rests on his role in the ARAB REVOLT against the Turks during World War I. Initially appointed to the Arab forces as an intelligence and liaison officer, he rose to a unique position of influence through his compelling personality, mastery of guerrilla tactics, and ability to adapt himself to Bedouin ways. The transformation of the historical Lawrence into the stuff of legend began soon after the war. The image of the romantic desert paladin was largely created by the US journalist Lowell Thomas (1892–1981), whose illustrated lectures played to huge audiences in 1919. Lawrence's sincere (if confused) attempts to escape the consequences of this fame, by entering the ranks of the RAF under an assumed name (**J. R. Ross** and later **T. E. Shaw**), only increased public fascination. To the image of the war hero was added that of the mystery man or psychological enigma. Further layers of myth have accumulated since Lawrence's death, notably the (historically untenable) view that he was a self-glorifying charlatan who invented most of his exploits. In particular, an aura of mystery has been created around the motorcycle accident in which Lawrence died (*see* BOANERGES). Suggestions of a murder conspiracy have hinged on sightings of a black car near the scene of the crash and false claims that at the time of his death Lawrence was seeking a private meeting with Adolf Hitler. Lawrence's life was the subject of a Terence Rattigan play, *Ross* (1960), in which Alec Guinness played Lawrence, and a David Lean film, *Lawrence of Arabia* (1962), with a script by Robert Bolt and Peter O'Toole in the title role.

lay Slang meaning to have sex with. Originally an Americanism from the early 1900s, it has, since the 1960s, been widely used in the UK. Originally, it was used by men of women, but by the 1970s it was also used by women. In 1987 Hanif Kureishi wrote the script for a film called *Sammy and Rosie Get Laid*. Although most common as a verb, the word is also used as a noun to mean a sexual act or a sexual partner, particularly a potential sexual partner. This usage often appears in such phrases as a **good lay** and an **easy lay**.

lay rubber US slang meaning to drive away very fast, especially from a stationary position. It describes the depositing of rubber from the tyres onto the road surface from the rapidly spinning wheels.

layered look A fashion style of the mid-1970s, in which casual clothes of various types and sizes were worn over each other to create a layered effect. Women might for example, wear a short skirt over jeans or leggings, a large open shirt over a dress or T-shirt, and swathes of overlapping shawls, scarves, sweaters, jackets, and coats. The effect was usually completed by a shoulder bag, ethnic jewellery, and some form of headgear. A version of the look was also adopted by some men. The name itself was coined as early as 1950 by the US fashion designer Bonnie Cashin.

LBJ Lyndon Baines Johnson (1908–1973), the 36th president of America, 1964–68. A Southern Democrat, Johnson became president after the assassination of John F. Kennedy, on 22 November 1963. Subsequently he pushed through his Great Society legislation, an unprecedented programme of civil rights and social welfare measures designed to allieviate some of the country's most pressing racial, social, and economic problems. As a result, he was re-elected as president in 1964 by the greatest majority of the popular vote in the country's history (15 million). However, his unsurpassed domestic achievements were overshadowed by his unwise escalation of the VIETNAM WAR, the economic and human cost of which destroyed his political credibility and crippled the Great Society programme. *See also* LADY BIRD.

LCD Liquid Crystal Display. A device using certain materials, known as liquid crystals, which are normally transparent but become opaque when an electric field is applied. They are used in digital watches, electronic calculators, etc.

LCT *See* LAST CHANCE TRENDY.

LDC Less Developed Country. A term used by some development economists in order to avoid the pejorative implications of describing countries as *under*developed or as belonging to the THIRD WORLD, both of which suggest backwardness. *See also* DEVELOPING COUNTRIES.

LDV Local Defence Volunteers. *See* HOME GUARD.

le. Le Bourget The former international Paris airport, now used only for internal domestic flights. Le Bourget was first used as a military aerodrome in 1917 and became Paris's airport after the end of World War I. It was at Le Bourget that Charles Lindbergh landed on 21 May 1927 after the first solo crossing of the North Atlantic. A new terminal was opened in 1937, which was regarded at the time as the best in the world. However, in the 1970s all major international operations were transferred to the new airport at Roissy-en-France (Charles de Gaulle airport) and to Orly. Besides handling domestic flights, Le Bourget remains the venue for the annual Salon de l'Aéronautique (Air Show), first staged there in 1953, and is also the home of a Musée de l'Air.

Le Corbusier Assumed name (literally 'the crow-like one') of the controversial Swiss-born French architect, Charles-Edouard Jeanneret (1887–1965). One of the dominant figures in the INTERNATIONAL STYLE of modern architecture, Le Corbusier is as renowned for his unfulfilled utopian urban planning, set out in his *The City of Tomorrow* (1924), as for his actual buildings, although his urban vision was partially achieved in his designs for Chandigarh, the new capital of the Punjab, India (1951–54). His early works were based on what he called 'Purism', which sought a pristine clarity of design as reflected in the private Villa Savoye (1929–31) at Poissy, a clean white cube raised on stilts, with open interiors, membranous stucco walls, and massive sliding windows. His tract *Towards an Architecture* (1923) contained his definition of a house as 'a machine for living in'. It also contained his revolutionary ideas on high-rise mass-produced housing, upon which he based his large-scale housing projects, Unité d'Habitation, at Marseilles (1946–52). After 1945 his style became more curvaceous and sculptural, as for example in the Chapel of Notre Dame Du Haut at Ronchamp (1950–55) and in the Parliament building at Chandigarh (begun 1951). These structures also reflected a move towards concrete BRUTALISM, the style with which British architects and town planners in the 1960s and 1970s created so much municipal ugliness.

Le Mans Capital city of the La Sarthe region in NW France, site of the first GRAND PRIX motor race in 1906. In 1923 a 24-hour event for four-seater touring cars was introduced and has been held annually in June ever since. Originally there was no outright winner: entrants qualified for the Rudge-Whitworth Triennial Cup, which was awarded to the car that covered the greatest distance over the first three annual runnings of the event. A Biennial Cup was introduced in 1924 (and survived until the 1955–56 events); in 1928 the event became, officially, a 24-hour race. From 1949, prototypes were allowed to race, as well as production models. The event was originally established to demonstrate the reliability of touring cars; however, the latest high-tech machines produced by German and Italian manufacturers, such as Porsche and Ferrari, bear little relation to the original touring models of the early years when such entrants as Bentley, Alfa Romeo, and Bugatti introduced their sporting cars. In 1955 it was the scene of a horrific crash, the worst in motor-racing history: three cars collided at 150 m.p.h. – one of them, a Mercedes, careered into the crowd, killing 80 people. The race organizers attracted intense criticism for not stopping the race.

LEA Local Education Authority. LEAs were first established by the Education Act (1902) to replace the old system of School Boards, introduced by the previous Act of 1870. Their numbers were then reduced and their functions more clearly defined by the Act of 1944, which also introduced a Minister of Education. LEAs are responsible for the provision of local primary, secondary, and further education as well as the recruitment and payment of teachers. However, the Education Reform Act (1988) has reduced the authority of the LEAs, devolving some of their powers to central government or to the schools themselves, in accordance with the Conservative government's drive in the 1980s for greater accountability and improved standards. For example, schools may now opt out of LEA control and be funded directly by central government; funding for further education is now the responsibility of the National Polytechnic and College Funding Council.

lead. Leadbelly The stage name of the US blues and folk singer Huddie Ledbetter (1888?–1949). The nickname, a corruption of his surname, has several possible origins: his physical strength, his temperamental toughness (he served prison terms for murder, attempted murder, and assault), or the buckshot wound in his stomach.

lead-free or **unleaded** Denoting petrol not treated with the antiknock agent tetraethyl lead. In the 1970s it was recognized that although **leaded petrol** increases the performance of petrol engines, the exhaust fumes produced were the principal cause of lead pollution in the atmosphere. Accumulation of lead in body tissues was linked with high blood pressure, brain damage, and the impairment of growth and learning abilities in children. In America, where the problem was acute, the phasing out of leaded petrol began in the mid-1970s and the production of lead additives fell by over 50% in the five years up to 1980. In the UK, lead-free petrol has been given a price advantage in carrying a lower duty than leaded petrol. Many car engines can be converted to accept lead-free petrol, but high-performance high-compression-ratio engines cannot.

Leaderene, the Nickname for Margaret Thatcher. *See* IRON LADY.

leading edge Literally, the foremost edge of an aeroplane wing or propeller blade. Metaphorically it came to mean advanced or innovative technological development of the 1980s. A **leading-edge development** is one involving the latest technology.

leaf (1) Slang for marijuana. (2) US slang for cocaine made from the leaf of the coca plant.

league. League against Cruel Sports An organization founded in 1924 to campaign for the protection of animals – in particular wild animals and birds 'persecuted for sport'. Among its primary objectives is the abolition of blood sports, especially those involving the use of hounds, such as foxhunting, staghunting, and hare coursing. It operates by means of public-awareness campaigns, peaceful demonstrations, and pressure groups, aimed particularly at lobbying members of parliament and local authorities. It has commissioned a considerable amount of scientific research into the life history and habits of the animals it seeks to protect. It has a membership of 20,000 and publishes a periodical entitled *Wildlife Guardian*. *See also* ANIMAL LIBERATION.

League of Nations An association of the world's nations having at one time about 60 members with headquarters at Geneva. Formed on 10 January 1920, after the end of World War I, it had the essential aim of preventing war as well as promoting other forms of international cooperation. From the outset it was weakened by the refusal of America to participate (although President Woodrow Wilson had played a major part in its foundation) and the exclusion of the Soviet Union. Its achievements were considerable in many fields, but it failed in its primary purpose. It last met on 18 April 1946, being replaced by the UNITED NATIONS, which had been established on 24 October 1945.

lean. lean-burn Said of an internal-combustion engine using a lean fuel mixture (an air-petrol ratio of more that 15:1). This promotes more efficient combustion to increase fuel economy and reduce pollution from such exhaust gases as carbon monoxide.

lean on one's chinstraps An army catchphrase, dating from World War I, meaning to be completely exhausted. For example, a long hard route march may be so draining that it leaves one's head drooping so that metaphorically, if not literally, one's chinstraps provide its only means of support. The phrase has persisted.

leap. leaper British slang for a stimulant drug, such as an amphetamine. It has the opposite effect to that of a **sleeper**, one of the slang names for a tranquillizing drug. Used in the 1960s, the word 'leaper' has largely dropped from use; **upper** or SPEED are the words now widely used for stimulants.

leaping lizards! An old-fashioned US expression of surprise. It was popularized by the heroine of Harold Gray's comic strip *Little Orphan Annie*, which began in 1924. As a 15-minute radio series it lasted into the 1940s. The curly-haired moppet revived the expression in the 1977 Broadway musical *Annie*, which ran for more than 2000 performances and was made into a film (1982; directed by John Huston).

learning curve or **experience curve** A business term for a graph plotting the progress of a trainee in performing a particular task against time. The curve tends to slope sharply at the beginning, as the trainee gains experience of a new production process or technology, then flattens off at the level of an experienced worker. The more complex a particular operation or technology, the steeper the learning curve before achieving the **learning plateau**.

least-worst Not very good but better than any available alternative. The combination of two superlatives adds to the emphasis, although grammatically the phrase should be 'least-bad'. It became popular in the late 1980s.

leather (1) British slang for a middle-aged male socialite with an all-year-round suntan from a life of leisure spent mostly at ski resorts and on fashionable beaches. It is occasionally also used of women. It is the old and lined skin, which becomes leathery in the sun, that gives rise to this unflattering epithet, although there is also the association with the expensive and well-cut leather clothes that such people often wear. (2) Underworld slang for a purse or a wallet.

leather boy (1) Slang from the 1960s for a motorcycle rider; a BIKER. (2) Slang for a young male homosexual or a male prostitute, both of whom often wear leather clothes.

Leather Lungs The nickname of the British singer and actress Elaine Page

(1957–), who appeared on the London stage in the musicals *Hair*, *Jesus Christ Superstar*, and *Grease*, before achieving stardom in the lead role in Andrew Lloyd Webber's *Evita* (1978). She is also a successful pop singer.

leatherneck A US marine. It derives from the custom of the US marine corps of facing the neckband of their uniform with leather.

Lebensraum A German word (room for living) applied especially to the territory desired by a nation for expansion, both for settlement and trade, to meet the population pressures in the mother country. The concept was latched onto by Adolf Hitler in the 1930s as a justification for the expansion of the territories coveted by Nazi Germany. The Nazi interpretation of the word included the forcible removal or murder of the existing non-German population, a policy that underlaid some of the worst atrocities of the period before and during World War II.

Leboyer A method of childbirth that emphasizes 'birth without violence'. It was devised by the French obstetrician Frédérick Leboyer (1918–). To create a peaceful and untraumatic atmosphere for the delivery, the birth takes place in a dark quiet room and the baby is then put in a bath kept at room temperature to simulate intrauterine conditions. This type of natural childbirth, in which the husband is an active participant, first became popular in the early 1970s.

> Birth may be a matter of a moment. But it is a unique one.
>
> F. LEBOYER: *Birth Without Violence*.

lech or **letch** Slang meaning to desire someone sexually, usually heard in the phrase **lech over** or **lech after**. As a noun, meaning a lecherous person, it is generally used contemptuously by women of men. The word is a shortening of 'lecherous'.

lecky British slang for electricity, as in 'If I don't put another 50p in the meter the lecky will go off'. Originally Liverpudlian, the word is now widely used throughout the UK, mostly by working-class speakers.

Leclerc Assumed name of Jean de Hautecloque (1902–47), the French general whose military fame during World War II was second only to that of Charles de Gaulle. A graduate of Saint Cyr Military Academy, he escaped to England soon after the Fall of France and joined the Free French forces under de Gaulle (*see* FIGHTING FRENCH). He then changed his name to Jacques-Phillipe Leclerc to protect his family in France from Nazi reprisals. He distinguished himself as commander of the Free French Army in Chad, fighting in Libya and supporting the allied campaigns in North Africa. He took part in the Normandy landings and achieved lasting fame when his tank division liberated Paris in August 1944. In March 1946 he was given command of the French forces in Indochina and campaigned vigorously against the VIET MINH, although he quickly perceived that a military solution to the guerrilla war was impossible. In July 1946 he was sent as inspector of the French forces to North Africa, where he was killed in a plane crash.

Lee. Bruce Lee (1940–73) US–Chinese film star renowned for his prowess as a practitioner of the martial arts in a series of action-packed low-budget movies, which proved to be an enormous box-office success and the inspiration behind the kung-fu cult. He was born in San Francisco, the son of a Chinese opera star, was brought up in Hong Kong, where he first received instruction in the martial arts, and later returned to America as a student. He worked briefly as a television actor in America but the films which brought his meteoric rise to fame were all made in Hong Kong, including *Fist of Fury* (1972), *Enter the Dragon* (1973), and *The Way of the Dragon* (1973). He died suddenly and in mysterious circumstances aged 33, after which he became something of a cult figure.

Gypsy Rose Lee Stage name of Rose Louise Hovick (1914–70), US striptease artist who was noted for the wit, sophistication, and style she introduced to her craft. Together with her sister (later the actress, June Havoc), she joined her mother on the vaudeville circuit at a very early age. At 14 she had her first engagement in burlesque; within two years she was on Broadway, heading the bill at Billy Minsley's Republic Theatre. Dubbed the 'Queen of Burlesque', she was lionized by some of New York's most celebrated writers and intellectuals, becoming a regular contributor to such publications as *Harper's* and *The New Yorker*. In 1937 she announced her retirement as a stripper; she then moved to Hollywood to make her film debut, in *You Can't Have Everything*. Over the next three decades she played in a further eight, generally rather mediocre, films including *Belle of the Yukon* (1944), *Screaming Mimi* (1958), and *The Trouble with Angels* (1966). She quite regularly emerged from retirement to make stage appearances and wrote two popular thrillers, *The G-string Murders* and *Mother Finds a Body*. Her autobiographical book, *Gypsy* (1957), formed the basis for a successful Broadway musical of the same name (1959) and later for a rather less successful film version (1962).

God is love, but get it in writing.
GYPSY ROSE LEE.

Lorelei Lee Archetypal gold-digging dumb blonde, the central character of Anita Loos' satire, *Gentlemen Prefer Blondes* (1925), and its sequel *But Gentlemen Marry Brunettes* (1928). Originally a novel, *Gentlemen Prefer Blondes* was adapted for the stage (1925) and for the silent screen (1928, directed by Mal St Clair); it was the basis for a stage musical (1949), and was updated for a musical film starring Marilyn Monroe (1953; directed by Howard Hawks).

left brain *See* RIGHT BRAIN.

leg. Four legs good, two legs bad The essence of 'Animalism' as described in chapter three of *Animal Farm* (1945), the political satire by George Orwell (1903–50). Animalism originally comprised seven commandments inspired by the teachings of old Major, the prize Middle White boar, and codified by one of the pigs, Snowball. These proved too difficult for some of the stupider farm animals to understand, so Snowball reduced the commandments to this single maxim, implying that all animals (four legs) are good and all humans (two legs) are bad. Here Orwell is parodying the reduction of complex issues to simple formulas or slogans in socialist societies, which he regarded as invidious and intellectually stultifying.

get one's leg over or **get one's leg across** Vulgar British slang euphemism meaning to have sex. It is used of men either by men ('Did you get your leg over last night?') or by women ('All he wants is to get his leg over').

leg it British slang meaning to run away or escape. Originally an expression popular with both the underworld and the police, it was used especially of running away from the scene of a crime. The expression acquired wider currency in the late 1980s among middle-class speakers, when it was fashionable to imitate earlier underworld idioms.

legless British slang for drunk, to the point of being totally incapacitated and unable to stand.

leg-opener Slang for an alcoholic drink, referring to its alleged seductive effects on women. It was coined, presumably by allusion to **eye-opener**, for the first drink of the day.

legwarmers A pair of thick stockings without feet, normally worn over tights or trousers and usually knitted in bright colours. They are worn during exercises, such as AEROBICS, and for ballet and other dance rehearsals.

legal aid Financial help from public funds given on an income-and capital-related scale to those who, unassisted, would not be able to meet the cost of legal advice or representation. This has enabled the poorer members of the community to make use of the processes of the law. Still unable to do so are the large number of people who earn too much or have too much capital to qualify for legal aid but for whom risking an expenditure of many thousands, or tens of thousands, of pounds is unthinkable. Litigation in the UK is now therefore restricted to the very rich and the very poor.

legionnaire's disease A form of pneumonia caused by the bacterium *Legionella pneumophilia*. It was first described after 182 delegates to an American Legion Convention in Philadelphia in July 1976 were struck down by a mystery illness, resulting in 29 deaths. The bacterium causing the illness was subsequently identified and named after its victims. Growth of the bacterium is encouraged by warm conditions (20–50°C), and the most common sources of infection are air-conditioning ducts, water tanks, and warm-water plumbing systems. The symptoms include headache, fever, cough, and possibly chest pain, nausea, vomiting and diarrhoea, following an incubation period of 2–10 days. Severe respiratory or renal complications may follow, especially in the sick or elderly. The illness can be successfully treated with antibiotics, especially erythromycin. Mass outbreaks are uncommon, especially now that architects and engineers are aware of the risk.

Lego The tradename for toy plastic bricks that can be fitted together with other plastic components, such as wheels, windows, and human figures, to construct buildings, vehicles, etc. Invented in Denmark in the 1930s and marketed throughout the world since the 1950s, it takes its name from the Danish words, *leg godt*, meaning play well. The tallest Lego tower ever made was constructed in Tel Aviv in 1990: 18.15 m (59.5 ft) high, it was composed of 221,560 bricks.

leisure centre A building or building complex, sometimes owned and run by a local council, offering facilities for a variety of sporting and leisure activities. The growth of leisure centres in the UK was a phenomenon of the 1980s.

lend-lease Reciprocal agreements made by America with the UK and the Allied forces in World War II to foster the pooling of resources. The policy began with the destroyers (*see* RUM RUNNERS) sent to the UK in return for naval and air bases in parts of the British Commonwealth, and was formalized by the Lend-Lease Act of March 1941. When lend-lease ended in 1945 America had received somewhat less than one-sixth, in monetary terms, of what she had expended in aid to her allies, over 60% of which went to the Commonwealth. Winston Churchill's original request for US aid – "Give us the tools, and we will finish the job" – was later paraphrased by the Ethiopian emperor Haile Selassie with reference to British aid to Ethiopia, which enabled the Ethiopians to liberate their country from the Italians in 1941:

> "We have finished the job, what shall we do with the tools?"

Lenin Adopted name of Vladimir Ilyich Ulyanov (1870–1924), Russian revolutionary and founder of the modern Soviet Union. Lenin was deeply scarred by the execution of his elder brother, Alexander, by Tsarist police in 1887, after he had attempted to assassinate the Tsar. As a result, after leaving university he became a professional revolutionary. In 1900 he joined other Marxists in exile in Europe, waiting and preparing for the ideal moment to launch the revolution in Russia. He placed his faith in the idea of the Party as the engine of revolutionary class consciousness and 'vanguard of the proletariat'. At a conference of the Russian Social Democratic Workers Party in London in 1903, the majority (BOLSHEVIKS) supported Lenin's proposals for the organization and revolutionary role of the party. After the collapse of the Tsarist government in March 1917, Lenin returned to Russia (with the connivance of Germany); with the aid of the Bolshevik-organized Red Guard, he overthrew the provisional government in October, seizing power in the name of the people. He suffered a stroke in 1922 and died in 1924, leaving behind in his writings a legacy of applied Marxism (*see* LENINISM) and a final 'Testament' (*see* LENIN'S TESTAMENT), warning colleagues against the choice of STALIN as his successor. His body lies in state in a mausoleum in Red Square in Moscow, where Russians and tourists daily queue up to file past the uncovered coffin.

Leningrad The name given in 1924 to Petrograd which, until 1914, was known as St Petersburg, the former capital of Tsarist Russia founded by Peter the Great in 1703.

Leningrad purge The purge of the Leningrad Communist Party organization in 1949–59 following the death of the Leningrad party boss Andrei Zhdanov on 31 August 1948. The purge was carried out by Abakumov, the ruthless head of SMERSH during World War II, and was probably initiated by Georgy Malenkov and P. Beria to eliminate supporters of Zhdanov, who had been Malenkov's chief rival for STALIN's favour. As well as A. A. Kuznetsov, a Central Committee member, and Nikolay Voznesensky, a Politburo member, over 2000 lesser functionaries from the Leningrad party were executed.

Leninism or **Marxist-Leninism** LENIN's ideological elaboration of Marxist political and economic thought and its practical adaptation to contemporary conditions of industrially underdeveloped and primarily agricultural societies, such as Russia in the early 20th century. In *Imperialism – The Highest Stage of Capitalism* (1916) he analysed the nature and origins of imperialistic monopoly capitalism; unlike Marx, he stressed the revolutionary potential of pre-capitalist societies and the importance of a worker-peasant alliance in achieving revolution. In *What is to be Done* (1902) he emphasized the indispensible role of a disciplined professional communist party as the "vanguard of the proletariat". *Left-wing Communism* (1920) has the benefit of Lenin's unique practical experience, emphasizing the importance of flexibility and pragmatism in achieving revolutions and then in sustaining communist authority. In this last book Lenin diverges significantly from the economic and historical determination of orthodox Marxism.

Lenin Prize An award granted for outstanding scientific, technical, and cultural achievements, established in 1950 as the Soviet counterpart to the NOBEL PRIZES. The winner of the Lenin Prize is announced on 1 May annually.

Lenin's Testament A two-part document intended as LENIN's final instructions to his colleagues in a future Communist Party Congress, dictated on 23–25 December 1922 and 4 January 1923. The first section contained advice on necessary political reforms and the second concise portraits of six party leaders (Stalin, Trotsky, Zinoviev, Kamenev, Bukharin, and Pyatakov). In the latter he warned against Stalin's accumulation of personal power, criticized him as being too rude, and advised that he be removed as secretary general of the party. After Lenin's death in January 1924 the Testament was made known to the Central Committee, who failed to act on its recommendations; Stalin then suppressed its wider dissemination within the Soviet Union. Thirty years later, Khushchev read the text to the 20th Party Congress on 25 February 1956, three years after Stalin's death, which marked the beginning of the process of DE-STALINIZATION.

Order of Lenin The highest decoration in the Soviet Union, established by the Presidium of the Supreme Soviet in 1930. It is conferred for outstanding service in various fields, including medicine, science and technology, defence, agriculture, education, fine arts, music, film, theatre, and literature. The recipient is presented with a gold medal and enjoys income-tax exemption, pension rights, transport privileges, and monthly payments.

Leopold and Loeb murder A US criminal case of 1924 involving the kidnap and murder of 14-year old Bobby Franks, the son of millionaire businessman Jacob Franks, by two teenage students from prominent families, Richard Loeb and Nathan Leopold. According to Loeb, who broke down under police questioning, Leopold had relished the intellectual challenge of committing the perfect murder undetected and then enlisted Loeb's aid in coolly executing his plan. The two were defended at their trial in July 1924 by the brilliant and controversial lawyer Clarence Darrow, who successfully appealed against the imposition of the death penalty. Loeb was killed in a homosexual brawl in 1936; Leopold served 33 years and was released in 1958.

> If I were not positive that my glasses were at home, I would say these are mine.
>
> NATHAN LEOPOLD, when shown his own glasses, which he had dropped at the scene of the crime.

lergi *See* LURGY.

les be friends An outrageous play on the word 'lesbian', probably first uttered in his inimitable camp voice by the British comedian, Kenneth Williams, in the BBC radio comedy series of the 1950s and 1960s, *Beyond Our Ken* and *Round the Horne*, in which he featured with Kenneth Horne.

letch *See* LECH.

Letraset Tradename for a transfer lettering system used by designers, artists, etc. It enables letters printed on a special backing to be transferred to another surface by the application of pressure to the backing sheet. The original product was introduced in 1963 by John Davis and Frederick Mackenzie of London. The name is loosely applied to other imitative products.

Let's blow, Crow US catchphrase used frequently by GIs and others in the 1940s, meaning 'Let's get out of this place'. 'Blow' meaning to leave dates back to the 1920s and, by the late 1940s the US radio detective Sam Space often talked of "blowing town". Another wartime phrase with the same meaning was **Let's take a powder**.

letter bomb, mail bomb, or **parcel bomb** A small explosive device hidden in, or disguised as, a letter or parcel. It is set to detonate when opened and posted to a victim. This tactic remains popular with such terrorist groups as the IRA, although the intended target is rarely the victim; more usually this is the secretary opening the mail or employees of the post office.

Lewis gun A type of gas-operated air-cooled light machine gun, taking its name from its inventor, US army officer Isaac Newton Lewis (1858–1931). It was used widely in World War I and was the first machine gun to be attached to an aircraft.

Leyte Gulf, Battle of the The sea and air battle on 23–26 October 1944, which crippled the Japanese Combined Fleet and enabled the US forces to recapture the Philippines. The battle was precipitated by the US amphibious assault on Leyte, the middle island in the Philippine group, on 20 October. The Japanese had formulated a plan, codenamed Sho-Go (Victory Operation), to split their fleet into four squadrons: two of these approached the Gulf through the Surigao Straits to the south, while another decoyed powerful elements of the US fleet away from the Leyte beaches allowing the remaining elements, commanded by Admiral Kurita, to attack the US invasion fleet through the San Bernardino Straits to the north. The plan nearly succeeded, but at the last moment Admiral Kurita retreated to salvage the remains of his forces, which had suffered heavy bombardment from the planes of the US navy; this enabled the superior US firepower to overwhelm the other elements of the Japanese fleet.

LGM Little Green Men. Mythical creatures from other worlds coming to visit the Earth in spaceships, usually FLYING SAUCERS or other UFOs. The phrase 'little green men' originated in the 1950s and was probably the result of illustrations in early science-fiction magazines. As science fiction became more sophisticated, the term became less common. However, in 1967 it came back into prominence in a more scientific environment – the radio-astronomy department at Cambridge University. Here the radio astronomer Antony Hewish (1924–) initiated a project to study the fluctuations of radio signals from space caused by ionized gas. His research student, Jocelyn Bell (1943–), was given the job of analysing the data from the university's radiotelescope. She noticed some unusual regular signals appearing – pulses of radio waves occurring every 1.337,301,13 seconds with a period measured to an accuracy better than one part in 100 million. One theory proposed at the time was that the source of the signals were LGM – 'little green men' from extraterrestrial civilizations attempting to make contact with the Earth. In fact, Jocelyn Bell had found the first example of a PULSAR (a 'pulsating star'). Hewish, together with the Cambridge astronomer Martin Ryle (1918–), shared the 1974 Nobel Prize for physics for this work. There was some controversy about the fact that Bell did not share in the prize. The first pulsar might once have been called 'Bell's star', but in fact is known as CP1919.

Liberal. Liberal Democrats *See* SOCIAL AND LIBERAL DEMOCRATIC PARTY.

Liberal Landslide The Liberal Party victory at the general election of January 1906, which represented an overwhelming public endorsement of the new Liberal government formed by Henry Campbell-Bannerman in December 1905. The Liberals, capitalizing upon the Conservative Party's disagreement on TARIFF REFORM, won 400 seats, giving them a technical majority of 130 over all other parties. However, they could also count on the support of the Irish Nationalist members (83) and those of the Labour Representation Committee (29), which gave the Liberals the largest working majority of any government since 1832.

Liberal Nationals or **National Liberals** Those Liberals who supported the NATIONAL GOVERNMENTS formed after the financial crisis of 1931 and remained in close cooperation with the Conservative Party. *See* NATIONAL LIBERAL PARTY.

Lib-Lab A Labour representative elected to parliament as a Liberal before the foundation of the LABOUR PARTY in 1906. The Lib-Labs were dominant in working-class politics during the period 1860–1880 but economic instability and unemployment, growing class-consciousness, the enfranchisement of manual workers in 1867 and 1884, and the failure of the Liberal Party to meet workers' aspirations, led to the foundation of the Labour Representation Committee in February 1900. This officially became the Labour Party after the election of 1906. The last Lib-Lab MPs joined the Labour Party in 1909, together with the Miners Federation, which sponsored them.

The name was revived in the late 1970s for the **Lib-Lab pact** (1977–78), an arrangement made between the Liberal Party under the leadership of David Steel and the minority Labour government of James Callaghan, in which the Liberals agreed to support the government in return for consultation rights.

liberation. Liberation Day The day (9 May) on which the Channel Islands celebrate their liberation in 1945 from German occupation. The anniversary is marked throughout the islands by an annual public holiday.

liberation theology A form of theology, most widely discussed in a South American context; it is based on the creation of links between the tenets of Catholicism and those of left-wing political theory. The most important proposition is that spiritual freedom should be linked to social and economic freedom. Because this suggests a formal connection between the

Catholic church and the Marxist movement, the Roman Catholic hierarchy has condemned liberation theology in spite of the good work done in its name.

Libermanism A series of liberal reforms of the Soviet economy proposed by Evsei Liberman of the University of Kharkov and published in a series of articles in *Pravda* in 1962. The measures were designed to shift the emphasis away from rigid centralized planning towards the operation of free market forces, allowing investment and production decisions to be based on costs and market forces, with workers and managers rewarded on the basis of profits. Libermanism was introduced in a hesitant and partial manner by Khrushchev and then later by Prime Minister Kosygin, but met with opposition from powerful vested interests and was effectively smothered by the early 1970s, until similar measures were introduced by Gorbachov in the late 1980s.

liberty. Liberty bodice A close-fitting sleeveless vestlike undergarment worn mainly by children. It was manufactured by R. & W. H. Symington and marketed in the 1900s under an agreement made with Liberty & Co., the London store. Apart from a modified ladies version, production of the Liberty bodice ceased in the 1960s.

Liberty Island The new name given in 1956 to Bedloe's Island in upper New York Bay. The 12-acre site is home to the Statue of Liberty, erected there in 1886. During the statue's 100th anniversary, 5000 new citizens were sworn in during a ceremony on Liberty Island. The American Museum of Immigration is also here. *See also* ELLIS ISLAND.

liberty ships Standardized prefabricated cargo ships of about 10,000 tons much used by America during World War II. At one point during the war liberty ships were being built in just four days.

Librium A tradename of the tranquillizer chlordiazepoxide, introduced in America in the 1960s by Roche Laboratories. The mock-Latin name has no meaning, but is sufficiently close to 'equilibrium' to provide the desired implications. The drug was widely prescribed in the 1960s and 1970s; **libs**, as the capsules were known among addicts, were also widely abused.

lick US drug-abusers' slang for smoking CRACK by sucking the smoke from a smouldering piece of crack through a small glass pipe.

lick one's chops Slang for showing great desire or anticipation. This original reference to the production of saliva in anticipation of eating something desirable is still predominant; it is also now applied to sexual and other desires.

licks In rock music, a short improvised solo that briefly interrupts the melody, such as electric-guitar licks. The word comes from 1920s use by JAZZ musicians and probably derives from a 'lick' meaning a try. *See also* RIFF.

> Crafty songwriting, plenty of little stories, and new bluesy licks.
>
> Review of a rock band in *The Independent*, 14 February 1991.

licorice stick US Black slang for a clarinet. This comparison to the popular sweet was first used by JAZZ musicians in the mid-1930s. The jazz clarinet was described by one enthusiast as "An ill woodwind that nobody blows good!"

Lidice A mining village in Czechoslovakia, NW of Prague, which was destroyed by the Germans on 10 June 1942 in reprisal for the assassination of Reinhard Heydrich, Reich Protector of Bohemia and Moravia, by the Czech underground. The assassins had no direct connection with Lidice, which was chosen at random to intimidate and subdue Czech resistance. The SS rounded up the population and shot 173 men and transported 198 women and 98 children to Ravensbrück concentration camp. Of these 98 children only 13 survived, being selected as racially pure and dispersed throughout Germany to be raised as Aryan Nazis. The village was then burned and dynamited and the area levelled. After the war one of the officials responsible for the atrocity, Karl Hermann Frank, Hitler's deputy in Prague, was executed, and another, Police General Kurt Dalvege, committed suicide in a Nuremburg jail. The site was made into a memorial garden after the war.

lie. lie detector A US invention that originally recorded the heartbeats of a person under questioning. It is based on the assumption that a human being cannot tell a lie without an increase in pulse rate. More modern instruments, called POLYGRAPHS, also measure blood pressure, respiration rate, and skin conductivity, changes in these parameters also being believed to accompany the stress that occurs when a lie is told. Lie detectors are not usually accepted as evidence in British courts of law.

lie down and I'll fan you A services catchphrase, particularly associated with the RAF, used to rebuff anyone making an unacceptably demanding or outrageous request. In use since the 1920s, it originated in India and alluded to the risks of feverish excitement in fellow servicemen in a hot climate. The colonial Britons employed punka wallahs to operate the large fans used for cooling their quarters; it is this practice that is thought to have inspired the phrase.

life. Life begins at forty *See under* FORTY.

lifeboat In financial jargon, a fund set up by dealers on an exchange, *e.g.* a stock exchange or commodity exchange, to rescue any firms in danger of insolvency in the event of a collapse in the market. If such a collapse occurs, the single insolvency of a main dealer could bring many other firms down with it. It is therefore in the market's interest to protect its members against the consequences of unexpectedly large falls in prices.

lifeboat ethics The ethical adjustments required in certain extreme situations, in which (it is claimed) practical good can only be achieved by setting aside one's normal humanitarian instincts. The phrase alludes to the plight of passengers in an overcrowded lifeboat, faced with the choice of throwing some of their number overboard or of all sinking together. A related concept is **triage**: the idea that when the ability to do good is limited, help should be given to those most likely to benefit from it rather than those in greatest need. Triage was orginally a World War I medical term (from French *trier*, to sort) for the practice of sorting battlefield casualties into those considered treatable and those quietly left to die. More recently, both phrases have been used to advocate a variety of apparently unsympathetic policies – notably withdrawing aid from poor countries on the grounds that their economies are beyond help and resources available could be better deployed elsewhere.

> At the very least, many Americans are now being forced to exercise "family triage". For example, a parent may save up to pay for a child's dental treatment before finding the money for his wife's mammogram.
>
> *The Times*, 3 May 1991.

Life Force *See* CREATIVE EVOLUTION; ÉLAN VITAL.

life is just a bowl of cherries A cliché now employed only with heavy irony; it started life as the title of a song by US composer Ray Henderson written to lyrics by Lew Brown for the Broadway show *George White's Scandals of* **1931**.

lifemanship A word and concept introduced by the British writer Stephen Potter (1900–69) in *Some Notes on Lifemanship* (1950). This applied GAMESMANSHIP to the practice of social relations. *Lifemanship* includes comical guidance on the art of Weekendmanship, Woomanship, and Newstatesmanship. *See also* ONE-UPMANSHIP.

> If you have nothing to say, or, rather, something extremely stupid and obvious, say it, but in a 'plonking' tone of voice – i.e. roundly, but hollowly and dogmatically.
>
> *Some Notes on Lifemanship.*

lifestyle A word that became popular in the 1980s to describe the manner in which people live their lives. It rapidly became a buzz word, much used by the media and advertisers trying to direct specific products at people with an appropriate lifestyle. The term 'lifestyle' is more often used to describe an affluent and successful way of life than to characterize the poor.

life wasn't meant to be easy A cliché widely heard in the late 1970s after its use by the Australian prime minister Malcolm Fraser, in reference to current government policies.

> It occurred to me that there are times when life is a little easier than it's meant to be.
>
> Speech to the Liberal Party, 1977.

liftoff The instant that a rocket blasts free from its launching pad. The term entered the language during the period of America's manned space flights in the 1960s. *See also* ALL SYSTEMS GO.

ligger British slang popularized in the 1970s for someone who is a gatecrasher, taking advantage of other people's hospitality, food, etc., especially in the rock-music and entertainment industry.

light. light pen (1) A penlike device with a photosensor in its tip that can be touched to a computer screen to draw diagrams and shapes or to select items from a displayed MENU. (2) A similar light-sensitive device used to read a BAR CODE, such as those found on magazines or packaged food products.

light pollution Extraneous light from street lighting, neon signs, etc., in populated areas. Of little interest to the public at large, it is regarded as 'pollution' by astronomers because it interferes with telescope observations of the night sky.

the light on the hill The oft-quoted objective of the Australian Labor Party, introduced in a speech by J. B. Chifley in 1949. It is synonymous with 'the light at the end of the tunnel', but in Australia, at least, acquired a particular relevance to socialism and became a standard phrase in the repertory of all that country's socialist leaders. It represents the ideal that no person should be deprived of the hope that hc can improve his lot in society.

like A word used in a number of unusual and ungrammatical contexts; it is added without meaning to a statement, such as 'The world is like crazy' or 'Like your argument is like useless'. It was first used by BEATNIKS and JAZZ musicians in the 1950s and then by HIPPIES in the 1960s and 1970s as part of their COOL philosophy of making detached and often not very profound or original assertions. It also enables speakers to gather their thoughts, in the same manner as 'uh' or 'you know'.

Likud A political coalition which, under the successive leadership of Menachem Begin and Yitzhak Shamir, was the outright governing power in Israel between May 1977 and November 1984, and since then, under Shamir, has formed a series of coalition governments. Formed in 1973, it consisted of various right-wing organizations, principally the Gahal bloc, comprising the Herut (Freedom) Party, which formally emerged in 1948 (the year of Israel's independence), and the Liberal Party, itself an amalgamation formed in 1961 of the former General Zionist and Progressive parties.

Li'l Abner The handsome hillbilly character of the long-running newspaper comic strip created by the US cartoonist Alfred G. Caplin in 1934, which continued into the 1970s. The character was played on screen by Granville Owen in a 1940 film and a later stage musical was also filmed in 1959 starring Peter Palmer in the title role.

Lili Marlene A German song of World War II (based on a poem written by a German soldier, Hans Leip, in 1917) composed by Norbert Schultze in 1938 and sung by the German singer Lale Andersen. It became increasingly popular during the 1940s, especially with the AFRIKA KORPS, and the recorded version was played nightly by Radio Belgrade from the late summer of 1941, virtually until the end of hostilities. Other German stations plugged it and it was picked up and adopted by the British Eighth Army, the English version of the lyric being by T. Connor. There were French, Italian, and numerous other renderings of what became the classic song of the war. It was featured, both in German and English, by the German-born star Marlene Dietrich (1901–), who emphasized its international appeal. Perhaps it was after hearing her sing 'Lili Marlene' that Ernest Hemingway wrote:

> If she had nothing but her voice, she could break your heart with it. But she also has that beautiful body and the timeless loveliness of her face.

See also BACKROOM BOYS.

Li-Lo An inflatable rubber mattress. Originally a registered (1936) tradename of P. B. Cow & Co. The word is now used loosely for any brand of airbed.

Lima Declaration A declaration by the Eighth International Pan-American Conference, which met in Lima, Peru, in December 1938, affirming American continental solidarity and collective security in the face of any foreign threat to its political or territorial integrity. The declaration was prompted by President Roosevelt's determination to secure the American republics against European totalitarianism, although many of the South American signatories harboured Fascist sympathies in preference to US democratic values.

limbo A West Indian dance, popularized in the 1950s, in which dancers bend backwards to pass beneath a horizontal bar that is lowered after each try. Often the dance continues until only one dancer remains.

Lime. Harry Lime The unscrupulous villain played by Orson Welles in *The Third Man* (1942), a remarkably poetic and exciting film directed by Carol Reed and scripted by Graham Greene (*The Third Man* was published by Greene as a novella in 1950). Lime, a shady figure who appears only briefly in the doorways, fairgrounds, and sewers of post-war Vienna, has a hospital contact who supplies him with penicillin, which Lime sells on the black market. As a result, the diluted penicillin left in the hospital fails to cure the sick children to whom it is administered. Lime justifies himself to his American friend Holly:

In Italy for 30 years under the Borgias they had warfare, terror, murder, bloodshed and they produced Michelangelo, Leonardo da Vinci and the Renaissance. In Switzerland they had brotherly love, 500 years of democracy and peace and what did they produce? The cuckoo clock.

It is said that Orson Welles himself added these lines to Graham Greene's script. The success of the film probably rested on the combination of a number of skills: the acting, the direction, the scriptwriting, the photography, and the haunting INCIDENTAL MUSIC of Anton Karas and his zither.

Lime Grove The old Rank Film Studios in Shepherd's Bush, London, which were acquired in November 1949 by the BBC. Lime Grove, a seven-storey building housing five studios, offered far superior facilities to the BBC's former cramped two-studio accommodation at Alexandra Palace. Broadcasting began from Studio D (Children's Programmes), the first of the new studios to open, in May 1950.

Limehouse or **Limehousing** Once commonly used for violent abuse of one's political opponents: so called from a speech by Lloyd George at Limehouse, London, on 30 July 1909, when he poured scorn and abuse on dukes, landlords, financial magnates, etc. In 1981 four former cabinet ministers (*see* GANG OF FOUR) issued the **Limehouse Declaration**, launching the Social Democratic Party.

limousine Originally, a large car in which the driver was separated from the passengers by a partition. Later it was used of any large and luxurious car, especially in North America, where it is often abbreviated to **limo**. It is derived from the French *limousine* (a cloak, originally a hooded cloak once worn by the inhabitants of the province of Limousin).

limousine liberal A derogatory term for a person with liberal political leanings, who also has a great deal of personal wealth. The implication is that it is easy to have liberal views in the back of a chauffeur-driven limousine. Largely a US expression, it has a British counterpart in **champagne socialist**.

limp-wristed A derogatory adjective used to describe a male homosexual. It is supposed to describe the CAMP and ineffectual wrist and hand movements of such a person.

Lincoln Center The Lincoln Center for the Performing Arts (1957–67), a complex in New York City that includes the Metropolitan Opera House (1966), New York Philharmonic Concert Hall (1962), New York State Theatre (1964; home to the NYC Opera, NYC Ballet and other groups), and the Juilliard School of Music (1967). The buildings flank a Michelangelo-style piazza, similar in concept to the Capitoline in Rome, and were designed by a team of architects including Philip Johnson, Max Abramovitz, and Eero Saarinen, coordinated by Wallace K. Harrison.

Lindbergh. Lindbergh baby murder A criminal case involving the kidnap and murder of the 20-month-old baby son of the US aviator Charles A. Lindbergh (1902–74) in March 1932. Lindbergh (or 'Lindy') had become enormously famous as a result of his first non-stop solo flight from New York to Paris (1927) in his monoplane SPIRIT OF ST LOUIS. The world was appalled by the case and a nationwide hunt resulted, with offers of help from the jailed Al CAPONE, among many others. In May the baby's body was found in a shallow grave – he had died from a blow to the head on the night of the kidnap. Painstaking investigation by the police led eventually to the arrest in September of a German-born carpenter, Bruno Richard Hauptmann, who had entered America illegally in 1923. Given Lindbergh's celebrity status, the trial in January 1935 was a media circus. Hauptmann was sent to the electric chair in April 1936. However, his conviction has been the subject of considerable controversy ever since and his innocence was argued by Ludovic Kennedy in his book *The Airman and the Carpenter* (1984). One theory is that the kidnap was staged by friends of Capone, seeking his release from prison. Whatever the truth was, 'Lindy' turned his back on US society and spent the next five years in Europe, an embittered man.

Lindbergh jacket A style of waist-length jacket, which was popular in the 1930s in imitation of the flying-jacket worn by the US aviator Charles A. Lindbergh.

lindy hop or **lindy** The vigorous JITTERBUG dance of the 1930s, named after transatlantic solo pilot Charles A. Lindbergh. The lindy hop version of jitterbugging was performed to JAZZ or SWING music and introduced the hip twists and pelvic gyrations that became a feature of many subsequent dances.

line British slang for a single dose of cocaine, or other drug in powder form, that is sprinkled in a straight line on a mirror, or similar hard flat surface, and sniffed into the nose through a straw or a rolled-up banknote.

Linear B script A syllabic version of Greek (also called Mycenaen Greek), dating from *c.* 1400 to *c.* 1150 BC, most examples of which have been discovered in recent years on fragments of tablet at Knossos in Crete, Mycenae, and areas of the Greek mainland. It was so named by Sir Arthur Evans (1851–1941) to distinguish it from the hieroglyphics which preceded the linear form. The script was deciphered in 1952 by the British architect Michael Ventris (1922–56) and is thought to be either derived from, or parallel to, Linear A (*c.* 2000–*c.* 1500 BC), which cannot yet be read.

linkage A political compromise in which unrelated issues and demands are discussed in an effort to resolve one or both of them. This was greatly used by Secretary of State Henry Kissinger during international negotiations in the 1970s. The most recent example was the effort during the 1991 GULF WAR by Iraq's Saddam Hussein to link his withdrawal from Kuwait with the question of an independent Palestinian state.

> The two countries [America and the Soviet Union] also offered to work together for peace between Arabs and Israelis after the war ends. Mr. Bessmertnykh [Soviet foreign minister] denied that there was "linkage" between the two issues.
>
> *The Times*, 30 January 1991.

Lion of Judah The title of Haile Selassie (1892–1975), emperor of Ethiopia from 1930 to 1974 except for the years of the Italian occupation of Ethiopia (1936–41), during which he lived in exile in the UK. In 1974 he was deposed by a military coup and Ethiopia was declared a socialist state. He is regarded by RASTAFARIANS as the Messiah, the incarnation of God. The name 'Rastafarian' comes from Haile Selassie's real name, Ras Tafari Makonnen. He assumed the title Haile Selassie, meaning 'Might of the Trinity', when he became emperor. The lion is the emblem of the tribe of Judah, Christ sometimes being referred to as 'the lion of the tribe of Judah'. Other titles of the emperor of Ethiopia have included Conquering Lion of the Tribe of Judah, King of Kings of Ethiopia, and Elect of God.

lip. lipstick US college slang from the 1970s for a fashionably and femininely dressed lesbian. A lipstick is the opposite of a **crunchie**, the more aggressive, austerely and masculinely dressed, lesbian.

lipsynch To pretend to sing or talk by silently moving the lips in synchronization to a recording. Long used by Hollywood, this became an acceptable mode in the 1960s for performing on stage and television. Singers could mime their own recorded songs in order to replay the original quality and retain studio sound devices, such as an echo chamber.

read my lips An expression meaning 'Listen very carefully to what I have to say'. It often implies that the speaker thinks that the listener is stupid. The phrase's present popularity began when George Bush used it in his nomination speech on 19 August 1988. He promised not to raise taxes whatever Congress tried to do to make him:

> I'll say no, and they'll push, and I'll say no, and they'll push again, and I'll say to them, 'Read my lips, no new taxes'.

The serious British press omitted this line from their transcripts of the speech, probably considering it another unfortunate example of Bush's low-brow speech patterns. However, it remains the enduring example of the use of this phrase, even though it is often misquoted as 'watch my lips'. In the UK the phrase had been used as an album title in 1978 by Tim Curry and it also appeared in several rock songs in the 1980s. Arnold Schwarznegger amusingly echoed this phrase with the slogan for the President's Council on Physical Fitness, of which he is head:

> Read my hips, no more fat.

liposuction A surgical method of slimming in which fat cells are permanently removed from such areas of the body as the stomach, hips, and upper arms, generally regarded with horror by all but the most obsessive slimmers. After administering a local anaesthetic, the surgeon makes a small incision and uses a syringe-like instrument to draw out the fat cells.

liquid. liquid crystal display *See* LCD.

liquidizer An electrical kitchen appliance with blades that can cut, purée, mix, and blend. It is also called a blender, especially in America, where it was first sold in the 1960s to mix crushed-ice alcoholic drinks, such as frozen daiquiris. Modern models can blend soups, chop nuts, purée vegetables or fruit, grate cheese, and make mousses and frothy sweets. *See also* URBAN LEGENDS.

listed building A building in the UK officially recognized as being of "special architectural or historic interest" according to the Town and Country Planning Act (1971). Under the act, such buildings are protected from demolition and their owners or occupiers are required to obtain consent from their local planning authority before carrying out any work that would affect the character of the building. There are three types of listing: Grade I for buildings of "exceptional interest" (about 1% of listed buildings); Grade II for "particularly important buildings of more than special interest" (about 4%); and Grade III for buildings of special interest that "warrant every effort being made to preserve them". Some of the more unusual 'buildings' to have been listed include PREFABS, ornate tombs, and various follies.

listeria A bacterium belonging to a genus named after the famous British surgeon, Joseph Lister. It usually refers to the species *Listeria monocytogenes*, which causes listeriosis in humans and animals and occurs widely in nature, for example in soil, faeces, silage, and the tissues of healthy animals. Infection in humans can cause three distinct forms of disease: a flu-like pattern of symptoms; septicaemia, caused by the organisms entering the bloodstream; and a form of meningitis. In pregnant women the organism can cross the placenta and affect the fetus, causing miscarriage, stillbirth, or birth defects. Occasionally, mass outbreaks of listeriosis occur, often traceable to contaminated food, such as soft cheeses, patés, etc. In most cases, however, infection is sporadic and from an unidentifiable source. Worries emerged in the 1980s over the risks of listeriosis caused by the presence of the highly resistant listeria organisms in COOK-CHILL food products inadequately reheated using microwave ovens. New guidelines were introduced in the UK in 1990 to combat this risk.

litterbug A person who drops litter in public places. The term was coined in about 1947 in America, where it is also used as a verb, meaning to drop litter. In colloquial usage the word *bug* is applied to someone with an enthusiasm for a particular activity, as in JITTERBUG, upon which this word is closely modelled. In the UK **litter lout** is more common. *See also* KEEP BRITAIN TIDY.

little. **Little America** *See* EISENHOWER PLATZ.

Little Bighorn British motor-cycle couriers' name for Hyde Park Corner in London. The reference is to the Battle of Little Bighorn (1876) in America, at which General Custer's troops were massacred by the Indians and Custer himself was killed, an episode known as Custer's Last Stand. For motorcyclists, Hyde Park Corner is seen as a likely place to be massacred.

Little Black Banda A derogatory nickname coined in the early 1960s for Dr Hastings Banda (1905–), prime minister of Malawi (then Nyasaland) from 1963 to 1966 and first president thereafter. The name is patterned on 'Little Black Sambo', a character in a children's story now considered racially offensive.

Little Entente The name given to the political alliance formed between Czechoslovakia, Yugoslavia, and Romania (1920–22). Originally intended to prevent the restoration of Habsburg power, it later became broader in scope. It was brought to an end by the destruction of Czechoslovakia after the Munich Agreement (1938).

Little Flower *See* LA GUARDIA.

little green men *See* LGM.

Little Miss Dynamite The stage name of the US singer Brenda Lee (1944–), who was one of the few successful female rock 'n' rollers of the late 1950s and 1960s. The nickname may have been partly inspired by the song 'Dynamite', a minor hit in 1957. In the 1980s she rebuilt her career as a country singer.

Little Mo The nickname of the US tennis champion Maureen Connolly (1934–69), which reflects the affection felt for her by the public. One of the great tennis stars of the early 1950s, she won her first championship at 16, took three Wimbledon titles between 1952 and 1954, and was the first woman to win the tennis grand slam, taking the British, US, Australian, and French singles championships in one year.

little rabbits have big ears A 20th-century Australian adaptation of the old proverb 'little pitchers have great ears' – an admonition to be circumspect when talking in front of children.

Little Red Book (of **Chairman Mao**) The collected *Quotations of Chairman Mao Tse Tung*, which was originally produced in 1964 for the indoctrination of the Red Army and then appeared in a regular edition in 1965. The pocket-sized book, bound in bright red plastic, contained a collection of political quotations, homilies, and aphorisms culled from

Mao's writings over the decades and designed to stimulate revolutionary awareness. It became a familiar sight during the upheavals of the CULTURAL REVOLUTION, when it was brandished aloft by zealous RED GUARDS and workers as they heeded Mao's call to root out revisionaries among the bureaucratic and intellectual elite. It also enjoyed a vogue among the New Left in Europe and America during the same period.

Every communist must grasp the truth, political power grows out of the barrel of a gun.

little ships *See* DUNKIRK.

Little Sparrow The nickname of Edith Piaf (1915–63), French cabaret singer whose real name was Edith Gassion; the stage name 'Piaf' is French slang for 'sparrow'. Many of her songs, 'Je m'en fous pas mal' ('I couldn't care less'), Je ne regrette rien' ('I regret nothing'), and La vie en rose' ('Life through rose-coloured glasses'), are a reflection of the drug- and alcohol-induced tragedies of her own short and chaotic life. Immensely popular in her native Paris, in which she had started as a street singer, she was mourned by virtually the whole population, which brought traffic to a standstill on the day of her funeral. When he heard the news of her death, her friend the writer and artist Jean Cocteau is said to have suffered a fatal heart attack.

Little Willie A nickname used by British troops in World War I of Friedrich Wilhelm, Crown Prince of Germany and eldest son of Kaiser Wilhelm II (*see* KAISER BILL). Commander of the German armies that attempted to capture Verdun, he was apparently unmoved by the enormous casualties sustained on both sides – hence another of his nicknames, the **Laughing Murderer of Verdun**.

too little, too late Cliché usually used in a political context. It was coined by the US historian Allan Nevias in an article in the May 1935 edition of *Current History*. Referring to the minimal offers made by the former allies to Germany, he said they were too little and came too late to prevent the disastrous rise of the Nazis.

The phrase was subsequently much used in politics. On one occasion, when the UK's chancellor, Norman Lamont, cut the interest rate by 0.5%, the shadow chancellor, John Smith, commented to the house:

Of course even a 0.5% cut is better than no cut. But there can be little doubt that it is too little too late . . .

The Independent, 14 February 1991.

live. Live Aid Two marathon rock concerts held on 13 July 1985 in Wembley Stadium, London, and JFK Stadium, Philadelphia, to raise funds for African famine relief. The concerts, featuring such stars as U2, David Bowie, Madonna, and Mick Jagger, were watched by an estimated one and a half billion people in 160 countries. Live Aid was also the name of the charity set up to administer these funds. The venture was masterminded by the Irish rocksinger Bob Geldof (1952–), who cajoled, bullied, and blackmailed everyone from superstars to heads of state in pursuit of his aims. Geldof had previously been the moving force behind a similar event, **Band Aid** (*see* BAND-AID), in response to harrowing TV footage of the Ethiopian famine of 1984. After Band Aid and Live Aid, the word 'Aid' was frequently incorporated into the titles of charity events.

I'm not interested in the bloody system! Why has he no food? Why is he starving to death?

BOB GELDOF in an interview, October 1985.

live-in The designation of a sexual partner with whom one shares one's living accommodation but to whom one is not married. Live-in boyfriends, for example, may or may not own, or partly own, the accommodation and are free to go when they choose to do so. In general, they have not achieved the status of common-law husbands, who might be regarded as boyfriends who have lived-in for some years and have probably entered into some property-sharing arrangements with their partners. It is interesting to note that, in the UK, in 1972 only 17% of wives had started their relationships with their husbands as live-in girlfriends. By 1987 this had risen to 57%.

lizards Slang for shoes or other footwear made from crocodile or snakeskin.

leaping lizards *See under* LEAP.

lounge lizard *See under* LOUNGE.

Llareggub The small fishing village in the play *Under Milk Wood* (1954) by the poet Dylan Thomas (1914–53), which was based on his own hometown of Laugherne in S Wales. Llareggub is 'buggerall' spelt backwards.

Lloyd George. Lloyd George Fund The controversial fund established and personally controlled by David Lloyd

George (1863–1945) as prime minister (1916–22) in order to finance a new Liberal Party organization after his split with Asquith's wing of the party. Lloyd George's blatant use of the honours system to reward wealthy contributors to the fund, such as the unscrupulous South African millionaire Sir James Robinson, without regard to their personal reputations or philanthropic credentials in other spheres of public life, provoked the 'Honours Scandal' of July 1922. A commission of inquiry was set up to investigate the propriety of Lloyd George's administration of the fund; his refusal to relinquish control of the fund contributed to the downfall of his coalition government.

Lloyd George knew my father A saying that has been immortalized by William Douglas Home's play of that name, which was first produced in London in 1972. The saying, however, was heard even before the death of the great Welsh Liberal prime minister in 1945. It is facetiously referred to as every Welshman's claim to fame. The originator of the phrase was reputedly Tommy Rhys Roberts QC (1910–75), of whom it was actually true as his father, Arthur Rhys Roberts, and Lloyd George had set up a solicitors' practice in London together in 1897. Tommy Rhys Roberts became famous for singing the lines 'Lloyd George knew my father, my father knew Lloyd George' to the hymn tune 'Onward Christian Soldiers' at the close of the after-dinner speeches at circuit dinners. This was the signal that a sing-song would follow. This practice was apparently also taken up by Welsh Rugby Clubs and by Welsh Liberal assemblies.

LMS (1) London, Midland & Scottish Railway. One of the big four railway companies created by the Railway Act of 1921 out of the 120 private concerns that formerly existed (the other three created under the Act being the LNER, SR, and GWR). At its creation the LMS was probably the largest joint-stock company in the world: covering 6900 miles of track, it operated 10,200 steam locomotives, 19,600 passenger carriages, and 207,000 freight wagons; its staff numbered 274,000. Its London termini were Euston and St Pancras; LMS operated the *Royal Scot* service between London and Glasgow. (2) Local Management of Schools. The control of a school's finances by its own board of governors, as established by the provisions of the Education Reform Act of 1988. *See* GERBIL.

LNER London and North Eastern Railway. The second largest, after LMS, of the big four railway companies created by the Railway Act of 1921. It had London termini at King's Cross, Marylebone, and Liverpool Street and ran the famous *Flying Scotsman* on the east-coast route from London to Edinburgh. *See also* GWR; SR.

load. loaded (1) US slang for being intoxicated by alcohol or high on drugs. In the 18th century in America, a 'load' was a single portion or drink of alcohol, as in '10 cents a load'. The alcoholic sense of being loaded was applied to heroin users by the 1950s and then to any drug user. (2) Slang for being extremely wealthy. Also originally a US expression, it is now common in all English-speaking countries.

> Is your Dad rich? . . . He's reasonably loaded.
> COLIN MACINNES: *City of Spades* (1957).

loadsamoney A colloquial expression coined in the UK in the 1980s by the comedian Harry Enfield, originally as a catchphrase and subsequently as the name of one of his comic characters. Loadsamoney (a plasterer who waves a wad of banknotes in other people's faces) satirizes the nouveau riche and YUPPIES who flaunt their newly acquired wealth with vulgarity (*see also* ESSEX MAN); Thatcherite Britain was consequently dubbed the **loadsamoney society** by its critics. *Loadsa-* also became a prefix attached to other words by analogy with loadsamoney. **Loadsabargains** are promised by shops advertising sales and comedy shows promise **loadsalaughs**. *See also* LOMBARD.

lobotomy Strictly, surgical incision into a lobe, although the term is generally used to describe an incision into a lobe of the cerebrum of the brain, a surgical procedure often also called leucotomy. In prefrontal lobotomy (prefrontal leucotomy) the nerve fibres connecting the extreme frontal (prefrontal) lobes with the thalamus are severed, using a cutting instrument (leucotome) introduced through a hole drilled in the skull. The technique was pioneered in 1935 by the Portuguese surgeon António Caetanio de Egas Moniz (1874–1955) and has been used to treat severe depression, schizophrenia, and other intractable emotional and behavioural disorders. Unfortunately, the operation had unpredictable and sometimes adverse effects on the patient, such as marked personality changes, and has long been a focus of controversy. It is still practised as a treatment of last resort.

local. Local Defence Volunteers *See* HOME GUARD.

Local Education Authority *See* LEA.

local radio A radio that serves a local area only. Usually broadcasting on a narrow FM band, local radio stations are designed – in addition to being broadly entertaining – to deal with local issues and to provide local information.

local yokel 'Yokel' is a derogatory term for a person living in the country and so thought to be unsophisticated. A local yokel, by rhyming association, is an equally derogatory term for a local resident. In US CB radio slang, a local yokel is a city police officer rather than a police officer attached to the state police or highway patrol.

Locarno Pacts A series of non-aggression agreements formulated at Locarno, in Switzerland, on 16 October 1925 and signed in London on 1 December 1925, which guaranteed the post-Versailles Treaty frontiers between Germany and France as well as those between Belgium and Germany. This settlement of Franco-German differences and the implied British and Italian military guarantee of French territorial integrity appeared to herald a new era of international peace and security (the **Locarno Spirit**). Germany was admitted to the LEAGUE OF NATIONS shortly afterwards (September 1926) but ten years later, in March 1936, Germany renounced Locarno and marched into the Rhineland.

Loch Ness Monster In April 1933, a London surgeon driving along the shore of Loch Ness, Scotland, saw (and photographed) a strange object at some distance out, subsequently described as being 30 ft long with two humps, a snake-like head at the end of a long neck, and two flippers about the middle of the body. This 'sighting' of some kind of monster renewed interest in a phenomenon that has persisted since St Adamnan's 7th-century biography of St Columba mentioned that he succeeded in banishing an *aquatilis bestia* from the depths of Loch Ness. After this revival in the 1930s it has been 'seen' by many others and featured in many newspapers, to whom it became known as 'Nessie'. Investigations have failed to provide convincing evidence to support the existence of a prehistoric monster but local traders, for whom the monster has been a fortuitous source of income, have done their best to keep the myth alive. The extreme depth of the loch combined with the murkiness of the water meant that underwater photographs of the monster in 1975 were indistinct; they were sufficient, however, to convince the leading naturalist Sir Peter Scott, among others, of the creature's existence. The Loch Ness Phenomena Investigation Bureau, set up in 1961, continues the quest. Sightings of a similar nature have been reported in other deep Scottish lakes.

lock. lockdown A US word used since 1974 for keeping a prison's inmates locked in their cells, usually for a day or more, following a disturbance in the prison or a warning of pending violence.

lock-in A form of organized protest in which the protesting group locks itself in a building. The lock-in was a tactic popular in America in the late 1960s, when it was used to gain concessions or as a means of passive demonstration. It subsequently spread to the UK, where it is sometimes used as a form of INDUSTRIAL ACTION. In this case the workers lock themselves into their workplace to prevent the management from closing the company down. *See also* LOCK-OUT.

lock-on To locate and track a target by means of a radar beam. A ground-based conically scanned radar beam can be made to lock onto an enemy aircraft, which enables a guided missile to be controlled so that its flight path coincides with the beam. When the missile reaches the apex of the cone it explodes, destroying the enemy aircraft.

lock-out During INDUSTRIAL ACTION, the closing of a factory or company by the management in order to pressure employees to negotiate or to accept workable terms. *See also* LOCK-IN.

Lockerbie disaster The UK's worst air disaster, in which a Pan American Boeing 747, en route from Frankfurt to New York via London, crashed over the small Scottish town of Lockerbie on 21 December 1988, killing all 259 passengers and crew and 11 people on the ground. The cause of the crash was the explosion of a terrorist bomb in one of the luggage holds; great public concern was aroused following the disclosure that warnings of terrorist attacks received some weeks earlier by airport authorities and others had neither been publicized nor heeded.

Lockheed A giant US aerospace corporation (headquarters at Burbank, California) that produces military aircraft (including the C-130 cargo planes and STEALTH bombers), satellites, and submarine-launched missiles. In the mid-1970s financial difficulties and an overseas pay-off scandal threatened to sink the company; it survived, however, and remains one of the world's largest weapons manufacturers. It was founded in 1913 by aircraft designers Malcolm and Allan Loughead (they later changed the spelling) but collapsed in 1931 and was then rescued without the Lockheed brothers by a Boston bank in 1932. In the 1960s Lockheed's decision to produce the L-1011 TriStar jet, coupled with severe cost overruns on the C-5 military transport, threatened to bankrupt the company; it was only kept solvent by massive injections of Federal funds. In 1975 it was revealed that as much as $24.5 million of this money was used to bribe foreign government officials to attract overseas contracts.

locust years Years of poverty or hardship. The term was applied by Sir Winston Churchill to the years of the GREAT DEPRESSION preceding World War II when rearmament should have taken place but did not. It is an allusion to the Bible, Joel 2:25: "And I will restore to you the years that the locust hath eaten . . . ". The phrase has also been used of the late 1960s in the UK, when the Labour government was in power.

logic. **logical positivism** A philosophical doctrine originating in Vienna (*see* VIENNA CIRCLE) in the 1920s and later popularized in the UK by Sir Alfred Ayer (1910–89) in his book *Language, Truth and Logic* (1936). At its core is the verification principle, which asserts that any statement that cannot be verified by empirical observation is literally meaningless. On this principle, only scientific knowledge can claim to be factual; all questions of metaphysics, ethics, and religion are rendered nonsensical. Ayer later modified his position in revised editions of his book (1946).
logic bomb A form of computer sabotage in which a system is made to break down by introducing into its memory a set of instructions that will become operative at some date in the future. By the time the breakdown takes place, the perpetrator is not readily identifiable and may even have left the organization concerned.

loi-cadre (Fr. draft law) Legislation enacted by the French National Assembly on 23 June 1956 to give French overseas possessions, except Algeria, a measure of political autonomy. French territories in West Africa, such as Senegal and Sudan, and Equatorial Africa, such as Gabon, were given territorial assemblies elected by universal suffrage. The territories could also send representatives to the French National Assembly, but France retained the power of veto over the local legislatures and retained control over foreign affairs, defence, and internal security.

loid Police and underworld slang for opening a locked door by using a piece of celluloid (now usually a credit card). This has been a popular method of illegal entry into houses and cars since the 1930s.

Lolita A sexually precocious adolescent girl under the age of sexual consent, who is attractive to men. The word derives from the title of a novel by Vladimir Nabokov (1899–1977) published in 1955, which deals with the seduction of a middle-aged academic antihero by the pubescent daughter of his landlady.

lollipop man or **lady** A schoolchildren's name for the traffic warden who conducts them across the road. It derives from the striped pole, surmounted by a brightly coloured disc, which he or she carries.

Loman, Willy The central character in the play *Death of a Salesman* (1949) by Arthur Miller (1915–). Loman, a failure as a salesman and father, kills himself in a car crash to raise money for his family. The play, a sad commentary on the failure of the AMERICAN DREAM, won a Pulitzer Prize.

> Attention, attention must be finally paid to such a person.
>
> *Death of a Salesman.*

Lombard An acronym for Loads Of Money But A Real Dickhead. This term is applied to people who have wealth but no intelligence. Earlier, a Lombard was an obsolete name for a banker or money-lender, so-called because of the number of bankers in London who came from Lombardy in N Italy. Lombard Street in the City of London, the home of many head-quarters of banks, is named after them. *See also* ESSEX MAN.

London. **London FOX** The London Futures and Options Exchange, formed in 1987 from the London Commodity Exchange. It is housed in a purpose-built exchange, which it shares with the International Petroleum Exchange in St Katherine Dock. The exchange deals in futures (promises to buy or sell at some specified future date at an agreed price) and options (the right to buy or sell at an agreed price in the future) in commodities, such as sugar, cocoa, and coffee.

London Group A society of artists founded in 1913 by a group of painters associated with Walter Sickert (1860–1942). Its aim was to break away from academic tradition and to draw inspiration from French post-impressionism.

London marathon A race over the classic marathon distance of 26 miles 385 yards held annually in London since 1981. The race, which starts at Blackheath and finishes over Westminster Bridge, passing through Dockland and the City, was the idea of former runners Christopher Brasher and John Disley and attracted a field of 7000 in its first year; of these 6255 finished within five hours. The men's race was won jointly by Dick Beadsley (America) and Inge Simonsen (Norway) in 2 hrs 11 mins 48 secs, and the women's race was won by Joyce Smith (UK) in 2 hrs 29 mins 57 secs. In addition to the races for able-bodied men and women, a wheelchair race for paraplegics was introduced in 1983. With some 26,000 starters in 1990, the race has become one of the most popular marathon fixtures, attracting serious athletes from all over the world as well as countless 'fun' runners, many of whom are sponsored on behalf of charities.

London Naval Conference A meeting between the UK, America, France, Italy, and Japan between 21 January and 22 April 1930, which enlarged the scope of the Washington Naval Agreements (1921–22) and agreed various new measures of naval disarmament. These included the regulation of submarine warfare, a five-year moratorium on the contruction of capital ships, and the limitation of US, British, and Japanese battleship tonnage to a ratio 10:10:7, respectively.

London season A period in summer and autumn of heightened social activity when debutantes (daughters of marriageable age of the aristocracy and upper middle classes) 'come out' and are introduced into society at a series of social, sporting, and charitable functions, such as the Alexandra Rose Ball and the Royal Academy Summer Exhibition. The practice of presenting debutantes at court – once an essential element of the London season – ceased in 1958; another, QUEEN CHARLOTTE'S BALL, ended in 1976 after 200 years. The London season was once an important part of English social life for the upper classes; it has now lost most of its glamour.

London to Brighton run (1) An annual run for VETERAN CARS (built before 1 January 1905) from the centre of London to the Metropole Hotel in Brighton (a distance of 53 miles, or 85 km). Organized by the RAC, it is held on the first Sunday in November and commemorates the Emancipation Run, held on 14 November 1896, over the same route to commemorate the raising of the speed limit from 4 m.p.h. to 12 m.p.h. Not a race, the run is intended to test the ability of the cars to arrive in Brighton under their own steam – an increasingly difficult task for cars approaching 100 years old. The British film *Genevieve* (1953), starring Kay Kendall and Kenneth More, stylishly popularized the event. (2) An annual road running race from London to Brighton, organized since 1951 by the Road Runner's Club. The race dates back to 1899 and an amateur running race organized by the South London Harriers, which was won by Frank Randell in a time of 6 hrs 58 mins 18 secs. The first runner to break the 6 hour barrier was Arthur Newton (5 hrs 33 mins 43 secs) in 1924. As a result of road changes the course of the race has varied considerably over the years, the current distance being 53½ miles (86.1 km).

Secret Treaty of London A secret alliance concluded on 26 April 1915 between the Triple Entente (the UK, France, and Russia) and Italy, which agreed terms for Italy's entry into World War I against Germany and Austria. Italy had been secretly courted by both sides after 1914; she eventually agreed to commit her forces to the Entente in return for specified territorial concessions at the end of the conflict. These included possession of S Tyrol, Trentino, Trieste, and portions of Dalmatia; recognition of Italian sovereignty over the Dodecanese; and enlarged holdings in Libya, Somalia, and Eritrea at Germany's expense. The text of the treaty was leaked by the BOLSHEVIKS in 1917 and later published by a Swedish newspaper, which caused a degree of embarrassment at the Paris peace conference in 1919.

lone. Lone Ranger The fictional masked law-enforcing hero of the American West. With his white horse, Silver, and Red Indian companion, Tonto, he was created in 1933 by scriptwriter Fran Striker and producer George W. Trendle for a radio series in America. A valiant crusader against injustice, he was the upright hero of 17 novels written by Fran Striker between 1936 and 1957; he was also the subject of comic strips, of cinema films – starting with *The Lone Ranger* (1938), with Lee Powell in the title role and Chief Thundercloud as Tonto – and of almost 200 television adventures (1949–57) starring Clayton Moore, with Jay Silverheels as the faithful Tonto. The radio series continued until 1954, and in 1956 and 1958 two large-screen spin-offs were made with Clayton Moore: *The Lone Ranger* (directed by Stuart Heisler) and *The Lone Ranger and the Lost City of Gold* (directed by Lesley Selander). The most recent full-length film, *The Legend of the Lone Ranger* (1981; directed by William A. Frakar), starred Klinton Spilsby. *See also* KEMO SABE.

Lone Wolf The central character of US writer Louis Joseph Vance's novel *The Lone Wolf* (1914) and numerous sequels published between 1918 and 1934. The gentleman-thief (Michael Lanyard) was the subject of a clutch of silent films and reappeared in over a dozen adventure movies made by Columbia in the 1930s and 1940s. The role of the Lone Wolf was played by a number of actors, including Melvyn Douglas in *The Lone Wolf Returns* (1935), Francis Lederer in *The Lone Wolf in Paris* (1938), Warren William in *The Lone Wolf Spy Hunt* (1939), *The Lone Wolf Strikes* (1940), and six others, and Gerald Mohr in *The Notorious Lone Wolf* (1946), *The Lone Wolf in London* (1947), and *The Lone Wolf in Mexico* 1947). The last film of the series, *The Lone Wolf and his Lady* (directed by John Hoffman), was made in 1949 and starred Ron Randell.

long. longhair A man perceived as having the characteristics associated with long hair. Since the 1960s long hair has been regarded as a distinguishing feature of the male HIPPIE. Prior to this it was the mark of the intellectual, musician, or artist, who wore his hair long to distinguish him from the 'short back and sides' haircut of the forces and the lower orders of the establishment.

long hot summer A journalists' cliché usually associated with the race riots in America in the summer of 1967. The phrase seems to have been created by William Faulkner in 1928 and used as the title of a 1958 film based on some of his stories. It was, however, Martin Luther King who made it famous:

> Everyone is worrying about the long hot summer with its threat of riots. We had a long cold winter when little was done about the conditions that create riots.

That a long hot summer unfortunately creates the ideal conditions for urban riots was borne out again in the summer of 1981, in the UK, with riots in Toxteth (Liverpool), Brixton (London), and elsewhere.

Long March The epic migration in 1934–35 of 100,000 Chinese communists from Kiangsi Soviet in SE China to a new base in Yenan in the NW. The GUOMINDANG Nationalist army under Chiang Kaishek had launched a series of offensives against the Kiangsi base after 1931; in October 1934 Mao Tse Tung, Chu Teh, and Lin Piao led a breakout through Nationalist lines and marched north. They arrived in October 1935, but after a trek of 6000 miles through rugged terrain, subjected to near starvation, freezing temperatures and Nationalist attacks, only 30,000 survived out of the original 100,000-strong Red Army. In Yenan, Mao consolidated his leadership of the Communist Party and prepared the military, economic, and political foundations for the eventual communist victory in 1949.

Long Range Desert Group A British military force of volunteers in World War II, who penetrated behind the enemy's lines in North Africa and carried out invaluable reconnaissance work through the uncharted desert. They helped to guide various forces to their objectives and facilitated the exploits of the SAS (*see also* POPSKI'S PRIVATE ARMY).

long time no see A greeting meaning it's a long time since we saw each other. It originates in the pidgin English phrases used by the colonial British and Americans in the Far East and dates probably from the beginning of the 20th century. Expatriots and sevicemen imported the phrase on their visits home, when it became well established on both sides of the Atlantic. It is now somewhat dated and used with caution. The variant 'long time no see – short time buckshee' (*i.e.* free) was how servicemen hoped they would be greeted by their favourite prostitute after a long absence.

Lonrho affair A financial scandal that shook the British establishment in 1973. The international mining and trading company Lonrho was accused of offering large bribes to business contacts, including a former Tory cabinet minister (Duncan Sandys), who accepted a golden handshake of £130,000 from the company for giving up his consultancy job. The money was to be paid into a tax-free account in the Cayman Islands. The transaction was not illegal but provided evidence of tax loopholes at the top end of the capitalist system.

> It is the unpleasant and unacceptable face of capitalism but one should not suggest that the whole of British industry consists of practices of this kind.
> EDWARD HEATH, replying to a question from Jo Grimmond in the House of Commons, 15 May 1973.

Lonsdale affair or **Portland Secrets Case** The trial of Gordon Arnold Lonsdale (real name Konan Trofimovich Molody, 1923–?70) in March 1961 for the theft of documents relating to nuclear-submarine warfare from the Admiralty Underwater Weapons Establishment at Portland in Dorset. Soviet-born Molody was a Soviet mole, who had been taken to Canada by his aunt at the age of 11 with a false passport in the name of Lonsdale, educated in California, served with the Red Army in World War II, and became a KGB spy in America in the early 1950s. He was posted to London in 1955, established a reputation as a playboy businessman, and recruited a network of agents, including naval clerk Harry Houghton, who stole the Portland documents, and the Krogers, from whose bungalow Lonsdale regularly radioed Moscow (*see also* KROGER AFFAIR). Lonsdale was sent to prison for 25 years, but was later exchanged for the British spy Greville Wynne in April 1964.

loon. loons or **loon pants** The tightly fitting bell-bottomed trousers worn by HIPPIES in the 1970s. They were usually purple and made of cotton, although velvet and canvas versions were also worn. This term, first heard in 1971, probably came from 'loon', a hippie word for a wild or unconventional person.

loony left A derogatory term originating in the 1980s to describe those members of the LABOUR PARTY, especially the Militant Tendency (*see* MILITANT), who were in favour of extreme left-wing policies. The phrase coincided with a split in the Labour Party, and the subsequent curtailment of the activities of the loony left by Neil Kinnock in his attempt to make the Labour Party an electable alternative to the Tories.

looping the loop The aerobatic manoeuvre that consists of describing a perpendicular circle in the air; at the top of the circle, or loop, the pilot is upside down. The term is derived from a switchback once popular at fairs in which a moving car or bicycle performed a similar circuit on a perpendicular track.

loose cannon US journalists' slang from the 1980s for an uncontrollable ally, a person who, despite being an ally, is not wholly reliable. The reference is to a cannon that is not properly secured to the deck of a ship, becoming a danger to thc crew as the ship pitches and rolls. Colonel Oliver North was referred to as a loose cannon in the Reagan administration in America.

loot US slang for money, especially a large amount; it derives from the English sense of the word, meaning military booty or blunder. It was first heard among JAZZ musicians in the 1920s, replacing the slang term 'coin', and became common during World War II.

Loran towers An abbreviation for *long-range navigation towers*, a system of marine and air navigation. A ship or aircraft's position (a 'fix') is calculated by noting time differences in the reception of synchronized pulses transmitted from widely dispersed broadcasting towers.

lord. Lord Haw-Haw Possibly the best known nickname to come from World War II, that of William Joyce (1906–46), who broadcast Nazi propaganda to the British people from Germany. The name was coined by Jonah Barrington, radio correspondent for the *Daily Express*, alluding to his exaggeratedly Oxford accent. Joyce's broadcasts, intended to threaten and demoralize, made him a figure of derision and loathing in the UK. Although he was hanged for treason after the war (despite the fact that he was of Irish descent), his wartime broadcasts, if they had any effect at all, probably did more to bolster British determination than to undermine it.

Lord Porn One of the nicknames of Frank Pakenham (1905–), 7th Earl of Longford, used by the British tabloid press (*see also* HOLY FOOL). A champion of moral causes, he led an unofficial inquiry into pornography in the UK and the state of the nation's morality in 1972. He campaigned for the banning of school sex eduction unless parental consent was obtained, the levying of higher penalties for offences that transgress the obscenity laws, and for a higher standard of morality to be upheld on films, television programmes and published material. *See also* MOORS MURDERS.

Lord's Taverners A cricket team, named after the *Tavern* at Lord's cricket ground, founded in 1950 by a small group of actors and their friends to raise money for charity. It is now a Commonwealth-wide organization of philanthropic 'good fellows' from the world of sport and entertainment. The money raised is administered by the National Playing Fields Association, which provides cricket fields and leisure facilities for boys' clubs, youth organizations, village teams, etc., and also sponsors overseas tours by junior cricket sides.

The Lord of the Rings The title of J. R. R. Tolkien's best-selling fantasy novel (1954–55). Within the book, the term – which occurs very rarely – refers to Sauron, a godlike personification of evil. The epithet stems from the events of an earlier time when Sauron had wished to gain control of the Rings of Power; to accomplish this, he had sacrificed much of his innate magical power to create one ruling ring. He had nevertheless been defeated and had lost this ring. It was later found, and *The Lord of the Rings* tells of the quest of the HOBBIT Frodo Baggins to destroy it, and with it Sauron himself.

Originally conceived simply as a sequel to Tolkien's children's story *The Hobbit, The Lord of the Rings* was a tale that "grew to the telling" (Foreword), deepening and darkening from a fairy tale into an epic saga of good versus evil. The book has acquired a cult following – many members of which attach significances to it never envisaged by Tolkien himself – and has become a benchmark against which all subsequent attempts at epic fantasy have been judged.

lorry. fell off the back of a lorry A euphemism for describing stolen goods. If someone is asked how he acquired a particular object, he may, if he does not wish to disclose the source, say that it fell off the back of a lorry, *i.e.* that he found it in the road. The implication is that he, or someone else, stole it.

Los Alamos project *See* MANHATTAN PROJECT.

loss leader A product or service offered for sale at a loss in order to attract customers to spend money on other more profitable items. The practice is technically illegal in the UK under the terms of the Resale Prices Act (1976), although 'special offers' and sales are a common feature in the retail trade.

Lost Generation A name sometimes applied to the young men, especially of the educated upper and middle classes, who lost their lives in World War I. Rupert Brooke became their symbol; he was 27 when he died (not in battle, but of blood-poisoning).

> That's what you are. That's what you all are. All of you young people who served in the war. You are a lost generation.
>
> GERTRUDE STEIN, 1926.

lotus position A cross-legged sitting position with the feet on the thighs and the arms resting on the knees, used for meditation and relaxation. The position became familiar to people in western countries from the early 1960s, as yoga and meditation became widely practised. The term is a translation from the Sanskrit *padmāsana*, from *padma*, lotus, plus *āsana*, posture. The lotus lily, a sacred plant to Hindus, symbolized the detachment or transcendence of the intellect from external matter and sensation. For most westerners, the lotus position is excrutiatingly uncomfortable; only after long practice can it become a relaxed position in which the intellect is free to do anything.

louie (1) British drug-users' slang for one sixteenth of an ounce of cannabis. It is named after King Louis XVI of France. This is the smallest quantity for sale by weight. *See also* HENRY. (2) US slang for a lieutenant.

lounge lizard Slang for a well-dressed man who frequents the restaurants, bars, and hotels in which the rich gather, with the aim of seducing a wealthy woman. Originating in the 1920s, the expression is still used. It reflects the cold and insinuating quality of reptiles. It perhaps also reflects the LIZARDS (shoes) that such a person may be expected to sport.

Louvain A town in Brabant province, Belgium, which suffered serious damage when invaded by Germany in both world wars. In August 1914 the Germans occupied the town, massacred hundreds of civilians as a reprisal for attacks on German soldiers, and then burnt large areas of the medieval town centre, including the 15th-century university library and Sint

Pieterskirche. These sites were seriously damaged again when the town was overrun by German forces in May 1942.

love. **Love and Marriage** A song written by the US lyricist Sammy Cahn (1913–) for a live NBC TV musical version of Thornton Wilder's play *Our Town* in 1955. The score included four songs with lyrics by Cahn and music by James van Deusen. *Love and Marriage* was written for the second act (also called 'Love and Marriage') and was sung by Frank Sinatra. The production was never shown again by special request of Wilder himself.

> Love and Marriage,
> Love and Marriage,
> Go together like a horse and carriage,
> This I tell ya brother,
> Ya can't have one without the other.

love beads Coloured beads worn, typically as a necklace, as a symbol of peace and love. Love beads were part of the dress of the FLOWER PEOPLE of the mid- and late 1960s.

love bombing A US term from the mid-1970s used to describe a style of recruitment used by some religious and pseudo-religious cults. Members bombard their potential, usually youthful, converts with intense (often insincere) feelings of oneness, care, and love. This loving approach is usually accompanied by exhortations deriding the materialistic society.

love-in A term from the late 1960s to describe a gathering of HIPPIES or FLOWER PEOPLE for the purpose of celebrating or expressing mutual love. This was one of many terms, such as SLEEP-IN, **laugh-in**, and **sing-in**, introduced in the 1960s by analogy with SIT-IN.

lovely grub A catchphrase, dating from service use during World War II, meaning anything agreeable or welcome, not only food.

make love, not war The ultimate pacifist slogan, coined in the mid-1960s to epitomize the philosophy of the FLOWER PEOPLE and the HIPPIE generation. It was taken as the slogan of the anti-VIETNAM WAR demonstrators and reappeared in January 1991 with the demonstrations against the GULF WAR.

low. **lower than a snake's hips (**or **belly)** A catchphrase meaning contemptible, in use since at least the 1930s; for example in Leonard Mann's *Flesh in Armour* (1932):

> 'It was a dirty trick. He knew about me and her.' 'Dirty! Lower than a snake's belly.'

It was still in use in Australia in the late 1970s. It should not be confused with the US slang expression **the snake's hips**, used in the 1920s and 1930s to describe a remarkable person, as in 'she was the snake's hips'.

low-involvement product *See* HIGH-INVOLVEMENT PRODUCT.

low-level language A type of computer programming language that is closer to MACHINE CODE – the actual sequence of digital instructions understood by the microprocessor itself – than to human language. In contrast to a HIGH-LEVEL LANGUAGE, a low-level language is much faster and more efficient in execution but can only be used by highly trained professional programmers.

low-level munchkin *See* MUNCHKIN.

low rider (1) US slang for someone who drives a customized car that has had its suspension lowered. It may also be used of the car itself. Low riders were popular during the 1970s and 1980s, especially among Hispanic youths in Los Angeles. Low riders would cruise slowly in packs showing off their customized vehicles. (2) Slang for an unpleasant person.

lox The Yiddish name for smoked salmon, eaten as a delicacy, usually on a bagel with cream cheese, in New York City and other US centres with a substantial Jewish population. Unlike Scottish smoked salmon, which is a luxury food in the UK, lox is either cured in salt (**Scandinavian lox**) or in sugar (**Nova Scotia lox**; sometimes called **Novey**). The Yiddish word is derived from the German *Lachs* (or Swedish *lax*), salmon. Although lox is usually regarded as a Jewish invention, it was unknown by the European Jews who emigrated to America and is hardly eaten in Israel. In fact, it is a delicacy that has been cultivated by the Jewish population of New York in the last 60 years. *See also* GRAVLAX.

LP Long Play. The standard format for gramophone records since the late 1940s, when they were introduced by the US broadcasting company CBS. They are normally 12 inches (30 cm) in diameter, revolve at 33⅓ r.p.m., contain an average of 250 grooves per inch on a vinyl plastic base, and play for about 25 minutes per side. The LP soon eclipsed the previous format (a shellac-based disc with around 100 grooves per inch, which was 10 or 12 inches in diameter and revolved at 78 r.p.m.). LPs lost favour to tape cassettes and are now being rapidly supplanted by the CD (compact disc). *See* DIGITAL RECORDING.

LSD (1) The former monetary units of the UK; pounds (Latin *libra*), shillings (Latin *solidus*), and pence (Latin *denarius*). They were introduced by the Lombard merchants. LSD was replaced by DECIMAL CURRENCY on 15 February 1971. (2) Lysergic Acid Diethylamide. A dangerous drug to abuse, its long-term use can cause schizophrenia-like conditions and even single doses can cause fear, anxiety, and confusion. Those who take this drug are said to have PSYCHEDELIC experiences.

LSE London School of Economics and Political Science. The LSE was founded in 1895 by the social reformer Sidney Webb (1858–1947) and admitted into the University of London in 1900, following the establishment of a Faculty of Economics and Political Science. The LSE occupies a small complex of buildings in Houghton Street, off the Aldwych, in central London.

LS/MFT One of America's most esoteric and successful advertising slogans. The American Tobacco Company first used LS/MFT for Lucky Strike cigarettes during the 1940s, when smoking was still regarded as acceptable and indeed encouraged by Hollywood films. The initials stand for 'Lucky Strike Means Fine Tobacco'. Two competitive cigarette slogans popular at the time were **Call for Philip Morris** and **I'd walk a mile for a Camel**.

Lublin Committee The Polish Committee of National Liberation. A group of left-wing Poles sponsored by the Soviets during World War II, as an alternative authority to the Polish government-in-exile in London. After the Red Army's liberation of E Poland in July 1944, the committee was installed in Lublin and recognized by the Soviet Union as the legitimate authority. A provisional government was proclaimed in December 1944 (of the 25 members 15 had been in the Lublin Committee), which was later recognized by the UK and America on 5 July 1945, two months after the end of the war in Europe.

Lubyanka prison One of Moscow's most notorious prisons, reserved for political prisoners only. Thousands of NKVD victims were imprisoned, interrogated, tortured, and executed here. The Lubyanka, in Dzerzhinsky Square, was the headquarters of an insurance company until it was taken over by the CHEKA in the 1920s. The NKVD offices occupied the outer section and the prison cells were located within an inner courtyard in a nine-storey building formerly used by the insurance company as a boarding house. There were around 110 small cells holding not more than 200 prisoners at a time. Executions were carried out in the basement.

Lucky A common nickname of people who appear to have more than the average share of good luck or who narrowly escape death or misfortune. Among its recipients in the 20th century are the Sicilian-born US gangster Savatore Luciano (1896–1962), a leader of organized crime, who survived having his throat cut by a rival and ended his days living in luxury in Naples; and the 7th Earl of Lucan (1934–) who disappeared without trace following the discovery of the body of his children's nanny. Widely suspected to be the murderer, he has been sought unsuccessfully by police forces all over the world; his friends maintained that he had committed suicide after the murder. To achieve a nickname prefaced with 'Lucky', it helps to have a surname beginning with 'L' – alliterative nicknames have always been popular.

Lucy Nickname given by palaeoanthropologists to skeletal remains discovered in 1974 in E Africa; the structure of the pelvis indicated that the remains were of a female. The fossil was identified as belonging to the species *Australopithecus afarensis*, an apelike hominid that lived at least 2 million years ago, probably coexisting with the earliest ancestors of modern humans.

Lucy ring A spy network based in Switzerland during World War II, which channelled details of the plans of the German High Command for the Eastern Front to Moscow on a daily basis. 'Lucy' was the codename of the key figure in the network, Rudolph Roessler, a German publisher who moved to Switzerland after Hitler came to power. The ring was actually a Soviet-controlled organization, which employed agents of several different nationalities to glean information from a variety of sources, including anti-Fascist freelance intelligence agencies. It also made use of Ultra intercepts of German signals, from the British Enigma code-breaking operation at Bletchley Park.

These were provided anonymously by the British and fed to STALIN indirectly through the Lucy ring because he mistrusted any intelligence that did not come from his own networks.

Luftwaffe The German airforce built up secretly after World War I and publicly unveiled to an astonished world in 1935. The Treaty of Versailles forbade the Germans to construct military aircraft; however, potential military designs, such as the Junkers 52 transport, were produced at Hugo Junkers' civilian aircraft factory at Dessau, Reichswehr personnel were trained at secret flying schools in the Soviet Union, and glider clubs were encouraged for pilot training in Germany. In 1935 the Luftwaffe was revealed as the most modern and best equipped air force in Europe, with 1888 aircraft and 20,000 trained officers and men.

luge A small one- or two-seater toboggan used for racing, with each rider lying on his or her back. Toboggan racing entered the Olympics in 1928 to be replaced in 1964 by luge racing, which was dominated for many years by the East Germans.

Lüger Various models of semi-automatic hand gun invented by the Austrian George Lüger in 1898 and first manufactured for both military and commercial use in 1900. The design was partly based on the first true automatic pistol, invented by Hugo Borchardt (1893), and was adopted as a regulation weapon by many countries, notably Nazi Germany. Production ceased in 1943, but some Lüger models were again manufactured commercially in the 1970s.

lumpectomy The surgical removal of a lump, especially from the breast. This technique is used in the treatment of breast cancer, and involves the excision of the tumour and surrounding tissues. Remaining breast tissue is left intact, in contrast to mastectomy, in which the entire breast is removed. Lumpectomy is thus a cosmetically preferable option. It is generally combined with high-energy radiotherapy to destroy residual cancer cells.

lunar. **Luna** A series of 24 Soviet moon probes launched during the years 1959–76. Luna 3 (October 1959) sent back the first pictures of the far side of the moon and Luna 9 achieved the first soft landing (3 February 1966). Luna 15 was launched on 13 July 1969 in an audacious attempt to retrieve samples of moonrock only days before the blast-off of Apollo 11, which placed the first men on the moon on 20 July 1969 (*see* APOLLO MOON PROGRAMME).

Lunar Orbiter A series of five US SPACE PROBES placed in orbit around the moon in 1966–67 to provide photographic details of the surface so that a landing site could be selected for the forthcoming APOLLO MOON PROGRAMME.

lunar rover or **lunar roving vehicle** A battery-driven four-wheeled vehicle used for exploratory travel on the moon's surface. Lunar rovers were used by the astronauts of Apollo missions 15, 16, and 17 in 1971 and 1972 and left behind on the moon after use. A remote-controlled television camera mounted on the vehicle beamed pictures of the lunar surface direct to Earth. Also called **moon car**, **moon crawler**, or **moon rover**.

Lunik The name of the first three Soviet LUNA moon probes launched during 1959.

Lunokhod (Russ. moonwalker) The name of two Soviet eight-wheeled unmanned vehicles used for scientific exploration of the lunar surface. The vehicles were landed by LUNIK spacecraft in 1970 and 1973. Powered by solar cells and directed by radio from Earth, they travelled across the moon's surface taking pictures and measurements. The first Lunokhod was operational for 10 months; Lunokhod 2 covered a distance of over 35 km in 4 months.

lunatic fringe An expression ascribed to the US president Theodore Roosevelt in 1913. It described a minority group of people, especially those in a large organization, who hold extreme or eccentric versions of the views held by the majority.

lunch. **luncheon vouchers** (LVs) Vouchers worth a fixed amount of money, which are issued to employees and can be used to pay for meals in certain restaurants. The original purpose was to offer employees an alternative to providing a canteen with low-priced meals. LVs above a certain annual value are subject to taxation in the UK.

lunchtime abortion An abortion carried out by vacuum aspiration in which a suction tube is used to remove the fetus. First heard in the early 1970s, it refers to the method's quick and relatively safe procedure: though full recovery may take one or two days, some women return to work the same day after the recommended minimum half-hour rest.

Lupin, Arsène Fictional criminal turned detective, who featured in the novels and stories of the French author Maurice Leblanc. He first appeared in *The Seven of Hearts* (1907) and has been compared to two famous characters of British fiction, the upper-crust criminal Raffles and the super-sleuth Sherlock Holmes. Films about the *cambrioleur* include a German-made series of five films starring Paul Otto in the leading role (1910–11), an early Hollywood silent movie (1917), various talkies made in the 1930s and 1940s, as well as a 1962 French film starring Jean-Claude Brialy. The character also featured in a 1970s French television series.

lurgy or **lergi** British slang for an unspecified infectious illness, often referred to as the **dreaded lergi**. This word, particularly popular with schoolchildren in the 1950s and 1960s, was an invention of the GOON SHOW. Its etymology is unknown but it may have been a corruption of 'allergy'.

lurker (1) British slang for an unpleasant person, a ne'er do well. It was adopted by the PUNKS in the 1970s to describe themselves. There was a punk band of that name in London in 1977. (2) British slang for an unauthorized street trader. (3) Australian slang for a petty criminal.

lush (1) US slang for a drunkard or drug addict. The word came into popular use in the 1920s for an alcoholic but goes back to the mid-19th century when a whisky bottle was also humorously called a 'lush Betty'. It was also a slang word for alcohol in late 18th-century England, probably after a London brewer named Lushington. (2) Abbreviated form of luscious, indicating that someone or something is eminently desirable or attractive.

Lusitania The Cunard liner sunk by a German U-BOAT off the south coast of Ireland on 7 May 1915, while en route from New York to Liverpool. The ship sank within 20 minutes with the loss of 1198 lives, including 124 Americans. Among the dead were the millionaire Alfred Vanderbilt and the theatre producer Carl Frohman. The sinking was greeted with horror and outrage by the US press and public and although, initially, the US government maintained its policy of neutrality, the tragedy was certainly a contributory factor in its decision to enter the conflict against Germany in April 1917. Years later controversy over the sinking continued with accusations that the *Lusitania* was carrying substantial amounts of ammunition and other war materials; there was some speculation that Winston Churchill and the other Lords of the Admiralty had deliberately put the liner at risk in the hope of bringing America into the war.

> To die will be an awfully big adventure.
>
> CARL FROHMAN, quoting from *Peter Pan* as he jumped into the sea from the *Lusitania*.

LVs *See* LUNCHEON VOUCHERS.

Lycra The tradename (registered by E. I. du Pont de Nemours & Co.) of a shiny man-made elastic polyurethane fibre and fabric used extensively for sportswear – swimming costumes, leotards, cycling shorts, etc. – and other tight-fitting clothing.

Lyme disease An infectious illness first identified in 1975 among children in the Connecticut town of Old Lyme. Lyme disease, which is carried by a bacterium, can in rare cases prove fatal; it is characterized by pains in the joints, high fever, a rash, and fatigue. Research has shown that the infection is spread to humans by the bites of infected ticks.

Lysenkoism or **Michurinism** A movement, based on the maverick ideas of the Soviet geneticist Trofim Denisovich Lysenko (1898–1976) and the horticulturalist I. V. Michurin (1855–1935), that caused ideological and political upheaval in Soviet science from the 1930s to the 1960s. Lysenko came to prominence in 1929 with his proposals for the vernalization of cereal seed. This involved partly germinating and chilling winter wheat seed to induce it to germinate after sowing in the spring. This had the benefit of eliminating seed losses in the field due to overwintering, a problem of pressing concern to Soviet agriculture at that time. Moreover, Lysenko claimed that such environmentally induced changes in the seed could be inherited by successive generations of the plant. This contradicted prevailing scientific orthodoxy – notably the genetic theories of Mendel and others – and harked back to the early 19th-century beliefs of Jean Lamarck.

STALIN, untroubled by the lack of scientific validity of Lysenko's ideas, gave his backing to the young geneticist, whose influence rapidly increased. The Lysenkoists integrated their theories of heredity with Marxist dogma and denounced the conflicting theories of orthodox geneticists as bourgeois and contrary to Marxist thinking. A notable critic of Lysenkoist theory was Nicolai Vavilov, president of the V. I. Lenin All-Union Academy of Agricultural Sciences; in 1938 Vavilov was succeeded in this post by Lysenko. Two years later Lysenko became director of the Genetic Institute of the Soviet Union and a key figure in Soviet agriculture and biology. Vavilov was exiled to Siberia in the same year and died in 1943. Many other dissenting Soviet geneticists shared his fate.

Lysenkoism reached its high point in 1948 with a report to the Academy of Agricultural Sciences entitled *The Position in Biological Science*. Approved by the Communist Party Central Committee, this set out the ideologically acceptable view of biology for Soviet science. Further, this meeting directed that textbooks and courses be changed in line with Lysenko's doctrines. After Stalin's death Lysenkoism still prevailed under Khrushchev, even though Soviet agriculture was demonstrably failing because of its ill-conceived notions. Only with the fall of Khrushchev in 1964 did Lysenko's star wane. A committee investigating his work uncovered evidence of fraud, and he was ousted from his key administrative posts. Soviet biology was at last allowed to rejoin the mainstream of genetics research.

The lesson that emerges from this sad episode in the history of science is that scientific theories make unsuitable bedfellows for political and religious systems. Today's scientific truth must, if the evidence is against it, be prepared to become tomorrow's scientific heresy. Political and religious systems encourage their followers to believe that their truths are perennial.

Lytton report A report condemning Japan's invasion of Manchuria (18 September 1931) published in September 1932 by a commission appointed by the LEAGUE OF NATIONS and headed by Lord Lytton. The Japanese completely ignored the commission's findings and the major European powers proved incapable of united action. This unfortunate episode exposed the inadequacy of the League of Nations in preventing aggression.

M

M The codename of the fictional service chief in the James BOND novels of Ian Fleming. The character may have been based on the head of Military Intelligence in the UK during World War II, Maj.-Gen. Sir Stewart Menzies (1890–1968).

Mo, M1, . . . M5 *See* MONEY SUPPLY.

Ma Bell The affectionate nickname of America's Bell Telephone System, which evolved from a company formed in 1877 by the telephone's Scottish-born US inventor, Alexander Graham Bell (1847–1922). The 22 regional operating companies, such as Southern Bell and Southwestern Bell, were owned by the American Telephone and Telegraph Co. until 1984, when the US government broke up the (80%) monopoly. The independent companies, however, remain 'Ma Bell' or – more commonly now – 'Baby Bell' to their users.

> Ma Bell's babies grow big away from home.
> *The Independent*, 19 February 1991.

Mac. Mac the Knife (1) Nickname of the British prime minister Harold Macmillan in 1962 after he had sacked seven cabinet ministers, among them the Lord Chancellor, in what became known as the NIGHT OF THE LONG KNIVES after the infamous Nazi killings of 1934. *See also* SUPERMAC. (2) The nickname of the businessman Ian MacGregor (later Lord MacGregor; 1912–), who earned the resentment of British trade unions in the 1980s after he was appointed to make the coal and steel industries profitable.

The name was originally coined by Bertolt Brecht for the villain in *The Threepenny Opera* (1929), celebrated in Kurt Weil's well-known song with this title.

Mac the Mouth *See* SUPERBRAT.

Macwonder *See* SUPERMAC.

Macavity The subject of the poem 'Macavity: The Mystery Cat', by T. S. Eliot (1888–1965), published in the collection OLD POSSUM'*s Book of Practical Cats* (1939). A leading member of the feline underworld, Macavity is described by Eliot as "the bafflement of Scotland Yard" and "the Napoleon of Crime". He is never found at the scene of the crime and always has an alibi:

> "Macavity, Macavity, there's no one like Macavity,
> For he's a fiend in feline shape, a monster of depravity.
> You may meet him in a by-street, you may see him in the square –
> But when a crime's discovered, then *Macavity's not there*!"

Macavity and the poem about him appear in the Lloyd Webber musical *Cats*, based on T. S. Eliot's book. In this production the poem is read in a stage whisper.

McCarthyism Political witch-hunting; the hounding of communist suspects to secure their removal from office and public affairs. So called after US Senator Joseph McCarthy (1909–57), who specialized in these activities during the early 1950s. His relentless investigation of many prominent figures in various walks of life, from writers and film stars to members of the Democratic Party, caused public disquiet. His claim to have names of communists employed by the State Department was never proved; when he tried to level criticism at President Eisenhower in 1954 he was censured by the Senate and sacked. Thereafter the witch-hunt ceased.

McDonald's The most successful FAST FOOD company in the world. About 96% of Americans eat at least once a year at McDonald's; it is also the largest such chain in the UK, Canada, Australia, and Japan. The company opened its first restaurant in Moscow in 1990. McDonald's was started in 1940 as a single drive-in restaurant in San Bernardino, California, by the McDonald brothers, Richard and Maurice. They perfected assembly-line production, selling their hamburgers for 15 cents each. The name and technique was bought in 1955 by Ray A. Kroc, who introduced the golden-arch logo and built a $40 million Hamburger University to train employees. Kroc's perfected technology has sold some 60 billion hamburgers. He died in 1984 but lived to see his company Americanize the global food-service industry.

Mace Tradename for a form of chemical nerve irritant used as a tear gas. Mace causes a burning sensation in the eyes, nose, and throat and temporarily incapacitates the recipient. It was used by police in America for crowd control in the late 1960s and early 1970s, being particularly associated with the suppression of demonstrations against the VIETNAM WAR. It has also been used, in aerosol form, as a means of personal protection; in the UK, Mace aerosols are considered to be offensive weapons and their use is illegal. The word is also used as a verb: 'to mace someone' is to render them inactive by spraying them with Mace. The name is probably taken from the spice obtained from nutmeg.

macguffin A word invented by the film director Alfred Hitchcock (1899–1980), who used it to describe something that starts off the action of one of his film plots but subsequently turns out to be irrelevant. It later spread to the general language, meaning something that sparks off a course of action or process but loses its importance as events proceed. Hitchcock is on record as saying that he took both the name and the idea from a Scottish shaggy dog story in which a train passenger carrying a large odd-looking parcel was asked by other passengers what it contained. He replied that it was a macguffin; he then went on to explain that a macguffin was a lion in the Highlands. When it was pointed out to him that there are no lions in the Highlands, he replied that there were no macguffins either.

machine. a machine for living in *See* LE CORBUSIER.

machine code The binary code sequence that is directly understood and executed by a specific microprocessor or computer central processing unit (CPU). Computers execute instructions in machine code much faster than if they were translated into a higher level programming language, such as BASIC or PASCAL. However, machine code programming is a painstaking process and requires detailed knowledge of the design of a particular microprocessor.

machine gun Drug-abusers' slang for a hypodermic syringe. It was also used in prison slang in the 1960s.

Mach number The ratio of the flight speed of a body, aircraft, etc., to the speed of sound. The concept was devised by the Austrian physicist and psychologist, Ernst Mach (1838–1916). An aircraft flying at Mach 2 is travelling at twice the speed of sound. The first aircraft to reach the speed of sound, *i.e.* Mach 1, was the US rocket plane Bell XS-1, in 1947, which reached Mach 1.015 (1078 k.p.h or 670 m.p.h). *See* SUPERSONIC.

macho Aggressively male and virile: from the Spanish for the animal sense of male, hence the emphasis on strength and virility. Macho is mostly used as an adjective. The noun for the concept is **machismo**. Zsa-Zsa Gabor, the Hollywood film star, is said to have remarked:

> Men who are macho aren't mucho!

Machu Picchu A ruined Inca city in Peru, built at the end of the 15th century, which existed only as a fable till it was discovered in a well-preserved condition in 1911 by Hiram Bingham. The excellent condition of the find is due to the fact that the Spaniards never found it. Built on a mountain ridge in the Urubamba valley, near Cuzco, the city contains a palace, temple, and other buildings constructed of stone blocks and is surrounded by agricultural terraces. Its original name is unknown: Machu Picchu is the name of the mountain that rises above it.

McKenna duties An import tax introduced during World War I by Reginald McKenna (1863–1943), Chancellor of the Exchequer, and abolished in 1924. The duties were intended to restrict the import of luxury items, such as cars and watches.

Maclean See BURGESS AND MACLEAN.

Maclean mission A World War II mission led by Major General Fitzroy Maclean (1911–). Maclean and his men parachuted into Yugoslavia in September 1943 to provide assistance to Tito and his partisans in their resistance to the German occupation of Yugoslavia.

McLuhanism The theories of the Canadian writer Marshall McLuhan (1911–80), concerning the impact of mass communication and modern technology on society. McLuhan envisaged the world as a GLOBAL VILLAGE, and predicted that the media through which information is transmitted would become more important than the information itself: "the medium is the message." The role of the printed word would be significantly reduced in this world of instant awareness, where electronic communications technology would alter perceptions of space, time, and personal identity. These controversial ideas were propounded in such books as *The Gutenberg Galaxy* (1962) and *Understanding Media* (1964).

McMahon. McMahon letters Secret correspondence (1915–16) between Sir Henry McMahon, British High Commissioner in Egypt, and Sherif Hussein of Mecca (*c.* 1854–1931). In the letters, which were published in 1938, Hussein demanded that certain Arab lands be granted independence in return for Arab help during World War I. These included what is now Saudi Arabia, Israel, Jordan, Iraq, Syria, and Lebanon. McMahon appeared to pledge British support for all but Lebanon and part of Iraq, but inserted a carefully worded get-out clause to preserve the UK's freedom of manoeuvre. His 'promise' was subsequently compromised by the BALFOUR DECLARATION and the SYKES-PICOT AGREEMENT; it was totally disregarded by the Allies after the war.

McMahon Line The boundary between NE India and Tibet, as agreed in the Simla convention (1914). The McMahon Line follows the crest of the Himalayas, the natural boundary between the two countries. The convention was signed by Sir Henry McMahon, who represented the UK at the Simla conference, and by the Tibetan representative, but the Chinese government refused to recognize the McMahon Line and subsequently laid claim to much of Arunachal Pradesh (formerly called the North-East Frontier Agency) on the Indian side of the boundary. Chinese troops made two unsuccessful attempts to invade this territory, crossing the McMahon Line in 1959 and in 1962 (*see* LADAKH CRISIS) and the boundary remains in dispute.

macroeconomics The study of economic systems at the level of the country or economic bloc. It may be seen as the study of KEYNESIANISM, MONETARISM, and any other economic theories that relate the MONEY SUPPLY, employment levels, interest rates, government spending, investment, and consumption with inflation. Macroeconomics assesses the role that governments should play in an economy. *See* MICROECONOMICS.

mad. all over the place like a madwoman's custard A colourful Australian catchphrase of the post-war period, meaning 'in total disarray'. Variants included 'all over the place like a madwoman's knitting' (or 'lunchbox').

He went mad and they shot him The facetious reply, often given by Australian troops during World War II, to a query (especially from an officer) as to someone's whereabouts. Another version was the more graphic 'He went for a crap and the sniper got him'.

MAD Mutual Assured Destruction. The acronym for the ultimate result of the strategy of nuclear deterrence, pursued by the superpowers since the 1960s. MAD maintains the balance of terror by virtue of the massive nuclear arsenals possessed by America and the Soviet Union. In the event of a pre-emptive missile strike by one side against the other, the victim is assumed to retain the capability for substantial retaliation against the aggressor. The result would be so devastating to both sides that, in theory and one hopes in practice, a nuclear strike becomes unacceptable as a military option.

mad cow disease The colloquial name for bovine spongiform encephalopathy (BSE), a disease of cattle caused by the same class of virus-like entity that causes scrapie in sheep. It results in degeneration of the brain tissue and is invariably fatal. Having a very long incubation period, it became a problem to British herds in the 1980s, probably as a result of the use of cattlefeeds containing the brains of sheep infected with scrapie. There is some evidence that the virus can affect other species and a lingering fear that it could cause human brain disease. Although there is as yet no evidence for this, there was a sharp fall in the consumption of beef in the UK in the late 1980s as a result of these fears.

Mad Jack The nickname of Jack Howard, 20th Earl of Suffolk and Berkshire. Renowned for his flamboyant behaviour, he was killed in 1941 while defusing a bomb; he was posthumously awarded the GEORGE CROSS.

Mad Mike Nickname of Mike Hoare, a South African mercenary leader who became notorious for his involvement in various escapades in the Congo in the 1960s with the WILD GEESE mercenaries. He was imprisoned in 1981 following a failed coup in the Seychelles. He and 43 fellow-mercenaries were detected after their cover as members of the 'Froth Blowers' club on a golfing holiday was blown – one of their golf bags came open to reveal a gun; they hijacked an Air India jet back to South Africa, where they were arrested and put on trial.

Mad Monk *See* RASPUTIN.

Mad Mullah Nickname of Mohammed bin Abdulla, a mullah who gave great trouble to the British in Somaliland at various times between 1899 and 1920. He claimed to be the Mahdi (the Islamic messiah) and made extensive raids on tribes friendly to the British. The Dervish power was not finally broken until 1920, when the Mad Mullah escaped to Ethiopia, where he died in 1921.

Mademoiselle from Armenteers In World War I Amentières in N France was held by the British until the great German offensive of 1918. The army song 'Mademoiselle from Armenteers, Parlez-vous', which became widely known, originated in 1916. It was a modification of the much earlier song and tune 'Three Prussian Officers Crossed the Rhine'. It readily lent itself to improvisation, especially of a scurrilous nature:

O Madam, have you any good wine?
Parlez-vous;
O Madam, have you any good wine?
Parlez-vous.
O Madam, have you any good wine?
Fit for a soldier of the line?
Inky-pinky, parlez-vous.

Madison. Madison Avenue A street in New York City in which many advertising firms were formerly situated. In the 1940s Madison Avenue became synonymous with the advertising business itself. This sense came into being when an article on the contribution of the advertising business to World War II appeared in *New Republic*, signed Madison Avenue. Most leading advertising firms have now left the Avenue.

Madison Square Garden murder The murder of Stanford White (1853–1906), the US architect who designed Madison Square Garden, an indoor sports stadium in New York. White was murdered by the millionaire Harry Thaw on 25 June 1906 in Madison Square Garden itself. The murder was apparently motiveless: at his trial, Thaw was found guilty but insane.

Mae West Nickname of the inflatable life-jacket or vest worn by aircrews in World War II. It was an allusion to the generously-proportioned film star Mae West. *See* COME UP AND SEE ME SOME TIME.

Mafficking Extravagant and boisterous celebration of an event, especially on an occasion of national rejoicing. From the uproarious scenes and unrestrained exultation that took place in the centre of London on the night of 18 May 1900, when the news of the relief of Mafeking (besieged by the Boers for 217 days) became known. The 'heroic' character of Baden-Powell's defence has been questioned, but the impact made at the time is not in dispute.

Mafia A network of Sicilian criminal organizations that became increasingly powerful during the 19th century and in the 20th century became the most powerful controlling force in the underworld. 'Protection' by blackmail, boycotting, terrorization, and the vendetta are characteristic methods, developed when Sicilian politics came to be dominated by the *mafiosi*. The mafia's power was largely broken in Italy under Mussolini in the 1920s but it has not been exterminated. Sicilian immigrants introduced it into America, where it became a growing nuisance from the 1890s; indeed, Mussolini's firm measures caused a fresh influx to America, where the *mafiosi* joined the BOOTLEGGERS and gangsters of the Al CAPONE era. These groups eventually adopted the name **Cosa Nostra** (Ital. our thing, our affair), controlling much of the drug racket, gambling, and prostitution in the big cities despite repeated campaigns to bring such organizations to justice.

Mafia is apparently an Arabic word denoting a place of refuge, dating from the Arab conquest of Sicily in the 9th century; many Sicilian families found a *mafia* in the hills, where they duly became peasant bandits, with patriotic and family loyalties. Their resistance continued after the Norman conquest of the 11th century and later control by Spain. After the liberation and unification of Italy the Mafia made crime its fulltime pursuit.

mafiaology The study of the MAFIA crime families. Since the 1960s mafiaology has been of interest to professional sociologists, criminologists, and historians investigating the origins and operation of organized crime. The activities of the Mafia have also inspired numerous popular books, films, and television programmes, which feed on the public's morbid fascination with violence and corruption. *See also* FAMILY; GODFATHER.

magic. magical mystery tour A long round-about journey, often when the driver is lost or taking a not very direct short cut. The phrase was used by the BEATLES for the title of their 1967 film. Before the Beatles adopted the phrase, a 'mystery tour' was a holiday excursion (usually lasting for a day) to an undisclosed destination offered by various coach companies. Passengers usually found themselves at a location they would not have dreamt of visiting in normal circumstances.

magic bullet A drug designed to destroy a specific bacterium, virus, or cancer cell, without damaging healthy cells or tissue in the host. The term was originally used in the 1960s to describe the efforts of the German biochemist Paul Ehrlich (1854–1915) to develop chemical agents that would selectively destroy disease-causing organisms. This led to his discovery in 1910 of the antisyphilitic drug arsphenamine (marketed as Salvarsan).

magic eye A photoelectric cell used to control a circuit. In the simplest form a beam of light is directed onto the cell. When this is interrupted the circuit operates. Magic eyes are used in security devices and for the automatic opening of doors.

magic mushroom Any of various species of mushroom that contain psilocybin, a hallucinogenic substance similar in effect to LSD. In the UK, eating these mushrooms is not an offence; for certain sections of the population, collecting native species of magic mushroom, such as the liberty cap, is a popular seasonal activity.

Maginot. Maginot Line A zone of fortifications built along the eastern frontier of France between 1929 and 1934 and named after André Maginot (1877–1932), French minister of war, who sponsored its construction. The line, essentially to protect the returned territories of Alsace-Loraine, extended from the Swiss border to the Belgium border and lulled the French into a belief that they were secure from any German threat of invasion. In the event, Hitler's troops entered France through Belgium in 1940, leaving the Maginot line intact but totally ineffectual. *See also* SIEGFRIED LINE.

Maginot mentality Belief in a strategy of static defence (as in the MAGINOT LINE); it is also used contemptuously of one whose tactics are regarded as out of date.

maglev *Mag*netic *lev*itation. A system of rail transport in which the carriages are suspended above the rails by the repulsive effects of magnetic fields. The advantage of maglev transport systems is that there is no friction between the vehicle and the rail. The disadvantage is that extremely strong electromagnetic fields are required to hold the carriages in position. These can only be produced by high electric currents, which, under normal circumstances, would require an energy input over and above that gained by reducing friction. The key to maglev transport is the use of superconducting magnets, in particular the possibility of using materials that exhibit SUPERCONDUCTIVITY at temperatures well above absolute zero. A number of small-scale maglev transport systems have been tried on an experimental basis. The maglev only supports the carriages above the rail; forward motion is obtained by using a linear motor.

magnet. Magnet A weekly paper for boys, in which the stories of the rotund and ever-hungry Billy BUNTER and his friends at Greyfriars School first appeared. The stories were written by Charles Hamilton (1876–1961), under the pen-name Frank Richards, from 1908 until 1940; they subsequently appeared in book form. The stories, glorifying the fagging system in English public schools, gave the impression that spending half one's school life being beaten by older boys and the other half beating younger boys was all good Christian fun, which could be relied upon to produce trustworthy leaders of men who would cope unflinchingly with adversity.

magnet school A school that concentrates on providing high-quality teaching in a related group of subjects, such as the sciences, rather than the whole curriculum. The schools originated in America, where the education authorities provided them in areas predominantly occupied by Black families in order to attract Black and White pupils both from within the catchment area and from outside it, the aim being to achieve an even racial balance. Later the emphasis changed so that the importance of the schools was their excellence in a narrow range of subjects rather than their racial balance. In the late 1980s it was suggested that similar schools be set up in the UK.

magnicide The murder of a great or prominent person, especially when the murderer has no intelligible grievance against his victim, who appears to have been selected for his or her celebrity alone. In such cases the killer's motive is thought to be a wish to share, however fleetingly, in his victim's fame. The term, coined from Latin *magnus*, great, and *homicide*, appeared in US newspapers in the late 1960s, following the assassination of John F. Kennedy (1963), Martin Luther King (1968), and Robert Kennedy (1968).

magnificent. Magnificent Five The name used by Soviet intelligence for the five British spies in the BURGESS AND MACLEAN case.

Magnificent Wildcat Nickname of the Polish-born US silent film actress Pola Negri (Appolonia Chalupek; 1897–1987). Her career was effectively ended by the arrival of sound films; her earlier successes included *Forbidden Paradise* (1924).

Magnox reactor *See* NUCLEAR REACTOR.

magnum force Extremely powerful. The phrase is derived from Magnum, a tradename for a powerful revolver patented in America in 1935. A 1973 film of this name starred Clint Eastwood.

Mahâtma (Sansk. great soul) The title particularly associated with Mohandas Karamchand Gandhi (1869–1948), the Hindu nationalist leader who identified himself with the poor, practised prayer and fasting, and sought to achieve his political ends by non-violence (*see* SATYAGRAHA) until he became himself the victim of an assassin's bullet. An ardent advocate of independence for India, he was imprisoned (1922–24) by the British for his policy of civil disobedience and again in 1930 for distilling salt from seawater in defiance of the government's salt monopoly. During World War II he described as "a post-dated cheque on a failing bank" the British offer of postwar independence in exchange for Indian cooperation in winning the war. Yet again imprisoned by the British, on his release he played a crucial part in the postwar decision by the British to grant independence, based on partition between India and Pakistan. When violence between the two newly independent nations broke out, Gandhi undertook a fast to try to bring about cooperation between Hindus and Muslims. This was resented by Hindu fundamentalists, one of whom assassinated this supreme Indian spiritual leader, who was widely regarded as a saint.

> Mahâtma is a well-known Sanskrit word applied to men who have retired from the world, who, by means of a long ascetic discipline, have subdued the passions of the flesh, and gained a reputation for sanctity and knowledge. That these men are able to perform most startling feats, and to suffer the most terrible tortures, is perfectly true.
>
> MAX MÜLLER: *Nineteenth Century*, May 1893.

Maigret The fictional detective created by the Belgian writer Georges Simenon (1903–89). Jules Maigret's rank in the Paris police was *commissaire*, roughly equivalent to the British rank of superintendent, but in English translations of the novels he is known as Inspector Maigret. He first appeared in the early 1930s and subsequently featured in some 100 stories, such as *La Marie du port* (1938) and *Maigret et le clochard* (1963). These have been translated into many languages, making the pipe-smoking detective a household name throughout the world.

Maigret's approach to solving crime was psychological, relying on insight into the criminal's motives rather than the scientific investigation of clues and logical deduction based on them. In the late 1950s and early 1960s the detective appeared on British television in the highly successful series *Maigret*, with Rupert Davies in the title role. The Maigret stories have also been adapted for the cinema in French, English, German, Italian, and other languages. Some of his character traits were borrowed from the author's own father.

mail. mail bomb *See* LETTER BOMB.

mailshot *See* JUNK MAIL.

main. Main Drag of Many Tears The nickname, since the 1940s, of 125th Street, Harlem, where poor and oppressed Blacks traditionally gathered to be distracted from their worries by cheap entertainment. Drag in US Black slang means street, a borrowing from Victorian Cockney slang.

mainframe Originally the name for the central processing unit (CPU) and primary memory of a computer; since the development of the MINICOMPUTER and MICROCOMPUTER, the mainframe has become the largest type of computer installation. These are used by such organizations as banks and insurance companies, which need to process massive amounts of data. Mainframes are bulky and expensive, require large clean air-conditioned rooms, have enormous storage capacities, support many input and output devices (terminals, printers, etc.), and need to be operated by highly trained personnel.

mainline Drug-abusers' slang meaning to inject an illegal drug intravenously. The main line is the main blood vessel in the arm; drugs injected here take immediate effect. The image derives from fast and powerful mainline trains. The word is sometimes used metaphorically, as in 'he's put on so much weight he must have been mainlining chocolate', indicating a love of eating chocolate that approaches addiction.

Main Street The principal thoroughfare in many of the smaller towns and cities of America. Sinclair Lewis's novel of this name (1920) epitomized the social and cultural life of these towns and gave the phrase a significance of its own.

make my day *See* GO AHEAD, MAKE MY DAY.

Malcolm X The assumed name of Malcolm Little (1925–65), US Black militant leader, an influential figure in the campaign for racial equality. The son of a Baptist minister, he was converted to the faith of the BLACK MUSLIMS in prison in 1952. Having changed his name to Malcolm X – he considered the surname Little to be a relic of slavery – he became actively involved in the work of the sect on his release the following year. In 1963, after a disagreement, he left the Black Muslims and founded a rival group, the Organization of Afro-American Unity, which endorsed the use of violence in the pursuit of racial equality. He was subsequently converted to orthodox Islam and took the name Malik El-Shabazz. The rivalry and hatred between the Black Muslims and the Organization of Afro-American Unity culminated in the assassination of Malcolm X at a rally in New York in 1965.

male chauvinist pig (MCP) A man who regards women as the inferior sex and wants them to keep to their traditional role in society, especially raising children, cooking, sewing, and looking after the home. His behaviour towards women is in accordance with these views; in particular, he sees nothing wrong with regarding women as sex objects. The term was coined shortly after the start of the WOMEN'S LIB movement in the late 1960s (*see also* FEMALE CHAUVINIST PIG).

> I enjoy fucking my wife. She lets me do it any way I want. No Women's Liberation for her. Lots of male chauvinist pig.
>
> JOSEPH HELLER: *Something Happened* (1974).

Mallaby-Deeleys A once popular term for off-the-peg clothes and suits; after Sir H. Mallaby-Deely, MP (1863–1937), who founded a firm for making cheap well-cut ready-mades for the middle classes after World War I. The venture ended in failure.

Mallard Famous British steam locomotive, which in 1938 established a long-standing record for the highest speed reached by a steam locomotive (202.8 k.p.h., 126 m.p.h.). Immediately recognizable by its distinctive streamlined design, this Gresley A4 Pacific engine was subsequently preserved in working order as an example of rail engineering excellence.

mallie or **mall rat** US slang for a female teenager who loiters in shopping malls, as somewhere to pass the time rather than a place to spend money. This phenomenon sprang up with the malls themselves in the 1980s.

Malvern Festival A theatre festival founded in 1929 at Malvern (now in Hereford and Worcester) by the British theatre manager and director Sir Barry Jackson (1879–1961). A number of George Bernard Shaw's plays, such as *The Apple Cart*, were first performed at the Malvern Festival. New productions also included plays by J. B. Priestley, James Bridie, and other contemporary writers. In 1939 the festival was discontinued; it enjoyed a brief revival in 1949 and was re-established in 1977 as a drama and musical festival featuring the works of Shaw and Sir Edward Elgar, who is buried at Malvern.

mamba Acronym for Middle-Aged Middle-Brow Accomplisher. It refers to an average middle-of-the-road person who manages to get things done and has made a success of his life. It was coined in the late 1980s when the fashion for acronyms was at its height.

mammoplasty Plastic surgery to alter the shape of the breasts. Small breasts may be enlarged by means of a silicone rubber implant. This is inserted into a pocket created behind the breast, made via an incision at the base of the breast, along the natural crease line. Some women develop scar tissue around the implant and may require further surgery to remove an excessive build-up. Improving the shape of a large or drooping breast is a more complex procedure, involving the removal of the necessary skin, fat, and underlying tissue, plus relocation of the nipple. This inevitably leaves scars, not only under the breast but also around the areola and vertically from the nipple to the base.

mamser *See* MOMZER.

man. a man's gotta do what a man's gotta do An expression used to emphasize the difficult and dangerous actions a man is forced to take in his life. It originated with John Wayne in *Stagecoach* (1939); paraphrases have since featured in many Westerns. Outside the context of the Wild West, however, it is invariably used facetiously.

Shortly before the GULF WAR of 1991 a US truck driver, William J. Brown, from Sioux Falls, South Dakota, decided he had to embark on a one-man peace mission to see Saddam Hussein personally. This he accomplished.

> In Sioux Falls a man's got to do what a man's got to do.
>
> *The Independent*, 20 March 1991.

A rather more remote paraphrase is also used in reply to a protest made about a dog fouling the pavement: **A dog's got to do what a dog's got to do.**

It's that man again! *See* ITMA.

man for all seasons A phrase used to describe an adaptable 'Renaissance man' of manners and accomplishments who can be regarded as dependable and competent in all situations. The phrase was popularized by Robert Bolt as the title for his 1960 play about Sir Thomas More. It was also the title of the 1966 film starring Paul Scofield. More had been described in these words by his contemporary, Robert Whittington.

Man from Missouri *See* GIVE 'EM HELL HARRY.

man from the Pru Part of the 1940s advertising slogan for the Prudential Assurance Company; the full slogan was: 'Ask the man from the Pru'. The company was founded in 1848 and a man *had* gone around collecting the insurance payments. Thus the phrase 'man from the Pru' was familiar in many households before it was used in the advertising slogan.

Man in Black The narrator of the BBC radio programme *Appointment With Fear*, first broadcast on 11 September 1943. The haunting tones belonged to Valentine Dyall and became a hallmark of this series of mystery and suspense stories, originally written for US radio by John Dickson Carr. Dyall's father, Franklin Dyall, narrated the second series, beginning in January 1944, but the Man in Black Junior returned to set spines tingling in later series. In 1949 Dyall was given his own series, *The Man In Black* – described as "famous tales of mystery and fear". *Appointment With Fear* returned in 1955 after a seven-year break, again with Dyall as narrator. The series was again resurrected in 1991, with Edward de Souza cast as the Man in Black.

Man in the Iron Mask A 20th-century equivalent of the historical prisoner made famous in the writings of Alexandre Dumas in the 19th century. It arose from a bet made in the National Sporting Club in London in 1907. With a stake of $100,000 offered by the US millionaire John Pierpont Morgan and the British sportsman Lord Lonsdale, the young and wealthy Harry Bensley agreed to attempt to walk round the world pushing a pram: he would start out with no more than £1 and wear an iron mask for the whole time. Other rules he had to observe included finding a wife (without showing his face) and paying for his journey by selling postcards. He set out on 1 January 1908 from Trafalgar Square wearing a 4½lb helmet. At Newmarket he sold a postcard to Edward VII for £5 but at Bexleyheath he only narrowly escaped imprisonment after he refused to remove his mask in the magistrates' court, having been arrested for selling postcards without a licence. By 1914 he had traversed 12 countries and turned down 200 offers of marriage. With the outbreak of World War I, however, Bensley had to give up the challenge as he wished to join up. The sporting peers agreed to allow him to do so and gave him a reward of £4000, which he gave to charity. Bensley himself survived the war but lost his fortune, most of which was invested in Russia. He died in reduced circumstances in Brighton in 1956.

Man of a Thousand Faces Nickname of the US film star Lon Chaney (1883–1930), who played numerous villains, usually in heavy disguise. His films included *The Hunchback of Notre Dame* (1923) and *The Phantom of the Opera* (1925). *Man of a Thousand Faces* was also the title of a biographical film about him made in 1957 and starring James Cagney.

> Don't step on that spider, it might be Lon Chaney.
>
> Joke from the 1920s.

Man of Steel The English rendering of the Russian name Stalin, adopted by the dictator Joseph Dzhugashvili (1879–1953). A BOLSHEVIK from 1903, he was frequently imprisoned and exiled in the years preceding the OCTOBER REVOLUTION of

1917. By 1922 he was general secretary of the Communist Party under Lenin; in 1929 he became dictator and began the reign of terror that made his assumed name synonymous with brutality and repression by the state (*see* FIVE-YEAR PLANS; STALINISM; YEZHOVSHCHINA). Treated circumspectly by the Soviet Union's allies during World War II, he became even more autocratic once the war was over, implacable in his hostility towards opposition both at home and abroad. After his death, psychiatrists conjectured for many years that the 'man of steel' had actually suffered from a variety of psychotic conditions. Long before the liberalization of Soviet society in the late 1980s he had been stripped of his almost legendary status as a great leader of the Soviet peoples.

> What could we do? There was a reign of terror. You just had to look at him wrongly and the next day you lost your head.
>
> NIKITA KHRUSHCHEV, 18 March 1956.

Man on the Wedding Cake Nickname of Thomas E. Dewey, governor of New York (1902–71), who was unexpectedly defeated by Harry S. Truman in the presidential election of 1948. The nickname was bestowed on him by Grace Hodgson Flandrau and much repeated by Alice Roosevelt. The nickname, with its overtones of ridicule and lack of character, was subsequently held to be partly responsible for Dewey's defeat. Truman's victory was a major surprise to the pollsters, who had predicted an easy win for Dewey: *The Chicago Tribune* had been so confident of Dewey's success it had gone to press with the headline 'Dewey defeats Truman'. *The Washington Post*, which had been similarly caught out, invited Truman and the pollsters to dinner to eat 'humble pie'.

man up! US street slang exclamation of alarm, warning of the arrival of the police. It is used by the lookouts posted to keep watch while a crime is committed. It is thought to derive from THE MAN, pejorative slang for a figure of authority.

man who rides the screaming gasser US Black slang from the 1940s for a policeman in a patrol car equipped with sirens.

man with headache stick US Black slang for a policeman, a 'headache stick' being a truncheon.

Man with the Golden Flute Nickname of the Irish flautist James Galway (1939–), in imitation of *The Man with the Golden Gun*, the title of a James BOND thriller by Ian Fleming. Galway was often pictured with his gold and silver flutes, which were made to his own specifications.

Man with the Orchid-Lined Voice Nickname of the Italian tenor Enrico Caruso (1873–1921). He was the first major opera star to be recorded and the first to make a wireless broadcast. Unfortunately his recordings were made in the pre-electric era and although electric remakes were produced much later, these were recorded not from live performances but from the pre-electric recordings. Nevertheless, the quality and amazing tone control of Caruso's voice can still be heard. When he died of peritonitis in Naples at the age of 48, New York's flags were flown at half mast.

Man you Love to Hate Catchphrase associated originally with the actor Erich von Stroheim (1885–1957), but subsequently with many other screen villains as well as others outside the cinema world. It was first used in publicity for the 1918 propaganda film *The Heart of Humanity*, in which von Stroheim played a particularly unpleasant and violent German officer. In 1979 a film, *The Man You Love to Hate*, commemorated the life and work of von Stroheim, who had gone on to become an admired Hollywood director.

one small step for man *See under* ONE.

the man (1) US slang for the police, the government, or the White establishment. Originally used contemptuously by Blacks to mean White authority in general, it is now used by disadvantaged social groups for any part of the establishment. (2) Slang for a dealer in illegal drugs, as in 'I'm waiting for my man', a song by the Velvet Underground rock band released in 1967.

The Man Who Never Was The title of a 1955 film relating the true story of a fictitious Royal Marines officer who played a key role in deceiving the Germans about the Allied invasion plans in World War II. The original book was written by a naval officer, the Hon. Ewen Montagu QC, who organized the whole affair. Montagu arranged for the body of a Major William Martin to be washed up in neutral Spain in 1943; when it was found that he was carrying apparently top-secret documents, local German agents quickly passed the word to the German High Command. Among the documents found on the dead Marine were a letter from the Vice-Chief of the Imperial General Staff to General Alexander and a letter from Lord

Mountbatten to Admiral of the Fleet Sir Andrew Cunningham, both of which suggested that Sardinia, not Sicily as expected, would be the target of the Allied assault. These letters, backed up by Martin's personal documents (including two theatre ticket stubs for London shows), convinced the German agents that they had stumbled upon genuine Allied invasion plans. When the Allies were finally handed back the body and the documents by the Spanish authorities, scientific analysis showed that the envelopes had been opened. The plan succeeded: when the Allies finally attacked Sicily, they were opposed by the Italians and only two German divisions; Allied losses were thus greatly reduced. His duty done, 'Major Martin' was buried with full military honours in a Spanish cemetery; his real identity was never revealed, in deference to the wishes of his family. All that is known about him is that he was a serviceman who had died in London of pneumonia.

Manassa Mauler Nickname of the US boxer Jack Dempsey (1895–1983). World heavyweight champion (1919–26), he acquired an almost legendary reputation for his ferocious punch before losing his title in controversial circumstances to Gene Tunney (*see* ROBBED, WE WUZ). His nickname was derived from Manassa, the town in which he was born.

Manchester school A group of dramatists associated with the Gaiety Theatre in Manchester. Notable members of the Manchester school included Stanley Houghton (1881–1913), whose controversial play *Hindle Wakes* was first performed at the Manchester Gaiety in 1912; Harold Brighouse (1882–1958), author of the comedy *Hobson's Choice* (1915); and Allan Monkhouse (1858–1936). The Gaiety Theatre company, the first modern English repertory company, was founded in 1908 by Miss Annie Horniman (1860–1937); its first production was Allan Monkhouse's *Reaping the Whirlwind.*

Manchukuo A puppet state created by the Japanese in 1932, after the MUKDEN INCIDENT, from the three provinces of Manchuria in NE China. The state was largely administered by the Chinese, but remained under Japanese control. Henry P'ui, the last emperor of the Manchu dynasty, returned from retirement to become the ruler of Manchukuo until 1945, when the state was dissolved after Japan's defeat in World War II. Manchuria was subsequently redivided into the provinces of Heilungkiang, Kirin, and Liaoning.

Manchurian candidate Someone who has been brainwashed by a foreign power to obey orders without thinking. The term is derived from the novel by Richard Condon (1915–), *The Manchurian Candidate* (1959), about a US POW who returns from Korea brainwashed as an assassin by the Chinese. This was made into a successful film (1962), directed by John Frankenheimer (1930–).

Mancini murder *See* BRIGHTON TRUNK MURDERS.

Mandates Commission An organization set up by the LEAGUE OF NATIONS after World War I to supervise the administration of the former overseas possessions of Germany and Turkey. These included Iraq, Syria, Palestine, and the African colonies of Tanganyika, the Cameroons, and Togoland. Mandatory powers over these territories were assigned to the UK, France, Belgium, and other countries, who submitted annual reports to the Mandates Commission. The Commission itself consisted of representatives from Belgium, France, Holland, Italy, Japan, Portugal, Spain, Sweden, and the UK; representatives from Germany, Norway, and Switzerland joined at a later date. In 1945 it was superseded by the UN Trusteeship System.

Mandelbaum Gate The control point for traffic passing from one sector of the divided city of Jerusalem to the other. The city was divided between Israel and Jordan in 1948 and the Mandelbaum Gate remained in operation until Israel took possession of the whole of the city in 1967 (*see* SIX-DAY WAR).

Manhattan. Manhattan eel US slang for a used condom. It is so called because of the large number of discarded condoms that can be seen floating in New York harbour.

Manhattan Project The codename given to a US project begun in the early 1940s with the aim of developing an atom bomb for use during World War II. Great secrecy and great haste were required in the race to construct such a bomb before the Germans, who were believed to be working on a similar project. Research and development took place at various laboratories, notably Los Alamos, New

Mexico, under the direction of the physicist J. Robert Oppenheimer. The Manhattan Project culminated in the testing of the first atom bomb on 16 July 1945 and its first use in war at HIROSHIMA on 6 August 1945. The total expenditure on the project from start to finish was around 2000 million dollars. *See* NUCLEAR WEAPON; OPPENHEIMER AFFAIR.

We knew the world would not be the same.
J. ROBERT OPPENHEIMER, 1945.

Manila Pact The treaty signed in Manila on 8 September 1954 on the creation of the South East Asia Treaty Organization (*see* SEATO). Signed by representatives of America, Australia, France, New Zealand, Pakistan, the Philippines, Thailand, and the UK, the treaty came into force on 19 February 1955 and was formally ended in 1977.

manky British slang meaning disgusting or filthy. It is derived from It. *mancare*, to be lacking, and is also influenced by 'mangy' and 'grotty'. It is used in the north of England to mean naughty or spoilt.

Mannerheim Line A line of fortifications built in the 1930s across the Karelian Isthmus, along the border between Finland and the Soviet Union. The line successfully protected Finland from invasion by Soviet forces at the beginning of the WINTER WAR (1939–40) but was breached in February 1940. The Mannerheim Line was named after Baron Carl Gustaf Emil Mannerheim (1867–1951), commander-in-chief of the Finnish defence forces during the Winter War and later president of Finland.

Mansion House speech A speech made by David Lloyd George in July 1911, at the Mansion House in London, in which he issued a strong warning to Germany that the UK would support France in any conflict that might arise out of the AGADIR CRISIS. This declaration was notable not only for its vehemence but also for its unexpectedness: as chancellor of the exchequer Lloyd George had been largely concerned with social reform and had shown little interest in foreign policy.

Manson gang A HIPPIE group living in a commune near Los Angeles, which in 1969 was responsible for a series of drug-crazed killings that shocked US society for their brutality. Led by the veteran convict and obsessive Charles Manson (1934–), members of the 'Family', as Manson called it, indulged in a quasi-religious and orgiastic lifestyle in which LSD played a major role. Their excesses reached an unacceptable climax when they carried out five murders in the house of the film director Roman Polanski; among the victims was Polanski's heavily pregnant wife (the actress Sharon Tate). In a previous incident they also killed supermarket millionaire Leno LaBianca and his wife. Manson's followers, after their arrest later in the year, claimed they were unaware of their victims' identities and had been inspired to kill after listening to the BEATLES song 'Helter-Skelter'. During the trial President Nixon attracted the judge's criticism when he was quoted in a newspaper to the effect that Manson was guilty, while Manson himself delivered tirades about the threat of race war; the four accused members of the gang were sentenced to death (in practice an indefinite life sentence).

Mao jacket *See* NEHRU JACKET.

maquis The thick scrubland in Corsica and Mediterranean coastal lands to which bandits formerly retreated to avoid capture.

In World War II French patriots, who formed guerrilla groups in the countryside during the German occupation (1940–45), attacking their patrols, depots, etc., were known as **the Maquis**. *See* FFI; RESISTANCE.

Marburg disease or **green monkey disease** A disease of vervet (green) monkeys and humans caused by a virus. It is named after the town of Marburg, Germany, where the first case was reported in 1967. The patient had contracted the disease from a consignment of vervet monkeys imported from Africa. Ticks, mites, or other arthropods may act as a reservoir of the virus, which can also be transmitted from person to person. This fact, coupled with the high mortality rate of around 30%, dictates stringent isolation measures for suspected cases. The incubation period is 3–9 days, followed by the development of fever, headache, muscle pain, nausea, and vomiting. Later, a skin rash appears and, in about 50% of cases, internal bleeding.

Marchioness disaster A tragedy that happened on the River Thames in London on 20 August 1989. The *Marchioness* pleasure boat carrying some 150 people, was rammed from behind by the dredger *Bowbelle* and sank within minutes, drowning 51 of her passengers. The accident happened near the Tower of London in the early hours of the morning. On board the *Marchioness* were partygoers celebrating the birthday of young City businessman, Antonio Vascancellas, who was among the victims, many of whom came from the capital's fashionable social set.

March on Rome The arrival in Rome of Mussolini and thousands of his BLACKSHIRTS (Fascist supporters) on 28 October 1922, shortly before the establishment of Italy as a Fascist state. Mussolini and his armed followers travelled to Rome by various means and entered the city with little or no opposition from military or civilian authorities. The head of the cabinet resigned and King Victor Emmanuel III invited Mussolini to form a new government.

Marconi affair A scandal in the career of David Lloyd George as chancellor of the exchequer. In 1912 Lloyd George had bought shares to the value of £2000 in the US Marconi company. He had obtained these shares at a preferential rate through the managing director of the company, Godfrey Isaacs, brother of the attorney general Rufus Isaacs (later 1st Marquess of Reading). Meanwhile, shares in the British Marconi company had enjoyed a sudden increase in value as the result of a government contract to build a chain of radio stations. Although the two companies were legally separate, there were inevitable rumours of corruption. The parliamentary committee set up to investigate the matter found Lloyd George and Isaacs not guilty of corruption, although the transaction was described as imprudent. Nevertheless, both ministers' reputations were damaged by the affair.

Marco Polo Bridge incident An incident that renewed hostilities between China and Japan at the beginning of the Sino-Japanese War. On 7 July 1937 Japanese and Chinese troops began firing at each other at the Marco Polo Bridge on the outskirts of Peking. This was followed by further clashes in the Peking-Tientsin area. The Chinese refused to withdraw their troops but a series of attacks and counter-attacks led to their expulsion by the Japanese at the end of July.

mardarse or **mardie** British slang for a mother's boy, a softie. It is particularly used in the north of England, where 'mardie' is also used as an adjective to mean bad-tempered or (of a child) spoilt.

Mareth Line A line of fortifications in S Tunisia. Originally built by the French to repel the Italians, the line was used by Rommel in the North African campaign of World War II. On 20 March 1943 the British Eighth Army under the command of Montgomery launched an attack on the Mareth Line, which led ultimately to the surrender of the AXIS forces in Tunisia.

marginalize To reduce the power, influence, or importance of a person or thing. For example, to marginalize a politician is to make him ineffective in the decision-making process. As with many such verbs it originated in America but became common in the UK in the second half of the 1980s.

Marienkirche frescoes A series of medieval wall paintings in a church in the German port of Lübeck, which in 1952 became the subject of a major art scandal. The Marienkirche was damaged by an incendiary bomb in 1942, revealing medieval frescoes previously hidden under a layer of whitewash. However, by the time work could begin on their restoration in the post-war period, they had suffered extensive damage from exposure. Dietrich Fey, owner of a firm of art restorers, was finally awarded a contract to restore the masterpieces (for a large sum) in collaboration with the artist Lothar Malskat. Gradually (out of the public gaze) the frescoes were restored to their former glory; in 1951 Fey himself showed the completed decorations to the West German Chancellor Konrad Adenauer. The German post office celebrated the restoration with a series of stamps depicting the frescoes. One year later, however, Malskat (who had received no money for his work) confessed that the frescoes were fabrications and bore no relation to the original paintings, which had been too faint to work from. Upon examination, some of the figures in the frescoes were recognized as likenesses of RASPUTIN, Marlene Dietrich, and members of Malskat's family. A sensational trial followed in which the German art establishment was deeply embarrassed; both Fey and Malskat were jailed.

Mariner A series of SPACE PROBES launched during US space programmes of the 1960s and early 1970s. Mariner 2, launched on 27 August 1962, passed within 22,000 miles of Venus, measuring the atmospheric and surface temperatures of the planet. Mariner 5, launched on 14 June 1967, came close to Venus, passing within 2500 miles of the planet. Mariner 4, launched on 28 November 1964, studied the atmosphere of Mars and photographed the surface of the planet; Mariners 6 and 7, launched in 1969, made further photographic and thermal investigations; and Mariner 9 went into orbit around the planet. Mariner 10, launched in 1974, passed Mercury three times. Mariners 11 and 12 were renamed and used in the VOYAGER programme (1977). Mariners 1, 3, and 8 failed to achieve their missions.

Marines. By the grace of God and a few Marines Catchphrase used in acknowledging that a difficult task has been fulfilled. It became widely known after General MacArthur's landing during the invasion of the Philippines in World War II; as he came ashore he was confronted by a sign put up by the US Marines, reading: "By the grace of God and a few Marines, MacArthur returned to the Philippines".

Maritime Trust A British charitable organization created in 1969 and dedicated to the restoration and upkeep of vessels that have played significant roles in the nation's maritime history. Several examples of such vessels are on public display in and around the River Thames in London, including the Trust's Historic Ship Collection, located near Tower Bridge, and the 19th-century tea clipper, *Cutty Sark*, permanently moored at Greenwich. Besides its own restoration work, the Trust provides grants to other bodies engaged in similar work, such as the MARY ROSE Trust.

market-maker A person who trades in shares and bonds on a stock exchange to make a profit, rather than to earn a commission. The role of the market-maker after the deregulation of the UK stock market (the BIG BANG of 1986) is roughly equivalent to that of the pre-1986 stockjobber. At the end of the 19th century a market-maker engaged in the slightly dubious activity of trading in a particular stock, with the sole intention of arousing the interest of potential buyers.

marleys Rhyming slang for piles, haemorrhoids; from Marley Tiles, a tradename for thermoplastic tiles made in a factory in Marley Lane, Riverhead, Kent.

> If it wasn't for my marleys I'd've given 'im what for.
>
> Elderly gentleman recovering in hospital from a mugging (quoted in *Evening Standard*).

Marlow, Captain The narrator of *Lord Jim* (1900), *Heart of Darkness* (1902), and other novels and short stories by the Polish-born British writer Joseph Conrad (1857–1924). Marlow provides a commentary on the events and characters of the story, performing a role similar to that of the chorus in Greek drama. Sometimes he is an observer, sometimes he intervenes in the action; his reminiscences contribute to the impressionistic style of Conrad's work.

Marlow is introduced at the end of the fourth chapter of *Lord Jim* as "a . . . man who sat apart from the others, with his face worn and clouded, but with quiet eyes that glanced straight, interested and clear". Most of the remainder of the novel consists of Marlow's narrative, related "later on, many times, in distant parts of the world, . . . at length, in detail and audibly".

Marlowe, Philip A fictional private detective created by the US writer Raymond Chandler (1888–1959), inspired by the hard-boiled heroes of the detective stories of Chandler's contemporary Dashiell Hammett. Marlowe first appeared in *The Big Sleep* (1939) and subsequently in a number of other novels, such as *Farewell, My Lovely* (1940) and *The Long Goodbye* (1954), many of which were adapted for the cinema.

Marlowe is a cool tough guy, attractive to women, and never short of a cynical wisecrack; he is often revealed, however, as a moral and lonely character. The film of *The Big Sleep* (1946) starred Humphrey Bogart as Marlowe and also featured Lauren Bacall; typical of Marlowe are the following lines from it:

> I don't mind if you don't like my manners. I don't like 'em myself. They're pretty bad. I grieve over 'em on long winter evenings.

marmalize British slang meaning to demolish completely, *i.e.* to punish. It is possibly related to 'marmalade', suggesting the fate of being cut up into tiny strips like orange peel in marmalade. It is usually used as a mock threat by adults to naughty children: 'If you do *that* again, I'll marmalize you'.

Marmite Tradename for a yeast and vegetable extract used as a spread and as an added flavouring to casseroles, etc. Marmite, which was first manufactured in 1902, is actually a French word for a type of cooking pot, a picture of which appears on the label of the Marmite jar. Marmite soon established itself as one of those necessaries much yearned for by expatriots abroad, being synonymous with memories of children's high tea.

Marne, Battles of the Two battles of World War I fought along the River Marne in NE France, both of which resulted in notable victories for the Allied armies. In the first battle of the Marne (5–9 September 1914) the British Expeditionary Force and French troops commanded by Joffre thwarted the advance of the Germans towards Paris, forcing them back across the River Aisne.

The second battle of the Marne (18 July 1918) was one of the last and most significant offensives of the war, consolidated by subsequent victories at Amiens and elsewhere. Foch's Allied forces succeeded in driving the Germans, commanded by Ludendorff, back to the HINDENBURG LINE; within three months Germany had begun peace negotiations.

Marple, Jane Fictional amateur detective created by the crime writer Agatha Christie (*see* QUEEN OF CRIME). Miss Marple, a matronly figure whose gentle manner disguises a capacity for powerful deductive reasoning, made her first appearance in *Murder in the Vicarage* (1930) and her last in *Sleeping Murder* (1976), although the latter was actually written in the 1940s. She has also featured in films, played by Margaret Rutherford amongst others, and a TV series, in which the veteran actress Joan Hickson endeared herself to many thousands of viewers in the title role.

Mars A series of SPACE PROBES launched by the Soviet Union in the 1960s: Mars 1 was launched on 1 November 1962. The probes were intended to study and investigate the planet Mars but their missions were largely unsuccessful.

Mars bar Tradename for a chocolate-covered bar with a creamy toffee-like filling, which is manufactured by Mars Confections Ltd, a company established in the UK in 1932 by Forrest Mars, an immigrant American. The Mars Bar immediately became popular and has remained so ever since.

> A Mars a day helps you work, rest and play.
>
> TV advert.

Martian invasion scare The result of a radio broadcast by Orson Welles based on H. G. Wells's science-fiction fantasy *The War of the Worlds*. The novel, first published in 1898, is the story of a Martian invasion of Britain. On 30 October 1938 the voice of Orson Welles was heard on US radio in an adaptation of the novel, in which the scene of the action was shifted to America and the invasion was reported in a simulated news broadcast. Listeners mistook this for a genuine news report of an actual Martian invasion of New Jersey and widespread panic ensued. Welles subsequently became known as 'the man who scared America to death'.

Marshall Plan The popular name for the European Recovery Programme sponsored by US Secretary of State G. C. Marshall, to bring economic aid to stricken Europe after World War II. It was inaugurated in June 1947. Most states, other than the Soviet Union and her satellites, participated. The UK ceased to receive Marshall aid in 1950. *See* LEND-LEASE.

Martini, shaken not stirred Catchphrase associated with James BOND, the hero of Ian Fleming's novels. It did not, however, appear in the books; it was a feature in the films made in the 1960s and 1970s, with the intention of epitomizing Bond's sophisticated lifestyle. It has been much parodied and ridiculed.

> There is no hint of the agent's shaken-but-not-stirred arrogance in the mature Connery's appearance or demeanour.
>
> Interview with Sean Connery, who played Bond, *The Independent*, 16 February 1991.

As an interesting footnote, shaking a dry martini, so the experts say, renders it unappetisingly opaque; it is, in fact, much better stirred.

Marx brothers The brothers Chico (Leonard Marx; 1886–1961), Harpo (Adolph Marx; 1888–1964), Groucho (Julius Marx; 1890–1977), Zeppo (Herbert Marx; 1901–79), and Gummo (Milton Marx; 1893–1977), who constituted one of the most famous of all comedy teams in the history of the cinema. Zeppo and Gummo were only involved in early productions, but the other three went on to make many films, until they disbanded in 1949. The legend that Harpo (named for his skill as a harpist) was dumb was, of course, merely put out to support the parts he played in their films. Many of Marx brothers' sharpest quips appeared in their films and were spoken by Groucho:

> One morning I shot an elephant in my pajamas.
> How he got into my pajamas I'll never know.
>
> *Animal Crackers* (1930).

I want to register a complaint. Do you know who sneaked into my room at three o'clock this morning?
Who?
Nobody, and that's my complaint.
Monkey Business (1931).

Look at me: I worked my way up from nothing to a state of extreme poverty.
Monkey Business (1931).

My husband is dead.
I'll bet he's just using that as an excuse.
I was with him to the end.
No wonder he passed away.
I held him in my arms and kissed him.
So it was murder!
Duck Soup (1933).

Don't point that beard at me, it might go off.
A Day at the Races (1937).

Hey boss, you got a woman in there?
If I haven't, I've been wasting thirty minutes of valuable time.
A Night in Casablanca (1945).

Many of the anecdotes told about the brothers are true; some are undoubtedly apocryphal. Groucho, again, was the greatest source of anecdotes. Resigning from a club, he sent a telegram:

I don't care to belong to any social organization which would accept me as a member.

One year he stayed at the Hotel Danieli in Venice. Descending in the lift from the fourth floor, the lift was stopped at the third floor. Three priests entered, one of whom, recognizing Groucho, told him that his mother was a great fan of his. "Really", said Groucho, "I didn't know you guys were allowed to have mothers."

But Chico also had his share of stories. It is said that when his wife caught him kissing a chorus girl, he protested that he wasn't doing any such thing – "I was only whispering in her mouth," he said.

Marxist-Leninism *See* LENINISM.

Mary. Mary Jane US slang for cannabis; it is derived from the direct translation of the Mexican word *marihuana*.

Mary of Arnhem The name used by Helen Sensburg in her Nazi propaganda broadcasts to British troops in NW Europe (1944–45). Her melting voice made her programmes very popular with the British, but without the results for which she hoped.

Mary Rose A warship in the English navy during the reign of Henry VIII that sank in 1545 in Portsmouth Harbour. One of the first true warships to be constructed (1509–10), she carried a crew of some 700 men. The cause of her sinking is unknown but may have been due to incompetent loading or handling. She went down with a full complement of crew and equipment, having just embarked to engage the French Navy off the Isle of Wight. In 1967 the hull was located in the mud and a rescue operation was launched to salvage the wreck. Many Tudor artefacts were recovered from the vessel, followed by the hull itself in 1982. These are now on display in a dry dock in Portsmouth. The Mary Rose Society was formed in 1978 to help finance restoration work and the upkeep of the vessel. *See also* VASA PROJECT.

maser *See* LASER.

M*A*S*H Mobile Army Surgical Hospital, also the title of a US (CBS) television comedy that satirized war through the wit of the staff of such a hospital during the KOREAN WAR. The series began in 1972 during the VIETNAM WAR, making obvious parallels. By 1974 *M*A*S*H*, starring Alan Alda, McLean Stevenson, and Loretta Swit, had won an EMMY as the year's outstanding comedy. The final episode, shown on 28 February 1983, was the top-rated programme in US television history, drawing more than 50 million viewers. The TV series was based on the 1970 film of the same name directed by Robert Altman. It has also been shown on British television, with several repeats.

Mason, Perry A fictional lawyer created by the US writer Erle Stanley Gardner (1889–1970) in a series of novels that combine courtroom drama with the mystery and suspense of a detective story. Perry Mason is a defence lawyer whose clients are always found innocent and whose investigations usually reveal the identity of the true guilty party. The character achieved widespread recognition and popularity on both sides of the Atlantic with the highly successful US television series *Perry Mason* (1957–65), based on Gardner's stories, in which Raymond Burr played the title role. In the final episode of the series, *The Case of the Final Fadeout*, Erle Stanley Gardner made a guest appearance as the judge.

mass production A system for producing large quantities of a standardized item. Mass production is usually automated and capital-intensive, the labour input being confined to simple and repetitive tasks on the assembly line. It was Henry Ford (1863–1947) who introduced the assembly line into car production in 1912. Using this technique, he had manufactured 15 million Model Ts (*see* TIN LIZZIE) by 1928.

master. masterclass A session of instruction in which a person who is a master of a specific art or a specific discipline gives advice to people who have achieved a high standard but who are still able to benefit from the master's experience. Much of the work in a masterclass takes the form of analysis and critical evaluation of the individual's work. Masterclasses in various musical disciplines and in acting have made very popular television programmes.

Mastermind *See under* START.

The Master Nickname of the British dramatist and entertainer Sir Noël Coward (1899–1973), who became one of the leading figures in the theatre of the 1930s. His status was established in the theatre with *The Vortex* (1924); subsequently his 'mastery' was confirmed both as a revue artist and in the film world. Coward himself disliked the nickname, possibly because it had already been given to the writer Somerset Maugham (1874–1965). It was also associated with the US film director D. W. Griffiths (1873–1948).

> I've over-educated myself in all the things I shouldn't have known at all.
>
> NOËL COWARD: *Wild Oats*.

Masters. Masters and Johnson A US research team that carried out the first comprehensive study of human sexual activity under laboratory conditions. William H. Masters (1915–), a physician, and Virginia Johnson (1925–), a psychologist, began their joint research in 1954 and 10 years later established the Reproductive Biology Research Foundation in St Louis. They published their influential book, *The Human Sexual Response*, in 1966 and were married in 1971. In their physiological studies Masters and Johnson observed the process of sexual arousal in 694 male and female volunteers in the age range 18 to 89. Their conclusions, acclaimed at the time as a breakthrough in our understanding of human sexuality, now appear somewhat trite – what is known by every normal man and woman accustomed to sexual relationships. For example, they concluded:

> . . . that the sexual response cycle of arousal and climax is a natural physiological property of the intact adult human being and responds predictably to adequate stimulation.

However, their physiological work did enable them to progress to sex therapy. The publication of their treatment results, with a success rate of over 80% and a relapse rate of only 5%, led to the establishment of large numbers of sex-therapy clinics throughout America and to very large sales for their book *Human Sexual Inadequacy* (1970). Some of this preoccupation of the public with sexual therapy arose from a prurient interest in Masters and Johnson's use of female 'surrogate' sexual partners as part of the therapeutic process for single males with sexual problems. Although they abandoned this form of therapy because of the "administrative and ethical problems involved", the concept had progressed sufficiently for some observers to wonder how their clinic was to be distinguised from a brothel. *See also* KINSEY REPORTS.

Masters tournament A US golf tournament played each spring at the Augusta National Golf Course, Georgia. Established in 1934, the Masters tournament is an open event at which leading international players are invited by the Augusta National Golf Club to compete for large prizes.

Mata Hari The pseudonym of Margaretha Zelle (1876–1917), a Dutch spy during World War I. Mata Hari, which means eye of the dawn, chose her pseudonym when she began to specialize as an exotic Indonesian dancer. She had a number of high-ranking Allied officers as lovers, gathered military classified information from them, and relayed it to the Germans, who had recruited her as a spy. In 1917 her spying activities were uncovered and she was executed by the French. Her trial attracted so much public interest that 'Mata Hari' has since become an epithet for any femme fatale who acts as a spy or betrays someone.

Matapan stew (Austr.) A meal concocted from left-overs, so called from the fact that the cook of HMAS *Perth* served a scratch hot meal during the Battle of Matapan, March 1941.

Matilda The central character in one of the best known of Hilaire Belloc's *Cautionary Tales* (1907). Her dreadful fate, with its allegorical message, has since become as familiar to succeeding generations of children as those of far older traditional nursery rhymes:

> Matilda told such Dreadful Lies
> It made one Gasp amd Stretch one's Eyes
> For every time she shouted "Fire"
> They only answered "Little Liar" . . .
> And therefore when her Aunt returned
> Matilda, and the House, were Burned.

Matteotti murder The assassination of the Italian socialist politician Giacomo Matteotti (1885–1924). On 30 May 1924 Matteotti made a speech in the Chamber of Deputies denouncing the Fascists; several days later he disappeared, having been murdered by six assassins who were alleged to have been hired by officials of the Fascist Party. The discovery of Matteotti's body on 16 August 1924 was a damaging blow for Mussolini's government. The assassins were brought to trial: three were found not guilty and the others were given light sentences, which were subsequently remitted. A retrial in 1947 resulted in sentences of 30 years' penal servitude for the three guilty men.

Maud Committee A committee set up in 1940 to investigate the possibility of using uranium fission to make an ATOM BOMB. Chaired by the British physicist Sir George Paget Thomson (1892–1975), the Maud Committee presented its positive findings on the feasibility of a uranium bomb to the British government in 1941. The project was then transferred to America for further development (*see* MANHATTAN PROJECT).

The committee is said to have been named after Maud Ray, the former English governess of the Danish physicist Niels Bohr. Bohr managed to send his friends in England a telegram immediately after the German occupation of Denmark in 1940. After assuring his friends that he was safe and well, he added at the end of the telegram " . . . please inform Cockcroft and Maud Ray, Kent". After hours of ingenious decoding of this apparently meaningless message, the decoders decided it was a message from Bohr telling Cockcroft to "make uranium day and night". The unfortunate Maud Ray never learnt that her former protegé was well.

Mau Mau A secret political society formed by the Kikuyu tribesmen of Kenya, possibly as early as the 1940s. Their chief aim was to drive the Europeans out of Kenya by terrorist means (the word *mau* means 'get out!'); the members were bound by oaths and dire threats if the oaths were broken. The existence of the society became known in 1952, when its members led a rebellion against the colonial government in Kenya, committing terrible acts of violence not only against White settlers but also against Blacks who refused to support the organization (*see* LARI MASSACRE). In 1953 Jomo Kenyatta, later president of Kenya, was sentenced to seven years' imprisonment as a suspected leader of the Mau Mau. The rebellion continued until 1960. For a time, to 'mau-mau' someone was consequently, in US slang, to harass or bully them.

Mau Mau bee *See* KILLER BEE.

mavin US slang for a nightclub host. It is derived from the Hebrew, meaning understanding, via Yiddish, in which it means an expert. In this slang sense it implies someone who knows the people who are allowed into the club.

maxi or **maxiskirt** *See* MINISKIRT.

Maximum John Nickname of the US judge John Sirica (1904–), who became widely known during the WATERGATE trial for pressing for severe punishment of the guilty parties.

mayday A phonetic form of the French *m'aidez*, translated into English as 'help me!' Mayday is an internationally recognized distress call for people requiring help, as set down by the International Radio Telegraph Convention in 1927.

May Economy Committee An extraparliamentary committee set up in 1931 by Philip Snowden, chancellor of the exchequer, to suggest economy measures. Its recommendations included drastic reductions in unemployment benefit and pay cuts for civil servants and members of the armed forces, which sparked off the INVERGORDON MUTINY. The unpopularity of these proposals resulted in a Cabinet rebellion and the subsequent collapse of Ramsay MacDonald's Labour government. MacDonald handed in his resignation as prime minister on 24 August 1931, but remained in office at the head of the newly formed NATIONAL GOVERNMENT.

Mayflower II A replica of the ship that carried the Pilgrim Fathers to America in 1620. In 1957 Mayflower II attempted to duplicate the Pilgrim Fathers' voyage, departing from Plymouth, England, on 20 April and arriving at Plymouth, Massachusetts, 53 days later (the original journey took rather longer). With a US designer and British builders, Mayflower II was a joint venture between America and the UK: the costs of constructing the 90-foot ship and the 5400-mile journey were met by contributions from both countries.

Maze prison A high-security prison built near Belfast in the early 1970s to hold terrorist suspects or convicted terrorists. Republicans in Ulster still refer to it by its original name, Long Kesh, or, simply, the Kesh. Both Loyalist and Republican prisoners were originally accommodated in Nissen huts – officially known as the Maze (Compound). In 1972 a group of Republican prisoners, led by Billy McKee, embarked on a hunger strike for prisoner-of-war status. Shortly afterwards the British government granted 'special status' to convicted prisoners in the Maze. This decision was reversed in 1976, from which time new inmates were held in eight new single-storey H-shaped blocks – the infamous **H-blocks**. Each wing of every H-block contained 25 cells, dining room, exercise yard, and recreation room. The crosspiece of the 'H' – paradoxically known as 'the Circle' – contained offices, medical room, classrooms, etc. Other facilities within the complex – known as the Maze (Cellular) and said at the time to be the most modern in Europe – included sports hall, workshops, hospital, and two all-weather sports pitches.

The Maze was now effectively two prisons, surrounded by a 17-ft high 2-mile concrete security wall overlooked by sentry posts. In the H-blocks, prisoners were segregated on sectarian lines. Shortly after the H-blocks were opened, Republican prisoners started a campaign for the reinstatement of special political status. A refusal to wear prison uniform led eventually to the so-called dirty protest, begun in 1978: prisoners confined themselves to the cells and resorted to smearing excrement over the cell walls. These protests culminated in 10 Republicans starving themselves to death in 1981. The first to die, on 5 May, was Bobby Sands, who had been elected to Parliament while in the Maze. His death, and that of Francis Hughes shortly after, sparked a wave of rioting in the province. Despite the protest, the British government refused to concede over the issue of political status for Maze prisoners. However, the prison, and in particular the H-blocks, remained a potent symbol of Republican opposition throughout the 1980s.

mazuma or **mazooma** US slang from the early 1960s for money. Originally from Yiddish, it reappeared in the late 1980s in the UK with a host of other slang words for money. It is said to derive ultimately from the Chaldean *m'zumon*, meaning ready, necessary. It appears in this form in the Talmud.

MBE *See* ORDER OF THE BRITISH EMPIRE.

MCP *See* MALE CHAUVINIST PIG.

me. ME Myalgic Encephalomyelitis. A viral disease affecting the nervous system, characterized by extreme fatigue, poor coordination, depression, and a general feeling of malaise. The disorder can be very long-term and has been called both **malingerer's disease** and **yuppie flu**, since there are often no physical symptoms. It is also known as **post-viral syndrome**.

me decade The description of the 1970s coined in a 1976 article in the *New Yorker* magazine by the US journalist Tom Wolfe (1931–). It refers to the narcissistic preoccupation with self-improvement and personal happiness, which he regarded as characteristic of the US culture in that decade. The phrase was also used in the UK of the Thatcherite values of the 1980s.

meals on wheels A UK welfare service that provides hot meals to elderly or housebound people, who are unable to shop or cook for themselves. The meals are prepared in central kitchens and transported by car or van to the homes of these people by voluntary workers organized by the WRVS (Women's Royal Voluntary Service). Recipients of the meals pay a token charge for the service, which is subsidized by the social services departments of local councils.

mean Slang for impressive, excellent. Originally Black slang dating from the 1940s.

mean machine Slang term of approval for a car or a motorcycle. It is also used of a very attractive male or of the male sex organ. Originally part of Black US slang of the 1960s, its use has spread to the UK.

mean! moody! magnificent! The advertising slogan for the film *The Outlaw* (1943), produced by Howard Hughes and starring his new find, Jane Russell. Despite the promise of the slogan and the censorship wrangle that ensued, the film that emerged shocked no one.

means test The principle of supplying evidence of need before qualifying for relief from public funds, *i.e.* a test of one's means. Such tests were introduced by the NATIONAL GOVERNMENT in 1931 for those whose unemployment benefit was exhausted, and the resulting inquisition was much resented by those concerned. It took note of any earnings by members of the household and all monetary assets, and penalized the provident. The regulations governing public assistance were modified after World War II but some non-contributary SOCIAL SECURITY benefits are still means-tested.

meathead One of the many slang names for a complete fool or idiot. The term originated in America in the 1940s but did not become common in the UK until the late 1980s. *See also* HEAD.

Mebyon Kernow (Sons of Cornwall) The society of Cornish nationalists, established in 1951. Their flag is the emblem of St Piran (a 5th-or 6th-century saint who discovered tin in Cornwall). The flag consists of a white cross, which symbolizes tin, on a black field, which represents the ground rock from which it is extracted.

Meccano The tradename of a construction set for children, first produced by Meccano Ltd of Liverpool in 1907. Meccano is a streamlined version of the original name 'Mechanics Made Easy', used by Frank Hornby for his invention in 1901. Hornby was also the inventor of Hornby model trains. The first Meccano sets consisted of green metal strips of various shapes and sizes with holes drilled in them, together with nuts, bolts, wheels, and other items that could be used to build a wide range of mechanical models of motor vehicles, cranes, etc. A plastic version, aimed at the junior end of the market, was introduced at a later date.

For more than 50 years, Meccano gave hours of educational enjoyment to generations of children and their parents and was even used in the field of engineering design. When Meccano Ltd ceased trading in the 1970s, the tradename passed through the hands of a number of other manufacturers and Meccano sets disappeared from the toyshops for several years, returning in the 1980s.

medallion man A 1970s heterosexual male with a predilection for fashion accessories, most typically the neck chain and medallion suspended from it. Many regard the 1978 film *Saturday Night Fever* as portraying the epitome of medallion man in John Travolta's mean Italian-American, who lives to dress and to dance, perfecting his rhythmic gyrations under the strobe lights of New York's discotheques. The trousers were tight and the shirt unbuttoned to reveal a bare but hairy (if possible) torso and the medallion – large, loud, and vaguely redolent of Olympian attributes. By the mid-1980s medallion man had been parodied into history.

> Singer Tom Jones . . . remains a macho sex symbol after 25 years, but now feels his Medallion Man image can be an embarrassment.
>
> *The Times*, 13 March 1991.

media Plural of *medium*: now widely used as a common name for the chief agencies that disseminate information in society, including newspapers, magazines, radio, and television. It is, of course, a shortened form of mass media. The communication explosion has been a 20th-century phenomenon. Before the advent of radio, telegraphy, etc., news travelled slowly. News of engagements in medieval wars could take weeks to reach the home country: in the 1991 GULF WAR, the media made sure that the British public knew what was happening more or less as it happened.

media event An event, usually in the world of politics, entertainment, or sport, arranged by public-relations personnel specifically to attract members of the media with the object of creating the maximum publicity.

Medicaid The US public-health programme to provide hospital and medical care for those who cannot afford it. This was established by Congress in 1965 as a joint state-federal plan in which the federal government funds 50–80% of a state's cost, depending on its citizens' average income. Each state must meet federal standards but may choose the services it wishes to provide. Any indigent person qualifies for Medicaid, and some states include the 'medically indigent', who are unable to pay medical bills that are incompatible with their earnings. *See also* FAMILY GANGING.

Medicare The US public-health insurance programme to provide hospital and medical care for persons aged 65 and older. Some disabled persons also qualify. The programme covers treatment at hospitals, nursing homes, and at home (after a deductible sum of over $500 is paid each year). It also pays 80% of physician and other medical costs not covered by the hospital insurance. This Congressional programme began in 1966. In 1988, Congress added the Medicare Catastrophic Coverage Act to expand coverage, but so many elderly Americans objected to the surtax to fund its cost (more than $32 billion over five years) that the Act was repealed the next year. Medicare is financed by a tax added to social security payments.

Meek, Private Napoleon Alexander Trotsky A character in the play *Too True to be Good* by George Bernard Shaw, first performed in 1932. Private Meek was based on T. E. Lawrence (*see* LAWRENCE OF ARABIA), a friend of Shaw's: the motorcycle (*see* BOANERGES) that was to cause Lawrence's premature death in 1935 also features in the play.

mega- Originally a Greek-derived prefix used to indicate a million, particularly in scientific SI UNITS: a megavolt is 10^6 volts, a megawatt is 10^6 watts, etc. In the 1980s *mega-* was also used more generally to mean very great or large; it was applied in general contexts, for example, **megabucks** (a great deal of money), **megacrowds** (a great many people), and **megastar** (a great film star).

megabyte (MB) In computing, loosely, one million bytes, or more accurately 1,048,576 bytes (one megabyte is 1024 kilobytes (KB) and one kilobyte is 1024 bytes). A byte is eight bits (binary elements), a bit being the basic unit of information in a computer. Memory capacity and the capacity of such storage devices as hard and floppy disks are measured in megabytes. The average microcomputer has a memory of at least one megabyte and the average hard disk will store 40 megabytes.

megadeath A unit representing the deaths of one million people; it was used by military bureaucrats at the height of the COLD WAR to calculate the likely effects of a nuclear exchange. The term is now used more loosely to mean an horrifically large number of deaths, as in a natural disaster.

megillah US slang, from Yiddish, for a long written screed or, more recently, for a long verbal account that omits no details, is probably repetitive, and will certainly bore the listener. It is used in such sentences as 'He wrote me a whole megillah . . . ' and 'Spare me a megillah, just tell me the facts'. The word came from the Hebrew, meaning scroll, and is often used in a religious context to refer to the Book of Esther.

Mein Kampf (Ger. My Struggle) The book by Adolf Hitler (1889–1945) that describes his political and racial theories and misreadings of history, which in due course became the Nazi 'Bible'. The first part was written when he was in prison after the abortive MUNICH PUTSCH of 1923. It was published in two parts (1925 and 1927). The original title was *Four and a Half Years of Struggle against Lies, Stupidity and Cowardice*, but the author was persuaded to think of something snappier. *See* HITLERISM.

Melba toast Toast that has been sliced down the centre and subsequently baked in the oven. According to tradition it was named after the Australian opera singer Dame Nellie Melba (Helen Porter Armstrong, née Mitchell; 1861–1931). While staying at the Savoy Hotel in London she was served dried-up fragile slices of toast that had been left too long in the oven. When the maître d'hotel apologized she cut him short, protesting how delicious it was. It was subsequently served to her, and to everyone else, in this state. *See also* PEACH MELBA.

mellow Slang for satisfying, cool. Originally Black slang dating from the 1930s, it is particularly associated with cool JAZZ. It was revived in 1991 in the military slang of the GULF WAR, when the mood of troops before the outbreak of hostilities against Iraq was described as 'mellow', meaning calm and collected.

meltdown Originally, the disastrous melting of the over-heated core of a nuclear reactor over which the operators have lost control, as happened at CHERNOBYL in the Soviet Union in 1986. The word has since entered the general language to describe a sudden economic collapse; it became particularly popular at the time of the crash of the world stock markets in 1987.

Melvin US slang of the 1950s for a dull person; based on the notion that anyone called Melvin must be extremely boring. The British equivalent is BRIAN.

men. men in grey suits Establishment figures who are unlikely to be seen in casual clothing and indeed are unlikely to be seen at all. They are the *éminences grises* of an organization, who make the ultimate decisions. It was the men in grey suits who were reputed to have persuaded Margaret Thatcher that her position as prime minister and leader of the Tory party was no longer tenable after the challenge from Michael Heseltine, so forcing her resignation on 22 November 1990.

Men's Lib An organization established in America in the late 1960s with the aim of freeing men from the burden of fulfilling the traditional image of the male role in society. It was, of course, intended as an answer to the more ubiquitous WOMEN'S LIB.

Menin Gate A giant war memorial erected in 1927 at Ypres in W Belgium. It stands in memory of the 55,000 British soldiers who died during World War I at the three battles that took place in and around Ypres. The names of the missing cover the entire edifice, while the graves of the identified dead stretch a great distance in all directions.

Mensa An international society for people who have a high IQ. Founded in the UK in 1946, the organization has no political or religious affiliations; members are of all ages and from all walks of life. Prospective members pay a small fee to take a supervised IQ test: those who achieve scores above a fixed level (approximately the top 2% of the population) are invited to join the society. Mensa organizes conferences and other events on a national basis and there are also local special-interest groups that enable members to form social and professional relationships with like-minded individuals. The name Mensa (Latin for 'table') was chosen to convey the image of a round table where all meet on equal terms.

Mensheviks (Russ. minority party) The moderate Russian social democrats who opposed the BOLSHEVIKS in the OCTOBER REVOLUTION of 1917.

menu In computing, a list of options that usually appears on the screen at the start of a programme, showing the commands and facilities available to the user, which can then be selected by a keystroke. Software making frequent use of menus is described as 'menu-driven'; it is usually much more USER-FRIENDLY than standard software. Even easier to use are computers with a **WIMP** (Windows, Icons, Menus, and Pointing devices) interface, which features 'drop-down' menus (extended lists accessed by a single menu title) to control virtually every aspect of their operation. Menu options are presented in the form of icons in individual windows on the screen, which can be selected by a pointer moved by a MOUSE.

MEP Member of the European Parliament. The parliament, which meets in Strasbourg or Luxembourg, has 518 MEPs who serve for a term of five years and are elected by universal suffrage by the 12 EC member states. The MEPs sit in political groupings (*e.g.* Communists, Socialists, Conservatives, Christian Democrats), not in national delegations, and deliberate on the legislative proposals of the EC Commission.

Mercedes The name of a car produced by the original German Daimler company. The name was that of a young girl, Mercedes Jellinek, whose father, Emil Jellinek, an Austrian diplomat, owned several Daimler cars, which he used for racing. In 1899 he entered one of his cars in the French Tour de Nice under the name 'Herr Mercedes'. After the Mercedes car had won the race, Jellinek bought a large number of identical cars, for which he was given the sole selling rights in Austria, Hungary, France and America, using the marque 'Mercedes'. It was not long, however, before all Daimler's cars were called Mercedes. When, in 1925, Daimler merged with Carl Benz's firm, the products of the merged company, Daimler-Benz, became known as **Mercedes-Benz** cars. Later Benz was dropped and the Merc, as it is called in the UK, became a highly successful post-war product of West Germany. The name Mercedes was much used for girls in 17th-century aristocratic Spanish circles but became more widely known in Europe after Dumas had so named the lover of Edmond Dantès in *The Count of Monte Cristo* (1844–45). It is said that Jellinek named his daughter after this Mercedes.

merchants of death Arms manufacturers and dealers. The epithet is derived from the title of a book (1920) by H. C. Engelbrecht and F. D. Hanighen, which investigated the suggestion that the arms merchants were to some extent instrumental in the start of World War I.

Mercury Project The first manned flight of the US space programme. The first Mercury spacecraft, named Freedom 7, was manned by Alan Shephard and launched on 5 May 1961, less than a month after the flight of the Soviet astronaut Yuri Gagarin, the first man in space. Freedom 7 and its successor Liberty Bell 7 reached altitudes of 116 miles and 118 miles, respectively, in ballistic flights lasting approximately 15 minutes. In 1962 the first US manned orbital flights were achieved by Friendship 7, Aurora 7, and Sigma 7. After the flight of Faith 7 in 1963 the Mercury project was replaced by the GEMINI programme.

mercy flight An aircraft or helicopter trip undertaken to relieve suffering or distress. This phrase, very much part of the 20th century, arose from the ability of aircraft to provide rapid access to the remotest regions, making it a favoured means of bringing urgent supplies to a disaster area or transporting victims away from such an area.

Meredith. We're in, Meredith A popular catchphrase derived from the very successful Fred KARNO sketch, *The Bailiff*, produced in 1907. It depicted the stratagems of a bailiff and his assistant, Meredith, attempting to enter a house for purposes of distraint. The phrase was used by the bailiff each time he thought he was on the verge of success.

merit. meritocracy Rule by those of superior intellect and talents. The term was popularized by Michael Young in his book *The Rise of the Meritocracy* (1958), in which he argued that educational achievements had replaced both noble birth and inherited wealth as the route to power in society.

Order of Merit *See* OM.

Merrill's Marauders A special infantry unit of US volunteers, organized by Brig.-Gen. F. D. Merrill (1903–55) in Burma during World War II. Trained in jungle warfare, they operated in the same way as the CHINDITS, using guerrilla tactics to harass the enemy. The Marauders set off in February 1944 to march several hundred miles through the Burmese jungle. Although weakened by disease, hunger, and exhaustion, they brought their campaign to a triumphant conclusion with the capture of Myitkyina in August 1944, establishing a vital air base along the supply route from India to China.

Mers el-Kébir A port near Oran on the Mediterranean coast of Algeria, which became a French naval base in 1935. A large number of French warships took refuge at Mers el-Kébir in June 1940, after the armistice between France and Germany. The British, anxious to prevent these vessels from falling into the hands of the AXIS forces, tried in vain to negotiate with the French commander, Admiral Gensoul. After the rejection of their final ultimatum on 3 July 1940, the British had no alternative but to attack the fleet, causing considerable damage and the loss of 1300 French lives.

Mersey sound (1) The characteristic POP MUSIC produced by the BEATLES and their contemporaries during the 1960s. The music was associated with the Merseyside area, notably Liverpool, birthplace of the Beatles and a number of pop groups of that era. (2) The work of the Liverpool poets, Adrian Henri, Roger McGough, and Brian Patten, who often gave readings together at the peak of their popularity in the 1960s. Their work was published together in Volume 10 of the Penguin Modern Poets series, under the title *The Mersey Sound* (1967).

meshugga (Heb. madness) US slang, from Yiddish, meaning crazy. A crazy person is a **meshuggener**. Like 'crazy' itself, meshugga can mean certifiably insane as well as foolish; for example: 'He's in a psychiatric hospital, poor fellow, hopelessly meshugga' or 'Don't let that meshuggener drive . . . '.

A specific kind of craziness – more particularly a foolishness – is a **meshugaas** (or **mishegaas**). It is often no more than a fairly harmless obsession: 'His meshugaas is that he believes that in order to stay alive he has to jog three miles every morning'. The Yiddish words entered the US language in New York around the turn of the century, with many other Yiddishisms.

mess. Here's another fine mess you've gotten me into Oliver Hardy's catchphrase from the LAUREL AND HARDY comedy films of the 1920s and 1930s. Hardy bemoans his fate of having such a hopeless partner as Stan Laurel. One of their films was actually called *Another Fine Mess* (1930).

message. message received loud and clear A standard phrase used in the early days of radio communications, meaning: I understand what you are telling me. It has since passed into more general use.

messenger RNA A molecule found in living cells that performs a crucial role as 'messenger' of the genetic information contained in the cell's genes. The cell manufactures proteins according to instructions carried by the genes. These instructions are in the form of a GENETIC CODE within the DNA molecule that constitutes the genes. The code is 'transcribed' with the formation of a messenger RNA molecule, very similar to the DNA of the genes, whose bases form a sequence complementary to that of the DNA, in effect a 'mirror image' of the code. The messenger

RNA molecules can move to different parts of the cell, where the message is 'translated' by another type of RNA – ribosomal RNA – and the corresponding protein is produced. The activities of the cell are determined by the proteins it produces, hence the vital importance of the RNA messengers to the life of the cell. The role of messenger RNA was elucidated in the 1950s and 1960s through the work of many biologists.

Messerschmitt Any of a number of aircraft designed by the German engineer Willy Messerschmitt (1898–1978). The Me-109 fighter, designed in 1935, won the world speed record in 1939 and was the most successful German aircraft of World War II: the Luftwaffe were supplied with some 33,675 Me-109s. The Me-262, capable of speeds up to 600 m.p.h., was the first jet fighter to be used in military action. Fortunately for the Allies, Hitler intervened in its development to give priority to jet bombers, delaying the introduction of the Me-262 until 1944. Other less successful Messerschmitt aircraft included the Me-110, which was outclassed by the HURRICANE and the SPITFIRE, and the single-jet Me-163.

Messina brothers Five members of an Italian family who were involved in procuring prostitutes and running brothels in London and other UK cities. For some 30 years the brothers made large profits from their work, at the expense of the women concerned. By the mid-1960s, after a period of imprisonment, all five had left the UK, either voluntarily or by deportation. However, some of their London brothels remained in operation, controlled from the brothers' new headquarters in Italy.

Meteor *See* GLOSTER METEOR.

meter maid Originally (in the 1950s) a US name for a policewoman employed to patrol metered parking areas and report offences; it was later applied to female traffic wardens in the UK. Owing to their uniforms and their ability to inflict summary punishment, women traffic wardens have acquired a special place in male mythology, featuring either as grim-visaged gorgons or as figures of sexual fantasy. The Beatles' song 'Lovely Rita, Meter Maid' ("When it gets dark you tow my heart away") appeared in 1967.

Method, the An acting technique developed from the theories of Konstantin Stanislavsky (Konstantin Alekstzev; 1863–1938) and taught from 1950 onwards at the Actors' Studio, New York, under the directorship of Lee Strasberg (1901–82). Strasberg was a former pupil of Richard Boleslavsky, who had brought Stanislavsky's ideas to America in the 1920s. The most important principle of the Method technique is the actor's total understanding of and identification with his character's motivations, which results in greater realism in his subsequent portrayal of the character. The technique was widely criticized, but remained an important influence on stage and screen acting in the latter half of the 20th century. Notable exponents of the Method include Marlon Brando and Dustin Hoffman.

metrication Conversion of any of a variety of units of measurement to those based on the decimal system. The metric system was first suggested in 1585 by Simon Stevin of the Low Countries but not used until it was promoted by Napoleon and established by French laws of 1795 and 1799. It came into general usage in Europe in the 1830s. In the UK it was authorized by law in 1864, although bills to make it compulsory were defeated in 1871 and 1907. The British stuck proudly to their own unwieldly and illogical hotchpotch of units, known as the Imperial System, until 1963, when the yard and the pound were given definitions by law in terms of metric units.

The metre, the cornerstone of the metric system, was originally defined (1791) as one ten-millionth of the length of the quadrant of the Earth's meridian passing through Paris. This piece of Gallic jingoism was replaced in 1927 by a definition relating the metre to the length of a platinum-iridium bar. This in turn gave way in 1960 to a scientific definition based on the wavelength of a particular kind of light, and in 1983 – to the distance travelled by light in a specified fraction of a second. It is on the basis of the 1960 definition of the metre that the British defined the yard: It is now 0.9144 metres exactly.

This break with the tradition of an isolated system of Imperial units was furthered by the setting up of a Metrication Board in 1969, with the target of completing metrication of British industry and commerce by 1975. Although DECIMAL CURRENCY was adopted in the UK in 1972, this surge towards an alien system of units predictably petered out in 1980, when the Metrication Board was disbanded with its targets unmet. Thereafter, it was decided, metrication should proceed, if at all, at its own pace and on a voluntary basis. In 1989 Parliament decided to retain Imperial units for such commodities as beer and milk and to keep the mile, yard, foot, and ounce until at least 2000. This has created a number of ridiculous anomalies. The price of petrol, for example, is quoted in pence per litre and measured at the pump in litres although almost all motorists think in terms of gallons. If the press comments on the cost of petrol it converts the price to pounds per gallon. Milk is sold in pint bottles, butter is sold in 250 gram packets; paint is sold by the litre but paint brushes are measured in inches; draught beer is sold by the pint but canned bear is sold in cans of 33 centilitres; spirits are sold in pubs in fractions of a gill but the bottles contain 750 millilitres; the scale of maps is now metric but land distances and signposts are all measured in miles, etc.

Only in science and engineering has reason prevailed: all measurements are now metric and expressed in SI UNITS.

Metro. Métro The universal name for the Parisian underground railway – the Chemin de Fer Métropolitain. The first Métro line, designed by Fulgence Bienvenuë, was opened in July 1900 to coincide with the 1900 World Exhibition. It ran east–west between Porte de Vincennes and Porte Maillot. Construction of an underground transit system was helped by the relatively shallow foundations of the capital's buildings and the wide boulevards, created during the rebuilding of central Paris in the late 19th century. Engineers adopted the cut-and-cover system of construction, building first the tunnel walls and roof from above. This means that the tunnels are relatively shallow and the trains easily reached from street level. The system now has 199 km (123 miles) of tunnels and some 430 stations; it is integrated with the Réseau Express Régional, opened in 1969 to provide a fast service between suburban Paris and the city centre. Métro stations reflect a range of 20th-century styles in architecture, including some prime examples of art nouveau, such as Porte Dauphine and Abbesses, as well as ART DECO. Other stations have design features that provide a foretaste of the district they serve; for instance, at Varenne the traveller is treated to exhibits from the nearby Rodin Museum, while Louvre Métro station shows items from the Louvre. Armchair enthusiasts of the Métro can enjoy its many delights on celluloid in the 1985 thriller *Subway*, directed by Luc Besson, in which the action takes place against the ticket barriers, tunnels, and trains of this world-famous network.

Metro-Goldwyn Mayer *See* MGM.

Metroland A nickname for the area covered by London's Metropolitan railway line, celebrated in the poetry of John Betjeman. The name was coined during the 1920s, when the newly built railway enabled commuting between the outer suburbs and the city and made the region easily accessible to Londoners. It was further popularized by the fictional character of Margot Metroland (originally Margot Beste-Chetwynde), who features in a number of Evelyn Waugh's novels, notably *Decline and Fall* (1928) and *Scoop* (1938).

Mexican wave An activity indulged in by an audience seated in the round – usually in sports stadiums – when they are waiting for something to begin or have become bored with the event they are watching. At a given moment, those people occupying the equivalent seats in every row stand up, raise their hands, and sit down again; as they near the high point of this cycle, their neighbours on one side begin to repeat it. The net effect is a wavelike motion that ripples round the stadium. Of course, the practical application of these rules is rather less tidy than this might suggest, but considerably more fun; the emphasis is on enthusiastic participation rather than precision. It is usual to cheer as one raises one's arms, and to boo those humourless individuals (usually in the better seats) who think it beneath their dignity to join in. A Mexican wave always seems to begin spontaneously (wherever one is sitting, it always begins somewhere else); it is never orchestrated but does not collapse in confusion (it is a mystery, for example, how it is decided whether the wave should go clockwise or anticlockwise); and it fades out when the participants lose interest. The origins of the activity are obscure, but it first came to world attention through television broadcasts of the 1986 Soccer World Cup finals from Mexico – hence the name.

mezoomas Slang for breasts, probably based on BAZUMAS, a corruption of bosom.

mezzanine Funding raised for the takeover of a company in which a number of minor unsecured loans are obtained at a high rate of interest on the understanding that these loans will only be repaid when the major loans have been repaid in case of bankruptcy. It is thus intermediate between making a straight loan and taking a share in the equity of the company, a mezzanine floor being intermediate between the ground floor and the first floor of a large building.

MFU *See* SNAFU.

MG The most popular and successful British sports car, originally manufactured by Morris Garages (William Morris's old business before he moved into manufacturing) under the direction of Cecil Kimber. MG's first model was launched in 1925 and in the next decade the company went on to produce a wide range of sports and sports racing cars, becoming the largest manufacturer of sports cars in the world. In 1930 production moved to a factory at Abingdon, near Oxford, where MGs bearing the famous octagonal badge continued to be produced for over 50 years until it was finally closed down by British Leyland in 1980. The marque continues, however, in the Metros, Maestros, and Montegos manufactured by the Austin Rover Company. In fact, the turbo versions of the 2-litre injection Maestros and Montegos are the fastest MGs ever made.

MGB Ministerstvo Gosudarstvennoi Bezopasnosti. The Soviet Ministry of State Security, or secret police, founded in 1946. The MGB was concerned with internal security, intelligence, and counter-intelligence. Its methods of investigation were more brutal than those of the KGB, which replaced it in 1954 after the downfall of Lavrenti Beria, head of Soviet secret police from 1938. Beria's execution in 1953 was the result of his attempt to achieve absolute political power for the MGB.

MGM Metro-Goldwyn-Mayer. A US film production company formed in 1924 when Marcus Loew's Metro Pictures Corporation merged with Goldwyn Pictures Corporation (founded in 1916 by Samuel Goldwyn; *see* GOLDWYNISMS) and a company run by Louis B. Mayer (1885–1957). Goldwyn left the merger and set up again as an independent; Mayer became head of the new company and, with his executive producer Irving Thalberg, rapidly established MGM's reputation for lavishly expensive and highly successful films, notably *Ben Hur* (1926; 1959), *Mutiny on the Bounty* (1935), *The Wizard of Oz* (1939), and *Doctor Zhivago* (1965). MGM's motto was "more stars than there are in heaven": these stars included Greta Garbo, Spencer Tracy, Judy Garland, and the Marx Brothers. Mayer retired from MGM in 1951.

MI5 Military Intelligence, section five. The former name (from 1916) of the British government's counter-intelligence agency (the Security Service). The name MI5 is no longer in official use but remains in the popular vocabulary. The work of MI5 involves the detection and surveillance of those known or suspected to be engaged in military or political espionage in the UK, with the aim of thwarting their mission. MI5 is answerable to the home secretary; ultimate control lies with the prime minister.

MI6 Military Intelligence, section six. The former name (from 1921) of the British government's intelligence agency (the Secret Intelligence Service, SIS). The name MI6 is no longer in official use but remains in the popular vocabulary. Members of MI6 are engaged in espionage and other intelligence activities abroad, using British agents and disaffected nationals of the countries in which they operate. Answerable to the foreign secretary, with ultimate control by the prime minister, MI6 is the British equivalent of the CIA in America.

Michigan Assassin Nickname of the US boxer Stanley Ketchel. Middleweight champion in the 1900s, he was renowned for totally demolishing his opponents.

Michurinism *See* LYSENKOISM.

Mickey. mickey finn Slang for a drugged drink given to an unsuspecting person, which renders the victim unconscious. It was usually made by mixing chlorine with alcohol. The term originated in the early 1900s in America and is thought to have been taken from the name of a Chicago barkeeper who practised this trick. The term is now sometimes used to mean any strong mixed drink used unknowingly to intoxicate the drinker. It is often shortened to mickey and can be used as a verb:

> Two men . . . had mickey-finned his drink.
> C. FRANKLIN: *Home Secretary Affair* (1971).

Mickey Mouse The mouse-like cartoon character created by Walt Disney (1901–

66). The term is now often used to describe something small, inferior, and trivial, for example, a Mickey Mouse project, salary, or car. This usage derives from the Mickey Mouse wristwatches introduced in America in the 1940s. These had a picture of Mickey Mouse on the dial with his outspread arms functioning as the watch-hands. This sort of gimmick set the tone for a number of inferior products which earned this epithet.

micro Colloquial term for something very small, such as a MICROCOMPUTER or a microskirt (*see* MINISKIRT). Though long known as a prefix (from the Greek *mikros*, small), its widespread use as a noun dates only from the mid-20th century, with the tendency towards miniaturization (especially in electronics and computing technology).

microcomputer A cheap compact computer, with a central processing unit (CPU) contained on one or more microprocessors, together with memory semiconductor chips and internal storage (floppy and/or hard disk drives), which can sit comfortably on a desk top. Microcomputers began to appear in the 1970s with the development of microchip technology and at first they were used for video games and by hobbyists for simple programming and home entertainment. They are now in the vanguard of the revolution in information technology and are in widespread use for wordprocessing, accounting, DESKTOP PUBLISHING, graphics, and design. The most advanced micros possess the equivalent in computing power of giant MAINFRAME computers of 20 years ago. *See also* PERSONAL COMPUTER.

microdot (1) A photographic image of a document reduced to the size of a pinhead for ease of transmission or for security reasons. (2) A small dose of LSD sold as a tiny blob on a piece of paper.

microeconomics The study of economic behaviour at the level of the individual or the firm. *See* MACROECONOMICS.

microfiche A flat rectangle of plastic film bearing greatly reduced photographs of text or printed pages. It is viewed through a reader, which magnifies the text and displays it on an illuminated screen. Microfiche are widely used to provide catalogues of parts, books, etc. Instead of reproducing a whole book for updating, only individual fiche need be updated.

microfilm A reel of film with reduced photographs of printed text, pages of books or newspapers, etc. It is viewed on a reader, which magnifies the text and displays it on an illuminated screen.

microskirt *See* MINISKIRT.

microsurgery Surgery of very fine structures requiring the use of an operating microscope. A microscope was first used as a surgical aid in 1921, for drainage of an ear infection; during the next 20 years ear surgeons developed various surgical treatments for deafness that depended on microscopy of the structures involved. The modern operating microscope was introduced in 1953 by the Carl Zeiss Company. Essentially it provides the surgeon with stereoscopic vision of the operating site, at magnifications in the range of × 4 to × 25. A beam splitter transmits the magnified image to the surgeon's eyepiece and often also to a camera and television monitor so that other theatre staff or students can follow the operation. The object field is illuminated by light transmitted through optical fibres; such fibres can also transmit laser light to make surgical incisions or destroy tissue. The microscope has enabled other micromanipulative techniques to emerge; these include the use of ultra-fine suture materials for sewing together blood capillaries, high-precision cutting techniques, and remote handling of instruments to eliminate wobble due to hand movements.

The last 30 years have seen enormous strides in microsurgery. Microtechniques are long established in ear surgery – they are now used in such operations as cochlear implants – and in eye surgery – for example cataract removal and corneal replacement. Plastic surgery has been revolutionized by modern microsurgical techniques: surgeons now successfully replace severed digits and limbs by joining blood vessels and nerves between the stump and the severed part. Similarly, progress in bone and skin grafting owes much to microsurgical restoration of blood and nerve supplies to the graft, while brain surgery now relies on microscopical techniques for precision repairs of damaged or burst blood vessels resulting from strokes.

microwave A form of electromagnetic radiation with a wavelength lying between that of infrared radiation and radio waves. Microwaves have a wavelength in the range 1 millimetre to 0.3 metre. They can be generated by electronic circuits and are used in radar systems, masers (*see* LASER), and in scientific experiments. Microwaves are also used in the **microwave oven** for cooking and heating food quickly. In a conventional oven the food cooks from the outside; heat is conducted into the centre of the food. Microwave cooking is different and much faster; the radiation penetrates the whole and the food is cooked evenly and quickly. Microwave ovens were first used by commercial caterers in the late 1960s but domestic use increased in the 1980s accompanied by the availability of CONVENIENCE FOOD suitable for microwave cooking. The use of microwave ovens has led to a number of modern myths (*see* URBAN LEGENDS).

middle. Middle America The majority of Americans, who believe in traditional values and reject extreme views or tastes. They also believe that they are the silent majority, as their opinions are rarely presented by the media, which tends to concentrate on either the west or east coast at the expense of the middle of the country. The term therefore has both a geographical and a sociological context. It was coined in 1968 by the US journalist Joseph Kraft, with reference to the people whom Richard Nixon regarded as his potential supporters. It came into prominence again in 1990 when the **mothers of Middle America** protested against the likely involvement of their sons in what was to become the GULF WAR of 1991.

Middle-earth A fantasy world created by J. R. R. Tolkien that forms the setting for the LORD OF THE RINGS trilogy (1954–55) and other works. Middle-earth, also known as Endor, was inhabited during the various ages of its existence by elves, dwarves, men, and HOBBITS: its mythology, geography, history, and languages were meticulously documented by Tolkien. Lying to the west of the Great Sea, Middle-earth contains regions with such poetic names as the Misty Mountains, the River Anduin, the elf-kingdom of Lothlórien, the eastern land of Hildórien (from where the first men came), and Mordor (or 'the Land of Shadow') – the realm of the evil Sauron.

middle management A term that originated in the 1950s to describe such managers as those responsible for running a single department within a large organization but who play no part in the development of policy for the organization as a whole.

middle-market Denoting goods or services aimed at the middle range of the market, *i.e.* somewhere between **down-market** (relatively inexpensive and unglamourous goods or services) and **up-market** (relatively expensive and luxurious goods or services).

middle-of-the-road Denoting those who tend to have moderate (rather than extreme) views and tastes. In politics, for example, middle-of-the-road party members are neither left-wing nor right-wing but hold the unadventurous solid views that provide the party with its stability. Because they are the most numerous, those with middle-of-the-road tastes have considerable commercial importance; in the music industry, for example, a new category exists to cater for their tastes, called **MOR**.

> We know what happens to people who stay in the middle of the road. They get run over.
>
> ANEURIN BEVAN, 1953.

midi Describing coats, skirts, and other garments that reach mid-calf level. Also used as a prefix and a noun, particularly for the **midiskirt** (*see* MINISKIRT).

midinette A young Parisian woman employed to make or sell clothes, hats, or other fashion accessories. In the early part of the century, the midinette's youth and independence encouraged the view, especially among Englishmen, that they were sexually available. The word is thought to derive from French *midi*, noon, and *dinette*, a light lunch: the implication being that the girls were too busy to eat more than a snack at midday.

midi system A compact stack of HI-FI equipment designed as a single unit. It plays tapes, records, and compact discs, although some are being made that do not play records.

midlife crisis A crisis of self-confidence that occurs with the onset of middle age; it is associated with the realization that one's youth lies behind one and what lies ahead is a decline into old age. It affects both sexes and usually passes fairly rapidly as the benefits of experience over youthful enthusiasm begin to become apparent.

Midway, Battle of A battle fought during World War II at the Midway Islands, a US military base in the Pacific Ocean. A major victory for the Allies, it marked an important turning point in the war in the Pacific. The battle began on 3 June 1942 and ended on 6 June with the retirement of the Japanese. Principally an engagement between US and Japanese carrier-based aircraft, the battle resulted in the loss of one US and four Japanese aircraft carriers, causing a significant reduction in Japan's naval strength.

Mif A word used by Nancy Mitford to describe people who pour tea into a cup after putting the 'Milk In First'. In her analysis of U AND NON-U language and behaviour, Mitford classified this habit as 'Non-U', a social blunder: members of the upper classes pour the tea in first. Although this kind of minor etiquette now has no significance for any class, the rationale dates back to the days in which wealthy ladies serving afternoon tea to their friends would pour the tea into the cup, which a maid would then offer to the guest on a tray containing a milk jug and a lump-sugar container. This enabled the guest to add milk and sugar to her own taste.

MiG Any of a series of Soviet aircraft designed by *Mi*koyan and *G*urevich. The MiG-15, a jet fighter, was used by the Chinese Communist Air Force during the KOREAN WAR in the early 1950s, but proved to be no match for the US F-86 Sabrejet. Other MiG aircraft include the supersonic MiG-19 and the MiG-21.

migrant worker A worker, often an agricultural worker, who leaves a poor country to work in a richer country. Migrant workers often send money home to support their families; this may constitute an important part of the foreign income of poor countries. *See also* GASTARBEITER.

mike Informal name for a microphone. *See also* LAVALIER.

militant (1) A person who is aggressive in putting his or her views or in achieving his or her aims. (2) A member of **Militant Tendency**, an extreme left-wing organization in the UK. Some members of Militant Tendency were previously members of the Labour Party but were expelled in the mid-1980s to make the party more acceptable to the MIDDLE-OF-THE-ROAD voter.

Military Cross A decoration inaugurated in December 1914 and awarded to captains, lieutenants, and warrant officers in the British Army. It was formerly also bestowed on members of the Colonial and Indian forces.

milk. milk round The visit paid by the personnel managers of large companies to universities to encourage the brightest of the year's graduates to join their organizations. In the sciences and engineering, particularly, there is strong competition for students who are likely to gain first-class degrees.

milk-run An expression common amongst Allied aircrew of World War II for any sortie flown regularly day after day, or a sortie against an easy target on which inexperienced pilots could be used with impunity – as simple as delivering milk.

milk's gotta lotta bottle *See under* BOTTLE.

Milk Snatcher Nickname of Margaret Thatcher. *See* IRON LADY.

milk the cow with a spanner To open a tin of evaporated or condensed milk with a tin-opener.

Mille Miglia A sports-car race formerly run in Italy, from Brescia to Rome and back, covering approximately 1000 miles on public roads (*mille miglia* is Italian for 'a thousand miles'). Inaugurated in 1927 and open to both amateurs and professionals, the Mille Miglia remained an immensely popular annual event for 30 years. The alarming number of deaths during the race caused it to be banned by Mussolini in the early 1940s, but the race continued after the war with ever-increasing risk and speed – up to 180 m.p.h. in close pursuit on badly maintained roads. The 1955 Mille Miglia was won by the British driver Stirling Moss, who covered the 1000-mile course in just 10 hours. In 1957, an accident that claimed the lives of the Spanish driver Alfonso ('Fon') de Portago, his co-driver, and 10 spectators finally brought the tradition of the Mille Miglia to an end.

Mills. Mills & Boon A British publishing house, which has become a byword for sentimental romance. Founded in 1908 by Gerald Mills and Charles Boon, it originally published a range of general fiction titles, including such authors as Jack London, Hugh Walpole, and P. G. Wodehouse. The historical romances of Georgette Heyer made their debut under the Mills & Boon imprint and during the early 1930s the company began its specialization in romantic novels. During the Depression these proved a very popular form of escapism, especially with subscribers to the commercial 'twopenny libraries' of that time. Storylines in the 1940s reflected the more prominent roles played by women – the war inspired the birth of the still-popular Doctor/Nurse series of medical romances. In the late 1950s a small Canadian paperback publisher, Harlequin, acquired the rights to Mills & Boon titles and launched its own series of paperback romances. Its success in North America prompted the British firm to start their own paperback series in 1960. In 1972 the two companies merged, and in 1981 this transatlantic combine was acquired by the Canadian Torstar group.

Mills & Boon now publish several different series of titles, each with its own particular formula but all containing the same essential ingredients – the vicissitudes of the hero and his heroine, which are eventually resolved by true love, which, or course, leads to a happy ending. The formula has been much derided but remains very popular. Little has changed since *Punch* described the work of one of Mills & Boon's first authors, Sophie Cole:

> Her tales should appeal to every reader who does not insist on battle, murder, and divorce as essential to the best romance.

Mills bomb A type of grenade developed by the British and used in both World Wars. The Mills bomb most widely used in World War I was a cast-iron fragmentation grenade weighing about 1½ pounds (700 g), designed for use against attacking infantry from a position of cover. It could also be fired from a rifle by employing a special discharger cup and projecting cartridge. The detonator was activated by a seven-second safety fuse. During World War II the equivalent Mills-type grenades were fired from 2-in mortars and had a four-second fuse. It was named after the engineer, Sir William Mills (1856–1932), whose Birmingham factory produced the grenades during World War I.

Milner's Kindergarten The nickname given to the notable group of young men gathered together by Sir Alfred (Viscount) Milner, High Commissioner for South Africa, for the work of reconstruction after the South African War (1899–1902). They were Robert Brand, Lionel Curtis, John Dove, Patrick Duncan, Richard Feetham, Lionel Hitchens, Philip Kerr, Douglas Malcolm, J. F. Perry, Geoffrey Robinson, and Hugh Wyndham. Among those associated with them were L. S. Amery, Basil Blackwood, John Buchan, and Basil Williams. They duly became advocates of closer imperial ties, both political and economic, and remained an important propagandist group for the imperial idea in the years before World War I. The name was probably invented by the lawyer, Sir William Marriott.

Milton Keynes A NEW TOWN in NE Buckinghamshire, England, founded in 1967; one of the most ambitious planned in the UK since World War II. Designed for a future population of 200,000, the town contains the headquarters of the OPEN UNIVERSITY, some light industry, and a number of innovative housing developments. Incorporated within the boundary of the new town, which covers an area of 9000 hectares, are the old village of Milton Keynes and the towns of Bletchley, Wolverton, and Stony Stratford. In the early years of its existence Milton Keynes, in common with many other similar developments, suffered a certain amount of reactionary criticism for the unimaginative design of some of its housing estates, its network of straight roads running parallel to each other or intersecting at right angles, and its general lack of character. Its 'concrete cows', an abstract sculptural group suggesting a herd of cattle, became famous after being ridiculed in the national press.

Minamata disease A form of mercury poisoning named after the Japanese town of Minamata on the island of Kyushu. Here, between 1953 and 1960, 111 people were affected by a mystery illness, resulting in 43 deaths. Symptoms began with tiredness and irritability and gradually progressed to headache, numbness, blurred vision, and wasting. Many of the sufferers came from fishing families; the cause was eventually traced to locally caught fish containing high levels of mercury. The fish were being contaminated by mercury waste discharged into the sea by a nearby plastics factory. The organic mercury ingested was affecting the victims' brain cells, causing the neurological signs of poisoning. A similar incident occurred on Honshu island in 1965, when five people died through eating mercury-contaminated fish.

mind. blow one's mind To have an exhilarating or shocking experience; especially, in the 1960s, as a result of the effects of hallucinogens, such as LSD.

MIND The UK's leading mental-health pressure group, formed in 1946 as the National Association for Mental Health. Its aims are "to represent the interests and uphold the rights of people with mental health problems and their families, and to promote mental health." Current priorities include ensuring adequate provision of community facilities for the mentally ill and handicapped and of support services for their families. The organization changed its name to MIND in 1970 as part of a 'new look' more radical approach, in part prompted by criticism of the NAMH, as well as deficiencies in state services for the mentally ill and handicapped.

minder Originally, criminal slang for a bodyguard; it has become much more widely used since the late 1970s and the popularity of a British TV series of that name, featuring the shifty Arthur Daley (George Cole) and his minder Terry (Dennis Waterman). Every small-time star now has a minder:

> Eddie Murphy was a nice guy . . . the first time he came in he had six huge minders guarding him.
> *The Sun*, 14 February 1991.

mindfuck Slang for a shattering (**mind-blowing**) experience or a state of extreme excitement or emotion.

mind mapping A technique used to develop a person's use of the right-hand side of the brain and thus his or her creativity. *See* LEFT BRAIN.

mind my bike! Catchphrase associated with the British film and television actor Jack Warner (1894–1981). Star of the long-running television police series *Dixon of Dock Green*, he first used the phrase in the *Garrison Theatre* radio programme during World War II and subsequently frequently repeated it in a wide range of contexts. *See also* EVENIN' ALL.

Ming Nickname of the Australian prime minister Sir Robert Menzies (1894–1978), coined by analogy with Ming the Merciless, a character in the FLASH GORDON comic strip series. The long period of Menzies' premiership (1939–41 and 1949–66) inevitably came to be known as the 'Ming dynasty'.

mini Extremely short or small – a 20th-century contraction of *miniature*. Also widely used as a prefix (as in MINIPILL and MINISKIRT) and as a noun (especially for the miniskirt).

Mini The Austin Mini, a popular small car designed by Sir Alec Issigonis (1906–88) and first unveiled on 26 August 1959. The Mini's revolutionary design featured front-wheel drive, small wheels, and a compact transverse-mounted engine, which allowed plenty of room for four adults and luggage despite measuring only 10 feet from bumper to bumper. The millionth Mini was produced in 1965 and by the mid-1980s altogether 5.6 million models had been sold, making it the fifth best-selling British-made car of all time. The Mini Cooper, a speeded-up version, was launched in 1961 and won the Monte Carlo Rally in 1964, 1965, and 1967.

> You can't tell one car from another – the only one that stands out is the mini.
> SIR ALEC ISSIGONIS.

miniskirt or **mini** A very short skirt, especially one in which the hemline is 4 inches or more above the knee. Although the mini first appeared in a collection by the French couturier André Courrèges (1923–), it is chiefly associated with the British designer Mary Quant (1934–), who marketed it in 1965. The mini quickly became ubiquitous, remaining one of the lasting symbols of 1960s style and mores. Perhaps it was the brazen thighs, often enhanced by KINKY BOOTS, that combined with the advent of the PILL to raise the sexual temperature in the late 1960s, although some have argued that the miniskirt was an effect, rather than a cause, of the SWINGING SIXTIES. To moralists the miniskirt was anathema; it was also a source of irritation to bureaucrats as under British tax law skirts less than 24 inches long were classed as children's wear and so exempt from purchase tax. In an attempt to forestall any loss of revenue, from 1 January 1966 the bust size of dresses was also taken into account, with any bust of 32 inches or more attracting tax. Nevertheless, undeterred by either the moralists or the Customs and Excise, skirts became progressively shorter as the decade wore on, approaching vanishing point with the **microskirt**, a garment that barely covered the pelvis. The inevitable reaction set in with the appearance in 1969 of the **maxiskirt** (or **maxi**), an ankle-length skirt that had the advantage of warmth as well as being more flattering to girls with indifferent legs. The **midiskirt** (or **midi**) was a calf-length skirt neither mini or maxi. The mini and the microskirt enjoyed a limited revival in the late 1980s and early 1990s.

mini-break Travel agents' jargon for a short holiday of two or three days, especially a weekend holiday. It later extended into the general language meaning any short break or pause.

minicomputer A type of computer intermediate in size and power between a MAINFRAME and a MICROCOMPUTER. In the early 1990s, due to the advances in microprocessor technology, the distinction between micros and minicomputers became blurred.

minipill A type of contraceptive pill that contains a progestogen hormone only, in contrast to the oestrogen plus progestogen of the combined PILL. The progestogen thickens the mucus lining the cervix making it difficult for sperm to pass into the womb. It also alters the lining of the womb so that implantation of any fertilized egg is made less likely. The minipill is slightly less effective than the combined pill and must be taken every day of the menstrual cycle. However, the side-effects are generally less, making it preferable for women who cannot tolerate the combined pill and for older women. Also, it can be taken by women who are breastfeeding, since it does not interfere with milk production.

minimal art A type of art, especially sculpture, that uses basic geometric forms and primary colours and is largely passive and inert, eschewing any expression of meaning or emotion. Also known as **reductivism**, minimal art began in New York in the late 1950s in reaction to the emotiveness of abstract expressionism and ACTION PAINTING. One of the movement's leading figures, the US sculptor Carl Andre (1935–), was responsible for the 'Tate Bricks' furore, when his *Equivalent VIII* (1976), a set of 120 bricks arranged two-deep in a rectangle, provoked severe criticism of the Tate Gallery for acquiring it at public expense. *See also* CONCEPTUAL ART.

minimum lending rate (MLR) Between 1971 and 1981, the minimum rate at which the Bank of England would lend to discount houses and thus the rate of interest that controlled the interest rate charged and paid by banks and building societies throughout the economy. Before 1971 this was known as the **bank rate**. After 1981 the minimum lending rate became known as the **base rate**, a change of name that was intended to signal a relaxing of government controls over the banking system. When the government suspended the MLR in 1981, it reserved the right to reintroduce it at any time if it felt it was needed. This it did for one day in January 1985. In the late 1980s and early 1990s, the government again increased interest rates in an attempt to control inflation and the balance of payments deficit.

Miniver, Mrs A fictional diarist created by Joyce Anstruther, writing under the pen-name Jan Struther. Mrs Miniver was an upper-middle-class housewife who recorded her personal reactions to events leading up to World War II, and life in England before and after the outbreak of war, in a diary subsequently published as *Mrs Miniver*. A Hollywood film of the same name, based on Mrs Miniver's diary and starring Greer Garson in the title role, was released in 1942. Despite its patent sentimentality and the conventional but inaccurate Hollywood image of rural England, it made a powerful contribution to the mythology of wartime Britain. The tone of the piece is summarized by the vicar's sermon in the bombed church as the film draws to a close:

> This is not only a war of soldiers in uniforms. It is a war of the people – of all the people – and it must be fought not only on the battlefield but in the cities and in the villages, in the factories and on the farms, in the home and in the heart of freedom. Well, we have buried our dead, but we shall not forget them. Instead they will inspire us with an unbreakable determination to free ourselves and those who come after us from the tyranny and terror that threaten to strike us down. This is the people's war. It is our war. We are the fighters. Fight it, then. Fight it with all that is in us. And may God defend the right.

minutemen A small secret ultra-right-wing US organization armed to conduct guerrilla warfare in the event of a communist invasion. The name was inspired from its adoption by American militiamen who, at the onset of the War of Independence, promised to take arms at a minute's notice. Hence, those who are similarly vigilant and ready to take prompt action. **Minuteman** is also the name of a US ICBM.

mips *M*illion *i*nstructions *p*er *s*econd. A measure of computing speed and power that became increasingly common during the 1980s. A fast microcomputer may achieve six mips, while a Cray-type supercomputer will operate at 100 mips.

miracle rice A type of high-yield hybrid rice developed in the 1960s to boost harvests in Asia and other areas of the developing world.

Miranda In America, police making an arrest must read the Miranda (Rule) to the suspect. It explains his or her legal rights during questioning, especially those of remaining silent or being represented by a lawyer. This protection is found in the Fifth and Sixth Amendments to the US

Constitution but became obligatory in 1966 after the Supreme Court reversed an Arizona court's conviction of Ernesto A. Miranda. He had confessed to kidnapping and rape but had not been advised of his rights.

MIRV *See* ICBM.

misery index A statistical term used as a measure of the economic problems in a particular county or society. It is based on the rates of inflation and unemployment.

mishegaas *See* MESHUGGA.

Miss. in Miss World Order In reverse order. This was the way that Eric Morley, who started the Miss World Beauty Contest in 1951, always gave the results. He would say, "I'll give you the results in reverse order."

Miss America The winner of America's annual beauty pageant, which began in 1922 – it is claimed to be the oldest in the world and is held each September in Atlantic City, New Jersey. It was discontinued in 1928 for five years and revived with more interest on talent and less on sexual beauty. It was derided during the HIPPIE era and picketed by advocates of WOMEN'S LIB. Other embarrassments included the 1984 resignation of the first Black Miss America, Vanessa Williams, for posing in the nude during her reign. Despite these problems, the nationally televised event remains a beloved US institution. Parallel contests run on similar lines have proliferated since 1922 with many states having a national contest; international versions include the **Miss World** competition, which is televised in many countries. There are several equivalent titles that are contested by men.

Miss Frigidaire Nickname of the US tennis player Chris Evert (1954–). Wimbledon singles champion in 1974, 1976, and 1981, she acquired the nickname from her cool manner on court.

Miss Lillian Nickname of Lillian Carter (1898–1983), mother of the US president Jimmy Carter. Of Southern stock, she became widely known for her outspoken support for her son.

Miss Otis regrets Catchphrase sometimes used in apologizing for not being able to attend a function, usually because the person invited does not wish to do so. It originated in Cole Porter's song of the same name (1934), in which Miss Otis's butler coolly passes on his mistress' tragic reason for not being able to attend a lunch to which she has been invited – she has been hanged.

missing mass *See* DARK MATTER.

Mission Impossible The title of a US TV espionage thriller series originally broadcast between 1966 and 1972; it was also seen in the UK. The phrase became a catchphrase for any impossible task.

> Madcap tube driver Cozmik Wilson cheers up depressed commuters . . . with a battery of quips taken from the cult sci-fi TV series . . . Cozmik says he's on a 'Mission Possible' and congratulates his audience for 'navigating through the company's ticket barriers'.
>
> *The Sport*, 5 April 1991.

mistake. Did you spot this week's deliberate mistake? A phrase that came to be used by broadcasters as a facetious way of covering up for an actual mistake in the programme. It first arose in 1938 on a BBC radio programme called *Monday Night at Seven*. After a mistake had occurred, the BBC was snowed under with listeners phoning in to make the correction. The producer decided to exploit the situation and the deliberate mistake became a feature of the programme. It has frequently been used since as a formula for small-prize competitions on radio programmes.

mister. Mr and Mrs Wood in front Theatrical catchphrase, first heard in the early 20th century, meaning that the auditorium is virtually empty, the performers being greeted with the sight of rows of empty wooden seats.

Mr Big A nickname for the boss or the leader of an underworld gang. The author Ian Fleming may have originated the phrase in *Live and Let Die* (1954). This novel features a gangster named Buonaparte Ignace Gallia, whose initials happen to spell Big, hence Mr Big.

Mr Charley US Black nickname for a White man. It became widespread in about 1960, with **Boss Charley** representing White authority figures. Older Black terms include **Whitey** and **ofay** for a White person and THE MAN for the White establishment or one of its members.

Mr Clean A nickname for someone who is above reproach on all levels. This epithet was originally the tradename of a US household cleaner.

Mr Magoo The short-sighted bumbling hero of animated cartoons and comic strips. The character was created by Stephen Bosustow for the *Mr Magoo* cartoon films produced in the early 1950s by

United Productions of America. The humour largely revolves around Mr Magoo's failure to recognize everyday objects and people: he talks to hatstands and mistakes the face in a portrait for his own reflection in a mirror, for example.

Mr Moto The hero of a popular Hollywood film series of the late 1930s, a Japanese detective, created by John P. Marquand. Peter Lorre, usually a classic villain, played Mr Moto. The first was *Think Fast Mr Moto* (1937); the last, *Mr Moto Takes a Vacation* (1939), proved prophetic since with PEARL HARBOR, America's interest in Japanese heroes disappeared overnight. (This opportunity provided a boost for the cinema's Chinese detective, CHARLIE CHAN, who turned out 47 films.) A nostalgic revival, *The Return of Mr Moto*, was released in 1965 with Henry Silva in the title role.

Mr Nice Guy An epithet used to characterize any man who wishes to be admired for his friendliness and compassion. It is often used of politicians, usually somewhat sneeringly.

Mr Speaker US Black slang from the 1940s for a handgun.

Mr Television Nickname of the US television comic Milton Berle (1908–), who became one of the stars of television in the 1950s.

Mistinguett The stage name of the French actress and singer Jeanne-Marie Bourgeois (1873–1956). Mistinguett was a star of the music halls of Paris between the wars, notably the Moulin Rouge and the Folies-Bergère, where she danced and sang with Maurice Chevalier. She also performed in comedy. Mistinguett was famous for her spectacular hats, her elaborate costumes, and her long shapely legs, which were said to be insured for a huge sum of money.

Mitford girls The five daughters of the eccentric and irascible second Baron Redesdale (1878–1958), who earned himself a reputation for outstandingly poor judgment by describing Hitler as:

> . . . a right-thinking man of irreproachable sincerity and honesty.

A demented father, who was seriously wounded in the Boer War, Redesdale's favourite sport was to hunt his terrified daughters with a bloodhound. He appeared as Lord Alconleigh, also known as Uncle Matthew, in the novels *The Pursuit of Love* (1945) and *Love in a Cold Climate* (1945) by his eldest daughter Nancy Mitford (1904–73). Nancy also wrote a number of other books describing the upper-class way of life in England, including *Noblesse Oblige* (1956), which contained the original paper on U AND NON-U behaviour (*see also* MIF), by Professor Alan Ross. Her *Wigs on the Green* (1935) consists of a pen portrait of Eugenia Malmains, based on her sister Unity Mitford (1914–48). Expelled from school three times, the wayward Unity, infected by her father's enthusiasm for Hitler, became a fanatical Nazi. Accosting Hitler in his favourite Munich restaurant, the *Osteria*, she became his close friend. When the UK finally declared war on Germany, Unity used the gun Hitler had given her to shoot herself in the head. The bullet lodged in her brain but failed to kill her; Hitler arranged for his wounded admirer to be sent in a special hospital train to Geneva, whence she returned to England. Eventually she died of her self-inflicted wound. The antisemitic strain seemed to run in the family: another sister, Diana Mitford (1910–), married Sir Oswald Mosley, the black-shirted failed politician who led the British Union of Fascists (*see* MOSLEYITES). The youngest of the Mitford sisters, Jessica (1917–), became a writer and a US citizen. She is best known for her books *Hons and Rebels* (1960; *see* HONS, THE) and her survey of US funeral habits, *The American Way of Death* (1963). The remaining sister, Deborah, was the only one not to achieve either fame or notoriety; their only brother, Tom, was killed in Burma in World War II.

Mitty, Walter A fictional character created by the US humorist James Thurber (1894–1961) in the short story *The Secret Life of Walter Mitty* (1939). Probably the most famous of Thurber's comic creations, Walter Mitty is a docile henpecked husband who escapes from his wife and from a world that seems perpetually to conspire against him by indulging in elaborate and heroic fantasies:

> Then, with that faint fleeting smile playing about his lips, he faced the firing squad; erect and motionless, proud and disdainful, Walter Mitty, the undefeated, inscrutable to the last.

The name of Walter Mitty has entered the English language as an epithet for anyone who takes refuge from reality in similar fantasies. *The Secret Life of Walter Mitty* was adapted for the cinema in 1947 with Danny Kaye in the title role.

mixed media The combined use of videotapes, photographs, music, and animation in an artistic or educational presentation. **Multimedia** is an associated term, which refers to the use of specialized computer software combining on-screen graphics, animation, music, and voice synthesis, for educational and other presentations.

MLR *See* MINIMUM LENDING RATE.

MMC *See* MONOPOLIES AND MERGERS COMMISSION.

Moaning Minnie (1) A World War II nickname for a six-barrelled German mortar, from the rising shriek when it was fired. (2) The air-raid warning siren used in the UK in World War II, from its repetitive wail. (3) A colloquial epithet applied to any constant moaner or habitual grumbler.

mob, the US slang for a criminal organization, notably the MAFIA. A member of such a gang is a **mobster**.

mock. mockers British and Australian slang for a curse, as in the expression 'to put the mockers on' meaning to ruin something. It has been used since the 1920s and is thought to derive either from the English *mock*, or from the Yiddish *makeh*, meaning plague or wound.

mock-up (1) A phrase originating in World War II for a trial model or full-size working model. (2) In the US Air Force, a panel mounted with models of aircraft parts and used for instructional purposes.

mod. mod cons Estate agents' shorthand for modern conveniences; used, especially in the phrase 'all mod cons', to confirm that a property has all the facilities (hot running water, central heating, etc.) expected in a modern home. It is sometimes used ironically of a derelict or insanitary dwelling.

mods and rockers Two British teenage cults in the 1960s whose contrasting mores led to rivalry and violence. The *mods* affected a COOL elitist image, setting great store by their smart suits and fastidious grooming. They rode scooters in their PARKAS, listened to rare US soul imports, and took PURPLE HEARTS. In total contrast were the leather-jacketed *rockers*, who rode powerful motorcycles and cultivated a filthy dishevelled appearance. In 1964 mutual resentment between the two groups culminated in Bank Holiday clashes at a number of seaside resorts, leading to hundreds of arrests. The violence was quickly suppressed but not before a wave of outrage had swept through parliament and the press. The mod style enjoyed a brief revival in the late 1970s, when there were even a few nostalgic riots (this time with the PUNKS).

Model T *See* TIN LIZZIE.

modem *Mo*dulator/*dem*odulator. An electronic device for converting digital signals from a computer into electrical signals that can be transmitted by a telephone line, and for converting these electrical signals back into digital form. Modems are used to transmit data between computers.

modernism (1) A movement in the Roman Catholic Church that sought to interpret the ancient teachings of the Church with due regard to the current teachings of science, modern philosophy, and history. It arose in the late 19th century and was formally condemned by Pope Pius X in 1907 in the encyclical *Pascendi*, which stigmatized it as the "synthesis of all heresies". (2) A movement in the arts towards the rejection of conventional subjects, attitudes, and techniques. Among the many innovations that can be labelled modernist are STREAM OF CONSCIOUSNESS in literature, SERIALISM in music, and FUNCTIONALISM in architecture. *See also* POSTMODERNISM.

mog or **moggie** British slang for a cat, although in the north of England a *mog* is a mouse. Some dictionaries suggest that the word is derived from a dialect word that was used as a pet name for a cow.

Mohole A US research project to obtain rock samples from the upper mantle of the Earth, which involved boring a 7-mile hole from the ocean floor, through the Earth's crust, to the Mohorovičić discontinuity (the boundary between the Earth's crust and upper mantle, named after its discoverer Andrija Mohorovičić; 1857–1936). Drilling began near Guadaloupe, off W Mexico, but the government-funded project was abandoned in 1966 because of spiralling costs and insurmountable technological difficulties.

mojo Black US slang for a magic spell or a lucky charm. It is thought to be derived from a W African word. It was frequently used in BLUES and ROCK 'N' ROLL songs of the 1950s and 1960s, one of the best known being Muddy Waters' 'Got my mojo working'. It is also often used as a euphemism for the male sex organ.

mole A spy or traitor who obtains a position of trust in an organization, especially a government department or intelligence service. The name reflects the hidden undermining activities of such agents. The most notorious of these moles was Kim Philby (1912–88), who worked for the Soviet Union with his fellow Cantabrigians Anthony Blunt, Guy Burgess, and Donald Maclean. *See* BURGESS AND MACLEAN; SLEEPER.

Molotov Alias of the Soviet statesman Vyacheslav Mikhailovich Seriabin (1890–1986), who adopted it in 1906 to escape from the Imperial Police. He later became prime minister of the Soviet Union (1930–41) and during and after World War II served as foreign minister. In 1956 he was expelled from the Communist Party over disagreements with Khrushchev.

Molotov breadbasket A canister of incendiary bombs which, on being launched from a plane, opened and showered the bombs over a wide area; named after the Soviet statesman MOLOTOV.

Molotov cocktail A home-made anti-tank bomb, invented and first used by the Finns against the Soviets in 1940 and developed in the UK as one of the weapons of the HOME GUARD. It consisted of a bottle filled with inflammable and glutinous liquid, with a slow match protruding from the top. When thrown at a tank the bottle burst, the liquid igniting and spreading over the plating of the tank. It was named after the Soviet statesman MOLOTOV.

moment of truth The moment of crisis when something or someone is put to the test. The phrase may have originated in Ernest Hemingway's novel *Death in the Afternoon* (1932), as a translation of the Spanish *momento de la verdad*, which refers to the moment in a bullfight when the matador kills the bull with his final sword-thrust.

momma Slang for a female member of a HELL'S ANGELS chapter. The epithet implies that the woman in question is not attached to any of the males in the group; if she was, she would be known as someone's 'old lady'. *See also* LAST OF THE RED HOT MOMMAS.

momzer or **mamser** US slang, from Yiddish, used to describe a person who is unlikable, stubborn, untrustworthy, or absolutely detestable. It came from the Hebrew, *mamzer*, meaning an illegitimate child. Thus, it is used, much like 'bastard', to describe either such a child or somebody unpleasant, who may or may not be illegitimate.

Monaco Grand Prix A motor race that takes place in May or early June on the streets of Monte Carlo. The Monaco Grand Prix is one of the few events of the Formula 1 World Championship to be raced on public roads rather than on a purpose-built track. The circuit is about 2 miles in length, including many sharp bends, narrow streets, and a long tunnel; it is comparatively slow by Formula 1 standards. The lap record for the fastest average speed stands at about 90 m.p.h. (as opposed to SILVERSTONE's 150 m.p.h.). Only 20 cars are allowed to start the race, which consists of 78 laps.

Mona Lisa theft The theft of Leonardo da Vinci's masterpiece from the Louvre in Paris, which took place on 21 August 1911. Three 'workmen', who had spent the night hidden in the museum, removed the painting with ease while the museum was closed. Subsequently the gang leader, an Italian criminal called Vincenzo Perugia, persuaded six US art collectors to part with $300,000 in the belief that they would acquire the masterpiece. Instead, they received copies painted by the master forger Yves Chaudron, who had already perpetrated a series of similar confidence tricks organized by the self-styled Marquis Eduardo de Valfierno. Chaudron and Valfierno had previously enjoyed great success with their fakes of paintings by Murillo and others; this time however, their plan went wrong when Perugia absconded with the money, attempted to sell the real painting to a dealer in Florence in November 1913, and was subsequently arrested. The painting was returned to the Louvre.

Monday Club An association of Conservatives from the right wing of the party, founded in 1961 by the Marquess of Salisbury, Julian Amery, and others. The club derives its name from the fact that the members originally met for lunch on Mondays.

monetarism The economic doctrine that sees the MONEY SUPPLY as the centre of policy in MACROECONOMICS. It was first formulated by David Hume (1711–76), but was revived in the 1970s as the main doctrine to combat KEYNESIANISM. In this form it expresses the view that an expansion of the money supply will tend to create inflation rather than employment.

money. Money Makes the World Go Around A song title from the musical *Cabaret* (1966) and the subsequent film (1972). It is, of course, a paraphrase of the traditional English proverb 'Love makes the world go round'.

moneyman A man whose work centres on finance, such as a company accountant, a stockbroker, or a banker. Originally a 16th-century word, it became popular in the UK in the 1980s, a decade much concerned with money-related matters.

money supply The amount of money available to the economy of a nation. Since the 1970s most western countries have accepted the central tenet of MONETARISM, that an increase in the money supply leads directly to inflation. In order to control the money supply it is first necessary to define it. This has been done in a variety of ways. In the UK seven definitions are used:

M0 The notes and coins in circulation plus banks' till money and balances with the Bank of England.

M1 The notes and coins in circulation plus private-sector current accounts and deposit accounts that can be transferred by cheque.

M2 The notes and coins in circulation plus non-interest-bearing bank deposits plus building society deposits plus National Savings accounts.

M3 (formerly called sterling M3) M1 plus all other private-sector bank deposits plus certificates of deposit.

M3c (formerly called M3) M3 plus foreign currency bank deposits.

M4 (formerly called private-sector liquidity 1; PSL1) M1 plus most private-sector bank deposits plus holdings of money-market instruments.

M5 (formerly called private-sector liquidity 2; PSL2) M4 plus building society deposits.

The choice of definition depends on the circumstances.

Monkees, The A US–British pop group whose success on a 1966 NBC Saturday-morning television series skyrocketed their first single, 'Last Train to Clarksville', to the top of the US charts. 'Monkeemania' went from strength to strength in 1967 with 'I'm a Believer' and the album *The Monkees*; for a time it seemed that the world had found the new BEATLES. The Monkees were, in fact, put together for the TV series, which was about the unlikely adventures of a mythical four-man pop group. Its members were the British former child star Davy Jones (1945–), the US former child star Mickey Dolenz (1946–), and the Americans Peter Tork (1945–) and Mike Nesmith (1942–). At first the group's members were allowed no say in the music (written by Neil Diamond and others) but eventually, led by Nesmith, they acquired some influence over their output before splitting up in 1968 after Tork left. They reformed in 1975 and again (minus Nesmith) in 1986, making a successful 20th anniversary comeback tour. The band's most significant effect was to identify a lucrative sub-teenage market, the needs of which dominated POP MUSIC for the next 20 years or more. Subsequent attempts to imitate the success of pop's first 'man-made' group included the creation of the bizarre punk rock group Sigue Sigue Sputnik in 1985. Their album *Flaunt It* (1986) was the first to have commercials between tracks; it was a dismal failure.

Monkey trial *See* DAYTON ANTI-DARWINIST TRIAL.

monohull A single-hulled sailing vessel, as opposed to a catamaran or trimaran, which have two and three hulls, respectively.

monokini A topless BIKINI, *i.e.* a pair of very brief pants used for swimming or sunbathing.

Monopoly One of the 20th century's most popular board games, in which players buy and sell property, charge rents, make a fortune – and ultimately force their oponents to go bust. It was devised in about 1930 by Charles B. Darrow, a US heating equipment engineer, who was made unemployed by the 1929 WALL STREET CRASH. The game proved so popular with his friends that Darrow started turning out sets full time, at $2.50 apiece. He took the street names from Atlantic City, the East Coast resort in which the Darrow family had spent their vacations. There are many similarities between Darrow's Monopoly and an earlier board game, 'The Landlord's Game', invented by Elizabeth M. Phillips of Virginia in 1924. Both games have the utilities (Electric Company and Waterworks), railway companies, and 'Go to Jail' corners. However, it was Darrow who exploited the popularity of Monopoly, producing 20,000 sets in 1934. In 1935 the US games manufacturer, Parker Brothers, bought the production rights from Darrow and were soon producing 20,000 sets a week of their own, slightly refined, version.

In 1935 the British firm John Waddington bought a licence to manufacture their English version of Monopoly, with London street names; for example, Pennsylvania Railroad was renamed Marylebone Station, while the most expensive property, Boardwalk, became Mayfair. Local placenames and currency are used in most of the many other national versions now produced. The game has nurtured its share of fanatics, willing to play Monopoly for days on end in the most unlikely places – in a lift, underwater, upside down on a ceiling, to name but a few. Many countries have national championships, and winners take part in the World Monopoly Championship, first held in 1973.

Monopolies and Mergers Commission (MMC) A commission established by the UK government in 1948 as the Monopolies and Restrictive Practices Commission. It took its present title in 1973. It investigates questions referred to it on the existence of unregistered monopolies relating to the supply of goods in the UK, mergers qualifying for investigation under the Fair Trading Act (1973), and any uncompetitive or restrictive-labour practices qualifying for investigation under the Competition Act (1980).

Monroe, Marilyn (1926–62) Stagename of a US film actress and international sex symbol, whose short and tragic life included rape as a child, marriage at 14, and death at 36 from an overdose of sleeping pills. Whether or not she intended to take her life was never established. Born Norma Jean Mortenson, later changed to Norma Jean Baker, she first won notice as a model and then in two 1950 films, *The Asphalt Jungle* and *All About Eve*. The decade that followed produced some of her best films: *The Seven Year Itch* in 1954, *Bus Stop* in 1956, *The Prince and the Showgirl* in 1957 (with Laurence Olivier), and *Some Like It Hot* in 1959. The director of some of these films, Billy Wilder, was not always charitable about the mythical creature he had helped to create.

> She had breasts like granite and a brain like Swiss cheese, full of holes. Extracting a performance from her is like pulling teeth.

Her marriage to baseball star Joe DiMaggio in 1954 lasted nine months. From 1956 to 1961 she was married to playwright Arthur Miller, who wrote *The Misfits* for her. This 1961 film with Clark Gable was her last. After her death Miller said of her:

> If she was simple it would have been easy to help her. She could have made it with a little luck.

Her extraordinary appeal seemed to lie in her quite unique beauty and her mixture of blatant sexuality and childlike innocence. Cybill Shepherd, another star, was generous:

> She had curves in places other women don't even have places.

Sharp, arch, and a natural comedienne, Marilyn Monroe was a product of her background and consequently hopelessly unstable; what little equilibrium she had was undermined by her success. Hollywood is often blamed for creating the myth, exploiting it, and failing to support the vulnerable and naïve little girl around whom the myth was constructed.

Perhaps the last line should be hers. Asked by a columnist if she had anything on for her famous calendar pose, she replied:

> Oh yes, I had the radio on.

Mons A town in Belgium: the scene of the first major engagement between the British Expeditionary Force and the Germans on the Western Front at the beginning of World War I (23 August 1914). Greatly outnumbered, the BEF failed to halt the Germans' advance across Belgium and were forced to retreat to the River Marne, where they took part in a more successful operation, the first Battle of the MARNE, on 5 September 1914.

The engagement at Mons gave rise to two catchphrases of World War I, used in response to the question 'Where's So-and-So?'. **Gassed at Mons** and **Hanging on the (barbed) wire at Mons** meant that the person's whereabouts were either unknown or secret: the troops had encountered no barbed-wire entanglements or gas attacks in the retreat from Mons. The British war medal (the 1914 Star) given for service in France or Belgium in 1914 was also known as the **Mons Star**. *See also* ANGELS OF MONS.

Monte. Monte Bello Islands A group of uninhabited islands off NW Australia, in the Indian Ocean: the scene of two British NUCLEAR WEAPON tests in the 1950s. The first British atom bomb was detonated in a ship on 3 October 1952; the second explosion took place in 1956.

Monte Cassino *See* ANZIO.

Montessori method A system of training and educating young children evolved by the Italian educationist, Dr Maria Montessori (1870–1952). The method is based on free discipline and the use of specially devised educational apparatus and didactic material. Dr Montessori's first school opened in Rome in 1907 and her method has since exercised considerable influence on work with young children. *See also* DALTON PLAN.

Montezuma's revenge or **Aztec Two-step** Diarrhoea as a result of eating foreign food – a common complaint of tourists. The phrase originated in America in the 1960s and related to travelling in Mexico; Montezuma (*c.*1480–1520) was an Aztec ruler of Mexico during the Spanish conquest and is greatly revered as a Mexican national hero. The phrase is now used internationally; local variants include Delhi Belly, Gyppy Tummy, and Spanish Tummy.

Montgomery. Montgomery beret The style of beret worn by the British commander Bernard Law Montgomery in World War II. His beret was easily distinguished because, contrary to usual practice, he always wore two cap badges. *See* MONTY.

Montgomery bus boycott A peaceful boycott of bus services in Montgomery, Alabama, by Blacks protesting against racial segregation on public buses. Organized by Martin Luther King, who had just begun his Baptist ministry in the town, the boycott began in December 1955. It is believed to have been sparked off by a White bus driver's offensive treatment of Mrs Rosa Parks, who refused to join her fellow Blacks at the back of the bus. The protest was successful not only in its primary aim – by the end of 1956 racial segregation on buses had been banned – but also in bringing the CIVIL RIGHTS MOVEMENT to the attention of the nation and encouraging King to take his place at the head of the campaign.

Montreux. Montreux Convention An agreement signed at Montreux on 20 July 1936, relating to the Turkish straits of the DARDANELLES and the Bosporus. The convention maintained the right of free passage through the straits for commercial vessels of all nations in peacetime. Restrictions were placed on warships, particularly those of countries other than the Black Sea states, and on the passage of commercial vessels in wartime. In addition, Turkey was authorized to begin work immediately on the refortification of the demilitarized straits zone. The Montreux Convention replaced the International Commission of the Straits and remained in force after World War II, despite an attempt by the Soviet Union to amend it in 1946.

Montreux Festival A television festival held annually at Montreux, Switzerland. The most prestigious award at the festival is the GOLDEN ROSE; Silver Roses and Bronze Roses are also awarded.

Monty Nickname of Bernard Law Montgomery (1887–1976), British commander in World War II. Under his direction the British Eighth Army was victorious at ALAMEIN and drove Rommel's forces back to Tunis (1943), making Montgomery a national hero in the UK. Subsequently he clashed with US military leaders over the command of allied forces in the D DAY campaign and lost face at home over the defeat at ARNHEM. His reputation recovered somewhat following his successful drive into Germany in 1945. His flamboyant manner and sometimes irascible relations with other commanders guaranteed him a lasting place in the public's affections.

> Indomitable in retreat; invincible in advance; insufferable in victory.
>
> WINSTON CHURCHILL, describing Montgomery.

He became 1st Viscount Montgomery of Alamein in 1946. After the war, he cultivated his reputation as a blimpish and reactionary old gentleman:

> This sort of thing may be tolerated by the French, but we are British – thank god.
>
> Reaction to a parliamentary bill to relax the laws against homosexuality, 1965.

Monty's double Nickname acquired by the British actor M. E. Clifton-James after he was employed to impersonate General Montgomery as part of an elaborate Allied hoax in World War II. The actor's physical similarity to the general, helped by some coaching in his mannerisms, enabled the British to mislead the Germans about Montgomery's whereabouts and plans.

Clifton-James subsequently told his story in a book, filmed as *I Was Monty's Double* in 1958, with Clifton-James recreating his impersonation.

Monty Python's Flying Circus A BBC television comedy series (1969–74) celebrated for its idiosyncratic blend of satire, absurdism, and elements of the English nonsense tradition. Written and performed by Graham Chapman, John Cleese, Eric Idle, Terry Jones, and Michael Palin, it also featured the distinctive work of the US animator Terry Gilliam. Favourite targets for its satire included bureaucracy, English reserve and deference, and the conventions of television itself. Introduced without fanfare in a late-night slot previously reserved for religious programmes, the show became an unexpected cult success, especially among students and the young. It later scored a still more unlikely success in America. The team made a number of films, including *Monty Python and the Holy Grail* (1975) and the spoof Bible epic *Life of Brian* (1979). The name of the show alluded to Baron Richthofen's Flying Circus, the World War I fighter group commanded by the famous RED BARON, but the relevance of this to the programme's content is as mysterious as the identity of Mr Python.

Monza A motor-racing circuit built in 1922 in the Royal Park of Monza, near Milan in N Italy. The Italian Grand Prix takes place annually at Monza in September. The scene of a number of legendary duels between some of the most famous names in motor sport, Monza is one of the fastest circuits in the Formula 1 World Championship; the lap record for the fastest average speed around the 3.6 miles of the track is over 146 m.p.h. The original elliptical course has been modified to an open L-shape, which includes such hazards as the Ascari bend and the Parabolica.

mooch A slow dance popular in the 1920s; the word was later extended to mean idling aimlessly about.

Moo-Cow A nickname given to the Morris-Cowley car, first built in 1925 by Morris Motors Ltd at Cowley, Oxford. The car was also known at the 'bull-nose' Morris, because of the shape of its radiator. A small reliable family car with an 11.9 HP engine, the Morris-Cowley was one of the earliest British cars produced for the mass market; at £200 it competed with Ford's Model T (*see* TIN LIZZIE).

Moog Tradename for a type of music synthesizer – an electronic keyboard that can emulate a variety of musical sounds. It is named after the US engineer who invented it, Robert A. Moog (1934–). Moog had developed the first synthesizers in the 1950s, but it was the success of Walter Carlos's *Switched on Bach* recording in 1969, which used a Moog, that made his name synonymous with synthesized electronic sound.

moolah or **moola** Slang for money. Originally an Americanism, it was adopted in the UK in the 1930s.

moon. moonchild A person born under the astrological sign of Cancer (June 21–July 21). It became a favoured sign of HIPPIES in the late 1960s and was often preferred to 'Cancerian', because of the association with the disease.

Moonies A religious sect, properly called the **Unification Church**, founded by Sun Myung Moon (1920–) in South Korea in 1954. It spread to America in the 1960s and subsequently to the UK, Australia, etc. Moon claims to be the Second Messiah and that his devotees will save mankind from Satan. Funds built up by his followers by selling artificial flowers and other items were used by Moon to create a large property and business organization in America, where he has lived since 1972. Tax avoidance led to his prosecution and imprisonment (1984–85).

mooning Slang for bending down and exposing one's buttocks to someone, usually as an insult. The practice originated in America in the 1950s. The derivation of the word is based on the supposed resemblance between the bare buttocks and the moon. Mooning is a traditional insult among the Maoris in New Zealand.

moonlighting *See* SUNLIGHTING.

moonrock Slang name for CRACK (a crystalline form of cocaine) laced with heroin.

moonwalk (1) An exploratory walk on the surface of the moon. (2) A type of dance step popularized by the US pop singer Michael Jackson.

over the moon *See under* OVER.

Moorgate disaster The worst disaster on London's Underground network, which occurred at Moorgate Station on 28 February 1975. 35 people died, including the traindriver, when a tube train crashed into the end of a dead-end tunnel: the first 15 feet of train telescoped to just two feet. Speculation about the cause of the crash ranged from the suggestion that the driver was drunk to the possibility that he had suffered a sudden 'brainstorm'; a verdict of accidental death was returned, but it seems the mystery will never be satisfactorily explained.

Moors murders A series of sadistic murders in the UK for which Myra Hindley and Ian Brady were sentenced to life imprisonment in 1966. At least three children were killed and buried on the Lancashire moors north of Manchester: some of the bodies were never recovered. The horrific nature of the crimes, in which the dying cries of the young victims were recorded on tape, shocked the nation. Campaigns for the early release of Myra Hindley have so far been unsuccessful, in spite of her reported conversion to Christianity and the support of Lord Longford (*see* HOLY FOOL).

mop The final beat at the end of a JAZZ number.

moped A lightweight motorized cycle – the name is a contraction of *mo*torized *ped*al cycle. Mopeds originated in Europe after World War II, when bicycles were modified and fitted with small engines to provide an economical means of transport in the lean postwar years. They are now popular not only in Europe but in many other parts of the world, often because of the generous tax concessions to owners and low legal age limit for the rider. Virtually all of them have 50 cc two-stroke engines, although the pedals are seldom now needed for pedalling.

Mopp, Mrs *See* ITMA.

MOR *See* MIDDLE-OF-THE-ROAD.

moral. moral majority The members of a country or society who hold what are generally regarded as traditional moral values. The phrase became popular in America during the Reagan administration, when it was used specifically of right-wing reactionaries opposed to liberal reforms, such as abortion and rights for homosexuals.

Moral Rearmament (MRA) A movement founded in 1938 by the US evangelist Frank Buchman (1878–1961), who had earlier founded the OXFORD GROUP. Its purpose was to counter the materialism of present-day society by persuading people to live according to the highest standards of morality and love, to obey God, and to unite in a worldwide association according to these principles.

Morel, Paul The hero of the largely autobiographical novel *Sons and Lovers* (1913) by D. H. Lawrence (1885–1930). Like Lawrence himself, Morel is the son of a sometimes violent and often drunk coalminer and his Puritan and better-educated wife. The novel deals with Morel's emancipation into a more cultured milieu, his loves, his mother's jealousy at the prospect of losing him, and his devastation when she finally dies. Lawrence's first major novel, it was soon established as one of the leading works of fiction of the 20th century, especially important because it was one of the earliest novels written by a working-class author about working-class life.

Morgenthau Plan A project relating to the future of Germany after World War II. It was drawn up by Henry Morgenthau (1891–1967), US Secretary of the Treasury, and the US Secretary of War Henry Stimson; it was put forward at the Quebec conference between Churchill and Roosevelt in September 1944. The Morgenthau Plan proposed "eliminating the war-making industries in the Ruhr and in the Saar" and "converting Germany into a country primarily agricultural and pastoral in its character". Churchill reluctantly accepted the proposal, which was later revoked.

morning-after pill A contraceptive PILL, containing high doses of oestrogen and progestogen hormones, that can be taken as a precautionary measure *after* unprotected intercourse. It may cause vomiting, and regular use is not recommended.

Mornington Crescent A panel game popularized during the 1980s by the BBC radio programme *I'm Sorry I Haven't A Clue*, featuring Humphrey Littleton, Barry Cryer, Tim Brooke-Taylor, Graeme Garden, and William Rushton. It is usually played by two teams, one of whom chooses a London underground station as a starting point; the two sides then alternate in making valid moves to other underground stations. The objective is to reach Mornington Crescent (a station on the Northern Line) and to prevent one's opponents from doing so. Newcomers to the game are expected to pick up the rules as they go along.

Moroccan crisis The arrival of the German emperor, Wilhelm II, in Tangier in 1905 to settle the conflicting interests of France, Spain, and Germany in Morocco. The Kaiser's intervention led to the international Algeciras conference (16 January–7 April 1906), which acknowledged Moroccan independence but resulted in the country's affairs being largely controlled by France, with Spanish cooperation. This culminated in the AGADIR CRISIS of 1911, which is sometimes called the second Moroccan crisis.

moron An adult with a mental age of between 8 and 12 years. This sense was coined by the US physician Henry Goddard in 1910 as a medical term, derived from the Greek *moros*, stupid (in medical terminology the word is now obsolete; such people are now described as suffering from a mild degree of mental subnormality). Later it came to be used generally of any mentally deficient person. It is now, however, widely used in the general language for anyone who does stupid things, without any implication of mental deficiency.

Morrison shelter The indoor air-raid shelter officially recommended by the home secretary Herbert Stanley Morrison (1888–1965) for use during the BLITZ. A not dissimilar shelter recommended for use against nuclear attack in a secret government information film made in the postwar years attracted considerable public derision when it was finally shown in the 1980s: essential features of the design included large amounts of tin foil and upturned mattresses. *See also* ANDERSON SHELTER.

MOS US cinematic slang used to indicate that a particular shot is silent. It is thought to derive from the guttural cry of the many German-born directors in the early years of Hollywood calling for a scene '*m*it *o*ut *s*ound'.

Moscow Conference A meeting between Churchill, Stalin, and the US ambassador Averell Harriman in Moscow (9–20 October 1944). The purpose of the conference was to discuss the partition of SE Europe at the end of World War II. The Soviet Union was given a controlling interest in Romania, Bulgaria, and Hungary; the UK was given a controlling interest in Greece; and Yugoslavia was to be a zone of counterbalanced Soviet and British influence. The last of these decisions proved to have little substance, with the rise of Tito.

moshing British slang for a type of dancing done in a packed auditorium or club to HEAVY METAL or HARDCORE music. The limited space means that moshing (with its echoes of the words squash and mash) amounts to making whatever sinuous movements are possible. This style of dancing took over in the 1980s from the antics of the HEADBANGERS of the 1970s.

Mosleyites The supporters of Sir Oswald Mosley (1896–1980), members of the British Union of Fascists (BUF), also known as BLACKSHIRTS (a nickname originally applied to Mussolini's Fascist supporters). The BUF was founded by Mosley in October 1932: its members took part in antisemitic demonstrations, which inevitably led to violence, in the East End of London and elsewhere. The Public Order Act (1936) restricted the activities of the Mosleyites, who are thought to have numbered about 20,000 at this time. The BUF was banned in 1940 and Mosley was interned (1940–43). He was married to Diana Mitford (*see* MITFORD GIRLS).

Mosquito A fast twin-engined aircraft manufactured by the de Havilland company and used by the RAF during World War II. A prototype Mosquito first took to the air on 25 November 1940, and the plane entered service as a light bomber with 105 Squadron in 1942. The lightweight wooden construction and Merlin engines gave it a top speed of over 400 m.p.h. (650 k.p.h). In the second half of the war, the Mosquito was cast in various roles, including reconnaissance plane, night fighter, fighter-bomber, and escort fighter. With a wingspan of 16.51 m (54 ft 2 in) and a length of 12.43 m (40 ft 6 in), the Mosquito could carry a payload of up to 1800 kg (4000 lb).

Mossad The Committee for Illegal Immigration – in full *Mossad le Aliyeh Beth* – an organization originally formed in 1937 as part of the Jewish defence force, HAGANAH, to arrange the illegal immigration of Jews into Palestine as part of the campaign to establish a Jewish homeland. The organization was revived after World War II and its activities expanded to direct the migration of Jews displaced by the horrors of the HOLOCAUST, initially to Allied refugee camps and thence to Palestine. This was performed by a network of Mossad agents working underground throughout Europe from a headquarters in Paris. Jewish migrants were carried from Mediterranean ports in chartered vessels and landed secretly on the Palestinian coast, in defiance of the British regulations under their Mandate. By 1948 members of Mossad were also engaged in smuggling arms and other covert activities. After the establishment of the state of Israel in 1948, Mossad formed the basis of the new country's intelligence service. As such, it has played a crucial role in Israel's struggle against Palestinian guerrilla organizations, such as the Palestine Liberation Organization (*see* PLO), as well as in the armed conflict with neighbouring Arab states.

most-favoured nation In a trade agreement between two countries, a most-favoured-nation clause is one that states that each country will give to the other the same treatment as regards quotas, tariffs, and import restrictions as they extend to the most-favoured nation with which each trades. This concept is included in the European Community trade agreements and also in GATT.

MOT The popular name for the test certificate issued by the UK's Department of Transport (originally *M*inistry *o*f *T*ransport) to road vehicles that have passed a mandatory test for roadworthiness. All cars and light goods vehicles over three years old are required to undergo an annual test at an authorized test centre – usually a garage. Such components as steering, brakes, tyres, suspension, and bodywork are examined and their condition noted. The owner is required to correct any defects before a certificate is awarded. Heavy goods vehicles must undergo similar annual tests, starting from one year old, at testing stations run by the DOT Vehicle Inspectorate. The MOT scheme was instituted by the Road Traffic Act 1960, when it applied to vehicles over five years old.

motel A hotel that caters especially for motorists by being situated close to a motorway or main road, providing car parking and specializing in one-night accommodation. The motel, which originated in America in 1925, became very popular in the 1950s, when the concept spread to the UK and elsewhere. Some motels consist of single chalet-like units, each with its own parking place. The word is a combination of *mo*tor and h*otel*.

mothball ships Ships placed in reserve, so called from the post-World War II practice of spraying a plastic covering or cocoon over gun-mountings and other working parts.

mother. Can you hear me, mother? *See under* HEAR.

Mother's Day The day on which mothers traditionally receive cards and gifts from their children. In the UK the name Mother's Day, imported from America during World War II, has become synonymous with the Christian festival of Mothering Sunday, the fourth Sunday in Lent, when servants, apprentices, and other young workers living away from home were traditionally given a day's holiday to visit their mothers. In America, Mother's Day falls on the second Sunday of May, established by the US Congress in 1914 as a secular festival in honour of mothers. The commercial potential of Mother's Day is exploited to the full on both sides of the Atlantic by florists and others. *See also* FATHER'S DAY.

Mother's Union A Church of England women's society to safeguard and strengthen Christian family life, to uphold the lifelong vows of marriage, and generally to play a proper part in the life of the Church. It was incorporated by Royal Charter in 1926 and generally operates as a parish institution.

Mother Teresa Yugoslavian-born nun (Agnes Gonxha Bejaxhui; 1910–), who has attracted worldwide attention for her charitable work amongst the poor of India. She has pressed her case for support for India's deprived with numerous heads of state, including Queen Elizabeth II and Pope John Paul II. She won the Nobel Peace Prize in 1979.

Some mothers do 'ave 'em Catchphrase from about 1920, implying that some mothers have stupid or clumsy sons. It was a catchphrase of the British radio comedy programme *The Jimmy Clitheroe Show* in the 1930s and was revived in the 1970s as the title of a popular television comedy series featuring the disaster-prone Frank Spencer (played by Michael Crawford).

motor. motorhead (1) Slang for a motorbike or car fan. The suffix *-head* is often used to indicate a particular interest in something (*see* HEAD). In the 1970s a heavy metal band of that name emerged. (2) Slang for a person who uses amphetamine drugs. This definition is related to the first, 'motor' denoting both speed and aggression.

motormouth US slang for someone who talks very fast or someone who 'shouts their mouth off' on a variety of subjects. It originated in the 1970s as part of Black slang but its use has spread to the UK. It has been used of RAP artists, DJs, and people who like the drug SPEED. The fast-talking British comedian Ben Elton, popular in the late 1980s and early 1990s, has also been called a motormouth.

motorway A main road for fast traffic with restricted access and dual carriageways, usually linking major centres of industry and population. The world's first motorway appeared in 1924 with the opening of the Milan–Varese Autostrade in Italy. In the following decades other countries, notably Germany and America, embarked on major motorway construction programmes. In the UK the Special Roads Act (1949) provided for the building of motorways. Construction eventually began on the M1 between London and Birmingham on 24 March 1958; the first section opened on 2 November 1959. By 1988 the UK had 1865 miles of motorway.

motorway madness The dangerous practice of driving too fast and too close to the car in front on a motorway, which is one of the major causes of accidents and multiple pile-ups, especially in bad weather with poor visibility.

Motown A kind of music with rhythm and blues elements, popular especially during the late 1960s and 1970s. It is so called because this is the nickname of Detroit, the US car-manufacturing town in which it originated. Motown is, of course, a combination of *mo*tor and *town*.

mouldy fig In JAZZ slang, someone who prefers traditional forms of jazz to modern styles.

mountain bike A type of sturdy bicycle designed for cross-country use in rough terrain. Its principal features are a strong frame, thick-rimmed wheels with heavy-duty tyres, and a large number (at least 16) of gears to cope with extreme gradients. In the 1960s the mountain bike was adopted by fashion-conscious YUPPIES as a healthy, ecologically sound, and status-enhancing means of getting to work. It remains an important status symbol among teenage boys.

Mountbatten *See* BATTENBERG.

Mount St Helens A volcano in the Cascade mountain range of Washington State, NW America. Its eruption in May 1980 was the biggest volcanic explosion witnessed in modern US history. The volcano, dormant since the 19th century, gave its first indication of renewed activity on 27 March 1980 with an eruption of steam. This was followed by several moderate eruptions with intervening quiet spells. However, in spite of intensive monitoring, the events of 18 May exceeded all predictions. An earthquake ruptured the entire north face of the volcano, triggering an avalanche and massive air blast, which carried ash and other debris over 20 km and felled vast swathes of the surrounding forest. Mudflows swept through nearby valleys, rivers steamed with the hot debris, and the sky filled with clouds of volcanic ash. The blast lifted ash to over 6000 m, causing it to spread across the continent and eventually around the globe, giving red sunsets and hazy skies throughout the N hemisphere. The eruption left over 60 people dead or missing and caused over $2 billion of damage. There was a second, but less severe, eruption on 25 May, after which, with its top literally blown off, St Helens quietened down.

mouse A device that controls the cursor on a computer screen. The name derives from the supposed resemblance to a mouse of the device, a small box with buttons on top and a lead connecting to a microcomputer.

Mouse A German tank developed on Hitler's orders in 1944, which at 180 tons was the heaviest tank ever built. Facing the overwhelming superiority of the Soviet Union's armour, Hitler commissioned Ferdinand Porsche to design a massive tank that could withstand virtually any assault. Powered by a 1500 horsepower engine, the prototype was capable of travelling underwater and ran on three foot-wide tracks. Unfortunately it was so heavy that it could only travel at 12 m.p.h., became bogged down on anything but the firmest ground, and shattered the roads on which it ran. The project was abandoned.

mouse-milking A US business expression used to describe any project that consumes time, money, and effort but yields very little profit. Clearly milking a mouse would be laborious and unproductive.

The Mousetrap A play by Agatha Christie (*see* QUEEN OF CRIME), which has enjoyed a record-breaking continuous run since its first performance at the Ambassador's Theatre, London, in 1952. In 1974 the play was transferred without a break to St Martin's Theatre, London, where it can still be seen. The British actor Richard Attenborough and his wife Sheila Sim were in the cast of the first production. *The Mousetrap* was originally written in 1947 as *Three Blind Mice*, a radio play for the 80th birthday of Queen Mary. It was subsequently published as a novel, under the original title, before being adapted for the stage.

Mouth, The *See* SUPERBRAT.

move. If it moves, shoot it, if it doesn't, chop it down A popular Australian saying, facetiously regarded as an informal national motto. It is an ironic echo of the pioneering spirit of the first Australian settlers.

Let's get America moving again A political slogan used in 1960 by President John F. Kennedy. It has been used elsewhere, by substituting the appropriate name of a country, party, etc.

movers and shakers US slang for people who are powerful and influential, people with the means to organize others and to make things happen. The term, although not with this specific meaning, derives from a poem by Arthur O'Shaughnessy (1874).

We shall not be moved A phrase used as a chant at demonstrations and sit-ins from the 1960s. It was originally a line from a negro spiritual.

mow the lawn US Black slang of the 1940s, meaning to comb the hair.

Mr *See under* MISTER.

muck. muckrakers The name given to US investigative journalists and writers at the beginning of the 20th century. Their use of sensationalism to increase circulation led President Theodore Roosevelt to call them "irresponsible". However, many reforms were brought about as a result of articles in such magazines as *Colliers* and *McClure's* and in newspapers, led by William Randolph Hearst's *New York Journal* and Joseph Pulitzer's *New York World*. Two effective muckrakers were Ira M. Tarbell (1857–1944), whose 1904 exposé of Standard Oil encouraged legislation on monopolies, and Lincoln Steffens (1866–1936), who exposed illegal political tactics in 1902. Upton Sinclair's book *The Jungle* (1906) gave many details of insanitary practices in the meat industry, which led to the Federal Food and Drugs Act later that year. The methods of the muckraking press were called **yellow journalism**, from Pulitzer's 'Yellow Kid' comic strip.

Sing 'em muck The advice allegedly given by the Australian soprano Dame Nellie Melba (1861–1931) to Clara Butt, who was about to carry out a tour of Australia:

> Still, it's a wonderful country, and you'll have a good-time. What are you going to sing? All I can say is – sing 'em muck! It's all they can understand!

The phrase has since been repeated in jaundiced tones by numerous entertainers about to tour 'remote' areas.

mud. Here's mud in your eye! A drinking toast of uncertain origin. Two possible explanations have been suggested. One is that the toast originated during World War I, when soldiers in the trenches would clearly prefer to get mud in their eyes than something more dangerous. Thus the toast was an expression of goodwill. The alternative context is the racecourse and the hope that one's own horse will be out in front kicking up mud into the eyes of the less successful horses following it. On the basis of this theory, the toast is not an expression of goodwill.

Mudros, Chios, and chaos A catchphrase heard from 1915 among the forces serving in the Mediterranean Expeditionary Force. It refers to the three main bases and commands in the area, two of them being on the islands of Mudros and Chios.

muesli-belt malnutrition A dietary paradox researched by Professor Vincent Marks of the University of Surrey. It appears that parents who feed their children on a supposedly healthy diet of high-fibre low-fat foods, such as muesli, brown bread, and raw vegetables, are doing them a disservice. Marks's research showed that because the food took so long to masticate, the children were not getting enough to eat. Children consuming food that was quicker to eat, such as fish fingers and chips, turned out to be better nourished.

mug. mugging The crime of assaulting and robbing people in the streets, on trains, in lonely parks, etc., especially at night. Muggers often hunt in packs and generally attack old or infirm people, young girls, etc., who are unable to protect themselves. This cowardly and vicious practice is a growing problem in urban environments. From the old slang use of *mug* meaning to rob or swindle.

mug shot Originally, US slang for a frontal photograph taken of a suspect by the police. It has since spread throughout the English-speaking world and it is now also used for any head-and-shoulders portrait.

Muhammed Ali The name adopted by the US boxer Cassius Clay (1942–   ) when he became a BLACK MUSLIM. Ali's professional career began after the 1960 Olympic Games in Rome, where he won a gold medal in the light-heavyweight class. In 1964 he defeated Sonny Liston to become world heavyweight champion, a title he held for three years, until his refusal to join the US army (because of his Black Muslim faith) caused him to be banned from the sport. He regained the title in 1974, lost it and won it back in 1978, and was finally defeated by Larry Holmes in 1980.

Ali is widely regarded as one of the greatest heavyweight boxers of all time. He is equally famous for his colourful personality and for his self-confident catchphrases "I am the greatest" (*see under* GREAT) and "Float like a butterfly, sting like a bee". *See also* ALI SHUFFLE.

mujaheddin (Arab. fighters) A loose coalition of rebel groups formed in Afghanistan to oppose the revolutionary government of the People's Democratic Party of Afghanistan (PDPA), which came to power after a military coup in 1978. This opposition intensified following the intervention in 1979 of Soviet forces in support of their PDPA allies. The mujaheddin comprise a wide range of political and ethnic factions, including Sunni and Shi'ite Muslims, Islamic traditionalists, and radical fundamentalists. Most mujaheddin attacks are led from across the border in neighbouring Pakistan, receiving arms and equipment from western countries, especially America, as well as China, Iran, Saudi Arabia, and Egypt. The political and religious diversity of the mujaheddin has frequently led to squabbling and factional fighting. However, some semblance of unity was achieved in 1985 with the creation of the Islamic Unity of Afghan Mujaheddin, encompassing seven of the guerrilla groups. In 1989 the same front formed a provisional Afghan government in exile. But, since the withdrawal of Soviet groops in 1989, the PDPA government led by Najibullah Ahmadzai has proved remarkably resilient to military pressure by the rebels.

Mukden incident An explosion on the South Manchurian Railway near the city of Mukden (now Shenyang) in NE China, on 18 September 1931. The Japanese blamed the explosion on the Chinese and used it as an excuse to attack and take control of the city. They set up a puppet administration there on 24 September 1931 and went on to drive the Chinese forces out of Manchuria, creating the puppet state of MANCHUKUO.

Mulberry harbour An artificial harbour created for the Allied invasion of Normandy in 1944. Mulberry was the codename of the engineering operation that produced two of these floating harbours: they were prefabricated in England, towed across the English Channel, and sunk into position on the French coast.

mule Slang for someone who smuggles drugs into a country. Originally it referred specifically to a smuggler of South American cocaine but its meaning has been extended to cover any drug smuggler.

multimedia *See* MIXED MEDIA.

multinational A large corporation that has many branches or divisions in different countries. Companies extend their activities overseas to exploit new markets, operate product service and distribution networks, secure supplies of raw materials, or to take advantage of lower taxes and cheaper labour.

munch. munchies Drug-users' slang for snacks craved after smoking marijuana. Users talk of 'having the munchies' for sweets, crisps, etc. This is a 1970s adaptation of the use of the word for any snack.

munchkin US slang for a sweet little child, taken from the name of the little people in the WIZARD OF OZ, written by L. Frank Baum (1856–1919) in 1900 and made into an immensely successful film in 1939, starring Judy Garland. The word can also be used patronizingly of low-level employees in an organization – sometimes as **low-level munchkins**.

Munich. another Munich A potentially disastrous, humiliating, or dishonourable act of appeasement or surrender. So called from the unfortunate act of appeasement, the **Munich Pact** or **Agreement**, concluded between the UK, France, Germany, and Italy (30 September 1938) in which the Sudetenland of Czechoslovakia was ceded to Germany. The British prime minister, Neville Chamberlain, who took part in this agreement, described it as achieving "peace in our time". Six months later Hitler invaded Czechoslovakia; in September 1939, World War II began. The best that can be said for Chamberlain and Deladier of France is that they bought a little time in which to rearm.

Munich air crash The accident on 6 February 1958 in which a BEA airliner crashed during take-off on a snow-covered runway at Munich airport. 23 of the 44 passengers were killed, including 12 players and staff belonging to Manchester United Football Club. The tragedy cut short the lives of several rising stars of British football – all members of the youthful Manchester team managed by Matt Busby and popularly known as BUSBY'S BABES. These included the England internationals Roger Byrne, Tommy Taylor, and David Pegg. Duncan Edwards, the English left-half, died in hospital 15 days later. The team was returning home from Belgrade after winning a European Cup semi-final place. Eight football journalists also died in the crash but manager Matt Busby recovered from his injuries to rebuild his shattered team.

Munich Putsch An abortive attempt by Adolf Hitler (12 November 1923) to take control of Bavaria. Often called the **beer-hall Putsch**, the incident took place in Munich's largest beer hall, the Burgerbraukeller, where Gustav von Kahr, the state commissioner, was speaking. Hitler broke in, supported by his BROWN SHIRTS, claiming that he had the support of the German war hero, Field Marshal von Ludendorff (1865–1937). Hitler and von Ludendorff were both arrested, Hitler subsequently spending time in prison, where he wrote MEIN KAMPF (My Struggle; 1925).

muppet (1) A felt puppet manipulated by a human operator, created by Jim Henson (1936–90), who coined the name from *m*arionette and p*uppet*. Muppets first appeared in the children's television series *Sesame Street* (1969 onwards) and subsequently graduated to their own show (1976–80), which was more adult-orientated, containing songs, sketches, and special guest stars. It featured such muppet favourites as KERMIT the Frog, Fozzie Bear, and Miss Piggy, who became major stars. (2) British derogatory slang for a mental-hospital patient or a person disadvantaged in some way. It is also used of unattractive teenagers by their peers. It is not known why the friendly puppets should have created this disagreeable slang sense.

muppie A facetious acronyn for *m*iddle-aged *u*rban *p*rofessional. Such acronyms were popular in the UK in the 1980s. *See* YUPPIE.

Murderers' Row The nickname of the batting line-up of the New York Yankee baseball team in the 1920s. Among its pinstripe uniforms were two all-time baseball greats, George Herman (BABE) Ruth and Lou Gehrig. Ruth hit a record 60 home runs in 1927 (no other player had more than 24 in a season) and retired in 1935 with 714. Gehrig, also a strong hitter, set a record of playing in 2130 consecutive games (1925–39). He died two years later from amyotrophic lateral sclerosis, now commonly called 'Lou Gehrig's disease'.

Murphy A confidence trick commonly played on men who pay to have sex with a prostitute. After payment has been made to a pimp, the punter is given a rendezvous to meet a woman, who does not turn up. The name is probably an allusion to the supposed gullibility of the Irish (Murphy being a common Irish surname). It has also been used of other 'con' tricks.

Bridey Murphy The name of the woman who was 'contacted' in a celebrated hypnotic regression of a US housewife in 1952. Under hypnosis by Morey Bernstein, who later recounted the experience in a bestselling book, the subject described the life of a person called Bridey Murphy in Ireland in the previous century. Among the scenes, Bridey recalled her own funeral and life after death before her 'rebirth' in 1923. All the facts produced were checked by the author, although subsequent investigators could find no record of Bridey's birth or death. Nevertheless, many of the details given during the regression were uncannily accurate and remain unexplained by various critics, who argued that most of Bridey Murphy's story was derived from the hypnotized woman's own subconscious, prompted by Bernstein's questions. Whatever the truth behind the regression, the story of Bridey Murphy greatly increased public interest in experiments on hypnosis. *See also* BLOXHAM TAPES.

Murphy's Law Of uncertain origin but with an Irish implication, Murphy's Law can be summed up by the saying: 'anything that can go wrong, will go wrong'. It is also known as **Sod's Law**. Some typical examples of its use are: you will always find something in the last place you look; the light at the end of the tunnel is the headlamp of an oncoming train. Exactly who Murphy is or was is not known for certain; however, the US Navy ran a series of cautionary cartoons featuring a fictitious character called Murphy, who could be relied on to get things wrong; such as attaching an aircraft propellor the wrong way round!

the Murphia A facetious name, a play on the word MAFIA, applied to a group of Irish broadcasters prominent in the UK in the 1980s. Murphy is, of course, a typical Irish surname. Similarly, the **Taffia** is used humorously for the Welsh old boys' network.

mushroom US police slang for a law-abiding member of the public who strays into the firing-line during a shoot-out with criminals. This slightly contemptuous term alludes to the way such people appear out of nowhere and cause unnecessary complications by getting themselves shot.

mushroom cloud The characteristic shape of the products of a nuclear explosion, particularly one occurring on or near the surface of the ground. The massive energy release of the explosion creates a shock wave and fireball, which render the air luminous in the form of a mushroom-shaped cloud. Such a cloud was first witnessed by scientists of the US MANHATTAN PROJECT, who detonated a prototype NUCLEAR WEAPON at the Alamogordo test site in New Mexico on 16 July 1945. The physicist Enrico Fermi described this first detonation:

> After a few seconds the rising flames lost their brightness and appeared as a huge pillar of smoke with an expanded head like a gigantic mushroom that rose rapidly beyond the clouds, probably to a height of the order of 30,000 feet.

Later that same year, America exploded nuclear weapons over the Japanese cities of HIROSHIMA and NAGASAKI. Thereafter, the mushroom cloud came to symbolize the nuclear threat overshadowing all life on the planet.

music. music centre An integrated home audio system that combines record turntable, cassette tape deck, radio tuner, amplifier, and speakers. It was introduced in the 1970s, made possible by the advent of the microchip and the consequent miniaturization of many audio components. The music centre's convenience, compactness, and competitive price made it popular, although HI-FI buffs remained loyal to more expensive systems comprising separate components. By the mid-1980s the music centre had been supplanted by the even more miniaturized MIDI SYSTEM.

music hall A popular form of variety entertainment that had its origins in the 'free and easy' of the public houses and in the song and supper rooms of early Victorian London. Music halls eventually became more numerous in London and the provinces than the regular theatres and such names as Palladium, Palace, Alhambra, Coliseum, Empire, Hippodrome, etc., proclaim their former glories. Their best days were in the early part of the 20th century, but in the 1920s the cinema eclipsed them to a considerable extent. Later, radio and – after World War II – television sealed their fate.

music, maestro, please A phrase used by the 1950s bandleader Harry Leader when inviting his band to strike up. It comes from a song by Magidson and Wrubel, used by Flanagan and Allen in their 1938 show *These Foolish Things*.

muso A musician. It was coined by association with the word 'wino', for one who is addicted to drink.

> Muso . . . a term normally used by very bad musicians to describe very good ones.
>
> *The Independent*, 5 February 1991.

mustard gas A highly poisonous war gas (dichlorodiethyl sulphide). Mustard gas attacks the respiratory tract but also causes eye damage and blisters the skin. It was first used by the German army during World War I, notably at PASSCHENDAELE (1917). The government of Iraq used mustard gas in 1988 against Kurdish dissidents in the north of the country.

Mutt and Jeff A married couple or two friends who are extremely unlike each other in physical appearance. The characters originated in a comic-strip cartoon drawn by the US cartoonist Bud Fisher (1884–1954) at the beginning of the 20th century. Mutt was a tall thin character, while Jeff was short and fat.

Muzak Tradename of a system for playing background music in such public places as shops, restaurants, hairdressers, doctors' waiting rooms, etc. The name was based on KODAK and music, Kodak being a short and successful tradename.

> If muzak be the food of love, no wonder it is commonly to be found . . . among the frozen mint-flavoured peas and the crinkle-cut chips.
> *The Times*, 29 November 1968.

MVD Ministerstvo Vnutrennikh Del. The Soviet police organization, the Ministry of Internal Affairs, which replaced the NKVD in 1946. The official duties of the uniformed members of the MVD included general police work, the control of labour camps, the supervision of border troops, the issue of passports and visas, etc. The MVD is also believed to have been involved in the secret trial and punishment of Stalin's opponents. In 1960 the MVD was replaced by the KVD.

MX Missile Experimental (Missile X). A sophisticated ICBM developed during the 1970s as part of a drive to modernize the ageing US arsenal of Titan and Minuteman III missiles. The MX was designed to carry 10 warheads and deliver them on target with pinpoint accuracy, using the latest INERTIAL GUIDANCE technology. It was also planned to be delivered from mobile launchers, so that it could survive a first attack; however, a successful and cost-effective method of concealing and moving the missiles underground could not be found and in 1983 the US Congress refused to vote more funds for mobile launch base development. The latest plan is to site a reduced number in Minuteman silos.

myalgic encephalomyelitis *See* ME.

My Lai A Vietnamese village, also known as Song My, situated in Quang Ngai province; it was the scene of one of the worst atrocities committed by US forces during the VIETNAM WAR. On 16 March 1968 C company of 1st Batallion 20th Infantry, led by Lieutenant William Calley, entered the village (designated My Lai 4 by the US Army). Several hundred unarmed villagers were shot dead, including women and children; many of the women were raped by US soldiers. Army officers conspired to conceal the truth, which only came to light the following year. In March 1969 Ronald Ridenhour, a soldier serving in Vietnam, who had heard about the incident, wrote an open letter to the US Army Department and to members of the Senate and Congress, calling for an investigation of the events at My Lai. Later in the year, photographs of the massacred villagers, taken by army photographer Ron Haeberle, were published in a newspaper, with Haeberle's eye-witness account. On 24 November the Army announced that Calley was to be court-martialled on murder charges.

25 men were charged with various crimes arising from incidents in My Lai, but only Calley was found guilty. In 1971 he was sentenced to a long prison term but after serving three years he was released on parole. Calley's defence rested on his claim that in 'following orders' the guilt lay with his army superiors and ultimately with the US people. For many Americans the My Lai killings confirmed their worst fears about US conduct in Vietnam. Others regarded Calley as the dupe of an incompetent and ill-disciplined command structure, or even as a martyr.

myxomatosis A disease of rabbits and hares that was deliberately introduced into wild rabbits in the UK and Australia in the 1950s in an attempt to restrict their ever-growing numbers. Caused by a virus, it is usually fatal but some rabbits have developed a degree of immunity to the disease. Its introduction was welcomed by farmers whose crops were suffering damage from the rabbits; it was less popular with the general public, who were distressed by the appearance of infected rabbits with large swellings on their faces, including the eyes, making them virtually blind. The disease reduced the wild rabbit population by about 90%, but numbers have since recovered.

N

NAACP National Association for the Advancement of Colored People. The US civil-rights organization that has campaigned for equal rights through legal actions and public protests. It was formed in 1909 and by the 1940s was using SIT-IN tactics to integrate White-only restaurants. The NAACP won a historic 1954 Supreme Court ruling that segregated schools for Whites and Blacks were unconstitutional. In 1955 it supported the MONTGOMERY BUS BOYCOTT, led by Martin Luther King, and took part in King's 1963 'March on Washington' by more than 200,000 people. Other strong organizations in the equal-rights movement have been the Congress of Racial Equality (CORE) and King's Southern Christian Leadership Conference (SCLC).

Naafi Navy, Army, and Air Force Institute. The body that organizes canteens for use by members of the British armed forces throughout the world. *See* NAFF; NAFFY MEDAL.

nab British slang, now obsolete, for the dole. It was an acronym for National Assistance Board, the official body that predated the DHSS, with the responsibility for paying the unemployment benefit.

Naderite A supporter or staff member of the campaigns of the US lawyer Ralph Nader (1934–), whose battles against dubious corporate and governmental practices have led to new legislation, such as improved automobile safety standards and stricter health laws. His 1965 book, *Unsafe at Any Speed*, indicted Detroit for putting profits before safety. His watchdog organization, Public Citizen Inc., has investigated pesticides, tax reform, health care, and the US Congress.

nadsat A word derived from the Russ. *pyatnádsat*, meaning fifteen; it is used to describe an invented form of teenage slang found as the narrative element in Anthony Burgess's novel *A Clockwork Orange* (1962), made into a film by Stanley Kubrick in 1972. The story-line is constructed round Alex, a renegade teenager from the near future who is locked up and forced to undergo psychological experiments known as Ludovic's Technique.

naff Slang for worthless, shoddy, in bad taste, or ostentatious: a term of general disapprobation. It has been suggested that naff is armed services' slang deriving from NAAFI, which was proverbial for providing indifferent food and poor-quality goods at its shops.

> Now comes this oddly naff book, a cross between Chekhov and Georgette Heyer.
>
> Book review, *The Independent*, 27 February 1991.

naff off A euphemism for 'fuck off'. The term was used in Keith Waterhouse's novel *Billy Liar* (1959) and in the BBC TV series *Porridge* (first shown 1974), starring Ronnie Barker, but owed its widespread popularity in the early 1980s to Princess Anne's reported use of it to a group of press photographers (*see* FOUR-LETTER ANNIE).

Naffy medal Colloquial name for both the 1939–45 Star and the Africa Star medals awarded during World War II. This is an ironic reference to the NAAFI.

Nagasaki A port in Japan, in W Kyushu, which was largely destroyed on 9 August 1945 by the dropping of the second atom bomb (*see* NUCLEAR WEAPON) in World War II. Damage was somewhat less severe than at HIROSHIMA, but nonetheless 75,000 people were killed or wounded, hastening the surrender of Japanese forces. The city was rapidly rebuilt after the war ended.

nail. another nail in my coffin A laconic catchphrase often uttered by smokers as they accept a cigarette offered to them. An apparent acknowledgment of the well-authenticated health risks associated with smoking, this phrase actually predates the link between smoking and cancer or heart disease. First heard in the 1920s, it originally referred to the hazard of a smoker's cough.

nailarium A US manicurist's salon, a much more common phenomenon in America than in the UK, where manicurists tend to be employed in beauty salons or hairdressers.

nail bomb A homemade explosive device packed with nails and other sharp metal objects. The nail bomb is a popular terrorist's weapon, being designed to inflict the maximum amount of injuries over the widest possible area.

naked ape A description of the human species, first popularized by the British zoologist Desmond Morris (1928–) in his study of human behaviour, *The Naked Ape* (1967). Morris justifies his choice of title in the book's introduction:

> There are one hundred and ninety-three living species of monkeys and apes. One hundred and ninety-two of them are covered with hair. The exception is a naked ape self-named *Homo sapiens*.

See also DAYTON ANTI-DARWINIST TRIAL.

'Nam *See* VIETNAM WAR.

Nana In the story of PETER PAN, the gentle and faithful old dog who always looked after the children in the Darling family. When Mr Darling played a trick on Nana by giving her unpleasant medicine, which he himself had promised to drink, the family did not appreciate his humour. This put him out of temper and Nana was chained up in the yard before he went out for the evening. As a consequence Peter Pan effected an entry into the children's bedroom.

Nansen passport A passport introduced in 1922 as a travel document for 'stateless' persons. It was named after the Norwegian explorer Fridtjof Nansen (1861–1930), who received the Nobel Peace Prize in 1922 for his humanitarian work on behalf of the LEAGUE OF NATIONS. It was Nansen who suggested such a passport as a measure towards the relief of international refugees.

napalm An explosive jelly used in incendiary bombs, which acquired a notorious reputation after its use by US forces in the VIETNAM WAR. Consisting of a mixture of *na*pathenic acid and *palm*itic acid, it was combined with petrol for use in bombs and in FLAME THROWERS. Napalm was used in World War II and the KOREAN WAR. Civilian casualties, suffering burns from napalm bombing in Vietnam, intensified demands for the withdrawal of US forces from the war.

Napier An early car, manufactured by a British company in 1902, which established a 24-hour motoring record at BROOKLANDS in 1907. The record remained unbroken until after World War I. The Napier Company went on to manufacture aeroengines, such as the Napier Lion, which gave valuable service in World War II.

napoo Military slang of World War I for something that is of no use or does not exist. It represents the French phrase *il n'y en a plus*, there is no more of it. It occurs in a popular song of 1917:

> Bonsoir old thing, cheerio, chin-chin,
> Nahpoo, toodle-oo, goodby-ee.
>
> WESTON and LEE: *Good-Bye-Ee.*

narc US slang for a narcotics agent, possibly by allusion to the 19th-century British slang 'nark', for an informer (from the Romany *nak*, a nose).

Narnia A magical kingdom created by C. S. Lewis in his children's novel *The Lion, the Witch and the Wardrobe* (1950) and further described in six sequels. When first seen, Narnia is ruled by the Evil White Witch, who has cast a spell so that it is "always winter but never Christmas"; it is rescued from this plight by four children from the real world and by the self-sacrifice of the Christlike lion **Aslan**. The Christian allegory, though never didactic, is obvious throughout: *The Magician's Nephew*, for example, has its own Garden of Eden and temptation scene involving an apple – although in this instance the temptation is refused; the series culminates with redemption at the end of the world in *The Last Battle*. The seven 'Chronicles of Narnia' have collectively become classics of children's literature that are also enjoyed by adults.

NASA National Aeronautics and Space Administration. The agency that, since its foundation in 1958, has coordinated America's space programme (excluding military projects). *See* APOLLO MOON PROGRAMME; SATELLITE; SKYLAB; SPACE PROBE; SPACE SHUTTLE.

Nasho Australian slang for national service (or someone fulfilling such service). National service ended in Australia in 1972. In the UK conscription was introduced during World War I (1916) and again in 1939; women were first recruited on a compulsory basis in 1941. The National Service Act (1947) allowed for the recruitment of a maximum of 150,000 men; it was abolished in 1962. In America conscription was introduced in both world wars and extended until 1973 (*see* VIETNAM WAR).

Nashville State capital of Tennessee, in America, also used in referring to COUNTRY-AND-WESTERN music. Country music began to evolve there during the 1920s with the success of a local hour-long radio programme, *WSM Barn Dance*, featuring banjo and fiddle music as well as Black and White gospel. In 1927 the programme was extended to three hours, renamed the *Grand Old Opry*, and broadcast live from a variety of venues. The first recording studios and music publishers were established in Nashville in the 1940s; with the growth of ROCK 'N' ROLL in the 1950s, other cities abandoned country music leaving Nashville the undisputed leader of the C & W recording and music-publishing industry.

Nassau conference A diplomatic meeting that took place in the Bahamas in 1962 between President John F. Kennedy and the British prime minister Harold Macmillan. Macmillan's decision during the conference to opt for the US POLARIS system rather than an Anglo-French alternative greatly angered the French leader Charles de Gaulle and intensified his distrust of the UK's attitude towards Europe.

Nasser, Lake *See* ASWAN HIGH DAM.

nasty. something nasty in the woodshed A secret horror or 'skeleton in the cupboard'. The phrase is sometimes applied to a child who is believed to be disturbed on account of having witnessed illicit sex within the family, *i.e.* 'has seen something nasty in the woodshed'. The phrase is derived from an incident in Stella Gibbons's parody *Cold Comfort Farm* (1932).

Natal, HMS A British cruiser that blew up without warning at anchor in Cromarty Firth on 30 December 1915, sparking off widespread speculation about a possible German sabotage campaign. The *Natal* sank in just three minutes with the loss of more than 350 lives; the immediate suspicion was that it had been attacked by a German U-BOAT. However, the discovery by divers that the Natal's hull had exploded from within ruled out this theory, although senior naval commanders refused to acknowledge that it was conceivable that security had been compromised. Others suggested that there might be a link with the loss of HMS *Bulwark* in suspicious circumstances in the Medway on 26 November 1914, shortly after the outbreak of World War I; it was also pointed out that German saboteurs had been proved to be active against allied shipping in New York, successfully planting an incendiary device in the munitions ship *Phoebus*, which blew up at sea in 1915. Nonetheless, the Navy still refused to act. Finally, on 14 July 1917, it was announced that HMS *Vanguard* had exploded at anchor in SCAPA FLOW. Among the debris recovered was a German bible and some letters written in German. Upon investigation it was learnt that two mysterious civilian fitters had visited HMS *Vanguard* only hours before it sank; one of them had also boarded HMS *Natal* shortly before it was lost. The naval establishment remained tight-lipped about the whole affair but rumours spread of a secret execution. The official verdict on the *Natal* sinking was that it had gone down due to "unavoidable causes of an uncertain nature".

Nation shall speak peace unto nation The motto of the BBC. It was conceived by a British schoolmaster, Montague John Rendall (1862–1950), in 1927 as the winning entry in a competition to provide a motto for the corporation.

national. National Curriculum A significant modification of the British educational system introduced by the Education Reform Act (1988). The Act established a curriculum of 10 subjects to be taken by the majority of children between the ages of 11 and 16 in England and Wales. Three of these – English, mathematics and science – form the *core* curriculum; the other seven – a modern language, history, geography, art, music, a technical subject, and physical education – are *foundation* subjects. The precise content of the subjects is determined by a series of working parties in consultation with the government. Attainment targets are specified in each subject at a series of levels.

National Front A militant racist organization founded in the UK in 1966. Professing neo-Nazi beliefs and provoking violent demonstrations in British cities, the party enjoyed a brief period of minor electoral success before splintering into numerous factions and disappearing from public view after humiliation in the general election of 1979. Adherents included many SKINHEADS.

National Governments The series of coalition governments in the UK from 1931 to 1940. The first National Government was formed on 24 August 1931 after the economic crisis had brought about the collapse of the previous Labour administration; it was headed by J. Ramsay MacDonald (1866–1937). Subsequent National Governments were formed under Stanley Baldwin (1867–1947) and Neville Chamberlain (1869–1940). Those Liberal and Labour MPs who supported these governments called themselves the NATIONAL LIBERAL PARTY and the NATIONAL LABOUR PARTY, respectively. The administrations became increasingly Conservative in character.

National Health Service (NHS) The 'Jewel in the Crown' of the social reforms introduced by Clement Attlee's post-war Labour government, which was established under the National Health Service Act (1946) and came into operation in July 1948. The envy of the world, it provided free primary and specialist medical care for all and was funded largely through general taxation. It was Aneurin (NYE) Bevan (1897–1960), the Minister of Health, who successfully unified the disorganized prewar network of local authority and voluntary hospitals into a single system and overcame the opposition of the medical establishment by allowing the continuation of private practice alongside the NHS. Bevan resigned in 1951 in protest at the government's proposals to introduce charges for false teeth and spectacles, which he regarded as a violation of the principle of an entirely free medical service. This principle has been gradually eroded since 1948. The basic problems of the NHS have been and continue to be financial. Contrary to Bevan's expectations, the cost of the service did not decline as the health of the nation improved. Instead, increasing demands were made on it by the patients whose lives it had prolonged and by the unexpected advances in medicine and surgery. The result is that the service has become a bottomless pit that consumes the vast amounts of money poured into it without emerging from its perennial dilemmas of growing waiting lists for treatment and a top-heavy infrastructure of administrators.

National Labour Party (NLP) Those Labour MPs who supported the coalition NATIONAL GOVERNMENT formed in 1931. The government was headed by Ramsay MacDonald; other prominent Labour members who joined the emergency cabinet included Philip Snowden, Sir John Sankey, and J. H. Thomas. The bulk of the Labour Party, however, remained in opposition to the new government; MacDonald and the other NLP members were branded as traitors to the Labour movement and expelled from the party. In September 1931 the NLP consisted of about 20 MPs; after the General Election of 27 October the numbers had dwindled to 13. MacDonald had hoped that the NLP would form the core of a new socialist party once the economic emergency had subsided. However, after 1931 his reputation, and that of the other National Labour members, suffered an irreversible decline and the party was wound up after the 1945 election.

National Liberal Party A group of 25 Liberal MPs, led by Sir John Simon (1873–1954), who broke away from the main party on the issue of free trade and joined the NATIONAL GOVERNMENT under Ramsay MacDonald, which had resolved on protectionist measures to help British industry weather the economic depression. The party was actually called the **Liberal National Group** until 1948, when it became the National Liberal Party. In 1966 the four remaining National Liberal Party MPs were incorporated into the Conservative Party.

national park An area of special scenic or scientific interest in England or Wales. Designated by the Countryside Commission, they include the Peak District, Snowdonia, and the Brecon Beacons. The Scottish equivalent is called a **national scenic area**. *See also* HERITAGE COAST.

National Plan A comprehensive statement of the Labour government's strategy for the British economy over the period 1965–70, devised by the newly formed Department of Economic Affairs under the direction of George Brown (1914–85). The plan specified a target of a 25% increase in national output by 1970 and indicated the changes in investment, expenditure, and consumption needed to achieve this target. Failure to meet the envisaged growth in exports over the period 1964–66 led to balance of payments difficulties, which prompted restrictions on domestic output after July 1966 and rendered most of the plan's other economic targets unattainable.

National Recovery Administration (NRA) One of the organizations set up during the so-called first 'Hundred Days' of President Roosevelt's NEW DEAL to tackle the social and economic crisis caused by the GREAT DEPRESSION. The role of the NRA was to promote industrial recovery through a series of nationwide regulatory codes to limit unfair competition, improve working conditions, establish a minimum wage, and guarantee the right to collective bargaining. Employers subscribing to the codes (which eventually amounted to 557 basic and 208 supplementary codes) were allowed to display a Blue Eagle emblem. Despite the plethora of codes and a certain confusion as to whether the NRA was intended to limit or promote corporate monopoly, it did achieve some notable successes, such as ending child labour in the cotton mills. By 1935, however, the New Deal came under increasing attack from Roosevelt's Republican opponents as 'creeping socialism', and the NRA was eventually declared unconstitutional by the Supreme Court on 27 May 1935 ('Black Monday'). Many of its provisions, however, were incorporated into later legislation.

National Security Agency (NSA) An organization that coordinates the communications systems of the US government. It was established under the Defense Department in 1952 to bring all the communications, cryptographical, and electronic-intelligence-gathering operations of the armed services, CIA, FBI, and other agencies under the control of a single body. The NSA is the most secret of all US intelligence agencies; its activities are excluded from public and press scrutiny to prevent penetration by foreign agents.

nationalization The purchase by the state of privately owned companies, for either political or economic reasons. In the 1950s and 1960s, UK Labour governments were strong advocates of nationalization both on the grounds that nationalization brought about a sensible rationalization of resources and that the profits earned by large industries, especially those with natural monopolies (such as the railways and the telephone service), should be shared by the population. In some cases companies were also nationalized to prevent them collapsing. These measures were opposed in the 1980s and 1990s by Conservative governments, which took the view that industries become inefficient in the absence of competition and of shareholders to ensure that profits are maintained at an acceptable level. PRIVATIZATION of many organizations, which had been nationalized under Labour, was undertaken by the Conservatives.

NATO North Atlantic Treaty Organization. An organization for collective military defence established by the North Atlantic Treaty of 4 April 1949 as a counterbalance to the power of the Soviet Union and its satellite states in E Europe. Its signatories included members of the Brussels Treaty organization (the UK, Belgium, Luxembourg, the Netherlands, and France) and Norway, Portugal, America, Canada, Denmark, and Iceland. Greece, Turkey, and West Germany joined in the early 1950s. Under the treaty members agreed to settle disputes by peaceful means and to adhere to the principle of collective security and resistance to armed aggression. The NATO military headquarters (Supreme Headquarters Allied Powers Europe – **SHAPE**) is at Chièvres, Belgium. France withdrew from NATO in July 1966 over fears that America could commit its European allies to conflict with the Soviet Union against their will. More recently tension has been growing between the European Community and America over 'burden sharing', with the Americans seeking a greater financial commitment by EC members to their own defence. The end of the COLD WAR has also destroyed the credibility of the Soviet threat and brings into question the necessity of NATO itself.

Nauecilus A German U-BOAT that was lost in a collision with a wreck on 15 November 1945. The sinking attracted unusual interest when, on 26 November 1946, a bottle containing a page apparently torn from the U-boat's log was found on the Danish coast. What really caused a sensation was that the log referred to a passenger named Adolf Hitler, suggesting that the FÜHRER had not after all died in his bunker but had perished at sea while attempting to escape war-ravaged Europe. The speculation was, however, brief and the message in the bottle was soon dismissed as a fake.

naughty but nice A phrase, easily memorized because of the alliteration, that conjures up visions of delicious cakes piled high with cream since it was used (1981–84) as a slogan in advertisements for fresh cream. It was, however, a well-established phrase before then, mostly used as an oblique reference to sex. It had also been used as the title of various films and songs.

Nautilus The first nuclear-powered submarine, which was launched in 1954. It was named after the submarine in the novel *Twenty Thousand Leagues under the Sea* (1873) by Jules Verne, although an earlier *Nautilus* had been built by the US engineer Robert Fulton in 1800, with finance from Napoleon. The submarine achieved the first submerged crossing of the Arctic in 1958. It was decommissioned in 1980 and put on permanent display in 1985.

Navicert Navigation Certificate. A method of ensuring that neutral merchant shipping was not supplying a belligerent nation with weapons, raw materials, etc., in defiance of a wartime blockade. The system, used in both world wars, involved the issue of a certificate to a merchant ship at its home port by the Naval Control of Shipping Officer, verifying that the cargo did not contain any such contraband material.

navy. The navy's here *See* ALTMARK, THE.

Nazi The shortened form of *National-Sozialist*, the name given to Adolf Hitler's party. *See* FASCISM; FÜHRER; HITLERISM; KRISTALLNACHT; MEIN KAMPF; NIGHT OF THE LONG KNIVES; NUREMBERG TRIALS; SWASTIKA.

NBC National Broadcasting Corporation. A US nationwide television network forming part of the sprawling RCA (Radio Corporation of America) empire. NBC was originally established in 1926 to create programming to encourage the sale of radio sets, which RCA manufactured. After experimenting with television broadcasts in the early 1930s, NBC decided in 1935 to invest $1 million in programming for television – to encourage sales of TV sets which RCA also manufactured; in the same year it began transmitting experimental programmes from a station in the EMPIRE STATE BUILDING. NBC's commercial debut was the broadcast of the opening ceremonies of the World's Fair in New York on 30 April 1939, during which Franklin D. Roosevelt became the first US president to appear on television.

NBG No Bloody Good. A dismissive tag frequently heard in its abbreviated form, especially among the armed services.

Neasden The NW London suburb known for its ordinariness and for being a target of the satirical magazine PRIVATE EYE:

> Why are we all beastly to Neasden?
> Just Because it lacks spires and dome?
> Or is it the curse of John Betjeman
> Who christened it Home of the Gnome.
>
> *The Times*, 11 May 1991.

In 1991 the Grange Museum, probably the only local museum to be virtually inaccessible on a roundabout around which London traffic roars, opened a section called Naff Neasden. *See* DISGUSTED, TUNBRIDGE WELLS; METROLAND; WIGAN.

nebbish US slang, from Yiddish, for an ineffectual person who is unable to stand up for himself and therefore merits one's sympathy. It is derived from the Yiddish *nebekh*, from Czech *nebohý*, unfortunate. It came into British English largely from American English, like many other Yiddish words. It is also used as an interjection conveying sympathy:

> He lost his job.
> Nebbish, with his handicap he'll never get another.

necessary. Is your journey really necessary? *See under* JOURNEY.

necessity knows no law The words used by the German chancellor Bethmann-Hollweg in the Reichstag on 4 August 1914, as a justification for the infringement of Belgian neutrality.

> Gentlemen, we are now in a state of necessity, and necessity knows no law. Our troops have occupied Luxembourg and perhaps have already entered Belgian territory.

necklace killing A particularly vicious style of unofficial execution in which a rubber tyre, often filled with petrol, is placed around the neck of the victim in the manner of a necklace and then set alight. This method of killing began in the Black townships of South Africa as a revenge against those thought to have betrayed the exponents of the Black cause.

Neddy The popular name for the National Economic Development Council set up by the UK government in 1962. The numerous Economic Development Committees for particular industries that subsequently appeared were called 'little Neddies'.

needle park Any public place in which drug addicts meet to purchase or inject drugs.

Nehru. Nehru dynasty The domination of Indian politics for more than 40 years by the family of the statesman Jawaharlal Nehru (1889–1964). A disciple of MAHÂTMA Gandhi, Nehru became president of the Indian National Congress in 1929 and was imprisoned nine times between 1921 and 1945 for his opposition to British rule. He became prime minister of independent

India in 1947 and remained in the post until his death, providing the political stability the new country desperately needed.

He groomed his daughter Indira Gandhi (1917–84) as his successor: although no relation to Mahatma Gandhi, the name gave added strength to her claim to power and undoubtedly helped her to become prime minister from 1966 to 1977 and again from 1980 to 1984. She too was determined to uphold the dynasty and prepared her son Sanjay Gandhi (1946–80) as her successor. When he died in an air crash she was forced to bring her other son, Rajiv Gandhi (1942–91), into the political limelight. When Indira Gandhi's suppression of Sikh unrest led to her assassination in 1984 by Sikh members of her bodyguard, she was immediately succeeded by Rajiv as prime minister.

Rajiv continued the Nehru dynasty's balancing act between rival religious and political factions until he lost office in 1989. In the third tragedy to strike the family, he was killed during the election campaign of 1991 by a terrorist bomb. By now Indian political life had revolved around the dynasty for so long that the leaders of the Congress (I) party immediately offered the post of party president to Rajiv's Italian-born widow, Sonia Gandhi (1949–), despite her lack of policial experience and despite the fact that she was not an Indian woman. She declined the offer, thus bringing the dynasty to an end.

> I do not know how to tell you and how to say it. Our beloved leader is no more.
>
> JAWAHARLAL NEHRU, announcing the death of Mahatma Gandhi.

Nehru jacket or **Nehru tunic** A long narrow tailored jacket, buttoned down the centre, with a high collar, as worn by the Indian prime minister Jawaharlal Nehru (1889–1964). It is commonly worn by Indian men, especially in Kashmir and the Punjab. The style became fashionable in London in 1967, the jackets usually being made of black crepe. A variation of the style, variously called the **Mao**, **oriental**, **meditation**, or **mandarin jacket**, was made from cotton, heavy linen, or velvet; this version was knee length and had side slits.

Neighbourhood Watch Since the early 1980s, any of the groups organized by residents, with police cooperation, in areas affected by increasing crime, especially burglary. Suspicious activities and circumstances are reported to the police. The idea was copied from similar schemes in America. *See also* GUARDIAN ANGELS.

Nell. And did he marry poor blind Nell? A catchphrase coined in the early years of the century, derived from a popular sentimental ballad of the period. The question begs the unspoken reply that 'he' certainly did not marry poor blind Nell; the phrase is generally used as a euphemism for 'like fucking hell'.

Nenni telegram The telegram of support sent by John Platts-Mills, Konni Zilliacus, and 20 other members of the Labour Party to the pro-communist socialist Signor Nenni at the time of the Italian general election of April 1948. The Labour Party officially supported the right-wing Italian socialists; as a result Platts-Mills was expelled from the party; Zilliacus was also subsequently expelled.

neo-. Neo-Destour *See* DESTOUR.

neorealism An Italian cinematic style of the 1940s, exemplified by Luchino Visconti's *Ossessione* (1942), Roberto Rossellini's *Open City* (1945), and Vittorio De Sica's *Bicycle Thieves* (1948). These films feature realistic contemporary settings with the characters – played by both actors and non-professionals – facing a range of social and economic problems; the films make use of unobtrusive camera and editing techniques. The style faded in the early 1950s but influenced the work of later Italian directors, such as Federico Fellini and Pier Paolo Pasolini, and Indian film makers, such as Sanjit Ray in his 'Apu' trilogy (1955–57). *See also* FILM NOIR.

NEP *See* NEW ECONOMIC POLICY.

nerd or **nurd** A term of general contempt loosely equivalent to fool or idiot. In 1970s US slang the word indicated a boring or conventional person.

> Some reviews you can classify as revenge of the nerds – hate mail.
>
> *The Independent*, 7 March 1991.

nervous. Not suitable for those of a nervous disposition *See under* DISPOSITION.

Net Book Agreement (NBA) An agreement that has been in force in the UK between publishers and booksellers throughout the 20th century. Its formulation was one of the first tasks of the Publishers Association, set up in 1896 by Sir Frederick Macmillan and other leading UK publishers. The NBA, dating from

1899, ensures that booksellers sell all 'net' books at their cover price without a discount. Certain ('non-net') books are allowed to be sold at a discount; these are mostly textbooks, specialist books, publishers' remainders, and books sold in a national book sale. The principle of the NBA is that if some large booksellers and other retail outlets (such as supermarkets and garages) are allowed to sell bestsellers at a discount, this will deprive small and specialist bookshops of the profitable sales that enable them to stock slow-moving books.

networking A concept that first appeared in the 1970s but achieved greater popularity in the 1980s. It involves groups of professional people trying to help each other in their careers by providing information, advice, and support. Forerunners of the system include the OLD-BOY NETWORK as well as various clubs and organizations, such as the Freemasons, which are available to men only. Modern networking has largely been undertaken by women, who did not enjoy the privileges of such social organizations.

Neue Kunstlervereinigung *See* BLAUE REITER.

Neuilly, Treaty of The post-war treaty between the Allies and Bulgaria signed on 27 November 1919. Bulgaria was forced to relinquish all territory occupied during the war, lost areas on her western border to Yugoslavia, and ceded Western Thrace to Greece (although she was guaranteed economic access to the Aegean). The Bulgarian army was limited to a volunteer force of 20,000 and the nation was also committed to pay massive reparations of 2,250,000,000 gold francs to the Allies over a period of 37 years. This claim was later reduced and eventually abandoned in 1932.

neutrino A type of fundamental particle with no electric charge and zero rest mass, thought to travel at the speed of light. The existence of neutrinos was first postulated in 1930 by the Austrian physicist Wolfgang Pauli (1879–1968). Definite evidence for their existence was first obtained in 1956. It is now known that there are three types of neutrino, depending on the radioactive decay process by which they are produced. Because of their low probability of interaction with matter, they are very difficult to detect. The US writer John Updike (1932–) was inspired to describe them in a poem *Cosmic Gall*:

Neutrinos they are very small
They have no charge and have no mass
And do not interact at all.
The earth is just a silly ball
To them through which they simply pass . . .

It is known that every second, millions of these particles are passing through the planet and through people. Physicists find this interesting Updike is less impressed:

At night they enter at Nepal
And pierce the lover and his lass
From underneath the bed – you call
It wonderful; I call it crass.

neutron One of the fundamental constituent particles of matter. A neutral particle with a mass 1840 times that of the electron, it is present in all atomic nuclei except for that of hydrogen. The neutron was discovered in 1932 by the British physicist James Chadwick (1891–1974); for this work he received the 1935 Nobel Prize for physics.

neutron bomb A type of tactical NUCLEAR WEAPON developed by America in the early 1970s. The neutron bomb is delivered by missiles or by artillery shells. The blast effects of the bomb are short-range, confined to a few hundred square yards, but the bomb is designed to throw off an intense flux of neutrons and gamma-ray radiation over a large area. The radiation can penetrate defences, in particular tank armour, and disable attacking troops who are killed instantly or die within days. The neutron bomb is regarded as a fairly 'clean' weapon in that there is very little general destruction or consequent radioactive contamination; it is, however, a very efficient means of killing people. It was developed as a strategic deterrent to discourage Soviet tank attacks in Europe. So far, it has never been used.

neutron star A type of star thought to have contracted under gravitational forces so that the matter within it is extremely dense. Typically, neutron stars have a diameter of about 20 km (12 miles) but a mass similar to that of the Sun. The matter within the star is largely in the form of neutrons. *See also* BLACK HOLE; PULSAR.

Neuve Chapelle A battle in World War I on the WESTERN FRONT on 10–13 March 1915, centred around the village of Neuve Chapelle, SW of Armentières, France. Field Marshall Sir John French decided to launch a British assault on Neuve Chapelle independently of the French; after a massive artillery bombardment of the area, British troops led by General Sir Douglas Haig pierced the German lines and captured the village on the first day. Before allied reserves could be brought up, however, the Germans, led by General Erich von Falkenhayn, managed to contain the breakthrough and recaptured the village a few days later. *See also* MADEMOISELLE FROM ARMENTEERS.

never. Never again! Slogan used after World War I, the war that was to end all wars. In the 1960s it was adopted by the Jewish Defence League as its slogan to commemorate the HOLOCAUST.

Never chase girls or buses (there will always be another one coming along soon) A catchphrase that dates from the 1920s. Perhaps sound advice in general; whether or not it is apposite in a particular circumstance may depend on what the girl looks like or how frequently the buses run.

Never knowingly undersold Advertising slogan for the John Lewis Partnership department stores that was coined by the founder John Spender in 1920. It means that, to the best of their knowledge, the goods in John Lewis shops cannot be purchased elsewhere at a lower price. As a catchphrase it is sometimes used as a basis for a set of variations:

> The industry secretary, Peter Lilley, was sparkier than usual, describing Labour's various policy proposals as 'never knowingly underlaunched'. Roy Hattersley (never knowingly underlunched) was not present to hear this, but Gordon Brown waited in his corner of the ring, jaw working, poised for the attack. Labour's industry shadow is never knowingly underpunched.
>
> Parliamentary Report, *The Times*, 26 March 1991.

never-never A colloquial name for the hire-purchase system. It is so called because, although the purchaser gets the article purchased immediately, payment for it continues for so long that it seems to be never-ending.

Never Never Land The land in which the Lost Boys and Red Indians lived and where Pirates sailed up the lake in J. M. Barrie's PETER PAN (1904). The phrase was also applied to the whole of the Australian outback, but since the publication of *We of the Never Never* (1908) by Mrs Aeneas Gunn, it has been restricted to the Northern Territory.

You've never had it so good *See under* GOOD.

new. New Age The philosophy, religion, and social attitudes of people seeking an alternative to the materialism common in the late 20th century. Such people tend to be interested in Eastern religions (such as Buddhism), meditation, ALTERNATIVE MEDICINE (especially homeopathy), HEALTH FOODS, ecological issues, and **New Age music**. This, unlike much of the modern music popular in the 1980s, was not POP MUSIC but mood music designed to promote meditation.

New Artists' Association *See* BLAUE REITER.

new brutalism *See* BRUTALISM.

new classical macroeconomics An economic theory of the 1970s that created the concept of rational expectations. According to this view, rational people will use the economic information available to them without systematic error to formulate their economic expectations. For example, if the government increases public expenditure to reduce unemployment, the expectations of taxpapers, that they will be called upon to pay for the increased expenditure by higher taxes, will persuade them to reduce their current expenditure in order to have the cash available to foot their higher tax bills. The theory that reflation of the economy will be anticipated by individuals, who will adjust their behaviour so that the economy remains unchanged in real terms, is contrary both to the macroeconomic theories of KEYNESIANISM and to MONETARISM.

New Deal President Roosevelt's policy of economic reconstruction announced in his first presidential campaign (1932):

> I pledge you, I pledge myself, to a new deal for the American people.

A relief and recovery programme known as the **First New Deal** was inaugurated in March 1933 and a **Second New Deal** concerned with social reform in January 1935. The **Third New Deal** of 1938 sought to preserve such gains made by its predecessors. *See* NATIONAL RECOVERY ADMINISTRATION.

New Deal Caesar *See* BOSS, THE.

New Economic Policy (NEP) A series of economic reforms introduced by Lenin to quell the widespread discontent with the BOLSHEVIK regime. The policy was announced at the Tenth Party Congress in March 1921 in the wake of urban riots, strikes, and the KRONDSTADT MUTINY; it amounted to a complete reversal of the previous economic strategy. Rigid centralized planning was replaced by a mixed economy; heavy industry and banking remained in state control but agriculture and the production of consumer goods were returned to the private sector, cash wages were reinstated for industrial workers, and the profit motive encouraged to promote economic expansion. The NEP was successful in reviving the economy and restoring popular support for the Bolshevik regime; the early years of the NEP (1921–28) were also associated with a flowering of Soviet art and culture. Stalin's seizure of absolute power in the period following Lenin's death in 1924, however, signalled the end of the NEP. In 1928 he announced the first of the FIVE-YEAR PLANS, which enforced a return to centralized planning, outlawed private enterprise, and began the collectivization of agriculture.

New Frontier A vague commitment to liberal reform in all areas of US society, made by John F. Kennedy (1917–63) during his 1960 presidential election campaign. The New Frontier programme, however, proved largely illusory and Kennedy's concrete domestic achievements were disappointing. This is largely explained by his concentration on foreign policy and the extremely narrow margin of his victory in 1960, which he believed deprived him of a popular mandate and Congressional backing for significant social and economic reforms.

New Look *See* DIOR.

New Man A man who does not conform to the traditional stereotype of a male as perceived by members of the Women's Movement. Responding to the changes in society recommended by the Women's Movement, the New Man has neither chauvinist nor sexist attitudes, is not MACHO, is concerned about the environment, and is prepared to play a full part in bringing up his children and running his house. The notion of the New Man is, however, largely a journalist's invention. In an age in which both parents are often required to work full-time in order to pay the mortgage on the family home, there is little alternative to both parents sharing the care of the children and the running of the household. Only if the wife remains at home all day and the husband works full-time is it reasonable for the husband to expect the wife to be responsible for those chores. In the rare cases in which the wife works and the husband stays at home the roles will obviously be reversed (*see* HOUSEHUSBAND).

> New Man must be careful – it's all very fine to be sensitive, but it would never do to be taken for gay.
> *The Independent*, 31 January 1991.

new morality A popular term of the 1960s implying that the hitherto publicly accepted canons of morality were no longer relevant to society, owing to the rapid spread of social and technological change, the advent of the PILL, and more enlightened attitudes generally. Some of the older and more reactionary members of society regarded these changes as unacceptable consequences of affluence, the diminishing of individual responsibility occasioned by the WELFARE STATE, the declining influence of Christian standards, and the championship of hedonism and self-indulgence by AVANT-GARDE writers. In the sphere of sexual behaviour it was dubbed by Lord Shawcross 'the old immorality'; others called it the 'sexual revolution'. 'Make love not war' became the cry of the decade: the **permissive society** had arrived. Divorce, remarriage, and one-parent families all increased. In 1961 85% of marriages were first marriages for both parties; by 1989 this had fallen to 64%. Between 1961 and 1989 the number of households consisting of a lone parent with dependent children had more than doubled. But by the 1980s a new factor – AIDS – had emerged and a more prudent 'new morality' began to evolve. Both men and women became much more cautious about having sexual relationships with people they did not know well. *See also* MORAL MAJORITY.

New Order in Europe The coordination of Europe under the domination of Germany as envisaged by Adolf Hitler. *See also* TRIPARTITE PACT.

New Orleans style The earliest style of ensemble JAZZ playing, originating in STORYVILLE, the redlight district of New Orleans at around the turn of the century. Classical New Orleans style featured collective improvisation by a front line of trumpet, clarinet, and trombone over a rhythm section of bass, drums, guitar, and piano. As the style was developed by such performers as Sidney Bechet (1897–1959) and Louis Armstrong (*see* SATCHMO), the solo instrumentalist gained greater prominence. It was superseded by SWING in the 1930s but has frequently been revived (*see* DIXIE; TRAD).

New Party A party established by Sir Oswald Mosley (1896–1980) in 1931 after his resignation from the Labour government when his *Memorandum*, containing radical proposals to tackle the economic crisis and reduce unemployment, was rejected by the party conference in October 1930. On 6 December the *Memorandum* was published and signed by 17 Labour MPs, six of whom then joined Mosley in forming the New Party in February 1931. The party failed to win any seats in the 1931 general election; all the sitting New Party MPs lost their deposits, except Mosley himself. In 1932 the New Party was renamed the British Union of Fascists. *See* MOSLEYITES.

newspeak Language in which the words change their meaning to accord with the official political views of the state. It was coined by George ORWELL in his 1984 (1949). *See* DOUBLETHINK.

new thing In JAZZ, slang for anything that appears to be challenging and original, especially the work of such innovative jazz musicians as John Coltrane during the 1960s.

new towns Specially designed towns, built in a single phase, that have been created since World War II to relieve overcrowding in large cities nearby (sometimes also known as **satellite towns**). In the UK The New Towns Act (1946) allowed for the development of 32 such towns, coordinated by development corporations and combining public and private investment. The largest project was MILTON KEYNES in Buckinghamshire, which was begun in 1967 and in many respects exemplified the ideals and problems shared by all the new towns. Among the disadvantages have been a lack of individuality in large-scale complexes and, perhaps as a consequence, difficulty in promoting a sense of community spirit. *See also* GARDEN CITY.

New Wave A new movement or fashion, particularly in the arts. It is a literal translation of the French, *Nouvelle Vague*, and is particularly used to describe a new movement in French film-making that began in the late 1950s. Highly original and individual in style, with minimal or cryptic dialogue, films of the New Wave include those of Francois Truffaut (1932–84), Claude Chabrol (1930–), and Jean-Luc Godard (1930–).

New Woman In the 19th century, a woman in favour of emancipation and female independence generally. In the late 20th century it was used to describe women who were able to make the most of the changes in the status of women brought about by the Women's Movement. New Woman was supposed to be able to enjoy not only enhanced career opportunities but also to indulge her femininity. In order fully to realize her potential, New Woman needed a NEW MAN. However, like New Man, New Woman turned out to be largely a journalist's invention.

news. news hole The part of a newspaper that is reserved for news stories. In America, this averages about 40%, with the remaining 60% being taken up with advertisements. By tradition, advertising space is sold first and determines the extent of the news hole. Rather than eating up news space, increased advertising sales produce more pages, which enables the paper to carry more news.

news junkies *See* REPORTAGE.

newsreels Short films (10–20 minutes long) covering news and other items of interest, which were a regular feature of cinema programmes until they were replaced by television news in the 1950s. News events had been recorded since the earliest days of film but the first actual newsreel (sequence of news items) appeared in France in 1908. The first sound newsreel was Fox Film Corporation's Movietone News, shown in 1927, which featured stories and interviews introduced by short titles and accompanied by a voice-over narrative. During World War II (and to a lesser extent in World War I), the newsreel was a valuable source of information as well as government propaganda.

newzak Repeated exposure by the media of scenes or reports of a disaster so that it loses its impact. The word was coined in 1986 with reference to the CHALLENGER DISASTER, in which seven US astronauts were killed. Frequent repetition of the film of the fatal explosion of the craft deprived the event of its horror. Formed by analogy with MUZAK, newzak becomes reduced to the status of background canned music in a restaurant or other public place. Newzak was not restricted to the Challenger disaster; it was applied with equal relevance to many other events, such as those occurring in the GULF WAR of 1991.

NIC *See* DRAGON.

nice. Have a nice day *See under* DAY.

It's turned out nice again The catchphrase of the Lancashire comedian George Formby (1904–61), with which he used to open his shows. It featured frequently in his films, especially as he rose to his feet and shook himself down after yet another mishap had befallen him.

nice guys finish last Catchphrase associated with the legendary US baseball manager Leo Durocher. The phrase was based on comments he made about the New York Giants team in 1948 and was widely hailed as the ultimate summary of Durocher's philosophy, and indeed that of any unscrupulous or determined sportsman, politician, etc.

nice little earner *See* EARNER.

Nice one, Cyril! A catchphrase of the 1970s. Originally a line from a 1972 TV commercial for Wonderloaf, it caught on as a phrase that could be used in almost any situation requiring a complimentary remark. It came into its own in 1973 with the popularity of the Tottenham Hotspur footballer Cyril Knowles, whose skilful moments on the field called forth from the terraces the chorus of the pop song with this title:

> Nice one, Cyril
> Nice one, son
> Nice one, Cyril
> Let's have another one.

This phrase was the obvious choice, in 1978, for the title of the autobiography of the comedian Cyril Fletcher. It had a new lease of life in 1989 when it was used by Access, the credit card company, which had already been promoted as 'the flexible friend' in commercials. The advertising hoardings featured the extremely large politician, Sir Cyril Smith, attempting to touch his toes, with the slogan: 'Nice one, Cyril . . . but Access is more flexible'.

Nice place you have here An observation referring ironically to any abode, however shabby. It was popularized around 1942 by the radio programme ITMA, apparently having been coined by Tommy Handley during a visit to Windsor Castle.

nickel. Don't take any wooden nickels Take care of yourself, don't let yourself be fooled. This well-wishing phrase was first heard in America in the 1920s and was also used in Canada.

nickelodeon The first cinema theatre called a Nickelodeon (because the admission price was only five cents) was that opened by John P. Harris and Harry Davis at McKeesport, near Pittsburgh, Pennsylvania, in 1905. The picture shown was *The Great Train Robbery*. It was the first real motion-picture theatre and thousands more nickelodeons soon sprang up throughout America. The name was later used for any form of cheap entertainment, particularly a JUKE BOX.

Niehan clinic A clinic in Switzerland run by Dr Niehan, which in the 1950s promised to halt, or at least delay, the inexorable ageing process. It was visited by many well-known personalities who parted with considerable sums of money, which may have made them feel better. They looked much the same.

Nielsen rating The most widely used rating system for television viewing in America. The Nielsen Survey is conducted by the A. C. Nielson Company, which samples 1200 US families to draw a profile of the nation's viewing habits. Sampling techniques have varied from asking viewers to keep a diary to attaching an electronic recording device to the television set. The Nielsen figures give ratings to individual shows, and these are used to set advertising rates. Programmes receiving poor Nielsen results are usually cancelled.

niet dobra! No good! A catchphrase widely heard during World War I after being adopted by members of the North Russian Expeditionary Force. It was taken directly from the Russian.

Nigel British slang for a certain type of arrogant upper-class male who often wears country tweeds and drives a sports car. Nigel was a popular name among the upper classes and in this context is always used pejoratively.

night. nightmare scenario *See* WORST-CASE.

Night of the Long Knives The night of 30 June 1934 when the leaders of the BROWNSHIRTS (SA) and some Catholic leaders were murdered by the GESTAPO, on Hitler's orders. The shootings (mainly in Munich and Berlin) actually began on the Friday night of the 29 June and continued until Sunday. The estimates of those killed vary between 60 and 400; Röhm and Schleicher were among them. Hitler had decided to rely on the Reichswehr rather than risk dependence on Röhm and the SA. Himmler presented the assassins with daggers of honour inscribed with his name.

George Borrow, referring to a treacherous murder of South British chieftains by Hengist in 472, says:

> This infernal carnage the Welsh have appropriately denominated the treachery of the long knives. It will be as well to observe that the Saxons derived their name from the saxes, or long knives, which

they wore at their sides, and at the use of which they were terribly proficient.

Wild Wales (1862).

See also MAC THE KNIFE.

-nik A suffix, copied from the Russian, that became popular in the late 1950s and 1960s following the launch of the Soviet satellite SPUTNIK in 1957. Neoligisms incorporating this suffix were often used in a derogatory sense and applied to anti-establishment individuals and movements, *e.g.* BEATNIK and **draftnik** (Vietnam draft dodger). *See also* REFUSENIK.

Nike A US army ground-to-air missile for use against high-flying attacking planes; named after the Greek winged goddess of victory.

nil carborundum or **illegitimi nil carborundum** A mock-Latin catchphrase meaning 'don't let the bastards grind you down'. 'Carborundum' is the tradename for an extremly hard form of silicon carbide used to make grinding wheels. The phrase nil carborundum, which was used by Henry Livings in 1962 for the title of a play, is an echo of the Latin tag from Horace's *Carmen*, *nil desperandum*, meaning never say die, despair of nothing. The catchphrase was widely used by the US General VINEGAR JOE Stilwell during World War II.

Nimby An acronym for *n*ot *i*n *m*y *b*ack*y*ard, coined in the UK in 1986 to describe people who were generally in favour of nuclear power but were strongly opposed to having either nuclear power stations or the resultant nuclear waste disposal units in the vicinity of their homes. The meaning has since been extended to cover other social issues. For example, a person of liberal views who petitioned against having an AIDS hospice in his street could be described as a Nimby.

Nimrod An airborne early warning system developed in the UK from the 1960s onwards as a possible key factor in NATO's future defences. The project became increasingly bogged down by technical difficulties and was eventually shelved in favour of a US system in the late 1980s. The name was derived from the biblical Nimrod, described as a "mighty hunter before the Lord" (*Gen.* x, 9). Pope says he was "a mighty hunter, and his prey was man" (*Windsor Forest*, 62); Milton similarly describes him in *Paradise Lost*, XII, 24, etc. The legend is that the tomb of Nimrod still exists in Damascus and that no dew ever falls upon it, even though all its surroundings are saturated.

nine. 1914 star *See* MONS.

1922 committee *See* CHANAK CRISIS.

1984 The nightmarish vision of a totalitarian future as depicted by George ORWELL in his last completed novel, *Nineteen Eighty-Four* (1949). In Orwell's future state human thought and action are rigidly controlled by a brutal regime that makes extensive and frightening use of propaganda and surveillance. The novel was intended as a warning against the authoritarian tendencies present in contemporary societies and 1984 was, until the actual year was reached, something of a 'doomsday' date. Orwell based some of the book on his experiences working in the Ministry of Information during World War II; he chose the year 1984 more or less at random by juggling the date 1948, the year in which he wrote the book. *See* BIG BROTHER IS WATCHING YOU.

19th Amendment The amendment made to the US constitution in 1920 under which women won the vote. *See* SUFFRAGETTES.

nineteenth hole The bar of the clubhouse of a golf course. The standard course has 18 holes, so the player who has played badly can lament his defeat at the nineteenth. The term was coined in America in the 1920s.

ninety days' wonder An altered version of nine days' wonder coined in World War I to describe officers emerging from military colleges after only 90 days' training. The obvious inference was that 90 days was not enough to turn them into soldiers. The original nine days' wonder originated in an old saying 'that there is no wonder so great that it lasts more than nine days'.

ninja Originally, a type of highly trained secret agent operating in feudal Japan. Their special role was to carry out tasks prohibited by the samurai code, such as spying, sabotage, and assassinations. *Ninjitsu*, the martial art of the ninja, taught the arts of deception and survival as well as more lethal skills. The term became generally known in the West as a result of the hype surrounding the TEENAGE MUTANT NINJA TURTLES, although ninja had previously featured in some comics and computer games. It is sometimes mistakenly applied to the tools of the ninja's trade – a variety of implements combining simplicity, discretion, and deadliness. Palestinians in the occupied territories now use the term to describe a kind of makeshift sabotage device for puncturing the tyres of Israeli military vehicles. This usually consists of a nail hidden in some harmless-looking object, such as an old boot or rotten vegetable.

nipple count The number of exposed female breasts appearing in a film or tabloid newspaper, used as an index of its downmarket appeal.

nippy Colloquial name for the waitresses at the popular teashops run by J. Lyons and Company from the 1920s. The waitresses were known for their cheerful and efficient service as they 'nipped' from table to table.

Nissen hut A semicylindrical corrugated-iron hut with a cement floor, originally used for military purposes in World War I. It takes its name from Lieutenant Colonel Peter Nissen (1871–1930), its inventor.

nitty-gritty A colloquial expression used to describe the basic facts of a situation, as in 'let's get down to the nitty-gritty'. It is probably derived from a combination of the words *nits* and *grits*, nits being the eggs of lice deposited in the hair and grits being slang for particles of excrement attaching to hairs near the anus.

Nivelle offensive A major French attack on the German defensive line on the River Aisne made in April 1917 during World War I. Led by the French General Nivelle, it resulted in enormous French losses and triggered a major mutiny in the French army. Nivelle was replaced by Pétain.

nixon US slang for an underhand or illegal deal, especially one to do with drugs. It is taken from the name of the former US president Richard Nixon (1913–), who was not famous for his honest dealings and who was forced, under threat of impeachment, to resign in 1974. *See* TRICKY DICKY; WATERGATE.

Nixon doctrine An informal statement to journalists made by President Richard Nixon in Guam in July 1969, that in future America would expect her overseas allies to provide for their own military defence, so that conflicts, such as the VIETNAM WAR, could be avoided. The statement was intended as a clarification of his policy of Vietnamization – the gradual removal of US troops from Vietnam and the transfer of responsibility for the war to the South Vietnamese. However, it was subsequently elevated into a general doctrine of US foreign policy by the Nixon White House.

NKVD (*Narodnyi Komissariat Vnutrennykh Dyel*; People's Commissariat for Internal Affairs) The Soviet agency responsible for state security from 1934 to 1943. Succeeding OGPU (*see* GPU), it was notorious for carrying out Stalin's PURGES. In 1943 its state security function was taken over by another agency, the **NKGB**, but it continued to manage internal affairs, becoming a ministry – the MVD – in 1946.

no. **no-claim bonus** A discount set against the annual premium of a motor insurance policy in which no claims for compensation have been made on the insurer for a specified period. Its purpose is to discourage motorists from making frequent claims for minor damage and to penalize those that do make claims. Insurers maintain that a no-claim bonus is not a no-blame bonus, *i.e.* a motorist who makes a claim forfeits his bonus, whether or not he is to blame for the accident that caused the claim. *See also* KNOCK FOR KNOCK.

no comment Stock phrase widely used as a method of evading the searching questions of journalists. It is equally freely used of political situations and personal relationships. It seems to have emerged in the 1940s as journalists became increasingly invasive. Churchill discovered it after a meeting, in 1946, with President Truman. More recently Marlin Fitzwater, a White House spokesman at the time of the GULF WAR of 1991, summed up the versatility of the phrase:

> No comment and you can feel free to use that no comment wherever you need it today.
>
> *The Guardian*, 21 February 1991.

no-fault A US term originally used to describe a form of car insurance in which the victim of an accident is compensated for damages by his own insurance company, whether or not the accident was his own fault (*see also* KNOCK FOR KNOCK). The term was later applied to a form of divorce in which neither party has to prove the other guilty of the marital breakdown.

no-go US slang for an unfavourable situation. In the UK it is used in several senses: a **no-go area** is barred to unauthorized individuals for security reasons; or it may be an area barricaded off from the police or military authorities by a paramilitary group or hostile crowd.

Certain deprived and crime-ridden areas of the inner cities are also described as no-go areas, implying that even the police are wary of entering the area except in substantial numbers.

no man's land The area between hostile lines of trenches in a ground war or any space contested by two opponents and belonging to neither.

no-win situation A set of circumstances in which a person is faced with alternative courses of action that all lead to unsatisfactory results. The term arose in the 1960s and originally came from the mathematical study of strategy known as GAME THEORY. *See also* CATCH-22.

Nobel Prizes International awards established under the will of Alfred Nobel (1833–96), the Swedish chemist who invented dynamite. First awarded in 1901, the prizes are presented annually in Stockholm for the most important achievements in Chemistry and Physics (both awarded by the Swedish Academy of Sciences), Physiology or Medicine (awarded by the Karolinska Institute), and Literature (awarded by the Swedish Academy). The Peace Prize is awarded by the Norwegian Parliament (Norway and Sweden were once united). A sixth prize, for economics, was established in 1968, based on a donation by the National Bank of Sweden, and is awarded by the Swedish Academy of Sciences. All the prizewinners receive an average of $185,000, a gold medal, and a diploma. Nobel Prizes are the most prestigious in the world; Nobel laureates are invariably men and women of exceptional achievement.

NOCD *See* NTD.

Noddy The somewhat simple 'nodding-man' in Enid Blyton's children's books. Created in 1949, this character's lack of brains is underlined by his name – a 'noddy' is a foolish person, an idiot.

noddy bike British slang name for the Velocette motorcycle that was used by police patrolmen until the end of the 1960s. It was considered a laughably inferior machine by the motorcycle police officers and bikers alike. High-ranking policemen, as well as members of the public, referred to the regular policeman on the beat as NODDY – a foolish person.

noddy suit A military garment worn by soldiers and other personnel to protect them against war gases and other chemical warfare. It is cumbersome to wear and inhibits freedom of movement. Such suits were in use in the GULF WAR of 1991. The connection with NODDY is that a person dressed in this garment looks somewhat foolish and even childlike.

noise pollution or **sound pollution** Contamination of the environment by noise, *i.e.* sound that is undesired by the recipient. Noise is an inevitable accompaniment to modern technological society and is now well recognized as a form of pollution, together with air and water pollution. It is not, however, entirely a modern phenomenon: Julius Caesar once tried to ban daytime chariot racing in ancient Rome because of the noise generated by flying hooves and rattling wheels. Excessive noise, especially with prolonged exposure, can cause hearing impairment and even deafness. In milder forms such symptoms as increased irritability, fatigue, and headache may arise. Levels of noise are measured in decibels, with 1 decibel (dB) corresponding to sounds just audible to the human ear. The scale is logarithmic, so an increase (or decrease) of 10 dB approximates to a doubling (or halving) in loudness. A refrigerator humming (at a distance of 2 metres) measures about 40 dB, while a pneumatic drill at 5 metres registers 100 dB. The UK's Noise Abatement Society, founded in 1959, is dedicated to reducing noise from all sources to tolerable and reasonable levels. Counterparts in America include the National Organization to Insure a Sound-Controlled Environment (NOISEP), a coalition of organizations and individuals founded in 1969 to combat jet aircraft noise.

Nomanhan incident The most serious of a total of 2800 separate clashes between Japanese and Soviet forces along the border between Siberia and Manchuria during the years 1932–39. The Japanese had invaded Manchuria and established the puppet state of MANCHUKUO in 1932, from which they threatened to invade Siberia. In May 1939 skirmishes between Mongolian and Manchukoan troops near the village of Nomanhan on the fringes of Outer Mongolia led to a full-scale invasion in July by the Japanese Kwantung Army in an attempt to inflict a crushing defeat on Mongolian and Soviet forces. Instead, the Japanese were led into a trap by the Soviet forces under Marshall Zhukov and suffered 17,000 casualties. An armistice was signed on 17 July 1940, which marked the end of Japan's ambitions to acquire Siberian territory.

non-. nonaerosol Containers that do not use a propellent, especially a CFC, under pressure to produce a fine spray of a liquid. These products are also described as 'ozone friendly', as the release of CFCs into the atmosphere from conventional aerosols is thought to be a major contributor to the depletion of the Earth's protective OZONE LAYER. Nonaerosol containers achieve their objective of producing a fine spray by means of a finger pump and a fine nozzle; this is often referred to as 'pump action'.

Non-Intervention Committee An international committee formed in 1936 to prevent other countries becoming involved in the SPANISH CIVIL WAR. As Germany and Italy, in particular, stepped up their participation in the conflict, the proceedings of the committee became increasingly irrelevant.

non-refoulement *See* DP.

nonstick A cooking utensil with a specially coated surface that prevents hot food from sticking to it. Nonstick saucepans are therefore easily cleaned. The most widely used nonstick coating is Teflon (*see* PTFE), a plastic discovered by a US engineer, Roy J. Plunkett, in 1938, although the process of using it to coat metal saucepans was not developed until 1954 (by Marc Gregoire).

non-U *See* U AND NON-U.

nookie Slang for sexual intercourse. It is probably derived from a 'nook', which the vagina may be thought to resemble. It has been common in America since the 1920s but was not used to any significant extent in the UK until the 1960s. Unlike the older four-letter words, nookie is not regarded as being taboo or offensive.

> Hendriks said he'd picked up with a skirt that was a warm baby and he was getting his nookie every night.
>
> J. DOS PASSOS: *42nd Parallel.*

NORAID See IRA.

norks Australian slang for breasts, which became known in the UK through the cartoon strip *The Wonderful World of Barry McKenzie* by Barry Humphries. This strip appeared in the satirical magazine PRIVATE EYE in the 1970s. The word was apparently coined from Norco, the name of a cooperative dairy company, which, in the 1950s, used a picture of a cow with a huge udder on the wrapping of its butter.

Norris, Arthur The central character in Christopher Isherwood's novel *Mr Norris Changes Trains* (1935). He was based on the flamboyant Irish-born Gerald Hamilton (1888–1970), a homosexual whose many notorious escapades included being gaoled in the UK for gross indecency and attempting to negotiate peace between Germany and the Allies in 1941 (he was arrested after being unmasked on his way to Ireland, disguised as a nun).

north. North Pole This was first reached on 6 April 1909 by the US explorer Robert Edwin Peary (1856–1920).

North Sea oil Oil reserves discovered below the North Sea in the late 1960s. The area is now divided into British, German, Norwegian, Danish, and Dutch sectors. The first government licences for the exploration of the British sector were issued to oil companies in 1964; the initial discoveries were of natural gas. The first oil field, Montrose, was discovered by Amoco in September 1969. The Shell-Esso partnership discovered the Brent field NE of Shetland in July 1971 and in the following year other major discoveries included Piper (Occidental) E of Orkney and Beryl (Mobil) and Thistle (Signal group) in the East Shetland Basin. Between 1964 and 1973, 266 wells were drilled in the British sector. By 1984 UK output had reached 125 million tons, enabling oil revenues to help the UK's balance of payments.

Northcliffe Press Newspapers owned or controlled by Alfred Harmsworth, Lord Northcliffe (1865–1922), the pioneer of popular journalism in the UK. Northcliffe was a flamboyant and controversial figure, who liked to be known as 'the Napoleon of Fleet Street'. The first issue of his *Daily Mail* appeared on 4 May 1896 and by World War I 'The penny newspaper for one halfpenny' had achieved a readership of one million. The *Daily Mirror*, which he founded in 1903, was aimed at female readers and reached the million mark in 1912, the first paper in the world to do so. In 1904 it was turned into a picture paper and pioneered the use of illustrations in Fleet Street. In these national papers, as in his earlier local papers, such as the *London Evening News* (1894) and *Glasgow Daily Record* (1895), Northcliffe tailored the content to satisfy a new lower-class newspaper readership with a taste for sensationalism. In 1905 he moved upmarket and acquired *The Observer*, which he then sold in 1911 to concentrate on *The Times*, which he had controlled since 1908. Fears, however, that he would cheapen *The Times* proved unfounded; he actually modernized the production process and turned the paper into a profitable concern. *See also* PRESS BARONS.

nose. nose job Slang for plastic surgery to alter the shape of the nose solely for cosmetic reasons.

The Nose Nickname of the US singer and film actress Barbra Streisand (1942–). The epithet has also been applied to the popular US singer Barry Manilow (1946–). *See also* SCHNOZZLE.

nosh Slang, from Yiddish (from Ger. *nachen*, to eat on the sly), for to eat, especially to eat surreptitiously between meals. Like many Yiddish words it came into British English in the 1950s from America. As a noun it may also be used for a meal – a good one might be described as a fine **nosh-up**.

Nostradamus The 16th-century French prophet whose predictions became a tool of Nazi propaganda during World War II. It was the wife of Josef Goebbels, Minister of Propaganda, who first realized that several of the Frenchman's prophecies could be adapted to current needs. She, and subsequently several other Nazi leaders, were impressed by Nostradamus' references to a German leader called 'Hister', although it was felt necessary to doctor his verses somewhat to ensure that his predictions left no doubt about an ultimate German triumph. In 1940 leaflets containing his prophecies were released over France and Belgium, predicting German victory; the Allies immediately countered with their own versions of the prophecies, which not unnaturally came to the opposite conclusion. The original verses referring to Hitler contained these lines:

> In the mountains of Austria near the Rhine
> There will be born of simple parents
> A man who will claim to defend Poland and Hungary
> And whose fate will never be certain.

Other predictions for the 20th century allegedly described air warfare, V-bomb attacks, the rise of Franco, and the ABDICATION CRISIS of 1936:

> For not wanting to consent to the divorce,
> Which afterwards will be recognized as unworthy,
> The king of the islands will be forced to flee
> And one put in his place who has no sign of kingship.

The ATOM BOMB was also apparently foreseen in his verses, which can be read to refer to the destruction of HIROSHIMA and NAGASAKI:

> Near the harbour and in two cities will be two
> Scourges the like of which have never been seen.

Most disturbing of all, Nostradamus also predicted a third world war in the 20th century, involving an alliance of Western powers against the East, following which the world will decline into a lengthy era of conflict and famine:

> In the year 1999 and seven months
> From the sky will come the great king of terror . . .
> Before and afterwards war reigns happily.

Notting Hill carnival An annual carnival, the largest in Europe, that takes place in the streets around Notting Hill Gate in London during the last weekend in August. The carnival began in the mid-1960s with local DJs playing a variety of Black music, including reggae, calypso, and jazz, from the backs of trucks, followed through the streets by an appreciative audience. Although it has been marred by periodic violence and muggings, the carnival survives as the major expression and celebration of Black music and culture in the UK.

nouveau roman (Fr. new novel) An experimental form of the novel that emerged in France in the 1950s (also called **anti-roman**). The new form was introduced in a series of literary essays by Alain Robbe-Grillet (1922–89), which were collected and published as *Pour un nouveau roman* in 1963. In his novels, and in those of a wide range of other modern French writers, including Nathalie Sarraute (1902–), Michel Butor (1926–), and Marguerite Duras (1914–), conventional characters, plot, dialogue, and narrative are rejected as alien to the reality of experience and replaced by descriptions of sensory impressions, mental perceptions, and an accumulated minutiae of impulses and gestures, the meaning of which the reader is left to decipher.

nouvelle. nouvelle cuisine (Fr. new cooking) A style of French cookery developed in the 1970s by several French chefs and gourmet food critics. Its protagonists tried to avoid the dangers of traditional cooking with its allegedly unhealthy ingredients, such as butter, sugar, starch, and cream. This health-protecting aspect of the cookery is called **cuisine minceur** (Fr. slimness cooking).

Nouvelle cuisine emphasizes fresh ingredients, light sauces, and quick cooking to retain the texture and colour of the food. The food is light, often with unusual combinations of ingredients. One of its features is that it is always arranged attractively on the plate. Portions are usually small, and it has been criticized as a highly expensive way of not getting enough to eat.

Nouvelle Vague *See* NEW WAVE.

now. now and for ever A phrase that has been used as a title for three different films (1934, 1956, 1983), perhaps to convey portentious echoes from the *Gloria* in the *Book of Common Prayer*: "As it was in the beginning is now and ever shall be . . .".

It was used in the late 1980s as an advertising slogan for *Cats*, the longest-running musical in London's West End.

Now Generation The young people of the 1960s who were preoccupied with contemporary fashion, music, events, issues, etc.

NTD Not Top Drawer. British slang meaning not well born. It is used, sometimes seriously, as a pejorative code word among snobbish people. Another example of this kind of thing is **NOCD**, not our class, dear.

nuclear. nuclear autumn *See* NUCLEAR WINTER.

nuclear energy *See* NUCLEAR REACTOR.

nuclear family A mother, father, and children, regarded as the standard social unit in modern industrial societies. The nuclear family is often contrasted with the **extended family**, which contains such extra members as grandparents, unmarried uncles and aunts, etc. The extended family is more common in traditional precapitalist cultures. Sociologists have suggested that the relationship between the nuclear family and capitalism is not accidental: the capitalist mode of production requires a degree of mobility in families that was not required of traditional families. Another social pressure that characterizes the nuclear family is the need for both parents to work in order to be able to afford the family home. Perhaps as a consequence, the stability of even the nuclear family is declining, as divorce, remarriage, and one-parent families become increasingly common.

nuclear fission A process in which the nucleus of a heavy chemical element, such as uranium or plutonium, is split into two fragments of roughly equal size. Usually it is induced by the impact of a NEUTRON and is accompanied by the evolution of large amounts of energy. Controlled nuclear fission is exploited in the NUCLEAR REACTOR; uncontrolled fission reactions are used in atom bombs (*see* NUCLEAR WEAPON). In spite of the fact that nuclear fission was one of the most important discoveries of the 20th century, opinions differ as to when it was first discovered, and by whom. It is generally accepted that the discovery was made in 1939 by the Austrian physicist Otto Frisch (1904–79) and his aunt Lise Meitner (1878–1968). Frisch did further work on fission at Birmingham University and wrote a report to Sir Henry Tizard (1885–1959), a scientific advisor to the British government, pointing out that an explosive chain reaction could be produced with a few pounds of uranium–235. He later worked on the resulting MANHATTAN PROJECT.

> MASTER They split the atom by firing particles at it at 5500 miles per second.
> BOY Good heavens! And they only split it?
>
> Exchange in the film *The Ghost of St Michael's* starring WILL HAY (1941).

nuclear fusion A process in which two light atomic nuclei are brought together to form heavier nuclei; for example, the fusion of two hydrogen nuclei to form a nucleus of helium. Over all, the reaction results in the evolution of a large amount of energy; however, very large energy inputs are necessary to initiate fusion reactions. Nuclear fusion is the process responsible for the energy produced by the sun and the stars. It is also the basis of the hydrogen bomb, first tested in 1952 (*see* NUCLEAR WEAPON). Considerable effort has been put into the development of a controlled fusion reactor for producing cheap energy (*see* NUCLEAR REACTOR). *See also* COLD FUSION.

nuclear reactor A device for producing energy from reactions involving the nuclei of atoms. Practical nuclear reactors depend on NUCLEAR FISSION as the source of energy. The fuel in a fission reactor is the element uranium, and early reactors used enriched uranium; *i.e.* uranium containing a high proportion of the isotope uranium–235. When bombarded with NEUTRONS of a suitable energy, these uranium nuclei can split into nuclei of lighter atoms with associated evolution of energy and the production of more neutrons. These additional neutrons cause fission of other uranium nuclei, releasing more neutrons, and so on – a self-sustaining chain reaction occurs and heat is produced. The heat can be extracted using a circulating liquid or gas (the coolant) and used to produce steam to drive a turbine, which generates electricity in the same way as a conventional power station produces energy. In atom bombs (*see* NUCLEAR WEAPON) the chain reaction is uncontrolled – the explosion depends on producing a large amount of energy in the shortest possible time. In a nuclear reactor the chain reaction is controlled by use of a moderator. This is a substance that can slow down neutrons. The slower neutrons have a higher probability of causing nuclear fission because they are not absorbed by the uranium–238 atoms, which is the most abundant isotope of uranium in natural uranium. The energies of these slower neutrons are comparable to those that would be produced at normal temperatures; the neutrons are called 'thermal neutrons' and reactors of this type are called **thermal reactors**. The first such nuclear reactor involving a controlled chain reaction was demonstrated in 1942 by a team of scientists led by the Italian physicist Enrico Fermi (1901–54) at the University of Chicago. Here, in the sports stadium, Fermi built what was then known as an **atomic pile** – a structure of about 40,000 blocks of pure graphite drilled with holes containing enriched uranium–235. At 2.20 p.m. on 2 December 1942 the pile 'went critical' producing a self-sustaining chain reaction lasting for 28 minutes. The British physicist, Sir Arthur Compton, reported by telephone to the management committee with the news that "the Italian navigator has just landed in the New World". He went on to say that the natives were friendly.

The first commercial power station using this principle was built at Calder Hall in Cumbria and opened in 1956 (*see* SELLAFIELD). Since then a number of different types of nuclear reactor have been developed. Thermal reactors are named according to the type of coolant used; e.g. **gas-cooled reactors**, **boiling-water reactors**, **pressurized-water reactors**, and **heavy-water reactors**. The **Magnox reactor** is a particular type of gas-cooled reactor in which the fuel rods are encased in Magnox (a tradename for a type of magnesium alloy). A different type of nuclear fission reactor is the **fast reactor**, in which no moderator is used. In these, the uranium fuel is enriched with plutonium–239. The core of the reactor is surrounded by a blanket of natural uranium which captures neutrons and is converted into plutonium, which can be further used as a fuel. Such reactors are known as **breeder reactors.**

Energy from fission reactors (**nuclear energy**) makes up 5.6% of the world's energy production. In 1988 it provided 30% of Europe's electricity (70% in France, 19.5% in the UK). It is, however, a contentious issue. Some regard nuclear reactors as a cheap and clean method of generating energy preferable to the use of coal and other fossil fuels (*see* GREENHOUSE EFFECT). Others point to the hidden costs involved in disposing of NUCLEAR WASTE and decommissioning reactors, as well as the environmental and health risks, particularly if there is an accident. They cite the problems caused at THREE MILE ISLAND and at CHERNOBYL.

In principle, NUCLEAR FUSION is a more promising method of producing nuclear energy. Fission reactors depend on uranium and there are only limited amounts available (uranium, in the jargon of energy science, is a 'non-renewable' resource). Fusion reactors would use hydrogen as their fuel, which could be obtained from water, and would lead to the availability of large amounts of cheap and 'clean' energy.

Many millions of pounds (as well as dollars and roubles) have been spent on research into fusion reactors – so far with little success. An early attempt was an apparatus built at Harwell in the 1950s called **ZETA** (Zero Energy Thermonuclear Apparatus). Modern research is based on a similar system called the **tokamak**, which was developed in the Soviet Union in the 1960s. *See also* COLD FUSION.

nuclear waste Radioactive material produced as an undesired by-product of NUCLEAR REACTORS and other radioactive processes. The safe disposal of nuclear waste has been a matter of considerable concern to environmentalists. Methods used have included sealing the waste in containers and dropping them in the sea, and underground burial. In the 1970s and 1980s, the UK developed an industry for reprocessing and disposing nuclear waste from other countries – leading to charges that the country had become the world's 'nuclear dustbin'.

nuclear weapon A type of weapon in which an explosion is produced by a nuclear reaction rather than by a chemical reaction (as in so-called 'conventional' explosives). Nuclear weapons are of two types:

Fission weapons depend on NUCLEAR FISSION for their effect; *i.e.* the explosive power comes from the splitting of heavy atomic nuclei, such as those of uranium and plutonium. The basic technique is to bring together sufficient quantities of fissile material (the critical mass) to allow a self-sustaining uncontrolled chain reaction to occur. The original fission bomb was tested in 1945 as a result of the MANHATTAN PROJECT. At 5.30 a.m. on 16 July the director of the project, J. Robert Oppenheimer (1904–67), saw the first MUSHROOM CLOUD and, as he later reported, thought of a quotation from the *Bhagavad Gita*:

> I am become Death, the shatterer of worlds.

At the time a number of senior scientists on the Manhattan Project were horrified at the monster that they had created and suggested that the bomb, known as the **atom bomb** or **A-bomb**, should be publicly tested to demonstrate the power of the weapon to the Japanese. Oppenheimer and senior US politicians opposed this and the atom bomb was first used at HIROSHIMA on 6 August 1945. Three days later another atom bomb was dropped on NAGASAKI, after which the Japanese capitulated. These are the only two occasions on which nuclear weapons have been used in warfare. Subsequently, several other countries developed and tested fission weapons: the Soviet Union first tested a nuclear bomb in 1949, the UK in 1952, France 1960, China 1964, and India 1974. These countries are known to have atomic weapons but it is thought that some other states may have nuclear weapons that they have not tested. These include Israel, Pakistan, South Africa, and possibly Brazil. Iraq was thought to be on the verge of developing a fission bomb before the GULF WAR (1991).

The second type of nuclear weapon is the fusion weapon, in which the energy of the explosion results from NUCLEAR FUSION; *i.e.* the joining together of small atomic nuclei, such as those of hydrogen, to form larger nuclei. The first **fusion bomb** (also known as a **hydrogen bomb**, **H-bomb**, or **thermonuclear weapon**) was tested by the Americans at ENIWETOK Atoll in the Pacific on 1 November 1952. Subsequent tests were conducted at BIKINI Atoll nearby. Other countries followed: the UK tested a fusion bomb in 1957, China in 1967, and France in 1968. Fusion bombs have never been used in warfare.

The power of nuclear weapons is measured by the equivalent explosive power of TNT. Typically, fission bombs have an explosive power measured in thousands of tons of TNT (kilotons); fusion bombs have a power measured in millions of tons (megatons). The effect of nuclear weapons is not confined to their blast, but also includes the effect of radioactive fallout. The principle of the bomb was a consequence of Einstein's equation $E = MC^2$, and Einstein himself once said:

> If I had known, I would have become a watchmaker.

See also CND; DOOMSDAY MACHINE; NEUTRON BOMB.

nuclear winter A period of darkness and cold weather postulated as the consequence of a thermonuclear war. The term was coined in 1983 by a group of US scientists that had been studying the possible after-effects of large-scale nuclear war. They suggested that nuclear weapons would, in a global war, cause uncontrolled firestorms. The smoke, particularly from plastics and other petroleum products in burning cities, would eventually cover a significant proportion of the Northern hemisphere, blotting out the sunlight for several weeks. According to the model, the low temperatures and lack of sunlight would result in widespread loss of plant and animal life. When associated with the destruction caused by the blast, and the consequent radioactive fallout, this would result in widespread loss of human life. The theory is contentious; some scientists have suggested that the results would be less extreme – more of a **nuclear autumn**.

nudge nudge, wink wink, say no more A catchphrase derived from the TV comedy show MONTY PYTHON'S FLYING CIRCUS, which was broadcast from 1969 to 1974. Laden with sexual innuendo, these words provided the answer to his own question when the prurient character played by Eric Idle asked people such things as "Is your wife a goer, then, eh, eh?", accompanied by much elbow nudging and prodding.

nudzh or **nudnik** US slang for a chronic complainer or pest. It was first popularly used in the late 1960s, coming from the Yiddish *nudyen*, to bore, from the Russian *nudnik*, a boring pest.

nuke Slang, meaning to attack with nuclear weapons: a shortening of 'nuclear'. Originally an Americanism of the 1970s, its use has now spread throughout the English-speaking world. It is also used in a more general sense, meaning to defeat or to annihilate; it is often applied in sporting contexts for an overwhelming defeat. In the noun sense it is an abbreviation for a nuclear weapon, as in the disarmament slogan 'no nukes!'.

Nullarbor nymph An unknown blonde woman who was widely reported in the Australian press in 1972 for her public appearances in a semi-dressed state. Speculation about her identity, after she was reportedly sighted, half-naked, feeding kangaroos in the bush near the town of Euda, was rife; she was tentatively identified as the missing 27-year-old daughter of a railway worker from Adelaide.

> If I've put my foot in it, I should probably be given a compulsory exit visa to the Antipodes and there find my name linked romantically in the best tradition with the naughty Nullarbor nymph.
>
> PRINCE CHARLES; speech at Australia Day dinner, 1973.

number. number 13 US teenage slang for marijuana. M (for marijuana) is the thirteenth letter of the alphabet. This name, which was common in the 1960s and 1970s, added an air of mystery and excitement to an illegal substance. *See also* POT.

number cruncher Originally, a person skilled at manipulating numbers or dealing with figures, *e.g.* an accountant. The term was later transferred to computing and is now applied to very large computers capable of performing complicated mathematical operations on large amounts of data.

numbers game or **numbers racket** An illegal lottery popular among the poorer sections of US society. Since the repeal of PROHIBITION in 1932 the numbers game has been controlled by organized crime on a massive scale; attempts by the authorities to stamp it out have proved ineffective. The person making the bet picks a three-digit number between 000 and 999. The bet, usually a minimum of 5 cents, and the slip is taken by the 'runners' (who work on a commission basis) to the area manager, known as the 'controller', who in turn is responsible to the 'banker', usually a syndicate appointee, who finances the operation. The winning number is picked from stock market figures or other suitable statistics published in the daily newspapers.

numerati A colloquial term for those employed in the financial world, particularly financial whiz kids. It was coined by analogy with *literati*, those who are familiar with literature.

Nunn May affair The arrest and trial of the British nuclear scientist Alan Nunn May (1911–) in 1946 for his involvement in the Soviet Canadian spy network exposed by the defection of Igor Gouzenco in 1945 (*see* OTTAWA SPY RING). A convinced communist since his days as a student and postgraduate at Cambridge University, May was included in a British scientific team pursuing atomic research in Canada (1944–45) and had passed information on the Allied development of the ATOM BOMB to the Soviet Union. He was sentenced to 10 years in prison, served six, and in 1962 took up the Chair of Physics at Ghana University.

Nürburgring The famous German motor racing circuit in the Eifel Mountains, centred around the village of Nürburg, south of Bonn. It was the site of the German Grand Prix from 1927 until 1976, when it was declared unsafe after the near-fatal accident suffered by Niki Lauda. It is now used for other races, rallies, and as a test track. The German Grand Prix is now held at Hockenheim, near Heidelberg.

nurd *See* NERD.

Nuremberg. Nuremberg rallies Massed gatherings and parades organized by the Nazi Party for propaganda purposes, which were first held in Nuremberg in January and August 1923 and then annually on Party Day (July) from 1926. The 1934 rally lasted a full week and was the subject of Leni Riefenstahl's *The Triumph of the Will*, perhaps the most impressive propaganda film ever made. Hitler reserved some of his most dramatic speeches for the rallies, which were carefully orchestrated to generate fervent, near hysterial, nationalistic support for the party and its leader; they were also intended to intimidate both internal and external opponents of the Nazis. During the 1930s the staging of the gatherings became increasingly elaborate, involving such special effects as massed torchlit parades and the use of powerful anti-aircraft searchlights to surround the audience in vertical columns of light. The design of the massive Nuremberg auditorium was entrusted to Hitler's architect Albert Speer in 1934, but the grandiose structure was never completed. It now remains a bleak monument to the evil of the Third Reich.

Nuremberg Trials The trials of 23 Nazi leaders conducted by an international military tribunal set up by the allies at Nuremberg after World War II (September 1945–May 1946). Three were acquitted. Göring, Ribbentrop, and nine others were condemned to death, and the remainder were sentenced to various terms of imprisonment. Amongst the most significant conclusions of the tribunal was the invalidity of the defence that the accused was simply following orders. Göring committed suicide in prison before being executed; Hess was sent to Spandau prison (*see* PRISONER OF SPANDAU). Hitler, Himmler, and Goebbels avoided retribution by committing suicide.

nursery slopes Easy hillsides on which beginners learn to ski.

nutmeg Slang used principally in soccer, for passing the ball between a player's legs and running round him to collect it, thus making him look foolish. The likely derivation of this sense is the connection with the slang meaning of 'nuts' for testicles.

Nye Shortened form of the Welsh name Aneurin, usually referring to the Welsh Labour politician Aneurin Bevan (1897–1960). As Minister of Health, he presided over the formation of the NATIONAL HEALTH SERVICE in 1948.

Nylon Tradename for the world's first synthetic fibre, introduced in 1938. With countless applications in spheres ranging from the clothing industry to engineering, nylon is a product of the polymerization of diamine with a fatty acid or the polymerization of a single monomer, thus forming a polyamide. The word Nylon was coined by the Du Pont company in 1938, but it is uncertain what reasons lay behind the choice. It has been suggested that 'nyl' was taken from the initials of New York and London, the word being formed by analogy with RAYON. A less likely derivation is that the name was created when one of the research chemists involved in developing nylon exclaimed: "*N*ow, *y*ou *l*ousy *o*ld *N*ipponese!" The commercial image of nylon was enhanced during World War II, when nylon stockings, as supplied by US servicemen arriving in the UK, became the last word in luxury and were much sought after.

NZEF New Zealand Expeditionary Force. A volunteer army raised and commanded by Major General Sir Alex Godley (1867–1957) during World War I. The NZEF fought valiantly at GALLIPOLI and in other theatres of the war; its actions contributed to the forging of a national identity for New Zealanders. By 1918, of the 100,444 men who had served overseas in the NZEF, 58,500 had been killed or wounded, a significant proportion of the male population of New Zealand, from which the country took many decades to recover.

O

O US Black slang for opium, dating from the 1930s.

007 *See* BOND, JAMES.

O and M Organization and methods. Increasing the efficiency of a business by studying and seeking to improve both office procedures and the ways in which these are controlled by the management.

o bop she bam US Black slang frequently heard in existential JAZZ vocalizations. Strictly meaningless, it represents an expression of exhilaration or excitement.

O level *See* GCE.

OAS *Organisation de l'Armée Secrète*. A French terrorist organization founded in 1961 to oppose the establishment of an independent Algerian state. Led by General Raoul Salan (1899–), the OAS conducted a campaign of bombings and other outrages in both France and Algeria, culminating in the attempted assassination of President Charles de Gaulle in September 1961. This incident inspired the thriller *The Day of the Jackal* (1970) by Frederick Forsyth, filmed in 1973. The OAS disintegrated in 1962 after Salan was captured.

oats. get one's oats British and US slang meaning to get sexual satisfaction, used usually of men, particularly outside marriage. It is related to the phrase 'sow one's wild oats' used of a man's sexual activities before he settles down in marriage.

> ... the bridegroom ... will not forget his wedding night ... He has spent the last two weeks behind bars – getting plenty of porridge, but no oats!
> *The News of the World*, 6 January 1991.

OAU Organization of African Unity. A supranational African organization, similar to the UN in its purpose and structure, which is supported by all the independent African nations. It was established in 1963 at a pan-African conference in Addis Ababa, Ethiopia, with the aim of defending the political and territorial sovereignty of its members, settling disputes by non-violent means, ending colonialism, and promoting economic, political, and cultural solidarity in Africa. The permanent secretariat of the OAU is based in Addis Ababa.

OBE *See* ORDER OF THE BRITISH EMPIRE.

Obie The annual theatre award, established in 1955 by *The Village Voice*, for OFF-BROADWAY productions.

Objective Burma A film made in Hollywood in 1945, which led to a crisis in Anglo-American relations at the close of World War II. The film, starring Errol Flynn, suggested that US forces had been solely responsible for the defeat of the Japanese in Burma. British anger at this notion led to the film being withdrawn from cinemas in the UK. *See also* FORGOTTEN ARMY.

objet trouvé (Fr. found object) An object displayed as a work of art, often with no contribution from the 'artist' beyond the act of selection. An object that has been tampered with or tidied up is sometimes called an *objet trouvé assisté*. The most celebrated *objets trouvé*s are probably the **ready-mades** of the French Surrealist Marcel Duchamp (1887–1968), who exhibited a number of mass-produced articles as sculpture. These included a bottle rack, a bicycle wheel, and a metal urinal (given the title 'Fountain' and signed R. Mutt).

Oboe Codename given to a secret British invention of World War II. A rudimentary direction-finding device used by RAF bombers, it operated by means of a constant note sounded in the pilot's headphones, which changed in character when the aircraft veered off its designated path.

Obscuranto A word coined by analogy with Esperanto, the artificial international language. It is used to describe the kind of pretentious language some people or organizations use to obscure rather than clarify.

occupational medicine The medical speciality concerned with the effects on health of work and the workplace. During the 20th century, many new industries have created particular health hazards, which has prompted a revolution in the research and practice of occupational medicine; to this end London's Royal College of Physicians founded its Faculty of Occupational Medicine in 1978. Industrial diseases are often slow to develop and the link with a specific material or process is hard to establish. For instance, asbestos has been used on a large scale since the late 1800s. It was first linked with the lung disease asbestosis in 1907, but was not identified as a cause of lung cancer until 1935; it was a further 30 or 40 years before the present stringent precautions for its manufacture and use were laid down. A similar pattern applies to radiation and radioactive materials. Many of the early radiologists suffered illness or death due to their work, including Marie Curie, who contracted bouts of radiation sickness and ultimately leukaemia; her husband and fellow radiologist, Pierre, was also affected by radiation sickness. Health in the workplace is now regulated by a host of laws and guidelines.

Ochrana or **Okhrana** (Russ. guard) The Russian Imperial secret police, a special division of the Department of State Police under the Ministry of the Interior, whose role was to protect the Tsar and the government from internal and external subversion. Its main task was the infiltration and exposure of revolutionary movements and the suppression of popular dissent; to this end its permanent elite corps of 15,000 gendarmes was supplemented by an extensive network of informers and agents provocateurs. Lenin had to flee to Switzerland from the Ochrana after the abortive revolution of 1905, and thereafter the Ochrana had considerable success in infiltrating the BOLSHEVIK movement – Lenin's close colleague, Roman Malinovskii, who was appointed the first editor of *Pravda* in 1912, was an Ochrana agent. As the hated symbol of Tsarist political oppression, the organization was liquidated in 1917 by Lenin but was soon replaced by the CHEKA, the Bolshevik's own revolutionary secret police, whose ruthlessness and efficiency far surpassed that of its predecessor.

ocker An Australian who lacks cultural awareness. A nickname of uncertain origin, it was attached to anyone with the surname Stevens. It was later applied more widely to any aggressive boorish native of Australia, following the success of a character so named in a series of television sketches in the 1970s (played by Ron Frazer).

OCR Optical Character Recognition. The process by which printed text is scanned, recognized, and translated into a form that can be read by a computer. Modern OCR systems use inexpensive flat-bed, or handheld, scanners attached to a microcomputer, driven by character-recognition software, which converts scanned text into a format that can be edited by any standard word-processing programme.

October. October Club A left-wing political club formed at Oxford in the 1930s by communist sympathizers; it took its name from the OCTOBER REVOLUTION.

October Manifesto The proclamation by Nicholas II, following the civil unrest of 1905, that he would allow the establishment of an elected DUMA, to participate in Russian affairs.

October Revolution In Russian history, the BOLSHEVIK revolution of October 1917 (November in the western Calendar), which led to the overthrow of Kerensky and the MENSHEVIKS and the triumph of LENIN.

> Ten days that shook the world.
>
> Book title, JOHN REED (1917).

Octobrists A constitutionalist centre party in Russia supported by the landlords and wealthy mercantile interests, prominent in the DUMA between 1907 and 1914. Its name derived from the Tsar's famous liberal manifesto published in October 1905. *See* OCTOBER MANIFESTO.

octopush A hockey-like game played underwater in swimming pools. The players – there are six on each side – use sticks to push a flat puck along the floor of the pool towards the opponents' goal. It was devised in the UK in the late 1960s and named by blending 'octopus' and 'push'.

OD Slang abbreviation, used since the 1960s, for an overdose of drugs, or to take an overdose. It is also used in the more general sense of over-indulging in something, as in 'I've OD'ed on chocolate milkshakes, I never want to see another.'

Oddjob The fictional Korean henchman of GOLDFINGER in the novels of Ian Fleming, one of the most formidable opponents of James BOND. His steel bowler hat, fitted with a sharpened rim, proved a lethal weapon.

Odeon Tradename of a cinema chain founded in the UK in 1933. Derived from the Greek *oideion*, meaning theatre, the word Odeon had become almost synonymous with cinema itself by the time the controlling company was taken over by the Rank Organization in 1941. The flagship of the chain was the Odeon in London's Leicester Square.

Oder-Neisse line The frontier between Germany and Poland following World War II. It was recognized by Poland and the former state of East Germany in 1950 but not by other powers until 1990, when it was formally agreed by the newly reunited Germany. The border itself follows the Rivers Oder and Neisse; it benefitted Poland by giving it a large slice of pre-war Germany.

ODESSA A secret Nazi organization that arranged for leading Nazis to escape from Germany at the end of World War II. In conditions of great secrecy, several notorious wartime commanders were spirited out of the country to South America and elsewhere, where the organization continued to protect their interests. Among those thus hidden was Adolf Eichmann (*see* EICHMANN TRIAL). The name itself was derived from *Organisation der SS-Angehörigen* (Organization of SS Members). Frederick Forsyth based his thriller *The Odessa File* (1972) on this shadowy group. ODESSA was disbanded in about 1952 and replaced by the *Kameradenwerke* (Comrade Workshop), which had similar aims.

Oerlikon A rapid-firing 20-mm anti-aircraft gun much used by both sides in World War II. It was named after the Swiss town in which it was made.

ofay Black US derogatory slang for a White person. It is thought to be derived either from a backslang rendering of 'foe', or from the Yoruba (Nigerian) *ofé*, meaning charm or fetish. The Black poet LeRoi Jones (1934–) uses the word in his rather bitter poem about the BEATS:

O, generation revered
above all others.
O, generation of fictitious
Ofays
I revere you . . .
You are all so beautiful.

off (1) US slang meaning to kill. It is thought to be an abbreviation of 'bump off'. It is also heard occasionally in the UK. During World War I the expression 'to off oneself' was used to mean to commit suicide. This usage is still heard. (2) US slang meaning to have sex with. This is probably an abbreviation of 'to have it off'.

off-Broadway US theatrical productions staged away from the commercial theatre of Broadway in the 1950s. Off-Broadway theatres became popular venues for creative low-budget plays by such dramatists as Tennessee Williams and Edward Albee, launching such stars as Geraldine Page. Inevitably, when the success of these off-Broadway productions was recognized, business interests moved in and its theatres (including the Circle in the Square) began staging more commercial plays. By the late 1960s a new **off-off-Broadway** theatre had developed to foster the original off-Broadway experimental spirit.

off-limits Out of bounds. An expression originating in military contexts that is now common in the UK in a general context.

off-piste Describing the practice of skiing on fresh snow, away from the pistes or regular ski slopes. Experienced skiers find this more challenging and relish the chance to escape from the crowds; it is, however, more dangerous. It was much favoured by younger members of the British Royal Family until a member of the Prince of Wales' skiing party was killed in an off-piste accident.

offshore fund Any sum of money held in a country that is not the country of residence of its owner. Offshore centres for such funds usually have low rates of taxation and simple exchange-control regulations. The British colony of the Cayman Islands is one of the most widely used offshore centres. Offshore funds may also be available for investors in the form of unit trusts based in a TAX HAVEN.

offside (1) The side of a car that is to the right hand of the driver. (2) A type of foul in various team games such as soccer, rugby, American football, and hockey. The rules vary with each game but the principle is that players should not gain an advantage by advancing too close to the opponents' goal in relation to the prevailing focus of play.

off-the-cuff Denoting a remark or speech that is unrehearsed, or a person who speaks in this way. The phrase derives from the practice by waiters of taking orders in restaurants by jotting down notes on their shirt cuffs.

off-the-shelf company A company that has been formed according to UK law, is registered with the Registrar of Companies, but is not trading and has no directors. Such companies can be bought from a business broker who specializes in this trade.

off the wall Eccentric or wildly creative: originally a US expression derived from such games as squash and handball, in which the ball bounces off a wall at an unpredictable angle.

officer. Officer in the Tower Nickname acquired by Lieutenant N. Baillie-Stewart, who was incarcerated in the Tower of London in 1933 after being accused of passing secrets to Nazi Germany. He returned to the Tower in 1946 to serve a second sentence for participating in propaganda broadcasts from Germany during World War II.

Officers' Plot *See* STAUFFENBERG PLOT.

official. Official Secrets Act A series of British parliamentary Acts (1911–89), designed to protect the country's security by outlawing activities deemed to be contrary to the national interest. Apart from encompassing a host of obviously essential areas, such as espionage and the collecting or passing on of information likely to be useful to an enemy of the state, the Acts before 1989 (notably Section 2 of the 1911 Act) were so broad and indiscriminate in their application that it was technically a criminal offence to disclose any information, however insignificant, contained in an official document. The lack of definition within Section 2 of the 1911 Act was finally underlined when the UK government failed to suppress publication of *Spycatcher* (1987), the memoirs of Peter Wright, a former secret-service agent. The offending section was replaced by the 1989 Act, which redefined and limited the classes of information to be protected from disclosure.

Official Unionists Members of the Official Unionist Party of Northern Ireland, who support continued union with the UK. It is descended from various Protestant political clubs of the late 19th century and provided a long sequence of prime ministers of Northern Ireland until direct rule was imposed in 1972.

oflag German name for prisoner-of-war camps for Allied officers, derived from *Offizier* (officer) and *lager* (camp). The most famous of these was undoubtedly COLDITZ.

OG US abbreviation, used by criminals, the police, etc., in the 1980s for 'Original Gangster', in the sense of a grand old man of the gang; a respected elder of the underworld.

OGPU *See* GPU.

O'Hara, Scarlett The heroine of Margaret Mitchell's blockbuster novel GONE WITH THE WIND (1936). Scarlett O'Hara, rejected by Ashley Wilkes and finally by the headstrong Rhett Butler, was based on the author's maternal grandmother, Annie Fitzgerald Stephens (1844–1934). She was the daughter of a Southern plantation owner and witnessed the burning of Atlanta in 1864 before returning to the neglected family farm. The casting of the role of Scarlett in the hugely successful film became part of Hollywood legend: after considerable speculation and wrangling between established film starlets, the part went to the relatively unknown Vivien Leigh. Unlike her heroine, Margaret Mitchell herself left her reckless first husband for a steadier man.

oik (1) British derogatory slang for an uncouth and uncultured youth, often used by public schoolboys for the boys at state schools or by officers in the services for other ranks. Working-class males, however, also use it deprecatingly of themselves. Its origin is uncertain but it is thought to have been coined as a reflection of uncultured vowel sounds. (2) Acronym for One Income and Kids. British slang of the 1980s, similar to YUPPIE and DINKIE. *See also* OINK.

oil. oilberg An oil-carrying supertanker: coined from 'oil' and 'iceberg'.

oily rag (1) British slang for an inexperienced or inept motor mechanic, *i.e.* one who might be given the task of wiping up the grease with a rag. (2) British rhyming slang from the 1950s for a fag, a cigarette.

oink Acronym of One Income No Kids. British slang of the 1980s similar to YUPPIE and DINKIE. *See also* OIK.

Okhrana *See* OCHRANA.

Okinawa The largest of the Japanese Ryukyu Islands, which in World War II became the scene of fierce fighting between Japanese and US forces. After a huge US amphibious operation, facing fanatical opposition from Japanese troops and attacks by KAMIKAZE pilots, America established control over this island. It was not returned to Japan until 1972.

old. Old Bill (1) *See under* BETTER. (2) *See* BILL.

Old Blood 'n' Guts Nickname of US General George Smith Patton (1885–1945), commander of the US Seventh and Third Armies in World War II. He was famous for the pearl-handled revolver he always wore and his bluff attitude towards fellow-commanders, especially Montgomery. His premature death resulted from injuries received in a car crash. The US Patton tank was named in his honour.

Old Blue Eyes Francis Albert Sinatra (1915–), known as Frank Sinatra and sometimes by the nicknames **Bones** or **the Gov'nor**. A US singer and film star, he is admired and loved throughout the world, in spite of sinister rumours of Mafia connections.

old boiled egg British facetious interpretation of the initials OBE (Officer of the ORDER OF THE BRITISH EMPIRE), an honour awarded for public services. This term has been used since the 1930s in the Civil Service.

old-boy network The long-established informal process by which old school-friends, ex-army colleagues, etc., gain employment or preferment by seeking favours based solely on the fact that they share the same background. Making use of the old-boy network is often now called **networking**.

Old Contemptibles *See under* CONTEMPTIBLES, OLD.

Old Crock Nickname of US General Anthony C. McAuliffe (1898–1975), who commanded US forces in the Battle of the Bulge (*see* ARDENNES OFFENSIVE) in 1944 with considerable success. He coined his own self-deprecating nickname but became very popular among his troops when, in reply to a German demand for his surrender, he responded simply "Nuts!"

Old Dutch Nickname of the singer and comedian Albert Chevalier (1861–1923), a star of the music-hall in the early years of the century. An informal Cockney expression for one's wife (an abbreviation of 'duchess'), it was associated with Chevalier after his success with the sentimental song 'My Old Dutch'. *See also* GIPPER.

Old Groaner Harry Lillis Crosby (1904–77), known worldwide as **Bing Crosby** and in German as **Der Bingle**. As a crooner, film star, and TV personality he became a US megastar. His record of Irving Berlin's *White Christmas* (1942) sold more copies than any other.

Old Possum The pseudonym adopted by T. S. Eliot as author of *Old Possum's Book of Practical Cats* (1939). The poems were years later enormously successful as the basis of the Lloyd Webber musical *Cats* (1981; *see* MACAVITY). The pseudonym was invented by Eliot's friend Ezra Pound, who referred to Eliot, the banker, as the poet 'playing possum', an idiom deriving from the possum's ploy of pretending to be dead or asleep when threatened.

Old Slow Hand Nickname of the British blues rock guitarist Eric Clapton (1945–), noted for his apparently effortless mastery of electric guitar technique.

Old soldiers never die, they simply fade away A proverb that was originally a line from a ballad popular in the British Army during World War I. It was, in fact, a parody of the gospel hymn 'Kind Words Never Die'.

Old Timber Nickname of the British conductor Sir Henry Wood (1869–1944), who founded the London Promenade concerts. Every year on the last night of the proms (*see* PROM), a garland is placed on the shoulders of a bust of Sir Henry Wood in the Albert Hall.

Old Tom The nickname given to a killer whale that established a remarkable relationship with the whalers of the township of Eden in New South Wales. Old Tom was the best known member of a pack of killer whales, who had learned to track down and weaken larger whales so that the whalers were able to kill them easily with their harpoons; the killer whales then fought over the prized tongue and lips of the carcass. Old Tom, who had made his first appearance as long ago as 1843, died in 1930, after which the collaboration ceased. Old Tom's skeleton is preserved in Eden's Museum.

Old Turkey Neck *See* VINEGAR JOE.

Old Vic The theatre in Waterloo Road, London, that became famous for its Shakespearean productions under the management of Lilian Baylis (1874–1937), who took over from her aunt, Emma Cons, in 1912. It was opened in 1818 as the Coburg and was renamed the Royal Victoria Hall in 1833. It became the temporary home (1963–76) of the National Theatre (*see* ROYAL NATIONAL THEATRE). In 1982 it was bought by the Canadian entrepreneur Ed Mirvish (1915–).

Oldsmobile The first US mass-produced car (1901–06), made by Ransom Eli Olds (1864–1950) at his factory in Lansing,

Michigan. The three horse-power curved-dash 'merry' Oldsmobile was little more than a motorized horse carriage with tiller steering, but at a price of $650 it was within the financial means of a large section of the US population and became the best-selling car in the world.

Olduvai Gorge A canyon in the Serengeti Plain of Tanzania, near the Ngorongoro crater, that has yielded a wealth of fossilized remains of prehistoric apes and the hominid ancestors of mankind. The most striking finds at Olduvai were made by the British anthropologists Louis and Mary Leakey. In 1959 Mary Leakey discovered the first remains of a sturdy ape, which they named *Zinjanthropus boisei*, now known as *Australopithecus boisei*. Further work by the Leakeys led to the discovery, announced in 1964, of *Homo habilis* (**Handy Man**), a probable ancestor of modern man. This early hominid was the likely user of the Oldowan tools found at the site – crude scrapers, choppers, and other artefacts made from chipped pebbles. The discovery of Handy Man and the other remains in Olduvai Gorge caused a radical re-evaluation of thinking about man's origins with the realization that man emerged much earlier than previously supposed and in Africa, rather than in Asia.

'ole, a better *See* A BETTER 'OLE *under* BETTER.

olim Jewish immigrants to Israel: a Hebrew plural noun meaning pilgrims (literally, 'those who ascend'). *See also* ALIYAH; CHOZRIM; YORDIM.

Olympic Games An international sporting contest held every four years. Modelled on the athletic festival of the ancient Greeks, held every fourth year at Olympia in July, the games were revived in their modern form in 1896, the first being held at Athens.

> The most important thing in the Olympic Games is not the winning but taking part . . . The essential thing in life is not conquering but fighting well.
> PIERRE DE COUBERTIN, founder of modern Olympics, 24 July 1908.

OM Order of Merit. A British order of chivalry established in 1902 by Edward VII on the occasion of his coronation. The order, which confers no title and is limited to 24 members and the sovereign, is open to both sexes and is awarded for special distinction in civil or military service or in a particular field.

Omaha Allied codename given to a beach NW of Bayeux, which was one of the main landing sites for US forces on D DAY. It became known as 'bloody Omaha' because of the fierce German resistance encountered there. *See also* GOLD; JUNO; SWORD; UTAH.

ombudsman (Swed. commissioner) An official appointed to protect the rights of the citizen against infringement by the government. The post originated in Sweden, which has had an ombudsman since 1809; Denmark has had one since 1955 and Norway since 1962. New Zealand was the first Commonwealth country to appoint such a commissioner (1962) and the UK appointed a **Parliamentary Commissioner for Administration** in 1967, commonly known as 'the Ombudsman'. In 1974 an ombudsman for local government was appointed and non-statutory ombudsmen have been set up for Insurance (1981), Banking (1986), Building Societies (1987), and Unit Trusts (1988).

Omega workshops A group of design workshops founded in 1913 by the British art critic Roger Fry (1866–1934). Following the example of William Morris, he hoped to bring a contemporary artistic sensibility to the production of useful everyday objects. Craftsmen were engaged to create furniture, textiles, pottery, etc., which were then decorated by a team of artists associated with the BLOOMSBURY GROUP (including Vanessa Bell and Duncan Grant). The workshops were run on a collective basis and the finished products identified only with an omega (Ω) sign. The project was a commercial failure and collapsed in 1919.

one. One and Only Nickname of the US strip-tease artiste of the 1940s Phyllis Dixey, since applied almost universally to show-business stars, regardless of their merits. The British comedian Max Miller was also known by this nickname.

one-armed bandit A gambling machine operated by the insertion of coins and the pulling of an arm or lever. So called because it frequently 'robs' one of loose change. It is also called a **fruit machine**, because pulling the lever gives random combinations of symbols representing different fruits on the display. Certain combinations win a prize.

One Day of the Year *See* ANZAC DAY.

one-hour dress A simple dress popular in the 1920s, consisting of a chemise with kimono sleeves and short skirt. It was so called because any competent dressmaker could, it was claimed, make this dress in just one hour.

One Nation group A group of liberal Conservatives, formed in 1950 soon after the general election to press for a greater financial commitment to the social services by the Conservative government. The pamphlet, *One Nation* (in homage to Disraeli's paternalistic conservativism), was published in October 1950 and, as intended, strongly influenced government social policy.

one-night stand A casual sexual encounter lasting only one night. It was a show-business expression that originally denoted an engagement by a theatrical touring company for one night only. A one-night stand is now regarded as a dangerous indulgence in view of the potential threat of AIDS.

one over the eight Drunk. Apparently eight pints of beer are considered a reasonable amount for the average man to drink – one more tips the balance.

one small step for man The words used by the US astronaut Neil Armstrong (1930–) at 3.56 a.m. British Summer Time on 21 July 1969, as he stepped off the ladder of the lunar module *Eagle*. Millions of television viewers throughout the world heard him say:

> That's one small step for man, one giant leap for mankind.

It is generally accepted that he intended to say "one small step for a man . . . " and that he had fluffed his lines. Armstrong himself, in his autobiography, later claimed that he had used the words "a man" rather than "man", but that the indefinite article had been lost in the radio transmission. President Nixon, phoning the astronauts to congratulate them on the successful mission, made the extravagant claim that:

> This is the greatest week in the history of the world since the Creation.

one-stop Denoting comprehensive shopping facilities provided in one large HYPERMARKET so that all one's shopping can be completed during one stop of the car. The meaning later extended to cover a comprehensive range of financial services provided by one organization and thence into more general contexts.

One-Take Nickname given to a number of public figures who were noted for giving flawless performances of one kind or another. Among those to receive this accolade were Bing Crosby (*see* OLD GROANER), who rarely needed to record anything twice, the child film actress Shirley Temple (*see* CURLY TOP), and Prince Charles.

one under British police slang for a person who has committed suicide by jumping under a train.

one-upmanship An expression coined by the British humorist Stephen Potter (1900–70) to describe the art of gaining an advantage over someone by psychological means; for example, by consciously setting out to make one's opponent feel inferior, irrespective of their ability. It is also the title of a book setting out the details of this ploy, which was published in 1952. *See also* GAMESMANSHIP; LIFEMANSHIP.

on-going situation *See* SITUATION.

onion boat, come over with the *See under* COME.

Oomph Girl Nickname of the US film actress Ann Sheridan (1915–67), who was a beauty queen before embarking on her film career. Her films include *Angels with Dirty Faces* (1938) and *The Man Who Came to Dinner* (1941).

op art Abstract art that exploits various forms of common optical illusion. The movement became popular during the 1950s and 1960s; its leading exponents, including Victor Vasarely (1908–) and Bridget Riley (1931–), use a variety of geometrical abstractions, such as fine grids and spirals that appear to pulsate or flicker when focused on, to stimulate visual perception.

OPEC Organization of Petroleum Exporting Countries. An international cartel of oil producers formed in 1960 to combat exploitation by western oil companies and encourage the nationalization of oil production in member countries. Current members include Venezuela, Iraq, Iran, Kuwait, Saudi Arabia, Indonesia, Libya, Qatar, United Arab Emirates, Algeria, Nigeria, Ecuador, and Gabon. OPEC has overseen a significant transfer of wealth from the industrialized nations to those DEVELOPING COUNTRIES with oil deposits.

open. open diplomacy The first of Woodrow Wilson's FOURTEEN POINTS, 'open covenants of peace openly arrived at, after which there shall be no private international understandings of any kind'. It is perhaps significant that the VERSAILLES TREATY was an 'open treaty' negotiated in secret, ultimately by President Wilson, Clemenceau, and Lloyd George.

open-heart surgery Surgery in which the heart is exposed, for instance to repair or replace diseased valves, to insert grafts into the coronary arteries (*see* BYPASS SURGERY), or to repair other heart lesions. Such operations require a bloodless and motionless heart; they have been made feasible by the development of the heart-lung machine, introduced in 1953.

open marriage A version of marriage that developed in the 1970s as women became more career-oriented and sexually liberated. In an open marriage both spouses have the right to an independent lifestyle in order to develop their individual potential. This includes the expression of honest feelings and sexual freedom.

open prison A low-security gaol for petty and non-violent offenders who are considered to be sufficiently trustworthy not to need to be locked up.

Open University A British university founded in 1969 with the express objective of providing further education opportunities for part-time (usually mature) students who, because of other calls upon their time or because of their lack of formal academic qualifications, would otherwise be unable to enrol at a conventional university or polytechnic. The courses are organized on a non-residential basis, students taking their instruction by means of correspondence courses, combined with radio and television lectures broadcast by the BBC. In addition to degree courses in both arts and sciences, the Open University also offers a variety of vocational and training courses. With an administrative centre at MILTON KEYNES, the Open University, originally called the 'University of the Air', was established during Jenny Lee's term of office as Minister of the Arts during the 1964–70 Labour administration. It was an inspired and innovative concept, which has since been adopted in other countries. *See also* UNIVERSITY OF THE THIRD AGE.

Operation Bernhard A clandestine Nazi plot to wreck the British economy, planned in the later stages of World War II. This attempt to stave off German defeat hinged on flooding the UK with some £140 million of fake banknotes. The forgeries needed to be of the highest quality. As Reichbank officials refused to cooperate, Himmler, head of the GESTAPO, assigned the task to a Major Bernhard Kruger, who gathered a team of engravers and printers from the concentration camps and set them to work, in exchange for various privileges, at Sachsenhausen Camp near Berlin. However, military events overtook the operation before its full effect could be felt. With Germany's collapse imminent, Himmler ordered the press to provide instead forged documents and cash for escaping Nazis. Much of this money was intercepted by the Allies – some of it being found floating in the Enns River in Austria – before it could be hidden to await collection. Kruger, the mastermind of the whole operation, which so very nearly succeeded, was never found.

opinion poll A means of attempting to predict public opinion by canvassing a random or representative sample of people. Probably the best known among the professional organizations that carry out such surveys are Gallup (*see* GALLUP POLL) and Moray; both organizations are associated mainly with sampling of political opinion. In an **exit poll**, those emerging from a polling station are asked how they voted in a political election. This usually gives a reliable indication of the way the voting has gone a few hours before the result is announced.

Oppenheimer affair A scandal involving the US physicist Julius Robert Oppenheimer (1904–67) in the early 1950s. Oppenheimer was a brilliant theoretical physicist who was effectively in charge of the MANHATTAN PROJECT to develop the atom bomb during World War II (*see also* NUCLEAR WEAPON). In 1942 Oppenheimer was investigated by the US security services – first as a matter of routine. Later, however, Colonel Pash, the director of security at Los Alamos, began to hear criticisms of Oppenheimer's loyalty.

Under interrogation, Oppenheimer finally admitted that he had been approached by Soviet agents but, at first, refused to name the person involved on the grounds that this person was no longer operating. Eventually, in 1943, he named Haakon Chevalier, Professor of Romance Languages at the University of California. Chevalier was never charged but his career was ruined. Oppenheimer was cleared to continue with the project, which was concluded in 1945.

After the war, Oppenheimer continued in government service, taking responsibility for the development of the hydrogen bomb. Accusations were then made that he was trying to obstruct the programme; in 1954 a Congressional commission investigated his loyalty, reporting that:

> Dr Oppenheimer did not show the support for the Superbomb program that might have been expected of the chief adviser of the Government.

Oppenheimer consequently lost his security clearance and returned to academic work. The truth of the matter has never been clearly revealed. (*see* MCCARTHYISM; REDS UNDER THE BED).

Opportunity Knocks The title of a British TV talent-spotting show that ran from 1956 to 1977 and was hosted by Hughie Green, who used the title as his catchphrase. It was taken from the proverb 'Opportunity seldom knocks twice' – untrue in this case, as the show was revived in the late 1980s as 'Bob Monkhouse says, Opportunity Knocks'.

Opus Dei (Lat. work of God) An international Roman Catholic organization, originally of lay people, whose members seek to demonstrate the principles of Christian living through the example of their own lives, in whatever career they have chosen. The organization was founded in Madrid in 1928 by José Mariá Escrivá de Balaguer, an Aragonese priest; two years later a women's branch was established.

OR Operational (or Operations) Research. The scientific analysis of managerial problems in civil and military organizations. It was first used by the RAF to improve radar efficiency in the early years of World War II. Similar techniques were adopted and refined by the US military establishment; in the late 1940s and 1950s they were extended to the management of civil industry. OR is now a major industry itself, employing quantitive techniques, such as linear programming and non-quantitive methods, such as modelling and game theory, to analyse man–machine relations to improve efficiency and productivity.

Oracle *See* CEEFAX.

Oradour massacre A tragic incident (10 June 1944) during World War II, in which German SS troops slaughtered 642 of the 652 people living in the French village of Oradour-sur-Glane, near Limoges. Germans gave the discovery of secret arms caches as justification for the massacre – not realizing that the Oradour they referred to was another village of the same name, where the RESISTANCE had been in operation. 21 of the 200 German troops responsible were tried in 1953: two men were executed. A new village was built nearby. *See also* LIDICE.

orange or **orange sunshine** US drug-users' slang of the 1960s for a type of homemade LSD tablet that was orange in colour. The LSD was reputedly unadulterated and very strong.

Orange, Agent *See* AGENT ORANGE.

Oranges and Lemons service A church service held annually at the end of March in St Clement Danes in the Strand, London. The first Oranges and Lemons service was held in 1920, following the restoration of the famous bells in the previous year. The service was attended by pupils of the nearby St Clement Danes primary school: after rendering 'Oranges and lemons, Say the bells of St Clements' on handbells, each child received an orange and a lemon. The tradition has continued ever since, interrupted only in World War II, when the church was badly damaged during an air raid. However, the St Clements referred to in the rhyme is almost certainly not St Clement Danes in the Strand, but St Clement in Eastcheap, which is close to the wharves into which cargoes of citrus fruits were once unloaded.

orbital or **orbital rave** British slang of the late 1980s for an ACID HOUSE party. RAVE was a 1960s term for a party; it was revived with the use of the drug ECSTASY, perhaps the most important ingredient of these huge gatherings of wildly dancing teenagers. The parties were held within reach of the London orbital motorway, the notorious M25, hence the name.

order. **Order of Merit** *See* OM.

Order of the British Empire The Most Excellent Order of the British Empire: an order of chivalry founded in 1917 by King George V, to reward distinguished wartime service by the military or civilians. Women were admitted on an equal basis in recognition of their role in the war effort. It is now conferred mainly for peacetime services. Senior positions include Sovereign of the order (the Queen), Grand Master (the Duke of Edinburgh), Prelate (the Bishop of London), King of Arms, Genealogist, and Gentleman Usher of the Purple Rod. There are five classes: Knights and Dames Grand Cross (KGBE and DGBE), Knights and Dames Commanders (KBE and DBE), Commanders (CBE), Officers (OBE), and Members

(MBE). Members of the two higher classes use the title 'Sir' or 'Dame'. The insignia carries the motto 'For God and Empire' and likenesses of George V and Queen Mary.

orders is orders Orders must be obeyed regardless of whether or not they are considered justifiable or acceptable. This phrase was first used by NCOs in the years following World War I; it soon passed into wider usage, however, although it lost something of its lighthearted tone after the war trials following World War II. In these trials many war criminals attempted to justify their actions by claiming that they were 'only obeying orders'. International law no longer permits the excuse of obeying orders to justify atrocities. *See* NUREMBERG TRIALS.

ordination of women The conferring of holy orders on women; outside the Nonconformist churches, this has become a contentious issue. The Roman Catholic Church has never wavered on the question, steadfastly refusing to countenance accepting women into the priesthood. Within the Church of England, however, a growing movement in favour of the ordination of women gathered momentum in the 1970s, when women began to be ordained in the Episcopal Church of America. The matter was given further impetus in the 1980s, when women were admitted into the Church of England as deacons; in this capacity they are permitted to fulfil all the ministerial functions of a priest, except for giving absolution and consecrating the bread and wine for Holy Communion (although they are allowed to administer it). However, although it was established at the General Synod that there are no theological grounds for excluding women from the ministry, the idea remains unacceptable to a considerable proportion of its members.

organization. organization and methods *See* O AND M.

organization man or **company man** A person who is totally devoted to the organization or company for whom he works, accepting its aims, methods of working, and values without question. Both expressions are therefore derogatory, being thought to describe someone who has no personal views of his own. The female equivalents are, of course, **organization** (or **company**) **women**.

orgasmatron A device that induces orgasm. The name derives from the Woody Allen film *Sleeper* (1973), in which people enter a capsule to achieve sexual satisfaction instead of using the traditional biological method.

Orient Express An extremely luxurious train that enabled those who could afford it to travel in comfort from Paris to Constantinople in around 82 hours. It was the creation of the entrepreneur Georges Nagelmackers (1845–1905), founder (at the age of 24) of the Compagnie Internationale des Wagons-Lits et Grands Express Européens. The first Express left the Gare de l'Est in Paris on 4 October 1883. There was a twice-weekly service in each direction and a daily service as far as Vienna was introduced in 1885. The train made a last trip in May 1977, but was revived in the mid-1980s in opulent form as a tourist attraction. Amongst the most famous works of fiction using the Orient Express as a setting are Agatha Christie's *Murder on the Orient Express* (1934) and Graham Greene's *Stamboul Train* (1932).

Orlando The central character of Virginia Woolf's novel (1928) of the same name. The extraordinary Orlando, whose sex changes as he moves from one historical context to another, was generally regarded as being based upon Woolf's friend Vita Sackville-West (1892–1962). Vita, wife of the critic Sir Harold Nicolson, had a remarkable relationship with Woolf, which is thought to have included lesbian activities. The precise nature of the friendship remained a subject of public fascination long after both women were dead; *Portrait of a Marriage* (1990), a controversial television dramatization of the Nicolsons' life together, which included an account of Vita's lesbian relationship with Violet Trefusis, revived this speculation.

> I enjoyed talking to her, but thought *nothing* of her writing. I considered her 'a beautiful little knitter'.
>
> EDITH SITWELL, referring to Virginia Woolf, 1940.

Orphism A movement in painting started by Robert Delaunay (1885–1941), characterized by patches and swirls of intense and contrasting colours. *See also* CUBISM; DADAISM; FAUVISM; FUTURISM; SURREALISM; SYNCHRONISM; VORTICISM.

Orwell, George The pseudonym adopted by Eric Arthur Blair (1903–50), Old Etonian and socialist; author of *The Road to Wigan Pier* (1937), ANIMAL FARM (1945), 1984 (1949), etc.

Orwellian Resembling or related to the totalitarian society described in Orwell's novel 1984. The use of Orwellian coinages, such as NEWSPEAK, DOUBLETHINK, THOUGHT POLICE, and BIG BROTHER IS WATCHING YOU, serve as a warning against the authoritarian tendencies in society.

Osborne House The country house near Cowes, on the Isle of Wight, in which Queen Victoria died in 1901. It was built in 1845 to designs by Prince Albert and was subsequently opened to the public.

Oscar A gold-plated figurine awarded annually by the American Academy of Motion Picture Arts and Sciences for the best film-acting, writing, or production of the year. Properly known as the Academy Award statuette, it is said to have earned its nickname from a long-forgotten secretary who said, when she saw the newly cast figure in 1927, that it reminded her of her uncle Oscar.

Oscar Slater case A famous case of wrongful imprisonment. Oscar Slater (*c.*1871–1948), a German fugitive from military service who lived by gambling and selling jewellery, was found guilty of the murder of an 82-year-old Glasgow woman, Marion Gilchrist, in 1909. Slater had been in Glasgow at the time of the murder and then sailed shortly afterwards to America on the *Lusitania*. A brooch he had pawned to pay for his passage was thought to have been owned by the victim; he was arrested on his arrival and returned to Scotland for trial. The brooch proved to have been Slater's for some time but this evidence was suppressed. As a result he was found guilty and sentenced to hang on the basis of circumstantial evidence and the dubious testimony of witnesses who claimed to have seen him outside Gilchrist's flat. After the trial 20,000 people signed a petition for clemency; his sentence was then commuted to life imprisonment. The campaign for his release was led by Sir Arthur Conan Doyle, who wrote *The Case of Oscar Slater* (1912) criticizing the verdict. Slater was finally released on appeal in 1927, after 18 years in prison. He was paid £6000 in compensation.

OSS Office for Strategic Services. The US espionage and sabotage organization, which was the forerunner of the CIA and the equivalent of the British wartime SOE (Special Operations Executive; *see* BAKER STREET IRREGULARS). The OSS was established in June 1942 by President Roosevelt and placed under the direction of General 'Wild Bill' Donovan (1883–1959), his intelligence adviser. Its role combined information gathering and analysis with covert operations against the enemy, including guerrilla warfare, the rescue of Allied servicemen, and the support of underground resistance movements. In this latter role, Donovan modelled the OSS on the SOE.

Ossewa-Brandwag (Afrikaans: Ox-Wagon Sentinels) South African pro-Nazi paramilitary organization that emerged in 1938 after the symbolic re-enactment of the Great Trek; it achieved popular support in the wake of German victories in the early years of World War II. An elite inner unit, called the *stormjaers* (stormtroopers), was dedicated to sabotaging the South African war effort. Led by Hans van Rensberg, the OB included in its ranks numerous prominent Afrikaners, such as John Vorster, later prime minister (1966–78), and Hendrik van den Bergh, who became head of the Bureau of State Security (BOSS). With the defeat of Germany, the OB disintegrated and its remnants were incorporated into the National Party.

Ostpolitik (Ger. eastern policy) The West German policy of normalizing relations with E European countries, which was adopted by the government (1969–74) of Willy Brandt. Previously, West German foreign policy had been constrained by the so-called **Hallstein doctrine**, prohibiting diplomatic relations with any country that recognized East Germany. *Ostpolitik* has also been used in a vaguer sense to mean any conciliatory policy by a western nation towards the (former) communist states of E Europe.

Oswald, Lee Harvey The suspected assassin of President John F. Kennedy. Oswald (1939–63), a former US Marine who turned to Marxism, lived in the Soviet Union from 1959 until 1962 and married a Russian. Kennedy was assassinated on 22 November 1963, in Dallas, by shots fired from a building in which Oswald worked. A Dallas policeman was shot the same day and witnesses identified Oswald as the murderer. He was then charged with Kennedy's death. Two days later, being moved to a more secure jail, Oswald was gunned down by a local club-owner, Jack RUBY, in full view of the television cameras. The government's **Warren Commission** concluded in 1964 that Oswald had acted alone; however, a 1974 House Select Committee on Assassinations thought that organized crime may have been involved. Oswald's wife, Marina, noted: "He wanted, by any means, good or bad, to get into history".

Other Club, The A dining club founded in 1911 by Sir Winston Churchill and F. E. Smith (Lord Birkenhead); it was said to be so called because they were not wanted at an existing fraternity known as *The Club*.

OTT OVER THE TOP. In the early 1980s a TV comedy show, which was considered outrageous, was entitled *O.T.T.* Thereafter the abbreviation became more popular than the full phrase in many informal contexts. For example, a particularly impassioned political speech, or a person who openly insults another or dresses in very bright colours, might be described as OTT.

Ottawa. Ottawa agreements The protectionist measures adopted at the Imperial Economic Conference in Ottawa (21 July–20 August 1932) at the height of the GREAT DEPRESSION. A series of bilateral agreements established a system of IMPERIAL PREFERENCE, by which the UK and her dominions and colonies exchanged tariff preferences to promote trade within the empire and exclude certain classes of foreign goods.

Ottawa spy ring An espionage network exposed in 1945 after the defection of a Soviet diplomat, Igor Gouzenko, from the Soviet Legation in Ottawa. Gouzenko, a GRU agent posing as a cipher clerk, had considerable difficulty in persuading the Canadian authorities to take him seriously because of their reluctance to embarrass their Soviet ally. A clumsy burglary at Gouzenko's apartment by the GRU finally persuaded the Canadian police to take him into custody. The documents handed over by Gouzenko revealed Soviet penetration of the Allied atom bomb programme and led to the immediate arrest of the British communist scientist Alan Nunn May and ultimately to the exposure of Klaus Fuchs and the Rosenbergs in America five years later. *See* NUNN MAY AFFAIR; ROSENBERG SPY CASE.

our. Our Gang The collective name of a group of child actors who appeared in several of the slapstick silent comedies made by Hal Roach in the 1920s. The team, with frequent changes of personnel, survived until the 1940s.

Our Ginny Nickname of the British tennis player Virginia Wade (1945–). Her victory in the women's singles championship in 1977, the year of Wimbledon's centenary and of Elizabeth II's silver jubilee, ensured her place in the affections of the nation.

Our Gracie Nickname of the British popular entertainer Gracie Fields (Dame Grace Stansfield; 1898–1979). Enormously popular in the 1930s, she starred in such films as *Sally in our Alley* (1931), *Sing As We Go* (1934), and *Keep Smiling* (1938). Of working-class origins herself, having started her working life as an employee in a cotton mill, she always sought to retain her image as the 'Lassie from Lancashire'. At the start of World War II she achieved great success with her song 'Wish Me Luck As You Wave Me Goodbye'; however, her subsequent departure to America with her Italian-born husband, Montie Banks, who became an undesirable alien when Italy came into the war, was widely regarded as an act of betrayal. *See also* FORCES' SWEETHEART.

Our Lady of Ballinspittle A statue of the Virgin Mary in the Irish village of Ballinspittle, near Cork, credited with miraculous powers of movement and gesture. On 22 July 1985, seven girls of the Daly and O'Mahony families were praying at the shrine when the statue – a life-sized concrete effigy weighing about half a ton – appeared to rock violently from side to side. After further reports of movements, visions, voices, and healings, crowds began to gather and an almost continuous vigil began, lasting the rest of the summer. To accommodate the daily influx of pilgrims, a stadium was built seating 7000 people. The events at Ballinspittle soon gained international publicity, much of it derisive. A variety of explanations was offered, most plausibly that the 'movements' were a hallucination produced by prolonged staring at the halo of electric lightbulbs above the Virgin's head. In 1987 it was estimated that half a million people have visited the shrine.

Our Lady of Fatima Apparitions of the Virgin Mary that appeared to three peasant children in the Portuguese hill town of Fatima in 1917. On 13 May, Lucia Santos (10) and her cousins Francesco (9) and Jacintha (7) reported meeting a 'shining lady' while out on the hills. The visitations recurred at monthly intervals and were accompanied by a number of solemn messages to mankind. By the time of the last appearance, on 13 October, a crowd of some 30,000 had gathered, many of whom reported strange lights in the sky and other unusual phenomena. The Catholic hierarchy was initially hostile, but showed the first signs of recognizing the visions in 1927, when a national pilgrimage was organized. A year later work began on a vast basilica at the scene of the apparitions; by the time this was completed, in 1953, Fatima had established itself as one of the great pilgrimage centres of the world.

Of the original witnesses only Lucia survived childhood, becoming a Carmelite nun and living into the 1980s. In her middle age she produced a full account of the messages received from the Virgin, but nothing was made public except a pious injunction to penance, recitation of the rosary, and devotion to the Immaculate Heart of Mary. The rest was placed under seal until the 1960s, when a decision was taken to postpone any further disclosures indefinitely. This reticence has inspired the usual crop of conspiracy theories, alleging that the so-called 'Secret of Fatima' concerns the date of the end of the world, the identity of the Antichrist, or details of some mysterious crime involving the Church leadership.

Our Lady of Knock An apparition of the Virgin Mary, accompanied by St Joseph and St John, that was reported to have been seen on the gable of the Catholic church in Knock, Co Mayo, Ireland. Although this vision occurred in 1879, Knock did not become an important centre for pilgrims until the 20th century. The original appearance was said to have preceded a number of miraculous cures. A new church, to accommodate 7500 people, was opened on the site in 1974, and five years later the Pope visited the church, during the first visit of any pope to Ireland. In 1986 a new international airport was opened nearby at Charlestown, to assist in bringing to Ireland the one million pilgrims who wish to visit the site each year.

Our Marie *See* QUEEN OF THE HALLS.

out. outasight Slang for something that is very highly regarded. Originally an Americanism from JAZZ musicians and BEATNIKS of the 1950s, it was used by HIPPIES interchangeably with 'far out' in the late 1960s. It is now only heard in America among Black musicians.

out-of-body A psychic experience in which the person concerned has the distinct impression of being outside his or her body, often looking down at it from another part of the room. Such experiences have been reported by many people, often during hospital operations or in other life-threatening situations, although critics are inclined to dismiss such experiences to the side-effects of drugs.

out of order (1) British slang meaning not following the rules as laid down by social custom. It is an extension of the familiar expression meaning not working, broken down. (2) British drug-users' slang meaning intoxicated or stoned.

> Do yourself a favour and take a little time off from the booze. It is really out of order . . .
>
> *The Sun*, 6 April 1991.

out to lunch Temporarily disorientated, stupid, or functioning below one's best. The phrase implies that one's mind has taken a break and gone out to lunch, leaving one's body to function as best it can without it.

> The captain of the team said he'd been batting pretty well this season but his bowling was out-to-lunch – and unlikely to return until next season.

outro The opposite of *intro*, a colloquial shortened form of introduction. Both terms are used in the music and entertainment industries, to denote, respectively, the closing or opening bars of a song or piece of music.

Outward Bound Trust A training organization that aims to help people aged 14 and over to expand their horizons and realize their potential through a wide variety of challenging activities designed to develop teamwork, self-discipline, and self-awareness. The trust was formed in 1946, following the introduction in 1941 of a course for merchant navy cadets in Aberdovey in Wales, which was designed to equip them for the rigours of wartime service.

Oval Office The oval-shaped room, in the west office wing of the White House, used as the office of the US president. Overlooking the Rose Garden, it was built for President Theodore Roosevelt. The elliptic design was copied from the White House's 'Blue Room'. The president's famous Oval Office desk, made from timbers of *HMS Resolute*, was a gift in 1878 from Queen Victoria to President Rutherford B. Hayes. Each president adds personal touches: on the desktop of President John F. Kennedy was the coconut shell bearing his own carved 'SOS' that led to his rescue during World War II. *See also* THE BUCK STOPS HERE *under* BUCK.

Ovaltine The tradename of a milk drink containing concentrated barley malt, cocoa, eggs and vitamins, originally developed in 1904 by Dr George Wander at his laboratory in Berne, Switzerland, and launched under the name Ovomaltine. When, in 1909, a factory was opened in England to manufacture Ovomaltine, the name was abbreviated to Ovaltine, reputedly because a clerical error was made at the time the company applied to register the name. The **Ovaltiney Club**, launched on Radio Luxembourg in 1935, was an immediate success with children; by 1939 there were five million members. The Sunday night broadcasts, heralded by the famous jingle 'We are the Ovaltineys', were brought to a halt by the outbreak of World War II but resumed in 1946 and continued for a number of years.

over. overkill The state in which something is overdone, usually by using considerably more effort and materials than are needed. An extravagant advertising campaign can be said to involve overkill. The term originated in the Kennedy administration with reference to the nuclear arms race: military overkill is having enough nuclear 'megatonnage' to annihilate the same enemy many times. One nuclear submarine, for instance, has more destructive power than all weapons used in World War II.

> There is a limit. How many times do you have to hit a target with nuclear weapons?
>
> JOHN F. KENNEDY.

Overlord The codename given to the Allied operation for the invasion of NW Europe, which began on D DAY 1944.

over-paid, over-fed, over-sexed, and over here A much-repeated catchphrase of World War II, referring to the presence of US forces in the UK. In fact, relations between the US troops and their British hosts were generally good, although the relatively high pay of the Americans and their sometimes brash manner, coupled with the competition they provided in the marriage market (*see* GI BRIDE), led to some irritation. The catchphrase was popularized by the British entertainer Tommy Trinder (1909–89). Subsequently it was also heard in Australia, when US forces were stationed there during the VIETNAM WAR.

overseas blue A shade of blue-grey adopted by the RAF for uniforms worn by personnel during World War II.

overseas cap A small military cap of the type worn by members of the US army in World War I.

over the moon A cliché used to express extreme pleasure or delight, implying that an almost impossible dream has come true. It is a particular favourite with the tabloid press. Its repetitive overuse by football players and managers, who declare themselves 'over the moon' at every victory, is a running joke in the satirical magazine PRIVATE EYE (*see also* SICK AS A PARROT; ROBBED, WE WUZ). This is now the best-known context for the phrase, though perhaps not for long. It was reported in the *Sun* newspaper (6 March 1991) that David Eyre, a lecturer at Norton College, Sheffield, had started a course for young footballers to improve their communication skills. He is reputed to have told the *Sun*:

> There is no reason on earth why they can't talk to cameras without resorting to soccer-speak.

Jimmy Greaves, the well-known football commentator, reacted enthusiastically to this news:

> If the course had been around in my playing days, I'd have been over the moon.

over the top An expression denoting that something goes beyond what is required or customary, excessive. It originated in World War I, when soldiers fighting trench warfare were described as going over the top when they climbed out of the trenches to attack the enemy. *See also* OTT.

Ovra Italian Fascist secret political police established in 1927 by Arturo Bocchini, Mussolini's Chief of Security (1926–40). The actual meaning of the term *Ovra* is a mystery; it may have been coined by Mussolini as a deliberately meaningless term to inspire fear in his opponents. The organization was used to spy on both anti-Fascist opponents and on many of the dictator's supporters, employed over 900 informers during its existence, and made frequent use of torture to terrorize its victims. Its activities, however, were never on the same scale as its German counterpart, the GESTAPO.

> To govern you need only two things, policemen, and bands playing in the streets.
>
> MUSSOLINI, on governing the Italians.

Owen gun A type of sub-machine-gun used by Australian forces in World War II. It was named after its inventor, Evelyn

Ernest Owen (1914–49), of Wollongong, New South Wales.

own goal In football, accidentally kicking the ball into one's own goal, thus scoring for one's opponents. This usage has broadened to include any event in which one accidentally does something that benefits one's enemies and is therefore to one's own detriment. In some cases there may not even be an enemy to benefit:

> It could be said that the Aids pandemic is a classic own-goal scored by the human race against itself.
> THE PRINCESS ROYAL; January 1988.

The expression has been further extended, especially by the British police, to include an act of suicide. This sense is thought to have originated with the British forces in Northern Ireland, who use it to describe the fate of a terrorist who blows himself up with his own bomb.

Oxbridge Colloquial term used to describe matters relating to both *Ox*ford and Cam*bridge* Universities. *See also* IVY LEAGUE.

Oxfam A charitable organization that aims to provide famine relief and other forms of aid, both emergency and long-term, wherever it is needed. Originally known as the Oxford Committee for Famine Relief (the truncated title was not officially adopted until 1965), it was founded in Oxford in 1942 in direct response to the plight of the starving civilian population of Greece during the German occupation of World War II.

Oxford US Black slang for a Black person whose skin colour is very dark; it is derived from *Oxford* shoe polish.

Oxford bags Very wide-bottomed flannel trousers first fashionable among Oxford undergraduates in the 1920s.

Oxford Group The name first adopted by the followers of US evangelist Frank Buchman (1878–1961), who had a considerable following at Oxford University in the 1920s. The group was evangelical in character and also became concerned with social, industrial, and international questions. It later developed into the MORAL REARMAMENT movement.

oxygen of publicity Glamour conferred on an organization or activity that is illegal, dangerous, or unacceptable as a result of being given undue publicity by the media. Margaret Thatcher is credited with having coined the phrase in 1985 in protest against the publicity given to terrorists, particularly the IRA.

Oz Colloquial name for Australia, used mainly by Australians.

Oz trial The trial (1971) of the editors of *Oz* magazine on charges including "conspiracy to corrupt the morals of liege subjects of Her Majesty the Queen by raising in their minds inordinate and lustful desires". The magazine – a heady mixture of satire, erotica, PSYCHEDELIC ART, and drug-related material – had been founded in Australia by Richard Neville, who brought it to London in 1966. Motivated principally by idleness and a lack of ideas, the editors turned the April 1970 issue over to their younger readers to write and edit for themselves: the result was the notorious 'Schoolkids Oz'. The involvement of legal minors gave the authorities the perfect excuse for action against the magazine. Articles cited by the prosecution included a piece on oral sex (such as might now appear in almost any women's magazine), a cartoon of RUPERT BEAR masturbating, and another showing a cane-wielding teacher with a visible erection. The trial, held at the Old Bailey, became a theatrical confrontation – greatly relished by both sides – between the HIPPIE underground and the guardians of traditional morality. The accused – Neville, Felix Dennis, and Jim Anderson – went for maximum publicity, posing in gymslips for the press and in the nude for a painting by David Hockney. Their supporters led a procession of chickens through the City of London (elephants having proved too expensive). Despite the evident hostility of the judge, the defendants were acquitted on the main charge (which carried a maximum life sentence). They were, however, found guilty on the two lesser counts of obscenity and sending indecent matter through the post. The judge's decision to gaol the defendants pending psychological reports was widely commented on, as were the short haircuts gleefully imposed by prison officers. Three weeks later prison terms of between 9 and 15 months were handed down, together with deportation orders on Neville and Anderson (who were Australians). When the case went to the Court of Appeal, only the minor charge of sending indecent matter through the post was upheld and the editors were released. The *Oz* trial is said to have provoked more letters to *The Times* than the SUEZ CRISIS.

Wizard of Oz *See under* WIZARD.

ozone. **ozone friendly** *See* -FRIENDLY.

ozone layer A region of the Earth's upper atmosphere, 10–50 km (6–30 miles) above the ground, in which the gas ozone (triatomic oxygen; O_3) forms in greatest concentration.

Ozone molecules themselves absorb the part of the Sun's ultraviolet radiation that is dangerous to life on Earth; the ozone layer is therefore an essential attribute of the planet. However, in recent years there has been widespread concern that the ozone layer is being depleted. The main culprit has been identified as the fluorinated hydrocarbons (*see* CFC) used as driver gases in aerosol cans and as refrigerants. These exceptionally stable compounds diffuse into the upper atmosphere, where they enter into photochemical reactions with the highly reactive ozone molecules, which break up and cease to function as ultraviolet absorbers. In the late 1980s holes were detected in the ozone layer over both the north and south poles. There is now an agreement that EC countries will cease to use harmful CFCs by the year 2000 and other countries have been urged to make similar commitments.

ozone sickness A condition caused by inhaling the poisonous gas ozone, characterized by headaches, drowsiness, chest pains, and inflammation. In the late 1970s, it was realized that ozone sickness was a hazard to the crews of high-flying aircraft because of ozone in the atmosphere seeping into the cabin.

Ozzie and Harriet US slang for the archetypal respectable middle-aged middle-class married couple epitomized by a TV show of that name.

P

pacemaker A device that provides electrical stimulation of the heart and so helps to correct an abnormal heart beat. The first internal pacemaker was designed in 1957; by the 1960s fully implantable units were available. These are inserted under the skin of the chest wall and connect to an electrode positioned on the surface of the left ventricle or inner wall of the right ventricle.

pacification The process, usually a military operation, of subduing or eliminating enemy or terrorist activity in an area by rendering the area inhospitable or unusable. Unlike **peacekeeping**, in which a military presence serves to enforce a truce, pacification is carried out during a time of hostilities in order to win peace and typically involves securing the cooperation of the local population or removing them from the area. Buildings, food supplies, crops, animals, and ground cover that could offer support or protection to the enemy may be destroyed. During the VIETNAM WAR US forces engaged in a policy of pacification to lower the morale of the VIET CONG soldiers and take rural areas from their control.

pack. package A collection or composite of various items or elements presented as or forming a complete unit. This usage derived from the idea of a parcel or package containing in one wrapping a number of different items; it comes from the notion that each component is an essential part of the whole. A **package deal** contains a number of conditions that must be accepted or rejected in their entirety; a **package holiday** includes all travel and accommodation arrangements in the overall price. In computer terminology a **package program** comprises all the programs and documentation necessary for a particular set of applications.

pack up your troubles in your old kit-bag The opening line of one of the most memorable choruses of World War I. It was written by George Asaf and composed by Felix Powell in 1915.

Pack up your troubles in your old kit-bag,
And smile, smile, smile.
While you've a lucifer to light your fag,
Smile, boys, that's the style, etc.

Pac-Man defence A business tactic undertaken to defeat an unwelcome takeover bid by making attempts to buy up the bidder. It derives from *Pac-Man*, an early popular computer game in which a rudimentary representation of a head tries to devour its enemies or predators by swallowing up 'power points'.

Pact of Steel A formal alliance between Germany and Italy, concluded in May 1939, which committed Italy to support Germany in the event of war. Mussolini coined the term 'pact of steel' after wisely abandoning his first choice, 'pact of blood'. The pact emerged from the closer ties between Italy and Germany, known as the Rome–Berlin AXIS. The Axis developed after Italy's invasion of Abyssinia in 1936 had made clear that Mussolini had only contempt for the LEAGUE OF NATIONS, whose authority both Hitler and Mussolini openly flouted until the outbreak of World War II.

pad Slang for a home. In the 17th century a pad was a sleeping mat, consisting of straw or rags, used by travellers. In America in the 1930s and 1940s, a pad was the couch in an opium den, or the place itself, in which illegal drugs were taken. This usage was extended by the BEATNIKS in the 1950s in America to include any room or home, a sense taken up by the HIPPIES in the 1960s and 1970s. It now sounds rather dated and would only be used self-consciously.

pad of galloping snap-shots Jaunty US Black slang for a cinema, first heard in the 1940s.

pad of stickers US Black slang for a hospital, first heard in the 1940s.

pad of stiffs US Black slang for a funeral parlour, first heard in the 1940s.

paddy wagon Slang for a police vehicle, usually a secure van of the type also known as a 'black Maria', although it can be used of a squad car. 'Paddy', a slang name for an Irishman, refers to the many Irish policemen in New York and the New England area, in which the term originated at the end of the last century. Its usage spread to Australia and the UK at the beginning of the 20th century.

paedophile A person who is sexually attracted to children. The 1980s saw heightened public awareness of its two largest manifestations: sexual abuse of children and the commercial distribution of child pornography. *See also* CHILD ABUSE.

page. **pager** *See* BLEEPER.

page-three girl A female model who poses topless, extremely scantily dressed, or nude, usually for newspaper photographs. The UK tabloid papers, especially the *Sun*, have traditionally reserved a slot on the third page of their papers for such a photograph. *See also* PIN-UP GIRL.

page-turner A particularly exciting or enthralling book. The inference is that the reader will want to turn the pages eagerly, reading the whole book at a single sitting. The expression is used by the promotional people involved in book publishing.

paintballing An adult game in which the members of two opposing teams try to hit each other with paint pellets fired from devices resembling guns. Points are gained by scoring hits and the winning team is the one that succeeds in capturing the other's flag. Before it became a sport, paintballing was used as a training exercise by the Canadian Mounted Police; it was then used as a management training technique by US and later British business firms. It has its origins in the practice of marking cattle in the American Mid-West by shooting pellets of paint at them from pistols powered by carbon dioxide.

pair bond A monogamous union or relationship existing between a male and a female animal of the same species. **Pair bonding** is the formation of this type of exclusive bond or the courtship and mating behaviour involved in establishing and reinforcing it. The phenomenon is relatively uncommon in the animal kingdom, a notable exception being birds, many of which form pair bonds that last throughout the mating season and often continue over a lifetime.

Paisleyite A supporter of the Rev. Ian Paisley (1926–), Presbyterian minister, Democratic Unionist MP, and militant leader of the Protestants in Northern Ireland. From the 1960s to the 1980s he presented the extreme Protestant stance, denouncing all efforts to draw together Catholics and Protestants and opposing any form of union with the Republic of Ireland. In the 1960s and 1970s the religious and political doctrines of Paisley and his followers, often referred to as **Paisleyism**, attained an almost cult status.

Pakistan The name of this state, which was formed in 1947, was coined by Chaudrie Rahmat Ali in 1933 to represent the units that should be included when the time came: P – Punjab; A – Afghan border states; K – Kashmir; S – Sind; Tan – Baluchistan.

Paki (1) British slang for a Pakistani. It has been in use since the 1960s and is often used pejoratively as a racist term of abuse. It is also applied to small supermarkets run by Pakistani families (or by people of other Asian nationalities), which stay open for long hours; in this context the use is merely descriptive, *e.g.* 'I'll just run round to the Paki to get some sugar, we've run out.' (2) British drug-users' slang for the black hashish from Pakistan, often known as **Paki black**. It is not particularly strong and has often been adulterated with other substances.

Paki bashing British slang term for the victimization and brutal attacking of Pakistanis and other Asian peoples by White racist youths. This began in the late 1960s and still occurs. There has been some criticism of the police, who in some cases have been accused of turning a blind eye to it.

pal. **dear old pals** A contemptuous catcall sometimes heard at boxing matches when it appears that the two opponents are not fighting with the aggression that the audience have paid to see. It was derived from the popular song 'Dear Old Pals, Jolly Old Pals'.

palimony US slang for alimony awarded in a court case involving an unmarried couple who break up after living together, usually in a long-term relationship. The word was coined during a 1979 case involving Hollywood star Lee Marvin; it is a combination of *pal* (*i.e.* friend) and *alimony*.

Palais Rose The first of many international conferences after World War II was held in the rose-decorated chamber of a Parisian mansion. The monotonous reiteration by the Soviet delegate of "No" to every suggestion put forward gave rise to the phrase 'another palais rose' to describe an abortive conference.

palm. Palm Beach Tradename for a lightweight fabric used in men's and women's summer suits, often with a striped design. It is named after Palm Beach, Florida, an exclusive tourist resort noted for its wealthy clientele. The famous palm trees appeared at the end of the last century, following the wreck of a ship with a cargo of coconuts.

Palme d'Or (Fr. Golden Palm) The major prize (called the Grand Prix until 1975) at the annual CANNES FILM FESTIVAL, which is awarded for the best film overall.

Palomares A nuclear accident that occurred on 17 January 1966, when four 20-megaton hydrogen bombs were lost from a US bomber, which collided while refuelling over the Spanish Mediterranean coast. Three of the bombs fell on land, close to the village of Palomares, two of them rupturing and spewing out radioactive plutonium. The fourth fell into the sea and was only located after a massive search operation had been mounted. Over 1000 tons of contaminated topsoil and vegetation were removed for disposal in America.

Panama Canal The canal that connects the Atlantic and Pacific oceans through the narrow isthmus of Panama, constructed by America during the period 1904–14. Vessels are towed through the 12 locks of the 50-mile (80 km) canal by locomotives on a cog railway; it takes an average of 28 hours to pass from one side to the other. Proposals for the canal had been in existence since the time of the great explorations in the 16th century, but it was not until the late 19th century that engineering expertise enabled construction to proceed. An attempt to build a sea-level canal began in 1880 by the French Panama Canal Company, founded by Ferdinand de Lesseps, who had supervised the construction of the Suez Canal. This was abandoned in 1891 after a financial scandal destroyed the consortium. In 1902 the Americans approved the Panama route for their own canal project; the Hay-Bunau-Vanilla treaty of November 1903, with the new Republic of Panama, provided for a US-controlled ten-mile-wide canal zone. Control over this zone eventually passed to Panama in 1979, but America retains responsibility for the management and defence of the canal itself until 1999. The privations suffered by the constructors of the canal, caused by malaria-carrying mosquitos, poor sanitary conditions, and consequently much disease, have passed into legend.

panda car A UK police patrol car of the 1960s. The name derives from the white and black paintwork used on the vehicles at this time, reminiscent of the markings of the giant panda.

Pangaea or **Pangea** The single supercontinent comprising all the Earth's land mass, first postulated by the German meteorologist, Alfred Wegener (1880–1930), in 1912. He argued that the present continents originated from the break-up of this supercontinent and cited their present shapes and distribution as evidence of this process. Wegener's hypothesis, initially derided by other scientists, is now accepted as the basis of PLATE TECTONICS. Pangaea is thought to have formed by coalescence of the Earth's crustal plates about 240 million years ago and to have broken up perhaps 50 to 100 million years later to form the southern supercontinent Gondwanaland and the northern supercontinent Laurasia, separated by the Tethys sea. These supercontinents in turn divided to produce the present continental land masses of the southern and northern hemispheres, respectively.

panic button The button pressed by test pilots to bring about an emergency ejection by parachute in the event of impending danger. In general language to **press the panic button** means to react, often to over-react, to a dangerous or unpredictable situation in a hysterical or hasty way. *See also* CHICKEN SWITCH.

pansy A male homosexual. This flower name was first used in this context in the 1920s. It is still used by older people but it has largely been superseded by GAY.

pants. pantsuit or **pants suit** A woman's or girl's suit of matching jacket and trousers. Pantsuits, more commonly called **trouser suits** in the UK, became fashionable in the mid-1960s. Smart and well-tailored, they helped to establish trousers as an acceptable alternative to a skirt or dress for women of all ages.

pantyhose or **pantihose** A combination of *pants* and *hose*, (*i.e.* stockings), invented in the early 1960s. Sales rocketed with the advent of the miniskirt in the latter half of the decade. Towards the end of the 1980s stockings made something of a comeback but as a glamour item rather than an everyday article of clothing. In the UK pantyhose are usually called **tights**.

paparazzo (Ital.) A freelance photographer who aggressively and intrusively pursues famous people in order to photograph them (or attempt to) wherever they go. Originating in Italy, where street photographers were commonly seen in pursuit of film celebrities, the term became current in the English-speaking world in the late 1960s, with the spread of this practice to other countries: the unfortunate targets now include not only film stars but any newsworthy victims. The word is usually used in the plural, **paparazzi**, as such pests tend to hunt in packs. The word came from the surname of such a photographer in Federico Fellini's 1959 film *La Dolce Vita*.

paper. All I know is what I read in the papers A catchphrase popularized by Will Rogers in 1926 and since heard not only in America, but also in the UK. In its original sense, it implies that the ordinary man in the street relies on the newspapers for all his information, which he expects to be true. It is now more often used as a defence for one's own views, on the grounds that they are so widely shared that they can be read in the newspapers.

paper tiger A person or object that appears to be both threatening and powerful but is neither; a paper tiger is, in fact, weak and powerless. The phrase is a translation of the Chinese *tsuh lao fu*, an expression made popular by Mao Tse-tung (1893–1976) in the mid-1940s, particularly to describe reactionaries.

Pap test The Papanicolaou smear test: a diagnostic test used in the early detection of cancer, especially cervical cancer. Two samples are taken – one of cells scraped from the wall of the cervix, the other of vaginal secretions; the latter may indicate malignancy of the endometrium or ovaries as well as the cervix. A smear of the flaked-off tissue cells is fixed in alcohol and examined under a microscope for signs of malignant change. The test can also detect cancerous changes in cell samples taken from the respiratory, digestive, and genitourinary tracts. The technique is named after the US physician, George N. Papanicolaou (1883–1962), who first recognized the diagnostic importance of changes in shed tissue cells.

para-. paracetamol The generic name in the UK for *para-acetylaminophenol*, a drug with mild pain- and fever-relieving properties. Widely available without prescription, paracetamol is used in the same circumstances as aspirin for the relief of headaches, rheumatic pains, and cold and influenza symptoms. Unlike aspirin, it has no adverse side effects on the stomach, but overdosage can cause serious liver damage. The American name is *acetaminophen*.

paragliding The sport, dating from the late 1960s, in which a person uses a wing-like parachute to glide from an aeroplane to a predetermined landing spot.

paramedic A health-care worker who supplements the work of doctors. It usually refers to trained personnel, such as nurses and medical technicians, who – acting under the direction of a doctor – perform routine assessments, administer injections, prepare diets, take X-rays, etc., and have direct responsibility for patient care. Used broadly, the term includes all who provide auxiliary clinical services, such as laboratory technicians, ambulance crews, and therapists.

paramilitary (1) Describing a semiofficial or secret organization run on military lines. The word was first used in the early 1970s for terrorist groups in Northern Ireland. A well-known US example was the BLACK PANTHER group, which came to the fore in the late 1960s. (2) Describing civil forces or organizations that legitimately support military forces.

Paraquat Tradename for a highly poisonous herbicide. A soluble yellow solid used in weedkillers, Paraquat is quick-acting but becomes inactive upon contact with the soil.

parasailing The sport in which a water-skier grasps the bar of a large kite or wears a parachute and is pulled by a speedboat until airborne. It was introduced in America in 1969; land versions (**parascending**) have been successfully developed using a car or other vehicle.

parcel bomb *See* LETTER BOMB.

Pardon me for living Retort to petty criticism that expresses the ultimate in humility with heavy irony.

Paris. Paris Club *See* GROUP OF TEN.

Paris Peace Conference The conference that took place in 1919–20 to arrange a peace settlement after World War I. Various treaties were concluded, the most famous being the VERSAILLES TREATY (28 June

1919) between the Allies and Germany. A series of other treaties were concluded to settle eastern Europe, the Soviet Union, and Turkey in the wake of the dissolution of the old Habsburg, Romanov, Hohenzollern, and Ottoman empires. Austria and Hungary were dismembered by the Treaty of St Germain and the Treaty of Trianon, respectively; the Bulgarian issue was settled by the Neuilly Treaty and the Turkish problems by the Treaty of Sevres. The Peace Conference also established the LEAGUE OF NATIONS to settle any remaining disputes or any that should arise in future.

Paris summit A superpower summit meeting between Dwight D. Eisenhower, Nikita Khrushchev, Harold Macmillan, and Charles de Gaulle, which was scheduled for 16 May 1960. All four leaders arrived in Paris, but the summit was abandoned at the last minute when Eisenhower refused to accede to Khrushchev's demand that he apologize for the U-2 incident.

Paris Treaty The treaty of 27 May 1952 between France, West Germany, Italy, Belgium, the Netherlands, and Luxembourg agreeing to the formation of the European Defence Community (EDC). Pacts were then agreed between NATO and the EDC and between the EDC and the UK. The purpose of the EDC was to incorporate West Germany into NATO, by means of a unified European military command, a formula devised by the French to enable German rearmament to become acceptable to French public opinion. After nearly two years of procrastination the French National Assembly refused to ratify the treaty, despite the efforts of the prime minister, Mèndes-France, and pressure from the Americans. Within a matter of months, however, a similar formula for Franco-German rapprochement, the Western European Union, was successfully adopted in its place.

parka A warm weatherproof thigh-length coat with a furry hood. It was originally an Eskimo garment made from caribou skin and seal fur, worn especially in Alaska and the Aleutian Islands (the name is Aleutian for 'skin'). The women's parkas had an extra hood, which could be used for wrapping a baby. In the 1930s the parka was adopted for skiing and winter sports, later passing into general outdoor use. It became an unlikely item of youth fashion in the 1960s, when the mods (*see* MODS AND ROCKERS) used it as a badge of identity.

park-and-ride A system, known as **park-ride** in America, enabling motorists, especially shoppers or employees, to leave their cars in designated areas on the outskirts of congested cities and to complete their journeys by bus. The idea originated in the mid-1960s in America, where suburban commuters drove to railway stations or other car parks and then transferred to public transport.

Parkinson's Law The business rule conceived by the British historian and author Cyril Northcote Parkinson (1909–), and described in his book with that title (1958), that work expands to fill the time available for its completion. One of the most often repeated of all 'laws' in the business world, it was only one of Parkinson's illuminatory and humorous views of commercial dealings.

> The rise in the total of those employed is governed by Parkinson's Law and would be much the same whether the volume of work was to increase, diminish or even disappear.
>
> *Parkinson's Law*, Ch. 1.

Parliamentary Commissioner *See* OMBUDSMAN.

parrot. sick as a parrot *See under* SICK.

party line (1) The official line, or policy, of a political party. To **toe the party line** is to follow or be coerced into following party policy. (2) A telephone line shared by two or more subscribers.

PASCAL A popular computer programming language named after the mathematician Blaise Pascal (1623–62) and devised by Niklaus Wirth of the Federal Institute of Technology, Zurich, in 1970. Because of its powerful, clear, and well-structured coding PASCAL has become the standard teaching language in computing science departments throughout the world.

Passchendaele A village in W Flanders, Belgium, the main objective of the final thrust of the Third Battle of Ypres (31 July–6 November 1917). The offensive to break out of the Ypres salient had progressed slowly throughout August and September, after the initial British advance had become bogged down, heavy rains turning the shell-cratered ground into liquid mud. On 30 October the Canadian Third and Fourth Divisions and British Fifty-Eighth and Sixty-Third Divisions, under Sir Douglas Haig, launched a bitter struggle with the Fifth and Eleventh Bavarian Divisions; on 6 November the Canadians succeeded in capturing the village, seven miles short of Ypres. British casualties were 380,000 and those of the Germans equally high.

pass. Pass Laws Legislation passed by the White South African government to regulate the movement of native Africans, by requiring them to carry documents authorizing their presence in restricted areas. Similar laws had been introduced in South Africa in the 18th century, obliging slaves to carry documents signed by their masters authorizing their absence from their master's premises. In the late 19th century passes were also used to regulate the movements of African workers at the Kimberley diamond mines; in the Transvaal similar laws were enacted to restrict the movement of rural Africans into urban areas, except as servants, to ensure an adequate supply of African labourers for White farmers. Under APARTHEID, after 1948, Pass Laws prevented rural Africans from visiting towns for longer than 72 hours without a special permit on pain of arrest and deportation. The number of those arrested for breaking these laws averaged 100,000 per annum, reaching a peak of 381,858 in 1976. The African National Congress (*see* ANC) organized periodic anti-Pass-Law campaigns throughout the 1950s and 1960s. In 1986 the South African government finally announced the scrapping of the hated laws as part of the movement towards the dismantling of apartheid.

They shall not pass! Famous rallying cry associated with Marshal Pétain during the fighting at VERDUN during World War I. In fact, it was uttered by his subordinate Robert Georges Nivelle. The phrase was revived during the SPANISH CIVIL WAR on the lips of the Spanish communist leader Dolores Ibarruri (1895–1989), better known as **La Pasionaria**.

passive smoking The inhalation of other people's cigarette, cigar, or pipe smoke. This became a recognized danger in the early 1970s; recent research shows that a nonsmoking worker in an office of smokers can inhale the equivalent of several cigarettes each day. Many communities have passed laws banning smoking in public places.

past. The past is a foreign country: they do things differently there The opening words of *The Go-Between* (1953), a novel by L. P. Hartley (1895–1972), which have come to rank among the best-known of all first sentences.

Patriot missile *See* SMART WEAPONS.

patsy A person who is easily deceived or exploited. The derivation of the word is uncertain but it has been suggested that it may have connections with the Italian *pazzo*, a fool. Originating in America, it became popular in the UK in the 1980s.

Pattie British student slang of the 1980s for a first class degree. It is a rhyming allusion to the US newspaper heiress Pattie Hearst (1954–), whose abduction by left-wing guerrillas and subsequent trial for complicity in their crimes was a *cause célèbre* in 1974–75. Her captors, a microscopic splinter-group styling themselves the Symbionese Liberation Army, kept her in a locked cupboard and subjected her to brutal and humiliating treatment. When revolutionary statements were issued in her name, coercion was naturally assumed. Doubts arose, however, when she was filmed taking an apparently active role in the armed robbery of a San Francisco bank. After several months on the run with the gang she was arrested by the FBI and charged with robbery and firearms offences. Her plea, that she had been brainwashed by her captors, was rejected and she received a seven-year sentence. The case, which went through several appeals, divided public opinion; it was argued on one side that the state was prolonging the ordeal of an innocent girl and on the other that any leniency would be an unwarranted concession to her youth, sex, and background. In 1979 she was released as a result of the intervention of President Carter. See STOCKHOLM SYNDROME.

Pauli exclusion principle A principle in physics first formulated by the Austrian–Swiss physicist Wolfgang Pauli (1900–58) in 1924. It states that, in an atom or other system, no two electrons (or similar identical particles) can have the same set of quantum numbers. The principle is one of the fundamental tenets of QUANTUM THEORY and, at the time, helped to explain the structure of the atom.

pavlova A meringue cake covered with fruit and whipped cream. It was named after Anna Matveyevna Pavlova (1881–1931), the Russian-born dancer considered by many to be the greatest ballerina of all time. She settled in the UK after making her London and New York debuts (1910), featuring her famous Dying Swan solo. The pavlova cake, like its namesake, is known for its lightness and graceful appearance. The distinction of inventing and naming the sweet is claimed by both Australia and New Zealand, where the name is often shortened to **pav**.

Pavlov's dog The subject of experiments by the Russian physiologist Ivan Petrovich Pavlov (1849–1936) into animal behaviour, which resulted in his discovery of conditioned reflexes. Pavlov's early research on dogs, concentrating on the physiology of digestion, had led to his discovery that the taste of food stimulates the release of gastric juices in the stomach. During his experiments he also noticed the phenomenon of 'psychic' salivation, in which a dog would salivate when confronted by a stimulus that customarily preceded feeding, *e.g.* the sight of the animal's food dish. He called this salivation response to a stimulus associated with food the conditioned reflex. Dogs were Pavlov's favoured subjects but he also used monkeys and mice, demonstrating that the conditioned reflex occurs in all animals, including humans, and can be activated by practically any environmental factor. His work is mainly important for its contribution to research on learning processes; in fact behavioural psychologists have claimed that all human behaviour is due to conditioning and reinforcement, although Pavlov himself rejected such an extreme interpretation of his work.

pay. PAYE Pay As You Earn. A method of collecting income tax in the UK introduced in 1944. The government then transferred the burden of collecting the tax to the taxpayer's employer. Each week or each month the employer has to deduct tax from its employees' wages or salaries and remit the proceeds to the Collector of Taxes. This also involves the employer in calculating the amount of tax to be deducted. From the gross pay, the employer deducts the free pay (given by a code number provided by the Inspector of Taxes), to obtain the taxable pay. The employer then uses the correct PAYE Tax Tables to arrive at the tax that has to be deducted in that week or month from the taxable pay. Large companies have to employ wages clerks at their own expense to provide this service for the government.

payload The goods or passengers carried in a ship, aircraft, etc., that pay for their carriage, as opposed to the crew and equipment, etc.

payola Slang for bribery. Consisting of the word 'pay' with the Spanish suffix -*ola*, meaning big or outrageous, it is mainly used in America and is especially related to the practice of making large payments to disc jockeys in order to secure extensive promotional air-time for one's records.

payphone A telephone provided for public use that requires a payment by the user. In the UK, where the term became current in the 1970s (it was originally US, dating back to the 1930s), payment may be made by inserting cash or a PHONECARD into the machine (in some telephones a credit card may be used). Alternatively, the caller may instruct the operator to reverse the charges (a transfer charge call) so that the receiver of the call pays for it on his or her telephone bill.

pazazz *See* PIZAZZ.

PBAB Please Bring A Bottle. A request appearing on invitations to bottle parties, etc. The less common **BYOG** translates as Bring Your Own Grog.

PBS Public Broadcasting Service. The US network of noncommercial television stations that comprise about a quarter of America's 1400 television stations. The system was established in 1967 when the US Congress created and funded an independent nonprofitmaking body, the Corporation for Public Broadcasting (CPB). It decides policy and gives grants to stations to produce programmes that PBS schedules and distributes. PBS also buys programmes from independent producers. The nonprofitmaking stations are funded primarily by viewer contributions raised during TELETHONS. In September 1990, PBS drew a record audience for its highly praised five-part documentary *The Civil War*, with an estimated 32% of the US population seeing some part of it. Most of the BBC's major productions shown in America have been on PBS, often as *Masterpiece Theatre*. CPB also oversees National Public Radio (NPR), which was created in 1971.

PC *See* PERSONAL COMPUTER.

PCB Polychlorinated Biphenyl. A type of organic chemical containing chlorine, first developed in the 1930s. PCBs are extremely stable compounds that have particular properties making them suitable for use as lubricants, dielectrics, plasticizers, etc. They were used extensively until the 1970s, when it became clear that they were damaging the environment. Because of their stability, they accumulated in soil and water and entered the food chain. They are extremely toxic, even in low concentrations, causing liver damage in humans. They may also be carcinogenic. In the 1970s restrictions were placed on their manufacture and use in many countries.

PCP Tradename for the drug phencyclidine (or phencyclohexylpiperidine), originally used in veterinary medicine, known as ANGEL DUST or HOG when used illegally.

peace. Peace Ballot A national ballot (27 June 1935) organized by the National Declaration Committee under the chairmanship of Lord Cecil (closely linked with the League of Nations Union), on certain questions of peace and disarmament. Over 11.5 million votes were in favour of adherence to the League of Nations and over 10 million voted for a reduction in armaments. The ballot was misinterpreted by the AXIS powers as a sign of British weakness.

Peace Corps An organization established by Executive Order of President John F. Kennedy in March 1961 and ratified by Congress in the Peace Corps Act (September 1961). The aim of the Peace Corps is to provide skilled manpower to aid DEVELOPING COUNTRIES (the first project, announced on 21 April, required engineers to help in road construction in Tanganikya) and to promote mutual understanding between the developed and developing world. Peace Corps volunteers, who work for subsistence wages, usually enter into a two-year contract of service and receive a brief training session before being sent abroad. About half the volunteers are teachers; the remainder are a mixture of agricultural experts, health workers, engineers, and those involved in community development projects.

peace dividend A fund of money that could be made available to international governments following the reduction in expenditure on weapons and defence after the end of the COLD WAR. The concept received a set-back on the outbreak of the GULF WAR (1991), although this had nothing to do with the Cold War.

peace in our time The unfortunate phrase used by Prime Minister Neville Chamberlain, on 30 September 1938, on returning from meeting Hitler in MUNICH. The optimism was shortlived. In less than a year Hitler had gone back on his assurances and the UK and Germany were at war. The words, which come from the versicle in Morning Prayer, 'Give peace in our time, O Lord', are sometimes used as a cynical rejoinder to any statement of undue optimism.

peacekeeping *See* PACIFICATION.

Peace Pledge Union A body pledged to renounce war, organized by Canon Dick Sheppard of St Martin-in-the-Fields in 1936.

peace sign A sign made with the palm of the hand facing outwards and the first two fingers upraised in the shape of a V, used as an expression of peace or desire for peace. Formerly, this was the V FOR VICTORY sign popularized by Winston Churchill. Its current use, dating from about 1969, derives from the symbol of the Campaign for Nuclear Disarmament (*see* CND) devised for the first BAN THE BOMB protest march at Aldermaston in 1958. This consists of a vertical line intersected by an upside-down V enclosed in a circle, the lines representing the semaphore signals for the letters N and D.

peace studies An educational course or programme concerning the role and legal status of peace in international relations. Such studies were introduced in the early 1950s and became a permanent part of courses in US colleges 20 years later.

peach melba A dessert consisting of half a cooked peach containing vanilla ice cream with a clear raspberry sauce (Melba sauce) poured over it. It is named after the Australian soprano Dame Nellie Melba (1861–1931). *See also* MELBA TOAST.

Peanuts A popular comic strip first created by the US cartoonist Charles M. Schultz in 1950. *Peanuts* features the exploits of the little round-headed boy CHARLIE BROWN, his pet beagle Snoopy (perhaps the world's most popular cartoon dog), and Snoopy's confidant Woodstock (a small bird). Their friends – including loud-mouthed Lucy, insecure Linus, Schroeder the pianist, and the tomboy Peppermint Patty – are all members of Charlie Brown's baseball team.

pearl. Pearl Harbor The Japanese surprise attack on the US Pacific Fleet at the Pearl Harbor naval base on the island of Oahu, Hawaii, on Sunday 7 December 1941, which brought America into World

War II. For over two hours 350 Japanese carrier-borne aircraft strafed, bombed, and torpedoed the US fleet at anchor, sinking or seriously damaging seven battleships and 16 other vessels; large numbers of aircraft on nearby airbases were also destroyed on the ground. America declared war on Japan on 9 December and on Germany and Italy on 11 December. The local military commanders' failure to act on advance reports of Japanese fleet, aircraft, and submarine movements was severely criticized by a subsequent government enquiry. Ever since then in US slang a person faced with a catastrophic turn of events is sometimes said to be 'meeting his Pearl Harbor'.

pearlies The coster 'kings', 'queens', 'princes', and 'princesses' of the London boroughs, so named from their glittering attire studded with innumerable pearl buttons. Since the FESTIVAL OF BRITAIN (1951), there has been a Pearly King of London. Originally elected by the street-traders of London to safeguard their rights from interlopers and bullies, they now devote their efforts to collecting and working for charities.

peck. peckerwood US Black slang for a woodpecker, also commonly used for poor White people. Black people adopted the blackbird as their own symbolic bird; the woodpecker was chosen to represent Whites, who 'peck' for a living. The existence of poor Whites (also called **White trash**), who lead even less successful lives than many oppressed Blacks, has always been an embarrassment to White supremacists in America; in recent years they have slowly been recognized as a poverty-stricken stratum of modern US society that has been long ignored.

pecking A style of JAZZ music of the 1950s in which such performers as Art Tatum played in a fast abbreviated manner. It is also a style of JITTERBUG popular in the 1930s, first seen at the COTTON CLUB.

pedalo A small pleasure boat driven by paddles, which are operated by foot-pedals. A common sight at the beach and on lakes from the 1920s pedalos have in recent years been largely superseded by the more exciting and athletic sports of water-skiing, windsurfing, and parascending (*see* PARAGLIDING).

pedal pushers Calf-length trousers worn by women and girls, originally for cycling. *See also* CLAM DIGGERS.

peel me a grape *See under* GRAPE.

Pegasus The winged horse on which Bellerophon rode against the Chimaera. In World War II, the horse, with Bellerophon on his back, in pale blue on a maroon ground, was adopted as the insignia of all British airborne troops.

Peking. Peking Man (*Sinanthropus pekinensis*) The name given to remains of a skull found near Peking in 1929, which in many respects showed resemblances to that of *Pithecanthropus erectus*; it is believed to be intermediate between Java and neanderthal man.

Pekingology or **Pekinology** The close observation of the politics and conduct of the Communist government of China, literally the study of Peking, the capital and seat of government of China. **Pekingologists**, who study and comment on Chinese affairs, are also known as 'China watchers'. The term, first used in the early 1960s, has largely fallen into disuse as the Wade-Giles transliteration *Peking* has been gradually superseded by the pinyin transliteration *Beijing*.

Pelé Popular name of the Brazilian footballer Edson Arantes do Nascimento (1940–), who is generally considered to have been the most widely admired footballer of the century. An inside forward, he played for Santos (1955–74), the New York Cosmos (1975–77), and Brazil, becoming a world star at the age of 17 when Brazil won the WORLD CUP. He scored over 1300 goals during his career.

Pelée, Mount A volcano on the island of Martinique in the Caribbean, which on 8 May 1902 erupted, causing the most severe volcanic disaster of the 20th century. It took only three minutes for the town of St Pierre to be devastated, with not a single building left standing. Of the population of 30,000 only two survived; one of them was a condemned prisoner who had ironically been protected by the robustness of his death cell.

pelican crossing A pedestrian crossing in the UK that is controlled by traffic lights, which the pedestrian operates by pressing a button. The crossing is marked with the black-and-white stripes of the uncontrolled **zebra crossing** or by two rows of metal studs. The name is a loose acronym taken from *pe*destrian *li*ght *con*trolled.

Penguin A publishing imprint founded in 1935 by Sir Allen Lane to issue the first paperback books in the UK. Lane believed that there was an unsatisfied demand for cheap editions of serious books and aimed to meet this market without sacrificing production standards. The first Penguins, all reprints of established fiction titles, sold for 6d each and proved an immediate success. Over the next decade the company expanded into most areas of general publishing, launching the topical Penguin Specials and the Pelican nonfiction series in 1937 and the Puffin children's books in 1941. Penguin dominated the market it had created to such an extent that, until the 1950s, 'Penguin' and 'paperbacks' were virtually synonymous in the UK. The company went public in 1961, following the runaway success of the unexpurgated edition of D. H. Lawrence's *Lady Chatterley's Lover*, which was legally published as a result of a famous obscenity trial (*see* LADY CHATTERLEY TRIAL). Lane is said to have become a millionaire overnight. The name Penguin was apparently suggested by a secretary and adopted because a highly effective penguin logo could be produced in black and white. Penguin Books Ltd, and several other publishers, are now owned by Pearson plc, a large conglomerate with banking, entertainment, and publishing interests. Penguin again became headline news in the late 1980s as a result of the Rushdie Affair (*see* FATWA).

penicillin The first of a whole range of antibiotic drugs that have saved millions of lives and eliminated an enormous amount of human suffering. That Sir Alexander Fleming (1881–1958) discovered penicillin is well-known and a firmly established item of modern folklore. What is perhaps less well known is the role of other scientists in revealing the true therapeutic value of the drug. Fleming's discovery came about by a curious accident. In 1928, working as a bacteriologist in St Mary's Hospital, London, he noticed that a dish of cultured staphylococcal bacteria had become contaminated by a mould, which had clearly destroyed the bacteria growing in its vicinity. He identified the mould as *Penicillium notatum* and demonstrated its effectiveness in killing a wide range of toxic bacteria in the test-tube by means of a metabolic product that he named 'penicillin'. From these tests, however, he concluded that penicillin (which he failed to isolate) would have little value as an antibacterial agent in living organisms. The publication of Fleming's discovery – which he himself regarded merely as a useful laboratory tool in preparing bacterial cultures – aroused little interest at the time.

It was not until 1940 that the Australian pathologist Howard Florey (1898–1968) and the German-born biochemist Ernst Chain (1906–79), working in Oxford in the search for an effective antibacterial drug, came across Fleming's paper and decided to test penicillin for this purpose. They eventually succeeded in isolating pencillin, which proved an immediate success in their first clinical trials (1941); however, they soon ran into problems with producing sufficient quantities of the drug for widespread clinical use. It was Florey and Chain who, by publicizing its enormous therapeutic potential in both the UK and America, succeeded in organizing large-scale production facilities; by 1943 penicillin was being used to save the lives of war casualties. Penicillin not only revolutionized the treatment of bacterial infections, the majority of which had hitherto relied mainly on skilled nursing care – usually with little success; it also paved the way for the isolation of a whole range of other antibiotics, enabling virtually all nonviral infectious diseases to become easily cured. When the results of pencillin treatment became widely known Fleming was hailed as a hero – he was knighted (1944) and shared the 1945 Nobel Prize (with Florey and Chain). Fleming's name will always be linked with penicillin: he was in the 1940s – and still widely is – regarded as the saviour of countless lives, while Florey and Chain, who were the first to understand the true significance of Fleming's discovery and who organized its manufacture, have been largely ignored.

penny share A security with a very low market value, although it is unlikely to be as low as one penny. Penny shares attract the small investor because a large number of shares can be bought for a small outlay and a rise in price of only a few pence can represent a large percentage profit. However, shares that are only worth a few pence are usually shares in unprofitable or near-bankrupt companies. Only if the company recovers, or if it is taken over on advantageous terms, is the investor likely to do well.

Pentagon A vast five-sided building erected in Washington, DC, to house government officials. It now houses the US Department of Defense and the word Pentagon is a synonym for the official US attitude in military matters.

Pentagonese A style of language characterized by euphemisms, circumlocution, and vagueness, frequently attributed to US politicians. It is intended to obscure rather than clarify the relevant facts.

Pentathlon An athletic contest of five events, usually the jump, javelin throw, 200-metre race, discus throw, and 1500-metre flat race. In the ancient OLYMPIC GAMES the contest consisted of running, jumping, throwing the discus and javelin, and wrestling.

people. Not many people know that A phrase made famous by the British actor Michael Caine (1933–) and always spoken by him in a cockney drawl. It is often used as a joke after the statement of a very well known fact. Michael Caine was connected with a book for charity called *Not a Lot of People Know That* (1984) and the phrase often appears in that form.

People's Budget The Budget introduced in April 1909 by David Lloyd George (1863–1941), so-called because it proposed to raise money for old-age pensions (and rearmament) by increasing the tax burden on the landed classes. Death duties were doubled, taxes on land and unearned income raised to unprecedented levels, and a new supertax levied on all income over £5000 p.a. The Budget provoked a violent outcry from Tory landowners, who denounced it as legalized robbery. Although its measures seem modest today, this was the first time that the Budget – previously an exercise in balancing the books and little else – had been used as a direct instrument of social policy.

The 1909 Budget also had important consequences for the balance of power between the two Houses of Parliament. In November the House of Lords, with its high inbuilt Tory majority, rejected the Budget. This had not happened for 250 years and was in clear breach of the unwritten convention that financial measures passed by the Commons should not be vetoed by the Lords. In January 1910 the Liberals went to the country seeking a popular mandate, not only for the Budget but also for the abolition of the Lords' right of veto (*see* VETO BILL). This **People v. Peers** election, as it became known, returned the Liberals to power and gave the Lords little choice but to pass the Lloyd George Budget, a year late, in April 1910. The interval represented some £5 million of lost revenue for the Treasury. This still did not resolve the constitutional crisis, as the Lords continued to block the Liberal measures curtailing their powers. It took a second general election (in December 1910) and a royal undertaking to end the stalemate, by creating enough Liberal peers to carry the bill, before the Lords accepted their defeat.

pep. PEP Personal Equity Plan. A UK government scheme introduced in 1989 to encourage private individuals to invest in UK companies. For a limited sum of money, dividends from the holdings are not subject to income tax if they are reinvested in the scheme and capital gains tax is not incurred on an investment if it has been held for at least one year.

pep pill A capsule or tablet containing a stimulant, usually a form of amphetamine, known in drug culture as **pep-em-ups**. The term arose in the 1940s for such mild stimulants as caffeine tablets; its use for amphetamines began in the 1960s. Other names used for these pep pills include **speed** and **uppers**.

Pepsi-Cola *See* COCA-COLA.

Pepsification The commercial exploitation by US firms of areas not previously commercialized. Introduced in the late 1980s, the concept originated with the introduction of FAST FOOD outlets in Moscow, following the relaxation of trading relations with the West under PERESTROIKA. The word is derived from Pepsi-Cola (*see* COCA-COLA).

Per ardua ad astra (Lat. Through difficulties to the stars) The motto of the RFC from 1913 and of the RAF from 1923.

Percy. point Percy at the porcelain To urinate. A euphemism from the comic strip *The Wonderful World of Barry McKenzie*, written by Barry Humphries, that appeared in the satirical magazine PRIVATE EYE in the 1970s. 'Percy' is a common personification for the penis; the porcelain is the lavatory bowl.

perestroika (Russ. restructuring) A policy, linked with GLASNOST, much publicized since 1986 when it became Mikhail Gorbachov's intention to introduce economic and political reform and allow greater freedom of expression, which included the publication of formerly banned books. Gorbachov became Communist Party leader in 1985 and president in

1988. Referring to the differences within his own politburo, he said:

> Every member of our leadership is deeply committed to the cause of perestroika.
> *Daily Telegraph*, 23 May 1988.

performance art A form of theatrical art that combines such media as drama, music, dance, film, photography, and painting. The performer mixes these various art forms into themes and provides a rambling commentary on them. Evolving from the 1960s HAPPENINGS, performance art first appeared at the beginning of the 1970s in America, the UK, and West Germany.

perm Short for permanent wave: treatment of the hair by heat or chemicals to give it a wavy appearance that will last for some weeks or months.

permissive society *See* NEW MORALITY.

peroxide A chemical compound containing two oxygen atoms linked together. The simplest such compound is hydrogen peroxide, H_2O_2, which is used as a mild antiseptic and as a bleach for hair. In the early part of the century 'peroxide' or 'peroxide blonde' came to be used for a woman who had bleached her hair in this way. It was not long before it had acquired a pejorative sense: such women were regarded as rather vulgar and common:

> An over-dressed, much behatted, peroxided young woman.
> BARONESS ORCZY: *Lady Molly* (1910).

A **platinum blonde** is a woman whose hair is treated to give a silvery colour popularized by the US film star Jean Harlow in the film *Platinum Blonde* (1931).

> It was a blonde. A blonde to make a bishop kick a hole in a stained-glass window.
> RAYMOND CHANDLER: *Farewell My Lovely* (1940).

Perrier water *See* DESIGNER WATER.

Pershing missile A US intermediate-range ballistic missile (IRBM), which first became operational in 1962. The Pershing II, developed during the late 1970s, has a range of 425 miles (680 km) and is ten times more accurate than its predecessor. They were deployed in W Europe in 1983 to counter the threat from Soviet medium range SS-20 missiles, but were later removed in accordance with the provisions of the US-Soviet INF (Intermediate Nuclear Forces) Treaty of 8 December 1987. They are named after US General John J. Pershing (1860–1948), who commanded the US forces in World War I.

persistent Describing substances, especially pesticides and other pollutants, that are degraded relatively slowly in the environment. Consequently any harmful effects on living organisms will tend to be long-lasting and widespread, reaching many different parts of the food chain. The best known examples are the organochlorine compounds, such as DDT, lindane, and dieldrin, formerly widely used as pesticides for crops and livestock. Their use resulted in a build-up of toxic residues in the tissues of many animals, especially carnivores, with such serious consequences as infertility or poor hatchability in birds. The use of persistent compounds is now restricted or banned in most western countries.

-person *See* CHAIR.

personal. personal column A newspaper or magazine column for private messages, announcements, and personal advertisements. These include invitations to share flats, charity appeals, marriage-bureau advertisements, and a range of private messages that are intelligible only to their intended audience. Birth, marriage, and death announcements (jokingly called the hatch, match, and dispatch columns) are usually separate.

personal computer (PC) A general-purpose MICROCOMPUTER for personal use that first came onto the market in the late 1970s and was used by home hobbyists for elementary programming and playing computer games. Such machines had limited memory and storage (most used portable cassette tape recorders) and used domestic television sets as monitors. As microchip technology progressed during the late 1970s and early 1980s, various manufacturers began producing more powerful PCs for business use. These models have larger memories, greater storage capabilities (such as hard disks), and their own monitors; they are now widely used commercially for wordprocessing, accounting, DESKTOP PUBLISHING (DTP), computer-aided design (CAD), and many other applications.

personal equity plan *See* PEP.

personal organizer *See* FILOFAX.

Perspex Tradename of polymethyl methacrylate (called Plexiglass and Lucite in America), a transparent plastic developed in 1924 and first marketed in 1934. Colourless, transparent, flexible, and hardwearing, it is manufactured in sheets or solid objects and is used for aircraft canopies, car windows, cheap camera lenses, spectacles, tail lights, etc.

perv (1) A sexual pervert. (2) To indulge in voyeurism.

Peter. Peterborough The column in the *Daily Telegraph* named after the newspaper's former office address in Peterborough Court, Fleet Street; their docklands address is now Peterborough Court, Marshwall. The column is a mixture of gossip, news, and comment, usually on politics and the arts, and is intentionally snobbish and superficial in tone. It first appeared on 17 February 1929 and was first signed 'Peterborough' in November of the same year. Perhaps Peterborough's greatest editor was Hugo Wortham, who ran the column from 1934 to 1959, peppering it with references to his favourite subjects, which included music, cricket, Eton, Egypt, horse-racing, and wine.

Peterlee A NEW TOWN in the mining area 10 miles (16 km) east of Durham, which was so designated on 10 March 1948. The town was intended to provide housing for a maximum of 30,000 people and to act as the commercial and social centre for 26 mining towns and villages in the region of the Durham coal fields. The establishment of new industries was also encouraged in the town to provide an alternative source of employment to the declining coal industry. It was named after a famous local miners' leader, Peter Lee (d. 1935), Secretary of the Durham Miners and later President of the Miners' Federation of Great Britain.

Peter Pan The little boy who never grew up, the central character of Sir J. M. Barrie's famous play of this name (1904). One night Peter entered the nursery window of the house of the Darling family to recover his shadow. He flew back to NEVER NEVER LAND accompanied by the Darling children, to rejoin the Lost Boys. Eventually all were captured by the pirates, except Peter, who secured their release and the defeat of the pirates. The children, by now homesick, flew back to the nursery with their new friends but Peter refused to stay as he did not wish to grow up. In their absence Mr Darling lived in the dog kennel as penance for having taken NANA away, thus making possible the children's disappearance in the first instance.

Frampton's statue of Peter Pan in Kensington Gardens was placed there by Barrie in 1912.

Peter Principle An observation put forward by the Canadian-born US educationalist Laurence J. Peter in 1966: in a hierarchy every employee tends to rise to his level of incompetence, *i.e.* people are promoted until they ultimately reach a job that they are incapable of doing.

Peter Rabbit The most popular of the animal characters created by Beatrix Potter in her children's stories. Towards the end of the century he had become firmly established as the chief figure in a lucrative array of merchandise, ranging from soft furnishings to china figures, based on the tales. He was, however, virtually unique in having (thus far) escaped vulgarization at the hands of television cartoonists.

Peters' projection The map projection that shows continents and oceans in their correct relative proportions. The older Mercator's projection gives the northern hemisphere two-thirds of the map space and thus emphasizes Europe and North America; Peters' projection gives proper attention to equatorial regions and the southern hemisphere. This revision was produced in 1973 by Arno Peters (1916–), a German cartographer and mathematician.

PET scanner *See* BRAIN SCANNER.

Peyton Place The first major US television SOAP OPERA, based on the 1956 bestseller by Grace Metalious about the salacious goings-on in a decayed textile town in New Hampshire. The half-hour twice-weekly series ran from 15 September 1964 to 2 June 1969 (1965–70 in the UK) and attracted an audience of 60 million avid viewers (8 million in the UK). British viewers could thank the success of their own CORONATION STREET for inspiring the US ABC network to produce the series. ABC eventually earned $62 million from *Peyton Place*, which also launched the film careers of two of its leading characters, 19-year-old Mia Farrow and 22-year-old Ryan O'Neill; it also spawned *Return to Peyton Place* (1972–74) and two films, *Murder in Peyton Place* (1977) and *Peyton Place: The New Generation* (1985).

PG Parental Guidance. A cinema certification in the UK and America for general-audience films containing some scenes unsuitable for children. They may attend at their parents' discretion. America also has a **PG-13** symbol, which strongly cautions parents about allowing children under that age to attend (*see also* G; R). The classifications for films are decided, respectively, by the British Board of Film Censors and the Motion Picture Association of America.

Phalangist A member of a Christian paramilitary organization in Lebanon, founded in 1936 on the fascist ideas of Spain's Falange movement.

Phantom Major Nickname of Colonel Sir David Stirling (1915–90), founder of the SAS in World War II. His concept of small highly trained teams operating behind enemy lines was controversial but turned out to be enormously successful. Stirling abandoned the usual conventions attached to rank in the British army and SAS members called each other by their first name and adopted a less than scrupulous attitude to details of uniform, etc. Stirling's nickname was coined by his victims in the German AFRIKA KORPS and alluded to his ability to conceal his men in the Western Desert. He was finally captured in 1943 and transferred to COLDITZ, having escaped four times from camps in Italy.

Philby, Kim *See* BURGESS AND MACLEAN.

phone. Phonecard A plastic card issued by British Telecom to enable members of the public to use a PAYPHONE designed to accept it. The cards are valid for a specified number of units and may be purchased at post offices, newsagents, etc.

phone freak (1) Someone who uses an electronic device to make free telephone calls. With the spread of US tone dialling in the early 1970s, phone freaks acquired equipment to imitate the tones to place calls, thus bypassing the recorded billing. A few practitioners can imitate the tones with their voices alone. Their activities are so costly that some telephone companies employ detectives to trace these illegal calls. (2) A person who phones a prostitute or other advertised source to listen to her pornographic monologue.

phone-in A broadcast programme, particularly a radio programme, in which listeners are invited to participate by telephoning the studio to ask questions or express their opinions on air. The phone-in began in America, where it is also known as a *call-in*, and was introduced into the UK at the beginning of the 1970s. It remains a standard item in many broadcasting stations, being both popular with the public and relatively cheap to produce.

phoney or **phony** Fraudulent, bogus, or insincere; a US colloquialism and slang term that became anglicized about 1920. It derives from *fawney*, an obsolete underworld name for the imitation gold ring used by confidence tricksters. During World War II, the period of comparative inactivity from the outbreak to the invasion of Norway and Denmark was characterized by US journalists as the **Phoney War**.

phosgene A poisonous gas (carbonyl chloride, $COCl_2$) with a smell of freshly cut hay. It was first used as a war gas in World War I. *See* CHEMICAL WARFARE.

photo. photo call The time set aside for press photographers to take pictures of a busy politician, actor, athlete, or other celebrity or group. This session is usually arranged and controlled by a PRO or information officer.

photodegradable Describing plastics, pesticides, and other synthetic chemicals that can be decomposed by sunlight. The use of photodegradable materials became popular in the 1970s as part of a general concern for protecting the environment. *See* BIODEGRADABLE.

photofinish The end of a race so closely contested that the winner can be discovered with certainty only by means of a photograph taken at the finish. Most racecourses are equipped to take such photographs.

Photofit The tradename for a police method of building up a composite photograph of a suspect's face, usually based on a description given by the victim or a witness. It was developed for Scotland Yard in 1970 by Jacques Penry. Witnesses choose facial features – nose, chin, mouth, eyes, forehead – from a range of different shapes to create the likeness. Photofit refined the IDENTIKIT system.

photojournalism News coverage dominated by photographs. Although newspapers create photographic essays, magazines have been the powerful medium of photojournalism because of their higher quality paper and earlier use of colour. As television proved later, public opinion can be forged by the power of realistic news images. This is vividly demonstrated during wartime: Mathew Brady's stark photography during the US Civil War; patriotic images of World War II, such as the IWO JIMA flag-raising by US

Marines; and the brutality of Eddie Adams' photo of the execution of a VIET CONG prisoner. Pioneers of photojournalism included the UK's *Picture Post* and America's *Life*. The latter announced:

> In using pictures first and foremost to inform, *Life* has made pictures not only a power, but a responsible new arm of journalism.

Photostat Tradename for an early make of photocopying machine, introduced in about 1912. The name has commonly been used to mean any photocopier or copy; since the 1950s, when XEROX machines were introduced, the two words have existed side by side as generic names. The suffix *-stat* is familiar from the names of scientific instruments, such as the thermostat, that cause something to remain constant; in the case of the Photostat it was presumably intended to suggest a scientific device that produced copies identical to the original.

Pianola Tradename of a type of **player piano** invented in 1897 by the US engineer Edwin S. Votey and marketed by the Aeolian Corporation. The Pianola, like other player pianos, functioned by suction generated by pedal-operated (or later electrically driven) bellows; the reduced air pressure made the keys move in accordance with the perforations in a paper roll. The more sophisticated types of roll were able to control tempo and expression and were used to reproduce performances by famous pianists and by such composers as Ravel and Gershwin. In bridge, a pianola is a hand so good that it plays itself.

PIAT *See* BAZOOKA.

picture. Every picture tells a story Catchphrase that originated as a trade slogan for Doane's Backache Kidney Pills in the early years of the 20th century. Although the original advertisements, featuring a man clutching his aching back, are no longer seen, the catchphrase has been adapted to many other situations. The pop singer Rod Stewart released an album with this title in the 1970s.

pie. There'll be pie in the sky when you die You will receive your reward in heaven. This US catchphrase was first heard in the early years of the 20th century; the implication is that there will be no reward at all.

piece of the action A US colloquialism for a share in the equity or profit of a venture. It originated with gamblers' slang in the 1920s, the 'action' being a gambling event, such as a game of poker or a spin of a roulette wheel. By the 1970s it had become business jargon on both sides of the Atlantic: 'If I sell you my business, I still want to keep a piece of the action'.

pig (1) Pejorative slang for a police constable. Originally an Americanism, this usage became widespread in the UK in the 1960s. It had, however, been used in the Victorian era, as underworld slang for a policeman. (2) Slang from the 1950s used by BEATNIKS to mean a girl. This was not, surprisingly, intended to be pejorative. (3) US slang college term from the 1980s for an ugly girl. Contests were held for the 'Pig of the Year' and the unfortunate winner awarded a prize. (4) Slang shortening of MALE CHAUVINIST PIG.

Pilgerism A derogatory term for a type of campaigning left-wing journalism, characterized (in the eyes of its detractors) by selective use of facts, tendentious arguments, and a tone of strident moral indignation. It was coined by the British writer Auberon Waugh (1939–) to express his distaste for the work of the Australian journalist John Pilger.

Pilkington Report A report on the future of British broadcasting produced by a committee headed by Sir Harry Pilkington and published on 27 June 1962. The report praised the 'professionalism' of the BBC, confirmed its position as the premier instrument of national broadcasting, and rejected advertising on that channel. The committee also accepted the BBC's claim to run a second channel on 625 lines UHF, which eventually became BBC 2. Commercial television, on the other hand, was heavily criticized by the committee, especially for the poor quality of its light entertainment.

> Those who say they give the public what it wants begin by underestimating public taste and end by debauching it.
>
> Pilkington Report, 1962.

Pill, the An orally administered preparation of synthetic sex hormones taken by women as a contraceptive (*see* BIRTH CONTROL). The female 'combined' pill consists of an oestrogen and a progestogen. Both suppress ovulation; the progestogen, moreover, alters the lining of the womb and causes mucus in the cervix to thicken, hence reducing the chances of successful fertilization in the event of ovulation. The so-called MINI PILL contains a progestogen only. The Pill was developed in the 1950s by Gregory Pincus and Min Chuch Chang of the Worcester Foundation for Experimental Biology in Massachusetts, in conjunction with obstetrician John Rock and pharmacologist Carl Djerassi. Following trials in Haiti and Puerto Rico, the Pill was approved by the US Food and Drug Administration in 1960. The first branded product, Enovid 10, manufactured by Searle Pharmaceuticals, went on sale in the same year.

For some women, the use of the Pill involves undesirable side-effects, such as nausea, headache, and weight gain; studies have also shown a slightly increased risk of blood clots and reduced fertility with prolonged use. However, the convenience and reliability of the Pill ensured its widespread popularity, adding a new dimension to the sexual liberation of women during the 1960s and 1970s (*see* NEW MORALITY). However, by the 1980s concern over the serious side-effects and the growing menace of AIDS prompted a return by many to barrier methods of contraception, particularly the condom, in an effort to prevent sexual transmission of the AIDS virus (*see* HIV). Various types of male contraceptive pill have been devised and tested, but none has yet entered general use. MORNING-AFTER PILLS are also being developed for those caught unprepared the night before.

pillock Mildly abusive British slang for a fool or an irritating person. It has been in use since the 1950s, but gained widespread popularity in the late 1970s and 1980s. Various etymologies have been suggested: *pillicock* is an obsolete Scottish and Northern English word for a penis; 'pillock' is also the country term for a rabbit dropping, in the sense of a little ball from the Latin, *pilula*; 'pill' and 'pillock' are slang terms for a ball, in the sense of testicle.

pillow. pillow-biter Slang for a male homosexual, especially the passive partner in the act of buggery. This expression is thought to have originated in Australia and to have been introduced in to the UK in the 1970s by the satirical magazine PRIVATE EYE.

pillow pigeons US Black slang for bedbugs, first heard in the 1940s.

Piltdown Skull or **Piltdown Man** In 1908 and 1911 Charles Dawson of Lewes 'found' two pieces of a highly mineralized human skull in a gravel bed near Piltdown Common, Sussex. By 1912 he and Sir Arthur Smith Woodward had discovered the whole skull. This was thought to be that of a new species of man and was called *Eoanthropus dawsoni*. It came to be accepted as such by most prehistorians, archaeologists, etc., although a few were sceptical. In 1953 J. S. Weiner, K. P. Pakley, and W. E. Le Gros Clark issued a report (*Bulletin of the British Museum* (Natural History), Vol. II, No. 3) announcing that the Piltdown mandible was a fake, in reality the jaw of a modern ape, the rest of the skull being that of *Homo sapiens*. The hoax, which took in most of the experts, was apparently planned by William Sollas, Professor of Geology at Oxford (1897–1937), through his dislike of Sir Arthur Smith Woodward.

pin. PIN Personal Identification Number. A number given to a customer of a bank or building society who has a cash card or a credit card. The number has to be memorized by the customer and is used in conjunction with the card to obtain cash from an automatic cash dispenser or to utilize electronic funds transfer at point of sale (*see* EFTPOS). It is necessary to keep one's PIN secret in order to avoid its misuse.

pinball A game of skill played on a pinball machine, whose inclined board has holes, bumpers, pins, channels, etc. A player shoots the ball to the top of the board and tries to keep it from rolling back by using automatic flippers to direct it into the obstructions. When the ball touches them, lights flash, bells ring, and scores are recorded. In the 1975 rock film, *Tommy*, Elton John played the 'Pinball Wizard'. Pinball arcades were popular until the advent in the mid-1970s of video games.

pindown A form of punishment used in residential homes on children held in care by the social services in Staffordshire. The children, some as young as nine, punished by this procedure were held, dressed only in nightclothes, in solitary confinement for long periods in their rooms, from which all personal belongings had been removed. Forbidden to talk to anyone, they had to ask permission to use the lavatory or to speak to a social worker. Some were given such absurd tasks as copying out the telephone directory.

The procedure, which was in use in four Staffordshire homes in the period 1983–89, was devised by a senior Staffordshire social worker, Tony Latham. Pindown was stopped by High Court order in 1989 when it was found that some children subjected to it had become clinically depressed, one girl attempting to commit suicide to escape the treatment by jumping out of the window.

The procedure, Tony Latham, and other senior social workers, as well as the Staffordshire social services were all roundly condemned by an independent report in 1991.

pin-up girl In World War II servicemen used to pin up in their quarters pictures of film stars and actresses (often scantily clad) or their own particular girlfriends. These were called pin-up girls. The most famous of them all during the war was the actress Betty Grable (1916–73), whose legs were reputed to be insured for $1 million. Any goodlooking girl, however clad and whether she is famous or not, may now be referred to as a pin-up girl. *See also* PAGE-THREE GIRL.

pina colada (Sp. strained pineapple) A drink made with rum, pineapple juice, and coconut milk, which became especially trendy during the late 1960s.

pine drape US Black slang for a coffin, first head in the 1940s.

ping-ponging In America, the practice of referring a patient, who attends a medical centre with one complaint, to a number of other specialists. It is a way in which doctors increase their fees from the US MEDICAID scheme. *See also* FAMILY GANGING.

pink (1) Slang for mildly left wing or influenced by communism. Red is the colour used to represent socialism. *See also* PINKO; REDS. (2) Slang for GAY, often used facetiously by homosexual males. It derives from the Nazis, who made known homosexuals wear a pink triangle in the same way that they made Jews wear a yellow star. Pink has always been a colour associated with femininity.

pink-collar Denoting occupations that are usually followed by women. These include secretarial and educational jobs as well as those in retail trades. The pink-collar label, which originated in America in the late 1970s, follows the earlier white-collar (1928) and blue-collar (1950) designations.

pinko (1) US slang for a person with political leanings to the left. *See also* PINK. (2) Australian slang for drunk on methylated spirits. This alcoholic substance is often dyed pink to warn people against drinking it.

pink triangle The pink cloth badge in the shape of a triangle that homosexuals were forced to wear by the Nazis as a means of identification. It has since been used voluntarily as a badge of identification by gays – sometimes the triangle is no bigger than a 5p piece.

pinta. Drinka pinta milka day *See under* DRINK.

Pio, Padre (1887–1968) Italian monk, who became world famous after his body showed the signs of the stigmata. The first occasion on which this occurred was 20 September 1915. Padre Pio never, himself, sought publicity but the repeated appearance on his hands, feet, and side of what were taken to be the wounds suffered by Christ on the Cross provoked a storm of interest. Although many famous instances of stigmatics have been recorded in previous centuries, that of Padre Pio, born of peasant stock in the village of Pietrelcina, near Benevento, became one of the best documented. Indeed, photographs were taken of his bleeding wounds, convincing many people that no deception was involved. Although medical experts suggested that stigmata were the product of some form of autosuggestion, pilgrims flocked to see Padre Pio, while many others offered him enormous sums of money. The Vatican twice suspended him from his duties in an attempt to prevent further embarrassment to the orthodox religious establishment. Nonetheless, tales spread of the monk's powers of clairvoyance, which included a prayer for George V even as the king, unknown to anyone in Italy, was on his deathbed. Padre Pio finally died on 28 September 1968; almost immediately a campaign began for his canonization.

Pioneer A series of US unmanned SPACE PROBES, designed to carry various scientific instruments for planetary investigation, the first of which was launched on 11 October 1958. The first five probes (1958–60) were used to study solar energy and to give advanced warning of solar flares to protect the astronauts on the moonflight programme. Pioneer 10 (launched March 1972) was the first spacecraft to fly beyond Mars, enter the Asteroid Belt, reach Jupiter (December 1973), and escape from the solar system into interstellar space (1983). Pioneer 11 (launched April 1975) flew three times closer to Jupiter and was the first spacecraft to reach Saturn (September 1979). Both Pioneer 10 and 11 carry a plaque with a diagram of the solar system showing Pioneer's route, plus drawings of a man (with his hand raised in a gesture of goodwill) and a woman, in case the probes should ever encounter intelligent life elsewhere in the universe. The final Pioneer probes, 12 (an orbiter) and 13, were launched in May and August 1978 towards Venus, the latter dropping four small probes before itself descending to the surface.

pip. pip emma Military usage in World War I for p.m. (post meridiem). Originally telephonese; 'ten pip emma' avoids any possibility of misunderstanding. In the same way **ack emma** stands for a.m. (ante meridiem).

pippy Person Inheriting Parents' Property. A loose acronym coined in the 1980s, on the basis of similar acronyms, such as YUPPIE, in recognition of the growing number of middle-aged people who inherited property from their parents as a result of the post-war boom in home ownership.

Pip, Squeak, and Wilfred A children's comic strip, about a penguin, a dog, and a rabbit, which appeared in *The Daily Mirror* between 1919 and 1946. It was drawn by A. B. Raine and written by B. J. Lamb. A feature of the strip was a bearded anarchist called **Popski**, whose sinister black broad-brimmed hat and orb-like bomb represented the evils of communism, atheism, and any other '-ism' that was likely to threaten the existing social order. In order to increase the pressure on parents to buy the paper, the *Mirror* organized a children's club, the members of which were called **Gugnunks**. These clubs were active in schools, holiday camps, and anywhere else that children might be expected to gather.

piss. piss-artist (1) British slang for a drunkard. **Pissed** means drunk; *-artist* is frequently used as a slang suffix for someone accomplished at their job. For example, a con-artist is a successful conman. (2) A boastful person who provides information that cannot be relied upon.

pissed off British slang for angry or bored. The US equivalent is **pissed**.

pisshead (1) British slang for a drunkard, a synonym for a PISS-ARTIST. (2) US slang for an unpleasant person.

piss-up British vulgar slang for a drinking session or a party with a liberal supply of alcohol. The expression **he couldn't organize a piss-up in a brewery** suggests the ultimate in ineptitude. Variants on these lines include 'he couldn't organize a fuck in a brothel', often used to describe an officer thought by his men to be peculiarly incompetent, and 'he couldn't sell iced-water in hell' for an unsuccessful salesman.

pit. pit bull terrier A strong and potentially dangerous dog that is a crossbreed between a bulldog and a terrier. It has a white coat and resembles a Staffordshire bull terrier, although it is larger. The name is also used for several crossbreeds and is therefore not recognized by kennel clubs. Originally bred for dog-fighting, the pit bull terrier was responsible for two-thirds of the deaths from dog bites in the 1980s in America. Some US communities have passed laws banning them or requiring them to be registered; in the UK, parliament banned their import in 1991 and discussed further measure, such as sterilization and muzzling, to curb pit bull terriers already in the country. *See also* ROTTWEILER.

the pits Slang for the lowest of the low, the most dreadful experience or the most awful person. Originally an Americanism, it is now widely used in the UK and elsewhere in the English-speaking world. It is thought to be a shortened form of 'armpits', an often malodorous and unattractive part of the body.

pizazz or **pazazz** US slang from the 1960s for flamboyant energy and style. Originally a show-business term, it is now applied to anyone or anything having glamour or flair. It is thought to derive from the sound of a racing car's engine.

placebo (Lat. I shall please) A substance given as medication to a patient although it has no physiological effect. Placebos may be prescribed for a patient who will feel cheated if he is not given a prescription. Indeed, in some instances the placebo may produce an improvement in the clinical condition of the person. This response, known as the **placebo effect**, was first documented in about 1950. Placebos are also given in the clinical trials of new drugs to assess the efficacy of the drug being tested. In a double-blind trial, neither the doctor nor the patient knows which is the drug and which is the placebo.

Placido British slang for £10, a *tenner*, coined in the late 1980s. The term derives from the Spanish operatic singer Placido Domingo (1941–), being a pun on the fact that he is a *tenor*.

Plaid Cymru (Welsh: Party of Wales) The Welsh nationalist party, set up in 1925 with the object of achieving Welsh home rule. Support grew in the 1960s and the party gained three seats in the House of Commons in 1974, but only two in 1979 and 1983 and three in 1987. Their major setback came in 1979 when the Welsh people rejected DEVOLUTION by an absolute majority in a referendum.

plan. planned obsolescence The policy of deliberately limiting the life of a product or component in order to force the consumer to replace it more frequently than he should need to. The practice can be regarded as an immoral exploitation of the consumer. Its practitioners, however, would defend it on two grounds. In the first place, in the modern world, technology advances so rapidly that very often a device, such as a camera or computer, is out-of-date long before it wears out. By designing the product in such a way that it will function well during its relatively short lifetime, the manufacturer is able to sell it more cheaply than if he had to design it to last so long that it would still function after it had become technically obsolete. Secondly, western economies depend on a vigorous consumer demand for durables, such as cars, washing machines, etc. If they were designed to last the consumer for his lifetime, demand would fall to such a low level that unemployment would reach unacceptable proportions.

planning blight A difficulty that arises in selling a property because it is either directly affected by a development plan or is adjacent to property that is so affected. For example, a residence may become unsaleable because a motorway is planned to pass close to it.

Planck constant A fundamental constant in physics named after the German physicist Max Planck (1858–1947). In his work on the emission of radiation, Planck suggested that the energy emitted or absorbed by a body would be proportional to the frequency of the radiation and would only occur in discrete amounts. Mathematically, $E = nh\nu$, where E is the energy, ν the frequency of the radiation, n is a whole number (1, 2, 3, etc.), and h is a constant, now known as the Planck constant. His theory was published in 1900 in a paper entitled 'On the Theory of the Law of Energy Distribution in the Continuous Spectrum'. The idea that energy could only be transferred in definite amounts ('quanta'), rather than continuously, was a fundamental break with the ideas of 19th-century science, leading to the development of QUANTUM THEORY. Planck's value for the constant: $h = 6.62 \cdot 10^{-27}$ erg·sec is engraved on his tombstone in Göttingen, Germany. A more up-to-date value in SI UNITS is $6.626\,076 \times 10^{34}$ J s.

plastic. plastic bullet *See* RUBBER BULLET.

plastic explosive Any of various high explosives produced in an adhesive mouldable form. The original plastic explosives were based on the substance RDX (research department explosive) mixed with various oils, waxes, and plasticizers. RDX (the chemical cyclotrimethylenetrinitramine, also called cyclonite) was invented in 1899 but was first used in World War II. Subsequently, plastic explosives became known because of their use by terrorist organizations. **Semtex**, which like RDX is a nitrogen-based plastic explosive, is an odourless substance, much favoured by terrorists; it was used in the LOCKERBIE DISASTER.

plastic money Credit cards. Often shortened to **plastic**, it is a manifestation of the cashless society that has grown up in western cultures since World War II. 'I don't have cash, will you accept plastic?' is a common question.

plate. Battle of the River Plate The scuttling of the German pocket-battleship GRAF SPEE in December 1939 in the estuary of the River Plate (Río de la Plata) off Montevideo, Uruguay. After a naval battle in the Atlantic the *Graf Spee* was damaged and took refuge in Montevideo Harbour. It was refused assistance by the Uruguayan government and was scuttled on Hitler's orders. The Captain, Commander Langsdorff, shot himself. The scuttling of the trapped and maimed German merchant-shipping raider disappointed many sightseers, who had hoped to see a classic naval engagement, including a party of US businessmen who had chartered a plane at the cost of £1,250 each.

plate tectonics In geology, the modern theory that the Earth's crust is composed of a number of plates that move relative to each other. The main plates correspond to the American, African, Antarctic, Eurasian, Indian, and Pacific continents;

where the edges of these plates meet, volcanic activity and earthquakes are common. It is the movement of these plates, either towards or away from each other, or over or under each other, that causes oceanic trenches, mountain ranges, and the formation of various other geological phenomena. *See also* PANGAEA.

platform sole A thick shoe sole, usually made of cork or wood, that raises the upper an inch or more off the ground. They became fashionable for both sexes in the early 1970s, when pop stars of the GLAM ROCK era took to wearing gaudy high-heeled shoes with built-up soles. **Wedges** (or **wedgies**) are shoes in which the heel and sole form a single solid block up to 4″ thick. They produced a grotesque hobbling gait in their wearers, who were chiefly teenage girls.

plating Slang for the act of fellatio. The term was used by rock-music groupies in the 1960s. It is thought to be a shortened version of 'plate of ham', the ham representing the penis. 'Plate of ham' is also rhyming slang for 'gam', also meaning to perform oral sex. 'Gam' is short for *gamahucher*, a 19th-century French term from the jargon of prostitutes; it is also an old English word for mouth.

platinum. platinum blonde *See* PEROXIDE.

platinum handshake A very lavish GOLDEN HANDSHAKE.

play. playgroup A group of preschool-age children, particularly in the UK, who regularly play together and receive nursery education under supervision. **Playschools**, which provide this service, are usually run on a part-time voluntary basis, by or with the help of the parents, using neighbourhood facilities such as the church hall or social centre. Some receive limited funding from local councils or charitable organizations.

Play it again, Sam A catchphrase that is supposed to come from the Michael Curtiz film *Casablanca* (1942), starring Humphrey Bogart (as Rick) and Ingrid Bergman (as Ilse). In fact, no such line exists, which is also well known. What Humphrey Bogart did say was "Play it Sam, Play 'As Time Goes By'". Nevertheless, the misquotation is better known and was well enough established by 1969 for Woody Allen to use it and have no fear that the reference would be lost as the title of his play (filmed in 1972) about a critic who is helped by the 'ghost' of Humphrey Bogart. Sam is the pianist in Rick's Casablanca war-time night spot, who plays and sings 'As Time Goes By' so evocatively that it reminds Rick and Ilse of their pre-war liaison in Paris. Sam is played by Dooley Wilson.

pleasure principle *See* REALITY PRINCIPLE.

Plexiglas *See* PERSPEX.

PLO Palestine Liberation Organization. A politico-military organization founded in 1964 to represent Palestinian Arab refugees and to re-establish a Palestine state. It has conducted terrorist campaigns against Israel, including the murder of 11 Israeli athletes at the Munich Olympic Games (1972). Since 1967 it has been dominated by the AL FATAH guerrilla group headed by Yasir Arafat (1929–). In 1988, the leadership declared the existence of a Palestinian state, renounced terrorism, and recognized Israel's right to exist within secure borders. However, the PLO continued to encourage violent tactics against Israeli occupation of the West Bank, home of 1.7 million Palestinians (*see* INTIFADA).

plonk A cheap wine for everyday or party consumption rather than for offering to wine buffs. It is thought to be a corruption of the French *vin blanc* (white wine) and dates back to World War I.

plonker (1) British vulgar slang for a penis. It has been used since the early years of the 20th century. (2) British vulgar slang for a stupid person. It became well known during the 1980s from its frequent use by the character Del Boy (David Jason) of his slightly dim but long-suffering younger brother Rodney (Nicholas Lyndhurst) in the BBC TV comedy series *Only Fools and Horses*.

> Dazzling Dave really made a change from most mumbling pop plonkers.
>
> *The Sun*, 6 March 1991.

(3) British slang for a mistake. (4) British slang for a big wet kiss, a smacker.

ploughman's lunch An informal lunch provided as a bar snack, usually consisting of bread and cheese with various trimmings, such as pickles and pickled onions; it is consumed with a glass of beer. Bread and cheese is regarded as having been the staple lunch of the medieval ploughman (hence the name), although what is now offered in most pubs as a ploughman's lunch would be unlikely to have sustained a manual worker. This modern-day version was promoted by the English Country Cheese Council in the 1970s.

Plowden Report A report, published in December 1964, on the reorganization of the British aircraft industry by a committee established by the Labour government and headed by Lord Plowden, chairman of Tube Investments. It recommended collaboration with European firms, purchases from America, and nationalization.

PLR *See* PUBLIC LENDING RIGHT.

PLU People Like Us. Slang abbreviation used as a signal of approval among snobbish British people. *See also* NTD.

plug. plugged in *Au fait* with the latest trends in fashion or popular trends generally. SWITCHED ON is similarly used; both are derived from electrical appliances.

plugumentary A film or television programme that appears to be a documentary but in fact is aimed at promoting a particular product or firm. A combination of *plug* (in the slang sense of publicity material) and 'documentary', it is a photographic version of the ADVERTORIAL common in newspapers and magazines for some time.

Plum Nickname of the British comic novelist P. G. Wodehouse (1881–1975): it is a contraction of his Christian name, Pelham. The cricketer and cricket writer Sir Pelham Francis Warner (1873–1963) was also known by this name. *See also* JEEVES; PSMITH; SPODE, RODERICK; WOOSTER, BERTIE.

plus fours Loose trousers overlapping the knee-band and thereby giving added freedom for active outdoor sports. They were particularly popular with golfers in the 1920s. The name derives from the four extra inches of cloth required below the knee to be tucked into long heavy socks.

Pluto (1) In World War II, the codename (from the initials of Pipe Line Under The Ocean) given to the pipelines to carry oil fuel laid across the bed of the English Channel – from Sandown to Cherbourg and from Dungeness to Boulogne. (2) Cartoon dog of early Walt Disney features.

PMT Premenstrual Tension. Irritability, nervousness, anxiety, depression, and emotional instability affecting some women for up to ten days before a menstrual period is due. Though probably not a 20th-century phenomenon, the condition was not recognized and named as part of a clinical syndrome until the 1920s. Associated with a premenstrual build-up of salt and water in the tissues, due to temporary hormonal imbalance, the symptoms disappear once menstruation begins.

pocket battleships Small battleships built by Germany after World War I. Forbidden to build warships of over 10,000 tons by the VERSAILLES TREATY (1919), Germany constructed several formidable so-called pocket battleships purporting to be within this limit.

POETS day Friday, *POETS* being an acronym for Piss Off Early Tomorrow's Saturday. As an explanation of what happens on Friday afternoons in many offices, it became current in the 1960s. A similar expression from that era was **TGIF** (Thank God It's Friday), which was used in various forms for the names of Friday radio and TV programmes.

pogo-dancing A form of dancing, originating as part of the PUNK culture, in which the participants jump up and down on the spot to music. It is derived from the **Pogo-stick**, a toy consisting of a spring-loaded stick with platforms for the feet, enabling a child to jump around.

point. on points A World War II expression relating to the system of rationing food, clothing, etc. Apart from direct rationing of meat, bacon, sugar, fats, and tea, miscellaneous groceries, etc., were given 'points' values and each ration-book holder was given a certain number of points to spend in an allotted period. Hence **it's on points** was a common reference to many commodities.

point man A person who spearheads a military, political, or business campaign. It is often used of someone appointed to handle the opposition to a particular programme. When President Ronald Reagan needed support in 1976 for his STAR WARS military policy, he sent Vice President George Bush to Europe as a point man to allay the gathering doubts. This US term of the early 1970s grew out of its World War II military usage, for the front soldier in a military patrol.

point of no return The point in an aircraft's flight at which it has not enough fuel to return to its point of departure and must continue. Hence its figurative application, a point or situation from which there is no turning back.

point of sale (POS) (1) The place at which a sale is made to a consumer. It may be a retail shop, petrol station, market stall, mail-order house, or the doorstep (in door-to-door selling). (2) The check-out in a departmental store, supermarket, etc., at which payments are made and sales recorded on a cash register linked to a central computer. A **point-of-sale display** is placed at such a check-out point in order to tempt customers to make a last-minute purchase of a magazine, confectionary, etc.

Poirot, Hercule The Belgian detective created by Agatha Christie (*see* QUEEN OF CRIME) in her first crime novel, *The Mysterious Affair at Styles* (1920). The dapper slightly plump ex-policeman is famous for his fastidious grooming of his waxed moustache and his insistence that crimes are best solved by the use of one's 'little grey cells'. He made his final appearance in *Curtain* (1975), after a career in 33 books and 56 stories. He has also featured in numerous films since the 1930s, being portrayed most recently by Albert Finney in *Murder on the Orient Express* (1974) and by Peter Ustinov in *Death on the Nile* (1978), *Evil under the Sun* (1982), and *Appointment with Death* (1988). David Suchet's portrayal in a recent television series (1990–91) is regarded by many Christie fans as the closest to their idea of the original.

poison pill A commercial spoiling tactic in which a company facing an unwanted takeover takes some action that will reduce the value of the company if the takeover succeeds. Examples of poison-pill measures include issuing securities with a conversion option that empowers the holder to buy the bidder's shares at a reduced price if the takeover goes through, or selling off a valuable asset to another organization at a low price on the understanding that they will sell it back if the bid fails.

poke (1) Slang for an act of sexual intercourse, or to have sexual intercourse. As a noun it is also used to mean the female partner, as in 'she was a good poke' – indicating a somewhat chauvinistic view of sexual relationships. (2) Slang for prison. This probably derived from the Old English *pocca*, a sack, thus an enclosed space.

Polaris A US submarine-launched ballistic missile (SLBM) developed during the late 1950s to help bridge the perceived missile gap between East and West. The first Polaris-equipped nuclear submarine, USS *George Washington*, was launched on 15 November 1960. In 1962 President John F. Kennedy offered Polaris technology to the British, to replace the V-bomber nuclear deterrent; the first British Polaris submarine, HMS *Renown*, was completed in 1968. The Americans replaced their Polaris with Poseidon in 1969, but the British updated their missiles with MIRV warheads under the Chevaline programme, completed in 1982; these updated Polaris missiles are now due to be replaced by the more advanced Trident SLBMs. *See* ICBM.

Polaroid (1) Tradename for a type of plastic manufactured by the US Polaroid Corporation and invented by the company's founder, Erwin Land (1909–91), in 1932. The plastic sheet contains crystals that are aligned in rows and has useful optical properties. 'Normal' light is a wave motion in which electric and magnetic fields vibrate at right angles to the direction of propagation. Because of the orientation of the crystals, Polaroid film only transmits light that is vibrating in one plane aligned with the crystal orientation (the light passing through the film is said to be 'plane-polarized'). Light polarized in other directions will not pass through the Polaroid filter. Light that is reflected from surfaces is also plane-polarized on reflection; Polaroid sunglasses are therefore used to cut the reflected light and thus reduce glare. (2) An INSTANT CAMERA manufactured by the Polaroid Corporation and invented by Land in 1947. The original model produced sepia prints 60 seconds after the picture has been taken. Later models produced fast black-and-white prints, and in the 1960s instant colour cameras were introduced. The full name is the **Polaroid Land camera**, also known as the **Land camera**.

pole position Figuratively, a position of advantage; from its use in motor and horse-racing to denote the most favourable starting position on the grid or line. On a racecourse or running track the pole is the inside boundary fence; thus a contestant nearest to the pole gains an advantage since opponents must cover a great distance. In motor racing the pole position is on the front row and on the inside of the first bend.

Polish Corridor The territory given to Poland by the VERSAILLES TREATY (1919) to give her access to the Baltic Sea west of Danzig. The Corridor cut off E Prussia from the rest of Germany and proved to be a bone of contention from the outset. It followed roughly the line of the Vistula.

Politburo Formerly, the chief policy-making body of the Communist Party in the Soviet Union, first formed in 1917. It examined matters before they were submitted to the government and consisted of five members. It was superseded by the PRESIDIUM of the Central Committee of the Communist Party in 1952.

Politics is the art of the possible The definition of politics popularized by the British Conservative politician R. A. (RAB) Butler (1902–82) in 1971. It may have been coined much earlier, possibly by the German leader Bismarck in the previous century.

poll tax *See* COMMUNITY CHARGE.

poly-. **poly bag** Short for polythene bag. The ubiquitous carrier bag provided or sold by supermarkets and shops to contain customers' purchases.

polychlorinated biphenyl *See* PCB.

polyester Any of a large number of synthetic polymers used in resins, plastics, synthetic fibres, etc. Polyesters, first developed in the 1930s, are extensively used, particularly in fabrics such as DACRON and TERYLENE.

polygraph To give someone a LIE DETECTOR test. The polygraph has been around since 1923, but this verb usage – 'The sheriff polygraphed two subjects' – only began in the early 1970s. Polygraphs are most frequently used in America by police and even by companies to screen potential employees.

polystyrene A type of synthetic polymer produced from the hydrocarbon styrene (phenylethylene). Polystyrene was first produced in the 1930s. The resin itself is a clear glasslike thermoplastic material, but is usually used in the form of a rigid foam (known as **expanded polystyrene**) for ceiling tiles, insulation, packing, etc.

polytetrafluoroethylene *See* PTFE.

polythene A synthetic plastic made by polymerizing the gas ethylene (ethene, $CH_2:CH_2$). The original form was made by the British company ICI in the late 1930s. There are two basic forms of the plastic: high-density polythene is a tough brittle material; low-density polythene is a softer more plastic material. Both forms are used for a variety of moulded articles. The name is a contraction of 'polyethylene'.

polyunsaturate An oil or fat in which the molecules are **polyunsaturated**; *i.e.* the chain of carbon atoms contains a number of double chemical bonds. Vegetable and fish oils have this type of structure. Animal fats, on the other hand, are saturated fats. In the 1960s research indicated that saturated fats could lead to a high level of cholesterol in the body and that this could cause atheroma (a degeneration of the walls of the arteries, often resulting in arterial obstruction causing heart conditions). As a result there was a general trend towards using vegetable oils for cooking (rather than lard or dripping) and replacing butter by margarine and vegetable-based spreads. *See* HEALTH FOOD.

polyurethane Any of a class of synthetic polymers used in adhesives, paints, varnishes, rubbers, and foams (in upholstery). Like many other such materials, polyurethanes were developed during the late 1940s.

polyvinyl chloride *See* PVC.

polywater A supposedly new form of water having different properties from ordinary water, first reported by Soviet scientists in 1968. It was said to be formed by condensing water vapour in fine glass or quartz capillaries. Its properties appeared to be very different from the normal properties of water; for example, it had much higher density, viscosity, boiling point, and freezing point. It was suggested that this was a polymeric form of water in which the water molecules had linked together in some way. It was also called **anomalous water**.

The initial report caused considerable interest and scientists all over the world hurried into print with their own reports on its properties. In the early 1970s there was even concern that the new form of water might induce a change in normal water, turning the oceans solid. Possibly this idea was influenced by the science-fiction novel *Ice Nine* by Kurt Vonnegut (1922–), in which a new high-melting crystalline form of ice was discovered. In fact, it was subsequently found that polywater was not a new polymeric form of water but impure water containing a high concentration of silicate ions from the glass or quartz surface of the capillary tubes. Many scientists were made to look rather stupid as a result of this finding.

pommy or **pommie** Australian derogatory slang for a British person. It is also used of British immigrants to Australia. It is now usually abbreviated to **pom**. The derivation is uncertain but two possibilities are offered. It could be a shortened form of pomegranate, a reference to the red cheeks thought to characterize the British. Alternatively, it could be derived from the acronym POME, meaning Prisoners of Mother England – a reference to the early British immigrants to Australia, who were convicts. The term has been in use since the beginning of the 20th century.

> Colin was a pom. He'd lived in Oz since he was 13 but that doesn't make any difference, if you're a pom, you're a pom.
>
> BEN ELTON: *Stark* (1989).

pongo (1) British derogatory slang for a Black man or a foreigner. (2) British military slang from World War I for a soldier or a marine. It is thought to derive from the Kongo word *mpongi*, ape, soldiers in uniform being thought to resemble monkeys. (3) Australian slang for a British person.

PONSI Person Of No Strategic Importance. Dismissive army slang from the GULF WAR of 1991 for any political visitor or other nonmilitary personnel at the front.

Pontiac fever A viral disease resembling flu and characterized by headaches, fatigue, breathlessness, and bouts of coughing. The term is derived from the city of Pontiac, Illinois, in which the first known outbreak was identified. The disease has since been diagnosed elsewhere, including the UK.

poof or **poofter** A homosexual, especially a CAMP one. The word was probably derived from 'puff', a 19th-century term for a homosexual.

> Now I'm that poof from the telly.
>
> JULIAN CLARY, *The Independent*, 31 January 1991.

pop. **pop art** Art that makes use of commonplace mass-produced objects and themes from popular culture as subject material, employing the imagery of advertising, television, comic strips, and magazines. The movement began in the late 1950s as a reaction to the elitism of traditional fine art and continued throughout the 1960s. Largely a British and US phenomenon, its exponents included Richard Hamilton in the UK and Jasper Johns and Andy Warhol in America.

popcorn market A derogatory term for that large section of the cinema-going public, chiefly teenagers, whose avid consumption of popcorn is only matched by their appetite for witless and disgustingly violent movies. The deliberate exploitation of this market began in the 1980s, when film-makers discovered that 16–24-year-olds now constituted a majority of the filmgoers. The result was a proliferation of raucous sex comedies and blood-spattered SPLATTER MOVIES, usually with increasingly feeble and repetitious sequels.

Popeye *See* SPINACH.

pop music Popular music, usually taken to mean the broad range of popular genres that have emerged since the ROCK 'N' ROLL era of the 1950s. The primary market for such music is the teenage market although much ROCK music is considered worthy of consideration by adults, who by tradition are expected by their offspring to decry such music as ephemeral, tuneless, repetitive, noisy, and unintelligent. At their most inane, pop records compete for places in the pop 'charts'. *See also* ACID HOUSE; ACID ROCK; DISCO; FOLK ROCK; HEAVY METAL; PUNK; RAP; SOUL; etc.

poppers Drug-abusers' slang for amyl nitrate capsules, so-called because the drug, a heart stimulant, comes in small glass bombs, the top of which is snapped off to enable the contents to be inhaled. A popular stimulant, it is supposed to increase sexual pleasure.

Poppy Day *See* REMEMBRANCE DAY.

Popski's Private Army A British raiding and reconnaissance force of some 120 men formed in October 1942 under Lt. Col. Vladimir Peniakoff, who had previously worked with the Libyan Arab Force. Familiarly known as 'Popski', he was born in Belgium of Russian parents, educated at Cambridge, and resident in Egypt after 1924. Popski and a small element of his force, together with the LONG RANGE DESERT GROUP, reconnoitred the route by which Montgomery conducted his surprise attack around the MARETH LINE; he subsequently operated in Italy and Austria. *See also* PIP, SQUEAK, AND WILFRED.

popular. **popular capitalism** A form of capitalism advocated by the British prime minister Margaret Thatcher (*see* IRON LADY) in the 1980s. It aimed to encourage people to become shareholders in various businesses, especially in previously nationalized industries that her government had privatized. Popular capitalism also encouraged people to own their own businesses; the Thatcher governments gave special tax incentives to small firms.

Popular Front A political alliance of left-wing parties (communists, socialists, liberals, radicals, etc.) against reactionary government, especially a dictatorship. The idea of an anti-Fascist Popular Front was proposed by the Communist International in 1935. Such a government was set up in Spain in 1936, but civil war soon followed. The French Popular Front government, set up by Blum in 1936, ended in 1938.

porcupine provisions *See* SHARK REPELLENTS.

pork. pork chop A style of slowly played JAZZ, popular in the 1900s.

porky or **porky pie** or **pork pie** British rhyming slang for a lie. The term gained popularity as a result of its use in the TV comedy series *Minder*, set in working-class South London.

porridge British slang for a term of imprisonment, chiefly used in the phrase to **do porridge**. Although the word has been in use from at least the 1950s, it became much more widely known from the mid-1970s with the popular television series *Porridge* (1974–77), a situation comedy of prison life, starring Ronnie Barker.

Porsche A German sports car, much prized for its speed, style, and high-quality engineering. The first Porsche, the 356, was introduced in 1948 as a sports version of the Volkswagon BEETLE, having a similar bug-like appearance. The Volkswagen's designer, Ferdinand Porsche (1875–1951), had been imprisoned by the French for his association with the Nazis, and production of the new car fell to his son, Ferry, who set up the Porsche Company for this purpose. Ferdinand was cleared in 1949 but died not long afterwards, a broken man. In 1963 Ferry and his son 'Butzi' produced the Porsche 911, a slimmed-down version of the 356 that became the classic Porsche model. Its elegant but idiosyncratic appearance has been compared to many things, including a half-used bar of soap, an old-fashioned steel roller skate, and a cross between a Messerschmidt and a dodgem car. In the 1980s the Porsche was much favoured by high-salaried YUPPIES and became a popular symbol of their lifestyle and values.

Porter, Jimmy The central character in John Osborne's play *Look Back in Anger* (1956), whose rantings were taken as typical of the ANGRY YOUNG MEN of the period. The frustrated product of a working-class background and a provincial university, Porter lived in a drab bedsit with his middle-class wife, Alison, who provided the butt for most of his invective.

> She's so clumsy. I watch for her to do the same things every night. The way she jumps on the bed, as if she were stamping on someone's face, and draws the curtains back with a great clatter, in that casually destructive way of hers. It's like someone launching a battleship. Have you ever noticed how noisy women are? Have you? The way they kick the floor about, simply walking over it? Or have you watched them sitting at their dressing tables, dropping their weapons and banging down their bits of boxes and brushes and lipsticks?

At the time, his self-pitying harangues were thought to articulate a general disillusionment with postwar Britain. The play's dingy milieu began the vogue for KITCHEN SINK drama.

Portland Secrets Case *See* KROGER AFFAIR; LONSDALE AFFAIR.

Porton Down Site of the Chemical Defence Establishment on a 7000-acre site near Salisbury Plain, Wiltshire. It was originally established in 1916 to provide the British war machine with gas and chemical weapons for use against the Germans. Attempts in the interwar period, and after 1945, to halt the research for moral and humanitarian reasons were not complied with on the grounds that research into offensive chemical and biological weapons had to proceed in order that the proper antidotes and countermeasures could be developed to protect British troops and, indeed, the British public in future conflicts.

post-. postmodernism A concept embracing all those tendencies in late 20th-century culture that seem to represent a break with the style and values of MODERNISM. It has also been applied to extreme avant-garde works that take Modernist principles to their *reductio ad absurdum*. Postmodernism was originally a label used in architecture as a reaction against the dogmas and ideas of the INTERNATIONAL STYLE. Postmodernist buildings are characterized by an eclectric borrowing from all cultures and periods, a delight in non-functional ornament, and a knowing flirtation with KITSCH. Phenomena as various as rock videos, the novels of Salman Rushdie, jeans commercials, and the HERITAGE INDUSTRY have all been described as postmodern. Attributes of postmodernist work are a playful ironic style, the embracing of cultural pluralism, and a concentration on style and presentation at the expense of substance and context. It is hard not to feel that the term has become a humpty-dumpty word meaning almost anything the user wishes it to mean.

post-traumatic stress disorder (PTSD) A set of symptoms suffered by a person who has been involved in a traumatic event, such as a major car or plane accident or a natural disaster. The symptoms vary but can include depression, mood swings, nightmares and other sleep disorders, personality changes, and feelings of guilt. One of the major problems is that these symptoms can recur, even years after the traumatic incident occurred. The expression was coined by US psychologists treating casualties of the VIETNAM WAR. *See also* SURVIVOR SYNDROME.

post-Vietnam syndrome *See* PVS.

post-viral syndrome (PVS) An alternative name for myalgic encephalomyelitis (*see* ME). Some people prefer this name since it emphasizes the likely cause of the illness.

pot Cannabis, when used as a drug for its euphoric relaxing properties. The term is used of both herbal cannabis (marijuana, grass, hemp) and cannabis resin (hashish, hash). It was the usual term in the BEAT culture of the 1950s and widely adopted by the 'straight' media a decade later – by which time it was considered rather old-fashioned by those who used the drug. The legalization of pot has been a perennial issue in the last 30 years – since its widespread use in America in the 1950s and in the UK in the 1960s. The main argument for its legalization is that it is harmless and that the law, by being so widely flouted, is brought into disrepute: moreover, the fact that pot can only be obtained illegally is likely to lead its users into a criminal subculture in which hard drugs are also available. On the other hand, the government, largely backed by medical and social workers, have adhered to the prohibition on the grounds that pot smoking is a stepping stone to more serious drug abuse and that if it were to be legalized supplies of the drug would have to be made available, which would be a breach of international law. In 1991 a report by lawyers, police, and psychiatrists recommended that cannabis should be reclassified as a lower-category drug, with reduced penalties for its production and supply.

pothead Slang for a person who habitually smokes marijuana (POT). *See also* HEAD.

Potato Jones Captain D. J. Jones, who died in 1962 aged 92. In 1937, with his steamer *Marie Llewellyn* loaded with potatoes, he tried to run General Franco's blockade off Spain but was prevented by a British warship. Two other blockade-running captains were called Ham-and-Egg Jones and Corncob Jones.

Potsdam Conference The last Allied wartime conference, held 17 July–2 August 1945, at Potsdam near Berlin; it was attended by Stalin, Truman, Churchill, and Attlee (who became prime minister after Labour's victory in the general election and took over from Churchill during the second round of discussions). The basis of the postwar settlement in Germany was agreed, involving the division of the country and of Berlin into four zones administered by the four occupying powers – the UK, America, the Soviet Union, and France. The Soviet occupation of E Germany after the fall of Berlin made many of the Potsdam arrangements unenforceable and marked the beginning of the COLD WAR.

Poujadists A short-lived French political party founded by the right-wing grocer-demagogue Pierre Poujade (1920–) in 1953. His party, Union de Défense des Commerçants et Artisans, was born out of a tax revolt by small shopkeepers and farmers in the Lot, who also felt increasingly threatened by the end of food rationing and the postwar growth of big retail businesses. His vitriolic attacks on the tax inspectorate and parliamentary government, his support for Algerie Français, and the quixotic demand for the calling of an 'estates general' to represent the voice of the little man attracted mass support. The 1956 election was fought on these principles and the Poujadists won a surprising 11.6% of the poll, amounting to 2.5 million votes, which returned 50 candidates to the National Assembly.

poverty trap An invidious situation in which low earners who manage to increase their income are worse off than they were before the increase, either as a result of loss of state benefits or of falling into a higher tax bracket.

powder one's nose A euphemism used mainly of women, meaning to go to the lavatory. The 'powder room' is itself a euphemism for the lavatory. It is thought to have first been used in the 1920s.

Powellism The political ideology espoused by the former Conservative MP Enoch Powell (1912–) since the 1960s. He is famous for his speech in Birmingham in April 1968, warning of the social consequences of unrestrained immigration:

> As I look ahead I am filled with foreboding. Like the Roman I seem to see 'The River Tiber foaming with much blood'.

As well as favouring strict immigration controls, Powellism embraced opposition to the maintenance of a British presence 'East of Suez' during the 1960s, emphasis on the necessity of cuts in government spending, belief in the unfettered working of the free market, opposition to British membership of the EC, and support for the Ulster Unionists. Dismissed from Edward Heath's shadow cabinet for his Birmingham speech, he was the United Ulster Unionist Council MP for South Down 1974–87.

power. power dance US Black slang for resistance to oppression, usually expressed in rioting and looting.

power dressing A style in women's fashions in the early 1980s, intended to convey such attributes as wealth, influence, and invulnerability, especially among businesswomen. It favoured sombre colours, limited use of jewellery, shoulder pads, and a 'carefully-managed' look. It was mastered by Margaret Thatcher among others. Actresses in US SOAP OPERAS rapidly took the fashion to extremes.

power sharing A shortlived attempt (1973–74) to find a solution to the problems of Northern Ireland by creating an executive assembly in which the Catholic minority would have a guaranteed share of the seats. In 1972 the STORMONT parliament, which had effectively excluded Catholics from any role in decision-making, was replaced by direct rule from Westminster. At the time, the intention was to reinstate some form of Northern Irish government, as soon as its constitution could be agreed by both communities. This approach seemed to bear fruit in 1973, when William Whitelaw (1918–), the Northern Ireland secretary in the British government, announced that Protestant and Catholic leaders had agreed to serve together in a new Northern Ireland Assembly responsible for all domestic matters, except security. His announcement was followed within weeks by the **Sunningdale Agreement**, which proposed a Council of All Ireland drawing its members from both the Irish Parliaments and the Northern Ireland Assembly. The Assembly opened in January 1974, under the leadership of Brian Faulkner (1921–77). From the start it faced a campaign of organized disruption by Protestant extremists, led by the Rev. Ian Paisley (*see* PAISLEYITE) who were determined to make it unworkable. In May 1974 this object was achieved by a general strike of Protestants, backed by widespread intimidation, which reduced the province to chaos. The Assembly resigned en masse and direct rule from Westminster was resumed.

Praise the Lord and pass the ammunition The title and chorus of a song by Frank Loesser, popular in America in 1942. A US navy chaplain is said to have used these words to a ship's gunner during the Japanese attack on PEARL HARBOR in 1941, although the identity of the chaplain has not been definitely established. During the BUZZ BOMB attacks on London in World War II, a common variation of the phrase was 'Praise the Lord and keep the engine running': when the engine died the bomb would shortly hit the ground.

prang RAF slang in World War II, meaning to bomb a target with evident success; to shoot down another aircraft or to crash one's own; and generally to collide with, or bump into, any vehicle. Hence, also, **wizard prang**, for a wonderful or extremely accurate hit, etc.

prawn. come the raw prawn To try to fool someone, a phrase common among Australian forces during World War II and more widely heard subsequently. It is presumably derived from the idea of someone being deceived into accepting a raw prawn, thinking it is cooked.

pre-. pre-emptive strike A military attack launched to forestall an imminent attack by the enemy.

prefab A small house or other building that has been erected from parts *prefabricated* away from its final site. This method of construction was widely practised after World War II to provide temporary housing as quickly as possible. Because the housing shortage persisted long after the end of the design life of these buildings, they have presented considerable problems as a result of water penetration, etc.

prequel A novel or film script based on the early lives and happenings of characters who have already appeared in an existing novel or film. This word is an adaption of 'sequel', which portrays events that follow those in a novel or film already published. The prequel is a way of extending the potential of a saga-like story, if the original story proves popular, especially if a sequel is not possible, *e.g.* if a major character dies in the core novel or film. Some novels and films have both prequels and sequels.

presoak A preparation added to water in which clothes are soaked before washing in order to loosen and remove dirt. Presoaks, which contain much the same ingredients as washing powder, were first marketed at the end of the 1960s. Modern washing machines now have a pre-wash programme, which serves the same purpose as the presoak process.

pre-teen Denoting a child between 10 and 12 years of age. This word originated in America in the affluent 1950s, when youngsters in this age group were recognized seriously as potential consumers.

preggers *See* HONKERS.

premium bond *See* ERNIE.

preppie or **preppy** A student or graduate of a US preparatory school, or 'prep', an expensive private secondary school that prepares students for college. The stereotype preppie – someone rich, pampered, and well-groomed – became known in the UK from the film *Love Story* (1970), based on a novel by Erich Segal, which was hugely successful on both sides of the Atlantic. It was described by the film critic Alexander Walker as "*Camille* with bullshit".

president. all the president's men Catchphrase embodying the notion of unquestioning loyalty to the president, frequently heard in US political circles. Originally coined by the German-born US politician and diplomat Henry Kissinger (1923–) in a discussion of US policy on Cambodia in 1970 it subsequently acquired a note of irony when used in the context of the WATERGATE scandal. It was the title of a film released in 1976 about the fall of Nixon, starring Dustin Hoffman and Robert Redford.

President Peanuts or **Jiminy Peanuts** Nickname of US President Jimmy Carter (1924–), who was born into a prosperous peanut-farming Georgia family.

Presidium The Presidium of the Supreme Soviet: in the Soviet Union, since 1936, a body elected by the Supreme Soviet that fulfils the role of constitutional head of the state. Its chairman is its representative in ceremonial affairs and it issues ordinances when the Supreme Soviet is not in session. *See* POLITBURO.

press. Press Barons Those newspaper proprietors who were raised to the peerage during the 20th century. They include Alfred Harmsworth (1865–1922), who was created a baron in 1905 and became Viscount Northcliffe in 1917 (*see* NORTHCLIFFE PRESS). Northcliffe's younger brother, Harold Sidney Harmsworth (1868–1940), was created a baron in 1914, becoming Viscount Rothermere in 1919; he took over the *Daily Mail* on his brother's death. William Maxwell Aitken (1879–1964) was created Baron Beaverbrook in 1917. This Scottish-Canadian self-made millionaire was the owner of the *Sunday Express*, the *Daily Express*, and the *Evening Standard*. James Gomer Berry (1883–1968), 1st Viscount Kemsley, was chairman of Kemsley Newspapers Ltd, which owned the *Sunday Times* and other papers. Roy Herbert Thomson (1894–1976), Baron Thomson of Fleet, acquired *The Scotsman* in 1953 and Kemsley Newspapers in 1959.

Press Council A UK body established in 1953 and composed of 18 lay and 18 professional individuals under an independent chairman. Its main purpose was to defend the freedom of the press and to consider complaints made by the public against the press. In 1991 the Council was replaced by the **Press Complaints Commission**, with the brief of determining the ethical behaviour of the press and to deal with complaints against it, but not to defend press freedom.

press the flesh To shake hands, a catchphrase first heard around 1910.

pressure group A group that tries to exert pressure on government officials, public opinion, etc., to promote their own special interests or causes. Their campaign, often aimed at new legislation, may be conducted through letter writing, lobbying, public information, or advertising.

Prestel A form of viewdata service provided by British Telecom.

preventive. preventive detention In UK law, the imprisonment of an offender under the Criminal Justice Act (1948) or its predecessor, the Prevention of Crime Act (1908). Under these Acts, the court could pass a further sentence of 5–14 years on a convicted offender found or admitting to be a habitual criminal, in order to prevent the repetition or continuance of his criminal activities. The 1948 Act was replaced in 1973, when the courts were authorized to extend a term of imprisonment if it was thought appropriate for the protection of the public.

In America, preventive detention refers to the imprisonment without bail of an alleged or suspected offender who, in the judge's view, may commit criminal acts before being brought to trial.

preventive medicine The branch of medicine concerned with identifying possible causes of disease and rectifying or eliminating them before the onset of disease. In its broadest sense, preventive medicine embraces all the activities of specialists in public or community health care and OCCUPATIONAL MEDICINE as well as the advice and treatment given by general practitioners and other health-care workers. In the West, most of the major communicable diseases have now been controlled or eliminated by the use of vaccines and strict quarantine regulations. One notable landmark was the announcement in 1980 by the World Health Organizaiton that smallpox had been effectively eradicated, nearly 200 years after Jenner introduced his cowpox vaccine against the disease. Vaccines developed in this century include those against tuberculosis (1908), whooping cough (1923), yellow fever (1939), measles (1953), polio (1957), and rubella (1965). In THIRD WORLD countries, however, many easily preventable diseases are still rife due to lack of resources and an appropriate health-care infrastructure. Infant mortality is a particular blackspot: in some African countries, for instance, up to 25% of all infants die before their fifth birthday, compared to 1–2% in the West. Preventive medicine in the West has slasher-switched emphasis in the late 20th century – to delaying the onset of non-infectious disease, such as cancer, heart disease, and stroke. This is achieved by screening and education. Regular medical check-ups are now recommended as a means of improving the early detection of disease and so increasing the chances of successful treatment. Mass screening programmes, e.g. for cervical and breast cancer, operate in some countries. People are encouraged to eat wisely, not to smoke, drink in moderation, and take exercise – in short, to tailor their lives to healthy living.

prices and income policy. A government policy that attempts to restrict rises in both the price of goods and individual earnings in order to control inflation. The policy is difficult to enforce and will only be effective if the inflation is caused by rising costs.

prick-teaser Vulgar slang for a female who misleads a man into thinking that she is a willing sexual partner. It is synonymous with **cock-teaser**.

primal. primal scene A child's first observation of sexual intercourse between his parents, as recalled by a patient undergoing Freudian analysis. The recollection, which may be either real or imaginary, is considered by some a major source of neurosis. *See also under* NASTY.

primal scream A type of psychotherapy in which a patient is encouraged, often in a group, to relive the sufferings of his infancy and to express violent emotions about parents or others in primitive screams or aggressive physical acts. Primal therapy was originated by Arthur Janov, a US psychologist who wrote a book with this name in 1970.

prime. Prime Minister of Mirth Nickname of the British actor and music-hall performer Sir George Robey (1869–1954). He became known as the **Darling of the Halls** for an act featuring such characters as Daisy Dilwater, the Mayor of Mudcumdyke, and a red-nosed vicar with staring eyes and a lewd smile. Robey later appeared in plays and films and was in great demand as a pantomime dame.

prime time The evening hours of television viewing approximately between 7 p.m. and 11 p.m. These are the peak viewing hours and therefore command the highest advertising rates. In America, the Federal Communications Commission restricted stations in large markets to three hours of prime-time network programming. This was intended to produce a variety of local programmes but has generally led to repeats of old films and game shows.

primordial soup or **prebiotic soup** A phrase derived from a conjectural description of the primeval oceans by the British biologist J. B. S. Haldane (1892–1964), first published in the 1920s as part of his theory for the origin of life. Haldane envisaged a starkly different oxygen-free atmosphere, containing methane, ammonia, hydrogen, and water. Energy sources, such as lightning and solar radiation, would have caused the formation of organic compounds which, he postulated, "must have accumulated until the primitive oceans reached the consistency of hot dilute soup". Further chemical reactions within this soup would lead eventually to the formation of rudimentary living cells. This theory, also derived independently by the Soviet biologist Alexander Oparin, prompted a famous experiment conducted in 1952 by Stanley Miller, a graduate student at the University of Chicago. Miller attempted to recreate these hypothetical conditions using a fully enclosed reaction vessel containing the supposed raw ingredients of the primitive atmosphere, and subjected them to repeated electric sparks. After one week he analysed the water in the flask to find that it contained, among many other materials, the amino acids glycine and alanine in appreciable amounts. As these are two of the essential building blocks of living organisms some have seized on the result as vindication of the Haldane–Oparin theory. Others have remained sceptical.

Prince of Wails Nickname of the US singer Johnnie Ray (1927–), whose maudlin style also earned him such sobriquets as the **Cry Guy** and the **Nabob of Sob**. He established his lachrymose reputation with the double-sided single 'Cry' and 'The Little White Cloud That Cried', a million-seller in 1952. He was also known for his stage performances in which he sobbed his way through many self-pitying numbers. Part Blackfoot Indian, he was sufficiently deaf to require a hearing aid.

pringle British slang for a young aggressive working-class male of the 1980s who wore expensive DESIGNER sportswear. Pringle is the tradename of an expensive type of woollen jumper, usually V-necked and most popular in such pastel colours as lemon and pale pink.

Prisoner of Spandau Rudolf Hess (1894–1987), Hitler's wartime deputy and a prisoner in Spandau Gaol, Berlin, from 1945 until his death. From 1966 he was the prison's sole inmate. Hess fell into Allied hands following his bizarre solo flight to Scotland in May 1941, apparently intending to discuss peace terms with the Duke of Hamilton. Churchill described this episode as:

> One of those cases where imagination . . . is baffled by the facts as they present themselves.

Berlin Radio announced that the Deputy Führer had been suffering from 'hallucinations'. In May 1945 the Nuremberg judges rejected his plea of insanity and Hess was sentenced to life imprisonment for war crimes. He appears eventually to have committed suicide. The epithet 'Prisoner of Spandau' is used mainly by those who insist that the prisoner was not Hess but a double, substituted by the Nazis at the time of the flight to Scotland or by the Allies at some later date. The charges are based on discrepancies in the medical record, the Allies' refusal to release the prisoner long after he had become harmless, and doubts about the circumstances of his death. The problems raised by this theory seem much greater than any it purports to solve. Hess, quite apart from any of his other claims to notoriety, was the last prisoner to be held in the Tower of London.

private. Private Eye A satirical magazine by Shrewsbury School and Oxbridge friends Christopher Booker, Richard Ingrams, Willie Rushton, and Peter Cook. The first issue (printed on yellow paper) appeared on Friday 25 October 1961. Booker edited it until 1963, then Ingrams (who wanted to call it *The Bladder*) took over until the present editor, Ian Hislop, replaced him in 1988. A product (and the only survivor) of the 1960s passion for satire, the magazine contains a mixture of gossip, satire, cartoons, and provocative articles exposing hypocrisy and corruption in the financial and political establishment. The *Eye* is famous as the persistent target of financially threatening libel suits brought against it by prominent victims. In 1966 the magazine nearly closed after it had to pay £5000 to Lord Russell of Liverpool and in 1977 it had to be helped out by readers' donations after the payment of £85,000 to businessman Sir James Goldsmith. In 1989 *Private Eye* was ordered to pay £600,000 damages to Sonia Sutcliffe, the wife of the Yorkshire Ripper. This was overturned and eventually *Private Eye* paid her £60,000 plus costs in an out-of-court settlement. In 1981 it was estimated that libel costs were running at £100,000 per annum.

privatization The selling of a publicly owned organization to private investors.

This may be done for economic or political reasons. Economically, privatization is only justified if it results in greater efficiency or an increase in competition. Politically, it can be used to increase the number of shareholders in the community by making share offers to the public on generous terms, thus widening support for the capitalist system.

Prix Goncourt The leading French literary prize, established in 1901 in accordance with the will of the writer Edmond de Goncourt (1822–96) in commemoration of himself and his brother Jules (1830–70). It is awarded annually for the best prose work in French. The winner receives a symbolic cheque for the sum of 50 francs, although the work is guaranteed to enter the bestseller lists.

prize money The net proceeds of the sale of enemy shipping and property captured at sea. Prior to 1914 the distribution was confined to the ships of the Royal Navy actually making the capture; since that date all prize money has been pooled and shared out among the navy as a whole. Prize money was paid at the end of World War II for the last time.

PRO Public Relations Officer. A person employed by a large firm, charity, or personality to deal with the media on their behalf and to provide information that shows them in a favourable light.

pro-. pro-am Denoting a sport or sporting event open to both professional and amateur players. It almost invariably refers to a golfing tournament. A special case of the pro-am event is the **pro-celebrity** match, in which professionals compete with well-known names from the entertainment world, usually for charity.

pro-life or **right-to-life** Describing people, groups, or movements that support the right of an unborn foetus to life. Pro-lifers therefore seek to limit or ban legal abortions; they also oppose experiments on embryos. The leading British anti-abortion organizations are the Society for the Protection of the Unborn Child (1966) and LIFE (1970). In America, the pro-life lobby is composed of the Catholic Church, such Protestant fundamentalist groups as the MORAL MAJORITY, and activists of such organizations as the National Right to Life Committee (1970), March for Life, and Right to Life. These activists were responsible for a series of fire-bomb attacks on birth-control and abortion clinics in America during the late 1970s and early 1980s. In 1989 President Bush supported pro-lifers who organized large marches immediately before the Supreme Court put new restraints on abortions.

professional foul A deliberate sporting offence committed to prevent an opponent scoring or winning. Originally, the expression referred to fouls committed by professional footballers but it has extended into the general language to describe tactics undertaken to prevent a rival's success, *e.g.* in business.

Profumo affair The resignation of John Profumo (1915–), Secretary of State for War in Harold Macmillan's Conservative government, in June 1963 because of his liaison with the call girl Christine Keeler. This lady was also sleeping with Lieutenant-Commander Yevgeny Ivanov, an assistant naval attaché at the Soviet Embassy in London, who was also suspected of being a GRU officer. Profumo had first encountered 19-year-old Keeler in July 1961, naked in a swimming pool at a party at Cliveden (*see* CLIVEDEN SET), the country estate of Lord Astor. The party was also attended by Dr Stephen Ward with whom Keeler lived. Ward, an osteopath with various famous patients to whom he occasionally supplied young women ('popsies'), had already introduced Keeler to Ivanov. MI5 learned of Profumo's association with Keeler through Ward, who was supplying them with information on the activities of Ivanov. Warned by a colleague of MI5's concern at the farcical implications of having a Secretary of State for War sharing a mistress with a Soviet agent, Profumo broke off his relationship with Keeler. After an unrelated shooting incident at her flat in December 1962, however, Keeler's activities began to attract the attention of the press and rumours of Profumo's relationship with her became rife. On 22 March 1963 he made a statement in the House of Commons that his relationship with Keeler was entirely innocent. Although subsequent pressure from the opposition on the security angle forced his resignation, it was his lie to the Commons that deprived him of support from his own party. MI5 and Harold Macmillan both declared themselves satisfied that no breach of security had taken place and this conclusion was also reached by the subsequent investigation into the affair by Lord Denning. Stephen Ward was brought to trial in July 1963, charged with various offences under the Sexual Offences Act (1956). When Lord Astor repudiated the evidence of Ward's mistress, the call-girl Mandy Rice-Davies, she replied somewhat archly: "He would, wouldn't he?" Ward committed suicide on 3 August with an overdose of Nembutal. Profumo subsequently devoted himself to social and charity work, was awarded the CBE in 1975, and in 1982 became administrator of Toynbee Hall in London.

> I am sorry to disappoint the vultures.
>
> Ward suicide note.

program A series of instructions, written in a particular computer programming language, which are executed by a computer to perform a specific operation. *See* FORTRAN; MACHINE CODE; PASCAL.

progressive rock *See* FOLK ROCK.

Prohibition The ban on the sale or consumption of intoxicating liquor introduced in America in 1919 by the passage of the Volstead Prohibition Act and enshrined in the Constitution under the 18th Amendment. The introduction of the 'noble experiment' was the result of decades of pressure from temperance groups and the church. By 1906 18 states had introduced some form of restriction or ban on the sale of alcohol and many counties and cities were also 'dry' by virtue of the 'local option' made available by state legislatures to local authorities. Prohibition, however, proved unenforceable; the supply of illicit liquor to a thirsty population by bootleggers spawned organized crime and widespread corruption among the police and politicians. It was finally repealed in 1933.

prom or **promenade concert** A concert in which some of the audience stand in an open area of the concert-hall floor. Promenade concerts date back to the days of the London pleasure gardens, such as Vauxhall and Ranelagh. Mansard had conducted similar concerts at Paris in the 1830s and from 1838 his example was followed at London. In 1895 Sir Henry Wood (see OLD TIMBER) began his famous Promenade Concerts at the Queen's Hall, which he conducted for over half a century and which became a regular feature of London life. In 1927 the BBC took over their management from Chapell's. The destruction of the hall by enemy action in 1941 caused a break in the concerts but they soon started again at the Royal Albert Hall and have continued there ever since. Each Prom season, from mid-July to mid-August, provides Londoners with a feast of serious music from all periods. Every concert is broadcast by the BBC; some are also televised. The **last night of the Proms** is devoted to British music and has become an immensely popular British institution. The second half of the concert always includes Elgar's LAND OF HOPE AND GLORY, Parry's 'Jerusalem', and Wood's 'Fantasia on British Sea-Songs', in which the audience participate with great gusto.

Protocols of the Elders of Zion Forged material published by Serge Nilus in Russia in 1905, based on an earlier forgery of 1903, purporting to outline secret Jewish plans for achieving world power by undermining Gentile morality, family life, and health and by securing a monopoly in international finance, etc. Their falsity was first exposed by Philip Graves, *The Times* correspondent in Constantinople, in 1921 and later judicially, at Berne (1934–35). Their influence in inciting antisemitism, notably among the Russians, and later providing Hitler and his associates with an excuse they knew to be a myth, provide tragic evidence of the power of a smear campaign.

Pru. the man from the Pru *See under* MAN.

Prufrock, J. Alfred The indecisive and introspective hero of the poem by T. S. Eliot (1888–1965), *The Love Song of J. Alfred Prufrock*, which was first published in the Chicago magazine *Poetry and Other Observations* (1917). The poem is in the form of a dramatic monologue, which reveals Prufrock (named after a St Louis furniture firm) as timid, sexually inhibited, bored with the Boston social round, and failing in his resolve to transform his life:

> I have measured out my life in coffee spoons . . .
>
> I grow old . . . I grow old . . .
> I shall wear the bottoms of my trousers rolled . . .
>
> Do I dare to eat a peach?

Prussianism The arrogance and overbearing methods associated with the Prussian military machine and governmental attitudes from the days of Frederick the Great (1712–86) until World War I. Unfortunately there was a return to Prussianism in Germany under the Nazis. *See* JACKBOOT; KÖPENICK HOAX.

> In its simplest form, Prussianism is blind submission. It is a philosophy of a military Order that sought primarily to maintain its position against the

possible revolt of the conquered. It is the spirit of an army carried over into a bureaucracy and into society itself . . . It is discipline – and servility. Standardized.

EDGAR MOWRER: *Germany Puts the Clock Back*, Ch. v.

pseud British slang for a pretentious pseudo-intellectual. The word became popular in the 1960s through its use in the satirical magazine, PRIVATE EYE, which featured a column called 'Pseuds Corner' – a collection of items from other publications containing elements of pretentiousness.

PSL Private-Sector Liquidity. *See* MONEY SUPPLY.

Psmith A character who appears in some of the earlier novels of P. G. Wodehouse, from *Enter Psmith* (1909) to *Leave it to Psmith* (1923). Psmith (originally named Smith – he adds the 'P' himself for effect) is not a monocled silly ass in the Bertie WOOSTER mould, and would be unlikely to join the DRONES' CLUB. Rather, he is an ingenious and resourceful manipulator, old beyond his years. He was based on Rupert D'Oyly Carte (1876–1948), a schoolfriend of the author's cousin, who later succeeded his father as proprietor of the D'Oyly Carte Company and became chairman of the Savoy Hotel.

psychedelic (Gr. *psychē*, soul, mind; *dēloun*, to reveal) Denoting experiences that are thought by some to be mind-expanding or involve heightened mental and sensory awareness. Psychedelic experiences are brought about by hallucinogenic drugs, such as LSD and mescaline. For those who do not take these drugs, psychedelic experiences appear to involve a distortion of reality rather than a more profound view of it. The term, from the jargon of the BEATNIKS and HIPPIES, was imported into the UK from America in the mid-1960s. Soon after, the word **psychedelia** had been coined to refer to the world of psychedelic drugs and the people and phenomena associated with it. The impact of psychedelic drugs on the senses, in particular the distorted images and sounds and kaleidoscopic patterns of light and colour, were imitated or reproduced in paintings, posters, fabric design, and music, which in turn came to be described as psychedelic.

psychedelic art A type of art popular in the late 1960s, characterized by complex swirling patterns of brilliant, often jarring, colours and involving elements of OP ART. In the summer of 1967 designs of this type proliferated in clothing, fabrics, posters, decor, album covers, and all kinds of fashionable bric-à-brac. They also featured prominently in multimedia events (*see* HAPPENING), which combined lightshows, 3D-art installations, and deafening psychedelic rock music to create a totally 'mind-blowing' experience. A favourite technique was to project slides containing coloured oils onto the walls and ceilings, producing vast drifting shapes like amoebas or imploding galaxies. Like other forms of psychedelic art, this was supposed to replicate the visual effects of LSD or other hallucinogens, and was perhaps best appreciated under the same influence.

psychodelicatessen *See* HEAD SHOP.

PTFE *P*oly*t*etra*f*luoro*e*thylene. A synthetic polymer containing the element fluorine, noted for its toughness, resistance to chemical attack, and its low coefficient of friction. It was developed in the 1940s and has a variety of uses; most people know it as the coating for NONSTICK frying pans. It is manufactured under the tradename **Teflon**.

PTSD *See* POST-TRAUMATIC STRESS DISORDER.

public. public access broadcasting US broadcasting channels legally reserved, since 1972, for public-service use. Since a cable system can carry more than 100 channels, many communities have public-access channels devoted to local government, which provide a forum for community organizations and individual comment. This freedom of speech has even occasionally been extended, with considerable controversy, to such groups as the racialist KU KLUX KLAN.

Public Broadcasting Service *See* PBS.

Public Enemy No. 1 The phrase used to describe the US bank robber and murderer John Dillinger (1903–34), who was active 1933–34 in Indiana and Illinois. He was given this impressive status by the Attorney General, Homer Cummings and was finally shot dead in Chicago by FBI agents, having escaped once from police custody. The phrase 'public enemy' is thought to have been coined by the president of the Chicago Crime Commission, Frank Loesch, in an attempt to alert the public to the dangerous nature of such gangsters and to dispel the aura of glamour that the press had created around them. By the 1930s the phrase had become part of the language both in America and in the UK, being applied to anything or anyone undesirable.

public health medicine *See* COMMUNITY MEDICINE.

public lending right (PLR) A UK government scheme, introduced in 1981, to enable authors to earn a small royalty when their books are borrowed from public libraries. Authors register with the PLR Registrar, who makes payments based on averages from some 30 libraries. Nearly 20,000 authors registered for the £4.75 million available for 1991–92. An annual upper limit (£6000 in 1991) on a single author's work is set to help less popular writers. Fiction accounts for nearly 70% of the money earned by authors. In 1990, only 55 authors, led by Catherine Cookson, received the top payment; 11,204 earned from £1 to £99.

public relations officer *See* PRO.

Pugwash An annual international scientific conference with the aim of promoting the constructive and peaceful uses of scientific knowledge. The first conference was held in July 1957, at the home of Canadian philanthropist Cyrus Eaton in Pugwash, Nova Scotia. It was inspired by the Einstein-Russell Memorandum, a document describing the appalling consequences for the human race of nuclear conflict, and called for a conference of scientists from both sides of the Iron Curtain. Subsequent meetings have been held in many different countries; subjects for discussion have included nuclear disarmament, environmental issues, and the problems of the developing world. The Pugwash movement, coordinated by an International Continuing Committee, has produced various reports over the years on arms control, which have contributed to the increase in disarmament since the 1970s.

Pulitzer Prizes Prizes for literary work, journalism, drama, and music, awarded annually from funds left for the purpose by Joseph Pulitzer (1847–1911), a prominent and wealthy US editor and newspaper proprietor.

pull one's finger out Slang for to get moving, to work efficiently. It is often used as a command or an exhortation to one dawdling or doing a job ineffectually. It is now widely heard, although it is regarded by some as too vulgar to use in polite society because of the possible position of the finger that needs pulling out.

pulsar An extremely dense star that emits short bursts of radio waves or other radiation at precise intervals. First discovered in 1968 (*see* LGM), over 300 pulsars have now been identified. It is thought that the strong magnetic field associated with the star focuses the radiation into two beams. The pulses detected are the result of the star's rotation sweeping the beams around, rather like the signal from a lighthouse.

pumpkin time The point at which a period of exceptional prosperity or happiness comes to an end with the status quo being suddenly re-established. The name refers to the time (midnight) when Cinderella's coach reverts to being a pumpkin after the ball.

pundit Hindi for a person learned in the Sanskrit disciplines. In English it is used to describe someone who is an authority on a particular subject. Pundits can be seen, for example, on television programmes giving their expert ideas on such subjects as economic policies or war strategy.

punk An archaic name for a prostitute; it later became a derogatory term for a person or thing considered worthless. In the late 1970s in the UK a youth cult arose known as punk. It began as an anarchic and rebellious movement against society with its adherents wearing spiky or extremely short hair, often dyed green or red; unusual accessories, such as safety-pins through the nose, were another hallmark. The punk movement was reflected on the musical scene with **punk rock**, the music being loud, energetic, and unsophisticated, with the lyrics often having some political content.

purges The systematic elimination of political opponents by Stalin (*see* MAN OF STEEL) from the 1930s to the 1950s. *See also* YEZHOVSHCHINA.

> You can't make an omelette without breaking eggs.
> Joseph STALIN, justifying his tyrannical methods.

Purple Heart (1) A US army medal awarded for wounds received as a result of enemy action while on active service. It consists of a silver heart bearing the effigy of George Washington, suspended from a purple ribbon with white edges. (2) The popular name of a stimulant pill (Drinamyl), so called from its shape and colour.

push. give someone the push To get rid of someone. The expression has a wide range of contexts; for example, it may be used when someone ends a relationship and gives his or her partner the push. It is most frequently used in an employment context, in which it means virtually the same as to sack someone.

push-button war A war fought with guided missiles controlled by pushing a button.

pusher Slang for someone who supplies illegal drugs, particularly someone who knowingly supplies addictive drugs in order to create a captive market. A supplier of non-addictive drugs is called a 'dealer'. The term 'pusher', however, is not used by the addicts themselves (who would probably use the term MAN), although it is widely used by the police and the tabloid press. Pushers are mostly male and many have become suppliers to finance their own drug addictions. Others are not themselves addicts; some combine being pushers with being pimps, supplying drugs to young women addicts in return for their earnings from prostitution.

pussy or **pussycat** (1) Slang for the female genitals, probably deriving from the resemblance of public hair to cats' fur. (2) Slang for a female, viewed as a sex object.

Pussyfoot Johnson W. E. Johnson (1862–1945), the temperance advocate. He gained his nickname from his 'cat-like' policies in pursuing law-breakers in gambling saloons, etc., in Indian territory when serving as Chief Special Officer of the US Indian Service (1908–11). After this he devoted his energies to the cause of PROHIBITION and gave over 4000 lectures on temperance.

put. put down To humiliate. A term widely used since the 1960s. In the noun form, **put-down**, it means a belittling remark or humiliating action.

> Isaak brought the audience round to his way of thinking with a swift "I remember my first drink" put-down.
>
> *The Independent*, 14 March 1991.

put the boot in British slang meaning to kick. It was a favourite 1960s expression of the SKINHEADS, who wore large DOC MARTENS boots. It is also used in a more general non-literal sense meaning to attack someone when they are particularly vulnerable.

PVC Polyvinyl Chloride. A synthetic plastic first developed in the 1930s and made by polymerizing the compound vinyl chloride (chloroethene, CH_2:CHCl). Commonly, the polymer is mixed with plasticizers, pigments, and other additives to give a flexible material used in packaging, electrical insulation, clothing (*e.g.* raincoats), etc. There is also a hard tough variety of the plastic known as **u-PVC** (unplasticized PVC), which is used as a building material (*e.g.* for door and window frames).

PVS (1) Post-Vietnam Syndrome. The emotional instability and serious psychological problems encountered by many US veterans (VETS) of the VIETNAM WAR (1954–75). Many of the US soldiers serving in Vietnam were young and inexperienced conscripts, who faced appalling conditions in which over 55,000 of their compatriots were killed, a fifth accidentally by their own troops. Readjustment to civilian life was made even more difficult by the mood prevailing in America on their return. The attitude of the US people to the war had become so hostile by 1973 that America was forced to begin a withdrawal. (2) *See* POST-VIRAL SYNDROME.

PWA Person With Aids. An abbreviation often used in preference to Aids patient or Aids victim when the number of diagnosed cases increased significantly in the late 1980s.

pylon Properly a monumental gateway (from Gr. *pulon*, a gateway), especially of an Egyptian temple, consisting of two massive towers joined by a bridge over the doorway. The word is now usually applied to the single structures that support the overhead cables that make up the electrical grid system.

Pylon Poets A derogatory nickname for the group of young British left-wing poets – principally W. H. Auden (1907–73), Stephen Spender (1909–), Louis MacNeice (1907–63), and C. Day Lewis (1904–72) – that emerged in the 1930s. It alludes to their sometimes naive enthusiasm for up-to-the-minute themes and imagery, seen at its most self-conscious, perhaps, in Spender's 1933 poem 'The Pylons'. Auden's idiosyncratic descriptions of industrial landscapes were widely imitated by other members of the group, giving their work a coterie flavour.

pyramid selling A method of selling a product using a pyramid-like structure of part-time salespeople. At the apex of the pyramid is the holder of a franchise empowering him to sell a particular product. He sells an agreed quantity of the product to a number of regional organizers who sell off their stock to district distributors, who in turn recruit door-to-door salesmen, each of whom takes a proportion of the distributor's stock. As the franchise holder can sell more goods to his regional organizers than are actually sold to consumers at the base of the pyramid, some participants in the structure are likely to be caught with unsold, and probably unsaleable, stock. Pyramid selling is therefore illegal in the UK.

Pyrex Tradename for a type of borosilicate glass, used domestically and in chemical apparatus for its heat-resistant properties. The name is often used generically for any kind of heatproof glassware. The first such article was produced in 1915; as it was a pie dish, the tradename 'Pie Right' was suggested: however, as the manufacturers already had a range of products with tradenames ending in *-ex*, the new dish was marketed as 'Pyrex'. Any connection with the Greek *pyr*, fire, seems to be coincidental.

Q

Q (1) The pseudonym of the British writer Sir Arthur Quiller-Couch (1863–1944). He compiled the influential first edition of the *Oxford Book of English Verse* (1900) and also wrote literary criticism, short stories, and adventure novels, such as *Dead Man's Rock* (1887). (2) The character in Ian Fleming's James BOND stories, who provides the secret agent with such sophisticated gadgetry as cars that convert into submarines.

Q-score A rating used in the US advertising world to indicate the popular appeal or prestige of a celebrity, hence the value of his or her name in publicity, product endorsements, etc. It is arrived at by marketing research. Fictional characters have been assessed in the same way: in 1990 advertising researchers correctly predicted only modest success for the film *Dick Tracy*, on the grounds that the hero had a Q-score of only 19 – some way below Wonder Woman and a children's puppet called Howdy Dowdy.

Q ships In World War I, the name given to GUNSHIPS camouflaged as tramps. These ships were used to lure U-BOATS to their destruction. Later in the century the UK police used so-called **Q-cars**, ordinary unmarked cars containing ununiformed police, to catch speeding motorists.

QE2 Queen Elizabeth 2. A passenger liner built for the British Cunard Company as the flagship and successor to the QUEEN ELIZABETH. Construction of the 293.52 m (963 ft)-long vessel began in September 1967; after completion the following year she had a gross tonnage of 65,863. She embarked on her maiden voyage in April 1969. The ship upheld the luxurious standards set by her Cunard predecessors, including four swimming pools, a casino, and a 24-hour FAST FOOD restaurant. Capable of carrying 1800 passengers, the QE2 has divided her year between plying the North Atlantic crossing and cruising to all parts of the globe. She remains the monarch of the UK's mercantile fleet and the epitome of stylish travel on the high seas. *See also* QUEEN MARY.

QSO Quasi-Stellar Object. *See* QUASAR.

quackerpuncture A US name for an incompetent or unqualified practitioner of acupuncture. It came into use in the early 1970s when this Chinese medical practice became fashionable in America. 'Quack' has been used to refer to unqualified doctors for more than 300 years.

quad (1) Short for **Quaalude**, a US tradename since 1973 for methaqualone, a sedative. Popular among university students as a sleeping pill, it is a depressant that acts on the central nervous system in much the same way as a barbiturate. (2) Short for QUADRAPHONIC.

Quadrant The codename of a conference that took place at the Citadel in Quebec (11–24 August 1943) between Franklin D. Roosevelt, Winston Churchill, and other Allied leaders. The aim of the conference was to discuss preparations for the Allied invasion of Europe, notably Operation OVERLORD; there were also debates on strategy and command.

quadraphonic The system, available since 1970, for recording music that can be played on four independent loudspeakers. The different voices and instruments are recorded by four microphones gathering the sound from different directions. The blended music on record or tape can then be separated into four channels for directional listening.

quality. quality of life A 1970s catchphrase that encompassed those aspects of everyday life that make it enjoyable or fulfilling. Annual rankings of US cities, employing different combinations of such criteria as weather, health care, education, population density, and pollution, have named such diverse cities as Seattle, Washington, and Pittsburgh as the metropolitan areas providing the best quality of life.

quality time A phrase that originated in America but is now also used in the UK to describe a limited period during the day of a very busy person, when they devote all their attention to the matter in hand. In middle-class families in which both parents work, it is often applied to the hour that follows their return from work, which they devote entirely to playing with their children. Conversely, it may refer to a short period early in the day, before the brain is addled by domestic or other pressures, which people can devote to whatever they want to do without interruption.

quandong An Australian colloquialism for a professional sponger and by extension anyone who accepts drinks, hospitality, etc., without returning the favour. It is often used contemptuously of a woman who allows herself to be entertained by a man but fails to provide the expected quid pro quo. *Quandong* is an Aboriginal name for the native peach, a small semiparasitic tree that depends on a larger tree for its food and shelter.

quango Quasi-Autonomous National (or Non-)Government Organization. An acronym for a body appointed by a minister in the British government to carry out some public duty at the public expense. Some members of a quango are usually civil servants but others are not. Although a quango is not a government agency, it is not entirely independent and is answerable to a minister. ACAS is an example of a quango.

quantum. quantum leap A sudden breakthrough, a significant advance. The phrase is borrowed from the field of physics (*see* QUANTUM THEORY). It has been used in this figurative way since the 1950s.

quantum theory A theory in physics that energy is not transferred continuously but in discrete amounts, called *quanta* (plural of *quantum*). It arose in 1900 as a result of work on the distribution of wavelengths of radiation emitted by hot bodies. At the time, scientists believed that they had the necessary theories to explain all phenomena and the fact that these experimental results were quite different from the theoretical expectations came as a great shock (called the **ultraviolet catastrophe**). In 1900 the German physicist Max Planck explained the result by introducing the idea of quanta of energy (*see* PLANCK CONSTANT). At around the same time, other phenomena were coming to light that needed a quantum explanation. In 1905, Albert Einstein explained the photoelectric effect (the ejection of electrons from matter by light or other electromagnetic radiation) by assuming that light was composed of a stream of particles (photons) having both particle-like behaviour and wave-like behaviour. In 1913, the Danish physicist Niels Bohr (1885–1962) explained the spectrum of the hydrogen atom by suggesting that the electron orbiting the nucleus could only have certain orbits and absorbed or emitted radiation by making a 'quantum jump' from one orbit to another. In 1923, the French theoretician Louis de Broglie (1892–1987) suggested that if light waves could sometimes behave as particles then particles could, under certain circumstances, behave as waves. 1927 saw the publication of HEISENBERG'S UNCERTAINTY PRINCIPLE. Subsequently, various mathematical formulations of the quantum idea were developed, known as **quantum mechanics**.

Quantum mechanics has been extremely successful in describing and predicting the behaviour of atoms and subatomic particles. It does, however, have profound and, as yet, unresolved philosophical problems associated with it. For example, the idea that electrons sometimes behave as waves and sometimes as particles, depending on the experimental conditions, has caused people to ask what electrons actually are. Sir Arthur Eddington once suggested that the electron was a particle on Mondays, Wednesdays, and Fridays, and a wave on Tuesdays and Thursdays. Niels Bohr, in 1927, formulated the **complementarity principle**, in which he said that there was no point in looking for the 'underlying reality'. The only reality was the result obtained by making an observation; different types of observation produce different types of result. Evidence from different observations may not be amenable to being presented in a single model and therefore different pieces of evidence gave complementary conclusions. A consequence of this view, and of the uncertainty principle, is that our knowledge of the universe can never be absolute but always depends on probabilities.

This view of quantum mechanics is known as the **Copenhagen interpretation** (after Bohr's university) and has been highly influential among physicists, even though it seems in some ways to be unacceptable on a commonsense basis. Bohr was once reputed to have admonished a student researching quantum theory by telling him:

> We all know that your ideas are ridiculous but some of us wonder whether they are ridiculous enough!

Not everyone agreed with this uncertain view of physics. Einstein, in particular, believed until the end of his life that there is an underlying explanation:

> God does not play dice with the Universe! He may be subtle, but He is not malicious.

Other physicists have pointed out paradoxes in the theory (*see* SCHRÖDINGER'S CAT).

quark A subatomic particle believed to be a fundamental building block of matter. The idea of quarks was first put forward by the US theoretical physicist Murray Gell-Mann (1929–) in 1964. He suggested that quarks have an electric charge that is a fraction of the electron's charge and that certain types of particle are composed of several quarks, of which there were originally three types. The name 'quark' was taken by Gell-Mann from a phrase in James Joyce's book *Finnegans Wake*, "Three quarks for Muster Mark". Protons, neutrons, and similar particles are composed of three quarks. Mesons are made of two quarks (a quark combined with an antiquark). Further extensions of the quark hypothesis have since been made, in which the quarks are characterized by various 'flavours' and 'colours'; they are held together by exchanging particles known as gluons (because they glue the quarks together).

Quark theory has been extremely successful in predicting and explaining the existence and properties of ELEMENTARY PARTICLES. The only problem is that, despite many efforts, nobody has ever detected the existence of a free quark or gluon. It is probable that the energies required to separate them are too large to be obtained in current particle accelerators.

quartz crystal A small crystal of quartz that is piezoelectric; *i.e.* a stress on the crystal produces an electric voltage between opposite faces. Crystals of quartz have a natural frequency of vibration and can be used to regulate the frequency of an electric circuit to a high degree of accuracy (a variation in timing of less than one tenth of a second in a year). Quartz crystal oscillators have many uses, particularly in regulating clocks and watches. Quartz watches driven by small batteries were first introduced in the 1960s, originally with a digital display but also with a conventional analog display. Their invention caused extensive redundancies in the Swiss watch industry.

quasar *Quas*i-Stell*ar* Object, or QSO. A distant astronomical object thought to be the nucleus of a galaxy. Quasars are the most distant observed objects in the universe, being up to 10^{10} light-years away. Discovered originally by radioastronomers, the US astronomer Allan Sandage (1926–) first observed one using an optical telescope in 1960. Quasars are pointlike objects that have very large REDSHIFTS. It is possible that they may be BLACK HOLES that are attracting matter in the surrounding galaxy.

Quatermass. It looks like something out of Quatermass An expression used to describe any weird and horrific creature. It is a reference to the three BBC TV science-fiction series, broadcast in the 1950s, called *Quatermass*, *The Quatermass Experiment*, and *Quatermass and the Pit*. Quatermass was the hero professor, played by the actor André Morell. In the first series, *Quatermass*, an astronaut returned from space slowly mutated into a spreading fungal plant. In the second series, *The Quatermass Experiment*, the scientists created a horrendous organic monster that needed a diet of corpses to survive. The expression is still heard today.

queen Slang for a male homosexual, especially one who is effeminate, or an older man affecting the female role. Both 'queen' and the earlier *quean* (derived from Old English *cwene*, woman) were formerly used to mean a whore; they were later applied to male prostitutes (who are often effeminate or transvestite), effeminate males, and then to male homosexuals generally.

Ellery Queen A fictional detective who is also the pseudonymous author of the stories in which he appears. These stories were actually written under the joint authorship of Frederic Dannay (1905–71) and Manfred Lee (1905–). *The Roman Hat Mystery* (1929) was followed by many more Ellery Queen stories; the popularity of the detective led to the launch of *Ellery Queen's Mystery Magazine* in 1941. Some of the stories were adapted for the cinema in the 1930s and 1940s. The US actor Jim Hutton played the role of the detective in a television series of the mid-1970s.

Queen Charlotte's Ball An annual event held at the Grosvenor House Hotel, London, to raise funds for Queen Charlotte's Hospital. Queen Charlotte's Birthday Ball was inaugurated in 1925 and held annually in May until 1976, as a major event of the London 'season', when debutantes 'came out' into society. It was revived in 1989 and is now held in September: around 150 debutantes are invited, together with representatives of the Royal Family and the media, celebrities from the world of entertainment and fashion, and consultants from Queen Charlotte's Hospital. A huge birthday cake is traditionally made for the occasion: the debutantes file past in a long procession, curtsying to the cake, before it is ceremonially cut.

Queen Elizabeth Either of two illustrious British vessels of the 20th century. The battleship HMS *Queen Elizabeth*, launched in 1913, saw action in both World Wars. This 183 m (600 ft)-long vessel, of 27,500 tons displacement, gave her name to a class of fast well-armoured battleships that included *Warspite*, *Valiant*, *Barham*, and *Malaya*, all launched between 1913 and 1915. *Queen Elizabeth* went into action at the DARDANELLES in February 1915; in November 1916 she became the flagship for the fleet's C-in-C, Admiral Beatty. The naval armistice with Germany was signed on board the *Queen Elizabeth* at Rosyth on 15 November 1918. After a reconstruction (1937–41) she was commissioned into the Mediterranean fleet and took part in the action to evacuate Crete in May 1941. In December she was struck by an Italian manned torpedo in Alexandria harbour and needed extensive repairs, but later re-entered the war to serve in home waters and the Far East. She was scrapped in 1948.

Her namesake, RMS *Queen Elizabeth*, was launched in 1938, built by the Cunard Steamship Company as a companion to their passenger liner, QUEEN MARY. However, war intervened, and in 1940 the new vessel sailed secretly to New York and thence to Singapore for fitting out as a troop carrier. Only when hostilities ceased was she converted to a passenger liner – the world's largest, with an original gross tonnage of 83,673 and a length of 314 m (1031 ft). She finally embarked on her first commercial voyage on 16 October 1946, sailing from Southampton to New York. In 1968, with her successor *Queen Elizabeth 2* (*see* QE2) being fitted out, Cunard sold her to a US company. A plan to convert her to a convention centre and tourist attraction fell through and in 1970 she sailed from her mooring at Port Everglades, Florida, to Hong Kong, under the ownership of Taiwanese shipping tycoon, C. Y. Tung. Again, fate intervened, this time on 9 January 1972, when several fires apparently started simultaneously swept the ship and gutted this one-time denizen of the world's sealanes. Ignominiously she sank, a victim of suspected arson, and was later cut up for scrap.

Queen Mary A luxury passenger liner built by the UK's Cunard Steamship Company and launched in September 1934, primarily for service on the company's transatlantic route. From 1938 until after the war she held the prestigious BLUE RIBAND OF THE ATLANTIC for the fastest transatlantic round trip, clocking up average speeds of 20.99 knots westbound and 31.69 knots eastbound. Like her younger companion ship, QUEEN ELIZABETH, the RMS *Queen Mary* served as a troop ship during World War II; during the latter half of the war, as a transatlantic ferry, she could carry up to 15,000 troops. Refitted as a liner after the war, she continued to offer passengers a unique blend of leisure and opulence. However, faced with growing competition from airlines, the company sold her in 1967, and she is now moored at Long Beach, California, as a floating museum and hotel.

Queen of Crime Nickname of the British detective-story writer Dame Agatha Christie (1890–1976). Born Agatha Mary Clarissa Miller, she wrote more than 70 novels and plays and created two popular amateur sleuths, Hercule POIROT and Miss MARPLE. Her works, many of which have been adapted for cinema and television, are characterized by complex plots in which the reader is constantly misled. They include the novels *Murder on the Orient Express* (1934) and *Death on the Nile* (1937) and the play THE MOUSETRAP (1952). Her private life created its own mystery. In 1914 she married Archibald Christie, whose name she used throughout her writing career, although they were divorced in 1928, two years after her own mysterious disappearance. She was finally found in a health resort, apparently suffering from amnesia. A full explanation of this episode has never been given; for some it was regarded as a publicity stunt, for others a genuine attack of amnesia, perhaps brought on by her failing marriage. In 1930 she married the archaeologist Max Mallowan.

Queen of the Air A press nickname for the British aviator Amy Johnson (1903–41). In April 1930 she piloted a second-hand Gypsy Moth aircraft from Croydon to Darwin in 19 days, becoming the first woman to fly solo from the UK to Australia. The 10,000-mile journey, undertaken at the age of 27 and with only a hundred hours previous flying experience, made her a national heroine and the darling of the press. She later made record-breaking flights from Siberia to Tokyo (1931) and from the UK to Cape Town (1932). In 1932 she married the aviator Jim Mollison (1905–59), with whom she flew the Atlantic in 1936, although the marriage later broke up. In 1941 she was flying a wartime mission for the Air Ministry when her plane disappeared over the Thames Estuary.

> Had I been a man I might have explored the Poles or climbed Mt Everest, but as it was my spirit found outlet in the air.

Queen of the Halls Nickname of the British music-hall artiste Marie Lloyd (1870–1922). Born Matilda Alice Victoria Wood, she was an immensely popular singer and comedienne: her alternative nickname, 'Our Marie', indicates the warmth of feeling with which she was regarded by the British public. Her most famous songs include 'Oh! Mr Porter' and 'A Little of What You Fancy Does You Good'. After a career of nearly 40 years Marie Lloyd collapsed on stage in 1922 and died a few days later.

Queen's Awards The Queen's Award to Industry, an award instituted by royal warrant in 1965, was given to a British firm for outstanding achievement. In 1976 it was replaced by two separate awards, **The Queen's Award for Export Achievement**, for a sustained increase in export earnings, and **The Queen's Award for Technological Achievement**, for a significant advance in technology. The awards are announced on the Queen's natural birthday (*see* QUEEN'S BIRTHDAY), are held for five years, and enable the winners to use a special emblem on their stationery and to fly a special flag.

Queen's birthday Either of two days in the calendar. The natural birthday of the monarch, currently 21 April, is celebrated by the hoisting of the Union flag over public buildings throughout the nation. A further ceremonial touch is shown by judges of the Queen's Bench Division, who mark this red-letter day literally, by wearing scarlet robes. However, full celebrations are deferred until the official birthday – not a fixed date but generally a Saturday in the middle of June (before 1958 it was fixed on the second Thursday in June). The centrepiece of the day is the trooping the colour ceremony on Horse Guards Parade in London, which until 1985 the Queen customarily attended on horseback. Announcement of the Birthday Honours list coincides with the Queen's official birthday. The official birthday was introduced during the reign of Edward VII (1901–10), who sensibly preferred to hold the outdoor ceremonials in mid-summer rather than on his natural birthday in November.

Queen's English *See* RECEIVED PRONUNCIATION.

Queen's Flight A fleet of aircraft used by the Queen, other members of the Royal Family, senior government ministers, and foreign dignitaries. The flight is maintained by the Ministry of Defence and stationed at RAF Benson, Oxfordshire. For short trips there are Wessex helicopters or Hawker-Siddeley Andovers; longer overseas flights are usually made by jet, either a BA 146-100 or a VC 10. Edward VIII created the first King's Flight in 1936; since then a special fleet has conveyed royalty at home and abroad. The royal craft are granted specially wide flight paths, known as 'purple corridors', to minimize the risk of collision with other aircraft. The sovereign and the heir to the throne never travel on the same aircraft.

Queen's Gallantry Medal A decoration for outstanding bravery bestowed on civilians or service personnel. It was introduced in 1974.

Queen's Guide A holder of the premier award of the GIRL GUIDES movement, open to Rangers aged between 16 and 18 years. The present syllabus generally takes about two years to complete; it involves undertaking various types of community service and an enterprise test. The badge of Queen's Guide must be earned before the entrant's 19th birthday. The award was instituted in 1945 for 1st Class Guides who demonstrated qualities of service, commitment, and conduct consistent with the ideals of the Guides' founder, Lord Baden-Powell.

Queen's Scout A holder of the highest award attainable by a Venture Scout, open to scouts of either sex, who already possess the Venture Scout Award. Candidates must fulfil various personal and practical requirements, including planning and successfully undertaking a 4–5-day cross-country expedition, and provide evidence of regular community and social service. Award-winners receive a gold crown uniform insignia and a special Royal Certificate from the Queen. The Award was introduced by King Edward VII, as the King's Scout Award. In 1934, watched by George V and other members of the Royal Family, the first annual National Scout Service and Review was held at Windsor, which Queen's Scouts (or King's Scouts) are privileged to attend.

queer (1) A slang name for a homosexual. This pejorative term has been largely replaced by GAY.

> Young American homosexuals want to be called queer rather than gay because it has more 'political potency'. They chant at rallies: 'We're here, we're queer – get used to it.' The trend, led by Militants Queer Nation, is also set to sweep Britain. Lesbian, Liza Powers, 34, said: 'Using a word that is offensive is a way of showing anger. Gay is white middle class.'
>
> *The Sun*, 9 April 1991.

(2) In underworld jargon, something of little value. (3) Ill or unwell, as in, 'he couldn't come to the office yesterday, he felt queer'.

queer-basher British 1960s slang for someone who physically attacks or victimizes male homosexuals. It can also be used figuratively for someone who is prejudiced against homosexuals.

Queer Hardie Nickname of the British Labour politician (James) Keir Hardie (1856–1915). A former coal miner and active trade unionist, he was a cofounder and chairman of the Independent Labour Party and the Labour Representation Committee, which became the LABOUR PARTY in 1906. His nickname relates to his eccentricity: on his first day in Parliament, for example, he arrived in the cloth cap that was to become his trademark. For the last 15 years of his life Hardie served as MP for Merthyr Tydfil. An ardent pacifist, he died disillusioned with the Labour Party's support for World War I.

queer-rolling British slang for robbing a male homosexual. **Rolling** was originally robbing someone who was drunk by rolling them over to go through their pockets. It is now used generally to mean rob.

> He himself rolled drunks on the subway for drug money.
>
> *The Independent*, 15 March 1991.

Quemoy crisis One of two periods of heightened international tension in the 1950s arising from the disputed sovereignty of Quemoy and Matsu islands, just of the E China coast. The islands had remained under Nationalist control after the Communist victory on the mainland in 1949, and in 1954 the Communist Chinese premier, Chou En-lai, declared his intention of ousting the Nationalists from their last strongholds of Taiwan and nearby islands. Communist forces started an artillery bombardment of Quemoy and Matsu in September 1954, which prompted the signing, in December, of a Mutual Defence treaty between the Nationalists and their principal ally, America. Early in 1955 Congress authorized US military action in the event of a threatened Communist invasion of the disputed islands. Crisis flared again in August 1958 with a renewed Communist bombardment of Quemoy, now home to a large Nationalist garrison. The Americans, wary of being drawn into a major conflict, criticized the Nationalists for their military build-up on Quemoy and effectively abandoned their policy of endorsing Nationalist hopes of recapturing the Chinese mainland. Although intermittent shelling continued on both sides, the confrontation was avoided.

question time The part of the timetable in both Houses of Parliament during which ministers reply to questions put by members or peers. In the House of Commons, question time commences at the start of the sitting every day except Friday, lasting for at least three-quarters of an hour, and ends not later than 3.30 p.m. Replies to questions of a complicated or personal nature are generally given in written form and sent to the member personally, besides being printed in Hansard. Members requiring oral answers must give at least two days' notice before the day on which the minister concerned is scheduled to appear. After the minister has read out the answer, the questioner usually asks one or more supplementary questions, with further responses from the minister. On Tuesdays and Thursdays, the prime minister appears to answer questions, commencing at 3.15 p.m. Often this takes the form of a set piece confrontation with the leader of the Opposition on a topic of current concern. A frequent ploy used in an effort to catch the prime minister off guard is to make the original question simply an innocuous enquiry about the prime minister's official engagements for the day. This provides the opportunity for a supplementary question on virtually any issue. With the advent of live broadcasting of Parliament, question time has assumed greater significance, with its lively but ritualized exchanges between the country's leading politicians.

quick. quick and dirty Denoting something that has been hastily put together and is therefore likely to be inaccurate or lacking in final polish. The phrase dates from about 1960, when it was used in US magazine publishing. In modern usage it might be applied to the initial printout of a computer program.

quickie (1) In film jargon, a cheaply produced film to catch the less discriminating and make a quick return on the money invested. *See* QUOTA QUICKIE. (2) In everyday speech, a quick drink, as in 'Come and have a quickie', or an impromptu and rapid act of sexual intercourse, as in 'We've just got time for a quickie'.

quid. not the full quid An Australian expression meaning not fully possessed of one's faculties; half-witted or mad. It dates from the time when the pound (quid) was still used in Australia and has many common variants, such as 'ten bob short of a quid', 'only tuppence in the quid', etc.

quiet. All quiet on the Western Front *See under* ALL.

quiff (1) British slang for a male hairstyle in which the hair at the front is worn long but brushed up and back. It usually needs to be held in place by some kind of hair preparation or by allowing the hair to remain greasy. It was a very popular style with the TEDDY BOYS and rockers (*see* MODS AND ROCKERS) of the 1950s and 1960s and is still worn today, especially by those who wish to imitate those styles.

> ... a quiff that looks as if it's been piped on like stiff black cream.
>
> *The Independent*, 13 March 1991.

(2) British slang for a male homosexual or an effeminate male. This sense is probably derived from a combination of QUEER and POOF.

quill driver A clerical member of the armed services, particularly the Royal Navy. In the 19th century it was a slightly derogatory term in standard English for a clerk but since then has survived only in services slang.

quisling Any traitor or fifth columnist. The name comes from Vidkun Quisling (1887–1945), the Norwegian admirer of Mussolini and Hitler, who acted as advance agent for the German invasion of Norway in 1940. He duly became puppet minister-president. He surrendered (9 May 1945) after the German defeat and was tried and shot (24 October).

quonset hut US name for a prefabricated building made of corrugated iron sheet. The UK equivalent is the NISSEN HUT. The name comes from Quonset Point, Rhode Island, where these buildings were first made in the early 1940s.

quota. quota hopping The practice of registering a business in an EC nation other than one's own in order to take advantage of that nation's more favourable production quotas. The best-known case in recent years involved Spanish fishing boats registering as British in order to benefit from the UK fishing quota. The Merchant Shipping Act (1989) was passed to prevent this abuse.

quota quickie In the 1920s and 1930s, a type of inferior B-MOVIE churned out by British studios in order to take advantage of the **quota system**. This was a well-intentioned measure requiring British cinemas to show a certain percentage of home-produced films. In practice, however, the dearth of good British material meant that cinemas could only make up the quota by accepting substandard products. As a result, poor-quality low-budget films acquired a distribution they would never have gained on their own merits; this made them commercially attractive to produce.

quota system A US equal-rights solution, dating from the mid-1960s, to the problem of ensuring that members of minority groups have a fair chance of being employed or educated. The quota system sets a minimum number or percentage of minorities to be hired by a company, accepted as students in a university, etc. This assistance to such groups as Blacks and women has been called REVERSE DISCRIMINATION by some, as more highly qualified candidates who are not members of a minority may be rejected to enable the quota to be met. *See* QUOTA QUICKIE.

qwerty or **QWERTY** The standard keyboard on an English-letter typewriter, wordprocessor, or computer. This name comes from the first keys of the top left row of letters. A 'querty keyboard' entered the language in the late 1920s, when it was designed, not to put the letters in the most convenient positions, but to slow the user down so that the old-fashioned mechanical typewriter did not jam as a result of being tapped too rapidly.

R

R Restricted. A cinema certification in America since 1968 for films that cannot be seen by persons under 17 unless accompanied by a parent or guardian. *See also* G; PG; X.

R & B *See* RHYTHM-AND-BLUES.

R & D Research and Development. A mainstay of competitive companies and international corporations, involving scientific research on both production methods and materials to enable products and processes to be developed and improved. Research began to be undertaken seriously at the start of the 20th century as scientists were brought into industry. Some of the first US research laboratories were opened at General Electric in 1900, Du Pont in 1902, and Bell Telephone in 1907. R & D is a major governmental expense in the development and updating of military hardware.

R and R Relaxation and Recreation. Army slang abbreviation still used by older people outside the army.

R101 British airship, the destruction of which, on 5 October 1930, signalled the end of airship development for many years. The R101 was the pride of the British aeronautical industry when it departed from England on its maiden non-stop journey to India. Bad weather, coupled with insufficient testing before the flight, caused the airship to crash in a wood near Beauvais in N France; 48 people died in the inferno resulting from the combustion of its 5½ million cubic feet of hydrogen. A curious postscript to the tragedy was a séance held in London three days later: a list of technical defects in the R101 was allegedly communicated through the medium; these were confirmed a year later when the results of the official enquiry were published.

raas Jamaican term of abuse, also used as an exclamation of anger or contempt. It is a shortened form of 'up your arse' or *raascla*, literally a cloth for wiping the arse.

Rab The nickname of the British Conservative politician Richard Austen Butler (1902–82), based on his initials. Butler held a number of important government posts, though he failed in both his attempts to become leader of the Conservative Party (Harold Wilson is said to have described him as 'the best prime minister we never had'). He is best remembered for his Education Act (1944), which introduced secondary education for all without payment.

Rab's Boys The bright young Tories who helped R. A. Butler to reshape Conservative social and economic policy after the party's electoral defeat in 1945. They were mostly members of the Conservative Research Department and the party's industrial policy committee, both headed by Butler. In particular, they are credited with changing the Conservatives' attitude to the WELFARE STATE, nationalization, and unemployment.

race. Race for the Sea The attempt by the Allied and German armies to achieve a decisive victory on the WESTERN FRONT in the autumn of 1914 by outflanking one another's lines to the north before reaching the coast of Flanders. The Battle of the Marne (5–10 September) had marked the final defeat of the famous SCHLIEFFEN PLAN, by which the Germans had hoped to outflank and encircle the French by advancing through Belgium. From mid-September, both sides attempted to extend their lines northwards through Flanders, fighting a series of bitter skirmishes, which culminated in the first Battle of YPRES, 20 October–18 November. The BEF suffered 50,000 casualties at Ypres and was virtually wiped out but the German attempt to break through and capture the Channel Ports was decisively frustrated. The Race for the Sea therefore ended in stalemate; from November 1914 the Western Front settled into static trench warfare, which persisted until the armistice in 1918. *See* PASSCHENDAELE.

race music From the 1920s to the 1940s, a euphemistic term for various musical styles, especially BLUES and RHYTHM-AND-

BLUES, played and appreciated by US Blacks. It was invented by record companies who, in the racial climate of the time, felt sensitive about advertising 'Negro' music. Until the 1950s most companies operated a type of musical segregation, putting out records by or appealing to Blacks on separate 'race' labels.

racism or **racialism** Belief in the genetic superiority of a particular race (invariably one's own), leading to prejudice or brutality towards people of other races. 'Racialism' is the older term, dating from the early years of this century, while 'racism' came into widespread use with the rise of Nazism in the 1930s. There is some disagreement as to whether the terms are exact synonyms. 'Racialism' is more likely to be used of pseudo-scientific theories purporting to show that moral or intellectual qualities are transmitted in the same way as physical characteristics, while 'racism' refers to the behaviour of those who practise racial discrimination. Racism itself became illegal in the UK with the passing of the Race Relations Acts (1965, 1968, and 1978). *See also* CIVIL RIGHTS MOVEMENT; APARTHEID.

In recent years racism, real or supposed, has become a highly contentious issue in such areas as education and local authority spending. LOONY LEFT councils have been charged with absurd oversensitivity to, for example, racial stereotyping in children's reading books and a sinister obsession with rooting out 'unconscious racism' among their employees. Upon investigation, some of the most notorious instances of this (such as the banning of 'Baa Baa Black Sheep' on racial grounds or the suspension of an employee for asking for 'black' coffee) have turned out to be URBAN LEGENDS or fabrications by tabloid journalists.

Rachmanism Extortion and general exploitation by a landlord of his tenants. After Peter Rachman (1920–62), a Polish immigrant whose undesirable activities of this kind in the Paddington area of London were brought to light in 1962–63.

racket jacket US Black slang for a type of thigh-length man's jacket with padded shoulders and narrow cuffs, usually worn as the top half of a ZOOT-SUIT. They were fashionable in the 1940s and had a somewhat raffish sleazy image. The name suggests noisy revelry, a 'loud' or flashy style, and involvement with the underworld.

RADA Royal Academy of Dramatic Art. The drama school founded in 1904 by Herbert Beerhohm Tree. Originally it was located at Her (then His) Majesty's Theatre, London, but moved to the present Gower Street site in 1905. For many years it was run by Sir Kenneth Barnes (1878–1957); its theatre, the Vanbrugh, opened in 1954 and was named after his actress sisters, Irene and Violet Vanbrugh. RADA's previous theatre was destroyed in a bombing raid in 1941. Many of the UK's leading actors and actresses learnt their craft at RADA; among its alumni are Margaret Lockwood, Richard Attenborough, Alan Bates, and Glenda Jackson.

radar An acronym formed from *ra*dio *d*etection *a*nd *r*anging; originally a means of detecting the direction and range of aircraft, ships, etc., by the reflection of centimetric radio waves. It is particularly valuable at night or in fog. It was first developed by Sir Robert Watson-Watt in 1934–35 (and independently in America, France, and Germany) and was of great importance during World War II, especially during the BATTLE OF BRITAIN. It has since been greatly extended so that automatic guidance and navigation of aircraft, missiles, ships, etc., can be achieved by computerized on-board radar equipment.

radar trap A section of road or motorway monitored by police radar to catch speeding morotists. Fixed radar speed traps first came into operation in the late 1950s, but with the increasing miniaturization of electronic components the latest police radar devices are easily portable and include vehicle-mounted and handheld continuous-wave radar guns. These devices, which monitor the speed of motorists from a patrolling police vehicle, are used in tandem with ancillary video equipment to record details of the speed and direction of offenders.

radical chic The fad in the late 1960s among members of high society to socialize and sympathize with radicals. The expression was coined by the US journalist and writer Tom Wolfe (1931–) in his 1970 book, *Radical Chic* (*Mau-Mauing the Flak Catchers*). These new social attitudes, Wolfe later recalled, created times in which:

> Manners and morals, styles of living, attitudes toward the world changed the country more crucially than any political events.

radio. radioastronomy The branch of astronomy concerned with detecting radio waves from sources in space. It began with the accidental discovery in 1932 by the US radio engineer Karl Jansky (1905–50), of radio sources outside the Earth. Jansky was at that time investigating static in a radio set and trying to track down its source. From the late 1940s, it became a major research field. *See* JANSKY; JODRELL BANK; LGM; PULSAR; QUASAR.

radiocarbon dating *See* CARBON DATING.

Radio Caroline The first UK offshore commercial 'pirate' radio station, which began broadcasting on Easter Sunday, 29 March 1964. The station was set up by Ronan O'Rahilly, a music agent, on an ex-Danish passenger ferry *Frederica*, which was equipped with two 10 kW transmitters and a 168 foot (51 m) radio mast; the *Frederica* was anchored outside British territorial waters, 3½ miles off Frinton-on-Sea, Essex, to evade the British government ban on commercial broadcasting. Within three weeks the pop station attracted nearly seven million listeners and could command a rate of £190 for 60 seconds air time from advertisers. In the wake of Radio Caroline's success, numerous other pirate stations of varying quality opened, such as Radio Scotland, Radio England, and Radio Sutch (run by 'Screaming Lord Sutch', ex-pop singer and eccentric by-election candidate). In July 1964, one of these rivals, Radio Atlanta, joined forces with Caroline to become Radio Caroline North, and was anchored 3½ miles off Ramsey, Isle of Man. All the pirate stations were outlawed by the Marine Broadcasting (Offences) Act, which came into operation in August 1967. In the same year the BBC introduced Radio One to satisfy the public appetite for non-stop pop music, employing young talents, such as Tony Blackburn, Johnny Walker, and Simon Dee, all of whom had begun their careers on Radio Caroline as pirate disc jockeys.

Radio City Part of the ROCKEFELLER CENTER in New York City. Radio City consists of five buildings in the W part of the Rockefeller Center, used by the National Broadcasting Company (NBC).

Radio Doctor Dr Charles Hill (1904–89), 'the doctor with the greatest number of patients in the world' (listener research once estimated his audience at 14 million), who broadcast regular five-minute radio talks dispensing advice on common medical problems from the 1930s to 1950s. He was well known for his distinctive deep broadcasting voice and the occasional outrageousness of his comments. Hill was secretary of the BMA (1944–50), became the Liberal Conservative MP for Luton in 1950, and as Lord Hill went on to become successively Chairman of the ITA (1963–67) and Chairman of the Governors of the BBC (1967–72).

> ... too much booze, causing you to flop down in bed like a sack of potatoes, usually on your back with your face to high heaven, and your beautifully expired air ascending to a heaven you'll never reach! Remedy obvious – the water wagon.
>
> THE RADIO DOCTOR on the causes and treatment of snoring.

radiopaging *See* BLEEPER.

radiophobia The fear of radioactivity shown by the public at large, especially those who live near nuclear installations. It is used pejoratively by those who make their living from the nuclear-power industry.

RAF Royal Air Force. The UK's principal military aviation service, formed on 1 April 1918 by amalgamation of the Royal Flying Corps (*see* RFC) and the Royal Naval Air Service. Headed by Viscount Trenchard, first Marshal of the RAF, the newly independent force was to play an important role in ending World War I by stepping up bombing raids on German industrial as well as military targets. After the end of the war, the RAF was slimmed down and set about securing a technically advanced aircraft manufacturing industry to supply its needs. The new craft were tested in record-breaking attempts and air races around the world, and in 1927 an RAF team gained the first of several victories in the SCHNEIDER TROPHY, flying planes specially built by R. J. Mitchell, who later designed the famous SPITFIRE. These Schneider-trophy aircraft were powered by Rolls Royce engines, which developed into the Merlin, used throughout the war in the Spitfire. Despite rearmament from the mid-1930s, the RAF entered World War II at a great numerical disadvantage to the LUFTWAFFE. Nevertheless, they soon distinguished themselves, notably in providing air cover for the evacuation of Allied troops from DUNKIRK in May 1940. Another critical test came in the late summer and autumn of 1940 – the BATTLE OF BRITAIN (*see also* FEW, THE).

Most of the theatres of war saw the RAF playing key roles – in the Mediterranean, North Africa, the North Atlantic, and the Far East. One outstanding action was the gallant air defence of Malta from mid-1940 to the end of 1942 by a force initially comprising three Gladiator biplanes, later reinforced by HURRICANES and Spitfires. At home, Bomber Command, led from 1942 by BOMBER HARRIS, intensified its strategic bombing of military and industrial targets in Germany and occupied countries. From 1943 huge bomber formations were regularly making night-time sorties over Germany. More controversially, civilian areas of German towns and cities were also targetted. RAF casualties in World War II were over 70,000 killed and nearly 23,000 wounded. Some 13,000 airmen were captured as POWs.

Since the war, the RAF has been an important element in the NATO defences of W Europe. Bomber and Fighter Commands were merged in 1968 to form Strike Command, which is now responsible for all strategic operations. Logistical support is provided by Maintenance Command, while personnel are supplied by Training Command. RAF aircrews and ground staff again went into action in the 1991 GULF WAR.

The Women's Royal Air Force (WRAF) was created in 1949 out of the Women's Auxiliary Air Force (WAAF). It provides a career structure for women in most sectors of the service, including ground-crew, aircrew, and officer branches.

rag. **raghead** A derogatory term for an Arab, referring to the characteristic head-dress (*ha'ik*) of Arab males. It was popularized by US troops stationed in Saudi Arabia during the build-up to the GULF WAR of 1991, grumbling about the privations of living in an Islamic country. Traditionally, Muslim Arabs have regarded the western style of brimmed hat as both ridiculous and disrespectful to God.

In the UK, the term is sometimes used offensively of Sikhs and other Asian males who wear turbans.

ragtime Medium tempo syncopated music of US Black origin, properly solo piano music although also played by bands. Scott Joplin's *Maple Leaf Rag* (1899) was one of the first of its kind to be written down. Ragtime, which was popular in the first 20 years of this century, had a substantial revival with the 1973 film *The Sting*, which featured Scott Joplin's rags, especially 'The Entertainer' (1902).

raider A person or organization that specializes in making takeover bids of companies with assets that are undervalued in their accounts. If a the bid is unwelcome to the company this is known as a hostile bid. The use of the word raider implies that such bids will be hostile.

rain. **If it was raining pea soup, I'd only have a fork** An Australian expression drawing attention to some outrageous piece of bad luck. There are many common variants, including 'If it was raining virgins, I'd end up with a poofter' and 'If it was raining palaces, I'd be hit on the head with the handle of a dunny door'.

rain check A receipt or the counterfoil of a ticket entitling one to see another baseball game if the original match for which the ticket was purchased is rained off. The phrase, which originated in America, is now in general use for a promise to accept an invitation at a later date, *e.g.* when invited and one cannot accept, one says, 'I'll take a rain-check on it'.

Rain is the best policeman A catch-phrase implying that rain keeps troublemakers at home. Presumably this is what every policeman hopes for before a big football match or any large and potentially troublesome gathering.

rainmaker US slang for an influential business executive or partner, often in a law firm, whose political connections could bring in business or advance company interests. Former leading political figures make natural rainmakers: Henry Kissinger, the US Secretary of State (1973–77), for example, soon joined a law firm. This 1968 usage derived from the American Indian medicine man, who chanted to the tribal rain gods, and the later fake US rainmakers, one of whom appeared in N. Richard Nash's play *The Rainmaker*, which was filmed in 1956.

rainbow. **Rainbow bomb** A US H-bomb detonated between 200 and 500 miles (320–800 km) above Johnston Island in the Pacific on 9 July 1962. Its name is derived from the spectacular aurora produced by the blast, which illuminated the Hawaiian Islands 750 miles to the southwest and was seen in New Zealand 4000 miles away. It was announced in August that radiation from the high-altitude blast had damaged the British satellite *Ariel*.

Rainbow Corner In World War II, a Lyons' Corner House in London was taken over and turned into a large café and lounge for US servicemen under this name; it became a general meeting place for Americans in London. The name was a reference to both the US Rainbow Division and the rainbow insignia of SHAEF (Supreme Headquarters Allied Expeditionary Forces).

Rambo The brutally brainless Hollywood hero played by Sylvester Stallone (1946–) after the part was turned down by Paul Newman and others. The original Rambo film was *First Blood*, a 1982 adaption of David Morrell's novel about a Vietnam veteran battling against a small-town sheriff. Although Morrell killed off his Rambo, Stallone continued through *Rambo: First Blood Part II* in 1985 (fighting the Soviets in Afghanistan) and the record $85 million *Rambo III* in 1988 (rescuing US prisoners-of-war from Vietnam), with more planned. Rambo became a folk hero when President Ronald Reagan praised the films. Even Iraqi leader Saddam Hussein chided America during the 1991 GULF WAR for having a Rambo mentality. The impact has been sufficiently vital to add two words to the language: **Ramboesque** and **Ramboism**.

ranch. Meanwhile back at the ranch A phrase that dates from the days of SILENT FILMS, when such phrases were used as captions to link the parts of a story. The implication is that while more exciting things go on elsewhere, life jogs on in its routine way at the ranch.

> Sioux Falls, South Dakota, is the place they mean when they say 'Meanwhile back at the ranch', it's America's slow-beating downhome heart.
>
> *The Independent*, 20 March 1991.

randy British slang meaning eager for sex, sexually excited, lustful. Now widely used, particularly in the tabloid press, in which 'Randy Andy' is the favourite epithet for any man called Andrew – from its widespread application to Prince Andrew in his bachelor days. It is rarely used in America because Randy is a popular Christian name, a shortened form of Randolph.

Rangers (1) Picked men in the US Army who worked with British COMMANDOS. They were named after Rogers' Rangers, an intrepid body of frontiersmen organized by Major Robert Rogers (1731–95). Rangers first appeared at the Dieppe Raid (1942), in which a small party went as armed observers. (2) *See* GIRL GUIDES.

Rank Organization A commercial enterprise that dominated the British film industry in the 1940s and 1950s, founded and headed by J. Arthur Rank (1888–1972). The product of a wealthy flour-milling family with strong Methodist convictions, Rank entered the film business partly because he saw it as the most effective way of spreading his beliefs. His earliest films were instructional aids for Sunday schools and he later used his influence to promote material of a religious or edifying character, often to the dismay of his accountants. During the 1930s and 1940s he extended his activities from film production into distribution and exhibition; by the time he founded the Rank Organization in 1946, he controlled not only the leading British film studios but also two of the three biggest cinema chains. The Organization later diversified into such areas as hotels, XEROX copying, etc. Rank himself never lost his early sense of mission, claiming that if he gave a full account of his experiences in the film world "it would be as plain to you as it is to me that I was being led by God." The Rank Organization's trademark, a huge metal gong, was in reality made of cardboard.

rap (1) Slang for a long and serious conversation, as in 'Sorry I'm late. I got in a rap with my neighbour'; it is also used as a verb, meaning to converse. A word much used by HIPPIES from the end of the 1960s, it was taken originally from the jargon of Blacks and BEATNIKS in America. The derivation is obscure. A **rap group** is US slang for a group of people who meet to discuss their problems. (2) A punishment for a crime. Originally a US usage, it is widely heard in such expressions as **take the rap**, meaning to take the punishment whether guilty or not; **beat the rap** means to escape the punishment. In America a **rap sheet** is slang for a criminal record. (3) A rhythmic monologue intoned over a prerecorded instrumental backing track. A highly popular style of music in the UK in the 1980s that originated among Black youths in the big cities in America. The songs often have a political, environmental, or social message and are very inventive in their use of language and imagery.

> London-based jazz-rapper Galliano is a White boy with West Indian inflections – no offence in itself – whose admirably wordy raps are handicapped by a fundamental lack of vocal charisma . . .
>
> *The Independent*, 28 March 1991.

Rapallo Treaty Either of two treaties signed after World War I at Rapallo, a coastal resort in NW Italy. The first

Rapallo Treaty, signed in November 1920, was between Italy and Yugoslavia: Italy renounced its claim to Dalmatia, the independence of Fiume was acknowledged, and the rights of Italians living in Yugoslav territory and Yugoslavs in Italian territory were established.

The second Rapallo Treaty was signed on 16 August 1922, during the Genoa Conference, by the foreign ministers of the Soviet Union and Germany. The treaty was hailed as a display of solidarity rather than an alliance: it paved the way for the immediate resumption of diplomatic relations between the two countries and enabled Germany secretly to develop and test new weapons – weapons banned by the VERSAILLES TREATY – on Soviet territory.

rapid eye movement *See* REM.

rapture of the deep Slang for the feelings of ecstacy deep-sea divers experience from breathing in compressed air that contains large amounts of nitrogen.

ra-ra skirt A type of short skirt with flounces, fashionable in the 1980s. Perhaps named after the short skirts of cheer leaders at American football games.

Rasputin Gregory Efimovitch (1871–1916), the Siberian monk notorious for his influence over the Russian monarchy in its last years. He was apparently so called by his fellow villagers: Rasputin means 'the dissolute' and he lived up to his nickname until the end. His conquests over women were furthered by his assertion that physical contact with him was itself a purification. Also known as the **Mad Monk**, his indecencies and coarseness did not prevent his excessive familiarity with the Empress Alexandra and Tsar Nicholas II, which arose from his apparent success in healing and sustaining the Tsarevich Alexis, a victim of haemophilia. Rasputin was first called to the palace in 1905 and his power increased steadily until his murder by Prince Yusupov and associates in 1916, itself a story reminiscent of Hollywood rather than real life – when attempts to poison him inexplicably failed, they shot him and threw his body into the River Neva.

Rastafarians Members of the *Ras Tafari*, a Black political and religious group originating in the 1920s in Jamaica. They recognized Haile Selassie (*see* LION OF JUDAH) as a god. They consider Blacks are superior to Whites, that Ethiopia is heaven, and that Haile Selassie will arrange that all of African origin will find a homeland in Ethiopia. *Ras* means duke and *Tafari* was a family name of Haile Selassie (Might of the Trinity). There are now Rastafarians, or **Rastas**, in the West Indies, America, Canada, and Europe, conspicuous by their long matted curls (dreadlocks).

rat. Rat A character in Kenneth Grahame's children's classic *The Wind in the Willows* (1908), best known for the opinion that "there is nothing – absolutely nothing – half so much worth doing as simply messing about in boats". The character was partly inspired by the rowing enthusiast Frederick James Furnivall (1925–1910), who introduced the first sculling-four and sculling-eight races to the UK and became president of the National Amateur Rowing Association. He was better known as a scholar and lexicographer, founding the Early English Texts Society (1864) and serving as one of the first editors of the *Oxford English Dictionary* (from 1861).

rat race The relentless struggle to get ahead of one's rivals, particularly in professional and commercial occupations.

> Just when you think you've got the rat race licked – Boom! Faster rats.
>
> DAVID LEE ROTH, US rock star.

rat run A minor road used by fast heavy traffic, either as a short cut or to avoid congestion on major roads. Rat runs often pass through villages or suburbs; their use by a volume of traffic they were never designed to carry, little of which makes any concession to the speed limit, infuriates residents and is the cause of frequent accidents. The term first appeared in the 1970s and was probably suggested by RAT RACE. It has more recently been used in a verbal sense, **rat-running**, *i.e.* availing oneself of such a route, especially during the rush hour.

ratted or **rat-arsed** British slang from the 1980s for drunk.

> The last four months have been knackering . . . the moment that theatre opens we're all going straight down the King's Head to get absolutely ratted.
>
> *The Independent*, 23 March 1991.

You dirty rat Always known as James Cagney's (1899–1986) catchphrase, it is used frequently as such by impersonators. In fact, he never said it. The closest he came to saying something like it was: 'a dirty double-crossing rat' (*Blonde Crazy*,

1931), and 'You dirty yellow-bellied rat' (*Taxi*, 1931).

rattlehead UK slang from the late 1980s for someone who listens to a personal stereo, especially on public transport. It refers to the annoying tinny noise that can be overheard by those sitting close by and which has been the subject of many irate letters to the press.

raunchy Earthy, bawdy, and sexually uninhibited. Originally a US slang term meaning shabby, cheap, or slovenly, the word developed strong sexual connotations in the 1960s, losing its pejorative flavour at the same time. In JAZZ and ROCK it is a term of approbation, meaning raw or unsophisticated. The back formation **raunch** now means sexually provocative behaviour or material (in a book, film, etc.), although some older speakers still use it in its former sense of untidiness. The word may derive from the Italian *rancio*, rotten.

rave or **rave-up** UK slang for a wild party, which usually involves alcohol and drugs and some wild behaviour. Originally used in the 1950s, it was adopted by the mods (*see* MODS AND ROCKERS) in the 1960s. In the late 1980s and early 1990s it was revived by the tabloid press to describe, among other things, acid-house parties (*see also* ORBITAL).

> As most raves didn't start until the wee small hours, the pub became the logical assembly point...
>
> *The Independent*, 7 March 1991.

Ravensbrück A Nazi concentration camp for women, situated 50 miles (80 km) north of Berlin. It was established in 1939, shortly after the outbreak of the war; women were transported there from all over occupied Europe and Germany. Between 1943 and 1945 over 92,000 Jews and non-Jews died there, 90% of them from Allied nations. In addition to executions and brutality by staff, the main causes of death were overwork, undernourishment, overcrowding, and disease. Medical experiments were also carried out, including bone grafts and transplants and the introduction of artificial gangrene into unnecessary amputations and other deliberate wounds. In 1944 mass gassings began of those 'unproductive' prisoners who were incapable of walking. One of the inmates who witnessed these horrors was Odette Sansom (Churchill), the SOE agent, who gave evidence against the Ravensbrück staff at the Hamburg War Crimes Tribunal in 1947 and was later awarded the George Cross for her wartime espionage services.

ray gun An imaginary weapon that shoots rays to paralyse or kill. This fictional device has long been a feature of the more juvenile science-fiction epics, vividly portrayed in cinema and television space operas. The Hollywood serials FLASH GORDON in 1936 and BUCK ROGERS in 1939 both starred Buster Crabbe (1908–83), who had to confront death rays and gamma bombs. Ray guns have also been revived since 1963 in the BBC series *Doctor Who*.

rayon A generic name for any artificial textile fibre made from cellulose. The oldest manmade fibre, rayon was first produced commercially in 1890 and generally known as 'artificial silk' until 1924, when the new name was invented by the Retail Drygoods Association. It alludes to the long filaments, or 'rays', in which the fibre emerges from the manufacturing process – the result of forcing cellulose solution through a finely perforated nozzle, or 'spinneret'. Although *rayon* is the French word for 'ray', it was probably created as a blend of 'ray' and 'cotton'. The name is fast becoming obsolete in the UK, having been replaced in general usage by a number of tradenames. *See also* NYLON.

Rayonism A Russian art movement founded in 1911 by Mikhail Larionov (1881–1964) and his wife Natalia Gonchorova (1881–1962); it specialized in semi-abstract compositions featuring ray-like lines of colour. There is no connection with the textile.

razoo (or **razzooh**) A US slang term, probably derived from *raspberry*, which is used to express ridicule or contempt. In Australia and New Zealand, a razoo is a nonexistent coin on no value; it is used in negative contexts in much the same way as 'brass farthing' is in British English.

RBT Random Breath Testing. The policy of stopping drivers at random in order to test for excess alcohol. Officially, British police can only stop a motorist for this purpose when his driving raises suspicions that he has been drinking. In practice, however, they can use a variety of pretexts to stop cars more or less as they please and then insist that the drivers take the breath test (*see* BREATHALYSER). Many local forces apply these procedures systematically over the Christmas and New Year period. Opponents of random testing (usually those who risk driving after having had a drink) claim to see it as a threat to civil liberties; supporters point out that its introduction in such countries as Sweden has led to a dramatic fall in deaths from drunken driving.

RCA Radio Corporation of America. Founded during World War I, RCA was an early leader in radio and one of four companies that created the National Broadcasting Company (*see* NBC) in 1926. When radio depressed the gramophone-record business, RCA bought the Victor company in 1929 and made RCA Victor a major producer of gramophone records and radio equipment. RCA also led the development of commercial television in America, launching its first important test at the 1939 World Fair in New York. RCA was bought in 1986 by General Electric, the US company that had cofounded it 70 years earlier. The NBC radio and television facilities occupy several floors of The General Electric Building (formerly RCA Building) in New York's ROCKEFELLER CENTER.

RCs, Parsees, Pharisees, and Buckshees A list of those who do not belong to the Church of England, or who differ from the majority in some other way. The phrase has existed in various forms in the British armed forces since the 1920s or 1930s: variants include 'Chinese, Japanese, RCs, Parsees, Standatease and One-Two-Threes' or 'Sudanese, Siamese, Breadancheese, Standatease'. It was sometimes used disparagingly to enumerate those who were not obliged to attend church parades.

re-. rebirthing A type of psychotherapy developed by Otto Rank, who thought that many people's difficulties and stresses in life were caused by traumatic experiences at birth. His technique of 'continuous breathing' enables the patient to relive the moment of birth and be 'reborn' without the attendant fear. It was popular in the mid-1980s but has since become less accepted.

rebop *See* BEBOP.

recall test A form of test used in marketing research to discover whether or not an advertisement has stuck in the minds of a group of consumers. In spontaneous tests, members of the group are asked how much they can remember about a particular advertisement, with no assistance. In a prompted test, the respondent is asked which advertisement they can remember from a series of advertisements in a campaign.

recombinant DNA DNA containing segments of DNA derived from a different species. It is produced by the techniques of GENETIC ENGINEERING and involves cleavage of the DNA molecule and subsequent recombination of its strands to incorporate the introduced DNA fragment.

recycling The process in which waste materials are salvaged, sorted, and treated in order that they may be reused for manufacturing or for some other purpose. Recycling has several benefits; notably it conserves raw materials, reduces the burden on waste-disposal facilities, and lessens various forms of environmental pollution. It can be practised with many types of waste, from household rubbish to factory effluents. For instance, many items found in household dustbins can be successfully recycled, including steel and aluminium cans, paper, textiles, and glass. Most towns and cities have introduced local recycling schemes involving bottle and paper banks. Pressure for recycling schemes has grown since the 1970s and 1980s with the greater awareness of the environmental ravages brought about by a modern consumer society and the huge amounts of waste it generates.

rejasing *Re*using *j*unk *as* someth*ing* else. US slang acronym for making use of old cast-off items, even rubbish, for some other purpose. Rejasing turns jam jars into paint containers and used tyres into playground obstacle courses. This movement was strong in the 1970s in reaction to the disposable society.

retread A colloquial term for something – such as a film, clothes style, or pop record – that reworks old ideas, either from poverty of imagination or as a calculated appeal to nostalgia. In Australia and New Zealand there is an older use of the term to mean a pensioner who returns to his or her former employment. It is especially used of retired teachers called back to the classroom to make up a temporary shortage. This usage seems to have originated in World War II, when 'retread' was services slang for a World War I veteran who enlisted to fight again.

The term derives from the idea of treading over the same old ground again but it is also an allusion to the car tyres known as retreads, in which a new tread is moulded onto the casing of a worn tyre.

reach for the sky Phrase often used in gangster and Western films meaning 'put your hands up'. However, the phrase is probably best known as the title of the 1954 film of Paul Brickhill's biography of Douglas Bader (1910–82), the RAF World War II hero, who continued his flying career after losing both his legs in a flying accident in 1931. In this instance the title must allude to the RAF motto, *Per ardua ad astra* (Through adversity to the stars). A similar catchphrase, **Reach for the Stars** was used as an advertising slogan for the *Star* newspaper in the late 1980s.

read. I'm sorry, I'll read that again A phrase used by radio newsreaders if they have made a mistake. It was used as the title of a radio comedy show (1964–73), starring John Cleese.

read 'em and weep A phrase uttered triumphantly or smugly as the winner of a card game (such as poker) lays the winning cards on the table. It originated in the early 20th century in America, where it was subsequently used in other gambling games. The phrase is also used in more general contexts, referring to anything written or printed that is likely to cause distress, such as bad reviews, bills, sales figures, etc.

Reader's Digest A pocket-sized monthly magazine first published in America in 1922. It is now published internationally, with a circulation of 28 million worldwide. There are eight English-language editions of the *Reader's Digest*, for the UK, America, Australia, New Zealand, and elsewhere, and 21 editions in 14 other languages, including French, German, Spanish, Italian, Norwegian, Chinese, Arabic, and Hindi. *Reader's Digest* is also a very successful publisher of books, especially manuals and reference books, that it sells principally to its captive magazine audience.

read my lips *See under* LIP.

read-only memory *See* ROM.

ready. readies British slang for bank notes rather than a cheque or PLASTIC MONEY. It is a shortened form of 'ready cash'. Those who hope to avoid or reduce the burden of tax on a payment often ask to be paid in readies.

ready-made *See* OBJET TROUVÉ.

ready-mix Commercial products, from cakes to concrete, that are blended in advance for quick and convenient use. The food industry has many preparations requiring only water or milk to be added. Ready-mix cakes were first rejected by US consumers because, market research showed, housewives felt they were contributing nothing to the recipe. When companies removed the eggs from the mixtures, requiring the housewives to add them, sales increased dramatically.

Reaganomics The economic policies adopted during the presidency (1980–88) of Ronald Reagan (1911–). Chief among these were big reductions in income tax, mandatory cuts in welfare provision and all areas of public spending except defence, and measures designed to weaken organized labour. The advocates of this programme asserted that any shortfall in government revenue resulting from tax cuts would be made up by the economic growth the cuts were sure to stimulate. In the event, the recession of 1982 was followed by only modest growth and the result was a massive federal deficit. By 1986 the national debt had more than doubled but Reagan persisted in his refusal to raise taxes. The term 'Reaganomics' was at first used derogatorily to imply that Reagan's economics were no economics at all; it was, however, later adopted by the President's supporters.

real. It's the real thing The advertising slogan used for the drink COCA-COLA, implying that all the other similar drinks are poor imitations.

real ale Draught beer brewed, stored, and served using traditional methods. In terms of flavour and texture, real ale is the antithesis of the bland fizzy bulk-packaged beers that have dominated the British market since 1950. These are fermented, then chilled, filtered, pasteurized, carbonated, stored in metal kegs and pumped to the bar using gas pressure. Watney's Red Barrel was the first of these 'convenience' beers with long shelf lifes to appear after the war, and other brewers, such as Bass, Courage, Whitbread, and Ind Coope, quickly followed with their own varieties. A spate of mergers in the 1950s and 1960s resulted in the domination of the brewing industry by the 'Big Six'; by 1976 63% of beer was in keg form, of which 20% was in the form of lager. The near disappearance of traditional ales and the resulting decline in consumer choice prompted the foundation of such interest groups as the Society for the Preservation of Beers from the Wood in the 1960s; by far the most successful of these groups has been the Campaign for Real Ale (CAMRA) founded in 1972. By the late 1970s CAMRA had a membership of 20,000; through its consumer campaigns and publications, such as *The Good Beer Guide*, it has persuaded the big brewers that real ales can be as profitable as their keg products.

Realpolitik (Ger.) Practical politics, political realism; politics based on national interests or material considerations as distinct from moral objectives.

reality. reality principle In Freudian psychology, the idea that external reality imposes certain constraints on one's instinctive urge to self-gratification. Its acceptance distinguishes the more-or-less sane adult from the infant or psychotic. According to Freudian theory, the reality principle governs the development of the ego, while the id is governed by the **pleasure principle**. The process by which the reality principle is learned forms the subject of Freud's *Beyond the Pleasure Principle* (1920).

reality therapy A method of psychotherapy introduced in the early 1970s to help people adjust to reality and cope with a hostile environment. The therapy is based on the REALITY PRINCIPLE.

Rebel Without a Cause Title of a 1955 film starring James Dean (1931–55) as a mixed-up teenager, whose affluent Californian background does nothing to prevent his slide into delinquency. The film opened only weeks after the star's death in a car crash – an event that transformed a talented (if increasingly mannered and typecast) young actor into an icon of youthful rebellion. Ever since, Dean's performance in this rather ordinary melodrama has been treated as if it embodied the essence of alienated and self-destructive youth. The legend has proved surprisingly enduring; the label 'rebel without a cause' is resuscitated by the press with each new wave of teenage rebellion and Dean's image continues to glower from advertisements and the bedroom walls of his teenage fans. It was even used by the National Westminster Bank in an attempt to persuade teenagers that opening a bank account is a cool and rebellious thing to do. In the 1980s a James Dean Foundation was set up by the actor's relatives to control the use of his name and image – even the imitation by others of his characteristic poses.

Received Pronunciation (RP) The pronunciation of English most widely accepted as standard in the British Isles and in some other parts of the world. It is the pronunciation used by British lexicographers in giving a pronunciation guide to the words in a dictionary. The term was coined by the English phonetician Daniel Jones (1881–1967) to describe the characteristic pronunciation of people educated in the public schools and universities in the south of England. Historically, RP is derived from the language spoken by Chaucer, the Middle English of London. In the 1930s, with the rise of sound broadcasting, this pronunciation was often referred to as **BBC English** or the **Oxford accent**. The diction of such announcers and news readers as Alvar Liddell and Leslie Phillips was impeccable and certainly served as a model for many native English speakers as well as those for whom English was a second language. In his Preface to the first edition of the *BBC Pronouncing Dictionary of British Names*, G. M. Miller writes that the BBC announcers used RP but that there was nothing exclusive to the BBC about this way of speaking:

> The good announcer remains, as far as the BBC is concerned, the pleasant unobtrusive speaker who does not distract attention from his subject matter by causing embarrassment, unwitting amusement, or resentment among intelligent listeners.

This policy now seems to have been relaxed, if not abandoned, with the introduction of news presenters and weather forecasters with a variety of regional dialects, reflecting the way people actually speak as opposed to the way some feel they ought to speak.

King's (or **Queen's**) **English** is another description often used for the pronunciation of southern England. In fact, the royal family and many members of the upper classes do not use RP. The Duke of Edinburgh, for example, refers from time to time to his 'trisers' (trousers); the Queen talks about the 'Hise of Lords', and Prince Charles calls the London tube 'the Undergrind'. Such speech idiosyncracies of small minorities occur throughout the class spectrum. It is therefore important that English dictionaries should maintain a strong hold on a standard of pronunciation. RP fulfils this function.

red *See* REDS.

better red than dead Living under a communist regime is preferable to being dead. The phrase was used as a slogan in the late 1950s by British campaigners for nuclear disarmament (*see* CND), inspired by the British philosopher and pacifist Bertrand Russell:

If no alternative remains except communist domination or the extinction of the human race, the former alternative is the less of two evils.

Supporters of the opposite point of view reversed the elements of the phrase, producing the slogan 'Better dead than red'.

Red Adair Nickname of Paul Adair, US consultant on oil-well disasters, chiefly known for putting out fires. In 1991 he was engaged to deal with the hundreds of oil-well fires deliberately started by Iraqi troops evacuating Kuwait. He was played by John Wayne in the film *Hellfighters* (1969).

Red Army Faction (RAF; Ger. *Rote Armee Faktion*) A West German terrorist group, known popularly as the **Baader-Meinhof gang**, born as the result of the violent release of Andreas Baader (1943–77) from prison on 14 May 1970 by Ulrike Meinhof (1934–76), Horst Mahler, and others. The group then launched a violent struggle against the political, economic, and military organs of the West German state, which they branded as the neo-Fascist 'Strawberry Reich'. They also targetted Nato and its military personnel as the international agency of US imperialism; their attacks on the European alliance during the 1970s and 1980s were organized in league with a European network of terrorist groups, including the French Action Directe and the Italian RED BRIGADES. Attacks within Germany escalated in violence during the 1970s and included bank raids, bombings, kidnappings, and the deliberate assassination of business leaders, police, and government officials. By 1972 the main leaders, Baader, Meinhof, and Gudrun Esslin, were in prison but violence continued unabated in an attempt to secure their release. In April 1977 the Attorney-General, Siegfried Buback, was murdered in revenge for the suicide in Stammheim prison of Meinhof; in October of the same year Red Army members collaborated with Palestinian Red Army terrorists in the hijacking of a Lufthansa jet with 91 hostages, during which the pilot was shot. As German anti-terrorist squads stormed the plane at Mogadishu airport in Somalia, it was discovered that Baader and Esslin had also committed suicide in Stammheim; another hostage, Hans-Martin Schleyer of Daimler-Benz, kidnapped in October, was murdered as a reprisal. After these events the revolutionary appeal of the group to German students and young radicals began to wane. By the early 1980s nearly all members were either dead or imprisoned. In 1985 membership was estimated at 20 hardcore activists, 200 militants willing to help in guerrilla attacks, and about 2000 supporters who would protect other members if required.

Don't argue – destroy.

Slogan of the Red Army Faction.

Red Arrows The RAF jet aircraft aerobatics display team, regarded as the finest in the world.

Red Baron Nickname of Manfred, Freiherr von Richtohofen (1892–1918), the most celebrated German fighter pilot of World War I, reflecting his aristocratic rank and his red Fokker triplane. From 1916 he commanded Fighter Group I of the German Imperial Air Force, known to Allied airmen as **Richthofen's Flying Circus** because of its brightly coloured and whimsically decorated planes and its innovative use of team tactics. He is thought to have shot down 80 enemy planes before being brought down himself by a combination of ground fire and the guns of a Sopwith Camel flown by the Canadian ace Captain A. Roy Brown during the second Battle of the Somme. Respected by the Allies, he was buried with full military honours by the British and Australians. The Red Baron's death was considered by Ludendorff the equivalent of losing 30 divisions. His command was taken over by Herman Göring; his niece, Frieda von Richthofen, married the novelist D. H. Lawrence.

redbrick A 19th-century British university, many of which were built in the redbrick gothic revival style of such architects as Alfred Waterhouse. The term is loosely applied to all English universities other than those of Oxford and Cambridge (*see* OXBRIDGE). The name was introduced by Bruce Truscot (Professor E. Allison Peers: d. 1952) in his book *Redbrick University* (1943). He was primarily dealing with the universities of Birmingham, Bristol, Leeds, Liverpool, Manchester, Reading, and Sheffield, and expressly excluded London.

There is nothing that makes me more angry than to hear the University of London associated with that hideous, snobbish term "Red Brick". The term itself ought not to be used but looking at this Senate House, or indeed at the classical portico of University College, I think it must be some flight of imagination that describes these, even architecturally, as "Red Brick".

SIR IFOR EVANS: *Address to Convocation (University of London)*, 9 January 1960.

Red Brigades (Ital. *Brigate Rosse*) The Italian left-wing terrorist group that was responsible for the kidnap and murder in March 1977 of Aldo Moro, the president of the Christian Democratic Party and ex-prime minister. The organization was established in 1969, initially with the aim of attacking leaders of large corporations, such as Fiat and Pirelli, who were regarded as 'enemies of the working class'. In subsequent years they have been responsible for a series of kidnappings, bombings, and the murders of police, judges, government officials, and business leaders with the aim of undermining the Italian state and initiating a Marxist revolution. The body of their most notable victim, Moro, was found in the boot of a car in Rome in May 1977, shot dead after the government refused to agree to the release of 13 Brigade leaders. The Brigades were also linked to other terrorist groups, including the German RED ARMY FACTION. In January 1982 the Italian police achieved a major success in freeing the US Brigadier-General James Dozier, a deputy NATO commander, who had been abducted in Verona in December 1981. Leading Brigade idealogues, such as Renato Curcio (1948–) and Alberto Fraceschini, as well as those responsible for the Moro and Dozier kidnappings, were captured and tried during the late 1970s and early 1980s. The last of the Moro kidnappers was sentenced in 1983; since then the authorities have had increasing success in penetrating and neutralizing the organization's cells in various parts of the country.

redcap (1) A colloquial term for British military police, whose caps have red covers. (2) In America, a porter at a railway or bus station.

redcoat *See* BUTLINS.

Red Dean Press nickname for Dr Hewlett Johnson (1874–1966), Dean of Canterbury and formerly Dean of Manchester. He attracted some controversy for his belief that communism, as practised in Stalin's Soviet Union, was a practical application of Christian ethics.

Red Devils (1) Nickname of the Special Air Service (*see* SAS). (2) Nickname of the Manchester United soccer team, founded in 1878, which wears a chiefly red and white strip.

red-eye (1) Slang for whisky or any other strong spirit that causes the drinker's eyes to become bloodshot. (2) US slang describing a flight that takes off late at night and arrives early the next morning, thus depriving the passengers of a good night's sleep. They arrive looking exhausted with bloodshot eyes. It is usually applied to coast-to-coast flights in America.

Red Friday Friday 31 July 1925, when a stoppage in the coal industry, planned to meet the threat of wage cuts, was averted by the promise of government subsidies to support wages, etc. It was so called by the Labour press to distinguish it from BLACK FRIDAY or 15 April 1921, when union leaders called off an impending strike of railwaymen and transport workers designed to help the miners, who were locked out.

Red Guards Young supporters of Mao Tse-tung during the CULTURAL REVOLUTION. The mobilization of the Red Guards began at a rally in Tiananmen Square, Peking, on 18 August 1966. These unruly mobs consisted chiefly of students from secondary schools, colleges, and universities: their task was to rampage the streets and the countryside of China and Tibet, harassing and attacking enemies and opponents of Mao Tse-tung, and destroying public and private property – anything that represented 'old' ideas, culture, customs, or habits. They wore red armbands and carried copies of Mao's LITTLE RED BOOK.

Red Ken Press nickname for the Labour politician Ken Livingstone (1945–), who achieved notoriety as the left-wing leader of the Greater London Council (1981–86). His outspoken views made him a bogeyman of the right-wing tabloids, one of which carried his photograph under the headline 'The Most Odious Man in Britain'. Livingstone skilfully countered this onslaught by presenting a soft-spoken downbeat image, visibly at odds with his press reputation. Meanwhile, his policies – which included handouts to unpopular fringe groups as well as a highly popular fare-cutting programme on London Transport – were increasingly seen as a deliberate provocation to central government. Margaret Thatcher's decision to abolish the Council, announced in October 1983, unexpectedly transformed Red Ken into something of a folk hero with Londoners, including many who had previously detested him. Following the abolition of the Council, Livingstone was elected to parliament representing Brent East. *See also* GLC.

Red Letter *See* ZINOVIEV LETTER.

redlining The US term for the systematic denial of loans, mortgages, and insurance to property owners, or prospective property owners, in the poorer sections of a city. Some banks and other financial institutions make use of this practice to minimize their risks, although it has been called racial discrimination, because it is in these areas that ethnic minorities usually reside. Redlining originated in the late 1960s and takes its name from the supposed practice of outlining such areas in red on a map.
redneck US derogatory slang for a person from a rural community who is poorly educated, narrow-minded, and right-wing. The word was originally used to describe White Southern farmers (the backs of whose necks would be red from working in the fields under the hot sun), but its use spread in the late 1960s to describe anyone with uneducated right-wing views. The word has been used in this way in the UK since the 1980s.
reds Colloquial name for socialists, radicals, or left-wingers of any kind, especially Soviet communists. The colour red has been associated with revolution since at least 1848, when the workers of Paris manned the barricades under red banners. The words to the socialist anthem, 'The Red Flag', date from 1889. 'Reds' became a general journalistic term for communists with the Russian Civil War of 1918–22, in which Trotsky's Red Army fought the conservative White Volunteer Force. Its use was especially prevalent during the McCarthy witch-hunts in America, when it was applied to alleged subversives of every kind. *See also* BETTER RED THAN DEAD; MCCARTHYISM; PINKO; REDS UNDER THE BED.
redshift An effect in physics in which the light (or other electromagnetic radiation) emitted by a body appears to have longer wavelength if the body is moving away from the observer. There is a shift in the position of lines in the spectrum from their normal position towards the red end of the electromagnetic spectrum. The converse effect – a blue shift – occurs if the body is moving towards the observer. Both are examples of the so-called **Doppler shift**, named after the Austrian physicist Christian Doppler (1803–53), who discovered the effect with sound waves in 1842.

The redshift is important in astronomy. In 1929 the US astronomer Edwin Hubble investigated the spectra of a number of distant galaxies and showed that their redshifts were proportional to the distance away of the galaxy. This provides the main evidence that the universe is expanding (*see* BIG BANG).
reds under the bed A reference to excessive suspicion of communists. The phrase dates from Senator McCarthy's witch-hunts of the 1950s in America, when supposed communist sympathizers were said to have been found in the most unlikely places (*see* MCCARTHYISM). Those who unreasonably or unjustifiably see a communist influence where none exists are said to be looking for 'reds under the bed'. In the UK, the phrase may refer to any left-wing activists seen as a threat to democracy or industrial harmony.

reductivism *See* MINIMAL ART.

reedsman A JAZZ musician, known as a **reedman** in America, who plays a variety of reed instruments, such as the clarinet or alto and tenor saxophone.

reefer Slang for a hand-rolled marijuana cigarette (*see* POT). It is now rarely heard, having been supplanted by JOINT in the late 1950s; the media nevertheless persisted in using the word well into the 1970s. There are two plausible etymologies; one derives from the nautical term *reef*, the gathered-in part of the sail, because of a similarity in shape between the furled sail and the hand-rolled cigarette. Others derive the word from *grifa*, Spanish slang for marijuana.

reffo In Australia, a derogatory term for any of the European refugees, predominantly Jewish, who arrived during or shortly before World War II. Australia was then a far more homogenous and culturally isolated society than it is today, and the reffos – also dubbed **reffujews** and **reff-raff** – provoked widespread resentment. Although the influx of refugees was unprecedented at the time, the numbers pale into insignificance beside the mass immigration that transformed Australian society in the post-war decades: between 1940 and 1964 some two million people, mainly from the UK and continental Europe, chose to start new lives in Australia. The government carefully referred to these incomers as **New Australians**, rather than immigrants, in the hope of easing assimilation. To the stubbornly xenophobic Old Australians, however, they were Naussies, Balts, emigrantos, micros, and wogs (subdivided into Pommie wogs, Yankee wogs, etc.).

reflexology A technique of foot massage used to relieve tension and promote general bodily health. Like acupuncture and shiatsu, reflexology claims an ancient pedigree; it is based on the theory that channels of energy course through the body in a network of nerves linking all the body's main organs and muscles. Reflexologists hold that this energy network terminates at tiny reflex points in the feet, which mirror the body's organs, and that compression or finger massage at these specific points can help restore healthy energy flow by removing crystalline deposits clogging the energy pathways. The techniques of modern reflexology were developed during the early 20th century by the US physician William H. Fitzgerald, who established the principles of 'zone therapy', using pressure points on different areas of the body to treat common ailments. The technique was pioneered in the UK by Doreen Bayly in the 1950s; since the 1980s Bayly clinics are the main source of reflexology practitioners treating the growing number of adherents of ALTERNATIVE MEDICINE. Reflexology does not find much support for its theories in the orthodox medical profession.

refuse. I'm going to make him an offer he can't refuse Originally the phrase meant that 'he' is about to be offered so much more than he expects that he will be unable to say 'no'. In Mario Puzo's book *The Godfather* (1969; filmed 1972), about the MAFIA, it takes on a much more sinister sense, implying the 'he' is about to be told to do something by a Mafioso and will certainly do whatever it is if he doesn't want to be killed. It is thus the ultimate in blackmail.

refusenik A Soviet citizen who has been refused an exit visa to emigrate to another country – most refuseniks are Jews wishing to emigrate to America or Israel. Until recently, under Soviet law, emigration was a state-granted privilege, although the Helsinki Accord (1975), to which the Soviet Union is a signatory, guarantees emigration as a basic human right. During the 1970s over 250,000 Soviet Jews were granted visas but many of those who were refused were branded as political dissidents and persecuted by the authorities. One of the most prominent refusenik campaigners was Anatoly Scharansky, imprisoned in 1978 for treason, who was eventually released and allowed to settle in Israel in 1986. Since his release, restrictions on the emigration of Soviet citizens are being gradually removed in accordance with Mikhail Gorbachov's policy of GLASNOST; large numbers of Soviet Jews have now been allowed to leave: 72,500 in 1989 and an estimated 200,000 in 1990 – a rate which, if it continues, will empty the Soviet Union of Jews. *See* -NIK.

reggae Popular music from Jamaica with a heavily accented upbeat in each bar of four beats. It has a strong bass line and a bluesy feel. In the UK its popularity spread from the largely urban West Indian communities to young Whites during the 1970s. The derivation of the word is uncertain, but it is thought to be connected to the Jamaican *rage-rage*, an argument.

Regulation 18b A provision of the British Emergency Powers (Defence) Acts (1939; 1940), which was amended by parliament in 1940 to give the Home Secretary the power to detain, without trial, members of any organization sympathetic to an enemy power. Defence Regulation 18b(1A) was specifically targetted at the British Union of Fascists and its leader, the MP Sir Oswald Mosley (1896–1980), who was arrested and imprisoned in Brixton on 23 May 1940. Altogether 763 BUF members (*see* MOSLEYITES) were rounded up, including Mosley's wife Diana (*see* MITFORD GIRLS), who was sent to Holloway, as well as many pro-German and pro-Italians. In all, 1769 British subjects were interned during the war, most of them in Peel Camp on the Isle of Man. Mosley remained in Brixton until November 1943, when he was released for health reasons.

Reichsmark (Ger. mark of the realm) Germany's standard monetary unit from 1924 to 1948, composed of 100 *Reichspfennig*. It is particularly associated with Adolph Hitler's THIRD REICH (1933–45). *Mark*, originally a measurement of precious metals, has been the name for German currency since 1871. *See* DEUTSCHMARK.

Reichstag fire The destruction by arson of the Reichstag parliament building in Berlin on 27 February 1933. The fire occurred at a crucial moment in 20th-century German history, enabling the Nazis to seize power and indirectly to enable Hitler to make himself FÜHRER. This was achieved by blaming the communists for the fire and so discrediting the left wing, who until then had blocked complete Nazi supremacy. A 24-year old

Dutchman, Marius van der Lubbe, was identified as the communist who had started the blaze; before the night of 27 February was over, 5000 known comunists had been arrested. The communists for their part accused the Nazis of staging the fire themselves with the object of blaming the communists. During the trials following the war, the German Chief of General Staff recalled hearing Göring boast: "The only one who really knows about the Reichstag is me, because I set it on fire." The one person who could have solved the mystery conclusively was der Lubbe himself, but he had been executed by the Nazis on 10 January 1934.

reinforcement therapy A psychiatric treatment that rewards a patient for normal behaviour. These rewards – money, food, encouragement, etc. – encourage repetition of the behaviour. Fears, such as flying, can often be eliminated through pleasant associations; for example, having a birthday party with friends in a plane. **Negative reinforcement** is the withdrawing of rewards. The term 'reinforcement therapy' was coined in 1969 to formalize early animal experiments by physiologists in Russia, the UK, and America and their adaptation to human behaviour by the US psychologist B. F. Skinner (1904–90) in the 1930s. Although reinforcement therapy has often proved successful, it is not a panacea. For example, in one study, which attempted to cure a child's fear of rabbits by giving it sweets while encouraging it to stroke a rabbit, the result was that thereafter the child invariably felt sick when given sweets.

Reis forgery An ambitious forgery that threatened the economy of Portugal and the reputation of a leading British printing company in 1924. It was planned by Arthur Virgilio Alves Reis, a member of the Portuguese colonial service, who capitalized on his discovery that Portuguese banknotes were printed by a British firm, Waterlow and Sons, which was less than scrupulous about checking for notes with accidental duplicate numbers. Reis's elaborate plan involved the forging of letters from the Portuguese Minister of Finance and other high officials commissioning the printing of huge numbers of 500-escudo notes (worth £5 each); these, he explained, would not need new serial numbers as they would later be overprinted 'Angola' for use in that country, which was then a colony of Portugal. The overprinting, however, never happened. Instead Reis exchanged the notes for foreign stock and built up a huge financial empire, even opening his own Bank of Angola and Metropole. Sooner or later, it was inevitable that the massive fraud would be detected. In mid-1925 notes with duplicate serial numbers were discovered in Reis's bank and he was arrested. Reis eventually confessed and was sentenced to 20 years in prison; he was released in 1945 and died ten years later. He was so poor that at his own request he was buried in a sheet to enable his son to inherit his only suit.

Reith lectures An annual series of radio broadcasts by leading thinkers, established by the BBC in 1947 in honour of John (Charles Walsham), 1st Baron Reith (1889–1971), the first Director-General of the BBC (1927–38).

relativity A theory in physics, first proposed by the German-born physicist Albert Einstein (1879–1955), in two parts. The first, known as the **Special Theory**, was published in 1905; it arose as a result of problems in the mathematics of relative motion, particularly with reference to the speed of light. Suppose, for example, that a car travelling at 40 m.p.h. approaches another travelling at 60 m.p.h.; each driver would know his speed relative to the road but would say that the other car was approaching at 100 m.p.h. This is the 'common-sense' view of relative motion, accepted also, until the early part of the century, by most physicists.

Common sense, however, is not always a good guide to reality in physics (*see also* QUANTUM THEORY). As Einstein once said:

> Common-sense is the collection of prejudices acquired by age eighteen.

In the 19th century light was regarded as a wave motion in an all-pervading weightless elastic medium known as the *ether*. If the Earth was moving through the ether it should be possible to confirm the existence of the ether by detecting a difference in the speed of light in the direction of the Earth's rotation compared to that at right angles to this motion. By 1887 the Michelson–Morley experiment had failed to detect this difference – a result that caused considerable uncertainty among physicists.

Einstein at the time was a technical expert (third class) in the Swiss Patent Office in Berne. As such, he was unaware of the Michelson–Morley experiment, but he was thinking about the speed of light and, in particular, the fact that the Scottish physicist James Clerk Maxwell (1831–79) had put forward in 1873 a set of equations describing light as electromagnetic waves travelling at a speed that did not depend on the relative motion of the source and observer.

At the turn of the century, mechanics – in the tradition of Galileo and Newton – was in a state of confusion. Einstein proposed that the best way to deal with the confusion was to assume that the speed of light is always the same, irrespective of the relative motion of the source and observer. For example, the drivers of the two cars approaching each other at 40 m.p.h. and 60 m.p.h. might add together their speeds to arrive at their relative speed (100 m.p.h.). However, the speed of the light emitted by their headlights would always be the same, irrespective of the speeds of the cars.

There were a number of unusual consequences to the Special Theory. For example, the mass of a body increases with its speed and becomes infinite at the speed of light, so that it is impossible to travel faster than the speed of light. Even more unusual is the idea of **time dilation**: time passes more slowly for a moving object than for a stationary object. This leads to the **twin paradox**, in which one of a pair of twins lives on Earth and the other lives in a spacecraft travelling at high speed. When they meet after many years the earthbound twin has aged in the normal way; the space traveller is still young because he has spent most of his life moving at a high speed, so time has passed more slowly.

The consequences of the Special Theory, unusual though they may seem in everyday life, have been completely verified by experiment but only give results that differ from classical mechanics when objects are moving at speeds close to the speed of light. However, one consequence of the theory *does* affect our lives; this is the principle of the equivalence of mass and energy put forward by Einstein in 1905 in the equation $E = MC^2$, which is the principle upon which NUCLEAR WEAPONS are based.

The Special Theory only applies to objects at rest or in uniform relative motion. By 1907 Einstein was able to incorporate acceleration into the scheme to produce his **General Theory**. In this, Einstein took the view that a body's inertial mass (measured by its resistance to being accelerated) and its gravitational mass (the force it experiences in a gravitational field) were identical and that there is an equivalence between accelerating forces and gravitational forces. The final form of the General Theory, published in 1916, used the ideas of the Russian-born German mathematician Hermann Minkowski (1864–1909), who postulated that the three dimensions of space and the dimension of time formed a continuum, called **space–time**. In the General Theory, gravitation is treated as a consequence of the fact that a mass warps space–time, leading to the concept of 'curved' space.

There have been many experimental verifications of the General Theory, the most spectacular in 1919. Einstein had earlier predicted that light could be deflected by a gravitational field; in a total eclipse of the Sun the deflection of starlight just grazing the Sun should be visible. In 1919 a group led by Sir Arthur Eddington observed a solar eclipse at Principe in West Africa and were able to verify Einstein's prediction.

The result caught the public's imagination – even *The Times*, in a rare editorial on scientific matters, commented:

> The scientific conception of the fabric of the universe must be changed.

The theory of relativity was widely regarded as being incomprehensible to all but a few physicists. It was said that only three people in the world could understand it (Eddington, on hearing this, asked "Who's the third?").

REM Rapid Eye Movement. A stage of sleep characterized by darting movements of the eyes beneath closed eyelids, irregular breathing, increased blood flow to the brain, and increased brain temperature. In humans, during normal sleep, short periods of REM sleep (5–15 minutes) alternate with longer periods (70–80 minutes) of heavier non-rapid eye movement (NREM) sleep. REM sleep is associated with dreaming and seems to be far more important for well-being than NREM sleep, although the reasons for this are still a mystery. Babies and infants may spend up to half their sleep in REM.

Remagen A town in Germany, on the River Rhine between Coblenz and Cologne: the scene of the first Allied crossing of the Rhine in World War II. On 7 March 1945 a division of the US army discovered that the railway bridge at Remagen was fit for use – other bridges across the Rhine had been blown up as the Allies approached – and they were able to establish the first bridgehead on the east bank of the river. Further bridgeheads were established later in March as planned (Remagen had not been part of the original strategy), facilitating the Allied advance towards Berlin.

REME Royal Electrical and Mechanical Engineers. A corp of engineers and technicians formed in May 1942 to maintain and repair the increasingly complex weaponry and equipment employed by the British Army. In previous wars these tasks had been performed by technicians from such units as the Royal Ordnance Corps and Royal Corps of Signals, but the need for a specialist corps became a matter of urgency; in 1942 these ROC and RCS technicians were transferred to the REME. In 1949 the REME's designation was changed to Corps of Royal Electrical and Mechanical Engineers.

remember. Remember I'm your mother and get up them stairs! A phrase first used during World War I by members of the British armed forces. In the 1940s it was a jocular command to a man who was about to go on leave, with the sexual connotations of taking his wife (or girlfriend) upstairs to bed. The phrase 'Get up them stairs!' retains these connotations in civilian usage.

Remember Pearl Harbor! A warning against overconfidence. A reference to the surprise Japanese attack on the US naval base at PEARL HARBOR during World War II, the phrase was first used in the 1940s by Australian, and subsequently by British and US, servicemen.

Remember there's a war on A phrase used during World War I in response to a request for something that was in short supply, or as a reprimand to those who were seen to be wasting time or resources or indulging in frivolous remarks or behaviour. During World War II the phrase reappeared in the form 'Don't you know there's a war on?' It was sometimes used ironically, as a justification for some undesirable state of affairs, as an encouragement to do something, or as a jocular response to any request.

Remembrance Day or **Remembrance Sunday** The day commemorating the fallen of both World Wars; also called **Poppy Day** from the artificial poppies (recalling the poppies of Flanders fields) sold by the British Legion in aid of ex-servicemen. From 1919 to 1945 it was called ARMISTICE DAY and observed on 11 November. From 1945 to 1956 Remembrance Day was observed on the first or second Sunday of November; in 1956 it was fixed on the second Sunday of November. *See also* TWO-MINUTE SILENCE.

remote control A system or device that enables a distant object to be controlled, usually by radio or electrical signals. Examples of remote-controlled objects range from toy cars, television sets, videocassette players, and garage doors on the domestic scale up to guided missiles, aircraft, or spacecraft on a global scale.

Reno divorce A divorce that can be easily obtained in Reno, Nevada, under the liberal laws of that state. Divorces are granted in Nevada on a wider range of grounds than elsewhere to applicants who have been resident in the state for as little as six weeks. Although these laws apply throughout the state, the city of Reno is particularly famous as the place in which a number of show-business celebrities have ended their marriages, being close to the border with California.

rent. rent-a-crowd A crowd that has been specially organized or paid to appear at a rally, demonstration, political occasion, etc. For example, such a group may be organized by a politician's campaign manager to mob the candidate during an election campaign to enable television audiences to see the successful and popular candidate being greeted by enthusiastic supporters. *See also* RENT-A-MOB.

rent-a-mob A crowd specially hired to cause a disturbance or riot. *See also* RENT-A-CROWD.

rent boy British slang for a young male prostitute, from the jargon of the GAY world. The 'rent' alludes to the payment received. It is an expression much favoured by the tabloid press.

> A top athletics club was rocked by a rent-boy sex scandal when their gay coach was convicted of a sex offence with a 14-year-old rent-boy.
>
> *The Sun*, 6 April 1991.

rent party or **house-rent party** In the 1920s to 1940s, a type of party held by US Blacks to raise money for the rent: 'guests' were charged at the door and for their food and drink. Especially common during the GREAT DEPRESSION, the practice was also stimulated by PROHIBITION, as it provided an environment in which alcohol could be freely consumed. Such parties often lasted for days on end and were famous for the spontaneous sessions of jazz and blues that developed. Many performers survived in hard times by travelling from one rent party to the next, playing for food, drink, and a bed. 'Rent party' or 'house party' became a term for a style of blues piano playing. *See also* RUGCUTTING.

rent strike An organized refusal by tenants to pay their rent; for example, to protest against the dilapidated conditions of a building, unfair rent rises, lack of services, and various restrictions. It was widely used in America in the 1970s, especially in large cities and among college students.

repent pad US Black slang of the 1940s for a bachelor PAD, because young women often repented for what occurred there.

repetitive strain injury (RSI) A painful condition of particular muscles and joints caused by repeated mechanical activity. The term is relatively recent, dating from the late 1980s, and embraces a wide range of disorders some of which, such as writer's cramp, have long been associated with certain jobs. All are the result of the prolonged repetition of specific tasks, typically performed using the hands, arms, or shoulders; common sufferers include musicians, hairdressers, machine operators, typists, and VDU operators.

reportage The reporting of current events by the media. Originally a 19th-century word meaning gossip, it acquired a 20th-century meaning as a result of the techniques of mass communication and the ability of journalists to provide instant information. Such news-gathering organizations as Cable News Network (CNN) offer 24-hour satellite reportage, which in the 1991 GULF WAR, for example, provided coverage of the war as it was happening. Many people became so addicted to the TV reportage that they sat in front of their sets almost all day and a good part of the night. These people became known as **news junkies**.

reserved occupation A civilian occupation that exempts those who work in it from military service. The need to prevent workers with certain essential skills from being recruited into the armed forces was first recognized by Lloyd George during the early months of World War I, when the high levels of voluntary enlistment threatened the supply of labour to crucial industries, such as coal mining, armaments, transport, and agriculture. As well as protecting these occupations during the period 1914–18, the British government also introduced measures to make more efficient use of skilled personnel, to open up skilled jobs to the semiskilled and unskilled, and to recruit large numbers of women into industry. The same concepts were used in World War II.

residents' association An organization of householders formed to act collectively on local issues, such as traffic regulation, approaching grant-making bodies for funding for property renovation, pressurizing the local council on planning issues, organizing a neighbourhood watch for crime prevention, etc. Called a **block association** in America.

Resistance An underground organization formed by the inhabitants of enemy-occupied territory in wartime: notably the French Resistance movement of World War II. The activities of the Resistance included sabotaging enemy operations, passing information about enemy movements to the Allies through clandestine radio communications, and hiding members of the Allied forces (such as airmen who had been shot down in action) and helping them to escape. From May 1943 the various Resistance groups – former army officers, political leaders, intellectuals, and workers – were coordinated as the Conseil National de la Résistance, led by Jean Moulin (until his arrest in June 1943, when he was succeeded by Georges Bidault). In February 1944 the MAQUIS, provincial guerrilla groups of Resistance fighters operating in the countryside, became part of the newly formed Forces Françaises de l'Intérieur (FFI), which played a vital role in the liberation of France (*see also* FIGHTING FRENCH). During World War II there were also active Resistance groups in Belgium, Holland, Denmark, Norway, Poland, Yugoslavia, Greece, and elsewhere.

Retail Price Index (RPI) An index showing how the price of goods and services in retail shops and other outlets changes on a monthly basis. In the UK the RPI is compiled by the Department of Employment and includes the prices of some 130,000 different items. The index is expressed in percentages and takes a base year as 100%, *e.g.* if 1975 is taken as 100, the RPI for 1988 was 286.3. In America the RPI is called the **consumer price index**.

retina identification Identification of a person by means of the unique pattern of veins in his or her retina. It has been investigated by banks as a means of improving security at cash-point machines and by hotels, etc., as an alternative to room keys. So far, the cost of installing machinery to read such 'eye-prints' has been found prohibitive.

Retreat? Hell, no! We just got here! A quotation attributed to the US army officer Lloyd S. William on his arrival at the Western Front towards the end of World War I. Captain William is said to have made this response to French troops, who were retreating and advised him to do likewise. The phrase was subsequently used in other situations, such as sporting competitions, by anybody defiantly rejecting advice to abandon what appears to be a lost cause.

retro-. retrorocket A rocket motor that acts in the opposite direction to the direction of motion of a spacecraft, probe, etc. Retrorockets are used to slow down the vehicle as it enters the atmosphere or lands.

retrovirus Any of a family of viruses that replicate in an unusual way. The genes of the retrovirus are in the form of RNA (rather than DNA); but what is remarkable is that by using an enzyme unique to themselves, called *reverse transcriptase*, retroviruses produce DNA versions of their own RNA genes. This is the reverse of the usual flow of genetic information – from DNA to RNA – hence the term retrovirus. This so-called DNA transcript can then combine with the DNA of the host cell, *i.e.* the cell which the virus is infecting, so that the viral genes are expressed with the genes of the host cell and are able to subvert the protein manufacturing apparatus of the host cell to assemble new virus particles. One important consequence is that certain retroviruses may introduce cancer-causing oncogenes into the host cell, transforming it into a cancer cell. These genes may be inherited by subsequent generations of the host organism, making the offspring of infected parents predisposed to certain cancers. The AIDS virus, HIV, is another type of retrovirus.

returned soldier In Canada, Australia, and New Zealand, a soldier returned from war. In Australia the Returned Services League (RSL) operates a nationwide network of local social clubs for ex-servicemen, and is similar in its aims and activities to the British Legion.

Reutenmark A new currency introduced on 20 November 1923 to stabilize Germany's economy and reduce inflation after World War I. Reutenmarks were issued in limited quantities for a temporary period, until the financial crisis showed signs of coming to an end. This drastic remedy was controversial but successful: in 1924 the new Reichsmark was introduced; it was worth 1,000,000,000,000 old marks.

reverse discrimination Discrimination against the majority group in society by giving preferential treatment in matters of employment, education, etc., to a member of a minority group, especially a racial minority or women. Such discrimination became an issue in America during the 1960s and 1970s, in the wake of the Civil Rights Act (1964) and associated legislation aimed at removing discrimination in employment. This legislation requires businesses and federally funded organizations to include a certain proportion of racial minorities, such as Blacks and Hispanics, among their employees. Such 'affirmative action programmes' have been attacked as imposing 'quotas', which are themselves discriminatory (*see* QUOTA SYSTEM). In the Bakke case of 1977, the Supreme Court ruled that affirmative action was legal, but that Alan Bakke, a White man who had been refused entry to the California University Medical School under a quota system, had been discriminated against. The exact ramifications of the Bakke decision, and the issue of the legality or otherwise of affirmative action legislation in America, is as yet unresolved.

revisionism A moderate version of socialism that is softer than orthodox Marxism. It was first advocated in 1899 in Germany by Eduard Bernstein, who wanted social reforms rather than revolution. He felt the socialist movement should include all classes and not be restricted to workers. This idea of revising and updating Marxist theory is recurrent within communism. Strict followers of Marxist-Leninist ideology have traditionally regarded any new interpretation of doctrine to be heretical and dangerous. For this reason 'revisionist' was a communist term of abuse before the introduction of PERESTROIKA by the Soviet leader Mikhail Gorbachov.

Revolt of the Four Generals A revolt in Algeria in 1961, led by four generals: Edmond Jouhaud, Raoul Salan, Maurice Challe, and André Zeller. The revolt was the culmination of a period of unrest in the country, resulting from President de Gaulle's Algerian policy. It began on 22 April and was quelled by the president within a few days.

Rexists A Belgian political party formed by Léon Degrelle in 1936 advocating Fascist methods. Markedly collaborationist during the German occupation of Belgium, it was accordingly suppressed when the Germans were expelled in 1944. The name is an adaptation of 'Christus Rex', Christ the King, the watchword of a Catholic Young People's Action Society founded in 1925. *See* FASCISM.

Reye's syndrome A rare but serious disease of children. First identified in 1963 by R. D. Reye (1912–77), the Australian physician after whom it was named, it typically develops during the recovery phase of a viral infection, such as influenza. Symptoms of brain damage (including swelling, delirium, and coma) are combined with those of liver failure: both require prompt treatment to prevent permanent damage to these organs. The cause has not been definitely established but recent evidence suggests that the disorder is caused by the toxic effects of ASPIRIN – given to relieve the original infection – on young children. For this reason aspirin should not be given to children under 12 years of age.

RFC Royal Flying Corps. The UK's first military aviation service and the forerunner of the RAF. It was created by royal warrant in 1912 from the Air Battalion of the Royal Engineers; it was originally intended to have both army and navy wings but the naval wing quickly separated to become the Royal Naval Air Service, leaving the RFC to the army. At first the pioneer airmen relied heavily on French-designed airframes and engines, owing to the rudimentary state of the home aviation industry. Furthermore, technical progress was hampered by the RFC's preoccupation with the biplane at the expense of the faster monoplane. At the outset of World War I, squadrons of the Corps were stationed in France, chiefly for reconnaissance of enemy positions. However, by the autumn of 1915 German aircraft armed with machine guns began to take an increasing toll of RFC craft; in retaliation the Corps began to fit some of its own planes with machine guns, as well as the rifle and pistol carried by the observer. Not until May 1916 did the RFC have its first squadron of effective fighter planes – Sopwith Strutters fitted with a synchronized machine gun firing through the propellor arc – capable of matching the German Fokkers. 1916 also saw an increased commitment to home defence by the Corps, in an effort to combat bombing raids by German Zeppelins. Casualties were high: in April 1917, for instance, the expected duration of service for a fighter crew on the Western Front was just two months.

Rhayader In Paul Gallico's sentimental story *The Snow Goose* (1940), a hunchbacked recluse with a love of wild birds. His character was based on Sir Peter Scott (1909–89), the ornithologist and wildlife artist, who illustrated the first edition of the book. The two men had once been rivals for the love of the same woman, a well-known figure skater.

Rhodes scholars Students holding a scholarship at Oxford under the will of Cecil Rhodes (1853–1902), whose wealth largely accumulated from his mining activities in South Africa. These scholars are selected from candidates in the Commonwealth, America, and Germany.

rhythm. rhythm-and-blues (R & B) The Black-American popular music that developed into ROCK 'N' ROLL. Born in the 1940s, rhythm-and-blues grew out of blues music to which a strong repetitious beat was added and electronically amplified. In the early 1950s, White teenagers began to buy R & B records, which critics described as 'sheer garbage' and 'as bad for kids as dope'. Early Black rock-'n'-roll stars who were first listed on the R & B charts included Fats Domino, Chuck Berry, Dinah Washington, Joe Turner, and The Platters.

rhythm section The instruments in a dance band, rock group, etc., that mainly provide the beat of the music. These are usually the double bass and drums but may also include the piano.

Ribbentrop-Molotov pact *See* HITLER-STALIN PACT.

ribbon development Single-depth building, chiefly houses, along main roads (arterial roads) extending out of built-up areas. Developments of this kind took place in the 1920s and 1930s but were stopped by the UK Town and Country Planning Act (1947).

Rice, Archie The central character in John Osborne's play *The Entertainer* (1957), a struggling survivor from the great days of music hall, partly based on the veteran comic Max Miller (1895–1963). The role was originally played by Laurence Olivier, in a notable departure from the classical repertory in which he had made his name.

Richard, Cliff The stage name of Harry Rodger Webb (1940–), the ROCK 'N' ROLL singer who dominated the UK charts in the 1960s and has endured to become 'Britain's Oldest Teenager'. Born in India, he worked as a factory clerk before performing in a London coffee bar with his backup group, The Drifters. He recorded his first single, 'Move It', at the age of 17 in 1958; it reached No. 3 on the charts. The next year, he received a gold disc for 'Living Doll' and The Drifters were renamed The Shadows. Together they made a series of film musicals: *The Young Ones* (1961), *Summer Holiday* (1963), and *Wonderful Life* (1964). Richards, once criticized for his 'revolting hip-swinging' and 'vulgar antics', became a BORN-AGAIN CHRISTIAN in the 1970s, after which he began to preach and carry out gospel tours. In 1989 he released his 100th single, 'The Best of Me'.

Richter scale The scale used to measure the strength of an earthquake. It was adopted in 1935 and named after its inventor, the US seismologist Charles Richter (1900–85). The scale ranges from 0 to 8, with each number representing a tenfold increase in energy measured by ground motion. The highest recorded earthquake was 8.9 in 1933 in Japan. The SAN FRANCISCO EARTHQUAKES were 8.3 in 1906 (earlier measurements converted to the Richter scale) and 6.9 in 1989. The Richter magnitude that measures the severity of an earthquake is not, of course, an indicator of the likely number of casualties; that is clearly also a function of the terrain experiencing the quake. For example, the 1985 Mexico City earthquake of 8.1 caused some 4200 deaths, while the 1988 earthquake in Armenia, registering 6.8 on the scale, caused more than 55,000 deaths.

Richthofen Flying Circus *See* RED BARON.

riddle. a riddle wrapped in a mystery inside an enigma Churchill's phrase for the ambiguities of Soviet policy in the early weeks of World War II. His words, used in a radio broadcast of 1 October 1939, were prompted by the Soviet invasion of E Poland on 18 September, some two weeks after the German invasion from the west. At the time, the Allies had little idea whether this represented active collaboration with the Nazis, an intention to resist them in some circumstances, or simple opportunism. In fact, the partition of Poland had been secretly agreed in the talks leading to the Nazi–Soviet Pact in August 1939.

Churchill's phrase has often been used out of historical context, as though it were a general comment on the Russian national character or the impenetrable secrecy of pre-GLASNOST Soviet politics.

ride. ride man US Black slang of the 1920s to 1940s for the lead soloist in a jazz band, especially one who improvises freely. The soloist can be said to 'ride' the accompaniment in the sense that he is carried along by it while at the same time controlling its speed and direction. The allusion is probably as much to the idea of a man 'riding' a woman in sexual intercourse as to any form of equestrianism.

A band or section of a band can also be said to 'ride' when it plays with an easy flowing rhythm. A **ride cymbal** is a cymbal used by jazz drummers to keep up a continuous rhythm, while the **ride-out** is the final chorus of a piece, usually taken in unison.

ride shotgun To sit in the passenger's front seat of a car. Popularized by US teenagers in the 1950s, this term was originally used, in the American West, for an armed guard who rode next to the driver of a stagecoach to provide protection against robbers, hostile Indians, etc.

riff In jazz and rock music, a simple ostinato figure used as a basis for improvisation. By extension, it has come to be used of speech or writing that resembles jazz riffing in its rhythms or improvisatory quality. It is also used in a derogatory sense to mean anything that is constantly reiterated, such as a phrase or argument.

The derivation is uncertain. Some accounts link it to the word 'riffle', meaning any kind of skimming or rippling motion; it may, however, be nothing more than a shortening of 'refrain'.

right. right brain The right hemisphere of the brain, which neuropsychological research has demonstrated to be dominant for spatial awareness, creative thinking, and the production of art, music, and literature. Creative individuals can therefore be described as 'right-brain thinking'. The **left brain** is usually dominant for verbal skills and mathematical and analytical thinking. Cerebral asymmetry and the localization of brain function became widely accepted in the 19th century with the discovery that damage to the left hemisphere resulted in speech impairment, whereas damage to the right had no discernible effect on speech abilities. In the early 20th century it was also discovered that the left side was dominant in controlling complex movements; the role of the right side remained unclear until the 1950s, when research demonstrated its importance in spatial analysis.

right on! (1) An expression of wholehearted agreement or encouragement that is chiefly associated with US Black slang. The phrase was already in use in the 1950s and gained wider currency in the 1960s and 1970s. (2) In the UK **right-on attitudes**, a phrase common in the late 1980s, are those attitudes characteristic of trendy members of the soft left. It now has an ironic self-righteous flavour.

right-to-life *See* PRO-LIFE.

the right stuff Army slang for the tough heroic quality regarded as necessary for officer material. The phrase, often heard in the 1930s, became popular again after the US writer Tom Wolfe used it as the title of his 1979 book about the first US astronauts.

righteous Black US JAZZ slang from the 1930s meaning either excellent or, if said disparagingly, typical of the Whites.

Rillington Place *See* CHRISTIE MURDERS.

ring. ring of steel A journalistic cliché for a circle of heavily armed troops. The 'ring' invokes the double images of encirclement and the sound made by clashing weapons.

ring road A main road that encircles a city centre so that heavy traffic and through traffic can bypass the city. London's M25, completed in the 1980s and glorying in its description as an orbital motorway, replaced an earlier ring-road network that was overtaken by the city's growth. The US name is **belt** or **beltway**. The beltway round Washington, DC, has become a local political catchphrase: 'outside the beltway' refers to public opinion in grass-roots America.

Ringo In full Ringo Starr, stage name of Richard Starkey (1940–), drummer with the BEATLES (1963–70) and subsequently a solo performer. He acquired the name in the early 1960s, when his habit of wearing several rings was far more unusual for a man than would be the case now. The surname Starr was adopted for an early stint at a Butlin's Holiday Camp.

Rintelen spy ring A group of German spies operating in America during World War I under the leadership of Kapitän Franz von Rintelen. The organization was highly successful, for a time, in its mission to sabotage US aid to the Allies. In August 1915 Rintelen was recalled from America by a false message; he was arrested when the Dutch ship on which he was travelling reached British waters.

Rin Tin Tin An Alsatian dog (also called a German shepherd dog) who became a star of the silent screen in the 1920s. Formerly a guard dog with the German army, Rin Tin Tin appeared in such films as *Jaws of Steel* (1927) and *A Dog of the Regiment* (1930), usually saving the day by means of a display of loyalty and resourcefulness. This remarkable dog died in 1932, aged about 16. *See also* LASSIE.

Riom trials The trials of a number of French politicians and military men, which took place in 1942 at a supreme court of justice set up by the VICHY government in the town of Riom, France. The defendants, opponents of the Vichy government, included such major figures as Edouard Daladier, Léon Blum, Paul Reynard, and Maurice Gamelin, who were blamed for the fall of France and imprisoned. The trials began in February 1942 and were suspended indefinitely in April of that year. The accused spent the remainder of World War II in prisons and concentration camps.

riot shield A defensive shield, made from tough plastic, carried by police or military forces during riot control. Riot shields have been used by British troops in Northern Ireland for riot control since the early 1970s and were first issued to police forces in the mainland after the Lewisham riots in the summer of 1977. The tactic of banging such shields to intimidate a foe was borrowed from the war customs of the Zulus and other earlier armies.

rip. ripcord A cord attached to a handle that is pulled to open a parachute from its pack during descent. The first parachutes in the late 18th century were dropped already opened from balloons. An American, A. L. Stevens, introduced the parachute pack and ripcord in 1908. This combination was perfected 10 years later by another American, Floyd Smith, for use in escaping from an aircraft.

rip off Slang meaning to steal, to swindle, to take advantage of. Originally a term from the Black street jargon of large US cities, it was taken up by the HIPPIES and has passed into more generally usage, being now heard in all parts of the English-speaking world.

> In Spain, tourists used to be ripped off by souvenir shops and property speculators: nowadays they are just ripped off.
>
> *The Independent*, 16 March 1991.

The noun form is also widely used, as in 'the price was a rip-off'. It is also used to imply that an idea has been stolen without attribution: 'His paper was a rip-off of mine!'

ripple effect A recent political catchphrase for repercussions that result from a single important event or situation. The easing of US-Soviet tensions had a ripple effect on military and domestic spending. The ripple effect of Salman Rushdie's novel *The Satanic Verses* (1989) included an Iranian FATWA on the author, western nations withdrawing ambassadors from Iran, West Germany halting its Iranian aid programme, and anti-Rushdie demonstrators being killed in India and Pakistan.

Ritz. Ritz Brothers A team of US comedians of the 1930s and 1940s, comprising Al (1901–65), Jim (1903–85), and Harry (1906–86) Ritz. Beginning in nightclubs, they later appeared in such film musicals as *The Goldwyn Follies* (1938) and *The Three Musketeers* (1939). Their original family name was Joachim.

ritzy Denoting an occasion, person, etc., that is fashionable and opulent. It is derived from the Ritz Hotel, Paris, and the Ritz Hotel, Piccadilly, London, which became identified with luxury and wealth. They were established by the Swiss hotelier, César Ritz (1850–1918). Hence 'to dine at the Ritz' may be considered to be the ultimate luxury in dining out. To **put on the Ritz** is to make an ostentatious display of opulence: the phrase predates the Irving Berlin song 'Putting on the Ritz', which was written in 1929.

RKO RKO Radio Pictures Inc., formerly one of the biggest Hollywood production and distribution companies. It was founded in 1921 when the Radio Corporation of America merged with the Keith-Orpheum cinema circuit. Notable RKO features included *Cimarron* (1931), *King Kong* (1933), and *Citizen Kane* (1941) but the company was best known for its low-budget and rather unsuccessful films; it was in continual financial difficulties. During World War II a popular West Coast joke ran 'In case of an air raid, go directly to RKO; they haven't had a hit in years'. In 1948 Howard Hughes acquired a controlling share of the stock, but he was unable to bring the company round; in 1953 the studios were sold off to a television company. The firm continues as RKO General, an umbrella organization controlling a number of radio and TV stations.

RNA Ribonucleic Acid. One of the fundamental molecules of life, responsible for interpreting the genetic information that resides in the genes of living cells. This it does in two stages: transcription and translation of the genetic message. RNA is chemically very similar to DNA; the essential difference is that it contains the sugar ribose (hence *ribo*nucleic) instead of the deoxyribose sugar of DNA. Cells contain several different types of RNA, including MESSENGER RNA, ribosomal RNA, and transfer RNA, which all have different roles in the manufacture of proteins by the cell. In some viruses RNA is also the genetic material. Discovery of the vital roles of RNA in protein synthesis came in the 1950s through the work of many scientists, including Francis Crick, Paul Berg, and Robert Holley.

RNAS Royal Naval Air Service. The air force of the Royal Navy, which was founded in 1914 to protect coastal ports and shipping and to carry out punitive raids on U-BOAT bases in the German-occupied Channel ports. After 1918, the RNAS was subordinated to, and controlled by, the RAF, although the Admiralty insisted that the navy should be allowed to maintain a separate specialist air service. In 1924 government permission was granted to establish the Fleet Air Arm, a carrier branch of the Royal Navy, although it was not until 1937 that the FAA was placed under sole Admiralty control.

road. Keep death off the road A slogan of the late 1940s and early 1950s in the UK exhorting drivers to take more care. It was used as the caption to an illustration of a haggard and distressed looking widow, who presumably represented both death itself and an unfortunate woman who had been bereaved by a road accident. It was criticized at the time as being too disturbing. *See also* CARELESSNESS KILLS.

one for the road One last drink before departing, formerly a popular call at the end of a party. However, since the introduction of strict drink-driving codes, this is rarely heard. *See* BREATHALYSER.

road hog Colloquial name for a selfish, reckless, and thrusting motorist. The term has been in common use since the early days of motoring.

roadhouse An inn or hotel by the roadside, usually at some distance outside a town, to which people in the 1930s went by car for meals, dancing, etc. Roadhouses ceased to be fashionable with the advent of strict drink-drive codes (*see* ONE FOR THE ROAD). Their other function, of providing overnight accommodation for travellers, has largely been taken over by MOTELS.

roadie Any of the individuals hired by touring musicians to transport, maintain, and erect equipment for their stage shows.

road movie A genre of film in which the central character takes to the road to escape the law, his own past, or a constricting home life. His experiences, and those of the people he meets, form the substance of the film. The hero's journey usually becomes a voyage of self-discovery or an exploration of the state of a society.

This mostly rather sombre genre should certainly not be confused with the 'Road' movies of Bob Hope, Bing Crosby, and Dorothy Lamour – a series of light comedies beginning conventionally enough with *The Road to Singapore* (1940) but later developing a zany ad-libbing style of its own.

road show (1) Originally a US term for a travelling show of actors, musicians, mountebanks, etc., now used of any kind of touring attraction, especially one requiring large amounts of equipment and personnel. It is commonly used of, for example, rock bands touring with their own sound and lighting equipment, campaigning politicians with their entourage and mobile back-up facilities, or a radio or TV programme that broadcasts live from a series of outside venues. (2) In the film business, the special 'pre-release' of a major feature in selected cities before its general distribution to local cinemas nationwide.

road tax A British tax on motor vehicles. The cost for private cars in 1991 was £100, which has remained unchanged for six years. It can be paid annually or every six months (£55), and drivers must display their **tax disc**, officially the *vehicle excise licence*, on the windscreen as proof of payment.

robbed. We wuz robbed A catchphrase that originated in the boxing world in America. In the 1927 world heavyweight fight between Gene Tunney and the challenger Jack Dempsey, Dempsey laid Tunney flat on the canvas – but it was six seconds before the referee could persuade Dempsey to retire to a neutral corner so that he could begin his count. The delay enabled Tunney to get to his feet, survive the round, and retain his title on points. Dempsey said afterwards, "I was robbed of the championship". This cry was echoed a little less grammatically by Joe Jacobs, the US manager of Max Schmeling, whom he believed had been cheated of victory in his 1932 fight against Jack Sharkey. "We wuz robbed", he shouted into a vacant microphone. Since the 1930s, the phrase has been used by the losers and their managers in many other sports, especially football. The *Sun*, reporting that footballers are being offered a course to help them avoid such clichés (*see* OVER THE MOON; SICK AS A PARROT), offered a more grammatical and gentlemanly alternative:

> We were humiliated by the vastly superior technical skills of the opposition.

robot (Czech *robota*, forced labour) An automaton with semi-human powers and intelligence. From this the term is often extended to mean a person who works automatically without employing initiative. The name comes from the mechanical creatures in Karel Capek's play *R.U.R.* (Rossum's Universal Robots), which was successfully produced in London in 1923. In its modern sense a robot is an automated and computer-controlled machine that is programmed to perform specific tasks that would otherwise be performed by a human being. Many functions in factories are now automated, *i.e.* performed by robots.

robot dancing or **robotic dancing** A dance popularized in the 1980s by Black Americans. Also called **robotics**, it has quick jerky movements in imitation of the mechanical actions of robots. *Robotic* (resembling a robot) was a word originally coined by the US biochemist and science fiction writer Isaac Asimov (1920–).

robug A remote controlled device used to clean, maintain, or photograph inaccessible parts of a tall building. It uses legs with adhesive suckers to crawl up vertical surfaces and across ceilings. Its name reflects its resemblance to a robotic spider. It was developed in the 1980s by Arthur Collie and Professor John Billingsley.

rock (1) US slang for cocaine, because of its crystalline form. This is the most widely used slang word for the drug. *See also* CRACK. (2) Slang for a diamond or any gemstone. (3) Electronically amplified music, encompassing many genres loosely descended from ROCK 'N' ROLL. It was used more-or-less interchangeably with POP until the early 1970s, when some critics began to insist on a distinction. Thereafter, 'rock' tended to be used of music that was (supposedly) more ambitious, more serious in intention, and less immediately commercial than the lightweight pop music that dominated the singles charts. In 1990 this distinction was the subject of a debate in the House of Lords, who had to rule whether a commercial radio franchise reserved for 'non-pop' broadcasting could be awarded to a company who planned to specialize in serious rock music. After a long and somewhat heated discussion, their lordships ruled that this was a distinction without a difference. Subdivisions of rock incude **soft rock** (a more melodic variety) and **hard rock** (based on pounding rhythms and high volume). *See also* ACID ROCK; FOLK ROCK; HEAVY METAL; PUNK; etc.

don't knock the rock A catchphrase of the 1950s, used in response to hostile criticism of ROCK 'N' ROLL music. It was the title of a 1957 film featuring the US group Bill Haley and the Comets: the title song reached seventh position in the British 'top ten' in the same year.

rockabilly A type of popular music, originating in America, that is a fusion between ROCK 'N' ROLL and hillbilly country music. Popular in the 1950s, it underwent a revival in the early 1990s.

rocker *See* MODS AND ROCKERS.

rock 'n' roll A type of POP music that emerged in the later 1950s, characterized by a heavily accented beat and simple repeated phrases. Essentially a commercialized version of RHYTHM-AND-BLUES, it was the first style of popular music to become a focus for youthful rebellion and parental panic. It was accompanied by a frenetic kind of JIVE dancing, also known as rock 'n' roll. The term was used from about 1953 by the US disc jockey Alan Freed, who found that the racial stigma attached to rhythm-and-blues prevented this music from being accepted by White audiences. Ironically, 'rock and roll' – like so many popular music terms – was originally Black slang for sexual intercourse. *See also* ROCK; TEDDY BOYS.

rock opera A drama set to ROCK music. The first of the genre to achieve artistic and commercial success was the HIPPIE musical *Hair* (1969). *Tommy*, written by Pete Townshend of The Who (also 1969) and filmed by Ken Russell in 1975, inspired a number of imitations. One of the more successful of these was *Jesus Christ Superstar* (1970) composed by Andrew Lloyd Webber and Tim Rice.

rock steady An early form of REGGAE music.

Rockefeller. Rockefeller Center New York City's 22-acre business and entertainment complex of 19 buildings. It includes the British Empire Building and the 70-storey 850-foot General Electric Building (the former RCA Building) housing the National Broadcasting Company (*see* NBC). The building's sunken Plaza, overlooked by a gilded statue of Prometheus, becomes a garden-terrace restaurant in summer and an ice-skating rink in winter crowned with "the world's largest Christmas tree". Superlatives also abound in Radio City Music Hall, whose indoor cinema (6200 seats), Wurlitzer organ, and chandeliers are all listed as "the world's largest". The Rockettes precision-dancing girls perform on the revolving stage. Radio City announced its closure in 1979 but was saved by a public campaign. The Rockefeller Center site – from 48th to 51st streets and from 5th Avenue to the Avenue of the Americas – was leased from Columbia University in 1928 by industrialist John D. Rockefeller Jr (1874–1960); the major buildings were constructed between 1931 and 1939.

Rockefeller Foundation A philanthropic foundation created in 1913 by the US industrialist John Davison Rockefeller (1839–1937) and his son John D. Rockefeller Jr (1874–1960). The purpose of the foundation was "to promote the well-being of mankind throughout the world". Initially concerned with public health and medical education, the work of the foundation diversified after 1928, providing generous financial support for scientific research and projects connected with the social sciences and humanities.

Rockhampton Rocket A press nickname for the Australian tennis player Rod Laver (1938–), referring to his speed about the court and his birth in Rockhampton, Queensland. Laver was the first player to win the grand slam of major tournaments twice, in 1962 and 1969; the interval represents the period during which he was barred from Wimbledon for his professional status. He was also the first player to earn £1 million in prize money.

Roger The word used to represent the letter R in a former version of the phonetic alphabet used in radiotelephony. 'Roger' also stood for 'received', indicating that a message had been received and understood. 'Roger and out' meant that the message had been received and there was no reply. 'Roger' has also been used as a general term of acknowledgment (meaning right, OK, or agreed) by British and US forces during World War II, and subsequently entered civilian language. In the modern phonetic alphabet the letter R and the word 'received' are represented by the word 'Romeo'.

role. role model A person whose behaviour in a particular role serves as a model for another to follow. For example, a father often functions as a role model for his son.

role play Playing the part of someone or something in a dramatic reconstruction of a real situation. Role play was originally developed as a therapeutic technique in psychodrama by the Austrian-born US psychiatrist Jacob Moreno (1890–1974). His patients were encouraged to act out a variety of social roles to gain insight into the motives, actions, and perspectives of others. The technique is now widely used in many forms of training to promote understanding and improve relationships.

Rolex Tradename for the watches produced by the Rolex Watch Co. Although meaningless in itself, the name may have been chosen to suggest the 'rolling' mechanism of a watch and the idea of *ex*cellence. This was one of the first tradenames to use the suffix *-ex*, which has since become ubiquitous. The famous **Rolex oyster**, introduced in 1926, was so-named because of its watertight design, at that time a unique feature. In the 1980s it became the YUPPIE watch par excellence, appearing regularly in the lists of designer accessories that fill the pages of S 'N' F novels from that era.

roll. roller British slang for a Rolls-Royce car. Originally a term from the underworld, its use became more widespread in the early 1980s.

> Duke's £38,000 bill to fix his roller.
>
> *The Sun*, 3 April 1991.

roller disco A form of disco dancing on roller skates that became a popular US pastime in the late 1970s. The most renowned performers were seen at the Empire Roller Disco in New York City's borough of Brooklyn. Indoor roller skating has remained popular in America since rinks proliferated in the 1870s.

rolling *See* QUEER-ROLLING.

Rolling Stones One of the three leading rock groups of the 1960s, the others being the BEATLES and The Who. The main members of the Stones were Mick Jagger (1943–), Brian Jones (1942–69), who was replaced by Mick Taylor (1948–) and then Ron Wood (1947–), Keith Richard(s) (1943–), Charlie Watts (1941–), and Bill Wyman (1936–). The group was heavily influenced by the RHYTHM-AND-BLUES movement of the early 1960s, the music of such blues singers as Muddy Waters, and the ROCK 'N' ROLL of Chuck Berry. Ironically, considering the battle between the Stones and the Beatles for the soul of British youth during the 1960s, their first top-ten hit was the Paul McCartney and John Lennon song 'I wanna be your man'. Their rebellious image led to strings of other hits in the mid-1960s; the group's success was sustained by establishment hostility reflected in a series of police raids, minor drug charges, and gaol sentences (quashed on appeal). The mid-1970s marked the end of their most creative period, with such albums as *Their Satanic Majesties' Request* (1967), *Beggars Banquet* (1967), *Let It Bleed* (1970), and *Exile on Main Street* (1972). Hit singles included 'Jumping Jack Flash' (1968) and 'Honky Tonk Woman', which reached No. 1 in 1969, the year Brian Jones drowned in his swimming pool.

Roll on, big ship A catchphrase used by members of the British armed forces towards the end of World War I, expressing an earnest desire for the war to be over. Variants of the phrase include 'Roll on, Blighty', 'Roll on, duration' (referring to the fact that volunteers had signed up for the duration of the war), 'Roll on, that boat' (used in the RAF from the 1920s), 'I heard the voice of Moses say, Roll on, my bloody twelve' (used in the Royal Navy, referring to the service period of 12 years), 'Roll on, death, and let's have a go at the angels' (an expression of boredom or frustration), and 'Roll on, time' (used by prisoners).

In general usage the phrase 'roll on' may be followed by anything that the speaker awaits with impatience, such as 'Roll on, pay-day', 'Roll on, Christmas', etc.

roll-on roll-off (RORO) Denoting a ferry that transports motor vehicles across a stretch of water and is so constructed that the vehicles can drive straight onto the vessel at the port of loading and off at the port of destination. Such vessels are widely used for transporting cars and heavy lorries across the English Channel. *See* HERALD OF FREE ENTERPRISE.

Rolls. It runs like a Rolls It runs perfectly and with the utmost smoothness. Usually said of a motor car or of other power-driven vehicles; a tribute to the traditional superiority and quality of Rolls-Royce cars. *See* BEST CAR IN THE WORLD.

ROM Read-Only Memory. A type of computer memory that cannot be written to, or erased by switching off the power. ROM is used for storing a program, such as that used in a wordprocessor, or the operating system (the computer program that controls the screen, keyboard, disk access, etc.) so that it becomes operative as soon as the computer is switched on. Because ROM is incorruptible, any changes to its contents, *e.g.* to fix errors in a program or to upgrade the operating system, have to be accomplished by replacing the ROM chips themselves.

roman candle British armed forces' euphemism for the fate of a parachutist when his parachute fails to open.

Rome–Berlin Axis *See* AXIS; PACT OF STEEL.

rooinek (Afrikaans, red-neck) A name given by the Boers to the British in the South African War; it was used later to mean any British or European immigrant to South Africa. *See also* REDNECK.

rookie In army slang, a recruit, a novice or greenhorn. In America, it is also used for a raw beginner in professional sport. It is probably a changed diminutive of 'recruit'.

rope Marijuana, which is derived from the hemp plant (*Cannabis sativa*), also the source of fibre for rope (hence the name). The term is usually applied to marijuana in the form of a JOINT, perhaps because in the 1930s and 1940s a 'rope' was a facetious term for a cigar. *See also* POT.

RORO *See* ROLL-ON ROLL-OFF.

Rorschach ink-blot test A test used in psychology, devised by the Swiss psychiatrist Hermann Rorschach (1884–1922). It consists of a series of ten ink-blots that form complex symmetrical shapes: five of the ink-blots are coloured, five are in shades of grey and black. The way in which the patients describe and interpret these shapes is supposed to reveal aspects of their personality and emotional stability (or instability); the results can be used to measure intelligence and diagnose psychological disorders. The validity of the test has been the subject of some controversy.

rort An Australian colloquialism for a riotous party or drinking bout. This usage seems to have originated among Australian servicemen in World War II, probably by back formation from the slang *rorty*, meaning lively or jolly. It seems to be unrelated to the older sense of 'rort' meaning a racket, dodge, or swindle. In the GREAT DEPRESSION a **rorter** was a tramp who made a precarious living by peddling trashy goods from door to door. The word is used more generally to mean a small-time conman or hustler.

rose. Rose Bowl A sports stadium in Pasadena, California, which is the venue of the annual post-season US college football game between a team representing the Pacific Eight and one representing the Big Ten Conference. The first of these games was held on 1 January 1902; it became officially known as the Rose Bowl game in 1923 and has been held annually there ever since. *See also* SUPER BOWL. The stadium is named after the Tournament of the Roses held there annually from 1890; this is based on the Battle of the Flowers, which takes place during the annual Lenten carnival in Nice on the French Côte d'Azur.

rose is a rose A phrase meaning that something is inexplicable yet somehow complete and perfect in itself. The phrase is a shortened version of a line from a poem by Gertrude Stein (1874–1946):

> Rose is a rose is a rose.
>
> 'Sacred Emily'.

'Rose' here is Sir Frederick Rose, a British painter whose work she loved.

Roseland South-east England outside London, regarded as a desirable place to live. *Rose* is here an acronym for 'Rest of South East', but also conveys the idea that life is rosy in this affluent and agreeable part of the country. The term first appeared in the mid-1980s, when the south-east enjoyed an economic boom (and a dramatic rise in property values) while other parts of the country were still struggling out of recession.

Rosenberg spy case The case of the US couple Julius (1918–53) and Ethel Rosenberg (1915–53), who were arrested in 1950 on suspicion of supplying the Soviet Union with atom bomb secrets. The case against them was based largely on the evidence of Harry Gold, a Soviet agent, and David Greenglass, Ethel Rosenberg's brother, who worked at the atomic research base at Los Alamos (*see* LOS ALAMOS PROJECT), both of whom had been eventually exposed by the arrest of Klaus Fuchs in 1945 (*see* FUCHS SPY CASE). Greenglass claimed that his espionage activities, which he admitted in return for leniency, were instigated and encouraged by the Rosenbergs, although both protested their innocence throughout their ordeal. The anti-communist hysteria generated by MCCARTHYISM at that time combined with the outbreak of the KOREAN WAR to give the Rosenbergs little chance of acquittal. They were sentenced to death in March 1951, although a series of appeals and stays of execution prolonged the agony until 19 June 1953, when they were electrocuted in Sing Sing despite appeals for clemency and public demonstrations throughout America and Europe on their behalf. They would have been reprieved if they had confessed to spying for the Soviet Union, which they steadfastly refused to do. The question of the guilt or innocence of the Rosenbergs has been the subject of controversy ever since. Not all the relevant FBI files have been released but the latest research indicates that Julius was guilty of espionage, but that Ethel was framed by the FBI in order to pressure her husband into revealing full details of his espionage activities.

> I can only say that, by immensely increasing the chance of an atomic war, the Rosenbergs may have condemned to death tens of millions of innocent people all over the world.
>
> PRESIDENT EISENHOWER.

Rotary Club A movement among business men which takes for its motto 'Service above Self'. The idea originated with Paul Harris, a Chicago lawyer, in 1905. In 1911 it took root in the UK and there are now clubs in most towns, membership originally being limited to one member each of any trade, calling, or profession. Lectures are delivered at weekly meetings by guest speakers. The name derives from the early practice of holding meetings in rotation at the offices of business premises of its members. The Rotary Clubs are now members of one association called Rotary International. The Inner Wheel club is a similar organization for the wives of Rotarians and Rotaract is for younger members.

rotodyne Tradename for a type of helicopter that has short fixed wings to provide additional lift. The first rotodyne was constructed in 1957 by the Fairey Aviation Co. (absorbed by Westland a few years later) but only one further machine was built before the project was suspended in 1962. Similar machines (also known as convertiplanes, compound helicopters, or tilt-rotors) have been produced by other companies.

The name combines 'rotor' with *aerodyne*, any heavier-than-air machine that uses aerodynamic forces to obtain lift.

rotor ship An experimental ocean-going vessel developed by Germany in 1925, which for a time promised to be a revolutionary step forward in sea transport. The *Baden-Baden*, designed by Anton Flettner, was propelled by two massive rotors, which responded to wind pressure in much the same way as a ball spinning in a breeze; Flettner claimed that it was capable of greater speeds than conventional sailing ships while being cheap and easy to run; it was also able to keep moving in the heaviest weather. It was confidently predicted that all the world's shipping would employ rotor power within years. However, the *Baden-Baden*'s dependence on the wind coupled with technical difficulties created by the continuous vibration caused by the rotors meant that even the prototypes had been scrapped within 20 years.

rotten One of many Australian colloquialisms meaning drunk. It presumably describes a more advanced state of intoxication than such terms as 'ripe' and 'over-ripe'.

rottweiler A breed of working dog with a stocky body and thick neck, named after the town of Rottweil in SW Germany.

Rottweilers are thought to have been brought there by the Roman legions and were traditionally used by local butchers to carry their moneybags to market. Their characteristics include strength and aggression, making them highly suitable as guard dogs. The rottweiler became notorious in the UK in the 1980s, following a series of attacks on children and others, some fatal. A press campaign to make the dog a controlled breed seems only to have increased its popularity, especially among those young men for whom its viciousness became the chief attraction.

The word 'rottweiler' is now frequently used to mean a brutally aggressive person with no scruples or sense of fair play. In some fields, such as politics or business, the usage may be half-admiring. The word is used in such common phrases as 'rottweiler tactics', 'rottweiler journalism', etc. *See also* BANDOG; PIT BULL TERRIER.

rough. rough cut The initial stage in the editing of a film. The rough cut is assembled by selecting one version of each shot and arranging them in a sequence that tells the basic story and preserves continuity. Many refinements are made before the film is released. *See also* RUSHES.

rough trade (1) British male homosexual slang of the 1950s for an uncouth and aggressive sexual partner, usually a younger man of a lower social group, often a manual labourer. It is also used in the same sense for the client of a male prostitute, or any casual male homosexual pick-up. More recently it has been used to describe a typical male homosexual pin-up – a MACHO and muscular youth. (2) An aggressive lower-class male client of a female prostitute. It is also used to describe a macho and muscular, but socially inferior, young boyfriend of a cultured older woman.

round. in the round In the theatre, the production of plays on a central stage surrounded by the audience as in an arena, without proscenium arch or curtains.

Round Table An international organization that provides men under the age of 40 with the opportunity for social gatherings, with a strong emphasis on community service, charitable works, and fund raising. It was founded in 1927 as a 'Club for Young Business and Professional Men' by Louis Marchesi, the son of a Swiss-born restaurateur living in Norwich, England. The origins of the name are somewhat confused: some have attributed it to a speech made by the Prince of Wales in which he urged:

> The young business and professional men of this country must get together round the table, adopt methods that have proved so sound in the past, adapt them to the changing needs of the times, and wherever possible improve them.

There are now over 1250 such local groups, or 'Tables', in the UK, with more than 30,000 members, known as Tablers. The organization is also established in some 70 other countries. Tablers retiring at 40 can seek solace in the '41 Club'. The first Ladies Circle, for members' wives, was formed in Bournemouth in 1930, and the National Association of Ladies Circles was set up in 1936.

Round-up The codename of the Allied landings in France in 1944, the planning of which began in June 1942. The cross-channel invasion was originally scheduled for April 1943, but was eventually postponed until March or April 1944. The codename was changed in May 1943 to 'Roundhammer' and in June 1943 to OVERLORD.

Roy Australian colloquialism for a rich fashionable man, especially one who drives a sports car, dresses in expensive leisure wear, and has an offensively smooth manner. He is despised by the OCKERS, who regard the Roys as idle, untrustworthy, and effeminate.

royal. Royal Air Force *See* RAF.

Royal Armoured Corps A British Army corps formed in April 1939 to amalgamate the former Cavalry of the Line, which was equipped with armour shortly before or during World War II, together with the mechanized Royal Tank Corps, which became the Royal Tank Regiment.

Royal Festival Hall A concert hall on the South Bank of the Thames designed by Sir Leslie Martin and Sir Robert Matthew for the FESTIVAL OF BRITAIN in 1951. It was the first significant British public building in the modern style.

Royal Flying Corps *See* RFC.

Royal Green Jackets An infantry regiment of the British Army comprising the 43rd, 52nd, King's Royal Rifle Corps, and Rifle Brigade. The regiment was created in 1966 through the amalgamation of the 1st Green Jackets, the 2nd Green Jackets (The King's Royal Rifle Corps), and the 3rd Green Jackets (The Rifle Brigade).

> Honi Soit Qui Mal y Pense
>
> Regimental motto.

Royal National Theatre The complex of three theatres on London's South Bank that houses the Royal National Theatre Company. It was designed by Sir Denys Lasdun and opened in 1976, when the Company moved from its earlier home at the Old Vic. The complex, with terraces overlooking the Thames, has been variously called "a great building", "a concrete fortress", and by Prince Charles:

> a way of building a nuclear power station in the middle of London without anyone objecting.

It houses the UK's most versatile and technically advanced drama facilities and stages a great variety of classic and experimental drama. The theatres are the Olivier, holding 1160 people in its fan-shaped auditorium; the Lyttleton, a proscenium theatre that accommodates 890 people; and the Cottesloe, whose flexible seating for up to 400 can be removed for experimental plays. The 'Royal' prefix was added to the theatre and the company in 1988.

Royal Observer Corps A volunteer civilian organization for tracking and identifying enemy aircraft flying over the UK. Since 1955 it has also been responsible for monitoring nuclear fallout and radiation levels in the event of a nuclear strike against the UK. The Observer Corps was formed in 1925, when it comprised a chain of observation posts in southern England. At the start of World War II the Corps' network of 1400 posts covered the entire country, a watch being maintained by some 32,000 trained volunteers. During World War II the Royal Observer Corps provided warnings of impending air attacks to enable the air-raid warnings to be sounded and the RAF to launch its counter-attacking fighters. The epithet 'Royal' was granted in 1941. After the war the Corps was stood down for two years, being re-formed in 1947. The present Corps is affiliated to the RAF and administered by the Ministry of Defence.

Royal Shakespeare Company (RSC) One of the world's leading theatre companies, originally formed in 1879 as the company of Stratford-upon-Avon's newly opened Shakespeare Memorial Theatre; it was incorporated by royal charter in 1925. The name of the theatre was changed in 1961 to the 'Royal Shakespeare Theatre' and the company then adopted its present title. Although the RSC now stages a wide variety of plays in its five auditoria, the company remains faithful to its prime role – performing the works of Shakespeare. The original Shakespeare Memorial Theatre was destroyed by fire in 1926 and replaced by the present building, which opened in 1932. The company established its first London base in 1960, at the Aldwych Theatre, followed by The Warehouse, a studio theatre opened in 1977. In 1982 both operations were transferred to the new Barbican Centre in the City of London, using the Barbican Theatre and The Pit. Meanwhile, Stratford had seen the opening of its own studio theatre for the RSC, The Other Place, in 1974; in 1986 this was joined by the Swan Theatre, built inside the shell of the original Shakespeare Theatre's auditorium.

Royal Victorian Chain A decoration instituted in 1902 by Edward VII in honour of his mother, Queen Victoria. It is bestowed, usually on foreign sovereigns, to mark special occasions.

RP *See* RECEIVED PRONUNCIATION.

RPI *See* RETAIL PRICE INDEX.

RSI *See* REPETITIVE STRAIN INJURY.

rubber. rubber bullet A projectile made from hard rubber fired from a special weapon, used in riot control. The rubber bullet, or 'baton round', was developed at PORTON DOWN especially for use in Northern Ireland and was based on the wooden police baton that could be fired from guns, which was used by the Hong Kong police for riot control in the late 1960s. The rubber bullet was supposed to be bounced off the ground as opposed to being fired directly into crowds, but it, and its successor the **plastic bullet** (a solid PVC cylinder), have been responsible for the deaths of 12 people, six of them children, in Northern Ireland since 1970.

rubber-chicken US slang from the 1950s for describing unappetizing banquet food, especially that served to lecturers, political candidates, etc., on their travels. It is generally used in such phrases as 'rubber-chicken circuit' and 'rubber-chicken banquet'.

rubberneck (1) Contemptuous slang for an unadventurous tourist, who travels by coach to see the world but who does little more than turn the neck to take in the sights as they are enumerated by the tour guide. Hence a **rubberneck wagon** is the coach or bus containing such people. (2) One who stares open-mouthed or gormlessly at some activity.

Rube Goldberg machine A complicated and contrived machine producing a simple result. The name comes from US cartoonist Reuben L. Goldberg (1883–1970), who for 40 years, starting in the 1920s, drew humorously intricate diagrams of such devices, teasing Americans about their love of gadgets. A Goldberg contraption designed to wipe a diner's chin with a napkin included such steps as lifting a spoon that pulled a string that jerked a ladle that threw a cracker biscuit past a parrot, who jumped and tilted its perch, etc., until a pendulum with a napkin attached swung past the chin. *See also* HEATH ROBINSON.

Rubik's cube A toy puzzle invented in 1975 by Professor Erno Rubik, a Hungarian teacher of architecture and design, which became a worldwide craze in the late 1970s and early 1980s. The puzzle was launched in the UK in 1979 and in the following two years sold three million (and 20 million worldwide). The 2½-inch cube is composed of 27 smaller cubes packed together; the aim is to restore the faces of the cube to single colours by rotating the individual layers of composite cubes. The numbers of permutations possible has been calculated as 43,252,003,274,489,856,000, but in the World Championships held during the craze, top contenders could manage a solution in less than 30 seconds. Some also fell prey to a painful medical condition, dubbed 'Cubists' (or Rubik's) Thumb', from obsessive manipulation of the toy. Rubik also invented the Magic Snake, a string of linked triangles described as a 'creative construction toy', and other brainteasing devices, but none exerted the same fascination as the cube.

Ruby, Jack The Dallas stripclub owner who shot Lee Harvey OSWALD at point blank range on 24 November 1963, while Oswald was being transferred from Dallas police station to the county prison after being charged with the assassination of President John F. Kennedy two days earlier. The killing took place in the basement of the police station in full view of a horrified television audience. Ruby was tried and sentenced to death in February 1964 but died of cancer in 1967, while appealing for a retrial. Although Ruby claimed to have shot Oswald to avenge the president's family, his links with organized crime have led to speculation by the ubiquitous Kennedy conspiracy theorists that he was hired by mobsters to silence Oswald, who was himself said to be the tool of a criminal conspiracy to destroy the Kennedy presidency. Conclusive evidence to support this theory has yet to be revealed.

rugcutting US Black slang for wild ebullient dancing, especially to JAZZ. The term originated in the practice of giving RENT PARTIES in one's own home. These attracted keen and often expert dancers, who were excluded from commercial dance halls because of their colour or lack of means. Their athletic jitterbugging could pose a real danger to the host's furnishings.

rumba or **rhumba** A ballroom dance adapted in 1930 from an Afro-Cuban dance called the *son*. The modern version is danced in one spot with the feet flat on the floor and with sinuous hip movements. Rumba music has a complex syncopated rhythm in 4/4 time. In the original Cuban form, widely used as a ballroom dance in Europe and America, the dancers covered a square pattern, with little bodily contact between them.

Rummidge The fictional industrial city in the West Midlands created by the British novelist David Lodge (1935–). Bearing a close resemblance to Birmingham, it is the home of Rummidge University, the setting for such comic novels as *Small World* (1984) and *Nice Work* (1988).

rumpie Rural Upwardly Mobile Professional. Slang acronym for a countrified YUPPIE. Rumpies typically buy large country properties after selling a smaller town house but still manage to commute to the large cities to work.

rum runners During the PROHIBITION era in America, those engaged in smuggling illicit liquor by speedboats across the lakes from Canada or from ships outside the **three-mile limit** (where US law ceased to have effect). The limit was subsequently increased to twelve miles by agreement with other powers and enforced by US Navy destroyers. These vessels, when over-age, were passed to the UK in 1940 under the LEND-LEASE arrangements. *See* BOOTLEGGER.

run. running dog Communist jargon for someone who carries out another's bidding, especially a capitalist lackey. It is a literal translation of the Chinese *zou gou*, used by the Chinese communist leader Mao Tse-tung. It was taken up with some of his other picturesque phrases, such as

PAPER TIGER, by readers of the LITTLE RED BOOK.

running shot In film-making, a shot in which a camera mounted on wheels follows the movement of an actor, vehicle, etc.

still running – like Charley's Aunt A phrase applied to any popular and long-running play or film. It refers to the farce *Charley's Aunt* by the British playwright Brandon Thomas (1857–1914), which was first performed in 1892 and was frequently revived throughout the 20th century. The phrase fell into disuse in the 1960s, when it was to some extent replaced with that other record-breaking theatrical production, 'still running – like the MOUSETRAP'.

You can run, but you can't hide *See under* HIDE.

Runnymede The site on the south bank of the Thames, near Egham in Surrey, where King John set his seal on Magna Carta in 1215. Owned by the National Trust since 1929, this historic setting has three memorials erected in the 20th century. The first, dedicated by Elizabeth II in 1953, commemorates the men of British and Commonwealth air forces who died in World War II. The second is a domed classical temple built in recognition of Runnymede's significance in establishing fundamental liberties and civil rights now enshrined in both British and US law; it was donated by the American Bar Association in 1957. The most recent is a memorial to the US president, John F. Kennedy. Set in 1.2 ha of land given to the American people, it was unveiled by the Queen in 1965. The name Runnymede means 'the meadow in council island', reflecting its use as an ancient meeting place.

Rupert Bear The subject of a long-running cartoon strip in the *Daily Express*. He was dreamt up by the wife of a news editor, when the *Express* needed a rival attraction to the *Daily Mail*'s cartoon bear, Teddy Tail. Mary Tourcel's creation, a young bear dressed in plaid trousers and matching scarf, made his debut in 1920 but did not achieve wide popularity until Alfred Bestall took the strip over in the 1930s. Rupert's adventures, summarized in rhyming couplets, were a feature of the paper until the 1980s.

ruptured duck The nickname in World War II for the US ex-service lapel button issued to all demobilized from the forces. The expression is also applied, not unkindly, to persons with some disablement.

rush. rushes In the film industry, the initial prints of a day's shooting, 'rushed' back from the laboratory and shown in a raw unedited form. *See also* ROUGH CUT.

rush hour The times during the morning and evening of a working day during which many people travel to or from their homes and workplaces in cars, trains, and buses. The term was used as early as 1898 for passenger traffic, but has become a nightmare for commuters on the roads, especially the main roads that lead from the centre of a town or city to the dormitory suburbs.

Rushdie Affair *See* FATWA.

Rushmore, Mount A mountain in the Black Hills of Dakota, which is the site of the huge carvings of the heads of four US presidents created by the US sculptor Gutzon Borglum (1867–1941). Work on this ambitious project began in the 1920s; it consists of the heads of Washington, Jefferson, Theodore Roosevelt, and Abraham Lincoln, each head measuring 60 feet from the chin to the top of the forehead. Upon completion, Mount Rushmore was rapidly established as one of the most frequented tourist attractions in America. It was also the scene of one of the US film industry's most memorable episodes: the final confrontation between Cary Grant and Eva Marie Saint with the villainous James Mason in Alfred Hitchcock's thriller *North by Northwest* (1959). Borglum also worked on another massive carving – of General Robert E. Lee, Stonewall Jackson, Jefferson Davis, and 1200 Confederate soldiers on Stone Mountain. However, this project was plagued by disagreements and Borglum died before it could be completed.

Russian Revolution *See* FEBRUARY REVOLUTION; OCTOBER REVOLUTION.

Russo-Japanese War (1904–05) The conflict in which the Japanese inflicted a crushing defeat on the Russians, helping to dilute, if not to destroy completely, the myth of White supremacy over the Oriental races. The Japanese were determined to crush all Russian power in Korea and Manchuria and to establish their own hegemony in the area. To this end, in February 1904 they launched a pre-emptive air strike against Port Arthur on the tip of Manchuria's Liaotung Peninsula, which inflicted serious damage on the Russian fleet at anchor there. Port Arthur was then besieged by Japanese land forces and surrendered in January 1905. The conflict between the opposing armies in central Manchuria was less decisive. However, in May 1905, in the Battle of Tsushima, the Japanese fleet under Admiral Togo inflicted severe losses on the Russian fleet, which brought the Russians to the conference table. By the Treaty of Portsmouth of September 1905, the Russians surrendered Port Arthur and half of Sakhalin to Japan as well as evacuating Manchuria.

> I have today seen the most stupendous spectacle it is possible for the mortal brain to conceive – Asia advancing, Europe falling back, the wall of mist and the writing thereon.
>
> LT-GEN SIR IAN HAMILTON on the Battle of Liaoyang, *A Staff Officer's Scrap Book during the Russo-Japanese War* (1907).

Ruth Draper garden A style of garden made famous by the US impressionist Ruth Draper (1884–1956) in a humorous dramatic monologue 'Showing the Garden'. An elderly English lady takes a visiting acquaintance on a tour of her country garden. Unfortunately, instead of a riot of colour, the borders are largely barren; as the tour progresses, excuse after hilarious excuse is made to explain the deficiencies. In short, a Ruth Draper garden is one that was as exquisite last month as it will be next month, although at the moment it is a shambles.

> That border was a dream in June, and it's going to be again in October . . . could you possibly come back in October?
>
> 'Showing the Garden'.

S

S. S & M Sadism and Masochism; sadomasochism. The abbreviation was originally a homosexual term in America and came into general use in the early 1960s. It is sometimes called **sadie-maisie**.

s 'n' f or **s 'n' s** Shopping and fucking, or sex and shopping. A type of popular women's fiction in which wealthy and glamorous heroines divide their time between these activities. The novels of Jackie Collins and Shirley Conran fall into this category.

> I spend most of the day going through a potential s 'n' s (sex and shopping) blockbuster that I've promised the author I will read in its entirety . . . The novel has everything – paedophiliac English aristocrats, long-lost French fathers, share scandals, a Russian love affair and boat chases in Monte Carlo.
>
> *The Independent*, 25 April 1991.

SA (1) Sex Appeal. Slang abbreviation formerly used by people who would be embarrassed by saying the word 'sex'. (2) *Sturmabteilung*. *See* BROWNSHIRTS; SS.

Sabin vaccine An oral polio vaccine developed by Dr Albert Sabin (1906–) of the Children's Hospital in Cincinnati in the 1950s. Sabin cultivated a preparation of live weakened (attenuated) strains of the polio virus that, when introduced into the body, did not cause the disease but did stimulate the production of antibodies to provide total long-term immunity. By the 1960s Sabin's vaccine had replaced the SALK VACCINE and remains the most effective protection against the disease.

sabotage Wilful and malicious destruction of machinery and plant, disruption of plans and projects, etc., by strikers, rebels, or fifth columnists. The term came into use after the great French railway strike in 1912, when the strikers cut the shoes (*sabots*) holding the railway lines.

saccharin A synthetic sweetener about 500 times as sweet as cane sugar. The white crystalline powder was discovered in 1879 by two US chemists and by the 1920s had become a common non-nutritive sugar substitute for diabetics. Sales boomed in the 1960s when its lack of calories appealed to a diet-conscious public. A health scare in the late 1970s prompted the US Congress to require labels saying, "Use of this product may be hazardous to your health. This product contains saccharin which has been determined to cause cancer in laboratory animals." *See* DELANEY AMENDMENT.

Sacco and Vanzetti Two Italian anarchists, Nicola Sacco and Bartolomeo Vanzetti, who were arrested for the murders on 15 April 1920 of a paymaster and his guard employed by a shoe factory in South Braintree, Massachusetts. The trial and conviction of the two immigrants by a Massachusetts court in July 1921 passed largely unnoticed by the US public but news of the case aroused the indignation of radicals in Europe, provoking a series of demonstrations and bomb attacks against US property in Europe and South America. This publicity transformed the plight of the two men into a *cause celèbre* in America, with public opinion divided between those convinced that the men were innocent and had been condemned for their political radicalism and those who believed that their political beliefs compounded their guilt. Compelling evidence that the two men were victims of mistaken identity was strengthened by the gentle and intelligent demeanour of the defendants themselves; it was given further credence by the statement of a member of the Joe Morelli gang in 1925, that Morelli had committed the crime. However, an independent investigatory commission appointed by the governor of Massachusetts upheld their conviction. They were refused clemency and executed on 23 August 1927, which provoked worldwide condemnation, mass demonstrations, and bomb explosions in New York City and Philadelphia. The executions inspired a series of paintings by US artist Ben Shahn.

SAD Seasonal Affective Disorder. A depressive condition experienced by some people in the winter months, thought to be caused by lack of sunlight. Symptoms vary from gloominess and lack of energy to manic anxiety. Although it is now a medically recognized condition, there is no agreed physiological explanation. Acute sufferers may be treated by exposure to artificial sunlight. SAD first received wide publicity in the early months of 1987, a period of particularly miserable weather in the UK; as a result, millions of people diagnosed themselves as sufferers.

sad sack US armed forces' slang for a pathetic case, a depressed or inept person. It was heard before World War II but not widely used until it was adopted as the name of a cartoon character by G. Baker in the 1950s.

safari. safari park A large enclosed park in which wild animals, such as lions, tigers, giraffes, monkeys, etc., roam freely and can be viewed by the public who ride through their large enclosures in their cars or coaches. This name for a 'reverse zoo', with humans caged in their vehicles, originated in the late 1960s. A popular venue for Londoners is Windsor Safari Park.

safari suit An outfit, usually of cotton or denim, modelled on the style of clothing worn on safaris, especially by the game wardens. It consists of a belted bush jacket with pleated pockets above and below the belt and matching trousers, shorts, or skirt.

safe. safe house An unobtrusive house, flat, or other premises used as a secret refuge, especially by members of intelligence or terrorist organizations. The buildings are used to hide agents, political refugees, or hostages, conduct meetings and interrogations, and plan operations. They have long existed, but safe house did not become a generally known name until the early 1960s. A well-publicized case was the guerrilla Symbionese Liberation Army's 1974 California kidnapping of Patricia (PATTIE) Hearst, who was moved from one safe house to another for over a year before being found. The IRA also have safe houses in London and other large cities.

safe sex *See under* SEX.

safety. Safety First The complacent slogan adopted by the Conservative prime minister Stanley Baldwin (1867–1947) during the general election of May 1929, which resulted in the formation of a minority Labour government under Ramsay MacDonald. Baldwin had hoped that despite the escalating economic depression and growing unemployment, the electorate would reject the radical economic reforms advanced by the opposition parties and allow the Conservatives to continue in power on the strength of his government's existing policies.

safety glass Strengthened glass, widely used for car windscreens. It was developed as the result of an accident in a French laboratory in 1904, when a scientist noted that after he had knocked a glass bottle off a shelf it had shattered but remained in one piece. Inside the bottle had been a collodion solution, which had evaporated and then served to hold the splinters together as a cellulose skin on the inside of the bottle. Since then, countless road-traffic accident victims have escaped disfigurement from flying glass due to the application of the process to car windscreens.

safety razor A shaving razor with a guarded cutting edge, first introduced in 1903. Before this men used the standard 'cut-throat' razor, with a long exposed blade, which could inflict quite serious wounds if not used with great care. The safety razor was invented by King C. Gillette, a Boston salesman, who had the idea of using a disposable blade in 1895 and spent the following eight years perfecting its design. It was a sensational success: within a year he had sold 90,000 razors and 12,400,000 blades.

saint. St Dunstan's An organization for the care of men and women blinded during military service in war or peacetime, or who become blind later in life as a result of injury. It was founded in 1915 at his home, St Dunstan's Lodge, by Sir Arthur Cyril Pearson (1866–1921), the newspaper proprietor, who himself became blind in 1910. The organization eschews residential care, providing instead the kind of help – such as employment retraining, the provision of special equipment, and financial support – that enables the blind to live as normal a life as possible within the sighted community.

St Ives group An association of artists that became a focus of national attention soon after it was founded in 1939. Chief among the members of the group, which made St Ives (in Cornwall) their centre, were such leading artists as Ben Nicholson, Barbara Hepworth, and Naum Gabo.

St Lawrence Seaway A vast system of canals, locks, channels, and natural waterways, stretching for 2342 miles (3769 km), that provides access for ocean-going vessels to the Great Lakes from the Atlantic. Construction of this massive engineering project began in August 1954 and was completed in April 1959; it is navigable from early April to mid-December and is serviced by 12 ports in Canada and 66 in America.

St Michael The brand name since 1928 of goods produced by Marks and Spencer. It was originally chosen to complement the St Margaret brand name on the Corah hosiery sold in Marks and Spencer stores (itself named after the church standing next to the main Corah factory in Leicester). Various saints' names were contemplated before the chairman, Simon Marks (1888–1964), decided on Michael, the name of his father, a refugee from E Europe who started the Marks empire when he set up a penny bazaar in Leeds market.

Saint Mugg The epithet applied, somewhat ironically, to British journalist, broadcaster, and writer Malcolm Muggeridge (1903–90) when, after a less than pious youth, he became an ardent Christian convert. A prolific writer on a variety of subjects, his books included *The Earnest Atheist, a Life of Samuel Butler* (1936), *Jesus the Man who Lives* (1975), *Conversion: A Spiritual Jouney* (1988), and several earlier autobiographies. He appeared frequently in current affairs and religious programmes, becoming an amusing TV guru; he made his own television series, *Muggeridge Ancient and Modern*.

St Nazaire Raid A British Commando raid on the port of St Nazaire, on the French Atlantic coast at the mouth of the Loire, on the night of 27–28 March 1942. The dry dock, then the largest in the world, was destroyed by ramming the lock gate with an old destroyer, HMS *Campbeltown*, which was packed with five tons of ammonal explosives timed to detonate later. Commandos then attacked the submarine pens and other repair facilities. Twelve hours after the start of the raid the *Campbeltown* exploded, killing 380 German officers and men exploring the wreckage of the ship. The operation, codenamed Chariot, successfully deprived the Germans of the only dry dock capable of accommodating such capital ships as the *Tirpitz*; the cost was heavy, however: 169 were killed and 200 captured out of a total force of 611. Five Victoria Crosses were awarded in the aftermath of the raid, the highest number for any single action in World War II.

St Trinian's The comical girls' school created by the cartoonist Ronald Searle (1920–) in the 1950s. The riotous adventures of the girls at the school inspired several successful films, starring Alastair Sim, Joyce Grenfell, and George Cole among others: *The Belles of Saint Trinian's* (1954), *Blue Murder at St Trinian's* (1957), *The Pure Hell of St Trinian's* (1960), and *The Great St Trinian's Train Robbery* (1966). The success of the films gave St Trinian's almost mythical status as the archetypal decayed and corrupt girls' private school.

St Valentine's Day Massacre The murder in America of seven members of George 'Bugsy' Moran's North Side gang on 14 February 1929, the horrific climax to a decade of slaughter that left Al CAPONE as head of the Chicago underworld. The mass killings took place at Moran's headquarters in a garage at 21222 North Clark Street. Capone's men, in the guise of uniformed and plainclothes police officers, raided the garage, lined up their victims against the wall, and then shot them to pieces with machine guns. Moran himself was late in arriving at his HQ and escaped death but his power in Chicago was effectively ended. Capone had retired to his estate in Miami, Florida, to establish an alibi, but he underestimated the impact of the massacre on public opinion, which prompted the federal authorities to redouble their efforts to convict Capone. Although he avoided capture for several more years, he was eventually imprisoned for tax evasion in 1931.

> I'm gonna send Moran a Valentine he will never forget.
>
> AL CAPONE.

The Saint The name used by Simon Templar, the debonair reformed British gentleman crook, who is the hero of a series of adventure novels by Leslie Charteris (1907–) starting with *Enter The Saint* (1930). A modern-day Robin Hood, who is customarily exposed to hair-raising risks, he is most familiar in his various screen incarnations, played most recently by Ian Ogilvie in a popular TV series (before that by Roger Moore). Earlier film versions date back to the 1930s, with Louis Hayward, Hugh Sinclair, George Sanders, and Tom Conway all taking their turn as The Saint. There was even a somewhat eccentric French version starring Jean Marais. The character of The Saint lent much to that of The FALCON. The Saint's trademark, left at the scenes of crimes, is a pin man with a halo.

Saki The pseudonym of H(ector) H(ugh) Munro (1870–1916), British humorist and author of *The Westminster Alice* (1902), *Reginald* (1904), *The Chronicles of Clovis* (1911), *The Unbeatable Bassington* (1912), and numerous other short stories, many featuring his snobbish Edwardian heroes Clovis and Reginald. He was killed in action in World War I.

Salerno landing Allied landings, codenamed Avalanche, in the Gulf of Salerno, south of Naples, on 9 September 1943. The US Fifth Army, commanded by Mark Clark and comprising the British 10th and US 6th Corps, managed to establish a beachhead but faced formidable opposition from German forces under Kesselring. On 15 September, forward units of the British Eighth Army under Montgomery, which had landed in the Calabrian peninsula 130 miles to the south a few days earlier, reached the Salerno area, forcing the Germans to withdraw to the north. *See* ANZIO.

sales promotion All the methods used to increase the sale of a product or service and to break down **sales resistance**, the negative attitude of a possible buyer, which hinders or prevents the sale of a commodity. A sales promotion may include a free-sample campaign; arranging demonstrations; offering price reductions; telephone, post, or door-to-door selling, etc.

Salk vaccine The first effective vaccine against polio, developed at the University of Pittsburgh School of Medicine in 1954 by Dr Jonas Edward Salk (1914–). Salk developed a trivalent 'killed' vaccine to cover the three known strains of the polio virus. The vaccine, which has to be injected, was first released for use in April 1955 but was later replaced by the oral SABIN VACCINE, made from living viruses, which provided more effective longer-term protection against the disease.

Salò, Republic of The short-lived fascist regime set up by Mussolini in 1943 following the defeat of Italian forces. Mussolini had been rescued from imprisonment by German paratroopers and established the new republic (with headquarters in the town of Salò) in an attempt to maintain control of that part of N Italy not yet in Allied hands. The republic collapsed ignominiously with Mussolini's death and the final defeat of the AXIS powers in 1945.

salsa A type of Latin American dance music popularized in New York City in the mid-1970s. The big-band sound, usually at a fast tempo, is dominated by brass, guitars, keyboards, and percussion instruments. It combines Puerto Rican, Afro-Cuban, and other Latin American music, such as the mambo, but adds the influence of JAZZ and ROCK. The dance itself is based on the rumba and related forms. The name comes from the American-Spanish word for a sauce.

SALT Strategic Arms Limitation Talks. Discussions initiated in 1969 between the US president, Lyndon Johnson, and the Soviet leader, Leonid Brezhnev, to limit the production of strategic NUCLEAR WEAPONS. The talks culminated in the **SALT I** accord (1972), signed by Brezhnev and President Nixon, which agreed limitation of the build-up of nuclear weapons by both sides and significantly slowed the pace of the arms race. Further discussion, mainly between Brezhnev and President Ford, resulted in **SALT II**, signed in 1979 by Brezhnev and President Carter but repudiated by America in 1986 after the Soviet invasion of Afghanistan.

salvage archaeology The urgent excavation of ancient sites to record the plans and purposes of buildings and to rescue artefacts in danger of being submerged by new construction projects or such natural disasters as floods. The name dates back to 1960, when emergency salvage work began on several building sites in London: archaeologists worked with developers who delayed work that threatened various Roman sites, including a basilica and forum, a public bath, and a palatial residence. Some sites have been preserved beneath the modern structures.

Salyut A series of Soviet space stations, starting with Salyut 1, an 18-tonne prototype launched on 19 April 1971. Crew members were ferried to and fro by SOYUZ spacecraft and spent long periods aboard, including a record-breaking 237-day stint in 1984. Salyut 7, the last to be launched, in April 1982, had a modular design, allowing the addition of further sections to increase its size. It was served by specially adapted unmanned 'Progress' space ferries, which automatically docked with the station. The Salyut series has now been superseded by the Mir space station.

Samaritans An organization founded by the Rev. Chad Varah (1911–) in the church of St. Stephen, Walbrook, London, in 1953, to help the despairing and suicidal. It now has 185 centres in the British Isles as well as many in overseas countries affiliated to its associated organization, Befrienders International. Trained volunteers, of whom there are 22,000 in the UK, give their help at any hour to those who make their needs known by telephone, letter, or by a personal visit.

samba A bouncy ballroom dance that evolved from a Brazilian folk-dance with African origins. It was first seen at the street carnivals in Rio de Janeiro. Samba dance music has a syncopated rhythm in duple time. It became very popular in the UK in the 1950s, being featured by such South American bands as that led by Edmundo Ros.

same-sex or **same-sexer** A neutral term suggested as a replacement for homosexual by those who object to the 19th-century view that homosexuality is a separate and life-long category of sexual identity (whether inborn or acquired) that has persisted unchanged throughout history in all cultures. It was the French philosopher Michel Foucault (1926–84) who suggested that the compulsion of 19th-century biologists and sexologists to categorize sexual acts has itself resulted in these separate watertight sexual categories.

> In the centuries of Rome's great military and political success, there was no differentiation between same-sexers and other-sexers; there was also a lot of crossing back and forth of the sort that those Americans who *do* enjoy inhabiting category-gay or category-straight find hard to deal with.
>
> GORE VIDAL: 'Pink Triangle and Yellow Star' (1981).

samizdat An underground press for publishing and disseminating dissident works in the Soviet Union. It is an abbreviation of the Russian *samizdatelstro*, self-publishing house. The word was first used in English in the mid-1960s.

sampling In the recording industry, the practice of editing snippets of earlier hits into one's own record. At its simplest, this involves straightforward quotation from a well-known hit, usually to provide a comment on the theme of the new song. However, since the mid-1980s more sophisticated and morally dubious forms of sampling have been employed. It is now possible for a producer to lift elements of a successful record – most commonly the rhythm track – and to work them into a new piece without acknowledgment or detection. For instance, the drum beat on David Bowie's song 'Let's Dance' (1983) is said to have reappeared on a dozen or so dance hits later in the decade. Computerized recording technology even allows a producer to 'sample' the style or sound of an earlier performance and to apply this to new material. In this way, it is possible to create an instrumental part to which the melody is new but the phrasing, tone, etc. are those of a master performer (who may even be dead). Defenders of sampling see it as a creative and legitimate use of the technology now available, while to others it is simple theft. The legal position has yet to be clarified.

sandbag (1) US slang meaning to hit, as if with a sack filled with sand. The word has been used in the business world since the 1980s in the sense of aggressively outdoing the opposition in order to win a contract. To HANDBAG, the feminine version of sandbag, became popular during this period being widely used by the press in the UK to describe Mrs Thatcher's technique for dealing with any opposition. (2) US gamblers' slang meaning to outmanoeuvre someone by pretending initially to be in a weak position. This is presumably derived from the image of hiding behind a sandbag wall and only showing oneself when the enemy has approached dangerously close. (3) US slang from the jargon of 'hot rod' racers, meaning to drive at full speed.

Sandinista A member of the Nicaraguan leftist political organization, the Sandinist National Liberation Front, that took power in 1979 and ruled until 1990. Named after August Cesar Sandino, an insurgent leader murdered in 1934, the movement was founded in 1962 as a guerrilla group opposing the regime of President Anastasia Somoza-Debayle, who was overthrown by the 1979 Sandinista offensive launched from Costa Rica and Honduras. The Sandinistas formed a ruling junta opposed by America, which supported guerrilla CONTRA groups in Honduras. Funds from a US secret arms sale to Iran were diverted to Contras after Congress had banned such aid, which created a national scandal known as the **Iran-Contra Affair**. It culminated in 1987 in Congressional hearings, during which President Ronald Reagan denied knowledge of the operation. The Sandinista government and the Contras held cease-fire talks in 1988. Free elections followed in 1990 and led to the defeat of President Daniel Ortega Saavedra by Violeta Barrios de Chamorro of the National Opposition Union. In his concession speech, Ortega said:

> We, the Sandinistas, have given Nicaragua this democracy and peace.

san fairy Ann Slang dating from World War I, meaning 'it doesn't matter'. It is an example of army slang based on an anglicized pronunciation of a French phrase, in this case *ça ne fait rien*, which has the same meaning.

San Francisco earthquake The earthquake on 18 April 1906 that razed the city of San Francisco, resulting in the deaths of 700 people. Many of the casualties were victims of the intensive three-day fires that followed the earthquake along the infamous San Andreas fault, where the Pacific and American continental plates collide. The tragedy etched itself upon the national consciousness but the residents refused to vacate the area; instead they rebuilt the city in the same place, instituted regular earthquake drills, and insisted that all new buildings comply with stringent safety standards. No one, however, has suggested that the entire city would survive another tremor on the same scale as 1906. A strong earthquake hit the city once more, in 1989, when about 70 people died, most of them as a result of the collapse of the double-tier Oakland Bay Freeway. The 1989 earthquake made worldwide news, but seismologists warned that it was not the long-awaited 'big-one', which could still strike at any time, virtually without warning.

Sansan In America, a name sometimes given to the affluent strip on the west coast between *San* Francisco and *San* Diego. *See also* BOSNYWASH; CHIPPITTS.

sapfu Surpassing All Previous Fuck-Ups. US acronym for a situation worse than SNAFU. Both terms were used by the forces during World War II. *See also* TABU.

Sapper The pseudonym of the writer Hermann Cyril McNeile (1888–1937), creator of Hugh 'Bulldog' Drummond, who first appeared in his popular thriller *Bulldog Drummond* (1920) – subtitled 'The Adventures of a Demobilized Officer who Found Peace Dull'. Many sequels followed; after McNeile's death the series was continued under the same pseudonym by G. T. Fairlie. Some 24 Bulldog Drummond films were made between 1922 (silent) and 1970. Perhaps *Bulldog Drummond* (1929), starring Ronald Colman, was the most authentic. *See also* BULLDOG BREED.

Sarah. The Divine Sarah Sarah Bernhardt (1845–1923), French actress of international repute. Her original name was Rosine Bernard. In 1915 she had a leg amputated, but this did not bring her career to an end – she continued to act until her death.

Sarajevo assassination The shooting of Archduke Franz Ferdinand, the heir to the Austro-Hungarian throne, and his wife in Sarajevo, the principal city of Bosnia, on 28 June 1914. The assassin was 19-year-old Gavrilo Princip (1895–1918), a member of a violent nationalist group that sought Serbian independence from Austria (Austria having annexed the province in 1908). The shooting is often described as 'the shot heard around the world', because it directly initiated a sequence of events that led to the outbreak of World War I. The Austrians, eager to expand their influence in the Balkans (*see* EASTERN QUESTION), with encouragement from Germany imposed a humiliating ultimatum on the Serbian government, which was only partially accepted. The Austrians then declared war on Serbia on 28 July. This in turn prompted the mobilization of Russia, which provoked a declaration of war by Germany on Russia (1 August) and France (3 August). Germany then invaded Belgium (in accordance with the SCHLIEFFEN PLAN), which prompted the British declaration of war on Germany on 4 August 1914, in defence of Belgian neutrality. *See* SCRAP OF PAPER.

SAS Special Air Service. The crack commando unit of the British Army, renowned worldwide for its expertise in undercover military operations and anti-terrorist activities. It was created in 1941 by David Stirling, a Scots Guards subaltern serving in North Africa who was subsequently nicknamed the PHANTOM MAJOR. Stirling persuaded his C-in-C, Claude Auchinleck, to authorize the formation of a small commando unit, initially of 66 men, to operate behind enemy lines. In spite of a disastrous initial parachute raid, on 16 November 1941, from which only 22 men returned, Stirling switched to the tactic of long-range overland infiltration and embarked on a successful campaign against Axis airfields, cratering runways and blowing up aircraft. Their success silenced critics and forced Rommel to deploy troops charged with intercepting this troublesome force. In October 1942, Stirling's unit was given full regimental status, as 1st Special Air Service. The SAS soon saw action in other theatres, notably during the Allied invasion of Italy and later in front-line penetration during the Normandy invasion.

The SAS was disbanded at the end of the war, but in 1947 it was re-formed as the 21st SAS Regiment. A special SAS unit, the Malayan Scouts, was created in 1951 to combat Communist insurgence in Malaya, becoming the 22nd SAS Regiment the following year. For the Malayan campaign the SAS developed new techniques, adapted both to the jungle setting and the type of operation, *i.e.* counter-insurgency. This resourcefulness also paid off later, in such diverse territories as Oman, Borneo, and Aden – all trouble-spots calling for the special talents of the SAS. In 1969 SAS personnel were sent to Northern Ireland, in response to the troubles; the province became a proving ground for a range of secret sophisticated counter-terrorist tactis. A vivid demonstration of their skills, and one witnessed by the world's media, was given on 5 May 1980 when SAS soldiers stormed the Iranian Embassy in Knightsbridge, London, to liberate the building and its staff; these had been seized at the end of April by an Iranian separatist group. A more controversial incident was the shooting by SAS soldiers of three suspected IRA terrorists in Gibraltar on 7 March 1988. The SAS cap badge incorporates the motto 'Who Dares Wins' surmounted by a winged dagger; both are attributed to Jock Lewis, one of Stirling's close comrades who was killed returning from a raid in late 1941.

Sasquatch *See* BIGFOOT.

Satchmo Nickname of the JAZZ trumpeter, singer, and bandleader (Daniel) Louis Armstrong (1900–71). It was derived from the Black slang **satchel-mouth**, meaning a person with a big mouth. His talented trumpet playing and his 'gravelly' singing voice, instantly identifiable, made him one of the most popular figures in the world of jazz.

satellite Any artificial or natural body, such as the Moon, that orbits a planet or other celestial body. The first artificial satellite was SPUTNIK 1, launched by the Soviet Union in 1957. Since then several thousand satellites have been sent into space for a wide range of purposes, both peaceful and military. One key role is the relaying of telecommunications and other signals (*see* COMMUNICATIONS SATELLITE). Another is to survey the Earth's surface from space, monitoring vegetation cover, pollution levels, mineral resources, and other aspects of global ecology. Such earth-resources satellites include the LANDSAT series. Satellites also provide scientists with information about space (*see* SPACE PROBE). Modern military strategists rely heavily on information about opposition forces gleaned from spy satellites, such as the US Big Bird series and some of the Soviet Cosmos satellites. Both the leading superpowers have drawn up plans for fighting wars using satellites as space-based weapons platforms (*see* STAR WARS).

satellite killer *See* KILLER SATELLITE.

satellite television The use of a COMMUNICATIONS SATELLITE to receive television signals from ground stations, which are then retransmitted to satellite dishes in viewers' homes. Each satellite covers an area on the surface of the Earth called a 'footprint'; in Europe these are large enough to cross national boundaries – the UK, for example, can pick up signals from some 25 satellites, each transmitting several television channels in various languages. Telstar, launched in 1962, was the first communications satellite to relay live television pictures across the Atlantic. The first (and to date only) British satellite television operation (after its merger with rival BSB) is Rupert Murdoch's Sky Television, which was launched in 1989. Sky leases six channels of the Astra medium-power 16-channel satellite launched in 1988, and offers 24-hour news and current affairs, films, sport, and light entertainment.

satellite towns *See* NEW TOWNS.

Saturday night special US slang for a small cheap handgun that is easily obtained, even by mail order. The name was coined in 1968 and refers to its use, most frequently on Saturday nights, in urban fights and robberies. It is normally .32 calibre or less and short-barrelled. Police statistics show such guns are used in about half of all gun-related crimes. Although the US Gun Control Act of 1958 banned their importation, the parts are often imported and then assembled.

Saturn rockets The two- and three-stage rockets, designed in America from 1958 onwards by the German rocket engineer Wernher von Braun (1912–77), that carried US command capsules into space during the 1960s and 1970s. Saturn 1 was successfully launched on 27 October 1961 and was followed by nine subsequent launches. The three-stage Saturn 5 was used for Apollo 8 and Apollo 11 manned space flights (*see* APOLLO MOON PROGRAMME). Weighing 3000 tons (with fuel) and, with the Apollo spacecraft in place, 360 feet tall, Saturn V included 11 main engines for upward thrust and another 22 for steering; the combined power of these engines was equivalent to that of 30 diesel locomotives, totalling 160 million h.p. The rocket was transported to the launch pad by huge 'crawlers', the world's largest land vehicles, travelling at 2 m.p.h. under the control of a crew of 10: the roadway on which they moved sank by an inch every time it was used. The Saturn 5 (carrying 12 million gallons of liquid hydrogen, liquid helium, and liquid oxygen) reached a speed of 6000 m.p.h. in the first stage, 15,000 m.p.h. in the second stage, and 25,000 m.p.h. in the third stage. The enormous cost of these unrecoverable giant rockets was the main reason for developing the SPACE SHUTTLE.

satyagraha (Hindi, from Sansk., literally truth grasping) Passive resistance. Mohandas Gandhi popularized this word during his nonviolent opposition to British rule in India, especially during the periods 1920–22 and 1930–34. *See* MAHÂTMA.

Save the Children Fund An international voluntary organization founded in 1919 to promote child health and welfare. It operates in 20 countries and has over 100 projects in Britain. Overseas its projects promote long-term health, nutrition, education, community development, and various welfare programmes. In the UK the Fund operates family centres and schemes for the underprivileged, the disabled, the support of the families of prisoners, etc. The Princess Royal (*see* FOUR-LETTER ANNIE) has done a great deal to promote the work of the Fund since she became its president.

Savoy Hill The street, off the Strand, in London in which the first studios of the British Broadcasting Company (1922) were situated; until 1932 it was the headquarters of the British Broadcasting Corporation.

say it ain't so, Joe *See* BLACK SOX SCANDAL.

SBS *See* SPECIAL BOAT SQUADRON.

scam Originally US slang for a swindle or a dubious business deal. It has been widely used in the UK since the middle 1970s and is often used specifically of a drug-smuggling run. The derivation is uncertain but it is thought to be connected with the 18th-century sense of the verb *scamp*, to be a highway robber (from the Middle Dutch *schampen*).

> He proposes to beat her with a towel filled with oranges – an old insurance scam . . . which if done correctly leaves ugly bruises and no damage.
>
> *The Independent*, 1 February 1991.

Scapa Flow A land-locked anchorage in the Orkney Islands, which was the site of the main British naval base until it was closed down in 1957. The Grand Fleet was based there during World War I, although the lack of security from submarine attack forced the fleet to remain at sea for long periods. This vulnerability was tragically demonstrated in the opening months of World War II, when a German submarine sank the battleship *Royal Oak* with the loss of 833 lives in October 1939. Scapa Flow was also host to the German fleet, interned there after the Armistice in November 1918. On 21 June 1919 the German crews scuttled their ships as an act of defiance during the Paris Peace Conference. *See also* NATAL, HMS.

Scarface *See* CAPONE, AL.

Scarlet Pimpernel The eponymous hero of a romantic novel by Baroness Orczy (Mrs Montague Barstow; 1865–1947), the Hungarian-born writer. Published in 1905, *The Scarlet Pimpernel* describes the adventures of Sir Percy Blakeney, leader of the League of the Scarlet Pimpernel, a group of Englishmen dedicated to the rescue of aristocratic victims of the Reign of Terror in Revolutionary France. The character appeared in ten sequels; his adventures have also been translated onto the big screen (1934; starring Leslie Howard), radio, and television (1982; starring Anthony Andrews). Blakeney's attractive and high-spirited wife, Marguerite, has also enjoyed a solo career in the novels of C. Guy Clayton published during the 1980s.

> They seek him here, they seek him there,
> Those Frenchies seek him everywhere.
> Is he in heaven or is he in hell,
> That demned elusive Pimpernel?

scarper British slang meaning to leave hastily, probably from the cockney rhyming slang *Scapa flow*, to go. It is also possibly influenced by an adaptation of the Italian *scappare*, to escape.

scat In JAZZ, a form of singing without words, using the voice as a musical instrument. Said to have been started by Louis Armstrong (*see* SATCHMO) in the 1920s, when he forgot the words or dropped the paper on which they were written while singing a number; JELLY ROLL Morton, on the other hand, claimed to have sung scat as early as 1906.

Schandband (Ger. shame band) The cloth badge bearing the six-pointed **yellow star** (magen David or Star of David), the traditional emblem of Judaism, which the Nazis forced Jews to wear after 1941. Hans Frank, the Governor-General of the 'Protectorate' of Bohemia and Moravia, first suggested the idea of introducing a system of identification for Jews within his territories in August 1941. Hitler approved the idea, and in a decree of 5 September ordered that the *Schandband* should be worn by all Jews throughout the Reich. To demonstrate his contempt for such antisemitic measures, King Christian X of occupied Denmark wore a yellow star himself, to the fury of his Nazi overlords. The yellow six-pointed cloth star subsequently became the badge of shame of the whole German people for the atrocities committed in the HOLOCAUST. *See also* PINK TRIANGLE.

Schicklgruber The surname of Adolf Hitler's stepfather, Alois Schicklgruber (1837–1903), a civil servant in the Austrian Imperial Customs Service. His mother, Maria Anna Schicklgruber, conceived him by Johann Georg Heidler, whom she eventually married in 1842. Alois, however, retained his mother's surname until he was nearly 40, when he adopted the name Hitler, based on the misspelling by a local priest of the name Heidler. Adolf Hitler went to considerable lengths to conceal the details of his ancestry, although they were dredged up by opponents of the Nazis during elections in the early 1930s. No concrete evidence has ever been discovered to substantiate the claim made by Hans Frank at the NUREMBERG TRIALS, that Hitler's father was the child of a Jew from Graz, named Frankenberger, in whose household Maria Anna Schicklgruber became pregnant while working as a maid.

> HEIL SCHICKLGRUBER!
>
> Headline in an Austrian newspaper during the German elections of July 1931.

schlemiel A consistently unlucky and foolish person. A Yiddish word that entered the English language in America early in the century, it is said to have originated from the Old Testament (Numbers 2): Shlumiel, the son of the leader of the tribe of Simeon, was an unfortunate general upon whom misfortune rarely failed to fall. The biblical Shlumiel was the antecedent of the modern schlemiel. Both merit some sympathy – but not as much as the NEBBISH. It is said that a schlemiel is a person who always knocks his glass over at the table; and the nebbish is the one who mops up the mess.

schlep To move in a tired and awkward way, often used in the phrase to **schlep around**. It derives from the German word *schleppen*, meaning to drag, and entered the English of New York from Yiddish. Schlep also means to carry or lug something around; the *New York Post* reported in 1957:

> Queen Elizabeth will schlep along 95 pieces of baggage on her trip here.

By extension, a **schlepper** is a slow foot-dragging incompetent or someone who is too tired or lazy to care for their appearance.

> She trudges, schleps, trains, drags her load.
>
> JAMES JOYCE: *Ulysses* (1922).

Schlieffen Plan A German war plan devised by Count von Schlieffen (1833–1913), the German Chief of Staff (1890–1906). The plan envisaged a war on two fronts, against France in the west and Russia in the east. Schlieffen's strategy for a quick victory was to hold off Russia with minimal forces and then overwhelm the French armies by a massive flanking movement through neutral Belgium, thereby avoiding the formidable natural and military defences along France's eastern border. The main German forces would then be free to confront the Russians to the east, who, it was assumed, would be slow to mobilize. The plan was put into operation in August 1914 by Helmuth Von Moltke, Schlieffen's successor, and was initially successful. Von Moltke, however, had modified Schlieffen's original plan by weakening the crucial right wing of the German advance from 90% to 60% of the total forces. At the Battle of the Marne in September, the Allied armies forced the retreat of the

German First Army under General Alexander von Kluck, thereby halting the main axis of the German advance. The subsequent trench warfare caused the total failure of Schlieffen's strategy; on 14 September the hapless Moltke was replaced by the German Minister of War, Erich von Falkenhayn.

> ... only make the right wing strong.
> Reputedly said by SCHLIEFFEN on his deathbed.

schlock A Yiddish word for anything shoddy, from the German *Schlag*, a blow – implying that the thing in question has been knocked around so much it has lost its value. It can also be used to describe an inferior work of art:

> This is a film that will make millions of sensible people weep, and still the word that best describes it is schlock. Tear ducts have no judgement. Tear ducts don't learn.
> *The Independent*, 15 March 1991.

schmaltz Originally a Yiddish word from the German *Schmaltz*, fat, especially chicken fat; it is now used of any exaggerated sentimentality, especially in the arts. Schmaltzy music is heavy with sweeping and weeping violins. Schmaltz in the cinema or the theatre is indigestibly rich, cloying, and mawkish. Not quite the same as SCHLOCK.

schmear To bribe, or a bribe. US slang from Yiddish, from the German *Schmiere*, grease or bribe, in the sense of 'to grease the palm' of somebody.

schmooze To chat or talk at length or, as a noun, a longish friendly talk. US slang, which entered American English early in the century from Yiddish, it ultimately comes from Hebrew *schmuos*, gossip.

schmuck A stupid clumsy person. It derives from the Yiddish *shmok*, penis. To avoid confusion with the taboo meaning it is often shortened to **schmo**.

Schneider Trophy An international race for seaplanes first held in Monaco on 16 April 1913. The race was established in December 1912 by the Frenchman Jacques Schneider, who offered a trophy worth £1000 and a prize of £1000 in an annual competition to promote the development of fast and reliable water-based aircraft. From 1919 the competition was dominated by the Americans, British, and Italians, who concentrated on developing increasingly faster and more powerful aero engines, as opposed to reliable transport. In September 1931 the UK won the trophy outright after the victory of Flight Lieutenant J. N. Boothman in a Supermarine S.6B51595, designed by R. J. Mitchell and powered by a Rolls Royce engine, the third successive British victory in a Supermarine. The SPITFIRE, the UK's famous World War II fighter, also designed by Mitchell, was a direct descendant of the Supermarine design, as was the Merlin engine.

schnorrer US slang for a sponger or a beggar. It derives from Yiddish and ultimately from the German *schnorren*, to beg. The semantic area covered by the word is wide, from the smoker who never seems to have a cigarette of his own to the out-and-out beggar who scrapes together a living by asking for money on the streets. A person does not have to be Jewish to be a schnorrer.

Schnozzle Nickname of the US comedian Jimmy Durante (James Francis Durante; 1893–1980), who was famous for his bulbous nose (his *Schnozz* or *schnozzle*) and his gravelly New York accent. He started his show-business career as a pianist, working first at Diamond Tony's Saloon on Coney Island. Later he teamed up with Eddie Jackson and Lou Clayton, and throughout the 1920s the trio worked New York's vaudeville and nightclub circuit. From the late 1920s he made periodic film appearances and in the 1940s his particular brand of unsophisticated humour, together with songs such as 'Ink-a-Dink-a-Doo' and 'It's my nose's boithday today', became familiar to thousands as a result of his regular radio performances in series that included *The Jimmy Durante Show*. In the 1950s he moved successfully into television (*see under* CALABASH).

school of hard knocks US expression for the experience of learning the hard lessons of life by experience rather than by formal education. Because 'school' is the US word for college, it is the US equivalent of the expression 'the university of life'. It is sometimes used defensively by those who were not fortunate enough to go to university.

Schrödinger. Schrödinger's cat An unfortunate cat that figured in a 'thought experiment' suggested by the Austrian physicist Erwin Schrödinger (1887–1961) and the Hungarian-born US physicist Eugene Wigner (1902–) to illustrate the philosophical problem known as the 'quantum measurement problem' in QUANTUM THEORY. In one interpretation of quantum mechanics, an object, such as an elementary particle, does not exist in particle form until it has been observed. Before that it has a potential existence described by a mathematical equation known as its *wavefunction*, which gives the probability of finding it at a particular point in space at a particular moment. When the observation is made, the properties of the entity become known and it exists as an object. In the jargon, the observation 'collapses' the wavefunction. But at what instant does the wavefunction collapse?

To answer this question Schrödinger suggested an experiment involving a box containing a piece of radioactive material, a Geiger counter to detect particles of radiation, and a cat. The counter is connected to a device that breaks a sealed tube of cyanide if a particle is detected, which kills the cat.

Nobody knows, according to quantum theory, exactly when a radioactive material will emit a particle, although it is known how many particles it will emit, on average, over a specific period of time. The experiment is run for a period that gives the cat a 50% probability of surviving. At the end of this period a person, known as **Wigner's friend**, looks in the box to observe whether or not the cat is dead. If the cat is dead, when did it die? Most normal people would answer that it died when the radioactive source caused the cyanide to be released. However, some interpreters of quantum mechanics would say that the cat, the cyanide, the detector, and the source were all part of the same system, which has its own wavefunction. This wavefunction collapses only when the observation is made, *i.e.* when Wigner's friend looks into the box. If this is the case, the cat has presumably been in an intermediate state up to this point. An additional complication is that Wigner's friend is also part of the system. Does he need an external observer to collapse his wavefunction? And so on . . .

Schrödinger wave equation A fundamental mathematical equation in quantum mechanics (*see* QUANTUM THEORY). It was developed in the 1920s by Erwin Schrödinger to describe the behaviour of systems in which particles also have a wavelike characteristic.

schtum Silent; especially in the phrase **to keep schtum**, to keep quiet, to say nothing. The word is of Yiddish origin, derived from the German *stumm*, dumb. It can also be used in the imperative, meaning 'keep quiet'.

Schweik The hero of the novel *The Good Soldier Schweik* (1921–23; English translation 1930), by Czech author Jaraslov Hasek (1883–1923). At his death Hasek had completed only four volumes of his projected six-volume satire on militarism, based largely on his own experiences in the Austro-Czech Army in 1915. The corpulent, drunken, and mendacious Schweik easily frustrates all authority and is the antithesis of a good soldier. The character became a hero to dissidents in E Europe after 1945. The book was banned in Czechoslovakia in the 1970s and was explicitly forbidden in the Czech, Polish, and Hungarian armies as 'detrimental to discipline'. The anarchic character fascinated Bertold Brecht, who paid homage to him in the drama *Schweik in the Second World War* (1943).

Scientology A quasi-religious cult developed in the 1950s by L. Ron Hubbard (1911–86), an author of pulp science fiction. In about 1949 Hubbard told a meeting of his fellow authors:

> Writing for a penny a word is ridiculous. If a man really wanted to make a million dollars, the best way to do it would be to start his own religion.

He took his first step down this road a year later, announcing the advent of a new "science of mental health", with the tradename **dianetics**, that constituted "a milestone for man comparable to his discovery of fire". Hubbard claimed to have found the source of all mental and many physical ills in 'engrams', images of painful experiences that could become lodged in the mind. A course of dianetic therapy, or 'auditing', could clear the mind of engrams, restoring the sufferer to perfect health. A success rate of 100% was claimed. Dianetics enjoyed a brief fashionable success in America in 1950–51, largely because it was cheaper and simpler to grasp than orthodox psychotherapy.

The conversion of dianetics into a fully fledged 'religion' dates from 1953, when Hubbard founded the first Church of Scientology. His chief motive seems to have been the tax-exempt status enjoyed by religious organizations, but megalomania was clearly another factor. The church preached a bizarre mixture of reincarnation and science fantasy, claiming that every individual had enjoyed millions of lives on a variety of planets. The aim of scientology was to restore the believer to his or her original status as a 'thetan', an omniscient immortal being outside the realm of space and time. Hubbard himself claimed to have visited heaven on two occasions, in about 23 trillion and 24 trillion BC.

In its heyday the Scientology movement claimed some six million followers worldwide and, as he had predicted, Hubbard became a millionaire. However, its use of dubious psychological techniques to gain and hold adherents soon attracted the attentions of the FBI and foreign governments. In 1965 an Australian report concluded that Scientology was "evil" and a "serious threat to the community"; three years later Hubbard and his followers were banned from entering the UK. Largely to avoid this scrutiny, Hubbard appointed himself 'commodore' of a private navy of scientologists and took to the high seas for some eight years from 1967. He also ordered his followers to infiltrate US government offices and steal or destroy all documents critical of Scientology. This proved an astonishing success: many thousands of classified documents passed into Scientologist control in the late 1970s. It also led to Hubbard's downfall. In 1979 the FBI arrested leading members of the organization, including Hubbard's wife, on multiple charges relating to the theft of government documents. When guilty verdicts were returned, Hubbard, who had managed to escape direct incrimination, simply disappeared. In 1986 the body of an elderly recluse, known to his neighbours simply as 'Jack', was identified as Hubbard's.

sci-fi Short for *science fiction*. This clipped version appeared in America in the mid-1950s, soon after *high-fidelity* became shortened to HI-FI.

Scone, Stone of The great coronation stone, the Stone of Destiny, on which the Scottish kings were formerly crowned at Scone, near Perth. It was removed by Edward I in 1296 and brought to Westminster Abbey, and has ever since been housed under the Chair of St Edward. It appeared in newspaper headlines when it was stolen on the night of 24–25 December 1950 by Scottish nationalists, who took it north of the border, where they wished it to remain. After its recovery it was restored to its place in February 1952.

It is also, traditionally, called **Jacob's Stone**. It is of reddish-grey sandstone and is fabled to have been once kept at Dunstaffnage in Argyll and removed to Scone by Kenneth MacAlpin in 843.

scoobs British army slang for beer, dating from the GULF WAR of 1991 (possibly derived from 'Scooby-doo', the name of a popular cartoon dog).

scorcher. Phew! What a scorcher! A phrase used to describe a very hot day. It was used in the satirical magazine PRIVATE EYE during the 1960s as a parody (or perhaps an actual quotation) of a tabloid newspaper headline during a heatwave. The phrase has now become such common usage that it is often written as one word. It is also used as an adjective, as in 'it's really phewwhatascorcher weather!'

score (1) British underworld slang for £20. (2) Slang for a successful act of seduction or a successful crime. (3) Slang for a purchase of an illegal drug.

Scotch tape Tradename for a brand of sticky tape, developed in America in 1952. It was the invention of some paint-sprayers who used it for masking purposes while at work. It acquired the name Scotch because of allegations that the adhesive was often applied too meanly and the tape refused to stick (by allusion to the traditional reputation of the Scottish for thrift).

Scottish National Party *See* SNP.

Scott of the Antarctic Captain Robert Falcon Scott (1868–1912), the leader of the ill-fated second Antarctic expedition of 1910–12 to the South Pole. As a lieutenant in the Royal Navy, Scott successfully commanded the scientific and exploratory Antarctic expedition of 1901–04 in HMS *Discovery*. In June 1910 he set off in the *Terra Nova* on a second expedition, with the aim of reaching the South Pole using both motorized sledges and ponies. The sledge party set off from Cape Evans on 24 October 1911; after a gruelling 900-mile trek, Scott and four companions (Dr E. A. Wilson, Captain Laurence Oates, Lieutenant H. R. Bowers, and Petty Officer Edgar Evans) reached the pole on 18 January 1912, only to discover that the Norwegian, Roald Amundsen, had beaten them by about a month. Murderous blizzards hampered the return journey; they ran out of food and fuel and eventually froze to death in their tent at the end of March, only eleven miles from supplies at One Ton depot. Their bodies were discovered by a relief party in November

1912, together with Scott's diary recording the harrowing last moments of the expedition. Evans had been killed in a fall on the Beardmore Glacier, and Oates, seriously ill and frostbitten, had sacrificed himself by leaving the tent in a blizzard (*see* FAMOUS LAST WORDS). Although he is usually regarded as a hero, some have recently questioned Scott's leadership and competence.

> I do not think we can hope for better things now. We shall stick it out to the end, but we are getting weaker, of course, and the end cannot be far. It seems a pity, but I do not think I can write more. For God's sake look after our people.
>
> Last entry in Scott's Diary, 29 March 1912.

Scottsboro trials Controversial trials of nine Black youths accused of raping two White women in a railway carriage in Scottsboro, Alabama. At their initial trial in April 1931, only three weeks after their arrest, the all-White jury found them guilty as charged, despite evidence from a doctor, who had examined the women, that no rape had occurred. The youths were then sentenced to death, which spurred protest from northern civil rights activists and other liberal and radical groups. The Supreme Court overruled the conviction in 1932, but various retrials, convictions, and successful appeals dragged on until the four youngest were freed and the others paroled, after spending six years in prison.

Scrabble A board game in which words made up from lettered tiles are interlocked like a crossword on a 15 × 15 grid, with each letter given different points values according to the frequency of occurrence. The game was developed in the early 1930s in America by Alfred M. Butts, who originally called his invention 'Criss-Cross'. The name was later changed to Scrabble; by the 1960s it had become established as one of the world's most popular and best-selling board games. World Tournaments have been held since the early 1970s. Top Scrabble champions have a wide knowledge of rare words containing Zs, Qs, Xs, and Js (the letters with the highest points values).

scramble An emergency takeoff of military aircraft to intercept and attack enemy aeroplanes approaching their area of defence. The word is also used to alert pilots and ground crews for the operation. It came into popular use in the RAF during World War II, especially during the BATTLE OF BRITAIN. It was later used by the US Air Force during the 1950–53 KOREAN WAR.

Scrap of Paper The description of the Treaty of London (1839) by the German Chancellor Bethmann Hollweg in August 1914. Under the terms of the Treaty, the UK was committed to defending Belgian neutrality, which was violated by the German invasion (in accordance with the SCHLIEFFEN PLAN) on 4 August after the German declaration of war against France and Russia. On 3 August the British government had informed the German government that it would stand by the London Treaty, which prompted Bethmann Hollweg's contemptuous comment. The German invasion allowed the UK government to justify the declaration of war on Germany as a defence of the integrity of Belgium and the Low Countries against unprovoked German aggression.

scratching In POP music of the 1980s, the incorporation of a scratching noise by rotating a record manually on the turntable, often done live by a disc jockey as an accompaniment to another record being played.

screwball US slang from the 1930s for a weird, slightly crazy, or eccentric person. The term has its origins in baseball, in which a screwball is a pitch having such a spin that its exact destination is uncertain.

Screwtape Letters A novel by C. S. Lewis (1893–1963) in which a devil, Screwtape, teaches a novice devil, Wormwood, how to lead human beings into damnation. The letters were first published in weekly instalments from May to November 1941 in *The Guardian*, a High Church weekly, and then collected in book form in 1942. The letters skilfully combine comic observations on human character with serious moral and religious content; the book remains one of Lewis's most popular works.

> A sensible woman once said . . . 'She's the sort of woman who lives for others – you can tell the others by their hunted expression.'
>
> *The Screwtape Letters*, XXVI.

scrubber British and Australian slang for a low-class prostitute or a promiscuous girl, widely used since the 1920s. Although this usage may derive from the menial activity of scrubbing floors, it is more likely to be related to scrubbing or scraping a living together.

scuba Self-Contained Underwater Breathing Apparatus. **Scuba-diving** is deep-sea diving using this type of apparatus, which was developed in America in the early 1950s.

scud In British army slang from the GULF WAR (1991), to inflict heavy damage on an enemy. This usage was inspired by the Soviet-designed Scud ballistic missiles, which proved the most feared (though still relatively easily knocked out) weapon in the Iraqi arsenal. During the Gulf War Scuds were used as a terror weapon against Israel and Saudi Arabia. *See* SMART WEAPONS.

scuzzy US teenage slang to describe a person who is dirty, shabby, or disreputable. Dating from the mid-1960s, it is either a shortening of *disgusting* or a blend of *scum* and *fuzz*.

sea. seagull Australian slang for a casual labourer employed in the docks, inspired by the seagull's scavenging habit.

Sea Lion (Ger. *Seelöwe*) The codename for the planned German invasion of S England in 1940, called for in Hitler's War Directive No. 16, issued on 16 July 1940, citing the UK's stubbornness in rejecting a negotiated settlement and refusal to recognize her hopeless military situation. Hitler instructed his army and navy chiefs to begin amassing an invasion fleet in the Channel ports; the Luftwaffe was given the task of destroying the RAF to secure air superiority. The defeat of the Luftwaffe in the BATTLE OF BRITAIN in August and September, however, made the invasion plans unworkable; by October Hitler had abandoned operation Sea Lion in favour of the invasion of the Soviet Union, codenamed BARBAROSSA.

Sealed Knot Society A British organization dedicated to the re-enactment of historical scenes from the English Civil War. Members engage in mock battles between 'Loyalists' and 'Parliamentarians', dressing in period costume and wielding replica muskets and other weapons. Founded in 1968 by Brigadier Peter Young, the society, and its sister group **The English Civil War Society**, has provided much harmless and entertaining spectacle in the name of 'living history'; derivative groups in America are based around such events as the War of Independence and the Civil War. Other groups re-enact battles of the Wars of the Roses, Viking raids, etc.

search-and-destroy A 1960s phrase from the VIETNAM WAR to describe intense military movements against guerrilla forces. Such an operation selects a limited area in which to locate the enemy and then directs concentrated firepower at this area.

Sears Tower A SKYSCRAPER in Chicago, which, at 1450 feet, is the tallest building in the world. 110 storeys high, it was completed in 1974 and replaced the World Trade Center in New York as the world's tallest building. 16,500 people work in the offices of the Sears Tower and power is provided by its own electricity substation below ground level. It was designed by Skidmore, Owings & Merril.

SEATO South East Asia Treaty Organization. An organization for mutual defence and economic cooperation, set up in Manila on 8 September 1954, whose members were Australia, the UK, France, New Zealand, Pakistan, the Philippines, Thailand, and America. SEATO was explicitly sponsored by America on the model of NATO to combat the spread of communism in SE Asia. The UK, France, and Pakistan largely abandoned their commitment after 1965 to avoid being involved in the VIETNAM WAR; in 1975, after the communist victories in Vietnam, Laos, and Cambodia, the members agreed to end the treaty. The remaining non-communist Asian nations then formed the Association of South East Asian Nations (ASEAN), a non-military non-political alliance for mutual economic aid.

second. Second Front The Allied invasion of German-occupied Europe, for which various plans were drawn up after 1941, although the eventual cross-channel invasion was delayed until 6 June 1944 (*see* D DAY). The establishment of a Second Front in the West was a matter of urgency for Stalin, who feared that his Allied partners were content to allow the Soviet Union and Germany to fight each other to extinction in the east. The Soviet Foreign Minister, Molotov, visited London and Washington in May 1942 and received promises that a Second Front for the relief of the Soviets would be opened soon. Churchill, however, told Roosevelt in June that US plans for an invasion of France in 1942 were unrealistic; in August he went to Moscow to explain to Stalin why these earlier promises could not be kept. Instead the Americans accepted British proposals for landings in North Africa, codenamed Operation Torch, which took place in November 1942. Churchill was determined that the invasion should not take place until success was assured and until sufficient British forces could be made available to play a major role in the campaign. At the Casablanca Conference in January 1943, plans for the invasion were postponed again, and the British plan for landings in Sicily adopted. A date for the European invasion – 1 May 1944 – was eventually agreed at the Quebec Conference in August 1943. By 1944, however, the Soviet Union had begun the drive west after the retreating German armies, so that as D Day approached, it became clear that America and the Soviet Union would play the decisive roles in the liberation and postwar settlement of Europe.

Second International *See* INTERNATIONAL.

second strike *See* FIRST STRIKE.

Second World *See* THIRD WORLD.

secret service The popular name for governmental intelligence, espionage, and counter-espionage organizations. *See* CIA; FBI; KGB; MI5; MI6.

Securitate The hated secret police of the Romanian dictator Nicolae Ceausescu (1918–89). They remained loyal to the dictator after his fall in December 1989, fighting running gun battles with the army (who had sided with the populace) and firing at random into crowded streets. They were eliminated after a week of fighting that is believed to have left more dead than any European conflict since World War II.

Securities and Investment Board (SIB) A regulatory body set up by the Financial Services Act (1986) to control London's financial markets. Each market has its own SELF-REGULATORY ORGANIZATION (SRO), which reports to the SIB. Members of the SIB are appointed jointly by the Secretary of State for Trade and Industry and the Governor of the Bank of England. The SIB has the overall responsibility of ensuring that investors in London markets are protected from fraud and that the markets comply with the rules established by their individual SROs.

security. security blanket Anything that provides emotional support and reduces anxiety, such as understanding parents, an inheritance, alcohol or drugs, or a handgun. This figurative use comes from the objects a young child clutches and carries for comfort and security, such as a small piece of blanket or a teddy bear. This habit was featured by Charles M. Schulz from 1962 onwards in his comic strip PEANUTS, in which the character Linus becomes paranoid without his blanket.

Security Council The main executive organ of the United Nations, which has the primary responsibility for the maintenance of international peace and security. The UK, America, France, the Soviet Union, and China are permanently represented while ten other nations serve two-year periods on the Council. The Council has proved more effective than the League of Nations in maintaining collective security because of its range of military, economic, and diplomatic sanctions for use against offending states. These powers have been only intermittently successful, however. During the Cold War effective action was often prevented by the use of the Veto (available to the permanent members) by the two superpowers to prevent action against their own interests. The UN intervention in the KOREAN WAR, for example, was only possible because of the Soviet Union's absence from the Council. In the first post-Cold War test of its effectiveness, the Council successfully mobilized sufficient military support from UN members in the GULF WAR to expel Saddam Hussein from Kuwait in March 1991.

security risk Governmental security is concerned with the prevention of leakages of confidential information; a security risk is someone of doubtful loyalty, whose background and associations make employment in state service inadvisable, especially in posts that involve access to confidential information likely to be of use to a potentially hostile government.

Seddon Murder The poisoning of Eliza Mary Barrow on 14 September 1911 by Frederick Henry Seddon, a District Superintendent with the London and Manchester Industrial Insurance Company. Seddon, who was obsessed with money, had rented out rooms in his large house in Islington to Barrow, a wealthy spinster. Having persuaded her to sign over most of her assets to him, he invited her to join his family on holiday to Southend, where he poisoned her with arsenic taken from a packet of Mather's Chemical Fly Papers, which his daughter had purchased for him at a local chemist's shop. A suspicious cousin demanded the exhumation of Barrow's body, and Seddon was arrested after traces of the poison were discovered in the tissues. Seddon was tried and convicted in March 1912, although many observers believed that the guilty verdict was influenced more by his cold and dispassionate demeanour in court than any conclusive evidence against him. He was hanged at Pentonville Prison on 18 April 1912.

Seeadler (Ger. Sea Eagle) A German warship of World War I, which was a great menace to allied shipping in the Atlantic from December 1916 to August 1917. What made the *Seeadler* so effective was its elaborate disguise as a Norwegian windjammer. Built in Glasgow as the *Pass of Balmaha* in 1888 and captured by the Germans in 1915, it appeared to be an entirely innocent vessel until it revealed its concealed 4.2 inch guns. To complete the deception, the ship sailed under the name *Maletta* (the name of a similar Norwegian cargo vessel) and the crew carried Norwegian papers. Only at the last moment was the *Seeadler*'s true identity revealed to its victims as a warship of the German Imperial Navy. In this way the *Seeadler* sank 12 allied ships, totalling 40,000 tons; in true buccaneering style all the prisoners were toasted with champagne and were well treated by the crew. The *Seeadler*'s end came in August 1917 when a freak wave, rather than an allied shell, wrecked the ship. *See also* Q SHIPS.

segue A link-word from the vocabulary of disc-jockeys. Pronounced 'seg-way', it is the Italian for 'now follows'.

self. self-determination In politics, the concept that every nation, no matter how small or weak, has the right to decide upon its own form of government and to manage its own affairs. The phrase acquired this significance during the attempts to resettle Europe after World War I.

Self-Regulatory Organization (SRO) One of five organizations set up in the UK under the terms of the Financial Services Act (1986) to enforce appropriate codes of conduct in the various branches of the investment business. The five SROs recognized by the SECURITIES AND INVESTMENT BOARD (SIB) are the Securities Association Ltd (TSA), which regulates the London International Stock Exchange; the Association of Futures Brokers and Dealers (AFBD), which regulates the London International Financial Futures Exchange (LIFE); the Life Assurance and Unit Trust Regulatory Organization (LAUTRO); the Investment Management Regulatory Organization (IMRO); and the Financial Intermediaries, Managers and Brokers Regulatory Organization (FIMBRA).

self service A largely mid-20th-century innovation in retailing in which the customer serves himself and passes through a cash point at which he pays for the goods he has taken. It is now widely used in supermarkets and petrol stations. The first supermarkets came from America to the UK at the beginning of the 1950s. They were opened by Premier Supermarkets, under the management of Patrick Galvani, who had been impressed with what he had seen in America. Very soon every high street in the country had its own supermarket, belonging to one of a few large chains. There are three basic principles underlying the supermarket: self service; buying one's groceries, fruit and vegetables, meat, fish, etc., all in one place instead of four or five; and paying a lower price than elsewhere. Sir Jack Cohen (1898–1979), the founder of the Tesco chain, used as his motto:

> Pile it high, sell it cheap.

In the 1980s the supermarket principle was extended to include the sale of a wider variety of goods in one very large out-of-town store (*see* HYPERMARKET).

sell-by date The date, as displayed on its packaging, after which a perishable food should not be offered for sale. It is now also used in an extended sense to mean the date beyond which something or somebody loses its freshness or appeal: a long-running TV series, an outmoded fashion, or a person thought to be no longer sexually attractive may all be described as past their sell-by date. *See also* SHELF LIFE.

Sellafield One of the UK's principal nuclear energy installations, located on the Cumbrian coast in NW England. The site was generally known as **Windscale** before 1981. In 1947 two air-cooled plutonium piles were built there, primarily to produce plutonium for the UK's atom bomb. They were joined by the country's first industrial nuclear power station, Calder Hall, which began supplying the national grid in 1956 and by 1958 comprised four Magnox reactors (*see* NUCLEAR REACTOR). A facility for reprocessing spent fuel from the reactors was started in 1952, with a second line opening in 1964 (the first closed in 1973). Still under construction at Sellafield is THORP (thermal oxide reprocessing plant), intended for reprocessing uranium oxide fuels, as used in AGR and PWR reactors. The site also contains storage tanks for high-level and intermediate-level nuclear waste and a fast-reactor fuel-assembly plant (manufacturing fuel for the DOUNREAY reactor); a vitrification plant for converting highly radioactive liquid wastes into a solid form is planned. Currently, low-level solid waste is dumped at the Drigg disposal site nearby.

The Sellafield/Windscale site has been dogged by accident and controversy. The worst accident was a reactor fire in October 1957, in which radioactive substances were released into the atmosphere and contaminated surrounding areas. Milk from farms covering an area of 500 sq km was deemed unfit for human consumption. The plant has also been censured for leaks of hazardous material from storage tanks into the soil and for radioactive discharges into the Irish Sea, attracting the attention of GREENPEACE and other environmental campaigners. Reports have also found an increased cancer incidence both among Sellafield workers and those living around the plant. *See also* CHERNOBYL.

Semtex *See* PLASTIC EXPLOSIVE.

send. Send in the clowns A phrase implying that whatever disasters have occurred, life must be seen to be continuing as usual. A similar phrase is 'the show must go on'. Both expressions come from the circus, where nobody could afford to let an accident or backstage drama ruin their reputation, and thus their livelihood. In the event of a catastrophe behind the scenes, the clowns would be sent out to entertain the audience and distract their attention from anything else that might be happening. It was used as a song title in Stephen Sondheim's *A Little Night Music* (1974).

That sends me An expression formerly used by JAZZ and POP enthusiasts to signify that the music sends them into raptures.

senior citizen A popular euphemism for an elderly person, especially one receiving a state retirement pension. This Americanism from 1938 was promulgated by advertisers and politicians. Although some older people regard it as patronizing, 'senior citizen' has become accepted on both sides of the Atlantic.

Senoussi A Muslim organization founded in the 19th century by Muhammad es-Senoussi in the region of North Africa occupied by modern Libya. It was the Senoussi Brotherhood, led by Idris Al Senoussi, which organized resistance to the Italian conquest of the provinces of Tripolitania and Cyrenaica from September 1911, and to Mussolini's African colonial regime from 1922 onwards. In 1934 Italy united Tripolitania and Cyrenaica and added a third province, Fezzan, to make up Libya. From Cairo, Idris coordinated resistance to the Italian settlement of Libya and to the Axis powers throughout World War II. When Libya was finally granted independence in December 1951, in accordance with the Allied postwar pledge of self-determination, Idris was proclaimed king. On 21 September 1969 the 70-year-old monarch was deposed in a coup by Colonel Muammar Gadaffi.

sense. You know it makes sense The line used in the late 1960s on road safety posters advising people to drive carefully. It was revived during the 1980s by Margaret Thatcher, as justification for some new policies.

sensitivity training or **bodbiz** Group psychotherapy in which a therapist attempts to guide individual members towards self-awareness by means of the psychodynamics of the group. They are encouraged to express their own feelings and to be aware of the feelings of others during touching sessions and by exchanges of intimate thoughts and experiences. Sensitivity training or bodbiz (short for body business) has driven some emotionally disturbed participants into medical treatment. This form of therapy was in vogue during the HIPPIE era and continued into the 1970s. A pacesetter was the National Training Laboratories, begun by US psychologist Kurt Lewin.

Sensurround Tradename for a film sound system using low-frequency sound waves to send detectable vibrations through a cinema audience. The effect was first used in the mid-1970s to give such films as *Earthquake* (1974) and *Rollercoaster* (1977) the flavour of unnerving realism. The name is a blend of *sense* and *surround*.

sent to dry us A catchphrase of the 1920s used with reference to PROHIBITION. It is, of course, a paraphrase of the expression 'sent to try us'.

septic Australian and New Zealand slang for an American, from rhyming slang *septic tank*, Yank. It was first used during World War II of the visiting US soldiers and is still heard.

seventeen

Seretse Khama affair In 1949, Seretse Khama (1921–80), chief-designate of the Bamangwato tribe of the British Protectorate of Bechuanaland in S Africa, returned to the province, after training as a barrister in London, with his English wife, a 24-year-old typist, Ruth Williams. This outraged the racial sensibilities of the South African government, which had been pressing the British government to allow the incorporation of the province into South Africa, under the terms of the South Africa Act (1909). As well as disconcerting the British and South Africans, Seretse's marriage was against the wishes of his uncle and regent, Tshekedi Khama. Despite the support of the tribe in general, it was decided by the British, South Africans, and the regent that he should be exiled for six years; he eventually returned to Bechuanaland in 1956, after renouncing the chieftainship. In 1965 he was elected head of government of the province and in 1966, when Bechuanaland became Botswana and was granted full independence, he became the first president of the new nation, which he remained until his death. He was knighted in 1966.

serial. serial imagery A genre in art that enjoyed a brief vogue in the 1960s. Works in this style consisted of the same object (or face) repeated several times with various changes in colour and treatment; among the best-known examples of the genre is Andy Warhol's multiple picture of Marilyn MONROE.

serialism An unconventional theory of 'time displacement' advanced by John William Dunne (1875–1949), aircraft designer, mathematician, and philosopher. Based on analysis of his own dreams, Dunne concluded that they offered glimpses of future experiences and that time itself was an unfolding of pre-ordained events. His *An Experiment with Time* (1927) explaining his observations and theory became a best-seller and started a fashion for recording dreams. In *The Serial Universe* (1934) he further refined his complex thesis; he produced two later works, *The New Immortality* (1938) and *Nothing Dies* (1940), containing a simplified explanation of serialism for the public at large. Serialism is not now taken seriously by the scientific community; there is no solid evidence for precognitive dreaming.

serial killer A murderer who kills on a number of occasions, usually picking subjects at random. The phenomenon became the subject of public attention in the 1960s (*see* ZODIAC MURDERS).

serious. serious money A large amount of money, a five- or six-figure salary, as in 'he's earning serious money now in the City'. A phrase much used during the materialistic Thatcher decade, the 1980s. A satirical play with this title was written by Caryl Churchill in 1987. Serious money is what you have to pay ambitious, thrusting, and successful executives. If you pay peanuts, so the saying goes, you get monkeys.

You cannot be serious *See* SUPERBRAT.

SERPS State Earnings-Related Pension Scheme. A UK government scheme that began in 1978 with the object of providing every employed person with an earnings-related pension in addition to the basic flat-rate pension. Contributions to the scheme came from National Insurance payments and the pension, payable at 65 for men and 60 for women, is calculated using a formula based on the person's earnings. Employees may contract out of SERPS provided that they subscribe to a personal pension scheme or an occupational pension scheme.

set In JAZZ slang, a session or series of songs or improvisations, subsequently also used in ROCK circles.

seven. seven-year itch The urge, especially on the part of husbands, to find a new sexual partner after seven years of marriage. George Axelrod, who wrote a play with this title in 1952 (filmed, starring Marilyn MONROE, in 1955), believed that it was his use of the phrase that gave it its modern marital connotation. Previously it had been used to describe various itching ailments, including scabies, that only disappeared after seven years of treatment. Itch however, has been used since the 17th century as a slang word for a sexual urge and seven years is a traditional period for change:

> Time's pace is so hard that it seems the length of seven years.
>
> WILLIAM SHAKESPEARE: *As You Like It.*

The Seven The original members of the European Free Trade Association (EFTA) formed in 1959, namely Denmark, Norway, Sweden, Austria, Portugal, Switzerland, and the UK. *See also* THE SIX.

seventeen. 17th Amendment An amendment to the Constitution of the United States of America, which came into effect on 31 May 1913, to provide for the direct election of senators, who until then had been chosen by the individual state legislatures. The 17th Amendment therefore reduced the power and status of state governments and increased popular control over the federal legislature.

17th Parallel The division between North and South Vietnam imposed by the Geneva Conference in May 1954, which was convened to arrange for an end to hostilities between the French and Vietminh forces in Indochina. Both sides agreed to regroup their forces north and south of the 17th Parallel, which was intended as a temporary dividing line pending nationwide elections promised in two years in July 1956 to determine the political settlement of the region. America later vetoed the elections, however, which effectively ensured the permanent division of Vietnam and shattered the Vietminh's dream of unification. US policy thus guaranteed continuing instability in the region and the eventual recurrence of hostilities between Ho Chi Minh's communist government in the North and the US-backed regime in the South (*see* VIETNAM WAR).

Seveso A town in N Italy, near Milan, which in 1976 became the scene of a major industrial accident when an explosion at a factory resulted in the discharge of a cloud of poisonous dioxin gas. The town had to be completely evacuated, domestic animals destroyed, and contaminated crops and other vegetation burned. Although the dioxin – a by-product in the manufacture of herbicides by the factory – caused no human deaths, many people heavily exposed to the gas developed chloracne, a disfiguring and persistent skin disorder.

sex. safe sex The 1980s catchphrase for sexual intercourse using a protective device, especially a condom, or non-penetrative means to prevent the spread of AIDS and other sexually transmitted diseases, such as gonorrhoea, syphilis, and herpes. These diseases, formerly known as venereal diseases, have increased in western countries in the wake of liberal attitudes to sex (*see* NEW MORALITY), but it took the Aids crisis to prompt large-scale governmental campaigns for safe sex.

sex bomb or **sex pot** British slang for a very sexy woman, someone who plays up their sexuality. A favourite with the tabloid press, it was first used in the 1960s and is still heard.

> They met . . . when they were both playing the classic sex bombs, the 'big boobed playthings' . . . who totter in on high heels . . .
>
> *The Independent*, 10 April 1991.

sexism Discrimination against and oppression of women, because they are women, by men. *See also* MALE CHAUVINIST PIG; SEXUAL POLITICS.

Sex Kitten The nickname of the French film actress, Brigitte Bardot (Camille Javal; 1933–). The daughter of an industrialist, she became a model and then appeared in a series of French-made sex-comedy films. However, it was with the release in 1956 of *Et Dieu créa la femme* (*And God Created Woman*) that she first attracted international notice and became the sex symbol of an epoch. Written and directed by her first husband, Roger Vadim, the film caused considerable moral outrage because it showed Bardot stripping on the beach at St Tropez; it was described by the Catholic Legion of Decency as "an open violation of conventional morality". Vadim, however, had this to say about it:

> It was the first time on the screen that a woman was shown as really free on a sexual level with none of the guilt attached to nudity or carnal pleasure.

Over the next 15 years there followed a further string of films, including *Viva Maria* (1965, with Jeanne Moreau), *Shalako* (1968), and finally *Don Juan* (1973).

Her private life – in particular her three marriages, the last of which (to Gunther Sachs) was dissolved in 1969 – was a continual target for scrutiny in the popular press, but with the end of her cinema career she withdrew from the public glare to devote her time to promoting animal rights and welfare.

sex 'n' drugs 'n' rock 'n' roll A phrase that was supposed to sum up all the ingredients of a good time for the young in the late 1960s and 1970s. It was the title of a song by Ian Dury and Chaz Jankel in 1977. It represents a world that every parent dreads their teenager entering.

sex object An attractive woman valued for her sex appeal by men who have little regard for her intelligence or abilities. Although these roles can be reversed, the disparaging term almost always describes a woman. This prompted Clare Boothe Luce, the US author and feminist, to complain in 1973:

> Altogether, the Male Establishment never lets women forget that they are all but valueless to society except as sex objects.

sex therapy *See* MASTERS AND JOHNSON.

Sex Thimble The nickname of the British comic actor, composer, and musician Dudley Moore (1935–). After leaving Oxford with degrees in arts and music, he was employed writing incidental music for productions at the Royal Court Theatre in London. His professional theatre debut came with BEYOND THE FRINGE, a successful revue that also featured former Oxbridge students Jonathan Miller, Peter Cook, and Alan Bennet. In 1964 he teamed up with Peter Cook for the first of three series of television comedy programmes entitled *Not Only . . . But Also*. He returned to the stage in 1970 in *Play It Again Sam* and again with Peter Cook in *Behind the Fridge* (1972–73). He made further appearances on Broadway, toured America in 1975, and became resident there. He has also appeared in many films in which he was promoted as a diminutive sex symbol (hence his nickname).

sexual politics The role of gender in political, business, and social institutions. Traditionally women have been discriminated against in the church, armed forces, law, medicine, and banking in relation to both employment and advancement. The US feminist Kate Millet introduced the phrase in her book *Sexual Politics* (1970). The **Women's Movement** maintains that the socio-cultural role of gender (*see* GENDER GAP) differs from the biological role of sex. It believes that sexual equality will change political and social structures for the better. In the UK the premiership (1979–90) of Margaret Thatcher was hailed as a breakthrough, but in practice it failed to mark a significant shift in sexual prejudice. *See also* FEMINISM; SUFFRAGETTES.

sexual revolution *See* NEW MORALITY.

Sexy Rexy The nickname of the British stage and screen actor Rex Harrison (1908–90). In the 1930s he pursued a successful career on the London stage, in plays such as *French without Tears* and *The Cocktail Party*; his prewar films included *The Citadel* (1938) and *Major Barbara* (1940). After wartime service in the RAF he returned to stage and screen; the highlight of his career was the Broadway production of *My Fair Lady* and the subsequent (1964) film.

A debonair and charming man, who was six times married, he was at his best in comedy; after seeing *Blithe Spirit* (1945), Noel Coward (its author) is reputed to have said to him:

> After me, you're the best light comedian in the world.

sez (says) you A contemptuous exclamation expressing disbelief in what someone has said. An expression of US origin, it was popular in the UK in the 1930s.

shack up To cohabit with someone to whom one is not married. Originally an Americanism dating from the 1930s, it was used mainly by itinerant workers who set up temporary homes in roughly built shacks. It has been widely used in English-speaking countries since the 1960s.

shades Originally Black slang for a pair of tinted sunglasses, an essential component of COOL gear since the 1950s.

shag (1) British and Australian slang meaning to have sex with, or an act of intercourse. It is thought to be related to the verb to shake, which has had sexual connotations since the 16th century. (2) British slang meaning to masturbate. (3) A short-lived teenage dance craze of the 1960s.

shagged Tired out by, or as if by, excessive indulgence in either intercourse or masturbation.

shaggy dog story A would-be funny story told at great length with an unexpected twist at the end. So called from the shaggy dog featured in many stories of this genre popular in the 1940s.

shamateurism The means by which an athlete maintains the amateur status necessary for competing in international events while accepting payments. This is usually achieved by setting up trust funds or by treating large sums of money received as 'expenses'. It is a combination of *sham* and *amateurism*.

shamus US slang for a private detective or a police officer, often used in crime fiction. It is thought to be derived from the Yiddish *shamos*, from the Hebrew *shamash*, a guardian of the synagogue. It is also possibly related to the popular Irish Christian name Seamus, which was applied to police officers (many of whom were Irish, particularly on the east coast of America).

Shangri La The hidden Buddhist paradise described in James Hilton's novel *Lost Horizon* (1933). The 1937 film starring Ronald Colman was hugely successful. The name was later applied to F. D. Roosevelt's mountain refuge in Maryland

and to the secret base used for the great US air raid on Tokyo in 1942.

SHAPE Supreme Headquarters of the Allied Powers, Europe. *See* NATO.

shark. sharkbait Australian slang for a swimmer who ventures further out to sea than other bathers, sometimes extended to anyone who takes more risks than might be wise.

shark repellents Measures taken by a company to deter unwelcome takeover bids. They include GOLDEN PARACHUTES, POISON PILLS, and other measures, such as staggered directorships, in which the company adds a resolution to its articles of association that the terms of office served by its directors are to be staggered and that no director can be removed from office without good cause. This ensures that a hostile bidder will be unable to gain executive control of the company for a number of years, even after it has acquired a majority shareholding. The measures are also known as **porcupine provisions**.

shark watcher A business consultant, especially one in New York or London, who is employed by a company to identify any share purchases or manoeuvres that may be a preliminary to a takeover bid for that company.

Sharon British slang from the late 1970s for a typical working-class girl. It is the female equivalent of Wayne, Gary, and KEVIN. Sharon became a very popular name among working-class families from the middle of the 1960s and thus was used for an easily identifiable stereotype. Sharon would typically wear snow-washed jeans with white high heels and have her hair streaked blonde in shoulder-length wet-look curls.

> Warren Clarke . . . is excellent as beer-swilling shop steward Albert (Vladimir). He's dug in so deep he's got kids called Gary, Wayne, and Sharon.
>
> Reviewing TV serial *Sleepers* in the *Sun*, 18 April 1991.

Sharpeville massacre The mass shooting of anti-PASS LAW demonstrators in a Black township 40 miles S of Johannesburg by the Transvaal police on 21 March 1960. 69 were killed (many shot in the back) and 180 injured, after the police panicked when 20,000 demonstrators without passes offered themselves for arrest at the local police station. The killings provoked worldwide condemnation and caused a state of emergency within South Africa. In the aftermath of the massacre, both the Pan-African Congress, which had called for the demonstration, and the African National Congress (*see* ANC) were banned; 18,000 people were summarily arrested and draconian powers introduced to suppress dissent, effectively transforming the country into a police state.

sharpie Australian slang for a SKINHEAD, first heard in the 1960s, from the bristly feel of closely cropped hair.

Shavian After the manner of George Bernard Shaw (1856–1950), or descriptive of his philosophy and style of humour.

Shaw, T. E. *See* LAWRENCE OF ARABIA.

She who must be obeyed A phrase used to describe an overbearing woman. It became popular through its use in John Mortimer's *Rumpole of the Bailey* stories (serialized on TV in the 1970s and 1980s) by the barrister Rumpole himself of his dragon of a wife. Denis Healey used it ironically with reference to Mrs Thatcher in 1984. The original source was H. Ryder Haggard's novel *She* (1887). *Compare* 'ER INDOORS.

sheep in sheep's clothing Weak through and through. A tongue-in-cheek alteration of the well-known proverb a 'wolf in sheep's clothing'. It is often attributed to Winston Churchill, supposedly making a reference to his successor, the Labour prime minister Clement Attlee. Churchill himself denied this; the British writer and critic Edmund Gosse (1849–1928) used it when referring to T. Sturge Moore. In another political jibe, Labour's Denis Healey described an attack on him by the Conservative Geoffrey Howe as being similar to being 'savaged by a dead sheep'.

shelf life The length of time that a commodity, such as a packaged food, can be kept before it deteriorates. The term is now applied metaphorically to other phenomena – fashions, ideas, media personalities – that are not expected to last: 'Today's pop stars have a very limited shelf life'. *See also* SELL-BY DATE.

shell. shell jacket A short tight-fitting undress military jacket reaching only to the waist at the back; also an officer's mess jacket.

shell shock A name that originated in World War I for the psychological illness, which may include loss of sight, loss of memory, terror dreams, depression, etc., resulting from prolonged exposure to exploding bombs and shells. A more modern name is **combat neurosis**.

sheltered accommodation A system of housing designed for the elderly and other vulnerable or at-risk groups, in which individuals or families live in their own self-contained flats or houses but are able to summon a warden for assistance should the need arise. Such accommodation is usually provided by local authorities or housing associations; it often has communal facilities, such as recreation rooms and laundry. Since the 1960s sheltered housing has become a popular method of enabling people, who might otherwise be forced into institutional care, to led independent lives in the community.

Shepperton studios Film studios on a 60-acre site at Shepperton, Middlesex, which were established in 1932 by Norman Loudon of the Sound City Film Production and Recording Company. By 1937 the lot contained seven stages, four of which could be converted to double size and had large water tanks. They were eventually taken over by the British Lion Film Corporation but closed in the early 1970s, leaving Pinewood and Elstree as the only British film studios still in use.

sherbert British army slang for beer, dating from the GULF WAR of 1991 (possibly by allusion to the Arabs' fondness for sherbert).

Sherman tank The 'General Sherman' M4, a US medium tank of World War II, which was produced in various versions from February 1942. The earliest Sherman carried most of the ammunition for its 75 mm gun in hull sponsons, which were extremely vulnerable to enemy fire; for this reason it was given the nickname 'Ronson' by the Germans, because it lit first time. This defect was remedied in later versions by placing the ammunition within the hull, and various other improvements were made to the armaments and the engine. In all, 30,346 Shermans were manufactured from July 1942 to February 1944; they formed an essential part of the Soviet and British, as well as the US, forces.

> We'll win the war with the M4.
>
> Allied slogan.

shicker US slang for an alcoholic drink or for a drunkard. It entered American English at the turn of the century from Yiddish and ultimately from the Hebrew, *shikor*. It is perhaps most widely used as an adjective, as in 'he is shicker'. The Anglicized form **shickered** is widely used in Australia.

shimmy A JAZZ dance that first became popular at the COTTON CLUB in the 1920s. Derived from the French *chemise*, shirt, the dance was so named because its energetic rhythms made shirts or blouses shake and shimmer.

Shock, horror! A phrase registering alarm and distaste, used as a parody of a tabloid newspaper headline in the satirical magazine PRIVATE EYE from the 1970s. It is now often used adjectivally, as in 'Mum had a real shockhorror reaction when I wanted to go on holiday with my boyfriend'.

shoot. Shoot! Go ahead; say what you have to say. Let's have it! In film studios it is the instruction for the cameras to begin turning.

shoot down in flames To refute the arguments of an opponent devastatingly and completely. A metaphor from aerial warfare.

shoot-'em-up Originally, a US slang term for a film, such as a Western, dominated by gunplay and multiple shootings. It is now mainly applied to video or computer games of the SPACE INVADERS type, in which the player attempts to obliterate a series of targets moving on the screen.

shooting gallery US drug-users' slang for any place in which addicts **shoot up**, *i.e.* inject themselves with drugs.

> Sid got worse till we had to drag him out of Linda's flat and bring him up to the office where Malcolm asked him if he was shooting up and stuff.
>
> *The Independent*, 13 April 1991.

shooting war A real war as distinct from a COLD WAR.

shop. closed shop A term, first used in America, to describe shops or factories from which non-union labour is excluded. It is also used more widely of any institution that has a reputation for not admitting outsiders.

the Shop In military slang, the former Royal Military Academy at Woolwich, which removed to Sandhurst in 1946; on the London International Stock Exchange it is the South African gold market.

short. sell short A commercial phrase meaning to sell stocks, shares, commodities, currencies, etc., that one does not at the moment possess, in the hope that they may be acquired more cheaply than at present before the date of delivery. It is also known as **bear selling**.

short-circuit To take a short cut, especially to bypass an official procedure or regulation. It derives from an electrical context in which a short circuit (or short) is an accidental connection between two points of different potential in which the load is bypassed.

short, fat, hairy legs One of the many catchphrases from the extremely popular *Morecambe and Wise Show*. The two British comedians, Eric Morecambe (1926–84) and Ernie Wise (1925–), began their career in variety and moved into television in the 1960s. Ernie was the small 'straight' man constantly ribbed by the much taller Eric about, among other things, his 'short, fat, hairy legs' and his hair-piece (which Ernie always vehemently denied wearing).

shoulder-pads Small pads inserted in the shoulders of women's blouses, jackets, or coats to raise the shoulder line, in imitation of male fashions. They were much used in fashion in the 1940s and 1950s and were reintroduced in the 1980s as the most characteristic element of POWER DRESSING.

show must go on, the *See under* SEND IN THE CLOWNS.

Shrieking Sisterhood *See* SUFFRAGETTES.

Shrimp, The Nickname of Jean Shrimpton (1941–), British fashion model of the 1960s. She was a close friend of the photographer David Bailey (1938–); it was his photographs of her that made her and her sister Chrissie Shrimpton (1943–) symbols of the SWINGING SIXTIES. Cecil Beaton, the leading fashion photographer of his time, called her 'the unicorn, the rare, almost mythological thing'. In 1969 Jean Shrimpton dropped out of the London fashion circus, eventually marrying and settling down as the owner of a small Penzance hotel. *See also* TWIGGY.

shrink *See* HEADSHRINK.

Shroud of Turin *See* TURIN SHROUD.

shuffle An early JAZZ dance involving a shuffling step, danced in 4/4 time. It dates from the 1900s.

shufti British army slang dating from the 1930s for a quick look. It is from the Arabic.

shut. a shut mouth never fills a black coffin US catchphrase heard during the gangster era of the 1920s and 1930s, enjoining an accomplice to silence or to risk being murdered as an informant.

Shut that door! The catchphrase of the British comedian, game-show host, and compère Larry Grayson (1930–) that he first used in 1970. He claims to have said it first on stage at the Theatre Royal, Brighton, in 1970 when he actually did feel a draught from the wings. The reaction was hilarity both from those in the wings and the audience so he decided to keep it in his act. It is usually spoken with a northern accent in imitation of Grayson.

shutterbug US slang for a keen photographer, especially an amateur.

shuttle diplomacy Negotiations conducted by a diplomat or politician who travels back and forth to mediate between hostile countries or parties. The name was first used to describe the personal life of the US Secretary of State, Henry Kissinger, during his Middle East negotiations in the 1970s. Several western nations and the Jordanian King Hussein attempted shuttle diplomacy in an attempt to avert the 1991 GULF WAR.

SIB *See* SECURITIES AND INVESTMENT BOARD.

sick. sick as a parrot A cliché used to describe extreme disappointment, as at some unexpected let-down or failure. It plays on sick meaning 'disgusted' and sick meaning 'diseased', parrots being notoriously prone to such ailments as the viral disease psittacosis (parrot fever). In the 1970s and 1980s it was a favourite expression of football players and managers, who routinely used it to describe their feelings on losing a match. This repetitive overuse was mercilessly guyed by the satirical magazine PRIVATE EYE and the phrase is now mostly used ironically. *See also* OVER THE MOON; WE WUZ ROBBED *under* ROBBED.

sick-building syndrome A mild affliction that spreads among employees housed in an air-conditioned office building. Pathogenic microorganisms are said to circulate and recirculate through the air ducts spreading infection throughout the workforce. The general symptoms include headaches and eye irritations.

sicko A psychopath or sexual deviant: a slang term used in America from the mid-1970s and in the UK from the later 1980s.

sick-out A form of industrial action by employees who stay away from work, claiming to be ill. A sick-out is used to achieve certain demands; it avoids a formal strike, which may be forbidden by law or result in penalties. Sick-outs have been used by various groups, including the police, teachers, postal workers, nurses, and air-traffic controllers.

Sid In the UK, an ordinary person who bought his or her first shares in one of the UK government's privatization schemes of the 1980s. It derives from the successful campaign to publicize the British Gas sell-off in 1986, which featured variants of the slogan 'Have you told Sid?' (*i.e.* about the share issue). The name was presumably chosen for its working-class associations, implying that anyone, even someone called Sid, could be a share-owner in the brave new world of Thatcherite Britain.

Sidney Street siege The siege by the police, Scots Guards, and Horse Artillery of a house at 100 Sidney Street, Stepney, London, on 3 January 1911. The house contained the Houndsditch Gang, who had killed three policemen three weeks previously after an unsuccessful raid on a jewellery shop in Houndsditch. The gang consisted of Latvian anarchists led by 'Peter the Painter', a sign-painter from Riga. The siege was witnessed personally by Winston Churchill, then Home Secretary, who had authorized the use of armed troops to flush out the gang. Two anarchists died; 'Peter the Painter' escaped.

SIDS *See* SUDDEN INFANT DEATH SYNDROME.

Siegfried Line The defences built by the Germans on their western frontier before and after 1939 as a reply to France's MAGINOT LINE. The British song, popular in 1939, began:

> 'We're gonna hang out the washing on the Siegfried Line
> If the Siegfried Line's still there.'

When Canadian troops penetrated the Line in 1945 they hung up a number of sheets with a large notice on which was written 'The Washing'.

signature tune A song or melody regularly used by or introducing a radio or television programme, dance band, singer, or other performer with which it becomes firmly associated. The US term is **theme song**. Examples include 'Calling All Workers' from British radio's wartime *Music While You Work*, 'Neighbours' from the Australian soap opera of that name, comedian Bob Hope's 'Thanks for the Memories', and bandleader Glenn Miller's 'Moonlight Serenade'. In America political examples include the Democratic Party's 'Happy Days Are Here Again'.

Sihanouk Trail *See* HO CHI MINH TRAIL.

silent. Silent Cal *See under* CHOOSE.

silent films The first commercially produced films before the advent of soundtracks. They were characterized by exaggerated facial expression and sweeping body actions to demonstrate emotions without the use of words. But they were not entirely silent: cinemas hired musicians to provide piano, organ, or violin mood-music below the screen. Early silent stars included Charlie Chaplin (*see* TRAMP, THE), LAUREL AND HARDY, Mary Pickford (*see* WORLD'S SWEETHEART), and Lillian Gish. Perhaps the most impressive silent film was D. W. Griffith's *The Birth of a Nation*, while the UK's outstanding contribution was John Grierson's 1929 documentary, *Drifters*. The first airline film was silent: *The Lost World* was shown on an Imperial Airways flight from London in 1925. Silent films virtually came to an end in 1927 when *The Jazz Singer*, with Al Jolson, became the first great TALKIE success.

> *The Jazz Singer* definitely established the fact that talking pictures are imminent. Everyone in Hollywood can rise up and declare that they are not, and it will not alter the fact. If I were an actor with a squeaky voice I would worry.
>
> WELFORD BEATON in *The Film Spectator* (1927).

Alfred Hitchcock produced the first British sound film, *Blackmail*, in 1929, by immediately reshooting his original silent version (both were released). Not everyone believed silent films would be supplanted:

> The talkie is an unsuitable marriage of two dramatic forms. We cannot believe that it will endure.
>
> *The Times* (1929).

silent majority The mass of the population who do not make protests, hold extreme views, or disagree publicly with the policies of the government. They are the people to whom any successful political candidate must have an appeal. The phrase is often associated with Richard Nixon (1913–), who did not coin it but used it in his election speech in October, 1970:

> It is time for the great silent majority of Americans to stand up and be counted.

Silicon Valley Colloquial name originally used for Santa Clara Valley, S of San Francisco in California. Many factories here make electronic equipment, including silicon chips. Many other 'silicon valleys' have appeared in America and the UK with the growth of the electronic industry.

silly. silly season A journalistic expression for the part of the year during which parliament and the law courts are not sitting (usually August and September), when, through lack of news, the papers have to fill their columns with trivial items.

Silly Symphony The title given by Walt Disney to all his cartoon shorts of the 1930s that did not feature MICKEY MOUSE, PLUTO, or DONALD DUCK.

silver. Silver Ghost The Rolls Royce car produced from 1907 to 1927. The 7 litre six-cylinder 40/50 hp model was first announced at the Motor Show in 1906 as 'the Best Six-Cylinder Car in the World'. It was exceptionally quiet, refined, and beautifully finished; from 1908 to 1925 it was the only model produced by the company. It had a top speed of 65 m.p.h. (105 k.p.h.).

Silver Star A US military decoration for gallantry in action. It consists of a bronze star bearing a small silver star in its centre.

Silverstone A motor-racing circuit near Towcester in Northamptonshire, opened in 1948 on track incorporating the runways and perimeter roads of a former airfield. The circuit hosted its first British Grand Prix in 1948 and has continued as a venue for this event ever since, alternating with the Aintree circuit from 1955, and with BRANDS HATCH between 1964 and 1986. Since 1987 all Grand Prix meetings have been held at Silverstone. The race lap record in 1991 was held by Nigel Mansell, who in a Ferrari averaged 149.977 m.p.h. (241.358 k.p.h.), making Silverstone one of the fastest circuits in the world. From 1991 a new, slightly longer and slower, circuit was used, designed for greater safety.

Sinatra doctrine The principle that, in the era of GLASNOST, the Soviet Union will allow the communist regimes of E Europe to find their own ways to socialism – they will be permitted to 'do it their way', alluding to the song 'My Way' made famous by Frank Sinatra (*see* OLD BLUE EYES). The phrase dates from 25 October 1989, when Gennady Gerasimov, the Soviet Foreign Ministry spokesman, used it to draw a contrast with the so-called BREZHNEV DOCTRINE. The Sinatra doctrine was quickly overtaken by the collapse of communism in E Europe in autumn 1989, but the phrase is still used to signify the principle of Soviet non-intervention in other eastern-bloc countries' affairs.

sin-bin British slang for a special unit within a school to which difficult or disruptive children are sent until they are able to reintegrate. The term originated in ice hockey, where a sin-bin is the area in which a fouling player must stay until the time penalty has elapsed.

sindonology *See* TURIN SHROUD.

Sindy Tradename of a girls' doll. First marketed in 1954, Sindy is blonde, slim, and long-legged with vacant model-girl looks. Her chief appeal is her extensive wardrobe, which contains outfits and accessories for every occasion, profession, and lifestyle. With the advent of feminism, business suits etc. have been added to the collection, but so far their popularity has not rivalled that of the wedding dress and nurse's outfit. A recent development is the manufacture of ethnic Sindy dolls. Her success led to the creation of the ACTION MAN for boys. The name was chosen on the basis of a survey in which 'Cindy' emerged as the favoured choice of girls shown a photograph of the doll and asked to choose a name. The spelling was changed to Sindy to permit its registration as a tradename. The name's suggestion of 'Sin', together with its evocation of doll-like cuteness and compliance, has led to its use as a pseudonym by many prostitutes.

sing. Singer's Singer *See* VELVET FOG.

Singing Capon *See* IRON BUTTERFLY.

Singing Cowboy Nickname of the US singer and film actor Roy Rogers (1912–), who starred with his faithful horse Trigger in such forgettable movies as *The Man from Music Mountain* (1944) and *Pals of the Golden West* (1953). He once said that when he died he would like to be skinned, made into a saddle, and put on Trigger's back "just as though nothing had happened". In the event, Trigger predeceased him in 1965. Roy Rogers should not be confused with Will Rogers (1879–1935), the film actor and humorist known as the **Cowboy Philosopher**, or Jimmie Rodgers (1897–1933), the yodelling country and western singer.

single A pop-music record, usually played at 45 r.p.m., that has one piece on each side. The **singles chart** has been used as the measure of commercial success in the pop world: in March 1964, the Beatles held down the top five slots in the Billboard singles chart. Sales of traditional vinyl single records have declined drastically, while purchases of cassette singles and albums have correspondingly increased. The **EP** (extended play) was a single-sized record with several songs on it, played at either 33⅓ r.p.m. or 45 r.p.m.

singles bar A bar used as a meeting place for unmarried people seeking partners for social, often sexual, relationships. It evolved in America with the new sexual freedoms of young swingers during the late 1960s. The danger of such casual contacts was the theme of the 1977 film *Looking for Mr. Goodbar*, based on a Judith Rossner novel about a young teacher murdered by a man she picked up in a singles bar.

sinkansen (Jap. new railroad) The Japanese system of high-speed bullet trains. Developed by Japanese National Railways, the passenger service began in 1964 with the opening of the New Tokaido Line, running between Tokyo and Osaka. The 16-car electric trains have a maximum speed of 210 k.p.h. (131 m.p.h) and an average speed of 166 k.p.h. (103 m.p.h.). Experimental research in Japan indicates that speeds of 501 k.p.h (310 m.p.h.) are feasible. *See also* TGV.

Sinn Fein (Irish, ourselves alone). The Irish nationalist movement formed in 1905, which set up the Irish Republic (1919) under De Valera and carried on guerrilla warfare with the British until the treaty of 1922. Disagreements over this settlement disrupted the party, which still aims to bring Ulster into the Republic. It is now the political wing of the Republican movement. *See also* IRA.

siren The loud mechanical whistle sounded at a factory, etc., to indicate that work is to be started or finished for the day. Sirens were employed in the UK in World War II to give air raid warnings – a rising and falling wail for the approach and a continuous note for the 'all clear' to signal the departure of hostile aircraft. *See also* KLAXON.

siren suit A one-piece lined and warm garment on the lines of a boiler suit, sometimes worn in London during the air raids of World War II. It was much favoured by Winston Churchill and so named because of the ease with which it could be slipped on over night clothes at the first wail of the SIREN.

SIS Secret Intelligence Service. The formal name for the British government's intelligence agency better known as MI6.

sissy bar US slang for a protective metal bar behind the seat of a motorcycle or bicycle. Shaped like an inverted U, it supports the back, keeps the rider from falling backwards, and acts as a rollbar.

sit. Are you sitting comfortably? *See under* COMFORTABLY.

sit-down strike A strike in which the workers remain at their workplace but refuse to work themselves or allow others to do so. A form of industrial action that was first used in the 1930s. *See also* SIT-IN.

sit-in A form of protest, usually applied to students occupying college premises, but boycotting lectures, etc., with the object of redressing grievances or dictating policy. Originally applied to a form of industrial action (*see* SIT-DOWN STRIKE), the term was first used in a non-industrial context in 1960, to describe the protest of Blacks in America at lunch counters that refused to serve them. *See also* LOVE-IN; SLEEP-IN.

sitcom *Sit*uation *com*edy. A comedy series on TV or radio, broadcast in a number of separate episodes in each of which the same group of characters take part in a variety of everyday situations.

Sittang River Disaster The virtual destruction of the 17th Indian Division by the demolition of the bridge over the Sittang River during the Japanese invasion of Burma on 23 February 1942. As the Japanese forces advanced towards Rangoon, the British and Commonwealth forces were ordered to fall back to the Sittang. The Japanese, having intercepted the radio transmission ordering the retreat, moved to cut them off at the bridge. Only a part of the Allied troops had crossed the bridge to the west when the Japanese attacked. A decision was taken to destroy the bridge to prevent it falling into Japanese hands, leaving those on the east bank cut off from retreat. Shelled by the Japanese, they tried to escape by crossing the treacherous and fast-flowing river. Hundreds were drowned or swept away and nearly all the division's transport, artillery, equipment, and personal weapons were lost. Many years later, Brigadier Noel Hugh-Jones, the commander who ordered the demolition, was driven to suicide by his own feelings of guilt.

situation A word added to a noun by a speaker or writer who feels that it adds authority when in fact it is usually unnecessary, cumbersome, and ungrammatical. It is a favourite in the sententious pronouncements of bureaucrats and politicians, who wish to disguise with superfluous words their inability to make a straightforward statement. 'Disasters' are called 'disaster situations' and a sports commentator was heard to report that 'England are in a five-yard scrum situation'. It is also used to form euphemistic or pretentious alternatives to straightforward nouns: military communiqués, for example, often refer to 'no-win situations' (*i.e.* defeats). In an unsuccessful attempt to curb this ugly misuse, the satirical magazine PRIVATE EYE has for some years run an 'On-going situations' column giving examples; this column also gives citations of the superfluous use of 'ongoing', 'at this point in time', and similar phrases. In 1989 Prince Charles used a selection of these phrases at the presentation of the Thomas Cranmer Schools Prize, in a parody of Hamlet's 'To be, or not to be' soliloquy:

> Well, frankly, the problem as I see it at this moment in time is whether I should just lie down under all this hassle and let them walk all over me, or whether I should just say OK, I get the message, and do myself in. I mean, let's face it, I'm in a no-win situation . . .

Sitzkrieg (Ger. 'sitting war') The period of comparative quiet and military inactivity at the outset of World War II (September 1939–April 1940). The word is a parody on the more familiar Blitzkrieg (*see* BLITZ). *See also* PHONEY.

SI units Système International de Unités. The international system introduced in 1960 by the General Conference on Weights and Measures for the use of scientists. It is a metric system (*see* METRICATION) based on the former metre-kilogram-second system. Its seven base units are the metre, kilogram, second, ampere, kelvin, candela, and mole; the radian and the steradian are treated as supplementary units. In Europe, including the UK, SI units are used exclusively by scientists and engineers; in America the system is used widely but not exclusively.

six. Les Six A group of French composers formed in Paris in 1918, under the aegis of Jean Cocteau and Erik Satie, in order to further their interests and those of modern music generally. The group lost its cohesion in the 1920s. Its members were Honegger, Milhaud, Poulenc, Durey, Auric, and Tailleferre.

six-bob-a-day tourist Australian slang for a soldier serving in World War I, derived from the daily rate of pay of the Australian private (higher than in other contemporary armies).

Six-Day War The short but bloody conflict between Israel and her neighbouring Arab states in 1967. Regional tension was raised in late 1966 and early 1967 by a series of political moves by Egypt's president, Gamal Abdel Nasser, and other Arab leaders, leading to heightened Israeli fears of concerted action against her. In May 1967 Nasser secured the removal of UN peace-keeping troops from the Egypt–Israel border zone, closed the Gulf of Aqaba to Israeli shipping, and signed a security pact with King Hussein of Jordan. These events prompted Israel to launch a pre-emptive strike against Egypt on 5 June, in which over 400 Egyptian airforce planes were destroyed on the ground by Israeli jets. With air supremacy established, there followed a swift advance by Israeli ground forces into Sinai. By 8 June Egyptian forces were in full retreat, and the following day Israeli tanks reached the Suez Canal, after which a ceasefire was agreed. Meanwhile, Israeli forces repulsed an attack by Jordan, occupying the Old City of Jerusalem and the WEST BANK of the River Jordan; they also defeated Syrian attacks, securing the Golan Heights. A UN-arranged ceasefire came into effect on 11 June. The overwhelming Israeli victory dealt a severe blow to Arab military and political aspirations and enabled Israel to establish tenable borders with her aggressive neighbours.

six-o'clock swill In parts of Australia bars formerly closed at 6 p.m. Drinkers leaving their jobs at 5.30 therefore tended to have a quick drink to beat the clock. This was termed the six-o'clock swill.

The Six The six countries – Belgium, France, Germany, Italy, the Netherlands, and Luxembourg, who were the original participants in three European economic communities. These were: the European Coal and Steel Community, 1951; the European Economic Community or Common Market, set up by the Treaty of Rome, 1957; and the European Atomic Energy Community or Euratom, 1957. *See also* THE SEVEN.

The Six Counties Another name for Northern Ireland, *i.e.* Armagh, Antrim, Down, Derry, Fermanagh, and Tyrone.

16th Amendment An amendment to the US Constitution legitimizing the imposition of a Federal income tax. A law of 1894 introducing income tax had been struck down as unconstitutional by the Supreme Court, but the importance of allowing the national government to impose an income tax to meet extraordinary expenses, such as those arising in time of war, was recognized by the vast majority of the general public and by Congress, who supported the 16th Amendment in 1913, overruling the Supreme Court's decision.

sixty. sixty-four thousand dollar question The last and most difficult question, the crux of the problem; from the stake money awarded in a US radio quiz for answering the final question. The expression is now used in all English-speaking countries.

62 Group An organization of Jewish ex-servicemen formed in 1962 to combat the threat from such fascist groups as the National Socialist Movement, established in the UK in the late 1950s.

ska Popular 1960s Jamaican dance music that was an early form of REGGAE. Dominated by saxophones and brass instruments, it blended calypso, jazz, bebop, and rhythm and blues in a syncopated rhythm.

Skegness is so bracing! The slogan from the advertisement for the North Eastern Railway Company used in 1909 recommending the seaside town of Skegness in Lincolnshire. The advertisement showed a smiling fisherman in a traditional striped jersey, drawn by John Hassall (1868–1948), which is still reproduced on postcards, posters, and mugs.

ski trip US slang for taking cocaine, or for a single dose of cocaine. It is based on the punning use of the words SNOW (cocaine) and TRIP.

skid row An originally US expression for the run-down area of a city where down-and-outs, vagrants, alcoholics, etc., end up. In the timber industry a skid row was a row of logs down which other felled timber was slid or skidded. Tacoma, near Seattle, flourished on its timber production and it was there that plentiful supplies of alcohol and brothels became available for loggers descending the skid row. This is said to be the origin of the expression, which is now used in all English-speaking countries, often in an even more metaphorical sense: 'You'll end up on skid row' is an admonishment that refers to an imminent state of penury and destitution rather than a transfer to an unpleasant area of a city.

skiffle (1) A style of JAZZ of the 1920s. (2) A POP music genre with elements of jazz, blues, and folk-music current in the UK in the late 1950s played by a skiffle group, consisting of guitar, drums, kazoo, washboard, and other improvised instruments.

skin. skin flick Slang name for a film in which nudity and sometimes explicit sex predominate. This late 1960s term refers to films shown in public cinemas, rather than the films not licensed for public showing (*see* BLUE MOVIES).

skin game A swindling trick. Presumably from the sense of *skin* meaning to fleece or strip someone of their money by sharp practice or fraud. John Galsworthy wrote a play (1920) with this title.

skinhead A young person, usually a member of a gang, with hair very closely cropped or shaved, heavy boots, and braces. They appeared first in the late 1960s and soon acquired a reputation for aggressive behaviour. *Compare* MODS AND ROCKERS; PUNK.

skinny-dip US slang for a naked swim. Skinny in this context means 'in one's skin' rather than thin. It was first used in the 1960s.

skive or **skive off** To avoid work, to shirk, or to play truant (of schoolchildren). The derivation of this British slang is obscure, but it may relate to 'skive', meaning to shave off a sliver of leather.

sky. skydiving The sport of parachuting from an aeroplane and free falling for as long as possible before opening the parachute. During free-fall, the participants perform tumbling or flying manoeuvres individually or in groups.

sky-jack *See* HIJACK.

Skylab The first US space station, launched on 14 May 1973. The station's solar panels, used to supply the craft with electricity, were damaged during the launch, threatening the mission's success at the outset. A three-man crew was launched on 25 May and, after docking with Skylab, were able to deploy a sunshield outside the craft, protecting it from overheating. They also freed a damaged solar panel, restoring adequate electricity to the station. After 28 days in space, performing telescopic observations of the Earth and other scientific investigations, the crew returned to Earth. They were followed in turn by two other crews, whose missions aboard Skylab lasted for 59½ days and 84 days, the last ending in February 1974. There were no further missions. On 11 July 1979 the 75-tonne space station burnt up as it re-entered the Earth's atmosphere, scattering debris over the Australian Outback.

skyscraper A very tall building, especially one in New York, Chicago, or some other city. Some of them run to a hundred floors, and more. The tallest in the world is the SEARS TOWER.

slam. slam dancing A style of dancing in which the participants fling themselves about so that they slam into each other, the walls, the stage, etc., to the strains of hard ROCK music.

slammer Slang for a prison, first used in America but now also widely heard in both the UK and Australia. It is derived from the slamming of the cell door.

slap-and-tickle British slang, often used in the form 'a bit of slap-and-tickle', a euphemism for sexual foreplay, first heard in the Edwardian era. It was popular in the 1950s and is still heard.

slasher movie A variety of horror film in which the central element is explicit violence, usually involving knives, claws, or other 'slashing' implements. Such films became a mainstay of the video library in the 1980s. *See also* SPLATTER MOVIE.

sleep. sleeper (1) An undercover agent who remains inactive and undetected within a society or organization until ordered to act by his superiors. The concept of the sleeper was much employed in the 'Red Scare' tactics of Senator Joe McCarthy and his associates in the 1950s (*see* MCCARTHYISM) and has since furnished writers of spy thrillers with much material: a BBC TV spy comedy, *Sleepers*, starring Warren Clarke and Nigel Havers, was broadcast in 1991. *See also* MOLE. (2) A cinematic term for a film that turns out to be more successful on release than had previously been expected. (3) Slang for a tranquillizing drug.

sleep-in A form of action in which a group stays overnight or sleeps in a public place to protest against something or to claim squatters' rights. This 1965 expression, like the hippie LOVE-IN, was formed on the model of SIT-IN.

sleeping policeman A low rounded hump built across a road, especially in a residential area, to deter motorists from speeding. Introduced in the 1970s, they are also known as **speed bumps** in America.

sleep-learning The intake of information while asleep, especially by playing audio tapes or records. The theory is that the subconscious mind can absorb some form of information while a person sleeps. This was first put into commercial practice in the early 1950s to employ the 'wasted hours' of sleep. Foreign languages have been the most popular subjects for sleep-learners. Other confidence-building ploys include tapes that repeat assertions that the sleeper is a talented and resourceful person whose every undertaking will meet with success. The effectiveness of sleep-learning has yet to be established.

sleep strike A type of industrial action in which employees deliberately go without sleep, to the point that they are unable to work efficiently or safely. It was used as a weapon by Greek air-traffic controllers in the summer of 1988.

slide guitar *See* BOTTLENECK.

Slimbridge A bird sanctuary founded by Sir Peter Scott (1903–89), painter and ornithologist, in 1946 along the River Severn. It contains the world's largest collection of waterfowl (such as geese, ducks, and swans) as well as flamingos, exotic ducks, and small birds. There are over 3000 species in all; the sanctuary is funded by the Severn Wild Fowl Trust and public attendance fees.

slimming pill *See* DIET PILL.

Sloane Ranger A young upper class person, usually a young woman, who wears informal but expensive country clothes and who lives in the vicinity of Sloane Square or in Kensington in London. The name was originated by Peter York, author of *Style Wear* (1982). *The Sloane Ranger Handbook* by Ann Barr and Peter York elaborated the theme. The name is a pun on LONE RANGER and Sloane Square.

slopperati British slang of the late 1980s for the wealthy young people who rebel by adopting sloppy dress and behaviour. It is coined from *sloppy* by analogy with *literati*. *See also* GLITTERATI.

Sloppy Joe Slang for a casual loose-fitting sweater popular, particularly among the young, since the 1940s.

> Huge bright orange and brown hand-knitted Sloppy Joes, worn over a leather jacket and trousers.
> *The Independent*, 7 February 1991.

slow. slow motion A technique used in making films and videotapes, which makes the action appear much slower than normal. In films, this is accomplished by either high-speed photography, in which frames are exposed at a higher rate to be projected at normal speed, or by filming at the usual speed and projecting more slowly. The effect can be created for television by videodisc equipment. Slow motion is used for action replay in televised sports and for various purposes in films, such as dream sequences. In America the term is often shortened to **slo-mo**.

Slow, slow, quick, quick, slow The rhythm of the quick-step as spoken by the dance-band leader and ballroom-dance teacher Victor Sylvester (1902–78) on the radio from 1941 and TV during the 1950s.

Slump *See* GREAT DEPRESSION.

slurb US slang from the 1960s for a sprawling extension of a suburb. It is a combination of *slum* and *suburb*.

slush fund Slang from the worlds of politics and big business for an undeclared fund of money used for making corrupt payments and bribes. In US sailor's jargon a slush fund is the money accumulated from selling slush (the waste fat from the galley), *i.e.* it is something gained on the side. This meaning is derived from the Norwegian *slusk*, slops.

smack Slang name used by addicts and others for heroin. It is derived from the Yiddish word *shmek*, sniff or taste, from the German *schmecken*, to taste.

small is beautiful Originally the title of a book (1973) by E. F. Shumacher (1911–77), which has become the slogan for those who are opposed to massive conglomerates in industry and centralization in government. Apparently, Shumacher himself did not coin the phrase, which was the combined inspiration of his publishers Anthony Blond and Desmond Briggs. It has now become part of the language and can be used in any context:

> Small is not beautiful down at Plough Lane.
> Article about crowd attendance at football matches, *The Independent*, 4 March 1991.

smart. smart card A plastic card issued by a bank, credit card company, etc., containing an integrated circuit that memorizes all transactions in which the card is used and the balance in the user's account. In shops with the required computer link it can be used to debit the customer's account directly from the checkout till (*see* EFTPOS). The smart card was developed in France in the 1980s. A **supersmart card** is equipped with its own miniature keyboard and display panel, allowing the user to check the balance of his or her account at any moment without reference to the bank.

smart house A house in which the electrical circuits, telephones and answering machine, TVs and video, thermostats, security system, etc., are connected into a single computerized network. As a result, these functions can be activated by remote control, by the sound of the owner's voice, or by telephone. The scope for disaster is presumably considerable. The concept was developed in America in the later 1980s.

smart weapons Bombs, missiles, or their delivery systems that operate by radar, laser, television, and computer technology. This US military slang began in the early 1970s with the **smart bombs** of the VIETNAM WAR; 'smart weapons' was an expression widely used during the 1991 GULF WAR. Examples of smart weapons are the RAF **Tornado** fighter-bomber, which uses a laser rangefinder to locate targets that appear on a head-up display (HUD) of an onboard computer screen; the **Patriot** missile, which intercepts and destroys incoming missiles (such as the SCUDS in the Gulf War), by using radar guidance and computer decisions on when and where to fire; the F11 7A STEALTH fighter, which operates through a combination of fibre optics and computers; the AH-64A *Apache* helicopter, which has infrared technology to find tanks in the dark; and the Tomahawk CRUISE MISSILE, which receives satellite data to evade enemy fire and has a video camera to help sharpen its aim by comparing its flightpath with maps programmed into its computer.

smear campaign A planned or organized attempt to tarnish someone's character or reputation.

SMERSH (Russ. *Smeart Spionam*, death to spies) The Section for Terror and Diversion of the KGB that specializes in eliminating enemies outside the Soviet Union. The term SMERSH ceased to be used after World War II but an organization with the same function has existed since the Bolshevik Revolution. During the COLD WAR, SMERSH was notorious for disposing of selected targets abroad, by murder, blackmailing, or kidnapping, using a variety of ingenious and lethal gadgets. Trotsky was murdered by a SMERSH agent in Mexico in 1940 under the direct orders of Stalin. SMERSH agents had less success in their encounter with the fictional British agent, James BOND, as described in the novel *From Russia with Love* (1957) by Ian Fleming.

Smiley, George A spymaster of studiedly nondescript manner who appears in several novels by John Le Carré (1931–), notably *The Looking-Glass War* (1965), *Tinker-Tailor-Soldier-Spy* (1974), and *Smiley's People* (1980). He is supposed to have been based on John Bingham, Baron Clanmorris (1908–), an intelligence officer who later wrote such spy thrillers as *Double Agent* (1965); his daughter is the writer Charlotte Bingham (1942–). Le Carré worked alongside Bingham at the Foreign Office in the early 1960s. Other traits are supposed to have been supplied by an academic, the Rev. Vivian Green (1915–), who taught the author at Sherborne School and later at Lincoln College, Oxford, where Green eventually became rector. In the UK, the character of Smiley is closely associated with Sir Alec Guinness's low-key performance in the role on television (1979, 1981).

Smith. Smith Act The Alien Registration Act, drafted by congressman Howard W. Smith of Virginia and passed by Congress on 28 June 1940. The outbreak of World War II having heightened fears of communist and fascist subversion, the Act required that all aliens should be registered and their fingerprints taken. The Act also made it illegal to belong to any organization advocating the overthrow of the US government. The constitutionality of the Act was upheld by the Supreme Court in *Dennis v. United States* (1951).

Smith-Connally Act A US wartime anti-strike Act passed in 1943, which gave the president authority to seize industrial plants threatened by strikes and to act against strikers. It was the first bill passed by congress to curb the power of the unions.

Smith Square A square in the City of Westminster; the location of the headquarters of the main political parties. *See* CENTRAL OFFICE; TRANSPORT HOUSE.

smog Polluted fog. The word, a combination of *smoke* and *fog*, was coined in 1905 by Dr Des Voeux to describe London's fog, which consisted largely of fog mixed with coal soot. The notorious London smog of 1952 caused the deaths of some 4000 people from respiratory diseases; it resulted in the Clean Air Acts (1956, 1968), establishing smokeless zones in urban areas. Much of today's smog results from the chemical reaction between vehicle emissions and sunlight; this so-called **photochemical smog** is a growing problem in such cities as Los Angeles and Tokyo, where cyclists and even pedestrians wear masks to protect them against respiratory ailments.

smoke. put up a smokescreen To take steps to conceal one's basic motives from one's opponents or rivals, or from the public at large. The original meaning was a cloud of smoke used to conceal military operations or movements from the enemy.

smoker's face A condition said to affect persistent heavy smokers, especially women. It takes the form of wrinkling about the mouth and eyes and deeper lines on the cheeks. Alleged sufferers include Princess Margaret and Brigitte Bardot (*see* SEX KITTEN).

smoke-stack industries *See* SUNSET INDUSTRY.

smokey bear or **smokey** US slang for a police officer. The name is derived from the cartoon character of the same name – a bear, dressed in a forest ranger's uniform resembling that of the police, who gave warnings about fire hazards, especially those caused by dropping lighted cigarette ends. In the 1970s the term was taken up by Citizens' Band (CB) radio enthusiasts as the codename for a police officer or a patrol car. Other CB codenames followed: **smokey beaver**, a female police officer, **smokey with camera**, police with radar; **smokey on rubber**, police in a moving patrol car; **smokey with ears**, police with CB radio.

Smokin' Joe The ring name of US heavyweight boxer Joseph Frazier (1944–), from his fiery aggressive style. Originally a slaughterman, he learnt to box at a police gymnasium and became Middle Atlantic Golden Gloves Heavyweight Champion in 1963–64. In 1964 he won the Olympic heavyweight title. The following year he turned professional, and in 1970 beat Jimmy Ellis to claim the vacant world heavyweight title. He defended the title successfully against MUHAMMAD ALI in 1971 but lost it to George Foreman in 1973. He lost two subsequent fights against Muhammad Ali (1974, 1975) and one more against Foreman before retiring.

Snafu *S*ituation *n*ormal, *a*ll *f*ucked *u*p (or *f*ouled *u*p). A coinage devised by British troops in World War II to describe the level of competence of their commanders. A variant form was **MFU**, Military Fuck-Up. *See also* TABU.

snarler Australian slang for a soldier who has been sent back from active service after proving of no worth in war. Shortened form of 'services no longer required'.

snatch squad In the UK since 1970, a police or special army detachment sent into a riot or public disturbance to identify and remove the most aggressive members of the crowd.

sneak preview An unexpected advance showing of a feature film before its general release. This enables a studio to measure the audience's reaction and gather written comments; it can also generate local interest for a 'coming attraction'. *Gone With The Wind*, however, received a top-secret sneak preview in 1939 to keep the press from reviewing it early. The audience in the Warner Theater at Santa Barbara, California, had come to see *Alexander's Ragtime Band*, but were told they were about to see 'the biggest picture of the year'. Once it started, security guards blocked the exits to prevent the audience from leaving or even making telephone calls.

snow (1) Slang for cocaine dating from the early 1900s. It derives from the powdery white form of the drug. (2) Australian derogatory slang for a blonde-haired male. (3) US slang meaning to confuse or complicate in order to prevent criminal detection, or to overwhelm with paperwork, information, etc., in order to confuse or conceal unwelcome information. Hence a **snow job** is the act of overwhelming someone with a torrent of insincere praise in order to manipulate or confuse them.
snowflake's chance in hell A phrase used to illustrate a situation in which something or someone has a very limited chance of survival. It originated in America at the turn of the century but is now in widespread use.

SNP Scottish National Party. It was founded in 1928 as the National Party of Scotland by a group of disaffected Independent Labour Party (ILP) members, journalists, intellectuals, and nationalist activists. The party remained insignificant until the late 1960s, when growing disenchantment with the failure of the established parties to halt the decline in the Scottish economy, and the discovery of NORTH SEA OIL, provoked increasing support among Scottish voters for independence. As a result, in the 1970 general election, the SNP achieved double their vote at any previous election and sent one MP to Westminster. SNP support grew steadily in the early 1970s, gaining 21% of the vote in Scotland and seven MPs in the general election of the February 1974, and 30% of the vote and eleven MPs in the October 1974 election. This threat to the traditional Scottish Labour vote prompted the Labour government to introduce DEVOLUTION legislation (1976) and a referendum. In the referendum of March 1979 less than the required 40% of the Scottish electorate voted in favour of the proposals. Since then support for the SNP has declined significantly; in the election of 1987 it gained only 14% of the vote and three MPs.

snuff movie or **snuff film** Slang for an underground pornographic film that has as its climax the murder of an unsuspecting actress or actor, usually a child. It is rumoured that these films began to appear in California in the late 1960s, although not one example has ever been verified. Faked snuff movies, however, have been made for commercial purposes.

so little done, so much to do *See* FAMOUS LAST WORDS.

soap opera A sentimental serialized domestic drama on radio or television. The name derives from the soap manufacturers who, in America, were the original sponsors of these programmes. It is often shortened to **soap**. Australian soaps, such as *Neighbours*, are very popular in the UK.

sob. sob sister A US journalist who conducts an 'answers to correspondents' column in a women's magazine. In the UK the more usual expression is AGONY AUNT.
sob stuff A film, newspaper article, or other story that makes use of highly sentimental, cheap, or tear-jerking pathos. *See also* SCHMALTZ.

social. Social and Liberal Democratic Party (SLD) A UK political party of the centre, formed in 1988 from a merger of the Liberal Party and the Social Democratic Party (*see* GANG OF FOUR). Known as the **Liberal Democrats**, their first leader was Paddy Ashdown.

social class At the turn of the century there still was a fairly well-defined class structure in the UK: essentially, society consisted of the aristocracy, the gentry, the upper middle class (professional), the lower middle class (trade), and the working class (both industrial and agricultural). Although this scheme is somewhat arbitrary, these broad divisions were accepted and most people knew to which stratum they belonged. As Mrs Alexander wrote:

> The rich man in his castle
> The poor man at his gate
> God makes them, high or lowly,
> And order'd their estate.

During the 20th century there have been significant changes in the British social structure. Traditional class barriers were undermined by the introduction of universal suffrage for men in 1918 and for women in 1928; but perhaps the strongest impetus for a new order resulted from the emergence of the Labour movement, which enabled members of the working classes to have their own members in parliament. In addition, the two world wars had a marked effect on social attitudes. Other factors have included a limited transfer of wealth to the former working class; in the 1980s the Conservative government made a considerable effort to persuade workers to own their own homes and to become shareholders in the privatized former state-owned industries (*see* SID).

The current classification of the British population was produced in 1962 by the Institute of Practitioners in Advertising, which commissioned a survey by Research Survey Ltd. It has since been used for a variety of social and commercial purposes:
A: upper middle class (3%; professional and managerial)
B: middle class (14%; administrative and professional)
C1: lower middle class (22%; supervisory and clerical)
C2: skilled working class (29%; skilled manual workers)
D: working class (18%; semi-skilled and unskilled)
E: lowest level (14%; state pensioners and casual workers)

Another, quite different, classification is based on the type of house or accommodation that people live in (*see* ACORN).

Although the advertisers' classification is almost entirely economic, it shows the influence of deep-rooted attitudes that date back to the last century. A particular example of this is the division of the C category into clerical and manual workers – why should a clerical officer in the Civil Service be regarded as in some way superior to a highly skilled lathe operator in an engineering company? The answer is that, even in the last few years of the 20th century, class distinctions are based not only on earnings, but also on how people see themselves, how they spend their money (*e.g.* private health care and private education), and their expectations for themselves and their children. Accent also remains important in perceptions of class (*see also* RECEIVED PRONUNCIATION):

> An Englishman's way of speaking absolutely classifies him
> The moment he talks he makes some other Englishman despise him.
>
> ALAN LERNER, *My Fair Lady*.

Despite these residual prejudices, most people would say that the UK has become less rigidly class-bound during the 20th century. When the romantic novelist Barbara Cartland was asked in a radio interview whether she thought that class barriers had broken down she replied:

> Of course they have, or I wouldn't be sitting here talking to someone like you.

Social Contract The agreement made in 1974 between the UK government and the trade unions; it was formulated by the prime minister, Harold Wilson. The government agreed to initiate economic and social policies to the advantage of union members; in return the unions promised to hold down demands for wage increases. Inflation continued to grow, however, and Wilson resigned in 1976. The term 'social contract' was coined in 1762 by the French philosopher Jean Jacques Rousseau.

social credit An economic doctrine based on the ideas of an English engineer, C. H. Douglas (1879–1952), which became influential in Canada after 1930. Douglas believed that money, or 'social credit', should be distributed to allow people to purchase the goods and services produced by a capitalist economy and that lack of such credit provoked economic instability. During the GREAT DEPRESSION the doctrine found enough willing adherents for a Social Credit Party to be victorious in Alberta in 1935; it won nine successive elections and remained in power until 1971. A Social Credit government was elected in British Columbia in 1952; the federal party continued to win seats and to be represented in the federal Parliament until 1980. Since then Social Credit has declined as a political force and the Alberta Party has been disbanded.

Social Democratic Party *See* GANG OF FOUR.

social realism Art that depicts the more sordid aspects of urban industrial society in a naturalistic manner, as practised by the ASH-CAN SCHOOL in America in the early 20th century.

socials British army slang for beer, dating from the GULF WAR of 1991.

social security A UK government system, run since 1988 by the Department of Social Security, for paying allowances to the unemployed (unemployment benefit) and the sick or injured (statutory sick pay) as well as state retirement pensions and benefit for pregnant women (statutory maternity benefit). It also includes the non-contributory benefits of income support for those in need as well as child benefits and family credits.

socialism. Socialism in Our Time The title of a policy statement issued by the Independent Labour party in 1927. The main proposal, based on the advice of the Keynesian economist J. A. Hobson, was that a future Labour government should introduce a 'living wage' to ensure adequate demand to maintain levels of economic output and production to provide full employment. Over the next two years constant pressure was placed on the Labour Party leader, Ramsay Macdonald, to adopt this policy but he favoured the more moderate policy statement, *Labour and the Nation*, adopted by the party conference in 1928. *See also* KEYNESIANISM.

socialist realism The approved theory and method of visual and literary composition in the Soviet Union from the 1930s, with the aim of building and glorifying the Socialist achievement. Although the application of the theory produced some interesting results in the early years, *e.g.* in the work of Andrei Goncharov (1903–), the style later degenerated into idealistic representations of the heroic successes of the Soviet economy and society, which are devoid of artistic or literary merit.

sock. Put a sock in it An instruction to be quiet. It comes from the days of the early gramophones, which had no mechanical volume controls; a convenient method of reducing the volume was to stuff a sock in the horn.

Sod's law *See* MURPHY'S LAW.

SOE *See* BAKER STREET IRREGULARS.

soft. soft drug *See* HARD DRUG.

soft focus In films or television, an image that is purposely shot slightly out of focus. The lack of sharpness is thought to create a romantic or dreamy atmosphere, as well as masking the age of some performers. Soft focus can be accomplished by placing a gauze over the lens or using such film-making devices as a diffusion disc. The technique is also sometimes employed by photographers for studio portraits.

soft landing A decelerated landing by an unmanned space probe on the moon or a planet, or by a manned spacecraft on the moon. Both the Soviet Union and America achieved unmanned soft landings on the moon in 1966, before Neil Armstrong set foot there three years later. Soft landings are important if delicate instruments are to survive the impact; soft landings were made by the Soviet and US probes in the 1970s to Mars.

soft porn A 1970s term for pornography that presents sex in a suggestive and titillating way rather than explicitly or violently. Soft porn is on open public sale in America and the UK, whereas the more explicit, deviant, and especially violent material is sold 'under the counter' – this is sometimes known as **hard** (core) **porn.**

soft rock *See* ROCK.

soft sell Selling by unobtrusive methods, usually by means of implication, rather than the challenging and repetitious methods that feature in the HARD SELL.

software Computer programs, as distinct from the equipment on which they are run, which is known as the HARDWARE.

solar power The use of light and other radiation from the Sun to produce usable energy (*see* ALTERNATIVE ENERGY). There are several ways of exploiting solar energy, the commonest being the direct heating of water in specially designed solar panels mounted on the roofs of buildings. Although the rise in temperature is not sufficient to produce water hot enough for washing or heating, it does reduce the cost of heating the water by other means. It is also possible to produce higher temperatures by focusing radiation by curved mirrors, to convert water into steam, which is used to drive an electric generator. At present, such solar generators are uneconomic. Another method of generating electricity from solar radiation is by direct conversion using a solar cell. This has been used in small-scale applications, such as spacecraft, marine warning beacons, pocket calculators, etc. Large-scale commercial exploitation of solar cells for producing electricity is uneconomic because of the high cost of the silicon used in the cells.

solid (1) Slang for trustworthy or true; it is used to describe anything impressive, especially JAZZ or ROCK music. It was first heard in the 1930s and revived in the HIPPIE era of the 1960s. (2) Slang for hashish, sold in solid blocks.

solvent abuse *See* GLUE SNIFFING.

somebody up there likes me A phrase used in the event of a miraculous escape or a lucky break. Both the autobiography of the World Middleweight Boxing champion (1947–48) Rocky Graziano, and the 1956 film made of his life, starring Paul Newman, had this title. Neil Kinnock, the leader of the Labour Party, used the phrase in 1983, after his escape from an overturned car on the M4 motorway.

somewhere in France Military coinage of World War I, used in soldiers' letters home to avoid the possibility of furnishing the enemy with details of Allied troop movements. It was subsequently used more widely, when someone was believed to be hopelessly lost, in hiding, or otherwise untraceable.

Somme, Battle of the The First Battle of the Somme, 1 July–13 November 1916, was one of the bloodiest battles of World War I. After months of preparation, the Allies launched a frontal attack on the German positions along a 21-mile stretch of the WESTERN FRONT, north of the River Somme. In the wake of a thundering seven-day artillery bombardment, 19 Divisions of the British Fourth Army, under General Sir Henry Rawlinson, and the Third Army, under General Edmund Allenby, went 'over the top' into a storm of machine gun fire from the entrenched German positions. The British suffered 60,000 casualties on the first day, including 19,000 killed, the greatest loss on a single day in the history of the British Army. Haig, the British Commander-in-Chief, had envisaged a swift breakthrough in the wake of the artillery barrage, with cavalry operating in open country to mop up the remnants of the shattered German positions. It quickly became apparent, however, that a breakthrough was impossible and the offensive deteriorated into five months of small but costly assaults on the well-defended German positions, which resulted in an advance of little more than eight miles. The Cavalry did get a taste of modern warfare in a British attack on 13 July (the last use of horse soldiers in such a way) but they were slaughtered by the German machine-gunners. On 15 September Haig authorized the use of British tanks for the first time in the war, but due to poor tactics, technical problems, and the unsuitable terrain they made little impact on the fighting. In this ultimately futile battle the British lost 418,000, the French 195,000 and the Germans 650,000 killed or wounded.

> I feel that every step in my plan has been taken with the Divine help.
>
> DOUGLAS HAIG, in his diary on the eve of the Battle of the Somme.

The Second Battle of the Somme, 21 March–5 April 1918, was the first battle of the last major German offensive of the war, by which the German commander, Erich Ludendorff, hoped to achieve a spring victory on the Western Front before the arrival of US troops to bolster the French and British forces. Three German armies struck at the British sector north of the Somme along a 60-mile-wide front between Arras and La Fère, preceded by a rolling artillery bombardment. The aim was to drive a wedge between the British and French but by the beginning of April the initial German breakthrough, which gained a 40-mile-deep salient, was halted by British reserves. The British lost 163,000, the French 77,000 and the Germans as many killed or wounded.

sonar A method of measuring the depth of water below a vessel or detecting underwater objects (submarines, shoals of fish, etc.). It is similar to RADAR, but uses pulses of ultrasonic sound waves rather than electromagnetic radiation. Originally developed in 1920 (*see* ASDIC), the name sonar (from *so*und *na*vigation and *r*anging) came into use later.

son et lumière (Fr. sound and light) Pageantry and dramatic spectacles presented after dark and, most advantageously, in an appropriate natural or historic setting. They are accompanied by, and dependent on, lighting effects, suitable music, and an eloquent narrative, often punctuated by sound effects; there may or may not be a cast of performers involved.

sonic boom The loud explosion created by an aircraft as it passes through the sound barrier (*see* SUPERSONIC).

Sonnenfeldt doctrine A US policy of not encouraging political revolts by citizens in communist E Europe in order to protect regional and world peace. The doctrine was proposed in 1976 by a US official, Helmut Sonnenfeldt. There had been a public outcry following the 1956 HUNGARIAN RISING in which some 7000 Hungarians were killed during Soviet military intervention. Congressional hearings were critical of US foreign policy and blamed Radio Free Europe for inciting Hungarians to rise up against their government. The 1968 Czechoslovakian attempt at liberalization was also crushed by troops from five Warsaw Pact countries; Sonnenfeldt's doctrine was thus a recognition of Soviet power. The policy began to erode under President Jimmy Carter's administration (1977–81).

Sooty A glove-puppet character on children's television in the UK, who first appeared (with the deviser Harry Corbett) in 1952. *The Sooty Show* can claim to be the longest-running show on British television; after Harry Corbett retired in 1975, his son Matthew took over. *See also* AMOS 'N' ANDY; ARCHERS, THE; BLUE PETER; CORONATION STREET; DESERT ISLAND DISCS.

Sopwith Camel The standard British fighter aircraft of World War I, built by the Sopwith Aviation Company Ltd, established in 1912 by Sir Thomas Sopwith (1896–1989). Sopwith produced a number of military aircraft for use by the RFC and RNAS during the conflict. The earliest was the Tabloid (1914), based on the design that won the SCHNEIDER TROPHY in the summer before the outbreak of the war. Subsequent Sopwith models that preceded the Camel included fighters, such as the Pup (1916) and the excellent but short-lived Triplane (1917); others were the Dolphin (1917), used mainly for escort and ground attack; the 1½-Strutter (1916), a fighter-bomber; the Baby (1917), a flying boat used for reconnaissance and as a light bomber; and the Cuckoo (1917), a torpedo-bomber. The Camel (so-called from the hump-shaped fairing over the twin Vickers machine guns in the nose) was a single-seater fighter developed by Herbert Smith in late 1916 and introduced into service in the following year. By April 1918, after the amalgamation of the RNAS and RFC into the RAF, the Camel was operated by 15 squadrons on the Western Front and claimed over 3000 enemy aircraft shot down in the last 18 months of the war. The Camel had a reputation as an extremely manoeuvrable but tricky aircraft to fly, due to the fierce torque produced by the powerful 110 hp Clerget 9-cylinder rotary engine. In all, 5490 Camels were built by Sopwith and eight other companies. Smith designed an even better fighter, the Snipe, to replace the Camel but only three squadrons had them by the Armistice in November 1918; it did, however, become the RAF's standard fighter in the years immediately after the war.

Sorge spy affair Dr Richard Sorge (1895–1944) was a German who spied for the Soviet Union and was executed by the Japanese in 1944. Sorge's brilliant assessment and analysis of military and political intelligence proved invaluable to Stalin. He had joined the German Communist Party in 1918, visited the Soviet Union as a journalist in 1925, and by 1929 was working for the GRU (Soviet military intelligence). He went to Japan in 1933 (after contriving to join the Nazi Party) as a correspondent of the *Frankfurter Zeitung*, and became friendly with Major-General Ott, the military attaché in the German Embassy in Tokyo. He also forged close links with Japanese military and political circles, and was thus able to provide crucial information to the Kremlin on both German and Japanese intentions in the period preceding the outbreak of World War II. He predicted, for example, that the Japanese would enter the war by an offensive in SE Asia, rather than an attack on the Soviet Union in Siberia, which allowed Stalin to divert troops from the east to support the major battles against the Germans in the west. Just before his exposure and arrest he had learned of the Japanese plan to attack PEARL HARBOR, but there is no evidence that he managed to communicate his discovery to Stalin or Roosevelt. In 1964, 20 years after his death, the Russians finally acknowledge Sorge's contribution to the Soviet war effort by making him a Hero of the Soviet Union and placing his image on a postage stamp.

SOS The Morse code signal (3 dots, 3 dashes, 3 dots, ...———...) used since the early years of the century by shipping, etc., in distress to summon immediate aid; hence any urgent appeal for help.

The letters, in Morse a convenient combination, have been popularly held to stand for *save our souls* or *save our ship*.

soul A genre of chiefly Black music characterized by moody sensual vocals and BLUES-based rhythms. Soul became a dominant form of POP music in the 1960s, especially in America, producing such stars as Aretha Franklin (called 'Lady Soul' by her fans), Otis Redding, and Stevie Wonder among many others.

soul food 'Southern-style' food that has come to be considered a distinct gastronomic entity since it first emerged in the diet of the poor Blacks of Southern United States. Its delicacies include chitterlings (pig intestines), corn bread, catfish, and pig's trotters.

sound. sound barrier *See* SUPERSONIC.

sound bite TV and radio jargon for a short burst of information. According to recent research, the amount of time for which a viewer or listener can be expected to concentrate and take in information is steadily decreasing; for example the typical TV advertisement now lasts less than 30 seconds. *See also* THREE-MINUTE CULTURE.

sound pollution *See* NOISE POLLUTION.

sound sculpture A piece of sculpture so constructed that it is able to produce sounds. This art form began during the HIPPIE era of the early 1970s. The sounds come either naturally from moving parts of metal, glass, etc. (as in a mobile) or are created artificially by electric or mechanical means.

souped-up Motor racing slang to describe a highly tuned engine. First heard in America it has been widely used in the UK. It is a shortening of the word 'supercharged'. Since supercharged engines are now called turbo-charged engines, 'souped-up' sounds rather old-fashioned.

south. South Bank The arts complex on the south bank of the River Thames in London, between Waterloo and Westminster bridges. The first modern building on the site was the Royal Festival Hall, built by the then London County Council under the direction of architect Sir Leslie Martin for the FESTIVAL OF BRITAIN in 1951. Other buildings include the National Film Theatre, under the southern arch of Waterloo Station, which was completed in 1958; the Hayward Gallery, Queen Elizabeth Hall, and the Purcell Room (linked together in a single group), which date from 1965–68; and the ROYAL NATIONAL THEATRE, which was opened in 1977. The brutal concrete style of the South Bank complex, especially the Hayward group, has attracted much criticism.

South Bank religion Journalists' label for the religious activities in the diocese of Southwark, on the south bank of the Thames in London, associated with Dr Arthur Mervyn Stockwood (1913–), Dr John Robinson (1919–83), Suffragan Bishop of Woolwich (1959–69), author of *Honest to God* (1963), and some of their diocesan clergy. It was characterized by outspokenness on moral and political issues, often from a socialist angle, and energetic attempts to bring the Church into closer relation to contemporary society. The epithet was often used disparagingly by opponents.

> That is rather the new idea inside the Church. I should definitely say you were a South Banker.
>
> AUBERON WAUGH: *Consider the Lilies*, Ch. 9.

southpaw In US usage, a left-handed baseball player, especially a pitcher; also sometimes applied to any left-handed person. In both US and British usage it describes a boxer who leads with his right hand.

Soviet. All power to the Soviets! Slogan adopted by BOLSHEVIK forces during the OCTOBER REVOLUTION of 1917, one of the most famous slogans of the new Soviet state.

soya *See* TVP.

Soyuz (Russ. union) A series of Soviet-crewed spacecraft, which began with Soyuz 1, launched on 23 April 1967. Each craft consists of an orbital module, in which the three-member crew live and work during the mission; an instrument assembly module, which contains the propulsion mechanism; and the descent vehicle, occupied by the crew during launch and descent and the only section to return to Earth. More advanced versions of this basic design were the Soyuz-T (introduced in 1981) and Soyuz-TM (1986). One of the principal tasks of the Soyuz craft has been carrying cosmonauts to and from orbiting space stations (*see* SALYUT). The good safety record of Soyuz craft was marred in 1971 when the Soyuz 11 reentry module depressurized during descent, killing three cosmonauts who were returning from the Salyut 1 space station.

space. **space age** The present era of exploration beyond the Earth's atmosphere. General agreement marks its beginning as 4 October 1957, when the Soviet Union launched SPUTNIK 1. The Americans followed three months later with their satellite, *Explorer 1*. Since then, there have been more than 3000 successful space launches. The first men went into space in 1961: Soviet cosmonaut Yuri Gagarin completed one orbit on 12 April and US astronaut Alan Shepard made a sub-orbital flight on 5 May. Other successful launchings have been military, weather, and communications satellites as well as SPACE PROBES, moon landings, and SPACE SHUTTLES and stations. The European Space Agency put up its *Spacelab* in 1983. The same year, NASA's PIONEER became the first spacecraft to leave the solar system, passing beyond the orbit of Neptune, a feat repeated in 1989 by VOYAGER 2.

Space travel was predicted by two French novelists, Cyrano de Bergerac in the 17th century and Jules Verne in his novel *From the Earth to the Moon* (1873). In 1901 H. G. Wells envisaged that Englishmen would be the first men in the moon in his novel of that name. The space age first loomed as a possibility in 1926 when physicist Robert Goddard (1882–1945) began his tests on liquid propelled rockets. Although he died before the space age began, the German wartime V2 rocket was largely based on his designs. It was developed into a reliable vehicle in Germany by the German rocket scientist Wernher von Braun (1912–77), who went to America after the war to work on the US space rockets, including the SATURN ROCKETS, which powered so many of the space-age achievements, including the APOLLO MOON PROGRAMME, as a result of which man set foot on the Moon.

spaced-out 1960s slang for the state of being dazed or intoxicated by a drug. It later came to mean disorientated or otherwise affected as a result of the impact of any moving experience, such as seeing a powerful film or listening to emotional music. The expression was originally heard in the drug culture, especially referring to the effects of LSD or other hallucinogens, which are said to make users feel out of touch with reality, as if flying through space. It was soon shortened to **spaced.** **Spacy** was added in the early 1970s to describe someone acting in a dreamy or stupefied way.

Space Invaders Tradename for a video war game in which a player attempts to shoot down hostile spaceships, which are attacking in different patterns across the screen.

space probe Any space vehicle or other device designed to investigate astronomical phenomena, either from Earth orbit or beyond. The first scientific satellites were launched in the late 1950s, starting with the Soviet SPUTNIK programme in 1957 and the US Explorer 1 in 1958. By orbiting above the Earth's atmosphere these early probes were able to monitor more accurately radiation from other parts of space, and so provide a wealth of new information. Since then space probes have travelled to other planets in the solar system, directed by remote control from Earth to transmit data back to Earth. Examples include the VOYAGER probes to Jupiter, the Viking missions to Mars, and the Pioneer spacecraft that passed close to Jupiter in the 1970s. *See also* MARINER.

Spaceship Earth The concept of our planet as a spacecraft that carries its inhabitants as passengers. The implication of the concept is that we are travelling through space alone, with our survival depending on a fragile ecology with limited natural resources and a polluted environment. This GREEN idea was popularized by the book *Operating Manual for Shapeship Earth* (1969), by R. Buckminster Fuller (1895–1983), the US architect who also developed the GEODESIC DOME.

space shuttle A re-usable manned space vehicle, designed to ferry personnel and equipment to and from space. The first space shuttles were introduced in the late 1970s and 1980s by NASA. The shuttle held the promise of reduced cost and increased payload, but NASA encountered formidable development hurdles, for example heatproofing the underside of the vehicle to withstand the high temperatures encountered during re-entry. The first shuttle into space was 102 (Columbia), launched on 12 April 1981, followed by 99 (Challenger), 103 (Discovery), and 104 (Atlantis). The delta-winged orbiter vehicle is launched vertically using its own engines and two rocket boosters; the latter are jettisoned at high altitude along with a large external fuel tank. Following re-entry, the orbiter performs a conventional runway landing. Besides a flight crew of four, up to four other persons can be accommodated. The shuttles have been used to deploy various payloads, perform experiments, and even repair broken satellites. In 1986 the programme came to an abrupt and tragic halt with the CHALLENGER DISASTER; flights did not resume until 1988, with the launch of Discovery on 29 September.

A Soviet space shuttle, Buran ('blizzard'), made its first unmanned space flight on 15 November 1988 but has yet to start regular flights.

space–time *See* RELATIVITY.

space walk *See* GEMINI.

spaghetti. spaghetti junction A junction of motorways, especially the Gravelly Hill interchange on the M6 in N Birmingham, which inspired this British nickname. An aerial view of the tangle of slip roads and flyovers suggests a plate of pasta.

spaghetti western A film about the US West made by an Italian director and Italian crew, often shot in Spain. The lead actors and actresses were usually American, with English dubbed in for the Italian members of the cast. The golden era of spaghetti westerns was the 1960s, the key director being Sergio Leone. Leone's cowboy discovery was Clint Eastwood, who starred in such hits as the Italian-German-Spanish 1964 co-production *A Fistful of Dollars (Per un Pugno di Dollari)* and *The Good, the Bad and the Ugly (Il Buono, il Brutto, il Cattivo)* in 1967. Other 'pasta stars' have included Claudia Cardinale, Lee Van Cleef, Eli Wallach, Charles Bronson, and Rod Steiger. Critics point out that spaghetti westerns converted the American genre into a parody.

Spam Tradename for a canned luncheon meat first marketed in the UK during World War II, when other meat was scarce. It was developed by George A. Hormel & Co. of Minnesota in 1936 and acquired its name as the result of a competition, for which the winner received $100; the name is short for *Sp*iced h*am*.

spammed British army slang for irritated, pissed off. Dating from the GULF WAR of 1991, it is possibly by allusion to the unpopularity of tinned luncheon meat or similar convenient but unappetizing items on the menus of army field kitchens.

Spandau *See* PRISONER OF SPANDAU.

Spanish. Spanish Civil War The bitter conflict (1936–39) in Spain between the Republican government and Nationalist rebels. For many contemporaries the war represented a classic struggle between the forces of good and evil: a democratically elected Popular Front government supported by urban workers, agricultural labourers, and much of the educated middle classes fought against a reactionary coalition comprising the army, Catholic Church, monarchists, industrialists, and wealthy landowners. Support for the insurgents from Hitler and Mussolini, and more limited backing for the Republicans from the Soviet Union and the left-wing volunteers from Europe and America in the INTERNATIONAL BRIGADES, broadened the conflict into a foretaste of the wider struggle to come between democracy and fascism. The military coup in July 1936, led by Nationalist Generals Franco and Mola, left the rebels in control of much of the south and northwest, but Barcelona and Madrid were saved for the government by the workers' militias. There ensued a war of attrition, with the Republican forces gradually succumbing to the superior military and economic resources of the Nationalists. The Republicans were effectively deprived of support from democratic European nations by the establishment of the Non-Intervention Committee by the UK and France, to minimize the danger of international conflict. Germany and Italy were openly contemptuous of the Committee; Hitler sent the fighters and bombers of the Condor Legion, and Mussolini 100,000 Italian troops, to fight on Franco's behalf – both dictators used Spain as a testing ground for their latest weaponry. Soviet aid and the support of the International Brigades was only sufficient to enable Madrid to survive the initial Nationalist assaults in the autumn of 1936. By October 1937 Bilbao and the Basque country in the north had been bombed into submission by the Nationalists (*see also* GUERNICA); they then drove eastwards to the Mediterranean, splitting the republic in two in April 1938. Catalonia was overrun by February 1939; fighting then erupted in Madrid between competing communist factions and on 28 March the city surrendered to Nationalist forces. Up to a million people were killed in the conflict; many were victims of massacres of opponents by both sides in their respective territories.

Spanish flu A pandemic of influenza, thought to have begun in Spain, which killed an estimated 15–20 million people throughout the world during the winter of 1918–19. Spanish flu killed more people than the number of dead from all nations in World War I.

Spanish pratices Industrial slang for restrictive practices, so called because of the punitive treatment meted out by the Spanish Inquisition. Although it was never widely used, the expression was applied to the restrictive practices of the print unions in the UK newspapers industry in Fleet Street, before mechanization and the move to Wapping.

spare-part surgery Surgery to replace diseased or damaged parts of the body with tissues or organs from a donor or with artificial prostheses. The transplantation of most organs only became feasible from the 1940s, when the mechanisms of graft rejection became known through the work of Sir Peter Medawar (1915–87) and other immunologists. The first successful kidney transplants were performed in 1958, while the world's first heart transplant was carried out by the South African surgeon Christiaan Barnard in 1967. Since then the scope of transplantation surgery has broadened to include combined heart-and-lung transplants, liver transplants, and bone marrow transplants. The bulk of spare-part surgery concerns smaller items, such as hip replacement, corneal grafts, and heart-valve replacement, often substituting precision-bioengineered parts for the real thing.

Spartacists An extreme socialist group in Germany that flourished between 1916 and 1919. It was founded by Karl Liebknecht who, with Rosa Luxemburg, led an attempted revolution in January 1919 in the suppression of which they were both killed. The movement was finally crushed by Ebert's government in April 1919. It took its name from the Thracian gladiator Spartacus, who in 73 BC led a slave rebellion against Rome.

speak. speak-easy A place in which alcoholic liquors were sold illegally in America in the years of PROHIBITION (1920–34). *See* BOOTLEGGER; CAPONE.

> The place of the saloon was taken by speak-easies which ranged all the way from dingy back rooms to palatial establishments, but all tolerated by the police.
>
> L. D. BALDWIN: *The Stream of American History*, Vol. II, Ch. xlv.

speaking clock The British Telecom service, officially *Timeline*, that gives callers a continuous recorded statement of the exact time at 10-second intervals. It recently acquired a commercial status:

> At the third stroke, the time sponsored by Accurist will be . . .

speak softly and carry a big stick Advice given by Theodore Roosevelt in 1901 in a speech at the Minnesota State Fair. This adage summarized Roosevelt's attitude to foreign policy, which he put into practice by intervening in Latin American affairs.

spear carrier Someone who assists or serves a more important person, or who has a subordinate role in an organization or activity. This early 1960s term was borrowed from the theatre, where such stage extras as spearholders in an opera chorus stand in the background.

special. Special Air Service *See* SAS.

Special Boat Squadron (SBS) A commando unit of the Royal Marines specializing in amphibious undercover operations. Prior to 1977 it was known as the 'Small Raids Wing' of the Royal Marines Amphibious School; the latter was created after World War II from various wartime units. The Squadron has served in several theatres of war, including Borneo and Oman. In 1972 a joint SBS-SAS team parachuted in mid-Atlantic to board and search the QE2 following a bomb threat; this turned out to be a hoax. The SBS should not be confused with the Special Boat Service, the amphibious arm of the SAS created during World War II.

special effects Cinema techniques, often called *trick photography*, to create sets and scenes that are otherwise realistically impossible, unsafe to film, or beyond a production budget. They are usually added last by a special-effects department. As early as 1906, Edwin Porter, a cameraman in Thomas Edison's studio, made trick movies, such as *Dream of a Rarebit Fiend*, featuring a flying bed. Hollywood's original techniques were simple and are still in use: breakaway bottles and chairs for fight sequences, double exposure to allow ghosts to materialize, clay miniature dinosaurs enlarged to tower over humans, and realistic models of warships that sink in a studio pond. Graphic techniques include dissolves, wipes, split screens, mattes (a mask to blank part of an image to enable another image to be superimposed), and microphotography. For the Atlanta fire sequence in *Gone With The Wind*, the buildings were a matte painting and the actors were filmed in front of a black backdrop. The fire, filmed weeks before, was added by special optical effects. In *Star Wars* (1979) Spielberg acquainted filmgoers with advanced special effects, including computer-linked cameras. British special-effects artists have dominated the profession in recent years.

speed or **whizz** Drug-abusers' slang from the 1960s for the amphetamine drug, methedrine. It was later applied to all amphetamines. The use of the word is a reference to the stimulant effects of these drugs, which appear to speed one up.

spend, spend, spend! The catchphrase of the Littlewood's football pools' winner Vivien Nicholson, who won £152,319 in September 1961 when she was 25 and who just wanted to spend her money after years of scrimping and saving to bring up her children on her husband's meagre wage as a coalminer. She used it as the title of her autobiography in 1977 and it was also adopted as the title of Jack Rosenthal's TV play about her. She claims that it was her reply when asked what plans she had for the money, but the phrase has stuck and is used almost as a celebration of profligate spending – Mrs Nicholson spent all her money, worth over £1 million today, in just four years.

Sperati forgeries Postage stamps forged by the Frenchman Jean de Sperati, which in 1942 became the subject of a widely reported trial. A respected philatelist, Sperati was accused of attempting to evade export duties when sending some extremely rare and valuable stamps to a Lisbon dealer: to Sperati's acute embarrassment the only way to escape severe punishment was to confess that he had forged the stamps himself and that they were thus valueless. It subsequently emerged that he had based his illustrious 30-year career on his forgeries, which had fooled all the most eminent philatelists. He was acquitted but failed to learn his lesson: in 1952 he was gaoled for two years for a further fraud. His forgeries are now much sought after by collectors and ironically change hands for large sums.

sperm bank A place in which a store of frozen human semen is kept for use in artificial insemination (*see* AI), especially by women whose husbands are infertile and who wish to be inseminated by an anonymous donor (*see* AID). The concept of sperm banks, or **semen banks** (the older name), dates back to the 1950s. The semen, which can be stored for years, is mainly provided by medical students for relatively small payments or in some cases by older men who have had their own families and wish to help infertile couples. It has also been known for college rugger clubs to donate sperm as a source of club funds. Several Nobel prizewinners have also donated semen to sperm banks. Sperm banks exist at infertility centres and clinics throughout the world.

spick Derogatory slang for anyone of Hispanic, Latin, or Italian origin, derived from the stock phrase allegedly used by such non-English speakers: 'No spick da Inglish'.

spinach A vegetable that has for generations been regarded as highly nutritious. In the 20th century the myth has been reinforced by the amazing effect it had on the film cartoon character **Popeye**, created by Max Flischer (1889–1972) in about 1933. When hero Popeye, the tough sailorman, needed to defend his girlfriend Olive Oyl against the villainous Bluto, he fortified himself with a tin of spinach. This ploy is said to have been inspired by the marketing department of a tinned-spinach manufacturer. The theory that spinach is a good source of iron is unfortunately untrue. It does contain 4 mg of iron per 100 g of leaf (high compared to 2.5 mg/100 g of haricot beans), but this iron combines with the oxalic acid in spinach to form an insoluble oxalate. While its presence accounts for the bitter taste of spinach, having activated the taste buds it passes through the body unchanged.

spin doctor A public relations expert whose job is to present unpopular decisions, political policies, etc., in the most favourable light (by allusion to the spin given to a ball in various sports in order to disguise its flight).

spine basher Australian slang for someone who is irredeemably lazy, *i.e.* one who spends all his time lying on his back.

Spion Kop A battle during the Boer War, on 24 January 1900; it was the second attempt by British forces, commanded by General Sir Redvers Buller, to break through the Boer lines on the Tugela River to relieve Sir George White besieged in Ladysmith (*see* RELIEF OF LADYSMITH *under* LADY). In the first attempt, at the Battle of Colenso on 15 December 1899, Buller had attempted to turn the left flank of the Free State General Louis Botha, but the British had suffered heavy losses from entrenched Boer sharpshooters. On 19 January, Buller sent Sir Charles Warren and 13,000 men to cross the Tugela with the aim of breaching the Boer lines west of Spion Kop, a summit at the centre of the Boer positions. Buller was to follow with the remainder of the British forces to exploit the planned breakthrough. Warren later decided on a surprise attack on the summit itself, which was successfully captured on the night of 23 January. It proved impossible, however, to reinforce the British positions with artillery, and Botha mounted a counterattack, driving the British from the summit. British casualties were 1500 killed, wounded, or captured, and Buller was forced to recross the Tugela where he had begun. Many of the British dead came from Liverpool; a stand at Liverpool football ground is called 'The Kop' in their honour and Liverpool's supporters are sometimes also called 'The Kop'.

spirit. Spirit of St Louis The aircraft in which Charles A. Lindbergh (1902–74) made the first non-stop solo flight across the Atlantic (20–21 May 1927). Lindbergh was sponsored by a group of businessmen in St Louis, Missouri, and the aircraft was a Ryan NYP single-engine monoplane, modified to Lindbergh's specifications and powered by a Wright Whirlwind 230 hp engine. It would normally have seated five people, but most of the space was taken up by extra fuel tanks giving it a range of 4100 miles (6600 km). The plane was returned to America by ship after the historic flight, and Lindbergh eventually donated it to the Smithsonian Institution in Washington, DC. *See also* LINDBERGH BABY MURDER.

The spirit of the troops is excellent A newspaper cliché dating from World War I, when it was regularly used in morale-boosting accounts of the latest fighting, regardless of how well things were really going. The public rapidly learnt to regard it as an empty cipher and it subsequently acquired a wider ironic usage.

Spitfire British fighter aircraft of World War II, one of the most successful all-round aircraft designs, which remained in operational service with the RAF into the 1950s. The design was based on the Supermarine seaplane, created by Reginald J. Mitchell (1895–1937) during the 1920s, which won the SCHNEIDER TROPHY outright in September 1931. The Spitfire's outstanding aerodynamics and powerful Rolls Royce Merlin engine (designed by a team led by A. G. Elliott) were based on Mitchell's experience in perfecting the Supermarine. The first model of the Spitfire, the MK1, went into production in 1937; by the time of the BATTLE OF BRITAIN in August 1940, Fighter Command was equipped with 19 Spitfire Squadrons, which played a crucial role in the defeat of the Luftwaffe (*see also* HURRICANE). The design was constantly modified and upgraded throughout the war to meet the challenge of different combat roles and to match improvements in German fighter designs. The MKXIV, for example, which was produced in 1944, was powered by the exceptional 2050 hp Rolls Royce Griffon engine; it could challenge the latest German jet fighters and was also used to intercept V-1 rockets. The Spitfire's last operational flight took place on 1 April 1954, but the aircraft remains one of the most cherished in the history of aviation.

splashdown The programmed landing of a space capsule on the sea. The word, also used as a verb, was first applied by NASA to the 1961 Atlantic splashdown of the suborbital flight by astronaut Alan Shepherd, America's first man into space. Many later landings occurred in the Pacific Ocean, always accompanied by NASA's live commentary of 'Splashdown!' or 'We have splashdown!'

splatter movie Journalistic slang for a gratuitously violent film in which an unnecessary number of people are killed for the sake of the technicolour blood and gore that film makers believe their audiences wish to see. *See also* SLASHER MOVIE; SNUFF MOVIE.

splitting the atom *See* CAVENDISH LABORATORY; NUCLEAR FISSION.

Spock baby One of the postwar generation of children brought up by parents influenced by the permissive approach to childcare espoused in *The Common-sense Book of Baby and Child Care* by the US pediatrician, Dr Benjamin Spock (1903–). Spock's best-selling book, published inexpensively in paperback in 1946, has sold over 30 million copies and was important for two main reasons: it was the first to counsel a flexible and gentle approach to childcare, as opposed to the prevailing hardline orthodoxy, and it was also the first popular medical textbook written by experts for the general public. During his career Spock was active in a variety of liberal causes, including nuclear disarmament and opposition to the war in Vietnam; his permissive theories of parenthood were blamed by some US conservatives for the 1960s student rebellion.

Spode, Roderick In P. G. Wodehouse's *The Code of the Woosters* (1938), a would-be dictator who leads an ineffectual band of fascists called the Black Shorts (so-named because every colour of shirt had already been claimed). A tall mustachioed bounder with "the sort of eye that can open an oyster at forty paces", he is clearly modelled to some extent on Sir Oswald Mosley (1896–1980; *see* MOSLEYITES), the founder of the BLACKSHIRTS. Spode is memorably denounced by Bertie Wooster as "a frightful ass . . . swanking about in footer bags . . . a perfect perisher". Wodehouse himself was heavily criticized during World War II after he broadcast from Berlin to America. After the war he settled in America, becoming an American citizen in 1955.

spook (1) US slang for a Black person. Perhaps because a Black person is difficult to see in a dark place and, like a ghost, only appears to have eyes. (2) US slang for a spy. This may be a reference to the fact that spies are supposed to be as invisible as ghosts.

spot. spot check A surprise check on the spot without notice being given; a random check to serve as a basis for conclusions on a wider basis.

spot dance A dance in which the couple focused in the spotlight when the music stops win a prize; or, when there is no spotlight, when the couple are on a particular spot on the floor not previously revealed to the dancers.

sprechgesang (Ger. speaking song) Vocal expression that blends singing and talking. It is heard in both opera music and religious chants. It is spoken in a monotone or preserving the natural inflexions of speech, its metre, and its rhythm. Schoenberg used it in various works, including *Pierrot Lunaire* (1912), and Walton made very effective use of it in *Façade* (1926).

Springer empire West German newspaper and magazine empire built up by the right-wing press magnate Axel Springer (1912–85) after 1945. His first publication was *Hör Zu!* (1946), a radio programme guide, and in 1952 he launched the tabloid *Bild Zeitung*, Europe's best-selling daily newspaper; in the following year he acquired *Die Welt*, an upmarket counterbalance to the *Bild*'s raucous populism. Springer's unbridled anti-communism and campaigns for law and order made him a target of the left during the 1960s; as a result his property was damaged in a series of attacks by terrorists of the RED ARMY FACTION.

Spruce Goose *See* FLYING BOAT.

Sputnik (Russ. travelling-companion) A Soviet man-made SATELLITE. Sputnik I, launched 4 October 1957, was the first satellite to be projected successfully into orbit round the Earth. Weighing 84.6 kg (186 lb), it orbited the Earth in 96 minutes and made various scientific measurements; it burnt up as it re-entered the Earth's atmosphere on 4 January 1958.

spy. spy satellite *See* EYE IN THE SKY.

The Spy Who Came in from the Cold *See* COME IN FROM THE COLD.

square Denoting a person who is old-fashioned in his views, dress, or habits, particularly one whose tastes in music are particularly conservative. There are several suggestions for the origin of these usages, which date from the 1930s and 1940s, none of which is particularly convincing; the most likely alludes to the patrons of the traditional square dance as opposed to the devotees of rock 'n' roll, jiving and twisting, etc.

Square Deal The ambitious programme of social and economic reform introduced (1901–09) by Theodore Roosevelt on behalf of the poorer sections of US society. The programme dictated extensive changes in working conditions, food production, and the control of monopolies; it is remembered as one of the most influential and beneficent political projects of the century.

> A man who is good enough to shed his blood for the country is good enough to be given a square deal afterwards. More than that no man is entitled to, and less than that no man shall have.
>
> THEODORE ROOSEVELT, speech at the Lincoln Monument, Springfield, Illinois, 4 June 1903.

squarehead Slang for a German. Germanic people supposedly have square-shaped heads as opposed to the rounder heads of the Anglo-Saxons. The haircut of German soldiers during World War II cut square across the back of the head and the square shape of the German helmet tended to emphasize this.

Squiffites Supporters of the former Liberal prime minister, Herbert H. Asquith (1852–1928), who followed him into the opposition to the new government after he was overthrown by Lloyd George in December 1916. Asquith had been head of a coalition government of Liberals and Conservatives since May 1915, but stalemate on the WESTERN FRONT progressively weakened his political standing, and on 5 December he resigned. Asquith refused to serve under Lloyd George, as did many of those Liberals who followed him onto the opposition benches, although Asquith refrained from attacks on government policy for the remainder of the war in the interests of national unity. The fragmentation of the Liberals into Squiffites, followers of Lloyd George, and Independents marked the effective end of the party as a force in British politics.

SR Southern Railway. British railway network in the S of England, formed after World War I. It disappeared during the nationalization of the railways in 1947, when British Railways (later BR) was formed. *See also* GWR; LMS; LNER.

SRO *See* SELF-REGULATORY ORGANIZATION.

SS *Schutzstaffel* (Ger. Protective Echelon), a corps of the Nazi Party that originated as part of Hitler's bodyguard in 1923 with the predominant SA (*see* BROWNSHIRTS). In 1929, Heinrich Himmler took on the SS, defining its duties as "to find out, to fight and to destroy all open and secret enemies of the FÜHRER, the National Socialist Movement, and our racial resurrection". During World War II SS divisions fought with fanatical zeal. The armed unit of the SS (Waffen-SS) included the notorious *Totenkopfverbände* (Death's-Head Battalions), responsible for administering the CONCENTRATION CAMPS.

stag (1) Denoting a social or other event, such as a prenuptial drinking session (stag party), to which only men are invited. (2) British army slang for sentry duty, dating from the GULF WAR of 1991 (possibly an allusion to the stag reindeer's alertness to movement).

stagflation An economic situation in which inflation is combined with a stagnation in output and employment. This combination of inflation and recession occurred in the 1970s.

stagnation theory The economic theory that depressions, and the TRADE CYCLE in general, arise in industrial societies because as people become more affluent in the boom periods, their savings increase but the opportunities from investing them decline, which leads to recession and eventually slump. The theory was proposed in the 1940s but was not widely accepted. The economists who favoured this theory advocated that investment in the boom period should be encouraged in such socially desirable ventures as slum clearance and improvements to the infrastructure.

Stakhanovite A follower of the system in the Soviet Union that encourages increased productivity of workers by giving increased rewards to the most efficient. It is named after Alexei Stakhanov (1906–77), a Donetz coal miner who substantially increased his daily output by rationalization. In 1935 Stalin held a conference of Stakhanovites in which he extolled the working man.

stalag German prisoner-of-war camp for NCOs and men. It is a shortened form of the German *Stammlager*, literally 'base camp'.

Stalin. Stalingrad Formerly Tsaritsyn, on the Volga, renamed to commemorate its defence by Stalin, in 1917, against the White Russians. Stalin died in 1953 and in 1962 the name was changed to Volgograd. In 1943 it was the scene of the bloody but decisive defeat of the German 6th Army. **Stalinism** The ruthlessly personalized version of Marxist-LENINISM forced on the Soviet Union for 30 years by Joseph Stalin (*see* MAN OF STEEL). His dictatorial methods included a personality cult; harsh suppression of dissidents and rivals in purges (*see* YEZHOVSHCHINA); and general political terror centred on a system of GULAG forced-labour camps. *See also* FIVE-YEAR PLANS.

Stanislavsky system *See* METHOD, THE.

star A top entertainer or performer in films, television, theatre, music, sports, etc. Although stars are talented people they rely heavily on clever promotion, as seen by the importance of Col. Tom Parker to Elvis Presley (*see* ELVIS THE PELVIS) and of Brian Epstein to the BEATLES. Sports stars were formerly known only through their performance but it is now common for them to employ such organizations as the International Management Group, which handles most star golfers, including the British Nick Faldo. The star system in films was created in the 1920s by Hollywood, especially by the director D. W. Griffith (1874–1948), whose stars included Lillian Gish, Mary Pickford, Douglas Fairbanks, and Charlie Chaplin (*see* TRAMP, THE). Before Griffiths, Hollywood film companies tended not to identify actors and actresses on screen in order to hold down their salaries. However, once the star system had been created it was instantly successful – child star Jackie Coogan was received by the pope and monarchs during a European trip, while such stars as Greta Garbo (*see under* ALONE) and Rudolph VALENTINO became 'legends in their own lifetimes'. In the 1930s, the studio system created a production line for new stars. Glamorous images were created by studio publicity departments, which even invented new names and new biographies for likely candidates. In the UK the first international star-maker was Alexander Korda (1893–1956), who made a hobby of finding star qualities among secondary performers; his successes included Merle Oberon, who also became his wife. With the collapse of the studio system, stars were able to escape from the kind of fixed images that kept Edward G. Robinson a gangster and Marilyn MONROE a sex queen. Hollywood stars, such as Meryl Streep, Faye Dunaway, and Dustin Hoffman, are now much more versatile although some, such as Sylvester Stallone, continue in set roles. *See also* STARLET; SUPERSTAR.

starlet A young film actress who seems to have star quality and is promoted and publicized by a studio in the hope that they can make her into a STAR.

star-studded Denoting an event that features many famous (and often less well-known) stars and entertainers. Films and plays advertise star-studded casts, and such events as the Command Performance and the Academy Awards are truly star-studded events.

Star Wars US nickname for the Strategic Defense Initiative (SDI), a system designed in the 1980s and backed by President Reagan for defending America, using laser-beam weapons orbiting in space programmed to shoot down the enemy's guided missiles. It was nicknamed *Star Wars* after the cult science-fiction film of that name, reflecting the sci-fi aspect of the project.

starkers *See* HONKERS.

start. I've started so I'll finish The catchphrase used by the chairman, Magnus Magnusson, of the BBC TV quiz programme *Mastermind* when one of his questions is interrupted by the buzzer, indicating that the time for the round is up. He then repeats the question, enabling the contestant to answer before the round is concluded. *Mastermind* was first broadcast in the 1970s and the expression has been widely used in a variety of contexts since then.

stash To hide something away, especially stolen goods, money, or drugs. The word was coined around the turn of the century, as *stache*, by combining 'stow' and 'store' with 'cache'.

Stasi Popular name for the former State Security Police (*Staatssicherheitsdienst*) in East Germany. Responsible for espionage, counterespionage, and the suppression of political dissent, they were notorious for their minute surveillance of the lives of East German citizens. They were disbanded in December 1989, a few weeks after the opening of the BERLIN WALL. Several prominent Germans were later accused of having been Stasi informers.

state-of-the-art A slang expression used to describe a top of the range, advanced, and up-to-date model. For example, 'his stereo is real state-of-the-art stuff with all those special refinements'.

Statue of Liberty sale The preposterous and very nearly successful 'sale' of the Statue of Liberty by the Scottish conman Arthur Furguson to an Australian tourist in 1925. The attempted sale of America's most famous landmark, beginning with a $100,000 deposit, was the culmination of an extraordinary career in such hoaxes. It began in London with Furguson's successful exchange of Nelson's Column (complete with Landseer's lions and fountains) to a wealthy American, for just £6000. Inspired by this success, Furguson went on charge £1000 for Big Ben, £2000 for Buckingham Palace, and, following his move to America, $100,000 for a year's lease of the White House. The Statue of Liberty sale, however, proved Furguson's downfall and he served a five-year sentence following his arrest and trial. In 1930 he was freed and, undaunted, began a whole new career based on similar hoaxes, successfully maintaining a luxurious lifestyle until his death in 1938.

statutory. statutory maternity pay *See* SOCIAL SECURITY.

statutory sick pay *See* SOCIAL SECURITY.

Stauffenberg Plot or **July Plot** or **Officers' Plot** The unsuccessful attempt to assassinate Hitler with a bomb on 20 July 1944. A briefcase containing the bomb was left by Count von Stauffenberg under a table at the Führer's headquarters in Rastenberg, E Prussia. A plan, known as 'Operation Valkyrie', had also been devised by the conspirators to seize key government installations in Berlin after Hitler's death. Hitler, however, escaped injury; not unexpectedly he immediately took savage revenge. Stauffenberg and three others were immediately shot, Rommel (*see* DESERT FOX), was forced to take poison and 7000 other suspects were arrested (and in many cases tortured), tried, and executed.

Stavisky affair The financial scandal surrounding the affairs of Serge Alexandre Stavisky (*c.* 1886–1934), a Russian-born French swindler, which came to a head in 1933–34 and precipitated a major crisis for the Fourth Republic. Stavisky, an adept at establishing fraudulent businesses, led an extravagant lifestyle, mixing with influential society in Cannes and Deauville, until he was exposed in a 500 million franc bond swindle involving the municipal pawnshop in Bayonne in December 1933. He fled to the luxury resort of Chamonix, where he was found dead in January 1934, supposedly by his own hand, although many suspected that he had been killed by the police to protect his influential patrons in the government, judiciary, and Sûreté Génerale itself. In February 1934 widespread suspicion of government corruption prompted violent anti-government and anti-parliamentary demonstrations in Paris led by the right-wing leagues, the Action Française and Croix Feu, which succeeded in bringing down the government and threatened the future of parliamentary democracy itself.

STD Subscriber Trunk Dialling. The telephone dialling system, now in use in most countries, that enables callers to dial any number at home or in any country overseas that uses the system, without reference to the operator.

steady-state theory A theory of cosmology first proposed in 1948 by the Austrian-born US astronomer Thomas Gold (1920–) and the Austrian-born British mathematician Hermann Bondi (1919–). The British astronomer Fred Hoyle (1915–) was a particular supporter of the theory. It depended on what is known as the 'perfect cosmological principle' – the idea that the universe looks the same from whatever point it is observed and moreover, at whatever time. According to the steady-state theory the universe had no beginning, will never end, and contains a constant density of matter. To account for the fact that the universe appears to be expanding (*see* REDSHIFT), Gold and Bondi made the controversial suggestion that matter was constantly being created from free space. In the 1960s it became apparent that there is a background of microwave radiation in the universe. This is best understood as a remnant of the BIG BANG. The big-bang theory of the origin of the universe is therefore the one currently accepted, while the steady-state theory has been discredited.

stealth In British army slang from the GULF WAR (1991), to kill someone. It was derived from the name of the US Stealth bomber (*see* SMART WEAPONS), developed in the 1980s and reputed to be virtually invisible to enemy radar on account of its innovative streamlined silhouette and HIGH TECH instruments. At a cost of £350 million each, its manufacture was under threat from the US government but it subsequently proved its worth in air raids on Iraqi strategic targets.

steaming British slang from the jargon of Black urban gangs of the late 1980s for a gang mugging. It is derived from the swift action of a group of muggers who 'steam in' on their prey.

Stellenbosch A town in South Africa, 40 miles (64 km) east of Cape Town, which was the location of the main British military base during the Boer War (1899–1901). To be 'Stellenbosched' became a popular term to describe the fate of those unfortunate senior officers who were relieved of their commands for incompetence in the field and sent back to the Cape in disgrace.

Stem van Suid-Afrika, Die (Afrikaans, *The Voice of South Africa*) The National Anthem of South Africa, which was introduced in 1936 and replaced the British anthem, *God Save The Queen*, in 1957.

Sten gun One of the most widely used British sub-machine guns of World War II. The name was coined with the introduction of the Mark I version in 1941, and derives from the initials of R. V. *S*hep-herd, in charge of small arms procurement in the Army, the gun's designer, J. J. *T*urpin, and *En*field, the site of the Royal Small Arms Factory. Designed for simplicity and ease of production, the early versions had a tubular skeleton stock, while the later Mark V had a wooden stock. More than two million Mark II Stens were produced; several underground resistance groups, as well as the Germans, produced their own copies despite the fact that the gun was dangerously difficult to aim accurately.

sterling area An association (also called the sterling bloc, or scheduled territories) that came into existence after the UK left the gold standard in 1931, when a large number of countries agreed to stabilize their currencies in terms of the pound and to hold sterling balances as part of their international reserves. These included the British Commonwealth nations (except Canada), Eire, Jordan, Iraq, Libya, Burma, and Iceland. The sterling area declined in importance after 1945, when the progressive devaluation of sterling made it less attractive as a reserve currency. Few countries, except some current and former members of the British Commonwealth, now hold sterling as a reserve, most preferring to maintain reserves in more stable currencies, such as German Deutschmarks or the Japanese yen.

Stern Gang A small anti-British Jewish terrorist organization, founded in Palestine in 1940, which concentrated on assassinating British personnel. It was named after an early leader, Abraham Stern (1907–42), who was killed in a gun fight with British police. On 6 November 1944 the gang murdered Lord Moyne, the Minister of State for Middle East Affairs, in Cairo, and from 1945 collaborated with two other terrorist groups, the IRGUN ZVAI LEUMI and HAGANAH, in a guerrilla campaign to force the establishment of a Jewish state in Palestine. Although denounced by the official Zionist leadership, the activities of the Stern Gang and other terrorist groups were effective in helping to secure the British withdrawal from Palestine, which eventually led to the foundation of Israel in May 1948. One of the leading members of the Stern Gang, Itzhak Shamir, became prime minister of Israel (1983–84; 1986–).

Stiffkey, Rector of The Rev. Harold Davidson, Rector of Stiffkey, a well-known figure of the 1930s in the UK. After a long and colourful trial at the Norwich Consistory Court in 1932, which exposed his amorous adventures to the delight of the press and public, he was unfrocked for immoral conduct. In order to make a living he then paraded his notoriety, appearing in cinemas and local fairs, even exhibiting himself in a barrel on Blackpool beach. He eventually joined a travelling menagerie and was killed by a lion in 1937.

stills *See* BUBS.

sting A robbery or con trick, especially one that is carefully planned. The use of the word in this context goes back to the turn of the century and derives from being 'stung for money', *i.e.* having to pay out a sum of money. By the 1930s it was in use among criminals and the police. The word was popularized in the 1970s by the film *The Sting* (1973) featuring Robert Redford and Paul Newman in an elaborate con trick on a gangster. The music of Scott Joplin (*see* RAGTIME) added considerable charisma to the 1920s Chicago setting.

> Top boxing manager Ambrose Mendy plotted to defraud companies of more than £650,000 in a complex bank sting . . .
>
> *The Sun*, 9 April 1991.

stir Slang for prison. It is thought to be derived from the Romany *stariben*, prison.

stir crazy Slang for being mentally disturbed as a result of being in prison (*see* STIR). A 1980 comedy film with this title made extensive use of all Hollywood prison clichés.

Stirling bomber The Short Brothers Ltd S 29 Stirling, a four-engined heavy bomber, which entered service with the RAF in August in 1940; it was at that time the RAF's only four-engined bomber. The Stirling was built to a 1936 specification, which limited the wing span to 100 feet (31 m) to allow it to pass through the standard width of hangar door. This drastically compromised its performance, preventing it from climbing to more than 12,000 feet (365 m) and making it vulnerable to anti-aircraft fire from the ground as well as to bombs from above dropped by the superior Lancasters and Halifaxes, which joined it in mass bombing raids. The Stirling was also sluggish, had poor manoeuvrability, and was unable to carry bombs heavier than 4000 lb. For these reasons, by 1943, it was used mainly as a transport and carrier of ECM (Electronic Counter Measure) and spoofing devices.

stockbroker belt The ring of leafy outer suburbs around London, from which many City businessmen commute daily to their offices.

Stockholm. Stockholm Appeal A petition to ban the atom bomb, allegedly signed by 500 million people in over 70 countries, which was launched at a meeting of the Stockholm World Peace Conference in March 1950.

Stockholm syndrome A psychological condition in which hostages identify with their captors' political or personal causes, even to the point of justifying their crimes and taking part in them. The syndrome's name comes from a 1973 bank robbery in Stockholm, Sweden, in which several hostages gave support to the robbers. *See also* PATTIE.

stock shot A film sequence that can be reused in different productions to save the time and expense of reshooting it. They are stored in the libraries of film studios and television stations or can be obtained from commercial film libraries. Stock footage is used for establishing shots, to introduce the locale (Southfork Ranch in the soap opera *Dallas*) or to add atmosphere (wildlife scenes in Tarzan films). Other topics may be western landscapes, police-car chases, aeroplane landings, etc. Stock shots were used even during the early years of cinema: Edwin Porter (*see* SPECIAL EFFECTS) made a 10-minute film in 1903, *The Life of an American Fireman*, in which he inserted stock film of fires and firemen taken from Thomas Edison's files.

Stokes mortar A type of light trench mortar, used in both world wars, which was invented by the civil engineer Sir Frederick Stokes (1860–1927). The weapon was originally rejected by the War Office in 1914, but Lloyd George persuaded an Indian maharajah to finance its manufacture enabling it to be introduced in the following year. The weapon consisted of a smooth-bored steel tube, 3–4 in (7–10 cm) in diameter. The projectile contained its own propellant charge, which was ignited automatically by dropping it down the tube onto a striker. The original design went through various improvements and was used for lobbing high explosives, smoke pellets, incendiary bombs, or gas into the enemy lines.

stomp A JAZZ dance that first became popular in the 1900s, characterized by much stamping of the feet and frenetic movement; the word 'stomp' later came to be used of any lively dance or session of dancing.

stone. stone ginger A certainty, from the New Zealand racehorse Stone Ginger, which won every race (*c.* 1910) for which it entered.

stoned Under the influence of drink, drugs, or some other stimulus. First heard among JAZZ musicians in the 1940s; in the 1960s it was applied especially to the effects of cannabis.

Stooges, The Three A US comedy team that became widely popular in a prolific series of films from the 1930s to the 1950s. The key to their success was their skill at slapstick, but their films, with a minimum of plot or character development, had a comparatively short life. The original trio, Larry Fine and Moe and Jerry Howard, transferred to HOLLYWOOD from vaudeville; there were various changes in personnel before the team finally broke up.

stop. stop-go A pejorative name for government economic policies that seek to reflate the economy when there is high unemployment and then employ restraining measures when there are signs that it is overheating. The use of the term implies that the government, incapable of long-term planning to control the economy, can only respond by short-term knee-jerk reflexes.

stop me and buy one Advertising slogan used by the manufacturers of Wall's ice-cream; first seen around 1923, displayed on placards attached to the tricycles ridden by the company's salesman.

stop yer tickling, Jock! Catchphrase used as a lover's admonishment in the first half of the 20th century, from the title of one of Sir Harry Lauder's most famous comic songs (1904).

Stopes clinic The UK's first BIRTH CONTROL clinic, opened by the pioneer birth control specialist, Marie Stopes (1880–1958), in 1922. Known as the Mothers' Clinic, it was originally housed at 61 Marlborough Road, Holloway, London, and catered mainly for married women from the capital's poorer districts. Initially the project was financed by Stopes and her husband, the aircraft manufacturer J. V. Roe (1878–1949). The clinic offered free advice and contraceptives; the most common devices were Stopes' own version of the cap and a sponge impregnated with olive oil, used as a suppository. The clinic moved to its present site, in Whitfield Street, in 1925. It is now a registered charity, with other clinics in Leeds and Manchester, and three nursing homes in London. The UK-based Marie Stopes International supports 42 birth control projects in 21 countries, mainly in the developing world.

storm. Stormin' Norman Nickname of US General H Norman Schwarzkopf (1935–), who was commander-in-chief of Operation DESERT STORM in the GULF WAR of 1991. His father, the police chief Herbert Norman Schwarzkopf (criticized in 1932 for his handling of the LINDBERGH BABY MURDER), gave him only the letter H as a first name because he disliked the family name Herbert. H Norman, credited with an IQ of 170, acquired his nickname shortly after entering the army for his ebullient manner and unpredictable temper (hence his other nickname, **The Bear**). He won two PURPLE HEARTS and three Silver Stars (for his courage in battle) during the VIETNAM WAR. Conversely, he also became known for his love of ballet, opera, and amateur conjuring. He was highly praised for achieving the success of Desert Storm at a minimal cost in casualties to the allied forces. In 1991 he was granted an honorary knighthood by Elizabeth II. He later commented:

> The single greatest honour I have received was that the British forces were put under my command.

stormtroopers *See* BROWNSHIRTS.

Stormont The seat of the Northern Ireland parliament and government, set amidst 300 acres of parkland some 6 miles east of Belfast. Centrepiece of the site is Parliament House, designed in the 'Official Classical' style by Sir Arnold Thornley and opened in 1932 by King George V. Nearby stands Stormont Castle, formerly the official residence of Viscount Craigavon, Northern Ireland's first prime minister; it now houses government offices. The other main administrative building is Dundonald House, designed by Gibson and Taylor and opened in 1963. From 1921 to 1972 the province had its own parliament, during which time Stormont came to symbolize Protestant domination in public affairs. The Northern Ireland government resigned in 1972 in protest at the British government's assumption of responsibility for law and order, since when the province has been governed by direct rule from Westminster. *See also* POWER SHARING.

Storyville The redlight area of New Orleans, in which JAZZ was born. Black musicians congregated in the area, where they could find employment playing for the customers of the many brothels in the neighbourhood.

strafe (Ger. *strafen*, to punish) A word borrowed in contempt from the Germans during World War I, one of their favourite slogans being *Gott strafe England!* It was applied to any sharp and sudden bombardment, and later used in World War II for the machine-gunning of troops or civilians by low-flying aircraft.

Straffen murders The crimes of a British child-murderer, John Thomas Straffen (1930–), a retarded 22-year-old who spent his early childhood in a school for the mentally deficient. In 1947, at the age of 17, he was institutionalized after an assault on a 13-year old girl. On his release at the age of 21 he moved to Bath, where he strangled two young girls, in order – as he said – to annoy the police (whom he hated). At his trial at Taunton assizes, in October 1951, he was declared unfit to plead and sent to Broadmoor asylum. Six months later he escaped, and during his brief period of freedom claimed the life of another young victim, Linda Bowyer. He was tried again in July 1952, this time at Winchester, and found guilty, but his death sentence was commuted to life imprisonment.

straight (1) Slang for honest, from the jargon of criminals who are known for 'bending the rules'. (2) Slang for heterosexual. (3) Drug-users' slang to describe a person who does not take drugs. (4) Slang from the jargon of cannabis smokers for an ordinary cigarette that does not contain cannabis.

Straker, Henry The chauffeur of John Tanner in the play *Man and Superman* (1903) by George Bernard Shaw (1856–1950). Straker is described as the 'New Man' of the polytechnic revolution. Skilled, confident, and a scientific socialist, he is superior in every respect to his master, whose gentlemanly class, Shaw believed, was doomed to extinction by the new economic and political forces embodied by Straker.

Strangelove A fanatic or insane militarist who advocates large-scale pre-emptive nuclear strikes. The name comes from Stanley Kubrick's 1963 black-comedy film, *Dr Strangelove*, in which the title role and two other parts were played by the British comedian Peter Sellers. An insane USAF general, played by George C. Scott, comments:

> I don't say we wouldn't get our hair mussed, but I do say no more than ten to twenty million people killed.

strangeness A property of certain ELEMENTARY PARTICLES first suggested by the US physicist Murray Gell-Mann (1929–) in 1953. It was recognized at the time that some mesons were 'strange' in that they had abnormally long lifetimes. Gell-Mann resolved the problem by introducing a new quantum property, strangeness, possessed by such particles. *See also* QUARK.

Stratofortress The US Boeing B-52 eight-engined strategic bomber, the long-serving symbol of US military might. There were eight basic variants of the initial design; the earliest version, the B-52A, went into service in August 1954, and the last, the B-52H, became operational in March 1961. The B-52D was modified for high-density bombing and used extensively during the VIETNAM WAR from bases in Guam and the Philippines. The B-52G and H are faster (maximum speed 595 m.p.h.), have a longer range (8500–10,000 miles), are equipped with the latest electronic weapons control and digital navigation systems, and can carry sophisticated air-to-air missiles or eight nuclear weapons, including air-launched cruise missiles.

streaking Running naked in a public place, so called because the **streaker** has to run like a streak of lightning to avoid being caught. This became something of a craze in the 1970s, especially at football and cricket matches.

stream of consciousness A technique of novel writing, first deliberately employed by Dorothy Richardson in *Pointed Roofs* (1915) and developed by James Joyce, particularly in his *Ulysses* (1922), and later by Virginia Woolf and William Faulkner. Using this technique the writer presents a view of the world formulated by the continuous stream of impressions that a person receives.

street credibility or **street cred** Slang from the 1970s for having a credible knowledge of the style, fashion, music, etc., of one's contemporaries on the street. It was a term of approval from the jargon of Black urban culture, implying a knowledge of how to handle oneself on the street in order to be accepted, but not outdone, by one's peers. To be seen wearing unfashionable clothes, for example, would seriously damage one's street cred.

Strength through joy *See* KRAFT DURCH FREUDE.

Stresa Front An agreement, signed in April 1935 at Stresa in Piedmont, between the UK, France, and Italy, to uphold the international status quo and to oppose further breaches of the Paris Peace settlement of 1919. The pact was concluded in response to Hitler's declaration of German rearmament in March; the three powers also agreed to defend the independence of Austria from the threat of German *Anschluss*. The Front presented no serious threat to German ambitions in Europe and collapsed only six months later, after Mussolini's invasion of Abyssinia.

strides Slang for trousers, first heard in the early years of the century; subsequently adopted in Australian and cockney slang.

Strike Command The RAF Command established on 30 April 1968 by the amalgamation of the historic Bomber and Fighter Commands, in accordance with a government proposal in a Defence White Paper of February 1967. In November 1968 Strike Command also absorbed the Coastal and Signals Commands, and in September 1972 Air Support Command was also incorporated. This reorganization of the structure of the RAF from four Commands to two was undertaken to improve efficiency and cut costs in the wake of the decline in the size of the RAF since 1945.

strip. **strip** *See* COMIC STRIP.

strip-tease A theatrical or cabaret performance in which an actress, called a **stripper**, slowly and provocatively undresses herself.

Structuralism An approach to such disciplines as linguistics, anthropology, psychology, and literature based in each case on an analysis of the structural relations between its elements. **Structural linguistics**, deriving from the work of Ferdinand de Saussure (1857–1913), regards language as a self-contained system that should be described and analysed without consideration of its comparative and historical aspects. **Structural anthropology**, deriving from the work of Claude Levi-Strauss (1908–), applies similar principles to the study of human cultures, which are analysed in terms of certain basic structures that are thought to underlie all human thought. **Structural psychology** offers an analysis of human thought processes in terms of the individual sensations and feelings of which they are constituted.

strut A slow and somewhat deliberate JAZZ dance that was popular from the 1900s, especially among those who could not dance well.

Student Nonviolent Coordinating Committee (SNCC) A civil rights organization founded by Black and White student activists in Raleigh, North Carolina, in April 1960. In the early 1960s the SNCC joined other civil rights groups, such as the Congress of Racial Equality (CORE) and Martin Luther King's Southern Christian Leadership Conference (SCLC) in organizing campaigns to desegregate lunch counters and other segregated facilities in the south; it also campaigned to encourage Black voter registration. The SNCC originally espoused the nonviolent integrationist philosophy of King but by 1966, under the leadership of Stokely Carmichael, it had abandoned these, embracing the militant chauvinist philosophy of BLACK POWER and supporting the revolutionary tactics of the BLACK PANTHERS. The organization collapsed in 1969 when Carmichael's successor, Hubert 'Rap' Brown, was convicted of armed robbery.

stuffed shirt A pompous and unnecessarily formal person, conjuring up the image of a slightly overweight man almost 'poured' into a starched dress shirt. Examples of its use in America go back to 1913, but it is often associated with Mrs Clare Boothe Luce (1903–87), who used it as the title of her first book (1933).

Stuka (short for *Stutzkampfbomber*) The Junkers JU-87, the German DIVE BOMBER, which saw action on all fronts during World War II. The first production version, JU-87 A-1, appeared in 1937; the aircraft became notorious during the first year of the war in support of the Blitzkrieg campaigns in Poland and France, when German ground and air superiority made the screaming Stukas appear to be invincible. Despite the accuracy of the dive-bombing technique, the JU-87's lack of effective armaments made it vulnerable to fighter attack and Stukas suffered severe losses during the BATTLE OF BRITAIN. The Stuka was less than popular among German aircrews, as the steepness of the dive often caused the pilot to lose consciousness.

stumer A swindle, or a swindler, a forged banknote or 'dud' cheque; a fictitious bet recorded by the bookmakers, and published in the papers, to deceive the public by running up the odds on a horse which is not expected to win. From 1914, in military parlance, a dud shell was called a stumer. The word is of unknown origin.

stuntman An athletic performer who is filmed in the dangerous scenes in a movie, normally replacing the leading actor or actress. There are also **stuntwomen**. Many early stars risked their own lives, taking pride in handling difficult work or succumbing to a director's enthusiasm for realism. D. W. Griffith floated Lillian Gish on a drifting ice chunk in *Way Down East* (1920), a daring scene that almost cost her her right hand. The ice floe sequence is famous for its excitement and realism. The comedian Harold Lloyd dislocated his shoulder in *Safety Last* (1923), when he hung outside a 12-storey building with only a projecting mattress for protection. Stuntmen, too, have been seriously injured and a few killed by stunts that misfired, as, for example, when a helicopter was brought down by ground explosions during filming of *Twilight Zone: The Movie* (1983). Stuntmen have become recognized MACHO figures in America and the subject of at least one major film, *Hooper* (1978), starring Burt Reynolds.

Stupenda, La The nickname of the Australian opera singer Joan Sutherland (1926–). She established her reputation in coloratura roles with her Lucia in *Lucia di Lammermoor* at Covent Garden in 1959. Thereafter she appeared in all the major opera houses of Europe and America giving outstanding performances as the heroines in *Norma*, *La Traviata*, and *La fille du régiment*.

stupid. so stupid he can't chew gum and fart at the same time Derisory catchphrase first heard around 1960 (often as 'so stupid he can't chew gum and walk straight at the same time'). It was revived in 1974 when Gerald Ford, who had acquired a reputation for making blunders, succeeded Nixon as president. According to the US economist J. K. Galbraith, it was first applied to Ford by Lyndon Johnson. *See also* PISS-UP.

subtitle In the cinema, the written dialogue superimposed at the bottom of the picture to translate a foreign-language film. Subtitles for silent films were not superimposed, but came in frames immediately after the unheard dialogue. They sometimes explained the action. Early subtitles also addressed the audience: "Please read the titles to yourself." One drawing depicted a man in the audience touching a woman's chin and advised: "If Annoyed When Here Please Tell the Management."

subtopia A word coined (from *suburb* and *Utopia*) by the British architectural critic Ian Nairn in 1954 to denote the sprawling suburban housing estates built to satisfy the town workers' desire for country surroundings without relinquishing the amenities of the town.

Suchow, Battle of The decisive battle between the communist People's Liberation Army and the Nationalist forces, which began in central China on 7 November 1948. With half a million men deployed by both sides, the 56-day struggle ended in the complete annihilation of Chiang Kai-Shek's military power. This led directly to the establishment of the Chinese communist regime in Peking in October 1949.

sudden infant death syndrome (SIDS) The medical name for the sudden and inexplicable death of an infant aged between 7 days and 2 years, typically while he or she is lying in the cot (hence **cot death** – the popular name). SIDS is diagnosed when no specific cause of death can be identified; suggested possible causes have included virus infections and allergies. One recent hypothesis implicates a build-up of toxic gases due to fungal action on certain plastic mattress coverings. There is evidence that the incidence of SIDS is lower in more affluent families and in breast-fed babies; it remains a significant cause of infant mortality.

Sudeten crisis The international crisis provoked by Germany's claim to the Czech Sudetenland and its German population, which was eventually conceded to Hitler at the Munich Conference in September 1938. The Sudeten Germans had been placed within Czechoslovakia by the Treaty of St Germain in 1919. However, agitation by the Sudeten German (Nazi) Party in the 1930s provoked increasing demands for regional autonomy and the redress of economic grievances, which were eventually conceded by the Czech government in April 1938. Because this failed to quell the pro-Nazi agitation, in September 1938 France, the UK, Italy, and Germany met in Munich; here, to avert war, they issued an ultimatum to the Czech government to cede the Sudetenland to Germany by 10 October. The Munich Agreement marked the zenith of appeasement. Within months Hitler had occupied Prague, making it clear that the policy of appeasement had failed and that a conflict was now unavoidable. After World War II the area was restored to the Czechs, who proceeded to expel most of the German population.

Suez crisis The crisis in the Middle East precipitated by the nationalization of the Suez Canal by the Egyptian president, Gamal Abdel Nasser, on 26 July 1956. Nasser had acted in the wake of America's refusal to help finance the ASWAN HIGH DAM, which they had formerly promised to do. This change of policy was a result of Egypt's growing affinity with the Soviet bloc. Nasser's seizure of the canal incensed the British and the French, who feared for the safety of oil supplies to western Europe. As diplomatic efforts continued to try to solve the crisis, the UK and France prepared secret plans for the military retrieval of the canal zone and the overthrow of Nasser, who was perceived by Anthony Eden, the British prime minister, as a new Hitler. They found ready allies in Israel, which had been in an almost continuous state of conflict with Egypt since its foundation in 1948. The Israelis invaded Egypt on 29 October 1956; British and French forces then landed at Port Said and Port Faud, on the pretext of supporting the UN call for a ceasefire, and moved to occupy the canal zone. The duplicity of the Anglo-French action distressed the Americans who threatened to support the UN's call for the imposition of economic sanctions. The British and French were therefore forced to withdraw on 22 December and the Israelis withdrew in March 1957. The episode served to underline the UK's postwar decline as an imperial power and the dependence of British foreign policy on America. It also raised Nasser to the status of an Arab nationalist hero, ensuring that British and French influence in the Middle East was deeply compromised. Egypt retained control of the Suez Canal and Eden was so widely criticized that he resigned shortly after the debacle.

suffragettes The militant women who agitated for a parliamentary vote, especially in the years 1903 to 1914. They included those who sought votes for women on the same property qualifications as applied to men at that time and those who demanded universal suffrage for all adults. From 1903 the militant members of the Women's Social and Political Union, led by Emmeline Pankhurst (1858–1928) and her daughter Christabel Pankhurst (1880–1958), chained themselves to railings, attacked property, refused to pay taxes, and held public meetings and demonstrations:

> We have taken this action, because as women . . . it is our duty even to break the law in order to call attention to the reasons why we do so.
>
> EMMELINE PANKHURST, speech in court 21 October 1908.

The suffragettes were repeatedly imprisoned (*see* CAT AND MOUSE ACT), where they endangered their lives by hunger strikes and had to endure brutal forcible feeding:

> We are not ashamed of what we have done, because, when you have a great cause to fight for, the moment of greatest humiliation is the moment when the spirit is proudest.
>
> CHRISTABEL PANKHURST, speech 19 March 1908.

With a few exceptions, the male members of the establishment behaved badly, while the women conducted themselves with determination and dignity:

> I see some rats have got in: let them squeal, it doesn't matter.
>
> LLOYD GEORGE, interrupting a speech when suffragettes entered the hall.

During World War I the women's organizations sensibly supported the war effort; in 1918 Lloyd George rewarded them by granting the vote to women over 30, subject to property qualifications. In 1928 these qualifications were removed and women became the political equals of men. The **Shrieking Sisterhood**, as their opponents called the suffragettes, had triumphed.

sugar. sugar daddy An elderly wealthy man who lavishes expensive gifts on a much younger woman in return for sexual favours. The female equivalent, **sugar mummy**, is rarely heard (*see* TOY-BOY).

Sugar Ray Robinson The ring name of US boxer Walker Smith (1920–90). A successful amateur, he acquired the name Ray Robinson when he used the amateur certificate of the real Ray Robinson in order to be able to take part in a contest. The epithet 'Sugar' was added later – a reference to his style, which was described as 'sweet as sugar'. In 1940 he turned professional, becoming world welterweight champion (1946–51) and middleweight champion (five times; 1951–60). He fought 202 professional contests and lost only 19 (12 of which were after he was 40).

suit A 1980s term for an executive or bureaucrat, suggesting dullness, anonymity, and time-serving. It seems to have spread from advertising agencies, where the casually dressed 'creatives' refer in this way to the expensively tailored executives who deal personally with clients. The term was popularized by Heath's cartoon strip 'The Suits' in PRIVATE EYE. An **empty suit** is an executive whose specious exterior, mastery of the latest professional jargon, and air of strenuous activity mask the fact that he is doing little or no useful work. *See also* MEN IN GREY SUITS.

Sultan of Swat *See* BABE, THE.

summer. Summerhill The experimental coeducational boarding school, established first at Lyme Regis in 1924 and subsequently at Leiston, Suffolk, by the controversial writer and educationalist Alexander Sutherland Neill (1883–1973). Neill's distrust of the conventional education system, derived from his own experience of teaching, led to his exploration of the progressive educational theories of such philosophers and psychologists as Rousseau, Freud, and Dewey. From these researches he distilled a theory of education that stressed the importance of absolute freedom from authority. Consequently, Summerhill is a self-governing community, where staff and pupils each have a vote on matters of policy and pupils can do exactly what they like as long as they do not infringe the rights of others. Neill's ideas and motivation are explained in a number of his books, including *A Dominie's Log* (1915), *That Dreadful School* (1937), and the autobiography *Neill! Neill! Orange Peel* (1973).

summer time *See* DAYLIGHT SAVING.

sun. a place in the sun A favourable position that allows for development; a share in what one has a natural right to.

The phrase achieved a particular significance when Wilhelm II of Germany (*see* KAISER BILL) spoke of his nation taking steps to ensure that "no one can dispute with us the place in the sun that is our due."

sunlighting Slang for doing two jobs at the same time. It is derived from **moonlighting**, doing two jobs but one in the day and one at night. High-powered sunlighters are also known as **two overcoat men**. They arrive at one office in the morning, hang up their overcoats to make it appear as if they are in the building, retire to their cars, and – armed with a second overcoat – make a similar display in the offices of their other employers. Some MEPs are said to be persistent offenders.

Sunny Jim *See under* JIM.

Sundance Kid *See* BUTCH CASSIDY AND THE SUNDANCE KID.

Sunday For centuries the first day of the week, dedicated to the sun since antiquity. In 1971 it became the seventh day, when the UK adopted the decision of the International Standardization Organization to call Monday the first day.

Sunderland flying-boat The Short Brothers Sunderland first appeared in 1938, remained in service throughout World War II, and continued to serve with the RAF until 1959. With its long-range capabilities and heavy armaments, including bombs, depth charges, and mines, the Sunderland specialized in convoy escort and anti-submarine warfare. it was the mainstay of Coastal Command's operations in the North Sea, Atlantic, and Mediterranean; it was also used during the BERLIN AIRLIFT in 1948 and during the KOREAN WAR.

Sunningdale Agreement *See* POWER SHARING.

sunrise industry High-technology industry, especially firms making electronic equipment with the help of computers and robots. It is the industry of the future, the era of which is just dawning. There is also an echo of Japan, the Land of the Rising Sun; many of these industries in the UK are Japanese-owned. *See also* SUNSET INDUSTRY.

sunset. ride off into the sunset A cliché for a happy and romantic ending. It derives from the era of silent films, which often ended with the hero and heroine riding off into the sunset to spend the rest of their days happily together. It is the visual equivalent of 'They lived happily ever after'.

sunset industry The industries that were the main stay of the British economy before the age of the new technology; for example, coal, steel, and shipbuilding. These are now called sunset industries because they are on the wane. Those sunset industries that have large 19th-century factories, such as steel works, cotton mills, and heavy engineering companies, are also known as **smoke-stack industries**. *See also* SUNRISE INDUSTRY.

super. Super Bowl In US professional football, the championship game held annually in late January between the best teams of the National Football League's two conferences, the American and National. Super Bowl I (Roman numerals are used) was played in 1967 in Los Angeles with Green Bay Packers defeating Kansas City Chiefs 35-10. For the first two years, the game was officially *The AFL-NFL World Championship Game*. The name 'Super Bowl' came from Lamar Hunt, the owner of Kansas City Chiefs, after he watched his daughter play with a *Super Ball*, and the title was adopted for the third game. About three out of every four Americans watch the telecast in addition to the millions more who are watching in other parts of the world. The price for at television commercial during ABC's 1991 Super Bowl broadcast was $850,000 for 30 seconds. *See also* ROSE BOWL.

Superbrat One of the many epithets applied to US tennis player John McEnroe (1959–); his other nicknames include **The Mouth** and **Mac the Mouth**. He became a professional in 1978, quickly establishing himself as one of the top international players, winning the Wimbledon singles title in 1981, 1983, and 1984. In 1986 he married the US actress Tatum O'Neal, missing Wimbledon for two years. He made a come-back in 1988, but he was unable to sustain his earlier form. His career has been marred by bouts of uncontrollable temper and lack of sportsmanship on court, which earned him his nickname: he was notorious for arguing with the umpire – 'You cannot be serious', a retort to an unfavourable decision, became his best-known catchphrase.

superconductivity The disappearance of electrical resistance in certain substances at very low temperatures (in the vicinity of absolute zero). The effect was discovered in 1911 and is now known to occur in 26 metals and many compounds and alloys. The so-called BCS theory explaining superconductivity is named after the three scientists who proposed it in 1957, J. Bardeen (1908–91), L. N. Cooper (1930–), and J. R. Schrieffer (1931–). According to this theory an electron moving through a crystal lattice can distort it sufficiently to affect a second passing electron. Thus, in superconductors the current carriers are not single electrons but bound pairs of electrons (called Cooper pairs). The BCS theory assumes that the flow of Cooper pairs is unchanged by interacting with the lattice and therefore continues indefinitely.

Superconducting coils can have large continuous currents passing through them creating powerful magnetic fields. These magnetic fields are made use of in some particle accelerators and other devices (*see also* JOSEPHSON EFFECTS).

In 1986 a different type of superconductivity was discovered in which a similar phenomenon occurs at much higher temperatures (as high as 100 K). This so-called **high-temperature superconductivity**, has not yet been explained.

supercontinent or **protocontinent** The putative huge land mass known as PANGAEA that, according to the geological theory of PLATE TECTONICS, formed about 240 million years ago and subsequently broke up to produce the Earth's present continents.

Superfortress The US B-29 high-altitude strategic bomber, which became operational in June 1944. The four-engined bomber set a new standard in terms of engine power, weight, armament, pressurization, and airborne control systems. The construction and delivery of over 3000 B-29s to the USAF by August 1945 marked one of the greatest feats in aviation history. *See* ENOLA GAY.

supergrass *See* GRASS.

supergroup A rock band made up of former members of other groups, especially during the HIPPIE era. In the late 1960s, a number of well-known musicians left their groups and several bands split up altogether. When the disengaged performers recombined, the new ensembles were called supergroups. The title proved hard to live up to, and the original supergroups flourished only into the mid-1970s. Perhaps the best known was Crosby, Stills and Nash, formed in 1969 by David Crosby of the Byrds, Stephen Stills of Buffalo Springfield, and Graham Nash of the Hollies. Later joined by Neil Young of Buffalo Springfield, they produced a 1970 hit album, *Deja Vu*. Other noted supergroups included Airforce, Blind Faith, Humble Pie, and Emerson, Lake and Palmer.

Supermac The cartoon characterization of the British Conservative prime minister Harold Macmillan (1894–1986) in the guise of SUPERMAN, the US comic-strip hero. These VICKY cartoons appeared in the London *Evening Standard* from 1958. *See also* MAC THE KNIFE.

Superman (1) A hypothetical superior human being of high intellectual and moral attainment. The term *Übermensch* was invented by the German philosopher Nietzsche (1844–1900) and the English translation was popularized in the UK by George Bernard Shaw's play, *Man and Superman* (1903). (2) A US comic-strip hero, who later featured on radio and television and (from 1978) in a series of blockbuster films starring Christopher Reeve. The character first appeared in *Action Comics* (1 June 1938) in a strip by Jerry Siegel and Joe Shuster. According to the story, the infant superhero was rescued from the planet Krypton shortly before it exploded and brought up on Earth by human parents. He soon discovers that he has superhuman powers, including X-ray vision, invincible strength, and the ability to fly "faster than a speeding bullet". While maintaining an outward identity as Clark Kent, a mild-mannered newspaper reporter, he adopts the guise of Superman to fight crime and uphold "truth, justice, and the American way." His Achilles' heel is his vulnerability to kryptonite, an element originating in the planet of his birth. An ironic subplot is provided by Kent's infatuation with a fellow reporter, Lois Lane, whose hero-worship of Superman leads her to slight her quiet colleague, Clark Kent. In 1991 DC Comics, publishers of the strip, announced that the two characters would finally marry, 52 years after they first met.

supermarket *See* SELF SERVICE; HYPERMARKET.

super rat A breed of rat that is immune to most poisons. It first appeared in America in the mid-1970s and has since been identified in Europe and Asia.

super realism or **hyper realism** A genre in art that developed chiefly in America in the 1970s. The aim of artists in the style was to imitate actual images with absolute verisimilitude. In painting this involved extensive use of photographs (photorealism) and in sculpture the making of casts direct from the human form.

supersonic Denoting an aircraft that can fly faster than the speed of sound in the medium in which it is flying. The **sound barrier** is an obstacle to supersonic flight that was first overcome by the US Bell XS-1 rocket aircraft in 1947. It occurs because the pressure waves created by the aircraft cannot escape in a forward direction as the supersonic aircraft is travelling faster than the waves; the result is that shock waves build up on the aircraft's wings causing instability. The barrier is overcome by greater streamlining and swept-back wings. CONCORDE became the first successful commercial supersonic aircraft when put into service in 1976.

superstar A very prominent, usually international, performer in the field of entertainment or sport. The word was coined in the 1920s. Current superstars include Frank Sinatra, Mick Jagger, Marlon Brando, and Luciano Pavarotti in the arts; Boris Becker, Diego Maradona, and Nick Faldo would qualify in sports.

superstore *See* HYPERMARKET.

supply-side economics The approach to MACROECONOMICS popular with economists in the 1970s and 1980s. It emphasizes the importance of the conditions under which goods and services are supplied to the market and reduces the influence of government. By allowing the free market to determine the level of employment and output, it aims to reduce the power of trade unions, cut government taxes and expenditure, and reduce unemployment benefits. It is a rejection of the early Keynesian measure (*see* KEYNESIANISM).

suprematism A genre of modern art in the 20th century. The first suprematist was the Russian artist Kasimir Malevich, whose earliest work in this new style (in 1913) consisted of a black square on a white background. The aim of such works, which have inspired much of the most impassioned debate about abstract art, was to employ geometric shapes to express pure emotion without objectivity.

Supreme Soviet The national legislature, elected every five years by citizens over the age of 18, which is notionally the supreme representative of the popular will in the Soviet Union. It consists of two chambers, the Council of nationalities (750 deputies elected by the various territories of the Soviet federation). Sessions take place twice a year, and matters of domestic and foreign affairs are considered by a series of elected standing commissions. The Supreme Soviet also elects the Council of Ministers (the Soviet government) and the Presidium (collective presidency). Although largely a 'rubber stamp' body for most of its existence, under Gorbachov the Supreme Soviet has been more assertive in pressing for reform at local and national level.

surrealism A movement in art and the literary world that began in 1924 and flourished between the wars under the leadership of the poet André Breton. In painting it falls into two groups: hand-painted dream scenes as exemplified by Chirico, Dali, and Magritte; and the creation of abstract forms by the practice of complete spontaneity of technique as well as subject matter by the use of contrast, seen in the works of Arp, Roy, Mirò, and Dali. They sought to express thought, uncontrolled by reason or aesthetic and moral concepts. *Compare* CUBISM; DADAISM; FAUVISM; FUTURISM; ORPHISM; SYNCHRONISM; VORTICISM.

surrender. We shall never surrender The climax to the speech delivered to the House of Commons on 4 June 1940 by Winston Churchill. With Germany over-running Europe and the UK facing an imminent invasion, Churchill's rallying cry was the epitome of the 'bulldog spirit' with which the British – erroneously or not – have long been credited:

> We shall not flag or fail. We shall go on to the end. We shall fight in France, we shall fight with growing confidence and growing strength in the air, we shall defend our island, whatever the cost may be, we shall fight on the beaches, we shall fight on the landing grounds, we shall fight in the fields and in the streets, we shall fight in the hills; we shall never surrender.

See also BLOOD, TOIL, TEARS AND SWEAT; DUNKIRK; FEW, THE; WINNIE.

surrogate motherhood An arrangement in which a woman agrees to undergo pregnancy in order to produce a child for another individual or a couple. The surrogate mother may be inseminated by the male of the couple (either by intercourse or by AI) or by sperm from another donor, for instance from a SPERM BANK. Such arrangements may be the only recourse for infertile childless couples and for gay couples, but they can be fraught with emotional and practical difficulties. In the UK, under the Surrogacy Arrangements Act (1985), all forms of commercial surrogacy service, *i.e.* those involving financial gain, are illegal and would-be surrogate mothers are unable to advertise their services. However, private surrogacy arrangements, even ones involving payment, are legal although they may prove difficult to enforce, since the biological mother has exclusive rights to the child. In America, legislation varies from state to state.

Surtsey An island that was spectacularly created off the S coast of Iceland on 14 November 1963. It was formed as the result of a powerful underwater volcanic eruption: within weeks the island had reached a height of 567 feet and a length of 1.3 miles. As soon as the eruption had abated the scientists arrived, realizing that this was a unique opportunity to study the processes by which flora and fauna become established. First to arrive were the birds; the seeds that came with them produced the first flower in June 1967. Within three more years four plant types and 18 mosses were found to be flourishing. The island itself was named Surtsey after a legendary Norse giant.

survive. survivable US military jargon for describing weapons systems, communications networks, etc., that are capable of surviving a nuclear attack and delivering a counterstrike. *See* FIRST STRIKE.

survivalist Someone who aims to survive the nuclear doom that he or she considers inevitable by taking to the wilderness, stockpiling food and equipment, and learning survival skills, including the use of deadly weapons. Determined to survive not only the immediate catastrophe but also the 'every-man-for-himself' world that will follow, US survivalist groups have built up impressive armouries and take part in exercises of an almost paramilitary nature. The movement's ethos combines nostalgia for the values of the US frontier with social Darwinism of the most virulent kind: some adherents seem to regard a nuclear disaster as nature's way of culling that part of humanity (the vast majority) too feeble to will its own survival. Such attitudes are often combined with religious FUNDAMENTALISM and an obsession with racial purity. In the 1980s, survivalism spawned a whole subculture of shops, suppliers, and 'how-to' literature, most of which lingered affectionately over the lethal properties of various types of weapon. Although many adherents are probably no more than overgrown boy scouts, the movement has an obvious appeal to the inadequate and deranged. Michael Ryan, who in 1987 shot 16 people dead in the village of Hungerford, was an avid student of survivalist literature (*see* HUNGERFORD MASSACRE).

survivor syndrome Symptoms exhibited by survivors of a natural disaster, plane crash, purge, etc., in which many others died. Psychological problems, such as guilt, anxiety, or depression can develop years after the event. This has been demonstrated by some survivors of the HOLOCAUST and by earthquake survivors. *See also* POST-TRAUMATIC STRESS DISORDER.

sus or **suss** British and New Zealand slang meaning to work out, discover. Thus to **suss out** someone or something is to discover that person's or thing's true nature or character, often by intuition. The word originated in the police jargon of the mid-1920s, being a shortened form of *suspect*; it became trendy among BEATNIKS in the early 1960s and has been common since the 1970s. A 1980s variation was **well-sussed**, *i.e.* having self-awareness. *See also* SUS LAW.

sus law Colloquial name for a former British law authorizing the arrest of a person *sus*pected of loitering with criminal intent in a public place. The original sus law formed part of the Vagrancy Act (1824; repealed 1981).

Susso Australian slang from the 1940s for someone who is claiming government sustenance.

Sutton Hoo treasure An Anglo-Saxon ship-burial of the early 7th century, discovered at Sutton Hoo near Woodbridge, Suffolk, in 1939. It is one of the richest ever found and the treasure, consisting of a sword and sheath, helmet, bowls and other objects in precious metals, is now in the British Museum. The find is of considerable archaeological and historical importance.

Suvla Bay *See* GALLIPOLI.

swap A **currency swap** is one that arises when a bank arranges for a borrower to exchange the type of funds he can raise as a loan (*e.g.* sterling) for the type of funds he needs (*e.g.* dollars). It may be that a US company has the opposite problem: the bank may be aware of this situation and enable the two companies to swap currencies. **Debt swaps** occur when borrowers exchange fixed interest rate debts for floating interest rate debts; these are common in eurocurrency markets.

swastika An elaborate cross-shaped design, also known as a gammadion or fylfot, used as a charm to ward off evil and bring good luck (the word is derived from Sanskrit *svasti*, good fortune). It was adopted by Hitler as the Nazi emblem in about 1920, probably from the German Baltic Corps, who wore it on their helmets after service in Finland, where it was used as a distinguishing mark on Finnish aeroplanes. It was described by Winston Churchill as the 'crooked cross' and came to symbolize the immense evil of Nazi Germany.

swat team Special Weapons And Tactics team. US slang for a military-style police unit brought in to deal with situations that cannot be controlled by regular police officers.

sweater girl A young woman with a well-developed bust, which is made apparent by the wearing of a clinging sweater.

Sweeney British rhyming slang for the Flying Squad (from Sweeney Todd), a high-powered division of the Metropolitan Police in London. Sweeney Todd was a fictional barber in a play by George Dibden Pitt (1799–1855), who murdered his customers. In the 1970s there was a popular TV police thriller series called *The Sweeney*, starring John Thaw and Dennis Waterman.

sweetheart agreement An agreement reached peaceably by direct negotiation between employer and employees, first heard in Australia but subsequently elsewhere.

swell Single Woman Earning Lots of Lolly. One of the more transient acronyms of the late 1980s that proliferated following the success of the word YUPPIE. This sense plays on the word's older usage, a rich swankily dressed person.

swine. swine flu A disease of pigs caused by a virus that is closely related to the human flu virus and may even have originated from humans. Infected animals show respiratory signs, such as coughing, loss of appetite, and fever. Outbreaks of the disease are confined to North America, usually occurring in the autumn and winter months.

swine vesicular disease A disease of pigs first identified in Italy in 1966 and appearing in the UK in 1972. It is caused by a virus and can be transmitted to humans. Affected animals develop blisters on the feet, which rupture, causing transient lameness. Because the signs are virtually identical to the much more serious FOOT-AND-MOUTH DISEASE, all cases of suspected swine vesicular disease have to be notified to the veterinary authorities in the UK.

swing A form of popular music derived from JAZZ, usually played by the big bands of the 1930s. *Compare* BOOGIE-WOOGIE; RAGTIME.

swinger (1) Slang for a fun-loving sophisticated sexually liberated person. (2) US slang for a wife-swopper or someone whose sexual appetites can swing both ways, *i.e.* a bisexual.

swinging Slang of the 1960s for lively or uninhibited. It also acquired a sexual relevance, reflecting the atmosphere of sexual freedom of the decade, and was often used in the context of wife-swapping or other unconventional sexual arrangements. The 1960s themselves are often recalled as the **Swinging Sixties**, although many survivors of the period subsequently questioned the reality of the popular concept (*see also* NEW MORALITY). In 1965 the US fashion journalist Diana Vreeland (*c.*1903–89) applied the term to London: **Swinging London** featured in *Time* magazine a year later, ensuring that the phrase caught on, and for a few years the capital of the UK was closely associated in the public imagination with the contemporary spirit of liberation in fashion, ideas, and sexual mores.

swing-wing An aircraft design, also called variable-geometry wing, that enables the position of the wings to be altered during flight so they can adopt the aerodynamically most favourable position. For take-off and landing the wings are set in the straight position, while for high-speed cruising they are moved to a swept-back position. The greater aerodynamic efficiency of the swing-wing design allows the aircraft to use a less powerful, hence lighter, engine, with a reduced fuel payload, giving a weight advantage that more than offsets the greater complexity of the swing-wing mechanism. Although the idea was pioneered by the British engineer Barnes Wallis (1887–1979), the world's first operational swing-wing aircraft was the General Dynamics F 111, introduced in the 1960s. The design has also been incorporatd in, among others, the European-built Tornado, and the Soviet MiG-23.

switched on (1) Aware of contemporary fashionable and popular cults, thoroughly up to date and responsive to current trends and tendencies. *See* PLUGGED IN. (2) Under the influence of drugs.

Both senses are 1960s slang, now rarely used.

Sword Allied codename given to a beach N of Caen, which was one of the main landing sites for British and Canadian forces on D DAY. *See also* GOLD; JUNO; OMAHA; UTAH.

SWOT Strengths, Weaknesses, Opportunities, and Threats. A nmemonic used in planning the marketing of a new product, for the areas a company has to assess. Internal strengths needed would be a good distribution system, a strong flow of cash to support the marketing, etc. Weaknesses that need attention might include inadequate servicing facilities or poor-quality testing. Opportunities might arise from a good demand that is known to exist in a particular area of the market. Threats might include government subsidizing of an overseas competitor.

Sydney Opera House The remarkable opera house in Sydney harbour that had become the subject of great controversy by the time of its completion in 1973. Undoubtedly the best-known building in Australia, it was designed by the Danish architect Joern Utzon (1918–), winner of an international competition, who planned a series of ten huge 'shells' of concrete, which – at 26,800 tons – constituted the heaviest roof in the world. The project should have been completed by 1961: endless delays and rocketing costs led to Utzon's resignation in 1966 with work still in progress. The finished building covers 4½ acres and contains a concert hall, a stage for opera and ballet, a theatre, a recording hall, and a cinema. Unfortunately the final result, considered to be one of the greatest abstract sculptures of the century, has been much criticized for its poor acoustic qualities.

Sykes-Picot agreement A secret pact, negotiated by Sir Mark Sykes of the UK and François Georges-Picot of France in January 1916, for dividing up the Ottoman Empire after World War I. France was given control of coastal Syria, Lebanon, and Mosul, while the UK would control southern Mesopotamia, including Baghdad, and the ports of Haifa and Akka. Palestine was to be placed under international control, and a number of independent Arab states were also to be created. The agreement was conditional on the approval of Russia, which was given in May 1916 in return for control over Turkish Armenia. The Italians had also been promised Ottoman territory in the Treaty of LONDON, and they eventually assented to the agreement in August 1917 after they were allotted portions of Anatolia. The agreement was a source of considerable embarrassment to the Allies when it was made public by the Bolshevik government late in 1917; unfortunately it contradicted British promises made to the Jews for a national home in Palestine (in the BALFOUR DECLARATION of 2 November 1917) and pledges to Hussein, the Sherif of Mecca (*see* MCMAHON LETTERS).

Sylvester Popular cartoon cat who appeared in Warner shorts from the 1940s to the 1960s, generally in vain pursuit of the distrusting bird **Tweetie Pie**. Sylvester's lisping voice, delivered by Mel Blanc, had many imitators.

synchronism A form of abstract art, resembling ORPHISM, begun by two Americans, Morgan Russell and S. MacDonald Wright, in 1913. It is characterized by the use of pure colour moving by gradations or rhythms from the primaries to the intermediary colours. Synchronist painting depended on colour and its immediate effects. *Compare* CUBISM; DADAISM; FAUVISM; FUTURISM; SURREALISM; VORTICISM.

syndicalism (Fr. *syndicalisme*, trade unionism) A trade-union movement originating about 1890 in France, where it was known as *syndicalisme révolutionnaire*. It was opposed to state socialism, the means of production being taken over by the trade unions and not by the state, and government was to be by a federation of trade-union bodies. The syndicalists aimed at achieving their objectives by widespread strikes, GO SLOWS, etc. Syndicalism played an important part in fomenting the trade-union unrest in the UK immediately preceding World War I, and syndicalists were a prominent element in Spain in the 1930s.

T

T-shirt or **tee-shirt** A casual short-sleeved shirt derived from the polo shirt, so-called from its T shape when laid down flat.

tabloid A newspaper that carries news in a condensed and easily readable form, with brash headlines, much of the space inside being devoted to gossip about film and television celebrities, PAGE THREE GIRLS, and titillating or sensational articles with the emphasis on violent crime and illicit sex. In the UK, the first tabloids to use these elements to appeal to a mass audience were the *Daily Mail* (1896) and the *Daily Mirror* (1903) published by the NORTHCLIFFE PRESS, although Northcliffe's titles were models of taste and sobriety compared to such current publications as *The Sun*. British tabloids have their counterparts in other countries, most notably Germany's *Bild Zeitung*, Europe's best-selling daily newspaper. Middle-market newspapers, such as the *Daily Express* and *Today*, also appear in tabloid form, and the format has also been experimented with by the British quality press, notably *The Independent on Sunday*. *See also* GUTTER PRESS.

Tabu *T*ypical *a*rmy *b*alls-*u*p: army slang dating from World War II. *See also* SNAFU.

tachisme (Fr. *tache*, spot) A style of modern painting in which dabs or blotches of colour are applied in a random intuitive manner to evoke a particular mood or image. Tachisme was part of the Art Informel movement as practised in Paris in the 1940s and 1950s by such artists as Hans Hartung, Karel Appel, Pierre Soulanges, and Georges Mathieu; it was partly inspired by the abstract expressionist movement in America, particularly ACTION PAINTING. Like Jackson Pollock and Willem de Kooning, whose style and technique they most closely resemble, the tachists created large canvases containing splashes, blobs, and sweeping strokes of colour, although with greater delicacy, discipline, and concern for line and form than their US counterparts.

tachograph (Gr. *takhos*, speed) A device used in a heavy goods vehicle to record its speed, distance covered, driver's name, etc., to ensure that the vehicle, driver, and owner are complying with regulations. Called by many drivers the 'spy-in-the-cab'.

Taffia *See* MURPHY.

Taff Vale Judgment The decision by the British courts in favour of the action for damages brought by the Taff Vale Railway Company against the Amalgamated Society of Railway Servants (ASRS) in 1900. In June 1900 striking ASRS members had picketed the Cardiff stations; in response, the general manager of the Taff Vale Company had brought an action against the secretary of the union, claiming that the picketing contravened the Conspiracy and Protection of Property Act (1875). The decision in favour of the company, which was upheld by the House of Lords in July 1901, meant that unions could be sued for damages arising out of the actions of its members in industrial disputes. In December 1902 the company was duly awarded £23,000, plus costs. This attack on the unions by the courts, backed by parliament, impressed on trade unionists that only by parliamentary action could they reverse the decision and redress their grievances. In the wake of Taff Vale, trade union affiliation to the Labour Party increased dramatically and the representation of the Party in parliament increased from 2 to 29 members during the period 1900–06. The Taff Vale decision was eventually reversed by the Trades Disputes Act (1906).

taffy Technologically advanced family. US journalists' acronym, in the style of YUPPIE and DINKIE, for a typically educated middle-class family all the members of which, including the children, are familiar with computers and word processors.

tag A type of spray-painted graffito consisting of a stylized signature or logo. Originating in the practice, common among US graffiti artists, of signing one's work with a nickname or personal symbol, tagging soon became an end in its own right. The object is to develop a stylish personal tag and to leave it in as many public places as possible, the more conspicuous or inaccessible the better. The craze began in America in the 1970s and has now spread to the UK and elsewhere. New York subways and London tubes have suffered mutilation as a result of this craze. It has spawned a flourishing subculture with its own vocabulary, conventions, and etiquette.

tail To follow someone so that they are never out of sight.

tail-end Charlie An RAF phrase in World War II for the rear-gunner in the tail of an aircraft; also for the aircraft at the rear of a group or the last ship in a flotilla. **Arse-end Charlie** and **arse-hole Charlie** were common variants.

Tailor of Gloucester The eponymous hero of Beatrix Potter's tale (1902), whose finest work is finished on time by mice. Potter was inspired to write the story after hearing of a notice in a tailor's window in Gloucester in 1894: 'Have your suits made by the Tailor of Gloucester, where the work is done by fairies.' Apparently, a local tailor had been startled to find unfinished work in the shop had been completed over the weekend by unknown hands: the truth finally emerged years later that early one Sunday some of his employees had remained in the shop after a lengthy drinking spree until the following evening because they were too embarrassed to reveal themselves in a dishevelled state to Gloucester's churchgoers. They completed the unfinished garments in order to pass the time as they waited for darkness to fall.

Taiwan 1980s student slang for an upper second degree ('two-one'). *See also* DESMOND; DOUGLAS; PATTIE.

take In the cinema, to record a scene on film, hence to 'go for a take'. If all goes to plan a single take is all that is required (*see* ONE-TAKE) but often a director insists on numerous takes before he is satisfied.

takeaway Ready-cooked food, or a whole meal, packaged to be taken and consumed away from its place of sale. Although fish-and-chip shops had been providing this service in the UK for many years, the term was only coined in the late 1960s as restaurants offering at first takeaway Chinese, then later Indian, food began to spring up in towns throughout the country. In America and Scotland the equivalent is a **carryout** which, in America, is bought from a **takeout** counter. In the UK the Chinese and Indian restaurants providing this service are known as Chinese and Indian takeaways. *See also* FAST FOOD.

take out To kill or destroy. Military slang first heard during the VIETNAM WAR, the expression subsequently achieved wide usage, particularly when HIGH TECH weapons were involved. Before that the term was occasionally heard in the context of winning something, *i.e.* 'taking out' the prize.

talk In JAZZ slang, to play an instrument as effortlessly as one can talk, *i.e.* communicating the emotion of the music with total authenticity. First heard in the 1920s.

talkies Commercial films with soundtracks. As all movies are now talkies the expression is no longer used, although it was in the years immediately following the 30 years of SILENT FILMS. The Hollywood transition to sound ruined such actors as John Gilbert, made a star of Al Jolson, and made no difference to some slapstick artists, such as LAUREL AND HARDY. Synchronized sound with film had been demonstrated as one-minute talkies in 1900 at the Paris Exposition. But it was not until 1926 that US audiences were exposed to background music provided with the film rather than by a cinema pianist (*e.g. Don Juan* with John Barrymore). In 1927, Fox Movietone newsreels had spoken sound, including covering of Charles Lindbergh's triumphal return from his solo Atlantic flight (*see* SPIRIT OF ST LOUIS). Four months later, Hollywood had its first box-office success with synchronized sound, Warner Brothers' *The Jazz Singer* with Al Jolson, which was first shown on 6 October 1927. It used Vitaphone's system of synchronized discs. In 1928, Walt Disney produced the sound cartoon, *Steamboat Willie*, featuring Mortimer Mouse (later renamed MICKEY MOUSE). The next year, the major studios had switched from synchronized discs to sound-on-film developed by Western Electric. Despite the reservations of the conservative, the era of silent films was over.

talking book Sound recordings of books and magazines read by professional actors, which were first produced in America in 1934 for use by the blind. Talking books were introduced in the UK the following year; a vast selection of recordings of books, magazines, and periodicals is now available on record and tape in libraries in many countries throughout the world.

talking head Originally, a broadcasting term for the televised 'head and shoulders' shot of a person talking, or for the type of programme produced in the studio that consists mainly of close-ups of a presenter or interviewer speaking directly to the camera. The phrase is now widely used, disparagingly, of the people who appear in such programmes and put forward their opinions on particular topics.

tall. tall, dark, and handsome A phrase used to describe the perfect hero of romantic fiction of the MILLS & BOON variety; it is now so over-used that it has become a cliché. It seems to have originated in the early years of the century but did not become really established until Mae West used it in the film *She Done Him Wrong* (1933) to describe Cary Grant.

tall poppy Australian colloquialism for a rich or prominent person. **Tall-poppy syndrome** is the tendency, said to be engrained in the Australian character, to cut such people down to size. The phrase has been current since 1931, when Jack Lang (1876–1975), the left-wing premier of New South Wales, described his egalitarian policies as 'cutting the heads off the tall poppies'. It derives from the legend that Tarquin, king of Rome, intimated his wishes respecting the captured city of Gabii by decapitating the tallest poppies in his garden; accordingly, the leading citizens were executed.

tamper-proof *See* CONSUMER TERRORISM.

Tanaka Memorial A Japanese blueprint for aggressive expansion in China, said to have been presented by the prime minister, General Tanaka Giichi (1864–1929), to the emperor in 1927. On becoming prime minister in April 1927, Tanaka convened a conference of top military and government officials to discuss policy towards the Asian continent, during which it was agreed that a strong stance in defence of Japanese interests in China was necessary. This conference was apparently the source of the belligerent Tanaka Memorial (memorandum), which was widely published throughout China in the late 1920s. The authenticity of the Memorial has yet to be proved, although Japanese aggression in China during the ensuing decade appears to conform to the strategy outlined in the document.

tango A ballroom dance in 2/4 or 4/4 time introduced into Europe from Argentina in the early years of the 20th century. The dance combines elements of Spanish flamenco, the *milonga*, a fast sensual dance popular in Buenos Aires in the 1880s, and the Cuban *habanera*, which was probably of African origin. It appears to have been created in the backstreets and bordellos of Buenos Aires, which, according to the Argentinian writer Jorge Luis Borges (1899–1986), was the only suitable place to dance it:

> ... how many other things would you willingly do in public that were first dreamed up by the clients of a Latin American brothel?
>
> JOE JOSEPH in *The Times*, 22 May 1991.

Nevertheless, by the 1920s the tango had spread from its native Argentina to North America and Europe; in America its popularity was greatly enhanced by such Mediterranean exponents as Rudolf VALENTINO, although for the British it never seemed entirely suitable – the English ex-public schoolboy finds it uncomfortable to look dark, Latin, and sexy, while the demure English rose is not at her best in fishnet stockings (at least not in public). By the 1950s the tango had become no more than a formal exercise for ballroom dance enthusiasts. However, in the early 1990s an Argentinian dance troupe toured the capitals of Europe with its highly successful *Tango Argentino*, bringing a revival of the dance to the grandchildren of its original devotees. Characterized by slow gliding movements broken by sudden changes of direction and pointing positions, the tango is very easy to caricature.

takes two to tango A common idiom dating back to the 1952 song with this title by Hofmann and Manning:

> There are lots of things you can do alone!
> But it takes two to tango.

It is often used in a sexual context when one partner is blamed for seducing the other; 'it takes two to tango' implies that the other partner was also willing. It is, however, now used more widely, especially politically, to imply that in order to achieve agreement between two parties, both may have to make concessions.

tank A heavily armoured motorized combat vehicle running on caterpillar tracks, which was first introduced on the battlefield by the British in the Battle of the

Somme (1916). It owes its name to *tank* being used as a code word for these vehicles in order not to arouse enemy suspicions and to achieve a complete surprise.

tank top A sleeveless pullover with a scoop neckline and wide shoulder straps worn by either sex, usually over a shirt or blouse. Tank tops, popular in the 1960s and 1970s, were named after *tank suits*, one-piece swimming costumes with wide shoulder straps worn in swimming pools (or 'swimming tanks').

Tannenberg The site in Poland (then East Prussia) of the battle fought between 26 and 30 August 1914, in which the Germans inflicted a crushing defeat on the Russians who had invaded at the start of August. The two invading Russian armies, the First Army under General Pavel K. Rennenkampf and the Second Army under Alexander Samsonov, were initially successful against the Germans, driving them back in the initial battles of Stallupönen (17 August) and Gumbinnen (20 August). On 22 August, Prittwitz was replaced as commander of the German Eighth army by General Paul von Hindenburg, with Erich Ludendorff as his chief of staff. Following a plan devised by Colonel Max Hoffman, Ludendorff ordered that one corps should be left to hold Rennennkampf north of the Masurian Lakes, while the bulk of the German forces were moved south against Samsonov in a region of forests and lakes, near the historic town of Tannenberg. The plan was so successful that by 29 August the Russian Second Army had been encircled and destroyed, with catastrophic losses of 125,000 men and 500 guns. Samsonov disappeared into the forest and shot himself.

Tannoy A type of public-address system originating in the 1920s. Tannoy was a tradename of the *Tannoy Audio Communications* company of America and its UK subsidiary. The name, which has subsequently been applied to any form of public-address system, is derived from an electrical rectifier device based on the element *tan*talum and a lead all*oy*.

Tante Yvonne (Fr. Aunt Yvonne) Yvonne de Gaulle, the wife of Charles de Gaulle, former president of France (1959–69), so called on account of her reputation for domesticity.

Taranto raid An attack by carrier-based British torpedo bombers on the main base of the Italian fleet in the Bay of Taranto on the night of 11 November 1940. Operation Judgment, as it was called, was a brilliant success: 21 Fairey Swordfish launched from the aircraft carrier *Illustrious* disabled three Italian battleships with the loss of only two aircraft. Half the Italian battlefleet was put out of action, which effectively removed the Italian naval threat in the Mediterranean. The success of the Taranto raid was carefully noted by the Japanese, who had invested heavily in the offensive potential of carrier-based forces.

target-rich environment US military jargon from the GULF WAR of 1991. It was used to describe an air sortie into an area in which the pilot had plenty of Iraqi tanks, missile launchers, or artillery pieces to destroy with his bombs or missiles.

Tariff Reform A political movement in the UK inaugurated in 1903 by Joseph Chamberlain (1836–1914) for the reintroduction of a tariff or scale of duties on imported goods, originally with the idea of strengthening the bonds of the British Empire on a basis of IMPERIAL PREFERENCE. Return to protection did not take place on any scale until 1932, following the financial crisis of 1931. *See also* LIBERAL LANDSLIDE.

Tarka The principal character in the popular animal saga *Tarka the Otter* (1927) by Henry Williamson (1895–1977). Williamson had published two previous natural history tales, *The Peregrine's Saga* (1923) and *The Old Stag* (1926), but it was *Tarka* (which won the Hawthornden Prize), with its sympathetic but unsentimental portrayal of the animal world, that made his enduring reputation.

Tarmac A material for surfacing roads, airport runways, car parks, etc., consisting of a mixture of crushed stone and tar or bitumen. The Scottish engineer John McAdam (1756–1836) had introduced the idea of using crushed stone as a road-surfacing material in the 19th century. In 1902, a civil engineer from Nottingham, Purnell Hooley, patented a material that he called *Tarmac*, made by mixing tar with crushed slag from blast furnaces. He later set up a company originally called the *TarMacadam Syndicate*. The name Tarmac has subsequently been used for any similar tar-based paving material and also for anything coated with this material, especially the area surrounding an airport terminal on which the planes stand for boarding and disembarking.

Tarzan The character in the jungle adventures of Edgar Rice Burroughs (1875–1950), who became one of the most enduring heroes in 20th-century cinema. The first Tarzan story was published in 1913 and the first film, *Tarzan of the Apes*, followed in 1918. By 1984, when the film *Greystoke* was released, the adventures of the 'apeman', born an aristocratic Englishman, orphaned, and brought up among wild apes, had inspired a long list of B-MOVIE directors. Among the actors to play Tarzan have been Johnny Weissmuller (an Olympic swimmer), Buster Crabbe, and TV's Ron Ely. His female companion, Jane, has been portrayed by Maureen O'Sullivan, Brenda Joyce, and Bo Derek among others. The name Tarzan has long been associated with MACHO posturing and has occasionally been bestowed on politicians or other public figures, who are seen to cultivate such an image (notably Conservative politician Michael Heseltine). Tarzan's halting approach to Jane, in the line "Me Tarzan, you Jane" has also become a part of 20th-century fable, familiar to three generations of cinemagoers.

Tasaday A small Stone Age tribe of about 25 people, said to have been discovered in the rain forests of Mindanao in the Philippines by neighbouring tribes in the mid-1960s; they were first encountered by anthropologists in 1971. The Tasaday were cave-dwellers, knew nothing of agriculture, lived on a diet of wild yams, bananas, frogs, and insects, wore only orchid-leaf loincloths, and used only the most primitive stone tools and bamboo implements. Their existence was hailed as a major discovery with profound implications for our understanding of Neolithic culture. In 1986, however, it was claimed that the whole affair was a hoax dreamed up as a publicity stunt by the regime of President Ferdinand Marcos. The Tasaday, it was said, were members of an advanced local tribe, who had been put up to adopting a Neolithic lifestyle by the Philippines' presidential assistant on national minorities.

Tass *Telegrafnoe Agentsvo Sovetskovo Soyuza.* The official Soviet news agency. It was established in 1925 to replace Rosta, the first Bolshevik news agency, which had taken over from the Tsarist counterpart in Petrograd during the Revolution. Tass is the main source of news for Soviet national newspapers, television, and radio. It also has bureaux in over 100 countries, serves all the major western wire services, and provides bulletins in a variety of major languages. Tass pronouncements reflect the Soviet government's offical line on domestic and international affairs.

Tassili cave paintings The accidental discovery of ancient cave paintings in the Saharan plateau of Tassili-n-Ajer in 1933 ranks as one of the most significant archaeological finds of the century. Found by a young French army lieutenant out on patrol, the paintings record in detail the family life, hunting parties, religious beliefs, and wars of an unknown ancient dark-skinned warrior race. Many of the animals they hunted are now extinct and it seems likely this long-forgotten people eventually succumbed to their harsh surroundings (once a lush and green land) and to invasion by paler-skinned neighbours.

tax. tax exile A wealthy person who chooses to leave his native country to live in a TAX HAVEN, in order to reduce the impact of taxation. Not all tax exiles would agree that a higher income in a tax haven brings greater happiness than a lower income in the country of one's birth. Tax exiles from the UK are allowed to spend only a limited amount of time in the British Isles. If they exceed this period they become liable for UK taxes.

tax haven A country in which a low rate of tax offers advantages to wealthy individuals (*see* TAX EXILE) and companies that can arrange for some of their income to pass through an office established in the tax haven. Monaco, Liechtenstein, and the Cayman Islands are well-known tax havens.

taxing Mugging a person and stealing some of his or her possessions, *i.e.* forcing the victim to pay a tax. In the 1980s this sense narrowed to mugging someone in order to steal his or her fashionable training shoes. In the later 1980s sports footwear became a potent status symbol among US teenagers, with price tag and brand name the crucial factors. As top-of-the-range products by Nike and Reebok sold for upwards of £100 a pair, many who coveted them turned to some form of crime. The vogue for expensive designer trainers was undoubtedly a factor in the rise in street crime and drug dealing in US cities at this time. In 1988–89 there was a rash of killings motivated purely by a desire to own the victim's shoes. The sports-shoe craze had spread to the UK by 1989 and the first shoe-related muggings were reported soon afterwards. In 1989 a London University survey concluded that the main cause of street crime was not drugs or unemployment but a craving for designer sportswear.

taxi (1) Short for *taximeter*, taxi is the accepted term for a motor-cab, which takes its name from the meter installed on French horse-drawn cabs or *fiacres* long before motor-cabs appeared on the road. In the UK it only became common with the introduction of motor-cabs and was thus associated with them. In London, and some other UK cities, taxis are purpose-built vehicles, the drivers of which have to demonstrate their KNOWLEDGE of the city before they are given a licence. With the emergence in the 1950s of minicabs (any small saloon car driven by an untrained driver), the purpose-built vehicles became known as **black cabs**, because they were originally all black (recently other dark colours have also been used). (2) Of an aircraft, to move along the ground under its own power.

teach-in An originally US name for a series of lectures and discussions on a particular theme led by experts. The expression became current in the UK in the 1960s. *See also* SIT-IN.

Teamsters Union The International Brotherhood of Teamsters, Chauffeurs, Warehousemen, and Helpers of America. The union was founded in 1899, and by 1940 had become America's largest, with over one million members. Persistent allegations of corruption and racketeering led to the union's expulsion from the American Federation of Labour–Congress of Industrial Organizations (AFL–CIO) in 1957, the year in which Jimmy Hoffa was elected leader. To the detriment of the rank and file of the union, it was Hoffa, more than any previous leader, who made the Teamsters synonymous with violence and corruption. Hoffa allowed his friends in organized crime to use the Teamsters as a legitimate front for their criminal activities; in return, Hoffa and the Teamsters became very wealthy, enabling Hoffa to use the money to forge links with corrupt politicians. Eventually, as a result of investigations led by the Attorney General, Robert Kennedy, Hoffa was imprisoned in 1967. He was paroled in 1971 by President Nixon, and in 1975 disappeared, presumably murdered by fellow gangsters. Since the mid-1970s, the Teamsters have made concerted efforts to purge themselves of their criminal elements and reform the basic structure and finances of the organization.

Teapot Dome scandal The long-running scandal in America during the 1920s resulting from the discovery that President Warren Harding's Secretary of the Interior, Albert B. Fall, had secretly leased government oil fields to a private company. The oil fields in question formed part of the Teapot Dome Naval Oil Reserves in Wyoming, which had been transferred to the Interior department in 1921. Fall then stealthily negotiated drilling rights with Harry F. Sinclair of the Monmouth Oil Company and granted similar rights in a reserve at Elk Hills, California, to an old friend, Edward L. Doheny. Fall retired from the cabinet in March 1923 but continuing Senate investigations into his activities resulted in a series of civil and criminal court actions, which kept the affair in the headlines for the rest of the decade and made the term 'Teapot Dome' synonymous with political corruption. In November 1929 Fall was eventually found guilty of receiving at least $404,000 in bribes and was sentenced to a one-year prison term, the first US cabinet officer ever convicted of a serious crime while in office.

> If Fall isn't an honest man, then I am not fit to be President.
>
> WARREN HARDING.

tear. tear gas A gas (or dispersed liquid or powder) that irritates the eyes and causes inflammation of the respiratory tract. Tear gas is used to disable people temporarily and for so-called 'crowd control'. *See* MACE.

tear-jerker or **weepie** A sentimental film, novel, or other narrative that is virtually guaranteed to bring a tear to the viewer's or reader's eye. The ultimate tear-jerker was probably the film *Love Story* (1970), about a dying newly wed, to which the audience was recommended to bring a box of tissues.

teaser In the publicity jargon of the cinema, a poster or other item that offers a glimpse of a forthcoming film in order to stimulate audience interest, without giving away much detail. The technique was widely used in the early years of the century when the first pornographic films were made.

Technicolor Tradename for a technique for making colour motion pictures. The original process in 1915 involved simultaneous projection of both red and green versions of the film. The first such films were tried in 1917–18 and in 1932 a new three-colour process was used in the Disney cartoon *Flowers and Trees*. In fact, many different colour processes have been used in the industry during this century, but 'technicolour' or 'technicoloured' has entered the general language to describe anything that is garishly colourful.

techno-. technobabble A derogatory term for abstruse technological jargon, especially when it seems designed primarily to impress or bamboozle the public. It is especially prevalent in such fields as computing and military technology.

technocracy A society controlled by technical experts (technocrats). A radical US political movement advocating the control of society and the economy by engineers and scientists adopted this name in the 1930s. The movement's ideology was derived from Thorstein Veblen's *The Engineers and the Price System* (1921), which sought to replace the irrationality of the free market by an economy planned by experts in science and technology. The movement lost impetus with the improvement in social and economic conditions brought about by the NEW DEAL after 1935.

technofear The anxiety brought on by having to use a piece of HIGH TECH equipment, such as a complex tape deck or a word processor. People who have technofears might self-deprecatingly describe themselves as 'low tech'.

technomania A mania or excessive enthusiasm for technology or its use. The technomaniac's zeal for modern technology in all possible situations often overrides other considerations, such as the consequences for the environment and society.

technophobia An exaggerated dislike of technology, particularly in relation to its potentially detrimental effects on the environment. The **technophobe** is contrasted with the **technophile**, who welcomes technology in everyday life. Technophobia is often used interchangeably with the later term, TECHNOFEAR.

teddy. teddy-bear A child's toy bear, said to have been named after Theodore (Teddy) Roosevelt, who was fond of bear-hunting. The toy acquired its name after a bearhunt arranged for the US president in 1903: to make sure that the president made a kill, the organizers stunned a small brown bear and tied it to a tree.

teddy-bear syndrome Jargon for a syndrome in which a person enters into a marriage or a relationship solely because he or she cannot bear to be alone and needs the constant presence of a comforter – the functions that a teddy bear fulfils for many during childhood.

teddy boys or **teds** Young men of the 1950s who affected an approximately Edwardian style of dress (they were sometimes jokingly referred to as **Edwardians**), including long jackets, DRAINPIPES, sideburns, and BROTHEL CREEPERS. Of working-class origin, they displayed an enthusiasm for ROCK 'N' ROLL music and the rowdier elements indulged in vandalism and violence. *See also* MODS AND ROCKERS.

Teenage Mutant Ninja Turtles The US televised cartoon series featuring four pizza-loving street-wise turtle heroes – Leonardo, Donatello, Raphael, and Michelangelo. Trained by Splinter the Rat, the foursome emerged from New York City sewers with their victory cry of *Cowabunga!* These figures became the number one children's fad of 1990, appearing in books, food and drink products, T-shirts, toothbrushes, etc. In the UK, where the name was changed to *Teenage Mutant Hero Turtles*, the buying surge of turtle paraphernalia during the recession was said to have saved the commercial Christmas season for some children's shops. *See also* NINJA.

teeny-bopper A girl in her early teens, who adopts current fashions in dress and is a devotee of pop music and its star performers. *See also* WEENY-BOPPER.

Teflon *See* PTFE.

Tehran Conference The Allied meeting in the Persian capital between 28 November and 1 December 1943; Churchill's and Roosevelt's first wartime meeting with Stalin. Churchill had hoped to delay the invasion of France, the SECOND FRONT, which Stalin had so long demanded, by a continuation of the Mediterranean strategy. Roosevelt however agreed with Stalin on the urgency of the cross-channel invasion; it was settled that OVERLORD should take place the following May and that diversionary Soviet offensives would be launched simultaneously in the east. Stalin also obtained Roosevelt's agreement to Soviet expansion into E Poland and the extension of Polish borders to include the German provinces of East Prussia and Danzig. The 'Big Three' also had inconclusive discussions on the zoning of the postwar Germany, debated the proposed nature of the United Nations Organization, agreed a commitment to postwar independence of Persia, and settled plans to increase Allied support for Tito's resistance movement in Yugoslavia.

tektite A small roundish glassy object of unknown origin found only on certain areas of the Earth's surface, known as **tektite fields**. Tektites range in size from a few millimetres to about 10 cm and their chemical composition is unrelated to the geological areas in which they occur. Their origin is the subject of much scientific debate in the 20th century: some geologists believe that they are extraterrestrial and possibly lunar in origin, while others think that they were formed on the Earth at an early stage of the planet's development.

tele-. telecide US slang (a combination of *television* and *suicide*) describing the downward spiral and death of an actor's career after he or she has made what turns out to be an unpopular appearance on television.

telecommuter A person who works from home with the aid of a computer or word processor and a telephone, fax, or MODEM.

Teleprompter *See* AUTOCUE.

Teletext *See* CEEFAX.

telethon A lengthy television programme or campaign to raise funds for a charity or some other cause. The programme invariably features noted entertainers, film footage of those needing help, appeals for funds, operators taking pledged donations over the telephone, and a running scoreboard on the total raised and how much is still needed to reach the stated goal. In America, local PBS stations conduct annual telethons to raise operating funds; the largest charity event is the annual 24-hour appeal for children with cerebral palsy and similar diseases. In the UK, the BBC's annual *Children in Need* campaign is broadcast on both television and radio. *Telethon* is a portmanteau word formed from *tele(vision)* and *(mara)thon*.

televangelists US evangelists who preach on television, often on their own cable networks. The *electronic church* tradition goes back to radio: Oral Roberts once regularly urged listeners to lay their hands on the radio to be healed. After Billy Graham and Cardinal Fulton J. Sheen demonstrated the power of religious messages on television in the 1950s, the screen became a growing tool of the church for three decades. In 1977, the Rev. Pat Robertson, head of the Christian Broadcasting Network, said: "We can't really be taken seriously unless we're a $1 billion-a-year operation." In the 1980s, however, financial and sexual scandals led to viewer disenchantment and falling revenues: Jim and Tammy Bakker, founders of the PTL (Praise the Lord) Club, lost their empire after Jim Bakker was jailed for financial misconduct and evangelist Jimmy Swaggart was caught with a prostitute. The bad publicity even affected Oral Roberts, who told viewers in 1987 that God would take him within the year if donation goals were not met (they were, and he survived). America's major religions also employ the television: in 1982, the US Catholic Conference began its National Catholic Telecommunications Network. As Pat Robertson noted: "It would be a folly for the church not to get involved with the most formative force in America."

television age The post-World War II period seen as an era dominated increasingly by television. Before World War II the television – invented in 1924 by the British electrical engineer John Logie Baird (1888–1946) – was a curiosity; although the BBC began regular TV broadcasts in 1936 there were a very small number of sets to receive them. By the 1960s, however, a television set ('the box') was an essential part of the living-room furniture in most British and US homes. In 1987 the total of homes with a television set throughout the world passed 500 million, with America leading with 89,130,000 sets. In 1988, however, Chinese officials announced the presence of no less than 100 million sets in their country. 98% of British households had a set in 1989 with half of these having two or more.

The effects of the penetration of television into homes throughout the world have long been the subject of anxious debate. In 1988 it was estimated that the average child in America has witnessed 26,000 murders on television by the age of 18. The average Briton watches 25 hours

21 minutes of television every week. Audiences across the world can be enormous: 1.6 billion people (one third of the world's population) tuned in to the LIVE AID concerts of 1985, while 2.65 billion people watched the 1990 World Cup finals in Italy between 8 June and 8 July.

The potential for television to influence huge numbers of people has led to strict control being placed on the medium, with measures ranging from total political censorship in some countries to regulations upon the degree of violence, foul language, etc., used on the small screen in democracies. There are also strict rules outlawing the transmission of 'sublimal messages', *i.e.* signals that are flashed on the screen so fast that the viewer is unaware that he has seen it, although his brain has registered its content.

To its advocates, television has broadened the range of public knowledge and provided more harmless enjoyment than any other medium of the 20th century. Critics say it trivializes everything, undermines family life, and contributes to the breakdown of moral codes. *See also* BLUE PETER; CORONATION STREET; SOOTY; THREE-MINUTE CULTURE; etc.

> Television? No good will come of this device. The word is half Greek and half Latin.
>
> C. P. SCOTT.

> Television is more interesting than people. If it were not, we should have people standing in the corners of our rooms.
>
> ALAN COREN; *The Times*.

telex A system for transmitting information over telephone lines using a keyboard and a printer. Originally developed in the late 1890s, the modern telex systems were developed in the 1930s and were widely used until the late 1980s, when FAX replaced them to a great extent. The name is a contraction of *tel(eprinter)* and *ex(change)*.

Telstar The COMMUNICATIONS SATELLITE launched in 1962 for relaying transatlantic telephone messages and television pictures.

ten. ten-four or **10-4** US slang for message received, message understood, message affirmed, or Yes, okay, affirmative, correct. It is equivalent to the military ROGER. The term was used first in the mid-1960s by CB radio operators and popularized in the 1970s by truck drivers, as depicted in films and country music *e.g.* 'That's a ten-four'. The terminology comes from the ten codes used by US police to save air time. Other examples are: **10-9** for repeat, **10-15** for civil disturbance, and **10-34** for trouble or emergency.

1066 and All That Catchphrase denoting anything historical or 'old hat'. It was taken from the title of a comical survey of British history by Robert Julian Yeatman and Walter Carruthers Sellar, published in 1930. The authors reduce British history from the Roman conquest to World War I to a breathless chronology of kings and queens, invasions, battles, wars, inventions, etc., summarized as either 'a Good Thing' or 'a Bad Thing' in a parody of traditional history textbooks familiar to every schoolchild. Familiar incidents and events are amusingly rendered; in Judge Jeffreys' notorious 'Bloody Assizes', for example:

> The Rebels were ferociously dealt with by the memorable Judge Jeffreys who . . . made some furious remarks about the prisoners known as "The Bloody Asides".

tennis. Anyone for tennis? Catchphrase of the 1920s, encapsulating the carefree and debonair concept of a period in which wealthy young men appeared to have nothing more pressing to do than to appear at house parties in their straw hats and white flannels, inviting their friends to play lawn tennis. The phrase became a cliché in various light comedies of the period.

Teresa, Mother *See* MOTHER TERESA.

terminological inexactitude A euphemism for a lie, attributed to Winston Churchill (1874–1965) after he used it in a speech in the House of Commons on 22 February 1906:

> It cannot in the opinion of His Majesty's Government be classified as slavery in the extreme acceptance of the word without some risk of terminological inexactitude.

It is contrary to parliamentary procedure for one MP to call another a liar. A more widely used phrase now, which is less of a mouthful, is ECONOMICAL WITH THE TRUTH.

Terrence Higgins Trust An organization that provides information, help, and advice on AIDS and HIV infection through its HELPLINE. The Trust was established in 1983 by the friends of Terrence Higgins, who in 1982 was one of the first people to die of Aids in the UK; it now has a government grant that covers about one quarter of its costs. The Trust's medical advice covers such issues as drug use, health education, and safe sex; its legal centre offers advice on the problems of employment, insurance, and mortgages; and its publicity department helps to promote public awareness and understanding of Aids and HIV infection through leaflets, campaigns in the media, lectures, and training courses. Its main contribution to Aids sufferers is its BUDDY system, in which some 400 volunteers provide practical and emotional support on a one-to-one basis for those dying of Aids.

Terylene Tradename for a type of synthetic POLYESTER used as a fibre and fabric. The material was developed in 1951 by ICI and named after the main constituents – *ter*phthalic acid and eth*ylene* glycol.

Tessa Tax Exempt Special Savings Account. A savings scheme in the UK introduced in 1991, which enables savers to invest £3000 in the first year and £1800 p.a. thereafter, up to a limit of £9000, in a bank or building society with tax-free interest, provided that the capital remains in the account for five years. Interest can be withdrawn but if the capital is withdrawn tax relief is forfeited.

test. Test-ban Treaty A treaty signed by America, the Soviet Union, and the UK on 7 October 1963 agreeing to a ban on the atmospheric (but not underground) testing of nuclear weapons. The treaty represented only a small step in the direction of nuclear disarmament but was a victory for environmentalists, who feared the damaging effects of radiation dispersal in the upper atmosphere. Later, over 100 other countries endorsed the treaty, France being a notable exception.

test marketing The launch of a new product in a restricted geographical area in order to test consumer reaction. It has the advantage of minimizing costs and enabling the product to be modified in the light of consumer reactions. The disadvantage is that competitors are able to see the product before its full launch.

test-tube baby *See* IVF.

Tethys Sea *See* PANGAEA.

Tet offensive The coordinated assault by 70,000 communist soldiers on more than 100 major cities and towns throughout South Vietnam, which was launched on 31 January 1968. The offensive broke the holiday (*Tet*, the lunar New Year) truce, took the US military by surprise, and came as a complete shock to the US public. For the first time in the VIETNAM WAR, television viewers witnessed US troops fighting the VIET CONG, not deep in the countryside, but in the streets of Hue and Saigon – even within the US Embassy itself. Since the US commitment of ground troops in 1965, the military had constantly assured the politicians, the press, and the general public that the communists were on the verge of collapse. The Tet offensive appeared to prove otherwise; as a result public support for the war, which had been diminishing significantly in recent months, declined even more rapidly. Walter Cronkite, 'the most trusted face' on network TV, reported from Saigon in February that the war was going badly, contrary to military optimism, and was bound to end in stalemate. Although the offensive was crushed with the communists suffering severe losses, Tet represented a decisive psychological victory for the Viet Cong. The offensive also represented the last nail in the coffin of Johnson's presidency. In March 1968, faced with the growing public and political opposition to the war, even among his own staff, he announced he would not seek re-election as the Democratic candidate in the forthcoming presidential contest.

TGV *Train à Grande Vitesse* (Fr. high-speed train). A French bullet train that can reach speeds of 170 m.p.h. (275 k.p.h.), the fastest in the world. The first TGV began service in 1983 on a specially built line between Paris and Lyon, cutting the 285-mile (460-km) journey time to two hours. A second TGV line, SW to Le Mans and Tours, was opened in 1990 and there are plans to extend the Lyon line to Marseille. It is also intended to link Paris by TGV with the CHANNEL TUNNEL to the west as well as to Brussels, Amsterdam, and Cologne to the east. *See also* SINKANSEN.

thalidomide A drug formerly used in medicine as a sedative and to prevent vomiting. Developed in the 1950s and marketed under the tradename Distaval, it was prescribed for pregnant women until its disastrous effects on the developing foetus became widely known. Women who had taken the drug early in pregnancy gave birth to babies with a range of abnormalities typically involving the absence of limbs, the fingers or toes being attached to the trunk by a short stump. Between 1959 and 1962 over 3000 so-called 'thalidomide babies' were born in the UK, West Germany, and Canada before the drug was withdrawn. The tragedy led to stricter controls in the testing of new drugs.

Thatcherism The economic and political ideology, as well as the personal style of leadership, associated with Margaret Thatcher (1925–), prime minister of the UK (1979–90). Broadly, Thatcher favoured the unhindered operation of the free market, the privatization of public utilities, the encouragement of share ownership, and the sale of council houses to further the 'enterprise culture' she stood for. Monetarism replaced KEYNESIANISM and the Thatcher government successfully embarked on the reform of the trade unions to curtail their power. In foreign affairs Thatcher was resolute in her support of America but resisted any move to greater unity with the European Community that would threaten the sovereignty of the UK or its economic independence. Irrespective of the success or popularity of these policies, it was Thatcher's confrontational style of leadership (*see* IRON LADY) and its divisive effect on the cabinet, especially over her hostility to Europe and her reforms of local government embodied in the poll tax (*see* COMMUNITY CHARGE), that brought about her downfall in November 1990.

Theatre Workshop An experimental left-wing drama group founded in Kendal in 1945 by a group of actors dissatisfied with the mainstream theatre. From 1953 the Workshop was based in the Theatre Royal, Stratford East, London, with Joan Littlewood (1914–) as artistic director, Gerald Raffles as general manager, and Ewan McColl (Littlewood's husband) as writer or adapter of many of the group's dramatic productions. Theatre Workshop sought to revitalize the British theatre with challenging adaptions of the classics and new works, especially working-class plays. Many of these later transferred to London's West End, including Brendan Behan's *The Quare Fellow* (1956) and Shelagh Delaney's *A Taste of Honey* (1958). In 1961 Littlewood left the group, disillusioned by the dilution of the radical content of its output as a result of the financial pressure for commercial success. She did, however, return to direct the occasional production, notably the musical *Oh, What a Lovely War!* (1963). She eventually left the UK in 1975 to work in France; the Workshop disbanded soon afterwards.

theme. themed Denoting a restaurant, pub, amusement park, etc., that is planned or designed around a single unifying theme, such as the Wild West or Sherlock Holmes. The concept arose with the advent of the **theme park**, a leisure site in which the various displays and buildings reflect a particular theme, usually a historic period or exotic place. The 1980s saw a vogue for 'theming' established pubs and restaurants with the aim of attracting a young wealthy clientele, generally to the disgruntlement of regulars. The practice has even spread to such areas as catering, so that it is possible to order a 'themed' meal for special occasions.

theme song A song that recurs during the course of a musical play or film generally reflecting the mood or theme of the production.

theory of games *See* GAME THEORY.

thermal reactor *See* NUCLEAR REACTOR.

thermonuclear weapon *See* NUCLEAR WEAPON.

Thermos Tradename for a brand of vacuum flask of the type invented by the Scottish physicist James Dewar (1842–1921) around 1872. The name dates from 1904.

think-tank A group of people with specialized knowledge and ability, set up to carry out research into particular problems (usually social, political, and technological) and to provide ideas and possible solutions. The original think-tank, officially the Central Policy Review Staff, was set up by Edward Heath in 1970 under the directorship of Lord Rothschild (1910–90). Its function was to provide the cabinet and individual ministers with advice on strategy. It was abolished in 1983 by Margaret Thatcher.

Thin Man The detective hero of the thriller novel *The Thin Man* by Dashiell Hammett, subsequently successfully filmed (with sequels) in the 1930s and 1940s and later as a TV series. The nickname became associated with the actor William Powell, who played the detective Nick Charles, although the Thin Man was originally the first of the murder victims in the book.

third. third age The years after middle age, a term borrowed from the French *troisième âge*. *See also* UNIVERSITY OF THE THIRD AGE.

third man A suspected third Soviet agent involved in the defection of BURGESS AND MACLEAN. In 1963, it became apparent that the third man was KIM Philby. The name alludes to the title of the Graham Greene and Carol Reed film *The Third Man* (1949). *See* LIME, HARRY.

Third Programme One of the three post-war BBC radio programmes (the others being the Light Programme and the Home Service), which went on the air for the first time on 29 September 1946. The Third Programme was devoted to serious, often avant-garde, music, drama, literature, lectures, and intelligent discussion. Exact programme timings were avoided to ensure a free-flowing schedule and items broadcast during the first week included Bach's *Goldberg Variations*, Shaw's *Man and Superman*, talks by Field Marshall Smuts and Max Beerbohm, and a humorous programme devised by Joyce Grenfell and Stephen Potter. The darling of intellectuals, 'the Third', as it was called, was sneered at by the uneducated and the pretentious:

> I have listened attentively to all programmes and nothing will confirm me more in my resolution to emigrate.
>
> EVELYN WAUGH.

Third Reich The offical name of the Nazi regime in Germany, from January 1933 to May 1945. The Third Reich was deemed to be the successor to two previous historical periods of German domination in Europe: the first being the medieval Holy Roman Empire and the second the German Empire (1871–1918).

Third Republic The government of France from the defeat of the Second Empire by Prussia in 1870 to the fall of France in 1940. The Third Republic was notable for its political instability, especially after 1918, when government ministries came and went with great rapidity. The period was also punctuated by a series of crises that threatened the French parliamentary system itself; these included the Dreyfuss Affair in the 1890s and the STAVISKY AFFAIR in the 1930s. In spite of these shortcomings, the Third Republic proved to be longest-lived of the French Republics since the French Revolution (1789).

Third World The underdeveloped countries of the world in which agricultural and industrial production are insufficient to sustain investment and economic growth (*see* DEVELOPING COUNTRIES). These countries, in Africa, Asia, and Latin America, are not aligned with either the capitalist western nations (the **First World**) or the communist bloc (the **Second World**), thus constituting a third, impoverished and independent, world.

Thirteen Plots of May 13 The dramatic and secretive plotting and counterplotting that returned Charles de Gaulle (1890–1979) to power in France in May 1958. De Gaulle had resigned the premiership in 1946 in disgust at what he perceived as the harmful vacillation and factionalism of parliamentary politics. By 1958, however, a powerful body of Gaullist supporters had begun secretly plotting to secure his return to power. They consisted of malcontents within the army and among White French settlers (*colons*) in Algeria, angered by what they regarded as inadequate political support from the mainland, and right-wing opponents of the government in metropolitan France. On 13 May, as a new prime minister, Pierre Pflimin, was about to be appointed, a large crowd attacked and occupied the government offices in Algiers, establishing a Committee of Public Safety. The army generals supported the Committee's call for de Gaulle's return to power, and on 15 May de Gaulle dramatically announced that he would be willing to assume power if invited. Meanwhile the rebellion in Algeria escalated; on 24 May Algerian-based troops occupied Corsica and it was widely rumoured that the generals were preparing to implement a plan to occupy Paris on 27 May. It was against this background of political crisis, heightened by fears of an imminent military coup and the threat of civil war, that Pflimin agreed to step down in favour of de Gaulle. On 1 June the national assembly confirmed de Gaulle's appointment as premier, gave him full powers for six months, and left him with the task of elaborating a new constitution. De Gaulle was certainly aware of the plots among his supporters to secure his return but he wisely refused to commit himself until the collapse of the Fourth Republic was certain; this enabled him to assume power on his own terms.

thirty. 38th Parallel The division between North and South Korea agreed by the Soviet Union and America in August 1945; it was intended as a temporary measure for the purpose of accepting the surrender of Japanese forces in the region. The Soviets would be responsible for the Japanese surrender north of the

38th Parallel and the Americans responsible south of the line. The division at the 38th Parallel was hastily suggested by the Americans as the Soviet forces moved into the north of Korea in the last days of the war. Stalin surprisingly agreed, although the absence of US forces in the area at that time would not have prevented him moving further south. As a result America was left in control of the capital Seoul, two-thirds of the population, and the main agricultural region, while the Soviet Union controlled the industrial north. As the wartime alliance between the Soviet Union and America dissolved into COLD WAR rivalry, the prospects for unification receded and civil war escalated into the full-scale international confrontation in the KOREAN WAR six years later. The division of Korea into North and South along the 38th Parallel remains.

thirty-something Any age between 30 and 40, when the conflicting impulses of youth and the growing awareness of oncoming middle age can precipitate a crisis of identity. The phrase is usually used to evade giving one's exact age; the overtones of spiritual crisis it evokes were reinforced in the 1980s when the phrase was used as the title of a highly successful US TV series about a group of affluent but troubled young people of this age.

Thought Police The sinister and murderous organs of Party security described by George Orwell (1903–50) in his novel *Nineteen Eighty-Four* (1949; *see under* NINE). In his nightmarish vision of a totalitarian future, society is divided into the Party and the Proles. The Proles are insignificant, but the Party is divided into the Inner Party, the privileged class, and the Outer Party, who are constantly monitored by the Thought Police for deviation from prescribed thinking. Those caught harbouring improper thoughts are arrested, tortured at the Ministry of Love, and then vaporized.

Thousand Days The three-year administration of President John F. Kennedy (1917–63), from his election on 9 November 1960 to his assassination on 22 November 1963. It was taken as the title of one of the best inside accounts of Kennedy's presidency, *A Thousand Days: John F. Kennedy in the White House* (1965), by the historian Arthur Schlesinger Jr, one of the 'Best and Brightest' whom Kennedy selected to implement his promised NEW FRONTIER. *See also* CAMELOT; OSWALD, LEE HARVEY.

thrash A type of ROCK music that combines the speed and violence of HARDCORE with the high-volume guitar style of HEAVY METAL. It originated in New York in the late 1980s. Exponents rejoice in such names as Anthrax, Napalm Death, and Millions of Dead Cops. It is also known as **speed metal**, **thrash metal**, **thrashcore**, and **deathcore**.

threatened species A species of animal or plant that is in danger of becoming extinct if nothing is done to halt the decline in its wild population. Reasons for the decline may include exploitation of the species (*e.g.* the killing of elephants to obtain their tusks) or destruction of its habitat (*e.g.* the burning of tropical rain forests). The International Union for the Conservation of Nature and Natural Resources (IUCN) has identified several categories of threatened species. These include (in ascending order of vulnerability): rare species (those with small populations considered to be at risk); VULNERABLE SPECIES; and ENDANGERED SPECIES. *See also* EXTINCT.

three. 3-D Three-dimensional cinematography. The film technique that creates realistic depth on the screen, introduced in 1936 in various short films. It was not, however, until competition from television became a serious threat in the 1950s that the technique came of age (with such tradenames as *Natural Vision 3-D* and *Dynoptic 3-D*). The first 3-D feature film, *Bwana Devil* in 1952, promised "A lion in your lap"; Warner Brothers' *House of Wax* (1953) was perhaps the most successful. The illusion of depth requires the audience to wear polarized glasses, which blend two superimposed images shot by separate cameras, requiring two projectors, and using a specially coated screen. The public's thrill at ducking spears and boulders soon waned in favour of well-scripted films that did not require glasses.

Three Mile Island The site near Harrisburg, Pennsylvania, of America's most serious NUCLEAR REACTOR accident. On 28 March 1979, due to human and technological failure, the fissionable core, normally immersed in water, became accidentally exposed to the air and began to melt, releasing radioactive gases into the air. Complete meltdown of the reactor core (*see* CHINA SYNDROME) was avoided but the accident provoked a national debate on the safety of nuclear power. This effectively brought the US nuclear reactor programme to a halt throughout the 1980s and provided support for the anti-nuclear power lobby elsewhere. *See also* CHERNOBYL.

three-mile limit *See* RUM RUNNERS.

three-minute culture A society in which the constant supply of information by means of television, magazines, etc., has led to the average viewer or reader being unable to concentrate on a single topic for more than three minutes. The high level of distractions offered by modern technological society is seen by critics as deeply damaging to popular culture, with only a small minority being prepared to study anything in depth. As evidence of the influence of the three-minute culture, these commentators point to the diminishing length of newspaper articles and the phenomenon of the SOUND BITE, etc.

throw. throwaway A disposable artifact, especially one designed to be discarded after (usually) a single use. Throwaway cameras, for example, are sold containing a film; after the film has been exposed and developed, the camera is thrown away. The proliferation of such items has led to accusations that the West has become a wasteful 'throwaway society'. A **throwaway remark** or **line** is one purposely underemphasized by delivery in a casual or offhand manner.

throw a wobby or **wobbler** To go into a fit of uncontrollable rage. Although a number of derivations have been suggested for this slang phrase (for example, referring to throwing a 'wobbly' ball in cricket), the simplest combines the idiom 'to throw a fit' with the idea of somebody trembling (wobbling) with anger. The term was popular with teenagers in the 1980s, who used it chiefly in an attempt to make the anger of parents or teachers seem ridiculous. It is sometimes used of other kinds of irrational or uncontrolled behaviour.

Thunderthighs A nickname for an obese or heavily built woman, especially one who is intimidating to men. In the late 1970s it was the press nickname for Christina Onassis, heiress of the Greek shipping magnate Aristotle Onassis (1906–75), referring to her evident weight problem. It presumably refers to 'thunder' in the sense of moving heavily or noisily.

Tiananmen massacre The massacre by the army of thousands of unarmed Chinese civilians in Peking's Tiananmen Square during pro-democracy demonstrations led by university students in June 1989. Protests had started in late April during the funeral of the liberal Hu Yaobang, a deposed former general secretary of the Chinese Communist Party. About 150,000 students gathered in Tiananmen Square shouting anti-government slogans. By mid-May more than one million demonstrators, including some government officials, held the largest protest gathering in communist China's history. This happened during a visit by the Soviet leader, Mikhail Gorbachov, interrupting his schedule, which included a wreath-laying ceremony in Tiananmen Square. Students occupied the square permanently and erected a Statue of Freedom based on New York's Statue of Liberty; some of them staged hunger strikes. Martial law was imposed on 20 May. On 3 June, about 10,000 troops of the People's Liberation Army entered the city. The next day they stormed Tiananmen Square, shooting at protesters with automatic weapons. Tanks and armoured personnel carriers then moved in to kill the retreating students. The massacre provoked worldwide condemnation and trade reprisals. However, Deng Xiaoping, China's conservative elder statesman, continued to crush the 'counter-revolutionary rebellion.' Mass arrests and executions followed.

ticker *See* BIRDER.

tidal power A method of generating electricity by using the ebb and flow of the tides. At high tide water is collected behind a barrage and released at low tide to drive a turbine, which in turn drives a generator. The first successful scheme to exploit tidal power was the Rance power station opened in 1967 in the Gulf of Saint-Malo in France. Several UK sites, especially the Severn estuary, are suitable for tidal power generation. *See also* ALTERNATIVE ENERGY.

Tiger A German heavy tank of World War II, introduced in August 1942. It had a reputation as one of the war's most formidable fighting machines: it's 88 mm gun could pierce 100 mm armour at a 1000 m (3280 feet) range, and its own 110 mm frontal armour was virtually impregnable. Despite its superb hitting power and protection, the Tiger's 56-ton weight limited its speed (23 m.p.h.; 37 k.p.h.) and manoeuvrability. 1354 were built before August 1944, by which time it was superseded by the Tiger II, which was armed with the 88 mm L/71 gun, capable of even greater penetrative power. It too suffered from poor engine performance and reliability but was virtually indestructible on the battlefield. 485 Tiger IIs were produced before the war ended.

tiger country Any remote thickly vegetated terrain that might be expected to be inhabited by tigers and other wild beasts. Tiger country is used more widely of any area that it would be dangerous to enter for whatever reason.

The Tiger The nickname of the French statesman and journalist Georges Clemenceau (1841–1929), who, as prime minister, negotiated the VERSAILLES TREATY (1919). A determined fighter, single-minded in achieving his objectives, he gained a reputation for destructive political power by bringing down one ministry after another, using his newspaper, *La Justice*, to carry his criticisms.

tights *See* PANTYHOSE.

time. **time and motion study** A widely used method of analysing a complex operation by breaking it into small steps and timing each step. This enables standards of performance to be set so that the operation can be incorporated into a larger process, which can be timed and costed accurately.

time capsule A box or other container enclosing items related to the present period, which is buried or hidden for rediscovery and reopening in the distant future. Such capsules, usually containing daily newspapers, coins, etc., have been 'planted' at numerous sites throughout the UK since the 1960s, often with civic ceremony. The ultimate in time capsules must, however, be the summaries of human achievement carried on board the PIONEER and VOYAGER space probes.

time dilation *See* RELATIVITY.

time-lapse photography A form of photography that records such slow processes as plant growth. A series of single exposures of the object is made using a ciné camera adapted to taking single shots. When this ciné film is projected at a normal speed the rate of change is greatly speeded up. For example, if one photograph per day is taken of a plant, the growth from seedling to mature plant over a period of several weeks can be seen in a few seconds.

time sharing (1) An arrangement for sharing ownership in a furnished holiday house or flat, with each owner occupying the property for a certain period during the year. Popularized in the mid-1970s, time sharing has since come into disrepute because of the high-pressure selling methods associated with it (*see* HARD SELL). A 1990 report by the UK Office of Fair Trading called for legislation to end abuses and in 1991 legislation by the European Commission was also under consideration. (2) The apparently simultaneous use of a central computer by operators at separate terminals. This is possible because of the computer's high speed of processing data.

tin. **tin fish** Naval slang for a torpedo.

tin hat A soldier's name for his protective metal helmet.

Tin Lizzie Nickname of the Ford Model T motor car, designed by Henry Ford and made by the Ford Motor Company in the early 20th century. The Model T was the first mass-produced motor car: 15 million had been manufactured and sold by 1927, when the model was discontinued. The first Model T car was made in 1908, and mass production began five years later on a specially designed assembly line housed in a purpose-built factory at Highland Park, Michigan. With its four-cylinder 2898 cc engine, the Model T was capable of speeds up to 40 m.p.h.; in accordance with Ford's specifications it was durable, easy to operate and maintain, and equally suitable for town and country driving. A reduction in the price of the Model T to $500, or £110, brought motoring within the reach of the average citizen in America and the UK. *See under* BLACK.

Tin-pan Alley The district of New York City, originally in the area of 14th Street, in which popular music is published. In England, Denmark Street, off Charing Cross Road, was so called as the centre of the popular music industry. The name has been said to derive from the rattling of tins by rivals when a performance was too loud and too protracted. The 'Alley' is now largely deserted by song writers and music publishers who have moved to bigger premises. *See* OLD GREY WHISTLE TEST *under* GREY.

TINA A nickname of Margaret Thatcher. *See* IRON LADY.

Tinker Bell In J. M. Barrie's children's play PETER PAN (1904), a female fairy who accompanies Peter and the Darling children on their adventures. When she 'dies', the audience is required to declare its belief in fairies in order to bring her back to life. The name is now sometimes applied to effeminate or sensitive males (often in the feminized form, Tinkerbelle). *See* NANA; WENDY.

tinsel town *See* HOLLYWOOD.

tip and run raid During World War II, a hurried and often indiscriminate air raid in which the enemy sped homeward after jettisoning their bombs. So called from the light-hearted form of cricket in which the batsman has to run every time he hits the ball.

Tipperary A song inseparably associated with World War I, composed by Jack Judge (d. 1938), of Oldbury, Birmingham. The words were by Harry J. Williams of Temple Balsall, Warwickshire, and the first line of the refrain was engraved on his tombstone. It was composed in 1912 in response to a bet that they could not write a song and perform it the same day and it was already popular in the MUSIC HALL by 1914; it was sung by troops embarking for France and on the front.

> It's a long way to Tipperary,
> It's a long way to go,
> It's a long way to Tipperary,
> To the sweetest girl I know,
> Goodbye, Piccadilly; farewell, Leicester Square;
> It's a long, long way to Tipperary,
> But my heart's right there.

tired and emotional A euphemism for drunk that has proved useful to the press who have to be mindful of the libel laws when reporting people's exploits. The expression is thought to have originated in the satirical magazine PRIVATE EYE in the 1960s, when it was used to describe George Brown's lapses (especially when he was foreign secretary). It is sometimes abbreviated to 't and e'.

Titanic The sinking of RMS *Titanic* on 14 April 1912 ranks as one of the most notorious shipwrecks of all time. The large number of deaths coupled with the shock caused by the loss of the world's newest and most luxurious ocean-liner on her maiden voyage left a scar on the national consciousness that has never faded. The *Titanic* set sail from Southampton with 3000 people aboard, including prominent members of British and US society. At 11.45 p.m. on 14 April, however, the claims that the ship was unsinkable were put to the severest test when she hit an iceberg, which tore a 300-foot gash below the waterline. When the *Titanic* went down two hours and 40 minutes later – its band still playing – 1513 people drowned, many because there were not enough lifeboats.

Curiously, the loss of the *Titanic* appears to have been foretold some years earlier, by Morgan Robertson in his novel *Futility*. In this work of fiction, a great liner on its maiden voyage – with many society figures among its 3000 passengers – sinks when it rams an iceberg: the death toll is high because there are not enough lifeboats. The *Titan* is also called 'unsinkable'.

This was not the only forewarning of the tragedy. The journalist and spiritualist W. T. Stead had in 1892 published yet another story closely parallel to the *Titanic*'s; he was one of those to die in the disaster in 1912.

The *Titanic* disaster was filmed in 1958 as *A Night to Remember*. An attempt at a sequel, *Raise the Titanic!* (1980) was such a disaster in cinematic terms that it nearly 'sank' its production company, costing $40 million and bringing in only $7 million. The wreck itself was located and photographed in 1985; divers recovered various items but talk of raising the vessel came to nothing.

> Over the mirrors meant
> To glass the opulent
> The sea-worm crawls – grotesque, slimed, dumb, indifferent.
>
> THOMAS HARDY; 'The Convergence of the Twain'.

Titan rocket A US liquid-fuelled ICBM developed during the 1950s and replaced by the Minuteman in the early 1960s. Titan I had a range of 8000 miles (12,800 km) and Titan II 9000 miles (14,400 km); both carried a 10 megaton nuclear warhead. The Titan was also modified as a two-stage space launch vehicle, proving to be one of the most reliable of NASA's rockets; Titan II successfully launched all ten of the Gemini two-man spacecraft in the early 1960s. Until the development of the SPACE SHUTTLE, the Titan IIIE-Centaur was the heaviest US launch vehicle, capable of placing 13,600 kg into Earth orbit. First tested in 1974, it was used to launch the Viking I spacecraft to Mars in August of the following year.

Titoism The pragmatic communist system implemented in Yugoslavia after 1945 by

Josip Broz Tito (1892–1980). Tito rejected the Soviet model of communist social and economic development, imposed by Stalin in the eastern bloc countries, believing instead in the possibility of 'separate roads to socialism'. His policies included decentralized profit-sharing workers' councils and a non-aligned stance in international affairs. Regarding Titoism as a dangerous threat to his authority, Stalin expelled Yugoslavia from the Cominform in 1948. A purge was then carried out of suspected Titoist heretics throughout the communist parties and governments of E Europe. Surprisingly, Tito survived Stalin's wrath, although similar national and reformist communist movements in Hungary and Czechoslovakia, which were partially inspired by the Yugoslavian example, were later crushed by Soviet tanks.

Toad One of the leading animal characters in the popular children's book, *The Wind in the Willows* (1908), by Kenneth Grahame (1859–1932). The work was later dramatised by A. A. Milne as *Toad of Toad Hall* (1929).

Tobruk The best harbour in Cyrenaica (Libya), North Africa, which was the scene of fierce battles during World War II. In January 1941 it was captured from the Italians by British and Australian troops; by February the whole of Cyrenaica was in British hands after the total collapse of the Italian forces. The Germans then entered the Mediterranean campaign and by April Tobruk was encircled by Rommel's Panzer divisions after German forces had met only thin resistance from the British as they drove eastward from El Agheila through Benghazi. The Royal Navy and the RAF managed to supply the besieged garrison with food, weapons, and fresh troops, until on 11 December the 242-day-long siege ended when Commonwealth troops broke out of the city to join with the British Eighth Army units at nearby Acroma. In his second offensive in Libya, Rommel inflicted another series of defeats on the Eighth Army, until on 20 June 1942 Tobruk was finally captured, along with 33,000 troops. In the following weeks the Eighth Army retreated all the way to El ALAMEIN, where Rommel's advance was finally halted in July.

Toc H The morse pronunciation of the letters T.H., the initials of Talbot House. The term originated during World War I, when the first Talbot House was founded, in December 1915, at Poperinghe in Belgium, in memory of Gilbert Talbot (1885–1915), son of the Bishop of Winchester, who had been killed at Hooge in the preceding July. The Rev. P. B. (Tubby) Clayton, MC (1885–1972), made it a famous rest and recreation centre. In 1920, he founded a similar centre in London, also known as Toc H, which developed into an interdenominational association for Christian social service. *See* PIP EMMA.

Today is the first day of the rest of your life A line attributed to the US founder of the anti-heroin clinic, Charles Dederich. Heroin addicts who are really determined to overcome their habit have to make a clean break with their past lives – refusing to see any of their addicted friends or drug sources, who will do all they can to undermine their reform. Entering a clinic, if it is to serve any purpose, needs to constitute a new start – the first day of a new life.

Todt Organization The Nazi construction organization headed by Fritz Todt (1891–1942), a civil engineer who had joined the Nazi Party in 1922. He was made inspector-general of the road and highway system in 1933, was put in charge of the Four-Year-Plan (1936–40), and was Reich Minister for Munitions from 1940 until his death in a plane crash. The Todt Organization was responsible for the construction of the AUTOBAHN system, the 400-mile long SIEGFRIED LINE, and the ATLANTIC WALL, the French coastal defences erected after the German occupation in 1940.

together Self-possessed, free of emotional problems. In the late 1960s this was a popular term in the HIPPIE lexicon, indicating a vague idea of being at peace with oneself and the world (especially in the exhortation **get it together**). In the work- and efficiency-obsessed 1980s its meaning dwindled to competent or well-organized.

tokamak *See* NUCLEAR REACTOR.

tokenism The practice by some companies, schools, sports teams, etc., of appearing to abide by equal-opportunity laws by accepting a token representation of a minority group, especially Blacks or women. This early-1960s Americanism spread to the UK in the decade following. A **showcase nigger** is Black slang for a token Black given high visibility in the company's front office.

> I was the showcase Jew with the agency. I tried to look Jewish desperately, used to read my memos from right to left all the time. They fired me finally 'cos I took off too many Jewish holidays.
>
> WOODY ALLEN.

tokus or **tochis** Bottom or backside, from the Yiddish *tokhes* and originally Hebrew *tahath*, under. A common expression in New York is **get off your tokus**, *i.e.* get up and do something. Like many other Yiddish words it has crossed the Atlantic since World War II.

Tokyo Rose The nickname given by US servicement to Iva Ikuko Toguri D'Aquino (1916–), a woman broadcaster of propaganda from Japan during World War II. Several American-born Japanese girls were suspected of taking part in these broadcasts but only D'Aquino was found guilty. *See also* LORD HAW-HAW.

Tom and Jerry Two cartoon characters, Tom, an accident-prone cat, and Jerry, a clever little mouse. They were created by William Hanna and Joe Barbera, who prepared many short cartoon films with them, starting with *Puss Gets the Boot* (1940).

They may have been named after a couple of roistering young men about town featured in Pierce Egan's *Life in London; or, The Day and Night Scenes of Jerry Hawthorn, Esq., and his Elegant Friend Corinthian Tom* (1821).

Tommy Nickname given to British soldiers fighting in World War I. In fact, Tommy or Tommy Atkins had been applied to the British soldiery for many years by then. From 1815 and throughout the 19th century *Thomas Atkins* was the name used in the specimen form, accompanying the official manual issued to all army recruits, supplied to show them how their own form, requiring details of name, age, date of enlistment, etc., should be filled in. *See also* FRITZ.

Tommy-cooker A small individual stove using solid fuel invented during World War I and issued to Allied troops in World War II. It was also the name given by the Germans to the SHERMAN TANK, which caught fire very easily when hit.

Tommy gun A Thompson short-barrelled sub-machine-gun.

tomography (Gr. *tōmos*, slice, section; *graphein*, to write) The technique of obtaining an X-ray picture of a specific plane of the body or of any other solid object. The X-ray machine is so designed that the radiation is focused only on a selected plane; clear images are obtained of structures in that plane, while overlying structures appear blurred. Tomography, which was developed in the 1930s, is widely used in medical diagnosis as it enables the imaging of soft and deep-seated tissues and organs, which cannot be visualized using conventional X-ray machines. It is often used in the form of computerized tomography (*see* CT SCANNER). *See also* BODY SCANNER; BRAIN SCANNER.

ton A speed of 100 m.p.h. In the late 1950s, 'doing a ton' became a goal for every young motorcyclist, being regarded as the ultimate test of both machine and rider. Organized speed trials were held on public roads, their illegality supplying an extra frisson of excitement. The activities of the **ton-up kids**, as they were dubbed, became the subject of outraged comment in the press.

In darts and cricket a ton is a personal score of 100, while in betting and underworld slang it means a sum of £100.

tong (Cantonese *tohng*, meeting place) Chinese fraternal organizations that originated in the benevolent and protective associations formed by Chinese immigrants to the West, especially America, in the second half of the 19th century. By the turn of the century, competition for scarce economic opportunities led to open warfare between the tong societies. During the 1930s, these 'tong wars' were serious enough for the US government to arrest and deport large numbers of Chinese. Although many of the tongs developed into fronts for criminal activities, including gambling, prostitution, and drug-pushing, the modern tong societies are largely respectable, unlike the MAFIA crime families, which remain criminal organizations. Their main function is promoting the economic and political well-being of the Chinese comunity.

Tonkin Gulf incident Attacks by North Vietnamese motor torpedo boats on the US destroyer *Maddox* on 2 August 1964, and on the *Maddox* and *C. Turner Joy* on 4 August off the North Vietnamese coast. The incident provoked America to bomb North Vietnamese oil refineries and naval bases in retaliation. On 7 August a receptive Congress approved the vaguely worded Southeast Asia Resolution (Tonkin Gulf Resolution), granting President Lyndon Johnson emergency powers to take any action necessary to repel or prevent any further attacks on US forces. This amounted to carte blanche to wage an undeclared war in Southeast Asia. It is now known that the *Maddox* was on a spying mission in North Vietnamese waters, gathering information to aid the clandestine campaign of commando raids against North Vietnamese coastal installations, which South Vietnamese forces (with US help) had been pursuing since partition in 1954. These had been stepped up since Johnson assumed office in late 1963. The action of the North Vietnamese MTBs against the *Maddox* on 2 August had therefore been largely defensive in nature. It is also highly likely that the attack of 4 August never took place, being the product of spurious sonar readings produced by atmospheric disturbances. It is also known that plans for bombing North Vietnam, implemented after the incident, had been drawn up in the early part of 1964, in anticipation of a major escalation in the US involvement.

Tontons Macoute (Creole 'Uncle Knapsack') A tonton macoute is a bogeyman who hunts naughty children and captures them in his sack (*macoute*). The name was applied to the fearsome private militia and secret police created by François 'Papa Doc' Duvalier (1907–71) as president of Haiti after 1957. The Tontons Macoute were Duvalier loyalists, who in return for weapons, and occasionally money, were licensed to terrorize, torture, and murder those perceived as enemies of the Duvalier regime. Many of the recruits (known officially after 1960 as the Volunteers for National Security – VSN) were ex-soldiers, many were criminals; all could be easily identified by their unofficial uniform – smart suit, dark glasses, and bulging hip holsters. Duvalier also encouraged the connection between the tontons and voodooism, in order to oppress and terrorize the population. When Duvalier died the tontons remained under his son, the new president, Jean-Claude 'Baby Doc' Duvalier, whose regime was toppled by a revolution in 1986.

Tony awards Broadway's best-known awards for the New York theatre season. Begun in 1947, Tonys are given each spring for performances that began the previous autumn. Special achievements are presented for the best play, musical, actors, actresses, directors, authors, designers, producers, etc. The award was named after Antoinette Perry (1888–1946), a Broadway producer and director.

Tonypandy riots Violent disturbances caused by striking miners in the village of Tonypandy in Rhondda Valley, S Wales, in November 1910. The episode is remembered as the source of the myth that Winston Churchill, then Liberal Home Secretary, authorized troops to fire on the strikers, killing a number of them. In fact, no miners died and it was Churchill who was largely responsible for preventing bloodshed. On 10 November the Chief Constable of Glamorgan had requested the local army commander to take military action to control the rioters. When Churchill was informed that a small force of troops were on their way to the area, he insisted that they be held in reserve and that extra unarmed constables be sent instead. The police then managed to restrain the rioters without causing serious injuries.

too much Outstanding or excellent; overpoweringly good. An expression originating in the Black JAZZ culture of the 1920s and 1930s, later adopted by HIPPIES as a favourite term of enthusiasm.

> One day 'too much' will sound as old-fashioned as 'ripping'.
>
> *Scottish Daily Mail*, January 1968.

top. go over the top *See* OTT; OVER THE TOP.

top-hat scheme A nickname for a pension plan for a senior executive of a company.

top secret Service or governmental information about which the greatest secrecy is to be observed. In service and civil-service jargon there is a hierarchy of epithets for information that is 'classified' (*i.e.* for restricted circulation): 'top secret' is for the eyes and ears of only a very few, 'secret' may be shared a little more widely, and 'restricted' is available to a larger number still.

topside of the rockpile US Black slang for the top floor of a SKYSCRAPER, first heard in the 1940s.

Top Twenty The top twenty best-selling pop records in the 'Hit Parade', now more commonly called 'The Charts'. Lists of sheet-music hits began appearing in *Billboard* in America in 1894, and in succeeding years the lists covered a variety of popular music from vaudeville to Country and Western, Rhythm and Blues, and soul. Today, *Billboard* features eight album charts (Rock, Black, Jazz, Top Pop, etc.) and 13 singles (Dance, Disco, Country, etc.). In the UK, the first hits chart listing the country's 'Top 12 Best-selling Records', was published in the *New Musical Express* in November 1952. There are now numerous charts in the UK covering a wide spectrum of musical tastes, from Classical to Rap, which are compiled and published by the music press, independent radio stations, and the BBC. The BBC 'Top 40' chart determines which artists will be invited to appear on BBC's influential *Top of the Pops*, the longest-running pop music show on British television.

topless Describing an item of women's clothing that leaves the breasts and upper part of the body uncovered. It is also used to describe a girl who is unclothed above the waist or a place in which girls are allowed to be topless (e.g. a **topless beach**). The permissive society of the 1960s saw the arrival of topless bars, nightclubs, etc., in which topless waitresses and entertainers were employed for the titillation of men; these contrast with the topless beaches, which enable women of all ages to obtain 'strapless' suntans.

topless radio Slang for a radio PHONE-IN programme that discusses sex. TOPLESS implies the sexually explicit nature of such a programme.

Torch The codename for the Allied plan for the North African landings which began on 8 November 1942.

torch song *See* CARRY A TORCH.

Tornado *See* SMART WEAPONS.

Torrey Canyon The oil tanker on charter to British Petroleum that ran aground on Seven Stones Reef, between Land's End and the Scilly Isles, on 18 March 1967. In an attempt to contain the leakage from her cargo of 120,000 tonnes of crude oil, naval vessels sprayed detergent onto the surrounding seas. On 26 March, however, she broke her back and thousands of gallons of oil polluted over 80 miles of the Cornish coastline. Subsequently Royal Navy Buccaneers were used to bomb the wreck to burn off the remaining oil and prevent further spillage.

Tortilla Curtain Slang for the fences along the US–Mexican border that are meant to keep illegal immigrants out of America. An echo of the phrase IRON CURTAIN, tortilla refers to the cornmeal pancake that is a staple of the Mexican diet.

Torvill and Dean The British ice dancers, Jayne Torvill (1957–) and Christopher Dean (1958–) who became heroes with the British public in the early 1980s after winning the World Ice Dance Championships three times in succession (1981–83), the European Championships in 1981–82 and 1984, and the gold medal in the 1984 Olympic Games in Tokyo. They subsequently became professionals.

Totenkopfverbände *See* SS.

Tour de France The world's most prestigious bicycle race, established in 1903 by Henri Desgrange (1865–1940), the French cyclist and journalist. The route covers some 4000 km (2500 miles) of flat and mountainous terrain, mostly through France and Belgium, and is divided into 21 daily stages. There are normally around 120 contestants in the annual competition, each stage of the race is timed, and the rider with the lowest aggregate time for all stages is the winner. Competitors ride in teams, which are sponsored by the manufacturer of a particular product; in addition to contending with the gruelling pace, riders are plagued by a flotilla of sponsors following behind them and an army of journalists and TV crews speeding just ahead of them and choking the race leaders with exhaust fumes.

toy. toy-boy The young male lover of an older woman. The term is usually derogatory, implying that the man is a brainless sexual athlete kept like a toy by the woman in return for his services. Its popularity in the 1980s reflected a social trend in which middle-aged female celebrities began to do what successful men had always done, *i.e.* use their wealth and status to attract younger lovers.

toyetic A word coined by toy manufacturers to describe a film or television character that readily lends itself to being made into a toy. To possess such a quality the character must have an unusual distinctive feature – the TEENAGE MUTANT NINJA TURTLES would be described as toyetic.

Trachtenberg System A system of speedy mathematical calculations based upon simple counting according to prescribed keys or formulae, which need to be memorized. It enables complicated calculations to be more easily and rapidly handled than by normal processes. The system was devised by Jakow Trachtenberg during his seven years in a Nazi concentration camp. He was born at Odessa and trained as an engineer, becoming a refugee in Germany after the Russian Revolution.

trad JAZZ in the traditional NEW ORLEANS STYLE, especially as revived by White musicians during the 'trad boom' of the late 1950s and early 1960s. *See also* DIXIE.

trade cycle or **business cycle** The cycle in an economy consisting of a boom, recession, depression, recovery, and boom. Although it first appeared in the 19th century, the 20th century has seen the greatest fluctuations and the most widespread consequences of the cycle. The GREAT DEPRESSION of the 1930s was a protracted world slump, causing great hardship in western democracies. There is no single clear theory to explain the phenomenon although the political influence has been stressed by a number of economists. Karl Marx suggested that during a boom workers became sufficiently powerful to demand higher wages, which capitalists countered by engineering a recession to create unemployment in order to undermine the workers' strength. More recent political theories highlight the stringent measures imposed by a government shortly after its election and the way in which such a government will tend to stimulate demand before the next election. These changes in governmental attitude can themselves make a strong contribution to the creation of a cycle. A simpler economic theory is that booms generate over-investment in new plant and equipment, which produces greater quantities of goods than the market can absorb. This causes price-cutting, redundancies, and a contraction in demand, as those made redundant cease to be affluent consumers. As more people are made redundant, the level of consumption falls, and more redundancies are required; this vicious circle leads to recession and eventually to slump. *See also* STAGNATION THEORY.

trading stamps Stamps given to customers by shops as an incentive to buy goods. They can be collected and later exchanged for goods or money. The trading-stamp company sells the stamps to the retailer, who gets his money back by the increased custom. The idea originated in America, where the company Sperry & Hutchinson produced what were popularly known as **green stamps**. In the UK a separate company produced **Green Shield stamps** from 1957. Trading stamps were extremely popular in the 1960s but their use has since declined.

trahison des clercs (Fr. treachery of the intellectuals) The betrayal of intellectual principles by the intelligentsia. In particular, the phrase refers to the incursion of the intelligentsia, who should be concerned with the pursuit of truth and be guided by abstract thought, into partisan politics and propaganda. It comes from the title of Julien Benda's work *La Trahison des Clercs* (1927) in which he attacked intellectuals who seek to govern the world.

trail. There's a long, long trail a-winding The refrain and title of one of the best-known songs of World War I. Peculiarly appropriate to the slogging warfare of the trenches, it was written by the then-unknown US songwriter Alonzo Elliott in 1913. The war he had in mind was not the terrible conflagration to come but Napoleon's retreat from Moscow in 1812.

Tramp, The The film character created by Charlie Chaplin (1889–1977), the British-born US comedian, film actor, and director. His portrayal of the shuffling downtrodden little vagabond with baggy trousers, bowler hat, moustache, and cane is one of the most endearing and enduring images in the 20th-century cinema. According to legend, Chaplin borrowed a pair of FATTY Arbuckle's trousers from a wardrobe in the male dressing room at the Keystone Studios in February 1914; this total misfit helped to create the character that developed over a period of years, from his first appearance in *Kid Auto Races at Venice, California* (1914) to the fully fledged character in *A Dog's Life* (1918).

tranny or **trannie** (1) Short for transistor radio; a type of light compact radio introduced in the late 1950s. Before long, cheap portable trannies were ubiquitous in the streets and on beaches, to such an extent that many regarded them as a public nuisance. The term is rarely heard now, although some disc jockeys continue to use it. The tiny outdoor tranny, with its small loudspeaker and tinny sound, has been superseded by the WALKMAN (with headphones) and the GHETTOBLASTER (with stereo and relatively large speakers). (2) Shortened form of photographic transparency, widely used by photographers and layout artists. (3) Shortened form of transexual or transvestite, used in GAY circles.

transcendental meditation (TM) A method of meditation and relaxation founded by the Maharishi Mahesh Yogi; he began to teach the method in India in 1955 but it did not become popular in Europe and America until the 1960s. The technique uses Sanskrit mantras repeated silently to distract thoughts from surface reality to a deeper level of consciousness. TM students are formally instructed by teachers, who then allocate them their mantras according to their temperament and lifestyle. The benefits of TM can, it is claimed, be obtained by two 20-minute meditation periods per day. The physical and mental benefits of the techniques of relaxation and meditation employed by TM are controversial. Advocates of TM claim meditation by large numbers of people can influence world events.

transformational grammar or **transformational-generative grammar** In linguistics, a system of grammar that devises rules for basic sentence structure and assumes that every possible sentence in the language can be generated from them. The system also indicates how intended meanings (the deep structure) are converted into specific language units (surface structures) by using these rules or transformations. The theory of transformational grammar was primarily developed by the US linguist, Noam Chomsky (1928–).

transgenic Denoting animals and plants whose genetic makeup has been altered by GENETIC ENGINEERING. Such organisms are created when genes from other species are inserted into the fertilized egg or very early embryo. The potential value of transgenic plants and animals in agriculture, the food industry, and medicine is considerable; for example in increasing meat, wool, or milk production, conferring resistance to disease, producing medically useful products, etc. However, the concept of genetic manipulation is widely associated with the creation of monsters and bizarre hybrids – five-legged sheep, goat-cow crosses, etc.; strict controls in such experimentation, which is still in the experimental stage, are being observed.

Transport House The headquarters of the British Labour Party, situated in Smith Square, Westminster. The building is also the headquarters of the Transport and General Workers' Union. *See also* CENTRAL OFFICE.

Trans-Siberian Railway The railway line between Moscow and Vladivostok, linking European Russia with the Pacific Coast across Siberia. The route runs for a distance of 9297 km (5778 miles), which takes about eight days to cover, the longest railway journey in the world both by distance and time. Construction began simultaneously from both ends in 1891 and was completed in 1904. The first line made use of the Chinese Eastern Railway from Chita to Vladivostock, but in 1916 an all-Russia line was completed via Khabarovsk. It was the construction of the railway that opened up Siberia to economic development and colonization.

travelogue A lecture or running commentary delivered to accompany a travel film.

Traven, B. The pen name of the author of best-selling adventure novels and short stories, the most popular of which are *The Death Ship* (1925), published in Germany, and *The Treasure of the Sierra Nevada* (1934), published in Mexico, which was filmed by John Huston in 1947. Because Traven avoided contact with his publishers and refused to provide any personal details, his true identity is still a mystery. According to W. Wyatt's *The Man who was B. Traven* (1980), Traven's real name was probably Albert Otto Max Feige (1882?–1969) – he also used the name Ret Marut. Born in the Polish town of Swiebodzin (then in Germany), Feige was an actor and radical pamphleteer, who was involved in the anarchist movement during the German Revolution of 1918–19 before moving to Mexico in 1924.

Treblinka Nazi CONCENTRATION CAMP opened in July 1942 at a railway junction on the Bug River in Poland, 45 miles (72 km) NE of Warsaw. The sole purpose of Treblinka was to systematically exterminate the Jews of central Poland (*see* FINAL SOLUTION; HOLOCAUST), including the 350,000 survivors of the Warsaw Ghetto, who were transported from there in batches of 5000 per day. The new arrivals were segregated by sex, stripped, and then herded along the Himmelstrasse ('Heavenly Way') towards the 30 chambers fed with carbon monoxide gas from diesel engines and later specially manufactured cyanide (Zyklon B). On 2 August 1943, about 700 of the Jewish forced labourers, whose task was to sort the clothes of the victims and burn corpses, rose in revolt. 15 Ukranian guards were shot, but most of the insurgents were killed in the camp;

of the 150 that managed to escape, all but 12 were hunted down and killed. It is estimated that 850,000 Jews were murdered at Treblinka before it was shut down in October 1943.

Treetops The most famous hotel in Kenya, built high in cape chestnut trees in the Aberdare National Park so that guests can observe the abundant wildlife in comfort and safety. The first Treetops Hotel, which was burned down by the MAU MAU in 1954, is famous as the place at which Princess Elizabeth, on vacation with Prince Philip in February 1952, learned of the death of her father and became Queen.

trench. **trench coat** A style of raincoat influenced by British army officers' uniform coats of World War I and later. These waterproof coats with various flaps and deep pockets have been popular for many years, becoming a fashion again in the 1950s in imitation of the battered trench coat frequently worn by Humphrey Bogart.

trench fever A remittent or relapsing fever affecting men living in trenches, dugouts, etc.; it is transmitted by the excrement of lice. It first appeared in World War I, in the static warfare on the WESTERN FRONT.

trendy Fashionable, up-to-date, following the latest trend or style. When first used in the 1960s, to be trendy was seen as a positive asset, often contrasted with being negatively SQUARE, or old-fashioned. In the 1980s it re-emerged as a derogatory epithet implying studied adherence to the latest fads and fashions. As a noun, it is almost always used scornfully, as in **middle-aged trendy** and LAST CHANCE TRENDY.

triage *See* LIFEBOAT ETHICS.

Trianon adventure The extraordinary experience of Charlotte Moberly, Principal of St Hugh's College, Oxford, and her companion Eleanor Jourdain, the Vice-Principal, while visiting the gardens of the Petit Trianon at Versailles on 10 August 1901. They claimed to have entered some form of time warp, which transported them back to 1789, and to have encountered a number of people in period dress, including a woman sketching, who, they decided later, was probably Marie Antionette. Their experience, which was described in a book, *An Adventure* (1911), provoked considerable contemporary debate.

trick. **trick cyclist** A derisive term for a psychiatrist, based on a mispronunciation of the word. It is common among the British police, who almost invariably refer to criminal psychiatrists in this way. *See also* HEADSHRINK.

trick or treat The traditional Halloween cry of US children who, disguised as ghosts, witches, monsters, etc., visit neighbouring houses to ask for sweets. Their friendly threat is to play a prank on any resident who does not fill their bags. In the early 20th century, teenagers often played such tricks as turning over lawn furniture and soaping windows. Little of this occurs today, however, largely because trick-or-treaters are now mostly preteenagers and households keep a supply of sweets for the occasion. The trick-or-treat custom found a foothold in the UK in the 1980s, with some householders treating with pennies in the tradition of Guy Fawkes Day (five days later).

Tricky Dicky A nickname of Richard Milhous Nixon (1913–), US president from 1969 until his resignation in 1974, when the WATERGATE scandal was disclosed. His part in the attempted cover-up of that affair and the discovery of a SLUSH FUND existing during his re-election campaign of 1972 led to a revival of the name, which had previously been used widely by those who suspected him of a degree of political manipulation bordering on illegality. He was first called 'Tricky Dick' by Helen Gahagan Douglas, his opponent in the 1950 senatorial election in California, whom he defeated in a campaign marked by innuendo about her communist sympathies.

> Would you buy a used car from this man?
> Caption to photograph of NIXON, c. 1952.

See also HOUDINI OF AMERICAN POLITICS.

Trident The codename of the wartime Anglo-American Washington Conference held between 12 and 25 May 1943. Churchill pressed for the continuation of the Mediterranean Strategy, with an attack on Sicily followed by an invasion of Italy. Roosevelt, on the other hand, insisted on a British commitment to the opening of the SECOND FRONT with a cross-channel invasion. A compromise was reached, with the Americans agreeing to preparations for an invasion of Italy, while Churchill was committed to the scheduling of OVERLORD for 1 May 1944. The US Pacific strategy against Japan was approved; a combined Anglo-American bombing offensive was also planned to destroy German military, industrial, and economic capabilities as a prelude to the cross-channel invasion. It was also secretly agreed that the development of the atom bomb should be a joint enterprise. *See* MANHATTAN PROJECT.

Trident missile US submarine-launched ballistic missile (SLBM) system developed as a replacement for Poisedon in America and POLARIS in the UK. Development of Trident I started in America in the late 1960s; by the early 1980s it had replaced the Poisedon SLBM, which had succeeded Polaris in 1969. It carries eight 100-kiloton MIRVs with a range of up to 6900 miles (11,000 km). Trident II, with greater accuracy and more powerful warheads, was developed for deployment by both the Americans and the British in the early 1990s.

triffid A large plant, either a houseplant or a garden weed, that seems to be growing unusually strongly and is threatening to take over. The word comes from the science-fiction novel by John Wyndham, *The Day of the Triffids* (1951), in which a species of plant, created by scientists, grew to gigantic proportions, moving about and stinging people to death.

trip A slang term coined in the 1960s to describe the hallucinatory experience – good or bad – undergone by someone who has taken LSD or a similar drug. By extension it was taken to mean any stimulating or 'mind-blowing' experience. In more recent use, a trip is an interest or enthusiasm that wholly occupies a person to an extent that amounts to obsession, as in **ego trip** or **health trip**.

Tripartite Pact The extension of the Rome-Berlin AXIS (formally concluded as the PACT OF STEEL in May 1939) to include Japan on 27 September 1940, which committed the signatories to a ten-year military alliance. Japan had initially refused Hitler's invitation to join the Axis powers in 1939 but reversed the decision after the outbreak of war, when German successes against France and Belgium rendered their Far Eastern colonies vulnerable to Japanese attack. Japan hoped that support from Germany and Italy would deter the Soviet Union and America from interfering in her plans for southern expansion. In the event, there was no attempt to coordinate German and Japanese strategy after 1940, although in March 1941 Hitler unwisely promised to support Japan if she attacked America. After PEARL HARBOR Germany declared war on America, which effectively guaranteed her defeat. Other countries that later joined the Axis were Hungary, Bulgaria, Romania, Slovakia, and Croatia.

Triple Entente The informal agreement between the UK, France, and Russia to seek means of settling their outstanding colonial differences. The agreement was based on the Anglo-French Entente Cordiale of April 1904, when the UK and France settled their colonial differences in Egypt and Africa, and the Anglo-Russian agreement in August 1907, which settled differences over Persia, Tibet, and Afghanistan. The Triple Entente became a military pact in 1914, forming the nucleus of the Allied powers in World War I.

Tripolitan War The conflict between Italy and Turkey in 1911–12, in which Turkey sought to conquer Libya and establish a presence in North Africa to counterbalance French colonial possession in Algeria, Tunisia, and Morocco. The Italians won fairly easy victories against Turkish forces, who were inferior both in numbers and training. By the Treaty of Ouchy (15 October 1912) Turkey was forced to cede Libya, Rhodes, and the Dodecanese to Italy.

trog A boorish or unintelligent person; a lout. The word is a shortened form of **troglodyte**, a caveman. In the 1950s it was JAZZ slang for someone who was considered unsophisticated or SQUARE, especially in his or her musical taste. The 1960s British rock group The Troggs played a deliberately basic form of ROCK 'N' ROLL, earning the encomium "They're so far behind, they're in front." The term is often used self-deprecatingly by potholers and speleologists.

Troika Plan The demand, first made by Premier Nikita Khrushchev on 23 September 1962, to replace the Secretary-General of the United Nations with a three-man *Troika*. Throughout the 1950s the Soviet Union regarded the UN as a tool of the capitalist West and the Secretary-General, Dag Hammarskjold, as a NATO puppet. Khrushchev's attempt to replace the Secretariat with a Troika, consisting of representatives of the West, the Soviet bloc, and the THIRD WORLD, was rejected as an assault on the concept of an impartial international body and a ploy to extend Soviet influence in the UN.

Trojan horse An apparently trustworthy computer program that, in reality, contains a hidden instruction designed to wreak havoc on the system in which it is used. The name comes from the wooden horse in which the Greeks concealed themselves in order to gain entry to the city of Troy. *See also* BUG; COMPUTER VIRUS.

troppo Deranged. The term originated among Australian troops in World War II, who applied it to cases of sunstroke or nervous collapse brought on by service in the tropics. It is mainly used in the phrase **to go troppo**, which can now refer to any kind of excessive behaviour (perhaps influenced by the French *trop*, too much).

Trot An informal term for a Trotskyite (see TROTSKYISM). In the UK it is applied rather loosely to any extreme left-wing activist, especially one who rejects the model of Soviet state communism. The epithet owes some of its derogatory implications to its resemblance to 'the trots', a British colloquialism for diarrhoea.

Trotskyism The theory of world revolution advanced by Leon Trotsky (1879–1940), in opposition to the theory of building 'socialism in one country', supported by Stalin. Trotsky held that the long-term success of the OCTOBER REVOLUTION could only be guaranteed by promoting revolutions in the nations of W Europe, to prevent the encirclement and isolation of the Soviet state by hostile capitalist nations. After his defeat by Stalin in their struggle for power following Lenin's death in 1924, Trotsky accused Stalin of betraying the world revolution in the interests of Russian nationalism and of creating an oppressive bureaucratic state based on the exploitation of the Soviet people. Trotsky was murdered in exile in Mexico by a Stalinist agent but various Trotskyite political parties continue to agitate for the implementation of his internationalist and anti-bureaucratic revolutionary ideas.

trouble. The Troubles The civil war in Ireland between January 1919 and April 1923. Sinn Fein, victors in the general election of 1918, set up an independent Irish parliament, the Dail, and elected as president Eamon De Valera, one of the survivors of the abortive EASTER RISING of 1916. Official British rule from Dublin Castle was ignored, and the Republican administration effectively extended its authority throughout the country. The peaceable rebellion turned into civil war in January 1919, when the newly constituted Irish Republican Army (*see* IRA), led by Michael Collins (another survivor of the Easter Rising), embarked on a terrorist guerrilla campaign against the British authorities. In 1920 the British introduced the BLACK AND TANS, a force of irregulars, to augment the regular army and the armed police, the Royal Irish Constabulary, in the fight against the IRA. The Black and Tans quickly established a reputation for brutality; as a result both sides indulged in an orgy of terrorism and murder in a bitter struggle, which was continued by a committed minority until 1923 (one year after the majority of Republicans had accepted partition with the formation of the IRISH FREE STATE).

> Things are being done in Ireland which would disgrace the blackest annals of the lowest despotism in Europe.
>
> LORD ASQUITH.

trouble-shooter Someone trained to locate a source of trouble and to give advice on how to repair the situation. The trouble may be of any kind, from mechanical failure to industrial relations.

trousersuit *See* PANTSUIT.

trucking A JAZZ dance step resembling an exaggerated strutting walk that originated at the COTTON CLUB in 1933. The term later came to mean walking in such a manner or walking generally. Because the dance could be kept up over long periods, it became a staple of the competitive dance marathons of the 1930s. This may be why the term came to acquire a further sense of persevering (*see* KEEP ON TRUCKIN'). In the late 1960s West Coast hippies used the term to describe a curious laid-back style of walking fashionable at the time: this involved taking long loping strides while leaning dangerously far backwards from the waist. It had no resemblance to the original dance.

Truman Doctrine An anticommunist doctrine formulated in 1947 by the administration of President Harry S Truman. US aid was guaranteed to countries that resisted communist intervention and aggression but the primary concern was to keep Greece and Turkey free of Soviet influence and dominance. Truman felt that the best defence against communism was to help in the financial rehabilitation of friendly nations weakened by World War II. The year before the doctrine was announced, Congress approved a loan of more than $3.7 million to the UK.

trunk Describing the main lines of railway, postal, and telephone systems, from which branch lines radiate. A **trunk call** was the former name for a telephone call on a trunk line from one town to another. A **trunk road** was a main highway between two principal towns, usually now a MOTORWAY.

truth In JAZZ slang, music that is regarded as being of the highest quality and communicating the essence of something. First heard in the 1940s.

truth drug The alkaloid scopolamine. A US doctor, R. E. House (1875–1930), used this drug to induce a state of lethargic intoxication in which the patient lost many of his defences and spoke the truth concerning matters about which he would normally have lied or prevaricated. The value of this and other truth drugs in penology has by no means been established.

Tschiffley's Ride A journey of 13,350 miles (21,484 km) undertaken by a Swiss-born Argentinian, A. F. Tschiffley, by horse between Buenos Aires and Washington DC between 1925 and 1927. He used only two horses on his epic journey in order to demonstrate the stamina of a certain Argentinian breed.

tsuris US slang for troubles or problems, from the Yiddish *tsores*, originally from the Hebrew *saroth*, troubles. The word was common in New York and Hollywood entertainment circles in the 1970s and has since crossed the Atlantic.

Tsushima A naval battle during the RUSSO-JAPANESE WAR on 27 May 1905, in which the Russian Baltic fleet, commanded by the incompetent Admiral Rozhdestvenski, was decisively defeated by the Japanese fleet commanded by Togo. The Russians lost all their eight battleships, seven out of eight cruisers, and four out of nine destroyers and suffered 10,000 casualties; the Japanese lost three torpedo boats and less than 1000 men.

TTFN Ta-Ta For Now. An abbreviation from the radio programme ITMA; it was the parting remark of the character Mrs Mopp, played by Dorothy Summers, and was widely used during the war years and after. A more recent version, popular during the 1960s, was the Radio 1 disc jockey Jimmy Young's **BFN** – bye for now – which he used at the end of his show.

TT races The Isle of Man Auto-Cycle Union Touring Trophy, the world's oldest motorcycle race and one of the most dangerous. The first competition was held in 1907 over the existing motor racing circuit, which was shortened and made easier for the purpose. There were two races, one for single-cylinder machines and the other for two-cylinder machines. In 1911 the race was run for the first time over the full length of the course round the island, which included the stiff climb up Snaefell mountain. Until the 1950s, British motorcycles, such as Nortons and Triumphs, largely dominated the event. In the 1960 race Honda made their first entry and the Japanese machines have dominated ever since.

tube (1) A television set; a colloquial name originating in America at the end of the 1950s. It is a shortening of *picture tube* or *cathode-ray tube*, which produces the images in a television set. (2) The London Underground railway system, from the tubular tunnels through which much of it runs.

Tube Alloys Codename of the committee established in October 1941 to supervise British research into nuclear power during World War II. It was constituted as a division of the Department of Scientific and Industrial Research, under the general direction of the Lord President of the Council, Sir John Anderson; the Tube Alloys committee itself was headed by Wallace Akers, Research Director of ICI, and his assistant Michael Perrin. At the TRIDENT Anglo-American wartime conference in May 1943 it was secretly agreed that the development of the atom bomb should be a joint effort between Tube Alloys and the US MANHATTAN PROJECT.

Tucker Report *See* BLUEBEARD OF EASTBOURNE.

Tuesday Club Regular meetings betwen UK civil servants, City journalists, economists, and representatives of finance and industry to exchange information and ideas on the direction of national economic policy. The Club evolved from dinner parties given by Oswald Toynbee Falk, a treasury official and friend of the economist John Maynard Keynes (1883–1946), who became a founder member. The first meeting took place on 19 July 1917 at the Café Royal; occasional Tuesday Club meetings in the Reform Club still take place.

tug of love A conflict of affections, especially a battle for the custody of a child. The term came into use in the 1970s.

tummy tuck Colloquialism for a cosmetic operation to tighten a sagging stomach; abdominal fat is removed, excess skin trimmed away, and what is left is sewn back into place.

Tum-Tum *See* BERTIE.

Tupperware Tradename for a range of moulded dishes, storage containers, etc., made of plastic. Introduced in America in 1945 by an engineer, Earl Tupper, the product was first sold in the UK in 1960. A feature of Tupperware is that it is sold directly by agents at **Tupperware parties**, held in people's homes.

Turing machine A hypothetical computer developed by Alan Mathison Turing (1912–54) in 1936. Its purpose is to determine whether or not a mathematical problem can be solved by algorithm (a computational procedure). It postulates a computer with an infinitely long tape storing characters in discrete locations. The computer passes through a series of active states scanning and altering characters until it settles into a passive state if the problem is soluble.

Turin Shroud The shroud of twill linen kept in Turin Cathedral and claimed to be that used to wrap the body of Christ after the crucifixion. The pope agreed to CARBON DATING in 1987 and in 1988 the Archbishop of Turin appointed the Oxford Research Laboratory for Archaeology, the Department of Physics of Arizona University, and the Swiss Federal Institute of Technology at Zurich to date the shroud, pieces of which were given to these institutes in April 1988. The results were announced on 13 October and the cloth was dated between 1260 and 1390. There is no historical evidence that it was known before the 14th century. The general conclusion is that the shroud is a medieval forgery, although the impressions it bears of a human body resembling the crucified Christ remain unexplained and are considered significant by those who continue to debate the shroud's origins (the science of **sindonology**).

turkey trot A US ballroom dance popular in the early 20th century; the precursor of the foxtrot. Danced to RAGTIME music, the modern contortions shocked many Victorian contemporaries. It was adapted in England as the *one-step*, having long quick steps.

turn. **turn-off** Something that repels, bores, or quenches sexual ardour; also used in the verb sense, to repel or discourage. The opposite of TURN-ON.

turn-on Something that is attractive, stimulating, or sexually arousing. In HIPPIE parlance, 'to turn on' meant to liberate one's mind from conventions, materialism, negative thinking, etc., especially through the use of mind-altering drugs. 'Turn on, tune in, drop out' was the slogan of the LSD-guru Dr Timothy Leary (1920–). The term derives from the idea of turning on a light or other electrical apparatus.

TVA Tennessee Valley Authority. The US federal corporation created in 1933 to develop the basin of the Tennessee River, mostly to build dams for flood control and to provide cheap electric power. It was one of President Franklin D. Roosevelt's first projects to reverse the GREAT DEPRESSION and tackle unemployment. Critics called it socialistic, which made TVA a controversial issue for many years; private electricity companies especially opposed the federal competition. It is now highly regarded, however: TVA's 39 dams on the Tennessee River and about 160 nonprofit-making electric power distributors provide cheap electricity (one-third less than the US average) to consumers within 210,000 sq km (80,000 sq miles). The river, which once flooded regularly, has been converted into a series of lakes along the Tennessee Valley, which extends 105,956 sq km (40,910 sq miles).

TV movie A film made specifically for showing on television rather than in the cinema. Such productions proliferated from the 1960s and have generally been distinguished by low standards in production and facile plots and characterization. The development of the genre did, however, do much to restore Hollywood's finances and helped the ailing careers of many minor stars. The quality of movies made for television has improved greatly in recent years since the introduction of more independent television companies.

TVP Textured Vegetable Protein (also called Textured Soya Protein, TSP). A meat substitute developed in the 1970s, TVP is similar in appearance, texture, and taste to meat but is generally cheaper. It comes in tins (sausages or slices) or in dried form (small lumps or granules), which usually has to be soaked before use. It is widely available in HEALTH FOOD stores and is also used in ready-made vegetarian meals and soup powders.

TVR Television rating. The popularity of a particular television programme as determined by equipment attached to sets in selected homes that records the times and channels during which the set is on. Diary panels are used to record the number of people watching a particular set. Audience research is clearly of great valuc to programme producers and advertisers. In the UK audience research is carried out by the Broadcasters Audience Research Board (BARB).

TW3 *That Was The Week, That Was*. A live late-night satirical BBC television programme first broadcast on Saturday 24 November 1962. TW3 was inspired by the satirical revue, *Beyond The Fringe*, featuring Dudley Moore, Peter Cook, Jonathan Miller, Alan Bennett, and others, which was a success at the EDINBURGH FESTIVAL in 1960 and transferred to London's West End in May 1961. The same year saw the launch of PRIVATE EYE and the opening of London's first satirical nightclub, *The Establishment*. Many of the comedy-writing talents involved in these ventures, such as Cook and Willie Rushton, produced material for TW3, the BBC's contribution to the comedy revolution of the early 1960s. The show was produced by Ned Sherrin and made stars of its leading performers, including David Frost (the compere), Bernard Levin, Lance Percival, and Millicent Martin. The material included merciless lampoons of leading political figures and humorous sketches and songs making fun of such sacrosanct topics as religion, the royal family, the police, and big business. The show was suspended in November 1963, due to the forthcoming general election, reappearing in the following year as *Not So Much a Programme, More a Way of Life*, also hosted by Frost.

twelve-tone music The atonal compositional system devised in the early 1920s by the Austrian composer Arnold Schoenberg (1874–1951), which had a profound impact on western music. Instead of orthodox keys, the system uses a series of twelve tones of the chromatic scale fixed in a particular order, from which the whole of a composition is derived. As long as the fixed sequence is maintained, the tones can be used harmonically (in chords) and melodically (successively), at different levels of pitch, and can also be transposed, inverted, and reversed. The principles of the system were later employed in the works of Schoenberg's disciples, Alban Berg and Anton Webern, and also to a certain extent by Igor Stravinsky. Despite the gradual integration of the method into the works of modern composers, however, atonality has yet to achieve any degree of popularity among the public.

twenty. 21st Amendment The 1933 amendment to the US Constitution that repealed PROHIBITION. It actually repealed the 18th Amendment, which in 1920 had banned the manufacture, sale, or transportation of intoxicating liquors. This 'Noble Experiment' had resulted in illegal distilling and brewing, the growth of SPEAK-EASY bars and nightclubs, and gangland warfare. As some states wished to keep Prohibition, the 21st Amendment promised federal help to enforce their anti-drinking laws. Various states still have 'dry counties', which are supposedly alcohol-free.

22nd Amendment The 1947 amendment to the US Constitution that limited the US president to two terms in office. This was in reaction to Franklin D. Roosevelt's successful election to four terms (though he died in the first year of the last term). No other president has served more than two terms. If a vice president or another person has served more than two years in place of an elected president, he can only be elected once thereafter. However, if he has replaced the president for only two years, his maximum time in office could be 10 years, which is the longest possible presidency under the 22nd Amendment.

Twenty Questions An immensely popular BBC radio panel game, whose audience rarely fell below 15 million, based on the parlour game in which someone chooses an object, which the others have to identify (animal, vegetable, or mineral, etc.) with only twenty questions. The programme was borrowed from US radio and first broadcast on 28 February 1947. The panellists included Richard Dimbleby, Joy Adamson, Jack Train, Anona Winn, Chairman Stewart MacPherson, and the Mystery Voice, Norman Hackforth, who all became celebrities. This family entertainment was a weekly ritual that helped to lighten the gloom of postwar Britain and eventually ran for over a quarter of a century.

two

Twickers *See* BILLY WILLIAMS'S CABBAGE PATCH.

Twiggy The professional name of Lesley Hornby (1946–), highly successful British model of the 1960s. She was born in NEASDEN in NW London. Her nickname is a reflection of her extreme thinness, which made her a world-famous hallmark of the 1960s look (*see also* SHRIMP, THE). Her exceptionally beautiful face enabled her to embark on a second career as a stage and film actress, in spite of her whiney Cockney accent, which she has always retained and indeed, cultivated. Her best-known film was *The Boy Friend* (1971).

twilight sleep A state of semiconsciousness produced by injection of scopolamine and morphine in which a woman can undergo childbirth with comparatively little pain. *See also* TRUTH DRUG.

twin paradox *See* RELATIVITY.

twist (1) A dance popular in the early 1960s, so called from the contortions performed by the dancers. (2) Slang for a girl. **Where the twist flops** is slang for 'where the girl lives'.

twitcher *See* BIRDER.

two. Two Cultures The controversial phrase coined by the scientist, novelist, and government administrator C. P. Snow (1905–80) to describe the division in western culture between those educated in the sciences and those educated in the humanities. The concept was first introduced in an article, 'The Two Cultures', in the *New Statesman* (1956); it was later expanded as *The Two Cultures and the Scientific Revolution*, delivered as the Rede Lecture at Cambridge University in May 1959, which was also published in book form. Snow asserted that science was fundamentally progressive and confident whereas the arts were reactionary and defensive, making communication between the two cultures practically impossible. This failure of communication, Snow believed, had serious consequences for western civilization, which he regarded as the product largely of scientific progress although it was still dominated politically by non-scientists. Snow criticized both sides for this state of affairs but his attack on the humanities provoked a fierce reaction, especially from literary critics, notably F. R. Leavis, whose counter-attack on Snow in the Richmond Lecture at Cambridge in 1962 was later published as *Two Cultures? The Significance of C. P. Snow*.

two-minute silence The period of silence when all traffic and all other activities stopped for two minutes at 11 am on 11 November to commemorate those who died in World War I. First observed in 1919, it remained a central feature of REMEMBRANCE DAY until World War II.

two-overcoat men *See* SUNLIGHTING.

Twopenny Tube The Central London Railway, so called because for some years after its opening (1900) the fare between any two stations was *2d*. In 1991 it was 80p.

Two-Ton Tessie The nickname of the variety artist Tessie O'Shea (1917–), an allusion to her size. In 1945 an RAF bomb weighing 22,000 lbs was named 'Ten-Ton Tessie' after her.

U

U A former category of film classification indicating that in the opinion of the British Board of Film Censors the film was suitable to be shown to both adults and unaccompanied children. Short for 'universal', the classification was dropped in the 1980s.

U and Non-U A distinction between social classes based on the usage of certain words. Devised by Professor A. S. C. Ross in an article 'Linguistic class indicators in present-day English' in 1954, it was publicized by Nancy Mitford (*see* MITFORD GIRLS). For example, it is 'U' (upper-class) to say luncheon, napkin, and cycle but 'Non-U' (non-upper-class) to say lunch (or worse, 'dinner'), serviette, and bike. This kind of snobbishness is not entirely serious. *See* SOCIAL CLASS.

U-boat A German submarine; from the German *Unterseeboot* (under-water vessel). *Compare* E-BOAT.

U-turn A U-shaped turn made by a vehicle, so that its direction is completely reversed. It is also used metaphorically of a total change of policy or opinion, as by a minister, government, etc. In November 1971 the phrase was widely used to describe the Heath government's decision to abandon its previous anti-inflationary policy and spend £160 million of public money in an attempt to reduce unemployment. In October 1980, Margaret Thatcher denied rumours that her government would perform a similar about-turn when she told the Conservative Party Conference:

> U-turn if you want to. The Lady's not for turning.

The phrase, inspired by the play title *The Lady's Not For Burning* (1948) by Christopher Fry, was supplied by the playwright Sir Ronald Millar, who wrote Mrs Thatcher's speech; he was knighted in the same year.

U-2 aircraft A US high-altitude photoreconnaissance aircraft built by the Lockheed company. The U-2 has a highly specialized lightweight design with some characteristics of a glider, allowing it to fly at 75,000 ft (22,860 metres) at a speed of about 500 m.p.h. (800 k.p.h.) It has a single-turbine engine with a range of about 3000 miles (4830 km). The U-2 was used from 1956 to 1960 by the CIA for photosurveillance of the Soviet Union and has been employed to gather data on the weather and on fallout from nuclear tests.

On 1 May 1960 a U-2 reconnaissance aircraft was shot down by the Soviet Union; its pilot, Francis Gary Powers, was captured and confessed to spying. This event (known as the **U-2 incident**) gave the first intimation of US spy missions over the Soviet Union, which President Dwight Eisenhower admitted had taken place for four years. It came a fortnight before representatives from America, the UK, France, and the Soviet Union were due to meet at the PARIS SUMMIT to discuss the status of Berlin. The Soviet leader, Nikita Khrushchev, first demanded Eisenhower's apology and a promise to punish those responsible for the flights. When this was refused, Khrushchev cancelled the conference and Eisenhower's coming visit to the Soviet Union. In 1962, the Soviets returned the U-2 pilot in exchange for a Soviet spy held in America.

U-65 haunting The alleged haunting of the ill-fated German U-BOAT U-65 by its second officer. U-65's short history was a series of misfortunes. These began even before its launch in 1916, when a falling steel girder killed two workmen. On the day of the launch itself, a further three workmen died when they inhaled poisonous fumes: no explanation for the accident was given at the subsequent inquest. Before the U-65's first dive, a rating went up on deck to check that all was secure – and simply stepped off the casing into the sea; the dive itself nearly ended in disaster for the entire crew when the submarine refused to return to the surface for 12 hours.

Subsequently, the second officer and four others died when a torpedo exploded. When members of the crew (including the captain) reported seeing the second officer's ghost on the casing, talk of a jinx rapidly spread. After docking in Bruges, the captain was killed in an air-raid. To stem the mounting panic, German officials held an inquiry followed by an exorcism of the vessel; this served only to convince the crew that something was seriously wrong.

U-65's career ended finally off the Irish coast, on 10 July 1918, when the US submarine L-2 spotted it on the surface. Before the L-2 could fire, the German target inexplicably blew up. Just before the explosion, the US commander reported seeing a lone figure on the casing, staring thoughtfully out to sea.

UB40 In the UK, a registration and attendance card formerly issued by the Department of Employment to those out of work and claiming unemployment benefit. It was also used as an informal name for someone in this position. A British REGGAE group of the 1980s adopted the name.

UCCA Universities Central Council on Admissions. An organization that handles applications to British universities. Candidates fill in a standard form (the **UCCA form**), supplying personal details, academic record with school references, and a list of the five universities, in order of preference, that the candidate would like to attend. UCCA passes copies of the application forms to the universities concerned, who then deal directly with the candidates. UCCA also acts as an emergency clearing-house, matching candidates who have failed to secure a place with any remaining vacancies.

UDI Unilateral Declaration of Independence. A declaration of independence made by a dependent state without reference to, or the agreement of, the controlling state. UDI specifically refers to the announcement of Southern Rhodesia's independence from the UK made by Ian Smith on 11 November 1965. Full official independence was not finally agreed until 1980.

UFO Unidentified Flying Object. An object, the exact nature of which is uncertain, that is claimed to have been sighted in the sky (*see also* FLYING SAUCERS) or picked up on radar screens. Study and observation of UFOs is known as **ufology** by its enthusiasts.

Ugandan discussions or **discussing Ugandan affairs** British euphemism for sex. The term first appeared in the gossip columns of the satirical magazine PRIVATE EYE in March 1973, becoming one of its longstanding jokes. It was reported that when a female journalist had to explain herself after being found upstairs in a compromising position with an African diplomat while at a party, she said, "We were discussing Ugandan affairs" (Uganda was a country much in the news at the time). In May 1981 *Private Eye* used the phrase to refer to homosexual sex. This usage is less common, however, and it is doubtful whether it is known outside the readership of *Private Eye*.

> That they should be there together doesn't surprise her. Everyone knows about them now: Rosemary has even been mentioned in *Private Eye* as 'discussing Ugandan Affairs with a gorgeous young American don'.
>
> ALISON LURIE: *Foreign Affairs* (1984).

Ulster. Ulster Covenant The pledge by Protestant Ulster Unionists led by Sir Edward Carson (1854–1935) to resist the imposition of all-Ireland Home Rule, signed in Belfast on 28 September 1912. The 'solemn covenant' echoed the earlier anti-Papist Solemn League and Covenant signed by Scottish Presbyterians in the early 17th century. The ceremonial signing at Belfast City Hall was led by Carson and two other prominent Unionists, Lord Londonderry and Sir James Craig MP; the queue of Ulster Protestants eager to add their names to the document stretched for three-quarters of a mile. The covenant eventually amassed 471,414 signatures, many inscribed in their authors' own blood. *See also* ULSTER VOLUNTEERS.

Ulster Volunteers A private army founded in 1913 by the lawyer and politician Sir Edward Carson (1854–1935) to resist Home Rule for Ireland. In 1912 Carson led a parliamentary campaign to obstruct the passage of the Home Rule Bill (1912), which would have granted independence to the whole of Ireland, and organized mass signings of the ULSTER COVENANT. In 1913 the Ulster Volunteer Force, who claimed over 100,000 members, began to drill publicly. Carson's threats convinced the British government that special provision would have to be made for the Protestant North; in 1914 the outbreak of World War I led to the whole question being shelved for the duration. The present-day Ulster Volunteer Force (UVF) is a Protestant terrorist organization, illegal since 1966. *See also* CURRAGH MUTINY.

ultra-. ultrasound scanner A device used to examine internal structures in the body using ultrasound, *i.e.* pressure waves with a frequency above 30,000 hertz (sound consists of pressure waves with a maximum frequency of 20,000 hertz). An ultrasound beam is directed into the body in such a way that reflections from the organ to be examined are used to form an electronic image on a screen, which can be photographed. The technique is widely used in pregnancy to examine the foetus without fear of the damage that could be caused by X-rays. It is also used to examine a number of other organs for abnormalities.

ultraviolet catastrophe *See* QUANTUM THEORY.

unacceptable face of capitalism *See* LONRHO AFFAIR.

unbundling Taking over a large organization with a view to keeping the central part of the business and selling off some of the more peripheral concerns in order to help pay for the takeover.

uncertainty principle *See* HEISENBERG'S UNCERTAINTY PRINCIPLE.

Uncle. Uncle Joe A British World War II nickname for Joseph Stalin, head of the Soviet Government (1941–53). *See* MAN OF STEEL.

Uncle Mac British rhyming slang from the 1970s for heroin, from *smack*, itself a slang name for heroin. Uncle Mac, a figure totally unconnected with this aspect of life, was a presenter of children's radio programmes from the 1930s to the 1960s.

under. under cover Working out of sight, in secret. An under-cover agent is someone, such as a spy or policeman, who pursues his enquiries or work unknown to any but his employer.

underground A political or military movement carried on in secret against an oppressor government or an occupying enemy administration, especially in World War II. *See* RESISTANCE.

underground mutton Australian slang for a rabbit.

under the counter *See under* COUNTER.

UNESCO United Nations Educational, Scientific, and Cultural Organization. An autonomous UN agency, based in Paris, that promotes an exchange among nations of ideas and achievements. This has included literacy programmes, teacher training, science conferences, and advice on how to preserve national monuments. The agency also helped found CERN. UNESCO was established in 1945 at a United Nations conference in London and began operating the next year with Julian Huxley as its first director-general. About 160 nations belong to it, but America withdrew in 1984 and the UK followed in 1985, both because of UNESCO's wasteful management and apparent bias against western nations.

unfair dismissal Under the UK Employment Protection Act (1978), employees have the right not to be dismissed unfairly if they have served 52 continuous weeks of full-time employment in a job and are not over the normal retirement age. Unfair dismissal does not apply if the employer can demonstrate the employee's incapability, bad conduct, or lack of qualifications; nor does it apply in cases of redundancy. The employer has an obligation to show that he has acted reasonably in dismissing an employee, otherwise the employee may apply to an industrial tribunal for reinstatement or compensation.

unflappable Imperturbable, remaining calm in a crisis; from *flap*, a state of excitement, panic, or confusion. The epithet was originally applied to the British prime minister Harold Macmillan (*see* SUPERMAC) in 1958, who was also referred to as a "legend of unflappability".

unhappy teddy British army slang from the GULF WAR of 1991 for a depressed soldier.

UNICEF United Nations Children's Fund; originally the United Nations International Children's Emergency Fund. An autonomous UN agency, established in 1946, to provide food, clothing, and medicine to children who became victims of World War II. It was made a permanent body in 1953 and now provides financial aid, education, and health care to children, young people, and mothers in more than 100 nations, especially in DEVELOPING COUNTRIES and in disaster areas. Its work includes help in family planning. It is based in the United Nations Building in New York but funding comes from voluntary contributions, with three-quarters being provided by governments. UNICEF was awarded the 1965 Nobel Peace Prize.

Unification Church *See* MOONIES.

unified-field theory A theory in physics that would encompass the four fundamental interactions (electromagnetic, gravitational, weak, and strong) in one set of equations. Unification has not yet been achieved although the **electroweak theory** (1967) of Steven Weinberg (1933–)

and Abdus Salam (1926–) has successfully combined the electromagnetic and weak interactions. It is not known whether or not complete unification is feasible; indeed problems remain in attempting to make use of relativistic quantum field theory to cover the four interactions and the known elementary particles.

Theories that seek to unite the strong, weak, and electromagnetic interactions are known as **grand unified theories** (GUTs). A number of such theories exist, most of which postulate that these interactions merge at energies over 10^{15} GeV, which is above the range of existing accelerators.

Union of Democratic Control (UDC) An ad hoc coalition of socialists, radicals, and pacifists formed in September 1914, shortly after the outbreak of World War I. The main aims of the UDC were to secure parliamentary control over foreign policy, to open negotiations for a peace settlement offering reasonable terms for all participants, and to promote more open conduct of international diplomacy to prevent a repetition of the secret alliances and agreements that had precipitated the conflict. Founding members of the UDC included Ramsay Macdonald, Bertrand Russell, E. D. Morel, Charles Trevelyan, and Joseph Rowntree. In the hysteria of the period, when pacifists and other opponents of the war were regarded as cowards and traitors, UDC public meetings were often broken up by soldiers on leave. Morel, the secretary, was imprisoned and Russell was fined for a pamphlet in which he allegedly discouraged recruiting. Much of the UDC platform was adopted by the Labour Party after 1917; the organization remained active until World War II.

unisex Not distinguishing or differentiating between the sexes; designed for or applicable to both males and females. The term was applied to the fashions of the late 1960s and early 1970s when women increasingly wore trousers or jeans, men had long hair, and unisex boutiques sold clothing that could be worn by either sex. The unisex style, while abhorred at the time by many of the older generation, has since become the norm, particularly for leisure wear.

unit. Unit One A group of British artists formed in 1933 to promote the ideas of international MODERNISM. Its leading members were Paul Nash (1889–1946), Henry Moore (1898–1986), Ben Nicholson (1894–1982), and Barbara Hepworth (1903–75). The writer and critic Herbert Read (1893–1968) became the chief spokesman for the group.

unit trust A trust that manages a substantial sum of money invested in stock-exchange securities, in which members of the public can buy units. Thus the unit trust provides the small investor with an opportunity to own a part of a diverse and professionally managed holding of securities. The trustees are usually a commercial bank and it is part of their responsibility to show that the terms laid down in the trust deed are rigidly adhered to by their managers. Many trusts are now available, including those investing in home companies and those making overseas investments; some trusts seek high income for their unit holders while others attempt to maximize capital gains.

UNITA *União Nacional para a Indepencia Total de Angola* (Port. National Union for the Total Independence of Angola). An Angolan guerrilla organization led by Dr Jonas Savimbi (1934–). In the 1960s it was in the forefront of the struggle against Portuguese rule in Angola. Since Portugal's withdrawal in 1975, it has fought a civil war against the rival MPLA, a Marxist group that gained control of the country in 1976. UNITA's acceptance of South African backing has discredited it in the eyes of many Black Africans. In 1990 talks began to end the civil war.

United Nations The successor to the LEAGUE OF NATIONS as a world organization primarily concerned with the maintenance of peace but with numerous other functions and agencies. It sprang from the DUMBARTON OAKS CONFERENCE (1944) between America, the UK, and the Soviet Union and was formally inaugurated on 21 October 1945 when 51 founder members joined it. Its headquarters is in New York City.

United Nations Day The birthday of the UNITED NATIONS; 21 October.

Universal Declaration of Human Rights A document adopted by the General Assembly of the UNITED NATIONS in 1948 setting forth basic rights and fundamental freedoms to which all are entitled. They include the right to life, liberty, freedom from servitude, fair trial, marriage, ownership of property, freedom of thought and conscience, and freedom of expression. They also include the right to vote, to work, and to be educated.

University of the Third Age (U3A) A 'university' for retired people, founded in France by Pierre Vellus in 1973. It was introduced into the UK by Peter Laslett in 1983 and now has some 100 thriving British branches. Learning is for pleasure; there are no qualifications, examinations, or age limits. Teaching and the organization of lectures, classes, etc., are on a voluntary basis.

unknown. The Unknown Prime Minister The nickname given to A. Bonar Law (1858–1923), who briefly held office as Conservative leader in 1922-23.

The Unknown Warrior The body of an unknown British soldier who died in Flanders in World War I. The body was chosen at random by a blindfolded senior officer from a number of unidentifiable corpses; it lies in soil brought from the battlefield to be "buried among the kings" in Westminster Abbey (11 November 1920). Part of the inscription on the gravestone reads:

> Thus are commemorated the many multitudes who during the Great War of 1914–1918 gave the most that man can give, Life itself . . .

Similar tombs were set up in the National Cemetery at Arlington, Virginia; beneath the Arc de Triomphe at Paris; and in the Unter den Linden, Berlin. In 1958 the bodies of two more unknown servicemen were placed in the **Tomb of the Unknowns** at Arlington – one who died in World War II, and one in the Korean War.

unleaded *See* LEAD-FREE.

unorthodox medicine *See* ALTERNATIVE MEDICINE.

unreal Fantastically good or outrageously bad, usually ascribed to behaviour, depending on intonation and context. Originally part of BEATNIK jargon, it was widely used by teenagers in America in the 1960s and later spread to the UK and Australia.

unsocial hours Hours of work outside the normal working day; the term is especially used by shift workers and others because of the disruptive effect working such hours has on family and social life. It has been used as a factor in pay bargaining between union representatives and employers.

up. up against the wall Catchphrase used by radical Black groups of the 1960s, usually with the word 'motherfucker' added. An imitation of the usual order of police officers when making an arrest or searching a suspect, it was chanted during demonstrations in defiance against racist oppressors.

up-and-under *See* GARRYOWEN.

upfront (1) Originally, open or honest; now widened to mean extrovert, or showing leadership qualities. Both senses derive from the idea of someone standing up boldly and openly in front of others. (2) Paid in advance, as in **money upfront**.

up-market *See* MIDDLE-MARKET.

upper *See* LEAPER.

uptight Originally US slang to describe a person in a tense, anxious, or irritable state. It can also be used to describe someone who is strait-laced or stiffly formal and, particularly in America, in financial difficulties.

upward mobility The ability or aspiration to move upwards in SOCIAL CLASS or economic position. Since its first use in 1949, as class structures have become less rigid, upward moblilty has come to be measured more and more in terms of financial success. The YUPPIE, who epitomized the 1980s concept of upward mobility, is primarily concerned with the enhanced status acquired through wealth.

urban. urban guerrilla One who employs the terrorist activities associated with guerrilla warfare in cities and towns. The term has been in use since the late 1960s to describe the members of organizations who use kidnapping, bombing, and other violent methods to intimidate and coerce governments.

urban legends A body of largely apocryphal stories that constitutes a major component of modern folklore. Such stories dwell on the macabre and often surreal, with just enough plausibility to ensure their retelling. Most are connected with the various technological innovations of recent years, such as cars, electric saws, microwave ovens (into which a baby is inadvertently placed), and liquidizers (into which a frog falls). Others are elaborations of actual events; for example, the discovery of venomous spiders in imported yucca plants and the presence of alligators in the sewers of New York. Perhaps the best-known urban legend relates to the family who take a motoring holiday in France with Granny. The heat proves too much for poor Granny, who expires in the car.

The family stop at the next town to report the death at the local police station, leaving the deceased Granny covered with a rug. When they emerge from the police station, they find that the car, and Granny with it, has been stolen. On their return home they are unable to inherit because they have no body with which to establish the death.

urban renewal The redevelopment of urban areas in response to changing economic and social needs. In principle, urban renewal programmes concentrate on the renovation and adaption of existing buildings, particularly substandard buildings in INNER CITY areas, rather than the wholesale demolition of slums. US in origin, the term was first used officially in the heading of Title I of the Housing Act of 1949: 'Slum Clearance and Urban Renewal'.

urban sprawl The expansion of urban areas into the surrounding countryside in a haphazard and largely uncontrolled manner (*see also* RIBBON DEVELOPMENT). A problem accentuated by car ownership, urban sprawl became a political and environmental issue in the 1960s. At its worst, urban sprawl results in piecemeal developments of houses, shopping complexes, and industrial sites on the outskirts of towns and cities. The result of this sprawling unplanned growth is that adjacent developments merge into a vast conurbation. *See also* GREEN BELT.

Urdd Gobaith Cymru (Welsh, The Order of the Hope of Wales) A Welsh youth organization whose members dedicate themselves to the service of Wales, humanity, and Christ. It is particularly concerned with preserving the Welsh language. Founded in 1922 by Sir Ifan al Owen Edwards (1895–1970), it now has some 40,000 members. It organizes eisteddfods and Welsh-language summer schools as well as the usual range of sporting and social events.

user-friendly Denoting a computer designed to be used by people who are not highly skilled in computer techniques. User-friendly systems can be relied upon to give the operator plenty of on-screen instructions, usually in the form of MENUS, and clear guidance on how to correct errors. *See also* -FRIENDLY.

USO United Service Organizations. *See* ENSA CONCERTS.

Utah Allied codename for a beach N of Carentan in Normandy, which was one of the landing sites for US forces on D DAY. *See also* GOLD; JUNO; OMAHA; SWORD.

utility The official name given during and after World War II to clothing, furniture, etc., made according to government specification and sold at controlled prices. The name was a sign of the austerity of the times, in which practical qualities were more important than ornamentation.

V

V. **V for Victory** On 14 January 1941, M. Victor de Lavaleye, a member of the exiled Belgian government in London, proposed in a broadcast to Belgium that the letter V, standing for Victory in all European languages, be substituted for the letters RAF, which were being chalked up on walls, etc., in Belgium. The plan was immediately adopted and the Morse Code V (...—) was featured in every BBC broadcast to Europe followed by the opening bar of Beethoven's 5th Symphony (which has the same rhythm). Colonel Britton (D. E. Ritchie), director of the BBC European news service, was responsible for the diffusion of the V-sign propaganda, which gave hope to those under the Nazi yoke. Winston Churchill greatly popularized the sign of two upraised fingers in the form of a V; it has subsequently been adopted by various movements all over the world. *See also* HARVEY SMITH.

V1 *See* BUZZ BOMB.

V2 A long-range rocket with an explosive warhead, projected against England by the Germans in autumn, 1944. V2s were so named because they were the second *Vergeltungswaffe* (reprisal weapon) devised by the Germans (*see also* BUZZ BOMB). The V2 weapons were designed by Wernher von Braun (*see* SATURN ROCKETS).

> It was very successful, but it fell on the wrong planet.
>
> WERNHER VON BRAUN, about the first V2 to reach London.

Valentine. **St Valentine's Day massacre** *See under* SAINT.

Valentine State One of the names by which Arizona is known, because it was admitted as a state of the USA on St Valentine's Day (14 February) 1912.

Valentino The screen-name of the legendary US star of SILENT FILMS Rodolpho de Valentina d'Antonguolla (1895–1926). Of Italian origin, he became a romantic idol for thousands of cinema-goers in such films as *The Four Horsemen of the Apocalypse* (1921), *The Sheik* (1921), *Blood and Sand* (1922), and *Son of the Sheik* (1926). His intense looks (before the TALKIES, 'looks' were very important) and sexual magnetism established the legend that surrounds his name. His sudden death from peritonitis led to national mourning and precipitated several suicides. His life and death have been the subject of many studies, including the film biography *Valentino* (1967), with Rudolf Nureyev in the title role.

> His acting is largely confined to protruding his large, almost occult eyes until the vast areas of white are visible, drawing back the lips of his wide, sensuous mouth to bare his gleaming teeth, and flaring his nostrils.
>
> ADOLPH ZUKOR, Hungarian-born early Hollywood film producer.

Valium A proprietary name for the drug diazepam, a tranquillizer and muscle-relaxant commonly prescribed for the short-term relief of tension and anxiety. The drug is potentially habit-forming and since its introduction in 1963 there have been several well-publicized cases of prolonged use leading to psychological dependence. *See also* LIBRIUM.

valley. **valley girl** A US pampered teenage girl from S California's San Fernando valley in the early 1980s. The quintessential valley girl came from a wealthy suburban background, often with parents in the music business or the media, and had sufficient money and leisure to indulge her passion for shopping. Her distinguishing characteristic was the idiosyncratic argot, VALSPEAK, with which she communicated with other valley girls. A passing phase in California's youth culture, the valley girl phenomenon is unlikely to have become widely known were it not for the commercial success of the satirical record 'Valley Girl' (1982), made by the rock musician Frank Zappa and featuring his daughter, Moon Unit, in an improvised monologue in Valspeak. The valley girl phenomenon was highlighted in the UK by an article in the magazine *Harpers and Queen* in 1983. In America, the girls have their own handbook, *The Valley Girl's Guide to Life*

(1982), by Mimi Pond. *See also* JEWISH AMERICAN PRINCESS *under* JEW; SLOANE RANGER.

Valley of Ten Thousand Smokes A volcanic valley in the region of Mount Katmai, Alaska. Shortly before Mount Katmai blew up on 6 June 1912 there were many bursts of molten matter in the valley; these fissures have since discharged hot gases, hence the name of the valley. It has been a National Monument since 1918.

valspeak US slang from the early 1980s for the jargon of the VALLEY GIRLS of S California. Based on a mixture of high-school slang and surf-talk, it is spoken in high-pitched lazy Californian drawl.

vamp A woman who uses her feminine charms and sexual attraction to entice and exploit men. The vamp (short for vampire) was a popular stock character of SILENT FILMS, the first screen vamp being the actress Theda Bara (1890–1955); vamps still frequently appear in television SOAP OPERAS.

Van Allen belts Radiation belts that surround the Earth, consisting of high-energy charged particles trapped in the Earth's magnetic field. The lower belt, containing electrons and protons, extends from 1000 to 5000 km above the equator. An outer belt, containing mostly electrons, extends from 15,000 to 25,000 km above the equator. They were discovered in 1958 by James Van Allen (1914–   ), as a result of radiation detectors carried by Explorer satellites.

Van de Graaff generator An electrostatic generator used to produce the very high voltages used in particle physics to accelerate electrons, protons, etc., for research purposes. It was invented by the US physicist R. J. Van de Graaff (1901–67).

Van Meegeren forgeries The notorious art forgeries perpetrated by the Dutch artist Hans Van Meegeren (1889–1947) in the 1930s and 1940s, which caused acute embarrassment to the numerous prominent art critics who had authenticated them. Van Meegeren's forgeries were exposed after the close of World War II, when a painting purporting to be Vermeer's *The Woman taken in Adultery* was found among the works of art looted by Herman Göring. The sale to Göring was traced to Van Meegeren, who ironically was paid the equivalent of £150,000 in forged banknotes. Accused of collaborating with the Nazis and facing a possible death sentence, the artist confessed to his long series of forgeries. It subsequently emerged that he had forged 14 masterpieces by such artists as Hals, Hooch, and Vermeer, including the latter's *Christ and the Disciples at Emmaus*, which had been hailed by the art establishment on its discovery in 1937. The critics dismissed his confession and challenged him to produce another Vermeer of equal quality. Van Meegeren was locked into a studio with a panel of experts and he began his *Young Christ Teaching in the Temple*. His mastery of forging the effects of time upon the painting was so sophisticated that he did not even have to complete the work to convince the judges. The collaboration charges were dropped but charges of falsifying signatures brought the artist a sentence of one year in prison: he died of a heart attack before he could begin his term. Van Meegeren's motivation, it emerged, had been to revenge himself upon the art establishment after his own work had been derided by a critic when, as a young man, he had refused to buy a good review with a bribe.

Vasa project The raising of the Swedish sailing ship *Vasa*, which sank in a sudden squall in Stockholm harbour before it began its maiden voyage in 1628. This feat of engineering, completed in 1961, was initiated by Anders Franzen, a salvage expert, who believed that the *Vasa* might well be largely intact on the seabed, the Baltic being free of the destructive shipworm (*teredo navalis*) that is prevalent elsewhere in the world. It took four years to find the wreck and a further five years to prepare the *Vasa* for its perilous ascent to the surface, using inflatable pontoons and hydraulic jacks. The ship was brought up in an extraordinary well-preserved condition; it was subsequently housed in a specially built museum, in which it was constantly sprayed to prevent the timbers warping. This triumph of marine salvage inspired several similar projects (*see* MARY ROSE; TITANIC).

VAT Value Added Tax. An indirect tax on goods or services calculated by adding a percentage (currently 17½% in the UK) to the value of a product at each stage in its production. Each trader has to remit the tax to the Customs and Excise after deducting the amount of tax he has paid for goods or services (but not labour costs). Thus the tax is not borne by traders but by consumers. It replaced **purchase tax** in the UK in 1973 to comply with the similar tax used in the European Community. Some products, *e.g.* food and books, are zero-rated for VAT.

Vatican. Second Vatican Council An ecumenical council of the Roman Catholic Church opened by Pope John XXIII in October 1962 and concluded by Paul VI in December 1965. It was concerned with the need for Christian unity. One special feature was the presence of observers from non-Roman Catholic Churches.

Vatican City State The area of Rome occupied by the city of the Vatican, recognized by the LATERAN TREATY (1929) as constituting the territorial extent of the temporal power of the Holy See. It consists of the Papal palace, the Library, archives and museums, the Piazza of St Peter, and contiguous buildings including a railway station, in all an area of just under a square mile. It has about 900 inhabitants and its own coinage. Certain other buildings outside the Vatican enjoy extraterritorial rights.

Vatican roulette Slang for the rhythm method of contraception, which is based on avoiding intercourse during the middle of the menstrual cycle when ovulation is most likely to occur. It is not a reliable method of contraception. The phrase is a reference to 'Russian roulette', a potentially suicidal game of chance played with a gun with only one bullet in the chamber. Each player spins the chamber, points the gun against his temple, and pulls the trigger. Vatican roulette is so called because the Vatican still forbids contraception by any other method. It is said jokingly that couples who play Vatican roulette are called 'parents'.

VC *See* VICTOR CHARLIE; VIET CONG.

VDU Visual Display Unit. The part of a computer system on which words, diagrams, etc., are displayed. It consists of a cathode-ray tube and is usually connected to a keyboard and personal computer, word processor, etc. In larger computer systems, however, the cathode-ray tube, its controlling electronics, and the keyboard may be referred to collectively as the VDU.

VE Day The end of hostilities in Europe after World War II, 8 May 1945. *See also* VJ DAY.

veganism A strict form of vegetarianism in which all food of animal origin is renounced. Vegans refuse not only meat but also eggs, dairy products, and even honey. Adherents of this strict regime coined the term in 1944, to distinguish themselves from mere vegetarians (sometimes referred to as **ovolactarians**, *i.e.* egg-and-milk eaters). Vegans argue that theirs is the only logical form of vegetarianism, since commercial production of milk and eggs could not be carried on without the market for beef and chicken. They use a milk-substitute manufactured from beans. The diet is not self-sufficient; vegans require certain dietary supplements to stay healthy.

Velcro Tradename for a 'touch and close' fabric fastener. The device was invented in 1957 in Switzerland by Georges de Mestral, who devised the name as a combination of the French words *vel*ours (velvet) and *cro*ché (hooked). It consists of two strips of nylon, one having a large number of tiny hooks and the other with an equal number of loops, into which the hooks fit when the two strips are pressed together.

Velvet Fog A nickname for the US singer Mel Tormé (1923–), in allusion to the smooth crooning style that characterized his singing of the late 1940s and 1950s. Another of his nicknames was the **Singer's Singer**.

Venlo incident The arrest of two British agents by German counter-intelligence in Venlo, on the German–Dutch border, on 8 November 1939. Their capture was a disaster for British intelligence and compromised its network of agents throughout Europe. The British agents, Captain Sigismund Payne Best and Major R. H. Stevens, were part of an MI6 network seeking contacts with the anti-Nazi movement in Germany, with the aim of removing Hitler from power and securing an end to the war. They were contacted by 'Captain Schaemmel', actually Major Walter Schallenburg of Nazi counter-espionage, who claimed to be a representative of the anti-Nazi movement. After several meetings, the MI6 agents agreed to arrange to airlift from Venlo to London the leader of the anti-Nazi movement who, Schallenburg claimed, wanted urgent talks with the British government. Hitler ordered that the British agents should be seized on Dutch soil, kidnapped, and transported to Germany, where they remained prisoners until released by US forces in 1945.

venture. venture capital Capital used by an investor to buy shares in a new company or an expanding business, when he is well aware that the investment carries a substantial risk. Venture capital is an investment rather than a loan.

Venture Scouts *See* BOY SCOUTS.

Verdun The fortress region in E France, site of the major German offensive of 21 February–18 December 1916 during World War I, which was intended to sap French resources. The initial German artillery barrage was one of the most devastating ever launched and enabled the German Fifth Army to advance through the outer defences and capture Fort Douaumont on 25 February. The French then mounted a counterattack using reinforcements transported to the front along the secondary road from Bar-le-Duc, which became known as the 'Sacred Way'. This halted the German advance and during March and April the German commander, Erich von Falkenhayn, focused his attacks on the eastern and western flanks; he had, however, given up hope of a swift breakthrough. The offensive settled into a war of attrition, with frequent attacks and counterattacks and the capture and recapture of territory around the Meuse Heights. At the nearest, the Germans came to within 5 km (3 miles) of Verdun but in October the French, under General Nivelle, mounted a series of counterattacks, which successfully recovered much of the lost territory, including Fort Douaumont (24 October) and Vaux (2 November). The long and bitter struggle became a symbol of French determination to resist and survive (*see under* PASS). The French losses were estimated at 542,000, against the Germans' 434,000.

Verdun pigeon A pigeon that performed invaluable service for the French army by carrying vital messages during the battle of VERDUN in 1916. Pigeons were a key factor in the Allied communications network in World War I; in World War II they were also dropped in crates by parachute to RESISTANCE fighters to facilitate the sending of secret messages to London. The Verdun pigeon won particular praise for its heroism in braving fierce artillery fire and was greatly mourned when it died from wounds received on one of these missions; in recognition of its courage, it was posthumously awarded the Legion d'Honneur.

Vereeniging Treaty The treaty that ended the second Boer War, signed in Pretoria on 31 May 1902, after the Boers had initially agreed to the British terms at Vereeniging. The South African Republic and the Orange Free State were placed under British military administration but were promised eventual self-government. A general amnesty was declared, the burghers were disarmed, and the sum of £3,000,000 was allocated for the payment of war debts and to provide for the economic reconstruction of the Transvaal. The issue of native voting rights was left for settlement after the granting of self-government, an ignoble concession by the British, which guaranteed African disfranchisement after the formation of the Union of South Africa in 1910 (*see* APARTHEID). *See* BOER WARS.

Versailles Treaty The peace treaty between the Allies and Germany concluded at the PARIS PEACE CONFERENCE in 1919; separate treaties were concluded between the Allies and the other defeated nations. The terms were fixed in Paris by President Wilson of America; Clemenceau, prime minister of France; Lloyd George, the British prime minister; and Orlando, the prime minister of Italy. There were no German representatives and the Germans were forced to sign under threat of the resumption of the war. The Versailles Treaty included the covenant of the LEAGUE OF NATIONS, as did all the other peace treaties. Germany lost one eighth of its European territory, including Alsace-Lorraine, the Rhineland, which was to be occupied by Allied troops, and the Saar, which was placed under League of Nations control for 15 years after which a referendum would decide the future of the population. Germany also lost Malmédy and Eupen to Belgium and North Schleswig to Denmark. The Poles were given access to the Baltic along a 'corridor' at the head of which was Danzig, declared a free city under League control. Austrian independence was assured and Germany also forfeited all her colonies, which became mandates of the League. The military terms were also harsh. Germany was to disarm, abolish military service, maintain an army of not more than 100,000 men, and reduce the size of her navy. In Article 231, the famous War Guilt Clause, Germany had to accept responsibility for the war and to pay reparations for the damages caused to Allied nations. The treaty was the focus for German disaffection throughout the life of the WEIMAR REPUBLIC, although the amount of reparations was reduced in later years, by the DAWES PLAN and the YOUNG PLAN, and various military clauses were circumvented, especially after Hitler came to power in 1933.

Vespa *See* LAMBRETTA.

vet A US abbreviation for 'veteran soldier'. It was often heard in the phrase **Vietnam vet**, widely used after the VIETNAM WAR (1954–75). *See also* PVS.

veteran. veteran car A car from the early days of motoring. The UK Veteran Car Club is interested in any car built before the end of 1918, although the strict definition of a veteran car is one built before the end of 1904. To qualify for the LONDON TO BRIGHTON RUN a car has to comply with this strict definition. Some enthusiasts call vehicles built between the beginning of 1905 and the end of 1918 **Edwardian cars**. *See also* VINTAGE CAR.

Veteran's Day *See* ARMISTICE DAY.

Veto Bill The controversial parliamentary bill, introduced by the Liberal Government and passed on 10 August 1911. The bill asserted the supremacy of the House of Commons, stipulated that bills passed by the Commons in three successive parliamentary sessions should become law in spite of the Lords' opposition, removed the authority of the Lords to veto money bills, and limited the Lords' powers to delay other legislation; it also reduced the duration of parliament from seven years to five. In July 1911 the Liberal prime minister, Asquith, secured the backing of King George V to the creation of 500 new peers if necessary to force the bill through the upper house. This finally persuaded the Lords to accept the legislation, thereby preserving the chamber from more radical changes in its constitution and function. *See also* PEOPLE'S BUDGET.

vette US abbreviation for a Chevrolet Corvette, the ultimate US sports car.

vibes (1) A slang shortening of 'vibrations', in the sense of an emotional atmosphere sensed intuitively and communicated by the aura emanating from a person, place, or thing. (2) In JAZZ, short for 'vibraphone', one who plays this instrument being known as a **vibrist**.

Vichy A town in the department of Allier, in central France, formerly fashionable on account of its thermal and medicinal springs. Vichy acquired a new significance during World War II as the seat of Marshal Pétain's collaborationist government (1940–44), after the German occupation.

Vicky The pseudonym of Victor Weisz (1913–66), the political cartoonist famous for his caricatures in the *Evening Standard* in the late 1950s and 1960s. He was born in Berlin of Hungarian parents, suffered harassment from the Nazis for his precocious political cartoons, and settled in England with his parents in 1935. He quickly learned English, became a self-taught expert on the nature of British humour, and in 1941, after a period freelancing, was given a job as a political cartoonist on the *News Chronicle*. Throughout the war he was frequently denounced by the political establishment as an enemy alien because of his mordant and satirical talents. After a spell on the *Daily Mirror* he joined the *Evening Standard* in 1958, for which he produced six cartoons a week, as well as a weekly cartoon for the *New Statesman*. His impudent caricatures of contemporary politicians and statesmen, such as de Gaulle, Churchill, Eden, and Macmillan (*see* SUPERMAC), became very well known. Despite his success, he committed suicide with an overdose of sleeping pills in February 1966.

Victor Charlie US military slang from the late 1960s for the VIET CONG or a Viet Cong guerrilla. *Victor* and *Charlie* are the communications code words for the letters V and C. The Viet Cong were later referred to simply as the **VC**.

> He . . . was told about being shot out of a helicopter by Victor Charlie.
>
> *New Yorker*, 18 June 1966.

victory. victory bonds *See* BOTTOMLEY CASE.

Victory Medal (World War I) A bronze medal with a winged figure of Victory on the obverse; awarded in 1919 to all allied service personnel who had served in a theatre of war, also to certain women's formations.

victory roll An aerobatic manoeuvre in which the pilot executes a complete roll of the aircraft; pilots in both world wars sometimes executed a roll to celebrate a 'kill' in the air.

video. video game *See* COMPUTER GAME.

video nasty A film, recorded on video, that is characterized by violence and horrific special effects, sometimes also having a strong pornographic content. *See also* SNUFF MOVIE.

video recorder A tape recorder for recording both the vision and sound signals of a film, TV programme, etc., on a magnetic tape contained in a closed plastic cassette. As the video (vision) signal contains frequencies in the megahertz range, a video tape cannot be used in the same way as an audio (sound) tape, in which the signals have kilohertz frequencies. To overcome this problem, avoiding excessive tape speeds, the signal is recorded diagonally on the tape (each diagonal line representing one line on the picture) and the tape runs slowly over a drum on which the recording and reading heads rotate rapidly. Since the early 1980s video recorders have been widely used by the British public; in the late 1980s nearly 60% of homes owned a recorder. **Video cameras** (camcorders) are also widely owned. Video cameras and video recorders playing through a domestic television set have now almost entirely replaced home movies on 8mm or 16mm film.

Vienna circle A group of philosophers, scientists, and mathematicians formed around the figure of Moritz Schlick (1882–1936), Professor of Philosophy at the University of Vienna, during the 1920s. The circle included Otto Neurath (1882–1945), Rudolph Carnap (1891–1970), Kurt Gödel (1906–78), Herbert Feigl (1906–), and others. In 1922 the group described themselves as logical positivists and dedicated their researches to separating true science from metaphysics. To this end they were influenced by the scientific phenomenalism of Ernst Mach, Schlick's predecessor in the chair of philosophy at the university, the New Logic developed by Frege, Bertrand Russell, and Alfred Whitehead, and by Wittgenstein's *Tractatus* (1921). The group issued a manifesto, *The Vienna Circle: Its Scientific Outlook* (1929); published a journal, *Erkenntnis*; and held a number of annual congresses in various European capitals. The circle made Vienna the centre of philosophy in the 1920s and early 1930s but with the rise of totalitarianism in Europe threatening a new Dark Age, its members (many of whom were Jewish) dispersed into exile after 1935. In 1936 Schlick was murdered on the steps of the university library by an insane student, a crime never fully investigated by the authorities, who reviled Schlick's empiricist and phenomenalist teachings. A radical version of the LOGICAL POSITIVISM of the Vienna circle was popularized by Alfred Ayer, who had studied in Vienna.

Viet Cong The communist guerrilla forces in South Vietnam, who fought from 1954 to 1975 in a successful effort to overthrow the government. After the GENEVA AGREEMENTS of 1954, which divided the country into north and south, about 10,000 communist VIET MINH insurgents stayed in the south and renamed themselves the *Viet Cong* to fight the VIETNAM WAR. Their political organization, the National Liberation Front (NLF), was established in 1960. The name is short for *Viet Nam Cong San* (Vietnamese for *Vietnamese Communists*). By the mid-1960s, US soldiers usually referred to the enemy as the **VC** (*see* VICTOR CHARLIE).

Viet Minh The communist-led Vietnamese military and political organization that resisted Japanese occupation during World War II and fought French rule after 1945. In 1957, its members in the south became VIET CONG guerrillas in the VIETNAM WAR against South Vietnam and, in the 1960s and 1970s, against the US forces defending it. The Viet Minh League was organized in 1941, a coalition of communist and nationalist parties headed by the communist leader Ho Chi Minh. In 1945, they ousted the Japanese-sponsored regime and, in 1954, defeated the French forces. They became the ruling government of the Democratic Republic of Vietnam (North Vietnam) and three years later began military support for the Viet Cong. The name *Viet Minh* is derived from *Viet Nam Doc-lap Dong Minh* (Vietnamese for the *Revolutionary League for the Independence of Vietnam*).

Vietnam War America's costly war of containment from 1965 to 1973 in support of South Vietnam against the VIET CONG communist guerrilla movement. America suffered about 58,000 combat deaths and 365,000 wounded during this unpopular war; South Vietnam and North Vietnam both had almost one million killed. America introduced support troops in 1961; they became combatants in 1965 against an enemy aided by North Vietnam, China, and the Soviet Union. Graphic television coverage, the US government's no-win containment policy, and a massive cost (which finally totalled around $150 billion) created an anti-war movement that began on college campuses, especially within the HIPPIE culture. The US military presence reached a maximum of 543,400 in April 1969; seven months later 250,000 anti-war activists demonstrated in Washington, DC. President Richard Nixon's administration signed a cease-fire agreement in 1973; after US troops withdrew, the South Vietnamese government finally fell on 30 April 1975.

The country was officially reunited on 2 July 1976, as the Socialist Republic of Vietnam. About 6.5 million refugees fled from South Vietnam, more than 165,000 being accepted into America. The Vietnam War has been said to have seen the end of America's innocence, with US soldiers massacring hundreds of civilians at MY LAI in 1968 and the government's secret bombing of Viet Cong in Cambodia. The war's legacy included hostile receptions for returning veterans (*see also* PVS), a continuing search for US bodies, and evidence that some US prisoners were still held in Vietnam. The weight of the guilt and the loss of idealism lingered for two decades; they prompted President George Bush's promises that the 1991 GULF WAR would not be another Vietnam. *See also* AGENT ORANGE.

Vimy Ridge A hill in N France, on the ridge of Nôtre Dame de Lorette, NE of Arras, which was captured by Allied troops in World War I during the Battle of Arras (9–14 April 1917). The capture of the German stronghold by the Canadian Corps under General Sir Julian Byng was the only success of the battle; it cost 11,285 lives.

Vinegar Joe The World War II nickname of General Joseph W. Stilwell (1883–1946), US Commander of troops in China. Another of his nicknames was **Old Turkey Neck**.

Vinland Map A supposedly 15th-century map showing the NE coast of America, as explored by the Vikings in the 10th century. According to the Norse Saga, *Flateyjarbók*:

> When spring came they made ready and left, and Leif named the land after its fruits, and called in *Vinland*.

The discovery of the map in 1957 was said to be the most exciting cartographic find of the century. Supposedly drawn about 1440, it substantially preceded the voyages of Columbus (1492) and of John Cabot (1497), thus conclusively establishing the extent of the Viking explorations. It was presented to Yale University by an anonymous donor in 1965. In 1974 Yale announced that it was a fake. The pigment of the ink with which it was drawn was found to contain titanium dioxide, first used in the 1920s.

vintage car Broadly, any car built between the beginning of 1905 (earlier models are called VETERAN CARS) and the start of World War II. However, the strict definition of a vintage car is one built between 1905 and 1930. The supreme example of a vintage car is the 1927 Bugatti Royale of which only six were sold. One survivor sold for £5.5 million pounds in 1987. The expression **classic car** is used for any sought-after model built after 1930 that had a good reputation in its day.

VIP Very Important Person. This now widespread usage was coined by a station commander of Transport Command in 1944, who was responsible for the movement of a plane-load of important individuals, including Lord Mountbatten, to the Middle East and so described them in his movement orders to avoid disclosing their identity.

Virgin Mary *See* BLOODY MARY.

virus *See* COMPUTER VIRUS.

vital statistics Properly, population statistics concerned with births, marriages, deaths, divorces, etc. It is also used to refer (in inches) to a girl's bust, waist, and hip measurements: 'Her vital statistics are 34-24-34'.

Viyella Tradename for a soft woven fabric used for shirts, blouses, etc. It is manufactured by William Hollins & Co., originally in the Via Gellia valley in Derbyshire. The Via Gellia was a Roman road that ran through the valley, between Buxton and Nottingham. Pronounced locally 'Vi Jella', this was the source for the tradename.

VJ Day The end of hostilities in Japan and the rest of the Far East, 15 August 1945. *See also* VE DAY.

Vogueing A style of dance of the late 1980s, in which participants strut and pose like models on a catwalk, a reaction in part to the POWER DRESSING fashion of the early years of the decade. It is named after the fashion magazine *Vogue*.

voice. Voice of America (VOA) The official overseas radio broadcasting network of the United States Information Agency. Founded in 1942 within the Office of War

Information for propaganda purposes, VOA now seeks to promote a favourable image of America by broadcasting balanced news and entertainment throughout the world. The programmes, originating from Washington, DC, are in English and 41 other languages. They reach an estimated weekly audience of 120 million people. VOA is often confused with Radio Free Europe/Radio Liberty, the Munich-based organization funded by Congress but run by private US citizens.

voice-over A background commentary accompanying pictures on a screen, spoken off-screen by an unseen narrator or announcer. The technique is common in television programmes and advertisements, which often feature the recognizable voices of well-known personalities. The unseen narrator is also sometimes called the voice-over.

voiceprint An electronically constructed graphic representation of a person's voice. A voiceprint, more formally called a *speech spectogram*, consists of a pattern of lines and whorls, showing distinctions in pitch, loudness, and duration of speech obtained by running a tape recording of a voice through a **sound spectrograph**. Like a fingerprint, a voiceprint pattern is said to be unique to each individual and of possible value in police work. They have been used as evidence in court cases but, like POLYGRAPHS, their validity has been challenged. The sound spectograph was devised in the 1940s by three US scientists at the Bell Research Laboratories; the US physicist Lawrence G. Kersta developed it for identification purposes.

The Voice *See* OLD BLUE EYES.

vorticism An artistic movement which began in the UK in 1914, somewhat akin to CUBISM and FUTURISM and embracing art and literature. It was iconoclastic and regarded the question of representation as irrelevant; its designs were in straight lines and angular patterns. Concern with machinery was also a feature. Among its representatives, P. Wyndham Lewis and Edward Wadsworth were the most notable. The name was bestowed by Ezra Pound. *Compare* DADAISM; FAUVISM; ORPHISM; SURREALISM; SYNCHRONISM.

Vostok (Russ. East) A series of six Soviet manned spacecraft launched during the two-year period 1961–63. Vostok 1, launched on 12 April 1961, took the first man into space: cosmonaut Yuri A. Gagarin made a single orbit of the Earth before re-entry, a total flight time of 1 hour 48 minutes. Vostok 2 (6 August 1961) carried Major Herman Titov in 17 orbits around the Earth; Vostok 3 and 4 (launched together on 11 August 1962) made 48 joint orbits, the first double manned flight. This mission also produced the first TV pictures from space and demonstrations of weightlessness seen by the public. Vostok 5, launched on 14 June 1963, was followed two days later by Vostok 6, which carried the first woman into spacc, Valentina V. Tereshkova.

Votes for Women *See* SUFFRAGETTES.

vox pop (Lat. *vox populi*, voice of the people) Public opinon, the popular verdict. The term was taken up by the British broadcasting media in the 1960s to refer to the opinions elicited from the man or woman in the street when stopped and questioned by reporters. The expression *vox populi* has been used since the mid-16th century and derives from the maxim *Vox populi vox Dei* (the voice of the people is the voice of God).

Voyager Two unmanned US SPACE PROBES designed for interplanetary travel and exploration of the outer solar system. Voyager 1 was launched on 5 September 1977, reached Jupiter in March 1979 and Saturn in November 1980. Data transmitted back from its planetary encounters included the discovery of three moons of Saturn, two moons of Jupiter, Jupiter's ring, and fine details of the structure of Saturn's ring system. Voyager 2 was launched on 20 August 1977, before its twin; travelling more slowly than Voyager 1, it passed Jupiter in July 1979, Saturn in August 1981, Uranus in January 1986, and Neptune in August 1989. Voyager 2 achieved the first flybys of Uranus and Neptune as well as discovering the 14th moon of Jupiter and 10 moons and two rings of Uranus. Both probes are now heading out of the solar system into deep space, carrying recordings of terrestrial culture, including Earth sounds, music, and greetings in 60 languages, should they ever encounter alien life forms.

VSO Voluntary Service Overseas. A UK organization founded in 1958 by Alexander Dickson (1914–   ) to allow skilled people to contribute voluntarily to improving the economic and social infrastructure of developing countries. VSO does not administer its own projects but provides volunteers with the desired qualifications in response to requests by the host countries. Skills required cover technical trades, education, agriculture, technology, and business development; volunteers are normally contracted for a period of two years. VSO pays travel expenses and offers certain grants and allowances, while the employer provides accommodation and wages at the local rates. As training is an important function of the VSO programme, volunteers are usually required to train a local person to take over from them when they leave.

VTOL Vertical Take-off and Landing. Denoting an aircraft, other than a helicopter or airship, that can take off and land vertically. Among fixed-wing aircraft with this facility, the most successful is the Harrier jump-jet, which uses swivelling exhaust nozzles to discharge the propellent jet downwards when taking off or landing. Other aircraft may be described as CTOL (conventional take-off and landing), STOL (short), and QSTOL (quiet short).

vulnerable species A category of THREATENED SPECIES identified by the International Union for the Conservation of Nature and Natural Resources (IUCN). Vulnerable species include those whose wild populations (1) are decreasing because of continuing destruction of their habitat, hunting, etc.; (2) have decreased but not yet recovered to their former levels; (3) are still abundant but are threatened by adverse factors. Vulnerable species are likely to become ENDANGERED SPECIES if the factors causing or threatening their decline continue to operate; they include:

gorilla (*Gorilla gorilla*)
grey wolf (*Canis lupus*)
polar bear (*Ursus maritimus*)
European otter (*Lutra lutra lutra*)
cheetah (*Acinonyx jubatus*)
ocelot (*Felis pardalis*)
jaguar (*Panthera onca*)
African elephant (*Loxodonta africana*)
pigmy hippopotamus (*Choeropsis liberiensis*)
Indian python (*Python molurus*)

W

WAAC Women's Army Auxiliary Corps. A body of women raised for non-combatant army service in World War I; members of the corps were known colloquially as **Waacs**. In World War II, the name of the corps was changed to Auxiliary Territorial Service and the girls were called **ATS**. The corps became the WRAC (Women's Royal Army Corps) in 1949.

WAAF Women's Auxilary Air Force. It was established in 1939, its members being known as **Waafs**, it became the WRAF (Women's Royal Air Force) in 1949. There was an earlier WRAF in World War I.

WAC Women's Army Corps. The US Army's women's force in World War II. It was equivalent to the British ATS (*see* WAAC). *See also* WAVES.

Wailing Wall *See* WESTERN WALL.

Wait and see A phrase often humorously used with reference to H. H. Asquith (Earl of Oxford and Asquith); thus 'What did Asquith say?' is another way of saying 'Wait and see'. Asquith used the phrase in answer to a question in the House of Commons on 4 April 1910 and took to repeating it subsequently when faced with an awkward question. Eventually the Opposition took it up and chanted it when questions were put to him.

Wakey-Wakey! The catchphrase of the British bandleader Billy Cotton (1899–1969). *The Billy Cotton Band Show* was an extremely popular radio and TV show first broadcast in 1949; it ran for 20 years. It opened with a short chorus from the band followed by a shout of 'Wakey-Wakey!' from the leader. The catchphrase is said to have arisen because the show originally went out early in the morning and on one occasion the musicians looked rather sleepy.

waldo (1) Slang for any remote-control device designed to manipulate objects, named after Waldo F. Jones, an inventor in a SCI-FI story by Robert Heinlein. (2) US teenage slang for a stupid person, a fool; equivalent to the British WALLY.

walk. walkabout In the Aboriginal culture of Australia, a long, solitary, and sometimes contemplative journey. The term acquired new relevance in the 1970s when it was applied to Elizabeth II's habit of making royal 'walkabouts', straying from her planned route to meet ordinary people who had come to see her during her tour of Australia. This unorthodox behaviour alarmed security men but subsequently did much to promote the popularity of the British monarch in Australia. Other celebrities are now also said to go on walkabouts when they depart from an official programme by mixing with crowds.

walkie-talkie A small portable short-range radio containing receiver and transmitter, as used by the fighting services, the police, etc.

walking bass In JAZZ slang, a bass line backing the main melody in BOOGIE-WOOGIE piano playing, consisting of ascending broken octaves. It is also used to describe a pizzicato accompaniment on a double base in regular crotchets moving up step by step in 4/4 time.

walking the dog A popular JAZZ dance of the post-World War II period.

Walkman Tradename for a portable cassette tape player (also called a personal stereo or personal hi fi) which is listened to through a small set of headphones. Walkman, although widely used as a generic name for any portable cassette player, actually refers to one of the first models on the market, manufactured by the Japanese firm Sony.

wall. off the wall *See under* OFF.

wall of death A fairground attraction consisting of a huge drum, round the inside of which a stunt motorcyclist rides his machine. The angular momentum enables the motorcycle to ride higher and higher up the inside wall, appearing to defy gravity.

Wall of Sound The distinctive musical accompaniment created for pop singers in the mid-1960s by Phil Spector (1940–), the US record producer. His expensive method of achieving this was to employ several musicians playing identical instruments in unison. He called the deep and full-bodied result his 'little symphonies for the kiddies'; this wall-of-sound technique enabled him to make hits for The Righteous Brothers ('You've Lost That Lovin' Feelin''), The Ronettes ('Be My Baby'), and Ike and Tina Turner ('River Deep – Mountain High'). Spector later produced John Lennon's *Imagine* album and one for George Harrison that included 'My Sweet Lord'.

wallpecker One of the many German citizens who assisted in the demolition of the BERLIN WALL with hammers, chisels, pickaxes, etc., following its opening in November 1989. While most wished simply to express their hatred of the wall or to gather a personal memento, others had more entrepreneurial intentions; by Christmas 'authentic' pieces of the wall were being sold at inflated prices through newspaper advertisements and on London markets. The term is a contraction of wall-woodpecker, a literal translation of the German term, *Mauerspecht*.

walls have ears A World War II security slogan from an advertising campaign designed to make people aware of the dangers of idle talk that might be useful to spies. *See also* KEEP IT DARK; KEEP IT UNDER YOUR HAT *under* HAT.

Wall Street Crash The collapse of the New York stock exchange on BLACK MONDAY, 28 October 1929, which plunged the world economy into the GREAT DEPRESSION. The crash came as the reaction to one of the greatest speculative booms in history, an orgy of gambling in shares whose values rose precipitously during the late 1920s and never seemed to reach a ceiling. The public's urge to speculate, helped by easy credit and the overweening optimism of the business community, was satisfied by a vast increase in the volume of shares available, especially from new investment trusts, the reckless issue of glamour stocks, and the marketing of securities to finance a flood of corporate mergers. Throughout the summer of 1929 share prices and the volume of trading rose inexorably; the underlying economy, however, was already entering a decline, with the indices of industrial production falling and unemployment rising. In the autumn, as this downturn became apparent, confidence in the market drained away and the frightened speculators sought to unload their holdings, causing the market to crash. On Thursday 24 October, panic selling resulted in 12,894,650 shares changing hands at disastrous prices, while hysterical crowds gathered outside the exchange. In the aftermath of the crash banks failed, businesses and factories closed down, and unemployment rose sharply. By 1933 the American GNP was one-third less than it had been in 1929, and one-quarter (13 million people) of the labour force was out of work. The crisis spread to the economies of all the other western nations and did not end until World War II boosted production and employment.

Wallenberg, Raoul (1912–47) A Swedish diplomat who was sent by his government to Hungary as a special envoy in 1944 to save the Hungarian Jews from the HOLOCAUST. A member of a well-known Swedish banking family, Wallenberg joined a foodstuff firm in 1939, the senior partner of which was a Jewish refugee from Budapest. As a frequent visitor to Budapest on business, he soon had a number of contacts with the Jewish community there. When the Swedish legation in Budapest decided in 1944 to try to protect Hungarian Jews from deportation to AUSCHWITZ, the Ministry of Foreign Affairs sent Wallenberg to the Budapest legation as he was then working as a diplomat. At great personal risk, Wallenberg issued thousands of protective Swedish passports to Jews and established a large number of Swedish houses to shelter them. By these means, it is estimated that he saved some 25,000 Jews in addition to the 70,000 lives he helped to save by his various actions on behalf of the inhabitants of Budapest's ghetto.

When the Red Army arrived in Budapest, Wallenberg approached the Soviet command in January 1945 to discuss further relief operations. He was arrested and taken to Moscow. Subsequent intensive inquiries failed to disclose either the reasons for the arrest or the fate of Wallenberg. In 1981, when it was still thought that Wallenberg was alive in a Soviet prison, he was made an honorary US citizen:

> Raoul Wallenberg considered his friends to be all those who suffered injustice. Each day he willingly jeopardized his own life so that others might live.

> In the face of the horror of evil, Raoul Wallenberg stood tall and unflinching.
>
> RONALD REAGAN, in a message to the Raoul Wallenberg Commemoration in 1985.

In Israel, Wallenberg is honoured at Yad Vashem, the Memorial to the Holocaust in Jerusalem, as the most outstanding of the Righteous Gentiles.

In 1989 the newly liberalized Soviet Union opened their files on Wallenberg in a determined effort to discover his fate. The conclusion reached was that he was shot in LUBYANKA PRISON in 1947.

Raoul Wallenberg was one of the true heroes of the 20th century; he proved that one man alone can challenge an entire empire of tyranny and evil.

wally Slang for a stupid unsophisticated person who can do nothing right; it became extremely popular in the late 1970s. It is thought to have originated in working-class London.

Wally blue A shade of light blue favoured by Wallis Simpson. It was the colour of her wedding dress when she married the Duke of Windsor in June 1937. *See also* ABDICATION CRISIS.

wanker Slang for a male masturbator. By extension it is used to describe any irritating and unpleasant man, especially one who is excessively self-indulgent.

> He would practise things like opening his zippo lighter with just one hand and throwing his cigarettes up in the air and catching them in his mouth. Strangely this did not make him look like a total wanker – it nearly did, but not quite.
>
> BEN ELTON; *Stark* (1989).

wannabee or **wannabe** Contemptuous slang for someone, usually a teenager, who slavishly imitates a film star or pop personality. The word is a corruption of the phrase 'want to be' and was first heard in America in the 1980s.

WAP *See* WHITE AUSTRALIA POLICY.

war. war baby A baby born in wartime; especially the illegitimate offspring of a serviceman. *See* BABY BOOM.

warhead The explosive head of a torpedo or bomb.

warnography A style of literature or film that glorifies war and stimulates aggression in the viewer or reader. The word was coined in the style of *pornography*; typical examples include such magazines as *Power Fire* and the RAMBO films. These films have a strong influence on the young; it is thought that some do actually inspire acts of aggression.

War of the Worlds scare *See* MARTIAN INVASION SCARE *under* MARS.

War Time *See* DAYLIGHT SAVING.

warb Australian slang for someone who is slovenly in appearance or simply unintelligent. It is a shortening of *warbie*, a maggot that breeds in the skin of cattle.

warehouse A US name for a large public facility that provides impersonal custodial care for persons who are mentally ill, orphaned, poor, aged, etc. The word originated in the early 1970s and is also used as a verb.

warehouse party A large professionally organized dance party for teenagers held in a warehouse, aircraft hangar, or similar site. Warehouse parties were closely associated with the ACID HOUSE craze of 1988–89 and became notorious for their wildness, deafening volume, and the open sale of drugs. The venue was usually publicized only by word of mouth to avoid the attentions of the police. *See also* ORBITAL RAVE.

Warminster Thing The sighting of UFOS on numerous occasions in the region of Warminster, Wiltshire. The frequency of these sightings in the area first attracted attention in the 1960s. The best-authenticated incident occurred on Christmas Day 1964, when an entire company of Welsh Guards was woken by the sound of inexplicable explosions all around them – although no sign of their source could be detected. Shortly afterwards a woman was pinned to the ground by what she described as a 'sonic blast wave', which also damaged houses in the town. These events were so regular and so well-publicized that the phrase 'The Warminster Thing' came to be used to refer to anything unusual. A more prosaic explanation might lie in the proximity of the School of Infantry, where experiments with new weapons are conducted. The first widely publicized CROP CIRCLES were seen in the vicinity of Warminster in the 1960s.

Warren Commission *See* OSWALD, LEE HARVEY.

Warsaw. Warsaw Pact The Warsaw Treaty of Friendship, Co-operation, and Mutual Assistance: a treaty signed in 1955 by the Soviet Union, Albania, Bulgaria, Czechoslovakia, East Germany, Hungary, Poland, and Romania. The Pact, organized in response to West Germany's admission to NATO, bound the COMMUNIST BLOC countries in a formal military alliance and created a single unified command based in Moscow. It also gave the Soviet Union the right to station troops on the soil of the other signatories and a pretext to suppress reform movements in these countries on security grounds (see BREZHNEV DOCTRINE; PRAGUE SPRING). Of the communist nations of E Europe only Tito's Yugoslavia declined to join (*see* TITOISM); Albania withdrew in 1968. Following the collapse of the communist regimes in E Europe in 1989 and East Germany's decision to leave the Pact, the remaining members agreed to wind up the organization over the next three years.

Warsaw Uprising (1) The Warsaw Ghetto Uprising. The revolt on 19 April 1943 by the Jews remaining in the Warsaw ghetto, into which the Germans had herded some 500,000 Jewish men, women, and children. From 22 July 1942 some 5000 Jews per day were transported from the ghetto to the gas chambers at TREBLINKA. When news of the fate awaiting them reached the Jews remaining in the ghetto from escapers from Treblinka, they staged an uprising on 18 January 1943. The Germans lost 50 men and withdrew, abandoning the deportations for four months. On 19 April Himmler launched a full-scale attack on the ghetto with tanks and artillery, in honour of Hitler's birthday on the following day. The 1500 Jewish guerrillas, under the command of Mordecai Anielewicz, managed to kill several hundred Germans before resistance ended on 16 May with the death of most of the guerrillas, many of whom, including Anielewicz, committed suicide to avoid capture. (2) The attempt by the Polish underground to seize control of Warsaw from the Germans before the arrival of the Red Army, which had advanced west of the River Vistula in July 1944 and was within striking distance of the capital. On 1 August 50,000 Poles of the Home Army, the communist-led People's Army, and armed civilians commanded by General Tadeusz Bor-Komorowski attacked the German forces and within three days had managed to capture two-thirds of the city. The Germans then went on the offensive and SS detachments proceeded to crush the insurgents with a maximum of brutality. Despite appeals to the Allies for help, the Soviets initially refused to allow their airfields to be used by Allied planes; it was 13 September before Stalin relented and the first drops of supplies into the city were made. By this time it was too late and the last of the Polish fighters were forced to surrender two weeks later. 15,000 of the Polish resistance fighters were killed during the fighting, while over 200,000 civilians were killed by the Germans afterwards in reprisal. The Germans lost an estimated 10,000 dead. Stalin's reluctance to support the uprising is explained largely by his determination that the largely non-communist Home Army should present no political or military threat to postwar communist domination of Poland through the Soviet-sponsored LUBLIN COMMITTEE.

Washington Conference (1) A conference of the major powers held on naval and Far Eastern affairs from November 1921 to February 1922. The UK agreed to parity in battleships with America (five each), while the Japanese agreed to three. The Anglo-Japanese alliance was also cancelled; the UK and America promised not to develop their bases in Hong Kong and in the Philippines. The naval agreement was the only effective measure of disarmament achieved between the wars and the conference also relieved tensions in the Far East, at least in the short term. (2) The first Allied conference (codenamed Arcadia) between Prime Minister Churchill and President Roosevelt (22 December 1941–12 January 1942). In the discussions of long-term strategy, Churchill secured a US commitment to the defeat of Germany in the Atlantic and European theatres before concentrating on Japan. A Combined Chiefs of Staff committee was established and plans implemented to boost US armaments productions. The conference also produced a Joint Declaration, formally announcing an alliance to defeat the Axis Powers, which was signed by 26 countries, including China and the Soviet Union. (3) *See* TRIDENT.

Washkansky transplant The first human heart transplant, carried out at Groote Schuur Hospital in Cape Town, South Africa, by Dr. Christiaan N. Barnard (1922–) and his team on 3 December 1967. Louis Washkansky, a 53-year-old grocer, was given the heart of Denise Darvall, a 25-year-old bank clerk, who had been killed in a road accident. Washkansky died 18 days after the operation, not from heart failure, as Barnard was keen to emphasize, but due to lung failure arising from double pneumonia. The transplant caused considerable controversy at the time but is now a fairly common procedure.

WASP White Anglo-Saxon Protestant. A US acronym that typifies the White middle-class attitudes that predominate in America, particularly in the upper echelons of society.

Wassermann test A blood-serum test for syphilis developed by the German scientist August von Wassermann (1866–1925) in 1906. Working at the Robert Koch Institute for Infectious Diseases in Berlin, Wassermann, together with the dermatologist Albert Neisser, developed a test for the antibody produced in the blood of persons infected by the syphilis bacterium. For many years the most commonly used test for diagnosing syphilis, it is now one of several indicators of the presence of the disease.

waste US street slang first heard in the 1950s meaning to kill.

> He prefers not to remember the night in 1978 when 'some English junkie wasted a broad'.
>
> *The Independent*, 27 April 1991.

wasted (1) Slang for exhausted. (2) Slang for intoxicated with drugs or drink. This is an extension of the slang sense of WASTE. Many words to describe intoxication are equally violent, *e.g.* bombed, smashed, blitzed.

watch. -watch A suffix that indicates organized or attentive monitoring of the subject specified. It is often used in the titles of TV programmes, newspaper columns, etc.: *Crimewatch* is a BBC programme that appeals to the public for help in defeating crime, while *Newswatch* is a news section of *The Observer*. The first coinage of this kind was **doomwatch**, a vogue term of the early 1970s referring to the expectation of imminent global catastrophe, nuclear or ecological. *See also* NEIGHBOURHOOD WATCH.

watchful waiting The phrase used by Woodrow Wilson in 1913 to describe his policy of non-recognition of the Mexican government of General Huerta. It did not last long as, in 1914, the Americans occupied Vera Cruz. The phrase was previously used by President Jackson in 1836.

Watergate In America, an area of flats and offices, etc., beside the river Potomac, Washington, which gave its name to a major political scandal. An illegal bugging attempt was made by Republicans at the Watergate headquarters of the Democratic Party during the 1972 elections followed by attempts to cover up the affair. The subsequent resignation and prosecution of senior White House officials and further evidence of corruption eventually led to the first resignation of a serving president; President Richard Nixon (*see* TRICKY DICKY) resigned when threatened with impeachment. President Ford granted him a free pardon after succeeding him as president.

> I let down my friends, I let down my country. I let down our system of government.
>
> RICHARD NIXON, 1977.

wave. wave power The generation of electricity by means of energy derived from sea waves (*see* ALTERNATIVE ENERGY). Various devices have been developed to effect this conversion, the best known being the nodding duck, consisting of a string of floats that bob up and down in the waves and turn a generator in so doing. However, the design of wave-power generators and the transmission of the current to the land involve difficult technical problems that have not yet found a practical solution.

WAVES (or **Waves**) Women Appointed for Voluntary Emergency Service. The women's section of the US Naval Reserve. *See also* WREN.

Wavy Navy The popular name for the former Royal Naval Volunteer Reserve (RNVR), whose officers wore gold distinction lace made in wavy lines instead of the straight lines worn on the sleeves of regular officers. The RNVR lost its separate existence, after a brilliant wartime record, in December 1957, when it was combined with the Royal Naval Reserve (RNR). *See also* HARRY TATE'S NAVY.

way. And that's the way it is The catchphrase of the US broadcaster Walter Cronkite (1916–), which he used at the end of the CBS TV Evening News programme between 1962 and 1981.

way-out Slang for eccentric or unusual. A term of approval first used by the JAZZ enthusiasts of the 1930s and taken up again by the BEATNIKS in the 1950s. By the 1960s it had become the type of word that an adult might use in an attempt to sound modern.

weasel words Words of convenient ambiguity, or an evasive statement from which the original meaning has been sucked or retracted. Theodore Roosevelt popularized the term by using it in a speech in 1916 when criticizing President Wilson:

> You can have universal training, or you can have voluntary training, but when you use the word *voluntary* to qualify the word *universal*, you are using a weasel word; it has sucked all the meaning out of *universal*. The two words flatly contradict one another.

Roosevelt was indebted to a story by Stewart Chaplin, 'Stained-Glass political Platform', which appeared in the *Century Magazine* in June 1900 in which this sentence occurs:

> Why, weasel words are words that suck the life out of the words next to them, just as a weasel sucks the egg and leaves the shell.

In America a politician who sits on the fence is sometimes called a *weasler*.

Weatherman A member of the Weather Underground, a US revolutionary terrorist group operating during the VIETNAM WAR. The youthful militants were responsible for a series of bombings; one in 1970 accidentally killed three people in New York City. Three Weathermen, including leader Kathy Boudin, were arrested in 1982 after two police officers and a security guard were killed during an attempted robbery of a Brinks armoured truck.

weaving. get weaving To set about a task briskly. A colloquial Services expression in World War II. Weaving implies dexterous movement, as when aircraft make rapid directional changes to escape enemy fire.

wedges or **wedgies** *See* PLATFORM SOLE.

weed (1) Slang for tobacco or a cigarette, often referred to as the 'evil weed' because of its toxic effects. (2) Slang for marijuana, either because it is smoked like tobacco or because it grows like a weed, *i.e.* prolifically in favourable conditions. *See* POT. (3) British schoolchildren's slang from the 1950s and 1960s for a weak, timid, and unsporty child, especially one who cries easily. It is still in use.

Wee Frees The minority of the Free Church of Scotland, which refused to join with the majority when the Free Church united with the United Presbyterian Church to form the United Free Church in 1900. The Wee Frees remain a powerful influence in certain areas of the Highlands and Islands of the West of Scotland, where strict observance of the Sabbath prevents Wee Frees from doing any kind of labour on a Sunday (even using scissors).

week. A week is a long time in politics A phrase attributed to Harold Wilson (Labour prime minister 1964–70, 1974–76) in 1966. It is most often used to mean that things may have changed by the end of the week for reasons of political expediency. However, Wilson himself has said that what he actually meant was that politics should be seen on a longer time-scale and should not be judged by day-to-day issues.

weeny-bopper A child, usually 8 to 12 years old, who is an avid fan of pop music and the latest fashions. The name is based on TEENY-BOPPER.

weepie *See* TEAR-JERKER.

weight-watcher A person who tries to control his or her weight, especially by following a diet. Weight Watchers International Inc. is an organization founded in America in 1964 to promote slimming through dieting: attenders at Weight Watchers clubs are given personal target weights and various incentives to meet them.

Weimar Republic The German federal republic established under the Constitution of 1919, which lasted until it was overthrown by Hitler in 1933. So called from the Thuringian town of Weimar, particularly associated with Goethe, in which the constitution was adopted by the National Assembly.

weirdo A strange or eccentric person. The term was originally used to mean somebody of unconventional appearance or lifestyle, such as a BEATNIK or HIPPIE. Until the mid-1960s, the usual British term was **weirdie**, the phrase **bearded weirdie** being especially common.

weisenheimer US slang from the 1900s for a know-all. It is formed from the German *weise*, wise, and the suffix *-heimer*, making it sound like a typical German surname.

welfare state The UK after the first post-war Labour government had implemented many of the recommendations of the Beveridge Report (1942), providing for nationwide social security services for sickness, unemployment, retirement, want, etc. It was essentially based on the National Insurance Act (1946). In the ensuing decade the British welfare state was greatly admired by other European countries.

wellie. green-wellie brigade *See under* GREEN.

wellie-wanging British slang for a child's game the object of which is to see who can throw a Wellington boot the farthest. Popular at country fêtes and other fund-raising events in the 1970s, it has since declined in popularity.

Welsh Wizard Nickname of the Welsh politician David Lloyd George (1863–1945), who was Liberal prime minister of the UK from 1916 to 1922. Regarded by many opponents as a political maverick (he supported the Afrikaners in the BOER WARS and was a proponent of Welsh nationalism) and a man of no fixed principles, he was also respected for his inventive mind. As Chancellor of the Exchequer (1908–15), he introduced the innovative PEOPLE'S BUDGET, while as prime minister he directed his small war cabinet with great effectiveness. Other landmarks included his introduction of old-age pensions (1908) and national insurance (1911). His private life was the subject of gossip, much of it relating to his long affair with his secretary Frances Stevenson (1888–1972), whom he married after his first wife died. He was made an earl in 1945, shortly before his death. *See also* COUPON ELECTION.

> Well, I find that a change of nuisances is as good as a vacation.
>
> LLOYD GEORGE, on being asked how he managed to remain cheerful in the face of political difficulties.

Wembley Stadium A large stadium built in the NW London suburb of Wembley in the early 1920s as part of the British Empire Exhibition; it was first used for the Football Association Cup Final on 29 April 1923. The FA Cup Final has been held there annually ever since. The stadium is also used for football internationals, Rugby League Cup Finals, and various other sports, including hockey, Gaelic Football, greyhound meetings, and even American baseball. It is also a popular venue for pop concerts and charity rock galas, such as LIVE AID in 1985.

wendy British schoolchildren's disparaging slang for a weak, inept boy. The name Wendy was originally invented by the playwright J. M. Barrie for a character in his children's play *Peter Pan*.

Wendy house A child's toy house that is large enough to enter; it is named after the little house constructed around the character WENDY in the play *Peter Pan* (1904) by J. M. Barrie.

West Bank The region on the west bank of the River Jordan, including Judaea, Samaria, and Jerusalem, which was occupied by Israel after the SIX-DAY WAR in June 1967 when Israel was attacked simultaneously by Egypt, Syria and Jordan. Formerly part of Palestine, the West Bank became part of Jordan after the ceasefire of 1949. Israeli military rule and the encouragement of Jewish settlements in the area has been a continuing source of tension with the Arab population and is central to the Palestinian-Israeli conflict. Roughly one million Palestinians live in the region, in towns, villages, and refugee camps. Over 60% of the land, however, is owned by Israelis, and although 150 settlements have been built since 1967 (encouraged by generous state subsidies) the Jewish population remains at around 50,000. In recent years large numbers of Soviet Jews (*see* REFUSENIK) have been encouraged to settle in an attempt to reduce this demographic disparity. *See also* INTIFADA.

western A story or film romanticizing America's Wild West and creating its own folk heroes, such as the LONE RANGER and the SINGING COWBOY.

Western Front The largely static ground across which Germany and the Allied Powers, including the UK and France, faced each other during World War I. The front extended from Nieuport on the Belgian coast, south through Ypres, Arras, Soissons, and Rheims to the area of VERDUN. Many thousands of Allied and Axis soldiers died in the trenches of the Western Front. *See* RACE FOR THE SEA.

Western Wall or **Wailing Wall** The high stone wall that forms a retaining structure along the western side of the **Temple Mount** in Jerusalem. The Temple Mount, traditionally the site upon which Jacob had his dream of angels ascending a ladder to heaven, is the foundation upon which both biblical Jewish temples were built. The Western Wall, all that remains of their Temples, is a holy site for Jews; until Israel achieved statehood in 1948 it was a shrine to which orthodox Jews came to bewail their absence of a national home in the Promised Land (hence the name, Wailing Wall, which is no longer used in Israel).

Unfortunately, according to Muslim tradition, the prophet Mohammed chose the Temple Mount as the place from which to ascend to Paradise in 632 AD. Some 60 years later Umayyad Caliph, Abd al-

Malik, built the Dome of the Rock, a Muslim mosque to commemorate this event, making it Islam's third most holy shrine (after Mecca and Medina).

Conflict between orthodox Jews and orthodox Muslims has persisted ever since. A fanatical Jewish sect annually (during the festival of Sukkoth) attempts to lay a cornerstone for a third Jewish temple, implying that the Muslim shrine will be demolished to make room for it. This provocative gesture, not surprisingly, causes a violent Arab reaction. In 1990, when the world's spotlights were already focused on the GULF WAR in the Middle East, the Israeli police were inadequately prepared for the ensuing conflict and shot dead some 20 protesting stone-throwing Arabs, causing widespread condemnation.

Westland affair The scandal in 1986 involving the Westland helicopter company, which brought about the resignation of the Defence Secretary, Michael Heseltine, and the Trade Secretary, Leon Brittan. Heseltine had backed the sale of Westland to a European company, while Brittan supported the sale to the US company Sikorsky. A letter, critical of Heseltine's role in the sale, was deliberately leaked to the press from the Department of Trade and Industry, sanctioned by Brittan himself, in order to discredit Heseltine – a fact that did not emerge immediately.

Journalists referred to the affair as **Westlandgate**, the name being coined – like those of other political scandals (*e.g.* IRANGATE) – by analogy with WATERGATE.

wet (1) In America, denoting states that did not support the PROHIBITION of the sale of alcoholic drinks. (2) Slang for stupid or feeble; thus 'he is pretty wet' means he is so feeble that he cannot be relied on; 'don't talk wet' means don't talk such nonsense, don't be silly. (3) Denoting the more liberal element in the Conservative party, which did not favour all the hard-line policies of THATCHERISM.

Also used as a noun in the last two senses.

wetback An illegal immigrant to America from Mexico. Such immigrants usually had to swim the Rio Grande.

wets Army slang from the GULF WAR of 1991 for alcoholic refreshment.

wet sell A salesman's slightly contemptuous slang for the technique of getting a potential client drunk over lunch while negotiating a deal in order to get the best terms.

wham-bam-thank-you-ma'am A phrase used mostly by women to describe a short and perfunctory act of sexual intercourse. It is now used contemptuously for any selfish act of male gratification at the woman's expense. It was originally used by the US forces during World War II.

wheel. wheel clamp *See* DENVER BOOT.

wheeler-dealer Slang for a businessman who negotiates his deals by smart manoeuvres that are not necessarily honest, typically wheeling in and out of a string of deals that finance each other.

wheelie A stunt on a bicycle or motorcycle in which the front wheel is raised and the rider balances for a short distance on the back wheel. A car being driven briefly on two wheels on the same side is also referred to as doing a wheelie, usually by professional stunt drivers.

whennies *See* BUBS.

Which? *See* CONSUMERS' ASSOCIATION.

whinge or **winge** To moan and complain in a whining voice, derived from a northern variant of the Old English *hwinsian*, to whine. It was widely used in Australia before being heard in the UK in the late 1970s. A **whingeing pom** is the Australian's favourite description of a typical British immigrant who does nothing but complain.

whiplash hustler US slang for someone who fakes injury from a car accident in order to claim the insurance money. Whiplash is a very common injury to the neck incurred in relatively mild traffic accidents; it is easy to fake as nothing is actually broken.

whistle British rhyming slang from the 1930s for a suit, from 'whistle and flute'. It was used by the mods (*see* MODS AND ROCKERS) in the 1960s and is still heard among working-class Londoners.

whistle-blower Slang for an informer. It derives from the phrase 'to blow the whistle on', meaning to stop a corrupt practice in the same way as a referee blows his whistle to stop play after a foul in football. A whistle-blower is usually someone in a business or a government office, who exposes a malpractice or a cover-up to the press. Often such a person is asked to leave his job.

white. White Australia Policy (WAP) The policy embodied in the Australian Immigration Restriction Bill (1901), which barred immigrants from non-White countries, especially Japan and China. In the last quarter of the 19th century, fear of economic and cultural competition from coloured immigrants was a powerful factor in the impetus towards federation, which took place in 1900. In the first Commonwealth parliament of 1901, all parties were agreed on the importance of preserving a predominantly European society in Australia. The Immigration Restriction Bill was duly introduced and excluded Asians by the simple device of a dictation test in a European language, which all immigrants were required to pass. The determination to preserve Australia for Whites was a significant feature of government policy from federation until the 1960s. Although the dictation test for immigrants was abolished in 1958, it was not until the mid-1960s that *The Bulletin*, a national newspaper, dropped the motto 'Australia for the White Man' from its masthead and the measures against Asian immigration were officially relaxed.

white goods A type of consumer durable that includes refrigerators, deep-freezers, washing machines, dishwashers, etc. They are so called because they have been traditionally finished in white enamel paint. However, they are sometimes now painted in a less stark colour, including various shades of brown, in order to make them harmonize with oak and other wooden kitchen fittings. *See also* BROWN GOODS.

white knight A firm or individual that rescues a company from an unwelcome bid by a **black knight**. A company under attack by a black knight might seek a white knight, whom it considers to be a more suitable owner, and encourage him to make an offer that will prove to be more attractive to the shareholders than that made by the black knight. A **grey knight** in such a takeover battle is a counterbidder whose ultimate intentions are unknown; he is therefore an intervener whose appearance is unwelcome to the company, the black knight, and the white knight.

White Russian An inhabitant of White Russia or Byelorussia (Russ. *byely*, white), one of the Soviet republics. (2) A counter-revolutionary or *émigré* at the time of the BOLSHEVIK revolution. The active counter-revolutionaries joined the so-called **White Army**.

White trash *See* PECKERWOOD.

Whitehall farce A series of popular plays produced by Brian Rix (1924–) at the Whitehall Theatre in London in the 1950s and 1960s. These included *Reluctant Heroes* (1950) by Colin Morris, John Chapman's *Dry Rot* (1954) and *Simple Spymen* (1958), Ray Cooney and Tony Hilton's *One For The Pot* (1961), and Ray Cooney's *Chase Me Comrade* (1964), all of which starred Brian Rix.

Whiteside, Sheridan The central character, a venomous theatre critic, in *The Man Who Came to Dinner* (1939) by George S. Kaufman and Moss Hart. The play was inspired by a visit by the notoriously outspoken US critic Alexander Woollcott (1887–1943) to the house of Hart's family.

Woollcott proved an impossible guest; among his many acid comments during his stay was the observation on Hart's home: "Just what God would have done if he had the money". Woollcott was surprisingly very amused by his stage re-creation and even toured in the role himself with great success.

whizz or **whiz kid** (1) A highly intelligent young person who achieves rapid success. *Whizz* implies rapid progress; alternatively it may have been based on *wizard*. (2) Another slang name for an amphetamine drug (*see* SPEED).

> Whizz or speed was the best until I got hold of ecstacy in Manchester.
>
> SHAUN RYDER, British pop star, in *The Sun*, 4 February 1991.

who. Dr Who *See* EXTERMINATE, EXTERMINATE.

Who dares wins *See* SAS.

whodunit A colloquial name for a detective story; the expression is probably of US origin.

wholefood Unprocessed food that retains all its natural attributes. For example, wholemeal bread is baked with flour made from the whole grain, *i.e.* it has not had the bran separated from it, unlike white flour, which has not only had the bran extracted but is often bleached. Wholefoods include cereals, grains, beans, pulses, dried fruits, natural fruit juices, sugarless jams, and fresh vegetables. Wholefoods first appeared in HEALTH FOOD shops in UK high streets in the late 1960s; once considered faddist, they are now widely available in supermarkets.

wicked Teenage slang for excellent or wonderful. A sense that became widespread among young Blacks in America in the 1980s; together with BAD, it was quickly copied by Whites and Blacks in the UK.

Wickedest Man in the World *See* BEAST 666.

wide boy A young male who is usually flashily dressed and lives, often dishonestly, on his wits. *See* FLASH HARRY.

widget Slang for a device or gadget the name of which is temporarily forgotten or unknown. It was used before World War II in America, but was not widely known in the UK until the late 1970s.

Wiesenthal Centre An organization dedicated to bringing Nazi war criminals to justice, which is run by Simon Wiesenthal (1908–), a survivor of the Nazi CONCENTRATION CAMPS. Originally an architect in Poland, Wiesenthal was imprisoned in a Nazi forced labour camp from 1941 to 1943, escaped, and was then recaptured and sent to Mauthausen in 1944. After the liberation of the camp by US forces in May 1945, Wiesenthal discovered that 89 members of his family had perished at the hands of the Nazis, although he was reunited with his wife, whom he had thought dead. After the war he worked with the Americans in collecting evidence against war criminals; in 1947 he and a group of volunteers founded the Documentation Centre on the Fate of the Jews and their Persecutors in Linz, Austria. The centre specialized in aiding Jewish refugees and collecting evidence against Gestapo agents, SS officers, and other perpetrators of the FINAL SOLUTION. In 1954 the Centre was closed and its files transferred to Israel. Wiesenthal continued to hunt for war criminals with the aid of the Israelis and managed to track down Adolf Eichmann (*see* EICHMANN TRIAL) in Argentina in 1959. This success prompted Wiesenthal to reopen the Jewish Documentation Centre in Vienna in 1961. Wiesenthal has been responsible for the identification of over 1000 other war criminals, notably Karl Silberbauer, the Gestapo officer who had arrested Anne FRANK.

Wigan A town in NW England (formerly in Lancashire, now in Greater Manchester). At the centre of a coalmining area, it used to be the archetypal northern industrial town and, as such, was the butt of jokes by many music-hall comedians, based on the fanciful notion that it had a seaside pier. The joke seems to have been inspired by the jetties on the Leeds–Liverpool Canal, which were used to load coal from rail trucks into barges. According to some, it was coined by George Formby Sr, father of the film entertainer. The pier was immortalized by George Orwell in the title of his romanticized account of northern working-class life, *The Road to Wigan Pier* (1937). In 1986 the Wigan Pier Heritage Centre (*see* HERITAGE INDUSTRY) was opened on the site of one of the original jetties. Wigan is still often taken as a typical northern provincial town by television producers, who ask 'How will that go down in Wigan?' *See also* DISGUSTED, TUNBRIDGE WELLS; NEASDEN.

wild Slang term of approval that was used by the BEATNIKS in the 1950s. It is still in use.

Wild Geese Nickname of a band of White, mainly European, mercenaries who in 1964 joined Congolese government forces in their struggle against the rebels led by Christophe Gbenye. Their exploits were viewed with some sympathy in the UK, as Gbenye's forces were notorious for their atrocities against Europeans, including the massacre of 15 British missionaries and a threat to grill 1500 White hostages alive. The leader of the Wild Geese was the South African MAD MIKE Hoare. In 1978 their exploits formed the basis of the film *The Wild Geese*, starring Roger Moore, Richard Burton, and Richard Harris.

The original Wild Geese were Irish Jacobites who, in the 18th century, joined the armies of the Continental powers to fight Britain.

wilding US Black slang for running about in a random, wild, and violent fashion, usually in a gang. It first came to public attention in 1989, when a young woman was raped by a gang and left in a coma in New York's Central Park by Black youths, who said they had been 'wilding'. She recovered to testify against them, which enabled them to be convicted.

wimp (1) Contemptuous slang for a weak and ineffectual person. It was first head in America in the 1970s among schoolchildren and students, later becoming known in the UK. Its derivation is obscure; some suggest it comes from *whimper*, others from *Mr Wimpy*, a character in the US carton *Popeye*.

> There's always been a place in pictures for David against Goliath, the wimp against the muscle man.
> *The Independent*, 30 January 1991.

(2) *See* MENU.

Wimsey, Lord Peter The aristocratic amateur detective in the novels of Dorothy L. Sayers (1923–73). The original model for this character was the schoolmaster and travel writer Eric Whelpton (1894–1981), for whom Sayers had an unrequited love at Oxford. In the novels, Wimsey finally falls for, and marries, his fellow-sleuth Harriet Vane, thought by many to represent Sayers herself.

wind. wind of change A new current of opinion, a markedly reformist or novel trend, etc. A phrase popularized by Harold Macmillan in his speech to the South African Parliament (3 February 1960), with reference to the social and political ferment in the African continent:

> The wind of change is blowing through this continent, and, whether we like it or not, this growth of national consciousness is a political fact.

wind power The generation of electricity by means of energy derived from the wind (*see* ALTERNATIVE ENERGY). The advantage of wind power is that it uses no fuel and creates no pollution. The disadvantages are that modern wind turbines take up a great deal of space and usually have to be sited away from the cities, in which the power is needed. In the UK a small number of wind turbines on the Atlantic coast are supplying power to the national grid. This number could be greatly increased; it is estimated that this renewable energy source could provide some 20% of the UK's electricity requirement if all the available sites were to be utilized.

windsurfing A watersport in which the participant stands up on a narrow moulded board equipped with a mast and sail. The craft, known as a **sailboard**, is steered with a hand-held boom to which the windsurfer also clings for support. So-called because the board resembles a surfboard, it is propelled by the wind rather than the waves.

Window The codename for the metallic chaff dropped during Allied bombing raids over Germany to confuse enemy radar in World War II. It was first used in a series of night raids over Hamburg (24 July–2 August 1943); its early success was demonstrated by the loss of only 12 out of 741 aircraft, which undertook the 24 July mission. Window disabled or confused ground and enemy fighter radar by producing spurious traces rendering accurate location and targeting of the bombing force impossible. The Germans developed their own version of Window and also evolved effective countermeasures, which rendered Window less effective during the latter stages of the conflict.

Windscale *See* SELLAFIELD.

Windsor The official name of the British royal family adopted in 1917, in deference to anti-German sentiment, to replace the existing name of Saxe-Coburg-Gotha, derived from Albert the Prince Consort. It was changed in 1960 to Mountbatten-Windsor for the descendants of Queen Elizabeth II, other than those entitled to the style of Royal Highness or of Prince and Princess. After his abdication, 11 December 1936, King Edward VIII was created Duke of Windsor.

wine lake *See* CAP.

winkle-pickers Shoes with very elongated and pointed toes, affected by some teenagers in the early 1960s. The allusion is to the use of a pin for picking winkles out of their shells.

Winnie Nickname of Sir Winston Churchill (1874–1965), whose leadership of the UK during World War II established him as one of the best-loved heroes of British history. His long, brilliant, and adventurous career, coupled with his inimitable style of oratory and ebullient manner, epitomizing the British 'bulldog breed', won him both the distrust of his political rivals and the affection of the nation. As a young man he served as a war correspondent in the BOER WARS and was praised for his resourceful escape from captivity. Entering parliament as a Conservative, he later served in both Liberal and Conservative cabinets in a variety of posts, including Home Secretary (1910–11), First Lord of the Admiralty (1911–16), and Chancellor of the Exchequer (1924–29). During the 1930s he was confined to the backbenches (his 'wilderness years') and became the foremost critic of the government's policy of appeasement. Towards the end of the 1930s it was suggested to Stanley Baldwin, the prime minister, that a post in the government should be offered to Churchill. Baldwin refused to do so saying, with remarkable foresight, that if war came, the nation would need Churchill – a Churchill unsullied by party politics. He was, in fact, recalled to the Admiralty at the outbreak of hostilities in 1939 and became head of the coalition government in 1940 after Chamberlain's resignation. It is in the role of war leader that he is best remembered, not only in the UK but throughout the free world. His defeat in the general election of 1945 caused him and his party considerable surprise; he was, however, elected prime minister again, as head of a Conservative government, from 1951 to 1955. His historical writings won him the Nobel Prize for Literature in 1953.

> The nation had the lion's heart. I had the luck to give the roar.
>
> SIR WINSTON CHURCHILL, on his 80th birthday.

See also ALAMEIN, BATTLES OF EL; BATTLE OF BRITAIN; BLOOD, TOIL, TEARS AND SWEAT; DUNKIRK; FEW, THE; IRON CURTAIN; JAW-JAW; LEND-LEASE; MONTY; RIDDLE; SIDNEY STREET SIEGE; SURRENDER; TERMINOLOGICAL INEXACTITUDE; V; etc.

Winnie-the-Pooh The TEDDY-BEAR character created by A. A. Milne in the stories he wrote for his son CHRISTOPHER ROBIN. Winnie-the-Pooh's adventures with his friends Piglet and EEYORE became enormously successful after publiction in the 1920s and the 'bear of very little brain' was soon established as a perennial children's favourite. He was not to every reader's taste, however. Dorothy Parker, in her 'Constant Reader' column, reported that:

> ... it is the word "hummy" ... that marks the first place in *The House at Pooh Corner* at which Tonstant Weader Fwowed up.

Winslow, Ronnie The young naval cadet at the centre of Terence Rattigan's play *The Winslow Boy* (1946). The story of the cadet's trial for petty theft was based on the case of the 13-year-old cadet George Archer-Shee, who was expelled from Osborne Naval College on the Isle of Wight in 1908 after being accused of stealing a postal order. The cadet's father engaged the famous barrister Sir Edward Carson to represent his son in suing the Admiralty. The case ended with George Archer-Shee receiving £7000 compensation from the Admiralty. He was killed at Ypres in World War I.

winter. Winterhilfe (Ger. winter aid) A Nazi charity to aid the less fortunate to which all Germans were supposed to contribute under veiled threats of violence or public humiliation. Workers' wages were docked 10% during the winter, industrialists sponsored special charity events, and families were supposed to restrict themselves to 'one-pot-meals' six times a year (an idea dreamed up by Goebbels) and add the savings to their donation. In 1937 about 10 million people received parcels of food and clothing or cash under the scheme.

Winter of Discontent *See under* DISCONTENT.

Winter War The Russo-Finnish War, fought between 30 November 1939 and 13 March 1940. After the division of Poland between the Soviet Union and Germany in September 1939, the Soviets, fearful of a German attack, sought to consolidate their position in the Baltic with a series of mutual defence pacts with Latvia, Estonia, and Lithuania, which effectively placed them under Soviet military control. Finland boldly resisted Soviet overtures and on 30 November the Soviet Union launched an air attack on Helsinki. The invasion that followed involved a force of nearly one million Soviet troops, which crashed into Finland from the east and southeast and in an amphibious operation across the Gulf of Finland. Opposing them were 300,000 Finnish soldiers, the majority reservists, commanded by Marshal Baron Carl Mannerheim, a veteran of three wars. The Finns successfully repulsed the Soviet advances along the eastern frontier, in battles at Kemijarvi, Suomussalmi, and at the MANNERHEIM LINE across the Karelian Isthmus, largely by virtue of their superior mobility, imperviousness to sub-zero temperatures, better organization, and indomitable fighting spirit. The UK and France prepared an expeditionary force to aid the Finns, but neutral Norway and Sweden refused to allow it to pass. By March a massive Soviet assault in the northwest, together with incessant attacks on the Mannerheim Line, effected a breakthrough. In the absence of Allied support, the Finns were forced to sue for peace and formally accepted the Soviet terms on 13 March 1940. The war cost the Soviet Union 200,000 men, 700 planes, and 1600 tanks, against Finnish losses of 25,000. The abysmal performance of the Red Army convinced Hitler that the Soviet Union could easily be defeated by his superior war machine; America and the UK had also miscalculated the fighting potential of the Red Army, which underwent a radical reorganization in the aftermath of the Winter War.

wire. live wire A wire through which an electric current is passing; hence, a very lively or energetic person.

wire-guided Describing a type of missile that is guided by electrical signals transmitted through a fine wire connecting it to the control device from which it is launched. The wire, which uncoils during the missile's flight, may be several miles long.

wireless The former name for a radio. When radio transmission was introduced by Guglielmo Marconi (1874–1937), who sent his first signal across the Atlantic in 1901, the word wireless was widely used. At that time it seemed like a miracle that messages could be transmitted without wires. Some members of the older generation still refer to 'the wireless'. 'Radio', however, is now much more common.

Wise forgeries A series of forgeries of rare Victorian first editions manufactured by Thomas James Wise (1859–1937), a prominent bibliographer and book collector. Wise loved the Romantic and Victorian poets and acquired a valuable collection of the first and early editions of their works. He was a founder member of the Browning and Shelley Societies, and compiled influential bibliographies, which included Browning (1897), Tennyson (1908), and the Brontës (1917). In addition to his legitimate bibliographical researches, however, Wise was also a talented forger. From 1880 he began forging whole editions, single poems, or short prose works by his favourite authors, using type facsimiles from genuine editions and the services of a printer, who remained innocent of his true purposes. The forgeries were entered into his bibliographies, copies were lodged with the British Museum to verify their existence, and others were sold for large sums as rare collectors' items. The operation was eventually exposed in 1934 by John Carter and Graham Pollard in their *Enquiry into the Nature of Certain Nineteenth-century Pamphlets*, a pioneering work of scholarly investigation using the latest scientific techniques accurately to date the forgeries. Wise died shortly afterwards, refusing to acknowledge his guilt.

with-it Slang for fashionable, up-to-date. Widely heard in the early 1960s, it is now used mainly by the older generation. It came from the Black musician's phrase of the 1930s and 1940s 'get with it', which was taken up by the BEATNIKS of the 1950s.

wizard. Wizard of Dribble Nickname of the British footballer Sir Stanley Matthews (1915–), whose skill at 'dribbling' the ball was proverbial. Playing at outside right, he represented Stoke City (1931–47; 1961–65), Blackpool (1947–61), and England, for whom he appeared 54 times. Possibly the most famous British footballer of the century, he finally retired at the age of 50, having played 886 first-class matches. In 1965 he became the first British footballer to receive a knighthood.

Wizard of Oz The central figure in the popular children's book, *The Wonderful Wizard of Oz* (1900), by Lyman Frank Baum (1856–1919), a well-known US journalist. The musical comedy of the same name (1901) was a great success, as was the 1939 film, which made a star of Judy Garland.

Wobblies Nickname of the Industrial Workers of the World (IWW), a radical labour movement, founded in Chicago on 7 July 1905 in response to the foundation of the conservative American Federation of Labor, which excluded the unskilled and craft unions. The movement was plagued from its inception by divisions between Syndicalists, such as William D. ('Big Bill') Haywood who advocated direct action to establish worker control over the means of production, and those who favoured more conventional political methods. At the height of its popularity, 1912–17, the movement had over 100,000 members, but violence by activists alienated popular support and allowed the government to arrest and suppress the membership, which by the mid-1920s had been hounded out of existence. The radical vision of the IWW lives on in popular folk songs, such as *Joe Hill*, commemorating the murdered IWW organizer; the phrase 'pie in the sky' derives from another song adapted for use by the movement.

Wolf Cub The original name for a member of the junior branch of the BOY SCOUTS, now called Cub Scouts (age range 8–11 years). The concept owes much to Kipling's *Jungle Books*.

womble British schoolchildren's slang for an unattractive and unstylish person. The Wombles of Wimbledon were a family of puppets featured in a children's TV programme in the early 1970s. Because it was enjoyed by very young children it tended to be ridiculed by older children.

women. Women's Lib *See* FEMINISM.

Women's Movement *See* SEXUAL POLITICS.

women's studies Courses of study related to women that were introduced in US colleges and universities in the late 1960s. Prompted by the feminist movement (*see* FEMINISM; SEXUAL POLITICS), academic departments offered courses on 'Women's Role in Society', 'Women in Literature', etc. Some of these courses remain but most of them were quietly dropped in the 1980s.

Woodbine. Packet of Woodbines Nickname of the Russian cruiser *Askold*, from its five long thin funnels – Woodbine cigarettes being thin and sold in packets of five. She was taken from the Bolsheviks after the OCTOBER REVOLUTION of 1917 and used by the Royal Navy against the revolutionaries in the White Sea.

Woodbine Willie Nickname of the Rev. Geoffrey A. Studdert-Kennedy (1883–1929), from the Woodbine cigarettes which he gave to the men in the trenches during World War I when serving as Chaplain to the Forces (1916–19). He was one of the best-liked and best-known padres of the war.

Woodstock A US rock music festival, held from 15 to 17 August 1969 on a 600-acre farmland near the small town of Woodstock, in the foothills of the Catskill Mountains in upstate New York. The 'Woodstock Music and Art Fair' was the best-documented and largest of the rock and folk music festivals in the 1960s and 1970s. Some half a million young people, many of them HIPPIES, survived 20-mile traffic tailbacks, inadequate facilities, rain, and copious quantities of mud to hear such singers and bands as Joan Baez, Jimi Hendrix, The Who, Creedence Clearwater Revival, The Grateful Dead, and Crosby, Stills, Nash Young.

Woolton Pie A pie making use of various leftovers and vegetables that was recommended during World War II as a means to make the greatest possible use of rationed food. Containing carrots, parsnips, turnips, and potatoes in a white sauce, it was one of the recipes publicized under the aegis of Frederick Marquis, First Earl of Woolton (1883–1964), who was Minister of Food (1940–43).

Woomera The rocket testing range in South Australia; appropriately, the name is an Aborigine word for a spear-throwing stick.

woopies An acronym current in the late 1980s for *w*ell *o*ff *o*ld *p*eople. It is applicable to less than 20% of retirement pensioners.

Wooster, Bertie The hapless young man-about-town created by P. G. Wodehouse in the story 'The Man with Two Left Feet' and subsequently the central character in a series of popular comic novels. Constantly in trouble, from which his manservant JEEVES always extricates him, he was based upon the comic actor George Grossmith Jnr. (1874–1935). Other traits were inspired by Anthony Bingham Mildmay, Second Baron Mildmay of Flete (1909–50), who was Wodehouse's son-in-law. Numerous actors have enjoyed success as Bertie both on stage and on the screen, among them Ian Carmichael, John Alderton, and Hugh Laurie.

word. word blindness *See* DYSLEXIA.

word processor A computerized typewriter consisting of a VDU, a keyboard, a printer, a disk backing store, and a control unit. With suitable programs (SOFTWARE) this device enables letters, documents, books, etc., to be created, edited, stored, and printed as justified and correctly hyphenated text.

work. workaholic *See* CHOCAHOLIC.

work ethic A system of values that emphasizes the moral and psychological importance of work and other productive activities. This basic tenet of Christianity (strongly espoused by the Puritan settlers in America) is also the mainstay of the capitalist economic system. The work ethic declined among young people in the 1960s and 1970s but returned with the materialism of the YUPPIE society and THATCHERISM.

work to rule A form of INDUSTRIAL ACTION in which all the regulations relating to a particular form of work are literally and pedantically obeyed, in order to bring about delays in working. It is a form of GO SLOW tactics.

world. World Bank The International Bank for Reconstruction and Development, established in accordance with agreements reached at the BRETTON WOODS CONFERENCE in July 1944. It began operations in 1947 to provide economic aid to member countries. Initially the Bank provided finance for the reconstruction of war-torn Europe but by 1949 its efforts were largely directed to funding aid projects in the developing countries. Most of its capital is provided by the developed nations, although the Bank also raises money on international capital markets. It operates strictly as a commercial entity, lending at commercial rates of interest to governments, or to private concerns with the government as guarantor, but only to countries capable of servicing and repaying debt. An affiliate agency, the International Development Agency, was established in 1960 to provide low-interest loans to poorer members.

World Cup Association Football's most prestigious competition, held every four years under the auspices of FIFA. National teams compete for the Jules Rimet Trophy, named after the honorary president of FIFA from 1921 to 1954, who first proposed the competition.

Winners:

1930 Uruguay
1934 Italy
1938 Italy
1950 Uruguay
1954 West Germany
1958 Brazil
1962 Brazil
1966 England
1970 West Germany
1974 Brazil
1978 Argentina
1982 Italy
1986 Argentina
1990 West Germany

World Disarmament Conference An international conference convened in Geneva on 2 February 1932 and attended by all major countries, including America and the Soviet Union (who were not members of the LEAGUE OF NATIONS). The conference had been planned at a time of considerable optimism in the wake of the YOUNG PLAN of August 1929; it was hoped to revive the spirit of Locarno, enabling relaxation in international tensions and agreement on disarmament to be achieved. By 1932, however, European affairs had deteriorated to such an extent that when detailed negotiations began, conflicts of interest between the participants destroyed any hope of progress. The irreconcilable interests of France and Germany proved the most intractable problem. France insisted on a guarantee of security from German invasion, either by an international police force or by the preservation of German military inferiority. Germany demanded equality; eventually the French offered equality after a trial period of four years during which Germany should prove herself. Meanwhile, as negotiations dragged on, the WEIMAR REPUBLIC was disintegrating as the Nazis rose to political dominance. Hitler was appointed Chancellor in January 1933; on 14 October Germany withdrew from the Conference and a week later from the League of Nations. The Conference lingered on into 1934 but by then most participants had concluded privately that only by vigorous rearmament could international security be guaranteed.

world music A genre in POP music of the 1980s in which the influence of folk music from around the world was incorporated into conventional ROCK rhythms and sounds.

World Service A BBC radio service, forming part of the External Services, first established as the Empire Service in 1932. During the middle years of World War II, the Empire Service became a universal service in English, broadcasting not only to Dominion and Colonial audiences but also to the British and Commonwealth troops throughout the various theatres of war. It was called variously the Overseas Forces Programme, the General Forces Programme, and the General Overseas Service, before becoming the World Service. During the same period its range was extended to cover North Africa, South America, the Pacific, and North America. The World Service now broadcasts in English 24 hours a day, offering a comprehensive programme of news, current affairs, drama, music, sport, and comedy; it is estimated to have an audience of over 25 million listeners.

World's Greatest Entertainer Nickname of the US singer and songwriter Al Jolson (Asa Yoelson; 1886–1950), who became the first major star of the TALKIES (*see also* SILENT FILMS) with the release of *The Jazz Singer* in 1927. His most successful song was 'Mammy', which he sang in his usual black make-up, in imitation of the old minstrel singers.

> It was easy enough to make Jolson happy at home. You just had to cheer him for breakfast, applaud wildly for lunch, and give him a standing ovation for dinner.
>
> GEORGE BURNS.

World's Sweetheart Nickname of the US film actress Mary Pickford (Gladys Mary Smith; 1893–1979), who became one of the great stars of SILENT FILMS in the 1920s. The wide-eyed heroine of such movies as *Pollyanna* (1919) and *Tess of the Storm Country* (1922) proved to be a shrewd business woman. In 1919 she co-founded United Artists Films with Charlie Chaplin, D. W. Griffiths, and Douglas

Fairbanks (her husband) and went on to become one of the wealthiest women in the world. When her career was still developing she was more modestly referred to as **America's Sweetheart**; victims of her financial acumen called her **Attila of Sunnybrook Farm**.

> I can't afford to work for only ten thousand dollars a week.
>
> MARY PICKFORD, to Adolph Zukor.

World Wars The wars of 1914–18 (World War I) and of 1939–45 (World War II), in which participation was worldwide.

wormhole A path through space that has been suggested as a drain down which energy from a BLACK HOLE passes to a so-called **white hole**.

worry. Don't worry, be happy *See under* HAPPY.

worst-case Indicating something that is or relates to the worst possible combination of circumstances. For example, a **worst-case scenario** is a hypothetical situation in which everything that could possibly go wrong does go wrong (also called a **nightmare scenario**); a **worst-case analysis** is planning that takes such a scenario into account, with the aim of producing an absolutely foolproof scheme, design, etc. The usage originated in military planning, in which it was used especially to refer to the possible outcome of a nuclear exchange.

Worth, Patience Pseudonym of Mrs J. H. Curran, US novelist who claimed that her books were 'communicated' to her from beyond the grave. The historical novel *Hope Trueblood* was particularly well received by critics, while other books varied widely in style and subject. *Telka*, set in medieval England, was praised for its authenticity – although Mrs Curran professed to know nothing of the period. The novels were, she claimed, dictated to her while in a trance, the first contact being made during a séance on 8 July 1913. Patience Worth, as the spirit responsible called herself, explained that she had been born in Dorset in the 17th century and had subsequently emigrated to America, where she died at the hand of an Indian war party. Whatever the truth behind the origin of the novels, literary commentators have never explained how the comparatively unimaginative and unacademic Mrs Curran managed to produce such apparently well-researched works.

would. Well, he would, wouldn't he? *See* PROFUMO AFFAIR.

WPA Works Progress Administration. An organization established by the US government in 1934 in an attempt to provide employment for the many artists unable to find work during the GREAT DEPRESSION. 5000 artists worked on various projects, including the decoration of public buildings with enormous murals. The artistic projects were closed down from 1939.

Wren A member of the Women's Royal Naval Service (WRNS). *See also* WAAC; WAC; WAAF.

Wright brothers The brothers Wilbur Wright (1867–1912) and Orville Wright (1871–1948) who, at 10.35 a.m. on 17 December 1903, achieved the first controlled and sustained powered flight. It took place at KITTY HAWK, North Carolina, and lasted just 12 seconds, with Orville at the controls. Before the day was ended the brothers had managed a further three flights, the fourth lasting 59 seconds and covering 852 feet. Their 12 h.p. chain-driven aircraft, *Flyer I*, recorded an air speed of 48 k.p.h. (30 m.p.h.); it is now preserved at the National Air and Space Museum at the Smithsonian Institute, Washington DC. The Wright brothers are usually credited with being the forerunners of the age of aviation; the first flight by a powered aircraft was, however, made on 9 October 1890 by the Frenchman Clément Ader (1841–1925), who flew 50m (164 feet) in his 20 h.p. steam driven aircraft *Eole*.

wrinklie or **wrinkly** British slang for an older person. As used by young people, it is not usually intended to cause offence (although it may well do so). It has been fashionable since the 1970s and is also used in the form of its common variants, **crinklie** or **crumblie** (or **crumbly**).

> Rod Stewart launched his first British tour for five years and proved he's still the liveliest wrinkly rocker around.
>
> *The Sun*, 27 March 1991.

WRVS Women's Royal Voluntary Service. Set up in 1938 as the Women's Voluntary Service (WVS), primarily to help with air-raid precautions, it became the WRVS in 1949. It does valuable social and welfare work with the aged and infirm and gives help in emergencies. It is particularly noted for its MEALS ON WHEELS service.

Wurlitzer organ The spectacular pipe organ that became a feature of the lavish picture theatres built in America and Europe during the early years of cinema. Also called the 'Mighty Wurlitzer', the organ was developed in Elmira, New York, in 1910 by the Wurlitzer family, long established in America as musical-instrument makers and dealers. The Wurlitzer was able to imitate a whole orchestra of instruments; although more were produced than any other model of a pipe organ in history, they are now difficult to find. Those that have survived are usually cherished and restored by dedicated enthusiasts.

wysiwyg Computer slang for 'What you see is what you get' *i.e.* what you see on the screen is exactly what will appear on the printout.

X, Y, Z

X A former category of film classification indicating that in the opinion of the British Board of Film Censors a film was unsuitable for showing to children under the age of 16. The category was introduced in 1951 and finally dropped in the 1980s. In America the equivalent of an X film was described as **X-rated**. X-rated is now used to describe anything considered shocking, *e.g.* 'X-rated language' or 'X-rated foul'.

X marks the spot An expression used to identify an exact location. It is derived from hypothetical treasure maps, in which the location of the treasure is marked with a cross. The term became widely used in 'spot the ball' competitions in newspapers, in which competitors are required to place a cross where they presume the ball to be in an action shot from a ball game.

Xerox Tradename for a type of copier for text, diagrams, etc., manufactured by the Rank-Xerox Corporation. The name, which is often used generically, comes from *xerography* – a process invented by the US scientist Chester Carlton in 1937. In this, copies are made by producing a photographic pattern of electric charge on a semiconducting surface. Carbon powder sticks to the charged areas of the surface and is then transferred to paper, where it is fixed by heat. The name comes from Greek *xeros*, dry. Xerox type copiers, which make copies on plain (i.e. untreated) paper, are now to be found in every office.

Xi An incident The kidnapping of the Chinese Nationalist (GUOMINDANG) leader Chiang Kai-shek in 1936. The seizure of the commander by two young marshals in Manchuria was a major factor in the forging of an alliance between the rival Nationalist and Communist forces to resist the Japanese invasion. Once the Japanese were defeated, however, the alliance soon broke up.

Y. **Y-front** Tradename for men's underwear by Lyle and Scott; from the design of their underpants, which have front seaming, allowing an opening, in the shape of an inverted Y. The name is now used generically for any garment of this type, although the company has taken legal action to prevent others from using it commercially. Despite their obvious convenience, Y-fronts were anathematized by style pundits in the 1980s; it was also suggested that their confinement of the testicles could cause, or at least contribute to, infertility. As a result, fashion-conscious young men with parental aspirations have abandoned them in favour of boxer shorts or briefs.

Y-gun A Y-shaped gun mounted in ships for firing a pair of depth charges.

yakkety-yak Idle chatter or gossip. It is an onomatopoeic extension of the US slang **yak**, to chatter. A pop-song of 1958 by the Coasters, written by Leiber and Stoller, had this title.

Yalta Conference The second Allied summit between Churchill, Roosevelt, and Stalin (the first was the TEHRAN CONFERENCE), held at the Yalta in the Crimea, 4–11 February 1945. Regarding the Allied military strategy, the ailing Roosevelt achieved his main aim in securing a Soviet commitment to enter the war against Japan three months after the end of the European conflict. It was agreed that Germany should be divided into four occupation zones, would have to pay reparations, and that war crimes would be investigated and punished. The precise details of the implementation of these measures were left to later discussions. Agreement was also reached on the use of the veto in the Security Council of the United Nations and on the allocation of three seats on the Council to the Soviet Union. Dominating much of the conference sessions was the issue of the Polish frontier settlement and the composition of the Polish government. Churchill and Roosevelt agreed to the extension of Poland's western border to the Oder and Neisse rivers and the ceding of territory in the east to the Soviet Union.

Stalin gave assurances that the Polish government would be reorganized to represent non-communist factions as well as the communist-backed LUBLIN COMMITTEE. He also promised that free democratic elections would be held in Poland and all the countries in E Europe currently under Red Army control. Subsequently, Stalin did not fulfil this commitment to free elections; as a result Churchill and Roosevelt have been accused of allowing E Europe to fall under Soviet control at Yalta. At the time, however, there was no reason to believe that Stalin would betray his promises. Moreover, given the occupation of the region by the Red Army, the West had the option of accepting Soviet assurances, or embarking on a Third World War.

yard. Yardbird *See* BIRD.

yardie (1) Jamaican slang for a Jamaican or sometimes any Caribbean person. **Yard** is the Jamaican name for Jamaica or home, as in the expression 'my own backyard'. (2) Jamaican slang for a member of a secret Jamaican criminal organization operating in the UK and America in the late 1980s and early 1990s.

> Yardies sent gunmen on drugs' quest.
> Headline in *The Independent*, 12 February 1991.

yarra Australian slang for insane. Yarra is the name of a mental hospital at Yarra Bend, Victoria.

yellow. yellow dog contracts A US name for agreements made by employers with employees to prevent the employees from joining labour unions. These contracts became invalid under an Act of 1932.

yellow flu US slang for the absence of students from schools, organized by families as a protest against the bussing of children to distant schools to achieve racial balance in the classroom. The term comes from the traditional yellow colour of US school buses.

yellow star *See* SCHANDBAND.

yes-man One who always expresses agreement with his superior, irrespective of his private opinions.

yeti Tibetan name for the ABOMINABLE SNOWMAN.

Yezhovshchina (Rus. Yezhof times) The period of the Great Terror in the Soviet Union in the late 1930s, when at least 10 million people were executed or deported to labour camps as part of Stalin's purge of supposed dissidents and opponents of the regime. From 1936 to 1938, the chief instigator of this purge was Nikolai Ivanovich Yezhof (1884–1940), head of the people's commissariat of internal affairs, the NKVD. Yezhof was a brutal man of low intelligence and small physical stature (he was barely five feet tall), who was described by a contemporary as a 'bloodthirsty dwarf'. He joined the Communist Party in 1917, became a political commissar in the Red Army, and from 1927 was a member of the party Central Committee. He replaced Yagoda as commissar for internal affairs in September 1936. One of his first actions was the purge of the NKVD itself; he then embarked on a purge of the high command of the army and was responsible for preparing the great show trials of the old Bolshevik leaders. Although these purges were orchestrated by Stalin, it was Yezhof whose name became synonymous with the Great Terror in the minds of contempories and it was Yezhof who was regarded as the principal agent of the policy. Yezhof himself fell victim to Stalin in December 1938, when he was arrested and replaced as head of the NKVD by Beria. He was probably shot two years later, a convenient scapegoat for the excesses of the Great Terror. However, the exact circumstances of his death are not known.

YHA Youth Hostels Association. A self-governing organization that provides cheap accommodation in order to promote the appreciation and understanding of the countryside, especially among students and other young people of limited means. The YHA was inspired by the German *Jugendherbergen*, a national system of cheap hostels started in 1909 by a school teacher, Richard Schirrmann, to provide overnight stays for pupils on school trips. The YHA was established in England and Wales in 1930 and in Scotland and Ireland in the following year. The first 12 hostels were open by Easter 1931 in N Wales, Yorkshire, and the Mendips and by 1939 the number had swelled to 297 with a membership of over 80,000. The YHA now has over 350 hostels throughout the UK and a membership of over 250,000. Members are also allowed access to 50,000 similar hostels run by National Associations in 45 other countries throughout the world, which are coordinated by the international YHA.

Yippie US slang for a politically active HIPPIE; the name is derived from the acronym for the Youth International Party. This anarchic left-wing party, founded by Abbie Hoffman and Jerry Rubin in 1968, put up a pig as presidential candidate at the Chicago Democratic convention, but was famous for little else.

yob British slang for an uncivilized youth; a lout, thug. One of the few examples of working-class and underworld back slang (for *boy*) to enter the general vocabulary. It has been widely used since the 1960s.

Yoknapatawpha Country The fictitious area of N Mississippi with the main town of Jefferson at its centre, which is the setting for many of the novels and short stories of the US author William Faulkner (1897–1962). These include *Sartoris* (1929); *Absalom, Absalom!* (1936); *The Hamlet* (1940), the first part of the trilogy dealing with the Snopes family, which he continued and concluded in *The Town* (1957) and *The Mansion* (1959); *Go Down, Moses* (1942), a collection of short stories; *Light in August* (1952); and *The Reivers* (1962), his last novel.

yomping Military slang for trekking across difficult terrain heavily laden with a full army pack. It emerged during the FALKLANDS CONFLICT (1982); the derivation is unknown.

yordim A derogatory term for Israeli citizens who emigrate to another country, generally America, in search of opportunities for advancement. They tend to be regarded as deserters by those who remain. Yordim is Hebrew for 'those who descend'; it is an ironic reversal of OLIM. *See also* CHOZRIM.

Yorkshire Ripper The press nickname for Peter Sutcliffe (1946–), a lorry driver from Bradford, Yorkshire, who murdered 13 women and attempted to kill seven others in the period 1975–80. The name arose from similarities to the Jack the Ripper killings of the 1880s. Both killers appeared to have a vendetta against prostitutes and both subjected their victim's bodies to horrific mutilation. Moreover, until Sutcliffe's belated arrest in 1981 it seemed as though the identity of the 20th-century Ripper might remain as much of a mystery as that of his 19th-century predecessor. Sutcliffe's plea of insanity – he claimed to have been acting on the orders of a supernatural voice – was rejected by the jury and he received a life sentence. After three years in prison he was transferred to Broadmoor (a secure hospital for the criminally insane).

young. Young England A play intended as a stirring morality tale, which opened at the Victoria Palace in September 1934 and convulsed audiences because of its unintentional comedy. Essentially a wholesome entertainment about young lovers beset by a variety of villains, the plot included a troop of Boy Scouts and Girl Guides, who foil the plans of a devious scoutmaster. The performances quickly degenerated into a riot of audience participation as theatregoers joined in or supplemented the dialogue. The author, Walter Reynolds, an 83-year-old dramatist and proprietor of the Theatre Royal, Leeds, used to sit in a box glaring at the audience as they joined in the Boy Scouts' Song or shouted lewd remarks at younger female characters. It is estimated that 250,000 people saw the play, before it finally closed in May 1935 after 278 performances.

> Away we go to camp and all its pleasures,
> A merry mob, a merry mob!
>
> Boy Scouts' Song.

Young Farmers An organization of clubs first established in the 1930s to provide social, educational, and leisure activities for young country people between the ages of 14 and 26. The original aim of the organization was to produce good farmers, good countrymen, and good citizens; however, the clubs are now open to everyone (not only young farmers) and their activities are tailored to suit the interests of the members.

young fogey British slang from the 1980s for a middle-class young male who espouses the traditional Conservative views, manners, and dress of a previous era. Like YUPPIES they aspire to wealth and a public school education for their children but they are against any ostentatious display of affluence, favouring traditional tweeds and corduroys in place of designer clothes. The novelist A. N. Wilson (1950–) is the personification of a young fogey. The term is a parody of 'old fogey', a familiar name for a member of the older generation, known for his tediously jingoistic right-wing views.

Young Plan An agreement negotiated at a series of conferences held in the Hague during 1929–30 between the Allied powers and Germany to reduce the amount of German reparations imposed by the VERSAILLES TREATY. It is named after the US banker, Owen D. Young (1874–

1962), then Chairman of the Allied Committee, and came into operation on 17 May 1930. German penalties were reduced by 75%, with the balance of 89 billion Reichsmarks to be paid in annuities until 1988 into a Bank for International Settlements. Allied control of German finances was removed, German securities taken into Allied hands were returned, responsibility for converting payments into foreign currency was transferred to Germany, the Reparations Commission abolished, and the Allied right to impose sanctions if payments were defaulted ended. Despite its many concessions, the Plan was vehemently attacked by German Nationalists and was no more successful than its predecessor, the DAWES PLAN, in settling the issue of the Allied war debt and their claim for reparations. In 1931, beset by the political and economic crisis caused by the GREAT DEPRESSION, Germany suspended repayments; after 1935 Hitler blocked any further Allied claims for reparations.

Young Turks Young up-and-coming men whose energy and ambition are likely to make them succeed. The expression derives from a Turkish reforming party of this name that transformed the decadent Turkish Empire into a modern European state. It had its origins in a committee formed in Geneva in 1891, which eventually deposed Sultan Abdul Hamid in 1908, and replaced him by his brother as Mohammed V. They remained the major force in Turkish politics until the end of World War I.

Your Country Needs You *See under* COUNTRY.

Yo-Yo Tradename for a toy consisting of a weighted spool attached to a string: the player holds the string in his or her hand and spins the spool up and down repeatedly. The Yo-Yo craze began in America in the late 1920s, reputedly in Chicago, reaching the UK a few years later. The device was first produced commercially by Louis Marx, who registered the name as a trademark in 1929. The term is used figuratively of anything that repeatedly rises and falls or fluctuates wildly between extremes, *e.g.* a 'yo-yo economy'. It also has a slang sense, meaning a foolish or insignificant person. The original yo-yo was a Filipino weapon consisting of two sticks and a thong: the name is thought to mean 'come come'.

Ypres A town in Flanders, Belgium, which was the site of bitter fighting during World War I. In mid-October 1914, after the RACE FOR THE SEA, the German armies commanded by Erich von Falkenhayn, launched a drive to capture the Channel Ports, which resulted in the First Battle of Ypres (20 October–18 November). Both sides experienced for the first time the true horrors of modern warfare, as reflected in the massive casualties inflicted by the devastating firepower of the opposing weaponry. In early November the Germans finally achieved a breakthrough but the breach was sealed before they could exploit their opportunity. The grim struggle resulted in 50,000 casualties for the BEF and marked the demise of the old British regular army. In the Second Battle of Ypres, 22 April–25 May 1915, the Germans launched an assault to divert Allied reinforcements from the offensives in Artois and Champagne. The Germans used chlorine gas for the first time but, despite initial successes against the French, British and Canadian reserves prevented any major German progress. For the Third Battle of Ypres, *see* PASSCHENDAELE.

yuppie A *y*oung *u*rban (or *u*pwardly mobile) *p*rofessional *p*erson. An acronym suffixed with *-ie* (on the model of HIPPIE etc.); it was coined in the late 1970s in America in response to the growing population of young ambitious career-minded materialists. Rapidly spreading throughout the English-speaking world, it was the first of a series of lifestyle acronyms that proliferated during the 1980s. *See also* DINKIE; PIPPY; RUMPIE; etc.

yuppie flu *See* ME.

Zabern incident A military incident in a small garrison town in Alsace in November 1913, which precipitated a political crisis in Germany. The Alsace region had been annexed from France by Germany after the Franco-Prussian War of 1870. In Zabern, repressive action by officers of the local garrison led to popular demonstrations; in response the colonel of the regiment, von Reutner, exceeded his authority in ordering the arrest and detention of a number of townspeople. In Germany, the incident was regarded as indicative of Prussian military arrogance; when Erich von Falkenhayn, the War Minister, and the Imperial Chancellor, Bethmann-Hollwegg, defended the actions of the military authorities, the left and centre parties in the Reichstag raised a storm of protest. On 13 December 1913, the government's actions were condemned by a vote of 293 to 54. The impact of the Zabern incident on German politics is regarded as indicative of the pre-revolutionary tensions between the ruling military class and the population, which were close to toppling the Hohenzollern regime before the outbreak of World War I.

zap (1) Slang meaning to destroy, to kill violently, from the language of comic-strip cartoons of the 1950s and 1960s in which 'zap' represented the sound of a laser gun. It is often used figuratively, meaning bombard (*e.g.* with witticisms).

> Madcap tube driver Cozmik Wilson cheers up depressed commuters . . . he zaps them with: 'I am to boldly go where only a man being paid double time would go'.
>
> *Daily Sport*, 5 May 1991.

(2) Gay slang from the 1970s meaning to bombard a particular organization with protests and political action, such as picketing. (3) Slang meaning to bypass the advertisement breaks in a television programme using a remote-control device (a **zapper**), either by switching to another channel or by operating the fast-forward control in a video recording. (4) Slang for power, lifeforce. A usage that reflects the idea of the power a gun gives its user.

> You get curious, especially if you've been past 41 yourself, which reminds you how your legs lose their spring and your reflexes their zap.
>
> *The Independent*, 10 April 1991.

Zapata moustache A type of bushy moustache that became fashionable in the 1960s and 1970s, especially among rock musicians. During the HIPPIE era it was sported by the BEATLES (especially during their *Sergeant Pepper* days), Alice Cooper, Frank Zappa, Jim Croce, and others. The moustache, which bends around and below the sides of the mouth, imitates that worn by the Mexican revolutionary Emiliano Zapata (1877–1919).

Zé Arigó (known in English as Joe from the Sticks) Nickname of José Pedro de Freitas, a poor Brazilian peasant who became world famous in the 1950s for his miraculous healing powers. Totally without medical training and using only an old kitchen knife, he is said to have performed intricate eye operations, restored the ability to walk to lame patients, and treated thousands of other poor Brazilians for a variety of disorders. He was twice prosecuted as a charlatan but none of his patients would testify against him. Arigó claimed that his remarkable powers originated in his spiritual contact with 'Dr Fritz', a German surgeon who died in World War I. It is said that he never accepted a fee for his work and that he predicted his own death, in a car crash, in 1971.

zebra crossing *See* PELICAN CROSSING.

zeppelin (1) A dirigible airship designed by Count Ferdinand von Zeppelin (1838–1917). Zeppelins were used for bombing and reconnaissance during World War I, but with the development of the aeroplane and the tragedy of the HINDENBURG airship in 1937, the more cumbersome and unsafe zeppelin was eclipsed. *See also* GRAF ZEPPELIN. (2) Slang for a large penis, because of its resemblance to a zeppelin.

zero. zero hour A military term (first used in World War I) for the exact time at which an attack, etc., is to begin. Subsequent operations are often timed in relation to zero hour, *e.g.* zero + 3 means 3 minutes after zero hour.

zero option President Reagan's proposal in the 1980s for the deal in which America would reduce to zero its stock of CRUISE MISSILES in Europe if the Soviet Union would no longer keep SS-20s. It has yet to be taken up.

ZETA *See* NUCLEAR REACTOR.

Ziegfeld Follies The spectacular revues first presented by the US theatre producer Florenz Ziegfeld (1867–1932) in 1907. The Follies, modelled on the Folies Bergère shows in Paris, became the last word in lavish entertainment, with a chorus line of beautiful girls, stunning sets, and appearances by the leading singers of the day. The shows are preserved in various film recreations, in which such stars as Fred ASTAIRE and Judy Garland appeared. The revues ran continuously from 1932 until 1957, after which they were periodically revived.

zilch (1) Nothing. Originally an Americanism of the 1960s, it was widely used in the UK a decade later. It seems to be an amalgam of 'zero', 'nil', and the Yiddish *nich*. It is also used to describe a person regarded as insignificant. A US magazine *Ballyhoo* in the 1930s featured a family of comic characters called the Zilches. (2) Slang for a diçe game.

Zinoviev Letter or **Red Letter Scare** A letter, which purported to be signed by the Soviet politican Grigori Zinoviev (1883–1936), president of the Presidium of the Third Communist International, summoning the British Communist Party to intensify its revolutionary activities and to subvert the armed forces of the crown; it was published on 25 October 1924, four days before a general election. It helped to promote a 'red scare' and possibly increased an almost certain Conservative majority. Many Labour leaders held it to be a forgery and its authenticity was denied by the Soviet Union. In December 1966 *The Sunday Times* published an article establishing that the letter was a forgery perpetrated by a group of WHITE RUSSIAN *émigrés*, at the same time suggesting that certain leaders at the Conservative Central Office knew that it was a fake, although the Conservative Party as a whole assumed it to be genuine.

Zionism The Jewish movement for the establishment of the 'national home' in Palestine. The Zionist movement was founded by Dr Theodore Herzl of Vienna in 1895, although it was the BALFOUR DECLARATION of 1917 that first recognized Zionist aspirations and gave them political teeth. From 1920 to 1948 Palestine was a British mandate, administered under great difficulties arising from the friction between Jews and Arabs. However, the HOLOCAUST provided Zionism with an unanswerable case and the independent state of Israel was established in 1948.

zip. zip code The US system used to differentiate the mail delivery zones based on five-digit numbers. The name 'zip' is derived from the initial letters of the name of the system, Zone Improvement Plan. The British post code composed of letters and numbers is a similar system.

zip fastener A type of fastener for clothing, bags, etc., consisting of two parallel strips with interlocking teeth opened or closed with a sliding clip. Although a fastener of this type was patented as early as 1893, the name did not appear until the 1920s, when the US company B. F. Goodrich marketed the 'zipper boot', a type of galosh fastened with a zip. The name – deriving from the verb to zip, *i.e.* to move briskly or hurriedly – was presumably chosen to highlight the quickness of the zip fastener as compared with buttons, etc. There may also be an allusion to the sound made when a zip is opened or closed.

zit Slang for a spot or a pimple. Originally an Americanism, it had become well known in the UK by the 1980s.

Zodiac murders A series of murders in California, which captured world headlines in the 1960s and were subsequently acknowledged as the first murders by a SERIAL KILLER. They began in 1968 with the motiveless shooting of two teenagers in a car near Vallejo, California. As the killings continued, the murderer maintained contact with the press in numerous cryptic messages, calling himself 'Zodiac' and explaining that he was acquiring 'slaves in the afterlife'. Panic was such that police officers accompanied school buses (threatened by 'Zodiac') and the authorities were plagued by letters and calls from hoaxers. The killer (or possibly a hoaxer) even rang a popular television chat show to say he was suffering from a mental illness. The killer has never been identified. As late as 1974 a message was received to the effect that 'Zodiac' claimed to have murdered 37 people. *See also* HUNGERFORD MASSACRE; YORKSHIRE RIPPER.

zoftig or **zaftig** US slang for delicious or attractive; it comes through Yiddish from the German *saft*, juice. It is typically used by men of women whom they find sexually attractive.

zoid Teenage derogatory slang for a dull and unpopular person, perhaps a shortening of such words as schizoid and zomboid.

zombie Slang for a dull-witted person, someone who cannot think for themselves. It is sometimes used as a mild term of abuse, as in 'He sits there like a zombie, never saying a word.' It is derived from the Kongo *zumbi*, a good-luck fetish; it was also the name of a python god in W Africa. From Africa it travelled with the slaves to Haiti and the West Indies, and thence to America.

> And, like a zombie, I found myself going into the shop and saying 'how much is it?' Which is not a question you are entitled to ask when you have not got a bean.
>
> *The Independent*, 20 May 1991.

zombie food US slang for JUNK FOOD. It is not certain whether 'zombie' in this case refers to the anticipated results of eating such food, the amount of intelligence required to prepare it (usually only opening the container), or to the kind of person who is willing to eat it. It is perhaps a combination of all three.

zonked Slang for incapacitated by drugs or alcohol. Zonk echoes 'bonk', a bang on the head, which has much the same effect as being zonked by alcohol. The meaning can also be extended to being incapacitated by tiredness.

zoo daddy US slang for a divorced father who has access to his children and typically takes them on a treat outing to the zoo when they visit him. There is a double implication in the term, first that he spoils his children and secondly that he doesn't know what else to do with them. There is sometimes a more ominous implication from the childrens' point of view – that their father is no better than some kind of animal for having broken up the home and brought such unhappiness to his children.

zoot-suit An exaggerated style of clothing adopted in the late 1930s by US HEP-CATS and followers of fashionable SWING music. It usually consisted of baggy trousers caught in at the bottom, a long coat resembling a frock coat, a broad-brimmed hat, and a flowing tie, all in vivid colours. An essential article of equipment was a vast key chain.

Zorro The sabre-wielding masked hero of numerous Hollywood B-MOVIES of the 1930s–1960s. This unlikely combination of swordplay and the Wild West was enormously successful, with Douglas Fairbanks the first to appear in the title role. Zorro first appeared in a comic strip in 1919; the first film was released a year later. Among Fairbanks' successors as the debonair Robin Hood of the West were Robert Livingston, John Carroll, Tyrone Power, Guy Williams, and Alain Delon. Zorro's trademark (known as the **mark of Zorro**) was a letter Z cut into the shirt of his opponent.